Southern Living®
ANNUAL RECIPES
MASTER INDEX

1979-1994

Oxmoor House®

©1995 by Oxmoor House, Inc.
Book Division of Southern Progress Corporation
P.O. Box 2463
Birmingham, Alabama 35201

Southern Living® is a federally registered
trademark of Southern Living, Inc.

Library of Congress Catalog Number: 79-88364
ISBN: 0-8487-1410-5
ISSN: 0272-2003

Manufactured in the United States of America
First Printing 1995

Oxmoor House, Inc.
    Editor-in-Chief: Nancy J. Fitzpatrick
    Senior Editor, Editorial Services: Olivia Kindig Wells
    Art Director: James Boone

Southern Living® *Annual Recipes Master Index 1979-1994*
    Southern Living® Foods Editor: Susan Dosier
    Senior Foods Editor: Susan Carlisle Payne
    Assistant Foods Editor: Whitney Wheeler Pickering
    Copy Editor: Donna Baldone
    Editorial Assistant: Keri Bradford

    Production and Distribution Director: Phillip Lee
    Production Manager: Gail Morris
    Associate Production Manager: Theresa L. Beste
    Production Assistant: Marianne Jordan

    Indexer: Mary Ann Laurens
    Designer and Illustrator: Carol Middleton

Introduction

We get countless calls from readers asking for help in finding recipes that have appeared in the magazine over the years, and we're glad for a chance to hear from them. This *Southern Living® Annual Recipes Master Index* is what we use to answer those questions. It helps us find every recipe we've printed since 1979. With this cumulative index, thousands of kitchen-tested recipes are at your fingertips.

To help you use the index, we've cross-referenced each recipe by the type of dish and the major ingredient in it. The page numbers of all microwave recipes are preceded by an "M." To quickly locate recipes, just look for the alphabetized guide word at the bottom of each page. If you're a fan of our light recipes, you'll find them under the "Living Light" category. The name of our light section has changed over time, and all the recipes from previous columns called "On the Light Side" and "Cooking Light" are now under the new heading.

Occasionally, you'll find the same recipe in different volumes of *Southern Living® Annual Recipes*. There's a simple reason: A recipe may appear in the magazine edition for one state before it appears in another state. To make sure you can find the recipes you seek, this index gives all of the page references to those bonus recipes that have run in more than one volume of *Southern Living® Annual Recipes*.

Readers tell us that the "From Our Kitchen To Yours" column is one of their favorites. This year we've added it as an index category to guide you to this useful information.

We hope you're pleased with this index of our recipes. Please call or write and let us know how we can make it easier for you to use and enjoy.

Susan Dosier

Master Index

All recipes are listed by their complete titles under a specific food category and ingredient. The volume is indicated in boldface followed by the page number. Microwave recipe page numbers are preceded by an "M."

Almonds

Asparagus, Almond, '83 86
Balls, Coconut-Almond, '84 256
Balls, Toasted Almond Chip, '84 240
Bars, Almond-Chocolate, '83 304
Beans Amandine, Green, '79 276;
 '82 M20
Beans with Almonds, Green, '84 253
Beans with Almonds, Italian Green,
 '81 207
Biscotti, Almond, '91 108
Biscotti, Almond-Anise, '93 266
Biscuits, Raspberry-Almond, '93 160
Braid, Almond, '89 86
Bread, Cocoa-Nut Swirl, '80 257
Brie, Almond-Raspberry, '94 M89
Broccoli with Almonds, Glazed, '80 12
Brownies, Date-and-Almond, '88 217
Brussels Sprouts Amandine, '79 213
Butter, Asparagus with Almond, '84 85
Butter-Nut Strips, '82 167
Cabbage with Almonds, Creamed, '79 4
Cake, Almond-Blueberry Coffee, '85 152
Cake, Almond-Butter, '86 107
Cake, Almond-Butter Wedding, '86 106
Cake, Almond Legend, '82 8
Cake, Almond Whipping Cream, '80 295
Cake, Apricot-Almond Coffee, '93 26
Cake, Chocolate-Almond, '91 248
Cake, Peach-Almond Pound, '89 86
Cake, Peachy Almond-Butter, '90 107
Cake Squares, Almond, '79 111
Cake Twist, Almond Coffee, '91 22
Cake with Cherry Filling, Chocolate-Almond,
 '84 225
Candied Nuts, '81 261
Candy, Almond Brittle, '80 255
Caramelized Almonds, '92 303
Casserole, Almond-Broccoli, '88 62
Casserole, Chicken-Almond, '94 199
Catfish Amandine, Mandarin, '84 183
Catfish Amandine, Spicy, '89 52
Celery Almondine, '85 116
Celery Amandine, Buttered, '82 98
Cheese, Almond, '88 173
Cheese Ball, Fruit-and-Nut, '91 251
Cheese Ball, Pinecone, '93 288
Cheesecake, Chocolate-Almond, '93 53
Chicken Almondette Fingers, '93 12
Chicken and Vegetables, Almond, '86 21
Chicken, Creamy Almond, '89 281
Chicken, Spicy Almond, '88 150
Chocolate Almond Velvet, '81 148
Cinnamon Stars, Swiss, '87 293
Cobbler, Blackberry-Almond, '81 132
Coffee, Chocolate-Almond, '84 54
Coffee Delight, Almond-, '84 115
Coleslaw with Grapes and Almonds, '83 59

Combs, Almond, '84 136
Confections, Almond Cream, '87 198;
 '90 310
Cookies, Almond, '83 22, 181; '91 51;
 '92 176
Cookies, Almond Butter, '79 52
Cookies, Almond Spritz, '82 306
Cookies, Chocolate-Almond Surprise,
 '88 M45
Cookies, Light Almond, '83 151
Cookies, Swedish Almond, '85 312
Cookies, Texan-Size Almond Crunch, '91 236
Cream, Chocolate-Almond, '91 108
Cream, Peach Almond, '82 108
Cream, Peaches 'n' Almond, '86 229
Cream with Fresh Strawberries, Almond,
 '87 93
Crêpes Gelée Amandine, '83 126
Crostini, Almond-Bacon-Cheese, '94 318
Crunch, Almond Butter, '80 301
Crunch, Vanilla Almond, '93 243
Curried Almonds, '82 297
Curried Almonds, Cauliflower and Peas with,
 '79 221; '80 82
Custard with Raspberries, Almond Crème,
 '88 174
Danish, Almond, '87 301
Dessert, Chocolate-Almond, '82 306
Dessert, Mocha-Almond, '80 289; '81 62
Dessert, Sour Cream-Almond, '92 120
Dip, Almond Delight, '90 226
Dip with Strawberries, Almond Cream,
 '92 164
Drops, Cherry-Almond, '81 20
Drops, Chocolate-Coconut Almond, '87 223
Eggplant with Almonds, '79 179
Filling, Almond, '87 301
Filling, Almond Cream, '85 320; '91 248
Filling, Ground Almond, '87 14
Filling, Nut, '91 35
Fish, Almond Baked, '88 270; '89 203
Fish Amandine, '85 179
Fish Amandine, Fillet of, '80 M54
Float, Nutmeg-Almond, '84 106
Flounder Amandine, '89 M196
Frosting, Almond-Butter, '86 107
Frosting, Chocolate-Almond, '83 241
Frozen Almond Crunch, '94 283
Fruit, Almond-Curried, '83 261
Glaze, Honey-Nut, '87 15
Ice Cream, Almond-Fudge, '93 205
Ice Cream Balls, Almond, '86 315
Ice Cream, Peach-Almond, '89 156
Leaves, Almond Holly, '86 319
Liqueur, Almond-Flavored, '81 287
Meringue Fingers, Chocolate-Almond,
 '84 158
Mousse, Chocolate-Almond, '93 316
Muffins, Almond, '90 87

Muffins, Banana-Honey-Nut, '88 62
Muffins, Peachy-Almond, '86 301
Nippy Nuts, '93 301
Olives, Almond-Stuffed, '88 95
Orange Lake Amandine, '80 99
Pastry, Almond, '85 177; '89 317; '92 30
Pastry Cups, Mushroom-Almond, '88 210
Pears, Almond-Stuffed, '83 207
Peas with Almonds, Curried, '88 M294
Petits Fours, Chocolate-Almond, '93 255
Phyllo Nests, Nutty, '87 277
Pie Amandine, Chocolate, '83 300
Pie, Apple-Amandine, '89 215
Pie, Creamy Chocolate-Almond, '85 102
Pie, Toasted Almond, '86 163
Pineapple-Almond Delight, '85 96
Pollo Almendrado, '81 193
Potatoes, Almond-Fried, '82 25
Potatoes, Broccoli-and-Almond-Topped,
 '83 3
Praline Sauce, '93 214
Pudding, Chocolate-Almond, '82 142; '88 24
Pudding, Mandarin-Almond, '85 M12
Puffs, Chicken Nut, '81 266
Quiche, Almond-Topped Crab, '79 127
Rice, Almond, '81 195; '85 M112; '89 100;
 '91 291
Rice, Almond Wild, '86 50
Rice with Almonds, Curried, '83 M285
Roca, Almond, '86 49
Rolls, Almond Crescent, '90 283
Rolls, Cherry-Almond, '84 M198
Rollups, Almond-Ham, '89 284
Salad Amandine, Chicken, '81 37
Salad, Cheesy Fruit-'n'-Nut, '87 56
Salad, Chicken-Almond, '81 133
Salad, Cucumber-Almond, '86 147
Salad Dressing, Almond, '81 37
Salad, Sesame-Almond, '89 123
Salad Shanghai, Almond-Chicken, '90 160
Sandwiches, Chicken-Almond Pocket,
 '81 240; '83 69
Sauce, Almond-Vanilla Custard, '88 M177
Sauce, Angel Food Cake with
 Amaretto-Almond, '90 199
Sauce, Asparagus with Almond, '91 117
Sauce, Cauliflower with Almond, '82 270
Sauce, Chicken in Orange-Almond, '79 219;
 '80 13
Sauce, Mandarin-Almond Cream, '84 183
Sauce, Shrimp-and-Almond, '87 282
Slaw, Pineapple-Almond, '92 171
Snaps, Almond, '92 273
Soup, Almond, '79 48
Soup, Chicken-Almond Cream, '92 21
Spread, Almond Cheese, '87 292
Squares, Cream Cheese-Almond, '85 68
Stir-Fry, Almond-Vegetable, '86 222
Sunburst, Almond, '94 245

Almonds (*continued*)

Syrup, Almond, '82 47
Tart, Almond, '89 232
Tarts, Almond Tea, '85 120
Tassies, Lucky Almond, '91 13
Tea, Almond, '85 43; '86 329; '89 212
Tea, Almond-Lemonade, '86 229
Tea, Ginger-Almond, '94 131
Toast, Almond-French, '88 62
Toast Amandine, Baked, '82 47
Toffee Crunch, Almond-, '88 285
Topping, Almond, '85 152; '86 200
Tortoni, Coffee-Almond, '81 30
Truffles, Almond, '83 298
Wafers, Almond-Filled, '88 120

Ambrosia

Anytime Ambrosia, '86 182
Baked Ambrosia, '83 303
Bowl, Ambrosia, '80 138; '84 313
Brunch, Ambrosia, '83 57
Cake, Ambrosia, '79 229
Cake Royale, Ambrosia, '89 335
Carrot-Marshmallow Ambrosia, '80 5
Chicken Salad Ambrosia, '85 216
Citrus Ambrosia, '82 287
Cookies, Ambrosia, '81 301; '82 110;
    '86 313
Cups, Sherbet Ambrosia, '82 159
Custard Sauce Ambrosia, '84 256
Easy Ambrosia, '92 45
Fantastic Ambrosia, '91 277
Fruit Ambrosia, Fresh, '88 184
Fruit Ambrosia, Mixed, '83 10
Grandma's Ambrosia, '90 254
Honey Bee Ambrosia, '83 267
Layered Ambrosia, '88 304
Mold, Ambrosia, '79 241
Mold, Ambrosia Cream Cheese, '79 249
Old-Fashioned Ambrosia, '80 5
Orange Ambrosia Supreme, '79 37
Pancakes with Orange Syrup, Ambrosia,
    '89 254
Peach Ambrosia, '83 53
Pie, Ambrosia, '79 284
Pie, Orange Ambrosia, '80 237
Pineapple-Orange Ambrosia, '88 252
Rhubarb Ambrosia, '88 93
Salad, Ambrosia, '83 231; '94 271
Salad, Carrot-Ambrosia, '81 252
Sauce, Hot Ambrosia, '89 335
Sherried Ambrosia, '84 324; '86 317
Spread, Ambrosia, '92 50
Tropical Ambrosia, '79 74

Anchovies

Appetizers, Zesty Anchovy, '83 93
Mayonnaise, Anchovy, '86 179
Tapenade, '92 194

Appetizers

Almond-Ham Rollups, '89 284
Almonds, Curried, '82 297
Anchovy Appetizers, Zesty, '83 93
Antipasto, Easy, '92 24
Antipasto Relish, '86 327
Apple-Phyllo Rolls, '88 213
Apple Quarters, Honey-Baked, '86 93
Artichoke-and-Shrimp Appetizer, '93 271
Artichoke Appetizer Frittata, '92 58
Artichoke Appetizer, Zesty, '80 146
Artichoke-Caviar Mold, '87 239

Artichoke-Cheese Bottoms, Baked, '94 61
Artichoke-Parmesan Phyllo Bites, '87 54
Artichokes, Marinated, '87 250
Artichokes, Spring, '86 62
Asparagus Croquettes, '85 265
Asparagus, Prosciutto-Wrapped, '91 98
Asparagus Rolls, '79 296; '80 31
Asparagus Rolls, Hot, '93 329
Asparagus Rollups, '79 63
Asparagus Roll-Ups, '84 270
Avocado-Crabmeat Cocktail, Sherried,
    '87 95
Bacon Appetizers, Hot, '80 248
Bacon-Chestnut Wraps, '84 M216
Bacon-Onion Appetizers, '94 290
Bacon Rolls, '84 270; '93 330
Bacon Rollups, '79 34
Bacon Swirls, '89 214
Bacon-Wrapped Crackers, '93 280
Bacon-Wrapped Pineapple Chunks, '84 25
Bacon-Wrapped Water Chestnuts, '79 63
Bagel Chips, '91 138
Bagel Chips, Cinnamon-and-Sugar, '91 139
Bagel Chips, Garlic, '91 139
Bagel Chips, Lemon-and-Herb, '91 139
Bagel Crisps, '86 278
Bean Burrito Appetizers, '94 226
Beef on a Stick, Marinated, '85 234
Beef Sticks, '93 331
Beefy Party Snacks, '80 249
Beets, Blue Cheese-Stuffed, '88 211
Black Bean Appetizer, '83 50
Black Bean Cakes with Greens and Apple
    Dressing, '92 216
Black-Eyed Pea Pinwheels, '85 300; '86 18
Broccoli-Cheese Appetizer, '92 265
Broccoli, Cocktail, '80 192
Broccoli Soup, Mock Cream of, '85 288
Brussels Sprouts, Marinated, '88 265
Burgers, Saucy Cocktail, '83 217
Burrito Rollups, '90 119
Burritos, Chinese, '87 181
Buzzard's Nests, '93 244
Canapé Bread, '89 292
Canapé Bread, Rye, '89 293
Canapé Bread, Whole Wheat, '89 293
Canapés, Cheesy Crab, '86 262
Canapés, Crab, '93 130
Canapés, Crabmeat, '88 150
Canapés, Fruit-Topped, '85 80
Canapés, Green Onion, '84 M216
Canapés, Hot Crab, '86 70; '87 239
Canapés, Hot Swiss, '83 259
Canapés, Lemon-Cheese, '87 93
Canapés, Mushroom, '80 285
Canapés, Party, '86 128
Canapés, Shrimp, '84 116
Canapés, Shrimp-and-Cucumber, '93 164
Canapés, Vegetable, '91 252
Caponata, '87 166
Caramel Corn, Oven-Made, '91 233
Caramel Good Stuff, Baked, '80 284
Caraway Wafers, '81 261
Carrots, Dilled Baby, '84 80
Carrots, Dill-Spiced, '87 200
Carrots, Pickled, '93 12
Catfish Appetizer, Layered, '92 209
Cauliflower, Crispy Fried, '80 220
Cauliflower, Dilled, '83 93
Cauliflower, French-Fried, '86 211
Cauliflower, Golden Fried, '82 78

Cauliflower, Pickled, '94 183
Cauliflower with Cheese Sauce, Fried,
    '87 231
Caviar Crown, '83 78
Caviar Mousse, '83 258; '85 86
Caviar Pie, '79 154
Caviar Potatoes, '84 80
Caviar Potatoes, Appetizer, '86 223
Caviar, Texas, '86 218
Caviar Tomatoes, '91 12
Celery, Creamy Stuffed, '82 102
Celery, Jalapeño Stuffed, '79 70
Celery, Stuffed, '82 98
Celery Trunks, Stuffed, '85 115
Cereal Bites, Buttery, '89 97
Cereal Nibblers, Great, '82 297
Cereal Snack, Toasted, '85 215
Ceviche (Marinated Raw Fish), '80 194
Ceviche, Mexican-Style, '88 115
Cheese
    Bagel Chips, Parmesan Cheese, '91 138
    Bake, Appetizer Cheese, '92 209
    Ball, Blue Cheese, '80 259; '84 221
    Ball, Blue Cheese-Olive, '82 248
    Ball, Bourbon Cheese, '81 57
    Ball, Brandied Blue Cheese, '85 283
    Ball, Carrot-Cheese, '86 325
    Ball, Cheese, '82 161; '91 200
    Ball, Cheese and Chutney, '87 247
    Ball, Cheese 'n' Beef, '83 230
    Ball, Chicken-Cheese, '93 216
    Ball, Chicken-Curry Cheese, '85 118
    Ball, Cocktail Cheese, '83 174
    Ball, Curried Shrimp Cheese, '86 135
    Ball, Deviled Pecan, '80 258
    Ball, Festive Cheese, '79 44; '94 279
    Ball, Fruit-and-Nut Cheese, '91 251
    Ball, Herbed Cheese, '89 246
    Ball, Holiday Cheese, '79 285
    Ball, Olive Cheese, '80 258
    Ball, Parmesan-Cream Cheese, '89 246
    Ball, Party Cheese, '84 258
    Ball, Party Pecan Cheese, '81 235
    Ball, Peanut Butter-Cheese, '86 136
    Ball, Pecan Cheese, '83 127
    Ball, Peppered Cheese, '79 100;
        '94 118
    Ball, Pimiento Cheese, '80 258
    Ball, Pineapple Cheese, '81 160
    Ball, Pineapple-Cheese, '84 26
    Ball, Pinecone Cheese, '93 288
    Balls, Bite-Size Cheese, '92 321
    Balls, Cheese and Mushroom, '79 63
    Ball, Shrimp-Cheese, '85 208
    Ball, Smoky Salmon Cheese, '82 247
    Balls, Olive-Cheese, '84 206
    Balls with Sun-Dried Tomatoes, Cheese,
        '94 317
    Ball, Tangy Cheese, '81 263, 287
    Bar, Savory Cheese, '91 98
    Bars, Bacon-Cheese Toast, '79 36
    Bars, Camembert, '86 58
    Bear Claws, '81 161
    Biscuits, Cheese, '79 296; '80 31
    Biscuits, Cheesy Sausage, '80 78
    Biscuits, Petite Ham and Cheese,
        '79 193
    Biscuits, Tiny Cheese, '80 192
    Bites, Benne Cheese, '80 121
    Bites, Cheese, '93 329
    Bites, Cheesy Pecan, '82 248

Appetizers, Cheese *(continued)*

Bites, Curried Swiss, '85 220
Bit-of-Brie Appetizer, '88 M8
Bonbons, Cheese, '87 93
Brie, Chutney-Bacon, '90 M292
Brie, Honey-Mustard, '91 252
Brie in Rye, Raspberry, '93 252
Brie, Kahlúa-Pecan, '92 289
Brie, Tropical Breeze, '94 M18
Brie with Fresh Fruit, Caramel, '90 266
Brie, Wrapped, '92 126
Brie Wrapped in Phyllo, '93 173
Caraway Cheese, '89 246
Chiles-Rellenos Squares, '91 161
Cracker Nibbles, Cheese, '84 328
Crackers, Cheddar, '84 236
Cream Cheese Appetizer, Baked, '92 58
Cream Cheese Round, Pesto-and-, '90 242
Crispies, Cheese-Bacon, '84 270
Crispies, Pecan-Cheese, '87 168
Croquettes, Hot Cheese, '89 182
Crostini, Almond-Bacon-Cheese, '94 318
Crostini, Mozzarella, '94 319
Crostini, Swiss-Blue Cheese, '94 318
Cucumber Slices, Cheesy, '84 80
Cups, Cottage Cheese-Spinach, '87 190
Cutouts, Sesame-Cheese, '82 296
Feta Cheesecakes, Little, '86 277
Fiesta Cheesecake, '93 273
Flaming Cheese, '84 187
Fondue, Cheese, '81 40
Fondue, Party Cheese, '92 20
Fondue, Swiss Cheese, '91 48
Fried Cheddar Cheese, '89 182
Fried Cheese Balls, '89 181
Fried Cheese Bites, '82 77
Fried Cheese, Italian-Style, '83 250; '89 182
Fried Ham-and-Cheese Balls, '84 221
Garnished Cheese, '91 98
Goat Cheese, Peppered, '94 128
Goat Cheese Rosemary, '89 270
Goat Cheese with Sun-Dried Tomatoes and Rosemary, '93 175
Herb Cheese, Pot-of-, '85 210
Herbed Cheese, '88 152
Kabobs, Peppered Cheese, '91 279
Little Bits, '79 196
Log, Cheesy Surprise, '82 247
Log, Garlic Cheese, '85 21
Log, Hawaiian Cheese, '89 246
Log, Roquefort Pecan, '89 247
Logs, Black Pepper Cheese, '90 61
Logs, East Indian Cheese, '88 173
Log, Toasted Pecan Cheese, '86 M288
Marinated Cheese, '90 244
Meat-and-Cheese Appetizers, '87 7
Mexicali Appetizer, Cheesy, '82 108
Mold, Blue Cheese, '85 210
Mold, Cheese-and-Wine, '84 197
Mold, Cream Cheese-Crabmeat, '90 71
Mold, Garlic-Chive Cheese, '85 210
Mousse, Roquefort, '82 71
Nuggets, Cheesy Ham, '81 290
Olive Appetizers, Cheesy, '85 113
Olive Appetizers, Cheesy-, '87 246

Olive Snack, Open-Faced Cheese-and-, '89 97
Pasta Bites, Pesto-Cheese, '87 251
Pastries, Cream Cheese, '80 250
Pastries, Date-Filled Cheese, '83 259
Pastry, Brie Wrapped in, '80 241
Pastry, Sausage Balls in Cheese, '80 248
Pastry Shells, Miniature Cream Cheese, '87 190
Patty, Lemon-Pepper Cheese, '84 117
Patty Shells, Cream Cheese, '82 249
Peachy Cream Cheese, '92 289
Pepper-Cheese Stacks, '87 80
Peppers, Cheesy Jalapeño, '80 195
Phyllo-Cheese Triangles, '87 246
Phyllo Cheese Triangles, '93 329
Phyllo Triangles, Cheese-Filled, '83 259
Pie, Cheesy Hors d'Oeuvre, '88 91
Pinwheels, Santa's, '91 275
Potato Skins, Cheesy, '82 78
Puffs, Bavarian Cheese, '80 191
Puffs, Cheese, '79 110
Puffs, Cheese-and-Spinach, '87 246
Puffs, Cream Cheese, '84 151
Puffs, Gouda-Shrimp, '79 234
Puffs, Ham-and-Cheese, '86 277
Puffs, Mexican Cheese, '87 8
Puffs, Surprise Cheese, '79 295; '80 31
Quesadillas, Green Chile, '90 121
Queso Blanco, '93 322
Quiches, Miniature Bacon-Cheese, '83 93
Quiches, Miniature Cheese, '80 150
Quick Cheese Snack, '89 98
Ring, Cheese, '81 261
Ring, Strawberry-Cheese, '86 14
Roll, Chili-Cheese, '84 114
Roll, Ham-and-Cheese, '79 234
Rollups, Ham-and-Swiss, '85 113
Round, Brie Appetizer, '82 41
Round, Herbed Cheese, '84 300
Rounds, Cheese, '86 262
Rounds, Parmesan, '85 131
Rounds, Parmesan Party, '82 248
Salami-Cheese Snacks, '88 96
Sandwiches, Cheese Tea, '92 276
Sandwiches, Cheshire Claret Cheese-and-Ham Striped Tea, '94 16
Sesame Cheese Bites, '89 24
Soufflé, Blue Cheese, '91 244
Sour Cream Appetizer, Cheesy, '84 51
Spinach-Cheese Bites, '94 23
Squares, Cream Cheese-Almond, '85 68
Squares, Green Chile-Cottage Cheese, '86 85
Squares, Jalapeño Cheese, '80 195
Squares, Quick Cheese, '84 191
Sticks, Parmesan, '82 297
Sticks, Parmesan Sesame, '81 39
Sticks, Peppery Cheese, '81 M289
Straws, Brie Cheese, '94 216
Straws, Cheese, '80 150; '82 137; '88 77
Straws, Chili-Cheese, '94 216
Straws, Easy-as-Pie Cheese, '94 216
Straws, Italian Cheese, '94 217
Straws, Parmesan Cheese, '94 216
Tartlets, Cheese, '88 211
Tarts, Blue Cheese Appetizer, '85 300; '86 18

Terrine, Italian Cheese, '93 64
Three-Cheese Appetizer, '80 174
Toast Treats, Cheese, '83 100
Turnovers, Cheesy Sesame Seed, '91 252
Twists, Double Cheese, '85 131
Wafers, Cheese, '80 151
Wafers, Hope Farm Cheese, '93 282
Wafers, Pecan-Cheese, '81 119
Wafers, Sage-Pecan Cheese, '93 12
Wedges, Cheesy Party, '84 84
Wonton Chips, Parmesan Cheese, '91 138
Wontons with Hot Sauce, Cheese, '83 74
Cherries, Stuffed, '85 81
Chicken Almondette Fingers, '93 12
Chicken Appetizers, Sesame, '89 61
Chicken Balls, Coconut Curried, '91 165
Chicken Balls, Curried, '91 98
Chicken Bites, Curried, '85 40
Chicken Bites, French-Fried, '85 160
Chicken Bites, Savory, '92 209
Chicken, Deep-Fried Walnut, '87 175
Chicken Drummettes, Down-Home, '93 157
Chicken Drummettes, Orange-Pecan, '93 158
Chicken Drummettes, Southwestern, '93 158
Chicken Little Fingers, '80 249
Chicken Liver and Bacon Roll-Ups, '80 200; '81 57
Chicken Livers, Party, '83 242
Chicken Liver Turnovers, '79 141
Chicken-Mushroom Appetizers, '88 210
Chicken Nuggets, Baked, '81 149
Chicken Nuggets, Lemon-, '87 283
Chicken Nuggets Supreme, '85 160
Chicken Nuggets with Pineapple Sauce, '84 236
Chicken Nut Puffs, '81 260
Chicken-Pecan Log, '81 290
Chicken Puffs, Appetizer, '85 72
Chicken Salad, Old-Fashioned, '83 79
Chicken Salad Tarts, '84 257
Chicken Tarts, Deviled, '94 14
Chicken Tempura Delight, '85 66
Chicken Terrine, Vegetable-, '83 224
Chicken Wings, Broiled, '80 149
Chicken Wings, Honey-Glazed, '91 251
Chicken Wings, Sweet-and-Sour, '90 206
Chicken Wings, Teriyaki, '85 300; '86 18
Chile-Sausage Squares, '86 297
Chiles Rellenos, Bite-Size, '87 246
Chili in Pastry Cups, '90 68
Chips with Guacamole Spread, Homemade Texas, '90 119
Chocolate-Almond Cream, '91 108
Chocolate Bites, Snowy, '90 47
Chocolate-Dipped Horns, '93 197
Chocolate-Peanut Butter Snacks, '90 226
Chocolate-Sesame Sticks, '91 316
Chutney Roll, '83 259
Chutney with Cream Cheese, Cranberry-Amaretto, '87 244
Cinnamon Wafers, '84 324
Clam Crisps, '80 151
Clam Puffs, '90 60
Clams Casino, '81 125
Clams Oreganata, '85 104
Cocktail Puffs, '91 106

Appetizers (*continued*)

Confetti Appetizers, **'84** 191
Corn Salsa, Spicy, **'93** 322
Crab Bites, Spicy, **'91** 165
Crab Casserole, Easy, **'93** 270
Crab Crisps, **'79** 63
Crab, Devilish Deviled, **'85** 264
Crabmeat Balls, **'88** 150
Crabmeat, Chafing Dish, **'89** 284
Crabmeat Hors d'Oeuvre, **'94** 236
Crabmeat Rémoulade, **'93** 280
Crabmeat Topping, **'91** 64
Crab Meltaways, Broiled, **'93** 287
Crab Mold, **'85** 318
Crab Puffs, **'80** 20; **'84** 269
Crab Snacks, **'83** 93
Crab-Zucchini Bites, **'84** M216
Cracker Bread, Sesame, **'87** 2
Crackers, Critter, **'93** 193
Crackers, Easy Bisque, **'83** 252
Crackers, Fennel-Rye, **'87** 2
Crackers, Florida, **'86** 179
Crackers, Hot Nut, **'90** 206
Cracker Snackers, **'86** 229; **'93** 197
Crackers, Oatmeal-Wheat Germ, **'84** 236
Crackers, Olive-Rye Snack, **'84** 191
Crawfish on Eggplant, Soft-Shell, **'88** 222
Crostini, Christmas, **'94** 318
Crostini, Hot Artichoke, **'94** 319
Crunchy Munchies, **'94** 196
Cucumber Delights, **'84** 117
Cucumber Fingers, Fried, **'86** 146
Cucumber Rounds, **'88** 78
Cucumber Sandwiches, **'94** 14
Cucumber Vichyssoise, **'94** 90
Date-Nut Ball, **'92** 326
Dates, Apricot-Stuffed, **'80** 250
Dips
  Almond Cream Dip with Strawberries, **'92** 164
  Almond Delight Dip, **'90** 226
  Antipasto Dip, **'93** 313
  Apple Dip, **'93** 205
  Apricot Dip, **'86** 178
  Artichoke Dip, Deluxe, **'80** 87
  Artichoke Dip in a Bread Basket, **'93** 13
  Artichoke Dip, Mexican, **'90** 292
  Artichoke Dip, Seasoned Mayonnaise, **'80** 87
  Artichoke-Seafood Dip, Hot, **'80** 241
  Artichoke Seafood Dip, Hot, **'85** M212
  Avocado Dip, **'80** 285; **'81** 57, 306
  Avocado Dip, "Bring-Home-the-Bacon," **'92** 80
  Avocado Dip, Zippy, **'82** 9; **'83** 69
  Bacon-and-Tomato Dip, **'90** 147
  Bacon Dip, **'82** 59
  Bacon Dip, Zesty, **'92** 156
  Bacon-Guacamole Dip, **'85** 25
  Basket, Dips and Dippers in a, **'83** 171
  Bean Dip, **'89** 97
  Bean Dip, Hotshot, **'87** 195
  Bean Dip, Prairie Fire, **'80** 195
  Beau Monde Dip in Rye Bread, Party, **'83** 127
  Beef Dip, Chipped, **'88** M8
  Beef Dip, Hot Cheesy, **'80** 85
  Black-Eyed Pea Dip, **'81** 8

Blue Cheese Dip, **'80** 285; **'83** 169; **'93** 313
Braunschweiger-and-Beer Dip, **'85** 69
Broccoli Dip, Cheesy, **'83** 92
Broccoli-Garlic Dip, **'82** 59
Brown Sugar Dip with Fruit, Buttery, **'90** 243
Cabbage, Dock Dip in, **'86** 179
Cheddar-Bacon Dip, **'89** M119
Cheese-and-Chile Dip, **'83** 31
Cheese and Crab Dip, Hot, **'81** 261
Cheese-Bean Dip, **'85** 208
Cheese-Crab Dip, **'91** 200
Cheese Dip, Hot, **'91** 171
Cheese Dip, Meaty, **'82** 59; **'92** 160
Cheese Dip, Seaside, **'85** 284
Cheese Dunk, Deviled, **'80** 265
Cheese-Garlic Dip, **'80** 192
Cheese-Herb Dip, **'89** 20
Chicken Dip, Hot, **'80** 86
Chile-Beef Dip, Hot, **'83** 218
Chile-Cheese Dip, **'87** 173
Chile con Queso, **'80** 194; **'81** 195
Chile con Queso Supreme, **'80** 265
Chile Dip, Hot, **'82** 248
Chile Sauce, Hot, **'92** 156
Chili-and-Black-Eyed Pea Dip, **'92** 155
Chili-and-Cheese Dip, **'89** 328
Chili-Cheese Dip, **'90** 225
Chili con Queso Dip, **'86** 81
Chili Dip, **'82** 161; **'88** 218; **'89** 47; **'91** 143
Chili Dip, Cheesy, **'80** 150
Chive-Cheese Dip, **'94** 62
Christmas Confetti Dip, **'92** 279
Clam Dip, **'79** 151; **'80** 265
Clam Dip, Hot, **'82** 59; **'89** 48
Clam Dip, Zesty, **'92** 25
Confetti Snack Dip, **'79** 107
Corn-and-Avocado Dip, Roasted, **'91** 279
Cottage Cheese Sun-Dried Tomato Dip, **'93** 13
Crab-and-Cheese Dip, Hot, **'94** 282
Crab Dip, Creamy, **'80** M135
Crab Dip, Festive, **'92** 285
Crab Dip, Hot, **'93** 269
Crab Dip, Oven-Baked, **'82** 59
Crab Dip, Tangy, **'83** 5
Crab Dip, Trawler, **'93** 238
Cranberry Fruit Dip, **'89** 60
Cranberry-Horseradish Dip, **'85** 65
Cream Cheese Dip, Fruited, **'88** 261
Cream Cheese-Onion Dip, **'79** 236
Creamy Texas Dip, **'94** 161
Crudité Dip, **'86** 105
Crudité Platter with Dip, **'84** 139
Cucumber Dipping Sauce, **'94** 47
Curried Dip, **'81** 262
Curry Dip, **'80** 84; **'81** 9; **'85** 132; **'86** 184; **'87** 25
Curry Dip and Vegetable Platter, **'89** 327
Curry Dip, Creamy, **'84** 206
Curry-Onion Dip, **'93** 313
Deviled Dip, **'87** 25
Dill Dip, **'80** 265; **'93** 330
Dilled Garden Dip, **'84** 324
Egg Dip, Festive, **'79** 285
Fiesta Dip, **'81** 206; **'92** 263
Fish Dip, Smoked, **'84** 46

Fondue, Nacho, **'94** 332
Fondue, Pub, **'94** 332
Fruit Dip, Coconut-Honey, **'84** 171
Fruit Dip, Creamy, **'84** 51
Fruit Dip, Fresh, **'80** 265
Fruit Dip, Heavenly, **'81** 160
Fruit Dip, Marshmallow, **'84** 171
Fruit Dip, Quick, **'90** 110
Fruit Dip, Sweet, **'89** 328
Garbanzo Dip, **'93** 94
Ginger Dip, **'94** 19
Grand Marnier Dip, **'86** 142
Green Goddess Dip, **'84** 159
Guacamole, **'79** 185; **'80** 74; **'83** 179; **'90** 205; **'91** 161
Guacamole, Black Bean, **'94** 277
Guacamole, Creamy, **'79** 91; **'83** 174
Guacamole Dip, **'86** 4
Guacamole in Shells, **'86** 74
Ham Dip, Creamy, **'93** 125
Herbal Dip, **'86** 14
Holiday Dip, **'83** 321; **'84** 289
Horseradish Dip, Creamy, **'94** 122
Hummas, **'92** 155
Hummus, Black-Eyed Pea, **'94** 123
Leek Dip, Creamy, **'86** 77
Lime-Dill Dip, **'92** 65
Mexican Appetizer, Chilled, **'87** 197
Mint Dip with Fresh Fruit, **'87** 146
Monster Mash Dip, **'93** 244
Mushroom Dip, Hot, **'89** 48
Nacho Dip, **'83** 239; **'93** M330
Nacho Dip, Layered, **'81** 261
Nacho Dip, Quick, **'90** 168
Olive-Relish Dip, **'84** 205
Onion Dip, **'94** 21
Onion Dip, Cheesy, **'83** 145
Onion Dip, Chunky, **'84** 257
Orange Cream, **'90** 126
Orange Dip, Creamy, **'84** 117; **'87** 247
Orange Dip, Spicy, **'85** 230
Orange Sour Cream Dip, **'79** 208
Oyster Dip, Smoked, **'79** 233
Parsley-Dill Dip with Fresh Vegetables, **'85** 79
Peach Dip, Creole, **'80** 142
Peachy Dip, **'92** 179
Peanut Butter Dip, **'86** 135
Peanut Butter-Honey Dip, **'85** 19
Peanut Butter Lovers' Dip, **'93** 162
Peas, Passion, **'89** 17
Pepperoncini-Cream Cheese Dip, **'91** 252
Pineapple Dip, Cheesy, **'80** 249
Pineapple-Ginger Dip, **'86** 104
Plantain Dip, **'92** 158
Ranch Dip, Skinny, **'93** 96
Ranch-Style Dip, **'90** 138; **'92** 148
Salsa, Chunky, **'90** 206
Salsa Cruda, **'87** 180
Salsa, Fresh Summer, **'87** 89
Salsa Picante, **'84** 108
Seafood Dip, **'79** 3
Seafood Dip, Hot Cheesy, **'84** 221
Seafood Dip, Super, **'90** 292
Shrimp Dip, **'86** 84; **'88** M261
Shrimp Dip, Hot, **'87** 190
Shrimp Dip, Quick, **'79** 153
Shrimp Dip, Zesty, **'80** 150
Six-Layer Dip, **'81** 160
Skinny Dip, Santa Fe, **'94** 137

Appetizers, Dips (continued)

Sour Cream Dip, '86 278
South-of-the-Border Dip, '81 235
Spinach-Cheese Dip, Hot, '89 48
Spinach con Queso, Easy, '88 101
Spinach Dip, '80 86; '86 159;
  '87 25, 214; '93 324
Spinach Dip, Cheesy, '82 59
Spinach Dip, Creamy, '88 132
Spinach Dip, Hot, '80 249
Spinach Dip in Cabbage, '82 155
Squash-Zucchini Dip, Yellow, '89 48
Sugar Snap Dip, '88 91
Summer Dip, '94 157
Taco Dip, Hot, '93 238
Tarragon Dip, '83 78
Tequila Dip, '91 166
Thick-and-Creamy Dip, '90 271
Tofu Dip, '86 109
Tostada Dip, '84 206
Tropical Dip for Fruit, '91 252
Tuna-Curry Dip, '84 31
Tuna Dip, Low-Cal, '87 25
Turnip Green Dip, '91 13
Turnip Green Dip with Jalapeño-Corn
  Muffins, Hot, '93 164
Vegetable Dip, '79 52; '82 161
Vegetable Dip, Creamy, '82 132;
  '83 99, 180
Vegetable Dip, Cucumber-Cheese,
  '83 128
Vegetable Dip, Fresh, '80 249
Vegetable Dip, Herb, '89 269
Vegetable Dip, Starburst, '82 248
Vegetable Dip, Tangy, '87 196
Vegetable Dip, Zippy, '84 256
Vegetable Garden Dip, '85 215
Water Chestnut Dip, '80 86; '86 183
Yogurt Dip, '94 21
Yogurt Dip, Fruited, '84 171
Yogurt Herring Dip, '80 232
Zesty Party Dip, '83 259
Drummettes, Ginger-Garlic Appetizer,
  '93 157
Eggplant Appetizer, '83 187
Eggplant Caviar, '88 262
Eggplant, Cheesy Fried, '90 75
Eggplant, Fried Parmesan, '87 166
Egg Rolls, '86 81
Egg Rolls, Chiles Rellenos, '86 296
Eggrolls, Shrimp and Pork, '82 240; '83 18
Egg Rolls, Vegetarian, '86 148
Empanadas, '92 156
Endive Boats, '84 80
Endive with Caviar, '93 118
Escargots Provençal, '82 238; '83 156
Eye-of-Round, Burgundy, '90 243
Fast Goodies, '84 206
Fondue, Fruitcake, '84 258
Frankfurter Appetizers, Bourbon, '85 207
Franks, Pickled Party, '83 174
Franks, Saucy Appetizer, '84 M12
Franks, Tipsy, '85 52
Frog Legs, Crispy, '80 99
Fruit and Cheese Tray, '83 171
Fruit Bowl, Sparkling Fresh, '80 146
Fruit Cascade, '86 104
Fruit Cup, Appetizer, '86 131
Fruit Kabobs, '86 181

Fruit Kabobs with Coconut Dressing, '87 251
Fruit with Curried Rum Sauce, Tropical,
  '91 164
Fruit with Dressing, Chilled, '85 222
Fruit with Honey-Sour Cream Dip, Fresh,
  '90 180
Gorp, Elf, '90 270
Gorp, Fancy, '89 253
Granola, '93 197
Granola, Fabulous, '92 213
Granola Gorp, '89 59
Granola, Nutty, '90 95
Green Onion Teasers, '82 42
Guacamole Mold, '86 184
Ham-and-Cheese Balls, Fried, '84 221
Ham Appetillas, '93 63
Ham-Filled Party Puffs, '84 116
Ham Rolls, '79 153
Ham Rolls, Party, '85 318
Ham Tapas, Garlic-, '92 175
Ham Turnovers, Chile-, '88 64
Ham Turnovers, Party, '82 39
Ham Twists, Deviled, '82 86
Hawaiian Dream Boats, '86 151
Hazelnuts, Curried, '93 301
Honey-and-Spice Crunch, '94 290
Horseradish Squares, Baked, '92 24
Hot Munch, Oriental, '87 8
Jalapeños, Fiery Fried Stuffed, '90 118
Jalapeños, Shrimp-Stuffed, '88 115
Jezebel Sauce, '93 331
June Bugs, '85 11
Lettuce Folds, Thai, '94 47
Links, Cocktail Smoky, '90 168
Meatballs
  Bacon-Wrapped Meatballs, '79 81
  Brandied Meatballs, '83 78
  Burgundy-Bacon Meatballs, '80 283
  Chafing Dish Meatballs, '81 260
  Chestnut Meatballs, '79 110
  Cocktail Meatballs, '79 63, 207
  Flavorful Meatballs, '84 206
  German Meatballs, Crisp, '92 326
  Ham Balls, '86 256
  Ham Balls, Appetizer, '82 39
  Polynesian Meatballs, '80 207
  Saucy Party Meatballs, '80 149
  Sauerkraut Meatballs, '86 257
  Spiced Meatballs, '79 284
  Sweet-and-Sour Meatballs, '82 247
  Sweet-and-Sour Party Meatballs,
    '79 233
  Tamale Meatballs, '80 194
  Venison Sausage Balls, '80 42
  Zesty Meatballs, '80 250
Melon Balls, Minted, '87 162
Melon, Berry-Filled, '86 93
Mints, Party, '81 119
Mirliton Balls, '90 217
Mix, Cereal Snack, '93 129
Mix, Creole Snack, '91 171
Mix, Crunchy Rice, '85 327
Mix, Crunchy Snack, '93 94
Mix, Dried Fruit, '92 22
Mix, Granola Snack, '86 229
Mix, Mexicali Snack, '86 230
Mix, Nutty Snack, '92 22
Mix, Party, '87 257
Mix, Quick Party, '83 92
Mix, Raisin-Nut Party, '83 60
Mix, Sea-and-Ski Cocktail, '90 319

Mix, Snack, '89 19
Mix, Snack-Attack Party, '84 328
Mix, Spicy Party, '81 M138
Mousse, Catfish, '92 327
Mousse, Caviar, '82 71; '83 258; '85 86
Mousse, Crab, '79 117
Mousse, Crabmeat, '90 190; '91 244
Mousse, Horseradish, '84 126
Mousse, Irresistible Salmon, '79 284
Mousse, Mustard, '84 127; '86 184
Mousse, Oyster, '81 245
Mousse, Salmon, '83 79
Mousse, Salmon Dill, '81 21
Mousse, Shrimp, '87 196, 251
Mousse, Smoked Oyster, '84 320
Mousse, Tuna, '80 275
Munchies, Reindeer, '91 276
Mushroom-Almond Pastry Cups, '88 210
Mushroom Appetizers, Stuffed, '88 210
Mushroom Caps, Crab-Stuffed, '84 160
Mushroom Caps, Marinated, '83 128
Mushroom Caps, Vegetable, '81 246
Mushroom Delight, Stuffed, '87 281
Mushroom Logs, '84 206
Mushroom Rollups, '85 318
Mushrooms, Black Olive-Stuffed, '86 258
Mushrooms, Cheese 'n' Bacon-Stuffed,
  '86 258
Mushrooms, Crab-Stuffed, '81 190
Mushrooms, Crawfish-Stuffed, '86 258
Mushrooms, Drunk, '83 174
Mushrooms, Easy Marinated, '86 217
Mushrooms, Elegant Cheese-Stuffed, '81 57
Mushrooms, Flavor-Stuffed, '85 288
Mushrooms, French-Fried, '82 78
Mushrooms, Italian Sausage-Stuffed, '83 127
Mushrooms, Marinated, '80 82, 270;
  '86 135; '91 306; '92 328
Mushrooms, Marinated Herb, '86 327
Mushrooms, Parmesan Stuffed, '83 115
Mushrooms, Pâté-Stuffed, '85 118
Mushrooms, Pecan-Stuffed, '84 261
Mushrooms, Pesto-Stuffed, '86 150
Mushrooms, Pistachio-Stuffed, '86 141
Mushrooms, Ricotta-Stuffed, '85 20
Mushrooms, Sausage-Stuffed, '80 248;
  '91 164
Mushrooms, Seasoned Stuffed, '84 206
Mushrooms, Shrimp-Stuffed, '80 M135
Mushrooms, Spinach-Stuffed, '86 81;
  '88 131, M261; '89 M133
Mushrooms, Stuffed, '79 212; '81 239;
  '83 13, 66, 126, 136; '93 172
Mushrooms Stuffed with Crab, '82 249
Mushrooms, Tipsy, '84 M216
Mushrooms with Stems, '86 258
Mushrooms with Tartar Sauce, French-Fried,
  '86 233
Mushroom Tarts, '88 161
Mushroom Tarts, Hot Sherried, '83 78
Nachos, Best-Ever, '79 91
Nachos, Chicken, '84 244
Nachos, Commissary Barbecue, '91 171
Nachos, Easy, '84 30
Nachos, Make-Ahead, '80 M135
Nachos, South Texas, '93 321
Nachos Supreme, '81 306
Nachos, Tex-Mex, '89 97
Nachos, Turkey, '90 118
Nectarine Cocktail, '85 107
Nibbles, Party, '90 249

Appetizers (*continued*)

Nuts, Chesapeake, '93 269
Nuts, Deviled, '93 118
Nuts, Hot Chili, '81 254
Nuts, Nippy, '93 301
Nuts, Sherry-Orange, '86 M289
Nuts, Spiced, '84 257; '91 M316
Nuts, Spicy, '82 161
Nuts, Spicy Curried, '82 250
Olive Quiche Appetizers, '86 159
Olives, Herb-Marinated, '92 176
Olives, Lemon-Garlic, '94 118
Onion Blossom, '94 226
Onion Crescent Crunch Sticks, '90 206
Orange-Berry Appetizer, '85 81
Orange Halves, Broiled, '85 288
Oyster Nachos, Texas, '87 39
Oysters à la Casino, '80 296
Oysters Annapolis, '89 195
Oysters, Barbecued, '82 247
Oysters Bienville, Baked, '90 27
Oysters Buccaneer, '87 40
Oysters Chesapeake, '92 254
Oysters, Crabmeat Stuffed, '94 328
Oysters, Creamed, '92 254
Oysters in Patty Shells, '85 257
Oysters Italiano, Baked, '89 97
Pasta Bites, Pesto-Cheese, '87 251
Pastry, Processor, '87 67
Pâtés
    Black-Eyed Pea Pâté, '91 12; '93 97
    Braunschweiger Pâté, '83 251
    Champignon, Pâté de, '93 171
    Cheese Pâté, Four-, '89 284
    Cheese Pâté, Layered, '86 105
    Chicken Liver Pâté, '79 153; '81 235;
        '83 108; '84 205; '88 M132
    Chutney-Cheese Pâté, '84 152
    Cognac, Pâté with, '86 159
    Country Pâté, '86 66
    Crab Pâté, '79 233
    Cream Cheese Pâté, '80 154
    Duck Liver Pâté, '79 227
    Duck Pâté, '79 226
    en Croûte, Pâté, '86 65
    Ham Pâté, '85 279
    Lentil Pâté, '92 285
    Liver-Cheese Pâté, '85 276
    Liver Pâté with Madeira Sauce, '93 323
    Maison, Pâté, '84 222
    Mock Pâté, '87 251
    Mushroom Pâté, '89 157
    Pastry, Pâté, '86 65
    Pork Pâté with Spinach and Cream,
        '83 224
    Shrimp Pâté with Dill Sauce, '85 39
    Spread, Quick Pâté, '84 117
    Turkey-Mushroom Pâté in Pastry,
        '92 327
    Vegetable-Chicken Pâté, '86 66
    Wine Pâté, '90 36
Pea Appetizers, Sugar Snap, '86 115
Peanuts, Sugared, '82 249
Pears, Pineapple-Honey, '86 94
Peas and Dip, Crunchy Snow, '86 62
Peas, Crab-Stuffed Snow, '85 288
Peas, Stuffed Snow, '84 80
Peas with Dip, Sugar, '86 170
Pecans, Barbecued, '83 222

Pecans, Buttery Toasted, '88 77
Pecans, Christmas Eve, '91 276
Pecans, Coffee 'n' Spice, '88 256
Pecans, Curried, '91 208
Pecans, Hot-and-Spicy, '89 161
Pecans, Hot Pepper, '85 4
Pecans, Orange, '87 292
Pecans, Pepper, '87 137; '93 79
Pecans, Southern Salted, '80 285
Pecans, Spiced, '79 296; '80 31
Pecans, Spicy, '93 279
Pecans, Sugar and Spice, '82 297
Pecans, Sugar-and-Spice, '86 121
Pecans, Sweet-and-Spicy, '92 321
Pecans, Toasted, '84 321; '86 229
Pecans, Toasted Chili, '85 154
Pepper Feet, '93 258
Pepperoni Rolls, Ground-, '83 244
Peppers, Marinated Roasted, '92 176
Peppers with Balsamic Vinaigrette, Roasted,
    '94 128
Pesto Rounds, Toasted, '94 289
Pickles, French-Fried, '82 77
Pickles, Fried Dill, '84 206
Pineapple and Strawberries, Skewered,
    '84 251
Pineapple Delight, Fresh, '79 111
Pineapple Spritz, '86 94
Piroshki, '92 84
Pita Bread Triangles, '88 211
Pita Chips, '89 19; '91 138
Pita Pizza Snack, '94 193
Pita Wedges, Garlic, '93 98
Pizza-Burger Snacks, '84 30
Pizza Horns, '89 214
Pizza Party Snacks, '86 262
Pizzas, Appetizer, '89 M118
Pizzas, Cocktail, '79 110
Pizza Slices, '84 269
Pizza Snacks, Tasty Little, '79 248
Pizzas, Pita, '89 19
Pizza Squares, '87 168
Pizzas, Quick Little, '88 227
Pizza Turnovers, Little, '85 327
Pizzettes, Party, '80 192
(Plantain Chips), Tostones de Plátano,
    '92 158
Pork Rounds, Sesame, '89 122
Pork Strips, Marinated, '92 219
Potatoes, Ham-Stuffed New, '88 211
Potato-Pea Soup, '94 90
Potato Shell Appetizers, '89 M119
Potato Skins, Baked, '86 81
Potato Skin Snack, '91 18
Pretzels, Chewy Soft, '87 159
Pretzels, Homemade, '84 159
Pretzels, Soft, '83 18
Pretzels, Whole Wheat, '89 20
Puff Nibbles, '84 191
Puffs, Cajun Hot, '94 277
Quiche, South-of-the-Border, '93 321
Quiche Squares, '84 222
Quiches, Tarragon Cocktail, '84 127
Raisin-Granola Treats, '92 22
Raspberry Party Puffs, '90 170
Ravioli, Sweet, '91 107
Relish Tree, Christmas, '84 257
Reubens, Party, '90 61
Riblets, Sweet-and-Sour, '85 276
Rice Balls, '81 51
Rosettes, Savory, '91 107

Rumaki, '80 136
Rye Appetizers, Party, '86 262
Salami Rollups, '90 226
Salmon Ball, '80 149; '86 262
Salmon, Drizzled Smoked, '88 91
Salmon Log, '81 22
Salmon Party Roll, '83 127
Samosas, '89 266
Samurai 'shrooms, '93 258
Sandwiches, Apple Party, '92 234
Sandwiches, Asparagus Spear, '84 165
Sandwiches, Bread Basket of, '86 126
Sandwiches, Calla Lily, '91 106
Sandwiches, Cucumber, '90 81
Sandwiches, Curried Tea, '91 314
Sandwiches, Dainty Cucumber, '81 119
Sandwiches, Double-Filled Party, '93 159
Sandwiches, Stacking, '86 127
Sandwiches, Victoria, '94 16
Sandwiches, Watercress, '90 82
Sandwich Wreath, Festive, '86 333
Sausage-Apple Balls, '90 85
Sausage-Bacon Rollups, '88 51
Sausage-Mushroom-Phyllo Bites, '89 284
Sausage Party Ryes, '89 315
Sausage Pinwheels, '80 209; '93 238
Sausage Quesadillas, '90 118
Sausage, Sweet-and-Sour, '88 296
Sausages with Mustard Sauce, Smoked,
    '81 56
Scallop Appetizer, '86 155
Scallop Appetizers, Flaky, '86 327
Scallops, Bacon-Wrapped, '87 94
Seafood Appetizer, Layered, '88 2
Seafood Mold, Chilled, '86 70
Seafood Tartlets, '87 247
Sesame Bites, '88 67
Seviche Cocktail, '83 258
Shrimp-and-Black Bean Tostadas, '93 204
Shrimp and Cucumber, Marinated, '91 166
Shrimp Balls, Curried, '94 180
Shrimp Bayou, '88 261
Shrimp Cocktail, '87 173
Shrimp, Coconut-Beer, '85 230
Shrimp Conga, Rock, '80 2
Shrimp, Dilled, '88 150
Shrimp Dippers, '84 324
Shrimp, Icy Marinated, '84 215
Shrimp-in-a-Pickle, '86 326
Shrimp Kabobs, '80 150
Shrimp Kabobs, Appetizer, '91 251
Shrimp, Key West, '94 278
Shrimp Manale, '86 268
Shrimp Miniquiches, '87 146
Shrimp Mold, '87 94
Shrimp Mold with Asparagus, '93 214
Shrimp, Pickled, '94 182
Shrimp-Pineapple Appetizer, '85 80
Shrimp Pizza Wedges, '89 158
Shrimp Rémoulade, '83 173
Shrimp, Salsa Picante with, '92 210
Shrimp, Sherried Garlic, '92 175
Shrimp, Spicy Boiled, '84 289
Shrimp Toast, '86 91
Shrimp Tree, '83 320; '84 288; '85 318
Shrimp with Cocktail Sauce, Boiled, '79 151
Shrimp with Herbed Jalapeño Cheese,
    '87 112
Shrimp, Zesty Marinated, '87 173
Snackwiches, '88 172
Spinach-Filled Phyllo Triangles, '84 52

Appetizers *(continued)*

Spinach Madeleine in Chafing Dish, **'85** 319
Spinach-Mushroom Cheesecake, **'92** 326
Spinach Quichelets, **'87** 67
Spinach Quiches, Miniature, **'82** 38
Spinach-Ricotta Phyllo Triangles, **'88** 212
Spinach Squares, **'88** 131
Spinach Strudels, **'93** 249
Spinach Supreme, Layered, **'82** 38
Spinach Tarts, **'82** 249
Spinach Triangles, Phyllo-, **'87** 53
Spreads and Fillings
   Aloha Spread, **'83** 93
   Antipasto Spread, **'81** 25
   Apple-Date Spread, **'91** 231; **'92** 67
   Apricot Brie Spread, **'86** 275
   Apricot-Cream Cheese Spread, **'82** 161;
     '87 158
   Artichoke-Crab Spread, Hot, **'85** 81
   Artichoke Hearts with Caviar, **'79** 142
   Artichoke-Parmesan Spread, **'92** 95
   Artichoke Spread, Chunky, **'89** 98
   Artichoke Spread, Hot, **'79** 110
   Beef Spread, Hot, **'83** 50; **'84** M216
   Beer Cheese Spread, **'81** 160; **'94** 123
   Beer-Cheese Spread, **'85** 69
   Black-Eyed Pea Spread, **'86** 77
   Blue Cheese Spread, **'90** 215
   Boursin Cheese Spread, Buttery,
     '94 301
   Boursin Cheese Spread, Garlic, **'94** 301
   Braunschweiger-Onion Spread, **'79** 82
   Broccamoli Curry Spread, **'88** 55
   Caraway Spread, **'85** 276
   Carrot Spread, Nutty, **'94** 123
   Caviar-Artichoke Mound, **'91** 244
   Caviar-Cream Cheese Spread, **'84** 256
   Caviar Spread, Creamy, **'92** 58
   Cheese-and-Orange Filling, **'93** 159
   Cheese-Horseradish Spread, **'84** 222
   Cheese-Olive Spread, **'79** 82
   Cheese Spread, **'86** 135
   Cheese Spread, Confetti, **'84** 256
   Cheese Spread, Creamy Sweet, **'79** 264
   Cheese Spread, German, **'79** 82
   Cheese Spread, Hawaiian, **'87** 158
   Cheese Spread, Make-Ahead, **'93** 324
   Cheese Spread, Mexican, **'90** 119
   Cheese Spread, Tipsy, **'80** 150
   Cheese Spread, Zippy, **'85** 4
   Cheesy Beer Spread, **'87** 196
   Chicken Salad Party Spread, **'88** M8
   Chicken Spread, Festive, **'87** 158
   Chicken Spread, Tasty, **'84** 193
   Chili Cheese Spread, **'93** 242
   Chive-Mustard Spread, **'91** 12
   Chocolate Chip Cheese Loaves, **'91** 299
   Chutney Spread, Curried, **'89** 283
   Clam Spread, Creamy, **'91** 274
   Coconut-Cranberry Cheese Spread,
     '92 328
   Corned Beef Spread, **'87** 196
   Crabmeat-Horseradish Spread, **'90** 292
   Crabmeat Spread, **'79** 81
   Crabmeat Spread, Layered, **'83** 127
   Crab Soufflé Spread, **'85** 4
   Crab Spread, **'93** 167
   Crab Spread, Baked, **'80** 86
   Crab Spread, Superb, **'81** 235

Cream Cheese Filling, **'90** 170
Cream Cheese Spread, Deviled, **'81** 235
Cream Cheese Spread, Fruited,
   '91 306; **'93** 79
Cream Cheese Spread, Nutty, **'89** 327
Cucumber Spread, **'79** 295; **'80** 31
Edam-Sherry Spread, **'84** 257
Egg Mound, Frosted, **'79** 33
Eggplant-Mushroom Spread, **'92** 156
Egg, Sour Cream, and Caviar Spread,
   '85 279
Fruit and Cheese Spread, **'81** 245
Fruit-and-Cheese Spread, Nutty,
   '87 246
Fruit Spread, **'85** 135
Garden Spread, **'86** 135
Garlic Spread, **'85** 111
Gouda Cheese Spread, **'90** 36
Green Onion-Cheese Spread, **'92** 24
Gruyère-Apple Spread, **'81** 160
Guacamole Spread, **'90** 119
Ham and Pimiento Spread, **'80** 285;
   '81 56
Ham Spread, Cold, **'82** 248
Ham Spread, Country, **'87** 8
Hearts of Palm Spread, **'90** 293
Herb-Cheese Spread, **'91** 124
Herb-Cream Cheese Spread, **'83** 24
Honey-Nut Spread, **'87** 157
Horseradish Spread, **'90** 243
Italian Spread, **'85** 135
Jalapeño-Cheese Spread, **'82** 248
Liver Spread, **'89** 161
Liver Spread, Sherried, **'80** 86
Mullet Spread, **'94** 159
Mushroom Spread, Hot, **'81** 190
Olive Spread, Creamy, **'81** 290
Olive Spread, Tomatoes with, **'85** 114
Oyster Spread, Smoked, **'91** 64
Party Bread Spread, **'82** 161
Peanut Butter Spread, **'92** 21
Pear-Cream Cheese Spread, **'93** 80
Pepper Spread, Roasted, **'94** 123
Pimiento Cheese, Hot, **'87** 173
Radish Spread, Fresh, **'84** 166
Raisin Spread, Creamy, **'90** 36
Salmon-and-Horseradish Spread,
   '87 146
Salmon Spread, **'81** 149
Salmon Spread, Smoked, **'84** 324
Seafood Spread, **'86** M58; **'87** 146
Shrimp Spread, **'81** 306; **'85** 135;
   '87 111; **'93** 205
Shrimp Spread, Chunky, **'85** 300;
   '86 18
Shrimp Spread, Curried, **'87** 158
Shrimp Spread, Tempting, **'79** 57
Shrimp Spread, Zippy, **'90** 36
Smoked Fish Spread, **'92** 305
Sombrero Spread, **'87** 111
Spinach-Bacon Spread, **'92** M310
Spinach Spread, **'88** 132
Spinach Spread, Savory, **'82** 180
Sweet 'n' Sour Spread, **'86** 184
Swiss Cheese Spread, **'90** 60
Tomato-Cheese Spread, **'81** 157
Tomato-Cheese Spread, Dried, **'90** 204
Tomato-Cheese Spread, Fiery, **'87** 196
Tomato Spread, **'94** 123
Tuna Spread, **'91** 305
Tuna Spread, Chunky, **'89** 147

Turkey Party Spread, **'83** 282
Turkey Spread, Curried, **'92** 16
Vegetable Party Spread, **'84** 166
Vegetable Sandwich Spread, **'85** 135
Vegetable Spread, **'90** 144
Vegetable Spread, Garden, **'93** 184
Watercress Spread, **'88** 103
Whitefish Spread, Smoked, **'92** 58
Squash Nosh, **'90** 147
Stalks, Splendid, **'93** 258
Steak-and-Chestnut Appetizers, Marinated,
   '84 323
Steak, Marinated Flank, **'83** 258; **'88** 262
Strawberries with Chocolate Cream, **'85** 81
Strawberries with Lemon Cream, **'90** 170
Strawberries with Walnuts, Stuffed,
   '85 122
Sugar Plums, **'92** 281
Sweet Potato Chips, **'91** 138; **'93** 332
Sweet Potato Chips with Blue Cheese,
   '93 290
Tabbouleh, **'88** 211
Taco Appetizer, Layered, **'84** 206
Tamale Balls, Tangy, **'89** 60
Tamales, Miniature, **'85** 154
Toasted Appetizers, **'94** 167
Toast Points, **'93** 270
Toast Strips, Seasoned, **'93** 98
Tomato Bites, **'84** 80
Tomatoes, Cucumber-Stuffed Cherry,
   '88 262
Tomatoes, Stuffed Cherry, **'84** 160;
   '88 95, 212; **'92** 25
Tomatoes, Tuna-Stuffed Cherry, **'89** 214
Tomato Soup, Appetizer, **'86** 258
Tomato Soup, Savory, **'94** 91
Tortilla Appetizers, Tex-Mex, **'86** 297
Tortilla Chips, **'91** 137
Tortilla Chips, Corn, **'91** 17
Tortilla Chips, Light, **'91** 257
Tortilla Dippers, Rolled, **'86** 4
Tortilla Española, **'92** 175
Tortilla Snacks, Pesto, **'89** 19
Tortilla Snack, Two-Cheese, **'90** 119
Tostados, Hot Chile Salsa with Homemade,
   '88 115
Tuna Mound, **'80** 276
Tuna-Pecan Ball, **'87** 94
Turkey Appetizers, **'91** 314
Turkey, Country-Fried Wild, **'94** 306
Turnovers, Meat, **'86** 326
Vegetable Appetizer, Tarragon, **'83** 277
Vegetable Juice Appetizer, Hot, **'93** 324
Vegetable Nachos, **'91** 17
Vegetable Party Tray, Fresh, **'82** 122
Vegetables Italian, Marinated, **'90** 242
Vegetables, Marinated, **'94** 183
Veggie Bites, **'91** 171
Venison Tenderloin Appetizers, **'88** 249
Walnuts, Chinese Fried, **'81** 254
Wings, Hot Buffalo, **'87** 176
Wings, Satan's, **'87** 214
Wonton Chips, Baked, **'91** 138
Wonton Chips, Cinnamon-and-Sugar, **'91** 138
Wonton Chips, Garlic, **'91** 138
Wonton Chips, Lemon-and-Herb, **'91** 138
Wonton Nibbles, **'85** 287
Zucchini Bites, Scalloped, **'91** 165
Zucchini Caviar, **'88** 212
Zucchini French Fries, **'82** 78
Zucchini Fries, **'90** 147

Appetizers (continued)

Zucchini Hors d'Oeuvres, '80 151
Zucchini Pizzas, '88 212
Zucchini-Shrimp Appetizers, '89 311
Zucchini with Cocktail Sauce, French Fried,
  '86 146

Apples

Aspic, Sunshine Apple, '81 73
Bake, Apple-Carrot, '93 304
Bake, Apple-Cheese, '92 225
Baked Alaska, Apple, '80 226
Baked Apple Quarters, Honey-, '86 93
Baked Apples, '79 276; '86 40
Baked Apples à l'Orange, '90 280
Baked Apples, Easy, '92 22, 238
Baked Apples, Honey-, '83 234; '84 244
Baked Apples, Imperial, '82 273
Baked Apples, Maple, '85 232
Baked Apples, Orange-Pecan, '85 45
Baked Apples, Stuffed, '89 217
Baked Apples with Orange Sauce, '84 314
Baked Ham and Apples, '82 M237
Baked Mincemeat-Filled Apples, '80 276
Bake, Squash and Apple, '79 210
Bake, Sweet Potato-Apple, '83 25; '86 282
Balls, Sausage-Apple, '90 85
Bars, Apple Butter, '84 153
Beets and Apples, '80 137; '88 155
Berry Sparkler, Apple, '94 100
Betty, Apple Brown, '83 213
Betty, Pineapple-Apple, '85 46
Blue Cheese-Apple Sunburst, '94 245
Brandied Apples, '81 248
Brandied Apples and Cream, '82 M237
Bread, Apple, '79 205; '80 226
Bread, Apple Butter, '84 49; '86 69
Bread, Apple-Nut, '79 12; '85 281
Bread, Apple Pull-Apart, '86 330
Bread, Apple Swirl, '85 4
Bread, Banana-Apple, '85 250
Bread, Fresh Apple-Nut, '87 256
Bread, Zucchini-Apple, '87 255
Breakfast Delight, '93 195
Brownies, Frosted Apple, '86 216
Burgers, Apple, '86 137
Butter, Apple, '79 200; '81 217; '92 311
Butter, Half-Hour Apple, '81 203
Cabbage and Apples, Red, '85 32
Cabbage with Apples and Franks, '87 42
Cake, Apple, '83 312; '84 262
Cake, Apple Cider Pound, '84 10
Cake, Apple Coconut, '80 226
Cake, Apple Coffee, '81 249
Cake, Apple-Ginger Upside-Down, '94 180
Cake, Apple-Nut, '87 76
Cake, Apple-Pecan, '92 167
Cake, Apple-Pecan Coffee, '84 242
Cake, Apple Pie, '82 226; '86 301
Cake, Apple Slice, '85 93
Cake, Apple Spice, '92 225

Cake, Apple-Walnut, '94 242
Cake, Covered Apple, '89 317
Cake, Dried-Apple, '79 13
Cake, Dried Apple Stack, '85 242
Cake, Fresh Apple Coffee, '92 32
Cake, Fresh Apple-Date, '83 300
Cake, Golden Apple-Oatmeal, '86 301
Cake Squares, Apple-Date Dream, '85 10
Cake Squares, Apple-Orange, '84 150
Candied Red Apples, '81 217
Candy Apple Creations, '94 256
Candy Apples, '84 243
Caramel Apples, '79 220; '89 M231
Caramel Apples, Old English, '85 231
Caramel-Peanut Apples, '93 M244
Casserole, Apple-Cheese, '84 287
Casserole, Apple-Egg, '85 44
Casserole, Apple Ham, '79 213
Casserole, Cranberry-Apple, '83 311
Casserole, Squash-Apple, '79 209
Casserole, Sweet Potato-and-Apple, '94 280
Casserole, Sweet Potatoes-and-Apple,
  '90 228
Cheesecake, Dieter's Apple, '86 318
Chicken, Apple, '85 57
Chutney, Apple, '92 309
Chutney, Pear-Apple, '89 141
Chutney, Tomato-Apple, '84 180
Cider, Apple-Orange, '92 20
Cider, December, '91 260
Cider, Holiday, '82 264
Cider, Hot Apple, '90 21, 225
Cider, Hot Mexican, '87 213
Cider, Hot Mulled, '79 205; '84 323
Cider, Hot Spiced Apple, '84 318
Cider Ice, '83 162
Cider, Mulled, '91 209; '94 227
Cider, Mulled Apple, '92 208
Cider Nog, Hot Apple, '84 42
Cider, Red Apple, '80 259
Cider Sauce, '87 224
Cider, Sparkling Apple, '88 276
Cinnamon Apples, Rosy, '87 M37
Cinnamon Apples with Brandied Date
  Conserve, '85 315
Cobbler, Apple-Pecan, '84 M198
Cobbler, Apple Walnut, '79 154
Cobbler, Apple-Walnut, '81 248
Cobbler, Cranberry-and-Apple, '84 306;
  '90 294
Cobbler, Easy Apple, '83 174
Cobbler for Two, Apple, '85 261
Cobbler, New-Fashioned Apple, '91 221
Coleslaw, Apple, '89 195
Conserve, Apple-Cranberry, '82 308
Cooked Apples, '93 338
Cookies, Apple Butter Spice, '79 291
Cookies, Apple-Filled, '92 311
Cookies, Apple-Nut, '80 228
Cookies, Apple-Oatmeal, '85 215; '90 218
Cookies, Fresh Apple, '84 36
Cooler, Apple, '90 14
Cooler, Minted Apple, '88 169
Crisp, Apple, '84 122
Crisp, Apple-Cheese, '92 235
Crisp, Delicious Apple, '82 303
Crisp, Granola Apple, '85 78
Crisp, Oatmeal Cherry-Apple, '90 M16
Crisp, Orange-Apple, '80 295
Crisp, Tart Apple, '92 226
Crumble, Whole Wheat-Apple, '90 M213

Crunch, Apple-Cranberry, '86 300; '87 178
Crunch, Apple-Nut, '82 M238
Cupcakes, Apple-Nut, '82 279
Curried Apples, '93 252
Danish, Deep-Dish Apple, '86 161
Date-Nut Ring, Apple-, '90 212
Delight, Apple, '80 109
Dessert, Cranberry Apple, '80 253
Dessert, Creamy Dutch Apple, '91 19
Dessert, Honey-Baked Apple, '90 M213
Dip, Apple, '93 205
Dressing, Apple, '92 216
Dressing, Sausage-Apple, '93 305; '94 296
Dried Apple Side Dish, '92 226
Dumplings, Apple, '82 273
Dumplings, Old-Fashioned Apple, '84 226
Dumplings with Orange Hard Sauce, Apple,
  '88 224
Fillets, Apple-Carrot Stuffed, '88 M192
Filling, Apple, '85 5
Filling, Apple-Date, '83 301
Filling, Dried Apple, '85 242; '87 229
Flambé, Hot Apples and Rum, '92 88
Flan, Apple, '81 309
Foldovers, Apple, '84 136
Fritter Rings, Apple, '88 44
Fritters, Apple, '81 105; '82 273; '85 14
Fritters, Apple Holiday, '86 314
Glazed Apples, Honey-, '90 125
Glazed Apples, Orange-, '82 51
Goblins, Apple, '94 256
Golden Apples, '82 254
Honey-Yogurt Apples, '92 46
Ice, Cranberry-Apple, '82 290
Jelly, Apple, '82 149
Jelly, Apple-Mint, '87 134
Jelly, Crabapple, '79 120; '81 217
Juice, Hot Apple, '86 270
Juice, Nectarines in Apple, '83 183
Juice, Perky Cinnamon-Apple, '90 22
Julep, Apple, '86 103, 215
Kuchen, Apple, '79 24
Lemonade, Apple, '89 212
Limeade, Pink Apple, '89 46
Loaf, Fresh Apple, '82 206
Loaf, Spiced Apple, '79 215
Marmalade, Apple, '79 120
Melting Apples, '88 19
Mold, Cranberry-Apple, '89 277
Mousse, Cran-Apple, '93 255
Muesli, '89 208
Muffins, Apple, '83 96; '84 193; '87 23
Muffins, Apple-Bran, '85 M89
Muffins, Apple-Carrot, '91 213
Muffins, Apple-Cinnamon Oat Bran, '89 106
Muffins, Fresh Apple, '84 264
Muffins, Spiced Apple, '79 60
Muffins, Spicy Apple-Oat, '86 45
Omelet Stack, Apple, '94 50
Pancake, Apple-Filled, '86 96
Pancakes, Apple-Topped, '93 339
Pancakes with Cider Sauce, Spicy Apple,
  '87 224
Pie, American Apple, '91 197
Pie, Apple-Amandine, '89 215
Pie, Apple-Cheese, '85 284
Pie, Apple Cider, '84 227
Pie, Apple-Cream Cheese, '81 247
Pie, Apple Custard, '88 236
Pie, Apple-Lemon Chess, '86 220
Pie, Apple-Mincemeat, '85 316

Apples (continued)

Pie, Apple-Pear, '83 249
Pie, Apple-Raisin Brandy, '89 58
Pie, Autumn Apple, '79 205
Pie, Berry-Apple, '88 251
Pie, Blackberry-Apple, '87 130
Pie, Brandy-Apple, '86 301
Pie, Brandy Raisin-Apple, '83 192
Pie, Caramel-Pecan Apple, '85 247
Pie, Cornbread-Sausage-Apple, '87 171
Pie, Cran-Apple, '92 304
Pie, Cranberry-Apple, '79 264
Pie, Cranberry-Apple Holiday, '81 M269
Pie, Dutch Apple, '81 105; '82 273
Pie, Easy-Crust Apple, '87 11
Pie, Fresh Apple, '84 178
Pie, Grandmother's Apple, '87 212
Pie, Grated Apple, '83 304
Pie, Holiday Apple, '87 260
Pie, Mexican Apple, '94 97
Pie, Natural Pear-Apple, '88 226
Pie, No-Crust Apple, '88 204
Pie, Old-Fashioned Apple, '82 M299; '88 94
Pie, Red Apple, '79 282
Pies, Delicious Fried, '83 84
Pies, Fried Apple, '81 217; '86 302;
  '88 112, 225; '94 61
Pie, Tart Lemon-Apple, '80 100
Pie, Upside-Down Southern Apple, '88 226
Pie with Hot Cinnamon Sauce, Apple, '88 210
Piggy Apple, '94 194
Pinwheel, Quick Apple, '85 42
Poached Apples, Spicy, '90 M141
Poached Lemon Apples, Chilled, '86 182
Poppyseed Dressing, Apple Wedges with,
  '86 131
Pork Chops and Apples, Baked, '81 10
Pork Chops, Apple, '91 198
Pork Chops, Apple-Crumb Stuffed, '81 234;
  '82 26
Pork Chops, Apple-Glazed, '84 212; '87 35
Pork Chops, Apple-Kraut, '84 50
Pork Chops, Apple-Stuffed, '79 125
Pork Chops, Glazed Apple, '86 300
Pork Chops, Sherry-Apple, '88 40
Pork Chops, Spicy Apple, '87 230
Pork Chops with Apples, Parmesan, '93 338
Pork Chops with Crabapple Peaches, Broiled,
  '81 83
Pork Cutlets, Apple-Glazed, '92 181
Pork Loin with Apples and Mushrooms,
  Roast, '92 218
Pork Tenderloin, Apple-Ginger, '86 75
Potatoes, Apple-Glazed Sweet, '82 303
Potatoes, Apple-Stuffed Sweet, '88 207
Potatoes Stuffed with Apples, Sweet, '82 228
Pot Roast, Spicy Apple, '83 7
Pudding, Apple-Raisin Bread, '88 175
Pudding, Apple Rice, '91 217
Pudding with Hot Rum Sauce, Apple-Nut,
  '79 86
Punch, Apple-Tea, '85 82
Punch, Hot Apple, '84 324
Punch, Hot Spiced, '80 250
Quiche, Crustless Sausage-Apple, '87 70
Relish, Apple-Celery, '89 141
Relish, Cran-Apple, '84 300
Relish, Spicy Apple, '84 M323
Ribs, Apple Barbecued, '80 111

Rice, Apple-Cinnamon, '86 249
Rings, Apple, '85 232
Rings, Cinnamon Apple, '82 M237; '90 250
Rings, Cinnamon-Apple, '85 107
Rings, Fried Apple, '81 209
Rings, Honey Apple, '80 243
Roll, Apple, '82 178
Rolls, Apple-Phyllo, '88 213
Rolls, Luscious Apple, '88 225
Salad, Apple, '87 233
Salad, Apple-Apricot, '88 121
Salad, Apple-Beet, '91 237
Salad, Apple-Carrot, '85 22
Salad, Apple Cider, '83 123
Salad, Apple Crunch, '84 232; '86 331
Salad, Apple-Nut, '80 226
Salad, Apple Snow, '81 224
Salad, Blue Cheese-Pear-Apple, '81 224
Salad, Cheesy Apple, '86 301
Salad, Cherry-Apple, '86 31
Salad, Chicken-Apple, '90 216
Salad, Congealed Apple, '85 252
Salad, Congealed Waldorf, '82 80
Salad, Creamy Waldorf, '87 311
Salad, Crunchy Apple, '80 138
Salad, Curried Apple-Raisin, '80 24
Salad, Deluxe Waldorf, '83 81
Salad, Double Apple, '84 227
Salad, English Pea-and-Apple, '87 24
Salad, Fresh Apple, '81 207
Salad, Frozen Apple-Cream, '82 80
Salad, Frozen Waldorf, '79 126; '82 145
Salad, Grapefruit-Apple, '89 41
Salad Greens with Apple and Brie, '93 241
Salad, Ham-and-Apple, '88 139
Salad, Jiffy Waldorf, '88 100
Salad, Lemony Apple-Bran, '86 223
Salad Mold, Apple Cider, '85 54
Salad, New Wave Waldorf, '92 36
Salad, Old-Fashioned Waldorf, '81 295
Salad, Peanut-Apple, '80 5
Salad, Pineapple Waldorf, '92 97
Salad, Southern Classic Waldorf, '92 36
Salad, Spicy Apple, '85 215
Salad, Spinach-Apple, '90 89; '92 13
Salad, Stuffed Apple, '92 266
Salad, Stuffed Apple Ring, '91 198
Salad, Summer Apple, '90 149
Salad, Swiss-Apple, '84 81
Salad, Triple Apple, '88 122
Salad, Tropical Waldorf, '89 12
Salad, Turkey-Apple, '88 123; '90 181
Salad, Waldorf, '89 278
Salad, Wild Rice-Green Apple, '92 90
Salad with Blue Cheese Dressing, Apple,
  '87 103
Sandwiches, Apple, '79 164; '80 130
Sandwiches, Apple Breakfast, '92 332
Sandwiches, Apple-Cinnamon Breakfast,
  '85 298
Sandwiches, Apple Party, '92 234
Sauce, Apple Ambrosia, '89 95
Sauce, Apple-Cinnamon, '93 42
Sauce, Apple Dessert, '87 M165
Sauce, Apple-Horseradish, '82 229
Sauce, Cranberry-Apple, '92 203
Sauce, Spicy Apple Dessert, '82 177
Sausage Patties, Apples on, '82 120
Sautéed Apples, Onions, and Pears over
  Spinach, '94 212
Scalloped Apples, '84 70; '87 156

Scallop, Yam-and-Apple, '91 199
Sesame-Apple Toss, '88 21
Shells, Sweet Potatoes in Apple, '85 206
Shortcake, Quick Apple, '93 42
Shrub, Shenandoah Apple Juice, '79 282
Slaw, Apple-Carrot, '92 243
Slaw, Apple-Pineapple, '79 241
Slaw, Fresh Apple, '81 63
Slaw, Nutty Apple, '88 216
Slaw, Red Cabbage-and-Apple, '87 31;
  '91 309
Sorbet, Cran-Apple Spice, '93 153
Soup, Creamed Butternut-and-Apple,
  '88 228
Spareribs, Apple-Barbecue, '90 160
Sparkler, Apple-Berry, '93 104
Spiced Apples, '93 123
Spiced Apple Slices, '83 289
Spiced Apples, Skillet, '83 234; '84 244
Spread, Apple-Date, '91 231; '92 67
Spread, Gruyère-Apple, '81 160
Squares, Apple, '92 311
Squares, Sour Cream Apple, '82 262
Squash, Apple-and-Pecan-Filled, '88 228
Squash, Apple-Stuffed, '85 206
Squash, Apple-Stuffed Acorn, '83 296;
  '84 285
Squash, Apple-Stuffed Butternut, '81 232
Stir-Fry, Apple-Sesame-Chicken, '92 226
Strudel, Apple, '85 259; '89 267; '92 269
Stuffed Apples, Peanutty, '85 25
Stuffing, Apple-Crumb, '81 234; '82 26;
  '83 39
Sugar-Crusted Apples in Walnut-Phyllo
  Baskets, '93 210
Sundae, Hot Apple Spice, '92 239
Sundaes, Spicy Apple Ice Cream, '86 M195
Syrup, Spiced Apple, '79 114
Tart, Apple Cream, '84 207
Tart, Apricot-Apple Crumb, '94 60
Tart, Creamed Apple, '94 17
Tart, Deluxe Apple, '84 227
Tarte aux Pommes, La, '80 125
Tarts, Apple-Pecan, '80 282
Tart with Cheese Pastry, Apple, '88 225
Tea, Cranberry-Apple, '88 169
Tea, Hot Apple-Cinnamon, '87 57
Tea, Johnny Appleseed, '85 23
Toast, Apple, '81 278
Topping, Apple, '89 107
Topping, Apple-Nut, '93 162
Topping, Spicy Apple, '87 125
Turnovers, Baked Apple, '93 338
Turnovers, Delicious Apple, '86 25
Turnovers, Fried Apple, '81 161
Turnovers, Puffy Apple, '87 276
Veal Chops, Apple, '87 220
Vinaigrette, Spinach Salad with Apple-Onion,
  '94 276
Applesauce
Applesauce, '90 255
Bread, Applesauce-Honey Nut, '87 300
Bread, Applesauce Nut, '81 305
Bread, Applesauce-Pecan, '90 66
Bread, Bran-Applesauce, '84 229
Butter, Half-Hour Apple, '81 203
Cake, Applesauce, '80 270
Cake, Applesauce Carrot, '81 202
Cake, Applesauce-Oatmeal, '92 119
Cake, Applesauce-Spice, '83 42
Cake, Applesauce Spice, '89 296

Applesauce *(continued)*

Cake, My Favorite Applesauce, **'87** 263
Cakes, Applesauce Snack, **'88** 215; **'89** 20
Cake Squares, Applesauce, **'86** 8
Cake with Bourbon Frosting, Applesauce, **'88** 236
Doughnuts, Applesauce, **'81** 203
Doughnuts, Applesauce Drop, **'90** 70
Dressing, Apple, **'83** 181
Fluff, Applesauce, **'91** 173
Fruitcake, Applesauce, **'83** 258
Gingerbread, Applesauce, **'94** 179
Loaf, Brandy Applesauce, **'81** 263
Muffins, Applesauce, **'84** 284; **'91** 141
Muffins, Applesauce Spice, **'88** 236
Muffins, Bite-Size Applesauce, **'82** 104
Oatmeal, Applesauce, **'89** 108
Pancakes, Applesauce, **'79** 114
Pudding, Applesauce-Graham Cracker, **'81** 34
Ribs, Apple Barbecued, **'80** 111
Spicy Applesauce, **'82** 296
Squares, Applesauce-Spice, **'86** 248
Sweet Potatoes, Applesauce, **'91** 292; **'92** 256

Apricots
Baked Apricots, Delicious, **'82** 10
Bake, Sweet Potato-Apricot, **'85** 206
Balls, Apricot, **'79** 274
Balls, Crunchy Apricot, **'89** 307
Bars, Apricot, **'81** 247
Bars, Apricot-Oatmeal, **'86** 216
Bars, Apricot-Raisin, **'87** 32
Bread, Apricot-Nut, **'79** 24
Bread, Apricot-Orange, **'92** 285
Bread, Pineapple-Apricot, **'84** 7
Bread, Tangy Apricot, **'81** 249
Breakfast Dish, Sausage-Apricot, **'82** 10
Butter, Apricot, **'82** 308
Cake, Apricot-Almond Coffee, **'93** 26
Cake, Apricot Brandy Pound, **'83** 267
Carrots, Apricot, **'84** 6
Carrots, Apricot Glazed, **'80** 89
Chicken, Apricot, **'92** 12
Chicken Breasts, Apricot, **'88** 301
Cobble Up, Apricot, **'82** 138
Coffee Cake, Apricot Lattice, **'94** 48
Cookie Rolls, Apricot, **'80** 282
Cookies, Frosted Apricot, **'81** 192
Cooler, Apricot, **'81** 100
Cooler, Apricot Mint, **'90** 165
Cornish Hens, Apricot-Glazed, **'80** 84; **'87** 306
Cornish Hens, Apricot-Stuffed, **'84** 6
Cream, Peachy-Apricot, **'86** 163
Crescents, Apricot, **'90** 181
Curried Apricots, **'91** 315
Dates, Apricot-Stuffed, **'80** 250
Delight, Apricot, **'81** 42
Dip, Apricot, **'86** 178
Divinity, Apricot, **'83** 297
Dressing, Honeydew Salad with Apricot Cream, **'84** 191
Filling, Apricot, **'83** 84; **'86** 107; **'93** 316
Filling, Lemon-Apricot, **'90** 105
Flip, Apricot Fruit, **'91** 18
Freeze, Apricot, **'82** 10
Frosting, Apricot, **'81** 192
Frozen Apricot Fluff, **'86** 242

Glaze, Apricot, **'80** 280; **'82** 8; **'86** 197
Glaze, Apricot-Kirsch, **'87** 14
Glaze for Ham, Apricot, **'85** 256
Glaze, Stuffed Pork Chops with Apricot, **'89** M36
Glaze, Sweet Apricot, **'82** 304
Glaze, Sweet Potatoes with Apricot, **'89** 331
Ham and Apricots, **'90** 53
Ham, Apricot Baked, **'84** 160
Ham Slice, Apricot-Glazed, **'93** 252
Ice, Apricot Yogurt, **'81** 177
Jam, Golden Apricot, **'80** 31
Kolaches, Apricot, **'83** 84; **'94** 291
Loaf, Apricot-Cranberry, **'79** 235
Loaf, Apricot-Nut, **'81** 8
Loaf, Tasty Apricot-Nut, **'82** 10
Mousse, Apricot, **'82** 72; **'91** 297
Nectar, Hot Apricot, **'81** 265
Nectar, Mulled Apricot, **'86** 229
Noodle Kugel, Apricot, **'92** 251
Pastries, Apricot, **'83** 297
Pie, Apricot Surprise, **'88** 99
Pie, Dried Fruit, **'83** 249
Pies, Apricot Fried, **'86** 269
Pies, Special Apricot, **'94** 60
Pie, Yogurt-Apricot, **'85** 132
Pinwheels, Apricot, **'87** 276
Pork Chops, Apricot-Sauced, **'85** 22
Pork Chops, Apricot-Stuffed, **'86** 76; **'92** 219
Pork Chops, Curried Apricot, **'89** 191
Pork Chops, Mustard-Apricot, **'89** 225
Pork Loin, Apricot-Pecan Stuffed, **'94** 274
Pudding, Apricot Bread, **'85** 24
Punch, Apricot Spiced, **'80** 269
Rolls, Cheese-Apricot Sweet, **'90** 195
Salad, Apple-Apricot, **'88** 121
Salad, Apricot, **'81** 251; **'83** 123
Salad, Apricot Fruit, **'82** 132
Salad, Apricot Nectar, **'83** 218; **'87** 236
Salad, Creamy Apricot, **'85** 263
Salad, Frosted Apricot, **'80** 248
Salad, Spinach-Apricot, **'94** 63
Sauce, Apricot, **'82** 212; **'87** 172
Sauce, Apricot Ice Cream, **'91** 57
Sauce, Apricot-Walnut Hard, **'88** 153
Sauce, Fresh Cranberry-Apricot, **'87** 243
Shake, Apricot, **'84** 115
Sherbet, Apricot, **'81** 177; **'92** 164
Slush, Apricot, **'93** 205
Slush, Apricot Brandy, **'91** 278
Slush, Apricot-Citrus, **'88** 82
Soufflé, Baked Apricot, **'88** 267
Spread, Apricot Brie, **'86** 275
Spread, Apricot-Cream Cheese, **'82** 161; **'87** 158
Sweet Potatoes, Apricot, **'82** 228
Sweet Potatoes, Apricot-Glazed, **'81** 295
Syrup, Apricot Fruit, **'82** 10
Tart, Apricot-Apple Crumb, **'94** 60
Tarts, Apricot, **'79** 282; **'88** 281
Tea Cakes, Brandied Apricot, **'91** 241
Tea, Hot Spiced Apricot, **'88** 248
Torte, Apricot-Filled Chocolate, **'90** 107
Torte, Apricot Sponge, **'90** 59
Turnovers, Fried Apricot, **'86** 24
Wassail, Pineapple-Apricot, **'83** 275
Wonders, Apricot, **'93** 316

Artichokes
Antipasto Spread, **'81** 25
Appetizer, Artichoke-and-Shrimp, **'93** 271
Appetizer, Zesty Artichoke, **'80** 146

Artichokes, **'92** 107
Aspic, Tomato-Artichoke, **'84** 320; **'86** 92
au Gratin, Crab, Shrimp, and Artichoke, **'90** 240
Avocado Acapulco, **'83** 2
Baked Artichoke-Cheese Bottoms, **'94** 61
Baked Chicken and Artichoke Hearts, **'82** 260
Bake, Tomato-and-Artichoke Heart, **'85** 81
Beef with Artichokes, Creamed Dried, **'85** 81
Beef with Tomatoes and Artichokes, **'92** 282
Bread, Artichoke, **'93** 140
Casserole, Alii Artichoke, **'93** 294
Casserole, Asparagus-Artichoke, **'86** 279
Casserole, Brussels Sprouts-and-Artichoke, **'94** 279
Casserole, Italian Green Bean-and-Artichoke, **'85** 81
Casserole, Mushroom-Artichoke, **'87** 241
Casserole, Spinach and Artichoke, **'81** 103
Casserole, Spinach-Artichoke, **'88** 252; **'93** 44
Caviar, Artichoke Hearts with, **'79** 142
Chicken, Artichoke, **'81** 97
Chicken with Artichoke Hearts, **'88** 54
Chicken with Artichokes and Mushrooms, **'90** 35
Chicken with Artichokes, Sherried, **'87** 143
Chilled Artichokes with Lemon-Pepper Dressing, **'87** 55
Crabmeat with Artichoke Hearts, Creamed, **'93** 26
Crostini, Hot Artichoke, **'94** 319
Dip, Deluxe Artichoke, **'80** 87
Dip, Hot Artichoke-Seafood, **'80** 241
Dip, Hot Artichoke Seafood, **'85** M212
Dip in a Bread Basket, Artichoke, **'93** 13
Dip, Mexican Artichoke, **'90** 292
Dip, Seasoned Mayonnaise Artichoke, **'80** 87
Dressing, Artichoke, **'84** 126
Eggs Sardou, **'92** 93
Frittata, Artichoke Appetizer, **'92** 58
Herb-Mayonnaise Dip, Artichokes with, **'84** 67
Lemon, Artichoke Hearts with, **'90** 98
Marinated Artichoke Hearts, **'88** 95
Marinated Artichokes, **'87** 250; **'88** 41
Marinated Cucumbers and Artichokes, **'82** 111
Mold, Artichoke-Caviar, **'87** 239
Mound, Caviar-Artichoke, **'91** 244
Pasta with Artichoke Hearts, **'86** 209
Pasta with Catfish and Artichokes, **'90** 123
Phyllo Bites, Artichoke-Parmesan, **'87** 54
Pie, Artichoke, **'79** 25
Pizza with Artichoke and Prosciutto, **'87** 182
Quiche, Artichoke, **'91** 71
Ragout, Veal-and-Artichoke, **'94** 43
Relish, Jerusalem Artichoke, **'89** 197
Salad, Artichoke, **'86** 333
Salad, Artichoke-Chicken-Rice, **'94** 132
Salad, Artichoke-Pasta, **'94** 180
Salad, Artichoke-Rice, **'80** 178; **'81** 41; **'85** 81
Salad, Artichoke-Stuffed Tomato, **'82** 101
Salad, Artichokes with Orzo, **'88** M193
Salad, Artichoke-Tomato, **'82** 239
Salad, Asparagus-Artichoke, **'85** 162
Salad, Italian, **'87** 145
Salad, Marinated Artichoke, **'83** 241
Salad with Artichoke Hearts, Rice, **'80** 232

Artichokes *(continued)*

Salad with Artichokes, Chicken, **'86** 186
Salad, Zucchini-Artichoke, **'91** 229
Soup, Artichoke, **'89** 269
Soup, Artichoke Cream, **'94** 62
Soup, Chicken, Artichoke, and Mushroom, **'92** 324
Soup, Cream of Artichoke, **'82** 232
Soup, Louisiana Oyster-and-Artichoke, **'92** 81
Spread, Artichoke-Parmesan, **'92** 95
Spread, Chunky Artichoke, **'89** 98
Spread, Hot Artichoke, **'79** 110
Spread, Hot Artichoke-Crab, **'85** 81
Spring Artichokes, **'86** 62
Steamed Artichokes, **'81** 59
Strata, Artichoke-Cheese, **'90** 236
Stuffed Artichokes, **'79** 76; **'82** 92; **'91** 117
Stuffed Artichokes, Shrimp-, **'84** 67; **'87** 55
Stuffed Artichokes, Shrimp, **'94** 62
Stuffed with Shrimp and Scallops, Artichokes, **'84** 174
Veal with Artichoke Hearts, Lemon, **'87** 219
Vinaigrette, Artichokes, **'88** 101
Whole Cooked Artichokes, **'94** 61

Asparagus
Almond Asparagus, **'83** 86
Almond Butter, Asparagus with, **'84** 85
Almond Sauce, Asparagus with, **'91** 117
Basil Butter, Asparagus with, **'85** 40
Basil Sauce, Asparagus with, **'86** 33
Beef with Asparagus, **'90** 100
Caesar, Asparagus, **'88** 133
Cashew Butter, Asparagus with, **'87** 56
Casserole, Asparagus-and-English Pea, **'86** 324
Casserole, Asparagus and Peas, **'80** 152
Casserole, Asparagus-Artichoke, **'86** 279
Casserole, Asparagus-Pea, **'88** M294
Casserole, Asparagus-Spaghetti, **'80** 77
Casserole, Cheesy Asparagus, **'82** 281; **'83** 32
Casserole, Chicken-Asparagus, **'83** 76; **'84** 71
Casserole, Creamy Asparagus, **'80** 76
Casserole, Easy Asparagus, **'83** 255
Casserole, Turkey-Asparagus, **'86** 284
Cheesecake, Ham-and-Asparagus, **'90** 174
Company Asparagus, **'85** 82
Cream Sauce, Asparagus with, **'90** 291
Croquettes, Asparagus, **'85** 265
Curry Sauce, Asparagus with, **'90** 17
Cutlets, Asparagus, **'80** 147
Delight, Asparagus, **'82** 269
Delight, Ham-Asparagus, **'86** 48
Dilly Asparagus, **'88** 180

Dinner, Ham-Asparagus, **'80** M10
Eggs à la Asparagus, Creamed, **'81** 201
en Papillote, Shrimp with Asparagus, **'86** 145
Fettuccine, Ham-and-Asparagus, **'94** 84
Fish-Asparagus Divan, **'87** 128
Fried Asparagus, French-, **'79** 66; **'83** 46
Goat Cheese Sauce, Asparagus with, **'93** 116
Goldenrod, Asparagus, **'79** 66
Guacamole, Mock, **'93** 36
Ham Rolls, Asparagus, **'91** 117
Holiday Asparagus, **'85** 260
Jeweled Asparagus, **'80** 42
Lemon Butter, Asparagus in, **'80** M123
Lemon Butter, Asparagus with, **'87** M151
Lemon Sauce, Asparagus with, **'86** 62
Lemon-Sesame Asparagus, **'91** 31
Loaf, Asparagus-Pimiento, **'84** 86
Marinated Asparagus, **'81** 108; **'83** 46; **'84** 67, 86; **'86** 92; **'87** 74
Marinated Asparagus and Hearts of Palm, **'90** 91
Marinated Asparagus, Easy, **'81** 148
Marinated Asparagus Medley, **'91** 105
Marinated Asparagus Spears, **'88** 130
Mayonnaise, Asparagus with Hot Wine, **'81** 83
Meringue, Asparagus, **'88** 131
Mold, Asparagus, **'80** 104
Mold, Asparagus-Cucumber, **'85** 252
Mushrooms, Asparagus and, **'85** 108
Mustard Sauce, Chilled Asparagus in, **'88** 130
Orange Butter Sauce, Asparagus with, **'85** 43
Orange Sauce, Asparagus with, **'83** 46
Pasta with Shrimp and Asparagus, Angel Hair, **'92** 100
Pickled Asparagus, **'83** 46
Pilaf, Turkey-Asparagus, **'88** 200
Pork Arlo, **'87** 229
Prosciutto-Wrapped Asparagus, **'91** 98
Quiche, Asparagus-Tomato, **'88** 198
Quiche, Springtime, **'83** 122
Rarebit, Uptown Welsh, **'87** 279
Rice and Asparagus, **'93** 324
Rolls, Asparagus, **'79** 296; **'80** 31
Rolls, Chicken-Asparagus, **'86** M211
Rolls, Ham-Asparagus, **'79** 41
Rolls, Hot Asparagus, **'93** 329
Rollups, Asparagus, **'79** 63
Roll-Ups, Asparagus, **'84** 270
Roulade, Asparagus, **'86** 102
Salad, Asparagus, **'88** 121; **'94** 67
Salad, Asparagus-and-Egg, **'86** 305
Salad, Asparagus-and-New Potato, **'86** 69
Salad, Asparagus-Artichoke, **'85** 162
Salad, Asparagus-Chicken, **'89** 83
Salad, Asparagus-Horseradish, **'87** 80
Salad, Asparagus Mousse, **'86** 252
Salad, Congealed Asparagus, **'83** 260
Salad, Crab-and-Asparagus, **'92** 141
Salad, Creamy Lemon-Asparagus, **'93** 116
Salad Cups, Asparagus, **'83** 47
Salad, Easy Asparagus, **'88** 131
Salad, Marinated Asparagus, **'79** 20
Salad, Peas-and-Asparagus, **'83** 141
Salad, Tart Asparagus, **'81** 203
Salad, Tomato-Asparagus, **'92** 79
Salad Vinaigrette, Asparagus, **'88** 56
Salad with Asparagus, Curried Chicken, **'81** 36
Salad with Crabmeat-and-Asparagus, Congealed, **'84** 86

Sandwiches, Asparagus-and-Ham Melt, **'88** M96
Sandwiches, Asparagus Grill, **'79** 164; **'80** 130
Sandwiches, Asparagus Spear, **'84** 165
Sauce, Asparagus White, **'80** 147
Sauté, Asparagus-and-Mushroom, **'93** 115
Sautéed Asparagus, **'79** 66
Shrimp Mold with Asparagus, **'93** 214
Soufflé, Asparagus, **'79** 66; **'83** 265; **'89** 89
Soup, Asparagus, **'84** 67
Soup, Asparagus-Potato, **'85** 23
Soup, Cream of Asparagus, **'84** 111
Soup, Creamy Asparagus, **'94** 225
Sour Cream, Asparagus with, **'83** 46
Squares, Asparagus, **'79** 161
Squash Rings, Asparagus in, **'87** 68
Steamed Asparagus, **'92** 211
Stir-Fried Asparagus, **'87** 52
Stir-Fry Beef and Asparagus, **'91** 124
Supreme, Asparagus, **'80** 77; **'89** 245
Supreme, Cauliflower and Asparagus, **'79** 287; **'80** 35
Sweet-and-Sour Asparagus, **'89** 159
Tangy Asparagus, **'84** 86
Tarragon Marinade, Asparagus with, **'83** 47
Tomatoes, Fresh Asparagus and, **'94** 162
Tomato Sauce, Asparagus with, **'83** 46
Toss, Asparagus-Carrot-Squash, **'91** 45
Vinaigrette, Asparagus, **'80** 77; **'90** 82, 138; **'93** 174
Vinaigrette, Light Asparagus, **'82** 50
Yogurt Dressing, Asparagus with, **'79** 66
Aspic
Apple Aspic, Sunshine, **'81** 73
Basic Aspic for Garnishing, **'84** 189
Beet Aspic, **'90** 123
Chicken Salad, Aspic-Topped, **'88** 88
Coating, White Aspic, **'85** 151
Cucumber-Curry Dressing, Aspic with, **'89** 178
Fish Aspic, **'84** 190
Fish 'n Aspic, **'84** 190
Gazpacho Aspic, **'89** 179
Grapefruit Aspic, **'80** 297; **'82** 112; **'83** 153
Madeira Aspic, **'86** 65
Orange-and-Carrot Aspic, **'86** 199
Shrimp-Coleslaw Aspic, **'79** 88
Shrimp-Cucumber Aspic, **'83** 108
Sunshine Aspic, **'80** 103
Three-Layer Aspic, **'88** 120
Tomato-Artichoke Aspic, **'84** 320; **'86** 92
Tomato Aspic, Bloody Mary-, **'81** 77
Tomato Aspic, Chicken in, **'84** 190
Tomato Aspic, Chili Sauce, **'85** 252
Tomato Aspic, Classic, **'91** 229
Tomato Aspic, Herbed, **'81** 73
Tomato Aspic, Layered, **'90** 99
Tomato Aspic, Light, **'85** 83
Tomato Aspic, Ranch, **'83** 218
Tomato Aspic, Spicy, **'81** 40; **'89** 288
Tomato Aspic, Tangy, **'83** 124
Tomato Aspic with Shrimp, **'79** 241
Tomato-Crab Aspic, **'85** 287
Two, Aspic for, **'83** 209
Vegetable Aspic, Cheesy, **'81** 73
Vegetable Aspic with Horseradish Dressing, Crisp, **'87** 152

Avocados

Acapulco, Avocado, '83 2
Baked Avocado-and-Crabmeat, '84 119
Broiled Crab and Avocado, '79 116
Chicken, Orange-Avocado, '80 38
Cocktail, Sherried Avocado-Crabmeat, '87 95
Crabmeat, Avocado with, '86 119
Cream, Avocado, '92 158
Dip, Avocado, '80 285; '81 57, 306
Dip, "Bring-Home-the-Bacon" Avocado, '92 80
Dip, Roasted Corn-and-Avocado, '91 279
Dip, Six-Layer, '81 160
Dip, Zippy Avocado, '82 9; '83 69
Dressing, Avocado, '80 15; '92 321
Dressing, Avocado Fruit Salad, '82 93
Filled Avocados, Shrimp-, '83 2
Guacamole, '79 185; '80 74; '83 179; '89 226; '90 205; '91 161; '94 116
Guacamole, Creamy, '79 91; '83 174
Guacamole Dip, '86 4
Guacamole Dip, Bacon-, '85 25
Guacamole Dressing, '92 64
Guacamole in Shells, '86 74
Guacamole Mexican Coleslaw, '82 302
Guacamole Mold, '86 184
Guacamole Salad, '80 14; '87 181
Guacamole Sandwiches, '82 9; '83 68
Guacamole, Spicy, '93 218
Guacamole Spread, '90 119
Guacamole Subs, '84 293
Guacamole-Tomato Salad, '81 302
Ice, Avocado, '83 179
Kabobs, Chicken-Avocado, '82 9; '83 68
Omelet, Yogurt-Avocado, '81 33
Pie, Mexican Cheese, '83 69
Potatoes, Avocado-Topped, '83 3
Relish, Avocado, '87 120
Salad, Avocado, '81 195; '82 9; '83 69; '92 246
Salad, Avocado-Chicken, '87 107
Salad, Avocado-Endive, '94 88
Salad, Avocado Fruit, '87 41
Salad, Avocado-Garbanzo, '81 33
Salad, Avocado-Grapefruit, '85 26; '93 282
Salad, Avocado-Melon, '82 164
Salad, Avocado-Orange, '91 44
Salad, Chicken-Avocado, '80 139
Salad, Citrus-Avocado, '82 265
Salad, Congealed Avocado, '84 266
Salad, Congealed Avocado Crunch, '85 26
Salad, Crab-Avocado, '81 114
Salad, Creamy Avocado and Zucchini, '79 208
Salad, Dude Ranch, '80 15
Salad, Fruited Chicken-Avocado, '82 101
Salad, Grapefruit-Avocado, '83 316; '84 16; '89 41
Salad, Green Spinach, '79 142
Salad in Avocados, Chicken, '85 216
Salad in Avocados, Fruited Chicken, '87 41
Salad on the Half Shell, Shrimp, '86 73
Salad Platter, Chicken-Avocado, '83 2
Salad, Rice-and-Avocado, '89 146
Salads, Congealed Avocado, '87 42
Salad, Shrimp and Avocado, '80 266
Salad, Spanish Avocado, '87 41
Salad Supper, Mexican, '82 9; '83 68
Salad, Tangy Romaine, '80 155
Salad, Tomato-Avocado, '86 74
Salad, Tossed Chicken-Avocado, '80 4

Salad with Honey-Yogurt Dressing, Avocado-Fruit, '93 172
Salsa, Avocado, '91 182
Salsa, Avocado-Corn, '94 201
Salsa, Tomato-Avocado, '94 83
Sandwiches, Avocado, Bacon, and Cheese, '87 279
Sandwiches, Avocado-Crabmeat, '83 2
Sauce, Avocado, '80 198; '83 200
Shells, Ceviche in Avocado, '81 33
Sherbet, Avocado, '83 162
Sherbet, Mexican, '79 155
Sorbet, Avocado, '88 117
Soup, Avocado, '88 160
Soup, Avocado-Banana-Yogurt, '80 78
Soup, Chilled Avocado, '81 34; '87 37; '93 108
Soup, Creamy Avocado, '79 107
Soup, Creamy Avocado-Mushroom, '85 25
Soup, Sherried Avocado, '84 181
Stuffed Avocados, Crab-, '86 73
Stuffed Avocados, Salmon-, '86 74
Stuffed Broiled Avocados, '88 246
Stuffed with Shrimp Salad, Avocado, '82 207
Tomatoes, Avocado-Stuffed, '82 101
Tomatoes, Crab-and-Avocado Stuffed, '94 141
Topping, Avocado, '93 309; '94 96
Tostadas, Crispy, '83 2
Whip, Avocado, '79 107
Yogurt with Candied Lime Strips, Frozen Avocado, '94 137

Bacon

Appetizers, Bacon-Onion, '94 290
Appetizers, Hot Bacon, '80 248
Bagel, Breakfast on a, '94 66
Bagels, Meal-in-One, '88 159
Bake, Lima-Bacon, '86 9
Bars, Bacon-Cheese Toast, '79 36
Beef-and-Bacon Twirls, '91 163
Biscuits, Bacon-Cheese, '88 84
Biscuits, Potato-Bacon, '94 214
Bread, Bacon-and-Cheese, '83 255
Bread, Bacon-Cheese French, '92 54
Bread, Bacon Monkey, '94 283
Breakfast Bake, '85 45
Breakfast Eye-Openers, '82 231
Breakfast, Farmer's, '84 44
Brie, Chutney-Bacon, '90 M292
Broccoli with Bacon, '92 302
Bundles, Bean, '80 246
Burgers, Cheesy Bacon, '81 29
Butternut and Bacon, Skillet, '85 9
Canadian Bacon, Lima Beans with, '83 219; '84 245
Canadian-Style Bacon, Glazed, '82 197
Carrots with Bacon and Onion, Glazed, '87 200
Casserole, Bacon and Egg, '81 225
Casserole, Egg-and-Bacon, '85 248
Champignons au Vin, '79 47
Cheesy BLT's, '85 92
Chestnuts, Bacon-Wrapped Water, '79 63
Chestnut Wraps, Bacon-, '84 M216
Chicken Bundles with Bacon Ribbons, '87 68
Chowder, Fresh Corn and Bacon, '93 203

Coleslaw, Bacon, '83 58
Cookies, Take-Along Breakfast, '84 59
Cornbread, Cowboy, '81 188
Crackers, Bacon-Wrapped, '93 280
Crispies, Cheese-Bacon, '84 270
Croissants, BLT, '93 158
Crostini, Almond-Bacon-Cheese, '94 318
Delight, Bacon-and-Egg, '85 143
Dip, Bacon, '82 197
Dip, Bacon-and-Tomato, '90 147
Dip, Bacon-Guacamole, '85 25
Dip, "Bring-Home-the-Bacon" Avocado, '92 80
Dip, Cheddar-Bacon, '89 M119
Dip, Zesty Bacon, '92 156
Dressing, Green Beans with Bacon, '85 147
Dressing, Hot Bacon, '84 12
Dressing, Potatoes with Hot Bacon, '88 M294
Dressing, Sweet Bacon, '93 108
Egg Salad, Bacon-Horseradish, '94 181
Eggs, and Hominy, Bacon, '85 143
Eggs, Bacon Deviled, '86 136
Eggs Benedict, Bacon-and-Tomato, '87 195
Franks, Bacon-Wrapped, '81 202
Green Beans, Bacon-Topped, '80 M123
Green Beans, Mushroom-Bacon, '91 291; '92 255
Green Beans with Bacon and Mushrooms, '92 13
Hoagies, Bacon, Pimiento, and Cheese, '90 144
Hush Puppies, Bacon, '91 201
Kabobs, Scallop-Bacon, '81 111
Linguine Carbonara, '87 108
Meatballs, Bacon-Wrapped, '79 81
Meatballs, Burgundy-Bacon, '80 283
Muffins, Bacon-and-Cheese, '89 205
Mushrooms, Cheese 'n' Bacon-Stuffed, '86 258
Mushrooms with Bacon, Stir-Fried, '80 123
Oysters, Bacon-Baked, '86 132
Oysters in Bacon, '83 211
Pancake, Maple-Bacon Oven, '89 255
Peas and Bacon, Sautéed, '89 331
Pie, Country Breakfast, '93 M328
Pineapple Chunks, Bacon-Wrapped, '84 25
Pita Pockets, BLT in, '93 158
Poor Boys, Oyster-and-Bacon, '87 40
Popcorn, Bacon-Cheese, '86 74
Pork Tenderloin, Spinach-and-Bacon Stuffed, '94 81
Potatoes, Bacon-Stuffed, '86 193
Potatoes, Bacon-Topped Blue Cheese, '79 46
Potatoes, Cheesy Bacon-Stuffed, '81 M61
Quiche, Bacon, '85 60
Quiche Lorraine, '80 M108
Quiche Lorraine, Classic, '81 131
Quiche Lorraine, Mushroom-, '86 242
Quiche Lorraine, Peppery, '81 228
Quiches, Miniature Bacon-Cheese, '83 93
Rice, Bacon-Chive, '83 129
Rice, Bacon Fried, '80 115
Rolls, Bacon, '84 270; '93 330
Rollups, Bacon, '79 34
Roll-Ups, Chicken Liver and Bacon, '80 200; '81 57
Rollups, Sausage-Bacon, '88 51
Rumaki, '80 M136
Rutabaga with Bacon, '83 243
Salad, Bacon-Topped Potato, '85 59
Salad, BLT Chicken, '87 144

Bacon (continued)

Salad, Endive, Bacon, and Pecan, **'89** 12
Salad, Escarole-and-Bacon, **'84** 85
Salad, Hot Bacon and Black-Eyed, **'85** 7
Salad, Spinach and Bacon, **'81** 143
Salad, Wilted Bacon-and-Lettuce, **'85** 69
Salad with Bacon, Rice, **'79** 52
Sandwiches, Avocado, Bacon, and Cheese, **'87** 279
Sandwiches, Bacon, Cheese, and Tomato, **'84** 14
Sandwiches, Breakfast, **'82** M123; **'89** M230
Sandwiches, Curried BLT, **'93** 158
Sandwiches, Grilled Bacon-Cheese, **'83** 242
Sandwiches, Open-Faced Breakfast, **'92** 140
Sandwiches, Open-Faced Cheesy Bacon, **'80** 78
Scallops, Bacon-Wrapped, **'87** 94
Scramble, Bacon-and-Eggs, **'80** M267
Soup, Bacon-Beer Cheese, **'87** M7
Soup, Bacon, Lettuce, and Tomato, **'91** 207
Soup, Bacon-Topped Cheese, **'80** M224
Soup, Bean and Bacon, **'83** 26
Soup, Potato-Bacon, **'84** M38
Spaghetti, Bacon, **'86** 213; **'87** 82
Spoonbread, Corn and Bacon, **'81** 129
Spread, Bacon-Cheese, **'83** 241
Spread, Spinach-Bacon, **'92** M310
Squash, Bacon-Flavored, **'82** 158
Steak, Bacon-Wrapped Flank, **'85** 59
Supper Supreme, Sunday, **'79** 76
Sweet Potatoes, Bacon-Stuffed, **'86** 224
Swirls, Bacon, **'89** 214
Tomatoes, Bacon-and-Egg-Stuffed, **'80** 162
Tomatoes with Bacon, Saucy Fried, **'81** 210
Vegetable-Bacon Bowl, Marinated, **'79** 191
Welsh Rarebit with Tomatoes and Bacon, **'92** M159

Bananas
Alaskas, Banana Split, **'87** 10
Baked Bananas, **'79** 103
Baked Bananas, Honey-, **'81** 268
Baked Bananas with Orange Sauce, **'79** 115
Bars, Banana Breakfast, **'79** 124
Berry Flip, Banana-, **'88** 215; **'89** 20
Bisque, Banana-Raspberry, **'93** 161
Boats, Banana, **'82** 50
Bread, Banana, **'87** 72
Bread, Banana-Apple, **'85** 250
Bread, Banana-Blueberry, **'81** 163
Bread, Banana Butterscotch, **'79** 116
Bread, Banana-Jam, **'84** 73
Bread, Banana-Nut, **'86** 8, 70
Bread, Banana-Nut-Raisin, **'81** 59
Bread, Banana Wheat, **'81** 14
Bread, Banana-Zucchini, **'85** 326
Bread, Chocolate Chip-Banana, **'90** 267
Bread, Cranberry-Banana, **'80** 281; **'90** 294
Bread, Hawaiian Banana Nut, **'79** 235
Bread, Honey-Banana, **'91** 68
Bread, Sour Cream-Banana, **'79** 190
Bread, Whole Wheat Banana, **'80** 88
Bread, Whole Wheat-Banana Nut, **'84** 50
Breakfast-in-a-Bowl, **'89** 87
Broiled Bananas with Honey, **'84** 175
Brownies, Chocolate-Banana, **'80** 160
Cake, Banana, **'84** 151
Cake, Banana-Blueberry, **'86** 247
Cake, Banana-Coconut, **'93** 154

Cake, Banana Coffee, **'81** 288
Cake, Banana Cream Coffee, **'85** 46
Cake, Banana-Nut, **'92** 120
Cake, Bananas Foster Crunch, **'93** 339
Cake, Banana-Sour Cream Coffee, **'80** 186
Cake, Banana Waldorf, **'85** 118
Cake, Chocolate-Banana, **'86** 138
Cake, Deluxe Light Banana, **'84** 314
Cake, Marvelous Banana, **'79** 115
Cake, Peanut Butter-Banana, **'80** 87
Candied Bananas, **'83** 179
Casserole, Sweet Potato-Banana, **'86** 276
"Concrete," All Shook Up, **'94** 114
Cookies, Banana Oatmeal, **'79** 217
Coolers, Banana, **'91** 308
Cream Pie, Chocolate-Banana-Pecan, **'94** 210
Crêpes Flambé, Banana, **'84** 262
Crush, Banana, **'80** 88; **'83** 142
Cupcakes, Banana-Cocoa, **'80** 130
Curried Bananas, Fillets with Horseradish Sauce and, **'85** 230
Dessert, Banana Cream, **'81** 180
Doughnuts, Banana-Nut, **'86** 137
Flambé, Banana-Peach, **'85** 316
Flip, Banana, **'83** 303
Flip, Orange-Banana, **'82** 48
Float, Strawberry-Banana, **'87** 160
Foster, Bananas, **'79** 18; **'83** M114; **'86** 139
Foster, Elegant Bananas, **'81** 59
Foster for Two, Bananas, **'80** 115
Foster, Orange-Glazed Bananas, **'91** 91
Foster, Tropical Bananas, **'79** 231
Fritters, Banana, **'79** 213
Frost, Banana-Strawberry, **'87** 199
Frostee, Banana, **'91** 66
Frosting, Banana-Nut, **'79** 115
Green Bananas Escabeche (Pickled Green Bananas), **'92** 169
Hawaiian, Bananas, **'89** 94
Ice Cream, Banana-Graham, **'91** 56
Ice Cream, Banana Split, **'80** 176
Ice Cream, Straw-Ba-Nut, **'80** 177
Ice Cream, Strawberry-Banana-Nut, **'88** 203
Ice Milk, Banana Yogurt, **'89** 199
Jam, Banana, **'82** 296
Jam, Rosy Peach-Banana, **'80** 142
Kabana, Banana, **'86** 316
Loaf, Banana-Oat Tea, **'87** 256
Loaf, Chocolate Chip-Banana, **'85** 115
Loaf, Hawaiian, **'80** 225
Malt, Banana-Chocolate, **'89** 170
Milkshake, Banana, **'85** 47; **'90** 179
Milk Shake, Banana-Pineapple, **'84** 59
Milk Shake, Chocolate-Banana, **'94** 113
Muffins, Banana, **'80** 88; **'84** 75
Muffins, Banana Bran, **'83** 48
Muffins, Banana-Chocolate, **'94** 197
Muffins, Banana-Honey-Nut, **'88** 62
Muffins, Banana-Nut, **'93** 140
Muffins, Banana-Oat, **'87** 188
Muffins, Banana Oat Bran, **'89** 106
Muffins, Banana-Oatmeal, **'84** 20
Muffins, Banana-Orange, **'84** 148
Muffins, Banana-Poppyseed, **'89** 205
Muffins, Banana-Raisin, **'89** 218
Muffins, Banana Surprise, **'82** 105
Muffins, Jumbo Banana-Chocolate Chip, **'93** 339
Muffins, Oat Bran-Banana, **'91** 18
Nog, Banana, **'82** 290

Nutty Bananas, **'79** 251
Pancakes, Island, **'87** 225
Pancakes, Wheat Germ-Banana, **'79** 114
Pie, Banana Cream, **'84** 48; **'87** 207
Pie, Blueberry-Banana, **'93** 115
Pie, Caramel-Banana, **'86** M165
Pie, Hawaiian Banana Cream, **'90** 105
Pie, Layered Banana Split, **'83** 189
Pie, Luscious Caramel Banana, **'79** 115
Pie, Strawberry-Banana Glazed, **'81** 181
Pie, White Chocolate-Banana Cream, **'94** 314
Pie with Hot Buttered Rum Sauce, Banana, **'88** 204
Pops, Banana, **'83** 60; **'84** 44
Pops, Orange-Banana, **'82** 129
Praline Bananas, **'84** 313
Pudding, Almost Banana, **'88** 174
Pudding, Banana, **'82** 53; **'84** 94; **'85** 255; **'88** 16, 32
Pudding, Banana-Mallow, **'86** 139
Pudding, Basic Banana, **'81** 59
Pudding, Creamy Banana, **'89** M130
Pudding, Delicious Banana, **'80** 9
Pudding, No-Bake Banana, **'91** 172
Pudding, Old-Fashioned Banana, **'92** 94
Pudding, Peanut Butter-Banana, **'93** 340
Pudding, Surprise Banana, **'86** 7
Regal Bananas, **'85** 46
Roll, Banana-Nut, **'85** 112
Salad, Banana, **'87** 80
Salad, Banana-Mixed Fruit, **'79** 270
Salad, Banana Split, **'91** 58
Salad, Frozen Banana, **'82** 80, 132
Salad with Celery Seed Dressing, Grapefruit-Banana, **'91** 237
Salsa, Banana Rum, **'94** 97
Sauce, Banana-Pineapple, **'83** 48
Sauce, Banana Sundae, **'84** 275
Sauce, Strawberry-Graham, **'81** 41
Shake, Pineapple-Banana, **'85** 215
Shake, Raspberry-and-Banana, **'89** 183
Shake, Strawberry-Banana, **'89** 35
Sherbet, Banana-Orange, **'83** 162
Shortcake, Banana-Pecan, **'93** 43
Slaw, Banana-Nut, **'86** 250
Slush, Banana, **'83** 56
Slush, Banana-Orange, **'80** 48; **'81** 155
Slush, Pineapple-Banana, **'90** 14
Smoothie, Banana, **'87** 160; **'93** 95
Smoothie, Banana-Blueberry, **'90** 104
Smoothie, Honey-Banana, **'89** 144
Smoothie, Quick Banana-Pineapple, **'93** 195
Smoothie, Strawberry-Banana, **'81** 59
Smoothie, Tropical, **'81** 50
Sorbet, Banana-Orange, **'88** 117
Soufflé, Banana Daiquiri, **'84** 317
Soup, Avocado-Banana-Yogurt, **'80** 78
Soup, Strawberry-Banana, **'86** 181
Splits, Cottage Cheese-Banana, **'87** 56
Supreme, Banana-Berry, **'81** 205
Supreme, Bananas, **'84** 256
Topping, Pound Cake with Strawberry-Banana, **'89** 200
Topping, Strawberry-Banana, **'87** 125
Tropical Delight, **'89** 182
Waffles, Banana-Ginger, **'86** 96
Waffles, Banana-Oatmeal, **'94** 206
Waffles, Banana Split, **'89** 205

Barbecue

Backbones, Smoked Country-Style, '82 162
Bannister's Barbecue, '92 166
Beans, Barbecued, '94 248
Beans, Barbecued Lima, '82 2
Beans, Barbecued Pork and, '79 100
Beans, Commissary Barbecue, '90 120
Beans, Skillet Barbecued, '93 217
Beef, Barbecued, '81 18
Beef Brisket, Barbecued, '83 11
Beef Brisket, Denton, Texas, Barbecued, '81 55
Beef Brisket with Sauce, Barbecued, '86 153
Beef Eye of Round, Grilled, '82 91
Beef Roast Barbecue, '79 159
Beef Roast, Barbecued, '82 96; '83 103
Beef Sandwiches, Barbecued, '81 25; '82 31; '83 34
Beef, Saucy Barbecued, '82 156
Beef Short Ribs, Barbecued, '83 178
Beef Shortribs Supreme, '79 14
Beef Tenderloin, Barbecued, '94 26
Bourbon Barbecue, '88 129
Brisket, Barbecued, '86 154; '88 218
Burgers, Barbecued, '82 168; '89 164
Burgers, Sausage, '83 212
Cabrito, Barbecued, '86 153
Catfish, Barbecued, '80 157
Catfish, Lemon Barbecued, '89 202
Catfish, Smoked, '84 47
Chicken Bake, Barbecued, '81 97
Chicken, Barbecue, '86 122
Chicken, Barbecued, '82 97, 106; '83 103; '85 144; '86 153; '89 167
Chicken, Barbecued Cranberry, '83 178
Chicken Breasts, Grilled, '84 172
Chicken, Carambola-Glazed Barbecued, '92 246
Chicken, Golden Barbecued, '83 136
Chicken, Grilled Barbecued, '81 154
Chicken, Grilled Yogurt-Lemon, '81 111
Chicken Legs and Thighs, Barbecued, '94 94
Chicken, Lemonade, '82 163
Chicken, Lemon Barbecued, '93 215
Chicken, Marinated Barbecued, '79 90
Chicken, Old South Barbecued, '82 97; '83 103
Chicken, Orange Barbecued, '88 123
Chicken, Oven-Barbecued Cranberry, '93 332
Chicken, Saucy Barbecued, '83 11
Chicken, Smoky Grilled, '85 160
Chicken, Tangy Barbecued, '86 186
Chicken, Zesty Barbecued, '80 M76
Chicken, Zippy Barbecued, '83 213
Corned Beef Sandwiches, Barbecued, '83 130
Cornish Hens, Smoked, '86 142, 154
Corn on the Cob, Barbecued, '81 128
Cups, Barbecue, '79 129
Dressing, Barbecue Salad, '80 74
Fish Fillets, Barbecued, '86 182
Flounder Fillets, Grilled, '83 213
Frank Barbecue, Tangy, '79 63
Frankfurters, Barbecued, '83 144
Frankfurters, Oven-Barbecued, '83 11
Franks, Barbecued, '85 192
Franks, Grilled Stuffed, '82 163
Grouper, Grilled, '86 185
Hamburgers, Flavorful Grilled, '81 110
Ham Slices, Barbecued, '81 110

Ham, Smoked, '86 92
Home-Style Barbecue, '88 145
Kabobs, Barbecued Steak, '79 89
Kabobs, Grilled Scallop, '83 101
Kabobs, Marinated Sirloin, '82 162
Kabobs, Pineapple-Beef, '83 212
Kabobs, Sea Scallop, '82 162
Lamb, Barbecued, '79 58
Lamb Chops, Barbecued, '79 89
Lamb Shanks, Barbecued, '92 128; '93 113
Liver, Barbecued, '85 219
Mackerel, Smoked Salmon or, '84 46
Meatballs, Oven Barbecued, '82 233
Meat Loaf, Barbecued, '80 60; '81 275; '87 216
Mullet, Smoked, '84 47
Nachos, Commissary Barbecue, '91 171
Outdoor Cooking, '82 109
Oysters, Barbecued, '82 247
Pork, Barbecued, '80 72
Pork Chops, Barbecued, '81 10
Pork Chops, Marinated Barbecued, '79 90
Pork Chops, Marinated Grilled, '81 110
Pork Chops, Oven-Barbecued, '81 234; '82 26; '83 40
Pork Loin Roast, Barbecued, '93 34
Pork Roast Barbecue, '82 97; '83 104
Pork Roast, Berry Barbecued, '80 288
Pork Shoulder, Barbecued, '81 111; '82 11
Pork Shoulder, Smoked, '82 225
Pork, Spicy Barbecued, '84 296
Potatoes, Barbecued, '91 311; '92 26
Pot Roast, Barbecued, '79 17; '83 319
Rabbit, Hickory Barbecued, '82 216
Ribs, Apple Barbecued, '80 111
Ribs, Barbecued, '80 111; '85 159; '91 205
Ribs, Barbecued Short, '90 148
Ribs, Country-Style Barbecued, '79 42
Ribs, Herbed Barbecued, '86 185
Ribs, John Wills's Baby Loin Back, '90 120
Ribs, Oven-Barbecued Pork, '88 132
Ribs, Saucy-Sweet, '81 166
Ribs, Smoky, '84 172
Ribs, Smoky Barbecued, '80 111
Ribs, Smoky Oven, '81 166
Ribs, Tangy Barbecued, '83 160
Roast, Barbecued Rib, '86 152
Roast, Grilled Pepper, '81 111
Salad, Barbecue Macaroni, '82 276
Salmon, Barbecued, '81 181
Salmon or Mackerel, Smoked, '84 46
Sauces
    Bannister's Barbecue Sauce, '92 166
    Barbecue Sauce, '84 172; '86 153; '88 218; '91 16, 205; '93 129; '94 27
    Barbecue Sauce, Baked Fish with, '84 92
    Basting Sauce, '90 120
    Beef Marinade, Tangy, '86 113
    Beer Barbecue Sauce, '84 173
    Blender Barbecue Sauce, Ribs with, '90 12
    Bourbon Barbecue Sauce, '85 90
    Brisket with Barbecue Sauce, Smoked, '85 144
    Dressed-Up Barbecue Sauce, '84 173
    Eastern-Style Barbecue Sauce, '88 145
    Easy Barbecue Sauce, '79 90; '82 178
    John Wills's Barbecue Sauce, '92 255

    Lemon Barbecue Sauce, Herbed, '94 154
    Lemony Barbecue Sauce, '88 M177
    Maple Syrup Barbecue Sauce, '94 154
    Mustard Barbecue Sauce, '84 173
    Orange Barbecue Sauce, Spareribs with, '83 11
    Oven Barbecue Sauce, '82 233
    Paprika Barbecue Sauce, '79 90
    Peanut Butter Barbecue Sauce, '81 233
    Piquant Barbecue Sauce, '79 159
    Savory Barbecue Sauce, '86 153
    Special Barbecue Sauce, '82 177
    Spicy Southwest Barbecue Sauce, '94 154
    Sweet-and-Sour Marinade, '86 113
    Sweet Sauce, '90 120
    Teriyaki Marinade, '86 114
    Thick and Robust Barbecue Sauce, '94 95
    Thick and Sweet Barbecue Sauce, '94 95
    Thin and Tasty Barbecue Sauce, '94 95
    Tomato Barbecue Sauce, Fresh, '84 172
    Western-Style Barbecue Sauce, '88 145
    White Barbecue Sauce, '94 95
    White Barbecue Sauce, Chicken with, '89 M84
    Zippy Barbecue Sauce, '92 166
Sausage, Barbecued, '86 153
Sausage, Smoked, '86 154
Shrimp, Barbecued, '82 74; '84 93; '90 28
Shrimp, Cajun Barbecued, '87 95
Shrimp, Grilled, '85 103
Spareribs, Apple-Barbecue, '90 160
Spareribs, Barbecued, '81 112; '82 12; '86 232
Spareribs, Barbecued Country-Style, '80 73
Spareribs, Easy Barbecued, '82 97; '83 104
Spareribs, Honey-Glazed, '82 163
Spareribs, Orange-Glazed, '84 296
Spareribs, Saucy Barbecued, '79 14
Spareribs, Southern Barbecued, '79 90
Spareribs, Spicy Barbecued, '84 93
Spareribs, Tangy Barbecued, '82 106
Steak, Barbecued Flank, '79 89
Steak, Grilled Black Pepper, '86 184
Steak, Grilled Flank, '80 152
Steak, Marinated Barbecued Chuck, '80 156
Steak, Marinated Flank, '82 162
Steak, Saucy Oven-Barbecued, '83 10
Steaks with Green Chiles, Grilled, '85 144
Steak Teriyaki, Flank, '81 110
Steak with Mushroom Sauce, '83 212
Trout, Smoked, '84 47
Trout with Ginger and Soy Sauce, Grilled, '85 228
Tuna, Barbecued, '80 275
Turkey Barbecue, '90 158
Turkey, Smoked, '79 293; '84 160
Venison Steaks, Grilled, '82 215

Barley
    Baked Barley, '91 133
    Casserole, Barley, '84 281
    Pilaf, Barley-Vegetable, '91 33
    Rolls, Wine-Sauced Beef-and-Barley, '87 269
    Salad, Barley, '92 212
    Salad, Barley-Broccoli, '90 135
    Salad, Black Bean-and-Barley, '94 174
    Soup, Turkey-Barley, '91 312
    Vegetables, Barley and, '91 81
Beans. *See also* Lentils.
    Appetizers, Bean Burrito, '94 226
    Bake, Cheesy Beef-and-Bean, '82 89
    Baked
        Barbecued Beans, '94 248
        Barbecued Pork and Beans, '79 100
        Beefy Baked Beans, '80 136; '84 149;
          '85 142
        Chuckwagon Beans, '81 188
        Crowd-Pleasing Baked Beans, '82 127
        Easy Baked Beans, '85 141
        Favorite Baked Beans, '86 210
        Franks, Beans and, '85 142
        Franks, Beany Kraut and, '79 64
        Franks, Hawaiian Baked Beans and,
          '80 136
        Genuine Baked Beans, '83 26
        Ham, Baked Beans with, '80 136
        Hawaiian-Style Baked Beans, '86 210
        Maple Heights Baked Beans, '91 223
        Meat Baked Beans, Three-, '86 210
        Medley, Baked Bean, '80 100
        Mixed Baked Beans, '87 92
        Molasses Baked Beans, '82 139;
          '84 327; '86 20
        More Beans, Baked Beans and, '92 173
        Old-Fashioned Baked Beans, '84 25
        Picnic Baked Beans, '83 143; '85 142
        Polynesian Beans-and-Franks, '84 M11
        Pork Chops with Baked Beans, '93 18
        Quick Baked Beans, '80 136
        Quintet, Baked Beans, '93 105; '94 100
        Rum-Laced Bean Bake, '82 283; '83 72
        Smoked Baked Beans, '79 150
        Spiced Baked Beans, '85 142
        Three-Bean Bake, '81 155
        White Bean Bake, Turnip Greens and,
          '94 246
    Barbecue Beans, Commissary, '90 120
    Barbecued Beans, Skillet, '93 217
    Beef-and-Bean Supper, '82 2
    Beefy Beans, '82 59
    Black Bean-and-Corn Salsa, '94 80
    Black Bean Appetizer, '83 50
    Black Bean Cakes with Greens and Apple
      Dressing, '92 216
    Black Bean Guacamole, '94 277
    Black Bean Pancakes with Gazpacho Butter,
      '92 86
    Black Beans, '93 28
    Black Bean Salsa, '93 155; '94 161
    Black Beans and Cilantro, Southwestern
      Scallop Broth with, '87 123
    Black Beans and Rice, '80 222; '89 178;
      '91 82
    Black Beans and Salsa, Poached Chicken with,
      '87 217
    Black Beans and Yellow Rice, Easy, '92 308
    Black Bean Sauce, '93 59
    Black Beans, Cuban, '88 196
    Black Beans, Marinated, '93 131

Black Bean Spaghetti, '92 217
Black Beans, Spanish, '84 327
Black Beans with Yellow Rice, '82 2
Black Bean Terrine with Fresh Tomato Coulis
    and Jalapeño Sauce, '93 230
Black Bean Terrine with Goat Cheese,
    '87 120
Black Bean-Tomatillo Relish, '87 121
Black Bean Tostadas, Shrimp-and-,
    '93 204
Burritos, Meat-and-Bean, '81 194
Butterbeans, '90 166
Casserole, Bean-and-Cornbread, '92 243
Casserole, Chuck Wagon Bean, '93 198
Casserole, Spicy Mexican Bean, '84 114
Casserole, Three-Bean, '88 56
Chili and Beans, Ranch, '79 270; '80 11
Chili Bean Roast, '87 268; '88 102
Chili Goes Southwest, Basic, '93 326
Chili, Mom's, '93 292
Chili Surprise, '82 229
Chili, Turkey-Bean, '88 M213
Chili, White, '91 284
Chili with Beans, Easy, '92 262
Chili with Beans, Meaty, '85 250
Chimichangas (Fried Burritos), '81 196
Chowder, Sausage-Bean, '83 20
Creole Beans and Rice, '80 223
Dip, Bean, '89 97
Dip, Cheese-Bean, '85 208
Dip, Hotshot Bean, '87 195
Dip, Layered Nacho, '81 261
Dip, Prairie Fire Bean, '80 195
Dip, South-of-the-Border, '81 235
Enchiladas, Spicy Bean, '88 18
Enchiladas, Three-Bean, '91 133
Franks, Jiffy Beans and, '91 M172
Franks 'n' Beans, Stove-Top, '88 201
Frijoles con Cerveza (Beans with Beer),
    '81 66
Garbanzo Dinner, Beef-and-, '84 31
Garbanzo Dip, '93 94
Green
    Almonds, Green Beans with, '84 253
    Amandine, Green Beans, '79 276;
      '82 M20; '85 156
    Appalachian Green Beans, '81 215
    au Gratin, Green Beans, '80 116
    Bacon and Mushrooms, Green Beans
      with, '92 13
    Bacon Dressing, Green Beans with,
      '85 147
    Bacon-Topped Green Beans, '80 M123
    Baked Green Beans, '91 159
    Barbecued Green Beans, '86 252
    Basil Beans and Tomatoes, '83 172
    Basil, Green Beans with, '82 96
    Beans, Green, '80 126; '87 M151
    Blue Cheese, Green Beans with, '88 57
    Bow-Tie Green Beans, '94 320
    Buffet Green Beans, '93 325
    Bundles, Bean, '80 246; '83 67
    Bundles, Green Bean, '83 180; '87 118
    Buttered Green Beans, '92 54
    Cashews, Green Beans with, '89 202
    Casserole, Chicken-Green Bean,
      '85 296
    Casserole, Corn-and-Bean, '90 208
    Casserole, Easy Green Bean, '87 284
    Casserole, Green Bean, '79 106;
      '84 145

Casserole, Green Bean-and-Corn,
    '88 123
Casserole, Italian Green
    Bean-and-Artichoke, '85 81
Celery, Green Beans and Braised,
    '84 254
Cheese-Topped Green Beans, '79 100
Cheesy Green Beans, '80 157
Creamed Green Beans, French-Style,
    '88 252
Cumin Green Beans, '82 90
Dilled Green Beans, '82 106; '86 157;
    '88 101; '89 203; '93 279
Dill Green Beans, '93 136
Dilly Green Beans, '80 116
Excellent, Green Beans, '94 321
French Green Beans, '90 208
French Quarter Green Beans, '80 298;
    '81 26
Fresh Green Beans, '79 122
Garlic Green Beans, '91 159; '94 273
Goldenrod Beans, '83 111
Greek Green Beans, '94 165
Herbed Green Beans, '83 M147, 177;
    '88 M190
Herb Green Beans, '89 321
Herbs, Green Beans with, '82 90
Indian-Style Green Beans, '88 265
Italian Green Beans, '85 147; '90 164;
    '92 183
Italian, Green Beans, '87 10
Italian Green Beans, Sesame, '82 174
Italian Green Beans with Almonds,
    '81 207
Italiano, Green Bean, '94 248
Italiano, Green Beans, '86 144
Lemon Green Beans, '89 275
Lemon-Walnut Green Beans, '93 304
Lemony Green Beans, '85 190
Marinated Beets, Green Beans, and
    Carrots, '88 162
Marinated Green Beans, '83 145
Marinated Italian Beans, '86 M226
Marinated Vegetables, '81 239
Marjoram, Fresh Green Beans with,
    '91 159
Mediterranean-Style Green Beans,
    '79 100
Medley, Green Bean, '85 108
Medley, Peppery Green Bean, '93 181
Minted Green Beans, '84 104
Mushroom-Bacon Green Beans,
    '91 291; '92 255
Mushroom Sauce, Green Beans in
    Sherried, '93 206
Mushrooms, Green Beans with, '82 21;
    '93 89
Mustard, Green Beans and Tomatoes
    with, '87 83
Nutty Green Beans, '88 M187
Oriental Green Beans, '88 43
Oriental, Green Beans, '91 158
Pecans, Green Beans with Buttered,
    '92 61
Pepper Strips, Green Beans and,
    '86 170
Pickled Beans, Dressed-Up, '86 251
Pole Beans, Old-Fashioned, '80 100
Potatoes, Down-Home Beans and,
    '85 254
Potatoes, Green Beans and, '91 221

Beans, Green (*continued*)

Potatoes, Green Beans with New, '87 164
Provençal, Green Beans, '81 182; '91 158
Red Peppers and Pearl Onions, Green Beans with Roasted, '93 260
Saucy Green Beans, '83 206
Savory Green Beans, '89 70, 235
Seasoned Green Beans, '88 304
Simple Green Beans, '92 100
Snap Beans, '86 218
Snap Beans, Simple, '85 148
Snap, or Wax Beans, Green, '85 105
Sour Cream, Green Beans in, '80 116
Sour Cream, Green Beans with, '82 90
Southern-Style Green Beans, '79 283
Spanish Green Beans, '80 116
Spanish-Style Green Beans, '84 128
Special Green Beans, '90 268
Squash, Beans, and Tomatoes, '83 148
Stir-Fried Green Beans, '85 148; '86 305
Surprise, Green Bean, '86 9
Sweet-and-Sour Beans, '87 197
Sweet-and-Sour Green Beans, '79 184; '81 158; '82 90; '91 250
Sweet-and-Sour Green Beans and Carrots, '83 6
Sweet-and-Sour Snap Beans, '89 173
Tangy Green Beans, '85 M142; '89 314, 332
Tarragon Dressing, Green Beans with Creamy, '93 191
Tomatoes, Bean-Stuffed, '84 34
Tomatoes, Green Beans with, '85 137
Tomatoes, Green Beans with Cherry, '86 177
Tomato Skillet, Bean-and-, '90 316
Vegetable-Herb Trio, '83 172
Vinaigrette, Green Beans, '93 120; '94 90
Vinaigrette, Kentucky Wonder Green Beans, '94 158
Walnut Dressing, Green Beans with, '94 279
Zucchini, Green Beans with, '84 128
Hot Dogs, Beany, '82 190
Hummas, '92 155
Kidney Bean Casserole, '90 136
Kidney Beans, Mexican, '90 205
Lasagna, Spinach-Bean, '92 96
Legumes, Marinated, '90 197
Lemon-Mint Beans, '88 22
Lima
Bake, Lima-Bacon, '86 9
Barbecued Lima Beans, '82 2
Beans, Lima, '80 127
Beef-and-Lima Bean Dinner, '84 292
Canadian Bacon, Lima Beans with, '83 219; '84 245
Casserole, Ham and Lima, '79 192
Casserole, Lima Bean, '79 189; '83 313; '86 225; '87 284
Casserole, Lima Bean Garden, '83 218; '84 246
Casserole, Spicy Lima Bean, '79 189
Casserole, Swiss Lima Bean, '80 191

Cheese and Limas in Onion Shells, '81 86
Cheese Limas, Spanish, '86 225
Chilly Lima Beans, '81 206
Combo, Hot Lima and Tomato, '83 219
Creole, Lima Beans, '80 191; '85 137
Deluxe, Lima Beans, '79 289; '80 26
Fresh Lima Beans and Scallions, '82 133
Marinated Limas, '86 225
Medley, Carrot-Lima-Squash, '80 123
Rancho Lima Beans, '80 191
Savory Lima Beans, '83 219; '84 246
Savory Sauce, Lima Beans and Carrots with, '84 196
Sour Cream, Lima Beans in, '79 189; '88 41
Spanish-Style Lima Beans, '83 25
Succotash, Easy, '80 165
Super Lima Beans, '79 189
Supper, Sausage-Bean, '86 52
Mogumbo, '93 32
Nachos, Best-Ever, '79 91
Nachos, Easy, '84 30
Nachos, Make-Ahead, '80 M135
Pinto
Beef and Bean Supper, '82 2
Chalupa, Bean, '80 223
Chalupas, Bean, '83 313
Chalupas, Pork, '83 160
Chili, Tex-Mex, '83 26
Cow Camp Pinto Beans, '94 28
Frijoles Rancheros, '88 148
Mexican Pinto Beans, '93 69; '94 30
Pie, Pinto Bean, '80 40
Pinto Beans, '87 303
Ranch Beans, Laredo, '81 75
Razorback Beans, '84 328
Sandwiches, Bean Salad, '81 243
Sausage, Hearty Pintos and, '88 296
Soup, Beanolla, '94 248
Southwestern Beans, '89 16
Spicy-Hot Beans, '89 17
Spicy Hot Pintos, '83 26
Sweet-Hot Pinto Beans, '86 114
Trailride Pinto Beans, '85 154
Red Beans and Rice, '80 58; '83 89; '84 37; '87 45; '90 27
Red Beans and Rice, Cajun, '83 26
Red Beans and Rice, Easy, '90 220
Refried Beans, '79 185
Rice, South Texas Beans and, '85 252
Salads
Black Bean-and-Barley Salad, '94 174
Black Bean-and-Cheese Salad, '92 217
Black Bean Salad, '89 217
Black Bean Salad, Caribbean Shrimp-and-, '93 143
Cannellini Bean Salad, Tuna-and-, '86 143
Chilled Bean Salad, '80 178
Cucumber-Bean Salad, '83 81
Five-Bean Salad, Hot, '81 149
Four-Bean Salad, '79 20; '84 82
Full o' Beans Salad, '81 38
Garbanzo Salad, '82 2
Garbanzo Salad, Avocado-, '81 33
Garden Medley Salad, '80 122
Green Bean-and-Tomato Salad, '86 180
Green Bean-Peanut Salad, '86 117
Green Bean-Potato Salad, '83 80
Green Bean Salad, '87 90

Green Bean Salad, Cold, '84 106
Green Bean Salad, Crispy, '82 239
Green Bean Salad, German, '92 169
Green Bean Salad, Hot, '86 298; '87 176
Green Bean Salad, Lettuce and, '80 79
Green Bean Salad, Molded, '85 252
Green Bean Salad, Paprika-, '86 191
Green Bean Salad, Pickled, '82 239
Green Bean Salad, Speedy, '84 283
Green Beans-and-Cheese Salad, '91 159
Green Beans Vinaigrette, '83 25
Hominy-Bean Salad, '88 266
Hot German-Style Bean Salad, '91 314
Kidney Bean-Salami Pasta Toss, '85 165
Layered Salad, '86 35
Lima Bean-Tomato Salad, '85 137
Marinated Bean-and-Rice Salad, '87 152
Marinated Bean-Pasta Salad, '94 167
Marinated Bean Salad, '85 137, 296; '89 314; '93 312; '94 167
Marinated Bean Salad, Crunchy, '84 197
Marinated Combo Salad, '82 267
Marinated Corn-Bean Salad, '87 9
Mexican Salad, '94 202
Mexican Tossed Salad, '81 280
Mixed Bean Salad, '83 217
Niçoise, Salad, '86 35
Overnight Fiesta Salad, '83 80
Pinto Salad, '86 169
Pole Bean-Potato Salad, Hot, '79 74
Pork-'n'-Bean Salad, '87 83
Potato-Bean Salad, '82 301
Quick Bean Salad, '89 128
Red Bean Slaw, '79 247
Rice-and-Bean Salad, '85 22
Rice Salad, Beans-and-, '91 44
Saucy Bean Salad, '84 18
Sausage Salad, Bean-and-, '91 313
Six-Bean Salad, Colorful, '87 82
Southwest Salad, '81 113
Sprout Salad, Bean, '82 113
Supreme Bean Salad, '91 202
Sweet-and-Sour Bean Salad, '85 198; '86 147
Sweet-and-Sour Beans with Sprouts, '86 32
Sweet-and-Sour Vegetable Salad, '81 25
Sauce, Pork-and-Onions with Bean, '85 76
Sausage, Beans, and Rice, Texas, '84 296
Shuck Beans, '81 216
Soup, Bean, '80 25
Soup, Bean and Bacon, '83 26
Soup, Bean and Pasta, '94 220
Soup, Bean-and-Turkey, '93 319
Soup, "Bean Counter," '92 80
Soup, Black Bean, '88 30, 266; '89 28; '93 231
Soup, Capitol Hill Bean, '80 222
Soup, Carolina Black Bean, '92 139
Soup, Chill-Chaser, '87 282
Soup, Chunky Navy Bean, '83 291
Soup, Cream of Green Bean, '84 111
Soup, Drunken Bean, '87 283
Soup, French Market, '92 49; '94 317
Soup, Guadalajara, '88 30
Soup, Ham-and-Bean, '84 4
Soup, Hearty Bean-and-Barley, '86 304
Soup, Leafy Bean, '86 223
Soup, Minestrone, '91 258
Soup Mix, French Market, '94 317

Beans *(continued)*

Soup Mix, Minestrone, **'91** 258
Soup, Navy Bean, **'84** 280
Soup, Sausage-Bean, **'85** 88
Soup, Savory Navy Bean, **'87** 282
Soup, Spicy Ham-and-Bean, **'94** 322
Soup, Spicy Sausage-Bean, **'83** 229
Soup, Spicy Three-Bean, **'91** 28
Soup, Spicy White Bean, **'94** 225
Soup, Three-Bean, **'89** 17
Soup, Vegetable-Bean, **'83** 317
Soup, White Bean, **'83** 229; **'90** 201
Tacos, Chicken-and-Bean, **'93** 293
Texas Ranch Beans, **'90** 198
White Bean Pot, **'86** 194
White Bean Relish, **'93** 229
White Beans, Caesar Salad with, **'93** 30
White Bean Spread, **'93** 30
Beef
Appetizers, Meat-and-Cheese, **'87** 7
Asparagus, Beef with, **'90** 100
Ball, Cheese 'n' Beef, **'83** 230
Barbecue, Bourbon, **'88** 129
Barbecued Beef, Saucy, **'82** 156
Bouilli, **'80** 58
Bourguignon, Beef, **'79** 104; **'82** 288
Bourguignon, Royal Beef, **'80** 106
Brisket, Barbecued, **'86** 154; **'88** 218
Brisket, Barbecued Beef, **'83** 11
Brisket, Denton, Texas, Barbecued Beef, **'81** 55
Brisket, Home-Style, **'87** 303
Brisket in Beer, Beef, **'93** 63
Brisket, Marinated, **'86** 129
Brisket, Smoke-at-Home, **'93** 192
Brisket, Smoked, **'89** 168
Brisket with Barbecue Sauce, Smoked, **'85** 144
Brisket with Sauce, Barbecued Beef, **'86** 153
Broccoli, Quick Beef and, **'91** 123
Broccoli with Chive Gravy, Beef and, **'88** 214
Burgoo, Five-Meat, **'87** 3
Burgoo, Kentucky, **'88** 235
Burgoo, Old-Fashioned, **'87** 3
Burgundy, Beef, **'82** 259; **'83** 125, 281; **'88** 25
Burgundy, Simple Beef, **'90** 234
Burgundy with Pearl Onions, Beef, **'81** 108
Burritos, Cheesy Beef, **'85** 193
Burritos, Meat-and-Bean, **'81** 194
Caldo de Rez (Mexican Beef Stew), **'89** 276
Carne Guisada, **'93** 68
Chalupa, Bean, **'80** 223
Chili, Chuck Wagon, **'81** 282; **'82** 57
Chili, Chunky, **'82** M282; **'86** 3
Chili con Carne, **'82** 310; **'83** 30; **'86** 2
Chili, Cowboy, **'86** 2
Chili, Firestarter, **'93** 34
Chili, North Texas Red, **'87** 303
Chili, Red, **'93** 108
Chili, South-of-the-Border, **'83** 283; **'91** 283
Chili, Texas Championship, **'81** 54
Chili, Zippy, **'87** 110
Chimichangas (Fried Burritos), **'85** 244; **'86** 114
Chimichangas, Oven-Fried Beef, **'92** 124
Chinese-Style Beef, **'87** 50
Chipped Beef and Toast, Creamy, **'79** 180

Corned Beef
Birming "Ham," **'94** 229
Brunch Bake, Corned Beef, **'82** 44
Cabbage au Gratin, Corned Beef and, **'83** 16
Cabbage, Corned Beef and, **'83** 104; **'93** 64
Cabbage, Corned Beef Squares and, **'82** 86
Cabbage, Quick Corned Beef and, **'79** 54
Dijon Glaze, Corned Beef with, **'87** 54
Dinner, Corned Beef, **'87** 54
Hash, Red Flannel, **'79** 191
Reuben Buns, **'88** 298
Reuben Casserole, **'90** 240
Reuben Cheesecake, **'90** 175
Reuben Meat Pie, **'80** 189
Reuben Sandwiches, **'80** M201
Reuben Sandwiches, Broiled, **'81** 240
Reuben Sandwiches, Crispy, **'85** 299
Reuben Sandwiches, Grilled, **'81** 206
Reuben Sandwiches, Open-Face, **'91** 199
Reubens, Party, **'90** 61
Reuben Turnovers, **'94** 253
Roll, Corned Beef, **'85** 66
Salad, Corned Beef, **'80** 104
Salad, Corned Beef-Cauliflower, **'83** 16
Salad, Corned Beef-Potato, **'85** 213
Salad, Molded Corned Beef, **'82** 86
Salad, Potato-Corned Beef, **'81** 36
Salad, Vegetable-Corned Beef, **'80** 148
Sandwich, Corned Beef and Cheese, **'79** 214
Sandwiches, Barbecued Corned Beef, **'83** 130
Sandwiches, Corned Beef, **'83** 291; **'85** 242; **'92** 23
Sandwiches, Grilled Corned Beef, **'87** 54
Sandwiches, Meal-in-One, **'80** 218
Soup, Corned Beef, **'83** 16
Soup, French Onion-Beef, **'87** 54
Spread, Corned Beef, **'87** 196
Creamed Beef and Chicken-Topped Potatoes, **'83** 210
Creamed Chipped Beef, **'92** 42
Creamed Dried Beef with Artichokes, **'85** 81
Cubes in Wine Sauce, Beef, **'79** 264
Curried Beef Dinner, **'83** 4
Dip, Chipped Beef, **'88** M8
Dip, Hot Cheesy Beef, **'80** 85
Élégante, Beef, **'80** 125
en Daube, Beef, **'79** 163
Eye of Round, Grilled Beef, **'82** 91
Fajitas, Beef, **'88** 233
Fajitas, Favorite, **'86** 114
Fillet of Beef with Blue Cheese Sauce, Pan-Roasted, **'94** 320
Goulash, Beef, **'83** 231
Goulash, Hungarian, **'81** 227; **'92** 227
Grillades and Grits, **'89** 47; **'93** 62
Gumbo, Texas Ranch-Style, **'82** 226
Gumbo z'Herbes, **'94** 239
Jerky, Beef, **'80** 269; **'81** 26
Kabobs, Barbecued Steak, **'79** 89
Kabobs, Beef, **'85** 110
Kabobs, Beef-and-Vegetable, **'91** 148
Kabobs, Chile-Beef, **'94** 251
Kabobs Deluxe, Beef, **'82** 182
Kabobs, Marinated Beef, **'82** 105; **'85** 159

Kabobs, Marinated Sirloin, **'82** 162
Kabobs, Marinated Steak, **'80** 184
Kabobs, Pineapple-Beef, **'83** 212
Kabobs, Saucy Beef, **'83** 109
Kabobs, Spirited Beef, **'87** 142
Kabobs, Steak, **'82** 4
Kabobs, Steak-and-Shrimp, **'80** 184
Kabobs, Teriyaki Beef, **'80** 207
Kabobs with Rice, Marinated Beef, **'84** 32
Kabobs with Vegetables, Beef, **'90** 148
Liver
Creamy Liver and Noodle Dinner, **'80** 11
Creole Sauce, Liver in, **'87** 33
French-Style Liver, **'80** 10
Gravy, Liver and, **'80** 10
Herbs, Liver with, **'81** 277
Kabobs, Liver, **'80** 185
Patties, Beef Liver, **'81** 277
Saucy Liver, **'81** 277
Sauté, Liver, **'81** 277
Spanish-Style Liver, **'80** 11
Stroganoff, Liver, **'79** 54
Sweet-and-Sour Liver, **'81** 277
Tasty Liver, **'83** 29
Mango-Beef and Rice, **'88** 138
Meatballs, Quick Processor, **'87** 111
Medaillons, Italian Beef, **'87** 305
Medaillons of Beef with Ancho Chile Sauce, **'87** 122
Medaillons of Beef with Horseradish Cream, **'90** 96
Mongolian Beef, **'85** 2, 75
Oriental, Beef and Cauliflower, **'80** 220
Oriental Beef and Snow Peas, **'79** 105
Oriental Beef with Pea Pods, **'86** M328
Pastichio, **'85** 194
Peppers, Beef and Green, **'79** 104
Pies, Carry-Along Beef, **'80** 224; **'81** 56
Pie, Shepherd's, **'92** 168
Pot Pie, Oriental Beef, **'92** 253
Pot Pies with Yorkshire Pudding Topping, Beef, **'93** 45
Ribs
Barbecued Beef Short Ribs, **'83** 178
Barbecued Short Ribs, **'90** 148
Hearty Beef Shortribs, **'79** 14
Supreme, Beef Shortribs, **'79** 14
Rice, Beef and Cauliflower over, **'93** 94
Roasts
Barbecue, Beef Roast, **'79** 159
Barbecued Beef Roast, **'82** 96; **'83** 103
Beer-and-Onion Sauce, Roast in, **'80** 124
Brisket Roast, Peppery, **'83** 319
Burgundy Roast, Beef, **'85** 291
Chili Bean Roast, **'87** 268; **'88** 102; **'89** 68
Chuck Roast, Fruited, **'91** 289
Chuck Roast, Marinated, **'80** 59
Chuck Roast, Orange Marinated, **'85** 179
Cola Roast, **'81** 298
Deli-Style Roast Beef, **'93** 15
Diablo, Beef, **'79** 17
Easy Beef Roast, **'89** M65
Easy Oven Roast, **'93** 64
Eye-of-Round, Burgundy, **'90** 243
Eye-of-Round Roast with Rice Gravy, Seasoned, **'89** 118
Eye Round Roast, Mexican, **'89** 190

Beef, Roasts *(continued)*

French-Style Beef Roast, **'89** 32
Grillades and Grits, **'88** 126
Grilled Marinated Beef Roast, **'93** 141
Grilled Pepper Roast, **'81** 110
Herbed Roast, **'91** 288
Java Roast, **'83** 319
Marengo, Beef, **'82** 284; **'83** 14
Marinated Roast, **'85** 3
Marinated Roast, Dijon Wine-, **'91** 289
New York Strip Roast, Spicy, **'93** 131
Patio Steak, **'87** 141
Pot Pie, Beef Roast, **'88** 296
Pot Roast, All-Seasons, **'86** 89
Pot Roast and Gravy, **'89** 234
Pot Roast and Gravy, Country-Style, **'94** 308
Pot Roast, Autumn Gold, **'83** 7
Pot Roast, Barbecued, **'79** 17; **'83** 319
Pot Roast, Basic, **'81** M208
Pot Roast, Bavarian-Style, **'79** 17
Pot Roast, Beef Brisket, **'93** 20
Pot Roast, Bloody Mary, **'86** 47
Pot Roast, Cardamom, **'79** 12
Pot Roast, Company, **'79** 162; **'88** M14
Pot Roast, Country, **'87** 216
Pot Roast, Dillicious, **'81** 187
Pot Roast, Easy Oven, **'86** 52
Pot Roast, Favorite, **'89** 118
Pot Roast, Fruited, **'90** 211
Pot Roast, Hawaiian, **'81** 298
Pot Roast, Indian, **'87** 215
Pot Roast in Red Sauce, **'87** 215
Pot Roast in Sour Cream, **'89** 117
Pot Roast in White Wine Gravy, **'81** 299
Pot Roast, Italian, **'81** 299; **'87** 95
Pot Roast, Marinated, **'85** 21
Pot Roast Medley, Vegetable-, **'83** 319
Pot Roast, Mushroom, **'79** 17
Pot Roast, Peppered, **'87** 215
Pot Roast, Perfect, **'83** 7
Pot Roast, Polynesian, **'80** 59
Pot Roast, Regal, **'79** 17
Pot Roast, Spicy Apple, **'83** 7
Pot Roast, Swedish, **'80** 59
Pot Roast, Sweet-and-Sour, **'83** 8
Pot Roast with Gravy, **'81** 298
Pot Roast with Herbed Red Sauce, **'88** 29
Pot Roast with Sour Cream Gravy, **'79** 17
Pot Roast with Spaghetti, **'80** 59
Pot Roast with Vegetables, **'80** 59; **'81** M208
Pot Roast with Vegetables, Marinated, **'88** M52
Pot Roast, Zesty, **'81** 206
Pressure-Cooker Roast, **'91** 289
Rib-Eye Beef, Spicy, **'84** 259
Rib-Eye Roast, Marinated, **'90** 318
Rib Roast, Barbecued, **'86** 152
Rib Roast, Standing, **'80** 246; **'84** 187
Rib Roast with Yorkshire Pudding, Standing, **'80** 252
Rump Roast, Easy, **'93** 217
Sauce, Chuck Roast in, **'91** 47
Sauerbraten Beef, Marinated, **'93** 16
Sauerbraten, Quick, **'80** 139
Simple Roast, **'81** 298

Sirloin Roast, Canary, **'89** 117
Sirloin Tip Roast with Mustard Cream Sauce, Herbed, **'88** 61
Supreme, Roast Beef, **'83** 8
Vegetables, Company Beef and, **'88** 234
Wellington, Beef, **'83** 319
Rolls, Stuffed Sherried Beef, **'79** 105
Rolls, Wine-Sauced Beef-and-Barley, **'87** 269
Roll-Ups, Mexican Beef, **'90** 176
Rollups with Rice, Royal Beef, **'79** 105
Roulades, Beef, **'83** 47
Roulades, Roquefort Beef, **'88** 215
Salad, Beef-and-Broccoli, **'87** 187
Salad, Beef Fajita, **'91** 70
Salad, Cucumber-Roast Beef, **'89** 162
Salad, Gingered Beef, **'88** 61
Salad, Peking Beef, **'88** 60
Salad, Roast Beef, **'80** 223; **'81** 56; **'90** 318
Salad, Tangy Beef, **'87** M218
Salad, Western-Style Beef, **'93** 321
Salad, Zesty Beef, **'79** 56
Sandwich, Beef-and-Kraut, **'91** 167
Sandwiches, Beef and Pork Tenderloin, **'80** 175
Sandwiches, Beef Salad Pocket, **'83** 267
Sandwiches, Dried Beef Pita, **'86** 160
Sandwiches, Wake-Up, **'84** 58
Sandwich, Roast Beef Hero, **'91** 167
Sandwich, Saucy Beef Pocket, **'80** 92
Seasoning Blend, Meat, **'88** 29
Shredded Beef over Rice Noodles, **'85** 74
Sirloin, Mustard Marinated, **'94** 41
Soup, Beefy Lentil, **'87** 282
Soup, Hearty Vegetable-Beef, **'84** 102
Soup, Vegetable-Beef, **'88** 296
Spaghetti, Meaty, **'82** 19
Spread, Hot Beef, **'83** 50; **'84** M216
Steaks
American Steakhouse Beef, **'93** 15
Appetizers, Marinated Steak-and-Chestnut, **'84** 323
au Poivre, Steak, **'88** 232
Bacon Twirls, Beef-and-, **'91** 163
Barbecued Beef, **'81** 18
Barbecued Steak, Saucy Oven-, **'83** 10
Bean Sprouts, Beef and, **'82** 281; **'83** 42
Benedict for Two, Steaks, **'85** 295
Blue Cheese Steaks, **'84** 171
Bourbon Steak, **'90** 148
Braised Steaks, Beer-, **'87** 96
Broiled Oriental Steaks, **'83** 110
Carne Guisada, **'94** 219
Carpetbagger Steak, **'84** 87
Chicken-Fried Steak, **'92** 214
Chuck Steak, Marinated Barbecued, **'80** 156
Continental, Steak, **'83** 178
Country-Fried Steak and Cream Gravy, **'84** 8
Country-Fried Steak, Mock, **'87** 163
Crêpes, Special Steak, **'91** 24
Curried Beef Steak, **'88** 60
Cutlets, Lemon-Flavored, **'79** 105
de Burgo, Steak, **'84** 117
Diane Flambé, Steak, **'79** 103
Diane, Steak, **'82** 275; **'92** 306
Dianne, Steak, **'83** 47
Fajita Crêpes, **'94** 116
Fajitas, **'84** 233
Fajitas, Plum Good, **'94** 115

Filet Mignon, Marinated, **'84** 171
Filet Mignon Tarragon, **'94** 46
Filet Mignon with Horseradish Gravy, **'92** 262
Filet Mignon with Mushroom Sauce, **'94** 250
Fillets au Vin, Beef, **'79** 137
Fillets with Horseradish Sauce and Curried Bananas, **'85** 230
Fingers, Golden Steak, **'85** 110
Flank Steak and Mushrooms, **'87** 61
Flank Steak, Bacon-Wrapped, **'85** 59
Flank Steak, Barbecued, **'79** 89
Flank Steak, Beer-Marinated, **'87** 35
Flank Steak, Ginger-Marinated, **'89** 25
Flank Steak, Grilled, **'80** 152; **'89** 168; **'91** 80; **'92** 166
Flank Steak, Herbed, **'92** 127
Flank Steak, Herb-Marinated, **'85** 275
Flank Steak, Marinated, **'82** 162; **'83** 35, 258; **'85** 86; **'88** 262
Flank Steak, Oriental, **'83** 178
Flank Steak Pinwheels, **'87** 141
Flank Steaks, Delicious Marinated, **'83** 110
Flank Steak Sukiyaki, **'88** 233
Flank Steak, Tangy, **'86** 184
Flank Steak, Tenderized, **'82** 105
Flank Steak Teriyaki, **'81** 110
Flank Steak, Texas, **'86** 185
Flank Steak with Black Bean-and-Corn Salsa, Grilled, **'94** 80
Flank Steak with Noodles, Stuffed, **'90** 101
Flank Steak with Sweet Peppers, Grilled, **'90** 138
French Quarter Steak, **'81** 17
Fried Steaks, Chicken-, **'88** 110
Garlic Steak, **'84** 8
Greek Pocket Steaks, **'81** 262
Grillades and Baked Cheese Grits, **'94** 240
Grilled Black Pepper Steak, **'86** 184
Grilled Steaks, Mesquite-, **'85** 154
Grilled Steaks with Green Chiles, **'85** 144
Grill, Steak Brunch, **'82** 44
Ham-and-Mushroom Sauce, Steak with, **'83** 109
Horseradish Steak, **'88** 39
Kabobs, Hot-and-Spicy, **'87** 193
Kabobs, Steak, **'93** 95
Korean Steak, **'89** 190
Lemon-Butter Steak with Brandy Sauce, **'85** 78
lo Mein, Steak, **'90** 100
London Broil, Grilled, **'92** 59
London Broil, Marinated, **'87** 32
London Broil, Peppercorn, **'88** 60
London Broil, Teriyaki, **'92** 282
Marinated Beef on a Stick, **'85** 234
Marinated Steak, **'88** 233
Marinated Steak, Mexican, **'88** 148
Mexican Steak, **'84** 76
Mushroom Sauce, Steak with, **'83** 212
Mush, Steak and Gravy with, **'81** 215
Oriental Beef, **'85** 20
Parmesan, Steak, **'93** 41
Parmigiana, Beef, **'84** 8; **'85** 234
Pepper-Beef Steak, **'85** 21
Pepper Cream, Steak in, **'94** 117

Beef, Steaks (continued)

Pepper Steak, '81 273; '85 57; '88 113
Pepper Steak and Rice, '81 17
Pepper Steak, Chinese, '82 236
Pepper Steak, Cold, '91 208
Pepper Steak, Cracked, '83 109
Pepper Steak Salad Cups, '86 206
Pepper Stir-Fry Steak, '81 240
Pies, Cornish Meat, '84 23
Pirate Steak, '79 89
Red Wine Marinade, Beef with, '91 46
Rib-Eye Steaks with Roquefort Glaze,
  '89 310
Ropa Vieja, '93 28
Roulades, Beef, '85 234
Round Steak, Braised, '87 35
Round Steak over Rice, Burgundy,
  '90 M33
Round Steak, Parmesan, '80 106
Round Steak, Red Pepper, '88 214
Round Steak, Savory Stuffed, '81 18
Round Steak, Skillet, '83 29
Round Steak, Tangy, '82 284; '83 14
Round Steak, Tender Grilled, '85 3
Salad, Greek Steak, '92 107
Salad, Grilled Sirloin, '94 129
Saltillo, Beef (Beef with Tomatillos),
  '82 219
Shrimp, Steak and, '88 123
Sirloin Steak, Secret, '81 110
Sirloin Supreme, Shrimp and, '81 131
Skewered Steak with Vegetables,
  '81 124
Skillet Steak in Red Wine Sauce, '85 21
Skillet Steak 'n Potatoes, '81 18
Smothered Beef and Onions, '85 293
Smothered Steak, '79 212
Smothered Steak, Onion-, '87 M189
Stick, Steak on a, '83 109
Stir-Fried Beef, '84 26
Stir-Fried Steak, Fast-and-Easy, '87 50
Stir-Fry, Beef-and-Vegetable, '87 22
Stir-Fry Beef-and-Vegetables, '84 141
Stir-Fry, Pepper Steak, '89 191
Stir-Fry, Steak-and-Vegetable, '84 8
Stuffed Steak, Italian-, '88 232
Stuffed Steak Rolls, '82 135
Stuffed Steaks, Cheese-, '81 17
Sweet-and-Sour Marinated Steaks,
  '83 110
Swiss Steak Cheese Skillet, '80 106
Swiss Steak, Deviled, '80 107
Swiss Steak, Oven, '85 234
Swiss Steak Surprise, '81 17
Swiss Steak with Vegetables, '81 273
Tartare, Steak, '83 78
Teriyaki Beef Broil, '92 56
Teriyaki, Marinated Steak, '84 50
Tomatoes and Artichokes, Beef with,
  '92 282
Tournedos Mouton, '83 262
Vegetables, Beef with Chinese, '81 211
Vegetables, Beef with Oriental, '84 140
Wellingtons, Individual Beef, '82 259
Zippy Steak and Gravy, '90 35
Stew, Bama Brunswick, '87 4
Stew, Beef, '86 51; '90 230
Stew, Beef-and-Onion, '87 18
Stew, Brown, '85 239

Stew, Burgundy Beef, '88 234
Stew, Company Beef, '83 85
Stew, Easy Brunswick, '92 280
Stew, Georgian Brunswick, '92 35
Stew, Irish, '90 64
Stew, Mexican, '82 231
Stew Olé, Mexican, '86 296
Stew, Oven Beef, '79 222; '80 64
Stew, Quick Beef, '92 71
Stew, Shortcut Vegetable-Beef, '89 218
Stew, Spicy Beef, '86 228
Stew, Sweet-and-Sour Beef and Vegetable,
  '85 87
Stew, Vegetable-Beef, '94 323
Stew, Virginia Ramsey's Favorite Brunswick,
  '91 16
Stew, White Wine, '82 228
Stew with Drop Dumplings, Burgundy,
  '83 125
Stew with Dumplings, Beef, '84 3
Stew with Noodles, Hungarian, '80 263
Stew with Parsley Dumplings, Beef, '81 76;
  '82 13; '85 M246
Stir-Fried Beef and Vegetables, '88 301
Stir-Fry Beef and Asparagus, '91 124
Stir-Fry Beef and Broccoli, '79 47
Stir-Fry, Beef-and-Broccoli, '91 46
Stir-Fry Beef and Pea Pods, '80 19
Stir-Fry, Beef-and-Shrimp, '93 32
Stir-Fry, Beef and Snow Pea, '82 98
Stir-Fry Beef and Snow Peas, '83 22
Stir-Fry, Beef-and-Vegetable, '81 211
Stir-Fry Broccoli and Beef, '83 110
Stir-Fry, Chinese Beef, '83 151
Stir-Fry, Hungarian, '93 64
Stir-Fry, Indian, '92 126
Stir-Fry, Lime-Ginger Beef, '92 65
Stir-Fry, Mongolian Beef, '89 25
Stir-Fry, Teriyaki, '83 110
Stock, Brown Meat, '90 31
Stroganoff, Beef, '79 163; '81 179; '91 134;
  '93 18
Stroganoff, Beef Burgundy, '85 31
Stroganoff, Light Beef, '86 36
Stroganoff, Liver, '79 54
Stroganoff, Quick Beef, '92 20
Stroganoff Sandwiches, Steak, '85 110
Stroganoff, Sirloin, '81 297
Stroganoff with Parslied Noodles, Steak,
  '85 31
Tacos al Carbón, '86 19
Tacos al Carbón, Tailgate, '79 185
Tamales, '80 195
Tempting Twosome, '81 240
Tenderloin, Barbecued Beef, '94 26
Tenderloin Bundles, Peppered Beef, '89 272
Tenderloin, Chutneyed Beef, '94 270
Tenderloin Deluxe, Beef, '85 109
Tenderloin, Easy Beef, '90 268
Tenderloin, Elegant Beef, '88 244
Tenderloin for Two, Beef, '90 295
Tenderloin, Grilled, '91 166
Tenderloin, Herb Marinated, '83 109
Tenderloin, Lobster-Stuffed Beef, '87 248
Tenderloin, Marinated, '80 146
Tenderloin, Marinated Beef, '81 246;
  '85 302; '93 215
Tenderloin Picnic Sandwiches, Beef, '90 91
Tenderloin, Spicy Beef, '88 29
Tenderloin, Spicy Marinated Beef, '83 262
Tenderloin, Spinach-Stuffed, '89 311

Tenderloin, Stuffed, '86 323; '88 50
Tenderloin with Mushroom Sauce, Beef,
  '88 3
Tenderloin with Mushrooms, Beef, '87 115
Tenderloin with Mushroom-Sherry Sauce,
  Beef, '87 306
Tenderloin with Peppercorns, Beef, '91 246
Tips and Noodles, Beef, '86 293
Tips on Rice, Beef, '85 87
Tournedos Diables, '87 60
Turnovers, Roast Beef, '88 273; '89 180
Tzimmes, Sweet Potato-Beef, '92 234
Tzimmes with Brisket, Mixed Fruit, '93 114
Vegetables in a Noodle Ring, Beef and,
  '85 285
Vegetables, Savory Beef and, '79 163
Wellington, Beef, '93 288
Beef, Ground
Appetizer, Cheesy Mexicali, '82 108
Barbecue Cups, '79 129
Bean Bake, Cheesy Beef-and-, '82 89
Bean Medley, Baked, '80 100
Beans, Beefy, '82 59
Beans, Beefy Baked, '80 136; '84 149;
  '85 142
Beans, Rancho Lima, '80 191
Beans, Three-Meat Baked, '86 210
Burgoo, Harry Young's, '87 3
Burritos, Chinese, '87 181
Burritos, Fiesta, '86 114
Cabbage-and-Beef Rolls, Easy, '88 49
Cabbage, Italian Stuffed, '84 294
Cabbage Rolls, '83 104
Cabbage Rolls, Beef Stuffed, '81 87; '82 7
Cabbage Rolls, Hungarian, '94 47
Cabbage Rolls, Spicy, '84 2
Cabbage Rolls, Stuffed, '84 217
Cabbage Rollups, Beef-and-, '80 63
Cabbage, Stuffed, '84 282
Casseroles
  Biscuit Casserole, Beef-and-, '83 75
  Cabbage Beef Bake, Zesty, '80 300
  Cavatini, '94 214
  Cheesy Ground Beef Casserole, '79 44
  Cheesy Mexican Casserole, '82 224
  Chili-Rice Casserole, '79 54
  Cornbread Casserole, '81 91
  Cornbread Skillet Casserole, '83 243;
    '84 101
  County Fair Casserole, '79 130
  Creamy Ground Beef Casserole, '81 142
  Crusty Beef Casserole, '82 88
  Easy Beef Casserole, '86 M58
  El Dorado Casserole, '81 140
  Enchilada Casserole, '87 287
  Enchilada Casserole, Firecracker,
    '80 260
  Enchilada Casserole, Sour Cream,
    '82 113
  Five-Layer Meal, '81 140
  Grits Italiano, '92 43
  Italian Cabbage Casserole, '87 42
  Italian Casserole, '80 81
  Layered Beef Casserole, '82 M203
  Layered Grecian Bake, '82 119
  Macaroni Bake, Beef-, '94 255
  Macaroni Combo, Beef-, '79 194
  Matador Mania, '86 19
  Mexican Casserole, '92 M22
  Mexican Casserole, Microwave,
    '90 M231

Beef, Ground, Casseroles *(continued)*

Mexi Casserole, **'83** M87
Moussaka Casserole, **'79** 179
Noodle Bake, Hamburger-, **'81** 140
Noodles Casserole, Beef-and-, **'84** 72
Pastitsio, **'87** 12; **'88** 11
Pizza Casserole, **'88** 273; **'89** 181
Pizza Casserole, Microwave, **'89** M248
Pizza Casserole, Quick, **'83** 266
Sausage Casserole, Ground Beef and,
  '80 260
Seashell-Provolone Casserole, **'80** 189
Sour Cream-Noodle Bake, **'79** 55
Spaghetti and Beef Casserole, **'79** 129
Spinach and Beef Casserole, **'79** 192
Spinach-Beef-Macaroni Casserole,
  '83 313
Taco Beef-Noodle Bake, **'81** 141
Taco Casserole, **'80** 33
Taco Squares, Deep-Dish, **'91** 88
Tortilla Bake, Texas, **'94** 285
Vegetable Casserole, Beefy, **'79** 248
Vegetable Chow Mein Casserole,
  Beef-and-, **'83** 313
Zucchini-Beef Bake, **'86** 146
Chiles Rellenos Egg Rolls, **'86** 296
Chili
  Basic Chili, **'82** M11; **'93** 326
  Basic Chili Embellished, **'93** 327
  Basic Chili Goes Southwest, **'93** 326
  Before-and-After Burner, Roy's,
    '89 316
  Cheese-Topped Chili, **'82** M11
  Cheesy Chili, **'82** 310
  Chili, **'87** 17; **'89** 143; **'93** 89
  Choo-Choo Chili, **'89** 316
  Company Chili, **'82** 311; **'83** 30
  con Carne, Beef and Sausage Chili,
    '83 284
  con Carne, Chili, **'84** 72
  con Carne, Favorite Chili, **'86** 293
  con Carne, Quick-and-Easy Chili, **'86** 2
  Dip, Chili, **'89** 47
  Double-Meat Chili, **'79** 269; **'80** 12
  Easy Chili, **'82** 310; **'83** 30
  Easy Texas Chili, **'90** 201
  Friday Night Chili, **'86** 228
  Hominy Bake, Chili, **'81** 282; **'82** 58
  Hot Texas Chili, **'80** 222; **'81** 77
  Hotto Lotto Chili, **'89** 316
  I-Cious, Chili-, **'89** 315
  "In-the-Red" Chili over
    "Rolling-in-Dough" Biscuits, **'92** 80
  Kielbasa Chili, Hearty, **'91** 28
  Lolly's Pop Chili, **'89** 316
  Lunchtime Chili, **'81** 230
  Meaty Chili, **'81** 282; **'82** 58
  Meaty Chili with Beans, **'85** 250
  Mexican Chili, **'89** 18
  Noodles, Chili with, **'81** 282; **'82** 57
  Pastry Cups, Chili in, **'90** 68
  Potato Chili, Savory, **'83** 284
  Potatoes, Chili-Topped, **'83** 3
  Quick-and-Easy Chili, **'92** 20
  Quick and Simple Chili, **'81** 282; **'82** 58
  Quick Chili, **'83** 283
  Ranch Chili and Beans, **'79** 270; **'80** 11
  Rice, Chili with, **'82** M11
  Roundup Chili, **'79** 269; **'80** 12

Sauce, Chili Meat, **'83** 4
Sausage-Beef Chili, **'86** 232
Sausage Chili, Beefy, **'82** M11
Simple Chili, **'79** 269; **'80** 11
Speedy Chili, **'92** 66
Spiced Chili, Hot, **'83** 214
Spicy Chili, Old-Fashioned, **'79** 269;
  '80 11
Texas-Style Chili, **'82** 311; **'83** 30
Tex-Mex Chili, **'83** 26
Tree-Hunt Chili, **'87** 292
Cornbread, Beefy Jalapeño, **'82** 142
Cornbread, Cheesy Beef, **'81** 242
Cornbread Tamale Bake, **'79** 163
Crêpes, Italian, **'90** 157
Crêpes, Sherried Beef, **'85** M29
Curried Beef and Rice, **'88** 164
Dinner, Beef-and-Garbanzo, **'84** 31
Dinner, Beef-and-Lima Bean, **'84** 292
Dinner, Beef-Cabbage, **'81** 179
Dinner, Beefy Sausage, **'80** M9
Dinner, Black-Eyed Pea Skillet, **'86** 6
Dinner, Fiesta, **'85** 110
Dinner, Ground Beef Skillet, **'82** 60
Dinner, Mexican Beef-and-Rice, **'88** 199
Dip, Hot Chile-Beef, **'83** 218
Dip, Meaty Cheese, **'82** 59; **'92** 160
Dip, Quick Nacho, **'90** 168
Dip, Tostada, **'84** 206
Eggplant, Baked Stuffed, **'81** 133
Eggplant, Beefy Stuffed, **'81** 204
Eggplant, Cheesy Stuffed, **'79** 188
Empanadas, **'92** 156
Enchiladas, American, **'81** 170
Enchiladas, Hot and Saucy, **'81** 141; **'82** 6
Enchiladas, Skillet, **'82** 89
Enchiladas, Sour Cream, **'87** 37
Enchiladas, Weeknight, **'93** 63
Fiesta, **'87** 180
Filet Mignon, Mock, **'80** 81
Filet Mignon Patties, Mock, **'82** M68
Fillets, Poor Boy, **'82** 106
Filling, Beef, **'80** 81
Flips, Pea, **'80** 7
Gumbo, Ground Beef, **'87** 283
Gumbo Joes, **'88** 158
Hamburgers
  Apple Burgers, **'86** 137
  au Poivre Blanc, Burgers, **'87** 186
  Bacon Burgers, Cheesy, **'81** 29
  Barbecued Burgers, **'82** 168; **'89** 164
  Beefburger on Buns, **'84** 71
  Beerburgers, **'79** 129
  Blue Cheese Burgers, **'89** M66
  Burgundy Burgers, **'80** 156
  Cheeseburger Biscuits, **'79** 194
  Cheeseburger Loaves, **'86** 19
  Cheeseburgers, Fried Green Tomato,
    '94 138
  Cheesy Beef Burgers, **'83** 217
  Chili Burgers, Open-Face, **'81** 24;
    '82 31; **'83** 33
  Cocktail Burgers, Saucy, **'83** 217
  Cracked Pepper Patties, **'89** M131
  Deluxe, Burgers, **'84** 125
  Favorite Burgers, **'89** 165
  Glorified Hamburgers, **'81** 73
  Grilled Hamburgers, **'93** 198
  Grilled Hamburgers, Flavorful, **'81** 110
  Hawaiian, Beefburgers, **'86** 137
  Mexicali Beef Patties, **'86** 137

  Mexicali, Hamburgers, **'93** 217
  Mushroom Burgers, **'89** 164
  Nutty Burgers, **'87** 185
  Old-Fashioned Hamburgers, **'79** 149
  Oven Burgers, **'83** 130
  Party Burgers, **'83** 164; **'84** 39
  Patties, Deviled-Beef, **'87** 22
  Patties, Hamburger, **'82** M172
  Pineapple Burgers, **'82** 169
  Pizza Burger, **'87** 185
  Pizza Burgers, **'80** M201; **'81** 73
  Pizza Burgers, All-American, **'92** 148
  Pizza Burgers, Easy, **'82** 169
  Sauce, Hamburgers with Tomato, **'81** 73
  Saucy Burgers, **'80** 93
  Saucy Hamburgers, Quick, **'82** 60
  Sausage Burgers, **'83** 212
  Seasoned Burgers, **'85** 158
  Seasoned Hamburgers, **'84** 230
  Seasoned Stuffed Burgers, **'86** 136
  Sour Cream Burgers, Grilled, **'87** 287
  Spirals, Burger, **'94** 139
  Sprouts, Burgers with, **'89** 164
  Steak-House Burgers, **'87** 186
  Steaks, Company Hamburger, **'82** 169
  Steaks with Mustard Sauce, Hamburger,
    '84 230
  Stuffed Burgers, **'85** 159
  Superburgers, **'79** 89
  Super Hamburgers, **'79** 129
  Super Supper Burgers, **'82** 110
  Surprise Burgers, **'82** 169
  Sweet-and-Sour Burgers, **'90** 128
  Tahiti Burgers, **'85** 179
  Teriyaki Burgers, **'81** 72
  Teriyaki, Hamburgers, **'89** 309
  Teriyaki Hamburgers, **'94** 138
  Tortilla Burgers, **'94** 138
  Triple-Layer Burgers, **'89** 165
  Vegetable Burgers, **'89** 164
  Vegetable Burgers, Beef-and-, **'84** 125
  Venison Burgers, **'87** 304
Kheema, Indian, **'81** 226
Kielbasa, **'92** 242
Lasagna, **'82** 119; **'83** M6
Lasagna, Beefy, **'80** 81
Lasagna, Cheesy, **'82** 224; **'88** 299
Lasagna, Cheesy Spinach, **'83** 204
Lasagna, Easy, **'92** M197; **'93** M24
Lasagna for Two, **'81** 91
Lasagna in a Bun, **'90** 176
Lasagna, Lots of Noodles, **'91** M127
Lasagna, Mexican, **'89** 63
Lasagna, Quick, **'84** 220
Lasagna, Quick 'n Easy, **'80** M10
Lasagna, Simple, **'81** 188
Lasagna, South-of-the-Border, **'84** 31
Lasagna Supreme, **'92** 198; **'93** 24
Lasagna, Vintage, **'79** 194
Log, Stuffed Beef, **'79** 71
Macaroni, Ground Beef and, **'85** 218
Macaroni, Skillet Beef and, **'82** 130
Madras, Beef, **'87** 284
Manicotti, Quick, **'79** 6
Manicotti, Saucy Stuffed, **'83** 288
Manicotti, Special, **'88** 50
Meatballs
  Bacon-Wrapped Meatballs, **'79** 81
  Barbecued Meatballs, Oven, **'82** 233
  Brandied Meatballs, **'83** 78
  Burgundy-Bacon Meatballs, **'80** 283

Beef, Ground, Meatballs *(continued)*

Chafing Dish Meatballs, **'81** 260
Charleston Press Club Meatballs,
   '93 129
Chestnut Meatballs, **'79** 110
Chinese Meatballs, **'83** 116; **'87** 194
Cocktail Meatballs, **'79** 63, 207
Creole, Meatball-Okra, **'83** 156
Creole, Meatballs, **'82** 233
Espanol, Meatballs, **'82** 110
Flavorful Meatballs, **'84** 206
Golden Nugget Meatballs, **'82** 233
Gravy, Meatballs in, **'79** 136
Hawaiian Meatballs, **'85** 86
Hawaiian Meatballs, Tangy, **'79** 129
Heidelberg, Beef Balls, **'83** 164; **'84** 39
Horseradish Dressing, Meatballs and
   Vegetables with, **'91** 32
Meatballs, **'89** 237
Paprikash with Rice, Meatballs, **'85** 31
Pineapple and Peppers, Meatballs with,
   '90 145
Pizza Meatballs, **'85** 86
Polynesian Meatballs, **'80** 207
Red Delicious Meatballs, **'85** 85
Royal Meatballs, **'87** 268; **'88** 102;
   '89 67
Sandwich, Giant Meatball, **'92** 196
Saucy Meatballs, **'85** 68; **'90** 122
Saucy Party Meatballs, **'80** 149
Sauerbraten Meatballs, **'85** 85
Spaghetti-and-Herb Meatballs, **'84** 75
Spaghetti with Meatballs, **'81** 38
Spiced Meatballs, **'79** 284
Spicy Meatballs and Sausage, **'79** 163
Stew, Meatball, **'79** 198
Stroganoff, Meatball, **'81** 297
Stroganoff, Mushroom-Meatball, **'85** 85
Swedish Meatballs, **'80** 80; **'86** 256
Sweet-and-Sour Meatballs, **'82** 233;
   '86 240
Sweet-and-Sour Party Meatballs,
   '79 233
Tamale Balls, Tangy, **'89** 60
Tamale Meatballs, **'80** 194
Zesty Meatballs, **'80** 250
Meat Loaf
   All-American Meat Loaf, **'92** 341;
      '93 46
   Barbecued Meat Loaf, **'80** 60; **'81** 275;
      '84 50; **'87** 216
   Basic Meat Loaf, **'88** M14
   Blue Cheese Meat Loaf Roll, **'93** 247
   Cheeseburger Loaf, **'81** 236, 276
   Cheesy Meat Roll, **'82** 136
   Chili Meat Loaf, **'81** 275
   Corny Meat Loaf, **'86** 68
   Crunchy Meat Loaf Oriental, **'79** 212
   Curried Meat Loaf, **'86** 43
   Easy Meat Loaf, **'88** M214
   Elegant Meat Loaf, **'89** 243
   Family-Style Meat Loaf, **'93** 18
   Fennel Meat Loaf, **'88** 46
   German Meat Loaf, **'87** 216
   Glazed Beef Loaf, **'86** 19
   Hurry-Up Meat Loaf, **'82** 21
   Hurry-Up Meat Loaves, **'88** 15
   Individual Meat Loaves, **'81** 279;
      '82 24; **'83** 154; **'92** 229

Italian Meat Loaf, **'79** 187
Meat Loaf, **'81** 170; **'89** 109
Mexicali Meat Loaf, **'81** 275
Mexican Meat Loaf, **'87** 217
Miniature Meat Loaves, **'85** 24
Mini-Teriyaki Meat Loaf, **'90** 69
Mozzarella-Layered Meat Loaf, **'79** 71
My-Ami's Meat Loaf, **'94** 229
Oriental Meat Loaf, **'81** M122;
   '83 M194
Parsleyed Meat Loaf, **'83** 35
Parsley Meat Loaf, **'87** 22
Pineapple Loaves, Individual, **'81** M121
Pizza Meat Loaf, Cheesy, **'81** M121
Roll, Meat Loaf, **'79** 129
Saucy Meat Loaves, **'79** 186
Savory Meat Loaf, **'87** 216
Southwestern Meat Loaf, **'93** 248
Special Meat Loaf, **'89** 70
Spicy Meat Loaf, **'79** 71
Sprout Meat Loaf, **'85** 51
Stuffed Beef Log, **'79** 71
Stuffed Meat Loaf, **'79** 187
Stuffed Meat Loaf, Rolled, **'80** 80
Sun-Dried Tomatoes and Herbs, Meat
   Loaf with, **'92** 192
Supreme, Meat Loaf, **'92** 33
Swedish Meat Loaf, **'81** M121
Tasty Meat Loaf, **'83** 213
Tex-Mex Meat Loaf for Two, **'90** 234
Triple Meat Loaf, **'79** 186
Vegetable Loaf, Beef-, **'79** 164
Vegetable Meat Loaf, **'85** M29
Wellington, Meat Loaf, **'79** 186; **'87** 284
Wrap, Meat Loaf in a, **'89** 122
Mix, Ground Beef, **'84** 71
Mix, Ground Meat, **'89** 143
Moussaka, **'87** 166; **'90** 68
Moussaka, Corn, **'87** 190
Mushrooms, Stuffed, **'83** 13
Noodle Dinner, Beefy, **'81** 179
Noodles, Easy Beef and, **'83** 288
Omelet, Beefy Vegetable, **'83** 188
Omelet con Carne, Tex-Mex, **'81** 209
Patties, Foo Yong, **'80** 223
Peppers, Beefed-Up, **'82** 186
Peppers, Beef-Stuffed, **'84** 154; **'85** 146;
   '91 M127
Peppers, Beefy Stuffed Green, **'81** 86
Peppers for Two, Stuffed, **'80** 84
Peppers, Mexican Green, **'80** 65
Peppers, Stuffed, **'81** 239; **'83** 66
Peppers Stuffed with Beef, **'84** 72
Picadillo II, **'93** 72
Picadillo (Spanish Hash), **'91** 87
Picadillo (Spicy Beef over Rice), **'80** 193;
   '84 118; **'85** 57
Picadillo Tarts, **'91** 279
Pie, Broccoli-Beef, **'83** 196
Pie, Cheese-Beef, **'85** 33
Pie, Cheeseburger, **'89** 121
Pie, Corn Burger, **'83** 156
Pie, Country, **'83** 155
Pie, Crescent Taco, **'80** 80
Pie, Double-Crust Taco, **'88** 272; **'89** 180
Pie, Enchilada, **'83** 155
Pie, Hamburger, **'81** 92; **'84** 13
Pie, Meat-and-Potato, **'84** 23
Pie, Mexicali Meat, **'81** 194
Pie, Mexican Burrito, **'87** 287
Pie, Old-Fashioned Meat, **'82** 110

Pie, Shepherd, **'83** 116
Pies, Individual Taco, **'82** M282
Pies, Natchitoches Meat, **'84** 21; **'91** 241
Pie, Sombrero, **'81** 140
Pie, Spaghetti, **'81** 32
Pies, Vegetable-Beef, **'80** 286
Pie, Taco, **'88** 256
Pitas, Curried Beef, **'85** 220
Pizza, Best Ever Homemade, **'80** 233
Pizza-Burger Snacks, **'84** 30
Pizza Cups, **'81** 215
Pizza, Double Cheesy Beef-and-Sausage,
   '86 77
Pizza Horns, **'89** 214
Pizza, Quick Hamburger, **'85** 243
Pizza Supreme, **'81** 214
Pizza, Tostada, **'81** 16; **'82** 13
Pizza, Upside-Down, **'91** 185
Potatoes, Taco-Topped, **'93** M18
Quiche, Green Chile, **'83** 31
Ravioli, Homemade, **'87** 230
Rice, Arabic, **'94** 200
Rice, Spanish, **'81** 51
Rice, Spiced Beef and, **'84** 285
Rice, Spicy Beef and, **'83** 231
Rolls, Italian Meat, **'86** 137
Rolls, Spicy Beef, **'85** 110
Roulades, Beef, **'80** 80
Salad Cups, Taco, **'85** M29
Salad, Dude Ranch, **'80** 15
Salad in a Shell, Mexican, **'86** 4
Salad, Mexican, **'81** 36
Salad, Mexican Chef, **'85** 84; **'92** 64
Salad, Mexican Olive, **'85** 84
Salad, Mexi-Pea, **'81** 7
Salad, Spicy Chili, **'86** 71
Salad, Spicy Taco, **'87** 287
Salad Supper, Mexican, **'82** 9; **'83** 68
Salad, Taco, **'79** 56; **'83** 145; **'84** 221;
   '85 84; **'90** 20
Salisbury Steak Deluxe, **'81** 170
Sandwiches, Barbecued Beef, **'81** 25;
   '82 31; **'83** 34
Sandwiches, Bavarian Pita, **'83** 31
Sandwiches, Beef-Eater, **'86** 72
Sandwiches, Hearty Pocket, **'80** 93
Sandwiches, Hot Pita, **'83** 217; **'87** M6
Sandwiches, Open-Face Pizza, **'82** 3
Sauce, Beer Spaghetti, **'85** 13
Sauce for 4, Easy Spaghetti Meat, **'92** 244
Sauce for 25, Easy Spaghetti Meat, **'92** 245
Sauce, Herbed Spaghetti, **'85** 13
Sauce, Italian, **'90** 67
Sauce, Italian Meat, **'83** 193
Sauce, Quick Spaghetti and Meat, **'94** 64
Shells, Cheesy Beef-Stuffed, **'83** 217
Shells, Mexican Stuffed, **'91** 87
Skillet, Vegetable-Beef, **'86** 172
Slice, French Beef, **'79** 125
Sloppy Joe Dogs, **'85** 192
Sloppy Joe Pocket Sandwiches, **'81** 200
Sloppy Joes, **'81** 279; **'82** 24; **'83** 153;
   '89 143; **'91** 172
Sloppy Joes, Easy, **'82** 31, 278; **'83** 34
Sloppy Joes, Pocket, **'85** M328
Sloppy Joes, Simple, **'82** 130
Sloppy Joes, Super, **'83** 130
Snacks, Beefy Party, **'80** 249
Soup, Beef-and-Barley Vegetable, **'89** 31
Soup, Beefy Black-Eyed, **'85** 6
Soup, Beefy Vegetable, **'79** 113; **'84** M38

Beef, Ground *(continued)*

Soup, Hamburger, **'80** 263
Soup, Quick Beefy Vegetable, **'80** 25
Soup, Spicy Vegetable-Beef, **'88** 11
Soup, Taco, **'94** 225
Soup, Vegetable-Burger, **'82** 6
Spaghetti, Black-Eyed Pea, **'81** 7
Spaghetti, Easy, **'83** M317; **'84** 72; **'92** 66
Spaghetti, Meaty, **'82** 19
Spaghetti, Quick Pepperoni, **'88** 40
Spaghetti, Real Italian, **'81** 233
Spaghetti Sauce, Thick, **'84** 118
Spaghetti, Thick-and-Spicy, **'83** 287
Spaghetti with Mushrooms, Spicy, **'85** 2
Spaghetti with Pizzazz, **'80** 85
Spaghetti, Zucchini, **'83** 160
Squash, Beef-Stuffed, **'83** 134
Squash, Stuffed Acorn, **'83** 15
Steak, Spanish, **'80** 80
Stew, Breeden Liles's Brunswick, **'91** 14
Stew, Campeche Bay Rib-Tickling, **'89** 317
Stew, Hamburger Oven, **'84** 4
Stew, Mixed Vegetable, **'84** 13
Stew, Quick Beef, **'86** 302
Sticks, Beef, **'93** 331
Stroganoff, Easy Hamburger, **'79** 208
Stroganoff, Ground Beef, **'84** 71
Stroganoff, Hamburger, **'82** 108, 110
Stroganoff, Quickie, **'81** 200
Stromboli, **'87** 283
Supper, Beef-and-Bean, **'82** 2
Supper, Beef-and-Eggplant, **'84** 291
Supper, Oriental Beef, **'79** 192
Supper, Quick Skillet, **'84** 69
Supreme, Beef, **'83** 196
Taco Joes, **'91** 167
Tacoritos, **'90** 133
Tacos, **'80** 196
Tacos, Basic, **'83** 199
Tacos, Corn Chip, **'81** 67
Tacos, Jiffy, **'83** M318
Tacos, Microwave, **'88** M213
Tacos, Soft Beef, **'91** 88
Texas Straw Hat, **'85** 293
Torta Mexican Style, **'89** 122
Tostada Compuestas, **'81** 194
Tostadas, Crispy, **'83** 2
Tostadas, Super, **'83** 199
Turnovers, Meat, **'86** 326
Wontons, Tex-Mex, **'87** 196
Zucchini, Beef-Stuffed, **'86** M139

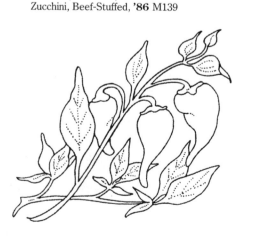

Beets
Apples, Beets and, **'80** 137; **'88** 155
Aspic, Beet, **'90** 123
Borscht, Crawfish, **'92** 84
Borscht, Ruby Red, **'83** 176
Cake, Chocolate Beet, **'80** 40
Cake with Almond Topping, Beet, **'86** 200
Chilled Beets and Cauliflower, **'80** 137
Creamy Beets, **'80** 136
Deviled Beets, **'84** 217; **'86** 252
Glazed Beets, Ginger-Marmalade, **'93** 35
Glazed Beets, Orange-, **'81** 167; **'85** 289; **'86** 187
Glazed Beets, Strawberry-, **'83** 234
Glazed Fresh Beets, **'81** 167
Harvard Beets, **'83** M195
Ivy League Beets, **'84** 122
Marinated Beets, Green Beans, and Carrots, **'88** 162
Orange Beets, **'91** 219
Orange Beets, Spicy, **'94** 280
Orange-Ginger Beets, **'80** 137
Pickled Beets, **'79** 276; **'81** 216; **'87** 163
Pickled Beets, Easy, **'80** 137
Pickles, Beet, **'81** 210
Pineapple, Beets with, **'79** 249; **'82** 204
Relish, Beet, **'84** 179
Relish, Colorful Beet, **'85** 136
Rice Ring with Beets, **'79** 225
Salad, Apple-Beet, **'91** 237
Salad, Beet-Nut, **'79** 74
Salad, Marinated Beet, **'83** 216
Salad Mold, Beet, **'82** 267
Salad, Orange-and-Beet, **'88** 43
Salad, Pickled Beet, **'83** 234
Salad, Red-and-Green, **'90** 55
Salad, Tangy Beet, **'86** 199
Slaw, "Think Pink," **'94** 247
Soup, Potato-Beet, **'88** 156
Sour Cream Dressing, Beets with, **'88** M295
Spiced Beets, **'79** 22
Stuffed Beets, **'88** 155
Stuffed Beets, Blue Cheese-, **'88** 211
Stuffed Beets, Potato-, **'83** 234
Sweet-and-Sour Beets, **'81** 167; **'82** 22; **'89** 314

Beverages
Alcoholic
Almond-Flavored Liqueur, **'81** 287
Amaretto, **'90** 272
Amaretto Breeze, **'83** 172
Amaretto Espresso, **'92** 263
Amaretto Slush, **'90** 322
Apricot Brandy Slush, **'91** 278
Apricot Slush, **'93** 205
Banana Flip, **'83** 303
Banana Kabana, **'86** 316
Bay Bloodies, **'93** 268
Bellinis, **'88** 77
Bellini Spritzers, **'90** 110
Bloody Mary, **'80** 221
Bloody Mary, Easy, **'84** 115
Bloody Marys, **'79** 33, 38; **'80** 51
Bloody Marys, Eye-Opener, **'82** 48
Bloody Marys, Overnight, **'81** 270
Bloody Marys, Pitcher, **'81** 198
Bloody Marys, Spicy, **'87** 173; **'90** 207
Blue Woo-Woo, **'94** 226
Bourbon Blizzard, **'92** 287
Bourbon Slush, **'84** 58
Bourbon Slush, Summertime, **'81** 101

Brandy Alexander, **'92** 283
Brandy Cream, **'84** 312
Brandy Slush, **'89** 110
Brandy Velvet, **'89** 170
Burgundy Bowl, Sparkling, **'83** 276
Café au Lait, German Chocolate, **'92** 264
Café Colombian Royal, **'80** M290
Café Cream, **'82** 312
Café Diablo, **'80** 259
Café Mexicano, **'92** 208
Café Mocha Cream, **'84** 54
Cafe Pontalba, **'92** 83
Café Royal, **'80** 259
Cappuccino Coffee Dessert, **'92** 264
Cappuccino, Flaming, **'79** 293
Champagne Delight, **'83** 304
Champagne Fruit Slush, **'90** 322
Champagne with Orange Juice, **'91** 71
Chocolate Deluxe, Hot, **'90** 272
Chocolate, Flaming Brandied, **'80** M290
Chocolate, Hot Laced Marshmallow, **'93** 53
Cider, December, **'91** 260
Cider, Hot Mexican, **'87** 213
Cider, Hot Mulled, **'84** 323
Cider, Red Apple, **'80** 259
Clam Diggers, **'91** 63
Coconut Frost, Pink, **'79** 174; **'80** 128
Coconut Nog, **'83** 275
Coconut-Pineapple Drink, **'83** 172
Coffee, After-Dinner, **'81** 262
Coffee, Brandied, **'81** 244
Coffee, Chocolate, **'82** 43
Coffee, Colonial, **'89** 290
Coffee Cream, Icy Rum, **'83** 172
Coffee, Creamy Irish, **'79** 232
Coffee Delight, Almond-, **'84** 115
Coffee, Flaming Irish, **'79** 293
Coffee-Flavored Liqueur, **'86** 266
Coffee Ice, Hazelnut-, **'94** 233
Coffee, Mexican, **'83** 175
Coffee Nog, Brandied, **'86** 329
Coffee Nog, Irish, **'84** 258
Coffee, Praline-Flavored, **'87** 69
Coffee Refresher, Velvet, **'79** 149
Cranapple Glogg, Hot, **'90** 22
Cranapple Wine, **'90** 272
Cranberry Cooler, **'86** 229
Cranberry-Rum Slush, **'84** 259
Cranberry Spritzer, **'91** 66; **'92** 265
Cranberry Spritzers, **'89** 213
Cranberry-Vodka Refresher, **'91** 210
Cranberry Wine Cup, **'85** 23
Cricket, **'89** 289
Daiquiris, Cranberry, **'81** 245
Daiquiris, Creamy Strawberry, **'91** 66
Daiquiris, Freezer Lime, **'79** 141
Daiquiris, Mint, **'89** 157
Daiquiris, Peach, **'90** 322
Daiquiris, Strawberry, **'90** 125
Daiquiri, Strawberry, **'81** 156
Daiquiritas, **'82** 160
Dessert, After Dinner-Drink, **'82** 100
Dessert Drink, Creamy, **'86** 131
Dessert Drink, Simply Super, **'83** 303
Eggnog, Blender, **'93** 341
Eggnog, Christmas, **'87** 242
Eggnog, Creamy, **'80** 259; **'83** 303
Eggnog Deluxe, Holiday, **'79** 232
Eggnog, Easy, **'91** 305

Eggnog, Edenton, '84 251
Eggnog, Thick and Creamy, '80 261
Frosty Sours, '81 156
Fruit 'ritas, '94 157
Fuzz Buzz, '82 160
Game-Cocktails, '93 214
Gin Cooler, Sparkling, '90 272
Ginger Beer, '84 159
Golden Dream, '82 100
Holiday Brew, '81 265
Irish Coffee Nog, '93 340
Irish Cream Nog, '82 312
Kahlúa Hummer, '91 176
Kahlúa Smoothie, '87 242
Kahlúa Velvet Frosty, '82 244
King Alfonso, '80 259
Lemonade, Claret, '93 72
Lemonade, Hot Buttered, '88 208
Lemon Cooler, '82 48
Lime Fizz, '81 172
Magnolia Blossoms, '87 72
Magnolias, '82 196
Margaritas, '92 210; '93 273
Margaritas, Frosted, '84 115
Margaritas, Frosty, '83 172
Margaritas, Lemon-Lime, '94 227
Margaritas, Pitcher, '83 175
Margaritas Supreme, Frozen, '80 160
Margaritas, Tart, '85 153
Melon Ball Cooler, '86 131
Mimosa Hawaiian, '85 44
Mimosas, '86 91
Minted Delight, '87 107
Mint Juleps, '81 155; '82 41; '85 40;
    '90 81
Mix, Bloody Mary, '89 110
Mix, Hot Wine, '81 287
Mix, Mulled Wine Spice, '85 266
Mocha Chocolate Fluff, '89 170
Mocha Deluxe Hot Drink, '82 289
Mocha Polka, '89 171
Mocha, Spirited Hot, '91 M260
Oklahoma Sunrise, '87 67
Old-Fashioneds, '86 270
Old-Fashioned Slush, '93 340
Orange Blossom Flips, '80 51
Orange-Champagne Cocktail, '79 39
Orange Liqueur, '81 287
Orange Milk Shake, '84 166
Peach Frosty, '81 156
Peach Petals, '90 104
Peach Smash, '88 161
Peppermint Flip, Hot, '86 329
Piña Coladas, Frosty, '83 176
Piña Coladas, Luscious, '81 134
Pineapple-Strawberry Slush, '94 227
Pink Palace, '93 293
Plum Slush, '84 139
Punch, Amaretto, '91 277
Punch, Anytime Wine, '79 232
Punch, Bourbon, '92 208
Punch, Bourbon-Citrus, '94 227
Punch, Bourbon-Tea, '87 57
Punch, Brandy Milk, '85 44; '88 83
Punch, Brandy Slush, '87 72
Punch, Champagne, '85 153, 257;
    '86 101
Punch, Champagne Blossom, '81 50

Punch, Chatham Artillery, '80 121
Punch, Coffee, '88 83
Punch, Coffee-Eggnog, '86 281
Punch, Coffee Eggnog, '92 264
Punch, Cranapple-Vodka, '87 72
Punch, Cranberry, '85 90
Punch, Cranberry Percolator, '88 248
Punch, Extra-Kick, '91 209
Punch, Festive, '94 289
Punch, Fruit, '83 52
Punch, Fruit Juicy Rum, '91 175
Punch, Gin, '80 160
Punch, Golden Gin, '79 233
Punch, Golden Spiked, '79 285
Punch, Health-Kick, '80 174
Punch, Hot Cranberry, '84 41
Punch, Hot Molasses-Milk, '86 329
Punch, Hot Pineapple, '82 264
Punch, Hot Wine, '85 265
Punch, Jefferson County, '86 267
Punch, Lemon Champagne, '94 176
Punch, Lime, '84 58
Punch, Milk, '79 38
Punch, New Orleans Milk, '81 50
Punch, Orange-Lime, '82 160
Punch, Party, '81 265
Punch, Perky Rum, '85 116
Punch, Pimms, '92 167
Punch, Piña Colada, '89 212
Punch, Pineapple, '79 174; '80 128
Punch, Raspberry-Rosé, '87 242
Punch, Red Velvet, '89 289
Punch, Refreshing Champagne, '84 259
Punch, Rum, '85 265
Punch, Sparkling Champagne, '84 58
Punch, Sparkling Holiday, '81 290
Punch, Spiked Tea, '86 101
Punch, Spirited Fruit, '81 100
Punch, Stormy Petrel Rum Thunder,
    '93 269
Punch, Strawberry Champagne, '90 315
Punch, Streetcar Champagne, '88 82
Punch, Tropical Fruit, '83 176
Punch, Vodka, '85 265
Punch, Wedding, '86 107
Punch, Whiskey, '90 64; '91 175
Punch, Whiskey Sour, '91 209
Punch, Wine, '93 331
Punch, Yacht Club Milk, '89 86
Raspberry Kir, '86 183
Red Roosters, '87 147
Red Ruby, '92 209
Rum, Hot Buttered, '80 259; '82 244;
    '88 247
Rum Slush, Easy, '79 174; '80 129
Sangría, '79 186; '81 67, 196; '82 121;
    '86 214
Sangría, Easy Citrus, '80 218
Sangría, Easy Frozen, '92 208
Sangría, Grapefruit, '89 92
Sangría, Orange, '81 237
Sangría, Pineapple, '91 176
Sangría, Punchy, '80 160
Sangría, Quick, '81 156
Sangría Slush, White, '90 322
Sangría, Spanish, '83 81
Sangría, Teaberry, '87 147
Sangría, Three-Fruit, '89 212
Sangría, White, '83 180; '94 289
Screwdrivers, '79 33
Sea Mist, '93 167

Sherry Sour, '87 74
Sipper, Sunshine, '86 179
Slush, Mexican, '83 176
Slush with a Punch, '90 322
Spritzers, Citrus, '91 231; '92 67
Spritzers, Spiced, '86 229
Strawberry-Banana Smoothie, '81 59
Strawberry Mimosa, Sparkling, '88 169
Sunny Morning, '93 295
Sunrise, St. Pete, '94 227
Syllabub, '81 265; '84 319
Tart Caribbean Cooler, '81 134
Tea, Sangría, '94 131
Tea, Southern Long Island Iced, '90 207
Tequila Slush, '83 176
Tequila Sunrise, '83 175
Toddy, Molasses Rum, '91 36
Tomato Bouillon, New Year's, '94 24
Tomato-Orange Juice Cocktail, '83 169
Tomato Sipper, Peppy, '94 227
Vodka, Frozen Pink, '89 170
Vodka-Orange Slush, '89 92
Vodka Slush, '88 82
Wassail, '83 311
Wassail, Bourbon, '86 270
Wassail, Four-Fruit, '90 22
Whiskey Sours, Frozen, '93 176
Whiskey Sours, Frozen Orange-, '92 67
Whisky Sour Slush, '86 183
Whispers, '86 317
Wine, Christmas Dreams in, '91 260
Wine Cooler, '82 41
Wine Cooler, Fruited, '86 176
Wine, Hot Mulled, '83 251
Wine, Hot Spiced, '84 41
Wine Spritzers, '81 94
Wine Welcomer, '81 100
Yellow Birds, '90 103
Apple-Berry Sparkler, '93 104
Apple Berry Sparkler, '94 100
Apple Cooler, '90 14
Apple Cooler, Minted, '88 169
Apple Juice, Hot, '86 270
Apple Juice, Perky Cinnamon-, '90 22
Apple Juice Shrub, Shenandoah, '79 282
Apple Julep, '86 103, 215
Apricot-Citrus Slush, '88 82
Apricot Cooler, '81 100
Apricot Fruit Flip, '91 18
Apricot Mint Cooler, '90 165
Apricot Nectar, Hot, '81 265
Apricot Nectar, Mulled, '86 229
Banana-Berry Flip, '88 215; '89 20
Banana-Blueberry Smoothie, '90 104
Banana-Chocolate Malt, '89 170
Banana Coolers, '91 308
Banana Crush, '80 88; '83 142
Banana Frostee, '91 66
Banana Nog, '82 290
Banana-Orange Slush, '80 48; '81 155
Banana-Pineapple Smoothie, Quick, '93 195
Banana Slush, '83 56
Banana Smoothie, '87 160; '93 95
Banana-Strawberry Frost, '87 199
Beach Brew, '91 177
Black Russian, Mock, '92 322
Bloodless Mary, '80 146
Bloody Mary Mix, '89 110
Breakfast Eye-Opener, '87 199
Brew, Quilter's, '85 43
Brew, Witch's, '93 244

Beverages *(continued)*

Bullshots, **'86** 91
Café Cappuccino, **'82** 253
Café Viennese, **'82** 254
Cappuccino, Chocolate Castle, **'84** 53
Carambola-Yogurt Calypso, **'90** 169
Carrot Cooler, **'89** 35
Champagne, Mock Pink, **'89** 46
Chocolate Malt, **'86** 183
Chocolate, Mexican-Style, **'81** 187
Chocolate Milk, French, **'79** 38
Chocolate-Mint Smoothie, **'84** 166
Chocolate Sipper, **'88** 83
Cider, Apple-Orange, **'92** 20
Cider, Cherry, **'94** 288
Cider, Holiday, **'82** 264
Cider, Hot Apple, **'90** 21, 225
Cider, Hot Mulled, **'79** 205
Cider, Hot Spiced, **'82** 290
Cider, Hot Spiced Apple, **'84** 318
Cider, Hot Spicy, **'84** 265
Cider, Mulled, **'91** 209; **'94** 227
Cider, Mulled Apple, **'92** 208
Cider Nog, Hot Apple, **'84** 42
Cider, Sparkling Apple, **'88** 276
Cider, Spiced Apple, **'85** 256
Cider, Spiced Cranberry, **'84** 261
Citrus Cooler, **'82** 160; **'93** 105
Citrus Float, **'89** 171
Citrus Slush, **'93** 198
Cocoa, Mocha, **'83** 318
Coco-Berry Calypso, **'89** 171
Coffee, Chocolate-Almond, **'84** 54
Coffee, Cocoa-, **'83** 55
Coffee, Creamy, **'81** 244
Coffee, Frosted, **'81** 244
Coffee, Holiday, **'90** 273
Coffee, Mexican, **'83** 275; **'91** 78; **'93** 310
Coffee Mix, Fireside, **'87** 241
Coffee, Mocha, **'85** M329
Coffee, Special Spiced, **'84** 284
Coffee, Spiced-Up, **'89** 92
Coffee, Viennese Orange, **'84** 54
"Concrete," Abaco Mocha, **'94** 114
"Concrete," All Shook Up, **'94** 114
"Concrete," Cardinal Sin, **'94** 113
"Concrete," Foxtreat, **'94** 113
Cooler, Spring, **'86** 214
Cranberry Cocktail, Hot, **'89** 310
Cranberry Drink, Mulled, **'92** 12
Cranberry Frappé, **'82** 263
Cranberry Juice, Sparkling, **'88** 275
Cranberry-Orange Soda, **'79** 148
Cranberry Smoothie, **'86** 183; **'91** 307
Eggnog, **'83** 318
Eggnog, Cooked Custard, **'91** 305
Eggnog, Sparkling, **'79** 232
Eggnog with Orange and Nutmeg, Mock, **'92** 323
Espresso, Italian Mocha, **'82** 254
Float, Frosty Fruit, **'87** 159
Float, Nutmeg-Almond, **'84** 106
Float, Pineapple Sherbet, **'79** 148
Floats, Maple-Coffee, **'86** 195
Float, Sparkling Cranberry, **'86** 195
Float, Strawberry-Banana, **'87** 160
Frappé, Hootenanny, **'89** 110
Fruit Beverage, Blender, **'83** 318
Fruit Cooler, Four-, **'86** 101

Fruit Drink, Three-, **'79** 38; **'80** 50; **'87** 199
Fruit Drink, Tropical, **'85** 43
Fruit Juice Cooler, **'92** 67
Fruit Juicy, Breakfast, **'86** 176
Fruit Refresher, **'91** 203
Fruit Refresher, Four-, **'79** 174; **'80** 129
Fruit Slush, Refreshing, **'82** 35
Fruit Slushy, **'80** 146
Fruit Smoothie, **'89** 87
Fruit Smoothie, Two-, **'89** 182
Fruit Whisper, Tropical, **'89** 212
Funshine Fizz, **'91** 66
Ginger-Mint Cooler, **'89** 92
Grapefruit Cooler, **'88** 81
Grapefruit Drink, **'90** 84
Grapefruit-Orange Refresher, **'82** 174
Grapefruit Refresher, **'88** 85
Grape Juice, Mulled, **'90** 21
Grape Juice, Spiced White, **'92** 320
Grape-Lime Cooler, **'94** 227
Hawaiian Crush, **'91** 66
Holiday Brew, **'90** 272
Honey-Banana Smoothie, **'89** 144
Honey-Yogurt Smoothie, Fruited, **'88** 231; **'89** 23
Hot Chocolate, **'94** 290
Hot Chocolate, Creole, **'80** M290
Hot Chocolate, Favorite, **'83** 55
Hot Chocolate, French, **'86** 328
Hot Chocolate, Old-Fashioned, **'85** 23
Hot Chocolate, Special, **'82** 5
Hot Chocolate, Spiced, **'80** 50
Hot Chocolate, Spicy, **'85** 278
Hot Cocoa, Quick, **'82** 5
Ice Bowl, **'83** 152
Ice Cream Ginger Fizz, **'83** 303
Ice Mold, Strawberry, **'91** 278
Ice Ring, Strawberry, **'94** 176
Jogger's Sunrise, **'93** 213
Kid's Cooler, **'90** 95
Kona Luscious, **'84** 54
Lemonade, Apple, **'89** 212
Lemonade, Berry Delicious, **'93** 205
Lemonade Concentrate, **'89** 110
Lemonade, Fresh Squeezed, **'81** 172
Lemonade, Front Porch, **'90** 156
Lemonade, Hot Buttered, **'94** 18
Lemonade, Pineapple, **'93** 194
Lemonade Slush, Pink, **'80** 151
Lemonade, Strawberry, **'80** 160
Lemonade with Frozen Tea Cubes, **'85** 161
Lemon Frappé, **'92** 44
Lemon Velvet, **'90** 15
Limeade, Pink Apple, **'89** 46
Lime Cooler, **'87** 160
Lime Fizz, Frosty, **'90** 104
Malt Special, **'85** 198
Mango Frappé, **'86** 216
Mango-Orange Smoothie, **'86** 216
Margaritas, Mock, **'88** 209
Melon Julep, Rainbow, **'80** 183
Milk, Santa Claus, **'92** 281
Milkshake, Banana, **'85** 47; **'90** 179
Milkshake, Fresh Strawberry, **'82** 113
Milkshake, Mocha, **'89** 35
Milkshake, Pineapple, **'87** 199
Milkshakes, Peanut Butter, **'85** 198
Mix, Beetle Cider, **'82** 308
Mix, Cappuccino, **'90** 87
Mix, Deluxe Hot Chocolate, **'80** M290
Mix, Hot Cocoa, **'81** 287

Mix, Hot Mocha-Cocoa, **'82** 296
Mix, Hot Spiced Cider, **'84** 42
Mix, Instant Cocoa, **'86** 332
Mix, Minted Hot Cocoa, **'91** 316
Mix, Mocha-Flavored Hot Cocoa, **'91** 316
Mix, Spicy-Hot Chocolate, **'85** 278
Mocha Frosty, **'92** 44
Mocha, Hot, **'84** 60
Mocha, Mexican, **'93** M341
Mocha, Quick Viennese, **'79** 232
Mocha, Swiss-Style, **'82** 253
Nog, Speedy Breakfast, **'82** 47
Orange-Banana Flip, **'82** 48
Orange Blush, **'80** 51
Orange Frosty, **'86** 101
Orange Juicy, **'90** 178
Orange-Lemon Mist, **'79** 288; **'80** 35
Orange Pick-Me-Up, **'80** 232
Orange-Pineapple Drink, **'89** 35
Orange Slush, **'82** 49
Orange Spiced Nog, **'82** 48
Patio Blush, **'92** 43
Peach Cooler, **'85** 198
Peaches 'n' Almond Cream, **'86** 229
Peach Frost, **'89** 155
Peach Frosty, **'83** 318
Peach Pick-Me-Up, **'89** 183
Peach Refresher, **'86** 103
Peanut Butter Cooler, **'84** 115
Piña Colada, Mock, **'92** 322
Piña Colada, Parson's, **'89** 46
Pineapple-Banana Slush, **'90** 14
Pineapple Cooler, **'90** 207
Pineapple Drink, Hot Buttered, **'91** 260
Pineapple Nectar, Hot, **'90** 21
Pineapple Slush, **'88** 82
Pineapple Soda, **'90** 179
Pineapple Sparkle, Spiced, **'92** 322
Pineapple-Yogurt Whirl, **'91** 132
Pink Soda, Blushing, **'90** 104
Punch. *See also* Beverages/Alcoholic.
   Apple Punch, Hot, **'84** 324
   Apple-Tea Punch, **'85** 82
   Apricot Spiced Punch, **'80** 269
   Autumn Punch, **'88** 209
   Berry Punch, **'92** 67
   Bubbling Jade Punch, **'79** 174; **'80** 129
   Cantaloupe Punch, **'81** 147
   Children's Punch, **'85** 322
   Christmas Eve Punch, **'86** 314
   Christmas Punch, **'84** 259; **'89** 330
   Cider Punch, Spiced, **'84** 258
   Citrus Party Punch, **'83** 141; **'92** 289
   Citrus Punch, **'85** 319; **'93** 99
   Citrus Punch, Budget, **'82** 121
   Citrus Punch, Fresh, **'85** 154
   Citrus Punch, Party, **'84** 117
   Coffee-and-Cream Punch, **'85** 116
   Coffee Punch, **'80** 50; **'83** 275
   Coffee Punch, Creamy, **'81** 50
   Coffee Punch, "Eye-Opener," **'92** 80
   Coffee Punch, Rich-and-Creamy, **'82** 121
   Cola Punch, **'91** 144
   Cranapple Punch, **'83** 142
   Cranberry-Cherry Punch, **'91** 176
   Cranberry-Cinnamon Punch, **'86** 270
   Cranberry Punch, **'83** 275
   Cranberry Punch, Holiday, **'85** 265
   Cranberry Punch, Hot, **'80** 288; **'84** 319; **'85** 265

Beverages, Punch (continued)

Cranberry Punch, Sparkling, **'85** 277
Cranberry Punch, Spiced, **'89** 290
Cranberry Punch, Tart, **'83** 318
Cran-Grape-Tea Punch, **'92** 209
Eggnog Punch, Holiday, **'86** 281
False-Kick Punch, **'82** 121
Frozen Punch Ring, **'83** 152
Fruit Punch, Can-Can, **'94** 122
Fruit Punch, Florida, **'92** 247
Fruit Punch, Golden, **'80** 299; **'83** 56
Fruit Punch, Holiday, **'79** 232
Fruit Punch, Holiday Hot, **'92** 286
Fruit Punch, Hot, **'83** 33
Fruit Punch, Mixed, **'90** 207
Fruit Punch, Party, **'82** 137
Fruit Punch, Passion, **'90** 169
Fruit Punch, Spiced, **'88** 2
Fruit Punch, Summertime, **'80** 160
Fruit Punch, Tropical, **'80** 51; **'90** 169
Fruit Slush Punch, **'91** 278
Ginger Ale-Nectar Punch, **'92** 171
Goblin Punch, **'88** 228
Golden Punch, **'85** 207
Grape Punch, Sparkling, **'82** 48
Holiday Punch, **'87** 252
Lemonade Punch, Sparkling, **'88** 276
Lemon Balm Punch, **'80** 42
Lime-Pineapple Punch, **'83** 142
Lime Punch, Foamy, **'82** 264
Lime Slush Punch, **'90** 273
Merry Christmas Punch, **'79** 285
Mocha Punch, **'84** 58, 166; **'86** 270
Mock Champagne Punch, **'93** 340
Morning Punch, **'88** 82
Nectar Punch, **'93** 283
Orange Blossom Punch, **'83** 142
Orange-Mint Punch, **'82** 121
Orange Punch, Refreshing, **'81** 39
Orange Sherbet Party Punch, **'83** 142
Orange Soda Punch, **'87** 214
Parsonage Punch, **'79** 148
Party Punch, **'91** 106, 278
Party Punch in a Pail, **'94** 289
Party Punch, Special, **'81** 119
Peppermint-Eggnog Punch, **'90** 273
Percolator Punch, **'91** 306
Percolator Punch, Hot, **'81** 288
Pineapple-Mint Punch, **'88** 209
Pineapple-Orange Punch, **'85** 236
Pineapple Punch, **'79** 174
Pineapple Punch, Frosty, **'91** 66
Pineapple Punch, Spiced, **'83** 33; **'92** 66
Pink Lady Punch, **'81** 100
Ponche de Piña, **'84** 58
Raspberry Sparkle Punch, **'84** 57
Rum Punch, Spiced, **'86** 179
Sherbet Punch, Double, **'79** 232
Spiced Punch, Hot, **'80** 250
Strawberry-Lemonade Punch, **'85** 116;
    '91 175
Strawberry Punch, **'90** 273
Strawberry Punch, Creamy, **'86** 195
Tangy Punch, **'83** 142
Tea Party Punch, **'87** 147
Tea Punch, **'90** 143, 207
Tea Punch, Citrus-, **'85** 116
Traders' Punch, **'87** 94
Tropical Punch, **'90** 207

Vegetable Punch, Hot, **'93** 12
Watermelon Punch, **'89** 204; **'92** 190
White Grape Punch, **'90** 15
Raspberry Cooler, **'89** 171
Raspberry Fizz, Rosy, **'90** 179
Sangría, Southern, **'88** 170
Sangría, Virgin, **'89** 46
Scarlet Sipper, **'90** 198
Shake, Amazin' Raisin, **'86** 195
Shake, Apricot, **'84** 115
Shake, Banana-Pineapple Milk, **'84** 59
Shake, Chocolate-Banana Milk, **'94** 113
Shake, Chocolate Mint, **'89** 170
Shake, Cranberry, **'83** 171
Shake, Date, **'92** 44
Shake, Frosty Fruit, **'87** 23
Shake, Papaya, **'90** 169
Shake, PBJ, **'93** 292
Shake, Peach-Coffee Milk, **'84** 284
Shake, Peach Melba Sundae, **'93** 134
Shake, Peachy Orange, **'81** 156
Shake, Peanut Butter, **'82** 48
Shake, Pep, **'79** 38
Shake, Pineapple-Banana, **'85** 215
Shake, Pineapple Milk, **'94** 113
Shake, Raspberry-and-Banana, **'89** 183
Shake, Strawberry-Banana, **'89** 35
Shake, Strawberry-Cheesecake, **'92** 44
Shake, Strawberry Milk, **'94** 113
Shake, Strawberry-Orange Breakfast,
    '87 186
Shake, Strawberry-Pear, **'92** 139
Shake, Strawberry-Pineapple, **'84** 166
Shake, Strawberry-Yogurt, **'87** 199
Shake, Summer, **'82** 161
Shake, Sunshine, **'79** 53
Shake, Tropical, **'87** 200; **'93** 212
Slush, Santa's, **'90** 271
Spiced Brew, Hot, **'91** 36
Spices, Barclay House Mulling, **'86** 289
Strawberry Cooler, **'83** 56; **'84** 51
Strawberry Coolers, **'92** 67
Strawberry-Mint Cooler, **'84** 57
Strawberry-Orange Slush, **'83** 172
Strawberry-Peach Smoothie, **'89** 182
Strawberry Refresher, Frozen, **'93** 213
Strawberry Slurp, **'81** 96
Strawberry Smoothie, **'86** 183
Strawberry Soda, **'84** 115
Strawberry Soda, Old-Fashioned, **'79** 49
Strawberry Spritzer, **'90** 14
Sunrise Smoothie, **'93** 139
Sunshine Fizz, **'92** 44
Syllabub, Plantation, **'79** 233
Syrup, Mint, **'90** 89
Tahitian Flower, **'87** 159
Tea, Almond, **'85** 43; **'86** 329; **'89** 212
Tea, Almond-Lemonade, **'86** 229
Tea, Bubbly Iced, **'81** 168
Tea, Christmas Fruit, **'83** 275
Tea Cooler, Citrus-Mint, **'92** 105
Tea Cooler, Fruited, **'94** 131
Tea Cooler, Spiced, **'83** 55
Tea, Cranberry, **'94** 131
Tea, Cranberry-Apple, **'88** 169
Tea, Easy Mint, **'91** 187
Tea, Frosted Mint, **'84** 161
Tea, Fruited Mint, **'88** 79; **'91** 81
Tea, Ginger, **'81** 100
Tea, Ginger-Almond, **'94** 131
Tea, Grapefruit, **'92** 67

Tea, Hawaiian, **'87** 57
Tea, Honey, **'81** 105
Tea, Hot Apple-Cinnamon, **'87** 57
Tea, Hot Citrus, **'83** 275
Tea, Hot Spiced, **'83** 244
Tea, Hot Spiced Apricot, **'88** 248
Tea, Hot Spiced Fruit, **'87** 242
Tea, Iced Citrus, **'85** 162
Tea, Iced Mint, **'83** 170
Tea, Johnny Appleseed, **'85** 23
Tea, Lemon, **'82** 156
Tea, Lemon-Mint, **'85** 162
Tea, Mint, **'87** 107; **'90** 89
Tea, Minted, **'86** 101; **'88** 163; **'92** 54
Tea Mix, Deluxe Spiced, **'88** 257
Tea Mix, Friendship, **'83** 283
Tea Mix, Spiced, **'86** 32
Tea Mix, Sugar-Free Spiced, **'91** 258
Tea, Pineapple, **'93** 165
Tea, Southern Sun, **'81** 168
Tea, Sparkling Strawberry, **'94** 131
Tea, Spiced Grape, **'79** 174
Tea, Spiced Iced, **'91** 209
Tea, Strawberry, **'88** 248
Tea, Summer, **'85** 162
Tea, Summertime, **'81** 167
Tea, White Grape Juice, **'87** 57
Tea, Yaupon, **'79** 31
Toddy, Jolly, **'86** 229
Toddy, Tasty, **'88** 82
Tofruitti Breakfast Drink, **'88** 26
Tomato Bouillon, **'83** 8
Tomato-Clam Cocktail, **'87** 252
Tomato Cocktail, **'83** M203
Tomato Juice Cocktail, **'79** 212; **'83** 230;
    '90 12
Tomato Juice Cocktail, Zesty, **'83** 289
Tomato Juice, Homemade, **'81** 50
Tomato Juice, Spicy, **'85** 189
Tomato Refresher, **'83** 318
Tomato Sipper, Peppy, **'94** 227
Tomato Sipper, Spicy, **'86** 229
Tropical Cooler, **'84** 120
Tropical Delight, **'89** 182
Tropical Ice, **'79** 174; **'80** 129
Tropical Refresher, **'85** 198
Tropical Smoothie, **'81** 50; **'90** 169
Vanilla Frosty, French, **'79** 148
Vegetable Cocktail, Fresh, **'82** 165
Vegetable Juice Delight, **'84** 58
Virgin Mary, Spicy, **'92** 323
Wassail, **'84** 259, 318; **'88** 248; **'90** 273
Wassail, Christmas, **'93** 295
Wassail, Cranberry, **'88** 289
Wassail, Holiday, **'89** 289; **'91** 260
Wassail, Pineapple-Apricot, **'83** 275
Watermelon-Berry Slush, **'90** 137
Zippy Red Eye, **'91** 209
Biscuits
Angel Biscuits, **'80** 49; **'90** 28; **'93** 270
Angel Biscuits, Ham-Filled, **'80** 159
Bacon-Cheese Biscuits, **'88** 84
Baking Powder Biscuits, **'82** 195; **'89** 144
Basil Biscuits, **'93** 160
Beaten Biscuits, **'86** 54
Beer-and-Cheese Biscuits, **'94** 215
Benne Seed Biscuits, **'79** 38
Biscuits, **'92** 31
Blueberry Buttermilk Biscuits, **'89** 210
Blue Cheese Biscuits, **'88** 83
Bran Biscuits, **'85** 228

Biscuits *(continued)*

Bread, Biscuit, **'84** 284
Buttermilk Biscuits, **'83** 208; **'85** 255, 321
Buttermilk Biscuits, Basic, **'94** 214
Buttermilk Biscuits, Deluxe, **'82** 130
Buttermilk Biscuits, Favorite, **'81** 191
Buttermilk Biscuits, Fluffy, **'84** 102
Buttermilk Biscuits, Old-Fashioned, **'80** 77
Buttermilk Biscuits, Quick, **'83** 311; **'88** 15;
  '92 269
Buttermilk-Raisin Biscuits, **'92** 338
Casserole, Beef-and-Biscuit, **'83** 75
Casserole, Biscuit-Topped Tuna, **'79** 113
Cheese Angel Biscuits, **'89** 211
Cheese Biscuits, **'79** 296; **'80** 31; **'81** 288;
  '83 253; **'85** 32; **'87** 78
Cheese Biscuits, Easy, **'81** 99
Cheese Biscuits, Lightnin', **'90** 283
Cheese Biscuits, Tiny, **'80** 192
Cheeseburger Biscuits, **'79** 194
Cheese-Chive Biscuits, **'94** 324
Cheese Dips, Butter, **'80** 46
Cheesy Biscuits, Hot, **'80** 186
Chicken in a Biscuit, **'79** 263
Cinnamon-Raisin Breakfast Biscuits, **'93** 159
Cloud Biscuits, **'87** 15
Cornmeal Biscuits, **'85** 228
Cornmeal-Jalapeño Biscuits, **'94** 214
Country Ham Biscuits, **'94** 215
Country Ham, Biscuits with, **'90** 93
Daisy Biscuits, **'90** 86
Dressing, Cornbread-Biscuit, **'79** 296
Elgin Biscuits, **'93** 281
Feather Biscuits, **'80** 78
Feather Light Biscuits, **'80** 246
Flaky Biscuits, **'84** 228
Grapefruit Juice Biscuits, **'83** 10
Ham and Biscuits, Southern, **'91** 12
Ham and Cheese Biscuits, Petite, **'79** 193
Ham 'n' Angel Biscuits, Kentucky, **'90** 83
Heart Biscuits, Country Ham in, **'86** 105
Heart Biscuits with Sausage, Angel, **'87** 156
Hearty Biscuits, **'83** 121
Herb Biscuits, Easy, **'90** 283
Herbed Biscuits, **'85** 228; **'93** 67
Hot Biscuits, **'86** 269
Light Biscuits, **'89** 53
Marmalade Biscuits, Carolina, **'85** 42
Marmalade Biscuit Squares, **'79** 193
Mile-High Biscuits, **'85** 41
Nannie's Biscuits, **'82** 156
Nutty Tea Biscuits, **'89** 210
Oatmeal Biscuits, **'89** 108
One-Step Biscuits, **'82** 173
Orange Biscuits, **'88** 85
Orange Puffs, Upside-Down, **'83** 57
Parker House-Style Biscuits, **'79** 162
Pepper-Cheese Biscuit Fingers, **'88** 283
Pepperoni Biscuits, **'84** 95
Potato-Bacon Biscuits, **'94** 214
Processor Biscuits, Easy, **'84** 218
Pudding, Biscuit, **'79** 86; **'93** 51
Pudding, Chocolate Biscuit Bread, **'94** 215
Quick Biscuits, **'89** 30
Raised Biscuits, Southern, **'82** 94
Raisin Biscuits, Glazed, **'89** 210
Raspberry-Almond Biscuits, **'93** 160
Rise-and-Shine Biscuits, **'89** 211
"Rolling-in-Dough" Biscuits, **'92** 80

Roquefort Biscuits, Herbed, **'84** 95
Rye Biscuits, **'84** 96
Sausage and Biscuits, Southern, **'82** 43
Sausage Biscuit Bites, **'84** 95
Sausage Biscuits, Cheesy, **'80** 78
Sausage Gravy, Biscuits and, **'92** 270; **'94** 20
Scones, Breakfast Drop, **'88** 83
Scones, Currant, **'84** 117
Snowflake Biscuits, **'90** 158
Sour Cream Biscuits, **'79** 128
Sour Cream Biscuits, Soft-as-a-Cloud,
  '86 138
Sourdough Biscuits, **'82** 201
Sweetened Biscuits, **'80** 42
Sweet Little Biscuits, **'85** 305
Sweet Potato Angel Biscuits, **'93** 312
Sweet Potato Biscuits, **'80** 287; **'84** 140;
  '89 210
Taco Biscuit Bites, **'91** 89
Tomato Biscuits, **'86** 72
Tomato-Herb Biscuits, **'94** 215
Topping, Biscuit, **'86** 157, 265
Up-and-Down Biscuits, **'88** 263
Velvet Cream Biscuits, **'92** 303
Wheat Bran Biscuits, **'81** 49
Wheat Germ Biscuits, **'86** 261
Wheat Quick Biscuits, **'85** 278
Whipping Cream Biscuits, **'80** 77
Whole Wheat Biscuits, **'83** 18; **'84** 60, 268;
  '85 227; **'88** 83; **'91** 222
Yeast Biscuits, **'87** 71, 301
Yeast Biscuits, Refrigerator, **'85** 48

Blackberries
Bars, Blackberry, **'87** 130
Bars, Blackberry-Filled, **'79** 124
Bars, Blackberry Jam, **'82** M185
Cake, Fresh Blackberry, **'81** 132
Cobbler, Blackberry, **'82** 139; **'83** 175
Cobbler, Blackberry-Almond, **'81** 132
Cobbler, Deep-Dish Blackberry, **'80** 186
Cobbler, Deluxe Blackberry, **'81** 132
Cobbler, Juicy Blackberry, **'89** 137
Cobbler, New-Fashioned Blackberry,
  '87 164
Cobbler, Southern Blackberry, **'81** 132
Dumplings, Blackberries and, **'86** 196
Flan, Blackberry, **'79** 182
Jam, Berry Refrigerator, **'89** 139
Jam, Blackberry, **'82** 149; **'89** 138
Jam, Freezer Blackberry, **'84** M181
Jelly, Blackberry, **'82** 149
Napoleons, Berry, **'94** 120
Parfait, Blackberries-and-Cream, **'87** 129
Pie, Berry-Apple, **'88** 251
Pie, Blackberry, **'84** 141; **'86** 152
Pie, Blackberry-Apple, **'87** 130
Pie, Blackberry Cream, **'81** 132

Pie, Creamy Blackberry, **'88** 179
Pie, Peach-and-Blackberry, **'89** 136
Roll, Blackberry, **'82** 178
Sauce, Berry, **'94** 130
Sauce, Blackberry, **'86** 152; **'94** 232
Sauce, Ducklings with Blackberry, **'82** 251
Tamales, Blackberry Dessert, **'94** 190
Tart, Cherry and Blackberry, **'83** 225
Tart, Pick-a-Berry, **'91** 118
Tarts, Berry Good Lemon, **'91** 119
Tarts, Blackberry Pudding, **'93** 200
Blueberries
à la Frederick, Blueberries, **'93** 123
Appetizer, Orange-Berry, **'85** 81
Basket, Summer Berry, **'84** 158
Berry Tartlets, Fresh, **'91** 98
Biscuits, Blueberry Buttermilk, **'89** 210
Bread, Banana-Blueberry, **'81** 163
Bread, Blueberry-Lemon, **'85** 190
Bread, Blueberry-Oatmeal, **'83** 139
Bread, Blueberry-Orange, **'87** 140
Bread, Blueberry-Orange Nut, **'84** 141
Bread, Hot Blueberry, **'81** 164
Buckle, Blueberry, **'85** 30
Buns, Deluxe Blueberry, **'81** 164
Cake, Almond-Blueberry Coffee, **'85** 152
Cake, Banana-Blueberry, **'86** 247
Cake, Blueberry Brunch, **'83** 183
Cake, Blueberry Coffee, **'82** 206; **'85** 326;
  '88 263
Cake, Blueberry-Sour Cream, **'90** 140
Cake, Blueberry Streusel, **'92** 144
Cake, Blueberry Streusel Coffee, **'88** 154
Cake, Fresh Blueberry Coffee, **'81** 164
Cheesecake, Blueberries 'n' Cream, **'87** 140
Cheesecake, Blueberry Chiffon, **'87** 76
Cobbler, Blueberry, **'83** 175
Cobbler, Blueberry Pinwheel, **'87** 140
Cobbler, Easy Blueberry, **'83** 183
Cobbler, Fresh Blueberry, **'80** 144
Cobbler, No-Dough Blueberry-Peach,
  '86 177
Cobbler, Peachy Blueberry, **'80** 143
Cointreau, Blueberries and, **'82** 100
Compote, Berry-Peach, **'82** 133
Compote, Peach-Berry, **'89** 112
Conserve, Blueberry, **'82** 149
Cream, Lemon-Blueberry, **'92** 153
Crisp, Blueberry, **'84** 177
Crumble, Blueberry, **'81** 84
Crunch, Fresh Blueberry, **'82** 143
Dessert, Easy Blueberry, **'89** M130
Dessert, Peach-Blueberry, **'92** 184
Dessert Squares, Chocolate-Blueberry,
  '87 299
Dream, Blueberry, **'88** 94
Fritters, Blueberry, **'85** 152
Glaze, Blueberry, **'83** 143
Huckle-Buckle Blueberry, **'86** 151
Ice Cream, Blueberry, **'88** 203
Jam, Blueberry, **'79** 120; **'85** 130
Jam, Blueberry Refrigerator, **'89** 139
Kuchen, Blueberry, **'80** 143
Lemon Curd with Berries, **'90** 102
Muffins, Blueberry, **'80** 143; **'91** 140, 203
Muffins, Blueberry-Bran, **'89** 23
Muffins, Blueberry Buttermilk, **'80** 16
Muffins, Blueberry-Cream Cheese, **'86** 14
Muffins, Blueberry Ice Cream, **'82** 143
Muffins, Blueberry-Lemon, **'79** 7
Muffins, Blueberry-Oat, **'92** 119

Blueberries *(continued)*

Muffins, Blueberry Oat Bran, **'89** 106
Muffins, Blueberry-Oatmeal, **'87** 24
Muffins, Blueberry Streusel, **'80** 46
Muffins, Easy Blueberry, **'81** 197
Muffins, Golden Blueberry, **'79** 235
Muffins, Old-Fashioned Blueberry, **'86** 161
Muffins with Streusel Topping, Blueberry,
　'88 129
Napoleons, Blueberry-Lemon, **'94** 122
Pancakes, Blueberry, **'85** 152; **'89** 138
Pancakes, Blueberry Buttermilk, **'79** 114
Pancakes, Blue Cornmeal-Blueberry, **'94** 115
Pancakes, Sour Cream Blueberry, **'81** 164
Pie, Blueberry-Banana, **'93** 115
Pie, Blueberry Cream, **'84** 142
Pie, Blueberry-Cream Cheese, **'88** 154
Pie, Blueberry-Peach, **'94** 158
Pie, Blueberry-Sour Cream, **'83** 183
Pie, Chilled Blueberry, **'89** 136
Pie, Fresh Blueberry, **'83** 183; **'85** 152
Pie, Fresh Blueberry Cream, **'80** 144
Pie, Fresh Blueberry Streusel, **'89** 137
Pie, Old-Fashioned Blueberry, **'89** 136
Pinwheels, Blueberry, **'82** 205
Pudding, Blueberry Bread, **'88** 154
Puree, Grapefruit with Pear-Berry, **'89** 213
Quick Blueberry Slump, **'91** 20
Raspberry Custard Sauce, Fresh Berries
　with, **'88** 163
Salad, Layered Berry, **'79** 173
Salad, Melon-Berry, **'90** 180
Sauce, Berry, **'94** 130
Sauce, Blueberry, **'80** 144; **'86** 248;
　'88 155; **'89** M130; **'94** 122
Sauce, Cinnamon-Blueberry, **'86** 11
Sauce, Melon Wedges with Berry, **'86** 178
Sauce, Peach-Berry, **'87** M165
Sauce, Peach-Blueberry, **'81** 170
Sauce, Peach-Blueberry Pancake, **'82** 177
Smoothie, Banana-Blueberry, **'90** 104
Snow, Berries on, **'82** 227
Sorbet, Blueberry-Kirsch, **'83** 120
Squares, Blueberry-Amaretto, **'83** 220
Tart, Pick-a-Berry, **'91** 118
Tarts, Berry Good Lemon, **'91** 119
Topping, Blueberry, **'87** 125
Trifle, Lemon-Blueberry, **'88** 210

Bok Choy
Stir-Fry, Bok Choy-Broccoli, **'84** 2

Boysenberries
Cobbler, Boysenberry, **'82** 133
Compote, Berry-Peach, **'82** 133
Cream Mold, Peachy Berry, **'83** 130
Cream Supreme, Boysenberries and, **'82** 133
Crisp, Berry, **'83** 130
Pie, Boysenberry, **'82** 133

Bran
Biscuits, Bran, **'85** 228
Biscuits, Wheat Bran, **'81** 49
Bread, Bran-Applesauce, **'84** 229
Bread, Honey-Oat, **'93** 232
Bread, Wheat-and-Oat Bran, **'92** 102
Bread, Whole Wheat Bran, **'79** 58
Chocolate-Bran Raisin Jumbos, **'91** 142
Crêpes, Bran, **'83** 70; **'86** 44
Cupcakes, Carrot-Bran, **'82** 16
Eggplant, Ratatouille-Bran Stuffed, **'86** 44
Muesli, Bran-and-Fruit, **'91** 134

Muffins, All-Bran Oat Bran, **'91** 134
Muffins, Apple-Bran, **'85** M89
Muffins, Apple-Cinnamon Oat Bran, **'89** 106
Muffins, Banana Bran, **'83** 48
Muffins, Banana Oat Bran, **'89** 106
Muffins, Blueberry-Bran, **'89** 23
Muffins, Blueberry Oat Bran, **'89** 106
Muffins, Bran, **'84** 53
Muffins, Bran-Buttermilk, **'85** 7
Muffins, Cranberry Oat Bran, **'89** 107
Muffins, Easy Bran, **'83** 55
Muffins, Ever-Ready Bran, **'81** 106
Muffins for Two, Bran, **'84** 211
Muffins, Freezer Bran, **'91** 141
Muffins, High-Fiber, **'85** 250
Muffins, Honey Bran, **'88** 171
Muffins, Honey-Bran, **'89** 250
Muffins Made of Bran, **'86** 103
Muffins, Maple-Bran, **'90** 66
Muffins, Oat Bran, **'89** 106
Muffins, Oat Bran-Banana, **'91** 18
Muffins, Oatmeal Bran, **'81** 236
Muffins, Oatmeal-Bran, **'91** 83
Muffins, Quick Bran, **'86** 85
Muffins, Raisin Oat Bran, **'89** 106
Muffins, Refrigerator Bran, **'79** 6
Muffins, Sour Cream-Bran, **'87** 98
Muffins, Spiced Bran, **'84** 229
Muffins, Whole Wheat Bran, **'88** M274
Pancakes with Cinnamon Syrup, Bran,
　'91 315
Rolls, Bran, **'85** 145
Rolls, Bran Yeast, **'87** 116
Salad, Lemony Apple-Bran, **'86** 223
Waffles, Oat Bran, **'92** 139

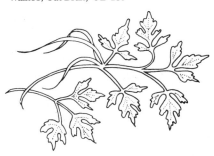

Breads. *See also* specific types.
Apple Bread, **'79** 205; **'80** 226
Apple Butter Bread, **'84** 49; **'86** 69
Apple Loaf, Fresh, **'82** 206
Apple Loaf, Spiced, **'79** 215
Apple-Nut Bread, **'79** 12; **'85** 281
Apple-Nut Bread, Fresh, **'87** 256
Applesauce-Honey Nut Bread, **'87** 300
Applesauce Loaf, Brandy, **'81** 263
Applesauce Nut Bread, **'81** 305
Applesauce-Pecan Bread, **'90** 66
Apricot Bread, Tangy, **'81** 249
Apricot-Cranberry Loaf, **'79** 235
Apricot-Nut Bread, **'79** 24
Apricot-Nut Loaf, **'81** 8
Apricot-Nut Loaf, Tasty, **'82** 10
Apricot-Orange Bread, **'92** 285
Artichoke Bread, **'93** 140
Asparagus Squares, **'79** 161
Bacon-and-Cheese Bread, **'83** 255
Banana-Apple Bread, **'85** 250

Banana-Blueberry Bread, **'81** 163
Banana Bread, **'87** 72
Banana Bread, Sour Cream-, **'79** 190
Banana Bread, Whole Wheat, **'80** 88
Banana Butterscotch Bread, **'79** 116
Banana-Jam Bread, **'84** 73
Banana-Nut Bread, **'86** 8, 70
Banana Nut Bread, Hawaiian, **'79** 235
Banana Nut Bread, Whole Wheat-, **'84** 50
Banana-Nut-Raisin Bread, **'81** 59
Banana-Nut Roll, **'85** 112
Banana-Oat Tea Loaf, **'87** 256
Banana Wheat Bread, **'81** 14
Banana-Zucchini Bread, **'85** 326
Batter Bread, Soft, **'84** 253
Batter, Primary, **'89** 192
Beer Bread, Easy, **'79** 213; **'84** 160
Biscuit Bread, **'84** 284
Blueberry Bread, Hot, **'81** 164
Blueberry-Lemon Bread, **'85** 190
Blueberry-Oatmeal Bread, **'83** 139
Blueberry-Orange Bread, **'87** 140
Blueberry-Orange Nut Bread, **'84** 141
Blue Cheese-Apple Sunburst, **'94** 245
Bourbon-Pecan Bread, **'93** 308
Bran-Applesauce Bread, **'84** 229
Breakfast Bread, Crunchy, **'93** 327
Breakfast Bread, Easy, **'83** 289
Brie Bread, **'87** 143
Brie Cheese Bake, **'87** 117
Brown Bread, **'84** 242; **'88** 63
Brown Bread, Eighteenth-Century, **'79** 72
Brown Bread, Steamed Buttermilk, **'86** 261
Buttermilk-Cheese Loaf, **'91** 52
Butternut-Raisin Bread, **'79** 25
Butternut Spice Loaf, **'92** 235
Calas, Easy, **'92** 89
Carrot Bread, **'89** 143
Carrot Bread, Tasty, **'84** 328
Carrot-Nut Loaf, **'83** 117
Carrot-Pineapple Bread, **'82** 210
Carrot Puffs, **'87** 200
Carrot-Walnut Bread, **'88** 284
Cheddar-Nut Bread, **'85** 41
Cheese Bread, **'82** 174
Cheese Bread, Dilly, **'83** 5
Cheese Bread, Easy, **'82** 74; **'86** 17
Cheese Bread, Quick, **'83** 9
Cheese-Herb Bread, **'85** 283
Cheese Loaf, **'87** 92; **'90** 93
Cheese Loaves, Little, **'86** 213
Cheese-Olive Bread, Spicy, **'84** 150
Cheese Puffs, Bavarian, **'80** 191
Cheesy Twists, **'84** 284
Cherry Nut Bread, **'81** 306; **'82** 36
Cherry Nut Bread, Maraschino, **'79** 234
Cherry-Nut Bread, Quick, **'85** 55
Chocolate Chip-Banana Bread, **'90** 267
Chocolate Date-Nut Bread, **'81** 284
Chocolate-Zucchini Bread, **'93** 308
Cinnamon Puffs, **'81** 209
Citrus-Nut Bread, **'83** 294
Coconut Bread, **'83** 140
Cranberry-Banana Bread, **'80** 281; **'90** 294
Cranberry Bread, **'79** 242
Cranberry Fruit-Nut Bread, **'79** 275
Cranberry-Orange Bread, **'87** 244
Cranberry-Orange Nut Bread, **'80** 288
Crouton Bread, Quick, **'90** 138
Croutons, **'86** M288
Croutons, Celery, **'79** 16

Breads (*continued*)

Croutons, Crispy Italian, '84 126
Croutons, Garlic-Flavored, '86 47
Croutons, Herb, '81 150
Croutons, Microwave, '86 M227
Croutons, Vegetable-Flavored, '84 148
Date-Nut Bread, '85 306
Date-Nut Loaf, '85 10
Date-Walnut Loaf, Blue Ribbon, '80 15
Easy Bread, '87 168
Eggnog Bread, '83 294
Feta Cheese-Spinach Roll, '91 22
Flatbread, Mexican, '80 197
Focaccia, Mustard-and-Onion, '90 321;
'92 97
French Bread, Bacon-Cheese, '92 54
French Bread, Cheesy, '88 172
French Bread, Chive-Garlic, '89 29
French Bread, Herbed, '82 174; '93 283
French Bread, Herb-Seasoned, '83 198
French Bread, Hot Garlic, '81 83
French Bread, Onion-Cheese, '89 29
French Loaf, Herbed, '87 243
Fruit-Nut Bread, Kahlúa, '79 235
Fruit-Nut Twists, '82 253
Fry Bread, '84 140; '85 155
Fry Bread, Indian, '81 56
Garlic Bread, '82 19; '89 282; '91 204
Garlic Bread, Cheesy, '84 150
Garlic Bread, Quick, '90 283
Garlic Breadsticks, '79 70
Gingerbread Loaf, '82 14
Gingerbread, Mocha, '81 207; '82 14
Gingerbread, Molasses, '88 203
Gingerbread, Old English, '79 265
Gingerbread, Old-Fashioned, '81 157, 207;
'82 14; '91 240
Gingerbread, Refrigerator, '80 52
Gingerbread, Spicy, '84 263
Gingerbread Squares, '84 16
Gingerbread, Very Moist, '86 261
Greek Bread, '89 200
Greek Sunburst, '94 245
Ham-and-Cheese Bread, '86 213
Hawaiian Loaf, '80 225
Herb-and-Cheese Pull Aparts, '87 143
Herb Bread, '86 17
Herb Loaf, Toasted, '84 150
Herbs-and-Cheese Bread, '93 56
Herb Sticks, '83 252
Herb-Vegetable-Cheese Bread, '88 172
Hobo Bread, '86 86
Honey-Banana Bread, '91 68
Irish Soda Bread, '90 214
Jam-and-Cheese Loaf, '89 246
Koulourakia, '90 193
Lemon Bread, '79 275; '87 256
Lemon-Cream Tea Loaf, '84 50
Lemon-Nut Bread, '79 24
Lemon-Pecan Bread, '83 54
Lemon Tea Bread, '92 268; '93 183
Mayonnaise Bread, '89 29
Mix, Quick Bread, '81 90; '86 8
Molasses-Nut Bread, '84 24
Monkey Bread, Bacon, '94 283
Monkey Bread, Cheese-Filled, '91 21
Monkey Bread, Quick, '81 306; '82 36
Mustard-Rye Ovals, '84 149
Nautical Knots, '93 168

Oatmeal Bread, '81 236, 300
Oatmeal Raisin Bread, '81 14
Onion Bread, Easy, '81 162
Onion-Cheese Bread, '79 180; '81 8
Onion-Cheese Supper Bread, '83 112
Onion-Herb Bread, Toasted, '83 266
Onion-Parmesan Bread, '84 284
Orange, Baba au, '86 138
Orange-Cranberry Bread, '85 266
Orange-Cream Cheese Bread, '82 210
Orange-Nut Bread, '82 75
Orange Nut Loaf, '80 226
Orange-Pecan Bread, '79 148
Orange-Pecan Bread, Glazed, '81 250
Orange-Pecan Loaves, '79 215
Orange Puffs, Upside-Down, '83 57
Orange-Pumpkin Bread, '87 300
Orange Tea Bread, '79 234
Papaya Bread, '88 138
Parmesan Herb Bread, '82 235; '83 41
Parmesan Rounds, '79 170
Parmesan Sesame Sticks, '81 39
Parmesan Twists, '83 239
Peach Bread, '82 170
Peach Bread, Georgia, '79 161
Peanut Bread, '87 184
Peanut Butter Bread, '88 64
Pear Bread, '80 218
Pepper Bread, '85 156
Persimmon Bread, '80 228
Persimmon Date-Nut Bread, '82 218
Pineapple-Apricot Bread, '84 7
Pineapple Bread, '83 139
Pineapple-Carrot Bread, '79 106
Pineapple-Nut Bread, '79 215
Pineapple-Pecan Loaf Bread, '87 256
Pita Triangles, Cheesy, '93 70
Pizza Sunburst, '94 245
Popover Puffs, Cheese, '85 6
Popover Ring, Cheesy, '80 45
Popovers, '94 43
Popovers, Cheddar Cheese, '85 41
Popovers, Cinnamon, '90 66
Popovers for Two, '81 304
Popovers, Giant Pecan, '83 208
Popovers, Good Old Southern, '79 138
Popovers, Jumbo, '83 225
Popovers, Muffin Tin, '79 138
Popovers, Parmesan, '90 66
Popovers, Perfect Blender, '79 53
Popovers, Pimiento, '79 138
Popovers, Seasoned, '86 86
Popovers, Whole Wheat, '90 66
Poppy Seed Bread, '83 140
Poppy Seed Loaf, Quick, '82 75
Poppy Seed-Swiss Cheese Bread, '91 52
Prune-Nut Bread, '87 255; '91 55
Pudding, Bread, '90 219
Puddings
    Amish Bread Pudding, '80 8
    Apple-Raisin Bread Pudding, '88 175
    Apricot Bread Pudding, '85 24
    Blueberry Bread Pudding, '88 154
    Bread Pudding, '89 M130
    Cheesy Bread Pudding, '83 68
    Chocolate Bread Pudding, '80 8
    French Bread Pudding, '85 231
    Lemon Bread Pudding, Old-Fashioned,
    '88 95
    Old-Fashioned Bread Pudding, '83 213;
    '88 175

    Old-Fashioned Bread Pudding with Rum
    Sauce, '88 32
    Peachy Bread Pudding, '88 175
    Raisin Bread Pudding, '94 215
    Soufflé, Creole Bread Pudding, '92 87
    Spiced Bread Pudding, '93 52
    Sweet Potato Bread Pudding, '94 241
    Tennessee Bread Pudding with Bourbon
    Sauce, '93 51
    Whiskey Sauce, Bread Pudding with,
    '80 58; '90 230; '92 93
Pumpkin Bread, '81 8
Pumpkin Bread, Harvest, '90 M215
Pumpkin Bread, Moist, '80 245
Pumpkin Bread, Spiced, '91 233
Pumpkin Bread with Cream Cheese and
    Preserves, '84 264
Pumpkin-Coconut Bread, '87 255
Pumpkin Loaf, Harvest, '85 232
Pumpkin-Nut Bread, '83 294
Pumpkin-Oatmeal Loaf, '81 49
Pumpkin-Pecan Bread, '87 221
Raisin-Cranberry Bread, '81 305; '82 36
Saffron Tea Bread, '85 26
Sally Lunn, Quick, '87 16
Salt-Rising Bread, '79 145
Santa Gertrudis Pan de Campo, '94 27
Sausage-Onion Squares, '83 112
Scones, Breakfast, '88 231; '89 22
Scones, Currant, '84 117; '92 332
Scones, Hazelnut, '94 16
Scones, Lemon-Raisin, '87 69
Scones, Orange-Pecan, '94 215
Seasoned Breadsticks, '81 84
Sesame Bread Twists, '84 283
Sesame-Cheddar Sticks, '81 150
Sesame Sticks, '83 9
Sesame Wheat Crisps, '81 106
Shortbread, '85 266
Sourdough Dill Bread, '89 192
Sourdough Starter, '89 192
Sourdough Wedges, '90 199
Spinach Bread, '83 121; '87 144
Spoonbreads
    Cheddar Spoonbread, '82 196
    Cheese Spoonbread, '86 261
    Corn and Bacon Spoonbread, '81 129
    Corn-Cheese Spoonbread, '88 9
    Dressing, Southwestern-Style
        Spoonbread, '94 273
    Garlic Spoonbread, '79 269; '80 14
    Golden Spoonbread, '83 286; '84 17
    Grits Spoonbread, '79 38
    Old Virginia Spoonbread, '84 102
    Spoonbread, '80 43; '81 138; '90 200
Squash Bread, '79 210
Squash Bread, Spicy, '83 121
Squash Bread, Yellow, '84 140
Stars, Bread, '93 286
Starter Food, '94 324
Stollen, '86 291
Strawberry Bread, '81 250; '83 140; '84 49
Strawberry Jam Bread, '79 216
Strawberry-Nut Bread, '79 24
Tacos, Navajo, '84 246
Three-C Bread, '81 284
Toast
    Apple Toast, '81 278
    Bacon-Cheese Toast Bars, '79 36
    Cheese Delights, Toasted, '79 37
    Cinnamon Toast, Buttery Skillet, '79 36

Breads, Toast (continued)

Orange Praline Toast, **'79** 36
Shrimp Toast, **'86** 91
Toast Points, **'93** 270
Toast Strips, Seasoned, **'93** 98
Tomato-Cheese Bread, Herbed, **'88** 143
Tortillas, Flour, **'81** 303
Tortillas, Never-Fail Flour, **'80** 198
Vegetable Bread, Breakaway, **'82** 74
Wampus Bread, **'81** 305
Wheat Loaf, Nutty, **'90** 65
Whole Wheat Cardamom Bread, **'86** 223
Whole Wheat Coffee Can Bread, Molasses-,
    '85 111
Whole Wheat Orange Bread, **'85** 5
Whole Wheat Quick Bread, **'82** 65
Wine-Date Nut Bread, **'82** 253
Yeast
    Almond Braid, **'89** 86
    Almond Danish, **'87** 301
    Anise-Orange Bread, **'83** 295
    Apple-Date-Nut Ring, **'90** 212
    Apple Pull-Apart Bread, **'86** 330
    Apple Swirl Bread, **'85** 4
    Armenian Thin Bread, **'94** 108
    Austrian Sweet Bread, **'83** 294
    Austrian Twists, **'80** 45
    Bagels, **'89** 266
    Bagels, Whole Wheat, **'84** 20
    Baguettes, **'85** 70
    Beer Bread, Best-Ever, **'82** 129
    Beer Bread, Hearty, **'87** 226; **'88** 133
    Beignets, **'84** 56
    Beignets, French Market, **'92** 88;
        '93 219; **'94** 319
    Binning Bread, **'80** 68
    Braided Bread, **'88** 76
    Braided Loaf, **'82** 17
    Braids, Festive, **'87** 297
    Braids, Holiday, **'83** 295
    Braid, Sweet Yeast, **'90** 46
    Break-Away Bread, **'86** 56
    Brioche, **'81** 122; **'89** 90
    Brioche Chicken Curry, **'88** 124
    Brioche Loaves, Vienna, **'87** 300
    Brown Bread, Light-, **'84** 268
    Bubble Bread, **'81** 107
    Bunny Bread, Glazed, **'92** 102
    Butter-Egg Bread, **'85** 269
    Butterhorns, **'84** 267
    Cake Bread, Golden, **'84** 269
    Canapé Bread, **'89** 292
    Caramel Bread, **'82** 75
    Caramel-Orange Coffee Ring, **'80** 45
    Caraway Breadsticks, **'89** 239
    Caraway Puffs, **'82** 174
    Caraway Seed Bread, Dark, **'80** 256
    Challah, **'92** 62
    Cheese Bread, **'83** 208; **'87** 11
    Cheese Bread, Cheddar, **'84** 268
    Cheese Bread, Crusty, **'86** 233
    Cheese Bread, Pimiento-, **'85** 223;
        '86 166
    Cheese Bread, Sour Cream-, **'85** 33
    Cheese Bread, Swiss, **'79** 60
    Cheese-Caraway Batter Bread, **'85** 33
    Cheese Crescents, **'82** 18
    Cheese-Dill Bread, Cottage, **'83** 154
    Cheese-Herb Bread, **'84** M144

Cheese Loaf, Jalapeño-, **'84** 76
Cheese Loaves, Processor Cream,
    '85 48
Cheese-Wine Bread, **'87** 254
Chocolate Loaf Bread, **'88** M188
Chocolate Pinwheel Loaf, **'80** 256
Christmas Bread, **'87** 296; **'88** 288
Christmas Bread, Norwegian, **'79** 234
Christmas Wreath, **'80** 280
Cinnamon Loaf, **'82** 18; **'85** 55
Cinnamon-Nut Bubble Bread, **'80** 22
Cinnamon-Oat Bread, **'90** 135
Cinnamon Raisin Bread, **'80** 22
Cinnamon Swirl Loaf, **'79** 23
Cinnamon Twists, **'83** 53
Cocoa-Nut Swirl Bread, **'80** 257
Coffee Ring, Filled, **'82** 18
Coffee Ring, Sugarplum, **'83** M37
Cornmeal Yeast Bread, **'89** 54
Cracker Bread, Sesame, **'87** 2
Cream Cheese Braids, **'82** 243
Crescents, Festive, **'80** 281
Croissants, **'83** 54; **'84** 188
Croissants, Flaky Butter, **'85** 42
Crust Bread, Country, **'80** 225
Dill-Oat Bread, **'91** 95
Dough, Basic Yeast, **'88** 74
Easter Bread, Golden, **'91** 54
Easter Egg Bread, **'84** 94
Easy Yeast Bread, **'79** 147
Egg Bread, County Fair, **'87** 68
Elephant Ears, **'84** 18
English Muffin Loaf, **'82** 96
English Muffin Loaves, **'85** 42
Figure-8 Bread, **'79** 171
Flat Bread, Italian-Style, **'82** 235;
    '83 41
Focaccia, Dried Tomato, **'94** 65
Focaccia, Onion, **'93** 77
French Bread, **'79** 158; **'87** 227; **'89** 54
French Bread, Easy, **'88** 299
French Bread, Glazed, **'88** 75
French Bread, Herbed, **'85** 222;
    '86 166
French Bread, New Orleans, **'80** 212
French Bread, Whole Wheat, **'88** 63
French Loaves, Crusty, **'85** 37
French Onion Bread, **'91** 90
Fruit-and-Cheese Braid, **'86** 214
Gingerbread Men, Yeast, **'92** 312
Golden Bread, **'90** 47
Gouda Bread, **'91** 59
Grittibanz (Swiss Bread Figure), **'93** 265
Ham Bread with Herb Butter, Country,
    '86 255
Heartland Loaves, **'89** 287
Herb Bread, **'84** 268
Herb Bread, No-Knead, **'81** 217
Herb-Cheese Bread, **'85** 70
Herbed Bread, **'89** 34
Herb Loaf, Butterflake, **'86** 261
Herb-Sour Cream Bread, **'85** 268
Herman Food, **'82** 200
Holiday Wreath, **'81** 284
Honey-Cinnamon Swirl Bread, **'88** 287
Honey-Curry Bread, **'89** 250
Honey-Granola Bread, **'86** 56
Honey Loaves, Hint o', **'81** 104
Honey-Oat Bread, **'89** 107; **'93** 232
Honey Twist, **'79** 80
Honey-Walnut Swirl, **'80** 21

Honey Wheat Bread, **'85** 18, 268
Honey-Wheat Bread, **'91** 223
Italian Bread, **'82** 297
Kolecz (Polish Bread), **'80** 29
Lightbread, Coffee Can, **'79** 59
Light Yeast Bread, **'81** 299
Loaf Bread, Hospitality, **'86** 299
Loaf Bread, Old-Fashioned, **'88** 75
Loaves, Sweet-Filled Yeast, **'90** 46
Mandelkrantz, **'92** 32
Marble Loaf, **'80** 230
Monkey Bread, **'82** 243
Monkey Bread, Easy, **'90** 214
Multi-Grain Bread, **'86** 236
Oat Bread, Caraway-Raisin, **'86** 44
Oatmeal Bread, **'81** 300; **'92** 212
Oatmeal Bread, Honey, **'80** 60
Oatmeal Bread, Round, **'84** 20
Oatmeal-Raisin Bread, **'83** 59
Oat-Molasses Bread, **'82** 139
Old-Fashioned Yeast Bread, **'79** 284
Olive Bread, **'93** 78
Olive-Dill Casserole Bread, **'92** 16
Onion-Dill Bread, Easy, **'85** 5
Onion-Herb Bread, **'90** 165
Onion Twist Loaves, **'84** 300
Pandoro, **'93** 267
Panettone, **'93** 266
Parmesan Bread, **'92** 19; **'93** 231
Party Bread, **'86** 218
Peanut Butter Bread, **'86** 171
Peanut Lover's Bread, **'93** 211
Pizza Batter Bread, **'85** 56
Pocket Bread, **'79** 58
Poppy Seed Loaf, **'83** 254
Portuguese Round Bread, **'83** 295
Potato Bread, **'85** 56
Potato Bread, Old-Fashioned, **'86** 57
Potato Lightbread, **'80** 225
Potato Loaves, **'86** 162
Pretzels, Chewy Soft, **'87** 159
Pretzels, Homemade, **'84** 159; **'91** 185
Pretzels, Soft, **'83** 18
Pretzels, Whole Wheat, **'89** 20
Pull-Apart Yeast Bread, **'94** 132
Raisin Batter Bread, Salt-Free, **'86** 33
Raisin Bread, Curried Chicken Salad on,
    '85 96
Raisin Bread, Homemade, **'87** 300
Raisin Bread, Round, **'89** 230
Raisin-Whole Wheat Bread, **'93** 77
Refrigerator Bread, No-Knead, **'83** 155
Rounds, Individual Bread, **'83** 159
Rye Bread, **'84** 21
Rye Bread, Swedish Orange-, **'85** 111
Rye Canapé Bread, **'89** 293
Rye Sandwich Bread, **'82** 65
Sally Lunn, **'81** 157; **'88** 163; **'94** 233
Sandwiches, Stacking, **'86** 127
Savarin, Holiday, **'80** 280
Sesame-Wheat Breadsticks, **'93** 114
Soft Breadsticks, **'83** 115
Sopaipillas, **'80** 197
Sour Cream Bread, **'79** 59
Sourdough Bread, **'82** 201
Sourdough Bread Dough, Potato,
    '94 324
Sourdough Bread, Potato, **'94** 325
Sourdough Starter, Herman, **'82** 200
Sourdough Starter, Potato, **'94** 324
"Sponge," **'93** 267

Breads, Yeast (continued)

Squares, Yeast Bread, '83 155
Starter Food, '94 324
Sugar Plum Bread, '80 256
Sweet Bread Wreath, Glazed, '90 192
Sweet Christmas Loaf, '84 278
Techniques of Breadmaking, '82 17
Trinity Feast Bread, '82 92; '83 83
Walnut Bread, '93 77
Wheat-and-Oat Bran Bread, '92 102
Wheat Bread, Buttermilk, '86 236
Wheat Bread, Pull-Apart Maple,
  '85 222; '86 166
White Bread, '79 275
White Bread, Cardamom, '82 236;
  '83 41
White Bread, Old-Fashioned, '81 285
White Bread, Special, '86 57
Whole Wheat Bran Bread, '79 58
Whole Wheat Bread, '83 17
Whole Wheat Bread and Rolls, Hearty,
  '79 92
Whole Wheat Bread, Anise-, '93 36
Whole Wheat Bread, Quick, '92 25
Whole Wheat Breadsticks, '84 228
Whole Wheat Canapé Bread, '89 293
Whole Wheat Honey Bread, '82 65;
  '83 106
Whole Wheat-Oatmeal Bread, '87 85
Whole Wheat-Rye Bread, '83 M37
Whole Wheat-White Bread, '82 130
Zucchini-Apple Bread, '87 255
Zucchini Bread, '85 111; '86 93
Zucchini Bread, Spiced, '79 161; '86 162
Zucchini Bread, Spicy, '81 305; '82 36
Zucchini-Carrot Bread, '83 190
Zucchini-Honey Bread, '89 143
Broccoli
Appetizer, Broccoli-Cheese, '92 265
au Gratin, Broccoli, '82 M20
au Gratin, Broccoli-and-Eggs, '85 289
au Gratin, Broccoli-Ham, '90 239
Bacon, Broccoli with, '92 302
Bake, Broccoli, '81 246; '89 279
Bake, Cheesy Broccoli, '83 255
Bake, Cheesy Italian Broccoli, '83 5
Bake, Company Broccoli, '83 279
Bake, Potato-Broccoli-Cheese, '80 114
Beef and Broccoli, Quick, '91 123
Beef and Broccoli with Chive Gravy, '88 214
Burritos, Broccoli, '83 200
Carnival Broccoli, '81 2
Casserole, Almond-Broccoli, '88 62
Casserole, Broccoli, '87 284; '88 M146, 265
Casserole, Broccoli-and-Egg, '86 324
Casserole, Broccoli-Blue Cheese, '85 260
Casserole, Broccoli-Cheese, '82 269; '84 9;
  '94 132
Casserole, Broccoli-Chicken, '82 33
Casserole, Broccoli-Corn, '83 313
Casserole, Broccoli-Rice, '81 101
Casserole, Broccoli-Swiss Cheese, '83 322;
  '85 M211
Casserole, Cheesy Broccoli, '84 293;
  '92 342
Casserole, Chicken-Broccoli, '79 48;
  '91 315
Casserole, Chicken Divan, '82 M203
Casserole, Crabmeat-Broccoli, '84 232

Casserole, Ham and Broccoli, '81 133
Casserole, Italian Broccoli, '82 6, 280;
  '83 32
Casserole, Quick Ham-Broccoli, '82 40
Casserole, Sausage and Broccoli, '80 33
Casserole, Tangy Tuna-Broccoli, '83 75
Casserole, Turkey-and-Broccoli, '86 332
Casserole, Winter Broccoli, '94 280
Cauliflower-Broccoli Crunch, '88 216
Cheese Sauce, Broccoli with, '82 107
Chinese Broccoli, '85 M12
Chowder, Broccoli, '79 16
Chowder, Swiss-Broccoli, '80 73
Cocktail Broccoli, '80 192
Crêpes, Royal Brunch, '81 44
Deluxe, Broccoli-Onion, '81 75
Dip, Broccoli-Garlic, '82 59
Dip, Cheesy Broccoli, '83 92
Dip, Santa Fe Skinny, '94 137
Divan, Chicken, '80 10; '87 M218
Divan, Creamy Turkey, '90 M34
Divan, Curried Chicken, '80 83
Divan, Easy Chicken, '94 310
Divan, Gourmet Chicken, '82 83
Divan, Overnight Chicken, '83 198
Divan Quiche, Chicken, '88 M125
Divan, Quick Turkey, '89 178
Divan, Sherried Chicken, '80 38
Divan, Turkey, '82 268
Eggs, Broccoli and Creamed, '83 84
Elegant, Broccoli, '81 267
Fettuccine, Broccoli-Parmesan, '93 55
Fettuccine with Broccoli, '90 97
Filling, Broccoli, '81 44
French Sauce, Broccoli with, '81 295
Frittata, Broccoli-Cheese, '81 243
Fritters, Cheesy Broccoli, '79 53
Garden Surprise, '83 112
Garlic Broccoli, '93 35
Glazed Broccoli with Almonds, '80 12
Herbed Broccoli, '88 101
Hollandaise Sauce, Broccoli with,
  '79 244, 276
Hollandaise Sauce, Broccoli with Mock,
  '82 272
Horseradish Sauce, Broccoli with, '81 2;
  '83 206; '84 33
Horseradish Sauce, Carrots and Broccoli
  with, '91 246
Italian-Style Broccoli, '88 41
Italienne, Broccoli, '82 300
Jade-Green Broccoli, '80 12
Lemon Broccoli, '81 119
Lemon-Broccoli Goldenrod, '84 M89
Lemon Cream, Broccoli with, '89 245
Lemon Dressing, Chilled Broccoli with,
  '88 270
Lemon Sauce and Pecans, Broccoli with,
  '86 71
Lemon Sauce, Broccoli with, '91 292;
  '92 256
Marinated Broccoli, '80 79; '81 40; '85 207;
  '86 157; '88 255
Marinated Broccoli, Tangy, '80 284
Marinated Fresh Broccoli, '81 M139
Medley, Broccoli, '81 206
Medley, Cauliflower-Broccoli, '81 69
Olive-Butter Sauce, Broccoli with, '83 118
Omelet, Broccoli-Mushroom, '85 45
Onions, Broccoli-Stuffed, '84 154
Orange Broccoli, Easy, '85 267

Orange Sauce, Broccoli with, '80 243
Pasta, Broccoli, '84 176
Pasta, Chicken-and-Broccoli, '87 286
Pasta with Broccoli and Sausage, '87 109
Pasta with Peppers and Broccoli, '91 69
Pickled Broccoli, '81 308
Pie, Broccoli-and-Turkey Pasta, '88 269
Pie, Broccoli-Beef, '83 196
Pie, Broccoli-Cheese, '84 235
Pimiento Broccoli, '86 268
Polonaise, Broccoli, '86 55
Potatoes and Broccoli, Creamy, '92 61
Potatoes, Broccoli-and-Almond-Topped,
  '83 3
Potatoes, Broccoli-Shrimp Stuffed, '92 M228
Potatoes, Broccoli-Topped Baked, '86 17
Puff, Broccoli, '81 94; '82 95
Quiche, Broccoli-Rice, '81 228
Quiche, Easy Broccoli, '82 34
Quiche, Italian Broccoli, '85 45
Quick-and-Easy Broccoli, '86 55
Red Pepper Rings, Broccoli in Sweet, '94 322
Rice, Holiday Broccoli with, '87 252
Rolls, Broccoli-Cheddar, '91 21
Rolls, Ham-and-Broccoli, '86 212; '87 82
Salad, Barley-Broccoli, '90 135
Salad, Beef-and-Broccoli, '87 187
Salad, Broccoli, '82 24; '85 249; '90 292
Salad, Broccoli and Cauliflower, '81 280
Salad, Broccoli and Red Pepper, '83 224
Salad, Broccoli-Cauliflower, '92 97
Salad, Broccoli-Cauliflower Pasta, '88 269
Salad, Broccoli-Chicken, '90 129
Salad, Broccoli-Corn, '87 24
Salad, Broccoli-Mandarin, '93 325
Salad, Broccoli 'n' Cauliflower, '90 32
Salad, Broccoli-Orange, '94 281
Salad, Broccoli-Peanut, '92 35
Salad, Cauliflower-Broccoli, '79 20
Salad, Congealed Broccoli, '84 124
Salad, Creamy Broccoli, '79 143
Salad, Creamy Broccoli and Cauliflower, '81 23
Salad, Creamy Broccoli-Raisin, '92 106
Salad, Crunchy Broccoli, '83 39
Salad, Curried Broccoli, '86 225
Salad, Fresh Broccoli, '82 34; '87 103
Salad, Hot Broccoli-Potato, '85 23
Salad, Marinated Broccoli, '83 240
Salad, Pepperoni-and-Broccoli, '83 216
Salad, Red, White, and Green, '90 18
Salad Supreme, Broccoli, '83 260
Salad, Warm Broccoli, '92 35
Sauce, Broccoli, '91 85
Sautéed Broccoli, '79 246
Savory Broccoli, '79 268; '80 14
Sesame Broccoli, '84 69; '85 8
Sesame, Broccoli with, '80 13
Sesame Seeds, Broccoli with, '82 34
Shrimp Sauce, Broccoli and Cauliflower with,
  '84 248
Slaw, Zesty Broccoli, '93 246
Soufflé, Broccoli, '81 24
Soufflé, Golden Broccoli, '84 283
Soup, Broccoli, '86 161, M194; '87 288
Soup, Broccoli-and-Chicken, '90 202
Soup, Broccoli-Swiss, '86 6
Soup, Cheese-and-Broccoli, '89 276
Soup, Cheesy-Broccoli, '86 258
Soup, Creamed Broccoli, '85 24
Soup, Cream of Broccoli, '79 130;
  '80 188, M225; '82 314; '83 66; '86 259

Broccoli (continued)

Soup, Cream-of-Broccoli, '88 56
Soup, Creamy Broccoli, '81 75; '82 13;
   '83 99; '91 307
Soup, Easy Broccoli, '81 307
Soup, Fresh Broccoli, '91 86
Soup, Hot Broccoli, '81 235; '83 44
Soup, Light Cream of Broccoli, '93 17
Soup, Mock Cream of Broccoli, '85 288
Sour Cream Sauce, Broccoli with,
   '87 127
Spears, Saucy Broccoli, '84 35
Spears, Zesty Broccoli, '79 152
Spread, Broccamoli Curry, '88 55
Stack-Ups, Jiffy Tomato, '80 161
Steamed Broccoli, '80 122
Steamed Broccoli with Tangy Chive Sauce,
   '83 101
Stew, Oyster-Broccoli, '89 242
Stir-Fried Broccoli, '83 227
Stir-Fry Beef and Broccoli, '79 47
Stir-Fry, Beef-and-Broccoli, '91 46
Stir-Fry, Bok Choy-Broccoli, '84 2
Stir-Fry Broccoli, '80 19
Stir-Fry Broccoli and Beef, '83 110
Stir-Fry, Chicken-Broccoli, '82 33
Stir-Fry, Turkey-Broccoli, '91 62
Strata, Ham and Broccoli, '80 261
Stroganoff, Chicken-and-Broccoli,
   '89 M248
Sunshine Sauce, Broccoli with, '84 248
Supreme, Broccoli, '82 34; '85 68
Supreme, Broccoli-Carrot, '89 331
Supreme, Creamy Broccoli, '82 287
Tomatoes, Broccoli-Stuffed, '83 136;
   '93 216
Toss, Broccoli, '86 294
Toss, Cauliflower-Broccoli, '82 54
Toss, Crunchy Broccoli and Cauliflower,
   '83 25
Toss, Italian Cauliflower-Broccoli, '88 269
Vinaigrette, Potato-Broccoli, '85 84
Walnut Broccoli, English, '89 68
Wine, Broccoli with White, '80 12
Wine Sauce, Broccoli with, '84 187
Brownies. See Cookies/Bars and Squares.
Brussels Sprouts
Amandine, Brussels Sprouts, '79 213
Beer, Brussels Sprouts in, '85 69
Brussels Sprouts, '89 278
Carrots and Brussels Sprouts, '82 300
Cashews, Brussels Sprouts with, '81 2
Casserole, Brussels Sprouts-and-Artichoke,
   '94 279
Casserole of Brussels Sprouts, '86 294
Celery, Brussels Sprouts and, '79 21
Cheese Sauce, Brussels Sprouts with,
   '79 246
Citrus Brussels Sprouts, Calico, '85 303
Creamed Brussels Sprouts and Celery,
   '83 322
Creamy Brussels Sprouts, '79 212
Deviled Brussels Sprouts, '84 248
Dilled Brussels Sprouts, '88 180
Fried Brussels Sprouts, '81 308
Glorified Brussels Sprouts, '86 282
Lemon Sauce, Brussels Sprouts in,
   '82 269
Lemon Sprouts, '85 288

Lemony Brussels Sprouts with Celery,
   '85 25
Marinated Brussels Sprouts, '88 265
Medley, Brussels Sprouts, '79 212; '85 267
Mustard Sauce, Brussels Sprouts in, '87 253;
   '90 228
Onion Sauce, Brussels Sprouts in, '81 308
Orange Brussels Sprouts, '84 34
Orange Sauce, Brussels Sprouts in, '86 55
Pierre, Brussels Sprouts, '84 248
Polonaise, Brussels Sprouts, '85 79
Rice, Brussels Sprouts and, '79 288; '80 26
Salad, Brussels Sprouts, '87 233
Salad, Cauliflower-Brussels Sprouts, '83 240
Sesame Brussels Sprouts, '86 55
Shallots and Mustard, Brussels Sprouts with,
   '85 258
Stir-Fry, Brussels Sprouts, '81 308
Tangy Brussels Sprouts, '88 40
Tarragon Brussels Sprouts, '83 291
Wine Butter, Brussels Sprouts in, '86 327
Bulgur
Tabbouleh, '93 70
Tabbouleh Salad, '94 174
Wild Rice Bulgur, '91 83
Burritos
Appetizers, Bean Burrito, '94 226
Breakfast Burritos, '84 57; '90 192
Broccoli Burritos, '83 200
Brunch Burritos, '91 77
Burritos, '80 196
Cheesy Beef Burritos, '85 193
Chimichangas (Fried Burritos), '81 196;
   '85 244; '86 114
Chinese Burritos, '87 181
Fiesta Burritos, '86 114
Meat-and-Bean Burritos, '81 194
Monterey Burritos, '84 292
Pie, Mexican Burrito, '87 287
Rollups, Burrito, '90 119
Vegetable Burritos, '80 197; '90 134;
   '92 138
Vegetable Burritos with Avocado Sauce,
   '83 200
Vegetarian Burritos, '93 319
Butter
Acorn Squash-and-Bourbon Butter, '94 266
Apple Butter, '79 200; '81 217; '92 311
Apple Butter, Half-Hour, '81 203
Apricot Butter, '82 308
Balls, Butter, '82 189; '89 90
Basil Butter, '87 171
Basil Butter, Asparagus with, '85 40
Cashew Butter, Asparagus with, '87 56
Cheese Butter, '84 114
Chervil Butter, '83 129
Chervil Butter, Swordfish Steak with,
   '91 147
Chili Butter, '82 219
Cinnamon Butter, '92 319
Cinnamon-Honey Butter, '89 281
Clarified Butter, '81 59
Clarifying Butter, '82 189
Curls, Butter, '82 51, 189; '89 90
Garlic Butter, '83 193; '84 108
Gazpacho Butter, '92 86
Ginger Butter, '91 26
Green Peppercorn Butter, '90 117
Herb Butter, '86 128, 255, 261, 306
Herb Butter, Cauliflower with, '81 2
Herb Butter, Corn-on-the-Cob with, '84 160

Herbed Caper Butter, '94 62
Herbed Unsalted Butter, '82 67
Honey Butter, '93 309; '94 206
Honey-Orange Butter, '79 36; '85 19
Horseradish-Chive Butter, '86 277
Lemon Butter, Asparagus with, '87 M151
Lime Butter, Chicken with, '84 68
Maple-Flavored Butter, Whipped, '79 36
Molds, Butter, '89 90
Nectarine Butter, '79 175
Olive Butter, '91 295
Onion Butter, '86 253
Onion Butter, Sweet, '93 124
Orange Butter, '81 8, 42; '90 323; '92 319;
   '94 115
Orange-Pecan Butter, '84 75
Peach Butter, '82 308
Peach Butter, Golden, '91 178
Pear Butter, '85 130
Pear Butter, Spiced, '80 218
Peppercorn Butter, Green, '88 60
Plum Butter, '88 152
Prune-Orange Butter, '92 49
Raisin Butter, '81 272
Sauce, Brown Butter, '91 65
Sauce, Garlic Buerre Blanc, '88 222
Sauce, Garlic-Ginger Butter, '94 89
Sauce, Pecan-Butter, '91 65
Sauce, White Butter, '92 107
Shrimp Butter, '92 91
Southwestern Butter, '92 320
Strawberry Butter, '79 36; '81 286;
   '91 71
Tomato Butter, '86 128
Tomato-Curry-Orange Butter, '93 159
Butterscotch
Bars, Butterscotch, '82 209; '83 297
Bars, Chocolate-Butterscotch, '81 197
Bread, Banana Butterscotch, '79 116
Brownies, Butterscotch, '85 248
Cake, Butterscotch, '91 270
Cake, Butterscotch-Pecan Pound, '92 153
Cheesecake, Butterscotch, '86 188
Cookies, Butterscotch, '87 58
Cookies, Butterscotch-Pecan, '84 36
Fantastic, Butterscotch, '83 76
Filling, Butterscotch, '91 271
Fudge, Butterscotch Rum, '88 256
Fudge, Four Chips, '92 318
Fudge Scotch Ring, '79 273
Mousse, Butterscotch, '93 254
Pie, Butterscotch Cream, '84 48; '87 207
Pie, Butterscotch Meringue, '83 158
Pinwheels, Butterscotch, '90 49
Pralines, Butterscotch, '81 253
Sauce, Butterscotch-Pecan, '82 212

C

Cabbage. See also Sauerkraut.
Apples and Franks, Cabbage with,
   '87 42
au Gratin, Cabbage, '83 279
Bake, Zesty Cabbage Beef, '80 300
Beef-Cabbage Dinner, '81 179
Bubbling Cabbage, '84 2
Caraway Cabbage, '85 32, 289
Caraway, Cabbage with, '93 181
Casserole, Cheesy Cabbage, '79 4
Casserole, Creamy Cabbage, '80 63
Casserole, Italian Cabbage, '87 42

Cabbage *(continued)*

Casserole, Savory Cabbage, '82 168
Chop Suey, Cabbage, '81 101
Chow-Chow, '82 196
Chowchow, '87 150
Chowder, Hearty Cabbage, '80 25
Colcannon, '90 64
Corned Beef and Cabbage, '83 104; '93 64
Corned Beef and Cabbage au Gratin, '83 16
Corned Beef and Cabbage, Quick, '79 54
Corned Beef Squares and Cabbage, '82 86
Country-Style Cabbage, '81 271
Creamed Cabbage with Almonds, '79 4
Creole Cabbage, '87 189
Frankfurter-Cabbage Skillet, '80 166
Hot Cabbage Creole, '87 42
Kielbasa and Cabbage, '85 67; '89 M196
Kielbasa, Cabbage, '87 42
Lemon-Butter Cabbage, '88 156
Medley, Cabbage, '80 64; '83 104
Piccalilli, Kentucky, '81 216
Red Cabbage and Apples, '85 32
Red Cabbage, German, '94 254
Red Cabbage, German-Style, '84 2
Red Cabbage, Pickled, '81 271
Red Cabbage, Sweet-Sour, '79 5
Relish, Cabbage, '83 260
Rolls, Cabbage, '83 104
Rolls, Crunchy Cabbage-Rice, '85 32
Rolls, Easy Cabbage-and-Beef, '88 49
Rolls, Hot-and-Spicy Cabbage, '84 249
Rolls, Hungarian Cabbage, '94 47
Rolls, Spicy Cabbage, '84 2
Rolls, Stuffed Cabbage, '88 18; '92 251
Rolls, Vegetarian Cabbage, '91 86
Rollups, Beef-and-Cabbage, '80 63
Salad, Cabbage, '87 120, 233
Salad, Cabbage and Fruit, '79 286
Salad, Chinese Cabbage, '81 271
Salad, Chinese Green, '88 48
Salad, Garden Cabbage, '81 210
Salad, Nutty Cabbage, '87 42
Salad, Overnight Cabbage, '79 83
Salad, Red Cabbage Citrus, '94 72
Salad, Tangy Cabbage, '82 55
Salad, Wilted Cabbage, '94 281
Sausage, Cabbage with Polish, '83 104
Sausage-Sauced Cabbage, '81 271
Sausage Surprise, '83 245; '84 42
Scalloped Cabbage, '82 269
Scalloped Cabbage, Cheese, '81 87; '82 7
Skillet Cabbage, '89 314; '90 229
Skillet, Cabbage-and-Tomato, '86 110
Slaws
    Apple-Carrot Slaw, '92 243
    Apple Coleslaw, '89 315
    Apple-Pineapple Slaw, '79 241
    Apple Slaw, Fresh, '81 63
    Apple Slaw, Nutty, '88 216
    Aspic, Shrimp-Coleslaw, '79 88
    Bacon Coleslaw, '83 58
    Banana-Nut Slaw, '86 250
    Blue Cheese Coleslaw, '89 13
    Broccoli Slaw, Zesty, '93 246
    Chicken Coleslaw, '84 2
    Chili Coleslaw, '80 178
    Chinese Cabbage Slaw, '89 312
    Coleslaw, '79 152; '82 135
    Colorful Coleslaw, '88 166

Confetti Slaw, '89 48
Corn and Cabbage Slaw, '79 135
Cottage Coleslaw, '80 64
Country-Style Coleslaw, '83 59
Creamy Coleslaw, '83 170
Crunchy Coleslaw, '86 295
Cucumber Slaw, Creamy, '89 49
Curried Coleslaw, '85 139
Freezer Coleslaw, '89 49
Freezer Slaw, '81 279; '82 24; '83 154
Fresh Cabbage Slaw, '85 139
Frozen Coleslaw, '82 102
Fruit Coleslaw, Three-, '86 250
Fruited Coleslaw, '83 209; '85 139
Grape-Poppy Seed Slaw, '86 225
Grapes and Almonds, Coleslaw with,
    '83 59
Guacamole Mexican Coleslaw, '82 302
Ham Coleslaw, '84 195
Healthy Slaw, '92 183
Hot-and-Creamy Dutch Slaw, '87 127
Hot-and-Sour Chinese Slaw, '85 139
Hot Slaw, '89 49
Kentucky Coleslaw, '81 216
Layered Coleslaw, '86 180
Layered Slaw, '93 214
Light and Creamy Coleslaw, '93 318
Make-Ahead Coleslaw, '81 155
Marinated Coleslaw, '79 135
Marinated Slaw, '91 229
Memphis Slaw, '91 28
Mexicali Coleslaw, '84 18
Mexican Coleslaw, '89 48
Mustard Slaw, Texas, '88 172
Nutty Cabbage Slaw, '88 218
Old-Fashioned Coleslaw, '80 120;
    '82 225
Old-Fashioned Slaw, '84 149
Old-Fashioned Sweet Coleslaw, '93 128
Orange Slaw, Cabbage-, '79 135
Overnight Cabbage Slaw, '81 88; '82 7
Overnight Coleslaw, '79 135
Overnight Slaw, '79 5; '92 280
Peach Slaw, Party, '86 250
Peanut Slaw, '85 139
Peanut Slaw, Chinese, '93 212
Pear Slaw, Peanutty-, '86 250
Pineapple-Almond Slaw, '92 171
Pineapple Coleslaw, Curried, '88 172
Pineapple Slaw, Cabbage-, '92 182
Pineapple Slaw, Colorful, '86 250
Polka Dot Slaw, '83 59
Red Bean Slaw, '79 247
Red Cabbage-and-Apple Slaw, '87 31;
    '91 309
Seafood Slaw, '79 56
Sea Slaw, Tomatoes Stuffed with, '89 96
Silks, Slaw, '93 236
Sour Cream Slaw, '87 10
Swedish Slaw, '79 135
Sweet and Crunchy Slaw, '79 104
Sweet-and-Sour Hot Slaw, '92 63
Sweet-and-Sour Slaw, '81 237
Sweet Cabbage Slaw, '79 76
Tangy Coleslaw, '83 59
Tomatoes, Coleslaw with, '80 34
Vegetable Slaw, '81 280
Zesty Slaw, '82 127
Zucchini Coleslaw, Fiesta, '91 168
Soup, Cabbage, '83 291
Soup, Sweet-and-Sour Cabbage, '89 314

Spinach Dip in Cabbage, '82 155
Stir-Fried Cabbage, '81 75, 271; '85 109
Stuffed Cabbage, '84 282
Stuffed Cabbage, Italian, '84 294
Stuffed Cabbage Rolls, '84 217
Stuffed Cabbage Rolls, Beef, '81 87; '82 7
Supper, Cabbage, '89 314
Supreme, Cabbage, '79 4; '83 206
Sweet-and-Sour Cabbage, '86 295; '87 189
Tex-Mex Cabbage, '80 63
Tomatoes, Cabbage and, '83 104
Tomatoes, Tasty Cabbage and, '86 72
Wedges, Saucy Cabbage, '83 86
Wedges, Smothered Cabbage, '81 87; '82 7
Wilted Cabbage, '80 64; '88 229

Cakes. *See also* Breads, Cookies.
Almond-Butter Cake, '86 107
Almond-Butter Cake, Peachy, '90 107
Almond-Butter Wedding Cake, '86 106
Almond Legend Cake, '82 8
Almond Whipping Cream Cake, '80 295
Amaretto Cake, Easy, '85 79
Ambrosia Cake, '79 229
Ambrosia Cake Royale, '89 335
Angel Food
    Amaretto-Almond Sauce, Angel Food
        Cake with, '90 199
    Chocolate Angel Cake, '88 128
    Chocolate Angel Food Cake, '87 21;
        '90 111; '91 55
    Chocolate Angel Food Cake with Custard
        Sauce, '88 259
    Coconut Angel Cake, Spiked, '85 279
    Deluxe Angel Food Cake, '86 121
    Ice Cream Angel Cake, '83 23
    Ice-Cream Angel Dessert, Triple Mint,
        '93 86
    Lemon Angel Cake, '80 147
    Orange-Coconut Angel Food Cake,
        '94 294
    Pineapple-Orange Sauce, Angel Cake
        with, '84 14
    Surprise, Angel Cake, '93 86
    Trifle, Pineapple Angel Food, '93 86
Apple Cake, '83 312; '84 262
Apple Cake, Dried-, '79 13
Apple-Date Cake, Fresh, '83 300
Apple-Ginger Upside-Down Cake, '94 180
Apple-Nut Cake, '87 76
Apple-Oatmeal Cake, Golden, '86 301
Apple-Pecan Cake, '92 167
Apple Pie Cake, '86 301
Applesauce Cake, '80 270
Applesauce Cake, My Favorite, '87 263

Cakes *(continued)*

Applesauce Cake with Bourbon Frosting, '88 236
Applesauce-Oatmeal Cake, '92 119
Applesauce Snack Cakes, '88 215; '89 20
Applesauce-Spice Cake, '83 42
Applesauce Spice Cake, '89 296
Apple Shortcake, Quick, '93 42
Apple Slice Cake, '85 93
Apple Spice Cake, '92 225
Apple Stack Cake, Dried, '85 242
Apple-Walnut Cake, '94 242
Banana-Blueberry Cake, '86 247
Banana Cake, '84 151
Banana Cake, Deluxe Light, '84 314
Banana Cake, Marvelous, '79 115
Banana-Coconut Cake, '93 154
Banana-Nut Cake, '92 120
Banana-Pecan Shortcake, '93 43
Bananas Foster Crunch Cake, '93 339
Banana Waldorf Cake, '85 118
Bars and Squares
    Almond Cake Squares, '79 111
    Apple-Date Dream Cake Squares, '85 10
    Apple-Orange Cake Squares, '84 150
    Applesauce Cake Squares, '86 8
    Applesauce-Spice Squares, '86 248
    Carrot-Lemon Squares, Golden, '80 40
    Carrot Squares, '79 256
    Cinnamon Cake Squares, '87 222
    Cream Cheese Cake Squares, '84 321
    Crumb Cake, Calico, '87 261
    Gingerbread Squares, '84 16
    Ginger Cake, '87 222
    Honey Cake Squares, '89 250
    Honey-Oatmeal Cake, '87 222
    Jam Squares, '81 M289
    Orange Cake Squares, '81 34
    Orange-Pumpkin Cake Squares, '83 242
    Pecan Squares, Easy, '81 230
    Pumpkin Cake Bars, '80 245
    Rhubarb Squares, '92 129
    Strawberry Shortcake Squares, '85 122; '86 124
    Zucchini-Carrot Cake, '93 20
Beet Cake with Almond Topping, '86 200
Birdhouse Cake, '93 284
Birthday Cake, Clowning Around, '94 52
Blackberry Cake, Fresh, '81 132
Blackberry Flan, '79 182
Blueberry-Sour Cream Cake, '90 140
Blueberry Streusel Cake, '92 144
Boston Cream Pie, '83 220
Bourbon-Pecan Cake, '84 25
Brown Mountain Cake, '84 39
Brown Sugar Meringue Cake, '81 70
Bûche de Noël, '84 304; '87 241
Bûche de Noël Cake, '82 262
Bunny Cake, '94 98
Butter Brickle Cake, '85 118
Butter Pecan Cake, '80 229
Butter Pecan Cake, Caramel-Filled, '88 278
Butterscotch Cake, '91 270
Cajun Cake, '87 138
Candy Bar Cake, '92 204
Caramel Cake, '89 55; '90 307
Caramel Layer Cake, Creamy, '81 71
Carolina Dream Cake, '88 278

Carrot Cake, '79 45; '82 137; '84 315
Carrot Cake, Applesauce, '81 202
Carrot Cake, Blue Ribbon, '81 70
Carrot Cake, Coconut-Pecan, '84 322
Carrot Cake, Easy, '83 215
Carrot Cake, Fresh Coconut-, '80 299
Carrot Cake, Frosted, '92 19
Carrot Cake, Old-Fashioned, '83 M232
Carrot Cake, Old-South, '80 120
Carrot Cake, Quick-and-Easy, '84 150
Carrot Cakes, Miniature, '90 94
Carrot Cake, Spiced, '87 296
Carrot Cake, Spicy Fruited, '85 117
Carrot Pudding Cake, '83 24
Carrot Snack Cake, Easy, '82 235
Chart, Cake Failure, '81 72
Cheesecakes
    Amaretto Cheesecake, '81 150
    Amaretto-Irish Cream Cheesecake, '90 266
    Apple Cheesecake, Dieter's, '86 318
    Black Forest Cheesecake, '84 74; '89 93; '94 21
    Blueberries 'n' Cream Cheesecake, '87 140
    Blueberry Chiffon Cheesecake, '87 76
    Brownies, Cheesecake, '85 249
    Brown Sugar-and-Spice Cheesecake, '89 93
    Butterscotch Cheesecake, '86 188
    Candy Bar Cheesecake, '85 298; '86 120
    Cherry Cheesecake, '79 50
    Cherry-Topped Cheesecake, '80 23
    Chicken Cheesecake, Curried, '90 174
    Chicken-Chile Cheesecake, '92 42
    Chocolate-Almond Cheesecake, '93 53
    Chocolate-Amaretto Cheesecake, '85 M294; '93 97
    Chocolate-Caramel-Pecan Cheesecake, '91 197
    Chocolate Cheesecake, '81 16; '82 305
    Chocolate Cheesecake, German, '87 265
    Chocolate Cheesecake, Rich, '84 74; '85 38
    Chocolate Cheesecakes, Tiny, '92 288
    Chocolate Cheesecake with Whipped Cream Frosting, '89 42
    Chocolate Chip Cheesecake, '85 114
    Chocolate Cookie Cheesecake, '91 298
    Chocolate Marble Cheesecake, '89 93
    Chocolate-Mint Baked Alaska Cheesecake, '94 142
    Chocolate-Mint Cheesecake, '91 104
    Chocolate-Raspberry Truffle Cheesecake, '91 270
    Chocolate Swirl Cheesecake, '84 295; '85 26
    Cottage Cheese Cheesecake, '80 24
    Cream Cheesecake, Rich, '83 270
    Crème de Menthe Cheesecake, '82 263; '89 93
    Daiquiri Chiffon Cheesecake, '88 66
    Deluxe Cheesecake, '80 23
    Feta Cheesecakes, Little, '86 277
    Fiesta Cheesecake, '93 273
    Frozen Cheesecake with Raspberry Sauce, '84 73
    Fruit-Glazed Cheesecake, '80 24; '90 162

    Glazed Cheesecake, '83 142
    Grasshopper Cheesecake, '80 191
    Ham-and-Asparagus Cheesecake, '90 174
    Individual Cheesecakes, So Easy, '85 30
    Kahlúa Cheesecake, Heavenly, '83 48
    Lemon Cheesecake, '86 194; '91 308; '92 24
    Lemon Cheesecake, Luscious, '90 M196
    Lemon Cheesecake with Orange-Pineapple Glaze, '81 60
    Light-and-Easy Cheesecake, '88 55
    Make-Ahead Cheesecake Pie, '81 233
    Marbled Cheesecake, '87 261
    Marble Mint Cheesecake, '84 152
    Margarita Cheesecake, '92 211; '94 142
    Mile-High Cheesecake, '86 334
    Miniature Cheesecakes, '82 305; '90 170
    Mocha-Chocolate Cheesecake, '88 258
    Mocha Swirl Cheesecake, '87 262
    Orange Cheesecake, '81 84; '85 38
    Passover Cheesecake, '91 53
    Peaches 'n' Cream Cheesecake, '88 137
    Peanut Butter Cheesecake, '94 142
    Pear-Berry Cheesecake, '82 M141
    Pear-Glazed Cheesecake, '79 67
    Pecan Cheesecake, '85 38
    Pecan Cheesecake, Butter, '86 61
    Peppermint Cheesecake, Frozen, '94 143
    Petite Cheesecakes, Holiday, '86 321
    Phyllo Cheesecakes, Little, '87 275
    Piña Colada Cheesecake, '92 70
    Pineapple Cheesecake, '81 32
    Pineapple Cheesecake, Ultimate, '85 38
    Praline Cheesecake, '83 270; '89 93
    Pumpkin Cheesecake, '80 254; '85 280
    Raspberry Sauce, Cheesecake with, '87 116
    Reuben Cheesecake, '90 175
    Shrimp-and-Gruyère Cheesecake, '92 57
    Sour Cream Cheesecake, '86 320
    Spinach-Mushroom Cheesecake, '92 326
    Spinach Pesto Cheesecake, '90 175
    Squares, Cheesecake, '84 151
    Strawberry Cheesecake, Almost, '86 32
    Sweet Potato Cheesecake, '80 287
    Tarts, Cream Cheese, '84 74
    Triple-Layer Cheesecake, Chocolate-Glazed, '86 315; '90 310
    Vanilla Cheesecake, Creamy, '89 93
    Vegetable Cheesecake, Layered, '91 62; '92 51
    White Chocolate Cheesecake, '87 44; '88 267; '94 180
    Yam Cheesecake, '81 224
Cherry Bourbon Cake, '82 287
Cherry Cake, '79 165
Cherry Cake, Quick, '81 238
Cherry Torte, Black Forest, '88 178
Cherry Upside-Down Cake, '82 56
Chocolate
    Almond Cake, Chocolate-, '91 248
    Almond Cake with Cherry Filling, Chocolate-, '84 225
    Banana Cake, Chocolate-, '86 138

Cakes, Chocolate *(continued)*

Banana Loaf, Chocolate Chip-, **'85** 115
Beet Cake, Chocolate, **'80** 40
Birthday Cake, Fishin'-for-Fun, **'93** 194
Black Forest Cake, **'81** 126; **'92** 174
Black Forest Cake, Six-Layer, **'85** 125
Black Forest Cherry Cake, **'83** 302
Black Forest Dump Cake, **'85** 13
Brownie Baked Alaska, **'80** 66
Brownie Delight, Chocolate, **'87** 224
Buttercream Cake, Chocolate, **'90** 108
Buttermilk Chocolate Cake, **'79** 13
Cameo Cake, **'94** 58
Candy Cake, Chocolate, **'81** 238
Caramel-Nut Cake, Chocolate-, **'83** 23
Carrot Cake, Brownie, **'92** 120
Cherry Cake, Chocolate-, **'84** 200;
   '86 239
Cinnamon Cake, Chocolate-, **'93** 154
Cocoa Crown Cake, **'90** 107
Coconut Cake, Chocolate-, **'83** 23
Cookies-and-Cream Cake, **'92** 163
Custard Cake, Chocolate, **'88** 175
Decadent Chocolate Cake, **'86** 142
Easy Chocolate Cake, **'80** 140
Father's Day Cake, **'92** 134
Frosting, Chocolate Cake with Double,
   '86 314
Fudge Cake, Best, **'83** 301
Fudge Cake, Brown Sugar, **'86** 316
Fudge Cake, Chocolate, **'80** 279
Fudge Cake for Two, **'81** 205
Fudge Cake, One-Foot-in-the-Fire,
   '90 252
Fudge Frosting, Chocolate Cake with,
   '89 56
German Chocolate Cake, **'81** 296;
   '83 M233
German Chocolate Chip Cake, **'86** 247
Grandma's Chocolate Cake, **'94** 133
Kahlúa Cake, Chocolate, **'91** 298
Kahlúa Chocolate Cake, **'81** 303
Marbled Cake, Cocoa, **'82** 265
Marshmallow Cake, No-Egg Chocolate,
   '87 M97
Mayonnaise Cake, Chocolate, **'83** 99
Mocha Cake, Belgian, **'84** 316
Mocha Cake, Double, **'84** 311
Mocha-Chocolate Cake, Dark, **'84** 311
Mousse Cake, Chocolate, **'87** 264
Nut Cake, Rich Chocolate-, **'86** 8
Pastry Cake, Chocolate, **'91** 196
Peanut Butter Cake, Chocolate-,
   '84 240
Peanut Butter Cake, Fudgy, **'85** 91
Peanut Cluster Cake, Chocolate-,
   '87 184
Perfect Chocolate Cake, **'82** 244;
   '90 307
Pound Cake. *See* Cakes/Pound.
Pudding Cake, Hot Fudge, **'88** 255
Pudding, Chocolate Cake, **'81** 99
Pudding, Hot Fudge Sundae Cake,
   '88 167
Queen's Chocolate Cake, **'89** 271
Raspberry Cake, Chocolate-, **'92** 173
Rich Chocolate Cake, **'89** 43
Rocky Road Cake, **'81** 178
Roll, Chocolate Cream, **'85** 317

Roll, Chocolate-Frosted Ice Cream,
   '84 200
Roll, Chocolate-Mocha Cream, **'84** 304
Roll, Chocolate Mousse, **'83** 290;
   '88 280
Roll, Chocolate-Orange, **'87** 21
Rolls, Chocolate Cake, **'94** 312
Royal, Chocolate Cake, **'86** 239
Rum Cake, Chocolate, **'79** 67
Sachertorte, **'84** 253
Snack Cake, Black Widow, **'93** 245
Snack Cake, Frosted Chocolate, **'90** 194
Sour Cream Cake, Chocolate-, **'87** 222
Sour Cream Cake, Chocolate Chip-,
   '85 115
Sour Cream Chocolate Cake, **'79** 282
Strawberry Shortcake, Chocolate-,
   '89 216
Swiss Chocolate Chip Cake, **'87** 85
Tic-Tac-Toe Cake, **'94** 52
Tiered Cameo Cake, **'94** 125
Toffee Cake, Chocolate-, **'89** 335
Torte, Apricot-Filled Chocolate, **'90** 107
Torte, Chocolate-Pecan, **'89** 42
Torte, Chocolate Praline, **'84** 165
Torte, Chocolate-Strawberry Ice Cream,
   '79 7
Torte, Chocolate Velvet, **'86** 316
Torte, Double-Chocolate, **'79** 67
Torte, Mocha Brownie, **'85** 102
Torte Royale, Chocolate, **'82** 263
Triangle Cake, Chocolate, **'85** 126
Truffle Cake, Chocolate, **'89** 43
Wedding Cake, Cameo, **'94** 124
Wedding Cake, Double Chocolate,
   '91 100
Whipped Cream Cake, Chocolate-Mint,
   '90 265
White Chocolate-Cherry Cake, **'88** 268
White Chocolate Mousse Cake, **'89** 160
Yule Log, **'79** 281; **'82** 289
Zucchini Cake, Chocolate, **'85** 156
Cinnamon Crumb Cake, **'85** 290
Cinnamon Streusel Cake, **'84** 151
Coconut
   Apple Coconut Cake, **'80** 226
   Cake, Coconut, **'92** 120
   Chocolate-Coconut Cake, **'83** 23
   Christmas Coconut Cake, **'82** 262
   Cream Cake, Coconut, **'81** 179; **'91** 269
   Creamy Coconut Cake, **'84** 43
   Fresh Coconut Cake, **'80** 289; **'82** 52;
      '85 281
   Holiday Coconut Cake, **'90** 308
   Layer Cake, Coconut-Pineapple,
      '80 140
   Layer Cake, Stately Coconut, **'81** 70
   Lemon-Coconut Cream Cake, **'81** 179
   Lemon-Coconut Sheet Cake, **'85** 117
   Pineapple Cake, Coconut-, **'89** 56
   Pineapple Cake Roll, Coconut-, **'84** 304
   Regal Coconut Cake, **'83** 299
   Rum-Orange Coconut Cake, **'88** 224
   Spice Cake, Coconut-, **'84** 255; **'87** 296
   Toasted Coconut Cake, **'86** 60
   Unforgettable Coconut Cake, **'90** 104
   White Chocolate-Coconut Cake, **'87** 263
Coffee Cakes
   Almond-Blueberry Coffee Cake, **'85** 152
   Almond Coffee Cake Twist, **'91** 22
   Almond Sunburst, **'94** 245

Apple Coffee Cake, **'81** 249
Apple Coffee Cake, Fresh, **'92** 32
Apple Loaf, Spiced, **'79** 215
Apple-Pecan Coffee Cake, **'84** 242
Apricot-Almond Coffee Cake, **'93** 26
Apricot Lattice Coffee Cake, **'94** 48
Banana Coffee Cake, **'81** 288
Banana Cream Coffee Cake, **'85** 46
Banana-Sour Cream Coffee Cake,
   '80 186
Blueberry Brunch Cake, **'83** 183
Blueberry Coffee Cake, **'82** 206;
   '85 326; **'88** 263
Blueberry Coffee Cake, Fresh, **'81** 164
Blueberry Streusel Coffee Cake,
   '88 154
Braid Coffee Cake, Daisy, **'82** 197
Breakfast Pullapart, **'81** 278
Butterflake Coffee Ring, **'79** 216
Buttermilk Coffee Cake, **'89** 50
Buttermilk Crumb Cake, **'79** 72
Caramel Bread, **'82** 75
Caramel Breakfast Rolls, **'79** 193
Caramel-Orange Coffee Ring, **'80** 45
Caramel Ring, Easy, **'85** M89
Cardamom Coffee Cake, **'83** 246;
   '84 17
Cheesecake Coffee Cake, Deep-Dish,
   '90 50
Cherry Blossom Coffee Cake, **'80** 21
Cherry Coffee Cake, **'94** 49
Chocolate-Chip Coffee Cake, **'79** 249
Chocolate Chip Coffee Cake, **'83** 231
Christmas-Tree Coffee Cakes, **'87** 298
Christmas Wreath, **'80** 280
Cinnamon-Buttermilk Coffee Cake,
   '80 45
Cinnamon Coffee Cake, **'83** M203
Cinnamon Crisps, **'81** 113
Cinnamon-Nut Bubble Bread, **'80** 22
Cinnamon-Pecan Coffee Cake, **'87** 69
Cinnamon-Raisin Coffee Cake, **'93** 180
Cinnamon Twist Coffee Cake, **'84** 322
Cinnamon Upside-Down Coffee Cake,
   '85 256
Coffee Cake, **'94** 167
Cora's Coffee Cake, **'91** 186
Cranberry-Coconut Coffee Cake,
   '93 332
Cranberry Coffee Cake, **'81** 14; **'90** 159
Cranberry-Nut Coffee Cake, **'81** 250
Cranberry-Orange Coffee Cake, **'82** 283
Cream Cheese Coffee Cake, **'86** 290
Crescent Coffee Cake, **'81** 229
Danish Coffee Ring, **'80** 20
Fig Coffee Cake, Easy, **'80** 116
Holiday Coffee Cake, **'84** 284
Holiday Wreath, **'81** 284
Honey Twist, **'79** 80
Lemon Coffee Cake, Lightly, **'81** 14
Macadamia Ring Coffee Cake, **'85** 326
Maple-Nut Coffee Twist, **'86** 290
Marbled Coffee Cake, **'86** 9
Mix, Quick, **'94** 167
Muffins, Coffee Cake, **'79** 7
Oatmeal-Coconut Coffee Cake, **'83** 312
Orange Breakfast Ring, **'81** 229
Orange Butter Coffee Cake, **'89** 229
Orange Coffee Cake, **'85** M88
Orange Marmalade Swirl Coffee Cake,
   '81 107

Cakes, Coffee Cakes *(continued)*

Orange-Pecan Coffee Cake, **'86** 86
Overnight Coffee Cake, **'80** 52; **'92** 213
Peach Flip, **'79** 217
Pecan-Topped Coffee Cake, **'81** 41
Pineapple-Coconut Coffee Cake, **'94** 49
Raisin Coffee Cake, Spicy, **'88** 63
Raspberry Coffee Cake, **'83** 112
Raspberry Tea Cake, **'91** 271
Ring, Coffee Cake, **'85** M89
Savarin, Holiday, **'80** 280
Snack Cake, Coffee, **'86** 247
Sour Cream Coffee Cake, **'81** 270;
  '93 154
Sour Cream-Walnut Coffee Cake,
  '79 209
Special Coffee Cake, Mama Cle's,
  '94 287
Strawberry Coffee Cake, **'85** 46
St. Timothy's Coffee Cake, **'91** 54
Sugar Cake, Moravian, **'87** 228
Sugar Cake, Polish, **'89** 267
Sugarplum Coffee Ring, **'79** 235;
  '83 M37
Sweet Roll Dough, **'79** 80
Tropical Coffee Cake, **'80** 232; **'90** 323
Walnut Coffee Cake, **'93** 124
Whole Wheat Coffee Cake,
  Crunchy-Topped, **'79** 93
Cola Cake, **'81** 238
Compromise Cake, The, **'90** 253
Cranberry Upside-Down Cake, **'87** 8
Cream Cheese Cake, Regal, **'80** 140
Cream Cheese Loaf Cake, **'84** 151
Crème de Menthe Cake, **'81** 178
Cupcakes
Apple-Nut Cupcakes, **'82** 279
A Tisket, a Tasket, **'92** 15
Banana-Cocoa Cupcakes, **'80** 130
Birthday Balloon Cakes, **'92** 15
Black Bottom Cups, **'82** 279
Brownie Cupcakes, **'82** 280
Carrot-Bran Cupcakes, **'82** 16
Chocolate Chip Cupcakes, Marble,
  '81 239
Chocolate Cupcakes, **'92** 14
Chocolate Surprise Cupcakes, **'85** 91
Cinnamon-Chocolate Cupcakes,
  '81 M139
Confetti Cupcakes, New Year's, **'92** 15
Cream Cheese Party Cupcakes, **'82** 279
Date Cupcakes, **'84** 7
Graveyard Grumblings, **'92** 15
Happy Day Cupcakes, **'80** 129
Ice-Cream Cone Cakes, Fourth-of-July,
  '92 15
Lemon Moist Cupcakes, **'82** 112;
  '83 153
Mocha Cupcakes, **'85** 250
Pumpkin Cupcakes, **'85** 121
Self-Filled Cupcakes, **'80** 129
Sweetheart Cupcakes, **'92** 15
Tannenbaum Temptations, **'92** 14
Turkey Talk, **'92** 15
Vanilla Cupcakes, **'92** 14
Vanilla Cupcakes, Golden, **'85** 121
Yellow Cupcakes, Easy, **'83** 241
Daffodil Cake, **'84** 161
Date Nut Cake, **'79** 176; **'80** 5

Date-Nut Cake Roll, **'89** 94
Decorating Techniques, Cake, **'83** 72, 240;
  '84 224
Easter Egg Cake, **'94** 98
Easter Rabbit Cake, **'94** 99
Éclair Cake, **'93** 42
Fig Cake, **'79** 32
Fig Preserve Cake, **'79** 140; **'84** 316
Fig Preserves Cake, **'89** 335
Friendship Cake, **'82** 250
Fruit-and-Cereal Brunch Cake, **'88** 263
Fruit-and-Nut Cake, Stately, **'84** 226
Fruitcakes
Applesauce Fruitcake, **'83** 258
Aronowitz Fruitcake, **'86** 285
Bourbon Fruitcake, **'85** 315
Brandy Fruitcake, **'82** 261
Burgundy Fruitcake, **'85** 292
Classic Fruitcake, **'91** 258
Favorite Fruitcake, Family, **'88** 284
Fondue, Fruitcake, **'84** 258
Japanese Fruitcake, **'83** 268; **'90** 252
Jeweled Fruitcake, **'88** 260
Kentucky Fruitcake, **'86** 266
Layered Fruitcake, **'87** 265
Lemon Fruitcake, **'83** 258
Light Fruitcake, **'90** 309
Mom's Fruitcake, **'85** 321
Old-South Fruitcake, **'79** 289
Regal Fruitcake, **'83** 257
Sherry-Nut Fruitcake, **'84** 266
Spice Cake, Fruit and, **'87** M97
White Fruitcake, **'80** 280; **'85** 316
Zucchini Fruitcake, **'88** 284
Fudge Cake, **'94** M293
Funnel Cakes, **'83** 250
Funnel Cakes, Nutty, **'91** 233
Gingerbread, Applesauce, **'94** 179
Gingerbread Cake Roll, **'89** 214
Gingerbread Cake Mix, **'92** 312
Gingerbread, No-Molasses, **'92** 313
Gingerbread, Old English, **'79** 265
Gingerbread, Old-Fashioned, **'91** 240
Gingerbread, Refrigerator, **'80** 52
Gingerbread, Spicy, **'84** 263
Gingerbread with Caramel Sauce, Pumpkin,
  '93 235
Ginger Shortcakes, **'94** 179
Graham Cracker Cake, **'79** 13
Grapefruit Cake, Fresh, **'89** 308
Holiday Cake, Favorite, **'81** 264
Honey Bun Cake, **'91** 214
Honey Cake, **'92** 250
Honey Cake, Southern, **'89** 251
Hummingbird Cake, **'82** 244; **'90** 305
Ice Cream Cake, **'86** 321; **'89** 71
Ice Cream Cake for Grown-Ups, **'88** M192
Ice Cream Cake, Fruity, **'87** 110
Ice Cream Yule Log, **'83** 253
Jam Cake, Spicy, **'89** 236
Jellyroll, Easy, **'82** 176
Jellyroll Layer Cake, **'85** 125
Jellyroll, Spiced, **'82** 176
Key Lime Cake, **'91** 214
King Cake, **'90** 20
Lady Baltimore Cake, **'90** 45
Lane Cake, **'80** 121; **'83** 269
Lane Cake, Nanny's, **'89** 55
Lemon Cake, Easy, **'83** 24
Lemon Cake, Glazed, **'86** 70
Lemon Cake, Luscious, **'93** 81

Lemon Cake Pudding, **'92** 96
Lemon Cake Roll, **'89** 312
Lemon Cake Roll, Elegant, **'80** 70
Lemon-Cheese Cake, Tart, **'88** 7
Lemon Gold Cake, **'83** 301
Lemon Layer Cake, Luscious, **'86** 61
Lemon Layer Cake, Old-Fashioned, **'85** 191
Lemon Meringue Cake, **'89** 296
Lemon Meringue Torte with Raspberry
  Sauce, **'93** 82
Lemon-Pineapple Cake, **'86** 60, 239
Lemon-Poppy Seed Cake, **'93** 154
Lemon Pudding Cake, **'83** 106
Lemon-Raspberry Cake, **'91** 247
Lemon Roll, Snow-Capped, **'79** 68
Lemon Sponge Cups, **'83** 10
Light Cake, Basic, **'90** 107
Lime Layer Loaf, **'85** 96
Lord Baltimore Cake, **'90** 45
Mandarin-Rum Cake, **'84** 150
Mango Cake, **'83** 150
Maraschino Nut Cake, **'83** 268
Mincemeat Spice Cake, **'79** 246
Molasses Snack Cake, **'86** 20
Neapolitan Cake, **'88** 168
Nutmeg Feather Cake, **'81** 238
Nutty Cakes, **'89** 50
Oatmeal Cake, Dutch, **'83** 95
Orange Cake, **'86** 61
Orange Cake, Fresh, **'83** 300
Orange Cake, Mandarin, **'83** 24
Orange Cake, Williamsburg, **'81** 120; **'82** 23
Orange Chiffon Cake, **'91** 56
Orange Chiffon Cake, Fresh, **'88** 179
Orange-Cranberry Cake, **'85** 314
Orange-Date Cake, **'94** 60
Orange-Lemon Cake, General Robert E. Lee,
  '88 92
Orange Liqueur Cake, **'87** 84
Orange Marmalade Cake, **'85** 53
Orange Meringue Cake, **'86** 336; **'87** 84
Orange-Nut Butter Cake, **'80** 254
Orange Nut Cake, **'80** 70
Orange-Pecan Crunch Cake, **'83** 10
Orange Rum Cake, **'79** 2
Orange Shortcake, Fresh, **'80** 100
Orange-Slice Cake, **'81** 264
Orange Streusel Cake, **'88** 10
Peach Cake, Fresh, **'85** 178
Peaches and Cream Cake, **'80** 142
Peach Shortcakes, Spicy, **'89** 154
Peach Upside-Down Cake, **'87** 8
Peachy Picnic Cake, **'79** 178
Peanut Butter-and-Jelly Cake, **'85** 34
Peanut Butter-Banana Cake, **'80** 87
Peanut Butter Cake, **'79** 51; **'83** M233
Peanut Butter Swirl Cake, **'86** 109
Peanutty Layer Cake, Super, **'83** 222
Pear Cake with Caramel Drizzle, **'86** 247
Pear Preserve Cake, **'85** 52
Pear Shortcakes, **'94** 215
Pecan Cake, Kentucky, **'84** 263
Pecan Cake with Praline Glaze, **'82** 196
Pecan Roulade, **'87** 183
Peppermint Candy Cake, **'89** 254
Persimmon Cake, **'79** 205
Petit Fours, Simple, **'92** 277
Petits Fours, **'79** 117
Petits Fours, Chocolate-Almond, **'93** 255
Petits Fours, Teatime, **'85** 119
Pineapple Cake, Heavenly, **'83** 303

Cakes *(continued)*

Pineapple-Pecan Upside-Down Cake, **'84** 25
Pineapple Upside-Down Cake, **'80** 102;
 '88 10
Pineapple Upside-Down Cake, Skillet,
 '85 242
Pineapple Upside-Down Cake, Stacked,
 '86 239
Popcorn-Gumdrop Cake, **'87** 262
Poppy Seed Cake, **'92** 174
Poppy Seed Cake, Plantation, **'79** 13
Poppy Seed Loaf Cake, **'81** 63
Poppy Seed Loaf, Quick, **'82** 75
Pound
  Apple Cider Pound Cake, **'84** 10
  Apricot Brandy Pound Cake, **'83** 267
  Black Walnut Pound Cake, **'92** 16
  Bourbon-Pecan Pound Cake, **'91** 270
  Brandied Pound Cake, **'89** 292
  Brown Sugar Pound Cake, **'82** 135
  Buttermilk Pound Cake, **'79** 285; **'85** 255
  Buttermilk Pound Cake, Old-Fashioned,
   '82 52
  Buttermilk Pound Cake, Spiced, **'84** 73
  Butter-Nut Pound Cake, **'86** 235
  Butterscotch-Pecan Pound Cake,
   '92 153
  Caramel Frosting, Pound Cake with,
   '87 39
  Carrot Pound Cake, **'87** 41
  Chocolate Chip Pound Cake, **'86** 178;
   '93 105; **'94** 100
  Chocolate Marble Pound Cake, **'88** 16
  Chocolate-Orange Pound Cake, **'89** 94
  Chocolate Pound Cake, **'82** 88; **'84** 10;
   '89 325; **'94** 288
  Chocolate Pound Cake with Frosting,
   '90 284
  Chocolate Pound Cake with Fudge
   Frosting, **'87** 296
  Chocolate-Sour Cream Pound Cake,
   '83 239; **'92** 153
  Coconut-Cream Cheese Pound Cake,
   '85 297; **'90** 305
  Coconut Cream Pound Cake, **'84** 10
  Coconut Pound Cake, **'82** 87; **'91** 224
  Cream Cheese Pound Cake, **'81** 290;
   '86 287
  Cream Cheese Pound Cake, Crusty,
   '89 124
  Croutons, Cinnamon Pound Cake,
   '93 161
  Daiquiri Pound Cake, **'93** 83
  Eggnog Pound Cake, **'90** 253
  Favorite Pound Cake, **'81** 132; **'92** 171
  Five-Flavor Pound Cake, **'87** 264
  Four-Flavor Pound Cake, **'91** 136
  Fruited Pound Cake, **'81** 265
  Glazed Pound Cake, **'89** 207
  Golden Pound Cake, **'90** 284
  I Remember Pound Cake, **'86** 180
  Irish Cream-and-Coffee Pound Cake,
   '92 287
  Lemon Pound Cake, **'82** 88
  Lemon-Sour Cream Pound Cake, **'87** 38
  Loaf, Pound Cake, **'85** 306
  Mahogany Pound Cake, **'89** 207
  Marbled Pecan Pound Cake, **'93** 313
  Milk Chocolate Pound Cake, **'90** 306

Million Dollar Pound Cake, **'90** 306
Mini Pound Cakes, **'86** 148
Old-Fashioned Buttermilk Pound Cake,
 '88 16
Old-Fashioned Pound Cake, **'80** 279;
 '82 88; **'93** 120
Orange-Pecan Pound Cake, **'93** 13
Orange Pound Cake, **'87** 84, 221;
 '92 69
Peach-Almond Pound Cake, **'89** 86
Pineapple Pound Cake, **'79** 148
Pound Cake, **'92** 94
Praline Pound Cake, **'82** 88
Problems to Avoid Chart, **'84** 319
Pumpkin Pound Cake, **'92** 235
Rose-Geranium Pound Cake, Mrs.
 Willoughby's, **'84** 318
Rum Pound Cake, Buttered, **'83** 220
Sandwich, Grilled Pound Cake Dessert,
 '94 171
Sour Cream-Orange Pecan Pound Cake,
 '89 207
Sour Cream Pound Cake, **'89** 56;
 '92 153
Sour Cream Pound Cake,
 Cinnamon-Topped, **'82** 43
Sour Cream Pound Cake, Elegant,
 '83 79
Southern Pound Cake, Smoothest,
 '93 237
Strawberry-Banana Topping, Pound
 Cake with, **'89** 200
Sweet Potato Pound Cake, **'83** 85
Whipping Cream Pound Cake, **'90** 284
White Chocolate Pound Cake, **'91** 101
Yogurt Pound Cake, **'84** 10
Praline Cake, **'81** 162
Praline Ice Cream Cake, **'80** 84
Prune Cake, **'85** 223
Prune Cake and Sauce, **'85** 118
Prune Cake, Spicy, **'79** 136
Pudding Cake, Danish, **'91** 269
Pumpkin Cake, **'81** 272; **'93** 303
Pumpkin Date Cake, **'79** 251
Pumpkin Kahlúa Cake, **'86** 292
Pumpkin Layer Cake, **'80** 245
Pumpkin Roll, **'79** 206; **'91** 297
Queen Bee Cake, **'81** 237
Raisin Layer Cake, Spicy, **'79** 230
Red Velvet Cake, **'93** 318
Satin Ribbon Cake, **'92** 68
Sauerkraut Cake, **'94** 254
Savarin, **'79** 171
Sorghum Cake, **'85** 239
Sorghum Tea Cakes, **'85** 239
Spice Cake, **'81** 162
Spice Cake, Buttermilk, **'81** 211
Spice Cake, Dark, **'82** 314; **'83** 43
Spice Cake, Old South, **'84** 263
Spice Cake, Sugar 'n, **'84** 226
Spice Cake with Caramel Frosting, **'82** 314;
 '83 42
Spice Cake with Chocolate-Coffee Frosting,
 '88 268
Spice Cake, Yule Log, **'85** 314
Spice Layer Cake with Coffee Frosting,
 '94 86
Sponge
  Chocolaty Sponge Cake, **'86** 60
  Coffee Sponge Cake, **'83** 229; **'91** 55
  Coffee Sponge Cake, Two-Day, **'86** 75

Daffodil Sponge Cake, **'79** 175; **'80** 6;
 '84 315
Passover Sponge Cake, **'90** 106
Strawberries 'n Cream Sponge Cake
 Roll, **'81** 95
Yellow Sponge Cake, **'80** 250
Squash Cake, **'86** 200
Stack Cake, Favorite, **'87** 228
Stack Cake, Old-Fashioned, **'81** 216
Strawberry Cake Roll, **'79** 49; **'83** 129;
 '84 305; **'85** 172
Strawberry Cream Cake, **'86** 61
Strawberry Crispy Shortcakes, **'93** 42
Strawberry Crunch Cake, **'79** 288;
 '80 35
Strawberry Delight Cake, **'85** 30
Strawberry Ice Cream Roll, **'84** 105
Strawberry Meringue Cake, **'86** 240
Strawberry Pinwheel Shortcake,
 '89 112
Strawberry Roll, **'82** 120
Strawberry Roll, Heavenly, **'82** 176
Strawberry Shortcake, **'81** 96; **'83** 122;
 '92 184; **'94** 162
Strawberry Shortcake, A Favorite,
 '88 136
Strawberry Shortcake, Elegant, **'88** 37
Strawberry Shortcake Jubilee, **'88** 209
Strawberry Shortcake Shells, **'88** 196
Strawberry Yogurt Layer Cake, **'94** 85
Sweet Potato Cake, **'79** 207; **'89** 295
Sweet Potato Loaf Cake, **'81** 224
Sweet Potato Log Roll, **'82** 227
Sweet Potato Surprise Cake,
 '80 287
Tea Cake, Lemon, **'82** 169
Tea Cakes, Mexican, **'81** 196
Teacakes, Old-Fashioned,
 '84 43
Teddy Bear Cakes, **'92** 278
Tipsy Squire, **'85** 41
Torte, Amaretto, **'82** 303
Torte, Apricot Sponge, **'90** 59
Torte, Black Forest, **'88** 209
Torte, Carob-Pecan, **'85** 218
Torte, Chocolate Mint, **'94** 86
Torte, Hazelnut, **'91** 248
Torte, Heavenly Pecan, **'81** 266
Torte, Mocha-Pecan, **'86** 26
Torte, Mocha Velvet, **'92** 318
Torte, Passover Linzer, **'90** 106
Torte, Spring, **'91** 57
Torte, Strawberry Meringue,
 '88 136
Torte, Sugar Cookie, **'79** 68
Torte, Toffee Meringue, **'87** 118
Twelfth Night Cake, **'93** 337
Upside Down Cake, Quick, **'90** 219
Upside-Down Sunburst Cake, **'87** 9
Vanilla Chiffon Cake, **'79** 266
Walnut Cake, Black, **'80** 253; **'84** 316;
 '90 308
Walnut Cream Roll, **'84** 192
White Cake, Buttermilk, **'86** 235
White Cake with Strawberries and Chocolate
 Glaze, **'87** 76
White Cake with Strawberry Frosting, Rich,
 '89 184
Yogurt-Lemon-Nut Cake, **'89** 169
Zucchini Cake, **'79** 24
Zuppa Inglese, **'85** 229

Candies

Almond Brittle Candy, '80 255
Almond Butter Crunch, '80 301
Almond Roca, '86 49
Almond-Toffee Crunch, '88 285
Apples, Candied Red, '81 217
Apples, Candy, '84 243
Apricot Balls, '79 274
Balls, No-Cook Candy, '85 14
Bourbon Balls, '81 254; '83 315; '90 83
Bourbon Balls, Chocolate, '84 298
Brandy Balls, '86 319
Brittle with Crushed Peanuts, '87 184
Buckeyes, '85 321
Butter Creams, '80 302
Buttermilk Candy, '80 302
Caramel Corn Candy, '84 243
Caramel Good Stuff, Baked, '80 284
Caramel-Peanut Squares, '85 247
Chocolate Brittle, '83 315
Chocolate Brittle, Quick, '82 114
Chocolate Caramels, '91 35
Chocolate-Coconut Almond Drops, '87 223
Chocolate-Covered Cherries, '81 286;
    '84 298
Chocolate-Covered Pecan Fritters, '79 205
Chocolate-Covered Pretzels, '82 295
Chocolate Drops, '84 111
Chocolate Greeting Card, '83 40
Chocolate-Marshmallow Squares, '92 M50
Chocolate-Nut Log Candy, '86 335
Chocolate Nut Teasers, '91 35
Chocolate-Peanut Butter Balls, '80 87
Chocolate-Peanut Butter Bites, '92 M317
Chocolate-Peanut Butter Drops, '92 322
Chocolate-Peanut Clusters, '81 16
Chocolate Peanutty Swirls, '94 M330
Chocolate Rum Balls, '80 302
Chocolate-Rum Balls, '88 285
Chocolates, Liqueur Cream-Filled, '87 258
Chocolate Spiders, '85 236
Chocolates, Spirited, '86 278
Chocolate, Tempered, '91 35
Chocolate Truffles, '85 114; '91 108
Chocolate Velvets, '84 298
Coconut-Almond Balls, '84 256
Coconut-Black Walnut Bonbons, '82 307
Coconut Candy, '79 272; '80 250
Corn Brittle, Crunchy, '85 208
Crème de Cacao Balls, '86 266
Crème de Menthe Chocolates, '91 36
Crystal Candy, '84 299
Date Candy, '89 308
Date Loaf Candy, '80 302
Date Logs, '79 274
Divinity, Apricot, '83 297
Divinity, Christmas, '81 286
Divinity, Peanut, '85 233; '87 M278
Divinity, Pink, '86 49
Divinity, Strawberry, '91 272
Frosting, Chocolate Candy, '81 238
Fruit Balls, '82 296; '84 299
Fudge
    Butterscotch Rum Fudge, '88 256
    Caramel Fudge, '91 273
    Cherry Nut Fudge, '83 315
    Chocolate Fudge, '82 20
    Chocolate-Peanut Butter Fudge,
        '87 257; '90 311
    Coffee-Chip Fudge, '86 74
    Cream Cheese Fudge, '84 111

Creamy Dark Fudge, '82 295
Creamy Fudge, '81 218
Diamond Fudge, '92 193
Double-Good Fudge, '79 M263
Double Good Fudge, '87 M278
Fast Fudge, '79 274
Four Chips Fudge, '92 318
Fudge, '86 266
Microwave Chocolate Fudge, '92 M50
Microwave Fudge, '91 M92
Mint Fudge, Dinner, '88 285
Mocha Fudge, Holiday, '84 298
Nut Fudge, Quick, '83 316
Nutty White Fudge, '81 253
Orange-Walnut Fudge, '92 288
Peanut Butter Fudge, '80 302; '89 307
Peanut Butter Fudge, Creamy, '92 240
Peanut Butter Fudge, Marbled, '88 65
Peanut-Fudge Bites, '91 M231;
    '92 M68
Peanut Fudge, Double, '85 91
Pecan Fudge, Creamy, '84 321
Penuche, '79 272
Pistachio Fudge, '83 298
Quick-and-Easy Fudge, '88 M190
Scotch Ring, Fudge, '79 273
Strawberry Fudge Balls, '93 80
Tiger Butter, '86 48
White Chocolate-Coffee Fudge, '94 232
White Chocolate Fudge, '92 317
Kentucky Colonels, '79 273
Lollipops, Colorful Molded, '81 218
Marzipan, '83 306
Millionaires, '79 M262
Mints, Cream Cheese, '93 79
Mints, Dinner, '88 66
Mints, Easy Holiday, '84 299
Mints, Party, '79 273; '81 119
Mint Twists, '86 106
Molded Candies, '84 40
Nut Clusters, '81 236
Nuts, Candied, '81 261
Orange Balls, '94 331
Orange Peel, Candied, '81 286
Peanut Brittle, '79 M263; '80 87; '84 298;
    '92 240
Peanut Brittle, Golden, '83 223
Peanut Brittle, Never-Fail, '79 273
Peanut Brittle, Orange, '80 302
Peanut Butter Candy, '93 166
Peanut Butter-Chocolate Balls, '80 269
Peanut Butter-Chocolate Candy Squares,
    '82 56
Peanut Butter Creams, '79 273
Peanut Butter Easter Eggs, '87 86
Peanut Butter Temptations, '84 29
Peanut Butter Yummies, '83 223
Peanut Clusters, '87 184; '92 288
Peanutty Clusters, '83 143
Pecan Brittle, '91 272
Pecan Clusters, '81 266
Pecan Clusters, Roasted, '85 233; '90 310
Pecan-Coconut Clusters, '86 M251
Pecan Pralines, Original, '81 11
Pecan Rolls, '79 285
Pecans, Brown Sugar, '81 266
Pecans, Glazed, '81 254
Pecans, Honeycomb, '84 300
Pecans, Orange, '84 299
Pecans, Spiced, '79 296; '81 286
Pecans, Spicy, '81 289

Pecans, Sugar-and-Honey, '86 319
Peppermint Patties, '86 278
Potato Candy, '79 273
Praline Clusters, Dark, '86 313
Praline Delights, Spicy, '84 299
Pralines, '79 272; '86 M288; '89 60; '90 48
Pralines, Basic, '92 313; '93 50
Pralines, Bourbon, '92 313; '93 51
Pralines, Butterscotch, '81 253
Pralines, Café au Lait, '92 313; '93 51
Pralines, Chocolate, '92 313; '93 51
Pralines, Chocolate-Mint, '92 313; '93 51
Pralines, Chocolate-Peanut Butter, '92 313;
    '93 51
Pralines, Creamy, '80 198; '92 289
Pralines, Dark, '83 52
Pralines, Hot Spicy, '92 313; '93 51
Pralines, Maple-Pecan, '83 222
Pralines, Mocha, '92 313; '93 51
Pralines, New Orleans-Style, '86 335
Pralines, Old-Fashioned, '89 318
Pralines, Orange, '92 313; '93 51
Pralines, Original Pecan, '81 11
Pralines, Peanut Butter, '92 313; '93 51
Pralines, Plantation Coffee, '86 241
Pralines, Southern, '79 M263
Pralines, Texas-Size, '79 186
Pralines, Vanilla, '92 313; '93 51
Quemada (Burnt-Sugar Candy), '87 38
Raisin Candy, Mixed, '84 111
Raspberry Cream Chocolates, '91 36
Red Rock Candy, '92 240
Rocky Road, '84 298
Rum Balls, '93 314
Strawberries, Christmas, '94 331
Taffy, Old-Fashioned, '80 302
Toffee, English, '79 273
Toffee, Microwave, '92 M317
Toffee, Nutty, '79 M263
Truffles, Almond, '83 298
Truffles, Amaretto Dessert, '86 319
Truffles, Bittersweet, '94 330
Truffles, Chocolate, '85 114; '89 43;
    '91 108
Truffles, Chocolate-Kahlúa, '92 285
Truffles, White Chocolate, '87 45
Truffles, Yule Street, '90 242
Turtle Candies, '93 M41
White Chocolate Salties, '92 50
White Chocolate Surprises, '91 36

Canning

Apple Rings, Cinnamon, '85 107
Asparagus, Pickled, '83 46
Bean Salad, Pickled Green, '82 239
Beans, Appalachian Green, '81 215
Beans, Dill Green, '93 136
Beans, Green, '80 126
Beans, Green, Snap, or Wax, '85 105

Canning (continued)

Beans, Lima, '80 127
Beets, Pickled, '81 216
Berries (except Strawberries), '80 128
Black-Eyed, Field, and Crowder Peas,
　'80 126
Catsup, Homemade, '85 188
Catsup, Spicy Tomato, '83 182
Chili Sauce, '81 175
Chili Sauce, Chunky, '85 188
Chow-Chow, '82 196
Corn, Cold-Pack, '81 216
Corn, Cream-Style, '80 127; '85 106
Corn, Whole Kernel, '85 106
Cranberry Conserve, '83 279
Fruit Juices, '85 107
Fruit, Unsweetened Mixed, '83 182
Mincemeat, Homemade, '79 245
Nectarines in Apple Juice, '83 183
Okra, '80 127
Peaches, '80 128
Peaches and Pears, '85 106
Peaches, Honey-Sweet, '85 107
Pear Mincemeat, '79 196
Piccalilli, Kentucky, '81 216
Sauerkraut, Homemade, '81 216
Squash, Summer, '80 127; '85 105
Succotash, '85 106
Tomatoes, '80 128; '85 106
Tomatoes, Stewed, '83 182
Tomatoes with Okra, '85 106
Tomato Juice, Spicy, '85 189
Tomato Puree, Seasoned, '83 182
Vegetable Soup, '80 128; '85 106
Cantaloupe. *See* Melons.
Caramel
Apples, Caramel, '79 220; '89 M231
Apples, Caramel-Peanut, '93 M244
Apples, Old English Caramel, '85 231
Baked Caramel Good Stuff, '80 284
Bars, Oatmeal-Caramel, '85 247
Bars, Yummy, '92 171
Bombe, Caramel-Toffee, '93 214
Bread, Caramel, '82 75
Brie with Fresh Fruit, Caramel, '90 266
Cake, Caramel, '89 55; '90 307
Cake, Caramel-Filled Butter Pecan, '88 278
Cake, Chocolate-Caramel-Nut, '83 23
Cake, Creamy Caramel Layer, '81 71
Candy, Caramel Corn, '84 243
Cheesecake, Chocolate-Caramel-Pecan,
　'91 197
Chocolate Caramels, '91 35
Cobbler, Peach-Caramel, '86 300; '87 178
Cookies, Caramel-Filled Chocolate, '92 319
Corn, Baked Caramel, '81 218
Corn, Caramel, '88 64
Corn, Nutty Caramel, '92 317
Corn, Oven-Made Caramel, '91 233
Crème d'Ange, '83 91
Dessert, Coconut-Caramel, '92 44
Drizzle, Caramel, '86 247
Filling, Caramel, '88 278
Flans, Caramel-Crowned, '90 227
Flan with Caramel, Baked, '92 231
Fondue, Caramel, '94 331
Frosting, Caramel, '81 278, M289; '82 314;
　'83 43; '84 39, 263; '86 239; '87 265;
　'89 55, 236; '90 307

Frosting, Creamy Caramel, '81 71
Frosting, Easy Caramel, '87 39
Frosting, Favorite Caramel, '83 106
Fudge, Caramel, '91 273
Helado, Caramel-Vanilla (Caramel-Vanilla Ice
　Cream), '81 67
Millionaires, '79 M262
Peaches, Caramel, '93 134
Pie, Burnt Caramel, '82 53
Pie, Caramel-Banana, '86 M165
Pie, Caramel Ice Cream, '82 181
Pie, Caramel-Nut Crunch, '94 244
Pie, Caramel-Peanut, '86 259
Pie, Caramel-Pecan, '88 282
Pie, Caramel-Pecan Apple, '85 247
Pie, Luscious Caramel Banana, '79 115
Pies, Coconut-Caramel, '87 260
Popcorn, Caramel, '79 219; '86 M212
Popcorn, Crispy Caramel, '83 92
Ring, Caramel-Orange Coffee, '80 45
Ring, Easy Caramel, '85 M89
Rolls, Caramel Breakfast, '79 193
Rolls, Caramel-Nut, '86 312
Rolls, Easy Caramel, '90 195
Sauce, Caramel, '79 79; '91 56, 180;
　'93 210, 235, 296; '94 234
Sauce, Caramel-Raisin, '88 127
Sauce, Easy Caramel, '87 38
Sauce, Toffee-Fudge, '89 95
Sauce, White Caramel, '92 195
Squares, Caramel-Peanut, '85 247
Squares, Chocolate-Caramel Layer, '79 83
Surprise, Caramel, '88 202
Syrup, Caramel, '82 43
Tart, Caramel Turtle Truffle, '93 M131
Tarts, Caramel, '82 43
Carrots
Aloha Carrots, '85 261
Ambrosia, Carrot-Marshmallow, '80 5
Apricot Carrots, '84 6
Aspic, Orange-and-Carrot, '86 199
Baby Carrots, Zucchini with, '88 24
Bake, Apple-Carrot, '93 304
Bake, Creamy Carrot, '85 67
Ball, Carrot-Cheese, '86 325
Balls, Carrot, '79 178
Bourbonnaise, Baby Carrots, '85 89
Braised Carrots and Celery, '86 327
Brandied Carrots, '87 253
Brandy Sauce, Carrots in, '83 86
Bread, Carrot, '89 143
Bread, Carrot-Pineapple, '82 210
Bread, Carrot-Walnut, '88 284
Bread, Pineapple-Carrot, '79 106
Bread, Tasty Carrot, '84 328
Bread, Three-C, '81 284
Bread, Zucchini-Carrot, '83 190
Brussels Sprouts, Carrots and, '82 300
Buttered Carrots and Celery, '89 44
Cake, Applesauce Carrot, '81 202
Cake, Blue Ribbon Carrot, '81 70
Cake, Brownie Carrot, '92 120
Cake, Carrot, '79 45; '82 137; '84 315
Cake, Carrot Pound, '87 41
Cake, Carrot Pudding, '83 24
Cake, Coconut-Pecan Carrot, '84 322
Cake, Easy Carrot, '83 215
Cake, Easy Carrot Snack, '82 235
Cake, Fresh Coconut-Carrot, '80 299
Cake, Frosted Carrot, '92 19
Cake, Old-Fashioned Carrot, '83 M232

Cake, Old-South Carrot, '80 120
Cake, Quick-and-Easy Carrot, '84 150
Cakes, Miniature Carrot, '90 94
Cake, Spiced Carrot, '87 296
Cake, Spicy Fruited Carrot, '85 117
Cake, Zucchini-Carrot, '93 20
Candied Carrots, '82 269; '83 225
Caprice, Carrots, '84 6
Cardamom Carrots, '89 271
Casserole, Carrot, '86 279; '87 285
Casserole, Carrot and Zucchini, '83 256
Casserole, Carrot-Pecan, '93 44
Casserole, Cauliflower-and-Carrot, '83 280
Casserole, Scrumptious Carrot, '84 328
Casserole, Squash-Carrot, '81 157
Celeriac and Carrots, '91 219
Cheese Scalloped Carrots, '94 36
Chowchow, Carrot, '93 218
Classy Carrots, '94 36
Combo, Carrot, '79 45
Cookies, Carrot, '82 137
Cookies, Carrot-Orange, '83 149
Cookies, Frosted Carrot, '81 7
Cooler, Carrot, '89 35
Cornbread, Carrot, '80 89; '81 163
Cupcakes, Carrot-Bran, '82 16
Curried Carrots and Pineapple, '90 228
Deviled Carrots, '83 322
Dilled Baby Carrots, '84 80; '92 145
Dilled Carrots, '85 24; '90 17
Dill-Spiced Carrots, '87 200
Dilly Carrots, '85 85
Fillets, Apple-Carrot Stuffed, '88 M192
Fried Carrot Balls, '82 16
Fried Carrots, Crispy, '94 36
Garden Surprise, '83 112
Ginger Carrots, '83 9; '85 139
Ginger-Cinnamon Carrots, '93 168
Gingered Carrots, '85 95; '92 302
Glazed Baby Carrots, '91 291; '92 256
Glazed Baby Carrots, Mint-, '89 102
Glazed Carrots, '81 304; '83 117; '85 258;
　'88 304; '89 106, 235
Glazed Carrots and Onions, '83 25; '87 128
Glazed Carrots and Peas, Mint-, '90 291
Glazed Carrots, Apricot, '80 89
Glazed Carrots, Ginger-, '87 68
Glazed Carrots, Honey-, '80 115; '84 121;
　'85 18; '92 229
Glazed Carrots, Lemon-, '84 16
Glazed Carrots, Light, '92 227
Glazed Carrots, Orange-, '79 12; '81 M165;
　'90 M98
Glazed Carrots, Peach-, '90 13
Glazed Carrots, Spice-, '83 M58
Glazed Carrots with Bacon and Onion,
　'87 200
Glazed Carrots with Grapes, '82 287
Golden Carrots, '85 267
Green Beans, Bow-Tie, '94 320
Harvard Carrots, '83 117
Herbed Carrots and Onions, '87 31
Honey-Kissed Carrots, '84 122
Horseradish Glaze, Carrots with, '85 66
Horseradish Sauce, Carrots and Broccoli
　with, '91 246
Julienne Carrots, How to Prepare, '84 120
Julienne Carrots, Sautéed, '82 91
Julienne Carrots with Walnuts, '84 188
Julienne, Tarragon Carrots, '84 329
Julienne, Turnips and Carrots, '86 295

Carrots (*continued*)

Julienne Zucchini and Carrots, **'90** 14
Lemon-Carrot Bundles, **'91** 80
Lemon Carrots, **'82** 300; **'83** 111
Loaf, Carrot-Nut, **'83** 117
Madeira, Carrots, **'80** 125; **'83** 281
Marinated Beets, Green Beans, and Carrots,
  '88 162
Marinated Carrots, **'86** 108, 111; **'91** 103
Marinated Carrots, Creamy, **'87** 200
Marinated Carrots, Crispy, **'81** 7
Marinated Carrot Strips, **'88** 176
Marmalade, Carrot-Citrus, **'81** 148
Marsala, Carrots, **'83** 56
Medley, Carrot-and-Leek, **'88** 102
Medley, Carrot-Lima-Squash, **'80** 123
Minted Carrots, **'81** 101
Minted Carrots, Saucy, **'82** 252
Muffins, Apple-Carrot, **'91** 213
Muffins, Carrot-and-Raisin, **'87** 24
Muffins, Carrot-Date-Nut, **'86** 262
Muffins, Carrot-Pineapple, **'81** 6
Muffins, Carrot-Wheat, **'88** 9
Muffins, Morning Glory, **'93** 327
Orange Carrots and Turnips, Sunset, **'94** 213
Orange-Fennel Carrots, **'92** 133
Orange-Raisin Carrots, **'80** 24
Orange Sauce, Carrots in, **'82** 107
Orange-Spiced Carrots, **'88** 18
Orangy Carrot Strips, **'89** 312
Parsleyed Turnips and Carrots, **'79** 253
Patties, Carrot, **'80** 89
Pecans, Carrots and Celery with, **'84** 254
Pickled Carrots, **'93** 12
Pie, Carrot, **'83** 117
Pie, Carrot Custard, **'79** 45
Pie, Carrot Ice Cream, **'86** 200
Pie, Cauliflower-Carrot, **'82** 191
Pineapple Carrots, **'83** 198
Polynesian, Carrots, **'79** 45
Pudding, Carrot-Potato, **'94** 279
Puff, Carrot, **'84** 328; **'89** 89
Puffs, Carrot, **'87** 200
Puree, Carrot-and-Sweet Potato, **'94** 56
Puree, Carrot-Sweet Potato, **'92** 90
Ring, Festive Carrot, **'82** 16
Ring, Rice-Carrot, **'79** 246
Roasted Carrots, **'92** 340
Roasted Potatoes, Carrots, and Leeks,
  '94 276
Rosemary Carrots, **'91** 219
Salad, Apple-Carrot, **'85** 22
Salad, Carrot, **'82** 137
Salad, Carrot-Ambrosia, **'81** 252
Salad, Carrot-and-Zucchini, **'83** 240
Salad, Carrot-Caraway, **'89** 105
Salad, Carrot-Pineapple, **'91** 83
Salad, Carrot-Raisin, **'83** 117; **'84** 174;
  '87 10
Salad, Carrot-Tangerine, **'83** 316; **'84** 16
Salad, Creamy Carrot-Nut, **'86** 331
Salad, Favorite Carrot, **'80** 33
Salad, Fruity Carrot-and-Seed, **'86** 223
Salad, Harvest Carrot, **'89** 128
Salad, Honey-Sweet Carrot, **'89** 161
Salad, Lime-Carrot, **'92** 65
Salad, Orange-Carrot, **'80** 89; **'84** 325
Salad, Shredded Carrot, **'80** 178
Salad, Simple Carrot, **'82** 101; **'84** 152

Salad, Sunshine Carrot, **'82** 132
Salad, Turkey-Carrot, **'86** 283
Salad, Turnip-and-Carrot, **'91** 212
Saucy Carrots, **'87** 41
Sauté, Carrot-Turnip, **'93** 241
Sautéed Zucchini and Carrots, **'92** 62, 99
Savory Sauce, Lima Beans and Carrots with,
  '84 196
Scalloped Carrots, **'81** 6
Scalloped Carrots-and-Celery, **'84** M112
Slaw, Apple-Carrot, **'92** 243
Soufflé, Carrot, **'79** 73
Soufflé, Carrots, **'83** 265
Soup, Carrot, **'80** 88; **'89** 146
Soup, Carrot Cream, **'90** 210
Soup, Carrot-Leek, **'86** 34
Soup, Carrot-Orange, **'79** 172
Soup, Cheesy Carrot, **'81** 262
Soup, Chilled Carrot-Mint, **'90** M168
Soup, Cream of Carrot, **'81** 307; **'88** 46;
  '91 69
Soup, Cream of Carrot-and-Tomato, **'94** 176
Soup, Creamy Carrot, **'92** 218
Soup, Curried Carrot, **'82** 157
Soup, Potato-Carrot, **'88** 297
Soup, Savory Carrot, **'84** 107
Special Carrots, **'81** 108; **'84** 6
Spiced Carrots Polynesian, **'88** 85
Spread, Nutty Carrot, **'94** 123
Squares, Carrot, **'79** 256
Squares, Golden Carrot-Lemon, **'80** 40
Steamed Carrots, Lemon-Dill, **'93** 180
Sticks, Carrot, **'89** 106
Stuffed Carrots, **'86** 324; **'87** 40
Sugar Snaps and Carrots, Creamed, **'93** 139
Sunshine Carrots, **'82** 16; **'83** 25
Supreme, Broccoli-Carrot, **'89** 331
Sweet-and-Sour Carrots, **'82** 137
Sweet-and-Sour Green Beans and Carrots,
  '83 6
Tarragon Carrots, **'83** 173
Tipsy Carrots, **'87** 40
Toss, Asparagus-Carrot-Squash, **'91** 45
Toss, Carrot-Fruit, **'82** 235
Tropical Carrots, **'84** 34
Veal and Carrots, Company, **'85** 22
Veal and Carrots in Wine Sauce, **'81** 31;
  '86 M139
Wine, Carrots in White, **'81** 109
Wine Sauce, Carrots in, **'80** 88
Zesty Carrots, **'84** 5
Zucchini and Carrots, Buttered, **'83** 252
Zucchini, Carrots and, **'84** 262

Casseroles

Apple-Cheese Casserole, **'84** 287
Apple-Egg Casserole, **'85** 44
Barley, Baked, **'91** 133
Barley Casserole, **'84** 281
Bean
  Baked Bean Medley, **'80** 100
  Baked Beans, Hawaiian-Style, **'86** 210
  Baked Beans, Maple Heights, **'91** 223
  Baked Beans Quintet, **'94** 100
  Baked Beans, Three-Meat, **'86** 210
  Baked Beans with Ham, **'80** 136
  Beef-and-Bean Bake, Cheesy, **'82** 89
  Chuck Wagon Bean Casserole, **'93** 198
  Cornbread Casserole, Bean-and-,
    '92 243
  Green Bean and Artichoke Casserole,
    Italian, **'85** 81

  Green Bean-and-Corn Casserole,
    '88 123
  Green Bean Casserole, **'79** 106;
    '84 145
  Green Bean Casserole, Easy, **'87** 284
  Green Bean Italiano, **'94** 248
  Green Bean Salad, Hot, **'86** 298
  Green Beans au Gratin, **'80** 116
  Green Beans, French Quarter, **'80** 298;
    '81 26
  Green Beans in Sour Cream, **'80** 116
  Green Beans, Italian, **'85** 147
  Green Beans Italian, **'87** 10
  Green Bean Surprise, **'86** 9
  Green Beans with Sour Cream, **'82** 90
  Kidney Bean Casserole, **'90** 136
  Lentils with Cheese, Baked, **'84** 113
  Lima-Bacon Bake, **'86** 9
  Lima Bean Casserole, **'79** 189; **'83** 313;
    '86 225; **'87** 284
  Lima Bean Casserole, Spicy, **'79** 189
  Lima Bean Casserole, Swiss, **'80** 191
  Lima Bean Garden Casserole, **'83** 218;
    '84 246
  Lima Beans Deluxe, **'79** 289; **'80** 26
  Lima Beans, Savory, **'83** 219; **'84** 246
  Lima Beans, Super, **'79** 189
  Lima Beans with Canadian Bacon,
    '83 219; **'84** 245
  Lima Casserole, Ham and, **'79** 192
  Limas, Spanish Cheese, **'86** 225
  Mexican Bean Casserole, Spicy, **'84** 114
  Three-Bean Bake, **'81** 155
  Three-Bean Casserole, **'88** 56
  White Bean Bake, Turnip Greens and,
    '94 246
Breakfast Casserole, **'91** 285
Broccoli-Ham au Gratin, **'90** 239
Brunch Casserole, Easy Cheesy, **'92** 91
Cannelloni, **'92** 17
Cavatini, **'94** 214
Cheese Bake, Continental, **'81** 89
Cheese Blintz Casserole, **'92** 251
Cheese Casserole, Feather-Light, **'79** 84
Cheese Casserole, Four, **'92** 170
Cheesy Breakfast Casserole, **'85** 247
Chile-Cheese Casserole, **'82** 90
Chile-Hominy Casserole, **'81** 29
Chile 'n' Cheese Breakfast Casserole, **'88** 57
Chiles Rellenos Casserole, **'79** 84; **'92** 18
Chili Casserole, **'90** 176
Chili-Rice Casserole, **'79** 54
Chili-Tamale Pie, **'83** 68
Cornmeal Puff, **'82** 42
Cranberry-Apple Casserole, **'83** 311
Egg-and-Cheese Casserole, **'84** 293
Egg-and-Cheese Puff, **'85** 45
Egg and Rice Bake, **'83** 119
Egg Casserole, **'83** 311
Egg Casserole, Brunch, **'86** 329
Egg Casserole, Cheesy, **'81** 244; **'86** 15
Egg Casserole, Saucy Scrambled, **'89** 213
Egg Casserole, Scrambled, **'80** 51; **'86** 241
Egg-Mushroom Casserole, **'83** 49
Eggs Bel-Mar, **'90** 92
Eggs, Bruncheon, **'83** 83
Eggs, Chile, **'88** 80
Eggs, Creole, **'82** 42
Egg Soufflé Casserole, **'83** 55
Enchilada Casserole, **'87** 287
Enchilada Casserole, Green, **'79** 76

Casseroles (continued)

Franks, Mexican, '93 78
Fruit Bake, Hot, '81 270
Fruit Casserole, Sherried, '80 284
Fruit, Gingered Baked, '81 232
Grits, Baked Cheese-and-Garlic, '83 292
Grits Casserole, Cheesy, '81 270
Grits Casserole, Garlic, '81 47
Grits, Garlic-Cheese, '86 180
Grits, Garlicky Ham-and-Spinach, '94 177
Grits Italiano, '92 43
Grits, Orange, '81 47
Grits, Swiss-and-Cheddar Baked, '91 71
Hominy Casserole, Cheesy, '83 170
Hominy-Chili Casserole, '86 255
Hominy, Gold Coast, '83 52
Hominy, Hot Cheese, '84 77
Hominy, Jalapeño, '82 51
Hominy with Chiles and Cheese, '86 78
Huevos Rancheros, '82 197
Italian Casserole, '90 238
Kale, Scalloped, '86 224
Lentils-and-Rice Casserole, '93 301
Macaroni and Blue Cheese, '93 248
Macaroni and Cheese, Creamy, '93 249
Macaroni and Cheese, Old-Fashioned,
    '92 215
Macaroni and Cheese, Thick-and-Rich,
    '84 329
Macaroni Bake, Jack-in-the-, '93 249
Macaroni Casserole, '84 220; '87 154
Macaroni, Glorious, '84 76
Macaroni-Mushroom Bake, Cheesy,
    '81 243
Meat. *See also* Casseroles/Pork.
    Beef-and-Bean Bake, Cheesy, '82 89
    Beef-and-Biscuit Casserole, '83 75
    Beef-and-Noodles Casserole, '84 72
    Beef-and-Vegetable Chow Mein
        Casserole, '83 313
    Beef Bake, Zesty Cabbage, '80 300
    Beef Bake, Zucchini, '86 146
    Beef Casserole, Crusty, '82 88
    Beef Casserole, Spinach and, '79 192
    Beef-Macaroni Bake, '94 255
    Beef-Macaroni Combo, '79 194
    Beef-Noodle Bake, Taco, '81 141
    Beef Supreme, '83 196
    Beefy Vegetable Casserole, '79 248
    Cheesy Mexican Casserole, '82 224
    Chiles Rellenos Casserole, '79 84;
        '84 31, 234; '92 18
    Chili Hominy Bake, '81 282; '82 58
    Cornbread Casserole, '81 91
    Cornbread Skillet Casserole, '83 243;
        '84 101
    Cornbread Tamale Bake, '79 163
    Corned Beef and Cabbage au Gratin,
        '83 16
    Corned Beef Brunch Bake, '82 44
    County Fair Casserole, '79 130
    El Dorado Casserole, '81 140
    Enchilada Casserole, Firecracker,
        '80 260
    Enchilada Casserole, Sour Cream,
        '82 113
    Five-Layer Meal, '81 140
    Frankaroni Potluck Dish, '88 201
    Franks 'n' Beans, Stove-Top, '88 201

Ground Beef and Sausage Casserole,
    '80 260
Ground Beef Casserole, Cheesy, '79 44
Ground Beef Casserole, Creamy,
    '81 142
Hamburger-Noodle Bake, '81 140
Hamburger Pie, '81 92
Hot Doggie Casserole, '88 200
Italian Casserole, '80 81
Layered Grecian Bake, '82 119
Matador Mania, '86 19
Moussaka, '87 166; '90 68
Moussaka Casserole, '79 179
Moussaka, Corn, '87 190
Pastichio, '85 194
Pastitsio, '87 12; '88 11
Pizza Casserole, '88 273; '89 181
Pizza Casserole, Quick, '83 266
Sour Cream-Noodle Bake, '79 55
Spaghetti and Beef Casserole, '79 129
Spaghetti Casserole, '84 241
Spinach and Beef Casserole, '79 192
Spinach-Beef-Macaroni Casserole,
    '83 313
Taco Beef-Noodle Bake, '81 141
Taco Casserole, '80 33
Taco Squares, Deep-Dish, '91 88
Tortilla Bake, Texas, '94 285
Veal and Wild Rice Casserole, '79 180
Veal Cutlet Casserole, '79 109
Venison-Vegetable Bake, '87 304
Ziti, Baked, '94 65
Microwave
    Asparagus-Pea Casserole, '88 M294
    Bacon-and-Eggs Scramble, '80 M267
    Beans-and-Franks, Polynesian, '84 M11
    Beans, Herbed Green, '83 M147
    Beef Casserole, Easy, '86 M58
    Beef Casserole, Layered, '82 M203
    Beefy Sausage Dinner, '80 M9
    Broccoli Casserole, '88 M146
    Broccoli-Swiss Cheese Casserole,
        '85 M211
    Carrots-and-Celery, Scalloped,
        '84 M112
    Chicken Divan, '80 M10
    Chicken Divan Casserole, '82 M203
    Chicken Mexicana, '91 M127
    Chicken Tetrazzini, Cheesy, '83 M87
    Ham-and-Potato Casserole, '83 M87
    Ham-Asparagus Dinner, '80 M10
    Ham Roll Casserole, '91 M127
    Macaroni-Ham Casserole, '81 M177
    Mexican Casserole, '92 M22
    Mexican Casserole, Microwave,
        '90 M231
    Mexi Casserole, '83 M87
    Okra and Tomatoes, Fresh, '81 M165
    Onion-Potato Bake, '83 M195
    Pineapple, Scalloped, '84 M323
    Pizza Casserole, Microwave, '89 M248
    Pork Casserole, Cheesy, '81 M74
    Potato Casserole, Creamy, '84 M113
    Potatoes, Parmesan, '90 M62
    Sausage and Rice Casserole, Oriental,
        '82 M123
    Sausage Casserole, Easy, '87 M189
    Sausage-Egg Casserole, '86 M12
    Sausage Jambalaya Casserole, '82 M203
    Spinach Delight, '84 M144
    Squash Bake, Cheddar-, '84 M113

Squash Casserole, Cheesy, '82 M21
Squash Casserole, Jiffy, '81 M144
Squash Medley, Fresh, '81 M165
Tuna Casserole, Easy, '82 M203
Turkey Casserole, Crunchy, '89 M282
Zucchini-Egg Casserole, '84 M113
Zucchini, Italian, '83 M147
Pineapple Bake, '79 251
Pineapple, Baked, '84 287
Pineapple, Scalloped, '79 106
Pork
    Bacon and Egg Casserole, '81 225
    Bacon Casserole, Egg-and-, '85 248
    Brunch Casserole, '82 124
    Brunch for a Bunch, '88 57
    Casserole, Pork, '83 116
    Chop Casserole, Peppered Pork,
        '81 235; '82 25; '83 39
    Chop Casserole, Pork, '94 255
    Chops and Potato Scallop, Pork, '82 114
    Chops Italiano, Pork, '80 72
    Chop-Vegetable Casserole, Pork,
        '90 208
    Fiesta Pork Bake, '79 265
    Frankfurter Casserole, Layered, '79 64
    Franks, Family-Style, '79 54
    Ham and Broccoli Casserole, '81 133
    Ham and Broccoli Strata, '80 261
    Ham-and-Cheese Casserole, '87 78
    Ham and Egg Casserole, Breakfast,
        '79 253
    Ham and Lima Casserole, '79 192
    Ham and Noodle Casserole, '80 300
    Ham-and-Potato Casserole, Cheesy,
        '84 326
    Ham-and-Rice Casserole, '84 75
    Ham and Turkey Bake, Layered, '79 252
    Ham Bake, Harvest, '79 210
    Ham-Broccoli Casserole, Quick, '82 40
    Ham Casserole, Apple, '79 213
    Ham Casserole, Golden, '82 119
    Ham Casserole, Macaroni-, '83 283
    Ham Casserole, Vegetable-and-, '84 91
    Ham Medley, Creamy, '84 90
    Ham Pie, Golden, '87 78
    Ham-Rice-Tomato Bake, '87 78
    Ham Strata, Baked, '83 283
    Ham Tetrazzini, '84 241
    Salami-Corn Casserole, '80 209
    Sausage and Broccoli Casserole, '80 33
    Sausage-and-Egg Casserole, '94 284
    Sausage and Noodle Casserole, '82 123
    Sausage-and-Rice Bake, Creole, '88 58
    Sausage and Wild Rice Casserole,
        '83 196
    Sausage Bake, Eggplant, '85 221
    Sausage Bake, Hominy-, '88 51
    Sausage-Bean Supper, '86 52
    Sausage Breakfast Casserole, '81 270
    Sausage Brunch, Italian, '88 57
    Sausage Casserole, '81 112; '82 12
    Sausage Casserole, Cheesy, '82 124
    Sausage Casserole, Country, '79 192
    Sausage Casserole, Crunchy, '81 288
    Sausage Casserole, Eggplant-, '84 215
    Sausage Casserole, Grits-, '84 75;
        '86 241
    Sausage Casserole, Ground Beef and,
        '80 260
    Sausage Casserole, Hawaiian, '85 42
    Sausage Casserole, Swiss, '80 209

Casseroles, Pork *(continued)*

Sausage-Cheese Bake, '88 58
Sausage-Chile Rellenos Casserole,
  '88 52
Sausage, Country Grits and, '83 54
Sausage Egg Bake, '81 225
Sausage-Egg Bake, Smoked, '85 248
Sausage Grits, '86 92
Sausage-Lasagna Rollups, '80 236
Sausage-Mushroom Breakfast
  Casserole, '86 95
Sausage-Noodle Bake, '81 92
Sausage-Potato Casserole, '86 217
Sausage-Rice Casserole, '82 50; '83 75
Sausages, Baked Zucchini and, '80 300
Sausage Strata, '83 243
Sausage, Wild Rice and, '86 268
Sausage-Wild Rice Casserole, '84 250
Spaghetti Bake, Pork, '81 11
Supper Supreme, Sunday, '79 76
Vegetable-Pork Combo, '85 113
Poultry
Chicken-Almond Casserole, '94 199
Chicken-and-Chiles Casserole, '93 107
Chicken-and-Dressing Casserole,
  '81 263
Chicken and Green Noodle Casserole,
  '80 32
Chicken and Rice Casserole, '80 260
Chicken-and-Shrimp Florentine, '89 64
Chicken-and-Spinach Enchiladas,
  '91 222
Chicken-Asparagus Casserole, '83 76;
  '84 71
Chicken Bake, Company, '80 301
Chicken Bake, Spicy, '85 251
Chicken Bake with Sweet Bacon
  Dressing, Vegetable-, '93 108
Chicken-Broccoli Casserole, '79 48;
  '91 315
Chicken-Brown Rice Bake, '91 314
Chicken Casserole, Broccoli-, '82 33
Chicken Casserole, Cheesy, '85 34
Chicken Casserole, Macaroni and,
  '80 260
Chicken Casserole, Make-Ahead,
  '84 241
Chicken Casserole, Mexi-, '93 69;
  '94 30
Chicken Casserole, Mexican, '82 143
Chicken Casserole, Pesto-, '94 231
Chicken Casserole, Quick, '81 91
Chicken Casserole, Rice-and-, '87 154
Chicken Casserole, Sunday, '83 290
Chicken Casserole, Swiss, '90 67
Chicken Chili Bake, '93 302
Chicken Chimichangas, '93 68
Chicken Dinner, Hot-and-Spicy,
  '94 M94
Chicken Divan, Easy, '94 310
Chicken Divan, Gourmet, '82 83
Chicken Divan, Overnight, '83 198
Chicken-Eggplant Parmigiana, '82 212
Chicken Enchiladas, '80 301
Chicken Enchiladas, Easy, '82 89
Chicken Florentine, '93 107
Chicken, Fontina-Baked, '90 64
Chicken, French Herbed, '86 89
Chicken, Garlic-Spinach, '92 56

Chicken-Green Bean Casserole, '85 296
Chicken-Macaroni Casserole, '85 219
Chicken-Noodle Casserole, '94 286
Chicken-Rice Casserole, '86 52
Chicken Salad, Baked, '86 297
Chicken, Scarborough, '80 38
Chicken Skillet Casserole, Spaghetti
  Squash and, '94 134
Chicken-Spaghetti Casserole, '84 15
Chicken, Spicy Mexican, '82 89
Chicken Superb Casserole, '89 83
Chicken Supreme Casserole, '84 219
Chicken Supreme, Hot, '81 76
Chicken Tetrazzini, '79 268
Chicken Thighs, Swiss, '94 282
Chicken Tortilla Bake, '82 89
Chicken Tortilla Casserole, '81 166
Chicken-Wild Rice Casserole, '84 241;
  '85 65
Cornish Hens-and-Rice Casserole,
  '92 267
Crêpes Divan, Elegant, '81 91
Duck and Wild Rice Casserole, '79 224
Pollo, Chilaquiles con, '81 66
Rice Casserole, Mexican, '83 31
Turkey-and-Broccoli Casserole,
  '86 332
Turkey-and-Shrimp Florentine
  Casserole, '92 122
Turkey-Asparagus Casserole, '86 284
Turkey Bake, Layered Ham and,
  '79 252
Turkey Casserole, '84 327
Turkey Casserole, Golden, '80 271
Turkey Casserole, Stuffed, '88 246
Turkey Florentine, '88 264
Turkey Noodle Bake, '93 243
Turkey-Noodle-Poppyseed Casserole,
  '90 239
Turkey-Olive Casserole, '87 268
Turkey Parmigiana, '87 193
Turkey Salad Bake, '79 253
Turkey Salad, Hot, '86 297
Turkey-Spinach Casserole, '84 71
Turkey-Swiss Casserole, '86 283
Turkey Tetrazzini, Herbed, '86 47
Provolone Casserole, Seashell-, '80 189
Ravioli, Mediterranean, '93 301
Reuben Casserole, '90 240
Rice-and-Cheese con Chiles, '89 99
Rice and Green Chiles, '83 152
Rice au Gratin Supreme, '86 78
Rice, Baked, '94 270
Rice Bake, Green, '79 43
Rice Casserole, '87 45
Rice Casserole, Brown, '87 118
Rice Casserole, Chili-, '79 54
Rice Casserole, Colorful, '82 199
Rice Casserole, Jalapeño, '81 66
Rice Casserole, Spanish, '79 192
Rice Casserole, Wild, '82 199
Rice Chantilly, '86 82
Rice, Easy Mushroom, '89 286
Rice, Fiesta, '84 76
Rice, Hot Pepper, '92 310
Rice Mélange, '87 240
Rice, Mexican, '85 147
Rice Pilaf, '86 82
Rice, Spanish, '81 51; '90 183
Rice, Spicy, '85 256
Rotini Romano, '87 193

Seafood
Crab-and-Mushroom Casserole, '89 96
Crab-and-Shrimp Casserole, '84 71
Crab and Spinach Casserole, Creamy,
  '80 3
Crab Bake, Quick, '87 192
Crab Casserole, '79 228
Crab Casserole, Deviled, '91 238;
  '92 27
Crab Casserole, Easy, '93 270
Crab, Dressed, '82 276
Crab-Egg Casserole, '80 260
Crab Imperial, '79 82, 116
Crab Imperial, Elegant, '83 245
Crabmeat-Broccoli Casserole, '84 232
Crabmeat Imperial, '82 311
Crabmeat with Artichoke Hearts,
  Creamed, '93 26
Crab Puff, '79 116
Crab, Shrimp, and Artichoke au Gratin,
  '90 240
Crawfish Lasagna, '91 89
Fish and Potato Bake, Herbed, '79 287;
  '80 34
Fish Casserole, Green Chile-and-,
  '84 32
Miss Hannah's Casserole, '92 236
Oyster-and-Corn Bake, '83 34; '84 44
Oyster-and-Spinach Casserole, '83 34;
  '84 44
Oyster-and-Wild Rice Casserole, '83 34;
  '84 44
Oyster Casserole, '79 228
Oyster Casserole, Wild Rice-, '86 256
Oysters Johnny Reb, '82 42
Oysters, Scalloped, '79 225; '84 213;
  '86 132
Salmon Casserole, '81 22
Salmon Florentine, '83 43
Scallop Casserole, '79 228
Seafood Casserole, '87 109; '89 63
Shrimp-and-Chicken Casserole, '91 102
Shrimp-and-Noodle Casserole, '90 240
Shrimp and Rice Casserole, '79 228
Shrimp-and-Rice Casserole, '94 328
Shrimp au Gratin, '85 79
Shrimp Casserole, '85 240
Shrimp Casserole, Chayotes and,
  '80 230
Shrimp-Crab Puff, '79 57
Shrimp Delight, '79 192
Shrimp Florentine Casserole,
  Turkey-and-, '92 122
Tuna and Peas in Wine Sauce, Baked,
  '83 196
Tuna-Broccoli Casserole, Tangy, '83 75
Tuna Casserole, '82 119
Tuna Casserole, Biscuit-Topped,
  '79 113
Tuna Casserole, Nippy, '84 241
Tuna Casserole with Cheese Swirls,
  '88 256
Tuna-Macaroni Treat, '82 131
Tuna Vegetable Casserole, '81 135
Shells, Southwestern Stuffed, '93 234
Tamale Casserole, Quick, '94 255
Tuna Chopsticks, '94 255
Vegetable. *See also* Casseroles/Bean.
Artichoke Casserole, Alii, '93 294
Asparagus-and-English Pea Casserole,
  '86 324

Casseroles, Vegetable *(continued)*

Asparagus and Peas Casserole, **'80** 152
Asparagus-Artichoke Casserole, **'86** 279
Asparagus Casserole, Cheesy, **'82** 281; **'83** 32
Asparagus Casserole, Creamy, **'80** 76
Asparagus Casserole, Easy, **'83** 255
Asparagus Delight, **'82** 269
Asparagus, Holiday, **'85** 260
Asparagus-Pea Casserole, **'88** M294
Asparagus-Pimiento Loaf, **'84** 86
Asparagus-Spaghetti Casserole, **'80** 77
Asparagus Supreme, **'89** 245
Broccoli-and-Egg Casserole, **'86** 324
Broccoli-and-Eggs au Gratin, **'85** 289
Broccoli Bake, **'81** 246; **'89** 279
Broccoli Bake, Cheesy, **'83** 255
Broccoli Bake, Cheesy Italian, **'83** 5
Broccoli Bake, Company, **'83** 279
Broccoli-Blue Cheese Casserole, **'85** 260
Broccoli Casserole, **'87** 284; **'88** M146, 265
Broccoli Casserole, Almond-, **'88** 62
Broccoli Casserole, Cheesy, **'84** 293; **'92** 342
Broccoli Casserole, Italian, **'82** 6, 280; **'83** 32
Broccoli Casserole, Winter, **'94** 280
Broccoli-Cheese Casserole, **'82** 269; **'84** 9; **'94** 132
Broccoli-Corn Casserole, **'83** 313
Broccoli Elegant, **'81** 267
Broccoli, English Walnut, **'89** 68
Broccoli-Onion Deluxe, **'81** 75
Broccoli Puff, **'82** 95
Broccoli-Rice Casserole, **'81** 101
Broccoli Supreme, **'82** 34; **'85** 68
Broccoli-Swiss Cheese Casserole, **'83** 322; **'85** M211
Broccoli with Lemon Cream, **'89** 245
Broccoli with Rice, Holiday, **'87** 252
Brussels Sprouts-and-Artichoke Casserole, **'94** 279
Brussels Sprouts, Casserole of, **'86** 294
Butternut Casserole, **'83** 280
Butternut Casserole, Sweet, **'83** 256
Cabbage au Gratin, **'83** 279
Cabbage, Caraway, **'85** 32, 289
Cabbage Casserole, Cheesy, **'79** 4
Cabbage Casserole, Creamy, **'80** 63
Cabbage Casserole, Italian, **'87** 42
Cabbage Casserole, Savory, **'82** 168
Cabbage, Cheese Scalloped, **'81** 87; **'82** 7
Cabbage, Scalloped, **'82** 269
Cabbage Wedges, Smothered, **'81** 87; **'82** 7
Cabbage with Apples and Franks, **'87** 42
Calabaza Mexicano (Mexican Squash), **'81** 196
Carrot and Zucchini Casserole, **'83** 256
Carrot Bake, Creamy, **'85** 67
Carrot Casserole, **'86** 279; **'87** 285
Carrot Casserole, Scrumptious, **'84** 328
Carrot-Pecan Casserole, **'93** 44
Carrot Puff, **'84** 328
Carrots, Scalloped, **'81** 6

Carrots, Zesty, **'84** 5
Cauliflower and Asparagus Supreme, **'79** 287; **'80** 35
Cauliflower-and-Carrot Casserole, **'83** 280
Cauliflower and Peas with Curried Almonds, **'80** 82
Cauliflower Casserole, **'86** 10, 279
Cauliflower Casserole, Easy, **'82** 204
Cauliflower Casserole, Festive, **'87** 232
Cauliflower Casserole, Herbed, **'79** 221
Cauliflower, Curried, **'91** 315
Cauliflower Italiano, Cheesy, **'82** 300
Cauliflower, Main-Dish, **'79** 221; **'80** 83
Cauliflower Medley, **'80** 220
Cauliflower 'n' Chiles Casserole, **'87** 285
Cauliflower-Pea Casserole, **'85** 260
Cauliflower Scallop, **'88** 270
Cauliflower, Spanish-Style, **'79** 21
Celery and Cheese Casserole, **'79** 178
Celery au Gratin, **'83** 38
Celery, Baked, **'82** 98
Celery Casserole, **'80** 246
Celery Casserole, Creamy, **'82** 98; **'83** 255
Celery, Creamed, **'79** 247
Celery, Exotic, **'83** 280
Celery Oriental, **'83** 206; **'85** 116
Celery, Saucy, **'83** 39
Chayote-Cheese Bake, **'80** 230
Cheesy Vegetable Casserole, **'81** 103
Chilaquiles, **'82** 220
Corn-and-Bean Casserole, **'90** 208
Corn and Cheese Casserole, **'81** 128
Corn-and-Green Chile Casserole, **'89** 68
Corn and Tomato Casserole, **'81** 127
Corn-and-Tomato Casserole, **'84** 145
Corn, Baked Scalloped, **'85** 290
Corn Casserole, **'79** 247; **'89** 126; **'93** 141
Corn Casserole, Chili-, **'88** 266
Corn Casserole, Fresh, **'80** 165
Corn Casserole, Jalapeño-, **'83** 256
Corn, Creamy Baked, **'90** 60
Corn, Elegant Scalloped, **'86** 268
Corn Pudding, **'86** 192
Corn, Scalloped, **'80** 164; **'81** 128; **'86** 111; **'88** 218
Corn with Sour Cream, Baked, **'86** 170
Corn-Zucchini Bake, **'79** 178
Curry Casserole, Vegetable-, **'91** 286; **'92** 27
Eggplant and Noodle Casserole, **'82** 230
Eggplant and Squash, **'83** 187
Eggplant-and-Tomato Casserole, **'83** 187
Eggplant and Zucchini, Italian-Style, **'79** 289; **'80** 26
Eggplant Bake, **'80** 82
Eggplant Casserole, **'81** 205; **'84** 217; **'93** 44; **'94** 214
Eggplant Casserole, Easy, **'80** 202
Eggplant Casserole, Elegant, **'82** 168
Eggplant Casserole, Flavorful, **'79** 92
Eggplant Casserole, Spicy Hot, **'93** 92
Eggplant Casserole, Super, **'80** 202
Eggplant Chiles Rellenos, **'91** 86
Eggplant Creole, **'86** 110
Eggplant, Heavenly, **'93** 293
Eggplant, Italian, **'84** 216
Eggplant Italiano, **'91** 212

Eggplant, Lebanese, **'81** 24
Eggplant, Mexican, **'83** 187
Eggplant Parmesan, **'83** 186; **'84** 215; **'92** 18
Eggplant Parmigiana, **'81** 19
Eggplant, Rolled Stuffed, **'80** 63
Eggplant, Scalloped, **'91** 223
Eggplant Supreme, **'79** 188; **'86** 170
Fresh Vegetable Casserole, **'82** 225
Garden Casserole, **'82** 168; **'88** 122
Garden Surprise, **'83** 112
Green-and-Gold Scallop, **'81** 159
Green Beans, Baked, **'91** 159
Greens Dinner Bake, Grits 'n, **'84** 281
Green Vegetable Medley, **'79** 287; **'80** 34
Hash Brown Cheese Bake, **'82** 50
Hominy, Mexican, **'91** 133, 162
Lasagna Casserole, Vegetable, **'92** 198; **'93** 25
Layered Vegetable Casserole, **'91** 286; **'92** 27
Lentils with Cheese, Baked, **'84** 113
Medley, Baked Vegetable, **'81** 75
Medley Bake, Vegetable, **'81** 268
Mixed Vegetable Casserole, **'83** 208, 256; **'86** 327
Mixed-Vegetable Casserole, **'87** 154
Mixed Vegetables, Scalloped, **'83** 5
Mushroom-Artichoke Casserole, **'87** 241
Mushroom Bake, Windsor, **'88** 132
Mushroom-Cheese Casserole, **'83** 216
Mushrooms Supreme, **'84** 214
Noodle Casserole, Vegetable, **'91** 30
Okra Casserole, **'79** 160
Okra-Tomato Bake, **'80** 298; **'81** 26
Onion Bake, Four, **'93** 304
Onion Casserole, Cheesy, **'79** 101
Onions, Baked Sweet, **'91** 79
Pea Casserole, Cheesy English, **'83** 216
Pea Casserole, Curry, **'87** 154
Pea Casserole, Quick Fresh English, **'84** 145
Pea Casserole, Reunion, **'87** 11
Pea Casserole Supreme, **'82** 281; **'83** 32
Pea-Pimiento Casserole, English, **'83** 207
Peas and Rice, **'88** 97
Peas, Cajun, **'88** 3
Peas, Chinese-Style Baked, **'86** 305
Peas, Mexi-, **'88** 3
Peas, Party, **'79** 102
Peas, Sweet-and-Sour, **'88** 3
Peas with Rice, Black-Eyed, **'83** 12
Potato Bake, **'83** 209
Potato Bake, Creamy, **'82** 201
Potato Breakfast Casserole, **'80** 52
Potato-Broccoli-Cheese Bake, **'80** 114
Potato Casserole, **'87** 190
Potato Casserole, Cheesy, **'80** 244; **'83** 53; **'92** 229
Potato Casserole, Easy, **'80** 114
Potato Casserole, Fluffy, **'80** 268
Potato Casserole, Hash Brown, **'81** 40
Potato Casserole, Holiday, **'92** 302
Potato Casserole, Irish, **'81** 263
Potato Casserole, Mashed, **'85** 296
Potato Casserole, Mushroom-, **'84** 5
Potato Casserole, Processor, **'86** 159

Casseroles, Vegetable (continued)

Potato Casserole, Saucy, '81 276
Potato-Cheese Casserole, '79 101
Potato-Egg Casserole, Cheesy, '84 5
Potato-Eggplant Casserole, '87 166
Potatoes and Eggs au Gratin, '79 107
Potatoes and Turnips, Scalloped, '85 235
Potatoes-and-Zucchini au Gratin, '84 5
Potatoes au Gratin, Shredded, '89 69
Potatoes, Cheesy New, '85 156
Potatoes, Cheesy Scalloped, '83 82
Potatoes, Christmas, '88 252
Potatoes, Cottage, '89 69
Potatoes, Double-Cheese, '86 6
Potatoes, Easy Oven-Baked, '82 202
Potatoes, Fix-Ahead Mashed, '89 70
Potatoes, Fluffy, '84 296; '85 196
Potatoes for Company, Saucy, '82 202
Potatoes, Garlic, '84 296; '85 196
Potatoes Gourmet, '80 114
Potatoes, Gruyère, '83 193
Potatoes, Hot Deviled, '84 296; '85 196
Potatoes, Italian-Style, '89 69
Potatoes, Jalapeño, '84 39
Potatoes, Jazzy Mashed, '87 192
Potatoes, Lemon and Nutmeg, '80 36
Potatoes, Light Scalloped, '89 311
Potatoes Lorraine, '87 190
Potatoes, Mexican-Style, '91 78
Potatoes, Missy, '85 259
Potatoes Moussaka, '93 44
Potatoes, Mushroom Scalloped, '87 191
Potatoes, Olive, '80 114
Potatoes, Parmesan, '82 270; '90 M62
Potatoes, Party Scalloped, '87 191
Potatoes, Scalloped, '82 300; '83 211;
    '92 48
Potatoes, Sour Cream, '84 39
Potatoes, Special Scalloped, '88 162
Potatoes, Two-Cheese, '80 114
Potatoes, Wayside Scalloped, '79 283
Potatoes with Feta Cheese, '84 295;
    '85 196
Potatoes with Ham Bits, Creamy,
    '87 191
Potatoes with Sweet Marjoram and
    Parmesan Cheese, Scalloped, '91 246
Potato-Tomato Bake, '86 17
Potato-Tomato Casserole, Saucy, '79 46
Potato Tuna Bake, Shoestring, '82 211
Pumpkin, Baked, '82 217
Spinach and Artichoke Casserole,
    '81 103
Spinach-and-Celery Casserole, '84 294
Spinach and Egg Casserole, '82 270
Spinach-Artichoke Casserole, '88 252;
    '93 44
Spinach Bake, Creamy, '89 68
Spinach Casserole, '79 265; '91 31
Spinach Casserole, Cheesy, '81 263
Spinach Casserole, Cottage
    Cheese-and-, '84 77
Spinach Casserole, Creamy, '86 111
Spinach-Cheese Bake, '88 10
Spinach-Cheese Casserole, '83 216;
    '89 64
Spinach-Cheese Puff, '84 96
Spinach, Cheesy Topped, '84 85
Spinach, Company, '89 280

Spinach, Creamy Lemon, '82 302
Spinach Fantastic, '93 173
Spinach, Gourmet Baked, '82 180
Spinach Parmesan, '93 72
Spinach-Parmesan Casserole, '82 281;
    '83 32
Spinach Rice, '85 146
Spinach Supreme, '84 77
Spinach Surprise, '82 42
Spinach with Cheese, Scalloped, '79 8
Squash and Apple Casserole, '79 209
Squash and Egg Casserole, '80 146
Squash, Bacon-Flavored, '82 158
Squash Bake, '82 107
Squash Bake, Cheddar-, '84 128
Squash Bake, Cheesy, '80 183
Squash-Carrot Casserole, '81 157
Squash Casserole, '87 163; '89 159;
    '90 161; '92 342
Squash Casserole, Baked, '83 149
Squash Casserole, Blender, '81 212
Squash Casserole, Butternut, '79 210
Squash Casserole, Calico, '90 290
Squash Casserole, Cheesy, '79 123
Squash Casserole, Company, '81 183
Squash Casserole, Crunchy, '84 293
Squash Casserole, Fresh, '82 204
Squash Casserole, Jiffy, '81 M144
Squash Casserole, Summer,
    '81 102, 184
Squash Casserole, Two-, '79 101
Squash Casserole, Yellow, '79 179;
    '85 135; '88 166
Squash Casserole, Zippy, '80 183
Squash, Country Club, '88 M16
Squash, Greek-Style, '91 285; '92 26
Squash, Mexican, '83 31
Squash Nicholas, '94 236
Squash, Posh, '81 159
Squash Puff, Butternut, '85 205
Squash, South-of-the-Border, '89 148
Squash, Tart Hubbard, '80 214
Sweet Potato-and-Apple Casserole,
    '94 280
Sweet Potato-Apple Bake, '83 25
Sweet Potato-Apricot Bake, '85 206
Sweet Potato Bake, '80 287
Sweet Potato Bake, Holiday, '90 291
Sweet Potato-Banana Casserole,
    '86 276
Sweet Potato Casserole, '79 289; '80 26;
    '85 256; '89 279
Sweet Potato Casserole, Glazed,
    '90 250
Sweet Potato Casserole, Pear-,
    '86 280
Sweet Potato Delight, '86 335
Sweet Potatoes-and-Apple Casserole,
    '90 228
Sweet Potatoes-and-Berries Casserole,
    '84 231
Sweet Potatoes, Bourbon, '86 324;
    '87 280
Sweet Potatoes, Candied, '86 111;
    '88 207
Sweet Potatoes Royale, '91 250
Sweet Potatoes with Sherry and Walnuts,
    '86 286
Sweet Potato-Rum Casserole, '84 231
Sweet Potato Supreme, '94 196
Sweet Potato Surprise, '81 267

Tomato-and-Artichoke Heart Bake,
    '85 81
Tomato Casserole, Scalloped, '88 144
Tomatoes, Herbed, '81 102
Tomatoes, Italian-Sauced Green,
    '85 214
Tomatoes, Scalloped, '84 142
Torta, Mexican, '88 149
Turnip Casserole, '83 242; '84 229
Turnip Casserole, Baked, '82 274
Turnips au Gratin, '84 229
Turnips, Scalloped, '79 254
Veggies Casserole, '88 123
Vidalia Deep Dish, '89 120
Yam-and-Apple Scallop, '91 199
Yams, Brandied, '94 273
Zucchini and Tomato Bake, '82 158
Zucchini-and-Tomato Casserole, '88 265
Zucchini, Baked, '83 209
Zucchini Casserole, '79 157; '87 154
Zucchini Casserole, Cheese-Egg-,
    '84 114
Zucchini Casserole, Cheesy, '82 168;
    '84 145
Zucchini Casserole, Italian, '85 59
Zucchini-Jack Casserole, '85 296
Zucchini-Rice Casserole Italiano,
    '89 146

Cauliflower
Almond Sauce, Cauliflower with, '82 270
au Gratin, Cauliflower, '82 204
Baked Swiss Cauliflower, '79 100
Beef and Cauliflower Oriental, '80 220
Beef and Cauliflower over Rice, '93 94
Beets and Cauliflower, Chilled, '80 137
Broccoli Crunch, Cauliflower-, '88 216
Casserole, Cauliflower, '86 10, 279
Casserole, Cauliflower-and-Carrot, '83 280
Casserole, Cauliflower 'n' Chiles, '87 285
Casserole, Cauliflower-Pea, '85 260
Casserole, Easy Cauliflower, '82 204
Casserole, Festive Cauliflower, '87 232
Casserole, Herbed Cauliflower, '79 221
Cheese-Frosted Cauliflower, '85 68
Cheese Sauce, Cauliflower with, '81 101
Cheesy Cauliflower Italiano, '82 300
Curried Cauliflower, '91 315
Dilled Cauliflower, '83 93
Festive Cauliflower, '84 34
Fried Cauliflower, '83 5; '84 248; '90 18
Fried Cauliflower au Gratin, French-,
    '79 221; '80 82
Fried Cauliflower, Crispy, '80 220
Fried Cauliflower, French-, '86 211
Fried Cauliflower, Golden, '82 78
Fried Cauliflower with Cheese Sauce, '87 231
Garden Surprise, '83 112
Goldenrod, Cauliflower, '79 21
Gratin, Cauliflower with Chinese Mustard,
    '94 45
Herb Butter, Cauliflower with, '81 2
Italian-Style Cauliflower, '92 36
Lemon Cauliflower, Easy, '83 322
Main-Dish Cauliflower, '79 221; '80 83
Medley, Cauliflower, '80 220
Medley, Cauliflower-Broccoli, '81 69
Medley, Cauliflower-Snow Pea, '87 305
Oriental Cauliflower, '81 75
Peas and Cauliflower, '82 288
Peas with Curried Almonds, Cauliflower and,
    '79 221; '80 82

Cauliflower *(continued)*

Pickled Cauliflower, **'94** 183
Pie, Cauliflower-Carrot, **'82** 191
Pimiento Sauce, Cauliflower with, **'87** 232
Quiche, Cauliflower, **'83** 86
Salad, Broccoli and Cauliflower, **'81** 280
Salad, Broccoli-Cauliflower, **'92** 97
Salad, Broccoli-Cauliflower Pasta, **'88** 269
Salad, Broccoli 'n' Cauliflower, **'90** 32
Salad, Cauliflower, **'79** 221; **'80** 83; **'81** 225;
   '84 291; **'85** 240, 279; **'92** 36
Salad, Cauliflower-Broccoli, **'79** 20
Salad, Cauliflower-Brussels Sprouts, **'83** 240
Salad, Cauliflower-Lemon, **'81** 23
Salad, Cauliflower-Pea, **'87** 231
Salad, Cauliflower-Vegetable, **'85** 158
Salad, Celery-and-Cauliflower, **'83** 39
Salad, Corned Beef-Cauliflower, **'83** 16
Salad, Creamy Broccoli and Cauliflower,
   '81 23
Salad, Creamy Cauliflower, **'82** 102
Salad, Crunchy Cauliflower, **'80** 4; **'82** 75
Salad, Crunchy Green, **'89** 321
Salad, Layered Cauliflower, **'83** 240
Salad, Marinated Cauliflower, **'82** 303;
   '84 232
Salad, Orange-Cauliflower, **'82** 266
Salad, Red, White, and Green, **'90** 18
Salad, Savory Cauliflower and Pea, **'81** 280
Salad, Sweet-and-Sour Cauliflower, **'81** 2
Sauté, Cauliflower, **'94** 67
Scallop, Cauliflower, **'88** 270
Shrimp Sauce, Broccoli and Cauliflower with,
   '84 248
Slaw, Cauliflower, **'92** 167
Soufflé, Cauliflower, **'82** 76; **'89** 279;
   '90 17
Soup, Cauliflower, **'90** 211
Soup, Cauliflower and Caraway, **'82** 264
Soup, Cream of Cauliflower, **'87** M7; **'88** 12
Soup, Cream of Cauliflower and Watercress,
   '83 126
Soup, Creamy Cauliflower, **'82** 76
Soup, Fresh Cauliflower, **'84** 279
Spanish-Style Cauliflower, **'79** 21
Supreme, Cauliflower and Asparagus,
   '79 287; **'80** 35
Toss, Cauliflower, **'85** 289
Toss, Cauliflower-Broccoli, **'82** 54
Toss, Cauliflower-Olive, **'85** 198; **'86** 147
Toss, Crunchy Broccoli and Cauliflower,
   '83 25
Toss, Italian Cauliflower-Broccoli, **'88** 269

Caviar
Artichoke Hearts with Caviar, **'79** 142
Crown, Caviar, **'83** 78
Eggplant Caviar, **'88** 262
Eggplant Caviar with Tapenade, **'92** 194
Endive with Caviar, **'93** 118
Homemade Cowboy Caviar, **'94** 64
Mold, Artichoke-Caviar, **'87** 239
Mound, Caviar-Artichoke, **'91** 244
Mousse, Caviar, **'82** 71; **'83** 258; **'85** 86;
   '92 83
Pie, Caviar, **'79** 154
Potatoes, Appetizer Caviar, **'86** 223
Potatoes, Caviar, **'84** 80
Spread, Caviar-Cream Cheese, **'84** 256
Spread, Creamy Caviar, **'92** 58

Spread, Egg, Sour Cream, and Caviar,
   '85 279
Texas Caviar, **'86** 218
Tomatoes, Caviar, **'91** 12
Zucchini Caviar, **'88** 212

Celery
Almondine, Celery, **'85** 116
Amandine, Buttered Celery, **'82** 98
Ants on a Float, **'91** 177
au Gratin, Celery, **'83** 38
Baked Celery, **'82** 98
Braised Carrots and Celery, **'86** 327
Braised Celery, Green Beans and, **'84** 254
Brussels Sprouts and Celery, **'79** 21
Brussels Sprouts with Celery, Lemony,
   '85 25
Buttered Carrots and Celery, **'89** 44
Carrots and Celery with Pecans, **'84** 254
Casserole, Celery, **'80** 246
Casserole, Celery and Cheese, **'79** 178
Casserole, Creamy Celery, **'82** 98; **'83** 255
Casserole, Spinach-and-Celery, **'84** 294
Chicken-and-Celery Skillet, **'88** 6
Creamed Brussels Sprouts and Celery,
   '83 322
Creamed Celery, **'79** 247
Croutons, Celery, **'79** 16
Curried Corn and Celery, **'86** 192
Dressing, Celery-Honey, **'80** 42
Dressing, Watermelon Salad with Celery-Nut,
   '80 182
Exotic Celery, **'83** 280
Orange Sauce, Celery in, **'79** 70
Oriental, Celery, **'83** 206; **'85** 116
Peas and Celery, **'93** 289
Peas and Celery, Deluxe, **'81** 267
Potatoes, Whipped Celery, **'94** 305
Potato Puffs, Celeried, **'89** 279
Relish, Apple-Celery, **'89** 141
Salad, Celery, **'79** 70
Salad, Celery-and-Cauliflower, **'83** 39
Salad, Chicken-Celery, **'81** 187
Salad, Overnight Alfalfa-Celery, **'82** 97
Salad, Pear-and-Celery, **'87** 56
Salad, Pineapple-Celery, **'85** 95
Sauce, Baked Fillets in Lemon-Celery, **'84** 91
Saucy Celery, **'83** 39
Scalloped Carrots-and-Celery, **'84** M112
Snow Peas with Celery, Skillet, **'84** 123
Soup, Burnet-Celery, **'84** 107
Soup, Celery-and-Potato, **'84** 279
Soup, Cream of Celery, **'79** 71; **'90** 210
Soup, Light Cream-of-Celery, **'82** 279
Soup, Tomato-Celery, **'83** M58
Splendid Stalks, **'93** 258
Stuffed Celery, **'82** 98; **'86** 324
Stuffed Celery, Creamy, **'82** 102
Stuffed Celery, Jalapeño, **'79** 70
Stuffed Celery Trunks, **'85** 115
Toss, Celery-Parmesan, **'84** 34

Chayotes
Bake, Chayote-Cheese, **'80** 230
Casserole, Chayotes and Shrimp, **'80** 230
Fried Chayotes, **'80** 230
Pickles, Chayote Squash, **'89** 197
Stuffed Chayote, **'92** 247

Cheese. *See also* Appetizers/Cheese.
Almond Cheese, **'88** 173
Almond-Raspberry Brie, **'94** M89
Apple-Cheese Bake, **'92** 225
Aspic, Cheesy Vegetable, **'81** 73
Bake, Brie Cheese, **'87** 117
Bake, Chicken, Ham, and Cheese, **'87** 217
Bake, Pineapple-Cheese, **'79** 106
Bake, Spinach-Ricotta, **'88** 97
Banana Splits, Cottage Cheese-, **'87** 56
Beef Parmigiana, **'85** 234
Beef Roulades, Roquefort, **'88** 215
Blintzes, Cheese, **'82** 146; **'83** 71; **'92** 84
BLT's, Cheesy, **'85** 92
Blue Cheese, Creamy, **'88** 173
Bobolis, Easy Cheesy, **'92** 278
Breads
   Bacon-and-Cheese Bread, **'83** 255
   Batter Bread, Cheese-Caraway, **'85** 33
   Biscuit Fingers, Pepper-Cheese,
      '88 283
   Biscuits, Bacon-Cheese, **'88** 84
   Biscuits, Beer-and-Cheese, **'94** 215
   Biscuits, Blue Cheese, **'88** 83
   Biscuits, Cheese, **'81** 288; **'83** 253;
      '85 32; **'87** 78
   Biscuits, Cheese Angel, **'89** 211
   Biscuits, Cheeseburger, **'79** 194
   Biscuits, Cheese-Chive, **'94** 324
   Biscuits, Easy Cheese, **'81** 99
   Biscuits, Herbed Roquefort, **'84** 95
   Biscuits, Hot Cheesy, **'80** 186
   Biscuits, Lightnin' Cheesy, **'90** 283
   Biscuits, Petite Ham and Cheese,
      '79 193
   Biscuits, Tiny Cheese, **'80** 192
   Blue Cheese-Apple Sunburst, **'94** 245
   Bobolis, Easy Cheesy, **'92** 278
   Brie Bread, **'87** 143
   Buns, Cheesy Onion, **'85** 5
   Buns, Hurry-Up Cheese, **'81** 300
   Buns, Onion-Cheese, **'88** 218
   Butter Cheese Dips, **'80** 46
   Buttermilk-Cheese Loaf, **'91** 52
   Cheddar Cheese Bread, **'84** 268
   Cheddar-Nut Bread, **'85** 41
   Cheese Bread, **'82** 174; **'83** 208;
      '87 11
   Cornbread, Cheddar, **'83** 285; **'84** 17
   Cornbread, Cheddar-Jalapeño, **'85** 3
   Cornbread, Cheesy Beef, **'81** 242
   Cornbread, Chile-Cheese, **'87** 171
   Cornbread, Cottage Cheese, **'80** 90
   Cornbread, Swiss Cheese, **'79** 60
   Cottage Cheese-Dill Bread, **'83** 154
   Cream Cheese Braids, **'82** 243
   Cream Cheese Bread, Orange-, **'82** 210
   Cream Cheese Loaves, Processor,
      '85 48
   Cream Cheese Pinches, **'87** 85
   Crescents, Cheese, **'82** 18
   Croissants, Cream Cheese, **'92** 159
   Crusty Cheese Bread, **'86** 233
   Delights, Toasted Cheese, **'79** 37
   Dilly Cheese Bread, **'83** 5

Cheese, Breads *(continued)*

Easy Cheese Bread, **'82** 74; **'86** 17
French Bread, Bacon-Cheese, **'92** 54
French Bread, Cheesy, **'88** 172
French Bread, Onion-Cheese, **'89** 29
Fruit-and-Cheese Braid, **'86** 214
Garlic Bread, Cheesy, **'84** 150
Gouda Bread, **'91** 52
Ham-and-Cheese Bread, **'86** 213
Herb-and-Cheese Pull Aparts, **'87** 143
Herb Bread, Cheese-, **'84** M144;
  '85 283
Herb Bread, Parmesan, **'82** 235; **'83** 41
Herb-Cheese Bread, **'85** 70
Herbs-and-Cheese Bread, **'93** 56
Herb-Vegetable-Cheese Bread, **'88** 172
Jalapeño-Cheese Loaf, **'84** 76
Jam-and-Cheese Loaf, **'89** 246
Lemon-Cream Tea Loaf, **'84** 50
Little Cheese Loaves, **'86** 213
Loaf, Cheese, **'90** 93
Monkey Bread, Cheese-Filled, **'91** 21
Muffin Mix, Cheese-and-Pepper,
  '89 330
Muffins, Bacon-and-Cheese, **'89** 205
Muffins, Blueberry-Cream Cheese,
  '86 14
Muffins, Caraway-Cheese, **'91** 213
Muffins, Cheddar, **'89** 15
Muffins, Cheddar-Raisin, **'91** 51
Muffins, Cheese-and-Pepper, **'84** 139
Muffins, Cheesy Cornbread, **'88** M275
Muffins, Cheesy Sausage, **'92** 252;
  '93 144
Muffins, Ham-and-Cheese, **'92** 252;
  '93 144
Muffins, Marvelous Cheese, **'83** 96
Muffins, Sausage-Cheese, **'86** 213
Muffins, Sesame-Cheese, **'86** 16
Olive Bread, Spicy Cheese-, **'84** 150
Onion-Cheese Bread, **'79** 180; **'81** 8
Onion-Cheese Supper Bread, **'83** 112
Onion-Parmesan Bread, **'84** 284
Parmesan Bread, **'92** 19; **'93** 231
Parmesan Sesame Sticks, **'81** 39
Parmesan Twists, **'83** 239
Pimiento-Cheese Bread, **'85** 223;
  '86 166
Pita Triangles, Cheesy, **'93** 70
Popover Puffs, Cheese, **'85** 6
Popover Ring, Cheesy, **'80** 45
Popovers, Cheddar Cheese, **'85** 41
Popovers, Parmesan, **'90** 66
Quick Cheese Bread, **'83** 9
Roll, Feta Cheese-Spinach, **'91** 22
Rolls, Broccoli-Cheddar, **'91** 21
Rolls, Cheese, **'80** 286
Rolls, Cheese-Apricot Sweet, **'90** 195
Rolls, Cottage Cheese, **'81** 78
Rolls, Ham-and-Cheese, **'82** 3
Rolls, Parmesan, **'79** 181
Rolls, Romano Sesame, **'87** 144
Sesame-Cheddar Sticks, **'81** 150
Sour Cream-Cheese Bread, **'85** 33
Spinach Bread, **'87** 144
Spoonbread, Cheddar, **'82** 196
Spoonbread, Cheese, **'86** 261
Spoonbread, Corn-Cheese, **'88** 9
Swiss Cheese Bread, **'79** 60

Swiss Cheese Bread, Poppy Seed-,
  '91 52
Toast Bars, Bacon-Cheese, **'79** 36
Toast, Cottage-Topped French, **'85** 49
Tomato-Cheese Bread, Herbed, **'88** 143
Twists, Cheesy, **'84** 284
Wine Bread, Cheese-, **'87** 254
Brownies, Cream Cheese Swirl, **'79** 51
Brownies, German Cream Cheese, **'80** 269
Brownies, Walnut-Cream Cheese, **'84** 240
Buns, Snack, **'87** 279
Burgers, Blue Cheese, **'89** M66
Burgers, Cheesy Bacon, **'81** 29
Burgers, Cheesy Beef, **'83** 217
Burritos, Breakfast, **'90** 192
Burritos, Cheesy Beef, **'85** 193
Butter, Cheese, **'84** 114
Cake, Coconut-Cream Cheese Pound,
  '85 297; **'90** 305
Cake, Cream Cheese Coffee, **'86** 290
Cake, Cream Cheese Loaf, **'84** 151
Cake, Cream Cheese Pound, **'81** 290;
  '86 287
Cake, Crusty Cream Cheese Pound, **'89** 124
Cake, Deep-Dish Cheesecake Coffee, **'90** 50
Cake, Regal Cream Cheese, **'80** 140
Cake Squares, Cream Cheese, **'84** 321
Cake, Tart Lemon-Cheese, **'88** 7
Cannoli, **'91** 20
Casseroles
  Apple-Cheese Casserole, **'84** 287
  Asparagus Casserole, Cheesy, **'82** 281;
    '83 32
  Bean Casserole, Swiss Lima, **'80** 191
  Beef-and-Bean Bake, Cheesy, **'82** 89
  Beef Casserole, Cheesy Ground, **'79** 44
  Blintz Casserole, Cheese, **'92** 251
  Breakfast Casserole, **'91** 285
  Breakfast Casserole, Cheesy, **'85** 247
  Broccoli Bake, Cheesy, **'83** 255
  Broccoli-Blue Cheese Casserole,
    '85 260
  Broccoli Casserole, Cheesy, **'84** 293;
    '92 342
  Broccoli-Cheese Casserole, **'82** 269;
    '84 9; **'94** 132
  Broccoli-Ham au Gratin, **'90** 239
  Broccoli-Swiss Cheese Casserole,
    '83 322; **'85** M211
  Brunch Casserole, **'82** 124
  Brunch Casserole, Easy Cheesy,
    '92 91
  Brunch for a Bunch, **'88** 57
  Cabbage au Gratin, **'83** 279
  Cabbage Casserole, Cheesy, **'79** 4
  Carrots, Cheese Scalloped, **'94** 36
  Celery and Cheese Casserole, **'79** 178
  Celery au Gratin, **'83** 38
  Chayote-Cheese Bake, **'80** 230
  Chicken Casserole, Cheesy, **'85** 34
  Chicken, Fontina-Baked, **'90** 64
  Chicken Tetrazzini, Cheesy, **'83** M87
  Chicken Thighs, Swiss, **'94** 282
  Chilaquiles, **'82** 220
  Chile-Cheese Casserole, **'82** 90
  Chile 'n' Cheese Breakfast Casserole,
    '88 57
  Chiles Rellenos Casserole, **'79** 84;
    '84 31, 234; **'92** 18
  Continental Cheese Bake, **'81** 89
  Corn and Cheese Casserole, **'81** 128

Corned Beef and Cabbage au Gratin,
  '83 16
Crab, Shrimp, and Artichoke au Gratin,
  '90 240
Egg-and-Cheese Casserole, **'84** 293
Egg Casserole, Cheesy, **'81** 244; **'86** 15
Eggplant Parmesan, **'83** 186; **'84** 215;
  '86 53
Eggplant Parmigiana, **'81** 19
Feather-Light Cheese Casserole, **'79** 84
Four Cheese Casserole, **'92** 170
Grits, Baked Cheese, **'80** 49, 99;
  '83 311; **'85** 41
Grits, Baked Cheese-and-Garlic,
  '83 292; **'84** 78
Grits Casserole, Cheesy, **'81** 270
Grits, Cheese, **'86** 242
Grits, Garlic-Cheese, **'80** 47; **'81** 197;
  '86 180
Grits, Swiss-and-Cheddar Baked, **'91** 71
Ham-and-Cheese Casserole, **'87** 78
Hominy Casserole, Cheesy, **'83** 170
Hominy with Chiles and Cheese, **'86** 78
Lasagna Maria, **'90** 191
Lentils with Cheese, Baked, **'84** 113
Limas, Spanish Cheese, **'86** 225
Macaroni and Blue Cheese, **'93** 248;
  '94 44
Macaroni and Cheese, Creamy, **'93** 249;
  '94 45
Macaroni and Cheese, Old-Fashioned,
  '92 215
Macaroni Bake, Jack-in-the-, **'93** 249;
  '94 45
Macaroni-Mushroom Bake, Cheesy,
  '81 243
Mexican Casserole, Cheesy, **'82** 224
Mexican Casserole, Microwave,
  '90 M231
Mushroom-Cheese Casserole, **'83** 216
Mushrooms au Gratin, **'81** 108
Onion Casserole, Cheesy, **'79** 101
Pea Casserole, Cheesy English, **'83** 216
Pineapple-Cheese Bake, **'79** 106
Pork Casserole, Cheesy, **'81** M74
Potato Casserole, Cheesy, **'80** 244;
  '83 53; **'92** 229
Potato-Cheese Casserole, **'79** 101
Potato-Cheese Dream, **'91** 307
Potato-Egg Casserole, Cheesy, **'84** 5
Potatoes and Eggs au Gratin, **'79** 107
Potatoes au Gratin, Shredded, **'89** 69
Potatoes, Cheesy Scalloped, **'83** 82
Potatoes, Cottage, **'89** 69
Potatoes, Double-Cheese, **'86** 6
Potatoes Gourmet, **'80** 114
Potatoes, Gruyère, **'83** 193
Potatoes, Mushroom Scalloped,
  '87 191
Potatoes, Scalloped, **'83** 211
Potatoes, Special Scalloped, **'88** 162
Provolone Casserole, Seashell-, **'80** 189
Reuben Casserole, **'90** 240
Rice-and-Cheese con Chiles, **'89** 99
Rice au Gratin, **'83** 129
Rice au Gratin Supreme, **'86** 78
Rice, Cheese-Parslied, **'89** 99
Rice Strata, Cheese-, **'81** 176
Sausage Brunch, Italian, **'88** 57
Sausage Casserole, Cheesy, **'82** 124
Sausage-Cheese Bake, **'88** 58

Cheese, Casseroles *(continued)*

Sausage-Chile Rellenos Casserole, **'88** 52
Spinach Casserole, Cheesy, **'81** 263
Spinach Casserole, Cottage Cheese-and-, **'84** 77
Spinach-Cheese Bake, **'88** 10
Spinach-Cheese Casserole, **'83** 216; **'89** 64
Spinach-Parmesan Casserole, **'82** 281; **'83** 32
Spinach Ring au Fromage, **'79** 8
Squash Bake, Cheddar-, **'84** M113, 128
Squash Casserole, Cheesy, **'79** 123; **'82** M21
Swiss Chicken Casserole, **'90** 67
Swiss Sausage Casserole, **'80** 209
Tuna Casserole with Cheese Swirls, **'88** 256
Turkey Parmigiana, **'87** 193
Turkey-Swiss Casserole, **'86** 283
Vegetable Casserole, Cheesy, **'81** 103
Zucchini Casserole, Cheese-Egg-, **'84** 114
Zucchini Casserole, Cheesy, **'82** 168; **'84** 145
Zucchini-Jack Casserole, **'85** 296
Catfish Parmesan, **'79** 184; **'86** 210
Catfish, Parmesan, **'92** 309
Cheesecake. *See* Cakes/Cheesecakes.
Chicken Alouette, **'91** 295
Chicken, Baked Parmesan, **'83** 320
Chicken Breasts, Cream Cheese, **'90** 234
Chicken Breasts Gruyère, **'80** 189
Chicken Breasts Romano, **'79** 218
Chicken Cordon Bleu, **'81** 304; **'82** 83; **'86** 37
Chicken, Crispy Parmesan, **'80** M76
Chicken Fiesta, Breast-of-, **'88** 151
Chicken Monterey, **'82** 275
Chicken, Oven-Fried Parmesan, **'81** 97; **'82** 148
Chicken Parmesan, **'83** 184
Chicken Parmesan, Baked, **'83** 137
Chicken Provolone, **'93** 323
Chicken Rollups, Cheesy, **'82** 44
Chicken, Roquefort, **'89** 320
Chicken Skillet, Cheesy, **'80** 115
Chiles Rellenos, **'88** 116; **'89** 226
Chiles Rellenos with Walnut Cream Sauce, Havarti-and-Corn-Stuffed, **'93** M275
Chili-Cheese Dogs, **'81** M176
Chili, Cheese-Topped, **'82** M11
Chili, Cheesy, **'82** 310
Chocolate-Cheese Cups, **'91** 142
Chunky Cream Cheese, **'85** 306
Coleslaw, Blue Cheese, **'89** 13
Coleslaw, Cottage, **'80** 64
Cookies, Cream Cheese, **'80** 282
Corn on the Cob, Parmesan, **'88** M187
Country Ham Puff, Cheesy, **'90** 88
Crab Bake, Quick, **'87** 192
Crabmeat au Gratin, **'86** 154
Crackers, Hot Nut, **'90** 206
Crackers, Taco-Cheese Animal, **'94** 197
Cream Cheese, Cranberry-Amaretto Chutney with, **'87** 244
Cream Cheese Frills, **'79** 291

Cream Puffs with Chicken Salad, Cheesy, **'86** 260
Cream-Style Cheese, **'85** 209
Crêpe Cups, Florentine, **'89** 44
Crêpes, Cheese and Mushroom, **'81** 88
Crêpes, Cheesy Sausage, **'82** 240; **'83** 71
Crêpes, Mushroom-Cheese, **'87** 289; **'88** 135
Crêpes, Spinach-Ricotta, **'81** 52
Crisp, Apple-Cheese, **'92** 235
Crispies, Pecan-Cheese, **'87** 168
Crostini, Feta-Tomato, **'92** 159
Crust, Cheese, **'80** 286; **'86** 264
Crust, Cheesy Crumb, **'88** 86
Crust, Chicken Pot Pie with Cheese, **'86** 264
Crust, Parmesan, **'94** 304
Crust, Parmesan Pizza, **'93** 58
Cupcakes, Cream Cheese Party, **'82** 279
Delight, Strawberry Cheese, **'79** 50
Dessert Cheese, Nutty Date, **'87** 299
Dessert, Creamy Cottage Cheese, **'87** 191
Dessert, Lemon-Cream Cheese, **'84** 95
Dessert, Strawberry-Cream Cheese, **'83** 123
Dressing, Blue Cheese, **'79** 69; **'82** 166; **'86** 233; **'90** 286
Dressing, Blue Cheese Salad, **'82** 94
Dressing, Cheese Fluff, **'91** 256
Dressing, Cheesy Barbecue Salad, **'92** 255
Dressing, Creamy Blue Cheese, **'81** 150; **'91** 307
Dressing, Creamy Blue Cheese Salad, **'86** 123
Dressing, Creamy Roquefort, **'84** 12
Dressing, Garden Salad with Tomato-Cream Cheese, **'79** 173
Dressing, Parmesan, **'86** 192
Dressing, Romano, **'80** 174
Dressing, Roquefort, **'79** 85; **'80** 74; **'93** 128
Dressing, Special Blue Cheese, **'80** 74
Dressing, Tangy Blue Cheese, **'87** 81
Dressing, Zesty Blue Cheese, **'79** 104
Dumplings, Chicken Ragout with Cheddar, **'94** 44
Egg Medley, Cheddary, **'81** M176
Eggs, Blue Cheese Stuffed, **'93** 87
Eggs, Cheddar, **'94** M141
Eggs, Chile-Cheese Deviled, **'93** 87
Eggs, Cottage, **'85** 44
Eggs, Cottage Cheese Scrambled, **'81** 142
Eggs, Cottage-Scrambled, **'80** 49
Eggs, Cream Cheese Scrambled, **'81** 287
Enchiladas, Cheese, **'81** 194; **'85** 154
Enchiladas, Cheesy Sour Cream, **'79** 25
Enchiladas, Meatless, **'93** 106
Enchiladas, Saucy Cheese, **'84** 220
Enchiladas, Vegetable-Cheese, **'94** 42
Fettuccine, Broccoli-Parmesan, **'93** 55
Fillets, Parmesan, **'86** M112
Flounder au Fromage, Baked, **'86** 234
Flounder, Cheesy Broiled, **'84** 69
Fondue, Nacho, **'94** 332
Fondue, Pub, **'94** 332
Fowl, Fancy, **'81** 76
French Toast au Fromage, **'88** 288
French Toast, Three Cheese Stuffed, **'93** 122
Fried Brie, Walnut-, **'86** 244
Frittata, Broccoli-Cheese, **'81** 243
Fritters, Cheesy Zucchini, **'88** 44
Frosting, Coconut Cream Cheese, **'86** 60

Frosting, Cream Cheese, **'79** 45; **'80** 140, 253, 299; **'82** 135, 244; **'83** 105, 215, M233; **'84** 201, 255, 315, 316; **'85** 118, 121; **'86** 217, 337; **'87** 58; **'90** 305, 308; **'92** 120; **'93** 20; **'94** 254
Frosting, Deluxe Cream Cheese, **'80** 120
Frosting, Fluffy Cream Cheese, **'80** 245
Frosting, Lemon-Cream Cheese, **'81** 157
Frosting, Nutty Cream Cheese, **'85** 117
Frosting, Orange Cream, **'82** 14
Frosting, Orange-Cream Cheese, **'81** 70; **'82** 16; **'92** 19
Frosting, White Chocolate-Cream Cheese Tiered Cake, **'94** 125
Frosting, White Chocolate-Cream Cheese, **'94** 58
Fruit, Cheese, and Nuts, **'93** 324
Fruited Cream Cheese, **'85** 306
Fruit with Cheese, Luscious Fresh, **'79** 153
Fudge, Cream Cheese, **'84** 111
Ginger Cheese, **'92** 163
Glaze, Cream Cheese, **'84** 150; **'94** 242
Goat Cheese and Greens, **'90** 54
Gratin, Pear-Blue Cheese, **'93** 328
Grits, Baked Cheese, **'94** 240
Grits, Cheese, **'90** 102
Grits, Garlic-Cheese, **'88** 126; **'89** 47
Grits, Good Morning, **'87** 156
Grits, Grillades and Baked Cheese, **'94** 240
Grits, Gruyère Cheese, **'81** 47
Grits, Jalapeño Cheese, **'85** 43
Grits, Quick Cheese, **'83** M203
Grits, Sausage-Cheese, **'90** 238
Grits, Sliced Cheese, **'84** 75
Ham-and-Cheese Bundles, **'93** 63
Ham-and-Cheese Flips, **'92** 46
Ham and Swiss in the Pocket, **'83** 31
Ham-and-Turkey Specials, Cheesy, **'84** 14
Ham-Cheese Chips, **'82** 34
Ham Dinner, Cheesy, **'84** 90
Ham, Frosted, **'89** 71
Ham Towers, Cheesy, **'82** M77
Hoagies, Bacon, Pimiento, and Cheese, **'90** 144
Hominy, Hot Cheese, **'84** 77
Hush Puppies, Cheesy Mexican, **'91** 201
Kabobs, Swiss-Ham, **'81** 124
Kuchen, Cheese, **'86** 84
Lasagna, Cheesy, **'82** 224; **'88** 299
Lasagna, Cheesy Spinach, **'80** 32; **'83** 204
Lasagna, Cheesy Vegetable, **'79** 84
Lasagna in a Bun, **'90** 176
Lettuce, Cheesy Stuffed, **'79** 175
Little Bits, **'79** 196
Loaf, Cheese, **'87** 92
Loaf, Cheeseburger, **'81** 236, 276
Loaf, Pepperoni and Cheese, **'82** 32
Loaves, Chocolate Chip Cheese, **'91** 299; **'92** 264
Loaves, Sausage-Cheese, **'88** 235
Macaroni and Cheese, **'83** M7; **'88** M147, M190; **'90** 30
Macaroni and Cheese, Baked, **'82** 199
Macaroni-and-Cheese Deluxe, **'79** 84
Macaroni and Cheese Deluxe, **'80** 236
Macaroni and Cheese Puff, **'79** 5
Macaroni-and-Cheese-Stuffed Peppers, **'80** 65
Macaroni and Cheese, Tasty, **'83** 288
Macaroni and Cheese, Thick-and-Rich, **'84** 329

Cheese *(continued)*

Macaroni-and-Cheese with Wine, '86 78
Macaroni, Double Cheese, '82 224
Manicotti, Cheesy, '83 216
Manicotti, Special, '88 50
Manicotti, Stuffed, '83 M6
Marinated Cheese, '90 244
Mayonnaise, Parmesan, '86 79
Meatballs, Golden Nugget, '82 233
Meatballs, Mock, '81 243
Meat Loaf, Mozzarella-Layered, '79 71
Meat Loaf Roll, Blue Cheese, '93 247
Mints, Cream Cheese, '93 79
Mold, Ambrosia Cream Cheese, '79 249
Mold, Cheesy Lemon, '79 241
Mold, Creamy Tuna-Cheese, '81 135
Molds, Heavenly Dessert Cheese, '85 209
Molds, Snowcap Cheese, '79 242
Noodles and Mushrooms, Cheesy, '79 84
Noodles, Cheesy Parmesan, '83 M7
Noodles, Ham and Swiss on, '87 108
Noodles, Parmesan, '83 118
Omelet, Cheddar-Vegetable, '83 205
Omelet, Cheesy Picante, '86 95
Omelet, Cheesy Vegetable, '85 49
Omelet, Ham and Cheese, '79 262; '80 123
Omelet, Herbed Cheese, '93 47
Omelet, Puffed Cheese, '89 227
Omelets, George's, '80 68
Omelet, Shrimp-and-Cheddar, '84 57
Omelet, Shrimp-and-Cheese, '94 31
Omelet, Spinach-Cheese, '83 119
Omelet, Swiss Oven, '80 189
Omelet, Zippy Cheese, '87 287
Orange Cream Cheese, '91 177
Pancakes, Cottage Cheese, '79 115
Pasta Stuffed with Five Cheeses, '88 197
Pastries, Cream Cheese, '80 250
Pastries, Date-Filled Cheese, '83 259
Pastries, German, '86 78
Pastry, Apple Tart with Cheese, '88 225
Pastry, Cheddar, '86 206
Pastry, Cheddar Cheese, '80 219; '82 194
Pastry, Cheese, '88 56
Pastry, Cream Cheese, '82 39; '86 78;
 '89 136
Pastry Shell, Cheese, '85 284
Pastry Shells, Cream Cheese, '86 13
Pastry Shells, Miniature Cream Cheese,
 '87 190
Pastry Tart Shells, Cheese, '85 216
Pâté, Cream Cheese, '80 154
Pâté, Liver-Cheese, '85 276
Patty Shells, Cream Cheese, '81 266;
 '82 249
Pears, Cheese-Filled, '81 268
Pears Stuffed with Cheese, '82 290
Perch, Parmesan-Crusted, '93 91
Pie, Apple-Cheese, '85 284
Pie, Apple-Cream Cheese, '81 247
Pie, Blueberry-Cream Cheese, '88 154
Pie, Breakfast, '86 242
Pie, Broccoli-Cheese, '84 235
Pie, Cheese-Beef, '85 33
Pie, Cheesy Mexican Chicken, '82 142
Pie, Chocolate-Cream Cheese, '80 69
Pie, Chocolate Cream Cheese, '92 240
Pie, Cottage Cheese, '82 85
Pie, Fruited Cheese, '92 228

Pie, Green Chile-Cheese, '84 234
Pie, Lemon Cheese, '81 136; '82 146
Pie, Lemon-Cottage Cheese, '79 44; '81 143
Pie, Mexican Cheese, '82 9; '83 69
Pie, Mincemeat-Cheese, '80 253
Pie, Onion-Cheese, '88 86
Pie, Quick and Cheesy Corn, '82 191
Pie, Tortilla, '85 M211
Pie, Turkey-Cheese, '88 264
Pie, Yogurt-Cheese, '82 121
Pie, Zucchini-Ham-Cheese, '80 272
Pimiento Cheese, Chunky, '88 91
Pineapple Gratin, '93 328
Pita Pockets, Ham-and-Cheese, '90 271
Pita, Stuffed, '89 87
Pizza, Breakfast, '88 288
Pizza, Cheese-and-Mushroom, '83 226
Pizza, Double Cheesy Beef-and-Sausage,
 '86 77
Pizza, Gruyère-Chicken, '87 182
Polenta Squares, Skillet, '94 22
Popcorn, Bacon-Cheese, '86 74
Popcorn, Sesame-Cheese, '79 220
Pork Chops, Cheese-Stuffed, '84 81
Pork Chops with Apples, Parmesan,
 '93 338
Pork Parmigiana, Easy, '94 57
Pork Tenderloin with Blue Cheese, '86 76
Preserves, Cream Cheese and Peach,
 '84 264
Pudding, Baked Cheese, '86 78
Pudding, Cheesy Bread, '83 68
Pudding, Corn-Cheese, '80 244
Puff, Egg-and-Cheese, '85 45
Puffs, Bavarian Cheese, '80 191
Puffs, Turkey-Cheese, '87 301
Quesadillas, Quick, '89 87
Quesadillas, Sausage, '90 118
Quesadillas with Shrimp and Brie, '94 173
Quiches
 Bacon-Cheese Quiches, Miniature,
  '83 93
 Benedict Quiche, '80 M107
 Blue Cheese Quiche, '84 52
 Cheddar-Leek Quiche, '88 198
 Eggless Quiche, '87 220
 Green Onion Quiche, Cheesy, '83 194;
  '84 42
 Ham-Cheese Quiche, '79 26
 Ham Quiche, Cheesy, '79 127
 Jalapeño Quiche, Cheesy, '84 31
 Lorraine, Perfect Quiche, '79 127
 Lorraine, Quiche, '79 40; '80 M108
 Miniature Cheese Quiches, '80 150
 Sausage-Cheddar Quiche, '79 26
 Sausage Quiche, Spicy, '80 M108
 South-of-the-Border Quiche, '93 321
 Spinach Quiche, Cheesy, '81 228
 Squares, Cheesy Hot Quiche, '79 124
 Swiss Alpine Quiche, '90 18
 Swiss-Zucchini Quiche, '82 49
 Tasty Quiche, '82 264
 Vegetable Quiche, Cheese-, '81 228
 Zucchini Quiche, Cheesy, '83 312
Ramekins, Three-Cheese, '79 26
Rarebit, Cheese, '86 78
Rarebit, Tangy Welsh, '88 159
Rarebit, Uptown Welsh, '87 279
Raspberry Brie in Rye, '93 252
Rice, Chili-Cheesy, '79 43
Roll, Cheesy Meat, '82 136

Rolls, Ham-and-Cheese Lettuce, '89 217
Rollups, Date-Cream Cheese, '83 298
Rounds, Parmesan, '79 170
Rounds, Turkey-Mozzarella, '82 3
Salad, Black Bean-and-Cheese, '92 217
Salad, Blue Cheese, '88 48
Salad, Blue Cheese Chicken, '94 81
Salad, Blue Cheese-Pear-Apple, '81 224
Salad, Blue Cheese-Potato, '91 208
Salad, Blue Cheese-Stuffed Lettuce, '94 202
Salad, Blue Cheese Tossed, '84 195
Salad, Cantaloupe-Cheese, '88 184
Salad, Cheddar-Pea, '84 82
Salad, Cheesy Apple, '86 301
Salad, Cheesy Fruit-'n'-Nut, '87 56
Salad, Cheesy Layered, '81 37
Salad, Cheesy-Vegetable Congealed, '86 199
Salad, Citrus-Blue Cheese, '92 220
Salad, Cottage Cheese-and-Fruit, '86 16
Salad, Cottage Cheese-Potato, '79 147, 285
Salad, Cottage-Tomato, '85 163
Salad, Cranberry-Cheese Ribbon, '79 241
Salad, Creamy Roquefort, '79 73
Salad, Crunchy-Creamy, '88 100
Salad, Different Cottage Cheese, '85 328;
 '86 22
Salad, Dilled Macaroni-Cheese, '86 208
Salad, Fresh Mozzarella-Tomato-Basil,
 '93 131
Salad, Frosted Lime-Cheese, '79 286
Salad, Green Beans-and-Cheese, '91 159
Salad, Ham-and-Cheese, '88 138
Salad, Ham-Pecan-Blue Cheese Pasta, '90 62
Salad, Hot Parmesan Potato, '79 78
Salad in Tomatoes, Cottage Cheese, '86 208
Salad, Lemon-Cheese, '85 240
Salad, Mexican, '81 36
Salad, Orange-Cottage Cheese, '79 44
Salad, Out-of-This-World Cottage Cheese,
 '79 44
Salad, Party Freeze, '82 145
Salad, Pear-Swiss Cheese, '91 237
Salad, "Pig in the Garden," '92 255
Salad, Quick Cheesy-Mushroom, '89 128
Salad, Spinach-Blue Cheese, '82 166
Salad, Swiss-Apple, '84 81
Salad, Swiss Tuna, '86 186
Salad, Tomato-Feta, '81 246; '91 168
Salad, Tomato-Mozzarella, '89 220
Salad, Ziti-Cheddar, '85 165
Salmon Patties, Cheesy, '89 99
Sandwich, Chicken Parmigiana, '94 65
Sandwich, Corned Beef and Cheese,
 '79 214
Sandwiches, Avocado, Bacon, and Cheese,
 '87 279
Sandwiches, Bacon, Cheese, and Tomato,
 '84 14
Sandwiches, Breakfast, '80 52
Sandwiches, Brown Bread-Cream Cheese,
 '87 M6
Sandwiches, Cheese Tea, '92 276
Sandwiches, Cheesy Breakfast, '90 140
Sandwiches, Cheesy Chicken, '82 190
Sandwiches, Christmas Tree, '92 279
Sandwiches, Creamy Blue Cheese-Ham,
 '87 279
Sandwiches, Fruit-and-Cheese Breakfast,
 '89 M21
Sandwiches, Gingered Tea, '84 116
Sandwiches, Grilled Bacon-Cheese, '83 242

Cheese *(continued)*

Sandwiches, Grilled Cheese, **'82** M172;
  '94 167
Sandwiches, Ham-and-Cheese Pita, **'87** 202;
  '88 44
Sandwiches, Hot Crab-and-Cheese, **'87** 279
Sandwiches, Hot French Cheese, **'82** 3
Sandwiches, Hot Ham-and-Cheese, **'85** 299
Sandwiches, Leafy Cheese, **'90** 56
Sandwiches, Open-Faced Cheesy Bacon,
  '80 78
Sandwiches, Open-Faced Cheesy Egg,
  '86 67
Sandwiches, Peanut-Cheese-Raisin, **'88** 140
Sandwiches, Pimiento Cheese, **'82** 278
Sandwiches, Sausage-Cheese Muffin,
  '92 M212
Sandwiches, Shrimp-Cheese, **'85** 242
Sandwiches, Tangy Ham-and-Swiss,
  '85 164
Sandwiches, Tasty Grilled, **'84** 30
Sandwiches, Toasted Chicken-and-Cheese,
  '85 242
Sandwiches, Yummy, **'81** 229
Sandwich, Fertitta's "Muffy," **'94** 34
Sandwich, Mexican Grilled Cheese, **'92** 63
Sandwich Round, Ham-and-Cheese, **'94** 326
Sandwich, Tex-Mex Ham-and-Cheese, **'86** 4
Sauces
  Blue Cheese Sauce, **'90** 142; **'94** 320
  Broccoli with Cheese Sauce, **'82** 107
  Brussels Sprouts with Cheese Sauce,
    '79 246
  Cauliflower with Cheese Sauce, **'81** 101
  Cheddar Cheese Sauce, **'91** 286
  Cheese Sauce, **'79** M156;
    '81 43, 44, 225; **'82** M123;
    '83 49, 138, 188; **'84** 57; **'85** 92;
    '86 241; **'88** 78, 272; **'89** 181, 229;
    '90 235; **'93** 48
  Cottage Cheese Sauce, **'87** 232
  Cream Sauce, Cheesy, **'82** 79
  Devonshire Sauce, Processor, **'86** 337
  Easy Cheese Sauce, **'79** 22
  Garlic-Cheese Sauce, **'84** M70
  Goat Cheese Sauce, Asparagus with,
    '93 116
  Guilt-Free Cheese Sauce, **'93** M95
  Ham and Eggs on Toast with Cheese
    Sauce, **'81** 43
  Lemon-Cheese Sauce, **'91** 24
  Lemony Cheese Sauce, **'84** 183
  Monterey Jack Sauce, **'84** 293
  Mornay Sauce, **'80** 120; **'81** 90;
    '89 195
  Mushroom-Cheese Sauce, **'83** 190;
    '86 48
  Parmesan Cheese Sauce, **'79** 165;
    '80 162; **'85** 143
  Parmesan Sauce, **'92** 17
  Potatoes with Cheese Sauce, Baked,
    '83 239
  Potatoes with Cheese Sauce, Stuffed,
    '87 192
  Rich Cheese Sauce, **'81** 89
  Roquefort Sauce, **'89** 321
  Rosemary-Parmesan Sauce, Tortellini
    with, **'92** 284
  Seafood Cheese Sauce, **'89** 240

  Swiss Cheese Sauce, **'79** 35; **'87** 289;
    '88 135
  Swiss Sauce, **'83** M195
  Swiss Sauce, Creamy, **'80** M53
  Tomatoes with Cheese Sauce over
    Toast, **'88** 159
  Topper, Vegetable-Cheese Potato, **'86** 6
  Tuna Salad, Cheese-Sauced, **'87** M124
  Turnips in Cheese Sauce, **'84** 229
  Vegetable-Cheese Sauce, **'85** M152
  Vegetable Sauce, Cheesy, **'92** M134
Scallops, Baked Gruyère, **'92** 57
Scallops, Chip and Cheese, **'80** 301
Scallops Mornay, **'80** 164
Schnitzel, Swiss, **'80** 189
Sebastian, The, **'94** 184
Shake, Strawberry-Cheesecake, **'92** 44
Shell, Rice-Cheese, **'82** 49
Shells, Cheesy Beef-Stuffed, **'83** 217
Shells, Cream Cheese, **'79** 2
Shrimp au Gratin, **'85** 79
Shrimp, Parmesan-Stuffed, **'85** 103
Soufflé, Blintz, **'88** 155
Soufflé, Blue Cheese, **'91** 244
Soufflé, Cheese, **'79** 72, 261; **'94** 116
Soufflé, Cheesy Spinach, **'81** 53
Soufflé, Corn-and-Cheese, **'88** 122
Soufflé, Cream Cheese, **'88** 11
Soufflé Cups, Hot, **'85** 284
Soufflé for Two, Cheese, **'81** 226
Soufflé, Rice-Cheese, **'79** 270
Soufflé, Rolled Cheese, **'89** 13
Soufflés, Individual, **'80** 190
Soufflés, Individual Frozen, **'80** 52
Soufflé, Three-Egg Cheese, **'87** 234
Soups
  Anytime Soup, Cheesy, **'81** 307;
    '82 314; **'83** 66
  Bacon-Beer Cheese Soup, **'87** M7
  Bacon-Topped Cheese Soup, **'80** M224
  Beer-Cheese Soup, **'84** 246
  Broccoli Soup, Cheese-and-, **'89** 276
  Broccoli Soup, Cheesy-, **'86** 258
  Broccoli-Swiss Soup, **'86** 6
  Carrot Soup, Cheesy, **'81** 262
  Cheddar Chowder, Hearty, **'79** 16
  Chicken Chowder, Cheesy, **'92** 21
  Corn and Cheese Chowder, **'80** 228
  Cream of Cheese Soup, **'83** 99
  Cream with Greens Soup, **'94** 277
  Favorite Cheese Soup, Uncle Ed's,
    '94 228
  Gazebo Cheese Soup, **'90** 158
  Gazpacho, Shrimp-Cream Cheese,
    '94 137
  Golden Cheese Chowder, **'80** 73
  Ham-and-Cheese Chowder, **'89** 15
  Ham 'n Cheese Chowder, **'79** 199
  Hearty Cheese Soup, **'84** 4
  Hot Cheese Chowder, **'89** 16
  Monterey Jack Cheese Soup, **'81** 112;
    '85 M211
  Onion-Cheese Soup, **'87** 81
  Onion Soup, Double-Cheese, **'85** 227
  Onion Soup, Double Cheese-Topped,
    '79 49
  Oyster-Cheese Soup, **'84** 213
  Potato-and-Wild Rice Soup, Cheesy,
    '89 16
  Roquefort Vichyssoise, Velvety, **'83** 223
  Swiss-Broccoli Chowder, **'80** 73

  Tomato Soup with Parmesan Cheese,
    Cream of, **'86** 161
  Vegetable-Cheese Soup, **'89** 15
  Vegetable-Cheese Soup, Creamy,
    '81 244
  Vegetable Cheese Soup, Creamy,
    '83 230
  Vegetable Chowder, Cheesy, **'80** 25;
    '83 20
  Vegetable Soup, Cheesy, **'80** 73
  Velvet Soup, Cheese, **'80** 74; **'92** 193
Spaghetti, Three-Cheese, **'83** 105
Spanakópita, **'86** 58
Spreads and Fillings
  Almond Cheese Spread, **'87** 292
  Aloha Spread, **'83** 93
  Apricot Brie Spread, **'86** 275
  Apricot-Cream Cheese Spread, **'82** 161;
    '87 158
  Artichoke-Parmesan Spread, **'92** 95
  Bacon-Cheese Spread, **'83** 241
  Beer Cheese Spread, **'81** 160; **'85** 69
  Beer Spread, Cheesy, **'87** 196
  Blintz Filling, **'92** 84
  Blue Cheese Spread, **'90** 215
  Boursin Cheese Spread, Buttery,
    '94 301
  Boursin Cheese Spread, Garlic, **'94** 301
  Caviar-Cream Cheese Spread, **'84** 256
  Cheese Filling, **'89** 91
  Chile-Cheese Spread, **'86** 297
  Chili Cheese Spread, **'93** 242
  Chocolate-Cheese Filling, **'90** 47
  Chocolate Cheese Spread, **'87** 292
  Cinnamon-Cheese Filling, **'90** 46
  Coconut-Cranberry Cheese Spread,
    '92 328
  Confetti Cheese Spread, **'84** 256
  Cottage Cheese Spread, **'87** 107
  Cottage-Egg Salad Spread, **'82** 146
  Crabmeat Spread, Layered, **'83** 127
  Crab Spread, Superb, **'81** 235
  Cranberry Cream, **'90** 66
  Cream Cheese Filling, **'90** 170
  Cream Cheese-Olive Spread, **'82** 35
  Cream Cheese Spread, Deviled, **'81** 235
  Cream Cheese Spread, Fruited,
    '91 306; **'93** 79
  Cream Cheese Spread, Peachy,
    '90 M215
  Cream Cheese Spread, Pear-, **'93** 80
  Cucumber and Cream Cheese Spread,
    '82 140
  Date Spread, Breakfast, **'84** 7
  Edam-Sherry Spread, **'84** 257
  Fruit and Cheese Spread, **'81** 245
  Fruit-and-Cheese Spread, Nutty,
    '87 246
  Garlic Pimiento Cheese Spread, **'79** 58
  German Cheese Spread, **'79** 82
  Gouda Cheese Spread, **'90** 36
  Green Onion-Cheese Spread, **'92** 24
  Gruyère-Apple Spread, **'81** 160
  Ham and Pimiento Spread, **'80** 285
  Hawaiian Cheese Spread, **'87** 158
  Herb-Cream Cheese Spread, **'83** 24
  Herbed Cheese Spread, **'87** 247
  Horseradish Spread, Cheese-, **'84** 222
  Jalapeño-Cheese Spread, **'82** 248
  Lemon-Cheese Filling, **'79** 68; **'88** 7
  Make-Ahead Cheese Spread, **'93** 324

Cheese, Spreads and Fillings *(continued)*

Mexican Cheese Spread, '90 119
Olive Spread, Cheese-, '79 82
Orange-Cheese Filling, '90 47
Orange Cheese Spread, '87 292
Orange Filling, Cheese-and-, '93 159
Parmesan-Spinach Spread, '93 55
Pimiento and Three Cheeses, '86 296
Pimiento Cheese, Chunky, '86 295
Pimiento Cheese, Creamy, '86 296
Pimiento Cheese Spread, '82 35;
  '83 93; '86 127
Pimiento Cheese Spread, Creamy,
  '92 159
Pimiento Cheese Spread, Low-Calorie,
  '85 215
Pimiento Cheese, West Texas, '84 9
Pineapple-Cheese Spread, '86 126;
  '91 167
Pineapple-Cream Cheese Spread, '82 35
Ricotta Filling, '80 58
Sandwich Spread, Benedictine, '80 299
Spinach-Ricotta Filling, '81 53
Swiss Cheese Spread, '90 60
Tomato-Cheese Spread, '81 157
Tomato-Cheese Spread, Fiery, '87 196
Tuna Spread, '83 174
Vegetable Sandwich Spread, '83 174
Waldorf Cheese Spread, '88 173
Zesty Cheese Spread, '82 140
Zippy Cheese Spread, '85 4
Squares, Lemony Cream Cheese, '82 159
Steak Cheese Skillet, Swiss, '80 106
Steak Parmesan, '93 41
Steak, Parmesan Round, '80 106
Steaks, Blue Cheese, '84 171
Steaks, Cheese-Stuffed, '81 17
Strata, Artichoke-Cheese, '90 236
Strata, Tomato-Cheese, '81 209
Stromboli, '88 272; '89 181
Stuffing, Catfish with Cream Cheese, '89 52
Supper Supreme, Sunday, '79 76
Sweet Potato Chips with Blue Cheese,
  '93 290
Tart, Dried Tomato-Cheese, '90 203
Tart, Ham-and-Cheese, '92 332
Tart, Herb-Cheese, '87 98
Tart Milan, '87 70
Tarts, Cranberry-Cream Cheese, '80 154
Tarts, Cream Cheese, '84 74; '90 312
Tart Shells, Cheese, '88 88
Tarts, Lemon-Cheese, '79 2
Tarts, Sausage 'n' Cheese, '88 51
Terrine, Italian Cheese, '93 64
Terrine with Goat Cheese, Black Bean,
  '87 120
Tiramisù, '91 21; '94 295
Topping, Blue Cheese Burger, '93 218
Topping, Cheese, '86 233
Topping, Yogurt-Cheese, '88 55
Tortillas, Cheesy, '81 62
Tortilla Snack, Two-Cheese, '90 119
Tortilla Stack, Cheesy Chicken-, '86 3
Tortilla Stack-Ups, '92 196
Toss, Ham and Cheese, '79 55
Trout Florentine, Cheesy, '85 53
Tuna Cheesies, '82 191
Turkey Parmesan, '82 268
Turnovers, Sausage-Cheese, '88 231; '89 22

Twists, Cheese, '92 125
Veal Parmigiana, '81 227
Vegetables
  Artichoke-Cheese Bottoms, Baked,
    '94 61
  Beans au Gratin, Green, '80 116
  Beans, Cheese-Topped Green, '79 100
  Beans, Cheesy Green, '80 157
  Beans with Blue Cheese, Green, '88 57
  Broccoli-and-Eggs au Gratin, '85 289
  Broccoli au Gratin, '82 M20
  Broccoli Fritters, Cheesy, '79 53
  Cabbage, Cheese Scalloped, '81 87;
    '82 7
  Cauliflower au Gratin, '82 204
  Cauliflower au Gratin, French-Fried,
    '79 221; '80 82
  Cauliflower, Baked Swiss, '79 100
  Cauliflower, Cheese-Frosted, '85 68
  Cauliflower Italiano, Cheesy, '82 300
  Chiles Rellenos (Stuffed Chiles),
    '82 220; '83 150
  Corn-and-Swiss Cheese Bake, '92 133
  Corn, Grilled Parmesan, '82 127
  Eggplant, Cheesy Fried, '90 75
  Eggplant, Cheesy Stuffed, '79 188;
    '82 208
  Eggplant, Fried Parmesan, '87 166
  Eggplant Parmesan, '82 230; '92 18
  Eggplant, Parmesan Fried, '79 189
  Eggplant Parmesan, No-Fry, '92 172
  Eggplant, Scalloped, '91 223
  Fries, Cheesy Oven, '91 187
  Hash Brown Cheese Bake, '82 50
  Lentils with Cheese, Baked, '84 113
  Limas in Onion Shells, Cheese and,
    '81 86
  Loaf, Pureed Vegetable-Cheese,
    '85 297
  Mushrooms, Parmesan Stuffed, '83 115
  Mushrooms, Ricotta-Stuffed, '85 20
  Okra with Cheese, '80 185
  Onion Bake, Cheese, '82 32
  Onion Bake, Romano, '90 98
  Onions, Cheese-Stuffed, '90 34
  Onions, Parmesan, '93 170
  Onions, Sherried Cheese, '82 32
  Pepper Toss, Parmesan, '93 208
  Potato-Broccoli-Cheese Bake, '80 114
  Potato Croquettes, Parmesan, '84 210
  Potatoes Alfredo, '89 204
  Potatoes-and-Zucchini au Gratin, '84 5
  Potatoes au Gratin, '93 90, 217
  Potatoes, Bacon-Topped Blue Cheese,
    '79 46
  Potatoes, Basil-Cheese, '90 M316
  Potatoes, Blue Cheese Mashed, '92 330
  Potatoes, Blue Cheese Stuffed, '81 276;
    '92 M228
  Potatoes, Blue Cheese-Stuffed, '89 69
  Potatoes, Cheesy, '82 211
  Potatoes, Cheesy Bacon-Stuffed, '81 61
  Potatoes, Cheesy Caraway, '86 17
  Potatoes, Cheesy Chive, '79 46
  Potatoes, Cheesy Chive-Stuffed,
    '91 128
  Potatoes, Cheesy Crab-Stuffed, '86 17
  Potatoes, Cheesy Frank-Topped, '83 3
  Potatoes, Cheesy New, '85 156
  Potatoes, Chicken-Cheese Stuffed,
    '86 55

Potatoes, Chili-Cheese, '90 M62
Potatoes, Chive-Cream Cheese Mashed,
  '92 330
Potatoes, Creamy Cheese, '88 M146
Potatoes, Feta Mashed, '92 330
Potatoes, Parmesan, '82 270; '90 M62;
  '92 M341; '93 M46
Potatoes Roquefort, '79 211
Potatoes, Two-Cheese, '80 114
Potatoes with Feta Cheese, '84 295;
  '85 196
Potatoes with Sweet Marjoram and
  Parmesan Cheese, Scalloped,
  '91 246
Potato Fans, Parmesan-, '88 M190
Potato Gratin, Dual, '93 328
Potato Skins, Cheese, '84 M239
Potato Soufflé, Cheesy, '89 332
Rice au Gratin, '83 129
Rutabaga au Gratin, '79 254
Spinach-Cheese Puff, '84 96
Spinach, Cheesy Topped, '84 85
Spinach Parmesan, '93 72
Spinach, Savory Parmesan, '85 68
Spinach with Cheese, Scalloped, '79 8
Spinach with Feta, Lemon, '85 190
Squash Bake, Cheesy, '80 183
Squash Boats, Parmesan-Stuffed,
  '79 156
Squash, Cheesy Stuffed, '82 134
Squash, Greek-Style, '92 26
Squash Soufflé, Cheesy, '82 146
Squash with Cheese Sauce, Stuffed
  Yellow, '80 162
Stalks, Splendid, '93 258
Summer Vegetables, Cheesy,
  '94 119
Swiss Chard Bundles, '94 48
Tomato Cheese Puffs, '81 48
Tomatoes, Baked Cheddar, '85 43
Tomatoes, Cheese Herbed-Topped,
  '86 108
Tomatoes, Cheese-Stuffed, '91 69
Tomatoes, Cheese-Topped, '81 160
Tomatoes, Cheesy Cherry, '83 135
Tomatoes, Cheesy Grilled, '79 150
Tomatoes, Cheesy Puff-Top, '86 187
Tomatoes, Cheesy Stuffed, '80 161
Tomatoes, Chile-Cheese Stuffed,
  '94 141
Tomatoes, Parmesan, '80 161
Tomatoes, Parmesan-Stuffed,
  '92 182
Tomatoes, Romano Broiled, '80 42
Turnip au Gratin, '79 289
Turnips au Gratin, '88 229; '89 244
Zucchini and Tomato au Gratin, '82 208
Zucchini, Ham and Cheese Stuffed,
  '79 157
Zucchini, Parmesan, '81 234
Zucchini Parmesan, '81 108;
  '82 103
Zucchini Pie, Cheesy, '82 103
Vermicelli, Shrimp and Feta Cheese on,
  '87 108
Vinaigrette, Blue Cheese, '90 55, 280
Vinaigrette, Garlic-Blue Cheese, '92 57
Wafers, Hope Farm Cheese, '93 282
Wafers, Italian, '87 36
Wafers, Sage-Pecan Cheese, '93 12
Walnut-Baked Brie, '93 241

Cheesecakes. *See* Cakes/Cheesecakes.
Cherries
à la Mode, Cherries, **'88** 202
Bars, Delightful Cherry, **'86** 217
Bread, Cherry Nut, **'81** 306; **'82** 36
Bread, Maraschino Cherry Nut, **'79** 234
Bread, Quick Cherry-Nut, **'85** 55
Cake, Black Forest Cherry, **'83** 302
Cake, Cherry, **'79** 165
Cake, Cherry Blossom Coffee, **'80** 21
Cake, Cherry Bourbon, **'82** 287
Cake, Cherry Upside-Down, **'82** 56
Cake, Chocolate-Cherry, **'84** 200; **'86** 239
Cake, Maraschino Nut, **'83** 268
Cake, Quick Cherry, **'81** 238
Cake, Upside-Down Sunburst, **'87** 9
Cake, White Chocolate-Cherry, **'88** 268
Cheesecake, Black Forest, **'89** 93; **'94** 21
Cheesecake, Cherry, **'79** 50
Cheesecake, Cherry-Topped, **'80** 23
Chocolate-Covered Cherries, **'81** 286;
 '84 298
Cider, Cherry, **'94** 288
Cloud, Cherry-Berry on a, **'79** 94
Cobbler, Berry-Cherry, **'83** 270
Cobbler, Cherry, **'82** 91, 139
Cobbler, Colossal Cherry, **'89** 137
Cobbler, Fresh Cherry, **'84** 178
Cobbler, Raspberry-Cherry, **'93** 230
Coffee Cake, Cherry, **'94** 49
Compote, Cherry, **'83** 139
Compote, Watermelon-Cherry, **'90** 180
"Concrete," Cardinal Sin, **'94** 113
Cookies, Cherry Bonbon, **'93** 52
Cookies, Cherry Pecan, **'82** 136
Cookies, Chocolate-Cherry, **'85** 324
Cookies, Christmas Cherry, **'88** 282
Cookies, Coconut-Cherry, **'79** 292
Cookies, Frosted Chocolate-Cherry, **'89** 294
Cream, Maraschino Russian, **'79** 231
Crêpes, Cherry, **'91** 67
Crêpes Flambé, Cherry, **'79** 18
Crisp, Cherry, **'91** 20
Crisp, Oatmeal Cherry-Apple, **'90** M16
Crowns, Cherry, **'92** 275
Dessert, Cherry Cordial, **'84** 312
Dessert, Holiday Cherry, **'80** 255
Drops, Cherry-Almond, **'81** 20
Filling, Cherry, **'83** 302; **'84** 225; **'88** 178
Frosting, Cherry, **'86** 217
Frosting, Chocolate-Cherry, **'89** 294
Fudge, Cherry Nut, **'83** 315
Glaze, Cherry, **'83** 143; **'93** 52
Ice Cream, Black Forest, **'88** 203
Ice Cream, Cherry, **'84** 184
Ice Cream, Cherry-Nut, **'86** 129
Ice Cream, Cherry-Pecan, **'88** 203
Jubilee, Cherries, **'79** 18; **'83** 139
Jubilee, Quick Cherries, **'82** M100
Jubilite, Cherries, **'86** 317
Kirsch, Melon Balls and Cherries in, **'91** 91
Muffins, Cherry, **'82** 105
Muffins, Cherry-Nut, **'90** 87
Muffins, Dried Cherry, **'94** 59
Nuggets, Cherry Nut, **'81** 286
Pie, Cherry-Berry, **'92** 316
Pie, Cherry-Pecan, **'92** 30
Pie, Coconut Crumb Cherry, **'92** 30
Pie, Easy Cherry, **'82** M299
Pie, Fresh Cherry, **'88** 178
Pie, Lemony Cherry, **'92** 30

Pie, No-Bake Cherry Confetti, **'93** 114
Pie, Prize-Winning Cherry, **'82** 57
Pie, Red Cherry, **'83** 192
Pie, Scrumptious Cherry, **'83** 250
Pie, Tart Cranberry-Cherry, **'87** 299
Pie with Almond Pastry, Cherry Cream,
 '92 30
Pork Roast, Cherry-Glazed, **'91** 84
Punch, Cranberry-Cherry, **'91** 176
Rolls, Cherry-Almond, **'84** M198
Sabayon, Cherries, **'88** 178
Salad, Best Cherry, **'82** 302
Salad, Cherry-Apple, **'86** 31
Salad, Cherry Cola, **'80** 104
Salad, Cherry-Cola, **'91** 224
Salad, Cherry Fruit, **'87** 236
Salad, Cherry-Orange, **'79** 74; **'82** 56
Salad, Congealed Cherry, **'89** 278
Salad, Delicious Frozen Cherry, **'81** 252
Salad, Elegant Cherry-Wine, **'82** 56
Salad, Festive Cherry, **'84** 265
Salad, Fresh Cherry, **'83** 120
Salad, Frozen Black Cherry, **'89** 163
Salad, Frozen Cherry, **'79** 126
Salad, Port Wine-Cherry, **'86** 11
Salad, Sweet Cherry, **'89** 326
Salad with Honey-Lime Dressing, Cherry,
 '83 139
Salad with Sherry Dressing, Cherry, **'79** 165
Sauce, Cherry, **'79** 91; **'83** 276; **'84** 91;
 '91 67
Sauce, Chocolate-Cherry, **'85** 189
Sauce, Chocolate Cherry, **'87** M165
Sauce, Elegant Cherry, **'79** M156
Sauce, Ham Balls with Spiced Cherry,
 '81 112; **'82** 12
Sauce, Roast Ducklings with Cherry, **'86** 312
Sauce, Roast Pork with Spiced Cherry,
 '89 324
Sauce, Royal Cherry, **'85** 224; **'86** 83
Sauce, Spicy Cherry, **'83** 244
Sherried Cherries, **'93** 289
Slump, Cherry, **'83** 139
Snow, Berries on, **'82** 227
Spread, Cherry, **'93** 309
Squares, Surprise Cherry, **'82** 57
Stuffed Cherries, **'85** 81
Syrup, Cherry-Lemonade, **'86** 214
Tart, Cherry and Blackberry, **'83** 225
Tarts, Cheery Cherry, **'80** 238
Topping, Cherry-Pineapple, **'87** 126
Torte, Black Forest Cherry, **'88** 178
Chicken
Acapulco, Chicken, **'84** 32
à la King, Chicken, **'79** 218; **'83** 137;
 '87 197; **'94** 41
à la King, Easy Chicken, **'93** 14
Almond Chicken and Vegetables, **'86** 21
Almond Chicken, Creamy, **'89** 281
Almond Chicken, Spicy, **'88** 150
à l'Orange, Chicken, **'84** 277
Alouette, Chicken, **'91** 295
Andalusia, Chicken, **'87** 103
Appetizers, Chicken-Mushroom, **'88** 210
Appetizers, Sesame Chicken, **'89** 61
Apple Chicken, **'85** 57
Apricot Chicken, **'92** 12
Apricot Chicken Breasts, **'88** 301
Ariosto, Shrimp and Chicken, **'79** 31
Artichoke Chicken, **'81** 97
Artichoke Hearts, Chicken with, **'88** 54

Artichokes and Mushrooms, Chicken with,
 '90 35
Bag, Chicken in a, **'86** M57; **'87** 23
Bake, Chicken-Brown Rice, **'91** 314
Bake, Chicken Chili, **'93** 302
Bake, Chicken, Ham, and Cheese, **'87** 217
Bake, Chicken-Italian Dressing, **'91** 199
Bake, Chicken-Tomato, **'83** 35
Bake, Chicken Tortilla, **'82** 89
Bake, Company Chicken, **'80** 301
Bake, Countryside Chicken, **'88** 39
Bake, Crispy Chicken, **'83** 115
Baked Breast of Chicken with Marinated
 Bermuda Onions, **'92** 194
Baked Chicken and Artichoke Hearts,
 '82 260
Baked Chicken and Dressing, **'79** 296
Baked Chicken, Breaded, **'81** 76
Baked Chicken Breasts, Creamy, **'83** 24
Baked Chicken Breasts, Sherried, **'79** 83
Baked Chicken Breasts, Wine-, **'83** 177
Baked Chicken, Citrus Herb, **'85** 303
Baked Chicken, Fancy, **'79** 85
Baked Chicken, Fontina-, **'90** 64
Baked Chicken, Herb-, **'82** 229
Baked Chicken in Wine, **'81** 109
Baked Chicken, Italian, **'82** 84
Baked Chicken Parmesan, **'83** 137
Baked Chicken, Tomato-, **'81** 281; **'82** 30
Baked Chicken with Tarragon Sauce, **'94** 126
Baked Chicken with Wine-Soaked Vegetables,
 '84 277
Baked Chile Chicken with Salsa, **'88** 147
Baked Italian Chicken, **'83** 184
Baked Lemon Chicken, **'85** 190
Baked Mustard Chicken, **'87** 10
Baked Parmesan Chicken, **'83** 320
Bake, Herb Chicken, **'82** 186
Bake, Individual Chicken, **'90** 279
Bake, Mushroom-Chicken, **'89** 147
Bake, Parslied Chicken, **'90** 65
Bake, Pineapple Chicken, **'82** 120
Bake, Saucy Chicken, **'84** 220
Bake, Seasoned Chicken, **'94** 278
Bake, Spicy Chicken, **'85** 251
Bake with Sweet Bacon Dressing,
 Vegetable-Chicken, **'93** 108
Ball, Chicken-Cheese, **'93** 216
Ball, Chicken-Curry Cheese, **'85** 118
Balls, Coconut Curried Chicken, **'91** 165
Balls, Curried Chicken, **'91** 98
Barbecued
 Bake, Barbecued Chicken, **'81** 97
 Breasts, Grilled Chicken, **'84** 172
 Bundles, Chicken-Mushroom, **'80** 157
 Charcoal Broiled Chicken, **'79** 90
 Chicken, Barbecue, **'86** 122
 Chicken, Barbecued, **'82** 97, 106;
  '83 103; **'85** 144; **'86** 153; **'89** 167
 Cranberry Chicken, Barbecued, **'83** 178
 Cumin Chicken, Grilled, **'87** 142
 Garlic-Grilled Chicken, **'87** 180
 Glazed Barbecue Chicken, Carambola-,
  '92 246
 Golden Barbecued Chicken, **'83** 136
 Grilled Barbecued Chicken, **'81** 154
 Legs and Thighs, Barbecued Chicken,
  '94 94
 Lemonade Chicken, **'82** 163
 Lemon Barbecued Chicken, **'93** 215
 Marinated Barbecued Chicken, **'79** 90

Chicken, Barbecued (*continued*)

Old South Barbecued Chicken, **'82** 97; **'83** 103
Orange Barbecued Chicken, **'88** 123
Oven-Barbecued Cranberry Chicken, **'93** 332
Saucy Barbecued Chicken, **'83** 11
Smoky Grilled Chicken, **'85** 160
Tangy Barbecued Chicken, **'86** 186
White Barbecue Sauce, Chicken with, **'89** M84
Yogurt-Lemon Chicken, Grilled, **'81** 111
Zesty Barbecued Chicken, **'80** M76
Zippy Barbecued Chicken, **'83** 213
Basil Chicken, **'87** 171
Bengalese Chicken, **'79** 12
Bird's-Nest Chicken, **'88** 152
Birds of Paradise, **'82** 224
Biscuit, Chicken in a, **'79** 263; **'80** 30
Bites, Curried Chicken, **'85** 40
Bites, Savory Chicken, **'92** 209
Bourbon Chicken with Gravy, **'94** 252
Braised Bourbon Chicken, **'86** 51
Braised Chicken Breast in Lemon Cream Sauce, **'94** 184
Brandado, Chicken, **'84** 195
Breaded Chicken Breasts, **'89** M196
Breast-of-Chicken Fiesta, **'88** 151
Breast of Chicken, Herbed, **'79** 100
Breasts, Island Chicken, **'84** 68
Breasts Lombardy, Chicken, **'82** 242
Breasts, Salsa-Topped Chicken, **'94** 144
Breasts, Saucy Chicken, **'83** 184; **'87** 167
Breasts with Herb Butter, Chicken, **'89** 120
Brioche Chicken Curry, **'88** 124
Broiled Chicken Breast Tarragon, **'89** 310
Broiled Chicken, Island, **'84** 288
Broth, Easy Microwave Chicken, **'90** M167
Bundles, Cheesy Chicken-and-Ham, **'84** 261
Bundles, San Antonio-Style Chicken, **'85** 251
Bundles with Bacon Ribbons, Chicken, **'87** 68
Burgers, Open-Faced Chicken-Onion, **'94** 139
Burgoo, Five-Meat, **'87** 3
Burgoo, Harry Young's, **'87** 3
Burgoo, Old-Fashioned, **'87** 3
Buttermilk-Pecan Chicken, **'89** 166
Cacciatore, Chicken, **'80** 39; **'83** 118; **'84** 9; **'86** 42
Cacciatore, Quick Chicken-and-Rice, **'88** 38
Cajun Chicken over Rice, **'87** 268; **'88** 102; **'89** 67
Cashew Chicken, **'79** 255; **'80** 8; **'83** 21
Cashew, Chicken, **'88** 38
Cashews, Chicken with, **'79** 207
Casserole, Broccoli-Chicken, **'82** 33
Casserole, Cheesy Chicken, **'85** 34
Casserole, Chicken-Almond, **'94** 199
Casserole, Chicken-and-Chiles, **'93** 107
Casserole, Chicken-and-Dressing, **'81** 263
Casserole, Chicken and Green Noodle, **'80** 32
Casserole, Chicken and Rice, **'80** 260
Casserole, Chicken-Asparagus, **'83** 76; **'84** 71
Casserole, Chicken-Broccoli, **'79** 48; **'91** 315
Casserole, Chicken-Green Bean, **'85** 296
Casserole, Chicken-Macaroni, **'85** 219

Casserole, Chicken-Noodle, **'94** 286
Casserole, Chicken-Rice, **'86** 52
Casserole, Chicken-Spaghetti, **'84** 15
Casserole, Chicken Superb, **'89** 83
Casserole, Chicken Supreme, **'84** 219
Casserole, Chicken Tortilla, **'81** 166
Casserole, Chicken-Wild Rice, **'84** 241; **'85** 65
Casserole, Macaroni and Chicken, **'80** 260
Casserole, Make-Ahead Chicken, **'84** 241
Casserole, Mexican Chicken, **'82** 143
Casserole, Mexi-Chicken, **'93** 69; **'94** 30
Casserole, Pesto-Chicken, **'94** 231
Casserole, Quick Chicken, **'81** 91
Casserole, Rice-and-Chicken, **'87** 154
Casserole, Shrimp-and-Chicken, **'91** 102
Casserole, Spaghetti Squash and Chicken Skillet, **'94** 134
Casserole, Sunday Chicken, **'83** 290
Casserole, Swiss Chicken, **'90** 67
Celery Skillet, Chicken-and-, **'88** 6
Chafing Dish Chicken, **'82** 284
Chalupas, Chicken, **'79** 185
Chalupas, Chicken-Olive, **'81** 227
Champagne Chicken, **'85** 251
Champagne Sauce, Chicken Breasts with, **'86** 49
Charcoal Broiled Chicken, **'79** 90
Charlemagne, Chicken, **'86** 293
Cheesecake, Chicken-Chile, **'92** 42
Cheesecake, Curried Chicken, **'90** 174
Chilaquiles con Pollo (Tortillas with Chicken), **'81** 66
Chili, White, **'91** 284
Chili, White Lightning Texas, **'92** 321
Chimichangas, Chicken, **'93** 68; **'94** 30
Chimichangas, Oven-Fried Chicken, **'90** 175
Chinese, Chicken, **'94** 33
Chinese Chicken and Vegetables, **'81** 212
Chinese Chicken, Lazy Day, **'81** 3
Chinese-Style Chicken Dinner, **'89** 247
Chinese-Style Dinner, **'84** 26
Chop Suey, Chicken, **'81** 227
Chowder, Cheesy Chicken, **'92** 21
Chowder, Chicken, **'83** 20
Chowder, Creamy Chicken-Vegetable, **'92** 20
Chowder, Curried Chicken-and-Corn, **'92** 21
Chow Mein, Chicken, **'90** 68
Chutney Chicken, **'86** 249
Coconut Chicken with Fresh Fruit, **'93** 294
Company Chicken, **'80** 39; **'83** 125
Continental, Chicken, **'82** 274
Cordon Bleu, Chicken, **'81** 304; **'82** 83; **'86** 37; **'93** 126
Cordon Bleu, Company Chicken, **'82** 274
Cordon Bleu in Mushroom Sauce, Chicken, **'86** 198
Corn Flake Chicken, **'91** 172
Country Captain Chicken, **'94** 252
Country Poulet, **'86** 292
Crabmeat Stuffing, Chicken Breasts with, **'85** 302
Cracked Wheat, "Fried," **'89** 31
Cream Cheese Chicken Breasts, **'90** 234
Creamed Chicken, **'82** 49, 284; **'83** 14
Creamed Chicken and Vegetables, **'91** 90
Creamed Chicken, Company, **'82** 84
Creamed Chicken in a Shell, **'79** 138
Creamed Chicken in Patty Shells, **'86** 123

Creamed Chicken over Confetti Rice Squares, **'81** 282; **'82** 31
Creamed Chicken over Cornbread, **'86** 231
Creamed Ham and Chicken, **'81** M74
Creole, Chicken, **'86** 231; **'89** 33; **'90** 146
Creole Chicken, **'94** 93
Creole Chicken and Rice, **'92** 262
Crêpes, Chicken, **'80** 39
Crêpes, Chicken-Vegetable, **'83** 70
Crêpes, Creamy Chicken, **'81** 200
Crêpes Divan, Elegant, **'81** 91
Crispy Chicken, **'84** 152
Croissants, Chutney-Chicken, **'92** 22
Croquettes and Mushroom Sauce, Chicken, **'91** 220
Croquettes, Chicken, **'81** 133
Croquettes, Crispy Chicken, **'88** 206
Curried Chicken, **'86** 43
Curried Chicken, Quick, **'89** 219
Curried Chicken, Regal, **'84** 110
Curry, Chicken, **'84** 110; **'85** 220; **'86** 21; **'89** 219
Curry, Turban Chicken, **'94** 266
Cutlets with Lemon, Chicken, **'85** 8
Dante's Chicken, **'88** 25
Deviled Chicken, Zesty, **'90** 232
Dijon Chicken, **'81** 156
Dijon Chicken with Pasta, **'90** 318
Dijon-Herb Chicken, **'89** 120
Dilled Chicken Paprika, **'86** 41
Dilly Chicken, **'90** 65
Dinner, Chicken-Mushroom, **'81** 3
Dinner, Chicken Peach, **'79** 77
Dinner, Healthful Chicken, **'83** 232
Dip, Hot Chicken, **'80** 86
Divan Casserole, Chicken, **'82** M203
Divan, Chicken, **'80** M10; **'87** M218
Divan, Curried Chicken, **'80** 83
Divan, Easy Chicken, **'94** 310
Divan, Gourmet Chicken, **'82** 83
Divan, Overnight Chicken, **'83** 198
Divan, Sherried Chicken, **'80** 38
Dixie Manor, Chicken à la, **'85** 3
Dressing, Chicken and Rice, **'79** 288
Dressing, Chicken Cornbread, **'90** 159
Dressing, Tipsy Chicken and, **'88** 151
Drummettes, Down-Home Chicken, **'93** 157
Drummettes, Ginger-Garlic Appetizer, **'93** 157
Drummettes, Orange-Pecan Chicken, **'93** 158
Drummettes, Southwestern Chicken, **'93** 158
Drumsticks, Cajun-Style, **'87** 159
Dumplings, Country Chicken and, **'85** 254
Dumplings, Easy Chicken and, **'86** 21
Dumplings, Old-Fashioned Chicken and, **'79** 55; **'83** 228; **'93** 302
Dumplings with Vegetables, Chicken and, **'85** M56
Easy Chicken, **'89** M129
Empanadas, **'92** 156
Enchiladas, Chicken, **'80** 301; **'86** 296; **'90** 121
Enchiladas, Chicken-and-Spinach, **'91** 222
Enchiladas, Creamy, **'93** 174
Enchiladas, Easy Chicken, **'82** 89; **'86** 231
Enchiladas Terrificas, **'84** 32
Enchiladas Verde, Chicken, **'93** 274
Enchiladas with Spicy Sauce, Chicken, **'84** 76

Chicken (*continued*)

Enchiladas with Tomatillo Sauce, Chicken, '94 231
English Muffin Delight, '82 45
en Papillote, Chicken and Vegetables, '86 145
Fajita Fettuccine, '94 84
Fajita in a Pita, '90 177
Fajitas, Chicken, '88 231; '89 100; '90 204
Fancy Fowl, '81 76; '82 13
Fettuccine, Chicken-and-Tomatoes over, '90 204
Fettuccine, Chicken-Pecan, '86 52
Fiesta Chicken, Spicy, '84 234
Filling, Chicken, '81 200
Filling, Chicken Divan, '81 91
Filling, Chicken-Olive, '81 227
Filling, Curried Chicken, '88 125
Filling Luau, Chicken, '79 81
Fingers, Buttermilk-Pecan Chicken, '93 165
Fingers, Chicken Little, '80 249
Fingers, Herb-Baked Chicken, '86 249
Fingers, No-Fry-Pan Chicken, '91 120
Fingers, Spicy Chicken, '91 162
Flautas, '83 199
Flautas with Guacamole, Chicken, '89 226
Florentine, Chicken, '93 107
Florentine, Chicken-and-Shrimp, '89 64
Florentine with Mushroom Sauce, Chicken, '87 250
Foil, Chicken in, '91 134; '94 93
Fried
  Beaumont Fried Chicken, '88 92
  Best Ever Sunday Chicken, '89 234
  Bites, French-Fried Chicken, '85 160
  Buttermilk Fried Chicken, Company, '86 177
  Cheese-Stuffed Chicken Thighs, Fried, '88 206
  Cream Gravy, Fried Chicken with, '85 241
  Crispy Fried Chicken Breasts, '80 155
  Curried Fried Chicken, '85 160
  Delicious Fried Chicken, '86 156
  Dixie Fried Chicken, '88 14
  Drummettes with Horseradish Sauce, Fried Chicken, '88 207
  Drumsticks, Buttermilk, '87 175
  Fingers, Chicken Almondette, '93 12
  Garlic-Flavored Fried Chicken, '79 147
  Garlic Fried Chicken, '82 148
  Herbed Fried Chicken, '87 91
  Herb-Seasoned Fried Chicken, '80 8
  Lemon-Fried Chicken, '79 77
  Lemon Fried Chicken, '82 275
  Mandarin Chicken, Crispy, '86 119
  Mexican Fried Chicken, '81 166; '87 176
  Nuggets, Golden Chicken, '80 159
  Nuggets, Lemon-Chicken, '87 283
  Oven-Fried Chicken, '84 118; '93 90
  Oven-Fried Chicken, Crisp, '94 220
  Oven-Fried Chicken, Crunchy, '87 163
  Oven-Fried Chicken, Crusty, '79 77
  Oven-Fried Chicken, Golden-Brown, '86 21
  Oven-Fried Chicken Legs, Jalapeño, '94 94
  Oven-Fried Chicken, Nutty, '85 160
  Oven-Fried Chicken, Southern, '86 37

Oven-Fried Chicken with Honey-Butter Sauce, '85 18
Oven-Fried Parmesan Chicken, '81 97; '82 148
Oven-Fried Pecan Chicken, '84 288
Oven-Fried Sesame Chicken, '79 77
Sesame Chicken, '82 148
Special Fried Chicken, '88 220
Spicy Country-Fried Chicken, '82 148
Spicy Fried Chicken, '83 5; '88 129; '94 162
Spinach-Stuffed Chicken Breasts, Fried, '88 206
Sunday Dinner Fried Chicken, '88 110
Super Fried Chicken, '82 148
Traditional Fried Chicken, '82 148
Walnut Chicken, Deep-Fried, '87 175
Wings, Hot Buffalo, '87 176
Fruited Chicken en Crème, '83 264
Garden, Chicken-in-a-, '80 18
Garlic-Spinach Chicken, '92 56
Ginger Chicken and Cashews, '85 M11
Ginger-Nut Chicken, '90 M33
Glazed Chicken, Fruit-, '80 211
Greek Lemon Chicken, '90 65
Grilled Basil Chicken, '93 201
Grilled Chicken, '89 200; '92 170; '94 167
Grilled Chicken Breasts, '84 172
Grilled Chicken, Garlic-, '87 180
Grilled Chicken, Smoky, '85 160
Grilled Chicken with Dill Sauce, '88 162
Grilled Chicken with Tabbouleh Salad, '91 70
Grilled Chicken with Vegetables Vinaigrette, '91 26
Grilled Cumin Chicken, '87 142
Grilled Ginger-Orange Chicken, '91 26
Grilled Jalapeño Chicken, '93 213
Grilled Lime-Jalapeño Chicken, '91 87
Grilled Teriyaki Chicken, '92 59
Grilled Yogurt-Lemon Chicken, '81 111
Gruyère, Chicken Breasts, '80 189
Gumbo, Chicken, '79 199; '90 26
Gumbo, Chicken and Oyster, '81 198
Gumbo, Chicken-and-Sausage, '89 275; '90 256; '94 20
Gumbo, Chicken-Ham-Seafood, '81 6
Gumbo, Combo, '81 198
Gumbo, Easy Chicken, '83 156
Gumbo, The Gullah House, '92 237
Gumbo, Wild Game, '91 290
Gumbo with Smoked Sausage, Chicken, '81 199
Gumbo Ya Ya, '87 210
Hawaiian Chicken, '82 274
Hawaiian, Chicken, '84 88
Hen with Cranberry Pan Gravy, Baked, '94 308
Herbed Chicken, French, '86 89
Herbed Chicken, Sunny, '86 156
Herbed Chicken, Tangy, '87 M302
Herb-Seasoned Chicken Breasts, '93 M325
Honey Chicken, '82 55; '88 67
Honey-Curry Chicken, '87 36
Honey Sauce, Chicken in, '89 82
Honolulu Chicken, '85 52
Hot-and-Spicy Chicken Dinner, '94 M94
Imperial Chicken, '81 238
Italian Chicken, '86 122; '91 206
Italian Chicken Cutlets, '89 82
Jambalaya, '90 26

Jambalaya, Chicken-and-Sausage, '88 200; '91 216
Jambalaya, Red Rice, '91 18
Kabobs, Chicken, '87 141
Kabobs, Chicken-Avocado, '82 9; '83 68
Kabobs, Good-and-Easy Chicken, '85 87
Kabobs, Hawaiian, '85 157
Kabobs, Marinated Chicken, '84 M144
Kabobs, Pineapple-Chicken, '86 M328
Kabobs, Sesame Chicken, '82 165
Kabobs, Soy-Chicken, '86 156
Kabobs Supreme, Chicken, '81 124
Kiev, Chicken, '80 39
Kiev, Cranberry Chicken, '87 250
Kiev, Oven-Baked Chicken, '86 37
Kiev, Oven Chicken, '82 83
King Ranch Chicken, '94 26
la France, Chicken, '86 248
Lasagna, Chicken, '87 M302; '88 90; '92 197; '93 25
Lemonade Chicken, '82 163
Lemon and Wine, Chicken in, '83 281
Lemon Chicken, '81 M138; '86 173
Lemon Chicken and Vegetables, '88 118
Lemon Chicken Breasts, '89 18
Lemon Chicken, Sweet, '79 218
Lemon-Chicken, Sweet, '84 69
Lemon-Dill Chicken, '93 19
Lemon-Dill Chicken Sauté, '91 186
Lemon-Frosted Chicken, '88 170
Lemon-Garlic Chicken, '89 M132; '90 35
Lemon-Herb Chicken, '85 127
Lemon-Pepper Chicken, '89 104
Lemon-Rosemary Chicken, '94 201
Lime Butter, Chicken with, '84 68
Livers
  Bits and Livers, Chicken, '84 222
  en Brochette, Chicken Livers, '84 222
  Italian Sauce, Chicken Livers in, '83 117
  Kabobs, Rumaki, '82 182
  Mushrooms, Chicken Livers with, '81 133
  Omelet, Chicken Liver, '82 44
  Orange Sauce, Chicken Livers in, '82 218
  Party Chicken Livers, '83 242
  Pâté, Chicken Liver, '79 153; '81 235; '83 108; '84 205; '88 M132
  Pâté Maison, '84 222
  Potatoes, Chicken Livers and, '82 218
  Rice, Chicken Livers with, '80 200; '81 58; '84 292
  Rice Dish, Chicken Livers and, '82 218
  Risotto, Chicken Livers, '82 218
  Roll-Ups, Chicken Liver and Bacon, '80 200; '81 57
  Rumaki, '80 M136
  Sautéed Chicken Livers, '80 200; '81 57
  Scrumptious Chicken Livers, '84 230
  Spread, Sherried Liver, '80 86
  Stroganoff, Chicken Livers, '80 200; '81 57
  Supreme, Chicken Livers, '81 298
  Turnovers, Chicken Liver, '79 141
  Wine Sauce, Chicken Livers in, '81 104
  Wine Sauce, Chicken Livers with Marsala, '81 76
Log, Chicken-Pecan, '81 290
Luzianne, Poulet, '86 197
Manicotti, Creamy Chicken, '85 60

Chicken (*continued*)

Marengo, Chicken, '92 70
Marinara, Chicken, '86 77
Marinated Breast of Chicken, '87 123
Marinated Chicken, '87 61
Marinated Chicken Breasts, '90 54
Marinated Chicken Strips and Vegetables,
   '90 110
Marsala, Chicken, '83 137; '89 237
Medaillons in Pepper Pesto, Chicken-Rice,
   '90 97
Mediterranean Chicken, '91 27; '94 72
Medley, Creamy Ham-and-Chicken, '92 272
Mexicana, Chicken, '91 M127
Mexican Chicken, '80 124
Mexican Chicken, Spicy, '82 89
Milano, Chicken, '84 220
Minted Chicken, '81 102
Mole, Chicken, '81 193
Mole Sauce, Chicken with, '93 34
Monterey, Chicken, '82 275
Mornay Sauce, Chicken Breasts in, '81 273
Murphy, Chicken, '89 82
Mushrooms, Chicken-Stuffed, '80 162
Mustard Chicken, '80 222; '86 293; '93 239
Mustard Cream Sauce, Chicken in, '92 181
Nachos, Chicken, '84 244
Nuggets, Baked Chicken, '81 149; '89 18
Nuggets, Golden Chicken, '80 159; '81 237
Nuggets, Lemon-Chicken, '86 337
Nuggets Supreme, Chicken, '85 160
Nuggets with Pineapple Sauce, Chicken,
   '84 236
Onion-Crusted Chicken, '88 40
Orange-Almond Sauce, Chicken in, '79 219;
   '80 13
Orange-Avocado Chicken, '80 38
Orange Chicken, '83 278; '86 M140
Orange Chicken Breasts with Parslied Rice,
   '87 242
Orange, Lime, and Ginger Sauce, Chicken
   with, '92 123
Orange Sauce, Chicken Breasts with, '79 77
Orange Sauce, Chicken in, '83 8
Orange Sauce, Skillet Chicken in, '94 252
Oriental Chicken, '80 40, 208; '82 131
Oriental Chicken with Peanuts, '82 236
Oriental Chicken with Pineapple, '86 42
Oriental Stuffed Pockets, '79 14
Paella, Chicken-Pork-Shrimp, '82 245
Paella, Chicken-Seafood, '88 68
Paella, Shrimp-and-Chicken, '94 168
Paella, Spanish, '85 26
Paella Valenciana, '82 246
Parmesan, Chicken, '83 184
Parmesan Chicken, Crispy, '80 M76
Parmigiana, Chicken, '80 190
Parmigiana, Chicken-Eggplant, '82 212
Pasquale, Chicken, '83 67
Pasta and Chicken, Taste-of-Texas, '92 78
Pasta and Garden Vegetables, '87 192
Pasta, Chicken-and-Broccoli, '87 286
Pasta Platter, Cold, '88 42
Pasta, Quick Chicken and, '93 14
Pastry, Chicken in, '86 122
Pâté, Vegetable-Chicken, '86 66
Peachy Chicken, '90 212
Peanut Butter-Marmalade Chicken, '81 282;
   '82 30

Peas, Chicken with Snow, '83 137
Pecan Chicken, '90 54
Pecan-Rice Dressing, Chicken with, '85 M57
Pecan-Sausage Stuffing, Chicken Breasts
   with, '94 212
Peppers, Chicken Breasts with Curried,
   '90 227
Peppers, Curried Chicken-Stuffed, '87 19
Peppers, Devilish Chicken, '80 65
Pesto Chicken and Pasta, '89 M132
Pesto Chicken with Basil Cream, '89 158
Phyllo, Chicken in, '87 286
Phyllo Pastry, Chicken Breasts in, '91 105
Piccata, Chicken, '83 35; '84 230
Piccata, Herbed Chicken, '88 28
Pie, Biscuit-Topped Chicken, '86 157, 264
Pie, Cheesy Mexican Chicken, '82 142
Pie, Chicken, '81 281; '82 31
Pie, Chicken Pot, '81 210; '82 114; '84 21
Pie, Chicken-Vegetable Pot, '81 281; '82 30
Pie, Deluxe Chicken, '88 298
Pie, Double-Crust Chicken, '87 111
Pie, Double-Crust Chicken Pot, '90 220
Pie, Easy Chicken Pot, '83 156; '89 218
Pie, Egg-Stra Special Chicken, '86 264
Pie, Greek Chicken Phyllo, '92 328
Pie, Montezuma Tortilla, '83 199
Pie, Nana's Chicken, '90 25
Pie, Old-Fashioned Chicken Pot, '92 271
Pie, Savory Southern Chicken, '90 24
Pie, Thick 'n' Crusty Chicken Pot, '87 267;
   '88 102; '89 67
Pie with Cheese Crust, Chicken Pot, '86 264
Pilaf, Chicken, '82 246
Piña Colada Chicken, '86 21
Pineapple Chicken, '83 M194; '85 3
Pineapple, Chicken and, '81 281; '82 30
Pineapple Chicken, Oriental, '84 288
Piquant Chicken, '86 76
Piquant, Chicken, '94 19
Pita, Oriental Chicken, '89 216
Pita, Peppery Chicken in, '93 62
Pitas, Acadian Stuffed, '90 177
Pizza, Chicken, '94 218
Pizza, Gruyère-Chicken, '87 182
Plum Sauce, Chicken with, '82 236
Poached Chicken Breast in Wine, '91 184
Poached Chicken Breasts, Wine-, '85 58
Poached Chicken Breast with Turned
   Vegetables and Chive Sauce, '94 309
Poached Chicken with Black Beans and Salsa,
   '87 217
Poached Chicken with Creamy Mustard
   Sauce, Champagne-, '94 24
Pollo Almendrado (Chicken in Almond Sauce),
   '81 193
Pollo con Calabacita (Mexican Chicken with
   Zucchini), '82 219
Pollo en Mole de Cacahuate (Chicken with
   Peanut Mole Sauce), '80 194
Pollo en Pipián, Mexican, '88 31
Poppy Seed Chicken, '94 108
Potatoes, Chicken-Cheese Stuffed, '86 55
Potatoes, Creamed Beef and
   Chicken-Topped, '83 210
Potatoes, Sweet-and-Sour-Topped, '83 4
Pot, Chicken in a, '81 3
Pot Pie, Chicken, '94 21
Pretzel-Crusted Chicken, '94 252
Primavera, Chicken-Pasta, '91 72
Princess Chicken, '86 122

Provolone, Chicken, '93 323
Puffs, Appetizer Chicken, '85 72
Puffs, Chicken Nut, '81 260
Quiche, Chicken Divan, '88 M125
Quiche, Chicken-Pecan, '91 206
Quiche Noël, '82 310
Quick Chicken, '90 117
Ragout with Cheddar Dumplings, Chicken,
   '94 44
Rice, Chicken Caruso and, '89 177
Rice Pilaf, Chicken Breasts with Fruited,
   '92 307
Rice, Shortcut Chicken and, '90 220
Rice, Spicy Chicken and, '88 200
Roast Chicken, '93 14
Roast Chicken and Brown Rice, '83 268
Roast Chicken and Vegetables, '81 3
Roast Chicken with Pineapple-Mustard Glaze,
   '89 83
Roasted Chicken, Herb-, '87 155
Roasted Chicken, Rice-Stuffed, '88 38
Rockefeller Chicken, '79 219
Rolls à la Swiss, Chicken-and-Ham, '92 42
Rolls, Chicken-Asparagus, '86 M211
Rolls, Crispy Chicken, '84 288
Rolls Élégante, Chicken, '80 210
Rolls, Hearts of Palm Chicken, '89 201
Rolls, Hearty Salad, '81 206
Rolls Jubilee, Chicken, '87 118
Rolls, Mexican Chicken, '93 242
Rolls, Pesto-Stuffed Chicken, '93 82
Rollups, Cheesy Chicken, '82 44
Rollups, Chicken, '85 179; '88 38
Rollups, Chicken and Spinach, '80 90;
   '82 M68
Rollups, Imperial Chicken, '80 217
Rollups in Gravy, Chicken, '83 184
Rollups, Sunshine Chicken, '85 251
Romano, Chicken alla, '83 M58
Romano, Chicken Breasts, '79 218
Romanoff, Chicken, '84 292
Roquefort Chicken, '89 320
Rotelle, Chicken and Tomato with, '87 108
Salads
   Almond-Chicken Salad Shanghai,
      '90 160
   Almond Salad, Chicken-, '81 133
   Aloha Chicken Salad, '80 297
   Amandine, Chicken Salad, '81 37
   Ambrosia, Chicken Salad, '85 216
   Apple Salad, Chicken-, '90 216
   Artichoke-Chicken-Rice Salad, '94 132
   Artichokes, Chicken Salad with, '86 186
   Asparagus-Chicken Salad, '89 83
   Aspic-Topped Chicken Salad, '88 88
   Avocado-Chicken Salad, '87 107
   Avocado Salad, Chicken-, '80 139
   Avocado Salad, Fruited Chicken-,
      '82 101
   Avocado Salad Platter, Chicken-, '83 2
   Avocado Salad, Tossed Chicken-, '80 4
   Avocados, Chicken Salad in, '85 216
   Baked Chicken Salad, '86 297; '87 176
   Basil-Chicken-Vegetable Salad, '92 162
   BLT Chicken Salad, '87 144
   Blue Cheese Chicken Salad, '94 81
   Broccoli-Chicken Salad, '90 129
   Celery Salad, Chicken-, '81 187
   Chicken Salad, '86 232, 261
   Chop Suey Salad, '81 37
   Chutney-Chicken Salad, '87 74

Chicken, Salads *(continued)*

Chutney Salad, Chicken, **'82** 108
Coleslaw, Chicken, **'84** 2
Cream Puff Bowl, Chicken Salad in,
 '86 232
Crunchy Chicken Salad, **'86** 157, 207
Curried Chicken-and-Orange Salad,
 '87 144
Curried Chicken-Rice Salad, **'92** 190
Curried Chicken Salad, **'79** 219; **'84** 66;
 '85 96; **'86** 131; **'89** 176
Curried Chicken Salad with Asparagus,
 '81 36
Dilled Chicken Salad, **'91** 212
Exotic Luncheon Salad, **'83** 210
Fancy Chicken Salad, **'79** 55
Filling, Chicken Salad, **'87** 106
Fruit, Chicken Salad with, **'82** 171
Fruited Chicken Salad, **'84** 25, 290;
 '88 88; **'90** 318
Fruited Chicken Salad in Avocados,
 '87 41
Fruit Salad, Chicken-, **'82** 79; **'90** 234
Fruity Chicken Salad, **'83** 157
Ginger Salad, Fried Chicken, **'93** 290
Grapes, Chicken Salad with, **'86** 117
Green Salad with Chicken, Mixed,
 '80 54
Hot Chicken Salad, **'81** 201; **'83** 196
Hot Chicken Salad, Country Club-Style,
 '86 10
Hot Chicken Salad, Crunchy, **'80** 138
Hot Chicken Salad Pinwheel, **'80** 139
Italian, Chicken Salad, **'89** 18
Layered Chicken Salad, **'89** 162
Macadamia Chicken Salad, **'80** 138
Macaroni-Chicken Salad, **'85** 296;
 '86 302
Macaroni-Chicken Salad, Dilled, **'92** 142
Mama Hudson's Chicken Salad, **'93** 238
Mandarin Chicken, Carousel, **'79** 88
Mango, Chicken Salad with, **'86** 215
Marinated Chicken-Grape Salad, **'85** 74
Marinated Chicken-Raspberry Salad,
 '93 190
Mexican Chicken Salad, **'85** 84; **'88** 272
Minted Chicken Salad, **'92** 104
Mold, Chicken-Cucumber, **'80** 175
Mold, Chicken Salad, **'83** 80; **'84** 163
Nectarine Chicken Salad, **'79** 175
Old-Fashioned Chicken Salad, **'83** 79
Oriental Chicken Salad, **'85** 216;
 '88 271; **'91** 43
Oriental, Chicken Salad, **'90** 146
Pasta-Chicken Salad, Tarragon, **'87** 155
Pasta Salad, Chicken, **'88** 89
Pasta Salad, Grilled Chicken-, **'94** 64
Pea Salad, Chicken-, **'83** 218
Persian Chicken Salad, **'81** 12
Pineapple-Chicken Salad Pie, **'80** 138
Pineapple-Nut Chicken Salad, **'83** 80
Pocket, Chicken Salad in a, **'88** 139
Polynesian Chicken Salad, **'88** 272
Poulet Rémoulade, **'87** 144
Rice Salad, Chicken-, **'81** 203
Rice Salad, Hot Chicken-and-, **'83** 22
Rice Salad, Nutty Chicken-, **'83** 157
Ring, Chicken Salad, **'90** 123
Ring Salad, Chicken Jewel, **'83** 282

Roasted Chicken Salad, **'93** 14
Rolls, Hearty Salad, **'81** 206
Sandwiches, Chicken-Salad Finger,
 '85 119
Southwestern Chicken Salad, **'88** 88
Spaghetti Salad, Chicken-, **'90** 146
Special Chicken Salad, **'85** 82; **'87** 183;
 '88 M193
Spinach Tossed Salad, Chicken-and-,
 '83 157
Spread, Chicken Salad Party, **'88** M8
Stack-Up Salad, Chicken, **'83** 80
Summer Chicken Salad, **'83** 145
Super Chicken Salad, **'82** 174
Supreme, Chicken Salad, **'79** 107, 152;
 '89 176
Taco Salad, Chicken, **'94** M136
Tahitian Chicken Salad, **'84** 120
Tarragon Chicken Salad, **'90** 199
Tarts, Chicken Salad, **'84** 257
Tortellini Salad, Chicken, **'87** 288
Tropical Chicken Boats for Two, **'82** 186
Tropical Chicken Salad, **'85** 216
Twist, Chicken Salad with a, **'84** 221
Vegetable-Chicken Salad, **'91** 287
Vegetable-Chicken Vinaigrette Salad,
 '86 135
Walnut-Chicken Salad, **'89** 14
Walnut Salad, Sunburst Chicken-and-,
 '93 91
Wild Rice-Chicken Salad, **'83** 146
Saltimbocca alla Romana, Chicken, **'80** 212
San Antonio-Style Chicken, **'81** 166
Sandwich, Chicken Parmigiana, **'94** 65
Sandwich, Crispy Chicken, **'81** 114
Sandwiches, Baked Chicken, **'79** 164;
 '80 130; **'84** 165
Sandwiches, Cheesy Chicken, **'82** 190
Sandwiches, Chicken-Almond Pocket,
 '81 240; **'83** 69
Sandwiches, Chicken Club, **'86** 160
Sandwiches, Hot Brown, **'80** 202
Sandwiches, Hot Chicken, **'83** 291
Sandwiches, Marinated Chicken, **'86** M45
Sandwiches, Puffed Chicken, **'82** 35
Sandwiches, Toasted Chicken-and-Cheese,
 '85 242
Sandwich, Marinated Chicken in a, **'86** 185
Sauce, Chicken Curry, **'90** 117
Sauce, Creamy Chicken, **'81** 91
Saucy Chick-Wiches, **'81** 25; **'82** 31; **'83** 34
Sautéed Chicken Breasts, **'87** 36
Sauté, Savory Chicken, **'88** 254; **'89** 120
Sauté, Sherry-Chicken, **'87** 218
Sauté, Sweet Pepper-Chicken, **'89** 104
Scallopini with Lemon Sauce, Chicken,
 '86 156
Scallopini with Peppers, Chicken, **'85** 78
Scarborough Chicken, **'80** 38
Scotch Cream, Chicken in, **'88** 42
Seasoned Browned Chicken, **'85** 25
Seasoned Chicken, Crunchy, **'87** 217
Seasoning Blend, Poultry, **'88** 28
Sesame Chicken, **'85** 252; **'86** 122
Sesame Chicken, Hawaiian, **'81** 106
Sesame Chicken with Noodles, **'88** M125
Sherried Chicken, **'79** 214
Sherried Chicken with Artichokes, **'87** 143
Sherry Chicken with Rice, **'81** 97
Skillet, Cheesy Chicken, **'80** 115
Skillet Chicken, **'81** 180

Skillet Chicken Dinner, **'86** 249; **'89** 247
Skillet Chicken, Spicy, **'94** 220
Skillet Company Chicken, **'82** 60
Snow Peas, Chicken with, **'83** 187
Soufflé, Chicken-Chestnut, **'79** 107
Soups
 Artichoke, and Mushroom Soup,
  Chicken, **'92** 324
 Broccoli-and-Chicken Soup, **'90** 202
 Chicken Soup, **'81** 98
 Chowder Sauterne, Chicken, **'84** 235
 Chunky Chicken-Noodle Soup, **'88** 12
 Cream of Chicken Soup, **'85** 243
 Cream Soup, Chicken-Almond, **'92** 21
 Curried Chicken Soup, **'86** 34
 Enchilada Soup, Chicken, **'86** 22
 Ham, and Oyster Soup, Chicken,
  '79 198
 Homemade Chicken Soup, **'82** 34
 Lime Soup, **'88** 31
 Mexican Chicken Soup, **'84** 234
 Noodle Soup, Chicken, **'80** 264
 Pepper-and-Chicken Soup, Roasted,
  '90 58
 Quick Chicken Soup, **'86** M72
 Rice Soup, Chicken-and-, **'88** 236
 Sopa de Lima, **'79** 211
 Vegetable Soup, Chicken-, **'88** 18
Soy and Wine, Chicken in, **'84** 26
Spaghetti, Chicken, **'83** 105; **'87** 221
Spaghetti, Chicken-Vegetable, **'92** 281
Special Occasion Chicken, **'91** 206
Spiced Chicken, Crunchy, **'85** M57
Spiced Fruited Chicken with Almond Rice,
 '81 195
Spicy Chicken Dish, **'87** 267; **'88** 103;
 '89 66
Spinach Fettuccine, Easy Chicken with,
 '88 89
Spinach Noodles, Chicken and, **'82** 19
Spread, Festive Chicken, **'87** 158
Spread, Low-Fat Chicken, **'82** 290
Spread, Tasty Chicken, **'84** 193
Steamed Dinner, Easy, **'83** M314
Stew and Dumplings, Chicken, **'84** 4
Stew, Bama Brunswick, **'87** 4
Stew, Breeden Liles's Brunswick, **'91** 14
Stew, Brunswick, **'80** 264
Stew, Brunswick Chicken, **'87** 4
Stew, Chili-Chicken, **'90** 319
Stew, Dan Dickerson's Brunswick, **'91** 16
Stew, Gay Neale's Brunswick, **'91** 17
Stew, Georgian Brunswick, **'92** 35
Stew, Jeff Daniel's Brunswick, **'91** 16
Stew, Sonny Frye's Brunswick, **'87** 4
Stew, Strader, **'89** 28
Stew, Van Doyle's Family-Size Brunswick,
 '91 14
Stew, Virginian Brunswick, **'92** 34
Stew, Virginia Ramsey's Favorite Brunswick,
 '91 16
Stir-Fried Chicken Curry, **'87** 51
Stir-Fried Chicken, Zesty, **'83** 82
Stir-Fry, Apple-Sesame-Chicken, **'92** 226
Stir-Fry Chicken à l'Orange, **'83** 82
Stir-Fry, Chicken and Vegetable, **'82** 237
Stir-Fry Chicken-and-Vegetables, **'86** 68
Stir-Fry Chicken and Vegetables, **'86** 249
Stir-Fry, Chicken-Broccoli, **'82** 33
Stir-Fry, Chicken-Vegetable, **'83** 151;
 '84 13, 141

Stir-Fry, Chicken-Zucchini, **'84** 50
Stir-Fry, Chinese Chicken, **'90** 100
Stir-Fry, Easy Chicken, **'91** 124
Stir-Fry, Herb-Chicken, **'89** 177
Stir-Fry, Hurry-Up Chicken, **'91** 124
Stir-Fry, Kyoto Orange-Chicken, **'87** 96
Stir-Fry, Mexican, **'92** 126
Stir-Fry, Orange-Chicken, **'84** 68
Stir-Fry, Pineapple-Chicken, **'89** 176
Stir-Fry, Shiitake-Chicken, **'89** 61
Stir-Fry Vegetables with Chicken, **'84** 195
Stock, Light Poultry, **'90** 31
Strips, Zippy Chicken, **'84** 205
Stroganoff, Chicken-and-Broccoli, **'89** M248
Stuffed Chicken Breasts, **'85** 291; **'87** 36;
 '88 50; **'89** 274
Stuffed Chicken Breasts, Peach-, **'79** 177
Stuffed Chicken Breasts Sardou, **'87** 269
Stuffed Chicken Breasts, Walnut-, **'85** 293
Stuffed Chicken Breasts with White Grape
 Sauce, **'80** 38
Stuffed Chicken, Crab-, **'84** 101
Stuffed Chicken in Puff Pastry, Spinach-,
 '92 125
Stuffed Chicken, Rice-, **'81** 4
Stuffed Chicken Rolls, Spinach-, **'86** 248
Stuffed Chicken Thighs, **'82** 84
Stuffed Chicken, Vegetable-, **'89** M65
Stuffed Chicken, Wild Rice-, **'79** 219
Stuffed Chicken with Sautéed Peppers and
 Mushrooms, Herb-, **'91** 26
Stuffed Chicken with Tomato-Basil Pasta,
 Basil-, **'94** M204
Sunshiny Chicken, **'81** 309
Supreme, Hot Chicken, **'81** 76
Suprêmes de Volaille à Blanc (Chicken
 Breasts in Cream Sauce), **'82** 83
Sweet-and-Sour Chicken, **'79** 106; **'83** 184;
 '84 218; **'86** 217, 240; **'90** 161; **'91** 202
Sweet-and-Sour Chicken Nuggets, **'90** 168
Sweet-and-Sour Chicken Wings, **'90** 206
Sweet-and-Sour Lemon Chicken, **'84** 93
Sweet-and-Sour Shrimp and Chicken,
 '87 267; **'88** 103; **'89** 66
Swiss Chicken Thighs, **'94** 282
Szechwan Chicken, **'83** 85
Szechwan Chicken with Cashews, **'81** 212
Tacos, Chicken-and-Bean, **'93** 293
Tahitian Chicken, **'84** 68
Tamales, Chicken, **'88** 151
Tangy Chicken, **'85** 251; **'86** 292; **'87** 35
Tarragon Chicken, **'86** 231
Tarts, Deviled Chicken, **'94** 14
Tempura Delight, Chicken, **'85** 66
Teriyaki, Chicken, **'80** M76
Teriyaki Chicken, **'91** 163
Teriyaki Chicken Wings, **'85** 300; **'86** 18
Terrine, Chicken-Vegetable, **'84** 131
Terrine, Cold Chicken-Leek, **'92** 145
Terrine Ring, Chicken, **'84** 132
Terrine, Vegetable-Chicken, **'83** 224
Tetrazzini, Cheesy Chicken, **'83** M87
Tetrazzini, Chicken, **'79** 268; **'80** M75;
 '83 288
Tomato Aspic, Chicken in, **'84** 190
Tortilla Stack, Cheesy Chicken-, **'86** 3
Toss, Quick Chicken, **'87** M124
Tostadas, Chicken, **'93** 204

Valencia, Chicken-and-Rice, **'85** 113
Vegetable Platter, Chicken-and-, **'88** M52
Vegetables, Chicken and, **'88** 165
Vegetables with Ginger-Soy Sauce, Chicken
 and, **'91** 32
Vermouth, Chicken and Vegetables,
 '87 M37
Véronique, Chicken, **'84** 260; **'85** 302
Waffles, Southern Chicken-Pecan, **'82** 231
Walnut Chicken, **'85** 126
Walnut Chicken and Vegetables, **'85** 194
Walnut Chicken, Crispy, **'90** 89
Wellington, Chicken Breasts, **'84** 22
Wild Rice, Chicken and, **'79** 248
Wild Rice, Chicken-Fried, **'89** 24; **'91** 132
Wild Rice, Elegant Chicken with, **'80** M76
Wild Rice Supreme, Chicken-, **'79** 77
Wine, Chicken in White, **'81** 97
Wine Sauce, Chicken and Mushrooms in,
 '81 109
Wine Sauce, Chicken in, **'80** 8
Wings, Broiled Chicken, **'80** 149
Wings, Honey-Glazed Chicken, **'91** 251
Wings, Satan's, **'87** 214
Wontons, Chicken, **'92** 284
Yogurt Chicken, Savory, **'91** 238; **'92** 28
Yogurt-Sesame Chicken, **'90** 216

Chili

Bake, Chili Hominy, **'81** 282; **'82** 58
Basic Chili, **'82** M11; **'93** 326
Basic Chili Embellished, **'93** 327
Basic Chili Goes Southwest, **'93** 326
Before-and-After Burner, Roy's, **'89** 316
Burgers, Open-Face Chili, **'82** 31;
 '83 33
Casserole, Chili, **'90** 176
Casserole, Chili-Rice, **'79** 54
Casserole, Hominy-Chili, **'86** 255
Cheese-Topped Chili, **'82** M11
Cheesy Chili, **'82** 310
Chili, **'87** 17; **'93** 89
Choo-Choo Chili, **'89** 316
Chuck Wagon Chili, **'81** 282; **'82** 57
Chunky Chili, **'82** M282; **'86** 3
Company Chili, **'82** 311; **'83** 30
con Carne, Beef and Sausage Chili, **'83** 284
con Carne, Chili, **'82** 310; **'83** 30; **'84** 72;
 '86 2
con Carne, Favorite Chili, **'86** 293
con Carne, Quick-and-Easy Chili, **'86** 2
Cowboy Chili, **'86** 2
Dip, Cheesy Chili, **'80** 150
Dip, Chili, **'82** 161; **'88** 218; **'89** 47;
 '91 143
Dip, Chili-and-Cheese, **'89** 328
Dogs, Chili-Cheese, **'81** M176
Double-Meat Chili, **'79** 269; **'80** 12

Easy Chili, **'82** 310; **'83** 30
Easy Chili with Beans, **'92** 262
Easy Texas Chili, **'90** 201
Eggplant Chili, **'85** 88
Firestarter Chili, **'93** 34
Friday Night Chili, **'86** 228
Hot Spiced Chili, **'83** 214
Hotto Lotto Chili, **'89** 316
I-Cious, Chili-, **'89** 315
"In-the-Red" Chili over "Rolling-in-Dough"
 Biscuits, **'92** 80
Kielbasa Chili, Hearty, **'91** 28
Lolly's Pop Chili, **'89** 316
Lunchtime Chili, **'81** 230
Manicotti, Chili, **'89** 247
Meat Loaf, Chili, **'81** 275
Meaty Chili, **'81** 282; **'82** 58
Meaty Chili with Beans, **'85** 250
Mexican Chili, **'89** 18
Microwave Chili, **'91** M232
Mom's Chili, **'93** 292
Noodles, Chili with, **'81** 282; **'82** 57
Pastry Cups, Chili in, **'90** 68
Pie, Chili-Tamale, **'82** 9; **'83** 68
Potato Chili, Savory, **'83** 284
Potatoes, Chili-Topped, **'83** 3
Potatoes, South-of-the-Border Stuffed,
 '86 54
Quick-and-Easy Chili, **'92** 20
Quick and Simple Chili, **'81** 282;
 '82 58
Quick Chili, **'83** 283
Ranch Chili and Beans, **'79** 270;
 '80 11
Red Chili, **'93** 108
Red Chili, North Texas, **'87** 303
Rice, Chili with, **'82** M11
Roundup Chili, **'79** 269; **'80** 12
Salad, Spicy Chili, **'86** 71
Sauce, Chili, **'81** 175; **'94** 287
Sauce, Chili Meat, **'83** 4
Sauce, Chunky Chili, **'85** 188
Sauce, Spicy Chili, **'87** 127
Sausage-Beef Chili, **'86** 232
Sausage Chili, Beefy, **'82** M11
Simple Chili, **'79** 269; **'80** 11
Soup, Chili Vegetable, **'94** 120
South-of-the-Border Chili, **'83** 283;
 '91 283
Southwestern Chili, **'91** 284
Spaghetti, Herbed Chili-, **'84** 222
Speedy Chili, **'92** 66
Spicy Chili, Old-Fashioned, **'79** 269;
 '80 11
Surprise, Chili, **'82** 229
Texas Championship Chili, **'81** 54
Texas Chili, Hot, **'80** 222; **'81** 77
Texas-Style Chili, **'82** 311; **'83** 30
Tex-Mex Chili, **'83** 26
Topping, Chili, **'84** 246; **'94** 22
Tree-Hunt Chili, **'87** 292
Turkey-Bean Chili, **'88** M213
Vegetable Chili, **'91** 28
Vegetarian Chili, **'84** 280, 327;
 '91 284
Venison Chili, **'82** 216; **'86** 3;
 '87 304
Venison Chili, Hot, **'91** 283
White Chili, **'91** 284
White Lightning Texas Chili, **'92** 321
Zippy Chili, **'87** 110

Chocolate

Banana Pops, **'84** 44
Bars and Cookies
    Almond Chip Balls, Toasted, **'84** 240
    Almond-Chocolate Bars, **'83** 304
    Almond Cream Confections, **'87** 198;
      '90 310
    Almond Surprise Cookies, Chocolate-,
      '88 M45
    Biscotti Cioccolata, **'93** 268
    Blond Nut Squares, **'82** 156
    Bonbons, Chocolate-Filled, **'89** 162
    Bran Raisin Jumbos, Chocolate-, **'91** 142
    Brazil Squares, **'82** 306
    Brownie Alaskas, **'83** 299
    Brownie Bars, Cinnamon, **'81** 230
    Brownie Chip Cookies, **'90** 320
    Brownie-Mint Dessert, **'82** 227
    Brownie Mix, **'82** 6
    Brownies, Amaretto, **'86** 246
    Brownies, Biscuit Mix, **'94** M51
    Brownies, Buttermilk Cake, **'87** 198
    Brownies, Candy Bar, **'92** 204
    Brownies, Chewy Marshmallow,
      '83 306
    Brownies, Chocolate-Banana, **'80** 160
    Brownies, Chocolate Chip, **'81** 162
    Brownies, Chocolate Chip-Peanut
      Butter, **'84** 73
    Brownies, Chocolate Ice Cream,
      '89 124
    Brownies, Chocolate-Kahlúa, **'93** 99
    Brownies, Chocolate-Mint, **'85** M294;
      '88 80
    Brownies, Chocolate-Nut, **'81** 129
    Brownies, Chocolate-Peanut Butter
      Chip, **'91** 306
    Brownies, Chocolate-Pecan, **'81** 64
    Brownies, Chocolate-Peppermint,
      '88 262
    Brownies, Chocolate Tea, **'83** 79
    Brownies, Chocolate-Walnut, **'89** 325
    Brownies, Choco-Mallow, **'87** 198;
      '90 309
    Brownies, Cream Cheese Swirl, **'79** 51
    Brownies, Crème de Menthe, **'83** 244
    Brownies, Crunch-Crust, **'87** 198
    Brownies, Easy, **'83** 245
    Brownies, Favorite, **'86** 158
    Brownies, Frosted Peanut Butter,
      '92 272
    Brownies, German Cream Cheese,
      '80 269
    Brownies, Heavenly Hash, **'83** 245
    Brownies, Heavenly Honey, **'79** 83
    Brownies, Macadamia-Fudge Designer,
      '94 51
    Brownies, Mint Julep, **'93** 165
    Brownies, Mississippi Mud, **'89** M25
    Brownies, Mocha, **'87** 93
    Brownies, Mother's, **'93** 239
    Brownies, No-Bake, **'94** 330
    Brownies, Nutty Blonde, **'81** 64
    Brownies, Nutty Cocoa, **'81** 64
    Brownies, Nutty Fudge, **'80** M171
    Brownies, Oat, **'89** 59
    Brownies, Oat 'n' Crunch, **'91** 233
    Brownies, Peanut Butter, **'87** 199
    Brownies, Pistachio-Mint, **'94** 50
    Brownies, Praline, **'93** 243
    Brownies, Quick, **'87** M302

Brownies, Quick and Easy, **'82** 6
Brownies, Raspberry, **'92** 274
Brownies, Rocky Road, **'86** 320
Brownies, Southern Chocolate-Mint,
    '93 216
Brownies, Triple Decker, **'92** 319
Brownies, Walnut-Cream Cheese,
    '84 240
Brownies, White Chocolate, **'89** 169
Brownies with Chocolate Chunks,
    Blonde, **'91** 271
Brownies with Mocha Frosting, **'94** 292
Brownie Waffle Cookies, **'86** 245
Butter Cookies, Chocolate-Tipped,
    '84 258; **'90** 312
Butter Pecan Turtle Bars, **'90** 70
Butterscotch Bars, Chocolate-, **'81** 197
By-Cracky Bars, **'84** 212
Caramel-Filled Chocolate Cookies,
    '92 319
Caramel Layer Squares, Chocolate-,
    '79 83
Cherry Cookies, Chocolate-, **'85** 324
Chess Squares, Chocolate, **'92** 45
Chewies, Chocolate, **'93** 216
Chewies, Easy Chocolate, **'93** 296
Chewy Chocolate Chip Squares, **'91** 175
Chewy Chocolate Cookies, **'80** 208
Chip Bars, Chocolate, **'81** 130
Chip Cookies, **'84** 120
Chip Cookies, Chocolate, **'86** 245;
    '90 193
Chip Cookies, Chocolate-Chocolate,
    '82 35
Chippers, Chocolate, **'92** 206
Chips Cookies, Loaded-with-, **'87** 223
Chip Squares, Chocolate, **'83** 170;
    '89 143
Chocolate Chip Cookies, Mom Ford's,
    '94 287
Cinnamon Bars, Chocolate, **'82** 209
Cocoa Drop Cookies, **'80** 217
Cocoa Kiss Cookies, **'85** 171
Coconut Squares, Chocolate-, **'90** 70
Crème de Menthe Bars, Chocolate-,
    '86 245
Crème de Menthe Bites, Chocolate,
    '88 285
Crème de Menthe Squares, **'93** 256
Crispies, Chocolate-Peanut, **'93** 80
Crispy Cookies, Chocolate, **'85** 115
Crumble Bars, Choco-, **'79** 292
Crunch Cookies, Chocolate, **'91** 316
Crunchies, Chocolate, **'92** 50
Date-Nut Chocolate Chip Cookies, Rich,
    '92 207
Deluxe Chocolate Chip Cookies,
    '79 216
Derby Brownies, Special, **'90** 94
Devil Doggies, **'84** 37
Different Chocolate Chip Cookies,
    '83 114
Double Chip Cookies, **'81** 301
Double Chocolate Chip Cookies, **'79** 217
Doubly-Good Chocolate Cookies,
    '82 M185
Dream Bars, Chocolate, **'79** 256;
    '82 298
Drop Cookies, Chocolate, **'84** 36
Easy Chocolate Chewies, **'94** 234
Forget 'em Cookies, **'83** 256

Frosted Chocolate-Cherry Cookies,
    '89 294
Fudge Bars, **'86** 93
Fudge Bars, Yummy, **'87** 158
Fudge Puddles, **'94** 292
German Chocolate Chess Squares,
    '94 51
Giant Chocolate Chip Cookies, **'84** 119
Gingerbread Cookies, Chocolate-,
    '94 293
Jumbo Chocolate Chip Cookies, **'82** 110
Keyboard Cookies, **'94** M330
Kissy Cookies, **'93** 331
Light Chocolate Chip Cookies, **'86** 46
Log Cookies, Chocolate-Tipped, **'87** 294
Lollapalooza, **'94** 194
Macaroon Cookies, Chocolate, **'88** 217
Macaroons, Chocolate, **'83** 300; **'87** 57
Meltaways, Chocolate, **'81** 302
Melt-Aways, Chocolate Chip, **'84** 118
Meringue-Chocolate Chip Bars, **'84** 118
Meringue Kiss Cookies, **'86** 121
Mint Chip Cookies, Chocolate-, **'86** 245
Mint Cookies, Chocolate-, **'92** 206
Mint Snaps, Chocolate-, **'83** 103; **'84** 96
Monster Cookies, **'84** 36
Nugget Cookies, **'79** 291
Nut Chews, Chocolate-, **'81** 92
Nut Freezer Cookies, Chocolate-,
    '88 217
Nutty Choco Snacks, **'83** 305
Nutty Oatmeal-Chocolate Chip Cookies,
    '82 M185
Oatmeal Bars, Chocolate-Topped,
    '86 110
Oatmeal-Chocolate Chippers, **'90** 218
Oatmeal Cookies, Chocolate-, **'80** 105
Oatmeal Cookies, Chocolate Chip-,
    '84 119
Oatmeal-Peanut Butter Chocolate Chip
    Cookies, **'92** 207
Orange-Chocolate Cookies, **'83** 113
Orange Delights, Chocolate-, **'93** 52
Peanut Butter and Chocolate Chunk
    Cookies, **'94** 169
Peanut Butter-and-Fudge Bars,
    '80 M172
Peanut Butter Bars, **'84** 243
Peanut Butter-Chocolate Chip Cookies,
    Freezer, **'86** 230
Peanut Butter-Chocolate Kiss Cookies,
    '86 49
Peanut Butter Cones, Chocolate-,
    '85 14
Peanut Butter Cookies, Chocolate-,
    '85 90
Peanut Butter Cups, Chocolate-, **'85** 14
Peanut Butter Fingers, **'79** 256
Peanut Butter Squares, Chocolate Chip-,
    '84 118
Peanut Chip Cookies, Choco-, **'92** 318
Peanut Cookies, Chocolate-, **'83** 223
Peppermint Squares, Chocolate-,
    '81 119
Pinwheel Cookies, **'93** 316
Pinwheel Cookies, Chocolate, **'86** 245
Pudding Cookies, Chocolate Chip-,
    '93 21
Pumpkin-Chocolate Chip Cookies,
    '93 235
Sandwich Cookies, Chocolate, **'81** 192

Sandwich Cookies, Choco-Nut, '84 200
Sandwiches, Chocolate Cookie Ice
   Cream, '87 147
Seashells, Chocolate, '91 178
Shortbread Wafers, Cocoa, '88 243
Snappers, Jumbo Chocolate, '81 218
Snowball Cookies, Chocolate, '82 295
Snowflake Cookies, Chocolate, '89 329
Sugar-Coated Chocolate Cookies,
   '92 274
Sugar Cookies, Double-Chocolate,
   '92 206
Super Chocolate Chunk Cookies,
   '88 217
Surprise Bonbon Cookies, '88 119
Surprise Cookies, Choco, '80 60
Teasers, Chocolate, '87 44
Toffee Treats, '89 330
White Chocolate Cookies, Chunky
   Macadamia Nut, '92 207
White Chocolate-Macadamia Nut
   Cookies, '94 315
Whoopie Pies, '86 246
Yummy Bars, '92 171
Baskets with Berry Cream, Chocolate,
   '92 118
Beverages
   Brandied Chocolate, Flaming, '80 M290
   Café au Lait, German Chocolate,
      '92 264
   Café Colombian Royal, '80 M290
   Café Mexicano, '92 208
   Cappuccino, Chocolate Castle, '84 53
   Cocoa Mix, Instant, '86 332
   Coffee, Chocolate, '82 43
   Coffee, Chocolate-Almond, '84 54
   Coffee, Cocoa-, '83 55
   Coffee, Mexican, '83 175, 275; '88 247;
      '91 78; '93 310; '94 97
   "Concrete," Abaco Mocha, '94 114
   "Concrete," Cardinal Sin, '94 113
   "Concrete," Foxtreat, '94 113
   Hot Chocolate, '94 290
   Hot Chocolate, Creole, '80 M290
   Hot Chocolate Deluxe, '90 272
   Hot Chocolate, Favorite, '83 55
   Hot Chocolate, French, '86 328
   Hot Chocolate Mix, Deluxe, '80 M290
   Hot Chocolate Mix, Spicy, '85 278
   Hot Chocolate, Old-Fashioned, '85 23
   Hot Chocolate, Special, '82 5
   Hot Chocolate, Spiced, '80 50
   Hot Chocolate, Spicy, '85 278
   Hot Cocoa Mix, '81 287
   Hot Cocoa Mix, Minted, '91 316
   Hot Cocoa Mix, Mocha-Flavored,
      '91 316
   Hot Cocoa, Quick, '82 5
   King Alfonso, '80 259
   Malt, Banana-Chocolate, '89 170
   Malt, Chocolate, '86 183
   Marshmallow Chocolate, Hot Laced,
      '93 53
   Mexican-Style Chocolate, '81 187
   Milk, French Chocolate, '79 38
   Milk Shake, Chocolate-Banana, '94 113
   Mocha Chocolate Fluff, '89 170
   Mocha Cocoa, '83 318

Mocha-Cocoa Mix, Hot, '82 296
Mocha Coffee, '85 M329
Mocha Cream, Café, '84 54
Mocha Deluxe Hot Drink, '82 289
Mocha Espresso, Italian, '82 254
Mocha Frosty, '92 44
Mocha, Hot, '84 60
Mocha, Mexican, '93 M341
Mocha Polka, '89 171
Mocha Punch, '84 58, 166
Mocha, Quick Viennese, '79 232
Mocha, Spirited Hot, '91 M260
Shake, Chocolate Mint, '89 170
Sipper, Chocolate, '88 83
Smoothie, Chocolate-Mint, '84 166
Bites, Snowy Chocolate, '90 47
Black-Bottom Goodies, '89 251
Bread, Chocolate Chip-Banana, '90 267
Bread, Chocolate Date-Nut, '81 284
Bread, Chocolate Loaf, '88 M188
Bread, Chocolate-Zucchini, '93 308
Bread, Cocoa-Nut Swirl, '80 257
Brickle Squares, Chocolate, '94 290
Buns, Chocolate-Cinnamon, '85 5
Buns, Chocolate Sticky, '81 300; '82 124
Cakes and Tortes
   Almond Cake, Chocolate-, '91 248
   Almond Cake with Cherry Filling,
      Chocolate-, '84 225
   Angel Cake, Chocolate, '88 128
   Angel Food Cake, Chocolate, '87 21;
      '90 111; '91 55
   Angel Food Cake with Custard Sauce,
      Chocolate, '88 259
   Apricot-Filled Chocolate Torte, '90 107
   Banana Cake, Chocolate-, '86 138
   Banana-Cocoa Cupcakes, '80 130
   Banana Loaf, Chocolate Chip-, '85 115
   Beet Cake, Chocolate, '80 40
   Birthday Balloon Cakes, '92 15
   Birthday Cake, Fishin'-for-Fun, '93 194
   Black Bottom Cups, '82 279
   Black Forest Cake, '81 126; '92 174
   Black Forest Torte, '88 209
   Brownie Cupcakes, '82 280
   Brownie Delight, Chocolate, '87 224
   Brown Mountain Cake, '84 39
   Bûche de Noël, '84 304; '87 241
   Bûche de Noël Cake, '82 262
   Buttercream Cake, Chocolate, '90 108
   Buttermilk Chocolate Cake, '79 13
   Candy Cake, Chocolate, '81 238
   Caramel-Nut Cake, Chocolate-, '83 23
   Carrot Cake, Brownie, '92 120
   Cheesecake, Black Forest, '84 74;
      '89 93; '94 21
   Cheesecake, Candy Bar, '86 120
   Cheesecake, Chocolate, '81 16; '82 305
   Cheesecake, Chocolate-Almond, '93 53
   Cheesecake, Chocolate-Amaretto,
      '85 M294; '93 97
   Cheesecake, Chocolate-Caramel-Pecan,
      '91 197
   Cheesecake, Chocolate Chip, '85 114
   Cheesecake, Chocolate Cookie, '91 298
   Cheesecake, Chocolate-Glazed
      Triple-Layer, '86 315; '90 310
   Cheesecake, Chocolate Marble, '89 93
   Cheesecake, Chocolate-Mint, '91 104
   Cheesecake, Chocolate-Mint Baked
      Alaska, '94 142

Cheesecake, Chocolate-Raspberry
   Truffle, '91 270
Cheesecake, Chocolate Swirl, '84 295;
   '85 26
Cheesecake, German Chocolate,
   '87 265
Cheesecake, Marbled, '87 261
Cheesecake, Marble Mint, '84 152
Cheesecake, Mocha-Chocolate, '88 258
Cheesecake, Mocha Swirl, '87 262
Cheesecake, Rich Chocolate, '84 74;
   '85 38
Cheesecakes, Tiny Chocolate, '92 288
Cheesecake, White Chocolate, '87 44;
   '88 267; '94 180
Cheesecake with Whipped Cream
   Frosting, Chocolate, '89 42
Cherry Cake, Chocolate-, '84 200;
   '86 239
Cinnamon Cake, Chocolate-, '93 154
Cinnamon-Chocolate Cupcakes,
   '81 M139
Cocoa Crown Cake, '90 107
Coconut Cake, Chocolate-, '83 23
Coconut Cake, White Chocolate-,
   '87 263
Coffee Cake, Chocolate-Chip, '79 249
Coffee Cake, Chocolate Chip, '83 231
Crumb Cake, Calico, '87 261
Cupcakes, Chocolate, '92 14
Custard Cake, Chocolate, '88 175
Decadent Chocolate Cake, '86 142
Double-Chocolate Torte, '79 67
Easy Chocolate Cake, '80 140
Father's Day Cake, '92 134
Frosting, Chocolate Cake with Double,
   '86 314
Fudge Cake, '94 M293
Fudge Cake, Best, '83 301
Fudge Cake, Brown Sugar, '86 316
Fudge Cake, Chocolate, '80 279
Fudge Cake for Two, '81 205
Fudge Cake, One-Foot-in-the-Fire,
   '90 252
Fudge Frosting, Chocolate Cake with,
   '89 56
German Chocolate Cake, '81 296;
   '83 M233
German Chocolate Chip Cake, '86 247
Grandma's Chocolate Cake, '94 133
Graveyard Grumblings, '92 15
Kahlúa Cake, Chocolate, '91 298
Kahlúa Chocolate Cake, '81 303
Marble Chocolate Chip Cupcakes,
   '81 239
Marbled Cake, Cocoa, '82 265
Marshmallow Cake, No-Egg Chocolate,
   '87 M97
Mayonnaise Cake, Chocolate, '83 99
Mint Torte, Chocolate, '94 86
Mocha Brownie Torte, '85 102
Mocha Cake, Belgian, '84 316
Mocha Cake, Double, '84 311
Mocha-Chocolate Cake, Dark, '84 311
Mocha Cream Roll, Chocolate-, '84 304
Mocha Cupcakes, '85 250
Mocha-Pecan Torte, '86 26
Mocha Velvet Torte, '92 318
Mousse Cake, Chocolate, '87 264
Mousse Roll, Chocolate, '88 280
Nut Cake, Rich Chocolate-, '86 8

Chocolate, Cakes and Tortes *(continued)*

Pastry Cake, Chocolate, **'91** 196
Peanut Butter Cake, Chocolate-,
  '84 240
Peanut Butter Cake, Fudgy, **'85** 91
Peanut Cluster Cake, Chocolate-,
  '87 184
Pecan Torte, Chocolate-, **'89** 42
Perfect Chocolate Cake, **'82** 244;
  '90 307
Petits Fours, Chocolate-Almond,
  '93 255
Pound Cake, Chocolate, **'82** 88; **'84** 10;
  '89 325; **'94** 288
Pound Cake, Chocolate Chip, **'86** 178;
  '93 105; **'94** 100
Pound Cake, Chocolate Marble, **'88** 16
Pound Cake, Chocolate-Orange, **'89** 94
Pound Cake, Chocolate-Sour Cream,
  '83 239; **'92** 153
Pound Cake, Mahogany, **'89** 207
Pound Cake, Marbled Pecan, **'93** 313
Pound Cake, Milk Chocolate, **'90** 306
Pound Cake, White Chocolate, **'91** 101
Pound Cake with Frosting, Chocolate,
  '90 284
Pound Cake with Fudge Frosting,
  Chocolate, **'87** 296
Praline Torte, Chocolate, **'84** 165
Pudding Cake, Hot Fudge, **'88** 255
Pudding Cake, Warm Chocolate, **'92** 324
Pudding, Chocolate Cake, **'81** 99
Queen's Chocolate Cake, **'89** 271
Raspberry Cake, Chocolate-, **'92** 173
Rich Chocolate Cake, **'89** 43
Rocky Road Cake, **'81** 178
Roll, Chocolate Cream, **'85** 317
Roll, Chocolate-Frosted Ice Cream,
  '84 200
Roll, Chocolate Mousse, **'83** 290
Roll, Chocolate-Orange, **'87** 21
Rolls, Chocolate Cake, **'94** 312
Roulage, Chocolate-Cranberry, **'94** 313
Roulage, Chocolate-Orange, **'94** 314
Roulage, Mint-Chocolate, **'94** 314
Royal, Chocolate Cake, **'86** 239
Royale, Chocolate Torte, **'82** 263
Rum Cake, Chocolate, **'79** 67
Sachertorte, **'84** 253
Self-Filled Cupcakes, **'80** 129
Snack Cake, Black Widow, **'93** 245
Snack Cake, Frosted Chocolate, **'90** 194
Sour Cream Cake, Chocolate-, **'87** 222
Sour Cream Cake, Chocolate Chip-,
  '85 115
Sour Cream Chocolate Cake, **'79** 282
Sponge Cake, Chocolaty, **'86** 60
Strawberry Ice Cream Torte,
  Chocolate-, **'79** 7
Strawberry Shortcake, Chocolate-,
  '89 216
Sugar Cookie Torte, **'79** 68
Surprise Cupcakes, Chocolate, **'85** 91
Swiss Chocolate Chip Cake, **'87** 85
Tannenbaum Temptations, **'92** 14
Toffee Cake, Chocolate-, **'89** 335
Triangle Cake, Chocolate, **'85** 126
Truffle Cake, Chocolate, **'89** 43
Turkey Talk, **'92** 15

Velvet Torte, Chocolate, **'86** 316
Wedding Cake, Double Chocolate,
  '91 100
Whipped Cream Cake, Chocolate-Mint,
  '90 265
White Chocolate-Cherry Cake, **'88** 268
White Chocolate Mousse Cake, **'89** 160
Yule Log, **'79** 281; **'82** 289
Zucchini Cake, Chocolate-, **'85** 156
Candies
Almond Roca, **'86** 49
Bourbon Balls, **'83** 315; **'90** 83
Bourbon Balls, Chocolate, **'84** 298
Brittle, Chocolate, **'83** 315
Brittle, Quick Chocolate, **'82** 114
Butter Creams, **'80** 302
Caramels, Chocolate, **'91** 35
Cherries, Chocolate-Covered, **'81** 286;
  '84 298
Coconut Almond Drops, Chocolate-,
  '87 223
Cream-Filled Chocolates, Liqueur,
  '87 258
Crème de Cacao Balls, **'86** 266
Crème de Menthe Chocolates, **'91** 36
Drops, Chocolate, **'84** 111
Fudge, **'86** 266
Fudge Balls, Strawberry, **'93** 80
Fudge Bites, Peanut-, **'91** M231;
  '92 M68
Fudge, Cherry Nut, **'83** 315
Fudge, Chocolate, **'82** 20
Fudge, Chocolate-Peanut Butter,
  '87 257; **'90** 311
Fudge, Coffee-Chip, **'86** 74
Fudge, Cream Cheese, **'84** 111
Fudge, Creamy, **'81** 218
Fudge, Creamy Dark, **'82** 295
Fudge, Creamy Pecan, **'84** 321
Fudge, Diamond, **'92** 193
Fudge, Dinner Mint, **'88** 285
Fudge, Double-Good, **'79** M263
Fudge, Double Good, **'87** M278
Fudge, Double Peanut, **'85** 91
Fudge, Fast, **'79** 274
Fudge, Four Chips, **'92** 318
Fudge, Holiday Mocha, **'84** 298
Fudge, Marbled Peanut Butter, **'88** 65
Fudge, Microwave Chocolate, **'92** M50
Fudge, Orange-Walnut, **'92** 288
Fudge, Peanut Butter, **'89** 307
Fudge, Pistachio, **'83** 298
Fudge, Quick-and-Easy, **'88** M190
Fudge, Quick Nut, **'83** 316
Fudge Scotch Ring, **'79** 273
Fudge, White Chocolate, **'92** 317
Fudge, White Chocolate-Coffee, **'94** 232
Greeting Card, Chocolate, **'83** 40
Kentucky Colonels, **'79** 273
Marshmallow Squares, Chocolate-,
  '92 M50
Millionaires, **'79** M262
Mints, Dinner, **'88** 66
Molded Candies, **'84** 40
Nut Clusters, **'81** 254
Nut Log Candy, Chocolate-, **'86** 335
Nut Teasers, Chocolate, **'91** 35
Peanut Butter Balls, Chocolate-, **'80** 87
Peanut Butter Bites, Chocolate-,
  '92 M317
Peanut Butter-Chocolate Balls, **'80** 269

Peanut Butter-Chocolate Candy Squares,
  '82 56
Peanut Butter Creams, **'79** 273
Peanut Butter Drops, Chocolate-,
  '92 322
Peanut Clusters, **'92** 288
Peanut Clusters, Chocolate-, **'81** 16
Peanutty Clusters, **'83** 143
Peanutty Swirls, Chocolate, **'94** M330
Pecan Clusters, Roasted, **'90** 310
Pecan Fritters, Chocolate-Covered,
  '79 205
Pralines, Chocolate, **'92** 313; **'93** 51
Pralines, Chocolate-Mint, **'92** 313;
  '93 51
Pralines, Chocolate-Peanut Butter,
  '92 313; **'93** 51
Pralines, Mocha, **'92** 313; **'93** 51
Pretzels, Chocolate-Covered, **'82** 295
Raspberry Cream Chocolates, **'91** 36
Rocky Road, **'84** 298
Rum Balls, Chocolate, **'80** 302
Rum Balls, Chocolate-, **'88** 285
Spiders, Chocolate, **'85** 236
Spirited Chocolates, **'86** 278
Tempered Chocolate, **'91** 35
Tiger Butter, **'86** 48
Toffee, English, **'79** 273
Toffee, Microwave, **'92** M317
Toffee, Nutty, **'79** M263
Truffles, Almond, **'83** 298
Truffles, Amaretto Dessert, **'86** 319
Truffles, Bittersweet, **'94** 330
Truffles, Chocolate, **'85** 114; **'89** 43;
  '91 108
Truffles, Chocolate-Kahlúa, **'92** 285
Truffles, White Chocolate, **'87** 45
Truffles, Yule Street, **'90** 242
Turtle Candies, **'93** M41
Velvets, Chocolate, **'84** 298
White Chocolate Salties, **'92** 50
White Chocolate Surprises, **'91** 36
Cannoli, **'80** 58
Charlotte Russe, Chocolate, **'87** 74
Cheese Cups, Chocolate-, **'91** 142
Cinnamon-Chocolate Cream, **'94** 199
Cocoa to Chocolate Equivalents, **'84** 200
Combo, Strawberry-Chocolate, **'85** 96
Cream, Chocolate-Almond, **'91** 108
Cream Dessert, Triple, **'94** 244
Cream, Heavenly Chocolate, **'88** 128
Cream, Strawberries with Chocolate, **'85** 81
Crêpes, Chocolate, **'86** 164
Crêpes, Chocolate Chantilly, **'82** 183
Crêpes, Chocolate Dessert, **'84** 84; **'85** 262
Crêpes, Chocolate Dream, **'86** 164
Crêpes, Chocolate-Orange, **'85** 263
Crêpes, Fruit-Filled Chocolate, **'89** 325
Crust, Chocolate, **'87** 264; **'90** M15
Crust, Chocolate-Coconut, **'87** 261
Crust, Chocolate Crumb, **'87** 261
Crust, Chocolate Wafer, **'89** 42, 93
Cups, Chocolate, **'80** 207
Cups, Chocolate Crinkle, **'93** 270
Cups, Chocolate Lace, **'87** 133
Cups, Chocolate-Mint, **'80** 71
Cups, Chocolate-Walnut, **'85** 213
Cups, Miniature Chocolate, **'87** 132
Custard, Chocolate, **'88** 258
Custard, Chocolate-Topped Amaretto,
  '87 M37

Chocolate (*continued*)

Date-Nut Delight, Chocolate, **'88** 168
Decadence, Chocolate, **'89** 183
Dessert, Chilled Chocolate, **'83** 177
Dessert, Chocolate-Almond, **'82** 306
Dessert, Chocolate-Coffee Frozen, **'85** 172
Dessert, Chocolate Dream, **'83** 198
Dessert, Chocolate Ladyfinger, **'86** 162
Dessert, Chocolate-Mint, **'82** 100
Dessert, Chocolate-Rum, **'81** 247
Dessert, Chocolate Truffle, **'88** 281
Dessert, Choco-Maple Frozen, **'86** 300;
   '87 178
Dessert, Cool Chocolate-Mint, **'80** 109
Dessert, Easy Chocolate, **'79** 75
Dessert, Frozen Chocolate, **'83** 76
Dessert, Fudge-Peanut Ice Cream, **'88** 167
Dessert, Layered Ice Cream, **'83** 189
Dessert, Peanut-Chocolate, **'80** 86
Dessert Squares, Chocolate-Blueberry,
   '87 299
Dessert with Kahlúa Cream, Fudge, **'91** 197
Dip, Chocolate, **'92** 50
Doughnuts, Chocolate, **'83** 95
Doughnuts, Chocolate-Covered, **'84** 55
Doughnuts, Chocolate-Glazed Potato, **'85** 6
Flan, Layered, **'89** 45
Fondue, Brandied Chocolate, **'93** 162
Fondue, Chocolate, **'91** 142
Fondue, Dessert, **'89** 281
Fondue, White Chocolate, **'92** 287
Frostings, Fillings, and Toppings
   Almond Frosting, Chocolate-, **'83** 241
   Buttercream, Chocolate, **'84** 156
   Butter Frosting, Chocolate, **'89** 271
   Candy Frosting, Chocolate, **'81** 238
   Cheese Filling, Chocolate-, **'90** 47
   Cherry Frosting, Chocolate-, **'89** 294
   Chocolate Frosting, **'80** M171; **'81** 265;
      '82 262; **'83** 79, 99, M233, 253;
      '84 200; **'85** 323;
      '86 8, 93, 138, 239, 314;
      '87 M97,198, 199, 293; **'89** M25;
      '90 194, 252, 265, 284, 309;
      '91 248; **'92** 319; **'93** 239; **'94** 133
   Cocoa Frosting, **'86** 60
   Coconut Chocolate Frosting, **'79** 13
   Coffee Frosting, Chocolate-, **'84** 36;
      '88 269
   Cream, Chocolate, **'94** 57
   Creamy Chocolate Frosting, **'85** 314;
      '86 316; **'87** 241
   Creamy Chocolate Glaze, **'82** 88
   Fluffy Chocolate Frosting, **'86** 336;
      '87 58
   Fudge Filling, **'94** 292
   Fudge Frosting, **'81** 303; **'87** 296;
      '89 56; **'94** 51
   Fudge Frosting, Chocolate, **'83** 105
   Fudge Frosting, Quick, **'81** 278
   Ganache, Chocolate, **'93** 255
   Ganache Cream, **'92** 318
   Glaze, Chocolate, **'81** 119; **'83** 220;
      '84 10, 55, 253; **'85** 6; **'86** 315, 316;
      '89 325; **'90** 310; **'91** M296; **'93** 52
   Glaze, White Cake with Strawberries and
      Chocolate, **'87** 76
   Honey Chocolate Frosting, **'79** 83
   Honey Glaze, Chocolate-, **'82** 306

Kahlúa Frosting, Chocolate, **'91** 298
Marshmallow Frosting, Chocolate-,
   '83 245
Mocha Butter Cream Frosting, **'79** 281
Mocha-Buttercream Frosting, **'86** 26
Mocha Cream, **'94** 47
Mocha Cream Filling, **'84** 305
Mocha Frosting, **'83** 301; **'84** 316;
   '87 224; **'94** 292
Mocha Frosting, Creamy, **'82** 289;
   '84 311; **'89** 248
Nut Frosting, Chocolate, **'80** 140
Peanut Butter Frosting, Chocolate-,
   '84 240; **'87** 222
Peanut Butter-Fudge Frosting, **'87** 184
Peanut Topping, Chocolate-, **'79** 222
Perfect Chocolate Frosting, **'90** 307
Rich Chocolate Filling, **'79** 68
Rich Chocolate Frosting, **'84** 304
Rum Frosting, Chocolate, **'79** 67
Satiny Chocolate Frosting, **'85** 126;
   '89 43
Truffle Filling, Chocolate, **'87** 69
Whipped Cream Frosting, **'89** 43
White Chocolate-Cream Cheese Tiered
   Cake Frosting, **'94** 125
White Chocolate-Cream Cheese
   Frosting, **'94** 58
White Chocolate Filling, **'89** 160
White Chocolate Frosting, **'88** 280;
   '91 101
Frozen Dessert, Nutty Fudgy, **'94** 28
Garnishes, Chocolate, **'85** 16
Garnishes, Lacy Chocolate, **'89** 43
Gâteau Panache, **'83** 269
Granola with Chocolate Morsels, **'86** 69
Grapefruit, Chocolate-Topped, **'89** 88
Horns, Chocolate-Dipped, **'93** 197
Ice Cream, Almond-Fudge, **'93** 205
Ice Cream Balls, Easy, **'84** 106
Ice Cream Balls, Nutty, **'89** 72
Ice Cream, Chocolate, **'80** 176; **'86** 129
Ice Cream, Chocolate Chunk-Peanut Butter,
   '85 297; **'86** 120
Ice Cream, Chocolate-Covered Peanut,
   '88 203
Ice Cream, Double-Chocolate, **'88** 203
Ice Cream, Mexican Chocolate, **'91** 162
Ice Cream, Mint-Chocolate Chip, **'88** 202
Ice Cream, Mocha, **'88** 202
Ice Cream Party Squares, **'91** 214
Ice Cream Sandwiches, Chocolate, **'89** 72
Ice Cream Squares, Mint-Chocolate Chip,
   '94 245
Kahlúa Delight, **'83** 67
Leaves, Chocolate, **'88** 281; **'89** 42
Loaf, Chocolate Pinwheel, **'80** 256
Loaves, Chocolate Chip Cheese, **'91** 299;
   '92 264
Log, Chocolate Cream, **'94** 220
Meringue Acorns, **'93** 284
Meringue Fingers, Chocolate-Almond,
   '84 158
Mexican Fiesta Confection, **'82** 223
Mint Freeze, Chocolate, **'88** 167
Mocha Alaska Dessert, **'84** 191
Mocha Chiffon, **'86** 75
Mocha Dessert, Frozen, **'84** 311
Mocha Freeze, Royal, **'84** 53
Mocha-Mallow Parfaits, **'80** 219
Mocha Squares, Frozen, **'81** 187

Mousse, Amaretto-Chocolate, **'86** 50
Mousse au Grand Marnier, Chocolate,
   '91 296
Mousse Baked Alaska, Chocolate, **'85** 195
Mousse, Blender Chocolate, **'82** 71
Mousse, Blender-Quick Chocolate, **'80** 269
Mousse, Brandy-Chocolate, **'85** 102
Mousse, Chocolate, **'88** 280
Mousse, Chocolate-Almond, **'93** 316
Mousse, Chocolate-Orange, **'81** 16, 205
Mousse, Chocolate Rum, **'86** 189
Mousse, Creamy Chocolate, **'87** 133
Mousse, Elegant Amaretto-Chocolate,
   '86 337
Mousse, Honeyed Chocolate, **'87** 223
Mousse, Kid-Pleasin' Chocolate, **'90** 271
Mousse, Mocha, **'94** 232
Mousse, Quick Chocolate, **'85** 87
Mousse, White Chocolate, **'91** 247;
   '93 315
Muffins, Banana-Chocolate, **'94** 197
Muffins, Chocolate Chip, **'90** 87
Muffins, Jumbo Banana-Chocolate Chip,
   '93 339
Muffins, Peanut Butter-Chocolate Chip,
   '94 167
Napoleons, Peanut Butter-and-Chocolate,
   '94 121
Parfait, Chocolate Mousse, **'94** 90
Parfaits, Chocolate-Crème de Menthe,
   '85 161
Parfaits, Chocolate-Mint, **'90** M15
Parfaits, Chocolate-Peppermint, **'88** 65
Parfaits, Speedy, **'83** 76
Parfait, White Chocolate-Raspberry Swirl,
   '93 315
Pies and Tarts
   Almond Pie, Creamy Chocolate-,
      '85 102
   Amandine, Chocolate Pie, **'83** 300
   Amaretto Heavenly Tarts, Chocolate-,
      '88 4
   Amaretto Mousse Pie, Chocolate-,
      '80 180; **'81** 30
   Banana-Pecan Cream Pie, Chocolate-,
      '94 210
   Bavarian Pie, Chocolate, **'89** 326
   Berry Pie, Heavenly Chocolate-, **'85** 102
   Best-Ever Chocolate Pie, **'88** M45
   Black Bottom Mocha-Cream Tart,
      '92 304
   Black Bottom Pie, **'82** 53
   Bluegrass Chocolate Tarts, **'90** 84
   Bourbon Pie, Chocolate, **'88** 99
   Brownie Pie, Crustless, **'82** 33
   Caramel Turtle Truffle Tart, **'93** M131
   Chess Pie, Chocolate, **'81** 161; **'86** 220;
      '92 13
   Chess Tarts, Chocolate, **'92** 214
   Chilled Chocolate Pie, **'88** 99
   Chip Pie, Chocolate, **'85** 114
   Cream Cheese Pie, Chocolate-, **'80** 69
   Cream Cheese Pie, Chocolate, **'92** 240
   Cream Pie, Chocolate, **'83** 192; **'84** 49;
      '87 208; **'94** 208
   Creamy Chocolate Pie, **'85** 298; **'86** 119
   Double Chocolate Pie, **'82** M282
   Easy Chocolate Pie, **'83** 158
   French Silk Pie, **'80** 247
   French Silk Tarts, **'79** 236
   Frozen Chocolate Pie, **'80** 154

Chocolate, Pies and Tarts (continued)

Frozen Chocolate Pie with Pecan Crust,
  '89 291
Fudge Pie, '87 168; '89 252
Fudge Pie, Sweetheart, '86 316;
  '90 313
German Chocolate Pie, '93 129
Heavenly Chocolate Pie, '87 260
Ice Cream Pie, Chocolate-, '87 224
Ice Cream Pie, Chocolate, '91 56
Ice Cream Pie, Chocolate-Mint, '81 144
Ice Cream Sundae Pie, '94 244
Kahlúa Pie, '83 191
Kentucky Derby Tarts, '79 102
Meringue Pie, Chocolate, '80 238;
  '82 206; '83 158; '92 216
Meringue Pie, Chocolate-Filled, '86 121
Microwave Chocolate Pie, '90 M15
Mocha Crunch Pie, Chocolate-, '81 136
Mocha Meringue Pie, '80 242
Mocha Pie, '94 168
Mousse Pie, Chocolate, '81 136
Mud Pie, Decadent, '89 252
Mud Pie, Mississippi, '89 26
Mud Pie, Tipsy, '80 255
Peanut Butter Pie, Chocolate-, '85 91
Peanut Butter Swirl Pie, Chocolate-,
  '87 262
Peanut Butter Tarts, Chocolate-,
  '92 277
Pecan Chess Pie, Chocolate-, '93 251
Pecan Pie, Choco-, '82 86
Pecan Pie, Chocolate, '80 237; '83 12;
  '90 184
Pecan Pie, Chocolate-, '91 272
Pecan Tart with Caramel Sauce,
  Chocolate-, '93 296; '94 234
Praline Pie, Chocolate-, '86 259
Silk Pie, Chocolate, '88 67
Strawberry-Chocolate Truffle Pie,
  '89 112
Tin Roof Pie, '85 91
Turtle Pecan Pie, '93 250
Whipped Cream Pie, Chocolate, '79 124
White Chocolate-Banana Cream Pie,
  '94 314
Pineapple with Raspberry Sauce,
  Chocolate-Drizzled, '90 57
Pizza, Chocolate, '91 298
Plunge, Chocolate, '94 332
Pots de Chocolat, Petits, '82 272
Pots de Crème, '81 15; '84 M145
Pots de Crème au Chocolat, '93 53
Pots de Crème, Chocolate, '93 296; '94 234
Pots de Crème for Two, '89 275
Pots de Crème, Mocha, '88 M45
Pots de Crème, Rum-Flavored, '85 102
Pudding, Brownie, '79 265; '80 295
Pudding, Chocolate-Almond, '82 142; '88 24
Pudding, Chocolate Biscuit Bread, '94 215
Pudding, Chocolate Bread, '80 8
Pudding, Creamy Chocolate, '83 106
Pudding, Hot Fudge, '81 208
Pudding, Hot Fudge Sundae Cake, '88 167
Pudding with Lemon Meringue, Chocolate,
  '88 258
Roulage, '90 266
Roulage, Chocolate-Mocha, '80 216
Roulage, Frozen Chocolate, '90 56

Roulage, White Chocolate, '92 230
Sack, Large Chocolate, '93 314
Sack, Small Chocolate, '93 314
Sauces
  Amaretto-Chocolate Sauce, '92 154
  Bittersweet Chocolate Sauce, '92 319
  Cherry Sauce, Chocolate-, '85 189
  Cherry Sauce, Chocolate, '87 M165
  Chocolate Sauce, '83 189; '84 208, 313;
    '86 322; '90 57; '91 56, 57; '93 276;
    '94 121
  Cinnamon-Fudge Sauce, '85 141
  Classic Chocolate Sauce, '85 207
  Creamy Chocolate Sauce, '88 M177
  Dark Chocolate Sauce, '93 296;
    '94 234, 283
  Dark Chocolate Sauce, Poached Pears
    with, '90 M141
  Double Chocolate Sauce, '83 79
  Easy Chocolate Sauce, '92 148
  Fudge Sauce, '91 174
  Fudge Sauce, Easy Hot, '94 194
  Heavenly Chocolate Sauce, '79 79;
    '82 167
  Honey-Chocolate Sauce, '89 251
  Hot Fudge Sauce, '82 181, 295; '84 143
  Hot Fudge Sauce, Easy, '84 69
  Hot Fudge Sauce, Quick, '82 212
  Kahlúa Chocolate Sauce, '85 155
  Mint Sauce, Chocolate-, '93 86; '94 314
  Mint Sauce, Quick Chocolate, '86 M58
  Orange Sauce, Chocolate-, '86 165;
    '94 314
  Peanut Butter Sauce, Chocolate-,
    '79 91, M156
  Peppermint Sauce, Chocolate-, '94 205
  Praline Sauce, Chocolate-, '85 M295
  Supreme, Chocolate Sauce, '85 189
  Toffee-Fudge Sauce, '89 95
  White Chocolate Sauce, '92 164
Shavings, Chocolate Hearts and, '86 26
Shell, Chocolate-Coconut Pie, '82 210;
  '83 100
Shell, Chocolate Pastry, '87 262
Shells with Kahlúa Cream, Chocolate,
  '88 195
Snacks, Chocolate-Peanut Butter, '90 226
Soufflé au Chocolat Cointreau, '94 56
Soufflé, Chocolate, '84 317; '94 46
Soufflé, Chocolate Mint, '81 16
Soufflé, Light Chocolate, '83 278
Spread, Chocolate Cheese, '87 292
Sticks, Chocolate-Sesame, '91 316
Strawberries Dipped in White Chocolate,
  '90 83
Sundae Dessert, Hot Fudge, '84 313;
  '86 322
Sundaes, Cocoa-Kahlúa, '83 M58
Supreme, Chocolate, '84 94
Torte, Frozen Viennese, '93 171
Trifle, Chocolate, '88 258; '93 326
Velvet, Chocolate Almond, '81 148
Waffles, Fudge, '94 205
Waffles with Strawberry Cream, Chocolate,
  '88 153
Whip, Chocolate, '89 326
Yogurt, Mocha Sauce with Chocolate, '92 243

Chop Suey
Cabbage Chop Suey, '81 101
Chicken Chop Suey, '81 227
Salad, Chop Suey, '81 37

Chowders
Bluefish Chowder, '84 282
Broccoli Chowder, '79 16
Cabbage Chowder, Hearty, '80 25
Cheddar Chowder, Hearty, '79 16
Cheese Chowder, Golden, '80 73
Cheese Chowder, Hot, '89 16
Chicken-and-Corn Chowder, Curried, '92 21
Chicken Chowder, '83 20
Chicken Chowder, Cheesy, '92 21
Chicken Chowder Sauterne, '84 235
Chicken-Vegetable Chowder, Creamy,
  '92 20
Clam-and-Sausage Chowder, '94 104
Clam Chowder, '79 182; '81 32; '85 9;
  '86 36; '89 95; '90 202
Clam Chowder, New England, '86 M72
Clam Chowder, Ocracoke, '79 31
Clam Chowder, Tomato-, '84 251
Corn and Bacon Chowder, Fresh, '93 203
Corn and Cheese Chowder, '80 228
Corn Chowder, '81 128; '83 20; '84 M38;
  '85 10; '90 202; '91 132
Corn Chowder, Delicious, '82 279
Fish Chowder, '79 152; '84 M38
Fish Chowder, Basque, '86 36
Fish Chowder, Chunky, '92 331
Fish Chowder, Creamy, '79 16
Fish Chowder, Tasty, '80 188
Ham-and-Cheese Chowder, '89 15
Ham and Corn Chowder, '79 16
Ham-and-Corn Chowder, '82 40
Ham Chowder, Creamy, '88 M53
Ham 'n Cheese Chowder, '79 199
Harvest Chowder, '83 317
Mushroom Chowder, '79 16
Mushroom-Potato Chowder, '92 331
Okra Chowder, Quick, '80 185
Oyster Chowder, '83 229
Oyster-Corn Chowder, '83 211
Potato-Corn Chowder, '94 66
Sausage-Bean Chowder, '83 20
Seafood Chowder, '85 9; '92 122
Seafood Chowder, Curried, '94 103
Seafood Chowder, Southern, '83 20
Shrimp and Corn Chowder, '79 199
Shrimp Chowder, '89 218
Snapper Chowder, Red, '85 217
Swiss-Broccoli Chowder, '80 73
Turkey Chowder, '85 10; '91 312
Turkey-Corn Chowder, '81 98
Vegetable Chowder, Cheesy, '80 25; '83 20
Vegetable Chowder, Hearty, '88 56

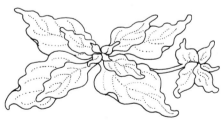

Chow Mein
Beef-and-Vegetable Chow Mein Casserole,
  '83 313
Chicken Chow Mein, '90 68
Noodles, Chow Mein over Crispy, '85 286
Pork Chow Mein, '80 208; '90 101
Shrimp Chow Mein, '82 30

Christmas. *See also* Cookies/Christmas.
Bread, Christmas, '87 296; '88 288
Bread, Norwegian Christmas, '79 234
Bread Stars, '93 286
Cake, Christmas Coconut, '82 262
Candy Canes and Wreaths, Braided, '92 276
Cinnamon Ornaments, '85 284
Coeur à la Crème, Christmas, '86 278
Coffee Cakes, Christmas-Tree, '87 298
Cookie Advent Calendar, '85 325
Cookie Cards, Christmas, '84 302
Cookie, Elf, '80 279, 303
Cookie, Mrs. Claus, '80 279, 303
Cookie, Rudolph, '80 279, 303
Cookie, Santa Claus, '80 278, 303
Cookies, Christmas Cherry, '88 282
Cookies, Christmas Date, '88 287
Cookies, Christmas Tree, '93 286
Cookies, Eggnog Christmas, '79 255
Cookies, Gingerbread, '80 278
Cookies, Jolly Reindeer, '91 273
Cookie, Sleigh, '80 279, 303
Cookies, Moravian Christmas, '91 282
Cookies, Painted, '86 322
Cookies, Spiced Christmas, '87 294
Cookies, Swedish Christmas, '79 290
Corn, Christmas, '93 325
Cottage, Quick-Fix Christmas, '91 280
Cottage, Sugarplum, '88 309
Cranberry Hearts, '93 286
Crostini, Christmas, '94 318
Dessert, White Christmas, '82 261
Dip, Christmas Confetti, '92 279
Divinity, Christmas, '81 286
Doughnuts, Snowy, '93 286
Fruit Squares, Christmas, '88 282
Gingerbread Bowl, Christmas, '93 266
Grittibanz (Swiss Bread Figure), '93 265
Jam, Christmas, '88 288
Jam, Christmas Brunch, '81 286
Jelly, Christmas Freezer, '86 M288
Lizzies, Christmas, '87 257
Loaf, Sweet Christmas, '84 278
Milk, Santa Claus, '92 281
Munchies, Reindeer, '91 276
Orange Baskets, '93 286
Ornaments, Edible, '94 316
Pandoro, '93 267
Panettone, '93 266
Peanut Butter Elf Bites, '91 275
Pecans, Christmas Eve, '91 276
Pie, White Christmas, '88 281; '93 289
Pinecones, Peanut Butter-Suet, '93 286
Pinwheels, Santa's, '91 275
Potatoes, Christmas, '88 252
Potpourri, Christmas, '94 317
Pretzel Garlands, '93 286
Pudding with Brandy Sauce, Baked
   Christmas, '88 279
Punch, Christmas, '84 259; '89 330
Punch, Christmas Eve, '86 314
Punch, Merry Christmas, '79 285
Reindeer Nibbles, '92 280
Relish Tree, Christmas, '84 257
Salad, Christmas, '88 249
Salad, Christmas Snow, '82 266
Salad, Cranberry Christmas, '79 243
Salad, Eggnog Christmas, '86 281
Sandwiches, Christmas Tree, '92 279
Sandwich Wreath, Festive, '86 333
Santa's Hat, '92 279

Santa's Whiskers, '85 323
Scent, Christmas, '84 325
Spices, Barclay House Mulling, '86 289
Strawberries, Christmas, '87 293; '94 331
Sugar Plums, '92 281
Tannenbaum Temptations, '92 14
Tea, Christmas Fruit, '83 275
Trees, Christmas, '89 294
Wassail, Christmas, '93 295
Wine, Christmas Dreams in, '91 260
Wreath, Christmas, '80 280
Wreath, Della Robbia Fruit, '87 294

Clams
Backyard Clambake, '81 92
Bisque, Clam, '86 228
Casino, Clams, '81 125
Casino, Maryland Clams, '89 196
Chase, Clams, '79 85
Chowder, Clam, '79 182; '81 32; '85 9;
   '86 36; '89 95; '90 202
Chowder, Clam-and-Sausage, '94 104
Chowder, New England Clam, '86 M72
Chowder, Ocracoke Clam, '79 31
Chowder, Southern Seafood, '83 20
Chowder, Tomato-Clam, '84 251
Cocktail, Tomato-Clam, '87 252
Crisps, Clam, '80 151
Dip, Clam, '79 151; '80 265
Dip, Hot Clam, '82 59; '89 48
Dip, Zesty Clam, '92 25
Fritters, Clam, '79 151; '86 71
Linguine, Quick Clam, '90 233
Oreganata, Clams, '85 104
Pizza, Baby Clam, '87 182
Puffs, Clam, '90 60
Quiche, Clam, '83 215
Sauce, Linguine in Clam, '81 83
Sauce, Linguine with Clam, '84 124; '88 90;
   '89 178
Sauce, Pasta with Clam, '84 291
Sauce, Tricolor Pasta with Clam, '93 272
Sauce, Vermicelli and Sprouts with Red Clam,
   '86 143
Sauce, Vermicelli with Clam, '85 295
Sauce with Linguine, Clam, '84 9
Shells, Baked Clam, '87 94
Soup, Clam Florentine, '85 23
Spread, Creamy Clam, '91 274
Steamed Clams Chesapeake, '89 196
Coconut
Ambrosia, Anytime, '86 182
Ambrosia, Baked, '83 303
Ambrosia Bowl, '80 138; '84 313
Ambrosia, Brunch, '83 57
Ambrosia Cake, '79 229

Ambrosia Cake Royale, '89 335
Ambrosia Cookies, '86 313
Ambrosia Cream Cheese Mold, '79 249
Ambrosia, Custard Sauce, '84 256
Ambrosia, Fantastic, '91 277
Ambrosia, Grandma's, '90 254
Ambrosia, Honey Bee, '83 267
Ambrosia, Layered, '88 304
Ambrosia, Mixed Fruit, '83 10
Ambrosia Mold, '79 241
Ambrosia, Old-Fashioned, '80 5
Ambrosia Pancakes with Orange Syrup,
   '89 254
Ambrosia, Peach, '83 53
Ambrosia Pie, '79 284
Ambrosia, Pineapple-Orange, '88 254
Ambrosia, Rhubarb, '88 93
Ambrosia Salad, '83 231
Ambrosia Sauce, Hot, '89 335
Ambrosia, Sherried, '84 324; '86 317
Ambrosia Supreme, Orange, '79 37
Ambrosia, Tropical, '79 74
Balls, Coconut-Almond, '84 256
Bars, Coconut Granola, '85 202
Bars, Golden, '84 255
Bars, Hawaiian, '84 153
Bonbons, Coconut-Black Walnut, '82 307
Bread, Coconut, '83 140
Bread, Pumpkin-Coconut, '87 255
Cake, Apple Coconut, '80 226
Cake, Banana-Coconut, '93 154
Cake, Chocolate-Coconut, '83 23
Cake, Christmas Coconut, '82 262
Cake, Coconut, '92 120
Cake, Coconut Cream, '81 179; '91 269
Cake, Coconut-Cream Cheese Pound,
   '85 297; '90 305
Cake, Coconut Cream Pound, '84 10
Cake, Coconut-Pineapple, '89 56
Cake, Coconut-Pineapple Layer, '80 140
Cake, Coconut Pound, '82 87; '91 224
Cake, Coconut-Spice, '84 255; '87 296
Cake, Cranberry-Coconut Coffee, '93 332
Cake, Creamy Coconut, '84 43
Cake, Fresh Coconut, '80 289; '82 52;
   '85 281
Cake, Fresh Coconut-Carrot, '80 299
Cake, Holiday Coconut, '90 308
Cake, Lemon-Coconut Cream, '81 179
Cake, Lemon-Coconut Sheet, '85 117
Cake, Oatmeal-Coconut Coffee, '83 312
Cake, Orange-Coconut Angel Food, '94 294
Cake, Pineapple-Coconut Coffee, '94 49
Cake, Regal Coconut, '83 299
Cake Roll, Coconut-Pineapple, '84 304
Cake, Rum-Orange Coconut, '88 224
Cake, Spiked Coconut Angel, '85 279
Cake, Stately Coconut Layer, '81 70
Cake, Toasted Coconut, '86 60
Cake, Unforgettable Coconut, '90 104
Cake, White Chocolate-Coconut, '87 263
Calypso, Coco-Berry, '89 171
Candy, Coconut, '79 272; '80 250
Chicken Balls, Coconut Curried, '91 165
Chicken with Fresh Fruit, Coconut, '93 294
Cloud, Coconut, '80 70
Clusters, Pecan-Coconut, '86 M251
Cookies, Chocolate Macaroon, '88 217
Cookies, Coconut-Cherry, '79 292
Cookies, Coconut Shortbread, '93 316
Cookies, Crinkle Sunflower, '83 149

Coconut *(continued)*

Cookies, Crisp Coconut, **'89** 162
Cookies, Crispy Coconut-Oatmeal, **'93** 80
Cookies, Oatmeal-Coconut, **'80** 218
Cookies, Peanut Butter-Coconut, **'83** 113
Cream, Orange-Coconut, **'84** 24
Crust, Chocolate-Coconut, **'87** 261
Crust, Coconut, **'89** 160
Custard, Coconut, **'86** 109
Dessert, Chilled Coconut, **'83** 116
Dessert, Coconut-Caramel, **'92** 44
Dessert, Macaroon-Sherbet Frozen, **'79** 212
Dip, Coconut-Honey Fruit, **'84** 171
Dressing, Coconut, **'87** 251
Dressing, Orange-Coconut, **'80** 158
Dressing, Tangy Coconut-Fruit, **'84** 171
Drink, Coconut-Pineapple, **'83** 172
Drops, Chocolate-Coconut Almond, **'87** 223
English Cherubs, **'83** 257
Filling, Coconut, **'81** 265
Filling, Coconut Cream, **'84** 200
Filling, Sour Cream-Coconut, **'92** 120
Frosting, Coconut, **'82** 262; **'91** 269
Frosting, Coconut Chocolate, **'79** 13
Frosting, Coconut Cream Cheese, **'86** 60
Frosting, Coconut-Pecan, **'81** 296;
  '83 M233; **'84** 43, 322
Frosting, Creamy Coconut, **'80** 287
Frosting, Lemon-Coconut, **'90** 253
Frosting, Nutty Coconut, **'86** 8
Frost, Pink Coconut, **'79** 174; **'80** 128
Fruit Bowl, Coconut, **'83** 111
Ice Cream, Coconut Fried, **'85** 141
Ice Cream, Fresh Coconut, **'79** 166
Kisses, Coconut, **'90** 106
Macaroon Charlotte, **'81** 296
Macaroons, Chocolate, **'83** 300
Macaroons, Coconut, **'79** 52
Macaroon-Stuffed Peaches, **'79** 178
Mousse, Coconut-Pineapple, **'94** 198
Muffins, Coconut-Molasses, **'82** 210
Nests, Strawberry Coconut, **'88** 136
Nog, Coconut, **'83** 275
Pears, Spicy Coconut, **'83** 207
Pecan Coils, Coconut-, **'90** 196
Pie, Blender Coconut, **'84** 236
Pie, Buttermilk-Coconut, **'94** 246
Pie, Coconut, **'93** 115
Pie, Coconut Chess, **'86** 220
Pie, Coconut Cream, **'80** 238; **'81** 136;
  '82 85; **'84** 49; **'87** 207; **'89** 236;
  '90 312
Pie, Coconut Crumb Cherry, **'92** 30
Pie, Coconut Crunch, **'90** 105
Pie, Coconut Custard, **'82** 33
Pie, Coconut Macaroon, **'88** 204
Pie, Coconut-Orange Chess, **'89** 169
Pie, Coconut Pecan, **'81** 161
Pie, Coconut-Pecan Chess, **'81** 248
Pie, Coconut-Pineapple, **'84** 256
Pie, French Coconut, **'90** 162
Pie, Fresh Coconut Cream, **'80** 289
Pie, Magic Coconut, **'79** 53
Pie, Mock Coconut, **'86** 200
Pie, Orange-Coconut, **'90** 90
Pie, Orange-Coconut Cream, **'94** 208
Pie, Pineapple-Coconut Chess, **'92** 214
Pie, Quick Coconut, **'83** 115
Pies, Coconut-Caramel, **'87** 260

Pie Shell, Chocolate-Coconut, **'82** 210;
  '83 100
Pie, Surprise Coconut Cream, **'92** 43
Pie, Toasted Coconut, **'90** 105
Puffs, Coconut, **'87** 277
Salad, Chunky Fruit-and-Coconut, **'84** 24
Sauce, Coconut-Orange, **'85** 189
Sauce, Creamy Light Coconut, **'82** 177
Shrimp, Coconut-Beer, **'85** 230; **'89** 23
Soufflé, Coconut, **'79** 73; **'85** 212
Spread, Coconut-Cranberry Cheese,
  '92 328
Spread, Coconut-Pineapple, **'93** 309
Squares, Chocolate-Coconut, **'90** 70
Sweet Potatoes, Coconut-Broiled, **'84** 231
Sweet Potatoes, Coconut-Orange, **'84** 252
Sweet Potatoes, Coconut-Stuffed, **'82** 204
Tropical Snow, **'86** 34

Coffee

After-Dinner Coffee, **'81** 262
Almond-Coffee Delight, **'84** 115
Brandied Coffee, **'81** 244
Cake, Coffee Sponge, **'83** 229; **'91** 55
Cake, Two-Day Coffee Sponge, **'86** 75
Cappuccino, Café, **'82** 253
Cappuccino, Chocolate Castle, **'84** 53
Cappuccino, Flaming, **'79** 293
Chocolate-Almond Coffee, **'84** 54
Chocolate Coffee, **'82** 43
Cocoa-Coffee, **'83** 55
Colombian Royal, Café, **'80** M290
Colonial Coffee, **'89** 290
Cookies, Java Shortbread, **'94** 233
Cream, Café, **'82** 312
Cream, Icy Rum Coffee, **'83** 172
Cream Puffs, Java, **'81** 187
Creamy Coffee, **'81** 244
Crêpes, Coffee Ice Cream, **'84** 85
Dessert, Cappuccino Coffee, **'92** 264
Dessert, Chocolate-Coffee Frozen, **'85** 172
Dessert Drink, Simply Super, **'83** 303
Dessert, Light Coffee, **'88** 260
Diablo, Café, **'80** 259
Espresso, Amaretto, **'92** 263
Floats, Maple-Coffee, **'86** 195
Frosted Coffee, **'81** 244
Frosting, Chocolate-Coffee, **'84** 36;
  '88 269
Frosting, Coffee, **'94** 86
Fudge, Coffee-Chip, **'86** 74
Fudge, White Chocolate-Coffee, **'94** 232
German Chocolate Café au Lait, **'92** 264
Granita, Coffee-Kahlúa, **'88** 118
Hazelnut-Coffee Ice, **'94** 233
Holiday Coffee, **'90** 273
Ice Cream, Coffee, **'88** 202
Ice Cream Crunch, Coffee, **'82** 182
Irish Coffee, Creamy, **'79** 232
Irish Coffee, Flaming, **'79** 293
Irish Coffee Nog, **'84** 258
Irish Cream Nog, **'82** 312
Kahlúa Delight, Make-Ahead, **'84** M89
Kona Luscious, **'84** 54
Liqueur, Coffee-Flavored, **'86** 266
Mallow, Coffee, **'80** 109
Meringues with Butterscotch Mousse,
  Coffee, **'93** 254
Mexican Coffee, **'83** 175, 275; **'88** 247;
  '91 78; **'93** 310; **'94** 97
Mexicano, Café, **'92** 208
Mix, Cappuccino, **'90** 87

Mix, Fireside Coffee, **'87** 241
Mocha Alaska Dessert, **'84** 191
Mocha-Almond Dessert, **'80** 289; **'81** 62
Mocha Brownies, **'87** 93
Mocha Brownie Torte, **'85** 102
Mocha Buttercream, **'89** 42
Mocha Butter Cream Frosting, **'79** 281
Mocha-Buttercream Frosting, **'86** 26
Mocha Cake, Belgian, **'84** 316
Mocha Cake, Double, **'84** 311
Mocha Chiffon, **'86** 75
Mocha-Chocolate Cake, Dark, **'84** 311
Mocha-Chocolate Cheesecake, **'88** 258
Mocha Chocolate Fluff, **'89** 170
Mocha Cocoa, **'83** 318
Mocha-Cocoa Mix, Hot, **'82** 296
Mocha Coffee, **'85** M329
Mocha "Concrete," Abaco, **'94** 114
Mocha Cream, Café, **'84** 54
Mocha Cream Filling, **'81** 187; **'84** 305
Mocha Cream Roll, Chocolate, **'84** 304
Mocha-Cream Tart, Black Bottom,
  '92 304
Mocha Crunch Pie, Chocolate-, **'81** 136
Mocha Cupcakes, **'85** 250
Mocha Deluxe Hot Drink, **'82** 289
Mocha Dessert, Frozen, **'84** 311
Mocha Espresso, Italian, **'82** 254
Mocha Filling, **'80** 55; **'82** 262
Mocha-Flavored Hot Cocoa Mix, **'91** 316
Mocha Freeze, Royal, **'84** 53
Mocha Frosting, **'83** 301; **'84** 316; **'87** 224;
  '94 292
Mocha Frosting, Creamy, **'82** 289; **'84** 311;
  '91 248
Mocha Frosty, **'92** 44
Mocha Gingerbread, **'81** 207; **'82** 14
Mocha, Hot, **'84** 60
Mocha Ice Cream, **'88** 202
Mocha-Mallow Parfaits, **'80** 219
Mocha Meringue Pie, **'80** 242; **'88** 163
Mocha, Mexican, **'93** M341
Mocha Milkshake, **'89** 35
Mocha Mousse, **'94** 232
Mocha Pie, **'94** 168
Mocha Polka, **'89** 171
Mocha Pots de Crème, **'88** M45
Mocha Pralines, **'92** 313; **'93** 51
Mocha Pudding, Pecan-, **'89** M130
Mocha Punch, **'84** 58, 166; **'86** 270
Mocha, Quick Viennese, **'79** 232
Mocha Roulage, Chocolate-, **'80** 216
Mocha Sauce with Chocolate Yogurt,
  '92 243
Mocha, Spirited Hot, **'91** M260
Mocha Squares, Frozen, **'81** 187
Mocha Swirl Cheesecake, **'87** 262
Mocha, Swiss-Style, **'82** 253
Mocha Velvet Torte, **'92** 318
Mousse, Coffee, **'84** 126
Mousse, Coffee-Nut, **'86** 319
Mousse, Quick-as-a-Wink, **'84** 311
Nog, Brandied Coffee, **'86** 329
Orange Coffee, Viennese, **'84** 54
Parfaits, Coffee Crunch, **'82** 159
Pecans, Coffee 'n' Spice, **'88** 256
Pie, Coffee Cream, **'94** 209
Pie, Coffee Ice Cream, **'79** 231
Pie, Coffee Pecan, **'82** 74
Pie, Decadent Mud, **'89** 252
Pontalba, Café, **'92** 83

Coffee *(continued)*

Praline-Flavored Coffee, **'87** 69
Pralines, Café au Lait, **'92** 313; **'93** 51
Pralines, Plantation Coffee, **'86** 241
Punch, Coffee, **'80** 50; **'83** 275; **'88** 83
Punch, Coffee-and-Cream, **'85** 116
Punch, Coffee-Eggnog, **'86** 281
Punch, Coffee Eggnog, **'92** 264
Punch, Creamy Coffee, **'81** 50
Punch, "Eye-Opener" Coffee, **'92** 80
Punch, Rich-and-Creamy Coffee, **'82** 121
Refresher, Velvet Coffee, **'79** 149
Royal, Café, **'80** 259
Shake, Peach-Coffee Milk, **'84** 284
Spiced Brew, Hot, **'91** 36
Spiced Coffee, Special, **'84** 284
Spiced-Up Coffee, **'89** 92
Tortoni, Coffee-Almond, **'81** 30
Tortoni, Creamy Coffee, **'88** 268
Viennese, Café, **'82** 254
Coleslaw. *See* Cabbage and Salads/Slaws.
Cookies
Almond-Anise Biscotti, **'93** 266
Almond Biscotti, **'91** 108
Almond Butter Cookies, **'79** 52
Almond Chip Balls, Toasted, **'84** 240
Almond Cookies, **'83** 22, 181; **'91** 51;
   '92 176
Almond Cookies, Light, **'83** 151
Almond Cookies, Swedish, **'85** 312
Almond Snaps, **'92** 273
Almond Spritz Cookies, **'82** 306
Apple-Filled Cookies, **'92** 311
Bars and Squares
   Almond Cake Squares, **'79** 111
   Almond-Chocolate Bars, **'83** 304
   Almond Cream Confections, **'87** 198;
      '90 310
   Apple Butter Bars, **'84** 153
   Apple Kuchen, **'79** 24
   Apricot Bars, **'81** 247
   Apricot-Oatmeal Bars, **'86** 216
   Apricot-Raisin Bars, **'87** 32
   Banana Breakfast Bars, **'79** 124
   Blackberry Bars, **'87** 130
   Blackberry-Filled Bars, **'79** 124
   Blackberry Jam Bars, **'82** M185
   Blondie Swirls, **'85** 248
   Blond Nut Squares, **'82** 156
   Brazil Squares, **'82** 306
   Brownie Alaskas, **'83** 299
   Brownie Bars, Cinnamon, **'81** 230
   Brownie-Mint Dessert, **'82** 227
   Brownie Mix, **'82** 6
   Brownies, Amaretto, **'86** 246
   Brownies, Biscuit Mix, **'94** M51
   Brownies, Buttermilk, **'85** 249
   Brownies, Buttermilk Cake, **'87** 198
   Brownies, Butterscotch, **'85** 248
   Brownies, Candy Bar, **'92** 204
   Brownies, Cheesecake, **'85** 249
   Brownies, Chewy Marshmallow,
      '83 306
   Brownies, Chocolate-Banana, **'80** 160
   Brownies, Chocolate Chip, **'81** 162
   Brownies, Chocolate Chip-Peanut
      Butter, **'84** 73
   Brownies, Chocolate Ice Cream,
      '89 124

Brownies, Chocolate-Kahlúa, **'93** 99
Brownies, Chocolate-Mint, **'85** M294;
   '88 80
Brownies, Chocolate-Nut, **'81** 129
Brownies, Chocolate-Peanut Butter
   Chip, **'91** 306
Brownies, Chocolate-Pecan, **'81** 64
Brownies, Chocolate-Peppermint,
   '88 262
Brownies, Chocolate Tea, **'83** 79
Brownies, Chocolate-Walnut, **'89** 325
Brownies, Choco-Mallow, **'87** 198;
   '90 309
Brownies, Cream Cheese Swirl, **'79** 51
Brownies, Crème de Menthe, **'83** 244
Brownies, Crunch-Crust, **'87** 198
Brownies, Date-and-Almond, **'88** 217
Brownies, Easy, **'83** 245
Brownies, Favorite, **'86** 158
Brownies, Frosted Apple, **'86** 216
Brownies, Frosted Peanut Butter,
   '92 272
Brownies, German Cream Cheese,
   '80 269
Brownies, Heavenly Hash, **'83** 245
Brownies, Heavenly Honey, **'79** 83
Brownies, Macadamia-Fudge Designer,
   '94 51
Brownies, Mint Julep, **'93** 165
Brownies, Mississippi Mud, **'89** M25
Brownies, Mocha, **'87** 93
Brownies, Mother's, **'93** 239
Brownies, No-Bake, **'94** 330
Brownies, Nutty Blonde, **'81** 64
Brownies, Nutty Cocoa, **'81** 64
Brownies, Nutty Fudge, **'80** M171
Brownies, Oat, **'89** 59
Brownies, Oatmeal, **'87** 199
Brownies, Oat 'n' Crunch, **'91** 233
Brownies, Peanut Butter, **'87** 199
Brownies, Pistachio-Mint, **'94** 50
Brownies, Praline, **'93** 243
Brownies, Quick, **'87** M302
Brownies, Quick and Easy, **'82** 6
Brownies, Raspberry, **'92** 274
Brownies, Rocky Road, **'86** 320
Brownies, Saucepan Pretzel, **'85** 171
Brownies, Southern Chocolate-Mint,
   '93 216
Brownies, Special Derby, **'90** 94
Brownies, Triple Decker, **'92** 319
Brownies, Walnut-Cream Cheese,
   '84 240
Brownies, White Chocolate, **'89** 169
Brownies with Chocolate Chunks,
   Blonde, **'91** 271
Brownies with Mocha Frosting, **'94** 292
Butter Pecan Pie Squares, **'81** 262
Butter Pecan Turtle Bars, **'90** 70
Butterscotch Bars, **'82** 209; **'83** 297
By-Cracky Bars, **'84** 212
Carrot-Lemon Squares, Golden, **'80** 40
Carrot Squares, **'79** 256
Cherry Bars, Delightful, **'86** 217
Cherry Squares, Surprise, **'82** 57
Choco-Crumble Bars, **'79** 292
Chocolate-Butterscotch Bars, **'81** 197
Chocolate-Caramel Layer Squares,
   '79 83
Chocolate Chess Squares, **'92** 45
Chocolate Chip Bars, **'81** 130

Chocolate Chip-Peanut Butter Squares,
   '84 118
Chocolate Chip Squares, **'83** 170;
   '89 143
Chocolate Chip Squares, Chewy,
   '91 175
Chocolate Cinnamon Bars, **'82** 209
Chocolate-Coconut Squares, **'90** 70
Chocolate-Crème de Menthe Bars,
   '86 245
Chocolate Crème de Menthe Bites,
   '88 285
Chocolate Dream Bars, **'79** 256;
   '82 298
Chocolate-Peanut Crispies, **'93** 80
Chocolate-Peppermint Squares, **'81** 119
Cinnamon Chews, **'84** 110
Cinnamon Sand Bars, **'91** 178
Coconut Granola Bars, **'85** 202
Coffee Bars, Frosted, **'79** 256
Crème de Menthe Squares, **'93** 256
Date Bars, **'84** 313
Date Bars, No-Bake, **'79** 256
Date Bars, Nutty, **'84** 153
Date-Nut Bars, **'80** 166
Date-Oat Bars, **'80** M172
English Cherubs, **'83** 257
Fudge Bars, **'86** 93
Fudge Bars, Yummy, **'87** 158
German Chocolate Chess Squares,
   '94 51
Golden Bars, **'84** 255
Granola Bars, **'83** 305
Granola Bars, Fruit and Nut, **'81** 49
Hawaiian Bars, **'84** 153
Honey Cake Squares, **'89** 250
Jam-It Bars, **'87** 159
Jam Squares, **'81** M289
Janhagel Cookies, **'86** 195
Layer Squares, Novelty, **'90** 70
Lemon Bars Deluxe, **'79** 35
Lemon Bars, Tangy, **'86** 217
Lemon-Pecan Squares, **'89** 124
Lemon Squares, **'81** 197
Lemon Yogurt Wheat Bars, **'79** 93
Lime Squares, **'79** 2
Marmalade Biscuit Squares, **'79** 193
Meringue-Chocolate Chip Bars, **'84** 118
Mincemeat-Spice Bars, **'88** 231; **'89** 22
Mystery Bars, **'93** 239
Nutmeg Logs, Frosted, **'85** 324
Nutty Choco Snacks, **'83** 305
Oatmeal Bars, Chocolate-Topped,
   '86 110
Oatmeal-Caramel Bars, **'85** 247
Oatmeal-Date Bars, Layered, **'85** 10
Peanut Bars, **'89** 307
Peanut Bars, Chewy, **'80** M172
Peanut Butter-and-Fudge Bars,
   '80 M172
Peanut Butter Bars, **'84** 243; **'93** 166
Peanut Butter Fingers, **'79** 256
Peanut Butter Frosts, **'84** 153
Peanut Butter-Jam Bars, **'94** 291
Peanut Butter Logs, No-Bake, **'84** 211
Peanut Butter 'n' Jelly Bars, **'83** 305
Peanut Butter Squares, **'83** 116
Pecan Bars, **'82** 209
Pecan Bars, Gooey, **'94** 133
Pecan Squares, **'79** 205; **'90** 69
Pecan Squares, Easy, **'81** 230

Cookies, Bars and Squares *(continued)*

Pecan Squares, Twice-Baked, **'79** 291
Pumpkin Bars, **'80** 40
Pumpkin Nut Bars, **'82** 217
Raisin Bars, **'94** 228
Raspberry Bars, **'82** 209; **'84** 212
Rhubarb Squares, **'91** 146
Rhubarb Squares, Rosy, **'79** 111
Shortbread, Orange, **'91** 272
Strawberry Bars, **'81** 301
Toffee Treats, **'89** 330
Tropical Bars, **'80** 284
Wheat Germ Squares, Spicy, **'80** 44
Yummy Bars, **'92** 171
Zucchini Bars, **'85** 77
Bird's Nest Cookies, **'93** 284
Biscotti Cioccolata, **'93** 268
Bonbon Cookies, Surprise, **'88** 119
Bourbon Balls, **'81** 254
Bourbon Dunkers, Crunchy, **'85** 90
Brutti Ma Buoni (Ugly but Good), **'93** 267
Butter Cookies, **'85** 322
Butter Cookies, Chocolate-Tipped, **'84** 258; **'90** 312
Butter Cookies, Holiday, **'92** 317
Butter Cookies, Melt-Away, **'81** 20
Butter-Nut Strips, **'82** 167
Butter Pecan Cookies, **'82** 139
Cheesecake Cookies, Chewy, **'82** 109
Cheese Straws, **'88** 77
Cherry Bonbon Cookies, **'93** 52
Cherry Crowns, **'92** 275
Cherry Nut Nuggets, **'81** 286
Chocolate-Cherry Cookies, Frosted, **'89** 294
Chocolate Chewies, Easy, **'93** 296; **'94** 234
Chocolate Chip Cookies, Giant, **'84** 119
Chocolate Chip Melt-Aways, **'84** 118
Chocolate Cookies, Caramel-Filled, **'92** 319
Chocolate Cookies, Sugar-Coated, **'92** 274
Chocolate Crunch Cookies, **'91** 316
Chocolate-Filled Bonbons, **'89** 162
Chocolate-Mint Snaps, **'83** 103; **'84** 96
Chocolate-Peanut Butter Cones, **'85** 14
Chocolate-Peanut Butter Cookies, **'85** 90
Chocolate-Peanut Butter Cups, **'85** 14
Chocolate Seashells, **'91** 178
Chocolate Snappers, Jumbo, **'81** 218
Chocolate Snowflake Cookies, **'89** 329
Chocolate-Tipped Log Cookies, **'87** 294
Choco-Nut Sandwich Cookies, **'84** 200
Christmas
Calendar, Cookie Advent, **'85** 325
Candy Canes and Wreaths, Braided, **'92** 276
Cards, Christmas Cookie, **'84** 302
Cherry Cookies, Christmas, **'88** 282
Date Cookies, Christmas, **'88** 287
Eggnog Christmas Cookies, **'79** 255
Elf Cookie, **'80** 279, 303
Fruit Squares, Christmas, **'88** 282
Gingerbread Bowl, Christmas, **'93** 266
Gingerbread Cookies, **'80** 278
Lizzies, Christmas, **'87** 257
Moravian Christmas Cookies, **'91** 282
Mrs. Claus Cookie, **'80** 279, 303
Ornaments, Edible, **'94** 316
Painted Cookies, **'86** 322
Reindeer Cookies, Jolly, **'91** 273
Rudolph Cookie, **'80** 279, 303

Santa Claus Cookie, **'80** 278, 303
Santa's Whiskers, **'85** 323
Sleigh Cookie, **'80** 279, 303
Spiced Christmas Cookies, **'87** 294
Strawberries, Christmas, **'87** 293
Swedish Christmas Cookies, **'79** 290
Tree Cookies, Christmas, **'93** 286
Trees, Christmas, **'89** 294
Cinnamon Balls, **'79** 23
Cinnamon Sticks, Italian, **'93** 204
Cinnamon Wafers, **'81** 192
Cocoa Kiss Cookies, **'85** 171
Coconut Cookies, Crisp, **'89** 162
Coconut-Oatmeal Cookies, Crispy, **'93** 80
Curled Cookies, French, **'87** 16
Drop
Ambrosia Cookies, **'81** 301; **'82** 110; **'86** 313
Apple Butter Spice Cookies, **'79** 291
Apple Cookies, Fresh, **'84** 36
Apple-Nut Cookies, **'80** 228
Apple Oatmeal Cookies, **'85** 215
Apple-Oatmeal Cookies, **'90** 218
Apricot Cookies, Frosted, **'81** 192
Banana Oatmeal Cookies, **'79** 217
Benne Seed Cookies, **'84** 318
Breakfast Cookies, Take-Along, **'84** 59
Brownie Chip Cookies, **'90** 320
Butterscotch Cookies, **'87** 58
Butterscotch-Pecan Cookies, **'84** 36
Candy Bit Cookies, **'81** 192
Carrot Cookies, **'82** 137
Carrot Cookies, Frosted, **'81** 7
Carrot-Orange Cookies, **'83** 149
Cashew Crunch Cookies, **'92** 17
Cherry-Almond Drops, **'81** 20
Chip Cookies, Double, **'81** 301
Chips Cookies, Loaded-with-, **'87** 223
Chocolate-Bran Raisin Jumbos, **'91** 142
Chocolate Chewies, **'93** 216
Chocolate Chip Cookies, **'84** 120; **'86** 245; **'90** 193
Chocolate Chip Cookies, Deluxe, **'79** 216
Chocolate Chip Cookies, Different, **'83** 114
Chocolate Chip Cookies, Double, **'79** 217
Chocolate Chip Cookies, Jumbo, **'82** 110
Chocolate Chip Cookies, Light, **'86** 46
Chocolate Chip Cookies, Mom Ford's, **'94** 287
Chocolate Chip Cookies, Nutty Oatmeal-, **'82** M185
Chocolate Chip-Oatmeal Cookies, **'84** 119
Chocolate Chippers, **'92** 206
Chocolate Chip-Pudding Cookies, **'93** 21
Chocolate-Chocolate Chip Cookies, **'82** 35
Chocolate Chunk Cookies, Super, **'88** 217
Chocolate Cookies, Doubly-Good, **'82** M185
Chocolate Crispy Cookies, **'85** 115
Chocolate Drop Cookies, **'84** 36
Chocolate Macaroon Cookies, **'88** 217
Chocolate Macaroons, **'87** 57
Chocolate-Mint Chip Cookies, **'86** 245
Chocolate-Mint Cookies, **'92** 206
Chocolate-Nut Chews, **'81** 92

Chocolate-Oatmeal Cookies, **'80** 105
Chocolate-Orange Delights, **'93** 52
Chocolate-Peanut Cookies, **'83** 223
Chocolate Sandwich Cookies, **'81** 192
Choco-Peanut Chip Cookies, **'92** 318
Cocoa Drop Cookies, **'80** 217
Coconut-Cherry Cookies, **'79** 292
Coconut Kisses, **'90** 106
Coconut Macaroons, **'79** 52
Cream Cheese Cookies, **'80** 282
Date-Nut Chocolate Chip Cookies, Rich, **'92** 207
Devil Doggies, **'84** 37
Forget 'em Cookies, **'83** 256
Fruitcake Cookies, **'79** 291; **'86** 320; **'88** 286
Fruitcake Cookies, Holiday, **'81** 301
Fruitcake Drop Cookies, **'92** 275
Fruit Cookies, Bourbon, **'86** 334
Fruit Cookies, Spicy Holiday, **'83** 298
Fruit Drops, Candied, **'89** 329
Gumdrop Cookies, **'79** 292
Jack-O'-Lantern Cookies, **'87** 214
Lace Cookies, **'86** 8
Lemonade Cookies, **'79** 51
Lemon Yummies, **'81** 301
Macadamia Nut White Chocolate Cookies, Chunky, **'92** 207
Macaroons, Chocolate, **'83** 300
Melting Moments, **'85** 191
Meringue Kiss Cookies, **'86** 121
Meringue Surprise Cookies, **'86** 320
Mincemeat Drop Cookies, **'79** 246
Molasses Cookies, Chewy, **'87** 257
Molasses Cookies, Crispy-Chewy, **'90** 218
Monster Cookies, **'84** 36
Nugget Cookies, **'79** 291
Oatmeal-Chocolate Chippers, **'90** 218
Oatmeal Cookies, **'92** 82
Oatmeal Cookies, Cinnamon, **'84** 72
Oatmeal Cookies, Crunchy, **'85** 202
Oatmeal Cookies, Easy, **'80** 105
Oatmeal Cookies, Nutty, **'81** 130
Oatmeal Cookies, Old-Fashioned, **'80** 106; **'85** 250
Oatmeal Cookies, Orange-Glazed, **'80** 60
Oatmeal Cookies, Peanutty, **'80** 106; **'83** 95
Oatmeal Cookies, Spicy, **'81** 197
Oatmeal Cookies, Toasted, **'92** 273
Oatmeal-Date Cookies, **'82** 109
Oatmeal Krispies, **'85** 115
Oatmeal-Peanut Butter Chocolate Chip Cookies, **'92** 207
Oatmeal-Peanut Butter Cookies, **'85** 171
Oatmeal-Raisin Cookies, **'87** 221; **'93** 127
Oatmeal-Raisin Cookies, Frosted, **'79** 290
Oatmeal-Spice Cookies, Giant, **'80** 105
Oatmeal Sunshine Cookies, **'89** 59
Oats-and-Peanut Cookies, **'89** 60
Orange-Chocolate Cookies, **'83** 113
Orange Cookies, Frosted, **'83** 114
Peanut Butter Cookies, No-Bake, **'94** 197
Peanut Butter-Oatmeal Cookies, **'81** 218

Cookies, Drop *(continued)*

Peanut Cookies, Salted, **'87** 92
Persimmon-Raisin Cookies, **'85** 232
Pineapple Cookies, **'79** 216
Potato Chip Cookies, **'86** 93
Praline Cookies, **'91** 271
Pumpkin-Chocolate Chip Cookies, **'93** 235
Pumpkin Drop Cookies, **'79** 206
Pumpkin-Walnut Cookies, Frosted, **'82** 217
Rainy Day Cookies, **'94** 168
Raisin Cookies, Alltime Favorite, **'80** 24
Raisin-Granola Treats, **'92** 22
Sour Cream Cookies, Southern, **'83** 113
Sour Cream-Nutmeg Cookies, **'85** 171
Sugar Cookies, Nutmeg, **'79** 136
Sugar Cookies, Stir-and-Drop, **'92** 174
Sunflower Cookies, Crinkle, **'83** 149
Tea Cakes, Dropped, **'90** 156
Toffee Crunch Cookies, **'93** 80
Walnut Spice Kisses, **'89** 295
White Chocolate-Macadamia Nut Cookies, **'94** 315
Eggnog Logs, **'92** 274
Ginger Cookies, **'85** 306
Ginger Crinkles, **'83** 149
Gingersnaps, **'79** 146; **'91** 299; **'92** 264
Gingersnaps, Best-Ever, **'79** 208
Hazelnut Cookies, **'84** 111
Hazelnut-Lemon Logs, **'84** 117
Heavenly Delights, **'85** 324
Keyboard Cookies, **'94** M330
Kissy Cookies, **'93** 331
Lace Cookies, Florentine, **'88** 120
Lemon Cookies, Sunshine, **'86** 69
Lemon Crinkle Cookies, **'81** 287
Lemon Zephers, **'81** 172
Lollipop Cookies, **'94** 196
Macadamia-Oat Snowballs, **'92** 274
Madeleines, Snow-Capped, **'85** 120
Mailing Cookies, Tips on, **'83** 305
Miracle Cookies, **'83** 149
Mix, Quick, **'94** 167
Molasses Crinkles, **'92** 276
Oat Cookies, Crispy, **'88** 203; **'90** 311
Oatmeal Cookies, Special, **'81** 236
Orange Fingers, **'87** 57
Peanut Butter and Chocolate Chunk Cookies, **'94** 169
Peanut Butter-Chocolate Kiss Cookies, **'86** 49
Peanut Butter-Cinnamon Cookies, **'84** 30
Peanut Butter Cookies, **'82** 56
Peanut Butter Cookies, Double-Chip, **'89** 169
Peanut Butter Cookies, Easy, **'92** 272
Peanut Butter Cookies, Quick, **'86** 109
Peanut Butter-Oatmeal Cookies, **'84** 72
Peanut Butter Temptations, **'84** 29
Peanut-Date Balls, **'81** 92
Peanut Truffle Cookies, **'93** 212
Pecan-Butter Cookies, **'83** 113
Pecan Crescent Cookies, **'85** 324
Pecan Pie Cookies, **'92** 289
Peppermint Candy Cookies, **'88** 286
Peppermint Sandwich Cookies, **'92** 277
Peppermint Wreaths, Melt-Away, **'85** 324
Pizzelles, **'83** 298
Pumpkin Cookies, Peppy, **'89** 253

Refrigerator
Almond Crunch Cookies, Texan-Size, **'91** 236
Apricot Kolaches, **'83** 84
Biscotti, Light, **'91** 310
Brown Sugar-Pecan Cookies, **'91** 236
Buckin' Bronco Cookies, **'90** 95
Butter Cookies, Valentine, **'81** 20
Cardamom Cookies, **'79** 12
Cheese Wafers, Hope Farm, **'93** 282
Cherry Pecan Cookies, **'82** 136
Chocolate-Almond Surprise Cookies, **'88** M45
Chocolate-Cherry Cookies, **'85** 324
Chocolate-Gingerbread Cookies, **'94** 293
Chocolate Meltaways, **'81** 302
Chocolate-Nut Freezer Cookies, **'88** 217
Chocolate Pinwheel Cookies, **'86** 245
Chocolate Snowball Cookies, **'82** 295
Chocolate Teasers, **'87** 44
Choco Surprise Cookies, **'80** 60
Crème de Menthe Cookies, **'86** 230
Crescents, **'85** 321
Date-Cream Cheese Rollups, **'83** 298
Date Nut Roll, **'79** 249
Fudge Puddles, **'94** 292
Gingerbirds, **'93** 283
Gingerbread Men, **'84** 299
Gingerbread Men, Miniature, **'84** 318
Ginger Icebox Cookies, **'93** 205
Gingersnaps, Raisin, **'85** 324
Holiday Garland Cookies, **'83** 299
Holiday Riches, **'83** 257
Memory Book Cookies, **'92** 45
Molasses Cookies, **'86** 20
Oatmeal Cookies, Crispy, **'89** 328
Oatmeal-Date Sandwich Cookies, **'83** 257
Orange Crispies, **'84** 205
Orange Refrigerator Cookies, **'86** 230
Orange-Slice Cookies, **'89** 294
Peanut Butter-Chocolate Chip Cookies, Freezer, **'86** 230
Peanut Butter-Coconut Cookies, **'83** 113
Peanut Butter Cookie Ice Cream Sandwiches, **'93** 199
Peanut Butter Cookies, **'87** 58
Peanut Butter Crisps, **'79** 50
Peanut Butter Slice-and-Bakes, **'82** M185
Peanut Butter Snaps, **'81** 237
Pecan-Cheese Wafers, **'81** 119
Pecan Crisps, Sugar, **'86** 230
Peppermint Rounds, **'94** 19
Pinwheel Cookies, **'93** 316
Raspberry Sandwich Cookies, **'82** 306
Ribbon Cookies, **'87** 293
Sandwich Cookies, Grandmother's, **'82** 306
Sesame-Cheese Cutouts, **'82** 296
Shortbread Cookie Crumbs, **'83** 298
Shortbread Cookies, **'87** 58
Shortbread Cookies, Crispy, **'83** 113
Snowball Surprises, **'93** 315
Sour Cream Cookies, Dutch, **'83** 149
Spice Cookies, Slice-of-, **'79** 290
Spice-Molasses Cookies, **'89** 289
Springerle, **'81** 251

Sugar Cookies, Crisp, **'84** 243
Sugar Cookies, Golden, **'88** 286
Sugar Cookies, Molasses, **'80** 270
Sugar Cookies, Red-, **'81** 21
Sugar Cookies, Symbol, **'91** 282
Sugar Cookies, Valentine, **'82** 20
Sugar 'n Spice Cookies, **'81** 21
Swedish Cookies, **'82** 306
Taco-Cheese Animal Crackers, **'94** 197
Tea Cakes, Old-Fashioned, **'91** 72
Tea Cookies, **'83** 170
Vanilla Crescents, **'82** 307
Vanilla Slice-and-Bake Cookies, **'85** 171
Wafers, Italian, **'87** 36
Walnut Cookies, **'81** 301
Watermelon Cookies, **'92** 179
Rolled
Almond-Filled Wafers, **'88** 120
Almond Holly Leaves, **'86** 319
Apricot Cookie Rolls, **'80** 282
Apricot Kolaches, **'94** 291
Apricot Wonders, **'93** 316
Bears, Red-Bellied, **'92** 277
Biscochitos, **'92** 230
Cheese Straws, **'82** 137
Chocolate Cookies, Chewy, **'80** 208
Cinnamon Stars, Swiss, **'87** 293
Cream Cheese Frills, **'79** 291
Crème de Menthe Cookies, **'80** 282
Cutout Cookies, Old-Fashioned, **'92** 273
Date-Filled Cookies, **'91** 95
Frosted Cutout Cookies, **'85** 236
Fruit Cookies, Rolled, **'80** 15
Fruit-Nut Twists, **'82** 253
Gingerbread Animal Cookies, **'86** 70
Gingerbread Cookies, **'80** 278; **'92** 343
Gingerbread Man Cookies, **'88** 227
Gingerbread Men, **'85** 259
Gingerbread Men Cookies, **'85** 319
Gingerbread People, **'92** 312
Ginger Cookies, Swedish, **'85** 323
Grandmother's Cookies, **'85** 319
Ice Box Filled Cookies, **'79** 112
Lemon Pecan Dainties, **'80** 208
Lemony Cutout Cookies, **'85** 323
Maple Sandwich Cookies, **'85** 322
Mincemeat Cookies, **'79** 51
Mincemeat Sweetheart Cookies, **'87** 293
Oat Crispies, **'83** 96
Oatmeal-Coconut Cookies, **'80** 218
Oatmeal Cookies, Date-Filled, **'86** 314
Oatmeal Cookies, Slice-and-Bake, **'80** 105
Oatmeal Nut Crispies, **'80** 208
Orange-Pecan Cookies, **'88** 119
Ornaments, Edible, **'94** 316
Peanut Butter Cookies, Double, **'80** 209
Peanuttiest Cookies, Crisp, **'88** 65
Pear Mincemeat Cookies, **'84** 264
Pecan Cookies, Easy, **'80** 208
Pumpkin Cookies, Great, **'91** 234
Raspberry Swirl Cookies, **'90** 111
Rugelach, **'92** 252
Scones, Currant, **'84** 117
Sherry Snaps, **'87** 94
Shortbread Cookies, Butter Pecan, **'80** 282
Shortbread Cookies, Coconut, **'93** 316
Shortbread, Easy Roll-Out, **'81** 21
Shortbread Sugarplums, Pecan-, **'83** 298

Cookies, Rolled (continued)

Snowflake Cookies, '92 278
Snow Flurries, '92 275
Strawberry Cookie Tarts, '89 112
Sugar Cookies, '94 271
Sugar Cookies, Crescent, '87 294
Sugar Cookies, Molasses, '80 270
Sugar Cookies, Moravian, '85 321
Sugar Cookies, Old-Fashioned, '86 313
Sugar Cookies, Orange, '89 329
Sugar Cookies, Rolled, '79 291
Sweetheart Cookies, '93 53
Tea Cakes, Back-Home, '90 156
Teacakes, Currant, '80 88
Tea Cakes, Decorative, '90 156
Tea Cakes, Grandma's, '90 156
Teacakes, Old-Fashioned, '84 43
Tea Cakes, Sorghum, '85 239
Sandwich Cookies, Viennese, '87 293
Sesame Cookies, Italian, '85 311
Shortbread, Brown Sugar, '93 331
Shortbread Cookie, Old-Fashioned, '88 242
Shortbread Cookies, Java, '94 233
Shortbread Cookies, Praline, '88 242
Shortbread Cookies, Spiced, '88 242
Shortbread Madeleines, Orange, '88 242
Shortbread, Scottish, '94 242
Shortbread Wafers, Cocoa, '88 243
Spice Cookies, '87 M278
Spider Cookies, '93 M166
Spritz Cookies, Butter, '91 175
Spritz Hearts, '91 107
Sugar Cookies, Cinnamon, '84 73
Sugar Cookies, Double-Chocolate, '92 206
Sugar Cookies, Molasses, '82 140
Sugar Cookies, Sour Cream, '79 51
Swedish Heirloom Cookies, '81 129; '90 311
Tea Cakes, Brandied Apricot, '91 241
Tea Cakes, Mexican, '81 196
Thumbprint Cookies, Childhood, '85 323
Thumbprint Cookies, Praline, '89 328
Turkey Treats, '93 256
Turtle Cookies, Snappin', '85 323
Waffle Cookies, Brownie, '86 245
Walnut Cookies, Simply, '91 236
Wedding Cookies, '82 M185
Whoopie Pies, '86 246
Cooking Light. See Living Light.

Corn
Bake, Corn-and-Swiss Cheese, '92 133
Bake, Corn-Zucchini, '79 178
Baked Corn, Creamy, '90 60
Baked Corn with Sour Cream, '86 170
Bake, Oyster-and-Corn, '83 34; '84 44
Balls, Zesty Corn Dressing, '82 307
Bisque, Crab-and-Corn, '87 137
Casserole, Broccoli-Corn, '83 313
Casserole, Chili-Corn, '88 266
Casserole, Corn, '79 247; '89 126; '93 141
Casserole, Corn-and-Bean, '90 208
Casserole, Corn and Cheese, '81 128
Casserole, Corn-and-Green Chile, '89 68
Casserole, Corn and Tomato, '81 127
Casserole, Corn-and-Tomato, '84 145
Casserole, Fresh Corn, '80 165
Casserole, Green Bean-and-Corn, '88 123
Casserole, Jalapeño-Corn, '83 256
Casserole, Salami-Corn, '80 209
Chiles Rellenos with Walnut Cream Sauce,
   Havarti-and-Corn-Stuffed, '93 M275
Chowder, Corn, '81 128; '83 20; '84 M38;
   '85 10; '90 202; '91 132
Chowder, Corn and Cheese, '80 228
Chowder, Curried Chicken-and-Corn, '92 21
Chowder, Delicious Corn, '82 279
Chowder, Fresh Corn and Bacon, '93 203
Chowder, Ham and Corn, '79 16
Chowder, Ham-and-Corn, '82 40
Chowder, Oyster-Corn, '83 211
Chowder, Potato-Corn, '94 66
Chowder, Shrimp and Corn, '79 199
Chowder, Turkey-Corn, '81 98
Christmas Corn, '93 325
Cob, Barbecued Corn on the, '81 128
Cob, Corn on the, '79 122
Cob, Foil-Baked Corn on the, '81 128
Cob, Foiled Corn on the, '80 165
Cob, Grilled Corn-on-the-, '90 166
Cob, Lemony Corn on the, '89 200
Cob, Microwaved Corn on the, '80 M122
Cob, Parmesan Corn on the, '88 M187
Cob, Seasoned Baked Corn on the, '82 134
Cob, Spicy Corn-on-the-, '84 149
Cob, Spicy Corn on the, '87 M151
Cob with Herb Butter, Corn-on-the-, '84 160
Cold-Pack Corn, '81 216
Combo, Zucchini-Corn, '86 218
Creamed Corn, Southern-Style, '81 M165;
   '92 201
Creamed Fresh Corn, '82 158
Cream-Style Corn, '80 127; '85 106
Creamy Corn, '79 213; '90 207
Creole Corn, '81 128
Creole, Corn-and-Okra, '89 127
Creole, Okra-Corn, '83 157
Curried Corn and Celery, '86 192
Custard, Fresh Corn, '89 127
Deviled Corn, '86 192
Dinner, Corn-and-Ham Skillet, '83 190
Dip, Roasted Corn-and-Avocado, '91 279
Escalloped Corn, '79 251
Flan, Corn-Chive, '94 172
Fresh Corn, Seasoned, '83 M147
Fried Corn, '89 127; '94 158
Fried Corn, Skillet, '83 190
Frittata, Corn-and-Squash, '89 144
Frittata, Skillet Corn, '87 90
Fritters, Corn, '86 192; '94 22
Fritters, Golden Corn, '80 165; '81 128

Fritters, Skillet-Fried Corn, '85 14
Grill, Corn on the, '94 161
Grilled Parmesan Corn, '82 127
Herb Butter Sauce, Corn with, '79 150
Hush Puppies with Corn, '83 286; '84 17
Limping Susan, '90 155
Macque Choux (Smothered Corn), '94 236
Meat Loaf, Corny, '86 68
Medley, Okra-Corn-Tomato, '81 159
Medley, Peas-and-Corn, '85 138
Medley, Skillet Corn, '86 192
Medley, Summer Garden, '84 158
Medley, Zucchini-and-Corn, '80 298; '81 25
Mexican Corn, '80 157, 165
Mexican Corn, Spicy, '93 90
Mexi-Corn, '82 M21
Moussaka, Corn, '87 190
Muffins, Corn-Oat, '89 108
Muffins, Tex-Mex Corn, '92 253; '93 144
Okra and Corn in Cream, '79 160
Okra, Corn, and Peppers, '87 M151
Pancakes, Corn, '93 43
Parslied Corn, '90 155
Peppers, Corn-Stuffed, '84 104
Peppers, Ham-and-Corn Stuffed, '81 87
Pie, Quick and Cheesy Corn, '82 191
Pudding, Baked Corn, '83 314
Pudding, Corn, '79 276; '81 128; '86 192;
   '90 219
Pudding, Corn-Cheese, '80 244
Pudding, Creamy Corn, '81 267
Pudding, Easy Corn, '83 280
Pudding, Fresh Corn, '80 157, 165; '89 172
Quiche, Jalapeño-Corn, '85 122
Quick Corn Fix-Up, '81 M4
Relish, Corn, '81 129, 175; '83 189;
   '84 107; '85 136; '87 120, 245; '92 241
Relish Dogs, Corn, '85 192
Relish, Easy Corn, '83 260
Relish, Quick Corn, '90 13
Relish, Summer Corn, '89 127
Relish, Sweet Corn, '93 119
Relish, Virginia Corn, '79 283
Roasted Red Pepper Corn, '91 122
Salad, Broccoli-Corn, '87 24
Salad, Chilled Corn, '79 20
Salad, Corn, '80 247; '81 139; '85 236;
   '91 27
Salad, Corn-and-Pea, '90 181
Salad, Corn-in-the-Shuck, '93 236
Salad, Festive Corn, '92 263
Salad, Fresh Corn, '91 126; '94 162
Salad, Garden Medley, '80 122
Salad, Marinated Corn, '89 126
Salad, Marinated Corn-Bean, '87 9
Salad, Shoepeg Corn, '81 23
Salad, Tangy Corn, '88 176
Salad, Tasty Corn, '84 289
Salad, Wheat Berry-and-Roasted Corn,
   '94 175
Salsa, Avocado-Corn, '94 201
Salsa, Black Bean-and-Corn, '94 80
Salsa, Mexi-Corn, '91 182
Salsa, Spicy Corn, '93 322
Salsa, Yellowfin Tuna with Corn, Pepper, and
   Tomato, '94 164
Sauté, Corn, '80 165
Sautéed Corn and Okra, '84 158
Scalloped Corn, '80 164; '81 128; '86 111;
   '88 218
Scalloped Corn, Baked, '85 290

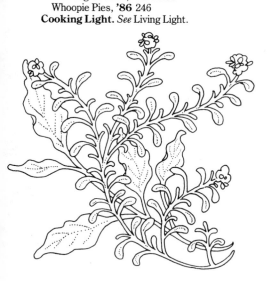

Corn *(continued)*

Scalloped Corn, Elegant, '86 268
Scalloped Corn for Two, '82 208
Slaw, Corn and Cabbage, '79 135
Smoked Corn, Hickory-, '85 145
Soufflé, Corn-and-Cheese, '88 122
Soufflé, Zucchini-and-Corn, '83 265
Soup, Corn, '80 56; '85 243; '87 156
Soup, Corn-and-Bourbon, '92 194
Soup, Cream of Corn, '90 210
Soup, Favorite Corn, '85 155
Soup, Fresh Corn-and-Crab, '92 183
Soup, Grilled Corn, '87 121
Soup, Pimiento-Corn, '89 126
Soup, Shrimp-and-Corn, '84 88
Spoonbread, Corn and Bacon, '81 129
Spoonbread, Corn-Cheese, '88 9
Succotash, Easy, '80 165
Timbales, Corn-and-Zucchini, '92 100
Tomatoes-and-Corn, Creole-Style, '84 142
Tomatoes, Corn-Stuffed, '82 270
Tomatoes with Corn, Baked, '80 161
Vinaigrette, Okra-Corn-and-Tomato, '90 173
Waffles, Corn-Chile, '94 206
Whole Kernel Corn, '85 106
Zucchini and Corn, '86 177
Zucchini and Corn, Dilled, '83 173
Zucchini, Corn and, '83 190

Cornbreads
Acorn Squash Puppies, '94 268
Bake, Cornbread Tamale, '79 163
Beef Cornbread, Cheesy, '81 242
Biscuits, Cornmeal-Jalapeño, '94 214
Bites, Corn Dog, '85 245
Buttermilk Cornbread, '79 34; '82 70
Carrot Cornbread, '80 89; '81 163
Casserole, Bean-and-Cornbread, '92 243
Casserole, Cornbread, '81 91
Casserole, Cornbread Skillet, '83 243; '84 101
Cheddar Cornbread, '83 285; '84 17
Cheddar-Jalapeño Cornbread, '85 3
Cheese Cornbread, Swiss, '79 60
Chicken over Cornbread, Creamed, '86 231
Chile-Cheese Cornbread, '87 171
Chile Cornbread, '86 254
Chile Cornbread, Green, '82 134
Confetti Cornbread, '94 170
Cornbread, '80 272; '86 231; '87 197; '92 324; '93 122
Cottage Cheese Cornbread, '80 90
Cowboy Cornbread, '81 188
Cracklin' Cornbread, '92 216

Cracklin' Cornbread, Southern, '80 119
Crackling Cornbread, '85 200
Crackling Cowboy Cornbread, '82 114
Crispy Cornbread, '92 340
Croutons, Cornbread, '93 192
Croutons, Honeyed Cornbread, '94 106
Crusty Cornbread, '85 255
Dieter's Cornbread, '87 164
Dressing, Chicken Cornbread, '90 159
Dressing, Cornbread, '86 286; '88 254; '92 267
Dressing, Cornbread-and-Sausage, '83 213
Dressing, Cornbread-Biscuit, '79 296
Dressing, Cornbread-Sage, '80 262
Dressing, Cornbread-Sausage, '82 307; '85 280
Dressing, Fruited Cornbread, '80 262
Dressing, Green Chile-Cornbread, '93 306; '94 296
Dressing, Herb-Seasoned Cornbread, '83 315
Dressing, Kentucky Cornbread, '86 281
Dressing, Light Cornbread, '92 324
Dressing, Old-Fashioned Cornbread, '84 321
Dressing, Quail Stuffed with Cornbread, '93 280
Dressing, Roast Turkey and Cornbread, '89 324
Dressing, Sage-Cornbread, '84 283
Dressing, Savory Cornbread, '88 303
Dressing, Texas Cornbread, '82 243
Dressing, Turkey with Sausage-Cornbread, '83 287
Easy Cornbread, '94 158
Fresh Cornbread, '80 165
Herbed Cornbread, '90 214
Hoecake, Hot Water, '81 56
Hoecakes, Green Onion, '88 112
Honey Cornbread, '83 286; '84 17
Hot Water Cornbread, '88 92
Hush Puppies, '84 102; '87 15; '92 168
Hush Puppies, Aunt Jenny's, '84 88
Hush Puppies, Bacon, '91 201
Hush Puppies, Baked, '89 53
Hush Puppies, Cheesy Mexican, '91 201
Hush Puppies, Cracker, '80 99
Hush Puppies, Easy, '81 191; '85 14
Hush Puppies, Fiery Beer, '86 233
Hush Puppies, Golden, '82 135
Hush Puppies, Mexican, '90 214
Hush Puppies, Onion, '85 14
Hush Puppies, Peppery, '80 221; '88 111
Hush Puppies, Tomato-Onion, '91 201
Hush Puppies, Topsail Island, '79 152
Hush Puppies with Corn, '83 286; '84 17
Jalapeño Cornbread, '85 200; '94 78
Jalapeño Cornbread, Beefy, '82 142
Jalapeño Pepper Bread, '83 121
Lacy Corncakes, '81 242
Lightbread, Corn, '81 137
Light Cornbread, Old Southern, '81 242
Loaf, Cornbread, '85 200
Menfolks' Cornbread, '82 156

Mexican Cornbread, '80 198; '81 137; '84 140, 242; '93 182
Mexican Cornbread, Hot, '83 286; '84 17
Mexican Cornbread, Quick, '81 242
Mexican Flatbread, '80 197
Muffins, Blue Corn, '89 145; '92 52; '94 114
Muffins, Cheesy Cornbread, '88 M275
Muffins, Corn, '82 M282; '84 16
Muffins, Cornmeal, '80 90; '88 92
Muffins, Cornmeal Yeast, '92 49
Muffins, Four-Grain, '80 46
Muffins, Jalapeño-Corn, '93 164
Muffins, Miniature Cornmeal, '93 119
Muffins, Quick Corn, '88 15
Muffins, Sage-Corn, '83 207
Muffins, Southern Cornbread, '85 201
Muffins, Spicy Cornbread, '90 59
Muffins, Tex-Mex Corn, '93 144
Muffins, Tomato Corn, '81 137
Mush, '81 215
Old-Fashioned Cornbread, '81 242
Onion Cornbread, '88 283
Onion-Topped Cornbread, '84 153
Oysters Casino on Cornbread, '79 34
Paprika Cornbread, '90 213
Pastry, Cornmeal, '81 140
Pecan Cornbread, '94 169
Picante Cornbread, '94 169
Pie, Cornbread-Sausage-Apple, '87 171
Pie, Cornbread-Tamale, '92 123
Pie, Sausage-and-Cornbread, '90 25
Puff, Cornmeal, '82 42
Quick-and-Easy Cornbread, '83 9
Quick Cornsticks, '81 192
Salad, Cornbread, '87 172
Seasoned Cornbread, '90 320
Serrano Chile Blue Cornbread, '94 114
Skillet Cornbread, '81 31; '84 102; '85 200; '90 13
Sour Cream Cornbread, '81 137
Southern Cornbread, '79 123; '81 56; '83 12
Southern Corncakes, '88 166
Spoonbread, '81 138
Spoonbread, Cheddar, '82 196
Spoonbread Dressing, Southwestern-Style, '94 273
Spoonbread, Golden, '83 286; '84 17
Spoonbread, Old Virginia, '84 102
Spoonbread, Ozark, '85 202
Sticks, Angel Corn, '84 20
Sticks, Blue Ribbon Corn, '84 102
Sticks, Buttermilk Corn, '80 120
Sticks, Corn, '79 275; '89 54; '90 214
Sticks, Cornbread, '87 15
Sticks, Favorite Corn, '85 202
Sticks, Firecracker Corn, '85 241
Sticks, Garlic-Thyme Corn, '93 242
Sticks, Golden Cornbread, '94 213
Sticks, Old-Fashioned Corn, '90 232
Sticks, Quick Corn, '88 15
Sticks, Savory Corn, '93 33
Sticks, Southern Corn, '81 242
Stuffing, Cornbread, '94 305
Supreme, Cornbread, '93 67
Toasted Cornbread, '82 174
Ultimate Cornbread, '80 90
Waffles, Cornbread, '79 265; '91 90
Waffles, Cornmeal, '85 201
Wampus Bread, '81 305; '82 36 .

Cornish Hens

Brandied Cornish Hens, '81 259
Brown Rice, Cornish Hens with, '82 275
Buttered Cornish Hens, Brandy-, '79 292;
'80 32
Casserole, Cornish Hens-and-Rice, '92 267
Chutney-Mustard Glaze, Game Hens with,
'93 66
Company Cornish Hens, '83 263
Cranberry Cornish Hens, '86 303
Cranberry-Orange Sauce, Cornish Hens with,
'86 119
Cranberry Sauce, Cornish Hens with,
'79 180
Elegant Cornish Hens, '80 227; '81 52
Flambé, Cornish Hens, '80 227; '81 52
Fruited Stuffing, Cornish Hens with, '90 191
Glazed Cornish Hens, Apricot-, '80 84;
'87 306
Glazed Cornish Hens, Jelly-, '89 193;
'93 251
Glazed Cornish Hens, Orange-, '83 267
Glazed Stuffed Cornish Hens, Orange-,
'84 M89
Grilled Cornish Hens, '88 243; '92 59
Grilled Cornish Hens, Orange-Glazed,
'86 250
Herbed Cornish Hens, '82 271
Marinated Cornish Hens, Sherry-, '91 148
Mesquite-Smoked Cornish Hens, '92 144
Orange Glaze, Cornish Hens with, '79 244
Port and Sour Cream, Cornish Hens in,
'86 323
Roast Cornish Hens, '86 89
Roasted Cornish Hens, Herb-, '88 29
Roasted Cornish Hens, Lemon, '82 260
Roasted Cornish Hens with Vegetables,
Tarragon, '94 79
Roasted Rock Cornish Hens, '82 66
Smoked Cornish Hens, '86 142, 154;
'88 168
Stuffed Cornish Hens, '85 261
Stuffed Cornish Hens, Apricot-, '84 6
Stuffed Cornish Hens, Rice-, '82 302
Tarragon, Cornish Hens with, '83 143
Teriyaki Cornish Hens, '86 198
Texas-Style Game Hens, '87 61
Vermouth, Cornish Hens in, '86 33
Wild Rice Stuffing, Cornish Hens with,
'79 222; '80 64; '82 136

Couscous

Salad, Basil-and-Tomato Couscous, '94 175
Salad, Curried Couscous, '91 44
Tabbouleh Salad, '91 70

Crab

au Gratin, Crabmeat, '86 154
au Gratin, Crab, Shrimp, and Artichoke,
'90 240
Avocados, Crab-Stuffed, '86 73
Avocado with Crabmeat, '86 119
Baked Avocado-and-Crabmeat, '84 119
Bake, Quick Crab, '87 192
Balls, Crabmeat, '88 150
Benedict, Crab, '92 63
Benedict, Lion, '93 121
Bisque, Crab, '88 251
Bisque, Crab-and-Corn, '87 137
Bisque, Crab-and-Leek, '94 104
Bites, Crab-Zucchini, '84 M216
Blue Crabs, Festive, '85 103
Blue Crabs, Spicy Steamed, '84 162

Blue Crabs, Steamed, '89 195
Broiled Crab and Avocado, '79 116
Broiled Crab Meltaways, '93 287
Burgers, Potato-Crusted Crab, '94 139
Cakes, Baltimore Crab, '92 117
Cakes, Chesapeake Bay Crab, '89 194
Cakes, Crab, '81 125; '90 71; '91 122
Cakes, Crispy Fried Crab, '80 119
Cakes, Down-East Crab, '79 151
Cakes, Gulf Coast Crab, '94 71
Cakes, Victoria Crab, '92 195
Cakes with Tomato Cream, Crab, '94 70
Canapés, Cheesy Crab, '86 262
Canapés, Crab, '93 130
Canapés, Crabmeat, '88 150
Canapés, Hot Crab, '86 70; '87 239
Casserole, Crab, '79 228
Casserole, Crab-and-Mushroom, '89 96
Casserole, Crab-and-Shrimp, '84 71
Casserole, Crab-Egg, '80 260
Casserole, Crabmeat-Broccoli, '84 232
Casserole, Creamy Crab and Spinach, '80 3
Casserole, Deviled Crab, '91 238; '92 27
Casserole, Easy Crab, '93 270
Chafing Dish Crabmeat, '89 284
Chicken, Crab-Stuffed, '84 101
Cocktail Puffs, '91 106
Cocktail, Sherried Avocado-Crabmeat,
'87 95
Cornbread, Crab with Chile, '86 254
Creamed Crabmeat with Artichoke Hearts,
'93 26
Crêpes, Crab, '79 165
Crêpes, Sautéed Crab, '84 84
Crisps, Crab, '79 63
Delight, Crab-and-Egg, '84 261
Deviled Crab, '85 104; '92 117
Deviled Crab, Devilish, '85 264
Dip, Cheese-Crab, '91 200
Dip, Creamy Crab, '80 M135
Dip, Festive Crab, '92 285
Dip, Hot Cheese and Crab, '81 261
Dip, Hot Crab, '93 269
Dip, Hot Crab-and-Cheese, '94 282
Dip, Oven-Baked Crab, '82 59
Dip, Tangy Crab, '83 5
Dip, Trawler Crab, '93 238
Dressed Crab, '82 276
Eggs New Orleans, Crabmeat and, '82 45
Eggs, Shrimp and Crab Scrambled,
'79 261
Étouffée, Crab-and-Shrimp, '89 96
Filling, Crab, '89 13
Flounder, Crab-Stuffed, '80 120
Fresh Crab, Preparing, '82 127
Gumbo, Crab and Shrimp, '81 200
Gumbo, Seafood, '83 90
Gumbo with Whole Crabs, Seafood, '85 2
Hors d'Oeuvre, Crabmeat, '94 236
Imperial, Crab, '79 82, 116; '89 194
Imperial, Crabmeat, '82 311; '83 72
Imperial, Easy Crab, '93 128
Imperial, Elegant Crab, '83 245
Imperial, Pineapple-Crab, '84 M286
Imperials, Individual Seafood, '84 162
Imperial, Speedy Crabmeat, '90 M112
Karen, Crabmeat, '93 49
Meunière, Soft-Shell Crab, '80 57
Mold, Crab, '85 318
Mold, Cream Cheese-Crabmeat, '90 71
Mousse, Crab, '79 117

Mousse, Crabmeat, '90 190; '91 244;
'94 159
Mushroom Caps, Crab-Stuffed, '84 160
Mushrooms, Crab-Stuffed, '81 190
Mushrooms on Toast Points, Crabmeat and,
'82 M91
Mushrooms Stuffed with Crab, '82 249
Oysters and Crabmeat, Creamy, '83 211
Oysters, Crabmeat Stuffed, '94 328
Pâté, Crab, '79 233
Peas, Crab-Stuffed Snow, '85 288
Pie, Hot Seafood, '80 32
Potatoes, Cheesy Crab-Stuffed, '86 17
Potatoes, Crabmeat-Topped, '83 3
Potatoes, Crab-Stuffed, '91 311; '92 26
Puff, Crab, '79 116
Puffs, Crab, '80 20; '84 269
Puff, Shrimp-Crab, '79 57
Quiche, Almond-Topped Crab, '79 127
Quiche, Crab, '82 M122, 243
Quiche, Quick Crab, '84 96
Quiche, Sherried Crab, '83 180
Quiche, Simple Crab, '85 207
Ravigote, Crabmeat, '82 250; '92 329
Rémoulade, Crabmeat, '93 280
Salad, Chesapeake Crab, '89 195
Salad, Crab-and-Asparagus, '92 141
Salad, Crab and Wild Rice, '79 116
Salad, Crab-Avocado, '81 114
Salad, Crabmeat, '91 169
Salad, Crabmeat Luncheon, '82 207
Salad, Crabmeat-Shrimp Pasta, '86 208
Salad, Crab-Stuffed Tomato, '80 148
Salad, Crab-Wild Rice, '86 207
Salad, Delightful Crab, '87 145
Salad, Macaroni-Crabmeat, '81 153
Salad, Marinated Crab-and-Endive, '93 22
Salad with Crabmeat-and-Asparagus,
Congealed, '84 86
Sandwiches, Avocado-Crabmeat, '83 2
Sandwiches, Crabmeat, '84 285
Sandwiches, Deluxe Crabmeat, '81 M74
Sandwiches, Hot Crab-and-Cheese, '87 279
Sandwiches, Open-Face Crab Tomato, '81 29
Sandwiches, Open-Faced Crab, '87 106
Sandwiches, Puffy Crab, '83 291
Sauce Piquante, Crab and Shrimp, '83 92
Sauce, Quick Crab Marinara, '85 M151
Sauce, Stone Crab Mustard, '80 3
Sauce, Tangy Stone Crab, '80 3
Sautéed Crabmeat, Roussos, '84 88
Sautéed Seafood Platter, '83 89
Seafood Boil, Low Country, '80 119
Shrimp Bundles, Crab-Stuffed, '81 176
Shrimp, Crab-Stuffed, '84 259
Snacks, Crab, '83 93
Soft-Shell Crabs, Chesapeake, '89 194
Soup, Beaufort Crab, '92 238
Soup, Crabmeat, '84 123
Soup, Cream of Crab, '88 302
Soup, Creamy Crab, '80 M224
Soup, Elegant Crab, '80 188
Soup, Fresh Corn-and-Crab, '92 183
Soup, Old-Fashioned Crab, '90 71
Soup, Plantation Crab, '92 237
Soup, Quick Crab, '84 279
Soup, Steamboat's Cream of Crab, '81 127
Soup with Marigold, She-Crab, '79 32
Spicy Crab Bites, '91 165
Spread, Baked Crab, '80 86
Spread, Crab, '93 167

Crab *(continued)*

Spread, Crabmeat, **'79** 81
Spread, Crabmeat-Horseradish, **'90** 292
Spread, Crab Soufflé, **'85** 4
Spread, Hot Artichoke-Crab, **'85** 81
Spread, Layered Crabmeat, **'83** 127
Spread, Superb Crab, **'81** 235
Stroganoff, Crab, **'79** 116
Stuffed Soft-Shell Crabs, **'83** 91
Stuffed Soft-Shell Crabs, Steamboat's, **'81** 127
Stuffing, Chicken Breasts with Crabmeat, **'85** 302
Stuffing, Crabmeat, **'94** 68
Supreme, Crab, **'79** 181
Tomatoes, Crab-and-Avocado Stuffed, **'94** 141
Tomatoes, Crab-Stuffed Cherry, **'82** 289; **'88** 78
Topping, Crabmeat, **'91** 64
Tostadas, Crab, **'93** 203
Veal with Crabmeat, New Orleans, **'86** 94

Crackers

Bacon-Wrapped Crackers, **'93** 280
Bread, Sesame Cracker, **'87** 2
Cheddar Crackers, **'84** 236
Cheese Cracker Nibbles, **'84** 328
Dessert Crackers, **'87** 3
Fennel-Rye Crackers, **'87** 2
Florida Crackers, **'86** 179
Hot Nut Crackers, **'90** 206
Hush Puppies, Cracker, **'80** 99
Oatmeal-Wheat Germ Crackers, **'84** 236
Olive-Rye Snack Crackers, **'84** 191
Pie, Cracker, **'79** 113
Snackers, Cracker, **'86** 229; **'93** 197

Cranberries

Apple Berry Sparkler, **'94** 100
Bake, Hot Cranberry, **'91** 250
Beach Brew, **'91** 177
Brandied Cranberries, **'86** 269
Bread, Cranberry, **'79** 242
Bread, Cranberry-Banana, **'80** 281; **'90** 294
Bread, Cranberry Fruit-Nut, **'79** 275
Bread, Cranberry-Orange, **'87** 244
Bread, Cranberry-Orange Nut, **'80** 288
Bread, Orange-Cranberry, **'85** 266
Bread, Raisin-Cranberry, **'81** 305; **'82** 36
Cake, Cranberry-Coconut Coffee, **'93** 332
Cake, Cranberry Coffee, **'81** 14; **'90** 159
Cake, Cranberry-Nut Coffee, **'81** 250
Cake, Cranberry-Orange Coffee, **'82** 283
Cake, Cranberry Upside-Down, **'87** 8
Cake, Orange-Cranberry, **'85** 314
Casserole, Cranberry-Apple, **'83** 311
Casserole, Sweet Potatoes-and-Berries, **'84** 231
Chicken, Barbecued Cranberry, **'83** 178
Chicken Kiev, Cranberry, **'87** 250
Chicken, Oven-Barbecued Cranberry, **'93** 332
Chutney, Cranberry, **'80** 243; **'83** 260; **'84** 265
Chutney, Cranberry-Orange, **'79** 292
Chutney, Orange-Cranberry, **'86** 266
Chutney with Cream Cheese, Cranberry-Amaretto, **'87** 244
Cider, Spiced Cranberry, **'84** 261
Cloud, Cranberry, **'90** 287

Cobbler, Cranberry, **'81** 275
Cobbler, Cranberry-and-Apple, **'84** 306; **'90** 294
Cobbler, Cranberry-Peach, **'92** 322
Cobbler, Easy Cranberry, **'86** 260
Cobbler Roll, Cranberry, **'80** 288; **'81** 248
Cocktail, Hot Cranberry, **'89** 310
Compote, Berry, **'81** 275
Conserve, Apple-Cranberry, **'82** 308
Conserve, Cranberry, **'79** 243; **'83** 279; **'85** 266
Cooler, Cranberry, **'86** 229
Cornish Hens, Cranberry, **'86** 303
Cream, Cranberry, **'90** 66
Crêpes, Cranberry, **'85** 262
Crisp, Cranberry-Pear, **'83** 207
Crunch, Apple-Cranberry, **'86** 300; **'87** 178
Cup, Berry Grapefruit, **'79** 242
Daiquiris, Cranberry, **'81** 245
Dessert, Cranberry Apple, **'80** 253
Dessert, Cranberry Surprise, **'79** 242
Dip, Cranberry Fruit, **'89** 60
Dip, Cranberry-Horseradish, **'85** 65
Dressing, Cranberry-Orange, **'91** 287
Dressing, Orange Salad with Honey-Berry, **'89** 250
Drink, Mulled Cranberry, **'92** 12
Float, Sparkling Cranberry, **'86** 195
Frappé, Cranberry, **'82** 263
Frosted Cranberries, **'82** 280
Fruit Bake, Cranberry-Mustard, **'90** 287
Gelatin Mold, Cranberry, **'92** 271
Glaze, Cranberry, **'84** 306; **'86** 171; **'88** 244
Glaze, Cranberry-Honey, **'89** 273
Gravy, Baked Hen with Cranberry Pan, **'94** 308
Ham, Cranberry Broiled, **'88** 301
Ham, Cranberry Glazed, **'88** 274
Ham, Cranberry-Orange Glazed, **'81** 295
Hearts, Cranberry, **'93** 286
Ice, Cranberry-Apple, **'82** 290
Ice, Tangy Cranberry, **'87** 305
Ice, Tart Cranberry-Orange, **'86** 317
Jam, Christmas, **'79** 288
Jam, Christmas Brunch, **'81** 286
Jelly, Cranberry-Wine, **'81** 290
Jubilee, Cranberries, **'85** 312; **'90** 293
Jubilee, Tasty Cranberry, **'84** 305; **'85** 189
Juice, Sparkling Cranberry, **'88** 275
Lamb, Cranberry Leg of, **'90** 52
Lemonade, Spiced Cranberry, **'87** 292
Loaf, Apricot-Cranberry, **'79** 235
Loaf, Cranberry-Ham, **'82** M77
Mexican Cranberries, **'94** 273
Mold, Cranberry, **'79** 250
Mold, Cranberry-Apple, **'89** 277
Mousse, Cran-Apple, **'93** 255
Muffins, Cranberry, **'81** 249
Muffins, Cranberry Oat Bran, **'89** 107
Muffins, Cranberry-Pecan, **'84** 269
Muffins, Cranberry Streusel Cake, **'88** M274
Muffins, Miniature Cranberry, **'90** 294
Orange Delight, Cranberry-, **'90** 168
Orange Surprise, Cran-, **'94** 143
Oriental, Cranberry, **'79** 126
Pie, Autumn Apple, **'79** 205
Pie, Berry-Apple, **'88** 251
Pie, Cran-Apple, **'92** 304
Pie, Cranberry-Apple, **'79** 264
Pie, Cranberry-Apple Holiday, **'81** M269
Pie, Cranberry-Pecan, **'92** 316

Pie, Cranberry-Raisin, **'80** 283; **'85** 316
Pie, Cran-Raspberry, **'87** 244
Pie, Festive Cranberry Freezer, **'84** 306
Pie, Frosty Cranberry, **'79** 249
Pie, Nutty Cranberry, **'82** M298
Pie, Peach-Cranberry, **'83** 249
Pie, Tart Cranberry-Cherry, **'87** 299
Pie, Walnut-Cranberry, **'87** 259
Pork Chops, Cranberry, **'80** 288; **'90** 53
Pork Chops, Orange-Cranberry, **'86** 335; **'87** 84
Pork, Cranberry, **'90** 293
Pork Roast, Berry Barbecued, **'80** 288
Pudding, Cranberry, **'84** 306
Punch, Cranberry, **'83** 275; **'85** 90
Punch, Cranberry-Cherry, **'91** 176
Punch, Cranberry-Cinnamon, **'86** 270
Punch, Cranberry Percolator, **'88** 248
Punch, Cran-Grape-Tea, **'92** 209
Punch, Holiday Cranberry, **'85** 265
Punch, Hot Cranberry, **'80** 288; **'84** 41, 319; **'85** 265
Punch, Hot Spiced, **'80** 250
Punch, Pink Lady, **'81** 100
Punch, Sparkling Cranberry, **'85** 277
Punch, Spiced Cranberry, **'89** 290
Punch, Tart Cranberry, **'83** 318
Red Roosters, **'87** 147
Refresher, Cranberry-Vodka, **'91** 210
Relish, Cran-Apple, **'84** 300
Relish, Cranberry, **'81** 275; **'83** 144; **'85** 258, 264; **'86** 283; **'87** 245; **'91** 257; **'92** 341
Relish, Cranberry-Nut, **'86** 275
Relish, Cranberry-Orange, **'81** M289; **'88** 254
Relish, Cranberry-Pear, **'85** 232
Relish, Holiday Cranberry, **'88** 304
Relish, Lemony Cranberry, **'79** 243
Relish, Old-Fashioned Cranberry, **'82** 297
Relish, Tipsy Cranberry, **'92** M310
Ring, Cranberry, **'90** 291
Ring, Spicy Peach-Cranberry, **'85** 264
Rolls, Cranberry-Pineapple, **'86** 275
Roulage, Chocolate-Cranberry, **'94** 313
Salad, Congealed Cranberry, **'90** 124
Salad, Cranberry, **'88** 250
Salad, Cranberry-Cheese Ribbon, **'79** 241
Salad, Cranberry Christmas, **'79** 243
Salad, Cranberry Congealed, **'91** 296
Salad, Cranberry Holiday, **'89** 277
Salad, Cranberry-Topped Green, **'87** 311
Salad, Cranberry-Whipped Cream, **'83** 261
Salad, Festive Cranberry, **'81** 264, 296
Salad, Frosted Cranberry, **'90** 288
Salad, Frozen Cranberry-Pineapple, **'91** 237
Salad, Holiday Cranberry, **'82** 266, 288
Salad, Holiday Jewel, **'81** 252
Salad, Jellied Cranberry, **'83** 279; **'85** 281
Salad, Layered Cranberry, **'84** 322; **'86** 325
Salad, Lemon-Cranberry Congealed, **'87** 311
Salad, Tart Cranberry, **'79** 286
Salad Ring, Cranberry, **'80** 247
Salsa with Sweet Potato Chips, Cranberry, **'93** 332
Sauce, Baked Cranberry, **'88** 257
Sauce, Baked Ham with Cranberry-Raisin, **'88** 244
Sauce, Cornish Hens with Cranberry-Orange, **'86** 119
Sauce, Cranberry, **'86** 278; **'88** 280; **'92** 269

Cranberries (continued)

Sauce, Cranberry-Apple, '92 203
Sauce, Cranberry Juice, '85 224; '86 83
Sauce, Cranberry Wine, '83 276
Sauce, Fresh Cranberry, '79 283; '84 275
Sauce, Fresh Cranberry-Apricot, '87 243
Sauce, Jalapeño-Cranberry, '92 310
Sauce, Tart Cranberry, '83 261
Shake, Cranberry, '83 171
Sherbet, Cranberry, '88 280
Slush, Cranberry-Rum, '84 259
Smoothie, Cranberry, '86 183; '91 307
Soda, Cranberry-Orange, '79 148
Sorbet, Cranberry, '82 251
Sorbet, Cranberry Juice, '85 259
Soufflé, Cranberry-Topped Holiday, '84 306
Sparkler, Apple-Berry, '93 104
Spiced Cranberries, '82 254, 287
Spread, Coconut-Cranberry Cheese, '92 328
Spritzer, Cranberry, '91 66; '92 265
Spritzers, Cranberry, '89 213
Squash, Cranberry-Filled Acorn, '81 M231
Stuffing, Crown Roast of Pork with Cranberry-Sausage, '88 49
Supreme, Cranberry, '85 280
Tart, Cranberry-Nut, '84 305
Tartlets, Fresh Cranberry, '87 244
Tarts, Cranberry-Cream Cheese, '80 154
Tarts, Cranberry Holiday, '83 279
Tarts, Cran-Raspberry Meringue, '92 286
Tea, Cranberry, '94 131
Tea, Cranberry-Apple, '88 169
Turkey Loaf, Cranberry-Glazed, '86 171
Vinegar, Cranberry, '91 288
Wassail, Cranberry, '88 289
Wild Rice, Cranberry-Pear, '83 279
Wine Cup, Cranberry, '85 23
Crawfish
Borscht, Crawfish, '92 84
Dressing, Louisiana Crawfish, '90 103
Étouffée, Crawfish, '83 91; '86 156; '90 103; '94 239
Mushrooms, Crawfish-Stuffed, '86 258
Salad, Dilled Crawfish, '83 126
Spaghetti, Crawfish, '85 104
Crème Fraîche
Fraîche, Crème, '85 39; '91 99
Sauce, Crème Fraîche, '79 281; '93 135
Crêpes
Amandine, Crêpes Gelée, '83 126
Amaretto-and-Orange Crêpes, '86 260
Banana Crêpes Flambé, '84 262
Basic Crêpes, '84 83; '86 38
Beef Crêpes, Sherried, '85 M29
Beef Roulades, '80 80
Blintzes, Cheese, '82 146; '83 71; '92 84
Bran Crêpes, '83 70; '86 44
Breakfast Crêpes, Country-Style, '79 22
Brunch Crêpes, Nutritious, '80 44
Brunch Crêpes, Royal, '81 44
Cannelloni Crêpes, '86 143
Cheese and Mushroom Crêpes, '81 88
Cheesy Party Wedges, '84 84
Cherry Crêpes, '91 67
Cherry Crêpes Flambé, '79 18
Chicken Crêpes, '80 39
Chicken Crêpes, Creamy, '81 200
Chicken-Vegetable Crêpes, '83 70

Chocolate Chantilly Crêpes, '82 183
Chocolate Crêpes, '86 164
Chocolate Crêpes, Fruit-Filled, '89 325
Chocolate Dessert Crêpes, '84 84; '85 262
Chocolate Dream Crêpes, '86 164
Chocolate-Orange Crêpes, '85 263
Coffee Ice Cream Crêpes, '84 85
Coquilles St. Jacques Crêpes, '83 13
Cornmeal Sombreros, '93 277
Crab Crêpes, '79 165
Crab Crêpes, Sautéed, '84 84
Cranberry Crêpes, '85 262
Crêpes, '82 38, 46, 146, 240; '83 13, 71, 122, 127, 205, 282; '84 186; '86 216; '87 126; '88 295; '89 44; '90 157; '91 24; '92 41, 88; '93 123; '94 116
Cups, Florentine Crêpe, '89 44
Dessert Crêpes, '84 84; '86 260; '87 290; '88 134
Dessert Crêpes, Basic, '82 183; '85 262; '86 275
Dessert Crêpes, Dixie, '79 222
Dessert Crêpes, Spicy, '84 262
Divan, Elegant Crêpes, '81 91
Entrée Crêpes, '79 264
Fajita Crêpes, '94 116
Florentine Crêpe Pie, '79 34
Florentine, Crêpes, '80 190
Fruit Crêpes, Tropical, '87 77
Fruit Filling, Crêpes with, '81 96
Ham-and-Egg Crêpes, '83 204
Ham-and-Egg Crêpes with Mushroom Sauce, '82 46
Italian Crêpes, '90 157
Lemon Crêpes with Fruit Filling, '82 46
Light Crêpes, '86 143
Low-Calorie Crêpes, '87 77
Mango-Pineapple Crêpes, '86 216
Mushroom-Cheese Crêpes, '87 289; '88 135
Orange Dream Crêpes, '82 183
Peach Crêpes, '82 184
Peach Crêpes, Fresh, '84 186
Plain Crêpes, '83 70
Processor Crêpes, Basic, '87 289; '88 135
Raspberry Crêpes, '87 126
Raspberry Crêpes with Yogurt Filling, Fresh, '93 123
Sausage Crêpes, '88 295
Sausage Crêpes, Cheesy, '82 240; '83 71
Sausage-Filled Crêpes, '79 39
Spinach-Ricotta Crêpes, '81 52
Steak Crêpes, Special, '91 24
Strawberry Dessert Crêpes, '83 122
Strawberry Ice Cream Crêpes, '87 290; '88 135
Suzette, Raspberry Crêpes, '84 84
Suzettes, Light Crêpes, '83 71
Tropical Crêpes, '86 275
Turkey Crêpes, '92 41
Turkey Crêpes, Elegant, '83 282
Virginia Crêpes, '79 264
Whole Wheat Crêpes, '80 44; '83 70
Zucchini Crêpes, '79 157
Croutons
Bagel Croutons, '93 192
Bourbon Croutons, '93 234
Bread Croutons, Hawaiian, '94 107
Celery Croutons, '79 16
Cinnamon Pound Cake Croutons, '93 161
Cornbread Croutons, '93 192
Cornbread Croutons, Honeyed, '94 106

Crispy Italian Croutons, '84 126
Crostini, '92 56
Croûtes, Croutons and, '93 30
Croutons, '86 M288
Dilled Croutons, '93 161
Egg Roll Fan, Sesame, '94 107
Garlic Croutons, '92 71
Garlic-Flavored Croutons, '86 47
Herb Croutons, '81 150
Microwave Croutons, '86 M227
Pita Croutons, '93 192
Pumpernickel Croutons, '94 62
Tortilla Triangles, '94 107
Vegetable-Flavored Croutons, '84 148
Cucumbers
Aspic, Shrimp-Cucumber, '83 108
Bisque, Shrimp-Cucumber, '79 172
Canapés, Shrimp-and-Cucumber, '93 164
Chips, Cucumber, '85 176
Combo, Cucumber-and-Pepper, '88 176
Cool Cucumbers, '84 152
Cooler, Simple Cucumber, '86 147
Creamy Cucumbers, '92 62
Delights, Cucumber, '84 117
Dilled Cucumber on Tomatoes, '84 142
Dills, Lazy Wife, '87 149
Dip, Cucumber-Cheese Vegetable, '83 128
Dressing, Creamy Cucumber Salad, '82 79
Dressing, Cucumber, '80 74; '90 144
Dressing, Cucumber-Curry, '89 179
Dressing, Cucumber-Mint, '87 153
Dressing, Tomato, Onion, and Cucumber in Italian, '81 83
Fried Cucumber Fingers, '86 146
Lemony Cucumbers, '89 102
Marinated Cucumbers and Artichokes, '82 111
Marinated Cucumbers and Squash, '86 146
Marinated Shrimp and Cucumber, '91 166
Mold, Asparagus-Cucumber, '85 252
Mold, Chicken-Cucumber, '80 175
Mold, Creamy Cucumber, '84 164
Mold, Lemon-Cucumber, '87 90
Mousse, Cucumber, '79 11; '88 121
Pickled Cucumber Rounds, Easy, '90 143
Pickles, Cucumber Sandwich, '81 174
Pickles, Dill, '81 174
Pickles, Mixed, '81 174
Pickles, Quick Sweet, '87 149
Pickles, Sour Cucumber, '85 176
Pickles, Sweet Icicle, '85 176
Relish, Cucumber, '85 176
Rounds, Cucumber, '88 78
Salad, Creamy Cucumber, '86 147; '92 97
Salad, Cucumber-Almond, '86 147
Salad, Cucumber-Bean, '83 81
Salad, Cucumber-Pineapple, '84 124
Salad, Cucumber-Roast Beef, '89 162
Salad, Cucumber-Tomato, '90 144
Salad, Cucumber-Yogurt, '87 33
Salad, Dilled Cucumber, '82 229; '92 72; '93 65
Salad, Dilled Cucumber and Tomato, '81 153
Salad, Grapefruit-Cucumber, '80 100
Salad, Marinated Cucumber, '82 111
Salad, Marinated Tomato-and-Cucumber, '92 216
Salad Mold, Cucumber, '82 111; '83 81, 253
Salad, Pineapple-Cucumber Congealed, '83 118
Salad, Tomato-and-Cucumber Summer, '93 141
Salad, Tomato-Cucumber, '86 218; '92 199

Cucumbers *(continued)*

Salad, Tomato-Cucumber-Onion, '81 239
Salad with Yogurt-Herb Dressing,
  Tomato-Cucumber, '92 96
Salad, Yogurt-Cucumber, '82 122
Sandwiches, Cucumber, '88 159; '90 81;
  '94 14
Sandwiches, Cucumber Pinwheel, '85 120
Sandwiches, Dainty Cucumber, '81 119
Sauce, Cucumber, '82 111; '84 M286;
  '92 41
Sauce, Cucumber Cream, '92 33
Sauce, Cucumber-Dill, '86 5; '91 62; '92 51
Sauce, Cucumber Dipping, '94 47
Sauce, Lemony Cucumber, '89 245
Scallions, Cukes and, '91 168
Sesame Cucumbers, '85 85
Slaw, Creamy Cucumber, '89 49
Slices, Cheesy Cucumber, '84 80
Slices, Fresh Cucumber, '86 177
Snapper Rolls, Cucumber-Stuffed Red,
  '83 176
Soup, Chilled Cucumber, '79 144
Soup, Cold Cucumber, '79 130; '81 130
Soup, Cold Minted Cucumber, '86 34
Soup, Cold Potato-Cucumber, '88 160
Soup, Cream of Cucumber, '81 98
Soup, Creamy Cucumber, '80 171
Soup, Cucumber-Yogurt, '82 157; '83 205
Soup, Dilled Cucumber, '90 M167
Sour Cream, Cucumber and Onion in, '81 69
Sour Cream, Cucumbers and, '93 203
Sour Cream, Cucumbers in, '79 52; '80 178
Spread, Cucumber, '79 295; '80 31; '93 158
Spread, Cucumber and Cream Cheese,
  '82 140
Spread, Shrimp-Cucumber, '79 81
Stuffed Cucumbers, '81 237
Tomatoes, Cucumber-Stuffed Cherry,
  '88 262
Topping, Lamb Pockets with Dilled
  Cucumber, '87 104
Tuna Boats, Cucumber, '83 136
Vichyssoise, Cucumber, '94 90
Vinaigrette Oriental, Cucumber-, '85 198;
  '86 147
Currants. *See* Raisins.
Curry
Almonds, Cauliflower and Peas with Curried,
  '79 221
Almonds, Curried, '82 297
Apples, Curried, '93 252
Apricots, Curried, '91 315
Bananas, Fillets with Horseradish Sauce and
  Curried, '85 230
Beef and Rice, Curried, '88 164
Beef Dinner, Curried, '83 4
Beef Pitas, Curried, '85 220
Beef Steak, Curried, '88 60
Bites, Curried Swiss, '85 220
Bread, Honey-Curry, '89 250
Butter, Tomato-Curry-Orange, '93 159
Carrots and Pineapple, Curried, '90 228
Casserole, Curry Pea, '87 154
Casserole, Vegetable-Curry, '91 286; '92 27
Cauliflower, Curried, '91 315
Cheese Ball, Chicken-Curry, '85 118
Cheese Ball, Curried Shrimp, '86 135
Chicken Balls, Coconut Curried, '91 165

Chicken Balls, Curried, '91 98
Chicken Bites, Curried, '85 40
Chicken Cheesecake, Curried, '90 174
Chicken, Country Captain, '94 252
Chicken, Curried, '86 43
Chicken, Curried Fried, '85 160
Chicken Curry, '84 110; '85 220; '86 21;
  '89 219
Chicken Curry, Brioche, '88 124
Chicken Curry, Stir-Fried, '87 51
Chicken Curry, Turban, '94 266
Chicken Divan, Curried, '80 83
Chicken, Honey-Curry, '87 36
Chicken, Quick Curried, '89 219
Chicken, Regal Curry, '84 110
Chicken-Stuffed Peppers, Curried, '87 19
Chops, Pineapple-Curry Glazed, '82 106
Chowder, Curried Chicken-and-Corn,
  '92 21
Chowder, Curried Seafood, '94 103
Coleslaw, Curried, '85 139
Coleslaw, Curried Pineapple, '88 172
Corn and Celery, Curried, '86 192
Dip and Vegetable Platter, Curry, '89 327
Dip, Curried, '81 262
Dip, Curry, '80 84; '81 9; '85 132; '86 184;
  '87 25
Dip, Curry-Onion, '93 313
Dip, Tuna-Curry, '84 31
Dressing, Cucumber-Curry, '89 179
Dressing, Curried, '84 115
Dressing, Curry, '80 242; '82 78
Eggs, Curried Deviled, '93 87
Eggs, Saucy Shrimp-Curried, '84 143
Filling, Curried Chicken, '88 125
Fish, Curried Baked, '87 5
Fish, Curry-Baked, '91 196
Fruit, Almond-Curried, '83 261
Fruit Bake, Curried, '87 241
Fruit, Hot Curried, '79 225; '81 264;
  '84 287
Ham and Peaches, Curried, '82 60
Ham Steak, Curried, '82 120
Ham with Rice, Curried, '80 111
Hazelnuts, Curried, '93 301
Hurry Curry, '79 103
Kheema, Indian, '81 226
Lamb Curry with Rice, '80 83; '81 10
Lamb with Rice Mold, Curried, '85 36
Meat Loaf, Curried, '86 43
Mushrooms, Curried, '84 214
Nuts, Spicy Curried, '82 250
Onions, Curried, '90 34
Peas with Almonds, Curried, '88 M294
Pecans, Curried, '86 326
Peppers, Chicken Breasts with Curried,
  '90 227
Popcorn Mix, Curried, '86 326
Pork Chops, Curried Apricot, '89 191
Pork Tenderloin, Curried, '86 76
Rice and Shrimp, Curried, '83 231
Rice, Curried, '90 183
Rice, Curry-Spiced, '86 M226
Rice Mix, Fruited Curry-, '86 326
Rice Mold, Curried, '85 36
Rice, Quick Curried, '86 81
Rice with Almonds, Curried, '83 M285
Rice with Curry, Raisin, '85 83
Rice with Pineapple, Curried, '79 142
Salad, Curried Apple-Raisin, '80 24
Salad, Curried Broccoli, '86 225

Salad, Curried Chicken, '79 219; '84 66;
  '85 96; '86 131; '89 176
Salad, Curried Chicken-and-Orange, '87 144
Salad, Curried Chicken-Rice, '92 190
Salad, Curried Couscous, '91 44
Salad, Curried Rice, '80 84; '85 147, 220
Salad, Curried Tuna, '86 208
Salad, Curried Turkey, '88 140
Salad, Curry Rice, '89 146
Salad, Curry Spinach, '80 242
Salad, Hot Indian Curry, '83 23
Salad with Asparagus, Curried Chicken,
  '81 36
Salad with Grapes, Curried Tuna, '87 201
Sandwiches, Curried BLT, '93 158
Sandwiches, Curried Tea, '91 314
Sauce, Asparagus with Curry, '90 17
Sauce, Chicken Curry, '90 117
Sauce, Curried Rum, '91 164
Sauce, Curried Sour Cream, '90 174
Sauce, Curry, '79 156; '83 138; '84 M71;
  '94 54
Sauce, Halibut with Orange-Curry, '87 91
Sauce, Pineapple-Curry, '79 252
Sauce, Turkey Slices with Curried Cream,
  '91 60
Shrimp Balls, Curried, '94 180
Shrimp, Curried, '84 110
Shrimp Curry, Creamy, '90 145
Shrimp Curry, Polynesian, '89 23
Shrimp Curry, Sour Cream, '80 83
Shrimp Curry, Sour Cream and, '81 10
Shrimp Malai Curry, '84 110
Shrimp, Quick Curried, '84 M198
Snapper, Honey-Curried, '85 181
Soup, Cold Curried Pea, '91 120
Soup, Curried, '81 130
Soup, Curried Carrot, '82 157
Soup, Curried Chicken, '86 34
Soup, Curried Mushroom, '84 M89
Soup, Curried Turkey, '86 332
Spread, Broccamoli Curry, '88 55
Spread, Curried Chutney, '89 283
Spread, Curried Shrimp, '87 158
Spread, Curried Turkey, '92 16
Spread, Curry, '93 159
Stir-Fry, Indian, '92 126
Tomatoes, Curried Green, '93 138
Turkey Pie, Crumb-Crust Curried, '86 265
Vegetables, Curried, '89 219
Vegetables with Curry, Stir-Fried, '87 51
Vinaigrette, Warm Curry, '93 107
Custards
Almond Crème Custard with Raspberries,
  '88 174
Amaretto Custard, Chocolate-Topped,
  '87 M37
Amaretto Custard, Range-Top, '87 77
Amaretto Custard with Raspberries, '86 152
Ambrosia, Custard Sauce, '84 256
Baked Custard, '80 219
Baked Custard, Creamy, '86 7
Baked Custard, Easy, '85 52
Baked Vanilla Custard, '82 129
Boiled Custard, Favorite, '81 181
Boiled Custard, Perfect, '81 34
Cake, Chocolate Custard, '88 175
Chocolate Custard, '88 258
Citrus Custard with Fresh Fruit, '93 70
Coconut Custard, '86 109
Corn Custard, Fresh, '89 127

Custards (*continued*)

Crema, **'80** 175
Crème Pâtissière, **'84** 207
Easy Custard with Nutmeg, **'90** 316
Filling, Creamy Custard, **'81** 180
Filling, Custard, **'82** 52, 298; **'85** 281
Filling, Egg Custard, **'87** 14
Flan, **'88** 247
Flan Almendra, **'80** 199
Flan, Blackberry, **'79** 182
Flan, Corn-Chive, **'94** 172
Flan de Leche (Flan with Milk),
  '92 169
Flan, Flaming, **'85** 313
Flan, Layered, **'89** 45
Flan, Luscious, **'90** 56
Flan, Orange, **'84** 95
Flan, Pumpkin, **'82** 217
Flans, Caramel-Crowned, **'90** 227
Flans, Individual, **'85** 52
Flan, Spanish, **'85** 51, 311
Flan with Caramel, Baked, **'92** 231
Lemon-Buttermilk Custards, **'89** 49
Lemon Custard in Meringue Cups, **'80** 295;
  '81 172
Mexican Custard, Light, **'88** 149
Napoleon Cream, **'84** 138
Orange Custard Pudding, **'88** 174
Peach Custard Dessert, Fresh, **'86** 162
Pears in Custard, Poached, **'88** 20
Pie, Apple Custard, **'88** 236
Pie, Carrot Custard, **'79** 45
Pie, Coconut Custard, **'82** 33
Pie, Custard Pecan, **'87** 184
Pie, Old-Fashioned Egg Custard, **'82** 261
Pie, Perfect Custard, **'82** 92
Pumpkin Custard, **'88** 279
Rice Custard, Baked, **'92** 308
Sauce, Custard, **'85** 41; **'88** 154, 251, 259;
  '89 291
Sauce, Fresh Berries with Raspberry
  Custard, **'88** 163
Squash, Custard-Filled Acorn, **'86** 334
Stirred Custard, **'92** 45
Stirred Custard, Old-Fashioned, **'85** 52
Stirred Custard over Fruit, **'84** 83
Tocino del Cielo, **'93** 29
Vanilla Cream, **'83** M115

Dates
Apple-Date-Nut Ring, **'90** 212
Ball, Date-Nut, **'92** 326
Balls, Date-Nut, **'85** 10
Balls, Peanut-Date, **'81** 92
Bars, Date, **'84** 313
Bars, Date-Nut, **'80** 166
Bars, Date-Oat, **'80** M172
Bars, Layered Oatmeal-Date,
  '85 10
Bars, No-Bake Date, **'79** 256
Bars, Nutty Date, **'84** 153
Bread, Chocolate Date-Nut, **'81** 284
Bread, Date-Nut, **'85** 306
Bread, Persimmon Date-Nut, **'82** 218
Bread, Wine-Date Nut, **'82** 253
Brownies, Date-and-Almond, **'88** 217
Cake, Date Nut, **'79** 176; **'80** 5

Cake, Fresh Apple-Date, **'83** 300
Cake, Orange-Date, **'94** 60
Cake, Pumpkin Date, **'79** 251
Cake, Queen Bee, **'81** 237
Cake Roll, Date-Nut, **'89** 94
Cake Squares, Apple-Date Dream, **'85** 10
Candy, Date, **'89** 308
Candy, Date Loaf, **'80** 302
Cheese, Nutty Date Dessert, **'87** 299
Chocolate Date-Nut Delight, **'88** 168
Conserve, Brandied Date, **'85** 315
Cookies, Christmas Date, **'88** 287
Cookies, Date-Filled, **'91** 95
Cookies, Oatmeal-Date, **'82** 109
Cookies, Oatmeal-Date Sandwich, **'83** 257
Cookies, Rich Date-Nut Chocolate Chip,
  '92 207
Cookies, Rolled Fruit, **'80** 15
Cupcakes, Date, **'84** 7
Dessert Squares, Date, **'89** 255
Dressing, Date, **'87** 57
Filling, Apple-Date, **'83** 301
Filling, Date, **'80** 15; **'83** 257; **'86** 314
Filling, Date Cream, **'81** 303
June Bugs, **'85** 11
Loaf, Blue Ribbon Date-Walnut, **'80** 15
Loaf, Date-Nut, **'85** 10
Logs, Date, **'79** 274
Muffins, Carrot-Date-Nut, **'86** 262
Muffins, Date, **'79** 142
Muffins, Date-Nut, **'84** 75
Muffins, Orange-Date, **'92** 119
Muffins, Surprise Date, **'79** 216
Pastries, Date-Filled Cheese, **'83** 259
Pie, Date-Pecan, **'80** 15
Pie, Dried Fruit, **'83** 249
Pudding, Steamed Date, **'79** 86
Roll, Date Nut, **'79** 249
Rollups, Date-Cream Cheese, **'83** 298
Salad, Festive Fruit, **'80** 16
Sandwich, Date-Nut Lettuce, **'94** 202
Sauce, Date-Nut Sundae, **'82** 167
Spread, Apple-Date, **'91** 231; **'92** 67
Spread, Breakfast Date, **'84** 7
Spread, Date-Walnut, **'87** 292
Squares, Date, **'90** 49
Stuffed Dates, Apricot-, **'80** 250

Desserts. *See also* specific types.
Alaska, Peachy Melba, **'88** 266
Alaskas, Brownie, **'83** 299
Almond Dessert, Sour Cream-, **'92** 120
Amaretto Cream Tortoni, **'85** 161
Ambrosia, Baked, **'83** 303
Ambrosia, Brunch, **'83** 57
Ambrosia, Easy, **'92** 45
Ambrosia, Honey Bee, **'83** 267
Ambrosia, Layered, **'88** 304
Apple Brown Betty, **'83** 213
Apple-Cheese Crisp, **'92** 235

Apple-Cranberry Crunch, **'86** 300; **'87** 178
Apple Crisp, Delicious, **'82** 303
Apple Crisp, Granola, **'85** 78
Apple Crumble, Whole Wheat-, **'90** M213
Apple Delight, **'80** 109
Apple Dessert, Creamy Dutch, **'91** 19
Apple Dessert, Honey-Baked, **'90** M213
Apple Dumplings, **'82** 273
Apple Dumplings with Orange Hard Sauce,
  '88 224
Apple Flan, **'81** 309
Apple Fritters, **'82** 273
Apple Kuchen, **'79** 24
Apple-Nut Crunch, **'82** M238
Apple Rings, **'85** 232
Apple Rings, Cinnamon, **'82** M237
Apples and Cream, Brandied, **'82** M237
Apples and Rum Flambé, Hot, **'92** 88
Apples, Baked Mincemeat-Filled, **'80** 276
Apples, Brandied, **'81** 248
Apples, Chilled Poached Lemon, **'86** 182
Apples, Cooked, **'93** 338
Apples, Golden, **'82** 254
Apples, Imperial Baked, **'82** 273
Apples, Melting, **'88** 19
Apples, Old English Caramel, **'85** 231
Apples, Orange-Pecan Baked, **'85** 45
Apple Squares, Sour Cream, **'82** 262
Apples with Brandied Date Conserve,
  Cinnamon, **'85** 315
Apples with Orange Sauce, Baked, **'84** 314
Apricot Cream, Peachy-, **'86** 163
Avocado Whip, **'79** 107
Banana-Berry Supreme, **'81** 205
Banana Cream Dessert, **'81** 180
Banana Flip, **'83** 303
Banana-Peach Flambé, **'85** 316
Bananas, Candied, **'83** 179
Bananas Foster, **'79** 18; **'83** M114; **'86** 139;
  '88 20
Bananas Foster, Elegant, **'81** 59
Bananas Foster for Two, **'80** 115
Bananas Foster, Tropical, **'79** 231
Bananas, Praline, **'84** 313
Bananas, Regal, **'85** 46
Bananas Supreme, **'84** 256
Bananas with Orange Sauce, Baked, **'79** 115
Bavarian Cream with Fresh Fruit, **'88** 137
Bavarian Cream with Raspberry Sauce,
  '91 180
Bavarian Dessert, Light, **'86** 6
Berried Treasure, **'89** 124
Berries on Snow, **'82** 227
Berries with Raspberry Custard Sauce,
  Fresh, **'88** 163
Berry Basket, Summer, **'84** 158
Berry Compote, **'81** 275
Berry Grapefruit Cup, **'79** 242
Berry-Peach Compote, **'82** 133
Biscotti, Light, **'91** 310
Biscuits, Sweet Little, **'85** 305
Blackberries and Dumplings, **'86** 196
Blackberry Dessert Tamales, **'94** 190
Blackberry Flan, **'79** 182
Blueberries and Cointreau, **'82** 100
Blueberry-Amaretto Squares, **'83** 220
Blueberry Crumble, **'81** 84
Blueberry Crunch, Fresh, **'82** 143
Blueberry Dessert, Easy, **'89** M130
Blueberry Dream, **'88** 94
Boysenberries and Cream Supreme, **'82** 133

Desserts *(continued)*

Brandy Alexander, '92 283
Brandy Float, Blazing, '85 314
Bread, Fry, '85 155
Brie, Almond-Raspberry, '94 M89
Brownie Ice Cream Sandwich Shells, '88 195
Brûlé, Petit, '93 219
Buñuelos, '80 199
Buñuelos, King-Size, '86 5
Butter-Nut Strips, '82 167
Butterscotch Fantastic, '83 76
Cakes, Funnel, '83 250
Cakes, Spanish Wind, '84 157
Cannoli, '80 58; '91 20
Cantaloupe Compote, '81 147
Cantaloupe Cream Delight, '82 179
Cantaloupe Delight, '89 204
Cappuccino Coffee Dessert, '92 264
Caramel Fondue, '94 331
Caramel Surprise, '88 202
Champagne Delight, '83 304
Charlotte, Macaroon, '81 296
Charlotte, Peach, '79 68
Charlotte, Pineapple, '90 288
Charlotte Russe, '80 71; '82 M142; '90 288
Charlotte Russe, Fresh Lemon, '80 13
Charlotte Russe, Lemon, '84 192
Charlotte Russe, Wine Jelly and, '82 305
Charlotte Russe with Strawberry Sauce, '92 85
Cheese Blintzes, '82 146; '83 71
Cheese, Chunky Cream, '85 306
Cheese Dessert, Creamy Cottage, '87 191
Cheese, Fruited Cream, '85 306
Cheese Kuchen, '86 84
Cheese Molds, Heavenly Dessert, '85 209
Cheese, Nutty Date Dessert, '87 299
Cheese Squares, Lemony Cream, '82 159
Cherries à la Mode, '88 202
Cherries Jubilee, '79 18; '83 139
Cherries Jubilee, Quick, '82 M100
Cherries Jubilite, '86 317
Cherries Sabayon, '88 178
Cherries, Sherried, '93 289
Cherry-Berry on a Cloud, '79 94
Cherry Compote, '83 139
Cherry Dessert, Holiday, '80 255
Chocolate
    Almond Dessert, Chocolate-, '82 306
    Almond Meringue Fingers, Chocolate-, '84 158
    Baskets with Berry Cream, Chocolate, '92 118
    Black-Bottom Goodies, '89 251
    Brickle Squares, Chocolate, '94 290
    Brownie-Mint Dessert, '82 227
    Buttercream, Chocolate, '84 156
    Charlotte Russe, Chocolate, '87 74
    Chilled Chocolate Dessert, '83 177
    Cinnamon-Chocolate Cream, '94 199
    Coffee Mallow, '80 109
    Cream, Heavenly Chocolate, '88 128
    Crêpes, Chocolate Dream, '86 164
    Crêpes, Fruit-Filled Chocolate, '89 325
    Cups, Chocolate, '80 207
    Cups, Chocolate Crinkle, '93 270
    Cups, Chocolate Lace, '87 133
    Cups, Chocolate-Mint, '80 71
    Cups, Miniature Chocolate, '87 132

Date-Nut Delight, Chocolate, '88 168
Decadence, Chocolate, '89 183
Dip, Chocolate, '92 50
Dream Dessert, Chocolate, '83 198
Easy Chocolate Dessert, '79 75
Fondue, Dessert, '89 281
Fondue, White Chocolate, '92 287
Fudge Dessert with Kahlúa Cream, '91 197
Ladyfinger Dessert, Chocolate, '86 162
Loaves, Chocolate Chip Cheese, '91 299; '92 264
Log, Chocolate Cream, '94 220
Mint Dessert, Chocolate-, '82 100
Mint Dessert, Cool Chocolate-, '80 109
Peanut-Chocolate Dessert, '80 86
Pizza, Chocolate, '91 298
Plunge, Chocolate, '94 332
Pots de Chocolat, Petits, '82 272
Pots de Crème, '81 15; '84 M145
Pots de Crème au Chocolate, '93 53
Pots de Crème, Chocolate, '93 296; '94 234
Pots de Crème for Two, '89 275
Pots de Crème, Mocha, '88 M45
Pots de Crème, Rum-Flavored, '85 102
Roll, Chocolate Cream, '85 317
Roll, Chocolate Mousse, '83 290
Roulage, '90 266
Roulage, Chocolate-Cranberry, '94 313
Roulage, Chocolate-Mocha, '80 216
Roulage, Chocolate-Orange, '94 314
Roulage, Mint-Chocolate, '94 314
Roulage, White Chocolate, '92 230
Rum Dessert, Chocolate-, '81 247
Sack, Large Chocolate, '93 314
Sack, Small Chocolate, '93 314
Shells with Kahlúa Cream, Chocolate, '88 195
Squares, Chocolate-Blueberry Dessert, '87 299
Strawberry-Chocolate Combo, '85 96
Sundae Dessert, Hot Fudge, '84 313
Supreme, Chocolate, '84 94
Trifle, Chocolate, '88 258; '93 326
Truffle Dessert, Chocolate, '88 281
Waffles with Strawberry Cream, Chocolate, '88 153
Cinnamon Crisps, '93 106
Coconut Cloud, '80 70
Coconut Dessert, Chilled, '83 116
Coeur à la Crème, Christmas, '86 278
Coffee-Almond Tortoni, '81 30
Crackers, Dessert, '87 3
Cranberries, Brandied, '86 269
Cranberries Jubilee, '85 312; '90 293
Cranberry Apple Dessert, '80 253
Cranberry Bake, Hot, '91 250
Cranberry Jubilee, Tasty, '84 305
Cranberry Supreme, '85 280
Cranberry Surprise Dessert, '79 242
Cream, Bavarian, '86 M165
Cream, Molded French, '85 311
Cream Puffs, Captivating, '81 180
Cream Puffs, Java, '81 187
Cream Puffs, Strawberry, '81 95
Cream Puffs, Tutti-Frutti, '79 231
Crème Celeste, '88 94
Crème d'Ange, '83 91
Crème Pâtissière, '84 207
Crêpes, Basic Dessert, '82 157; '86 275

Crêpes, Dessert, '86 260; '87 290; '88 134
Crêpes, Dixie Dessert, '79 222
Crêpes Flambé, Cherry, '79 18
Crêpes, Strawberry Dessert, '83 122
Crêpes Suzettes, Light, '83 71
Custard Dessert, Fresh Peach, '86 162
Date Dessert Squares, '89 255
Date-Nut Balls, '85 10
Doughnuts, Orange Spiced, '79 136
Drink, Creamy Dessert, '86 131
Drink, Simply Super Dessert, '83 303
Éclair Cake, '93 42
Éclairs, Minted Miniature, '88 66
Éclairs, Pistachio-Cream, '91 296
Éclairs with Pecan Sauce, '83 219
Flan de Leche (Flan with Milk), '92 169
Frappé, Hawaiian, '81 178
Frozen
    After Dinner-Drink Dessert, '82 100
    Almond Crunch, Frozen, '94 283
    Amaretto Chantilly, '89 14
    Amaretto Freeze, '82 182
    Amber Bombe, '80 255
    Applesauce Fluff, '91 173
    Apricot Fluff, Frozen, '86 242
    Apricot Freeze, '82 10
    Baked Alaska, '84 105; '85 295
    Baked Alaska, Apple, '80 226
    Baked Alaska, Brownie, '80 66
    Baked Alaska, Chocolate Mousse, '85 195
    Banana Pops, '83 60; '84 44
    Banana Split Alaskas, '87 10
    Banana Split Pie, Layered, '83 189
    Bombe, Ice Cream, '90 269
    Bombe with Raspberry Sauce, Creamy, '89 322
    Cantaloupe Cream, Frozen, '82 159
    Cantaloupe Whip, '89 198
    Caramel-Toffee Bombe, '93 214
    Charlotte, Spumoni, '90 193
    Cherry Cordial Dessert, '84 312
    Chocolate Almond Velvet, '81 148
    Chocolate-Coffee Frozen Dessert, '85 172
    Chocolate Dessert, Frozen, '83 76
    Chocolate Mint Freeze, '88 167
    Chocolate Roulage, Frozen, '90 56
    Chocolate-Walnut Cups, '85 213
    Chocolate Whip, '89 326
    Choco-Maple Frozen Dessert, '86 300; '87 178
    Cinnamon Ice Cream Sombreros, '93 276
    Citrus Cup, Snowball, '79 2
    Coconut-Caramel Dessert, '92 44
    Coffee Dessert, Light, '88 260
    Coffee Ice Cream Crunch, '82 182
    Coffee Tortoni, Creamy, '88 268
    Cookies 'n' Cream Dessert, Gold-Dusted, '94 271
    Cream Dessert, Triple, '94 244
    Elegant Ending, '86 145
    Fruit Cream Freeze, '82 144
    Fruit Cups, Frozen, '93 197
    Fruit Freeze, Holiday, '88 283
    Fruit Ice, Mixed, '88 85
    Fruit Pops, '87 168
    Fudge-Peanut Ice Cream Dessert, '88 167
    Fudgy Frozen Dessert, Nutty, '94 28

Desserts, Frozen *(continued)*

Grand Marnier Cream, '84 312
Grapefruit Freeze, '93 242
Grasshopper Freeze, Creamy, '81 180
Hazelnut-Coffee Ice, '94 233
Honeydew Granita, '87 162
Ice-Cream Angel Dessert, Triple Mint, '93 86
Ice Cream Bombe, '82 305
Ice Cream Delight, '80 69
Ice Cream Dessert, Decadent, '91 56
Ice Cream Dessert, Layered, '83 189; '84 94, 105; '86 163
Ice Cream Dessert, Mint, '88 66
Ice Cream Party Squares, '91 214
Ice Cream Sandwiches, Chocolate Cookie, '87 147
Ice Cream Treats, Crunchy, '86 300; '87 178
Lemon-Chiffon Frozen Yogurt, '85 54
Lemon Cream, Frozen, '83 118
Lime-Mint Refresher, '82 144
Lime Whip, '89 199
Little Bits, '79 196
Macaroon-Sherbet Frozen Dessert, '79 212
Mimosa Ice, '94 24
Mint Patty Alaska, '80 219
Mocha Alaska Dessert, '84 191
Mocha Dessert, Frozen, '84 311
Mocha Freeze, Royal, '84 53
Mocha Squares, Frozen, '81 187
Orange Alaska, '83 177
Orange-Banana Pops, '82 129
Orange Dessert, Frozen, '92 44
Oranges Grand Marnier, '92 82
Ozark Pudding, Frozen, '88 127
Peach Freeze, Creamy, '82 144
Peach Torte, Frozen, '93 135
Peanut Butter Delight, Frozen, '88 137
Pineapple Delight, Fresh, '79 111
Pineapple-Orange Bars, '82 129
Pineapple-Yogurt Pops, '91 173
Pops, Deep Blue Sea, '94 143
Pops, Hawaiian Orange-Pineapple, '94 143
Praline Freeze, '89 60
Pumpkin Dessert, Frozen, '88 167
Rainbow Delight, Frozen, '84 105
Raspberry Dessert, Frozen, '84 192
Raspberry Fluff, '89 198
Sherbet Ambrosia Cups, '82 159
Sherbet Dessert, Layered, '87 109
Strawberry Cups, Frozen, '91 173
Strawberry Delight, Frozen, '82 112, 174
Strawberry Frost, '82 24; '83 154
Strawberry Popsicles, Smoothie, '82 112
Strawberry Puff, '82 5
Strawberry Whip, '89 198
Texas Tornadoes for Grown-Ups, '94 143
Toffee Ice Cream Dessert, '87 110
Torte, Frozen Viennese, '93 171
Tropical Paradise, Frozen, '89 206
Vanilla Almond Crunch, '93 243
Vanilla Frozen Yogurt, '87 125

Vanilla Soufflé, Frozen, '79 230; '82 173
Watermelon Frost, '86 196
Fruit. *See also* specific types.
Amaretto Crème on Fresh Fruit, '93 176
Bake, Nutty Fruit, '83 127
Bowl, Fresh Fruit, '89 137
Caribbean Fruit Dessert, '84 314
Cheese, and Nuts, Fruit, '93 324
Cheese, Luscious Fresh Fruit with, '79 153
Chilled Fruit with Dressing, '85 222
Combo, Fresh Fruit, '86 178
Compote, Baked Fruit, '80 276; '84 314
Compote, Baked Mustard Fruit, '85 47
Compote, Champagne Fruit, '81 309; '82 124
Compote, Chilled Fruit, '83 123
Compote, Fresh Fruit, '79 162; '82 197, 272; '84 82; '94 190
Compote, Fruit, '86 330
Compote, Gingered Fruit, '88 184
Compote, Hot Fruit, '81 203; '83 53
Compote, Jicama-Fruit, '92 49
Compote, Mixed Fruit, '93 123
Compote, Peach-Berry, '89 112
Compote, Warm Praline Fruit, '85 260
Compote, Wine Fruit, '81 272
Crisp, Fruit, '94 168
Cup, Fruit, '81 141; '91 202
Cup with Rum, Fruit, '83 55
Flame, Sherried Fruit, '85 313
Flaming Fruit Dessert, '83 302
Fondue, Fruitcake, '84 258
Gingered Fruit, '83 151
Glazed Fruit, '85 83
Hot Fruit Delight, '83 281
Kabobs with Mint Marinade, '82 157
Lemon Curd, Fresh Fruit with, '88 21
Medley, Chinese Fruit, '83 22
Medley, Fancy Fruit, '84 82
Medley, Fresh Fruit, '81 141
Medley, Frosty Fruit, '82 226
Medley of Fruit, Tropical, '86 53
Meringue Shells, Fruited, '87 32
Orange, Fruit Dessert, '84 314
Rainbow Fruit Dessert, '85 108
Soup Dessert, Fruit, '79 172
Spiced Fruit Delight, '82 229
Spiced Fruit Dessert, '82 50
Tequila, Fruit in, '82 223
Turnovers, Fruit, '79 150
Gâteau Panache, '83 269
Glacé, Sabayon, '89 306
Golden Dream, '82 100
Grahams, Praline, '92 239
Grape Juice-Fruit Refresher, '86 182
Honeydew-Berry Dessert, '83 120
Honeydew Melon with Grapes, '91 91
Ice Cream Ginger Fizz, '83 303
Kahlúa Cream, '87 134
Kahlúa Delight, '83 67
Kahlúa Delight, Make-Ahead, '84 M89
Kahlúa Velvet Dessert, '85 M294
Kiwi and Cream in Meringue Cups, '81 279
Kiwi-and-Orange Dessert, '93 295
Kiwi-Berry Pizza, '86 198
Kiwifruit Pizza, '89 306
Kiwi Jubilee, '83 120

Kugel, Apricot Noodle, '92 251
Kugel, Sweet, '90 254
Lemon Angel Rolls with Raspberry Sauce, '94 294
Lemon-Cream Cheese Dessert, '84 95
Lemon Cups, Baked, '87 128
Lemon Curd, '87 139; '89 334; '94 315
Lemon Curd with Berries, '90 102
Lemon Delight, '82 227
Lemon Dessert, Layered, '88 134
Lemon Solid, '93 279
Little Nothings, '79 135
Lollapalooza, '94 194
Madeleines, '88 79
Mango Dessert Tamales, '94 190
Mango Pan Dowdy, '83 150
Maple Nut Dessert, '81 84
Maraschino Russian Cream, '79 231
Melon Ball Compote, '85 157
Melon Balls and Cherries in Kirsch, '91 91
Melon Balls in Watermelon Sauce, '79 177
Melon-Mint Julep, '86 196
Melons in Mint Sauce, '85 164
Melon Wedges with Berry Sauce, '86 178
Meringue Cream Cups, Lemon, '84 23
Meringue Flowers, '84 156
Meringue, Piping, '84 156
Meringues, Baked Pear, '85 232
Meringues, Strawberry, '84 188
Mocha-Almond Dessert, '80 289; '81 62
Mocha Chiffon, '86 75
Nectarines Royale, '85 132
Oatmeal Cherry-Apple Crisp, '90 M16
Orange-Apple Crisp, '80 295
Orange Baskets, '81 308
Orange Chantilly Cream, '84 156
Orange Chiffon Dessert, '93 295
Orange-Coconut Cream, '84 24
Orange Cream, '81 12
Orange Cream Dessert, '80 254; '84 165
Orange Dip, Creamy, '84 117
Orange Elegance, Baked, '80 13
Orange Flambé, Dessert, '85 313
Orange Molded Dessert, '83 302
Oranges, Champagne, '93 83
Oranges, Frosted, '83 270
Orange Slices, Burgundy-Spiced, '93 294
Oranges, Wine-Poached, '84 M323
Orange-Tapioca Crème, '82 M283
Orange Tapioca Fluff, '87 31
Pancakes, Dessert Ginger, '88 153
Pancakes, Luau Dessert, '88 154
Parfaits
Blackberries-and-Cream Parfait, '87 129
Chocolate-Crème de Menthe Parfaits, '85 161
Chocolate-Mint Parfaits, '90 M15
Chocolate Mousse Parfait, '94 90
Chocolate-Peppermint Parfaits, '88 65
Coffee Crunch Parfaits, '82 159
Eggnog Bavarian Parfait, '79 255
Family, Parfait, '94 130
Kiwi Parfait, '86 199; '87 55
Lime Parfaits, '80 153
Mocha-Mallow Parfaits, '80 219
Orange Cream Parfaits, '94 198
Orange Parfaits, Chilled, '80 219
Peach Parfait, '82 166
Peanut Butter Parfaits, Crunchy, '79 176; '80 6
Peppermint Parfait, '93 315

Desserts, Parfaits *(continued)*

Pineapple Parfait, **'84** 83
Speedy Parfaits, **'83** 76
Strawberry-Lemon Parfaits, **'84** 198
Strawberry Parfait, **'79** 99
Strawberry Parfaits, Frosty, **'85** 213
Strawberry Parfait, Surprise, **'86** 151
Strawberry-Yogurt Parfait, Crunchy, **'79** 124
Surf-and-Sand Parfaits, **'93** 169
Tropical Trilogy Parfait, **'92** 247
White Chocolate-Raspberry Swirl Parfait, **'90** 315
Pavlova, **'92** 101
Peach Almond Cream, **'82** 108
Peach-Blueberry Dessert, **'92** 184
Peach Cardinale, **'89** 155
Peach Cream, Bavarian, **'82** 171
Peach Crisp, **'92** 13
Peach Dessert, Quick, **'85** 178
Peach Dessert, Spiced, **'83** 9
Peach Dumplings, **'85** 177
Peaches, Baked, **'92** 179
Peaches, Brandy, **'85** 275
Peaches, Caramel, **'93** 134
Peaches Champagne, **'79** 146
Peaches Foster, **'86** 240
Peaches, Gingersnap, **'85** M329
Peaches in Wine Sauce, **'79** 184
Peaches, Macaroon-Stuffed, **'79** 178
Peaches, Marinated, **'91** 91
Peaches 'n' Cream, Honeyed, **'93** 134
Peaches with Ginger, Oven-Baked, **'82** 170
Peaches with Nutty Dumplings, Spiced, **'87** 164
Peaches with Rum, Ginger, **'84** M323
Peach Halves, Stuffed, **'86** 196
Peach Melba, **'81** 83; **'83** M114
Peach Split, **'85** 277
Peach Trifle, **'92** 179
Peachy Melt-Away Dessert, **'87** 298
Peanut Butter Dessert, **'92** 164
Peanut-Buttery Dessert, Crunchy, **'92** 204
Pear-Blue Cheese Gratin, **'93** 328
Pear Fans with Raspberry-Orange Sauce, Poached, **'88** 22
Pears, Almond-Stuffed, **'83** 207
Pears Belle Helene, **'86** 164
Pears, Crème de Menthe, **'94** 50
Pears Elegant, Baked, **'91** 48
Pears Flambé, Orange-Poached, **'85** 313
Pears, Flaming, **'84** 313
Pears in Custard, Poached, **'88** 20
Pears in Red Wine, **'82** 254
Pears in Wine, Poached, **'82** 194
Pears, Lemon Poached, **'82** 74
Pears, Maple-Sugared, **'81** 232
Pears Poached in Red Wine, **'83** 302
Pears, Spicy Coconut, **'83** 207
Pears, Vanilla Poached, **'90** 57
Pears with Berry Sauce, Wine-Poached, **'86** 144
Pears with Crème Chantilly, Holiday, **'91** 297
Pears with Dark Chocolate Sauce, Poached, **'90** M141
Pears with Honey-Yogurt Sauce, Poached, **'92** 306
Pears with Meringue, Amaretto, **'90** M58

Pears with Raspberry Sauce, Poached, **'84** 213; **'87** 69; **'88** 223
Pecans, Sugared, **'82** 167
Peppermint Bavarian, **'80** 153
Peppermint Fondue, **'94** 332
Peppermint Wafer Dessert, **'79** 176; **'80** 7
Pineapple-Almond Delight, **'85** 96
Pineapple Dessert Chimichangas, **'86** 4
Pineapple, Meringue-Topped, **'84** 178
Pineapple 'n' Cream, **'88** 202
Pineapple, Scalloped, **'79** 106; **'82** 254
Pineapple with Natillas Sauce, Baked, **'83** 179
Pineapple with Raspberry Sauce, Chocolate-Drizzled, **'90** 57
Pizzelles, **'83** 298
Plum Crunch, Layered, **'86** 174
Port Wine Jelly with Whipped Cream, **'84** 254
Pots de Crème, Easy, **'93** 281
Profiteroles, **'84** 208
Prune Bavarian, **'86** 223
Pumpkin Chiffon, **'82** 216; **'86** 283; **'88** 260
Pumpkin Chiffon Dessert, **'88** 128
Pumpkin Mold, **'82** 311
Pumpkin-Orange Delight, **'86** 321
Pumpkin Swirl, Easy, **'93** 234
Raspberry Dream, **'83** 108
Raspberry-Jellyroll Dessert, **'85** 95
Raspberry Jellyrolls, **'93** M255
Raspberry-Pear Crisp, **'89** 109
Raspberry Prunes, **'82** 124
Raspberry-Strawberry Bavarian, **'89** 15
Rhubarb Crisp, **'91** 146; **'92** 130
Rhubarb-Strawberry Bavarian, **'86** 140
Rhubarb Whip, **'79** 112
Rice Cream with Mandarin Oranges, **'85** 317
Roulage, Toffee-Pecan, **'94** 312
Rum Balls, **'93** 314
Sabayon, **'93** 272
Santa's Hat, **'92** 279
Sauces
Almond-Vanilla Custard Sauce, **'88** M177
Amaretto-Chocolate Sauce, **'92** 154
Amaretto-Cinnamon Sauce, **'93** 171
Amaretto-Strawberry Sauce, **'87** M165
Ambrosia Sauce, Hot, **'89** 335
Apple Ambrosia Sauce, **'89** 95
Apple-Cinnamon Sauce, **'93** 42
Apple Dessert Sauce, **'87** M165
Apple Dessert Sauce, Spicy, **'82** 177
Apple Topping, Spicy, **'87** 125
Apricot Ice Cream Sauce, **'91** 57
Apricot Sauce, **'82** 212
Apricot-Walnut Hard Sauce, **'88** 153
Banana-Pineapple Sauce, **'83** 48
Banana Sundae Sauce, **'84** 275
Berry Mimosa Sauce, **'90** 315
Berry Sauce, **'87** 290; **'88** 135; **'94** 130
Bittersweet Chocolate Sauce, **'92** 319
Blackberry Sauce, **'86** 152; **'94** 232
Blueberry Sauce, **'88** 155; **'89** M130; **'94** 122
Blueberry Topping, **'87** 125
Bourbon Praline Sauce, **'81** 170
Bourbon Sauce, **'93** 51
Brandied Hard Sauce, **'80** 264; **'83** 250; **'85** 313
Brandy-Butter Sauce, **'79** 230
Brandy-Macadamia Sauce, **'82** 311
Brandy Sauce, **'88** 279

Brown Sugar Sauce, **'90** 314
Buttered Rum Sauce, **'83** 249
Buttered Rum Sauce, Hot, **'88** 204
Butter Pecan Sauce, **'91** 174
Butterscotch-Pecan Sauce, **'82** 212
Caramel-Raisin Sauce, **'88** 127
Caramel Sauce, **'79** 79; **'91** 56, 180; **'93** 210, 235, 296; **'94** 234
Caramel Sauce, Easy, **'87** 38
Caramel Sauce, White, **'92** 195
Cherry-Pineapple Topping, **'87** 126
Cherry Sauce, **'79** 91
Cherry Sauce, Elegant, **'79** M156
Chocolate-Cherry Sauce, **'85** 189
Chocolate Cherry Sauce, **'87** M165
Chocolate-Mint Sauce, **'93** 86; **'94** 314
Chocolate Mint Sauce, Quick, **'86** M58
Chocolate-Orange Sauce, **'86** 165; **'94** 314
Chocolate-Peanut Butter Sauce, **'79** 91, M156
Chocolate-Peppermint Sauce, **'94** 205
Chocolate-Praline Sauce, **'85** M295
Chocolate Sauce, **'83** 189; **'84** 208, 313; **'86** 322; **'90** 57; **'91** 56, 57; **'93** 276; **'94** 121
Chocolate Sauce, Classic, **'85** 207
Chocolate Sauce, Creamy, **'88** M177
Chocolate Sauce, Dark, **'93** 296; **'94** 234, 283
Chocolate Sauce, Double, **'83** 79
Chocolate Sauce, Easy, **'92** 148
Chocolate Sauce, Heavenly, **'79** 79; **'82** 167
Chocolate Sauce Supreme, **'85** 189
Cinnamon-Blueberry Sauce, **'86** 11
Cinnamon-Fudge Sauce, **'85** 141
Coconut-Orange Sauce, **'85** 189
Coconut Sauce, Creamy Light, **'82** 177
Cranberry Jubilee, Tasty, **'85** 189
Cranberry Sauce, **'86** 278; **'88** 280
Crème Anglaise, **'92** 164
Crème Fraîche Sauce, **'79** 281; **'93** 135
Custard Sauce, **'85** 41; **'88** 154, 251, 259; **'89** 291
Date-Nut Sundae Sauce, **'82** 167
Fig Sauce, **'79** 140
Fruit Dessert Sauce, Hot, **'87** 299
Fruit Puree, **'94** 190
Fruit Sauce, Golden, **'89** 281
Fruit Sauce, Quick, **'82** 212
Fudge Sauce, **'91** 174
Fudge Sauce, Easy Hot, **'84** 69; **'94** 194
Fudge Sauce, Hot, **'82** 181, 295; **'84** 143
Fudge Sauce, Quick Hot, **'82** 212
Golden Sauce, **'88** 267
Hard Sauce, **'80** 265; **'82** 14
Hard Sauce, Special, **'86** 318
Honey-Chocolate Sauce, **'89** 251
Honey-Orange Sauce, **'85** 108
Honeyscotch Sundae Sauce, **'82** 167
Honey-Yogurt Sauce, **'92** 307
Hot Cinnamon Sauce, Apple Pie with, **'88** 210
Kahlúa Chocolate Sauce, **'85** 155
Lemon Cream Sauce, **'93** 200
Lemon Dessert Sauce, **'87** M165
Lemon Sauce, **'84** 258, 306; **'85** 77, 190; **'91** 240
Lemon Sauce, Tart, **'85** 191

Desserts, Sauces *(continued)*

Mandarin Dressing, **'89** 137
Mandarin Orange Sauce, **'89** 204
Mango Sauce, **'83** 120
Marshmallow Sauce, **'91** 91
Melba Sauce, **'87** 77
Mint Sauce, Party, **'82** 212
Orange Dessert Sauce, **'87** 58
Orange Hard Sauce, **'88** 225
Orange Sauce, Fresh, **'85** 209
Peach-Berry Sauce, **'87** M165
Peach-Blueberry Pancake Sauce, **'82** 177
Peach Blueberry Sauce, **'81** 170
Peach-Praline Sauce, **'85** 161
Peach Sauce, **'84** 144
Peach Sauce, Creamy, **'85** 189
Peach Sauce, Fresh, **'87** 167
Peanut Butter Ice Cream Sauce, **'84** 30
Peanut Dessert Sauce, **'86** M251
Pear Sauce, **'92** 164
Pecan Sauce, **'83** 219
Piña Colada Topping, Chunky, **'87** 125
Pineapple Ice Cream Sauce, **'81** M289
Pineapple-Rhubarb Sauce, **'88** 94
Pineapple-Rum Sauce, **'84** 275
Plum Sauce, Fresh, **'94** 129
Praline Ice Cream Sauce, **'85** 189
Praline Ice Cream Sauce, Southern, **'86** M227
Praline Sauce, **'83** 25; **'84** 143; **'89** 95; **'92** 282; **'93** 214; **'94** 206, 312
Raspberry-Amaretto Sauce, **'88** 130
Raspberry-Orange Sauce, **'88** 22; **'92** 154
Raspberry-Peach Topping, **'87** 126
Raspberry Sauce, **'82** 289; **'83** 108; **'84** 73, 213; **'87** 69, 117, 183; **'88** 267; **'89** 183, 322; **'91** 96, 180, 270; **'92** 130; **'93** 82, 99, 315; **'94** 295
Raspberry Sauce, Crimson, **'79** 91; **'85** 30
Raspberry Sauce Dessert, **'80** 147
Raspberry Sauce Flambé, **'84** 142
Raspberry Sauce, Fresh, **'93** 120
Rhubarb Sauce, Chilled, **'88** 94
Rum-Butter Sauce, **'86** 301
Rum-Fruit Sauce, **'84** 312
Rum-Raisin Sauce, **'84** 7; **'94** 295
Rum Sauce, **'88** 32; **'94** 241
Rum Sauce, Brown Sugar-, **'85** 231
Rum Sauce, Hot, **'79** 86
Rum Sundae Sauce, **'93** 162
Sherry Sauce, **'84** 109
Spicy Sauce, **'93** 52
Strawberries Arnaud Sauce, **'93** 50
Strawberry-Banana Topping, **'87** 125
Strawberry-Peach Sauce, **'92** 154
Strawberry Sauce, **'84** 144; **'87** 93, 198; **'92** 85; **'94** 121
Strawberry Sauce, Brandied, **'88** 196
Strawberry Sauce, Fresh, **'82** 177
Strawberry Sauce, Old-Fashioned, **'94** 130
Strawberry Sauce, Peaches with, **'85** 8
Strawberry Sauce with Crunchy Topping, **'81** 170

Strawberry Sauce with Dumplings, **'84** 314
Taffy Dessert Sauce, **'86** 20
Tea-Berry Sauce, **'94** 130
Toffee-Fudge Sauce, **'89** 95
Toffee Sauce, **'94** 72
Vanilla Crème Sauce, **'94** 243
Watermelon Sauce, Melon Balls in, **'79** 177
Whiskey Sauce, **'90** 230; **'92** 87, 93
White Chocolate Sauce, **'92** 164
Savarin, **'79** 171
Sherbet-Cantaloupe Surprise, **'91** 105
Sherbet Cooler, Peachy, **'91** 187
Sopaipillas, **'80** 197; **'88** 112; **'91** 78
Sopaipillas, Pineapple, **'83** 179
Soufflé, Banana Daiquiri, **'84** 317
Soufflé, Brandy Alexander, **'82** 173; **'83** M114
Soufflé, Chilled Devonshire, **'88** 279
Soufflé, Chilled Orange, **'84** 317; **'86** 189
Soufflé, Chocolate-Mint, **'81** 16
Soufflé, Coconut, **'85** 212
Soufflé, Cold Lemon-Lime, **'84** 24
Soufflé, Elegant Daiquiri, **'80** 69
Soufflé, Frozen Orange, **'79** 211
Soufflé, Frozen Vanilla, **'79** 230; **'82** 173
Soufflé, Grand Marnier, **'79** 281
Soufflé, Grasshopper, **'81** 248; **'86** 188
Soufflé, Kahlúa, **'82** 173
Soufflé, Lemon, **'82** 170
Soufflé, Light Chocolate, **'83** 278
Soufflé, Orange Dessert, **'83** 206
Soufflé, Pineapple Dessert, **'80** 153
Soufflé, Raspberry, **'86** 188
Soufflé, Raspberry-Topped, **'85** 317
Soufflé, Tart Lemon, **'85** 82
Soup, Sherry-Berry Dessert, **'91** 180
Spumoni and Berries, **'91** 204
Strawberries, Almond Cream with Fresh, **'87** 93
Strawberries and Cream, **'82** 100
Strawberries Arnaud, **'93** 50
Strawberries, Deep-Fried, **'84** 109
Strawberries, Dipped, **'94** 17
Strawberries Jamaica, **'85** 161; **'93** 239
Strawberries Juliet, **'84** 82
Strawberries Marsala, **'88** 171
Strawberries 'n' Cream, **'90** 30
Strawberries, Old-Fashioned Rock Cream with, **'90** 125
Strawberries Romanoff, **'84** 108; **'88** 95; **'91** 126
Strawberries, Ruby, **'82** 100
Strawberries Sabayon, **'79** 94
Strawberries with Brandied Orange Juice, **'82** 160
Strawberries with French Cream, **'83** 191
Strawberries with Strawberry Cream, **'84** 108
Strawberries with Walnuts, Stuffed, **'85** 122; **'86** 124
Strawberries Zabaglione, **'81** 95
Strawberry Carousel, **'91** 247
Strawberry Cheese Delight, **'79** 50
Strawberry Coconut Nests, **'88** 136
Strawberry-Cream Cheese Dessert, **'83** 123
Strawberry Delight, **'81** 85
Strawberry Dessert, **'83** 123

Strawberry Dessert, Chilled, **'84** 164
Strawberry Dessert, Glazed, **'84** 33
Strawberry Dessert, Summer, **'92** 143
Strawberry Dessert, Sweet-and-Sour, **'92** 54
Strawberry Frost, **'81** 279; **'82** 24; **'83** 154
Strawberry-Lemon Dessert, **'86** 162
Strawberry Napoleons, **'81** 126
Strawberry Pizza, **'79** 94
Strawberry Shortcake Squares, **'85** 122
Strawberry Swirl, **'84** 108
Strawberry Yogurt Delight, **'85** 77
Strawberry-Yogurt Dessert, **'90** 295
Sundae, Cantaloupe, **'89** 166
Sundae Dessert, Hot Fudge, **'86** 322
Sundae, Hot Apple Spice, **'92** 239
Sundaes, Cocoa-Kahlúa, **'83** M58
Sundaes Flambé, Peach, **'81** 88
Sundaes, Hot Strawberry, **'81** M5
Sundaes, Mauna Loa, **'80** 126
Sundaes, Quick Pear, **'86** 71
Tiramisù, **'91** 21; **'94** 295
Toffee Dessert, English, **'88** 136
Tortilla Baskets, **'94** 97
Trifle, Angel Food, **'91** 184
Trifle, Easy Strawberry, **'88** 201
Trifle, English, **'93** 289
Trifle, Island, **'92** 238
Trifle, Lemon-Blueberry, **'88** 210
Trifle, Pineapple Angel Food, **'93** 86
Trifle, Raspberry, **'88** 259
Trifle, Rum, **'86** 322
Trifle, Savannah, **'80** 121
Trifles, Easy Individual, **'92** 239
Trifle, Toffee, **'94** 168
Tropical Snow, **'86** 34
Vacherin Moka, **'80** 55
Vanilla Cream, **'83** M115
Vanilla Sherry Dessert, Glorified, **'81** 85
Waffles, Banana Split, **'89** 205
Waffles with Mandarin Orange Sauce, Dessert Pumpkin, **'89** 204
Waffle, Whole Wheat Dessert, **'79** 92
White Christmas Dessert, **'82** 261
Wine Jelly, Rosy, **'85** 306
Yule Log, **'79** 281; **'82** 289
Dips. *See* Appetizers/Dips.
Doughnuts
Applesauce Doughnuts, **'81** 203
Applesauce Drop Doughnuts, **'90** 70
Banana Doughnuts, **'86** 137
Beignets, **'84** 56
Cake Doughnuts, Quick, **'82** 226
Chocolate-Covered Doughnuts, **'84** 55
Chocolate Doughnuts, **'83** 95
Cinnamon Puffs, **'81** 209
Dutch Doughnuts, **'81** 50
Fry Bread, **'84** 140
Glazed Doughnuts, **'83** 94
Jelly-Filled Doughnuts, **'84** 55
Orange Spiced Doughnuts, **'79** 136
Pineapple Drop Doughnuts, **'83** 95
Potato Doughnuts, Chocolate-Glazed, **'85** 6
Potato Doughnuts, Old-Fashioned, **'84** 56
Puffs, Doughnut, **'86** 85
Puffs, Wheat Quick Doughnut, **'85** 278
Pumpkin Doughnut Drops, **'90** 323
Snowy Doughnuts, **'93** 286
Spice Doughnuts, **'84** 56
Sufganiyot (Jelly-Filled Doughnuts), **'90** 255
Whole Wheat Doughnuts, **'84** 56

Dove
Enchiladas, Dove, **'85** 270
Gumbo, Dove and Sausage, **'81** 199
Roasted Doves, Pan-, **'87** 240
Sherried Doves, **'91** 290
Dressings. *See* Stuffings and Dressings or
Salad Dressings.
Duck and Duckling
Baked Duck, Sherried, **'79** 224
Blackberry Sauce, Ducklings with, **'82** 251
Blackened Duck Breasts, **'93** 259
Breasts with Raspberry Sauce, Duck,
'87 240
Casserole, Duck and Wild Rice, **'79** 224
Enchiladas with Red Pepper-Sour Cream,
Smoked Duck, **'87** 121
Foxfire Duck, **'89** 241
Grilled Duck with Orange Sauce, **'94** 305
Gumbo, Duck, Oyster, and Sausage, **'79** 226
Gumbo Ya Ya, **'87** 210
Holiday Duckling, **'80** 251
Kabobs with Almond Rice, Grilled Duck,
'91 291
Marinated Duck Breasts, Charcoaled,
'79 226
Orange Duck, Chafing Dish, **'79** 226
Orange Gravy, Duck with, **'81** 259
Pâté, Duck, **'79** 226
Pâté, Duck Liver, **'79** 227
Pecan Stuffing, Wild Duck with, **'85** 269
Pot Pie with Parmesan Crust, Game,
'94 304
Prairie Wings Mallard, **'83** 252
Roast Ducklings with Cherry Sauce,
'86 312
Roast Duckling with Orange Sauce, **'81** 125
Roast Duckling with Tangerine Stuffing,
'90 16
Roast Duckling with Wine Jelly, **'88** 243
Roast Duck with Sweet Potato-Eggplant
Gravy, **'83** 90
Roast Long Island Duckling, **'84** 87
Roast Wild Duck with Orange Gravy,
'89 323
Smoked Duck Breasts, **'87** 121
Wild Duck, Buffet, **'86** 268
Dumplings
Apple Dumplings, **'82** 273
Apple Dumplings, Old-Fashioned, **'84** 226
Apple Dumplings with Orange Hard Sauce,
'88 224
Beef Stew with Dumplings, **'84** 3
Blackberries and Dumplings, **'86** 196
Cheddar Dumplings, Chicken Ragout with,
'94 44
Chicken and Dumplings, Country, **'85** 254
Chicken and Dumplings, Easy, **'86** 21
Chicken and Dumplings, Old-Fashioned,
'79 55; **'83** 228; **'93** 302
Chicken and Dumplings with Vegetables,
'85 M56
Chicken Stew and Dumplings, **'84** 4
Cornmeal Dumplings, Turnip Greens with,
'82 211
Drop Dumplings, Burgundy Stew with,
'83 125
Old-Fashioned Dumplings, **'81** 191
Parsley Dumplings, Beef Stew with, **'81** 76;
'82 13; **'85** M246
Peach Dumplings, **'80** 143; **'85** 177
Peas and Dumplings, Green, **'80** 102

Potato Dumplings, Venison Stew with,
'87 304
Shrimp with Dumplings, Stewed, **'79** 31
Strawberry Sauce with Dumplings,
'84 314
Tomato Dumplings, **'88** 144

Eggnog
Blender Eggnog, **'93** 341
Bread, Eggnog, **'83** 294
Breakfast Nog, Speedy, **'82** 47
Cake, Eggnog Pound, **'90** 253
Christmas Eggnog, **'87** 242
Coconut Nog, **'83** 275
Coffee Nog, Brandied, **'86** 329
Cooked Custard Eggnog, **'91** 305
Cookies, Eggnog Christmas, **'79** 255
Creamy Eggnog, **'80** 259; **'83** 303;
'85 300
Easy Eggnog, **'91** 305
Edenton Eggnog, **'84** 251
Eggnog, **'83** 318
Holiday Brew, **'81** 265
Holiday Eggnog Deluxe, **'79** 232
Irish Coffee Nog, **'84** 258; **'93** 340
Irish Cream Nog, **'82** 312
Mock Eggnog with Orange and Nutmeg,
'92 323
Orange Spiced Nog, **'82** 48
Parfait, Eggnog Bavarian, **'79** 255
Pie, Eggnog, **'80** 254; **'83** 205; **'86** 317;
'87 295
Pie, Eggnog Chiffon, **'86** 281
Pie, Fluffy Eggnog, **'81** M269
Punch, Coffee-Eggnog, **'86** 281
Punch, Coffee Eggnog, **'92** 264
Punch, Holiday Eggnog, **'86** 281
Punch, Peppermint-Eggnog, **'90** 273
Salad, Eggnog Christmas, **'86** 281
Sparkling Eggnog, **'79** 232
Tarts, Creamy Eggnog, **'79** 255
Thick and Creamy Eggnog, **'80** 261

Eggplant
Almonds, Eggplant with, **'79** 179
Appetizer, Eggplant, **'83** 187
Bake, Eggplant, **'80** 82
Bake, Eggplant-Sausage, **'85** 221
Caponata, **'87** 166
Casserole, Easy Eggplant, **'80** 202
Casserole, Eggplant, **'81** 205; **'84** 217;
'93 44; **'94** 214
Casserole, Eggplant and Noodle, **'82** 230
Casserole, Eggplant-and-Tomato, **'83** 187
Casserole, Eggplant-Sausage, **'84** 215
Casserole, Elegant Eggplant, **'82** 168
Casserole, Flavorful Eggplant, **'79** 92
Casserole, Moussaka, **'79** 179
Casserole, Potato-Eggplant, **'87** 166
Casserole, Spicy Hot Eggplant, **'93** 92
Casserole, Super Eggplant, **'80** 202
Caviar, Eggplant, **'88** 262

Caviar, Homemade Cowboy, **'94** 64
Caviar with Tapenade, Eggplant, **'92** 194
Chiles Rellenos, Eggplant, **'91** 86
Crawfish on Eggplant, Soft-Shell, **'88** 222
Creole Eggplant, **'82** 107; **'83** 86
Creole, Eggplant, **'86** 110
Dressing, Eggplant, **'90** 236
Easy Eggplant, **'87** M151
Fried Eggplant, **'79** 178; **'83** 187; **'88** 111
Fried Eggplant, Cheesy, **'90** 75
Fried Eggplant, French-, **'81** 204
Fried Eggplant, Parmesan, **'79** 189
Fried Parmesan Eggplant, **'87** 166
Fritters, Eggplant, **'91** 211
Gravy, Roast Duck with Sweet
Potato-Eggplant, **'83** 90
Grilled Eggplant, **'80** 202; **'89** 174
Heavenly Eggplant, **'93** 293
Italian Eggplant, **'84** 216
Italiano, Eggplant, **'91** 212
Italian-Style Eggplant and Zucchini, **'79** 289;
'80 26
Jackstraw Eggplant, **'82** 230
Julienne, Eggplant, **'85** 221
Lebanese Eggplant, **'81** 24
Main Dish, Sausage-Eggplant, **'80** 211
Medley, Eggplant-Shrimp, **'79** 188
Mexican Eggplant, **'83** 187
Mexicano, Eggplant à la, **'82** 229
Moussaka, **'87** 166; **'90** 68
Moussaka, Potatoes, **'93** 44
Oven-Fried Eggplant, **'91** 187
Parmesan, Eggplant, **'82** 230; **'83** 186;
'84 215; **'86** 53; **'92** 18
Parmesan, No-Fry Eggplant, **'92** 172
Parmigiana, Chicken-Eggplant, **'82** 212
Parmigiana, Eggplant, **'81** 19; **'82** 186
Patties, Eggplant, **'83** 186
Pizza, Eggplant, **'85** 221
Provençal, Eggplant, **'92** 82
Ratatouille, **'84** 105, 243
Ratatouille, Eggplant-Zucchini, **'81** 205
Ratatouille Niçoise, **'81** 22
Ratatouille, Quick-and-Easy, **'80** 212
Salad, Eggplant, **'90** 99
Sandwiches, Baked Eggplant, **'82** 230
Sautéed Eggplant and Zucchini, **'82** 96
Scalloped Eggplant, **'91** 223
Slices, Quick Eggplant, **'90** 75
Soup, Eggplant Supper, **'85** 221
Soup, Herbed Eggplant, **'90** 173
Spaghetti Squash with Sesame Eggplant,
'92 252
Spanish Eggplant, **'79** 21
Spread, Eggplant, **'86** 278
Spread, Eggplant-Mushroom, **'92** 156
Squash, Eggplant and, **'83** 187
Stacks, Eggplant, **'91** 211
Stuffed Eggplant, **'80** 158
Stuffed Eggplant, Baked, **'81** 133
Stuffed Eggplant, Beefy, **'81** 204
Stuffed Eggplant, Cheesy, **'79** 188; **'82** 208
Stuffed Eggplant Creole, **'82** 230
Stuffed Eggplant, Ham-, **'80** 162
Stuffed Eggplant, Italian-, **'90** 74
Stuffed Eggplant, Mushroom-, **'83** 136
Stuffed Eggplant, Ratatouille-, **'83** 187
Stuffed Eggplant, Ratatouille-Bran, **'86** 44
Stuffed Eggplant, Rolled, **'80** 63
Stuffed Eggplant, Sausage, **'81** 204
Stuffed Eggplant, Sausage-, **'91** 211

Eggplant (continued)

Stuffed Eggplant, Seafood, '79 187
Stuffed Eggplant, Shrimp-, '92 99
Supper, Beef-and-Eggplant, '84 291
Supreme, Eggplant, '79 188; '86 170
Tophats, Eggplant, '79 188

Eggs

au Gratin, Broccoli-and-Eggs, '85 289
au Gratin, Potatoes and Eggs, '79 107
Bake, Breakfast, '85 45
Baked Egg Crisps, '83 57
Baked Eggs Florentine, '86 M12
Baked Eggs in Spinach Nests, '82 70
Baked in Mushroom Sauce, Eggs, '93 47
Bake, Egg and Rice, '83 119
Bake, Sausage Egg, '81 225
Bake, Smoked Sausage-Egg, '85 248
Bedeviled Eggs, '86 67
Bel-Mar, Eggs, '90 92
Benedict, Bacon-and-Tomato Eggs, '87 195
Benedict, Easy Eggs, '80 M268
Benedict, Eggs, '79 40, 254; '85 49
Benedict, Light Eggs, '93 M68
Benedict, Lion, '93 121
Benedict with Cheese Sauce, Eggs, '81 225
Brandied Cream Sauce, Eggs in, '82 70
Bread, Butter-Egg, '85 269
Bread, County Fair Egg, '87 68
Bread, Easter Egg, '84 94
Breakfast Eye-Openers, '82 231
Breakfast, Farmer's, '81 44
Brunch Eggs, '85 44
Bruncheon Eggs, '83 83
Brunch, Texas, '82 70
Bunwiches, '80 92
Burritos, Brunch, '91 77
Casserole, Apple-Egg, '85 44
Casserole, Bacon and Egg, '81 225
Casserole, Breakfast Ham and Egg, '79 253
Casserole, Broccoli-and-Egg, '86 324
Casserole, Brunch Egg, '86 329
Casserole, Cheese-Egg-Zucchini, '84 114
Casserole, Cheesy Egg, '81 244; '86 15
Casserole, Cheesy Potato-Egg, '84 5
Casserole, Crab-Egg, '80 260
Casserole, Egg, '83 311
Casserole, Egg-and-Bacon, '85 248
Casserole, Egg-and-Cheese, '84 293
Casserole, Egg-Mushroom, '83 49
Casserole, Egg Soufflé, '83 55
Casserole, Saucy Scrambled Egg, '89 213
Casserole, Sausage-and-Egg, '94 284
Casserole, Sausage Breakfast, '81 270
Casserole, Sausage-Egg, '86 M12
Casserole, Spinach and Egg, '82 270
Casserole, Squash and Egg, '80 146
Casserole, Zucchini-Egg, '84 M113
Cheddar Eggs, '94 M141
Chile Eggs, '88 80
Cottage Eggs, '85 44
Crabmeat and Eggs New Orleans, '82 45
Creamed Eggs à la Asparagus, '81 201
Creamed Eggs, Broccoli and, '83 84
Creamed Eggs in Patty Shells, '80 M267
Creamed Eggs in Toast Cups, '83 83
Creole Eggs, '82 42
Creole, Eggs, '92 86
Creole, Skillet Eggs, '85 143
Crêpes, Ham-and-Egg, '83 204

Crêpes with Mushroom Sauce,
    Ham-and-Egg, '82 46
Croissant Eggwiches, '91 160
Croquettes, Tuna-Egg, '80 275
Delight, Bacon-and-Egg, '85 143
Delight, Crab-and-Egg, '84 261
Delight, Mushroom-Egg, '83 14
Dip, Festive Egg, '79 285
Dressing, Egg, '86 79
Featherbed Eggs, '93 122
Florentine, Eggs, '79 39; '83 56
Florentine-Style Eggs, '82 38
Foo Yong, Egg, '80 19; '86 232
Foo Yong Patties, '80 223
Foo Yong, Shrimp Egg, '83 22
Frittata, Broccoli-Cheese, '81 243
Frittata, Corn-and-Squash, '89 144
Frittata, Firecracker Pasta, '94 230
Frittata, Fresh Vegetable, '93 140
Frittata, Potato, '89 145
Frittata, Spinach, '81 53
Frittata, Vegetable, '92 48; '93 183
Ham and Eggs à la Swiss, '88 158
Ham and Eggs, Creamed, '82 40
Ham and Eggs, Creamy, '87 286
Ham and Eggs on Toast with Cheese Sauce,
    '81 43
Ham and Eggs, Savory, '82 231
Hard-Cooked Eggs, '82 280
Hash Brown Skillet Breakfast, '82 5
Herb Sauce, Eggs in, '88 80
Hominy, Bacon, Eggs, and, '85 143
Huevos Rancheros, '82 197; '91 77
Medley, Cheddar Egg, '81 M176
Mexicana, Eggs, '82 146
Migas, '87 180; '94 26
Mound, Frosted Egg, '79 33
Mushroom Eggs, Sherried, '83 49
Mushrooms and Eggs in Patty Shells,
    '85 143; '88 197
Mushrooms and Eggs, Saucy, '79 138
Nests, Fluffy Egg, '79 128
Omelets
    Apple Omelet Stack, '94 50
    Baked Omelets, '94 50
    Broccoli-Mushroom Omelet, '85 45
    Cheese Omelet, Herbed, '93 47
    Cheese Omelet, Puffed, '89 227
    Cheese Omelet, Zippy, '87 287
    Cheesy Picante Omelet, '86 95
    Chicken Liver Omelet, '82 44
    Country Omelets, '91 228
    Creole Sauce, Omelets with, '89 228
    Fines Herbes, Omelette aux, '92 82
    Fluffy Omelet, '84 56
    George's Omelets, '80 68
    Ham and Cheese Omelet, '79 262;
        '80 123
    Italian Omelet, '92 47
    Mexican Omelet, '79 128; '81 225
    Mexican Omelet, Easy, '88 114
    Mushroom Omelet, Rolled, '82 70
    Mushroom Sauce, Puffy Omelets with,
        '85 40
    Olé Omelet, '87 M124
    Olé, Omelet, '94 31
    Oyster Omelets, Smoked, '84 96
    Potato Omelet, Family-Size, '94 31
    Potato-Sprout Omelet, '79 128
    Primavera, Omelet, '87 71
    Rising Sun Omelet, '82 281; '83 42

    Rolled Omelet, '89 228
    Sandwich, Omelet, '86 95
    Sausage Filling, Omelet with, '81 43
    Sausage Omelet, Puffy, '80 M268
    Shrimp-and-Cheddar Omelet, '84 57
    Shrimp-and-Cheese Omelet, '94 31
    Sour Cream-Ham Omelet, '79 261
    Spanish Omelet, '81 201; '83 243;
        '84 101
    Spanish-Style Omelets, '83 188
    Spinach-Cheese Omelet, '83 119
    Strawberry-Sour Cream Omelet,
        '89 229
    Sunrise Omelet, '83 289
    Swiss Oven Omelet, '80 189
    Tarragon Omelet, '89 144
    Tex-Mex Omelet con Carne, '81 209
    Vegetable Omelet, Beefy, '83 188
    Vegetable Omelet, Cheddar-, '83 205
    Vegetable Omelet, Cheesy, '85 49
    Vegetable Omelet, Fresh, '84 211
    Vegetable Omelet, Golden, '82 M123
    Vegetable Omelet, Puffy, '83 188
    Vegetarian Omelet, '84 114
    White Wine Omelet, '79 103
    Yogurt-Avocado Omelet, '81 33
    Zucchini Omelet, '81 99
Paint, Egg Yolk, '86 322
Peanut Butter Easter Eggs, '87 86
Pickled Eggs, Beet, '84 287
Pickled Eggs, Rosy, '86 68
Pickled Eggs, Spiced, '84 288
Pie, Country Breakfast, '93 M328
Pie, Egg-Stra Special Chicken, '86 264
Pie, Old-Fashioned Egg Custard, '82 261
Pillows, Egg, '92 332
Pizza, Breakfast, '85 44
Pizza, Ham-and-Eggs Crescent, '93 47
Poached Eggs, '92 87, 93; '93 121
Poached Eggs, Basic, '82 58
Poached Eggs, French-Style, '82 58
Potatoes with Eggs and Meat, '91 311;
    '92 25
Potato Nests, Mashed, '94 141
Puff, Egg-and-Cheese, '85 45
Rancheros, Easy Eggs, '88 81
Rice, Egg Fried, '79 252; '80 19
Roll-Ups, Spicy Egg, '90 140
Roulade with Mushroom Filling, Egg, '88 84
Salad, Asparagus-and-Egg, '86 305
Salad, Bacon-Horseradish Egg, '94 181
Salad, Deviled Egg, '83 124
Salad, Egg-Rice, '84 18; '86 169
Salad, Green Vegetable and Egg, '79 191
Salad, Ham-and-Egg Potato, '86 84
Salad, Ham 'n Egg, '81 36
Salad Sandwiches, Shrimp-and-Egg, '94 182
Salad Tacos, Mexican Egg, '94 181
Salad, Tossed Shrimp-Egg, '80 4
Salad, Tuna-Egg, '81 135
Salad, Yolkless Egg, '94 181
Sandwiches, Breakfast, '82 M123; '89 M230
Sandwiches, Confetti, '79 236
Sandwiches, Eggsclusive, '79 164; '80 130
Sandwiches, Eggs-Tra Special, '81 240;
    '83 69
Sandwiches, Open-Faced Cheesy Egg,
    '86 67
Sandwiches, Open-Face Egg, '83 292;
    '84 78; '86 160
Sandwiches, Saucy Egg, '91 160

Eggs *(continued)*

Sardou, Eggs, **'92** 93
Saucy Eggs, **'83** 84
Saucy Eggs on Toast, **'81** 209
Scotch Eggs, **'79** 261; **'83** 289
Scrambled
    Bacon-and-Eggs Scramble, **'80** M267
    Buttermilk Scrambled Eggs, **'79** 72
    Casserole, Scrambled Egg, **'80** 51;
      '86 241
    Cottage Cheese Scrambled Eggs,
      '81 142
    Cottage-Scrambled Eggs, **'80** 49
    Country Eggs, **'86** 330
    Country-Style Scrambled Eggs, **'79** 22
    Cream Cheese Scrambled Eggs,
      '81 287
    Creamy Scrambled Eggs, **'90** 82
    Home-Style Scrambled Eggs, **'84** 66
    Mexican-Style Scrambled Eggs,
      '85 50
    Migas, **'87** 180; **'94** 26
    Onion Scrambled Eggs, Creamy,
      '83 M203
    Shrimp and Crab Scrambled Eggs,
      '79 261
    Sonora, Eggs, **'80** 196
    Spanish Scrambled Eggs, **'83** 49;
      '84 60
    Special Scrambled Eggs, **'81** 103
    Supreme, Scrambled Eggs, **'79** 39
    Tostadas, Scrambled Egg, **'86** 95
    Wild Rice, Scrambled Eggs with, **'80** 42
Soufflés, Little Egg, **'83** 57
Soufflé, Three-Egg Cheese, **'87** 234
Soup, Egg Drop, **'83** 21; **'86** 16
Soup, Egg-Drop, **'85** M12
Soup, Egg Flower, **'81** 307; **'82** 313;
  '83 65
Soup, Lemon-Egg Drop, **'93** 81
Spread, Cottage-Egg Salad, **'82** 146
Spread, Egg Salad, **'86** 127
Spread, Egg, Sour Cream, and Caviar,
  '85 279
Spread, Ham-and-Egg, **'79** 59
Spread, Vegetable-Egg, **'87** 106
Strata, Cheese-Rice, **'81** 176
Strata, Sausage, **'84** 101
Strata, Tomato-Cheese, **'81** 209
Stuffed
    Blue Cheese Stuffed Eggs,
      '93 87
    Creamed Eggs, **'86** 67
    Creamy Stuffed Eggs, **'84** 143
    Crunchy Stuffed Eggs, **'86** 67
    Deluxe, Eggs, **'82** 79
    Deviled Eggs, **'86** 176; **'94** 161
    Deviled Eggs, Bacon, **'86** 136
    Deviled Eggs, Best, **'80** 159
    Deviled Eggs, Chile-Cheese,
      '93 87
    Deviled Eggs, Creamed, **'82** 79
    Deviled Eggs, Curried, **'93** 87
    Deviled Eggs, Easy, **'82** 127
    Deviled Eggs, Nippy, **'80** 217
    Deviled Eggs, Pimiento-, **'84** 143
    Deviled Eggs, Saucy, **'82** 80
    Deviled Eggs Surprise, **'79** 83
    Deviled Eggs, Sweet, **'93** 88

    Deviled Eggs with Smoked Oysters,
      '84 161
    Deviled Eggs, Zesty, **'84** 205
    Devil's Island Eggs, **'82** 79
    Eggs, Stuffed, **'80** 155; **'88** 95
    Ham Devils, **'93** 88
    Herb-Sour Cream Stuffed Eggs, **'93** 87
    Mustard Eggs, Spicy, **'84** 143
    Pecan-Stuffed Eggs, **'80** 78
    Shrimp-Curried Eggs, Saucy, **'84** 143
    Stuffed Eggs, Easy, **'93** 87
    Tomato Slices, Stuffed Eggs-and-,
      '84 152
    Tuna-Stuffed Eggs, **'83** 83
Substitute, Homemade Egg, **'92** 47
Sunny-Side-Up Eggs, **'79** 38
Tacos, Breakfast, **'80** 43
Tomatoes, Bacon-and-Egg-Stuffed,
  '80 162
Tortillas, Chorizo and Egg, **'81** 193
Tortillas, Egg-and-Sausage, **'83** 246;
  '84 42
Tulsa Eggs, **'87** 95

Enchiladas
American Enchiladas, **'81** 170
Bean Enchiladas, Spicy, **'88** 18
Bean Enchiladas, Three-, **'91** 133
Casserole, Enchilada, **'87** 287
Casserole, Firecracker Enchilada, **'80** 260
Casserole, Green Enchilada, **'79** 76
Casserole, Sour Cream Enchilada, **'82** 113
Cheese Enchiladas, **'81** 194; **'85** 154
Cheese Enchiladas, Saucy, **'84** 220
Chicken-and-Spinach Enchiladas, **'91** 222
Chicken Enchiladas, **'80** 301; **'86** 296;
  '90 121
Chicken Enchiladas, Easy, **'82** 89;
  '86 231
Chicken Enchiladas Verde, **'93** 274
Chicken Enchiladas with Spicy Sauce,
  '84 76
Chicken Enchiladas with Tomatillo Sauce,
  '94 231
Creamy Enchiladas, **'93** 174
Dove Enchiladas, **'85** 270
Duck Enchiladas with Red Pepper-Sour
  Cream, Smoked, **'87** 121
Green Chile-Sour Cream Enchiladas,
  '84 234
Hot and Saucy Enchiladas, **'81** 141; **'82** 6
Meatless Enchiladas, **'93** 106
New Mexican Flat Enchiladas, **'85** 244
Pie, Enchilada, **'83** 155
Sauce, Enchilada, **'81** 194
Sauce, Red Chile Enchilada, **'85** 245
Skillet Enchiladas, **'82** 89
Soup, Chicken Enchilada, **'86** 22
Soup, Shrimp Enchilada, **'94** 103
Sour Cream Enchiladas, **'83** 200;
  '87 37
Sour Cream Enchiladas, Cheesy,
  '79 25
Spinach Enchiladas, **'83** 60; **'84** 14
Terrificas, Enchiladas, **'84** 32
Weeknight Enchiladas, **'93** 63

Escargots
Provençal, Escargots, **'82** 238;
  '83 156

Escarole
Cooked Escarole, Easy, **'84** 85
Salad, Escarole-and-Bacon, **'84** 85

Fajitas
Beef Fajitas, **'88** 233
Beef Fajita Salad, **'91** 70
Chicken Fajitas, **'88** 231; **'89** 100;
  '90 204
Crêpes, Fajita, **'94** 116
Fajitas, **'84** 233
Favorite Fajitas, **'86** 114
Fettuccine, Fajita, **'94** 84
Pita, Fajita in a, **'90** 177
Plum Good Fajitas, **'94** 115

Fettuccine
Alfredo, Fettuccine, **'80** 236; **'86** 158
Broccoli, Fettuccine with, **'90** 97
Broccoli-Parmesan Fettuccine, **'93** 55
Chicken-and-Tomatoes over Fettuccine,
  '90 204
Chicken-Pecan Fettuccine, **'86** 52
Creamy Fettuccine, **'92** 283
Fajita Fettuccine, **'94** 84
Ham-and-Asparagus Fettuccine, **'94** 84
Parsley, Fettuccine with, **'83** 115
Poppy Seeds, Fettuccine with, **'91** 48
Primavera, Fettuccine, **'89** 238; **'94** 85
Salmon Fettuccine, **'90** 123
Shrimp Fettuccine, **'94** 84
Shrimp with Dried Tomato Pesto, Fettuccine
  and, **'94** 249
Spinach Fettuccine, **'82** 179
Spinach, Fettuccine and, **'88** 90
Spinach Fettuccine, Easy Chicken with,
  '88 89
Spinach Fettuccine, Fresh, **'83** 60
Spinach Fettuccine with Mustard Greens,
  '94 247
Spinach Sauce, Fettuccine with, **'84** 329
Supreme, Fettuccine, **'83** 288; **'86** 333
Vegetable Fettuccine, **'83** 312

Figs
Cake, Easy Fig Coffee, **'80** 116
Cake, Fig, **'79** 32
Cake, Fig Preserve, **'79** 140; **'84** 316
Cake, Fig Preserves, **'89** 335
Cobbler, Cajun Fig, **'94** 196
Cobbler, Fig, **'79** 140
Cobbler, Super Fig, **'86** 206
Ice Cream, Fig, **'87** 139
Jam, Fig, **'86** 206
Muffins, Fig, **'86** 206
Pickled Figs, **'79** 140
Preserves, Fig, **'79** 140; **'82** 150;
  '89 140
Sauce, Fig, **'79** 140
Snacks, Sliced Fig, **'86** 206

Fillings. *See* Frostings.
Fish. *See also* specific types and Seafood.
Amandine, Fillet of Fish, **'80** M54
Amandine, Fish, **'85** 179
Amandine, Orange Lake, **'80** 99
Amberjack Sandwiches, Grilled, **'91** 195
Asparagus Divan, Fish-, **'87** 128
Aspic, Fish 'n, **'84** 190
Baked Fillets, Creamy, **'84** 91
Baked Fillets in Lemon-Celery Sauce, **'84** 91
Baked Fish, Almond, **'88** 270; **'89** 203
Baked Fish, Curried, **'87** 5
Baked Fish, Curry-, **'91** 196
Baked Fish Fillets, Creamy, **'85** 217
Baked Fish Fillets, Crunchy, **'85** 217
Baked Fish, Southern, **'82** 73

Fish *(continued)*

Baked Fish with Barbecue Sauce, **'84** 92
Bake, Fast Fish, **'85** 218
Bake, Saucy Fish, **'79** 75
Beer-Batter Fish, **'85** 68
Bluefish Chowder, **'84** 282
Breaded Herbed Fish Fillets, **'91** 121
Broiled Fish Fillets Piquante, **'84** 91
Broiled Herb Fish Fillets, **'79** 99
Caesar's Fish, **'90** 76
Cakes, Fish, **'85** 54
Captain's Spicy One, **'81** 125
Casserole, Green Chile-and-Fish, **'84** 32
Catfish Amandine, Mandarin, **'84** 183
Catfish Amandine, Spicy, **'89** 52
Catfish and Artichokes, Pasta with, **'90** 123
Catfish Appetizer, Layered, **'92** 209
Catfish, Baked, **'94** 67
Catfish, Barbecued, **'80** 157
Catfish Cajun-Style, Grilled, **'90** 129
Catfish Cakes, **'94** 70
Catfish, Crisp Fried, **'82** 242
Catfish, Crisp-Fried, **'88** 110
Catfish, Crown Room's Shrimp-Stuffed,
   '84 182
Catfish Eldorado de Colorado, **'84** 183
Catfish Fingers, Crackermeal, **'89** 53
Catfish, Fried, **'82** 135; **'83** 169
Catfish Fry, **'84** 184
Catfish, Golden Fried, **'80** 99
Catfish Gumbo, **'90** 278; **'91** 216
Catfish Kiev-Style, **'84** 184
Catfish, Lemon Barbecued, **'88** 271; **'89** 202
Catfish Louisiana, **'93** 291
Catfish Meunière, **'80** 57
Catfish, Microwave, **'89** M52
Catfish, Middendorf's Broiled Manchac,
   '84 183
Catfish Mousse, **'92** 327
Catfish Parmesan, **'79** 184; **'86** 210
Catfish, Parmesan, **'92** 309
Catfish Pecan, **'85** 53
Catfish Pilaf, **'94** 171
Catfish Sesame, **'81** 106
Catfish, Smoked, **'84** 47
Catfish, Soufflé-Stuffed, **'84** 183
Catfish, Southern Oven-Fried, **'87** 163
Catfish, Spicy-Seasoned, **'89** M66
Catfish Stew, Cajun-Style, **'88** 12
Catfish Stir, **'84** 184
Catfish with Cream Cheese Stuffing, **'89** 52
Catfish with Creole Sauce, Breaded, **'90** 28
Catfish with Red Salsa, Grilled, **'90** 172
Catfish with Relish, Grilled, **'92** 54
Ceviche in Avocado Shells, **'81** 33
Ceviche (Marinated Raw Fish), **'80** 194;
   '82 220
Ceviche, Mexican-Style, **'88** 115
Chart, Fat and Lean Fish, **'85** 180
Chowder, Basque Fish, **'86** 36
Chowder, Chunky Fish, **'92** 331
Chowder, Creamy Fish, **'79** 16
Chowder, Fish, **'79** 152; **'84** M38
Chowder, Tasty Fish, **'80** 188
Corned Fish, **'79** 32
Crawfish Étouffée, **'83** 91; **'94** 239
Crawfish Lasagna, **'91** 89
Crawfish on Eggplant, Soft-Shell, **'88** 222
Crawfish Salad, Dilled, **'83** 126

Crawfish Spaghetti, **'85** 104
Crawfish Stroganoff, **'91** 89
Creole Fish, **'87** M79
Crust, Fish in a, **'84** 294
Delight, Fish, **'86** M212
Dinner, Fish-and-Vegetable, **'91** 196
Dinner, Jollof Rice, **'91** 230; **'92** 325
Dip, Smoked Fish, **'84** 46
en Papillote, Fish with Snow Peas, **'86** 144
Fillet of Fish à l'Orange, **'89** 180
Fillets, Apple-Carrot Stuffed, **'88** M192
Fillets, Lemon-Coated, **'80** M53
Fillets, Pan-Fried Fish, **'91** 196
Fillets, Parmesan, **'86** M112
Fillets, Spanish-Style, **'86** M112
Fillets Tomatillo, **'94** 135
Florentine, Fish, **'86** 35
Florentine in Parchment, Fish, **'87** 22
Flounder Amandine, **'89** M196
Flounder Ambassador, **'86** 234
Flounder au Fromage, Baked, **'86** 234
Flounder, Baked, **'79** 31; **'90** 316
Flounder, Broiled, **'88** 28; **'89** 310
Flounder, Cheesy Broiled, **'84** 69
Flounder, Crab-Stuffed, **'80** 120; **'81** 176
Flounder, Creole-Style, **'85** 180
Flounder, Crispy Fried, **'84** 93
Flounder Dijon, **'85** 95
Flounder Fillets, Grilled, **'83** 213
Flounder Fillets in Shrimp Sauce, **'83** 227
Flounder Fillets, Royal, **'91** 128
Flounder Fillets, Stuffed, **'86** 234
Flounder, Grand Lagoon Stuffed, **'94** 68
Flounder-Grapefruit Broil, **'85** 53
Flounder in Wine Sauce, Fillet of, **'80** 179;
   '81 30
Flounder Nicole, **'85** 217
Flounder, Pesto Broiled, **'86** 150
Flounder, Quick Crunchy, **'90** 76
Flounder Rolls, Vegetable-Stuffed, **'87** 6
Flounder Rolls with Citrus Sauce, Stuffed,
   '85 180
Flounder, Seasoned Fried, **'79** 214
Flounder, Sesame, **'89** 33
Flounder Stuffed with Shrimp, **'88** 51
Flounder Supreme, Baked, **'79** 75
Flounder Thermidor, **'85** 190
Flounder-Vegetable Medley, **'85** 217
Flounder with Hollandaise-Shrimp Sauce,
   '86 234
Fresh Fish, Preparing, **'82** 127
Fried Fish, **'79** 151
Fried Fish, Crispy, **'84** 92
Fried Fish Fillets, Oven-, **'79** 75
Fried Fish, Golden, **'82** 134
Fried Fish, Southern, **'92** 168
Gourmet Fish, **'86** 71
Greek Fish with Vegetable Sauce, **'82** 72
Grilled Fish and Vegetables, **'89** 179
Grilled Fish, Easy, **'91** 194
Grilled Fish with Heather Sauce, Catfish
   Inn's, **'84** 182
Grill Fish, How to Charcoal-, **'84** 48
Grouper, Creamy Baked, **'85** 292
Grouper Fillets, Breaded, **'89** M36
Grouper, Garlic-Basil Marinated, **'94** 160
Grouper, Grilled, **'86** 185
Grouper, Grilled Marinated, **'90** 166
Grouper, Hot Spicy, **'94** 78
Grouper Macadamia, **'85** 127
Grouper Sauté, Shrimp-and-, **'87** 91

Grouper Spectacular, **'84** 163
Grouper with Confetti Vegetables, **'88** M189
Grouper with Sautéed Vegetables, **'90** M233
Grouper with Vanilla Wine Sauce, Pan-Fried,
   '94 241
Gumbo, Easy Fish, **'81** 6
Haddock, Baked, **'80** 179; **'81** 30
Haddock Fillets in White Wine, **'90** 76
Haddock Fillets with Zucchini Stuffing,
   '88 M191
Haddock Italiano, **'81** M4
Halibut, Chinese-Style Fried, **'80** 179;
   '81 30
Halibut Steaks Italiano, **'88** M191
Halibut Steak, Wine-Herb, **'94** 171
Halibut with Champagne Sauce, Baked,
   '90 29
Halibut with Cider, **'79** 182
Halibut with Orange-Curry Sauce, **'87** 91
Halibut with Swiss Sauce, **'83** M195
Hash, Smoked Fish, **'92** 306
Herb-Coated Fish, **'86** M112
Herbed Fish and Potato Bake, **'79** 287;
   '80 34
Heroes, Neptune, **'84** 281
Herring Dip, Yogurt, **'80** 232
Huachinango à la Veracruzana (Veracruz-Style
   Red Snapper), **'80** 193
Italian Fish, **'88** 270; **'89** 203
Italian Fish, Easy, **'86** M112
Mackerel Creole, **'80** 126
Mackerel, Lemon-Baked, **'79** 182
Mackerel, Rosemary-Garlic, **'92** 200
Mackerel, Smoked Salmon or, **'84** 46
Mahimahi in Grape Sauce, **'91** 218
Mahi Mahi, Macadamia, **'88** 164
Marinated Beer-Battered Fish, **'86** 180
Monkfish, Greek-Style, **'87** M79
Monterey, Fish, **'84** 293
Mullet, Festive, **'79** 75
Mullet, Smoked, **'84** 47
Mullet Spread, **'94** 159
Orange Roughy-and-Vegetable Stir-Fry,
   '91 50
Orange Roughy Fillets with Herb Sauce,
   '91 29
Orange Roughy, Kiwi, **'87** 193
Orange Roughy, Vegetable-Topped, **'93** 67
Orange Roughy with Spinach Pesto,
   '88 M192
Orange Roughy with Vegetables, Basil-,
   '92 98
Oven-Fried Fish, **'91** 172; **'94** 172
Oven-Fried Fish, Mexi-Style, **'90** 76
Papillote, Ocean, **'84** M287
Perch Fillets, Buttery Baked, **'81** 134
Perch, Parmesan-Crusted, **'93** 91
Pizza, Shellfish, **'91** 224
Poached Fish in Creamy Swiss Sauce,
   '80 M53
Poached Fish with Greek Sauce, **'91** M183
Poached Fish with Vegetables, **'89** 332;
   '90 18
Pollock with Summer Squash Relish, **'92** 200
Potatoes, Fish-Stuffed, **'92** 306
Potato Platter, Fish-and-, **'89** M248
Redfish Court Bouillon, **'83** 290; **'84** 93
Rolls, Vegetable-Filled Fish, **'86** M251
Rollups, Shrimp-Stuffed, **'82** 234
Roughy with Brown Butter Sauce, Pecan,
   '91 64

Fish *(continued)*

Salad, Smoked Fish-Potato, '84 233
Salad, Smoky Seafood, '84 46
Salmon Mousse, Irresistible, '79 284
Salmon or Mackerel, Smoked, '84 46
Salmon Steaks, Baked, '85 54
Sautéed Seafood Platter, '83 89
Scamp, Tangy Broiled, '87 5
Seasoning Blend, Fish-and-Seafood, '88 28
Seviche Cocktail, '83 258
Shad Roe with Lemon-Butter Sauce, Baked, '84 252
Shark, Marinated, '79 151
Skillet Fish Dinner, '88 199
Smoked Fish, '92 305
Smoked Fish Log, '85 144
Snapper à l'Orange, Baked, '85 181
Snapper and Stuffing, Baked, '82 72
Snapper, Blackened Red, '90 27
Snapper, Caribbean, '87 5
Snapper Chowder, Red, '85 217
Snapper, Company Red, '82 72
Snapper Destin, '88 222
Snapper Gumbo, Savannah, '94 105
Snapper, Honey-Curried, '85 181
Snapper in Wine Sauce, Red, '85 138
Snapper Louisiane, Red, '85 217
Snapper, Orangy, '88 23
Snapper, Oven-Fried, '90 75
Snapper, Poached, '83 101
Snapper, Poached Red, '85 127
Snapper Provençal, '91 M170
Snapper Rolls, Cucumber-Stuffed Red, '83 176
Snapper Rome, Fillet of, '80 57
Snapper, Southwestern, '91 195
Snapper, Spicy, '89 179
Snapper, Stuffed, '87 138
Snapper Veracruz, Red, '88 149; '92 142
Snapper with Creamy Dill Sauce, Peppered, '94 42
Snapper with Dill, '84 190
Snapper with Julienne Vegetables, Yellowtail, '93 31
Snapper with Lime, Stuffed Red, '83 246
Snapper with Tarragon Stuffing, Baked, '82 136
Sole Divan, '87 21
Sole Fillets, Herbed, '82 21
Sole Fillets in Wine Sauce, '81 109
Sole in Papillote, '82 22
Sole Provençal, Fillet of, '85 78
Sole Royale, '89 104
Sole, Saucy, '82 M68
Sole Véronique, '85 181
Sole with Cucumber Sauce, '84 M286
Soup with Garlic Mayonnaise, Rich Fish, '92 56
Sour Cream, Fish with, '89 180
Spread, Smoked Fish, '92 305
Steaks, Soy Fish, '86 M112
Steamed Fish and Vegetables, '91 32
Stew, Fish-and-Vegetable, '87 220
Stock, Homemade Fish, '92 237
Surprise, Fish, '84 231
Sweet-and-Sour Fish, '80 M54
Swordfish, Foil-Baked, '87 5
Swordfish, Skewered, '86 256

Swordfish Steaks, Orange-Ginger Marinated, '93 271
Swordfish Steak with Chervil Butter, '91 147
Tomato Sauce, Fish in, '85 75
Trout Cakes with Lemon-Butter Sauce, Mountain, '92 337
Trout Delmonico, '80 57
Trout Florentine, Cheesy, '85 53
Trout in Wine Sauce, '80 180; '81 31
Trout Laurie, '88 270; '89 202
Trout, Smoked, '84 47
Trout Spread, Smoked, '84 47
Trout, Stuffed Rainbow, '93 121
Trout, Sunshine, '84 M286
Trout with Ginger and Soy Sauce, Grilled, '85 228
Two, Fish for, '92 60
Vegetables, Cheesy Fish and, '94 254
Veracruz Fish with Shrimp, '86 130
Whitefish Spread, Smoked, '92 58

Food Processor

Appetizers
Artichoke-Caviar Mold, '87 239
Black-Eyed Pea Pinwheels, '85 300
Cheese Bites, Sesame, '89 24
Cheese Croquettes, Hot, '89 182
Cheese Ring, Strawberry-, '86 14
Dip, Blue Cheese, '80 285
Dip, Cheese-Garlic, '80 192
Dip, Herbal, '86 14
Dip, Hot Cheesy Beef, '80 85
Dip, Spinach, '86 159
Dip, Sugar Snap, '88 91
Dip, Yogurt Herring, '80 232
Guacamole, '90 205
Guacamole in Shells, '86 74
Mousse, Salmon Dill, '81 21
Mousse, Shrimp, '87 251
Olive Quiche Appetizers, '86 159
Pasta Bites, Pesto-Cheese, '87 251
Pastry, Processor, '87 67
Pâté, Chicken Liver, '81 235; '88 M132
Pâté, Mock, '87 251
Pâté, Mushroom, '89 157
Pâté with Cognac, '86 159
Pâté with Dill Sauce, Shrimp, '85 39
Salsa Cruda, '87 180
Sandwiches, Dainty Cucumber, '81 119
Shrimp Pizza Wedges, '89 158
Shrimp Toast, '86 91
Spread, Country Ham, '87 8
Spread, Fiery Tomato-Cheese, '87 196
Spread, Liver, '89 161
Spread, Sherried Liver, '80 86
Spread, Shrimp, '87 111
Spread, Sombrero, '87 111
Spread, Superb Crab, '81 235
Spread, Tipsy Cheese, '80 150
Tortilla Snacks, Pesto, '89 19

Beverages
Coffee, Praline-Flavored, '87 69
Lemonade, Strawberry, '80 160
Milkshake, Banana, '85 47

Breads
Apple-Nut Bread, '85 281
Baguettes, '85 70
Biscuits, Beaten, '86 54
Biscuits, Easy Processor, '84 218
Biscuits, Refrigerator Yeast, '85 48
Cheese Bread, Crusty, '86 233
Cream Cheese Loaves, Processor, '85 48

Muffins, Blueberry-Cream Cheese, '86 14
Muffins, Cinnamon-Pecan, '84 219
Butter, Green Peppercorn, '88 60
Crêpes, Basic Processor, '87 289; '88 135
Crêpes, Mushroom-Cheese, '87 289; '88 135
Desserts
Apple Crisp, '84 122
Cake, Fresh Coconut, '85 281
Cake, Fresh Coconut-Carrot, '80 299
Candy, Date, '89 308
Cheesecake with Orange-Pineapple Glaze, Lemon, '81 60
Cheesecake, Yam, '81 224
Cheese, Nutty Date Dessert, '87 299
Coconut Puffs, '87 277
Crêpes, Dessert, '87 290; '88 134
Crêpes, Strawberry Ice Cream, '87 290; '88 135
Crust, Pecan, '86 317
Cupcakes, Mocha, '85 250
Flan, Apple, '81 309
Frosting, Cream Cheese, '80 299; '86 337; '87 58
Frosting, Fluffy Chocolate, '86 336; '87 58
Frosting, Snow Peak, '85 281
Ice, Apricot Yogurt, '81 177
Ice Cream, Mango, '86 216
Ice Cream, Peach, '86 15
Ice, Peach, '81 178
Mousse, Elegant Amaretto-Chocolate, '86 337
Pastry Shells, Cream Cheese, '86 13
Phyllo Nests, Nutty, '87 277
Pie, Apple-Amandine, '89 215
Pie Dough, Quick Food Processor, '84 219
Pie, Pumpkin-Pecan, '85 233, 282
Pie, Quick Peach, '89 252
Pies, Miniature Pecan, '86 13
Raspberry Fluff, '89 198
Sherbet, Instant Fruit, '85 158
Sherbet, Pineapple, '89 199
Sorbet, Avocado, '88 117
Sorbet, Banana-Orange, '88 117
Sorbet, Cranberry Juice, '85 259
Sorbet, Pear-Lemon, '88 116
Sorbet, Strawberry, '88 117
Strawberry Whip, '89 198
Sweet Puffs, '89 91
Tart Shells, '88 4
Dressing, Cornbread-Sausage, '85 280
Dressing, Pecan-Sage, '80 262
Eggs, Scotch, '83 289
Fruit Nuggets, Dried, '86 326
Main Dishes
Chicken Pie, Double-Crust, '87 111
Chili, Zippy, '87 110
Meatballs, Quick Processor, '87 111
Oysters St. Jacques, '80 103
Pasta, Creamy Turkey-Basil, '89 216
Pizza, Deep-Dish Mediterranean, '80 163
Pizza, Pesto, '87 182
Pizza Supreme, '81 214
Pizza, Vegetarian Processor, '89 225
Spareribs, Peach-Glazed, '86 14
Steak, Herb-Marinated Flank, '85 275
Turkey, Galantine of, '85 150

Food Processor (continued)

Marmalade, Delicious Fruit, '81 285
Oil, Fresh Basil, '89 174
Pancakes, Pumpkin, '80 228
Pancakes, Strawberry, '84 219
Relish, Cranberry, '85 258, 264; '86 283
Relish, Cranberry-Nut, '86 275
Relish, Cranberry-Pear, '85 232
Relish, Easy Tomato, '80 126
Relish, Jerusalem Artichoke, '89 197
Relish, Mango, '89 198
Salad Dressings
    French Dressing, Creamy, '81 60
    Lemon Dressing, Creamy, '88 M193
    Pesto Salad Dressing, '86 150
    Poppy Seed Dressing, '86 305
    Russian-Style Salad Dressing, '86 305
Salads
    Cranberry Holiday Salad, '89 277
    Cranberry Salad, Jellied, '85 281
    Guacamole Salad, '87 181
    Relish Salad, '84 121
    Spinach-Mustard Twist, '86 209
    Tomato-Artichoke Aspic, '86 92
    Tortellini Salad, '89 237
Salsa, Hot Mexican, '85 136
Salsa Picante, Homemade, '81 67
Sauces and Gravies
    Berry Sauce, '87 290; '88 135
    Dessert Sauce, Orange, '86 337; '87 58
    Devonshire Sauce, Processor, '86 337; '87 58
    Green Sauce, Herbed, '86 244
    Homemade Picante Sauce, '90 205
    Peanut Hot Sauce, '86 305
    Pesto, Fresh, '86 150
    Pesto, Pepper, '89 103; '90 97
    Pizza Sauce, '80 163
    Pumpkin Seed Sauce, '88 246
    Raspberry Sauce, '89 322
    Seafood Sauce, '86 304
    Tomato Sauce, Italian-Style, '87 182
    Tomato Sauce, Refrigerator, '85 188
Soups and Stews
    Avocado Soup, Chilled, '81 34
    Bean Soup, '80 25
    Brunswick Stew, '80 264
    Brunswick Stew, Blakely, '87 4
    Cauliflower Soup, Creamy, '82 76
    Gazpacho, '80 266
    Melon Soup, Swirled, '87 162
    Mushroom Soup, Cream of, '85 93, 261
    Strawberry Soup Supreme, '81 M144
    Tomato Soup, '89 217
    Tomato Soup with Parmesan Cheese,
        Cream of, '86 161
Spread, Benedictine Sandwich, '80 299
Spread, Corned Beef, '87 196
Terrine with Goat Cheese, Black Bean,
    '87 120
Vegetables
    Asparagus Soufflé, '89 89
    Asparagus with Basil Butter, '85 40
    Carrot Puff, '89 89
    Carrots, Honey-Glazed, '84 121
    Cauliflower Soufflé, '90 17
    Loaf, Pureed Vegetable-Cheese,
        '85 297
    Okra and Tomatoes, Fresh, '81 M165

Peppers, Ham-and-Corn Stuffed, '81 87
Potato-Apple Bake, Sweet, '86 282
Potato Casserole, Processor, '86 159
Potato Pancake, '85 20
Ratatouille Niçoise, '81 22
Squash Casserole, Jiffy, '81 M144
Tomatoes, Crab-Stuffed Cherry, '88 78
Tomatoes, Spinach-Stuffed Baked,
    '86 14
Waffles, Crunchy Walnut, '85 48

Frankfurters
Appetizer Franks, Saucy, '84 M12
Appetizers, Bourbon Frankfurter, '85 207
Bacon-Wrapped Franks, '81 202
Barbecued Frankfurters, '83 144; '84 M12
Barbecued Frankfurters, Oven-, '83 11
Barbecued Franks, '85 192
Barbecue, Tangy Frank, '79 63
Beans and Franks, '85 142
Beans and Franks, Hawaiian Baked, '80 136
Beans and Franks, Jiffy, '91 M172
Beans-and-Franks, Polynesian, '84 M11
Beans, Stove-Top Franks 'n', '88 201
Beany Hot Dogs, '82 190
Cabbage with Apples and Franks, '87 42
Casserole, Hot Doggie, '88 200
Casserole, Layered Frankfurter, '79 64
Chafing Dish Franks, '83 143
Chili-Cheese Dogs, '81 202
Corn Dog Bites, '85 245; '93 79
Corn Dogs, Favorite, '83 144
Corn Relish Dogs, '85 192
Crusty Franks, '80 166
Delicious, Hot Dogs, '81 202
Family-Style Franks, '79 54
Grilled Stuffed Franks, '82 163
Hash Browns, Franks and, '80 166
Hawaiian Franks, '81 202
Jubilee, Hot Dog, '81 113
Kraut and Franks, Beany, '79 64
Mexicali Hot Dogs, '82 131
Mexican Franks, '93 78
Pickled Party Franks, '83 174
Pizzas, Hot Dog, '93 78
Potatoes, Cheesy Frank-Topped, '83 3
Potatoes, Frank-Filled, '84 M11
Potluck Dish, Frankaroni, '88 201
Sandwiches, Frankfurter, '84 M11
Sauce, Hot Diggity Dog, '93 198
Saucy Franks, '88 201
Skillet Dinner, Frankfurter, '80 166
Skillet, Frankfurter-Cabbage, '80 166
Skillet, Hot Dog and Spaghetti, '83 144
Sloppy Joe Dogs, '85 192
Soup, Split Pea and Frankfurter, '79 64
Spanish Frankfurters, '80 166
Spicy Frankfurters, '81 202
Stuffed Franks and Potatoes, '81 202
Supper, Hot Dog, '93 78
Tipsy Franks, '85 52

French Toast
Almond French Toast, '88 62
Amandine, Baked Toast, '82 47
au Fromage, French Toast, '88 288
Baked French Toast, Oven-, '82 47; '90 192
Caribbean French Toast, '92 46
Cinnamon French Toast, '84 211
Cottage-Topped French Toast, '85 49
Easy French Toast, '82 M172
Grand Marnier Fruit Sauce, French Toast
    with, '90 93
Macadamia French Toast, '86 96
Orange Butter, French Toast with, '81 42
Orange French Toast, '83 292; '84 78;
    '86 329
Orange Sauce, French Toast with, '82 47
Oven-Baked French Toast, Easy, '93 195
Overnight French Toast, '89 227
Overnight French Toast Deluxe, '79 216
Pain-Perdu Po-Boy, '93 291
Peanut Butter French Toast, '93 166
Potato-Crusted Texas Toast, '94 142
Sandwiches, Strawberry-French Toast,
    '91 160
Slender French Toast, '86 103
Stuffed French Toast, Three Cheese, '93 122
Waffled French Toast, '82 47
Fritters
Apple Fritter Rings, '88 44
Apple Fritters, '81 105; '82 273; '85 14
Apple Holiday Fritters, '86 314
Banana Fritters, '79 213
Blueberry Fritters, '85 152
Broccoli Fritters, Cheesy, '79 53
Buñuelos, '93 29
Clam Fritters, '79 151; '86 71
Corn Fritters, '86 192; '94 22
Corn Fritters, Golden, '80 165; '81 128
Corn Fritters, Skillet-Fried, '85 14
Eggplant Fritters, '91 211
Ham Fritters, '82 39
Ham Fritters with Creamy Sauce, '81 105
Okra, Fritter-Fried, '86 218
Okra Fritters, '79 160
Orange Fritters, Puffy, '81 169
Oyster Fritters, '79 31
Pear Fritters, Ol' Timey, '86 51
Pecan Fritters, Chocolate-Covered, '79 205
Pineapple Fritters, '88 112
Squash Fritters, '89 68
Sweet Potato Fritters, '88 44
Sweet Potato Fritters, Golden, '79 9
Zucchini Fritters, '81 163
Zucchini Fritters, Cheesy, '88 44
Frog Legs
Crispy Frog Legs, '80 99
Fried Frog Legs, '88 110
From Our Kitchen To Yours (FOKTY)
Alcohol
    substituting in recipes, '92 314
Apples, '84 227, 228
    amounts to buy, '84 228
    preventing browning after cutting,
        '84 228
    selecting for cooking, '84 227, 228
    selecting for eating, '84 227, 228
    storing, '84 228
Appliances, kitchen. See FOKTY/Kitchen,
    Dishwasher, Food processor, Freezer,
    Microwave oven, Oven, Refrigerator.
Arrowroot, as a thickening agent, '83 147

Barbecue, **'94** 155. *See also* FOKTY/Grilling.
  chicken, **'94** 155
Beans, dried, **'88** 4
  buying, **'88** 4
  cooking, **'88** 4
  soaking, **'88** 4
  storing, **'88** 4
Beef, **'83** 38; **'92** 65, 66; **'94** 140
  browning, **'83** 38
  buying, **'83** 38; **'90** 276; **'92** 65
  cooking methods, **'83** 38
  fat content of, **'92** 65, 66; **'94** 140
  handling properly, **'87** 208; **'94** 140
  making gravy from pan drippings, **'83** 38
  storing, **'94** 140
  tenderizing, **'83** 38
Beverages, **'83** 191; **'90** 276, 277. *See also*
  FOKTY/Alcohol, Buttermilk, Eggnog, Ice,
  Tea, Wines.
  determining amounts to buy for
    entertaining, **'90** 276, 277
  freezing, **'92** 314
  ice molds, **'86** 331
  placement of in basic table setting, **'90** 182
  placement of when entertaining, **'90** 277
  substituting for alcohol in recipes,
    '92 314
Biscuits, **'89** 211, 212; **'92** 52. *See also*
  FOKTY/Breads, Rolls, Yeast.
  baking, **'89** 211, 212
  cutting dough, **'89** 211
  freezing, **'89** 212
  kneading, **'92** 52
  making dough for, **'89** 211; **'92** 52
  reheating, **'89** 212
  storing leftovers, **'89** 212
  using food processor to make,
    '89 211, 212
Breads, **'82** 198; **'84** 92; **'89** 268; **'92** 52,
  102, 314; **'93** 183. *See also*
  FOKTY/Biscuits, Rolls, Yeast.
  cutting, **'91** 144, 145
  doubling recipes, **'91** 22
  freezing, **'89** 268; **'90** 315; **'91** 95;
    '92 102
  as gifts, **'91** 95
  metal dough scraper, **'90** 126; **'92** 52
  microwave oven, **'89** 268
  quick breads, **'84** 92; **'89** 268
  rising procedures, **'87** 12; **'89** 268
  testing for doneness, **'84** 92; **'92** 314
  yeast breads, **'84** 92; **'87** 12; **'89** 268;
    '92 314
  yeast rolls, **'83** 323
Broccoli, **'84** 249
  cutting, **'93** 132
  preparing, **'84** 249
  selecting, **'84** 249
Broths. *See* FOKTY/Soups.
Brussels Sprouts, **'84** 249
  preparing, **'84** 249
  selecting, **'84** 249
Butter, **'82** 189
  availability of, **'82** 189
  balls, how to make, **'82** 189
  clarifying, **'82** 189
  curls, how to make, **'82** 189
  fat content of, **'82** 189

  storing, **'82** 189
  substituting for in baked goods, **'90** 314
Buttermilk, freezing, **'92** 314
Cactus (Nopales), **'94** 29
  cooking, **'94** 29
  selecting, **'94** 29
  storing, **'94** 29
Cakes, **'89** 57, 58; **'91** 144, 200, 201;
  '92 154, 155, 314; **'94** 59
  baking techniques, **'89** 57
  cheesecakes, eliminating cracks in,
    '91 300
  cooling, **'92** 155
  cutting, **'91** 144; **'92** 314
  decorating, **'94** 59
  dry ingredients, **'87** 12; **'92** 155
  freezing, **'89** 58; **'90** 314, 315
  frosting, **'89** 57, 58
  greasing pans, **'92** 314
  jellyroll cakes, **'92** 314
  mixing procedures, **'89** 57;
    '92 154, 155
  pan sizes, **'92** 154, 314
  pound cakes, **'84** 92, 319 (baking tips
    chart); **'92** 154, 155
  as snacks, **'91** 200, 201
  storing, **'89** 57, 58; **'92** 155
  substituting flours, **'92** 155
  testing for doneness, **'84** 92; **'92** 155
Campsite cooking, **'86** 172
  cleaning up, **'86** 172
  making lists, **'86** 172
  packing, **'86** 172
  planning, **'86** 172
Canning fruits and vegetables, **'84** 180;
  '89 141, 142; **'93** 136, 137. *See also*
  FOKTY/Paraffin.
  boiling water bath, **'84** 180; **'89** 141,
    142; **'91** 300; **'93** 136, 137
  equipment, **'93** 137
  packing, **'84** 180; **'89** 141, 142
  safety, **'84** 180; **'89** 141, 142; **'91** 300;
    '93 137
  steam pressure method of, **'84** 180;
    '89 141, 142
Casseroles
  doubling recipes, **'91** 22, 23, 96
  freezing, **'90** 314; **'91** 96
  preventing spoilage of, **'87** 208
Cast-iron cookware, **'93** 33
  caring for, **'93** 33
  seasoning, **'93** 33
Cauliflower, **'84** 249
  cutting, **'93** 132
  preparing, **'84** 249
  selecting, **'84** 249
Centerpieces, **'90** 205
Champagne. *See* FOKTY/Wines.
Cheese, **'82** 109
  buying, **'85** 210; **'90** 276
  cooking with, **'85** 210; **'87** 12
  freezing, **'82** 109; **'85** 211
  handling properly, **'87** 208
  serving, **'85** 210, 211
  as snacks, **'91** 200, 201
  storing, **'85** 210
Cheesecakes. *See* FOKTY/Cakes.
Chicken, **'87** 12; **'88** 39; **'94** 155, 253
  barbecuing, **'94** 155
  boning, **'88** 39
  cooking, **'87** 12; **'88** 39

  cutting up, **'94** 253
  handling properly, **'87** 208
  microwaving, **'88** 39
  packaging of, **'88** 39
  preparing for stir-frying, **'91** 160
Children, in the kitchen, **'91** 92; **'92** 102, 207
China, **'88** 301
  removing marks from, **'88** 301
  storing, **'88** 301
  washing, **'88** 301
Chinese cooking, **'85** 76
  equipment, **'85** 76
  garnishing, **'85** 76
  preparing food for, **'85** 76
Chocolate, **'86** 246, 247; **'92** 314; **'93** 317
  dipping, **'86** 330, 331
  garnishing with, **'86** 247; **'93** 317;
    '94 59
  illustrations for chocolate sacks, **'93** 317
  kinds of, **'86** 246, 247
  melting, **'92** 314; **'93** 317
  substitutions, **'86** 246, 247
  white chocolate, **'86** 246, 247; **'94** 59
Cholesterol, **'90** 72
  and food labels, **'90** 72
Cookies, **'91** 234; **'92** 207, 208
  baking, **'92** 208
  cooling, **'92** 208
  equipment, **'92** 208
  freezing, **'90** 314; **'92** 207, 208
  as gifts, **'91** 95
  mixing procedures, **'92** 207
  storing, **'92** 208
  testing for doneness, **'84** 92
Cooking directions, basic, **'87** 12, 208. *See
  also* FOKTY/Handling food properly,
  Recipe preparation.
  chicken, **'87** 12
  shrimp, **'87** 12
Cooking spray. *See* FOKTY/Vegetable
  cooking spray.
Cookware, **'85** 329; **'86** 227; **'90** 50;
  '93 33, 183, 220. *See also*
  FOKTY/Cast-iron cookware.
  caring for, **'85** 329; **'93** 33, 183
  for microwave, **'86** 227
  selecting, **'85** 329; **'86** 227; **'93** 220
Cornbread, **'87** 16
  cornmeal, **'87** 16
  ingredients in, **'87** 16
  making cornbread, **'87** 16
Cornmeal, **'87** 16
  making cornbread, **'87** 16
  understanding the label, **'87** 16
Cornstarch, **'83** 146, 147
  as a thickening agent, **'83** 146, 147
Cranberries
  buying, **'92** 314
  freezing, **'92** 314
  frosted cranberries (garnish), **'82** 280
Crystal, **'88** 300, 301
  removing discolorations and stains,
    '88 300, 301
  repairing chips, **'88** 300
  storing, **'88** 300
  washing, **'88** 300, 301
Custards
  preparing and storing properly,
    '87 208 (chart)
  testing for doneness, **'84** 92
  thickening, **'83** 147

From Our Kitchen To Yours *(continued)*

Cutting boards, **'87** 208
    acrylic, **'87** 208
    cleaning, **'87** 208
    and food safety, **'87** 208
    wooden, **'87** 208
Dishwasher, **'87** 130
Drying foods, **'93** 23
    cherry tomatoes, **'93** 23
    equipment, **'93** 23
    safety, **'93** 23
    uses for, **'93** 23
Eggnog, freezing, **'92** 314
Eggs, **'83** 147, 214; **'89** 26. *See also*
  FOKTY/Meringue.
    cooking methods, **'83** 214
    handling properly, **'87** 208 (chart)
    pasteurized egg substitute, **'89** 26
    preventing curdling, **'82** 198; **'83** 147
    using raw egg whites, **'91** 300
    using raw egg yolks, **'89** 26
    yolks, thick and lemon colored, **'83** 214
Entertaining, **'84** 122, 123; **'88** 276;
  '90 182, 276, 277; **'91** 300; **'94** 17, 18
    determining amounts of food to buy,
      '90 276 (chart)
    determining traffic flow, **'84** 122, 123;
      '86 191; **'90** 276, 277
    making preparations for, **'84** 122;
      '86 191; **'94** 17, 18
    outdoors, **'86** 191
    presenting food, **'84** 122; **'88** 276
    selecting menus for, **'84** 122; **'86** 191;
      '88 276; **'90** 276
    serving food safely, **'91** 300
    setting up a bar for, **'90** 277
    table setting, **'90** 182 (illustration), 276
Equivalents of ingredients, **'91** 22, 23
Etiquette, **'90** 225
    basic manners at the table, **'90** 225
Fat, dietary, **'82** 189; **'90** 72; **'91** 200, 201;
  '92 65, 66; **'93** 207
    in beef, **'92** 65, 66
    in butter, **'82** 189; **'90** 314
    eliminating in snacks, **'91** 200, 201
    and food labels, **'90** 72; **'92** 65;
      '93 207
    in margarine, **'82** 189; **'90** 314
    storing, **'82** 189
Fish, **'84** 48; **'87** 79, 80; **'90** 130; **'94** 105,
  106. *See also* FOKTY/Seafood, Shrimp,
  Surimi.
    buying, **'84** 48; **'87** 79, 80; **'90** 130;
      '94 106
    cooking, **'87** 80
    eliminating odors on hands, **'82** 109
    fat fish, **'87** 79
    freezing, **'87** 80
    grilling, **'84** 48; **'92** 52
    handling properly, **'87** 208
    lean fish, **'87** 79
    market forms of, **'87** 79
    selecting fish for grilling, **'84** 48;
      '90 130
    storing, **'87** 80; **'90** 130;
      '94 105, 106
    substituting, **'90** 130
    thawing, **'87** 80; **'90** 130
    transporting fresh, **'94** 105, 106

Flour, **'82** 197, 198
    all purpose, **'82** 197, 198; **'87** 12
    cake flour, **'82** 197, 198; **'87** 12
    cracked wheat, **'82** 197, 198
    sifting, **'82** 197, 198; **'87** 12
    storing, **'82** 197, 198
    types of, **'82** 197, 198
Flowers, edible, **'94** 59
    crystallizing, **'94** 59
Food processor, **'82** 109; **'86** 13
    chopping nuts, **'92** 314
Food safety. *See* FOKTY/Handling food
  properly.
Freezer, **'83** 14, 15; **'86** 50, 51;
  '87 112, 208; **'93** 83, 84
    amount of food to store in, **'87** 112
    casseroles in, **'87** 112
    cleaning, **'84** 11; **'87** 112
    constant freezer temperature, **'86** 50
    defrosting, **'87** 112
    foods that freeze well, **'86** 50; **'87** 112;
      '90 314, 315
    fruits in, **'87** 112
    labeling foods in, **'84** 11; **'86** 51;
      '87 112
    leftovers, freezing safely, **'87** 112
    organizing foods in, **'87** 112
    and power loss, **'83** 14, 15; **'93** 83, 84
    preventing sogginess of particular foods
      to be frozen, **'87** 112
    refreezing foods, **'83** 15; **'93** 83, 84
    reheating frozen foods, **'87** 112
    sausage, **'87** 238
    vegetables in, **'87** 112
    wraps and containers for freezing foods,
      '86 50, 51; **'87** 112
Fruitcakes, **'83** 285; **'86** 331
    storing, **'83** 285; **'86** 331
    purchasing candied fruit for, **'92** 314
Fruits, **'83** 94; **'85** 233; **'89** 141, 142;
  '92 248, 249, 250. *See also* FOKTY/Apples,
  Mangoes, Melons, Pears.
    canning, **'84** 180; **'89** 141, 142
    in centerpieces, **'90** 205
    exotic fruits, **'92** 248, 249, 250
    fall fruits, **'85** 233
    freezing, **'87** 112
    nutritive values of, **'92** 248, 249, 250
    preparing, **'92** 248, 249, 250
    selecting, **'84** 186, 187;
      '92 248, 249, 250
    as snacks, **'91** 200, 201
    storing, **'83** 94; **'92** 248, 249, 250
Frying foods, **'84** 211; **'88** 112, 113
    cooking fat to use, **'88** 113
    equipment, **'88** 113
    safety, **'90** 22
    techniques, **'88** 113
Garlic, **'93** 182
    baker, **'94** 332
    press, **'94** 332
Garnishes, **'82** 138, 280; **'89** 100; **'90** 108;
  '93 317; **'94** 59
    chocolate sacks, **'93** 317
    curling garnishes, **'89** 100
    eggs, hard-cooked, **'82** 280
    flowers, crystallized edible, **'94** 59
    fruit garnishes, **'82** 280
    illustrations, **'89** 100; **'90** 108;
      '93 317
    making ahead, **'89** 100

    piped garnishes, **'82** 280; **'86** 330;
      '90 108
    utensils for creating, **'89** 100; **'90** 108
    vegetable garnishes, **'82** 280;
      '89 100, 243
    whipped cream, **'86** 330
Gelatin, **'83** 124, 125; **'91** 300
    chilling, **'83** 124; **'86** 13
    molds, determining size of, **'82** 313
    softening, **'91** 300
    unmolding, **'83** 124, 125; **'86** 330
    using fresh fruits and vegetables in,
      '91 300
Gifts of food, **'86** 289; **'91** 95, 96
    containers for, **'86** 289; **'91** 95, 96
    freezing, **'91** 95, 96
    mailing, **'86** 289
    storing, **'91** 95, 96
    wrapping, **'86** 289
Gingerroot, **'94** 29
    cooking with, **'92** 314; **'94** 29
    selecting, **'94** 29
    in stir-frying, **'92** 314
    storing, **'92** 314
Gravies, **'83** 38; **'86** 330
    serving and storing properly,
      '87 208 (chart)
Grilling, **'82** 109; **'83** 191; **'84** 48; **'86** 172;
  '88 145, 146; **'92** 202; **'93** 103, 104
    avoiding flare-ups, **'88** 145; **'92** 202
    basting, **'82** 109; **'88** 146; **'93** 103
    charcoal, **'82** 109; **'93** 103, 104
    cleanup, **'93** 104
    direct/indirect cooking methods,
      '88 145; **'93** 103, 104
    equipment, **'82** 109; **'88** 146; **'92** 52;
      '93 103
    flavoring with wood chips, **'88** 145;
      '93 103
    kabobs, **'88** 146; **'93** 103
    temperature of fire, **'82** 109;
      '88 145, 146
    thermometer, **'93** 103, 104
Grocery shopping, **'84** 11; **'91** 187, 188
    best time for, **'84** 11
    comparative shopping, **'91** 188
    determining best values,
      '91 188 (chart)
    making lists for, **'82** 312; **'83** 284;
      '84 11
    planning menus, **'82** 312; **'83** 284;
      '84 11
    saving time and money, **'91** 187, 188
    stocking up, **'91** 188
    using coupons, **'91** 188
Ham, **'89** 333, 334; **'90** 276
    cooking in microwave oven, **'89** 333, 334
    determining amount to buy for
      entertaining, **'90** 276
    freezing, **'89** 334
    preparing, **'89** 333, 334
    selecting, **'89** 333
    storing, **'89** 334
Handling food properly, **'87** 208; **'89** 26;
  '91 300; **'92** 202; **'93** 23, 83, 84. *See also*
  FOKTY/Beef, Canning, Chicken, Eggs,
  Fish, Turkey.
    chart, **'87** 208
    egg whites, raw, **'91** 300
    egg yolks, raw, **'89** 26
    when entertaining, **'91** 300

From Our Kitchen To Yours *(continued)*

Herbs, **'85** 58; **'89** 121. *See also*
FOKTY/Seasonings, Spices.
    amounts to use, **'89** 121
    chart, **'89** 121
    cooking with, **'85** 58
    drying, **'85** 58
    freezing, **'85** 58
    gathering fresh, **'85** 58;
      '89 121
    storing, **'85** 58; **'89** 121
Ice
    dry ice, **'83** 14, 15
    molds, **'86** 331
Ice cream, **'82** 171; **'86** 215
    adding fresh fruit to homemade,
      '82 171
    homemade, **'82** 171
    varieties of, **'86** 215
Kitchen, **'83** 191; **'84** 10, 11, 148, 149;
    '90 22, 50; **'93** 220; **'94** 332
    appliances, **'87** 130
    basic equipment, **'90** 50; **'93** 220;
      '94 332
    cookware, **'85** 329; **'90** 50; **'93** 220
    countertops, **'84** 148, 149
    gadgets, **'86** 13; **'90** 126; **'94** 332
    keeping cool in summer, **'83** 191
    knives, **'91** 144, 145
    organizing, **'84** 10, 11
    safety in, **'84** 37; **'90** 22
    shears, **'91** 160; **'92** 52
Knives, **'84** 11; **'91** 144, 145
    buying, **'91** 144, 145
    sharpening, **'91** 144, 145
    storing, **'84** 11
    using properly, **'86** 13; **'91** 144, 145
    varieties of, **'91** 144, 145 (illustration)
Labels, food, **'90** 72; **'93** 207; **'94** 140
    chart, **'90** 72
    sample label, **'93** 207
    understanding, **'90** 72; **'93** 207
Lamb, **'88** 59
    buying, **'88** 59
    cooking, **'88** 59
    selecting, **'88** 59
    storing, **'88** 59
Leftovers, **'82** 313; **'87** 112, 208;
    '92 314
    bread slices, **'82** 313
    buns, **'82** 313
    freezing, **'87** 112, 208; **'92** 314
Lettuce, **'86** 80
    coring, **'86** 80
    selecting, **'86** 80
    storing, **'86** 80
    types of, **'86** 80 (illustration)
    yields, **'86** 80
List making, **'82** 312; **'83** 284; **'84** 11, 122;
    '86 172
    and grocery shopping, **'88** 165;
      '91 188
    and meal planning, **'82** 312; **'83** 284;
      '84 11; **'91** 188
    telephone numbers for emergencies,
      '84 37
Mailing food, **'86** 289
Mangoes, **'94** 192
Manners. *See* FOKTY/Etiquette.

Margarine, **'82** 189
    availability of, **'82** 189
    diet margarine, **'82** 189
    fat content of, **'82** 189; **'90** 314
    storing, **'82** 189
    substituting in baked goods, **'90** 314
Marinating, **'88** 165
    containers to use, **'87** 208
Masa harina, **'94** 192
Meal planning, **'82** 312, 313; **'83** 191, 284;
    '84 122, 123; **'86** 13; **'88** 165, 276. *See*
    also FOKTY/Snacks.
    advance planning, **'82** 312, 313; **'86** 172
    for a crowd, **'82** 313; **'86** 191
    for holidays, **'83** 284
    making lists, **'82** 312; **'83** 284;
      '84 11, 122; **'86** 172
    party menus, **'82** 313; **'84** 122, 123;
      '86 191; **'88** 276
Measuring, **'85** 192, 193; **'86** 13
    butter, **'85** 192, 193
    determining cup measurement of dish,
      '85 193
    dry measuring utensils, **'85** 192, 193
    how to measure accurately, **'85** 192, 193
    liquid measuring utensils, **'85** 192, 193
    sifting ingredients for, **'82** 197, 198;
      '85 192, 193; **'87** 12
    solid shortening, **'85** 192, 193
Meats, **'89** 191, 192; **'91** 300; **'92** 202. *See*
    also FOKTY/Beef.
    handling properly, **'87** 208
    meat-cure mix, **'91** 300
    serving safely, **'87** 208; **'91** 300
    standing time, **'89** 192
    suggested cooking temperatures,
      '89 191, 192; **'92** 202
    using a meat thermometer,
      '89 191, 192; **'92** 202
Melons, **'88** 183
    cantaloupe, **'88** 183
    honeydew, **'88** 183
    selecting, **'88** 183
    storing, **'88** 183
    watermelon, **'88** 183
Meringue, **'83** 214
    baking, **'83** 214
    equipment, **'83** 214
    humidity, effects of, **'83** 214
    making, **'83** 214
    powder, **'92** 314
    preventing weeping, **'83** 214
Microwave oven, **'83** 191; **'84** 211;
    '86 113, 227; **'87** 130; **'91** 92;
    '92 176
    cleaning, **'87** 130
    cookware for, **'86** 227
    features, **'86** 113
    roasting peppers in, **'92** 176
    safety when using, **'91** 92
    sizes, **'86** 113
    variations of, **'86** 113
    wattage, **'86** 113
Mushrooms
    as garnish, **'82** 280
    storing, **'92** 314
Nopales. *See* FOKTY/Cactus.
Nutrition, **'90** 72; **'91** 200, 201;
    '92 65
    food labels, **'90** 72; **'92** 65
    snacks, **'91** 200, 201

Olive oil, **'89** 175
    flavored, **'89** 175
    selecting, **'89** 175
    storing, **'89** 175
    varieties of, **'89** 175
Onions, **'88** 87
    chopping, **'92** 314
    cooking with, **'88** 87
    eliminating odor on hands, **'82** 109;
      '94 332
    extracting onion juice, **'88** 87
    grating, **'92** 314
    selecting, **'88** 87
    varieties of, **'88** 87 (illustrations)
Outdoor cooking. *See* FOKTY/Campsite
    cooking and Grilling.
Ovens, **'83** 191; **'84** 211; **'86** 113;
    '87 130
    cleaning, **'87** 130
    convection, **'86** 113
    conventional, **'86** 113
    microwave, **'83** 191; **'84** 211; **'86** 113;
      '87 130
    preheating, **'86** 13
Paraffin, **'89** 244
    as a seal in canning, **'84** 180; **'89** 142;
      '91 300
Pastas, **'87** 177
    basic categories, **'87** 177
    cooking, **'87** 177
    measuring, **'87** 177
    reheating, **'87** 177
    storing, **'87** 177
    substituting, **'87** 177
Pastry. *See* FOKTY/Piecrust.
Peanuts, **'83** 228, 229
    boiling, **'83** 228
    chopping, **'83** 229
    roasting, **'83** 228
Pears, **'85** 233
    cooking, **'85** 233
    peeling, **'85** 233
    ripening, **'85** 233
    selecting, **'85** 233
Peas, dried, **'88** 4
    buying, **'88** 4
    cooking, **'88** 4
    soaking, **'88** 4
    storing, **'88** 4
Pecans, **'83** 228, 229; **'94** 59
    chopping, **'83** 229
    as garnish, **'94** 59
    toasting, **'83** 228
Peppers, **'85** 4; **'92** 176; **'94** 29
    freezing, **'85** 4
    as garnish, **'82** 280; **'89** 100
    removing skins of, **'85** 4
    roasting, **'92** 176
    selecting, **'94** 29
    storing, **'94** 29
    substituting, **'85** 4
    types of, **'85** 4
    working with hot peppers, **'85** 4;
      '94 29
Persimmons, **'85** 233
    freezing, **'85** 233
    preparing, **'85** 233
    selecting, **'85** 233
Pickles, **'87** 150
    pickling vegetables, **'87** 150
    spoilage, **'87** 150

Piecrust, **'82** 234, 235; **'92** 52, 314;
  '94 210
  equipment, **'82** 234; **'94** 332
  finishing, **'82** 234
  glazing, **'82** 235
  mixing, **'82** 234; **'92** 52
  preventing overbrowning, **'92** 314
  preventing sogginess, **'86** 330; **'91** 300;
    '92 314
  rolling, **'82** 234; **'92** 314
  variations of, **'82** 234, 235
Planning meals. *See* FOKTY/Meal planning.
Poaching, **'85** 127
  eggs, **'85** 127
  equipment, **'85** 127
  fish, **'85** 127
  fruits, **'85** 127
  liquid to use, **'85** 127
Potatoes, **'84** 210, 211. *See also*
  FOKTY/Sweet Potatoes.
  preparing, **'84** 210, 211
  selecting, **'84** 210, 211
  storing, **'84** 211
Poultry. *See* FOKTY/Chicken, Turkey.
Pound cakes. *See* FOKTY/Cakes.
Puddings, **'86** 330. *See also*
  FOKTY/Custards.
  preventing "skin" from forming,
    '86 330
Pumpkins, **'85** 233
  preparing for cooking, **'85** 233
  selecting, **'85** 233
  storing, **'85** 233
Raspberries, making sauce, **'92** 314
Recipe preparation, **'86** 13; **'91** 22, 23;
  '93 235. *See also* FOKTY/Cooking
  directions, Handling food properly,
  Substitutions.
  cleaning up, **'86** 13
  determining solutions to problems,
    '93 235
  doubling recipes, **'91** 22, 23;
    '92 66
  equipment, **'86** 13
  measuring, **'86** 13
  planning menus, **'86** 13
  preparing ingredients, **'86** 13
  substitutions, **'92** 314, 344
  utensils, **'86** 13
Recycling, **'92** 28
  items to be recycled, **'92** 28
  packaging of products, **'92** 28
  setting up home recycling center,
    '92 28
  the three R's, **'92** 28
Refrigerator, **'83** 94; **'87** 130
  canned foods (opened), **'83** 94
  cleaning, **'84** 11; **'87** 130
  dairy products, **'83** 94
  food storage chart, **'83** 94
  meats, **'83** 94
Rice, **'87** 46
  flavoring, **'87** 46
  forms of, **'87** 46
  preparing, **'87** 46
  reheating, **'87** 46
  storing, **'87** 46
  types of, **'87** 46

Rolls, **'83** 323. *See also* FOKTY/Biscuits,
  Breads, Yeast.
  glazing, **'83** 323
  variations of, **'83** 323
  yeast, **'83** 323
Roux, **'87** 211, 212
  color of, **'87** 211, 212
  cooking temperature, **'87** 211
  cooking times, **'87** 211
  ingredient amounts, **'87** 211
  microwave roux, **'87** 211, 212
  oven roux, **'87** 211
  reducing fat in roux, **'87** 212
  utensils to use, **'87** 212
Safety, **'84** 37, 180; **'90** 22; **'91** 92, 300. *See
  also* FOKTY/Handling food properly.
  canning fruits and vegetables, **'84** 180;
    '91 300
  first aid for burns, **'90** 22
  in the kitchen, **'84** 37; **'90** 22
  preventing burns in the kitchen, **'84** 37;
    '90 22
  when serving food, **'91** 300
  when using the microwave, **'91** 92
Salads, **'82** 313
  congealed, **'82** 313; **'91** 300
  equipment, **'94** 332
Sauces, **'83** 146, 147; **'92** 314; **'94** 274
  chilling quickly, **'86** 13
  reduction sauces, **'94** 274
  thickening, **'83** 146, 147
Sausage, **'87** 238
  classifications of, **'87** 238
  freezing, **'87** 238
  meat-cure mix, **'91** 300
Seafood, **'90** 130. *See also* FOKTY/Fish,
  Shrimp, Surimi.
Seasonings, **'92** 121, 344; **'93** 182. *See also*
  FOKTY/Herbs, Spices.
  in recipes, **'91** 22
  recipes for seasoning blends, **'92** 121
  storing, **'82** 198; **'84** 11; **'92** 121
  substitutions, **'92** 344
Shellfish, **'94** 105, 106
  buying, **'94** 106
  transporting fresh, **'94** 105, 106
Shelf life, **'83** 65
  of canned foods, **'83** 65
  chart, **'83** 65
  of packaged mixes, **'83** 65
  of staples, **'83** 65
Shopping. *See* FOKTY/Grocery shopping.
Shrimp, **'87** 12; **'94** 105, 106
  cooking, **'87** 12
  deveining, **'92** 52
  grilling, **'92** 52
  selecting, **'94** 106
  transporting fresh, **'94** 105
Sifting, **'82** 197, 198; **'85** 192, 193;
  '87 12
  flour, **'82** 197, 198; **'87** 12
  powdered sugar, **'85** 192; **'87** 12
Silver, **'88** 300
  avoiding spotting and pitting, **'88** 300
  cleaning, **'88** 300
  removing tarnish, **'88** 300
  storing, **'88** 300
Snacks, **'91** 200, 201
  nutritious, **'91** 200 201
  planning, **'91** 200, 201
  recipes for, **'91** 200, 201

Sodium, **'90** 72
  content of in surimi, **'90** 130
  and food labels, **'90** 72
Soufflés, **'84** 92
  testing for doneness, **'84** 92
Soups, **'89** 30
  broths, **'89** 30
  freezing, **'89** 30
  as gifts, **'91** 95
  reheating, **'89** 30
  removing surface fat, **'89** 30
  stocks, **'89** 30
  storing, **'89** 30
Spices, **'87** 297. *See also* FOKTY/Herbs,
  Seasonings.
  amounts to use, **'87** 297
  buying, **'87** 297
  checking for freshness, **'84** 11; **'87** 297
  grinding your own, **'87** 297
  storing, **'82** 198; **'84** 11; **'87** 297
  substituting, **'87** 297
  whole spices, **'87** 297
Squash, winter, **'88** 229, 230
  cooking, **'88** 229, 230
  determining amount to buy, **'88** 229
  selecting, **'88** 229, 230
  storing, **'88** 229, 230
  types of, **'88** 229, 230
Stocks. *See* FOKTY/Soups.
Strawberries, **'82** 109
  buying, **'82** 109
  as garnish, **'82** 138
Substitutions, **'92** 344
  alcohol, **'92** 314
  emergency substitutions,
    '92 344 (chart)
Sugar, **'85** 19
  making colored sugar, **'86** 331
  measuring, **'85** 19; **'87** 12
  powdered sugar, **'87** 12
  preventing brown sugar from drying out,
    '85 19
  sifting powdered sugar, **'85** 192;
    '87 12
  substitutions, **'85** 19
  types of, **'85** 19
Surimi, **'90** 130
Sweet potatoes, **'88** 208. *See also*
  FOKTY/Potatoes.
  cooking, **'88** 208
  handling, **'88** 208
  selecting, **'88** 208
  storing, **'88** 208
  substituting canned for fresh,
    '88 208
  yams, **'88** 208
Table setting, **'90** 182, 225
  centerpieces, **'90** 205
  for formal entertaining, **'90** 182
  illustration, **'90** 182
Tamales, **'94** 192. *See also* FOKTY/Masa
  harina.
  making tamale dough, **'94** 192
Tapioca, as a thickening agent, **'83** 147
Tea, **'85** 120, 121
  brewing, **'85** 120, 121
  storing, **'85** 121
  types of, **'85** 120, 121
Thawing food, **'83** 14, 15; **'86** 330;
  '87 208; **'88** 165
  turkey, **'83** 284; **'86** 330

From Our Kitchen To Yours *(continued)*

Thermometers, **'89** 191, 192; **'92** 202;
   '93 103, 104
   deep-fat frying, **'84** 37
   instant-read, **'89** 191, 192; **'92** 202,
     314; **'93** 104
   meat, **'89** 191, 192; **'92** 202
   storing, **'89** 192; **'92** 202
   testing for accuracy, **'89** 192; **'92** 202
Thickening agents, **'83** 146, 147. *See also*
   FOKTY/Arrowroot, Cornstarch, Eggs,
   Tapioca.
Tomatoes, **'85** 181, 182; **'93** 23
   drying cherry tomatoes, **'93** 23
   as garnish, **'82** 280; **'89** 100
   peeling large amount of, **'82** 138;
     '85 181, 182
   recipe, Marinated Dried Cherry
     Tomatoes, **'93** 23
   ripening, **'85** 181
   seeding, **'85** 182
   selecting, **'85** 181
   slicing, **'85** 181, 182
   storing, **'85** 181
   stuffing, **'85** 182
Turkey, **'83** 284, 285; **'93** 306, 307
   carving, **'93** 306, 307
   chart, **'83** 285
   cooking, **'83** 284, 285; **'86** 330
   determining amounts to buy for
     entertaining, **'90** 276
   handling properly, **'87** 208
   leftovers, storing, **'83** 285
   stuffing, **'83** 284
   thawing, **'83** 284; **'86** 330
U.S. Department of Agriculture (USDA),
   '89 142; **'90** 72; **'92** 65, 202; **'93** 83
Vegetable cooking spray, **'92** 208
   cleanup, easy, **'82** 198, 314; **'84** 48;
     '92 314; **'93** 104
Vegetable oil, **'82** 189; **'84** 211;
   '88 112, 113
   deep-fat frying thermometer, **'84** 37;
     '88 113
   preventing fire, **'84** 37; **'88** 112, 113
Vegetables, **'82** 138; **'83** 94;
   '84 180, 211, 249; **'86** 140, 141;
   '89 243, 244; **'92** 344; **'93** 132; **'94** 29, 92.
   See also FOKTY/Broccoli, Brussels
   sprouts, Canning, Cauliflower, Garnishes,
   Lettuce, Mushrooms, Onions, Peas,
   Peppers, Potatoes, Pumpkins, Squash,
   Sweet Potatoes, Tomatoes.
   basic cooking methods, **'82** 138;
     '84 249; **'94** 29, 92 (chart)
   canning, **'84** 180; **'93** 136, 137
   cutting, **'86** 13; **'92** 52; **'93** 132; **'94** 29
   determining amounts to buy for
     entertaining, **'90** 276
   freezing, **'87** 112
   grilling, **'83** 191; **'92** 52
   microwaving, **'82** 138; **'83** 191
   preparing, **'86** 140, 141; **'89** 243, 244
   seasoning, **'94** 92 (chart)
   selecting, **'84** 249; **'86** 140, 141;
     '89 243, 244; **'94** 29
   stir-frying, **'82** 138; **'83** 191
   storing, **'83** 94; **'84** 211; **'86** 140, 141;
     '89 243, 244; **'94** 29

substitutions, **'92** 344
   winter vegetables, **'84** 249; **'88** 229
White chocolate. *See* FOKTY/Chocolate.
Wines, **'85** 292, 293
   champagne, **'85** 293
   selecting, **'85** 292
   serving, **'85** 292, 293
   storing, **'85** 292
Wok cooking, **'85** 76
   equipment, **'85** 76
   preparing food for, **'85** 76
Yams. *See* FOKTY/Sweet Potatoes.
Yeast, **'89** 268. *See also* FOKTY/Biscuits,
   Breads, Rolls.
   kinds of, **'89** 268

Frostings, Fillings, and Toppings

Almond-Butter Frosting, **'86** 107
Almond Cream Filling, **'85** 320; **'91** 248
Almond Filling, **'87** 301
Almond Filling, Ground, **'87** 14
Almond Topping, **'85** 152; **'86** 200
Amaretto Filling, **'87** 241
Amaretto Frosting, **'86** 246
Apple-Date Filling, **'83** 301
Apple Filling, **'85** 5
Apple Filling, Dried, **'85** 242; **'87** 229
Apple-Nut Topping, **'93** 162
Apples, Cooked, **'93** 338
Apple Topping, **'89** 107
Apricot Filling, **'83** 84; **'86** 107; **'93** 316
Apricot Frosting, **'81** 192
Apricot Glaze, **'80** 280; **'82** 8; **'86** 197
Apricot Glaze for Ham, **'85** 256
Apricot Glaze, Sweet, **'82** 304
Apricot-Kirsch Glaze, **'87** 14
Avocado Topping, **'93** 309; **'94** 96
Banana-Nut Frosting, **'79** 115
Bananas Hawaiian, **'89** 94
Beef Filling, **'80** 81
Berry Glaze, **'83** 225
Biscuit Topping, **'86** 157, 265
Blintz Filling, **'92** 84
Blueberry Glaze, **'83** 143
Blue Cheese Burger Topping, **'93** 218
Boiled Frosting, **'90** 45; **'92** 14; **'93** 318
Bourbon Frosting, **'88** 236
Brandy Cream Frosting, **'86** 239
Brandy Glaze, Powdered Sugar-, **'86** 291
Broccoli Filling, **'81** 44
Brown Sugar Frosting, **'79** 13; **'87** 296;
   '91 236
Brown Sugar Glaze, **'83** 312
Brown Sugar Meringue Frosting, **'81** 70
Brown Sugar Topping, **'81** 162
Buttercream Frosting, **'85** 322; **'92** 230;
   '93 53, 285
Butter Cream Frosting, **'88** 279
Buttercream Icing, **'83** 73

Buttercream, Spiced, **'84** 226
Butter Frosting, **'80** 129
Butter Frosting, Browned, **'86** 248
Butter Frosting, Williamsburg, **'81** 120;
   '82 23
Buttermilk Frosting, **'85** 249
Buttermilk Glaze, **'79** 140; **'81** 70; **'84** 316
Butter Pecan Frosting, **'80** 229
Butterscotch Filling, **'91** 271
Caramel Drizzle, **'86** 247
Caramel Filling, **'88** 278
Caramel Frosting, **'81** 278, M289; **'82** 314;
   '83 43; **'84** 39, 263; **'86** 239; **'87** 265;
   '89 55, 236; **'90** 307
Caramel Frosting, Creamy, **'81** 71
Caramel Frosting, Easy, **'87** 39
Caramel Frosting, Favorite, **'83** 106
Caramel Glaze, **'85** 320
Carob Frosting, **'85** 218
Carolina Dream Frosting, **'88** 278
Catsup Topping, **'81** 170
Chantilly Cream, **'83** 91
Chantilly Crème, **'80** 280
Cheese-and-Orange Filling, **'93** 159
Cheese Filling, **'89** 91
Cheese Topping, **'86** 233
Cherry Filling, **'83** 302; **'84** 225; **'88** 178
Cherry Frosting, **'86** 217
Cherry Glaze, **'83** 143; **'93** 52
Chicken Divan Filling, **'81** 91
Chicken Filling, **'81** 200
Chicken Filling, Curried, **'88** 125
Chicken Filling Luau, **'79** 81
Chicken-Olive Filling, **'81** 227
Chicken Salad Filling, **'87** 106
Chili Topping, **'94** 22
Chocolate-Almond Frosting, **'83** 241
Chocolate Buttercream, **'84** 156
Chocolate Butter Frosting, **'89** 271
Chocolate Candy Frosting, **'81** 238
Chocolate-Cheese Filling, **'90** 47
Chocolate-Cherry Frosting, **'89** 294
Chocolate-Coffee Frosting, **'84** 36; **'88** 269
Chocolate Cream, **'94** 57
Chocolate Filling, Rich, **'79** 68
Chocolate Frosting, **'80** M171; **'81** 265;
   '82 262; **'83** 79, 99, M233, 253; **'84** 200;
   '85 323; **'86** 8, 93, 138, 239, 314;
   '87 M97, 198, 199, 293; **'89** M25;
   '90 194, 252, 265, 284, 309; **'91** 248;
   '92 319; **'93** 239; **'94** 133
Chocolate Frosting, Creamy, **'85** 314;
   '86 316; **'87** 241
Chocolate Frosting, Fluffy, **'86** 336; **'87** 58
Chocolate Frosting, Perfect, **'90** 307
Chocolate Frosting, Rich, **'84** 304
Chocolate Frosting, Satiny, **'85** 126; **'89** 43
Chocolate Fudge Frosting, **'83** 105
Chocolate Ganache, **'93** 255
Chocolate Glaze, **'81** 119; **'83** 220; **'84** 10,
   55, 253; **'85** 6; **'86** 315, 316; **'89** 325;
   '90 310; **'91** M296; **'93** 52
Chocolate Glaze, Creamy, **'82** 88
Chocolate-Honey Glaze, **'82** 306
Chocolate Kahlúa Frosting, **'91** 298
Chocolate-Marshmallow Frosting, **'83** 245
Chocolate Nut Frosting, **'80** 140
Chocolate-Peanut Butter Frosting, **'84** 240;
   '87 222
Chocolate-Peanut Topping, **'79** 222
Chocolate Rum Frosting, **'79** 67

Frostings, Fillings, and Toppings *(continued)*

Chocolate Truffle Filling, **'87** 69
Cinnamon-Cheese Filling, **'90** 46
Cinnamon-Cream Frosting, **'84** 311
Cinnamon Frosting, Buttery, **'81** M139
Cinnamon Glaze, **'88** 83
Cinnamon-Pecan Topping, **'85** 277
Citrus Glaze, **'82** 128; **'89** 205
Cocoa Frosting, **'86** 60
Coconut Chocolate Frosting, **'79** 13
Coconut Cream Cheese Frosting, **'86** 60
Coconut Cream Filling, **'84** 200
Coconut Filling, **'81** 265
Coconut Frosting, **'82** 262; **'91** 269
Coconut Frosting, Creamy, **'80** 287
Coconut Frosting, Nutty, **'86** 8
Coconut-Pecan Frosting, **'81** 296; **'83** M233;
    '84 43, 322
Coffee Frosting, **'94** 86
Cola Frosting, **'81** 238
Colored Frostings, **'90** 21
Crab Filling, **'89** 13
Crabmeat Topping, **'91** 64
Cran-Apple Mousse, **'93** 255
Cranberry Glaze, **'84** 306; **'86** 171; **'88** 244
Cranberry-Honey Glaze, **'89** 273
Cream Cheese Filling, **'90** 170
Cream Cheese Frosting, **'79** 45;
    '80 140, 253, 299; **'82** 135, 244;
    '83 105, 215, M233;
    '84 201, 255, 315, 316;
    '85 118, 121; **'86** 217; **'87** 58;
    '90 305, 308;
    '92 120; **'93** 20; **'94** 254
Cream Cheese Frosting, Deluxe, **'80** 120
Cream Cheese Frosting, Fluffy, **'80** 245
Cream Cheese Frosting, Nutty, **'85** 117
Cream Cheese Glaze, **'84** 150; **'94** 242
Cream Filling, **'83** 220; **'84** 37; **'87** 198;
    '90 311
Cream, Luscious Pastry, **'82** 304
Cream, Mock Devonshire, **'81** 288
Cream Topping, Spicy, **'85** 177
Crème Chantilly, **'87** 9; **'91** 297
Crème de Menthe Frosting, **'86** 245;
    '93 256
Crème Fraîche, **'91** 99
Crème Pâtissière, **'83** 225
Crumb Topping, **'83** 183; **'88** 216
Custard Filling, **'82** 52, 298; **'85** 281
Custard Filling, Creamy, **'81** 180
Custard Filling, Egg, **'87** 14
Daiquiri Glaze, **'93** 83
Date Cream Filling, **'81** 303
Date Filling, **'80** 15; **'83** 257; **'86** 314
Decorating Techniques, Cake, **'83** 72, 240
Decorator Frosting, **'82** 20, 307; **'83** 106;
    '87 86; **'91** 282; **'93** 285
Decorator Frosting, Creamy, **'79** 117
Decorator Frosting, Green, **'93** 286
Decorator Frosting, Yellow, **'93** 283
Divinity Frosting, **'79** 229
Drizzle Glaze, **'87** 94
Drizzling Icing, **'91** 35
Fluffy Filling, **'81** 192; **'86** 246
Fluffy Frosting, **'79** 246; **'86** 235; **'88** 268;
    '89 254; **'90** 308
Fluffy White Filling, **'90** 252
Fluffy White Frosting, **'90** 105
Fondant, Rolled, **'92** 69

Fruit Dressing, Nutty, **'88** 68
Fruit Filling, **'94** 245
Fruit Filling, Crêpes with, **'81** 96
Fruit Fluff, Tropical, **'88** 68
Fruit-Nut Filling, **'80** 289
Fruit Topping, **'81** 42; **'87** 225; **'89** 50
Fruity Dessert Topping, **'82** 167
Fudge Filling, **'94** 292
Fudge Frosting, **'81** 303; **'87** 296; **'89** 56;
    '94 51
Fudge Frosting, Quick, **'81** 278
Ganache Cream, **'92** 318
Ginger Cream Topping, **'84** 312
Glaze, Dijon, **'87** 54
Glaze, Topping, **'87** 69
Grapefruit Frosting, **'89** 308
Hazelnut Whipped Cream, **'94** 16
Heavenly Frosting, **'80** 140
Honey Chocolate Frosting, **'79** 83
Honey Filling, **'88** 287
Honey Glaze, **'88** 287
Honey-Nut Glaze, **'87** 15
Honey Topping, **'83** 154
Honey-Walnut Filling, **'80** 21
Horseradish Cream, **'90** 96
Irish Cream Glaze, **'92** 287
Kahlúa Cream, **'91** 197
Kahlúa Glaze, **'86** 292
Ketchup, Hoisin, **'94** 138
Lane Cake Filling, **'89** 55
Lemon-Apricot Filling, **'90** 105
Lemon-Blueberry Cream, **'92** 153
Lemon Buttercream Frosting, **'83** 301;
    '86 61; **'91** 247
Lemon-Butter Cream Frosting, **'85** 117
Lemon-Cheese Filling, **'79** 68; **'88** 7
Lemon-Coconut Frosting, **'90** 253
Lemon Cream, **'82** 237; **'91** 119
Lemon-Cream Cheese Frosting, **'81** 157
Lemon Cream Filling, **'84** 23; **'87** 14
Lemon Curd, **'87** 139; **'94** 315
Lemon Filling, **'81** 172; **'84** 137; **'85** 191;
    '86 235; **'87** 293; **'89** 312; **'90** 308;
    '94 122
Lemon Filling, Creamy, **'80** 70
Lemon Frosting, **'85** 191; **'86** 217; **'93** 81
Lemon Frosting, Creamy, **'79** 93
Lemon Glaze, **'79** 285; **'86** 194; **'87** 41;
    '92 269; **'93** 154, 183
Lemon-Orange Filling, **'81** 71
Lemon-Pineapple Topping, **'86** 60
Lime-Rum Cream, **'93** 169
Maple Frosting, **'82** 217; **'85** 322
Meringue, Cooked, **'86** 130
Meringue, Easy Cooked, **'82** 207; **'83** 158
Meringue Frosting, **'86** 336; **'87** 84
Mint Cream Frosting, **'93** 216
Mint Frosting, **'88** 80
Mint Syrup, **'90** 89
Mocha Buttercream, **'89** 42
Mocha Butter Cream Frosting, **'79** 281
Mocha-Buttercream Frosting, **'86** 26
Mocha Cream, **'94** 47
Mocha Cream Filling, **'81** 187; **'84** 305
Mocha Filling, **'80** 55; **'82** 262
Mocha Frosting, **'83** 301; **'84** 316; **'87** 224;
    '94 292
Mocha Frosting, Creamy, **'82** 289; **'84** 311;
    '91 248
Mushroom Filling, **'81** 89; **'88** 84
Napoleon Cream, **'84** 138

Never Fail Frosting, **'86** 314
Nut-and-Fruit Filling, **'84** 263
Nut Filling, **'91** 35
Nutty Topping, **'85** 256; **'86** 16
Oat Crunch Topping, **'89** 108
Olive Salad, Doodles, **'94** 35
Olive Salad, Italian, **'94** 35
Omelet Filling, Greek, **'80** 68
Omelet Filling, Spanish, **'80** 68
Orange Buttercream Frosting, **'80** 70
Orange Butter Frosting, **'83** 300
Orange Butter Glaze, **'90** 194
Orange-Cheese Filling, **'90** 47
Orange-Cream Cheese Frosting, **'81** 70;
    '82 16; **'92** 19
Orange Cream Frosting, **'81** 207; **'82** 14
Orange Filling, **'79** 229; **'86** 336; **'87** 84;
    '88 224; **'89** 287
Orange Frosting, **'81** 7; **'86** 61; **'88** 119
Orange Frosting, Creamy, **'83** 24, 241
Orange Glaze, **'79** 2; **'80** 257; **'81** 34, 107;
    '82 75, 206; **'83** 33, 114, 140, 267;
    '84 161; **'86** 298; **'92** 263
Orange Glaze, Nutty, **'80** 45
Orange-Lemon Frosting, **'88** 92
Orange-Mallow Cream, **'94** 295
Orange-Pineapple Glaze, **'81** 60
Orange Topping, Whipped, **'80** 254
Paint, Egg Yolk, **'86** 322
Panocha Frosting, **'89** 296
Papaya Topping, **'86** 181
Peach Filling, **'89** 154; **'90** 107
Peach Topping, **'94** 22
Peanut Butter Frosting, **'83** 223; **'84** 153;
    '85 34
Peanut Butter-Fudge Frosting, **'87** 184
Peanut Butter Swirl Frosting, **'86** 109
Peanut Filling, **'93** 211
Peanut Frosting, Creamy, **'80** 87
Pear Whip, **'89** 94
Pecan Frosting, **'86** 86
Pecan Topping, **'94** 36
Peppermint Birthday Cake Frosting, Pink,
    '92 269
Peppermint Filling, **'81** 119; **'89** 254
Pepper Topping, Rainbow, **'90** 117
Pesto, **'89** 158
Pimiento Topping, **'83** 93
Pineapple Filling, **'80** 140; **'83** 179; **'84** 153;
    '89 57
Pineapple Glaze, **'83** 143; **'85** 38
Pineapple Topping, **'86** 239
Piping Icing, **'92** 69
Potato Topping, Mashed, **'89** 243
Powdered Sugar Glaze, **'79** 24; **'82** 92, 283;
    '83 83, 295; **'85** 55; **'90** 95
Praline Filling, **'89** 328
Praline Glaze, **'82** 196
Quick Pour Frosting, **'85** 119
Raisin Filling, **'90** 86
Raspberry Filling, **'90** 111
Raspberry Topping, **'85** 317
Red Pepper Puree, **'93** 275
Ricotta Filling, **'80** 58
Royal Icing, **'80** 278; **'81** 21; **'83** 73;
    '84 303; **'85** 323; **'87** 295; **'88** 309; **'91** 281
Rum Cream, **'88** 154, 224
Rum Cream Topping, **'80** 255
Rum Glaze, Buttered, **'83** 220
Salad Mix, Muffy, **'94** 34
Sea Foam Frosting, **'81** 211; **'91** 271

Frostings, Fillings, and Toppings
(continued)

Seven-Minute Double Boiler Frosting, '81 278
Seven-Minute Frosting, '80 289; '83 299, 301; '87 296; '89 55, 57; '94 98, 99
Shrimp Filling, '89 320
Shrimp Salad Filling, '87 106
Shrimp Topping, '93 291
Snow Peak Frosting, '82 53; '85 281
Snowy Glaze, '82 295
Sour Cream-Coconut Filling, '92 120
Sour Cream Topping, '85 298; '86 120
Southwestern Dressing, '91 195
Spiced Cream, '89 215
Spinach-Mushroom Filling, '80 215
Spinach-Ricotta Filling, '81 53
Strawberry-Banana Topping, Pound Cake with, '89 200
Strawberry Cream, '88 153
Strawberry Frosting, '89 184
Strawberry Glaze, '80 35; '83 142
Strawberry Topping, '86 32; '90 142
Streusel, '85 326
Streusel Topping, '88 154, M275; '94 280
Sugar Glaze, '86 161; '90 47
Sugars, Colored, '90 21
Teriyaki Glaze, '94 82
Tips for Piping Icing, '84 302
Toffee Frosting, English, '85 125
Turkey-Vegetable Topping, '94 22
Vanilla Buttercream Frosting, '92 239; '94 99
Vanilla Cream, '81 248
Vanilla Frosting, '84 36; '85 236; '92 14, 274
Vanilla Glaze, '85 M89; '89 211
Vanilla-Rum Frosting, '85 324
Vegetable Topping, '79 79
Whipped Cream Filling, '90 265, 307
Whipped Cream Frosting, '83 229; '85 125; '87 263; '89 43; '93 86
Whipped Cream Topping, '87 264; '89 154
Whipped Topping, Reduced-Calorie, '85 55
White Buttercream Frosting, '93 337
White Chocolate-Cream Cheese Tiered Cake Frosting, '94 125
White Chocolate-Cream Cheese Frosting, '94 58
White Chocolate Cream Filling, '92 230
White Chocolate Filling, '89 160
White Chocolate Frosting, '88 280; '91 101
White Frosting, '83 268
White Frosting, Fluffy, '81 278
White Frosting, Lemony, '88 7
White Frosting, Luscious, '81 71
Yogurt-Cheese Topping, '88 55

Fruit. *See also* specific types.
Amaretto Crème on Fresh Fruit, '93 176
Bake, Cranberry-Mustard Fruit, '90 287
Baked Fruit, Gingered, '81 232
Baked Fruit, Ginger-Orange, '93 313
Baked Fruit Medley, '81 297
Baked Spiced Fruit, '89 305
Bake, Hot Fruit, '81 270
Bake, Mustard Fruit, '90 291
Bake, Nutty Fruit, '83 127
Balls, Fruit, '82 296; '84 299
Bars, Fruit and Nut Granola, '81 49
Bavarian Cream with Fresh Fruit, '88 137
Beverage, Blender Fruit, '83 318
Boats, Honeydew Fruit, '81 147
Bowl, Fresh Fruit, '89 137
Bowl, Sparkling Fresh Fruit, '80 146
Braid, Fruit-and-Cheese, '86 214
Brandied Fruit, Hot, '80 48
Brandied Fruit Starter, '82 249
Bread, Cranberry Fruit-Nut, '79 275
Bread, Kahlúa Fruit-Nut, '79 235
Brie, Tropical Breeze, '94 M18
Brie with Fresh Fruit, Caramel, '90 266
Brown Sugar Dip with Fruit, Buttery, '90 243
Cake, Fruit-and-Cereal Brunch, '88 263
Cake, Fruit and Spice, '87 M97
Cake, Fruited Pound, '81 265
Cake, Fruity Ice Cream, '87 110
Cake, Spicy Fruited Carrot, '85 117
Cake, Stately Fruit-and-Nut, '84 226
Canapés, Fruit-Topped, '85 80
Canning and Preserving
    Apple Rings, Cinnamon, '85 107
    Berries (except Strawberries), '80 128
    Conserve, Dried Fruit, '82 308
    Dehydration Chart, Fruit and Vegetable, '84 147
    Freezing Chart, Fruit, '85 187
    Juices, Fruit, '85 107
    Mixed Fruit, Unsweetened, '83 182
    Peaches, '80 128
    Peaches and Pears, '85 106
    Peaches, Honey-Sweet, '85 107
    Syrup, Fruit, '86 176
Cascade, Fruit, '86 104
Chafing Dish Fruit, '89 305
Cheese, and Nuts, Fruit, '93 324
Cheese Ball, Fruit-and-Nut, '91 251
Cheesecake, Fruit-Glazed, '80 24; '90 162
Cheese, Fruited Cream, '85 306
Chicken en Crème, Fruited, '83 264
Chicken, Fruit-Glazed, '80 211
Chicken with Almond Rice, Spiced Fruited, '81 195
Chicken with Almond Sauce, Spiced Fruited, '81 195
Chicken with Fresh Fruit, Coconut, '93 294
Chilled Fruit with Dressing, '85 222
Chuck Roast, Fruited, '91 289
Chutney, Autumn Fruit, '88 M230
Cobbler, Quick Fruit, '91 20
Combo, Fresh Fruit, '86 178
Compote, Amaretto-Hot Fruit, '90 250
Compote, Baked Fruit, '80 276; '84 314; '87 228
Compote, Baked Mustard Fruit, '85 47
Compote, Champagne Fruit, '81 309; '82 124
Compote, Chilled Fruit, '83 123
Compote, Festive Fruit, '94 279

Compote, Fresh Fruit, '79 162; '82 197, 272; '84 82; '94 190
Compote, Fresh Fruit Pudding, '86 151
Compote, Fruit, '86 330
Compote, Gingered Fruit, '88 184
Compote, Hot Fruit, '81 203; '83 53; '86 324; '90 124
Compote, Jicama-Fruit, '92 49
Compote, Mixed Fruit, '93 123
Compote, Warm Praline Fruit, '85 260
Compote, Wine Fruit, '81 272
Compote with Raspberry Puree, Fruit, '88 81
Conserve, Dried Fruit, '82 308
Cookies, Bourbon Fruit, '86 334
Cookies, Fruitcake, '79 291; '86 320; '88 286
Cookies, Fruitcake Drop, '92 275
Cookies, Holiday Fruitcake, '81 301
Cookies, Rolled Fruit, '80 15
Cookies, Spicy Holiday Fruit, '83 298
Cooler, Four-Fruit, '86 101
Cooler, Fruited Wine, '86 176
Cooler, Fruit Juice, '92 67
Cream Freeze, Fruit, '82 144
Cream Puffs, Tutti-Frutti, '79 231
Crêpes, Fruit-Filled Chocolate, '89 325
Crêpes, Tropical, '86 275
Crêpes, Tropical Fruit, '87 77
Crisp, Fruit, '94 168
Cup, Appetizer Fruit, '86 131
Cup, Fruit, '81 141; '91 202
Cup, Mixed Fruit, '94 60
Cups, Honeydew Fruit, '82 179
Cup, Snowball Citrus, '79 2
Cups, Royal Fruit, '81 146
Cup, Tipsy Fruit, '81 268
Cup, Vanilla Fruit, '80 183
Curried Fruit, Almond-, '83 261
Curried Fruit Bake, '87 241
Curried Fruit, Hot, '79 225; '81 264; '84 287
Curried Rum Sauce, Tropical Fruit with, '91 164
Custard over Fruit, Stirred, '84 83
Custard with Fresh Fruit, Citrus, '93 70
Delight, Fruit, '86 131
Delight, Winter Fruit, '80 243
Dessert, Caribbean Fruit, '84 314
Dessert, Flaming Fruit, '83 302
Dessert, Rainbow Fruit, '85 108
Dip, Coconut-Honey Fruit, '84 171
Dip, Cranberry Fruit, '89 60
Dip for Fruit, Tropical, '91 252
Dip, Fresh Fruit, '80 265
Dip, Fruited Cream Cheese, '88 261
Dip, Fruited Yogurt, '84 171
Dip, Heavenly Fruit, '81 160
Dip, Marshmallow Fruit, '84 171
Dip, Quick Fruit, '90 110
Dip, Sweet Fruit, '89 328
Dressing, Avocado Fruit Salad, '82 93
Dressing, Baked Fruit, '87 253
Dressing, Fluffy Fruit, '79 69
Dressing for Fruit, Salad, '86 40
Dressing for Fruit Salad, '87 81
Dressing, Fresh Fruit, '87 134
Dressing, Fruit-and-Pecan, '84 252
Dressing, Fruited Cornbread, '80 262
Dressing, Fruit Salad, '79 69; '93 184
Dressing, Lime-Honey Fruit Salad, '87 81

Fruit *(continued)*

Dressing, Marmalade-Fruit, **'84** 171
Dressing, Nutty Fruit, **'88** 68
Dressing, Tangy Coconut-Fruit, **'84** 171
Dressing, Whipped Cream Fruit, **'79** 270
Drink, Three-Fruit, **'79** 38; **'80** 50; **'87** 199
Drink, Tropical Fruit, **'85** 43
Drops, Candied Fruit, **'89** 329
Elegant Fruit, **'91** 91
Filling, Crêpes with Fruit, **'81** 96
Filling, Fruit, **'94** 245
Filling, Fruit-Nut, **'80** 289
Filling, Lemon Crêpes with Fruit, **'82** 46
Filling, Tutti-Frutti, **'79** 231
Flip, Apricot Fruit, **'91** 18
Float, Frosty Fruit, **'87** 159
Frappé, Hootenanny, **'89** 110
Freeze, Holiday Fruit, **'88** 283
Fresh Fruit, Mint Dip with, **'87** 146
Fresh Fruit with Cheese, Luscious, **'79** 153
Fresh Fruit with Lemon Sauce, **'82** 290
Fresh Fruit with Lemon-Yogurt Dressing, **'93** 17
Frozen Fruit Cream, **'94** 129
Frozen Fruit Cups, **'93** 197
Fruitcakes
  Applesauce Fruitcake, **'83** 258
  Aronowitz Fruitcake, **'86** 285
  Bourbon Fruitcake, **'85** 315
  Brandy Fruitcake, **'82** 261
  Burgundy Fruitcake, **'85** 292
  Classic Fruitcake, **'91** 258
  Favorite Fruitcake, Family, **'88** 284
  Fondue, Fruitcake, **'84** 258
  Japanese Fruitcake, **'83** 268; **'90** 252
  Jeweled Fruitcake, **'88** 260
  Kentucky Fruitcake, **'86** 266
  Layered Fruitcake, **'87** 265
  Lemon Fruitcake, **'83** 258
  Light Fruitcake, **'90** 309
  Mom's Fruitcake, **'85** 321
  Old-South Fruitcake, **'79** 289
  Regal Fruitcake, **'83** 257
  Sherry-Nut Fruitcake, **'84** 266
  White Fruitcake, **'80** 280; **'85** 316
  Zucchini Fruitcake, **'88** 284
Garnishes, **'82** 280; **'85** 339
Gingered Fruit, **'83** 151
Glazed Fruit, **'85** 83
Goose, Fruit- and Pecan-Stuffed, **'83** 268
Goose, Fruited Stuffed Wild, **'88** 248
Goose, Fruit Stuffed, **'83** 320
Granola, Fruity, **'84** 148
Ham Slice, Fruited, **'83** M317
Hawaiian Fruit Dish, **'82** 112
Honey-Sour Cream Dip, Fresh Fruit with, **'90** 180
Hot Fruit Delight, **'83** 281
Ice Cream, Tutti-Frutti, **'86** 129
Ice, Fruit, **'86** 176
Ice, Mixed Fruit, **'81** 178; **'88** 85
Ice Tropical, **'79** 174
Juicy, Breakfast Fruit, **'86** 176
Kabobs, Fruit, **'86** 181; **'89** 85
Kabobs, Fruity Mermaid, **'91** 177
Kabobs, Turkey-and-Fruit, **'88** 140
Kabobs, Winter Fruit, **'89** 34
Kabobs with Coconut Dressing, Fruit, **'87** 251

Kabobs with Mint Marinade, Fruit, **'82** 157
Lemon Curd, Fresh Fruit with, **'88** 21
Lemon Freeze, Fruity, **'82** 145
Marinated Fruit, **'91** 67
Marinated Fruit Bowl, **'80** 297
Marmalade, Delicious Fruit, **'81** 285
Medley, Chilled Fruit, **'84** 60
Medley, Chinese Fruit, **'83** 22
Medley, Fancy Fruit, **'84** 83
Medley, Fresh Fruit, **'81** 141
Medley, Frosty Fruit, **'82** 226
Medley, Fruit, **'89** 235
Medley, Fruit Cup, **'85** 47
Medley, Midsummer Fruit, **'88** 182
Medley, Minted Fruit, **'80** 182
Medley of Fruit, Tropical, **'86** 53
Mélange Delight, Fruit, **'81** 302
Mélange, Fruit, **'88** M295
Mélange, Melon, **'84** 139
Meringue Shells, Fruit-Filled, **'86** 151
Minted Marinated Fruit, **'92** 138
Mix, Dried Fruit, **'92** 22
Mixed Fruit, Unsweetened, **'83** 182
Muesli, Bran-and-Fruit, **'91** 134
Muesli, Homestyle, **'91** 315
Muffins, Fruited Wheat, **'79** 93
Nuggets, Dried Fruit, **'86** 326
Oatmeal, Fruited, **'88** 19
Parfait, Tropical Trilogy, **'92** 247
Pick, Fruit-on-a-, **'90** 179
Picks, Fruit on, **'80** 159
Pie, Crispy-Crust Fruit, **'88** 68
Pie, Fruitcake, **'80** 237
Pie, Fruited Cheese, **'92** 228
Pie, Fruit-Topped Vanilla Cream, **'84** 49
Pie, Japanese Fruit, **'80** 238
Pies, Baked Fruit, **'84** 7
Pizza, Peanut Butter-Fruit, **'94** 60
Pops, Fruit, **'87** 168
Pork Chops, Fruited, **'87** 194
Pork Chops, Fruited Stuffed, **'86** 197
Pork Chops, Fruit-Stuffed, **'82** 136
Pork Chops, Fruit-Topped, **'94** 41
Pork Chops with Rice, Fruit-Glazed, **'82** 73
Pork Pilaf, Fruited, **'82** 246
Pork Tenderloins, Fruit-Stuffed, **'87** 270
Pot Roast, Fruited, **'90** 211
Pudding, Fruited Rice, **'86** 95
Puff, Giant Fruit, **'85** 72
Puff Pastry Baskets, Tropical, **'93** 177
Punch, Can-Can Fruit, **'94** 122
Punch, Florida Fruit, **'92** 247
Punch, Fruit, **'83** 52
Punch, Fruit Juicy Rum, **'91** 175
Punch, Fruit Slush, **'91** 278
Punch, Golden Fruit, **'80** 299; **'83** 56
Punch, Holiday Fruit, **'79** 232
Punch, Holiday Hot Fruit, **'92** 286
Punch, Hot Fruit, **'83** 33
Punch, Mixed Fruit, **'90** 207
Punch, Party Fruit, **'82** 137
Punch, Passion Fruit, **'90** 169
Punch, Spiced Fruit, **'88** 2
Punch, Spirited Fruit, **'81** 100
Punch, Summertime Fruit, **'80** 160
Punch, Tropical Fruit, **'81** 51; **'83** 176; **'90** 169
Puree, Fruit, **'94** 190
Refresher, Four-Fruit, **'79** 174
Refresher, Fruit, **'91** 203
Refresher, Grape Juice-Fruit, **'86** 182

Rhapsody, Fruit, **'80** 158
Rice, Far East Fruited, **'81** 175
Rice Mix, Fruited, **'90** 267
Rice Mix, Fruited Curry-, **'86** 326
Rice Pilaf, Chicken Breasts with Fruited, **'92** 307
Rice Pilaf, Fruit-and-Vegetable, **'84** 196
'ritas, Fruit, **'94** 157
Salads
  Ambrosia, Fantastic, **'91** 277
  Ambrosia, Fresh Fruit, **'88** 184
  Apricot Fruit Salad, **'82** 132
  Avocado Fruit Salad, **'87** 41
  Avocado-Fruit Salad with Honey-Yogurt Dressing, **'93** 172
  Banana-Mixed Fruit Salad, **'79** 270
  Cabbage and Fruit Salad, **'79** 286
  Cantaloupe, Fruit-Filled, **'83** 120
  Carrot-and-Seed Salad, Fruity, **'86** 223
  Carrot-Fruit Toss, **'82** 235
  Chef Salad, Fruited, **'85** 222
  Chef's Fruit Salad, **'86** 35
  Cherry Fruit Salad, **'87** 236
  Chicken-Avocado Salad, Fruited, **'82** 101
  Chicken-Fruit Salad, **'82** 79
  Chicken Fruit Salad, **'90** 234
  Chicken Salad, Fruited, **'84** 25, 290; **'88** 88; **'90** 318
  Chicken Salad, Fruity, **'83** 157
  Chicken Salad in Avocados, Fruited, **'87** 41
  Chicken Salad with Fruit, **'82** 171
  Citrus-Cilantro Dressing, Fruit Salad with, **'93** 310; **'94** 97
  Citrus Dressing, Fruit Salad with, **'88** 6
  Coconut Fruit Bowl, **'83** 111
  Coconut Salad, Chunky Fruit-and-, **'84** 24
  Coleslaw, Fruited, **'83** 209; **'85** 139
  Coleslaw, Three-Fruit, **'86** 250
  Colorful Fruit Bowl, **'91** 58
  Colorful Fruit Salad, **'82** 113
  Cottage Cheese-and-Fruit Salad, **'86** 16
  Cottage-Fruit Split, **'86** 169
  Cream Dressing, Fruit Salad with, **'89** 277
  Creamy Fruit Salad, **'84** 265
  Creamy Holiday Fruit Salad, **'90** 251
  Curried Fruit Salad, **'85** 107
  Date Dressing, Fruit Salad with, **'87** 57
  Dressed-Up Fruit, **'82** 5
  Easy Fruit Salad, **'80** 221
  Easy Patio Fruit Salad, **'88** 184
  Fall Salad with Ginger Dressing, **'82** 194
  Festive Fruit Salad, **'80** 16
  Fresh Fruit Cup with Mint Dressing, **'80** 183
  Fresh Fruit Salad, **'82** 165
  Fresh Fruit Salad with Celery-Honey Dressing, **'80** 42
  Fresh Fruit Salad with Poppy Seed Dressing, **'91** 168
  Frisky Fruit Salad, **'85** 46
  Frozen Fruit Salad, **'83** 110
  Frozen Fruit Salad, Dreamy, **'79** 126
  Frozen Fruit Salad, Luscious, **'81** 204
  Frozen Fruit Salad, Summertime, **'89** 111
  Frozen Salad Christmas Wreath, **'79** 241
  Fruit Salad, **'83** 209; **'89** 277

Fruit, Salads (continued)

Glazed Fruit Salad, '83 48; '84 290
Green Fruit Salad with Honey-Lime
    Dressing, '93 71
Ham Salad, Fruited, '81 36, 146
Heavenly Salad, '81 252
Holiday Fruit Salad, '87 236
Honeydew Fruit Bowl, '84 186
Honey Dressing, Fruit Salad with,
    '87 129
Honey Fruit Salad, '80 276
Honey-Lemon Dressing, Fruit Salad with,
    '93 21
Hurry-Up Fruit Salad, '87 236
Jicama-Fruit Salad, '86 83
Layered Fruit Salad, '84 290; '89 277;
    '91 58
Lemonade Fruit Salad, '84 24
Lettuce and Fruit Salad with Poppy Seed
    Dressing, '80 152
Main Dish Fruit Salad, '83 119
Marinated Fruit Deluxe, '81 146
Melon-Citrus Mingle, '79 177
Mint-Gin Fruit Salad, '92 92
Mint Sauce, Fruit Salad with, '88 M96
Mixed Fruit Cup, '87 233
Mold, Sherried Fruit, '90 124
Multi-Fruit Salad, '93 184
Nut Salad, Cheesy Fruit-'n'-, '87 56
Old-Fashioned Fruit Salad, '82 80
Orange Cream, Fresh Fruit Salad with,
    '90 126
Orange Fruit Cup, '91 277
Oriental Dressing, Fruit Salad with,
    '91 277
Pasta Salad, Fruited, '92 108
Peachy Fruit Salad, '89 206
Persimmon Fruit Salad, '79 206
Pineapple Cream Dressing, Fruit Cups
    with, '83 81
Pineapple Dressing, Fruit Salad with,
    '85 207
Pineapple-Fruit Salad, Icy, '87 9
Platter, Fresh Fruit Salad, '92 213
Platter, Fruit Salad, '83 261
Poppy Seed Dressing, Fruit Salad with,
    '88 78
Potato Salad, Fruity, '85 214
Quick-and-Easy Fruit Salad, '81 99
Raspberry Fruit Mounds, '79 35
Refreshing Fruit Salad, '85 92
Rum, Fruit Cup with, '83 55
Sangría Fruit Cups, '89 34
Shrimp Salad, Fruited, '86 156
Sour Cream Fruit Salad, '80 138
Sparkling Fruit Salad, '82 266
Spiced Autumn Fruit Salad, '87 228
Springtime Fruit Salad, '81 96
Summer Fruit Salad, '82 164; '92 171
Summer Salad, Favorite, '80 158
Sunny Fruit Salad, '91 58
Sweet-and-Sour Fruit Salad, '80 13;
    '84 125
Tossed Fruit Salad, '92 106
Tropical Fruit Salad, '89 306
Tropical Fruit Salad with Fresh Mint
    Dressing, '84 126
Turkey-Fruit Salad, '79 56
Turkey Fruit Salad, '83 233; '84 244

Turkey Salad, Fruit-and-, '89 176
Turkey Salad, Fruit-and-Spice, '94 325
Turkey Salad, Fruitful, '84 197
Watermelon Fruit Basket, '84 161
Winter Fruit Salad, '80 248; '82 23
Wreath, Della Robbia Fruit, '87 294
Yogurt Fruit Salad, '81 114
Yogurt-Granola Fruit Medley, '91 58
Sandwiches, Fruit-and-Cheese Breakfast,
    '89 M21
Sandwiches, Glazed Breakfast Fruit, '93 178
Sangría, Three-Fruit, '89 212
Sauce for Fruit, Tangy, '90 161
Sauce, Fruit, '81 177
Sauce, Golden Fruit, '89 281
Sauce, Grand Marnier Fruit, '90 93
Sauce, Hot Fruit Dessert, '87 299
Sauce, Quick Fruit, '82 212
Sauce, Rum-Fruit, '84 312
Shake, Frosty Fruit, '87 23
Shake, Tropical, '93 212
Shells, Fruited Meringue, '87 32
Sherbet, Freezer Fruit, '86 334
Sherbet, Frozen Fruit, '79 155
Sherbet, Fruit Punch, '86 129
Sherbet, Instant Fruit, '85 158
Sherried Fruit Casserole, '80 284
Sherried Fruit Flame, '85 313
Sherried Fruit Mélange, '80 158
Slush, Champagne Fruit, '90 322
Slush, Refreshing Fruit, '82 35
Slushy, Fruit, '80 146
Smoothie, Fruit, '89 87
Smoothie, Fruited Honey-Yogurt, '88 231;
    '89 23
Smoothie, Two-Fruit, '89 182
Soup, Chilled Fresh Fruit, '88 160
Soup, Cold Fresh Fruit, '87 157
Soup Dessert, Fruit, '79 172
Soup, Dried Fruit, '79 23
Soup, Fruit, '87 98
Soup, Swedish Fruit, '82 313; '83 65
Soup, Yogurt Fruit, '86 176
Spareribs, Fruit-Stuffed, '79 14
Spiced Fruit, '79 23
Spiced Fruit, Cold, '90 269
Spiced Fruit Delight, '82 229
Spiced Fruit Dessert, '82 50
Spiced Fruit, Warm, '86 39
Spiced Winter Fruit, '83 262
Spread, Fruit, '85 135
Spread, Fruit and Cheese, '81 245
Spread, Fruited Cream Cheese, '91 306;
    '93 79
Spread, Nutty Fruit-and-Cheese, '87 246
Spread, Sugarless Fruit, '84 60
Squares, Christmas Fruit, '88 282
Squash, Fruited Acorn, '85 235
Squash, Fruit-Stuffed Acorn, '81 295
Strudel, Fruit Basket, '87 276
Stuffing, Cornish Hens with Fruited, '90 191
Stuffing Mix, Fruited, '89 331
Summer Fruit Fantasy, '91 178
Syrup, Apricot Fruit, '82 10
Syrup, Fruit, '86 176
Tart, Fancy Fruit, '82 128; '91 119
Tart, Fresh Fruit, '84 178; '90 58
Tartlets, Fresh Fruit, '93 96
Tart, Open-Face Fruit, '84 207
Tart, Rainbow Fruit, '82 304
Tarts, Bowl-Me-Over Fresh Fruit, '93 200

Tea, Christmas Fruit, '83 275
Tea Cooler, Fruited, '94 131
Tea, Fruited Mint, '88 79; '91 81
Tea, Hot Spiced Fruit, '87 242
Tequila, Fruit in, '82 223
Topping, Fruit, '81 42; '87 225; '89 50
Topping, Fruity Dessert, '82 167
Tropical Fruit Fluff, '88 68
Tropical Fruit Tray, '93 72
Tropical Fruit Whisper, '89 212
Turnovers, Fruit, '79 150
Twists, Fruit-Nut, '82 253
Tzimmes with Brisket, Mixed Fruit,
    '93 114
Wine, Fruit in White, '81 48
Winter Fruit with Custard Sauce, '88 251
Wontons, Fruit-Filled, '85 287

G

ame. *See also* specific types.
Birds in Wine Marinade, Game, '94 306
Chili, Double-Meat, '80 12
Dove and Sausage Gumbo, '81 199
Dove Enchiladas, '85 270
Doves, Pan-Roasted, '87 240
Doves, Sherried, '91 290
Duck and Wild Rice Casserole, '79 224
Duck, Buffet Wild, '86 268
Duck, Foxfire, '89 241
Duck Kabobs with Almond Rice, Grilled,
    '91 291
Duckling, Holiday, '80 251
Duckling, Roast Long Island, '84 87
Ducklings with Blackberry Sauce, '82 251
Ducklings with Cherry Sauce, Roast, '86 312
Duckling with Orange Sauce, Roast, '81 125
Duckling with Wine Jelly, Roast, '88 243
Duck, Oyster, and Sausage Gumbo, '79 226
Duck, Sherried Baked, '79 224
Duck with Orange Gravy, '81 259
Duck with Orange Gravy, Roast Wild,
    '89 323
Duck with Orange Sauce, Grilled, '94 305
Duck with Pecan Stuffing, Wild, '85 269
Duck with Sweet Potato-Eggplant Gravy,
    Roast, '83 90
Goose, Fruited Stuffed Wild, '88 248
Goose with Currant Sauce, Wild, '87 240
Gumbo, Wild Game, '91 290
Mallard, Prairie Wings, '83 252
Pepper Feet, '93 258
Pheasant Muscatel, '85 269
Pot Pie with Parmesan Crust, Game,
    '94 304
Quail Breasts, Southern, '85 270
Quail, Foxfire, '89 240
Quail, Fried, '82 45
Quail, Grilled, '92 90
Quail, Grilled Breakfast, '88 220
Quail, Hawkeye-Stuffed, '89 241
Quail, J.W., '89 240
Quail, Magnificent, '82 214
Quail, Marinated, '80 221
Quail, Seasoned Fried, '88 220
Quail, Smoked, '93 236
Quail Stuffed with Cornbread Dressing,
    '93 280
Quail Superb, '81 303
Quail with Cornbread Stuffing, Baked,
    '94 305

Game *(continued)*

Quail with Gravy, Georgia, **'87** 240
Quail with Mushrooms, **'85** 138
Quail with Mushrooms, Baked, **'81** 259
Quail with Onion Gravy, Fried, **'82** 214
Quail with Red Plum Sauce, **'80** 48
Rabbit, Hickory Barbecued, **'82** 216
Rabbit, Santa Fe Spanish, **'94** 307
Squab, Baked Stuffed, **'82** 260
Stew, Hunter's, **'85** 270
Turkey, Country-Fried Wild, **'94** 306
Venison and Tomatoes, **'85** 270
Venison Burgers, **'87** 304
Venison Chili, **'82** 216; **'86** 3; **'87** 304
Venison Chili, Hot, **'91** 283
Venison, Country-Fried, **'81** 233
Venison Kabobs, **'82** 215; **'88** 249
Venison Loin, Mushroom-Crusted, **'94** 302
Venison Reduction Sauce, **'94** 303
Venison Roast, **'82** 226
Venison Roast, Grilled, **'93** 278
Venison Roast, Lillie Bell's, **'89** 242
Venison Roast with Red Wine Gravy, **'85** 270
Venison Sausage Balls, **'80** 42
Venison Sausage Stew, **'87** 238
Venison Soup, **'82** 216
Venison Steak, Country-Fried, **'83** 262
Venison Steaks, Country-Style, **'82** 215
Venison Steaks, Grilled, **'82** 215
Venison Stew, **'86** 294
Venison Stew with Potato Dumplings, **'87** 304
Venison Stock, **'94** 302
Venison Tenderloin Appetizers, **'88** 249
Venison-Vegetable Bake, **'87** 304
Venison with Chutney-Mustard Sauce,
    Bostick, **'89** 242

Garnishes
Broccoli Bouquet, **'87** 115
Butter Balls, **'82** 189; **'89** 90
Butter Curls, **'82** 51, 189; **'89** 90
Butter Molds, **'89** 90
Carrot Curls, **'85** 338
Carrot Flowers, **'85** 338
Celery Fans, **'85** 339
Chocolate Crinkle Cups, **'93** 270
Chocolate Curls, **'85** 338
Chocolate Garnishes, Lacy, **'89** 43
Chocolate Hearts and Shavings, **'86** 26
Chocolate Leaves, **'88** 281; **'89** 42
Chocolate Sack, Large, **'93** 314
Chocolate Sack, Small, **'93** 314
Citrus Cups, **'85** 339
Citrus Cups, Notched, **'82** 280
Cranberries, Frosted, **'82** 280; **'85** 339
Eggs, Hard-Cooked, **'82** 280
Grapes, Frosted, **'82** 51; **'85** 339
Green Onion Fans, **'85** 339
Green Pepper Cups, **'85** 339
Guide, Garnishing, **'82** 138
Lemon Peel, Candied, **'94** 199
Lemon Roses, **'82** 280; **'85** 338
Lemon Slices, Fluted, **'82** 51
Marinade, Dill, **'87** 115
Marinade, Garlic-and-Oregano, **'87** 115
Marinade, Sweet-and-Sour, **'87** 115
Mushrooms, Aztec, **'82** 51
Mushrooms, Fluted, **'82** 280; **'85** 338
Onion Mum, **'85** 339
Onion Rose, **'87** 114

Orange Rose, **'85** 338
Piped Garnishes, **'82** 280
Radish Rose, **'85** 339
Squash Buttercup, **'87** 114
Tomato Cups, **'85** 339
Tomato Flower, Marinated Pasta in, **'87** 115
Tomato Rose, **'82** 51; **'85** 338
Vegetable and Fruit Garnishes, **'82** 280
Zucchini Fan, **'87** 114

Glazes. *See* Frostings, Fillings, and Toppings.

Goose
Stuffed Goose, Fruit-, **'83** 320
Stuffed Goose, Fruit- and Pecan-, **'83** 268
Wild Goose, Fruited Stuffed, **'88** 248
Wild Goose with Currant Sauce, **'87** 240

Granola
Bars, Coconut Granola, **'85** 202
Bars, Fruit and Nut Granola, **'81** 49
Bars, Granola, **'83** 305
Bread, Honey-Granola, **'86** 56
Chocolate Morsels, Granola with, **'86** 69
Crisp, Granola Apple, **'85** 78
Crunchy Granola, **'81** 218; **'84** 144
Easy Granola, **'81** 49
Fabulous Granola, **'92** 213
Fruit Medley, Yogurt-Granola, **'91** 58
Fruity Granola, **'84** 148
Gorp, Granola, **'89** 59
Granola, **'79** 190; **'93** 197
Homemade Granola, **'84** 58
Mix, Granola, **'94** 168
Mix, Granola Snack, **'86** 229
Nutty Granola, **'90** 95
Orange Granola, Sunny, **'84** 212
Pancakes, Granola-Squash, **'94** 267
Peanut Butter Granola, **'82** 296
Peanut Granola, Crunchy, **'90** 48
Reindeer Nibbles, **'92** 280
Sunshine Granola, **'79** 37
Toasty Granola, **'79** 37
Treats, Raisin-Granola, **'92** 22
Whole Wheat Granola, **'82** 167

Grapefruit
Aspic, Grapefruit, **'80** 297; **'82** 112; **'83** 153
Biscuits, Grapefruit Juice, **'83** 10
Broiled Grapefruit, **'85** 7
Broiled Grapefruit, Holiday, **'88** 251
Broiled Grapefruit, Sherried, **'80** 50
Broil, Flounder-Grapefruit, **'85** 53
Cake, Fresh Grapefruit, **'89** 308
Chocolate-Topped Grapefruit, **'89** 88
Compote, Spicy Grapefruit-Berry, **'91** 19
Cooler, Grapefruit, **'88** 81
Cup, Berry Grapefruit, **'79** 242
Delight, Winter Fruit, **'80** 243
Dressing, Grapefruit French, **'80** 101
Dressing, Grapefruit Salad, **'84** 262
Drink, Grapefruit, **'90** 84
Drink, Three-Fruit, **'80** 50

Freeze, Grapefruit, **'93** 242
Frosting, Grapefruit, **'89** 308
Ice, Grapefruit, **'91** 122
Ice, Pink Grapefruit, **'85** 304
Marmalade, Combination Citrus, **'80** 50
Marmalade, Grapefruit, **'82** 308
Minted Grapefruit, **'88** 81
Pear-Berry Puree, Grapefruit with, **'89** 213
Refresher, Grapefruit, **'88** 85
Refresher, Grapefruit-Orange, **'82** 174
Salad, Avocado-Grapefruit,
    '85 26; **'93** 282
Salad, Congealed Grapefruit, **'84** 325;
    '85 279
Salad, Grapefruit, **'83** 124; **'84** 325;
    '88 122
Salad, Grapefruit-and-Shrimp, **'88** 5
Salad, Grapefruit-Apple, **'89** 41
Salad, Grapefruit-Avocado, **'83** 316; **'84** 16;
    '89 41
Salad, Grapefruit Combo, **'80** 50
Salad, Grapefruit Congealed, **'83** 190
Salad, Grapefruit-Cucumber, **'80** 100
Salad, Grapefruit-Orange, **'91** 276
Salad, Grapefruit Winter, **'84** 24
Salad, Orange-Grapefruit, **'93** 294
Salad with Celery Seed Dressing,
    Grapefruit-Banana, **'91** 237
Sangría, Grapefruit, **'89** 92
Sorbet, Grapefruit-Mint, **'93** 153
Supreme, Grapefruit, **'80** 50
Tea, Grapefruit, **'92** 67

Grapes
Carrots with Grapes, Glazed, **'82** 287
Chicken Véronique, **'84** 260; **'85** 302
Cooler, Grape-Lime, **'94** 227
Frosted Grapes, **'82** 51; **'85** 339
Granita, Grape, **'88** 118
Green Grapes Supreme, **'88** 81
Ham Véronique, **'85** 90
Honeydew Melon with Grapes, **'91** 91
Ice Cream, Scuppernong, **'88** 216
Ice, Grape, **'83** 162
Ice, Muscadine, **'82** 202
Jelly, Grape, **'89** 140
Jelly, Grape-Burgundy Freezer, **'85** 130
Jelly, Quick Grape, **'89** M156
Jelly, Thyme-Grape, **'89** 193
Jelly, Wild Muscadine, **'79** 32
Juice, Mulled Grape, **'90** 21
Mold, Double Grape-Cantaloupe,
    '79 173
Pie, Grape, **'85** 212
Pie, Grape Juice, **'79** 123
Pie, Muscadine, **'82** 202
Pie, Scuppernong, **'88** 216
Punch, Sparkling Grape, **'82** 48
Punch, White Grape, **'90** 15
Refresher, Grape Juice-Fruit, **'86** 182
Salad, Marinated Chicken-Grape, **'85** 74
Salad Mold, Grape, **'83** 120
Salad Véronique, Macaroni, **'85** 164
Salad with Grapes, Chicken, **'86** 117
Sauce, Pears in Muscadine, **'88** 216
Sauce, White Grape, **'80** 38
Scallops Véronique, **'83** 144
Slaw, Grape-Poppy Seed, **'86** 225
Sole Véronique, **'85** 181
Tart, Green Grape, **'87** 77
Tea, White Grape Juice, **'87** 57
Tuna Salad with Grapes, Curried, **'87** 201

Gravies. *See also* Sauces.
Black-Eyed Pea Gravy, **'87** 12
Chive Gravy, Beef and Broccoli with, **'88** 214
Cranberry Pan Gravy, Baked Hen with, **'94** 308
Cream Gravy, **'88** 15
Cream Gravy, Country-Fried Steak with, **'84** 8
Cream Gravy, Fried Chicken with, **'85** 241
Currant Gravy, **'83** 276
Dill-Cream Gravy, Pork Chops with, **'84** 81
Fried Ripe Tomatoes with Gravy, **'82** 180
Giblet Gravy, **'79** 283; **'88** 253
Giblet Gravy, Roast Turkey and, **'94** 308
Gravy, **'88** 303
Ham with Gravy, Virginia, **'86** 15
Horseradish Gravy, Filet Mignon with, **'92** 262
Mushroom Gravy, Baked Quail with, **'89** 273
Onion Gravy, Fried Quail with, **'82** 214
Orange Gravy, **'81** 259; **'89** 323
Red-Eye Gravy, Country Ham with, **'79** 37
Redeye Gravy, Country Ham with, **'86** 254
Red-Eye Gravy, Ham and, **'88** 221
Sausage Gravy, **'92** 271; **'94** 20
Sour Cream Gravy, **'92** 301
Sour Cream Gravy, Pot Roast with, **'79** 17
Sweet Potato-Eggplant Gravy, Roast Duck with, **'83** 90
Tasso Gravy, **'92** 236
Tomato Gravy, **'93** 18
Turkey Gravy, **'91** 255; **'94** 306
White Wine Gravy, **'89** 322
Wine Gravy, Pot Roast in White, **'81** 299
Wine Gravy, Venison Roast with Red, **'85** 270

Greens. *See also* specific types.
Bake, Grits 'n Greens Dinner, **'84** 281
Chard, Buttered, **'83** 36
Chard with Tomatoes, Swiss, **'83** 36
Collard Greens, Seasoned, **'82** 211
Collards, **'79** 32
Collards and Sausage, Pasta with, **'94** 230
Collards, Southern-Style, **'82** 107
Collards, Uptown, **'92** 23
Escarole-and-Bacon Salad, **'84** 85
Escarole, Easy Cooked, **'84** 85
Gumbo z'Herbes, **'94** 239
Kale, Scalloped, **'86** 224
Kale, Sweet-and-Sour, **'80** 298
Kale with Salsa, Southwest, **'94** 246
Kale with Tomato and Onion, **'92** 244
Mustard Greens and Potatoes, **'86** 224
Mustard Green Soup, Cream of, **'93** 280
Mustard Greens, Spinach Fettuccine with, **'94** 247
Stir-Fried Greens, **'94** 33
Turnip-and-Carrot Salad, **'91** 212
Turnip-and-Collard Greens, **'92** 215
Turnip Green Dip, **'91** 13
Turnip Green Dip with Jalapeño-Corn Muffins, Hot, **'93** 164
Turnip Greens, **'90** 13, 232
Turnip Greens and Ham Hock, Southern, **'80** 119
Turnip Greens and White Bean Bake, **'94** 246
Turnip Greens, Fresh, **'92** 339
Turnip Greens, Old-Fashioned, **'85** 255
Turnip Greens, Saucy, **'83** 12
Turnip Greens with Cornmeal Dumplings, **'82** 211

Turnip Greens with Turnips, **'84** 230
Turnip Salad, **'85** 235
Turnips, Braised, **'91** 219
Watercress-and-Mushroom Salad, **'88** 104
Watercress Mousse, **'88** 104
Watercress Soup, **'88** 104
Watercress Spread, **'88** 103

Grits
Bake, Grits 'n Greens Dinner, **'84** 281
Cakes, Southwestern Grits, **'93** 61
Casserole, Cheesy Grits, **'81** 270
Casserole, Garlic Grits, **'81** 47
Casserole, Grits-Sausage, **'84** 75; **'86** 241
Cheese-and-Garlic Grits, Baked, **'83** 292; **'84** 78
Cheese Grits, **'86** 242; **'90** 102
Cheese Grits, Baked, **'80** 49, 99; **'83** 311; **'85** 41; **'94** 240
Cheese Grits, Garlic, **'80** 47; **'81** 197
Cheese Grits, Grillades and Baked, **'94** 240
Cheese Grits, Gruyère, **'81** 47
Cheese Grits, Jalapeño, **'85** 43
Cheese Grits, Quick, **'83** M203
Cheese Grits, Sliced, **'84** 75
Country Grits and Sausage, **'83** 54
Creamy Grits, **'92** 237, 238; **'93** 60
Dressing, Grits, **'93** 306; **'94** 296
Eggs Creole, **'92** 86
Fried Grits, **'83** 292; **'84** 78
Garlic-Cheese Grits, **'86** 180; **'88** 126; **'89** 47
Good Morning Grits, **'87** 156
Grillades and Grits, **'88** 126; **'89** 47; **'93** 62
Ham-and-Spinach Grits, Garlicky, **'94** 177
Italiano, Grits, **'92** 43
Nassau Grits, **'81** 47
Orange Grits, **'81** 47
Pan-Fried Grits, **'93** 62
Patties, Grits, **'83** 52
Pie, Crustless Grits-and-Ham, **'86** 103
Pie, Grits Fiesta, **'92** 43
Quiche, Ham-and-Grits Crustless, **'94** 89
Sausage-Cheese Grits, **'90** 238
Sausage Grits, **'86** 92
Scrambled Grits, **'80** 48
Shrimp Stew and Grits, **'80** 118
Shrimp Stew over Grits, **'89** 47
Soufflé, Grits, **'80** 30
Soufflé, Mexican Grits, **'79** 55
Spoonbread, Grits, **'79** 38
Stew over Grits, Shrimp, **'88** 126
Swiss-and-Cheddar Baked Grits, **'91** 71
Timbales, Chives-Grits, **'90** 172
Timbales, Grits, **'88** 223

Gumbos
Beef Gumbo, Ground, **'87** 283
Catfish Gumbo, **'90** 278; **'91** 216
Chicken and Oyster Gumbo, **'81** 198
Chicken-and-Sausage Gumbo, **'89** 275; **'90** 256; **'94** 20
Chicken Gumbo, **'79** 199; **'90** 26
Chicken Gumbo, Easy, **'83** 156
Chicken Gumbo with Smoked Sausage, **'81** 199
Chicken-Ham-Seafood Gumbo, **'81** 6
Combo Gumbo, **'81** 198
Crab and Shrimp Gumbo, **'81** 200
Creole Gumbo, **'86** 228
Creole Gumbo, Quick, **'82** 87
Dove and Sausage Gumbo, **'81** 199

Duck, Oyster, and Sausage Gumbo, **'79** 226
Fish Gumbo, Easy, **'81** 6
Gullah House Gumbo, The, **'92** 237
Ham and Seafood Gumbo, **'81** 199
Mogumbo, **'93** 32
Okra Gumbo, **'86** 210; **'91** 206
Okra Gumbo, Deep South, **'79** 48
Okra Gumbo Freezer Mix, **'86** 210
Seafood Gumbo, **'79** 198, 286; **'80** 34; **'81** 5; **'83** 90; **'84** 87, 92; **'87** 210; **'90** 154
Seafood Gumbo, Cajun, **'94** 238
Seafood Gumbo, Champion, **'86** 293
Seafood Gumbo, Creole, **'82** 278
Seafood Gumbo, Spicy, **'91** 207
Seafood Gumbo with Whole Crabs, **'85** 2
Seafood-Okra Gumbo, Light, **'86** 155
Shrimp Gumbo, **'81** 199
Shrimp Gumbo, Quick, **'86** 71
Snapper Gumbo, Savannah, **'94** 105
Southern Gumbo, **'82** 242
Texas Ranch-Style Gumbo, **'82** 226
Turkey Gumbo, **'82** 268; **'85** 258
Wild Game Gumbo, **'91** 290
Ya Ya, Gumbo, **'87** 210
z'Herbes, Gumbo, **'94** 239

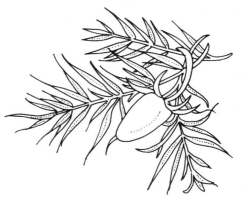

Ham. *See also* Pork.
Appetillas, Ham, **'93** 63
Appetizers, Meat-and-Cheese, **'87** 7
Apricots, Ham and, **'90** 53
au Gratin, Broccoli-Ham, **'90** 239
Bake, Chicken, Ham, and Cheese, **'87** 217
Baked
    Apples, Baked Ham and, **'82** M237
    Apricot Baked Ham, **'84** 160
    Burgundy Ham, Baked, **'94** 326
    Cranberry-Honey Glaze, Baked Ham with, **'89** 273
    Cranberry-Raisin Sauce, Baked Ham with, **'88** 244
    Festive Baked Ham, **'83** 263
    Glazed Ham, Molasses-, **'84** 24
    Glazed Ham, Sunshine-, **'84** 252
    Glazed Stuffed Ham, **'84** 321
    Maple-Raisin Sauce, Baked Ham with, **'83** 215
    Marinated Baked Ham, **'86** 94; **'88** 133
    Orange-Honey Glaze, Baked Ham with, **'86** 294
    Orange Sauce, Baked Ham with, **'86** 294

Ham, Baked *(continued)*

Pineapple-Baked Ham, '86 48
Plum Ham, '80 110
Royale, Ham, '84 260
Slice, Baked Ham, '83 12
Strata, Baked Ham, '83 283
Bake, Ham-Potato-Pineapple, '93 302
Bake, Ham-Rice-Tomato, '87 78
Bake, Harvest Ham, '79 210
Bake, Layered Ham and Turkey, '79 252
Balls, Appetizer Ham, '82 39
Balls, Fried Ham-and-Cheese, '84 221
Balls, Ham, '84 91; '86 256
Balls with Spiced Cherry Sauce, Ham, '81 112; '82 12
Barbecued Ham Slices, '81 110
Beans with Ham, Baked, '80 136
Birming "Ham," '94 229
Biscuits, Ham-Filled Angel, '80 159
Biscuits, Kentucky Ham 'n' Angel, '90 83
Biscuits, Petite Ham and Cheese, '79 193
Biscuits, Southern Ham and, '91 12
Bread, Ham-and-Cheese, '86 213
Broiled Ham, Cranberry, '88 301
Bundles, Ham-and-Cheese, '93 63
Cakes, Hawaiian Ham, '79 252
Casserole, Apple Ham, '79 213
Casserole, Breakfast, '91 285
Casserole, Breakfast Ham and Egg, '79 253
Casserole, Cheesy Ham-and-Potato, '84 326
Casserole, Golden Ham, '82 119
Casserole, Ham and Broccoli, '81 133
Casserole, Ham-and-Cheese, '87 78
Casserole, Ham and Lima, '79 192
Casserole, Ham and Noodle, '80 300
Casserole, Ham-and-Potato, '83 M87
Casserole, Ham-and-Rice, '84 75
Casserole, Ham Roll, '91 M127
Casserole, Macaroni-Ham, '81 M177; '83 283
Casserole, Quick Ham-Broccoli, '82 40
Casserole, Vegetable-and-Ham, '84 91
Cheesecake, Ham-and-Asparagus, '90 174
Cheese Chips, Ham-, '82 34
Cheese Toss, Ham and, '79 55
Cheesy Chicken-and-Ham Bundles, '84 261
Cheesy Ham-and-Turkey Specials, '84 14
Cheesy Ham Dinner, '84 90
Cheesy Ham Nuggets, '81 290
Cheesy Ham Towers, '82 M77
Chowder, Creamy Ham, '88 M53
Chowder, Ham-and-Cheese, '89 15
Chowder, Ham and Corn, '79 16
Chowder, Ham-and-Corn, '82 40
Chowder, Ham 'n Cheese, '79 199
Citrus-and-Spice Ham, '88 40
Coleslaw, Ham, '84 195
Cordon Bleu, Chicken, '81 304; '82 83; '93 126
Cordon Bleu, Company Chicken, '82 274
Cordon Bleu, Veal, '87 219
Country Ham
Biscuits, Country Ham, '94 215
Biscuits, Country Ham in Heart, '86 105
Biscuits with Country Ham, '90 93
Bread with Herb Butter, Country Ham, '86 255

Brown Sugar Coating, Country Ham with, '90 88
Brown Sugar Glaze, Smithfield Ham with, '86 253
Chips, Country Ham, '92 338
Cider-Baked Country Ham, '82 195
Cider, Country Ham in Apple, '80 251
Cornbread, Crab with Chile, '86 254
Kentucky Hot Brown, '86 254
Kentucky Jack, '86 254
Loaves, Country Ham, '86 255
Oven-Braised Country Ham, '90 87
Oysters and Ham, Edwards', '86 253
Puff, Cheesy Country Ham, '90 88
Quiche, Country Ham, '87 287
Red-Eye Gravy, Country Ham with, '79 37
Redeye Gravy, Country Ham with, '86 254
Roasted Country Ham, Edwards', '86 253
Sauce, Country Ham, '90 117
Sotterley Plantation Country Ham, '93 270
Spread, Country Ham, '87 8
Stuffed Country Ham, '90 317
Stuffed Country Ham, Maryland, '88 49
Swirls, Veal-and-Smithfield Ham, '86 253
Virginia Ham with Gravy, '86 15
Wine, Country Ham in, '81 260
Creamed Ham and Chicken, '81 M74
Creamed Ham and Eggs, '82 40
Creamy Ham Medley, '84 90
Creamy Ham Towers, '79 138
Crêpes, Ham-and-Egg, '83 204
Crêpes with Mushroom Sauce, Ham-and-Egg, '82 46
Croquettes, Ham, '82 119
Cured Ham and Biscuits, '85 320
Curried Ham and Peaches, '82 60
Curried Ham Steak, '82 120
Curried Ham with Rice, '80 111
Delight, Ham-Asparagus, '86 48
Deviled Delight, '83 130
Deviled Ham Twists, '82 86
Devils, Ham, '93 88
Dinner, Corn-and-Ham Skillet, '83 190
Dinner, Ham-Asparagus, '80 M10
Dinner, Ham Skillet, '85 179
Dip, Creamy Ham, '93 125
Eggplant, Ham-Stuffed, '80 162
Eggs à la Swiss, Ham and, '88 158
Eggs, Creamy Ham and, '87 286
Eggs on Toast with Cheese Sauce, Ham and, '81 43
Eggs, Savory Ham and, '82 231
Fettuccine, Ham-and-Asparagus, '94 84
Flips, Ham-and-Cheese, '92 46
Fritters, Ham, '82 39
Fritters with Creamy Sauce, Ham, '81 105
Frosted Ham, '89 71
Fruited Ham Slice, '83 M317
Glazed Ham, Cranberry, '81 274
Glazed Ham, Cranberry-Orange, '81 295
Glazed Ham, Currant-, '91 249
Glazed Ham, Honey-Orange, '83 320
Glazed Ham, Marmalade-, '89 M196
Glazed Ham, Orange-, '89 324
Glazed Ham Slice, Apricot-, '93 252
Glazed Ham Slice, Honey-, '81 104

Glazed Ham, Strawberry-, '91 84
Glazed Ham, Sweet-and-Sour, '88 M15
Glazed Ham, Sweet-Sour, '83 311
Griddle Cakes, Ham, '89 255
Grilled Ham, Easy, '92 134
Grilled Ham, Golden, '79 90
Grilled Ham, Hickory-, '92 81
Grits, Garlicky Ham-and-Spinach, '94 177
Gumbo, Chicken-Ham-Seafood, '81 6
Gumbo, Combo, '81 198
Gumbo, Ham and Seafood, '81 199
Hideaways, Ham, '81 29
Hopping John with Ham, '81 7
Hot Rods, Ham, '86 136
Jambalaya, Creole, '87 210
Jambalaya de Covington, '87 211
Kabobs, Honey Ham, '80 156
Kabobs, Swiss-Ham, '81 124
Loaf, Cranberry-Ham, '82 M77
Loaf, Glazed Ham, '79 187; '90 212
Loaf, Ham, '79 180; '80 272
Loaf, Hawaiian Ham, '79 71
Loaf, Pineapple Upside-Down Ham, '79 253
Loaf, Saucy Ham, '86 M328
Loaf, Spicy Ham, '80 110
Loaf, Supreme Ham, '79 242
Loaf, Upside-Down Ham, '82 40
Loaves, Ham, '90 235
Medley, Creamy Ham-and-Chicken, '92 272
Muffins, Ham-and-Cheese, '92 252; '93 144
Muffuletta, Doodles, '94 35
Noodles, Ham and Swiss on, '87 108
Omelet, Ham and Cheese, '79 262; '80 123
Omelet, Rolled, '89 228
Omelet, Sour Cream-Ham, '79 261
Omelets with Creole Sauce, '89 228
Pain-Perdu Po-Boy, '93 291
Pâté, Ham, '85 279
Patties, Ham, '81 99
Patties, Ham-Sprout, '85 51
Patties, Pineapple-Ham, '80 110
Patties, Spicy Ham, '90 235
Peas and Ham, Southern, '85 138
Peas with Ham Hocks, Black-Eyed, '79 122
Peppers, Ham-and-Corn Stuffed, '81 87
Peppers, Ham-Stuffed Green, '80 65
Peppers with Rice and Ham, Stuffed, '82 131
Pie, Crustless Grits-and-Ham, '86 103
Pie, Golden Ham, '87 78
Pie, Ham Pot, '90 25
Pie, Spaghetti-Ham, '93 19
Pie with Cheese Crust, Ham, '80 286
Pie, Zucchini-Ham-Cheese, '80 272
Pilaf Mold, Ham, '86 222
Pineapple-Flavored Ham, '87 160
Pinwheels, Ham, '90 235
Pita Pockets, Ham-and-Cheese, '90 271
Pita, Stuffed, '89 87
Pizza, Ham-and-Eggs Crescent, '93 47
Pocket, Ham and Swiss in the, '83 31
Potatoes, Ham Stuffed, '79 210
Potatoes, Ham-Stuffed New, '88 211
Potatoes, Jalapeño-Ham Stuffed, '81 M61
Potatoes with Ham Bits, Creamy, '87 191
Praline Ham, '85 302
Prosciutto, Party Pasta with, '94 176
Prosciutto, Pizza with Artichoke and, '87 182
Prosciutto Salad, Melon-and-, '92 191
Prosciutto-Wrapped Asparagus, '91 98
Puffs, Ham-and-Cheese, '86 277
Puffs, Ham-Filled Party, '84 116

Ham *(continued)*

Quiche, Cheesy Ham, '79 127
Quiche, Cheesy Jalapeño, '84 31
Quiche, Crustless Ham, '84 235
Quiche, Ham, '80 110
Quiche, Ham-and-Grits Crustless, '94 89
Quiche, Ham-and-Mushroom, '81 11
Quiche, Ham-and-Vegetable, '84 326
Quiche, Ham-Cheese, '79 26
Raisin Ham, '80 124
Raisin Sauce, Ham with, '82 M76
Red-Eye Gravy, Ham and, '88 221
Rice, Savannah Red, '80 119
Rice Toss, Ham-, '82 40
Ring, Chili-Sauced Ham, '81 M122
Ring, Ham, '84 91
Roast, Peachy Ham, '86 118
Roll, Ham-and-Cheese, '79 234
Rolls à la Swiss, Chicken-and-Ham, '92 42
Rolls, Asparagus Ham, '91 117
Rolls, Ham, '79 153
Rolls, Ham-and-Broccoli, '86 212; '87 82
Rolls, Ham-and-Cheese, '82 3
Rolls, Ham-and-Cheese Lettuce, '89 217
Rolls, Ham-Asparagus, '79 41
Rolls, Hearty Salad, '81 206
Rolls, Rice-Stuffed Ham, '83 190
Rolls, Spinach-Ham, '88 78
Rollups, Almond-Ham, '89 284
Roll-Ups, Ham and Spinach, '81 143
Rollups, Ham-and-Swiss, '85 113
Rollups, Spinach-and-Ham, '86 84
Salad Boats, '80 93
Salad, Colorful Ham-and-Rice, '90 319
Salad, Congealed Ham, '81 36
Salad, Crunchy Baked Ham, '83 23
Salad, Fruited Ham, '81 36, 146
Salad, Ham-and-Apple, '88 139
Salad, Ham-and-Cheese, '88 138
Salad, Ham-and-Egg Potato, '86 84
Salad, Ham and Macaroni, '79 220
Salad, Ham-and-Pasta, '90 128
Salad, Ham and Potato, '80 272
Salad, Ham-Dijon Pasta, '92 191
Salad, Ham 'n Egg, '81 36
Salad, Ham-Noodle, '85 249
Salad, Ham-Pecan-Blue Cheese Pasta, '90 62
Salad, Hawaiian Ham-Sweet Potato, '82 232
Salad, Hearty Ham, '82 40
Salad, Macaroni-Ham, '85 218
Salad, Mandarin Ham-and-Rice, '87 145
Salad, Spicy Italian Ham, '85 74
Salad, Tropical Ham, '89 175
Salad with Ham, Pasta, '92 108
Sandwiches, Asparagus-and-Ham Melt, '88 M96
Sandwiches, Baked Ham, '81 29
Sandwiches, Cheshire Claret Cheese-and-Ham Striped Tea, '94 16
Sandwiches, Creamy Blue Cheese-Ham, '87 279
Sandwiches, Croissant, '89 161
Sandwiches, Denver Pita, '86 M12
Sandwiches, Double-Decker Club, '91 231; '92 68
Sandwiches, Ham-and-Cheese Pita, '87 202; '88 44
Sandwiches, Hot Ham, '79 214
Sandwiches, Hot Ham-and-Cheese, '85 299

Sandwiches, Meal-in-One, '80 218
Sandwiches, Monte Cristo, '83 134
Sandwiches, Open-Faced, '79 214
Sandwiches, Open-Face Ham, '82 40; '85 8
Sandwiches, Tangy Ham-and-Swiss, '85 164
Sandwiches, Virginia Ham, '80 155
Sandwiches, Yummy, '81 229
Sandwich Loaf, Pineapple-Ham, '91 167
Sandwich Round, Ham-and-Cheese, '94 326
Sandwich, Tangy Ham Salad, '80 272
Sandwich, Tex-Mex Ham-and-Cheese, '86 4
Sauce, Steak with Ham-and-Mushroom, '83 109
Sebastian, The, '94 184
Skillet Ham-and-Vegetables, '84 90
Skillet, Ham-Noodle, '87 78
Skillet, Ham Spaghetti, '83 283
Slice with Cinnamon Apple Rings, Holiday Ham, '90 250
Smoked Ham, '86 92
Soufflé, Virginia Ham Breakfast, '93 121
Soufflé with Cucumber Sauce, Ham, '92 41
Soup, Chicken, Ham, and Oyster, '79 198
Soup, Ham-and-Bean, '84 4
Soup, Hearty Ham, '82 4
Soup, Spicy Ham-and-Bean, '94 322
Spread, Cold Ham, '82 248
Spread, Deviled Ham, '79 81
Spread, Ham, '86 126
Spread, Ham-and-Egg, '79 59
Spread, Ham and Pimiento, '80 285; '81 56
Spread, Ham Salad, '87 92
Spread, Hawaiian Ham, '87 106
Spread, Horseradish-Ham, '91 167
Squash, Ham-Stuffed Acorn, '81 239; '83 66
Steak, Glazed Ham, '91 13
Stew, Blakely Brunswick, '87 4
Stew, Ham-and-Black-Eyed Pea, '93 20
Stir-Fry, Easy Ham, '86 332
Stir-Fry, Ham and Zucchini, '79 47
Strata, Ham and Broccoli, '80 261
Stroganoff, Ham, '82 40
Stromboli, '88 272; '89 181
Stuffed Ham, '86 323
Superburgers, '79 89
Supper, Top-of-Stove, '86 332
Tapas, Garlic-Ham, '92 175
Tart, Ham-and-Cheese, '92 332
Tart Milan, '87 70
Tart, Supreme Ham, '84 22
Tetrazzini, Ham, '82 M77; '84 241
Turnip Greens and Ham Hock, Southern, '80 119
Turnovers, Chile-Ham, '88 64
Turnovers, Party Ham, '82 39
Véronique, Ham, '85 90
Waffles, Ham, '80 44
Zucchini, Ham and Cheese Stuffed, '79 157

Hearts of Palm
Chicken Rolls, Hearts of Palm, '89 201
Marinated Asparagus and Hearts of Palm, '90 91
Salad, Different Vegetable, '82 143
Salad, Hearts of Palm, '81 252; '89 276
Salad, Hearts-of-Palm, '87 138
Salad with Basil-and-Garlic Dressing, Hearts of Palm, '94 55
Sandwich, Hearts of Palm, '92 191
Spread, Hearts of Palm, '90 293

Hominy
Bacon, Eggs, and Hominy, '85 143
Bake, Chili Hominy, '81 282; '82 58
Bake, Hominy-Sausage, '88 51
Casserole, Cheesy Hominy, '83 170
Casserole, Chile-Hominy, '81 29
Casserole, Hominy-Chili, '86 255
Caviar, Texas, '86 218
Cheese Hominy, Hot, '84 77
Chiles and Cheese, Hominy with, '86 78
Gold Coast Hominy, '83 52
Jalapeño Hominy, '82 51
Mexican Hominy, '86 255; '91 133, 162
Salad, Hominy-Bean, '88 266
Skillet, Hominy-Sausage, '81 29
Soup, Southwest, '86 255

Honey
Ambrosia, Honey Bee, '83 267
Apple Quarters, Honey-Baked, '86 93
Apples, Honey-Baked, '83 234; '84 244
Apples, Honey-Yogurt, '92 46
Bananas, Honey-Baked, '81 268
Bread, Applesauce-Honey Nut, '87 300
Bread, Honey-Banana, '91 68
Bread, Honey-Cinnamon Swirl, '88 287
Bread, Honey-Curry, '89 250
Bread, Honey-Granola, '86 56
Bread, Honey-Oat, '89 107; '93 232
Bread, Honey Oatmeal, '80 60
Bread, Honey Wheat, '85 18, 268
Bread, Honey-Wheat, '91 223
Bread, Whole Wheat Honey, '82 65; '83 106
Bread, Zucchini-Honey, '89 143
Brie, Honey-Mustard, '91 252
Brownies, Heavenly Honey, '79 83
Buns, Honey Oatmeal, '83 154
Butter, Cinnamon-Honey, '89 281
Butter, Honey, '93 309; '94 206
Butter, Honey-Orange, '79 36; '85 19
Cake, Honey, '92 250
Cake, Honey-Oatmeal, '87 222
Cake, Southern Honey, '89 251
Cake Squares, Honey, '89 250
Carrots, Honey-Glazed, '80 115; '84 121; '85 18
Carrots, Honey-Kissed, '84 122
Chicken, Honey, '82 55; '88 67
Chicken, Honey-Curry, '87 36
Chicken Wings, Honey-Glazed, '91 251
Cornbread, Honey, '83 286; '84 17
Crunch, Honey-and-Spice, '94 290
Dip, Coconut-Honey Fruit, '84 171
Dip, Peanut Butter-Honey, '85 19
Dressing, Celery-Honey, '80 42
Dressing, Dijon-Honey, '89 45
Dressing, Fruit Salad with Honey-Lemon, '93 21
Dressing, Honey, '79 242; '83 146; '87 129
Dressing, Honey French, '87 81
Dressing, Honey-Lime, '83 139; '93 71
Dressing, Honey-Mustard, '90 55, 111, 146
Dressing, Honey-Walnut, '93 107
Dressing, Honey-Yogurt, '93 172
Dressing, Lime-Honey, '92 213
Dressing, Lime-Honey Fruit Salad, '87 81
Dressing, Orange Salad with Honey, '89 14
Dressing, Orange Salad with Honey-Berry, '89 250
Dressing, Spinach Salad with Honey, '90 16
Dressing, Tomato-Honey French, '81 105
Filling, Honey, '88 287

Honey *(continued)*

Filling, Honey-Walnut, **'80** 21
Frosting, Honey Chocolate, **'79** 83
Glaze, Chocolate-Honey, **'82** 306
Glaze, Cranberry-Honey, **'89** 273
Glaze, Honey, **'88** 287
Glaze, Honey-Nut, **'87** 15
Ham, Honey-Orange Glazed, **'83** 320
Ham Slice, Honey-Glazed, **'81** 104
Kabobs, Honey Ham, **'80** 156
Leeks, Honey-Glazed, **'86** 62
Lemon Honey, **'94** 16
Loaves, Hint o' Honey, **'81** 104
Marinade, Garlic-Honey, **'93** 102
Marinade, Honey-Mustard, **'93** 103
Mousse, Honeyed Chocolate, **'87** 223
Muffins, Banana-Honey-Nut, **'88** 62
Muffins, Honey Bran, **'88** 171
Muffins, Honey-Bran, **'89** 250
Muffins, Honey-Oatmeal, **'84** 229
Muffins, Honey-Wheat, **'83** 96; **'88** 263
Muffins, Oatmeal-Honey, **'83** 95
Muffins, Orange-Honey, **'88** 284
Muffins, Peanut Butter-Honey, **'82** 56
Mustard, Hot Honey, **'93** 240
Onions, Honey, **'81** 86
Onions, Honey-Paprika Sweet, **'92** 52
Pancakes, Honey, **'91** 139
Peaches, Honey-Sweet, **'85** 107
Peaches 'n' Cream, Honeyed, **'93** 134
Pear Honey, **'90** 159
Pears, Honey-Baked, **'93** 47
Pears, Pineapple-Honey, **'86** 94
Pecans, Honeycomb, **'84** 300
Pecans, Sugar-and-Honey, **'86** 319
Pork Chops, Honey-Lime, **'91** 33
Preserves, Honeyed Peach, **'85** 130
Rice, Honey, **'85** 83
Rings, Honey Apple, **'80** 243
Rolls, Dilled Honey-Wheat, **'83** 254
Rolls, Honey Wheat, **'83** 278
Rolls, Super Honey, **'80** 115
Rutabaga, Honey, **'91** 220
Salad, Honey Fruit, **'80** 276
Sauce, Chicken in Honey, **'89** 82
Sauce, Cinnamon-Pecan-Honey Pancake, **'88** 46
Sauce, Honey-Butter, **'85** 18
Sauce, Honey-Chocolate, **'89** 251
Sauce, Honey-Lemon Mustard, **'84** 275
Sauce, Honey-Lime, **'82** 85
Sauce, Honey-Mustard, **'85** 13
Sauce, Honey-Orange, **'85** 108
Sauce, Honey-Poppy Seed, **'93** 13
Sauce, Honeyscotch Sundae, **'82** 167
Sauce, Honey-Yogurt, **'92** 307
Sauce, Smoked Ribs with Honey-Mustard, **'92** 168
Shrimp, Tangy Honeyed, **'94** 32
Smoothie, Fruited Honey-Yogurt, **'88** 231; **'89** 23
Smoothie, Honey-Banana, **'89** 144
Snapper, Honey-Curried, **'85** 181
Spareribs, Honey-Glazed, **'82** 163
Spread, Honey, **'81** 229
Spread, Honey-Nut, **'87** 157
Stir-Fry, Honey-Butternut, **'93** 184
Swirl, Honey-Walnut, **'80** 21
Syrup, Maple-Honey-Cinnamon, **'85** 19

Tea, Honey, **'81** 105
Topping, Honey, **'83** 154
Turkey Salad, Honey-Mustard, **'92** 309
Twist, Honey, **'79** 80
Vegetables, Honey-Mustard Marinated, **'93** 236
Vinaigrette, Honey-Mustard, **'94** 249
Vinaigrette, Honey-Orange, **'91** 255
Whip, Peaches with Honey-Lime, **'85** 108
Yogurt, Orange Slices with Honey, **'91** 68
Honeydew. *See* Melons.
Hors d'Oeuvres. *See* Appetizers.
Hot Dogs. *See* Frankfurters.

Ice Creams and Sherbets

Alaska, Apple Baked, **'80** 226
Alaska, Baked, **'84** 105; **'85** 295
Alaska, Brownie Baked, **'80** 66
Alaska, Mint Patty, **'80** 219
Alaskas, Banana Split, **'87** 10
Almond-Fudge Ice Cream, **'93** 205
Amaretto Freeze, **'82** 182
Ambrosia Cups, Sherbet, **'82** 159
Apricot Sherbet, **'81** 177; **'92** 164
Apricot Yogurt Ice, **'81** 177
Avocado Ice, **'83** 179
Avocado Sherbet, **'83** 162
Avocado Sorbet, **'88** 117
Balls, Almond Ice Cream, **'86** 315
Balls, Easy Ice Cream, **'84** 106
Balls, Nutty Ice Cream, **'89** 72
Banana-Graham Ice Cream, **'91** 56
Banana-Orange Sherbet, **'83** 162
Banana-Orange Sorbet, **'88** 117
Bananas Foster, Elegant, **'81** 59
Banana Split Ice Cream, **'80** 176
Banana Split Pie, Layered, **'83** 189
Banana Yogurt Ice Milk, **'89** 199
Berry Sorbet, Very, **'90** 85
Beverages
    Almond Float, Nutmeg-, **'84** 106
    Amaretto Breeze, **'83** 172
    Apple Juice Shrub, Shenandoah, **'79** 282
    Banana Flip, **'83** 303
    Banana-Pineapple Milk Shake, **'84** 59
    Banana Smoothie, **'87** 160
    Brandy Cream, **'84** 312
    Champagne Delight, **'83** 304
    Chocolate-Mint Smoothie, **'84** 166
    Coffee Floats, Maple-, **'86** 195
    Coffee Punch, Creamy, **'81** 50
    Coffee Refresher, Velvet, **'79** 149
    Cranberry Float, Sparkling, **'86** 195
    Cranberry-Orange Soda, **'79** 148
    Cranberry Shake, **'83** 171
    Fruit Float, Frosty, **'87** 159
    Ginger Fizz, Ice Cream, **'83** 303
    Golden Dream, **'82** 100
    Kahlúa Velvet Frosty, **'82** 244
    Lime Cooler, **'87** 160
    Lime Fizz, **'81** 172
    Lime-Pineapple Punch, **'83** 142
    Mocha Punch, **'84** 166
    Orange Milk Shake, **'84** 166
    Orange Shake, Peachy, **'81** 156
    Orange Sherbet Party Punch, **'83** 142
    Peach Frosty, **'81** 156

    Peanut Butter Milkshakes, **'85** 198
    Peanut Butter Shake, **'82** 48
    Pineapple Sherbet Float, **'79** 148
    Pineapple Soda, **'90** 179
    Pink Soda, Blushing, **'90** 104
    Punch, Double Sherbet, **'79** 232
    Punch, Parsonage, **'79** 148
    Raisin Shake, Amazin', **'86** 195
    Raspberry Fizz, Rosy, **'90** 179
    Rum Coffee Cream, Icy, **'83** 172
    Shake, Pep, **'79** 38
    Strawberry-Banana Float, **'87** 160
    Strawberry Milkshake, Fresh, **'82** 113
    Strawberry-Pineapple Shake, **'84** 166
    Strawberry Punch, Creamy, **'86** 195
    Strawberry Smoothie, **'86** 183
    Strawberry Soda, Old-Fashioned, **'79** 149
    Tahitian Flower, **'87** 159
    Vanilla Frosty, French, **'79** 148
    Whispers, **'86** 317
Black Forest Ice Cream, **'88** 203
Blueberry Ice Cream, **'88** 203
Blueberry-Kirsch Sorbet, **'83** 120
Bombe, Amber, **'80** 255
Bombe, Ice Cream, **'82** 305; **'90** 269
Bombe with Raspberry Sauce, Creamy, **'89** 322
Bourbon Ice Cream, **'87** 139
Brownie Dessert, Special-Occasion, **'87** 139
Brownies, Chocolate Ice Cream, **'89** 124
Butter Crisp Ice Cream, **'92** 132
Buttermilk Sherbet, **'84** 184
Butter Pecan Ice Cream, **'80** 176; **'86** 129; **'88** 202
Cake for Grown-Ups, Ice Cream, **'88** M192
Cake, Fruity Ice Cream, **'87** 110
Cake, Ice Cream, **'86** 321; **'89** 71
Cake, Ice Cream Angel, **'83** 23
Cake, Praline Ice Cream, **'80** 84
Candy Crunch Ice Cream, **'79** 166
Cantaloupe Ice Cream, **'79** 177
Cantaloupe Sherbet, **'88** 183
Cantaloupe Sherbet, Frosty, **'82** 144
Caramel-Vanilla Helado (Caramel-Vanilla Ice Cream), **'81** 67
Champagne Ice, **'90** 315
Cherry Ice Cream, **'84** 184
Cherry-Nut Ice Cream, **'86** 129
Cherry-Pecan Ice Cream, **'88** 203
Chocolate Chunk-Peanut Butter Ice Cream, **'85** 297; **'86** 120
Chocolate-Covered Peanut Ice Cream, **'88** 203
Chocolate Ice Cream, **'80** 176; **'86** 129
Chocolate Ice Cream, Mexican, **'91** 162
Cider Ice, **'83** 162
Cinnamon Ice Cream Sombreros, **'93** 276
Coconut Ice Cream, Fresh, **'79** 166
Coffee Ice Cream, **'88** 202
Coffee Ice Cream Crunch, **'82** 182
Coffee-Kahlúa Granita, **'88** 118
Cookies and Cream Ice Cream, **'88** 203
Cran-Apple Spice Sorbet, **'93** 153
Cranberry-Apple Ice, **'82** 290
Cranberry Ice, Tangy, **'87** 305
Cranberry Juice Sorbet, **'85** 259
Cranberry-Orange Ice, Tart, **'86** 317
Cranberry Sherbet, **'88** 280
Cranberry Sorbet, **'82** 251
Crêpes, Coffee Ice Cream, **'84** 85

Ice Creams and Sherbets (continued)

Crêpes, Strawberry Ice Cream, '87 290
Delight, Ice Cream, '80 69
Dessert, Decadent Ice Cream, '91 56
Dessert, Layered Ice Cream, '83 189;
  '84 94, 105; '86 163
Dessert, Layered Sherbet, '87 109
Dessert, Mint Ice Cream, '88 66
Double-Chocolate Ice Cream, '88 203
Fig Ice Cream, '87 139
Frangelica Cream, '89 291
Fried Ice Cream, Coconut, '85 141
Fried Ice Cream, French-, '85 141
Fried Ice Cream Puffs, '85 141
Fruit Cream, Frozen, '94 129
Fruit Ice, '86 176
Fruit Ice, Mixed, '81 178
Fruit Punch Sherbet, '86 129
Fruit Sherbet, Freezer, '86 334
Fruit Sherbet, Frozen, '79 155
Fruit Sherbet, Instant, '85 158
Fudge-Peanut Ice Cream Dessert, '88 167
Galore and More, Ice Cream, '91 144
Grapefruit Ice, '91 122
Grapefruit Ice, Pink, '85 304
Grapefruit-Mint Sorbet, '93 153
Grape Granita, '88 118
Grape Ice, '83 162
Hawaiian Frappé, '81 178
Honeydew Granita, '87 162
Italian-Style Ice Cream, '79 245
Kiwi Ice, '84 315
Lemonade Ice Cream, '88 202
Lemon Cream Sherbet, '79 114
Lemon Ice Cream, '79 142; '83 170; '91 65
Lemon Ice Cream Tarts, '80 152
Lemon Sherbet, '91 309
Lemon Sorbet, '93 153
Lime Sherbet, '82 159; '89 202
Lime Sherbet, Creamy, '84 165
Loaf, Pink Lemonade Ice Cream, '88 202
Log, Ice Cream Yule, '83 253
Macaroon-Sherbet Frozen Dessert, '79 212
Making Ice Cream, About, '82 171
Mango Ice Cream, '86 216
Mango Sorbet, '86 196
Merlot Ice, '93 323
Mexican Sherbet, '79 155
Mint-Chocolate Chip Ice Cream, '88 202
Mint-Chocolate Chip Ice Cream Squares,
  '94 245
Mint Ice-Cream Angel Dessert, Triple,
  '93 86
Mint Sherbet, Fresh, '88 23
Mocha Ice Cream, '88 202
Muscadine Ice, '82 202
Nectarine Sherbet, '89 199
Orange Granita, '88 118
Orange-Pineapple Ice Cream, '86 117
Orange Sherbet, '79 155
Orange Sherbet Salad, '81 154
Orange Sherbet with Blackberry Sauce,
  '94 232
Orange Sorbet, Fresh, '92 143
Parfaits, Chocolate-Crème de Menthe,
  '85 161
Parfaits, Coffee Crunch, '82 159
Parfait, Strawberry, '79 99
Parfait, Surprise Strawberry, '86 151

Peach-Almond Ice Cream, '89 156
Peach Ice, '81 178
Peach Ice Cream, '81 184; '82 171; '83 159;
  '86 15; '93 135
Peach Ice Cream, Creamy, '85 177
Peach Ice Cream, Deluxe, '80 176; '90 314
Peach Sherbet, '90 179
Peach Sorbet, '93 153
Peach-Yogurt Ice, '84 83
Peanut Butter Ice Cream, '81 103;
  '88 64, 203
Peanut Ice Cream, '92 132
Pear-Lemon Sorbet, '88 116
Peppermint Ice Cream, '80 176; '86 129
Pie, Absolutely Divine Ice Cream, '82 181
Pie, Caramel Ice Cream, '82 181
Pie, Carrot Ice Cream, '86 200
Pie, Chocolate-Ice Cream, '87 224
Pie, Chocolate Ice Cream, '91 56
Pie, Chocolate-Mint Ice Cream, '81 144
Pie, Coffee Ice Cream, '79 231
Pie, Double-Delight Ice Cream, '89 72
Pie, Heavenly Ice Cream, '82 181
Pie, Ice Cream Sundae, '94 244
Pie, Kona Ice Cream, '83 189
Pie, Lemon Ice Cream, '80 70
Pie, Nutty Ice Cream, '91 180
Pie, Peanutty Ice Cream, '82 56
Pie, Peppermint Candy-Ice Cream, '87 260
Pie, Pumpkin Ice Cream, '81 272
Pie, Pumpkin-Ice Cream, '87 243
Pie Spectacular, Ice-Cream, '90 314
Pie with Meringue-Pecan Crust, Ice Cream,
  '88 127
Pie with Rum-Fruit Sauce, Ice Cream,
  '84 312
Piña Colada Ice Cream, '91 181
Pineapple-Mint Ice Cream, '84 186
Pineapple Sherbet, '81 177; '84 83; '89 199
Pineapple Sherbet, Creamy, '79 155
Pineapple Sherbet, Easy, '92 199
Praline Freeze, '90 48
Praline Ice Cream, '89 318
Pralines and Cream Ice Cream, '82 184;
  '83 159
Rainbow Candy Ice Cream, '88 202
Raspberry Ice, '92 268
Raspberry Ice Cream, '80 176
Raspberry Ice Cream, Fresh, '86 152
Raspberry Liqueur Granita, '88 117
Raspberry Sherbet, '83 162
Roll, Chocolate-Frosted Ice Cream, '84 200
Roll, Strawberry Ice Cream, '84 105
Salad, Ice Cream, '79 126
Sandwiches, Chocolate Cookie Ice Cream,
  '87 147
Sandwiches, Chocolate Ice Cream, '89 72
Sandwiches, Oatmeal Crispy Ice Cream,
  '93 199
Sandwiches, Peanut Butter Cookie Ice
  Cream, '93 199
Sandwich Shells, Brownie Ice Cream, '88 195
Scuppernong Ice Cream, '88 216
Snow Ice Cream, '88 10
Squares, Ice Cream Party, '91 214
Straw-Ba-Nut Ice Cream, '80 177
Strawberries and Cream, '92 132
Strawberry-Banana-Nut Ice Cream, '88 203
Strawberry-Champagne Sorbet, '83 162
Strawberry Ice, '84 175; '85 108
Strawberry Ice Cream, '80 177

Strawberry Ice Cream Crêpes, '88 135
Strawberry Ice Cream, Fresh, '89 111
Strawberry Ice Cream, Homemade, '84 184
Strawberry Ice Cream, Old-Fashioned,
  '79 94
Strawberry Ice Cream, Very, '81 155
Strawberry Ice Milk, Fresh, '92 94
Strawberry Margarita Sorbet, '89 111
Strawberry-Orange Ice, '86 196
Strawberry Sherbet, '82 112, 160
Strawberry Sorbet, '88 117; '93 153
Sundae Dessert, Hot Fudge, '84 313
Sundaes, Cocoa-Kahlúa, '83 M58
Sundaes Flambé, Peach, '81 88
Sundaes, Hot Strawberry, '81 M5
Sundaes, Mauna Loa, '80 126
Sundaes, Quick Pear, '86 71
Sundaes, Spicy Apple Ice Cream,
  '86 M195
Tea Granita, Mint, '88 117
Toffee Ice Cream, '88 202
Toffee Ice Cream Dessert, '87 110
Treats, Crunchy Ice Cream, '86 300;
  '87 178
Tropical Paradise, Frozen, '89 206
Tutti-Frutti Ice Cream, '86 129
Vanilla Custard Ice Cream, '92 148
Vanilla Ice Cream, '80 176; '86 129;
  '91 174
Vanilla Ice Cream, Basic, '88 202
Vanilla Ice Cream, Country, '82 143
Vanilla Ice Cream Spectacular, '82 166
Watermelon Ice, '91 173
Watermelon Sherbet, '79 155; '92 124
Watermelon Sherbet, Light, '81 147
Watermelon Sorbet, '92 190
Wine Ice, '83 163
Icings. *See* Frostings, Fillings, and Toppings.

Jams and Jellies
Apple-Cranberry Conserve, '82 308
Apple Jelly, '82 149
Apple Marmalade, '79 120
Apple-Mint Jelly, '87 134
Apricot Jam, Golden, '80 31
Banana Jam, '82 296
Basil Jelly, '82 301
Berry Refrigerator Jam, '89 139
Blackberry Jam, '82 149; '89 138
Blackberry Jam, Freezer, '84 M181
Blackberry Jelly, '82 149
Blueberry Conserve, '82 149
Blueberry Jam, '79 120; '85 130
Blueberry Refrigerator Jam, '89 139
Carrot-Citrus Marmalade, '81 148
Champagne Jelly, '90 248
Chile Piquín Jelly, '94 28
Christmas Brunch Jam, '81 286
Christmas Jam, '88 288
Citrus Marmalade, '80 101
Citrus Marmalade, Combination, '80 50
Citrus Marmalade, Mixed, '81 43
Crabapple Jelly, '79 120; '81 217; '89 139
Cranberry Conserve, '79 243; '85 266
Cranberry-Wine Jelly, '81 290
Di-Calcium Phosphate Solution, '89 138
Fig Jam, '86 206
Fig Preserves, '79 140; '82 150; '89 140
Freezer Jelly, Christmas, '86 M288

Jams and Jellies (continued)

Fruit Conserve, Dried, '82 308
Fruit Marmalade, Delicious, '81 285
Grape-Burgundy Freezer Jelly, '85 130
Grapefruit Marmalade, '82 308
Grape Jelly, '89 140
Grape Jelly, Quick, '89 M156
Grape Jelly, Thyme-, '89 193
Green Tomato Jam, '79 121
Jalapeño Jelly, '92 230
Kumquat Marmalade, '90 48
Lime Jelly, '94 23
Mango-Pineapple Preserves, '79 137
Mint Jelly, '79 121; '82 301
Muscadine Jelly, Wild, '79 32
Onion Jelly, '93 135
Orange Marmalade, '81 42
Orange-Pineapple Marmalade, '82 150;
    '89 M156
Peach-Banana Jam, Rosy, '80 142
Peach Conserve, '79 120
Peach Jam, '93 135
Peach Jam, Freezer, '83 182; '84 M182
Peach-Orange Marmalade, '82 150
Peach-Plum Freezer Jam, '85 130
Peach Preserves, '81 147; '89 140
Peach Preserves, Honeyed, '85 130
Peach Preserves, Old-Fashioned,
    '82 150
Pear Jam, Paradise, '84 300
Pear Marmalade, '79 196
Pear Preserves, '82 195
Pepper Jelly, '79 121
Pepper Jelly, Unusual Green, '82 132
Pineapple Jam, '81 147
Pineapple-Orange Mint Jelly, '92 105
Plum Jam, Freezer, '89 M156
Plum Jelly, '82 150
Plum Refrigerator Jam, '89 139
Port Wine Jelly with Whipped Cream,
    '84 254
Raspberry Freezer Jam, '84 M181
Red Pepper Jelly, '89 M156
Rose Geranium Jelly, '82 301
Rosemary Jelly, '82 301
Sage Jelly, '82 301
Sangría Jelly, '93 341
Strawberry Freezer Jam, '84 M182
Strawberry Jam, '89 138
Strawberry Jelly, '81 147
Strawberry-Pineapple Marmalade,
    '85 130
Strawberry Preserves, '79 120; '81 96
Strawberry Preserves Deluxe, '82 150
Strawberry Preserves, Freezer, '82 112
Thyme Jelly, '82 301
Watermelon Preserves, '79 120
Wine Jelly, '88 243
Wine Jelly, Rosy, '85 306

Jicama
Compote, Jicama-Fruit, '92 49
Fried Jicama, French-, '81 88
Parsleyed Jicama, '81 88
Salad, Jicama, '87 123
Salad, Jicama-and-Orange, '88 246
Salad, Jicama-Fruit, '86 83
Salad, Jicama-Orange, '86 83; '90 122
Tomatillo Soup with Crunchy Jicama,
    '92 245

Kabobs
Antipasto Kabobs, '94 144
Beef-and-Vegetable Kabobs, '91 148
Beef Kabobs, '85 110
Beef Kabobs, Chile-, '94 251
Beef Kabobs Deluxe, '82 182
Beef Kabobs, Marinated, '82 105; '85 159
Beef Kabobs, Pineapple-, '83 212
Beef Kabobs, Saucy, '83 109
Beef Kabobs, Spirited, '87 142
Beef Kabobs, Teriyaki, '80 207
Beef Kabobs with Rice, Marinated, '84 32
Beef Kabobs with Vegetables, '90 148
Cantaloupe Wedges, Grilled, '87 162
Cheese Kabobs, Peppered, '91 279
Chicken-Avocado Kabobs, '82 9; '83 68
Chicken, Garlic-Grilled, '87 180
Chicken Kabobs, '87 141
Chicken Kabobs, Good-and-Easy, '85 87
Chicken Kabobs, Marinated, '84 M144
Chicken Kabobs, Pineapple-, '86 M328
Chicken Kabobs, Sesame, '82 165
Chicken Kabobs, Soy-, '86 156
Chicken Kabobs Supreme, '81 124
Chicken Livers en Brochette, '84 222
Duck Kabobs with Almond Rice, Grilled,
    '91 291
Fruit Kabobs, '86 181; '89 85
Fruit Kabobs, Winter, '89 34
Fruit Kabobs with Coconut Dressing, '87 251
Fruit Kabobs with Mint Marinade, '82 157
Fruity Mermaid Kabobs, '91 177
Ham Kabobs, Honey, '80 156
Ham Kabobs, Swiss-, '81 124
Hawaiian Kabobs, '85 157
Hot-and-Spicy Kabobs, '87 193
Lamb Kabobs, '85 159; '86 90; '92 129
Lamb Kabobs, Rosemary Marinated, '93 203
Lamb Kabobs, Saucy, '89 167
Lamb Kabobs, Savory, '80 184
Lamb Shish Kabobs, '79 142; '93 70
Liver Kabobs, '80 185
Oysters Brochette, '80 56
Pepper Kabobs, Pretty, '90 166
Pork Kabobs, Spicy, '82 182
Rumaki Kabobs, '82 182
Salmon Kabobs, '81 182
Scallop-Bacon Kabobs, '81 111
Scallop Kabobs, Grilled, '83 101
Scallop Kabobs, Sea, '82 162
Scallops en Brochette with Vegetables,
    '80 163
Seafood Brochette, '87 96
Shish Kabobs, '82 182; '85 M112
Shish Kabobs, Overnight, '81 124
Shish Kabobs Teriyaki, '85 37
Shrimp-and-Scallop Kabobs, Grilled,
    '92 210
Shrimp, Barbecued, '90 28
Shrimp, Grilled Marinated, '87 173
Shrimp Kabobs, '80 150, 184
Shrimp Kabobs, Appetizer, '91 251
Shrimp Kabobs, Marinated, '84 276;
    '85 158
Shrimp, Marinated and Grilled, '87 141
Sirloin Kabobs, Marinated, '82 162
Steak-and-Shrimp Kabobs, '80 184
Steak Kabobs, '82 4; '93 95
Steak Kabobs, Barbecued, '79 89
Steak Kabobs, Marinated, '80 184

Steak on a Stick, '83 109
Steak with Vegetables, Skewered, '81 124
Turkey-and-Fruit Kabobs, '88 140
Vegetable Kabobs, Fresh, '81 158; '92 101
Vegetable Kabobs, Grilled, '93 170
Vegetable Kabobs, Marinated, '83 M195
Vegetable Kabobs, Tangy Marinated, '88 142
Vegetable Skewers, Grilled, '94 160
Venison Kabobs, '82 215; '88 249
Watermelon, Sherried, '92 117

Kiwifruit
Chutney, Kiwifruit-Onion, '93 125
Dessert, Kiwi-and-Orange, '93 295
Glacé, Sabayon, '89 306
Ice, Kiwi, '84 315
Jubilee, Kiwi, '83 120
Meringue Cups, Kiwi and Cream in,
    '81 279
Muffins, Kiwifruit, '87 255
Orange Roughy, Kiwi, '87 193
Parfait, Kiwi, '86 199; '87 55
Pizza, Kiwi-Berry, '86 198; '87 55
Pizza, Kiwifruit, '89 306
Salad, Peach-and-Kiwi, '90 180
Salad, Spinach-Kiwifruit, '87 305
Salsa, Hot Kiwifruit, '94 82
Tart, Kiwifruit, '89 232
Tart, Kiwifruit-Peach, '88 20

Lamb
Barbecued Lamb, '79 58
Burgers, Mesquite-Grilled Lamb, '88 59
Burgoo, Five-Meat, '87 3
Casserole, Moussaka, '79 179
Chops, Barbecued Lamb, '79 89
Chops, Broiled Lamb, '85 22
Chops Dijonaise, Gourmet Lamb, '82 93
Chops, Dijon Lamb, '84 277
Chops, Grilled Lamb, '91 163
Chops, Orange Lamb, '83 35
Chops, Peppercorn-Crusted Lamb,
    '92 142
Chops Teriyaki, Lamb, '85 109
Chops, Teriyaki Lamb, '87 60
Chops with Herbs, Lamb, '90 164
Chops with Shrimp, Lamb, '88 58
Curried Lamb with Rice, '82 93
Curried Lamb with Rice Mold, '85 36
Curry with Rice, Lamb, '80 83; '81 10
Fillets of Lamb with Vegetables, '85 36
Glazed Lamb, Honey-Mustard, '90 52
Grape Leaves, Stuffed, '94 48
Hawaii, Lamb, '81 58
Kabobs, Lamb, '85 159; '86 90; '92 129
Kabobs, Lamb Shish, '79 142; '93 70
Kabobs, Overnight Shish, '81 124
Kabobs, Rosemary Marinated Lamb, '93 203
Kabobs, Saucy Lamb, '89 167
Kabobs, Savory Lamb, '80 184
Kabobs, Shish, '82 182; '85 M112
Kabobs Teriyaki, Shish, '85 37
Leg of Lamb, '86 90
Leg of Lamb, Cranberry, '90 52
Leg of Lamb, Glazed, '86 90
Leg of Lamb, Greek-Style, '93 170
Leg of Lamb, Half of, '86 90
Leg of Lamb, Roast, '87 96
Leg of Lamb, Stuffed, '82 93; '87 248
Leg of Lamb with Mustard Sauce, '89 71

Lamb (continued)

Meatballs with Yogurt Sauce, Lamb, '85 132
Meat Loaf, Minted Lamb, '93 248
Moussaka, '87 166
Pie, Lamb, '90 26
Pilaf, Hearty Lamb, '83 101
Pockets with Dilled Cucumber Topping, Lamb, '87 104
Quenelles, Veal-Vermicelli Soup with, '94 14
Rack of Lamb, '89 270
Rack of Lamb, Marinated, '94 55
Rack of Lamb with Herb Mustard Glaze, '81 260
Roasted Lamb Rosemary, '88 244
Roasted Rosemary Lamb, '86 89
Roast, Garlic-Rolled Lamb, '92 128; '93 113
Roast of Lamb, Crown, '81 58
Salad, Spinach-Lamb, '85 58
Shanks, Barbecued Lamb, '92 128; '93 113
Shanks Milanaise, Lamb, '82 93
Steak, Destin Lamb, '92 129; '93 113
Steaks with Béarnaise Sauce, Lamb, '85 37
Stewed Lamb with Five Spices, '92 72
Stew-in-a-Loaf, Lamb, '85 37
Stew, Lamb, '79 293; '88 58
Stew with Popovers, Lamb, '94 43
Stir-Fry, Indian, '92 126

Lasagna

Beefy Lasagna, '80 81
Bun, Lasagna in a, '90 176
Cheesy Lasagna, '82 224; '88 299
Chicken Lasagna, '87 M302; '88 90; '92 197; '93 25
Crawfish Lasagna, '91 89
Easy Lasagna, '92 M197; '93 M24
Florentine, Creamy Lasagna, '91 94
Florentine, Lasagna, '88 196
Garden Lasagna, '83 119
Lasagna, '82 119; '83 M6
Lean Lasagna, '86 37
Maria, Lasagna, '90 191
Mexican Lasagna, '89 63
Noodles Lasagna, Lots of, '91 M127
One-Step Lasagna, '89 M129
Pizza, Lasagna, '85 285
Quick Lasagna, '84 220
Quick 'n Easy Lasagna, '80 M10
Rolls, Pepper-Topped Lasagna, '89 M36
Sausage Lasagna, '83 288
Sausage-Lasagna Rollups, '80 236
Sausage Pinwheels, Lasagna, '79 6
Simple Lasagna, '81 188
South-of-the-Border Lasagna, '84 31
Spaghetti Squash Lasagna, '84 127
Spinach-Bean Lasagna, '92 96
Spinach Lasagna, '79 25; '81 243
Spinach Lasagna, Cheesy, '80 32; '83 204
Supreme, Lasagna, '92 198; '93 24
Tofu Lasagna, '83 312
Tuna Lasagna, '83 44; '84 123
Turkey Lasagna, '83 239; '91 130
Two, Lasagna for, '81 91
Vegetable Lasagna, '84 201; '93 320
Vegetable Lasagna Casserole, '92 198; '93 25
Vegetable Lasagna, Cheesy, '79 84
Vegetable Lasagna, Colorful, '87 19

Vintage Lasagna, '79 194
Zesty Lasagna, '87 M188
Zucchini Lasagna, '85 194

Leeks

Bisque, Crab-and-Leek, '94 104
Dilled Lemon-Butter, Leeks in, '90 M98
Dilly Leek Combo, '82 26
Dip, Creamy Leek, '86 77
Glazed Leeks, '82 26
Glazed Leeks, Honey-, '86 62
Medley, Carrot-and-Leek, '88 102
Orange Sauce, Leeks in, '88 86
Quiche, Cheddar-Leek, '88 198
Roasted Potatoes, Carrots, and Leeks, '94 276
Soup, Carrot-Leek, '86 34
Soup, Leek-and-Potato, '84 112
Soup, Leek-Vegetable, '86 304
Soup, Watercress-and-Leek, '86 161
Tarragon Leeks, '84 66
Terrine, Cold Chicken-Leek, '92 145

Lemon

Apples, Chilled Poached Lemon, '86 182
Artichoke Hearts with Lemon, '90 98
Asparagus, Lemon-Sesame, '91 31
Beans, Lemon Green, '89 275
Beans, Lemon-Mint, '88 22
Beans, Lemony Green, '85 190
Beverages
    Apple Lemonade, '89 212
    Berry Delicious Lemonade, '93 205
    Buttered Lemonade, Hot, '88 208
    Claret Lemonade, '93 72
    Concentrate, Lemonade, '89 110
    Cooler, Lemon, '82 48
    Cranberry Lemonade, Spiced, '87 292
    Frappé, Lemon, '92 44
    Fresh Squeezed Lemonade, '81 172
    Front Porch Lemonade, '90 156
    Hot Buttered Lemonade, '94 18
    Margaritas, Lemon-Lime, '94 227
    Mist, Orange-Lemon, '79 288; '80 35
    Orange-Mint Lemonade, '88 82
    Pineapple Lemonade, '93 194
    Punch, Lemon Balm, '80 42
    Punch, Lemon Champagne, '94 176
    Punch, Sparkling Lemonade, '88 276
    Punch, Strawberry-Lemonade, '85 116
    Sipper, Sunshine, '86 179
    Slush, Pink Lemonade, '80 151
    Strawberry Lemonade, '80 160
    Syrup, Cherry-Lemonade, '86 214
    Tea, Almond-Lemonade, '86 229
    Tea Cubes, Lemonade with Frozen, '85 161
    Tea, Lemon, '82 156
    Tea, Lemon-Mint, '85 162
    Velvet, Lemon, '90 15
Bread, Blueberry-Lemon, '85 190
Bread, Lemon, '79 275; '87 256
Bread, Lemon-Nut, '79 24
Bread, Lemon-Pecan, '83 54
Bread, Lemon Tea, '92 268; '93 183
Broccoli Goldenrod, Lemon-, '84 M89
Broccoli, Lemon, '88 119
Brussels Sprouts with Celery, Lemony, '85 25
Butter, Asparagus in Lemon, '80 M123
Butter, Asparagus with Lemon, '87 M151
Butter, Shrimp in Lemon, '84 163
Cabbage, Lemon-Butter, '88 156

Canapés, Lemon-Cheese, '87 93
Carrot Bundles, Lemon-, '91 80
Carrots, Lemon, '82 300; '83 111
Carrots, Lemon-Dill Steamed, '93 180
Carrots, Lemon-Glazed, '84 16
Catfish, Lemon Barbecued, '88 271; '89 202
Cauliflower, Easy Lemon, '83 322
Cheese Patty, Lemon-Pepper, '84 117
Chicken and Vegetables, Lemon, '88 118
Chicken, Baked Lemon, '85 190
Chicken Breasts, Lemon, '89 18
Chicken Cutlets with Lemon, '85 8
Chicken, Greek Lemon, '90 65
Chicken, Grilled Yogurt-Lemon, '81 111
Chicken in Lemon and Wine, '83 281
Chicken, Lemon, '81 M138; '86 173
Chicken, Lemonade, '82 163
Chicken, Lemon Barbecued, '93 215
Chicken, Lemon-Dill, '93 19
Chicken, Lemon-Fried, '79 77
Chicken, Lemon Fried, '82 275
Chicken, Lemon-Frosted, '88 170
Chicken, Lemon-Garlic, '89 M132; '90 35
Chicken, Lemon-Herb, '85 127
Chicken, Lemon-Pepper, '89 104
Chicken, Lemon-Rosemary, '94 201
Chicken Nuggets, Lemon-, '86 337; '87 283
Chicken Piccata, Herbed, '88 28
Chicken Sauté, Lemon-Dill, '91 186
Chicken, Sweet-and-Sour Lemon, '84 93
Chicken, Sweet Lemon, '79 218
Chicken, Sweet Lemon-, '84 69
Chips, Lemon-and-Herb Bagel, '91 139
Chips, Lemon-and-Herb Wonton, '91 138
Cornish Hens, Lemon Roasted, '82 260
Corn on the Cob, Lemony, '89 200
Cream, Broccoli with Lemon, '89 245
Cream, Strawberries 'n Lemon, '85 120
Crêpes with Fruit Filling, Lemon, '82 46
Cucumbers, Lemony, '89 102
Cutlets, Lemon-Flavored, '79 105
Desserts
    Apples, Chilled Poached Lemon, '86 182
    Bars Deluxe, Lemon, '79 35
    Bars, Lemon Yogurt Wheat, '79 93
    Bars, Tangy Lemon, '86 217
    Cake, Easy Lemon, '83 24
    Cake, General Robert E. Lee Orange-Lemon, '88 92
    Cake, Glazed Lemon, '86 70
    Cake, Lemon Angel, '80 147
    Cake, Lemon-Coconut Cream, '81 179
    Cake, Lemon-Coconut Sheet, '85 117
    Cake, Lemon Gold, '83 301
    Cake, Lemon Meringue, '89 296
    Cake, Lemon-Pineapple, '86 60, 239
    Cake, Lemon-Poppy Seed, '93 154
    Cake, Lemon Pound, '82 88
    Cake, Lemon Pudding, '83 106
    Cake, Lemon-Raspberry, '91 247
    Cake, Lemon-Sour Cream Pound, '87 38
    Cake, Lemon Tea, '82 169
    Cake, Lightly Lemon Coffee, '81 14
    Cake, Luscious Lemon, '93 81
    Cake, Luscious Lemon Layer, '86 61
    Cake, Old-Fashioned Lemon Layer, '85 191
    Cake Roll, Elegant Lemon, '80 70
    Cake Roll, Lemon, '89 312
    Cake, Tart Lemon-Cheese, '88 7

Lemon, Desserts *(continued)*

Cake, Yogurt-Lemon-Nut, **'89** 169
Candied Lemon Peel, **'94** 199
Charlotte Russe, Fresh Lemon, **'80** 13
Charlotte Russe, Lemon, **'84** 192
Cheesecake, Lemon, **'86** 194; **'91** 308;
  '92 24
Cheesecake, Luscious Lemon,
  '90 M196
Cheesecake with Orange-Pineapple
  Glaze, Lemon, **'81** 60
Cookies, Lemonade, **'79** 51
Cookies, Lemon Crinkle, **'81** 287
Cookies, Lemony Cutout, **'85** 323
Cookies, Sunshine Lemon, **'86** 69
Cream Cheese Dessert, Lemon-, **'84** 95
Cream, Frozen Lemon, **'83** 118
Cream, Lemon, **'82** 237; **'91** 119
Cream, Lemon-Blueberry, **'92** 153
Cream Puffs, Lemon, **'93** 254
Cream Puffs, Strawberry-Lemon, **'87** 75
Cream, Strawberries with Lemon,
  '90 170
Cupcakes, Lemon Moist, **'82** 112;
  '83 153
Cups, Baked Lemon, **'87** 128
Curd, Fresh Fruit with Lemon, **'88** 21
Curd, Lemon, **'87** 139; **'89** 334;
  '94 315
Curd with Berries, Lemon, **'90** 102
Custard in Meringue Cups, Lemon,
  '80 295; **'81** 172
Custards, Lemon-Buttermilk, **'89** 49
Dainties, Lemon Pecan, **'80** 208
Delight, Lemon, **'82** 227
Filling, Creamy Lemon, **'80** 70
Filling, Lemon, **'81** 172; **'84** 137;
  '85 191; **'86** 235; **'87** 293; **'89** 312;
  '90 308; **'94** 122
Filling, Lemon-Apricot, **'90** 105
Filling, Lemon-Cheese, **'79** 68; **'88** 7
Filling, Lemon Cream, **'84** 23; **'87** 14
Filling, Lemon-Orange, **'81** 71
Frosting, Creamy Lemon, **'79** 93
Frosting, Lemon, **'85** 191; **'86** 217;
  '93 81
Frosting, Lemon Buttercream, **'83** 301;
  '86 61; **'91** 247
Frosting, Lemon-Butter Cream, **'85** 117
Frosting, Lemon-Coconut, **'90** 253
Frosting, Lemon-Cream Cheese,
  '81 157
Frosting, Lemony White, **'88** 7
Frosting, Orange-Lemon, **'88** 92
Fruitcake, Lemon, **'83** 258
Glaze, Lemon, **'79** 285; **'86** 194;
  '87 41; **'92** 269; **'93** 154, 183
Ice Cream, Lemon, **'79** 142; **'83** 170;
  '91 65
Ice Cream, Lemonade, **'88** 202
Layered Lemon Dessert, **'88** 134
Loaf, Lemon-Cream Tea, **'84** 50
Logs, Hazelnut-Lemon, **'84** 117
Melting Moments, **'85** 191
Meringue, Chocolate Pudding with
  Lemon, **'88** 258
Meringue Cream Cups, Lemon, **'84** 23
Mousse, Lemon Cloud, **'90** 90
Mousse, Strawberry-Lemon, **'82** 128

Mousse with Raspberry Sauce, Lemon,
  '91 96; **'92** 130
Napoleons, Blueberry-Lemon, **'94** 122
Parfaits, Strawberry-Lemon, **'84** 198
Pastry Shell, Lemon in, **'84** 137
Pears, Lemon Poached, **'82** 74
Pie, Angel, **'79** 123
Pie, Apple-Lemon Chess, **'86** 220
Pie, Best-Ever Lemon Meringue,
  '94 208
Pie, Buttermilk Lemon, **'81** 120; **'82** 23
Pie, Buttermilk-Lemon, **'88** 297
Pie, Buttermilk-Lemon Cream, **'88** 99
Pie, Deluxe Lemon Meringue, **'81** 172;
  '90 313
Pie, Frozen Lemonade, **'92** 101
Pie, Frozen Lemon Cream, **'82** 86
Pie, Lemonade, **'91** 42
Pie, Lemon-Buttermilk, **'91** 272
Pie, Lemon Cheese, **'81** 136; **'82** 146
Pie, Lemon Chess, **'79** 32; **'82** 196
Pie, Lemon-Cottage Cheese, **'79** 44
Pie, Lemon Cottage Cheese, **'81** 143
Pie, Lemon Fluff, **'92** 342; **'93** 46
Pie, Lemon Ice Cream, **'80** 70
Pie, Lemon Meringue, **'85** M112;
  '86 130
Pie, Lemon-Orange, **'85** 172
Pie, Lemon Parfait, **'94** 310
Pie, Lemon-Pecan, **'93** 251
Pie, Lemon-Sour Cream, **'82** 169
Pie, Lemon Sponge, **'83** 192
Pie, Lemon-Strawberry, **'88** 127
Pie, Lemon Twirl, **'84** 94
Pie, Lemony Cherry, **'92** 30
Pie, Slice of Lemon, **'84** 23
Pie, Tart Lemon, **'91** 275
Pie, Tart Lemon-Apple, **'80** 100
Pie, Whipped Lemon, **'79** 124
Pops, Deep Blue Sea, **'94** 143
Pudding, Layered Lemon, **'82** 128
Pudding, Lemon, **'79** 86; **'81** 99
Pudding, Lemon Cake, **'92** 96
Pudding, Lemon Fluff, **'85** 304
Pudding, Old-Fashioned Lemon Bread,
  '88 95
Roll, Snow-Capped Lemon, **'79** 68
Rolls with Raspberry Sauce, Lemon
  Angel, **'94** 294
Sauce, Lemon, **'84** 258, 306;
  '85 77, 190; **'91** 240
Sauce, Lemon Cream, **'93** 200
Sauce, Lemon Dessert, **'87** M165
Sauce, Tart Lemon, **'85** 191
Sherbet, Lemon, **'91** 309
Sherbet, Lemon Cream, **'79** 114
Solid, Lemon, **'93** 279
Sorbet, Lemon, **'93** 153
Sorbet, Pear-Lemon, **'88** 116
Soufflé, Cold Lemon-Lime, **'84** 24
Soufflé, Lemon, **'82** 170, 252; **'94** 199
Soufflés, Quick Lemon Sauce, **'88** 43
Soufflé, Tart Lemon, **'85** 82
Soufflé with Raspberry-Amaretto Sauce,
  Frozen Lemon, **'88** 130
Sponge Cups, Lemon, **'83** 10
Squares, Golden Carrot-Lemon, **'80** 40
Squares, Lemon, **'81** 197
Squares, Lemon-Pecan, **'89** 124
Squares, Lemony Cream Cheese,
  '82 159

Strawberry-Lemon Dessert, **'86** 162
Tarts, Berry Good Lemon, **'91** 119
Tarts, Dainty Lemon, **'82** 304
Tarts, Golden Lemon, **'85** 191
Tart Shells, Lemon, **'88** 195
Tarts, Lemon, **'82** 156; **'83** 79
Tarts, Lemon-Cheese, **'79** 2
Tarts, Lemon Ice Cream, **'80** 152
Tarts, Lemon-Sour Cream, **'81** 304
Tart, Strawberry-Lemon, **'89** 111
Topping, Lemon-Pineapple, **'86** 60
Torte with Raspberry Sauce, Lemon
  Meringue, **'93** 82
Trifle, Lemon-Blueberry, **'88** 210
Yogurt, Lemon-Chiffon Frozen, **'85** 54
Yummies, Lemon, **'81** 301
Zephers, Lemon, **'81** 172
Dressing, Chilled Broccoli with Lemon,
  '88 270
Dressing, Creamy Lemon, **'88** M193
Dressing, Fruit Salad with Honey-Lemon,
  '93 21
Dressing, Green Salad with Lemony French,
  '85 67
Dressing, Lemon-and-Herb, **'92** 108
Dressing, Lemon Cream, **'82** 170
Dressing, Lemon-Herb Salad, **'82** 67
Dressing, Lemon-Pepper, **'87** 55
Dressing, Lemon Salad, **'79** 8
Dressing, Lemon-Yogurt, **'93** 17
Dressing, Tomato Slices with Lemon,
  '87 167
Fillets, Lemon-Coated, **'80** 53
Flounder Thermidor, **'85** 190
Freeze, Fruity Lemon, **'82** 145
Green Beans, Lemon-Walnut, **'93** 304
Honey, Lemon, **'94** 16
Knots, Glazed Lemon, **'86** 290
Linguine with Garlic and Lemon, **'88** 91
Mackerel, Lemon-Baked, **'79** 182
Marinade, Lemon-Soy, **'91** 194
Marmalade, Citrus, **'80** 101
Mayonnaise, Lemon-Cream, **'85** 264
Mold, Cheesy Lemon, **'79** 241
Mold, Lemon-Cucumber, **'87** 90
Muffins, Blueberry-Lemon, **'79** 7
Muffins, Fresh Lemon, **'79** 161
Muffins, Lemon, **'88** 119, M275
Muffins, Lemon-Raspberry, **'92** 119
Olives, Lemon-Garlic, **'94** 118
Pork Chops, Lemon-Herb, **'84** 81; **'89** M132
Pork Chops, Lemony, **'88** 118
Pork Piccata, **'94** 57
Potatoes, Herbed Lemon Mashed, **'93** 208
Potatoes, Lemon and Nutmeg, **'80** 36
Potatoes, Lemon-Buttered New, **'84** 149;
  '90 268
Potatoes, Lemon-Herb Stuffed, **'83** 173
Potatoes, Lemon-Steamed, **'86** 177
Potatoes, Lemony New, **'82** 158
Potatoes, Oregano-and-Lemon Skillet, **'93** 54
Potato Wedges, Lemon, **'88** 21
Potato Wedges, Lemony, **'90** M61
Punch, Strawberry-Lemonade, **'91** 175
Relish, Lemony Cranberry, **'79** 243
Ribs, Lemon Baked, **'81** 166
Ribs, Lemon Grilled, **'81** 154
Rice, Lemon, **'89** 166
Roses, Lemon, **'82** 280
Salad, Cauliflower-Lemon, **'81** 23
Salad, Congealed Lemon-Tomato, **'89** 178

Lemon *(continued)*

Salad, Creamy Lemon-Asparagus, '93 116
Salad, Lemonade Fruit, '84 24
Salad, Lemon-Cheese, '85 240
Salad, Lemon-Cranberry Congealed, '87 311
Salad, Lemon-Cream, '88 250
Salad, Lemon-Onion, '85 252
Salad, Lemon-Vegetable Congealed, '85 22
Salad, Lemony Apple-Bran, '86 223
Sauce and Pecans, Broccoli with Lemon, '86 71
Sauce, Asparagus with Lemon, '86 62
Sauce, Baked Fillets in Lemon-Celery, '84 91
Sauce, Braised Chicken Breast in Lemon Cream, '94 184
Sauce, Broccoli with Lemon, '91 292; '92 256
Sauce, Brussels Sprouts in Lemon, '82 269
Sauce, Herbed Lemon Barbecue, '94 154
Sauce, Honey-Lemon Mustard, '84 275
Sauce, Hot Lemon-Herb, '91 286
Sauce, Lemon, '82 290
Sauce, Lemon-Butter, '84 252; '92 337
Sauce, Lemon-Cheese, '91 24
Sauce, Lemon Meunière, '88 222
Sauce, Lemon Parsley, '81 106
Sauce, Lemon-Parsley, '93 48
Sauce, Lemony Barbecue, '88 M177
Sauce, Lemony Cheese, '84 183
Sauce, Lemony Cucumber, '89 245
Sauce, New Potatoes with Lemon, '86 130
Sauce, Shrimp in Lemon Garlic, '83 67
Scones, Lemon-Raisin, '87 69
Shrimp, Lemon-Garlic Broiled, '82 29; '86 182
Shrimp, Luscious Lemon, '88 150
Slaw or Salad Dressing, Lemon-Yogurt, '88 54
Slices, Fluted Lemon, '82 51
Soup, Lemon-Egg Drop, '93 81
Spareribs, Lemony Sweet, '80 73
Spinach, Creamy Lemon, '82 302
Spinach with Feta, Lemon, '85 190
Spirals, French Lemon, '81 94
Sprouts, Lemon, '85 288
Steak with Brandy Sauce, Lemon-Butter, '85 78
Sugar Snap Peas with Basil and Lemon, '93 66
Turkey Picatta, '91 137
Veal, Lemon, '93 35
Veal Piccata, '92 181
Veal Piccata, Lemon, '86 118
Veal with Artichoke Hearts, Lemon, '87 219
Vegetables, Lemon, '93 83
Vermicelli, Lemon, '84 329
Vinaigrette, Lemon-Basil, '94 205
Vinegar, Lemon-Mint, '85 124
Vinegar, Raspberry-Lemon, '87 134
Vinegar, Spicy Oregano-Lemon, '85 124
Wild Rice, Pecan-Lemon, '92 211
Zucchini, Lemon-Garlic, '89 226

Lentils
Baked Lentils with Cheese, '84 113
Casserole, Lentils-and-Rice, '93 301
Pilaf, Rice-and-Lentil, '88 17
Salad, Lentils-and-Rice, '90 197
Sauce, Lentil Spaghetti, '90 198
Soup, Beefy Lentil, '87 282
Soup, Lentil, '83 292; '86 304; '91 28
Stew, Lentil-Rice, '82 232
Supper, Lentil-and-Rice, '84 202
Tacos, Lentil, '88 197
Light Cooking. *See* Living Light.
Lime
Apple Limeade, Pink, '89 46
Butter, Chicken with Lime, '84 68
Cake, Key Lime, '91 214
Candied Lime Strips, '94 137
Chicken, Grilled Lime-Jalapeño, '91 87
Cooler, Grape-Lime, '94 227
Cooler, Lime, '87 160
Cream, Lime-Rum, '93 169
Daiquiris, Freezer Lime, '79 141
Dip, Lime-Dill, '92 65
Dressing, Honey-Lime, '83 139; '93 71
Dressing, Lime, '79 2; '83 120
Dressing, Lime-Honey, '92 213
Dressing, Lime-Honey Fruit Salad, '87 81
Dressing, Lime-Parsley, '85 131
Dressing, Lime Sherbet, '80 221
Dressing, Spinach Salad with Chili-Lime, '94 63
Fizz, Frosty Lime, '90 104
Fizz, Lime, '81 172
Fuzz Buzz, '82 160
Jelly, Lime, '94 23
Loaf, Lime Layer, '85 96
Margaritas, Frosted, '84 115
Margaritas, Frosty, '83 172
Margaritas, Lemon-Lime, '94 227
Margaritas, Pitcher, '83 175
Marmalade, Citrus, '80 101
Mousse Freeze, Luscious Lime, '81 173
Mustard, Key Lime, '94 278
Parfaits, Lime, '80 153
Parfaits, Surf-and-Sand, '93 169
Pie, Key Lime, '91 42
Pie, Lime Chiffon, '86 130
Pie, Lime Fluff, '84 43
Pies, Lime Party, '92 65
Pork Chops, Honey-Lime, '91 33
Punch, Foamy Lime, '82 264
Punch, Lime, '84 58
Punch, Lime-Pineapple, '83 142
Punch, Lime Slush, '90 273
Punch, Orange-Lime, '82 160
Refresher, Lime-Mint, '82 144
Rice, Lime-Flavored, '84 175
Salad, Emerald, '81 143
Salad, Frosted Lime-Cheese, '79 286
Salad, Lime-Carrot, '92 65
Salad, Pear-Lime, '84 152
Salad, Pineapple-Lime, '84 320
Salad, Snowy Emerald, '87 311
Sauce, Chicken with Orange, Lime, and Ginger, '92 123
Sauce, Honey-Lime, '82 85
Sauce, Lime Hollandaise, '93 121
Sauce, Lime-Saffron, '94 71
Sauce, Sour Cream-Lime, '91 286
Sherbet, Creamy Lime, '84 165
Sherbet, Lime, '82 159; '89 202

Snapper with Lime, Stuffed Red, '83 246
Sopa de Lima, '79 211
Soufflé, Cold Lemon-Lime, '84 24
Soup, Lime, '88 31
Squares, Lime, '79 2
Stir-Fry, Lime-Ginger Beef, '92 65
Tart in Coconut Crust, Key Lime, '89 160
Tart, Lime-Pineapple, '88 6
Tornadoes for Grown-Ups, Texas, '94 143
Turkey Tenderloins, Lime-Buttered, '92 127
Veal, Amaretto-Lime, '93 54
Vinaigrette, Cilantro-Lime, '94 77
Whip, Lime, '89 199
Whip, Peaches with Honey-Lime, '85 108
Linguine
Carbonara, Linguine, '87 108
Chicken, Taste-of-Texas Pasta and, '92 78
Clam Linguine, Quick, '90 233
Clam Sauce, Linguine in, '81 83
Clam Sauce, Linguine with, '84 124; '88 90; '89 178
Clam Sauce with Linguine, '84 9
Garlic and Lemon, Linguine with, '88 91
Mussels Linguine, '90 M112
Pasta Verde, '84 201
Pesto and Pasta, '92 98
Red Pepper Sauce, Linguine with, '93 127
Salad, Pasta, '84 139
Seafood Linguine, '79 227
Seafood Sauce, Linguine with, '83 232
Shrimp and Linguine, Spicy, '92 34
Spinach, Linguine with, '91 30
Tomato-Cream Sauce, Linguine with, '86 158
Vegetables, Traveling Linguine with Roasted, '93 178
Whole Wheat Linguine, '84 177
Liver
Barbecued Liver, '85 219
Beef Liver Patties, '81 277
Calf's Liver with Vegetables, '85 219
Chicken Liver and Bacon Roll-Ups, '80 200; '81 57
Chicken Liver Omelet, '82 44
Chicken Liver Pâté, '79 153; '81 235; '83 108; '84 205
Chicken Livers and Potatoes, '82 218
Chicken Livers and Rice Dish, '82 218
Chicken Livers en Brochette, '84 222
Chicken Livers in Italian Sauce, '83 117
Chicken Livers in Orange Sauce, '82 218
Chicken Livers in Wine Sauce, '81 104
Chicken Livers, Party, '83 242
Chicken Livers Risotto, '82 218
Chicken Livers, Sautéed, '80 200; '81 57
Chicken Livers, Scrumptious, '84 230
Chicken Livers Stroganoff, '80 200; '81 57
Chicken Livers Supreme, '81 298
Chicken Livers with Marsala Wine Sauce, '81 76
Chicken Livers with Mushrooms, '81 133
Chicken Livers with Rice, '80 200; '81 58; '84 292
Chicken Liver Turnovers, '79 141
Creamy Liver and Noodle Dinner, '80 11
Creole Liver, '85 219; '86 108
Creole Sauce, Liver in, '87 33
Duck Liver Pâté, '79 227
French-Style Liver, '80 10
Gravy, Liver and, '80 10
Herbs, Liver with, '81 277
Italiano, Liver, '85 219

Liver *(continued)*

Kabobs, Liver, **'80** 185
Loaf, Skillet Liver, **'80** 11
Pâté, Country, **'86** 66
Pâté, Liver-Cheese, **'85** 276
Pâté with Cognac, **'86** 159
Pâté with Madeira Sauce, Liver, **'93** 323
Rumaki, **'80** M136
Rumaki Kabobs, **'82** 182
Saucy Liver, **'81** 277
Sauté, Liver, **'81** 277
Spanish-Style Liver, **'80** 11
Spread, Liver, **'89** 161
Spread, Sherried Liver, **'80** 86
Stroganoff, Liver, **'79** 54
Sweet-and-Sour Liver, **'81** 277

Living Light *(formerly On The Light Side)*
Andouille, **'92** 242
Appetizers
Ambrosia, Sherried, **'84** 324
Apple-Phyllo Rolls, **'88** 213
Artichokes, Marinated, **'87** 250
Artichokes with Herb-Mayonnaise Dip,
   '84 67
Beets, Blue Cheese-Stuffed, **'88** 211
Buzzard's Nests, **'93** 244
Carrot-Cheese Ball, **'86** 325
Cheese Tartlets, **'88** 211
Chicken-Mushroom Appetizers, **'88** 210
Chicken Wontons, **'92** 284
Chips, Bagel, **'91** 138
Chips, Baked Wonton, **'91** 138
Chips, Cinnamon-and-Sugar Bagel,
   '91 139
Chips, Cinnamon-and-Sugar Wonton,
   '91 138
Chips, Corn Tortilla, **'91** 17
Chips, Garlic Bagel, **'91** 139
Chips, Garlic Wonton, **'91** 138
Chips, Lemon-and-Herb Bagel, **'91** 139
Chips, Lemon-and-Herb Wonton,
   '91 138
Chips, Light Tortilla, **'90** 278; **'91** 257
Chips, Parmesan Cheese Bagel, **'91** 138
Chips, Parmesan Cheese Wonton,
   '91 138
Chips, Pita, **'89** 19; **'91** 138
Chips, Sweet Potato, **'91** 138
Chips, Tortilla, **'91** 137
Crudité Platter with Dip, **'84** 139
Dip, Cheese-Herb, **'89** 20
Dip, Creamy Ham, **'93** 125
Dip, Curry, **'87** 25
Dip, Deviled, **'87** 25
Dip, Dilled Garden, **'84** 324
Dip, Festive Crab, **'92** 285
Dip, Garbanzo, **'93** 94
Dip, Low-Cal Tuna, **'87** 25
Dip, Monster Mash, **'93** 244
Dip, Quick Fruit, **'90** 110
Dip, Ranch-Style, **'90** 138
Dip, Santa Fe Skinny, **'94** 137
Dip, Skinny Ranch, **'93** 96
Dip, Spinach, **'87** 25
Dip, Tofu, **'86** 109
Dip, Vegetable Garden, **'85** 215
Fruit Kabobs with Coconut Dressing,
   '87 251
Fruit with Lemon Sauce, Fresh, **'82** 290

Mix, Crunchy Snack, **'93** 94
Mix, Snack, **'89** 19
Mousse, Shrimp, **'87** 251
Mushroom-Almond Pastry Cups,
   '88 210
Mushroom Appetizers, Stuffed, **'88** 210
Mushrooms, Spinach-Stuffed, **'89** M133
Nectarine Cocktail, **'85** 107
Orange Halves, Broiled, **'85** 288
Oysters Bienville, Baked, **'90** 27
Oysters Italiano, Baked, **'89** 97
Pasta Bites, Pesto-Cheese, **'87** 251
Pâté, Black-Eyed Pea, **'93** 97
Pâté, Lentil, **'92** 285
Pâté, Mock, **'87** 251
Pears Stuffed with Cheese, **'82** 290
Peas, Crab-Stuffed Snow, **'85** 288
Pita Bread Triangles, **'88** 211
Pita Wedges, Garlic, **'93** 98
Pizzas, Pita, **'89** 19
Popcorn, Chili, **'91** 17
Popcorn Mix, Curried, **'86** 326
Popcorn with Pizzazz, **'93** 245
Potatoes, Ham-Stuffed New, **'88** 211
Potato Skin Snack, **'91** 18
Pretzels, Whole Wheat, **'89** 20
Quesadillas, Green Chile, **'90** 121
Scallop Appetizer, **'86** 155
Shrimp Dippers, **'84** 324
Spinach-Ricotta Phyllo Triangles,
   '88 212
Spread, Artichoke-Parmesan, **'92** 95
Spread, Broccamoli Curry, **'88** 55
Spread, Low-Fat Chicken, **'82** 290
Spread, Smoked Salmon, **'84** 324
Steak-and-Chestnut Appetizers,
   Marinated, **'84** 323
Tabbouleh, **'88** 211
Tomatoes, Crab-Stuffed Cherry,
   '82 289
Tomatoes, Stuffed Cherry, **'88** 212
Tortilla Snacks, Pesto, **'89** 19
Vegetable Appetizer, Tarragon, **'83** 277
Vegetable Nachos, **'91** 17
Zucchini Caviar, **'88** 212
Zucchini Pizzas, **'88** 212
Zucchini-Shrimp Appetizers, **'89** 311
Apple-Cheese Bake, **'92** 225
Apples, Baked, **'86** 40
Apple Side Dish, Dried, **'92** 226
Apples, Stuffed Baked, **'89** 217
Apples with Orange Sauce, Baked, **'84** 314
Barley, Baked, **'91** 133
Beverages
Apple Cooler, **'90** 14
Apple Julep, **'86** 103
Apricot Fruit Flip, **'91** 18
Apricot Mint Cooler, **'90** 165
Banana Coolers, **'91** 308
Banana Nog, **'82** 290
Banana Smoothie, **'93** 95
Bellini Spritzers, **'90** 110
Black Russian, Mock, **'92** 322
Bourbon Blizzard, **'92** 287
Brew, Witch's, **'93** 244
Carrot Cooler, **'89** 35
Cider, Hot Spiced, **'82** 290
Cocoa, Mocha, **'83** 318
Cranberry Cocktail, Hot, **'89** 310
Cranberry Smoothie, **'91** 307
Eggnog, **'83** 318

Eggnog with Orange and Nutmeg, Mock,
   '92 323
Fruit Beverage, Blender, **'83** 318
Fruit Refresher, **'91** 203
Fruit Shake, Frosty, **'87** 23
Fruit Smoothie, **'89** 87
Grapefruit Refresher, **'88** 85
Lemon Velvet, **'90** 15
Milkshake, Mocha, **'89** 35
Mocha, Hot, **'84** 60
Orange Juicy, **'90** 178
Orange-Pineapple Drink, **'89** 35
Orange Slush, **'82** 49
Peach Cooler, **'86** 6
Peach Frosty, **'83** 318
Peach Refresher, **'86** 103
Piña Colada, Mock, **'92** 322
Pineapple-Banana Slush, **'90** 14
Pineapple Sparkle, Spiced, **'92** 322
Pineapple-Yogurt Whirl, **'91** 132
Punch, Apple-Tea, **'85** 82
Punch, Citrus, **'93** 99
Punch, Holiday, **'87** 252
Punch, Holiday Hot Fruit, **'92** 286
Punch, Hot Apple, **'84** 324
Punch, Tart Cranberry, **'83** 318
Punch, White Grape, **'90** 15
Scarlet Sipper, **'90** 198
Shake, Strawberry-Banana, **'89** 35
Shake, Strawberry-Orange Breakfast,
   '87 186
Shake, Strawberry-Pear, **'92** 139
Strawberry Cooler, **'83** 56
Strawberry Spritzer, **'90** 14
Tea Mix, Spiced, **'86** 32
Tea Mix, Sugar-Free Spiced, **'91** 258
Tofruitti Breakfast Drink, **'88** 26
Tomato-Clam Cocktail, **'87** 252
Tomato Refresher, **'83** 318
Vegetable Cocktail, Fresh, **'82** 165
Virgin Mary, Spicy, **'92** 323
Watermelon-Berry Slush, **'90** 137
Breads
Apricot-Orange Bread, **'92** 285
Banana Bread, **'87** 72
Biscuits and Sausage Gravy, **'94** 20
Biscuits, Angel, **'90** 28
Biscuits, Cheese-Chive, **'94** 324
Biscuits, Herbed, **'93** 67
Biscuits, Light, **'89** 53
Biscuits, Oatmeal, **'89** 108
Biscuits, Orange, **'88** 85
Biscuits, Whole Wheat, **'84** 60; **'91** 222
Biscuits, Yeast, **'87** 71
Caraway Breadsticks, **'89** 239
Cinnamon-Oat Bread, **'90** 135
Cornbread, **'92** 324
Cornbread, Dieter's, **'87** 164
Cornbread, Jalapeño, **'94** 78
Cornbread, Mexican, **'93** 182
Cornbread Supreme, **'93** 67
Cornmeal Yeast Bread, **'89** 54
Corn Sticks, **'89** 54
Cranberry-Banana Bread, **'90** 294
Crouton Bread, Quick, **'90** 138
French Bread, **'89** 54
Garlic Bread, **'82** 19; **'91** 204
Herbed Bread, **'89** 34
Honey-Oat Bread, **'89** 107
Hush Puppies, Baked, **'89** 53
Muffins, All-Bran Oat Bran, **'91** 134

Muffins, Apple, '84 193
Muffins, Applesauce, '91 141
Muffins, Banana-Oat, '87 188
Muffins, Banana-Raisin, '89 218
Muffins, Blueberry, '91 140, 203
Muffins, Bran-Buttermilk, '85 7
Muffins, Cornmeal, '91 19
Muffins, Cornmeal Yeast, '92 49
Muffins, Corn-Oat, '89 108
Muffins, Freezer Bran, '91 141
Muffins, Honey Bran, '88 171
Muffins Made of Bran, '86 103
Muffins, Miniature Cranberry, '90 294
Muffins, Oat Bran, '89 106
Muffins, Oat Bran-Banana, '91 18
Muffins, Oatmeal-Bran, '91 83
Muffins, Spicy Apple-Oat, '86 45
Muffins, Spicy Cornbread, '90 59
Muffins, Yogurt, '88 55
Oat Bread, Caraway-Raisin, '86 44
Onion-Herb Bread, '90 165
Pumpkin-Pecan Bread, '87 221
Rolls, Dinner, '89 312
Rolls, Honey Wheat, '83 278
Rolls, Old-Fashioned Cinnamon, '92 226
Rolls, Parsley-Garlic, '93 319
Rolls, Vegetable Salad, '82 278
Rolls, Whole Wheat, '90 111
Rolls, Yogurt Crescent, '91 123
Sourdough Wedges, '90 199
Spoonbread, '90 200
Toast, Cottage-Topped French, '85 49
Toast, Slender French, '86 103
Toast Strips, Seasoned, '93 98
Whole Wheat Cardamom Bread, '86 223
Breakfast-in-a-Bowl, '89 87
Chorizo, '92 241
Crêpes, Basic, '86 38
Crêpes, Bran, '83 70; '86 44
Crêpes, Ham-and-Egg, '83 204
Crêpes, Light, '86 143
Crêpes, Low-Calorie, '87 77
Crêpes, Plain, '83 70
Crêpes Suzettes, Light, '83 71
Crêpes, Whole Wheat, '83 70
Croutons, Bagel, '93 192
Croutons, Cornbread, '93 192
Croutons, Garlic, '92 71
Croutons, Pita, '93 192
Crust, Whole Wheat, '94 78
Desserts
    Alaska, Orange, '83 177
    Alaska, Peachy Melba, '88 266
    Ambrosia, Baked, '83 303
    Ambrosia, Layered, '88 304
    Apple Crisp, Tart, '92 226
    Apples à l'Orange, Baked, '90 280
    Applesauce Fluff, '91 173
    Apples, Caramel-Peanut, '93 M244
    Apples, Melting, '88 19
    Bananas Foster, '88 20
    Bananas with Honey, Broiled, '84 175
    Bars, Apricot-Raisin, '87 32
    Bars, Pineapple-Orange, '82 129
    Bavarian Dessert, Light, '86 6
    Biscotti, Light, '91 310
    Blackberries and Dumplings, '86 196
    Blintzes, Cheese, '83 71

Blueberry Crisp, '84 177
Brownies, Chocolate-Kahlúa, '93 99
Brownies, Chocolate-Walnut, '89 325
Cake, Apple-Nut, '87 76
Cake, Apple Spice, '92 225
Cake, Banana-Coconut, '93 154
Cake, Black Widow Snack, '93 245
Cake, Blueberry Streusel, '92 144
Cake, Chocolate Angel Food, '87 21;
    '90 111
Cake, Chocolate-Cinnamon, '93 154
Cake, Chocolate Custard, '88 175
Cake, Chocolate Pound, '89 325
Cake, Deluxe Light Banana, '84 314
Cake, Four-Flavor Pound, '91 136
Cake, Frosted Carrot, '92 19
Cake, Heavenly Pineapple, '83 303
Cake, Lemon-Poppy Seed, '93 154
Cake, Orange-Coconut Angel Food,
    '94 294
Cake, Orange Pound, '87 221
Cake, Pound, '92 94
Cake, Pumpkin, '93 303
Cake, Red Velvet, '93 318
Cake Roll, Lemon, '89 312
Cake, Strawberry Yogurt Layer, '94 85
Cake, Warm Chocolate Pudding, '92 324
Cake with Amaretto-Almond Sauce,
    Angel Food, '90 199
Cake with Coffee Frosting, Spice Layer,
    '94 86
Cake with Custard Sauce, Chocolate
    Angel Food, '88 259
Cake with Pineapple-Orange Sauce,
    Angel, '84 14
Cake with Strawberries and Chocolate
    Glaze, White, '87 76
Cantaloupe Whip, '89 198
Cheesecake, Almost Strawberry, '86 32
Cheesecake, Black Forest, '94 21
Cheesecake, Blueberry Chiffon, '87 76
Cheesecake, Chocolate-Amaretto,
    '93 97
Cheesecake, Dieter's Apple, '86 318
Cheesecake, Lemon, '91 308
Cheesecake, Light-and-Easy, '88 55
Cherries Jubilite, '86 317
Chocolate-Bran Raisin Jumbos, '91 142
Chocolate-Cheese Cups, '91 142
Chocolate Cream Log, '94 220
Chocolate Cream Roll, '85 317
Chocolate Fondue, '91 142
Chocolate Glaze, '89 325
Chocolate-Orange Roll, '87 21
Chocolate Whip, '89 326
Chocolat, Petits Pots de, '82 272
Cobbler, Cranberry-and-Apple, '90 294
Cobbler, Fresh Cherry, '84 178
Cobbler, New-Fashioned Apple, '91 221
Cobbler, New-Fashioned Blackberry,
    '87 164
Cobbler, Peach, '84 178
Cobbler, Raspberry-Cherry, '93 230
Coffee Cake, Sour Cream, '93 154
Coffee Dessert, Light, '88 260
Compote, Baked Fruit, '84 314
Compote, Fresh Fruit, '82 272; '84 82
Compote, Jicama-Fruit, '92 49
Compote, Melon Ball, '85 157
Cookies, Almond, '91 51
Cookies, Apple-Oatmeal, '85 215

Cookies, Light Almond, '83 151
Cookies, Light Chocolate Chip, '86 46
Cookies, Oatmeal-Raisin, '87 221;
    '93 127
Cranberries Jubilee, '90 293
Cream Puffs, Strawberry-Lemon, '87 75
Crêpes, Fruit-Filled Chocolate, '89 325
Crêpes, Tropical Fruit, '87 77
Crust, Gingersnap, '90 296
Crust, Graham Cracker, '86 32; '88 55;
    '91 308
Crust, Lattice, '90 294
Custard, Baked Rice, '92 308
Custard, Baked Vanilla, '82 129
Custard, Coconut, '86 109
Custard, Light Mexican, '88 149
Custard over Fruit, Stirred, '84 83
Custard, Range-Top Amaretto, '87 77
Custard with Raspberries, Almond
    Crème, '88 174
Filling, Lemon, '89 312
Flambé, Banana-Peach, '85 316
Flan, Luscious, '90 56
Frosting, Boiled, '93 318
Frosting, Coffee, '94 86
Frosting, Orange-Cream Cheese, '92 19
Fruitcake, Classic, '91 258
Fruitcake, Jeweled, '88 260
Fruit Cup, '91 202
Fruit Dessert, Caribbean, '84 314
Fruit Dessert, Flaming, '83 302
Fruit Dessert Orange, '84 314
Fruit Dessert, Rainbow, '85 108
Fruit Dessert, Spiced, '82 50
Fruit, Gingered, '83 151
Fruit, Glazed, '85 83
Fruit Medley, Fancy, '84 82
Fruit with Lemon Curd, Fresh, '88 21
Glaze, Lemon, '93 154
Grapefruit-Berry Compote, Spicy,
    '91 19
Grapefruit Ice, '91 122
Honeydew-Berry Dessert, '83 120
Ice, Cranberry-Apple, '82 290
Ice, Kiwi, '84 315
Ice Milk, Banana Yogurt, '89 199
Ice Milk, Fresh Strawberry, '92 94
Ice, Mixed Fruit, '88 85
Ice, Peach-Yogurt, '84 83
Ice, Strawberry, '84 175; '85 108
Ice, Strawberry-Orange, '86 196
Ice, Tangy Cranberry, '87 305
Ice, Tart Cranberry-Orange, '86 317
Ice, Watermelon, '91 173
Kiwi Jubilee, '83 120
Lemon Angel Rolls with Raspberry
    Sauce, '94 294
Lemon Curd with Berries, '90 102
Lime Strips, Candied, '94 137
Lime Whip, '89 199
Melon Mélange, '84 139
Melon-Mint Julep, '86 196
Meringue Shells, Fruited, '87 32
Meringues, Peach Melba, '87 76
Mocha Sauce with Chocolate Yogurt,
    '92 243
Mousse, Coffee-Nut, '86 319
Mousse, Peach, '85 54
Mousse, Strawberry-Lemon, '82 128
Orange-Mallow Cream, '94 295
Orange Molded Dessert, '83 302

Living Light, Desserts (continued)

Oranges and Pineapple, Glazed, '86 318
Parfait, Peach, '82 166
Parfait, Pineapple, '84 83
Pastry, Light, '92 95
Peach-Blueberry Dessert, '92 184
Peach Dessert, Spiced, '83 9
Peaches with Honey-Lime Whip, '85 108
Peaches with Nutty Dumplings, Spiced, '87 164
Peaches with Strawberry Sauce, '85 8
Peach Halves, Stuffed, '86 196
Pear Fans with Raspberry-Orange Sauce, Poached, '88 22
Pears in Custard, Poached, '88 20
Pears in Orange Sauce, Poached, '82 19
Pears Poached in Red Wine, '83 302
Pears, Vanilla Poached, '90 57
Pears with Berry Sauce, Wine-Poached, '86 144
Pears with Honey-Yogurt Sauce, Poached, '92 306
Pears with Meringue, Amaretto, '90 M58
Pie, Buttermilk, '92 95
Pie, Chocolate Bavarian, '89 326
Pie, Eggnog, '83 205
Pie, Fresh Apple, '84 178
Pie, Fruited Cheese, '92 228
Pie, New-Fashioned Pumpkin, '90 296
Pineapple, Meringue-Topped, '84 178
Pineapple with Raspberry Sauce, Chocolate-Drizzled, '90 57
Pineapple-Yogurt Pops, '91 173
Plum Slush, '84 139
Pops, Orange-Banana, '82 129
Prune Bavarian, '86 223
Pudding, Almost Banana, '88 174
Pudding, Apple-Raisin Bread, '88 175
Pudding, Layered Lemon, '82 128
Pudding, Lemon Cake, '92 96
Pudding, Light Plum, '86 318
Pudding, Old-Fashioned Banana, '92 94
Pudding, Old-Fashioned Bread, '88 175
Pudding, Orange Custard, '88 174
Pudding, Peachy Bread, '88 175
Pudding, Raisin-Pumpkin, '84 315
Pudding with Whiskey Sauce, Bread, '90 230
Pumpkin Chiffon, '86 283; '88 260
Raspberry Fluff, '89 198
Raspberry-Pear Crisp, '89 109
Rice Cream with Mandarin Oranges, '85 317
Roulage, Frozen Chocolate, '90 56
Sherbet, Easy Pineapple, '92 199
Sherbet, Fresh Mint, '88 23
Sherbet, Instant Fruit, '85 158
Sherbet, Lemon, '91 309
Sherbet, Nectarine, '89 199
Sherbet, Peach, '90 179
Sherbet, Pineapple, '84 83; '89 199
Sherbet, Watermelon, '92 124
Shortcake, Strawberry, '92 184
Sorbet, Blueberry-Kirsch, '83 120
Sorbet, Fresh Orange, '92 143
Sorbet, Mango, '86 196
Soufflé, Baked Apricot, '88 267
Soufflé, Light Chocolate, '83 278
Soufflé, Orange Dessert, '83 206

Soufflé, Raspberry-Topped, '85 317
Soufflé, Tart Lemon, '85 82
Spumoni and Berries, '91 204
Strawberries Juliet, '84 82
Strawberries Marsala, '88 171
Strawberries 'n' Cream, '90 30
Strawberry Cups, Frozen, '91 173
Strawberry Dessert, Glazed, '84 33
Strawberry Dessert, Summer, '92 143
Strawberry Puff, '82 5
Strawberry Whip, '89 198
Strawberry-Yogurt Dessert, '90 295
Tapioca Fluff, Orange, '87 31
Tart, Fancy Fruit, '82 128
Tart, Fresh Fruit, '84 178; '90 58
Tart, Green Grape, '87 77
Tart, Kiwifruit-Peach, '88 20
Tartlets, Fresh Fruit, '93 96
Tart, Pear, '92 72
Tarts, Cran-Raspberry Meringue, '92 286
Tart Shell, '87 77; '88 20
Tiramisù, '94 295
Topping, Blueberry, '87 125
Topping, Cherry-Pineapple, '87 126
Topping, Chunky Piña Colada, '87 125
Topping, Raspberry, '85 317
Topping, Raspberry-Peach, '87 126
Topping, Reduced-Calorie Whipped, '85 55
Topping, Spicy Apple, '87 125
Topping, Strawberry, '86 32
Topping, Strawberry-Banana, '87 125
Torte, Apricot Sponge, '90 59
Torte, Chocolate Mint, '94 86
Trifle, Angel Food, '91 184
Trifle, Raspberry, '88 259
Truffles, Chocolate-Kahlúa, '92 285
Wafers, Cinnamon, '84 324
Watermelon Frost, '86 196
Yogurt, Frozen Fresh Peach, '90 139
Yogurt, Lemon-Chiffon Frozen, '85 54
Yogurt, Vanilla Frozen, '87 125
Yogurt with Candied Lime Strips, Frozen Avocado, '94 137
Di-Calcium Phosphate Solution, '89 138
Dressing, Light Cornbread, '92 324
Dressing, Savory Cornbread, '88 303
Eggs and Omelets
  Benedict, Eggs, '85 49
  Benedict, Light Eggs, '93 M68
  Cheddar-Vegetable Omelet, '83 205
  Florentine, Eggs, '83 56
  Italian Omelet, '92 47
  Primavera, Omelet, '87 71
  Roulade with Mushroom Filling, Egg, '88 84
  Scrambled Eggs, Mexican-Style, '85 50
  Scrambled Eggs, Spanish, '84 60
  Substitute, Homemade Egg, '92 47
  Vegetable Omelet, Cheesy, '85 49
Enchiladas, Three-Bean, '91 133
Fettuccine and Spinach, '88 90
Fettuccine Primavera, '89 238
Filling, Chicken Salad, '87 106
Filling, Mushroom, '88 84
Filling, Shrimp Salad, '87 106
Fruit Kabobs, Winter, '89 34
Fruit Medley, Chilled, '84 60
Fruit, Minted Marinated, '92 138
Fruit Nuggets, Dried, '86 326

Fruit-on-a-Pick, '90 179
Fruit, Warm Spiced, '86 39
Fruit with Lemon-Yogurt Dressing, Fresh, '93 17
Glaze, Cranberry-Honey, '89 273
Glaze, Teriyaki, '94 82
Grapefruit, Broiled, '85 7
Grits, Cheese, '90 102
Guacamole, Mock, '93 36
Ham-and-Cheese Lettuce Rolls, '89 217
Jam, Berry Refrigerator, '89 139
Jam, Blackberry, '89 138
Jam, Blueberry Refrigerator, '89 139
Jam, Plum Refrigerator, '89 139
Jam, Strawberry, '89 138
Jelly, Crabapple, '89 139
Jelly, Grape, '89 140
Kielbasa, '92 242
Linguine with Garlic and Lemon, '88 91
Linguine with Red Pepper Sauce, '93 127
Low Sodium
  Applesauce, Spicy, '82 296
  Asparagus with Basil Sauce, '86 33
  Beans, Minted Green, '84 104
  Beef and Rice, Spicy, '83 231
  Beef Burgundy, '83 281
  Beef Goulash, '83 231
  Beef Roast, French-Style, '89 32
  Biscuits, Flaky, '84 228
  Bread, Bran-Applesauce, '84 229
  Bread, Salt-Free Raisin Batter, '86 33
  Breadsticks, Whole Wheat, '84 228
  Brussels Sprouts, Calico Citrus, '85 303
  Butter, Herbed Unsalted, '82 67
  Carrots Madeira, '83 281
  Catsup, Spicy Tomato, '83 182
  Cereal Snack, Toasted, '85 215
  Chicken à l'Orange, '84 277
  Chicken-and-Vegetables, Stir-Fry, '86 68
  Chicken, Citrus-Herb Baked, '85 303
  Chicken, Creole, '89 33
  Chicken Dinner, Healthful, '83 232
  Chicken, Herb-Baked, '82 229
  Chicken in Lemon and Wine, '83 281
  Chicken Piccata, '83 35
  Chicken-Tomato Bake, '83 35
  Chicken with Wine-Soaked Vegetables, Baked, '84 277
  Chili Surprise, '82 229
  Cookies, Sunshine Lemon, '86 69
  Cornish Hens in Vermouth, '86 33
  Cornish Hens, Roasted Rock, '82 66
  Dressing, Basil, '88 24
  Dressing, Lemon-Herb Salad, '82 67
  Dressing, Orange-Yogurt, '85 304
  Fish, Curried Baked, '87 5
  Flounder Rolls, Vegetable-Stuffed, '87 6
  Flounder, Sesame, '89 33
  Fruit Delight, Hot, '83 281
  Fruit Delight, Spiced, '82 229
  Fruit, Unsweetened Mixed, '83 182
  Ice, Pink Grapefruit, '85 304
  Jam, Banana, '82 296
  Jam, Freezer Peach, '83 182
  Lamb Chops, Dijon, '84 277
  Lamb Chops, Orange, '83 35
  Linguine with Seafood Sauce, '83 232
  Meat Loaf, Corny, '86 68
  Meat Loaf, Parsleyed, '83 35
  Mocha-Cocoa Mix, Hot, '82 296

Living Light, Low Sodium *(continued)*

Mousse, Orange, '86 69
Muffins, Honey-Oatmeal, '84 229
Muffins, Spiced Bran, '84 229
Mustard, Lower Sodium Horseradish,
    '86 325
Nectarines in Apple Juice, '83 183
Onions, Glazed, '84 104
Orange Scampi, '85 303
Pastry Shell, Sesame, '82 67
Peppers, Corn Stuffed, '84 104
Pie, Nutty Pumpkin, '82 67
Pork, Roast Loin of, '84 276
Pork Tenderloin with Brown Sauce,
    Grilled, '89 32
Potato Bake, Chive-, '82 229
Potatoes, Yogurt-Stuffed, '88 24
Pretzels with Lower Sodium Horseradish
    Mustard, Herb, '86 325
Pudding, Chocolate-Almond, '88 24
Pudding, Lemon Fluff, '85 304
Ratatouille, '84 105
Rice and Shrimp, Curried, '83 231
Rice, Calico Brown, '86 33
Rolls, Low-Sodium Refrigerator, '82 67
Rolls, Low-Sodium Yeast, '84 228
Salad, Asparagus-and-New Potato, '86 69
Salad, Citrus Green, '85 304
Salad, Dilled Cucumber, '82 229
Salad Mold, Golden Citrus, '85 303
Salad, Mushroom-and-Pepper, '86 68
Salad, Sesame-Citrus Green, '86 33
Salmon, Poached, '83 35
Salmon Steaks, Marinated, '87 6
Sauce, Apple-Horseradish, '82 229
Sauce, Brown, '89 32
Sauce, Green Herb, '83 36
Sauce, Seafood, '83 36
Scallops, Sherried, '83 281
Scamp, Tangy Broiled, '87 5
Seasoning Blend, '82 296
Shake, Pineapple-Banana, '85 215
Shrimp Kabobs, Marinated, '84 276
Shrimp, Special Boiled, '83 36
Snapper, Caribbean, '87 5
Snapper, Orangy, '88 23
Soup, Chunky Chicken-Noodle, '88 12
Soup, Chunky Mushroom, '88 12
Soup, Cream of Cauliflower, '88 12
Soup, Spicy Vegetable-Beef, '88 11
Spaghetti, Veal, '84 276
Squash Sauté, '82 67
Squash, Vegetable-Stuffed, '84 104
Steak, Marinated Flank, '83 35
Stew, Cajun-Style Catfish, '88 12
Stew, White Wine, '82 228
Stuffing, Low-Sodium, '82 66
Swordfish, Foil-Baked, '87 5
Tomatoes, Stewed, '83 182
Tomato Puree, Seasoned, '83 182
Tropical Snow, '86 34
Veal, Savory, '83 281
Vegetable Stir-Fry, '84 104
Waffles, Whole Wheat, '84 228
Zucchini, Herbed, '84 104
Zucchini with Baby Carrots, '88 24
Macaroni and Cheese, Baked, '82 199
Macaroni with Pesto, Whole Wheat,
    '89 238

Main Dishes
Asparagus Roulade, '86 102
Beans and Rice, Red, '90 27
Beef, American Steakhouse, '93 15
Beef-and-Barley Rolls, Wine-Sauced,
    '87 269
Beef and Cauliflower over Rice, '93 94
Beef-and-Rice Dinner, Mexican, '88 199
Beef and Vegetables, Company, '88 234
Beef-and-Vegetable Stir-Fry, '87 22
Beef Burgundy, '88 25
Beef Chimichangas, Oven-Fried,
    '92 124
Beef, Chinese-Style, '87 50
Beef Fajitas, '88 233
Beef Kabobs, Chile-, '94 251
Beef Kabobs, Spirited, '87 142
Beef Kabobs with Rice, Marinated,
    '84 32
Beef, Marinated Sauerbraten, '93 16
Beef Medaillons, Italian, '87 305
Beef Patties, Deviled-, '87 22
Beef Stir-Fry, Chinese, '83 151
Beef Stroganoff, '91 134
Beef Stroganoff, Light, '86 36
Beef Tenderloin Bundles, Peppered,
    '89 272
Beef Tenderloin for Two, '90 295
Beef with Asparagus, '90 100
Black Beans and Rice, '91 82
Black Beans and Yellow Rice, Easy,
    '92 308
Burgers, Barbecued, '89 164
Burgers, Favorite, '89 165
Burgers, Mushroom, '89 164
Burgers, Pizza, '89 165
Burgers, Seasoned, '85 158
Burgers, Triple-Layer, '89 165
Burgers, Vegetable, '89 164
Burgers, Walnut, '89 163
Burgers with Sprouts, '89 164
Burritos, Cheesy Beef, '85 193
Cabbage Rolls, Stuffed, '88 18
Cannelloni, '92 17
Carne Guisada, '94 219
Casserole, Bean-and-Cornbread,
    '92 243
Casserole, Breakfast, '91 285
Casserole, Chiles Rellenos, '92 18
Casserole, Crab-and-Mushroom, '89 96
Casserole, Turkey-and-Shrimp
    Florentine, '92 122
Catfish, Baked, '94 67
Catfish, Parmesan, '92 309
Catfish, Southern Oven-Fried, '87 163
Catfish with Creole Sauce, Breaded,
    '90 28
Chicken à la King, '94 41
Chicken and Dumplings, Old-Fashioned,
    '93 302
Chicken and Rice, Spicy, '88 200
Chicken-and-Sausage Jambalaya,
    '88 200
Chicken and Spinach Noodles, '82 19
Chicken and Vegetables, Stir-Fry,
    '86 249
Chicken and Vegetables, Walnut,
    '85 194
Chicken and Vegetables with Ginger-Soy
    Sauce, '91 32
Chicken Bake, Individual, '90 279

Chicken Breast in Wine, Poached,
    '91 184
Chicken Breasts Sardou, Stuffed,
    '87 269
Chicken Breasts, Wine-Baked, '83 177
Chicken Breasts with Fruited Rice Pilaf,
    '92 307
Chicken Cacciatore, '86 42
Chicken Chili Bake, '93 302
Chicken, Chutney, '86 249
Chicken Cordon Bleu, '86 37; '93 126
Chicken, Creamed, '82 49
Chicken Croquettes and Mushroom
    Sauce, '91 220
Chicken, Crunchy Oven-Fried, '87 163
Chicken, Curried, '86 43
Chicken Curry, Stir-Fried, '87 51
Chicken Cutlets with Lemon, '85 8
Chicken, Dante's, '88 25
Chicken Dinner, Skillet, '86 249
Chicken Enchiladas, '90 121
Chicken Fingers, Herb-Baked, '86 249
Chicken Fingers, No-Fry-Pan, '91 120
Chicken-Fried Wild Rice, '91 132
Chicken Gumbo, '90 26
Chicken in a Bag, '87 23
Chicken in Foil, '91 134
Chicken in Orange Sauce, '83 8
Chicken Kabobs, Sesame, '82 165
Chicken Kiev, Oven-Baked, '86 37
Chicken la France, '86 248
Chicken Lasagna, '88 90
Chicken-Leek Terrine, Cold, '92 145
Chicken, Lemon-Frosted, '88 170
Chicken Marengo, '92 70
Chicken Marsala, '89 237
Chicken, Orange, '83 278
Chicken, Oven-Fried, '93 90
Chicken Paprika, Dilled, '86 41
Chicken, Pineapple, '83 M194
Chicken Pot Pie, '94 21
Chicken Rolls, Spinach-Stuffed, '86 248
Chicken, Southern Oven-Fried, '86 37
Chicken Spaghetti, '87 221
Chicken Stir-Fry, Apple-Sesame-,
    '92 226
Chicken Stir-Fry, Chinese, '90 100
Chicken Strips and Vegetables,
    Marinated, '90 110
Chicken, Sweet-and-Sour, '91 202
Chicken-Vegetable Stir-Fry, '83 151;
    '84 13
Chicken with Artichoke Hearts, '88 54
Chicken with Artichokes, Sherried,
    '87 143
Chicken with Mole Sauce, '93 34
Chicken with Orange, Lime, and Ginger
    Sauce, '92 123
Chicken with Pineapple, Oriental, '86 42
Chicken with Salsa, Baked Chile,
    '88 147
Chicken with Spinach Fettuccine, Easy,
    '88 89
Chicken with Tabbouleh Salad, Grilled,
    '91 70
Chicken with Tomato-Basil Pasta,
    Basil-Stuffed, '94 M204
Chiles Rellenos, Light, '93 156
Chiles Rellenos with Tomatillo Sauce,
    Roasted, '94 203
Chile Verde, Light, '88 148

Living Light, Main Dishes *(continued)*

Chili, '93 89
Chili, Firestarter, '93 34
Chili, Hot Venison, '91 283
Chili, South-of-the-Border, '91 283
Chili, Southwestern, '91 284
Chili, Vegetarian, '91 284
Chili, White, '91 284
Cornbread-Tamale Pie, '92 123
Cornish Hens, Herbed, '82 271
Cornish Hens, Mesquite-Smoked,
    '92 144
Cornish Hens, Orange-Glazed Grilled,
    '86 250
Cornish Hens with Vegetables, Tarragon
    Roasted, '94 79
Crab-and-Shrimp Étouffée, '89 96
Crab Cakes, '91 122
Crabmeat au Gratin, '86 154
Cracked Wheat, "Fried," '89 31
Crawfish Étouffée, '86 156
Crêpes, Cannelloni, '86 143
Crêpes, Chicken-Vegetable, '83 70
Eggplant Parmesan, '92 18
Enchiladas, Spicy Bean, '88 18
Fajita Fettuccine, '94 84
Fajita in a Pita, '90 177
Fettuccine and Shrimp with Dried
    Tomato Pesto, '94 249
Fettuccine, Ham-and-Asparagus,
    '94 84
Fettuccine Primavera, '94 85
Fettuccine, Shrimp, '94 84
Filet Mignon with Mushroom Sauce,
    '94 250
Fillets, Apple-Carrot Stuffed, '88 M192
Fillets, Tomatillo, '94 135
Fish and Vegetables, Steamed, '91 32
Fish Dinner, Skillet, '88 199
Fish Fillets, Breaded Herbed, '91 121
Fish Florentine, '86 35
Fish Florentine in Parchment, '87 22
Fish with Greek Sauce, Poached,
    '91 M183
Flank Steak with Black Bean-and-Corn
    Salsa, Grilled, '94 80
Flank Steak with Noodles, Stuffed,
    '90 101
Flank Steak with Sweet Peppers, Grilled,
    '90 138
Flounder, Creole-Style, '85 180
Flounder Rolls with Citrus Sauce,
    Stuffed, '85 180
Frijoles Rancheros, '88 148
Frittata, Vegetable, '92 48
Game Hens with Chutney-Mustard
    Glaze, '93 66
Goulash, Hungarian, '92 227
Grits-and-Ham Pie, Crustless, '86 103
Grouper, Grilled Marinated, '90 166
Grouper, Hot Spicy, '94 78
Haddock Fillets with Zucchini Stuffing,
    '88 M191
Halibut Steaks Italiano, '88 M191
Halibut with Champagne Sauce, Baked,
    '90 29
Halibut with Swiss Sauce, '83 M195
Hamburger Pie, '84 13
Ham-Potato-Pineapple Bake, '93 302

Ham with Cranberry-Honey Glaze,
    Baked, '89 273
Hopping John with Grilled Pork
    Medaillons, '93 229
Jambalaya, '90 26
Jambalaya, Black-Eyed Pea, '92 70
Jambalaya, Red Rice, '91 18
Kabobs, Hawaiian, '85 157
Lamb Chops, Broiled, '85 22
Lamb Chops, Peppercorn-Crusted,
    '92 142
Lamb Chops with Herbs, '90 164
Lamb with Five Spices, Stewed, '92 72
Lasagna, Cheesy Spinach, '83 204
Lasagna in a Bun, '90 176
Lasagna, Lean, '86 37
Lasagna, Spinach-Bean, '92 96
Lasagna, Vegetable, '84 201
Lasagna, Zucchini, '85 194
Lentil-and-Rice Supper, '84 202
Lentils-and-Rice Casserole, '93 301
Linguine with Clam Sauce, '88 90
Liver, Creole, '86 108
Liver in Creole Sauce, '87 33
Lobster Tails with Spiced Orange Sauce,
    '86 155
London Broil, Marinated, '87 32
Mackerel, Rosemary-Garlic, '92 200
Manicotti, Spinach, '82 199
Meatballs and Vegetables with
    Horseradish Dressing, '91 32
Meat Loaf, '89 109
Meat Loaf, Curried, '86 43
Meat Loaf, Oriental, '83 M194
Meat Loaf, Parsley, '87 22
Orange Roughy-and-Vegetable Stir-Fry,
    '91 50
Orange Roughy, Vegetable-Topped,
    '93 67
Orange Roughy with Spinach Pesto,
    '88 M192
Pasta, Creamy Turkey-Basil, '89 216
Pasta Primavera, Almost, '86 38
Pasta Salad, Main-Dish, '82 199
Pasta Verde, '84 201
Pastichio, '85 194
Pear Breakfast Treat, '87 72
Peas and Red Pepper, Sesame Snow,
    '84 175
Peppers Stuffed with Shrimp-and-Orzo
    Salad, '91 203
Perch, Parmesan-Crusted, '93 91
Pie, Italian Meat, '89 109
Pizza, Breakfast, '90 178
Pizza, Garden, '89 108
Pizza, Turkey-Vegetable, '90 139
Pizza, Vegetable, '94 218
Pizza, Veggie, '94 78
Pizza, Whole Wheat, '84 33
Polenta with Black Bean Salsa, Grilled,
    '93 155
Pollock with Summer Squash Relish,
    '92 200
Pork-and-Noodles Skillet Dinner,
    '88 199
Pork, Chinese Roast, '91 308
Pork Chop Dinner, '88 25
Pork Chops, Apricot-Sauced, '85 22
Pork Chops, Creole-Style, '91 49
Pork Chops, Fruit-Topped, '94 41
Pork Chops, Honey-Lime, '91 33

Pork Chops in Gravy, '91 137
Pork Chow Mein, '90 101
Pork, Cranberry, '90 293
Pork Loin Roast, Barbecued, '93 34
Pork Medaillons, Grilled, '93 229
Pork Roast, Oven-Barbecued, '91 50
Pork Roast, Stuffed Crown, '89 272
Pork, Stir-Fried, '87 51
Pork, Sweet-and-Sour, '85 34, 194
Pork Tenderloin, Marinated, '84 175
Pork Tenderloins, Fruit-Stuffed, '87 270
Pork Tenderloin, Spinach-and-Bacon
    Stuffed, '94 81
Pork Tenderloin with Orange
    Marmalade, '91 49
Pot Roast, Marinated, '85 21
Quail with Mushroom Gravy, Baked,
    '89 273
Quesadillas, Quick, '89 87
Quiche, Eggless, '87 220
Quiche, Fiesta, '92 47
Quiches, Individual Spinach, '86 38
Quiche, Spinach, '85 49; '91 204
Quiche, Swiss-Zucchini, '82 49
Ravioli, Mediterranean, '93 301
Red Snapper, Blackened, '90 27
Red Snapper Veracruz, '92 142
Rice-and-Lentil Pilaf, '88 17
Roast Beef, Deli-Style, '93 15
Salmon Fillets with Red Wine Garlic
    Sauce, '94 250
Salmon Loaf with Cucumber-Dill Sauce,
    '86 5
Salmon-Pesto Vermicelli, '92 200
Salmon with Horseradish Sauce,
    Poached, '91 183
Sausage, Dieters' Spicy, '85 49
Scallop Kabobs, Grilled, '83 101
Scallops in Vegetable Nests, '91 70
Scallops with Cilantro-Lime Vinaigrette,
    Grilled Orange, '94 77
Shrimp, Barbecued, '90 28
Shrimp, Beer-Broiled, '87 142
Shrimp Cancun en Papillote, '91 136
Shrimp Étouffée, '90 229
Shrimp Skillet, Quick, '87 50
Shrimp, Sweet-and-Sour, '83 278
Shrimp with Peanut Sauce, '93 303
Sirloin, Mustard Marinated, '94 41
Snapper à l'Orange, Baked, '85 181
Snapper, Honey-Curried, '85 181
Snapper, Poached, '83 101
Snapper Rolls, Cucumber-Stuffed Red,
    '83 176
Snapper Veracruz, Red, '88 149
Snapper with Creamy Dill Sauce,
    Peppered, '94 42
Sole Divan, '87 21
Sole Véronique, '85 181
Spaghetti, Meaty, '82 19
Steak au Poivre, '88 232
Steak Diane, '92 306
Steak, Fast-and-Easy Stir-Fried, '87 50
Steak in Red Wine Sauce, Skillet, '85 21
Steak, Italian-Stuffed, '88 232
Steak Kabobs, '82 4; '93 95
Steak lo Mein, '90 100
Steak, Marinated, '88 233
Steak, Mexican Marinated, '88 148
Steak, Mock Country-Fried, '87 163
Steak, Pepper-Beef, '85 21

Living Light, Main Dishes *(continued)*

Steak Sukiyaki, Flank, **'88** 233
Stew, Burgundy Beef, **'88** 234
Tacoritos, **'90** 133
Tenderloins, Honey-Grilled, **'92** 199
Tenderloin, Spinach-Stuffed, **'89** 311
Tofu, Stroganoff, **'84** 202
Tomato with Tuna Pasta, Stuffed, **'88** 54
Tuna Croquettes with Parsley Sauce, **'86** 108
Tuna Steaks on Mixed Greens with Lemon-Basil Vinaigrette, Seared, **'94** 205
Tuna with Poblano Salsa, Grilled, **'91** 135
Tuna with Rosemary, Broiled, **'93** 127
Tuna with Tangy Mustard Sauce, **'92** 201
Turkey-Asparagus Pilaf, **'88** 200
Turkey Breast and Gravy, Roast, **'88** 303
Turkey Breast, Stuffed, **'87** 270
Turkey Breast with Special Gravy, Roast, **'86** 282
Turkey Cutlets, Oven-Fried, **'91** 121
Turkey Cutlets with Pepper Salsa, Spicy, **'88** 26
Turkey Lasagna, **'91** 130
Turkey, Lazy Day, **'93** 93
Turkey Picatta, **'91** 137
Veal and Carrots, Company, **'85** 22
Veal, Lemon, **'93** 35
Veal Marsala, **'91** 310
Veal Picante, **'87** 31
Veal Picatta with Capers, **'87** 142
Veal Scallopini, **'83** 8
Vegetarian Supper, **'86** 222
Vermicelli and Sprouts with Red Clam Sauce, **'86** 143
Vermicelli, Scallop-Vegetable, **'87** 143
Zucchini Frittata, **'86** 103
Meatballs, **'89** 237
Meatballs, Turkey, **'89** 237
Meat Mixture, Basic, **'92** 241
Muesli, Bran-and-Fruit, **'91** 134
Oatmeal, Applesauce, **'89** 108
Oatmeal, Fruited, **'88** 19
Pancakes, Honey, **'91** 139
Pancakes, Oatmeal, **'89** 107
Pancakes, Shredded Wheat, **'84** 59
Pancakes, Whole Wheat-Oat, **'93** 16
Pasta-Basil Toss, **'87** 33
Pasta, Garden, **'82** 199
Pasta Provençale, **'88** 90
Pasta, Tomato-Basil, **'94** 204
Peaches, Spicy Baked, **'86** 39
Pizza Crust, Special, **'90** 139
Pizza Crusts, Skillet, **'94** 218
Pizza on a Bagel, **'93** M94
Preserves, Fig, **'89** 140
Preserves, Peach, **'89** 140
Relish, Cranberry, **'86** 283; **'91** 257
Relish, Holiday Cranberry, **'88** 304
Relish, Papaya-Basil, **'94** 82
Relish, White Bean, **'93** 229
Rice and Mushrooms, Wild, **'83** 278
Rice, Apple-Cinnamon, **'86** 249
Rice Bulgur, Wild, **'91** 83
Rice Casserole, Colorful, **'82** 199
Rice-Cheese Shell, **'82** 49

Rice, Herb, **'91** 257
Rice, Lime-Flavored, **'84** 175
Rice Mix, Fruited Curry-, **'86** 326
Rice, Orange, **'82** 200
Rice, Peppered, **'82** 4
Rice Pilaf, Brown, **'90** 136; **'91** 82
Rice Pilaf, Browned, **'87** 305
Rice, Seasoned Onion, **'82** 166
Rice, Southwestern, **'90** 121
Rice, Spicy Mexican, **'88** 149
Rice with Black-Eyed Peas, **'93** 66
Rice with Tofu, Spanish, **'88** 26
Rice, Yellow, **'91** 136
Salad Dressings
Blue Cheese Dressing, **'82** 166
Blue Cheese Dressing, Creamy, **'91** 307
Blue Cheese Vinaigrette, **'90** 280
Caper Vinaigrette, **'91** 310
Cilantro-Lime Vinaigrette, **'94** 77
Coconut Dressing, **'87** 251
Creamy Dressing, **'93** 318
Cucumber-Mint Dressing, **'87** 153
Cucumber Salad Dressing, Creamy, **'82** 79
Curry Dressing, **'82** 78
French Dressing, Miracle, **'82** 79
Fruit, Salad Dressing for, **'86** 40
Herb Salad Dressing, **'86** 40
Honey-Mustard Dressing, **'90** 111
Horseradish Dressing, **'87** 152; **'91** 32
Lemon-Basil Vinaigrette, **'94** 205
Lemon-Yogurt Dressing, **'93** 17
Lemon-Yogurt Slaw or Salad Dressing, **'88** 54
Lime Dressing, **'83** 120
Orange-Poppy Seed Dressing, **'87** 187
Pineapple-Poppy Seed Dressing, **'85** 55
Raspberry Dressing, **'87** 153
Soy-Sesame Dressing, **'87** 153
Spicy Southwestern Dressing, **'94** 136
Spring Garden Dressing, **'85** 157
Stay Trim Dressing, **'86** 40
Sweet-and-Sour Dressing, **'87** 305
Tangy Dressing, **'83** 9
Thousand Island Dressing, Special, **'82** 79
Wine Vinegar Dressing, **'93** 126
Yogurt Dressing, **'85** 59, 215; **'88** 27
Yogurt Dressing, Sweet-Hot, **'86** 40
Yogurt-Herb Dressing, **'92** 96
Yogurt-Honey Poppy Seed Dressing, **'83** 177
Salads
Ambrosia, Brunch, **'83** 57
Apple-Apricot Salad, **'88** 121
Apple-Bran Salad, Lemony, **'86** 223
Apple Cider Salad Mold, **'85** 54
Apple Salad, Spicy, **'85** 215
Apple Salad, Triple, **'88** 122
Apple Toss, Sesame-, **'88** 21
Asparagus, Marinated, **'84** 67
Asparagus Salad, **'88** 121; **'94** 67
Asparagus Vinaigrette, Light, **'82** 50
Aspic, Light Tomato, **'85** 83
Aspic, Three-Layer, **'88** 120
Aspic, Tomato-Crab, **'85** 287
Aspic with Horseradish Dressing, Crisp Vegetable, **'87** 152
Barley-Broccoli Salad, **'90** 135
Bean-and-Rice Salad, Marinated, **'87** 152

Bean Salad, Marinated, **'85** 137, 296
Bean Salad, Supreme, **'91** 202
Beans with Sprouts, Sweet-and-Sour, **'86** 32
Bean-Tomato Salad, Lima, **'85** 137
Beef-and-Broccoli Salad, **'87** 187
Beef Fajita Salad, **'91** 70
Black Bean-and-Barley Salad, **'94** 174
Black Bean Salad, **'89** 217
Black-Eyed Pea Salad, Marinated, **'93** 190
Broccoli-Corn Salad, **'87** 24
Brown Rice Confetti Salad, **'94** 174
Caesar Salad, **'92** 71
Cantaloupe, Fruit-Filled, **'83** 120
Carrot-and-Seed Salad, Fruity, **'86** 223
Carrot-Pineapple Salad, **'91** 83
Carrot-Raisin Salad, **'84** 174
Cauliflower-Vegetable Salad, **'85** 158
Cheesy Italian Salad, **'84** 33
Cherry-Apple Salad, **'86** 31
Cherry Salad, Fresh, **'83** 120
Chicken-and-Walnut Salad, Sunburst, **'93** 91
Chicken-Fruit Salad, **'82** 79
Chicken Pasta Salad, **'88** 89
Chicken-Raspberry Salad, Marinated, **'93** 190
Chicken Salad, Blue Cheese, **'94** 81
Chicken Salad, Crunchy, **'86** 207
Chicken Salad, Special, **'85** 82
Chicken Taco Salad, **'94** M136
Chile-Tomato Salad, Spicy, **'88** 121
Citrus Salad, Tangy, **'89** 34
Coleslaw, Crunchy, **'86** 295
Coleslaw, Light and Creamy, **'93** 318
Composé, Salad, **'93** 126
Corn Salad, **'85** 236
Cottage Cheese Salad in Tomatoes, **'86** 208
Couscous Salad, Basil-and-Tomato, **'94** 175
Crab-and-Asparagus Salad, **'92** 141
Crab-Wild Rice Salad, **'86** 207
Cucumber Mousse, **'88** 121
Cucumber Salad, Dilled, **'92** 72
Cucumber-Yogurt Salad, **'87** 33
Freezer Salad, **'94** 118
Fruit Cups, Sangría, **'89** 34
Fruit, Dressed-Up, **'82** 5
Fruit Salad, Chef's, **'86** 35
Fruit Salad, Curried, **'85** 107
Garden-Patch Salad Molds, **'86** 283
Garden Salad, Summer, **'87** 153
Gazpacho Molded Salad, **'92** 323
Grapefruit Salad, **'88** 122
Grape Salad Mold, **'83** 120
Green Beans with Creamy Tarragon Dressing, **'93** 191
Green Salad, Mixed, **'90** 230
Greens, Crimson, **'87** 153
Greens with Blue Cheese Vinaigrette, Mixed, **'90** 280
Hominy-Bean Salad, **'88** 266
Jicama-Orange Salad, **'90** 122
Layered Salad, **'86** 35
Legumes, Marinated, **'90** 197
Lentils-and-Rice Salad, **'90** 197
Lettuce, Confetti-Stuffed, **'87** 24
Lettuces with Mustard Vinaigrette, Baby, **'93** 67

Living Light, Salads *(continued)*

Macaroni-Cheese Salad, Dilled, **'86** 208
Macaroni-Chicken Salad, Dilled, **'92** 142
Macaroni-Tuna Salad, Whole Wheat, **'84** 193
Mandarin Salad Molds, **'85** 54
Meal-in-One Salad, **'86** 43
Melon Ball Bowl with Cucumber-Mint Dressing, **'87** 153
Mushroom-Zucchini Salad, **'85** 8
Niçoise, Salad, **'86** 35
Oriental Salad Bowl, **'87** 153
Paella Salad, **'86** 207
Pasta-and-Tomato Salad, Herbed, **'92** 144
Pasta Salad, **'84** 139; **'89** 217
Pasta Salad, Garden, **'86** 188
Pea-and-Apple Salad, English, **'87** 24
Peaches in a Garden Nest, **'87** 154
Pork Salad, Oriental, **'92** 140
Potato Salad, **'90** 122
Potato Salad, Hot-and-Light, **'93** 90
Potato Salad, New, **'84** 139
Potato Salad, Pesto, **'90** 164
Potato Slices, Marinated, **'93** 98
Rice-and-Vegetable Salad, **'86** 42
Rice-and-Vegetable Salad, Brown, **'84** 202
Rice-Shrimp Salad, **'92** 142
Romaine with Caper Vinaigrette, Hearts of, **'91** 310
Salmon-and-Wild Rice Salad, Oriental, **'94** 173
Seafood Salad Sussex Shores, **'93** 98
Shrimp-and-Rice Salad, **'92** 307
Shrimp Salad, Fruited, **'86** 156
Shrimp Salad, Marinated, **'85** 82
Slaw, Apple-Carrot, **'92** 243
Slaw, Cabbage-Pineapple, **'92** 182
Slaw, Chinese Cabbage, **'89** 312
Slaw, Healthy, **'92** 183
Slaw, Red Cabbage-and-Apple, **'87** 31
Spinach-Blue Cheese Salad, **'82** 166
Spinach-Kiwifruit Salad, **'87** 305
Spinach Salad, Citrus, **'90** 59
Spinach Salad, Wilted, **'93** 125
Spinach Salad with Orange Dressing, **'87** 187
Sprout Salad, **'90** 137
Steak Salad Cups, Pepper, **'86** 206
Strawberry Salad, Frozen, **'94** 119
Tabbouleh Salad, **'91** 70; **'94** 174
Tarragon Chicken Salad, **'90** 199
Tofu Salad, **'88** 27
Tomato-Cucumber Salad, **'92** 199
Tomato-Cucumber Salad with Yogurt-Herb Dressing, **'92** 96
Tomatoes Stuffed with Sea Slaw, **'89** 96
Tortellini Salad, **'89** 237
Tuna-and-Cannellini Bean Salad, **'86** 143
Tuna Chef Salad, **'82** 78
Tuna-Mac in Tomatoes, **'87** 188
Tuna-Pasta Salad, **'92** 141
Tuna Salad, Curried, **'86** 208
Turkey Waldorf Salad with Yogurt Dressing, **'88** 53
Turnip Salad, **'85** 235
Vegetable Salad, Crispy Marinated, **'84** 193

Vegetable Salad, Grilled, **'94** 203
Vegetable Salad, Italian, **'82** 19
Vegetable Salad, Marinated, **'84** 13
Vegetable Salad, Minted, **'88** 23
Vegetable Salad, Tarragon-, **'85** 288
Vegetable Salad, Winter, **'86** 42
Vegetables, Zesty Marinated, **'82** 272
Wheat Berry-and-Roasted Corn Salad, **'94** 175
Wild Rice Salad, **'93** 191
Sandwiches
Bagel, Breakfast on a, **'94** 66
Breakfast Sandwiches, Open-Faced, **'92** 140
Chicken Pita, Oriental, **'89** 216
Chicken Sandwiches, Marinated, **'86** M45
Crab Sandwiches, Open-Faced, **'87** 106
Garden Sandwiches, Open-Faced, **'87** 105
Ham Sandwiches, Open-Face, **'85** 8
Heroes, Healthy, **'90** 177
Lamb Pockets with Dilled Cucumber Topping, **'87** 104
Open-Face Sandwiches, **'84** 13
Pimiento Cheese Sandwiches, **'82** 278
Pitas, Acadian Stuffed, **'90** 177
Pita Sandwiches, **'84** 139
Pita, Stuffed, **'89** 87
Pizza Sandwiches, Open-Face, **'85** 22
Shrimp Salad Sandwiches, **'90** 178
Sloppy Toms, **'91** 51
Tofu-Veggie Sandwiches, Open-Face, **'86** 5
Turkey-in-the-Slaw Sandwich, **'90** 177
Turkey-Roasted Pepper Sandwiches, Smoked, **'94** 66
Vegetable Pockets, **'85** 215
Vegetarian Melt, Open-Faced, **'87** 106
Vegetarian Pita Sandwiches, **'84** 193
Sauces and Gravies
Alfredo Sauce, **'94** 84
Apple Dessert Sauce, Spicy, **'82** 177
Barbecue Sauce, Easy, **'82** 178
Barbecue Sauce, Special, **'82** 177
Basil-Brown Butter Sauce, **'93** 92
Champagne Sauce, **'90** 29
Cheese Sauce, Guilt-Free, **'93** M95
Chocolate Sauce, **'90** 57
Coconut Sauce, Creamy Light, **'82** 177
Creole Sauce, **'90** 28
Cucumber-Dill Sauce, **'86** 5
Custard Sauce, **'88** 259
Dill Sauce, Creamy, **'94** 42
Ginger-Soy Sauce, **'91** 33
Golden Sauce, **'88** 267
Gravy, **'88** 303
Greek Sauce, **'91** 183
Hard Sauce, Special, **'86** 318
Hollandaise Sauce, Mock, **'85** 49; **'93** 68
Honey-Orange Sauce, **'85** 108
Honey-Yogurt Sauce, **'92** 307
Horseradish Sauce, **'91** 183
Jalapeño Sauce, **'93** 230
Lemon-Chive Sauce, **'86** 249
Lemon Sauce, **'82** 290
Mandarin Sauce, **'84** 60
Mango Sauce, **'83** 120
Marinade, Tangy Light, **'82** 178

Marinara Sauce, **'82** 178; **'89** 239; **'92** 18
Mediterranean Sauce, **'94** 83
Melba Sauce, **'87** 77
Mushroom Sauce, **'83** 205; **'91** 221
Mushroom Sauce, Spicy Sherried, **'89** 239
Mustard-Hollandaise Sauce, Mock, **'87** 269
Mustard Sauce, **'87** 22
Mustard Sauce, Easy, **'94** 83
Mustard Sauce, Light, **'82** 178
Mustard Sauce, Tangy, **'92** 201
Parmesan Sauce, **'92** 17
Parsley Sauce, **'86** 108
Pesto, Dried Tomato, **'94** 249
Picante Sauce, Processed, **'91** 257
Pineapple-Orange Sauce, **'84** 14
Pizza Sauce, **'84** 33
Rancheros Sauce, **'88** 148
Raspberry-Orange Sauce, **'88** 22
Raspberry Sauce, **'88** 267; **'93** 99; **'94** 295
Red Chile Sauce, **'94** 251
Red Wine Garlic Sauce, **'94** 250
Rum-Raisin Sauce, **'94** 295
Salsa, **'88** 147
Salsa, Black Bean, **'93** 155
Salsa, Black Bean-and-Corn, **'94** 80
Salsa Cruda, **'88** 148
Salsa, Fiesta Onion, **'94** 82
Salsa, Hot Kiwifruit, **'94** 82
Salsa, Pepper, **'88** 26
Salsa, Poblano, **'91** 135
Salsa, Tomato-Avocado, **'94** 83
Sauerbraten Sauce, **'93** 16
Sausage Gravy, **'94** 20
Seafood Sauce, **'89** 239
Spaghetti Sauce, Lentil, **'90** 198
Swiss Sauce, **'83** M195
Tarragon Sauce, **'83** 56
Tomato Sauce, **'85** 193, 244
Tomato Sauce, Spicy, **'88** 19
Vegetable-Cheese Potato Topper, **'86** 6
Whiskey Sauce, **'90** 230
White Sauce, Low-Calorie Medium, **'87** 26
Zesty Sauce, **'94** 82
Zippy Sauce, **'86** 44
Sausage, Country, **'92** 242
Sausage, Italian, **'92** 242
Soups and Stews
Asparagus Soup, **'84** 67
Bean-and-Pasta Soup, **'94** 220
Bean-and-Turkey Soup, **'93** 319
Bean Soup, Black, **'88** 266
Bean Soup, Carolina Black, **'92** 139
Bean Soup, Leafy, **'86** 223
Bean Soup, Navy, **'84** 280
Beef-and-Barley Vegetable Soup, **'89** 31
Beef Stew, **'90** 230
Beef Stew, Quick, **'92** 71
Bisque, Squash, **'84** 280
Borscht, Ruby Red, **'83** 176
Bouillon, Tomato, **'83** 8
Broccoli Soup, Creamy, **'91** 307
Broccoli Soup, Light Cream of, **'93** 17
Broccoli Soup, Mock Cream of, **'85** 288
Broccoli-Swiss Soup, **'86** 6
Cantaloupe Soup, **'83** 120
Carrot-Leek Soup, **'86** 34

Living Light, Soups and Stews *(continued)*

Chicken, Artichoke, and Mushroom Soup, **'92** 324
Chicken Soup, Curried, **'86** 34
Chicken-Vegetable Soup, **'88** 18
Chili Vegetable Soup, **'94** 120
Chili, Vegetarian, **'84** 280
Chowder, Basque Fish, **'86** 36
Chowder, Clam, **'86** 36; **'89** 95
Chowder, Corn, **'91** 132
Chowder, Potato-Corn, **'94** 66
Chowder, Seafood, **'92** 122
Corn-and-Crab Soup, Fresh, **'92** 183
Crab Soup, Cream of, **'88** 302
Cucumber Soup, Cold Minted, **'86** 34
Cucumber-Yogurt Soup, **'83** 205
Fish-and-Vegetable Stew, **'87** 220
French Market Soup, **'92** 49
Gazpacho, Chilled, **'84** 138
Gumbo, Catfish, **'90** 278
Gumbo, Chicken-and-Sausage, **'94** 20
Gumbo, Light Seafood-Okra, **'86** 155
Ham-and-Bean Soup, Spicy, **'94** 322
Hot-and-Sour Soup, **'91** 50
Mex-Tex Soup, **'90** 278
Minestrone Soup, **'86** 144; **'91** 258
Minestrone Soup Mix, **'91** 258
Okra-and-Shrimp Soup, **'94** 323
Peach Soup, **'83** 120
Pepper-and-Chicken Soup, Roasted, **'90** 58
Pepper Soup, Spicy, **'93** 98
Plum Soup, **'85** 107
Seafood Stew, **'84** 280
Spinach Soup, Oriental, **'83** 151
Split Pea Soup, **'90** 198; **'94** 322
Tomato Soup, **'89** 217
Tomato Soup, Easy, **'84** 14
Tomato Soup Plus, **'88** 170
Tortilla Soup, **'94** 136
Turkey-Tomato Stew, **'90** 279
Vegetable-Beef Stew, **'94** 323
Vegetable Soup, **'86** 187; **'88** 266
Vegetable Soup, Light, **'84** 280
Vegetable Stew, Mixed, **'84** 13
Sour Cream, Mock, **'83** 71, 205
Spice Mix, Tex-Mex, **'94** 135
Spread, Cottage Cheese, **'87** 107
Spread, Hawaiian Ham, **'87** 106
Spread, Light Strawberry, **'85** 55
Spread, Low-Calorie Pimiento Cheese, **'85** 215
Spread, Peachy-Raisin, **'86** 326
Spread, Sugarless Fruit, **'84** 60
Spread, Tasty Chicken, **'84** 193
Spread, Vegetable-Egg, **'87** 106
Syrup, Maple, **'93** 16
Topping, Apple, **'89** 107
Topping, Oat Crunch, **'89** 108
Topping, Yogurt-Cheese, **'88** 55
Tortellini with Rosemary-Parmesan Sauce, **'92** 284
Tortilla Rollups, **'89** 87
Vegetables
Acorn Squash, Fruited, **'90** 228
Artichokes, Shrimp-Stuffed, **'84** 67
Artichokes Stuffed with Shrimp and Scallops, **'84** 174
Asparagus, Company, **'85** 82

Asparagus, Stir-Fried, **'87** 52
Asparagus Vinaigrette, **'90** 138
Barley and Vegetables, **'91** 81
Beans, Lemon-Mint, **'88** 22
Beans, Texas Ranch, **'90** 198
Beets, Ginger-Marmalade Glazed, **'93** 35
Beets, Harvard, **'83** M195
Beets, Orange, **'91** 219
Beets, Orange-Glazed, **'86** 187
Beets, Pickled, **'87** 163
Black Bean Terrine with Fresh Tomato Coulis and Jalapeño Sauce, **'93** 230
Black-Eyed Peas, **'93** 180
Black-Eyed Peas, Seasoned, **'85** 138
Black-Eyed Peas, Spicy Hot, **'90** 135
Broccoli Casserole, **'88** 265
Broccoli, Easy Orange, **'85** 267
Broccoli, Garlic, **'93** 35
Broccoli, Sesame, **'85** 8
Broccoli Toss, **'86** 294
Broccoli with Horseradish Sauce, **'84** 33
Broccoli with Tangy Chive Sauce, Steamed, **'83** 101
Brussels Sprouts, Casserole of, **'86** 294
Brussels Sprouts, Glorified, **'86** 282
Brussels Sprouts in Mustard Sauce, **'90** 228
Brussels Sprouts, Marinated, **'88** 265
Brussels Sprouts Medley, **'85** 267
Bundles, Vegetable, **'93** 181
Burritos, Vegetable, **'90** 134; **'92** 138
Butterbeans, **'90** 166
Butternut-Orange Bake, **'86** 295
Cabbage, Skillet, **'90** 229
Cabbage, Sweet-and-Sour, **'86** 295
Cabbage with Caraway, **'93** 181
Carrots and Onions, Herbed, **'87** 31
Carrots and Pineapple, Curried, **'90** 228
Carrots, Dilled Baby, **'92** 145
Carrots, Ginger, **'83** 9
Carrots, Glazed, **'88** 304
Carrots, Golden, **'85** 267
Carrots, Lemon-Dill Steamed, **'93** 180
Carrots, Light Glazed, **'92** 227
Carrots, Marinated, **'86** 108
Carrots Marsala, **'83** 56
Carrots, Orange-Spiced, **'88** 18
Carrots Polynesian, Spiced, **'88** 85
Carrots, Rosemary, **'91** 219
Carrot Strips, Orangy, **'89** 312
Carrots, Tropical, **'84** 34
Cauliflower Sauté, **'94** 67
Cauliflower-Snow Pea Medley, **'87** 305
Celeriac and Carrots, **'91** 219
Celery-Parmesan Toss, **'84** 34
Corn Casserole, Chili-, **'88** 266
Corn, Creamy Baked, **'90** 60
Corn-on-the-Cob, Grilled, **'90** 166
Corn Pudding, Fresh, **'89** 172
Corn, Roasted Red Pepper, **'91** 122
Corn, Southern-Style Creamed, **'92** 201
Corn, Spicy Mexican, **'93** 90
Crêpes, Vegetable-Filled Bran, **'86** 44
Eggplant Casserole, Spicy Hot, **'93** 92
Eggplant, Ratatouille-Bran Stuffed, **'86** 44
English Pea Medley, **'85** 236
English Peas, Deluxe, **'84** 68
French Fries, Oven, **'91** 122
Green Bean Medley, Peppery, **'93** 181

Green Beans and Potatoes, **'91** 221
Green Beans, Herbed, **'83** 177
Green Beans, Indian-Style, **'88** 265
Green Beans, Italian, **'90** 164; **'92** 183
Green Beans Italiano, **'86** 144
Green Beans, Seasoned, **'88** 304
Green Beans with Mushrooms, **'93** 89
Green Beans with New Potatoes, **'87** 164
Green Beans with Tomatoes, **'85** 137
Grilled Vegetables, **'92** 124
Grilled Vegetables, Italian-Style, **'92** 143
Hominy, Mexican, **'91** 133
Kabobs, Marinated Vegetable, **'83** M195
Kale with Tomato and Onion, **'92** 244
Kidney Bean Casserole, **'90** 136
Lima Beans Creole, **'85** 137
Marinated Vegetables, **'88** 170
Medley, Chinese Vegetable, **'84** 33
Mixed Vegetables, **'83** M195
Mushrooms, Flavor-Stuffed, **'85** 288
Mushrooms, Savory Fresh, **'85** 268
New Potatoes, Herbed, **'83** 9
New Potatoes, Roasted, **'90** 138
New Potato Medley, **'90** 279
Okra-and-Tomato Bake, **'89** 173
Okra, Oven-Fried, **'91** 121
Onion-Potato Bake, **'83** M195
Onion Rings, Crispy Baked, **'93** 247
Onions and Wine, Stuffed, **'85** 268
Onions, Stuffed Vidalia, **'89** 172
Onions Stuffed with Peas, **'84** 68
Parsnips, Glazed, **'91** 220
Peas-and-Corn Medley, **'85** 138
Peas and Ham, Southern, **'85** 138
Peas and Peppers, Stir-Fried, **'87** 51
Pepper Kabobs, Pretty, **'90** 166
Peppers, Stuffed, **'84** 202
Pilaf, Barley-Vegetable, **'91** 33
Potato-Cheese Dream, **'91** 307
Potatoes and Turnips, Scalloped, **'85** 235
Potatoes au Gratin, **'93** 90
Potatoes, Cottage, **'93** M92
Potatoes, Double-Cheese, **'86** 6
Potatoes, Herbed, **'91** 220
Potatoes, Light Scalloped, **'89** 311
Potatoes, Mexican-Stuffed, **'91** 131
Potatoes, Mushroom-Dill-Topped, **'86** 41
Potatoes, Scalloped, **'92** 48
Potatoes, Stuffed, **'89** 173
Potatoes, Twice Baked Cottage-Style, **'91** 135
Potatoes, Vegetable-Topped Stuffed, **'85** 235
Potato, Twice-Baked, **'90** M295
Potato Wedges, **'94** M119
Potato Wedges, Lemon, **'88** 21
Ragout, Vegetable, **'89** 172
Red Cabbage-and-Apple Slaw, **'91** 309
Rice Toss, Vegetable-, **'91** 309
Rice, Vegetables and, **'93** 91
Rutabaga, Honey, **'91** 220
Rutabagas, Mashed, **'86** 295
Sautéed Vegetable Medley, **'83** 101
Sauté, Tossed Vegetable, **'92** 138
Snap Beans, Sweet-and-Sour, **'89** 173
Snow Peas with Red Pepper, **'90** 102
Spinach Quiche, **'85** 49; **'91** 204

Living Light, Vegetables (continued)

Spinach Soufflé, **'86** 108
Squash Casserole, **'87** 163
Squash, Fruited Acorn, **'85** 235
Squash Stuffed with Spinach Pesto,
 '89 M133
Squash with Nutmeg, Acorn, **'85** 267
Steamed Garden Vegetables, **'93** 155
Steamed Herbed Vegetables, **'93** M303
Steamed Vegetable Medley, **'90** 29
Stir-Fried Vegetables, **'90** 136
Stir-Fried Vegetables with Curry, **'87** 51
Stir-Fry, Almond-Vegetable, **'86** 222
Sugar Snap Peas with Basil and Lemon,
 '93 66
Summer Vegetables, **'91** 136
Summer Vegetables, Cheesy, **'94** 119
Sweet Potato-Apple Bake, **'86** 282
Sweet Potatoes-and-Apple Casserole,
 '90 228
Sweet Potato Puff, **'85** 235
Sweet Potato Puree, **'92** 306
Tomato Coulis, Fresh, **'93** 230
Tomatoes and Okra, **'87** 164
Tomatoes, Bean-Stuffed, **'84** 34
Tomatoes, Cheese Herbed-Topped,
 '86 108
Tomatoes, Cheesy Puff-Top, **'86** 187
Tomatoes, Green, **'89** 174
Tomatoes, Grilled, **'85** 158
Tomatoes, Oven-Fried Green, **'91** 122
Tomatoes, Parmesan-Stuffed, **'92** 182
Tomatoes, Spinach-Topped, **'88** 265
Tomatoes, Stuffed Scalloped, **'90** 29
Tomato Slices, Herbed, **'89** 173
Torta, Mexican, **'88** 149
Turnips and Carrots Julienne, **'86** 295
Turnips, Braised, **'91** 219
Zucchini-and-Tomato Casserole, **'88** 265
Zucchini and Tomato with Herbs,
 '92 182
Zucchini-Basil Delight, **'85** 267
Zucchini-Basil Scramble, **'87** 34
Zucchini Dressing, **'86** 282
Zucchini Fans, **'91** 33
Zucchini Spears, Oven-Fried, **'91** 121
Zucchini, Stuffed, **'86** 187; **'89** M133
Zucchini with Pecans, **'87** 31
Vinegar, Raspberry Wine, **'93** 191
Vinegar, Shallot-Tarragon-Garlic, **'93** 191
Waffles, Light, **'91** 139
Waffles, Oat Bran, **'92** 139
Waffles, Oatmeal, **'89** 107
Yogurt Snack, **'88** 55

Lobster
Beef Tenderloin, Lobster-Stuffed, **'87** 248
Clambake, Backyard, **'81** 92
Creamy Lobster, **'79** 181
How to Cook Lobster, **'81** 169
Medaillons in Garlic-Chive Butter Sauce,
 Lobster, **'90** 96
Orange Sauce, Lobster Tails with Spiced,
 '86 155
Salad, Lobster, **'89** 249; **'90** 69
Salad, Lobster and Orange, **'82** 207
Soup, Spicy Thai Lobster, **'94** 102
Taco with Yellow Tomato Salsa and Jicama
 Salad, Warm Lobster, **'87** 122
Thermidor, Lobster, **'85** 103

Macaroni

Bake, Jack-in-the-Macaroni, **'93** 249;
 '94 45
Beef and Macaroni, Ground, **'85** 218
Beef and Macaroni, Skillet, **'82** 130
Beef-Macaroni Bake, **'94** 255
Beef-Macaroni Combo, **'79** 194
Blue Cheese, Macaroni and, **'93** 248;
 '94 44
Casserole, Chicken-Macaroni, **'85** 219
Casserole, Macaroni, **'84** 220; **'87** 154
Casserole, Macaroni and Chicken, **'80** 260
Casserole, Macaroni-Ham, **'81** M177;
 '83 283
Casserole, Spinach-Beef-Macaroni, **'83** 313
Cheese, Baked Macaroni and, **'82** 199
Cheese, Creamy Macaroni and, **'93** 249;
 '94 45
Cheese Deluxe, Macaroni-and-, **'79** 84
Cheese Deluxe, Macaroni and, **'80** 236
Cheese, Macaroni and, **'83** M7;
 '88 M147, M190; **'90** 30
Cheese Macaroni, Double, **'82** 224
Cheese, Old-Fashioned Macaroni and,
 '92 215
Cheese Puff, Macaroni and, **'79** 5
Cheese, Tasty Macaroni and, **'83** 288
Cheese, Thick-and-Rich Macaroni and,
 '84 329
Cheese with Wine, Macaroni-and-, **'86** 78
Cheesy Macaroni-Mushroom Bake, **'81** 243
Dinner, Sausage Skillet, **'83** 29
Glorious Macaroni, **'84** 76
Oysters with Macaroni, Scalloped, **'80** 297
Peppers, Macaroni-and-Cheese-Stuffed,
 '80 65
Salad, Acini di Pepe, **'83** 163
Salad, Barbecue Macaroni, **'82** 276
Salad, Confetti Macaroni, **'82** 132; **'85** 297
Salad, Crunchy Macaroni, **'82** 24
Salad, Dilled Macaroni, **'89** 161
Salad, Dilled Macaroni-Cheese, **'86** 208
Salad, Dilled Macaroni-Chicken, **'92** 142
Salad, Festive Macaroni-Shrimp, **'85** 165
Salad for Two, Macaroni, **'81** 31
Salad, Garden Macaroni, **'84** 290; **'92** 64
Salad, Gourmet Macaroni, **'81** 253
Salad, Ham and Macaroni, **'79** 220
Salad, Hearty Macaroni, **'84** 90
Salad, Macaroni, **'87** 92
Salad, Macaroni-Chicken, **'85** 296; **'86** 302
Salad, Macaroni-Crabmeat, **'81** 153
Salad, Macaroni-Ham, **'85** 218

Salad, Macaroni-Salmon, **'82** 232
Salad, Macaroni Shell, **'87** 38
Salad, Macaroni-Shrimp, **'85** 121
Salad, Macaroni-Vegetable, **'86** 209
Salad, Olive Clubhouse, **'81** 114
Salad, Overnight Pasta, **'82** 276
Salad, Pineapple Macaroni, **'79** 220
Salad, Refreshing Macaroni, **'80** 177
Salad, Salmon-and-Macaroni, **'81** 114
Salad, Shell Macaroni, **'92** 163
Salad, Shrimp Macaroni, **'79** 220
Salad, Shrimp-Macaroni, **'85** 219
Salad, Spiral Macaroni, **'82** 276
Salad, Sweet-and-Sour Macaroni, **'85** 166
Salad, Taco Macaroni, **'85** 165
Salad, Tuna Macaroni, **'83** 44, 145
Salad, Tuna-Macaroni, **'84** 66
Salad, Turkey Macaroni, **'83** 282
Salad Véronique, Macaroni, **'85** 164
Salad, Whole Wheat Macaroni-Tuna, **'84** 193
Supper Supreme, Sunday, **'79** 76
Tomatoes, Tuna-Mac in, **'87** 188
Toss, Corkscrew Macaroni, **'83** 163
Treat, Tuna-Macaroni, **'82** 131
Whole Wheat Macaroni with Pesto, **'89** 238

Mangoes
Beef and Rice, Mango-, **'88** 138
Cake, Mango, **'83** 150
Chutney, Mango, **'89** 141
Crêpes, Mango-Pineapple, **'86** 216
Dessert Tamales, Mango, **'94** 190
Frappé, Mango, **'86** 216
Ice Cream, Mango, **'86** 216
Orange Smoothie, Mango-, **'86** 216
Pan Dowdy, Mango, **'83** 150
Pie, Green Mango, **'79** 137
Pie, Mango-Ginger, **'88** 138
Preserves, Mango-Pineapple, **'79** 137
Relish, Mango, **'89** 198
Salad, Fresh Mango, **'84** 126
Salad, Mango, **'79** 137
Salad with Mango, Chicken, **'86** 215
Salsa, Mango, **'91** 182
Sauce, Mango, **'83** 120
Sauce, Mango-Spiced Rum, **'86** 215
Slaw, Mango, **'93** 31; **'94** 71
Sorbet, Mango, **'86** 196

Manicotti
Cheesy Manicotti, **'83** 216
Chicken Manicotti, Creamy, **'85** 60
Chili Manicotti, **'89** 247
Quick Manicotti, **'79** 6
Seafood Manicotti, **'94** 195
Special Manicotti, **'88** 50
Spinach Manicotti, **'82** 199
Stuffed Manicotti, **'83** M6
Stuffed Manicotti, Saucy, **'83** 288
Stuffed Manicotti, Spinach-, **'88** 255
Zucchini Manicotti, **'84** 194

Marinades. *See* Sauces.

Marshmallows
Ambrosia, Carrot-Marshmallow, **'80** 5
Brownies, Chewy Marshmallow, **'83** 306
Brownies, Choco-Mallow, **'87** 198; **'90** 309
Brownies, No-Bake, **'94** 330
Cake, No-Egg Chocolate Marshmallow,
 '87 97
Chocolate, Hot Laced Marshmallow, **'93** 53
Coffee Mallow, **'80** 109
Cream, Orange-Mallow, **'94** 295
Dip, Marshmallow Fruit, **'84** 171

Marshmallows *(continued)*

Frosting, Chocolate-Marshmallow, **'83** 245
Parfaits, Mocha-Mallow, **'80** 219
Popcorn Balls, Marshmallow, **'90** 226
Pudding, Banana-Mallow, **'86** 139
Sauce, Marshmallow, **'91** 91
Squares, Chocolate-Marshmallow, **'92** M50

Mayonnaise

Aioli (Garlic Mayonnaise), **'88** 221
Anchovy Mayonnaise, **'86** 179
Citrus Mayonnaise, Creamy, **'92** 107
Dill-Garlic Mayonnaise, **'92** 320
Dip, Artichokes with Herb-Mayonnaise,
  '84 67
Dip, Seasoned Mayonnaise Artichoke, **'80** 87
Dressing, Mayonnaise, **'86** 11
Flavored Mayonnaise, **'94** 167
Garlic Mayonnaise, **'92** 56
Herbed Mayonnaise, **'82** 85, 192
Homemade Mayonnaise, **'80** 155; **'90** 81
Homemade Mayonnaise, Easy, **'84** 12
Italian Herbed Mayonnaise, **'92** 320
Lemon-Cream Mayonnaise, **'85** 264
Parmesan Mayonnaise, **'86** 79
Russian Mayonnaise, **'80** 137
Sauce, Herb-Mayonnaise, **'85** 73
Tasty Mayonnaise, **'82** 192
Watercress Mayonnaise, **'93** 119
Wine Mayonnaise, Hot, **'81** 83

Meatballs

Bacon Meatballs, Burgundy, **'80** 283
Bacon-Wrapped Meatballs, **'79** 81
Beef Balls Heidelberg, **'83** 164; **'84** 39
Brandied Meatballs, **'83** 78
Chafing Dish Meatballs, **'81** 260
Charleston Press Club Meatballs, **'93** 129
Chestnut Meatballs, **'79** 110
Chinese Meatballs, **'83** 116; **'87** 194
Cocktail Meatballs, **'79** 63, 207
Creole, Meatball-Okra, **'83** 156
Creole, Meatballs, **'82** 233
Español, Meatballs, **'82** 110
Flavorful Meatballs, **'84** 206
German Meatballs, Crisp, **'92** 326
Golden Nugget Meatballs, **'82** 233
Gravy, Meatballs in, **'79** 136
Ham Balls, **'84** 91; **'86** 256
Ham Balls, Appetizer, **'82** 39
Hawaiian Meatballs, **'85** 86
Hawaiian Meatballs, Tangy, **'79** 129
Lamb Meatballs with Yogurt Sauce, **'85** 132
Meatballs, **'89** 237
Mock Meatballs, **'81** 243
Mushroom-Meatball Stroganoff, **'85** 85
Oven Barbecued Meatballs, **'82** 233
Pineapple and Peppers, Meatballs with,
  '90 145
Pizza Meatballs, **'85** 86
Polynesian Meatballs, **'80** 207
Processor Meatballs, Quick, **'87** 111
Red Delicious Meatballs, **'85** 85
Royal Meatballs, **'87** 268; **'88** 102; **'89** 67
Sandwich, Giant Meatball, **'92** 196
Saucy Meatballs, **'85** 68; **'90** 122
Saucy Party Meatballs, **'80** 149
Sauerbraten Meatballs, **'85** 85
Sauerkraut Meatballs, **'86** 257
Spaghetti-and-Herb Meatballs, **'84** 75
Spaghetti with Meatballs, **'81** 38

Spiced Meatballs, **'79** 284
Spicy Meatballs and Sausage, **'79** 163
Stew, Meatball, **'79** 198
Stroganoff, Meatball, **'81** 297
Swedish Meatballs, **'80** 80; **'86** 256
Sweet-and-Sour Meatballs, **'82** 233, 247;
  '86 240
Sweet-and-Sour Party Meatballs, **'79** 233
Tamale Balls, Tangy, **'89** 60
Tamale Meatballs, **'80** 194
Turkey Meatballs, **'89** 237
Veal Meatballs, European, **'85** 30
Venison Sausage Balls, **'80** 42
Zesty Meatballs, **'80** 250

Meat Loaf. *See* Beef, Ground/Meat Loaf.

Melons

Balls and Cherries in Kirsch, Melon, **'91** 91
Balls, Fiery Sweet Melon, **'92** 311
Balls, Mellowed-Out Melon, **'88** 182
Balls, Minted Melon, **'87** 162
Bowl with Cucumber-Mint Dressing, Melon
  Ball, **'87** 153
Cantaloupe-Cheese Salad, **'88** 184
Cantaloupe Compote, **'81** 147
Cantaloupe Cooler Salad, **'79** 176
Cantaloupe Cream Delight, **'82** 179
Cantaloupe Cream, Frozen, **'82** 159
Cantaloupe Cream Pie, **'79** 177
Cantaloupe Delight, **'89** 204
Cantaloupe, Fruit-Filled, **'83** 120
Cantaloupe Green Salad, **'91** 126
Cantaloupe Ice Cream, **'79** 177
Cantaloupe Meringue Pie, **'88** 182
Cantaloupe Mold, Double-Grape, **'79** 173
Cantaloupe-Pecan Salad, **'86** 178
Cantaloupe Pie, **'86** 163
Cantaloupe Punch, **'81** 147
Cantaloupe Salad, **'86** 182
Cantaloupe Sherbet, **'88** 183
Cantaloupe Sherbet, Frosty, **'82** 144
Cantaloupe Soup, **'83** 120; **'88** 160
Cantaloupe Soup, Chilled, **'81** 156
Cantaloupe Soup, Fresh, **'84** 190
Cantaloupe, Southern Plantation, **'82** 179
Cantaloupe Sundae, **'89** 166
Cantaloupe Surprise, Sherbet-, **'91** 105
Cantaloupe, Sweet Pickled, **'89** 197
Cantaloupe Wedges, Grilled, **'87** 162
Cantaloupe Whip, **'89** 198
Citrus Mingle, Melon-, **'79** 177
Compote, Melon Ball, **'85** 157
Cooler, Melon, **'81** 146
Cooler, Melon Ball, **'86** 131
Filled Melon, Berry-, **'86** 93
Fruit Bowl, Sparkling Fresh, **'80** 146

Fruit Cup with Mint Dressing, Fresh, **'80** 183
Fruit Deluxe, Marinated, **'81** 146
Fruited Ham Salad, **'81** 146
Fruit Medley, Minted, **'80** 182
Honeydew-Berry Dessert, **'83** 120
Honeydew Fruit Boats, **'81** 147
Honeydew Fruit Bowl, **'84** 186
Honeydew Fruit Cups, **'82** 179
Honeydew Granita, **'87** 162
Honeydew Melon with Grapes, **'91** 91
Honeydew Salad with Apricot Cream
  Dressing, **'84** 191
Julep, Melon-Mint, **'86** 196
Julep, Rainbow Melon, **'80** 183
Mélange, Melon, **'84** 139
Minted Melon Cocktail, **'81** 146
Mint Sauce, Melons in, **'85** 164
Salad, Avocado-Melon, **'82** 164
Salad, Congealed Melon Ball, **'84** 125
Salad, Georgia Summer, **'92** 179
Salad, Melon-and-Prosciutto, **'92** 191
Salad, Melon-Berry, **'90** 180
Salad, Summertime Melon, **'82** 101
Salad with Dill Dressing, Melon, **'88** 182
Soup, Melon, **'80** 182
Soup, Swirled Melon, **'87** 162
Sweet-and-Hot Melon, **'92** 163
Watermelon-Berry Slush, **'90** 137
Watermelon-Cherry Compote, **'90** 180
Watermelon Cookies, **'92** 179
Watermelon Frost, **'86** 196
Watermelon Fruit Basket, **'84** 161
Watermelon Ice, **'91** 173
Watermelon Mousse, Frozen, **'91** 96;
  '92 130
Watermelon Preserves, **'79** 120
Watermelon Punch, **'89** 204; **'92** 190
Watermelon Rind Pickles, **'81** 174
Watermelon Salad with Celery-Nut Dressing,
  '80 182
Watermelon Sauce, Melon Balls in, **'79** 177
Watermelon Sherbet, **'79** 155; **'92** 124
Watermelon Sherbet, Light, **'81** 147
Watermelon, Sherried, **'92** 117
Watermelon Sorbet, **'92** 190
Watermelon Sparkle, **'84** 191
Wedges with Berry Sauce, Melon, **'86** 178

Meringues

Acorns, Meringue, **'93** 284
Asparagus Meringue, **'88** 131
Baked Pear Meringues, **'85** 232
Bars, Meringue-Chocolate Chip, **'84** 118
Basket, Summer Berry, **'84** 158
Cake, Brown Sugar Meringue, **'81** 70
Cake, Orange Meringue, **'86** 336; **'87** 84
Cakes, Spanish Wind, **'84** 157
Coconut Kisses, **'90** 106
Coffee Meringues with Butterscotch Mousse,
  '93 254
Cooked Meringue, **'86** 130
Cooked Meringue, Easy, **'82** 207;
  '83 158
Cookies, Forget 'em, **'83** 256
Cookies, Meringue Kiss, **'86** 121
Cookies, Meringue Surprise, **'86** 320
Cran-Apple Mousse Filling, Meringues with,
  '93 254
Cups, Kiwi and Cream in Meringue, **'81** 279
Cups, Lemon Custard in Meringue, **'80** 295;
  '81 172
Cups, Lemon Meringue Cream, **'84** 23

Meringues (continued)

Fingers, Chocolate-Almond Meringue, '84 158
Flowers, Meringue, '84 156
Frosting, Brown Sugar Meringue, '81 70
Frosting, Meringue, '86 336; '87 84
Holiday Meringues, '88 280
Meringue, '87 207; '94 208
Pavlova, '92 101
Peach Melba Meringues, '87 76
Pears with Meringue, Amaretto, '90 58
Pineapple, Meringue-Topped, '84 178
Piping Meringue, '84 156
Shell, Cinnamon Meringue, '82 263
Shells, Fruited Meringue, '87 32
Shells, Fruit-Filled Meringue, '86 151
Strawberry Meringues, '84 188
Strawberry Meringue Torte, '88 136
Toffee Meringue Torte, '87 118
Vacherin Moka, '80 55
Microwave. Includes microwave conversions.
Appetizers
Bacon-Chestnut Wraps, '84 M216
Brie Appetizer, Bit-of-, '88 M8
Brie, Chutney-Bacon, '90 M292
Brie, Tropical Breeze, '94 M18
Canapés, Green Onion, '84 M216
Cheese Log, Toasted Pecan, '86 M288
Cheese Sticks, Peppery, '81 M289
Crab-Zucchini Bites, '84 M216
Dip, Cheddar-Bacon, '89 M119
Dip, Chili-and-Cheese, '89 M328
Dip, Chipped Beef, '88 M8
Dip, Creamy Crab, '80 M135
Dip, Hot Artichoke Seafood, '85 M212
Dip, Mexican Artichoke, '90 M292
Dip, Nacho, '93 M330
Dip, Shrimp, '88 M261
Franks, Saucy Appetizer, '84 M12
Mix, Spicy Party, '81 M138
Mushrooms, Shrimp-Stuffed, '80 M135
Mushrooms, Spinach-Stuffed,
'88 M261; '89 M133
Mushrooms, Tipsy, '84 M216
Nachos, Make-Ahead, '80 M135
Nuts, Sherry-Orange, '86 M289
Nuts, Spiced, '91 M316
Pâté, Chicken Liver, '88 M132
Pecans, Spicy, '81 M289
Pizzas, Appetizer, '89 M118
Popcorn, Caramel, '86 M212
Popcorn, Garlic, '83 M315
Potato Shell Appetizers, '89 M119
Potato Skins, Cheese, '84 M239
Rumaki, '80 M136
Spread, Artichoke-Parmesan, '92 M95
Spread, Chicken Salad Party, '88 M8
Spread, Hearts of Palm, '90 M293
Spread, Hot Beef, '84 M216
Spread, Seafood, '86 M58
Spread, Spinach-Bacon, '92 M310
Apples, Honey-Glazed, '90 M125
Apples, Rosy Cinnamon, '87 M37
Apples, Spicy Poached, '90 M141
Beverages
Café Colombian Royal, '80 M290
Chocolate, Creole Hot, '80 M290
Chocolate, Flaming Brandied, '80 M290
Chocolate Mix, Deluxe Hot, '80 M290

Coffee, Mocha, '85 M329
Mocha, Mexican, '93 M341
Mocha, Spirited Hot, '91 M260
Tomato Cocktail, '83 M203
Blanching Chart, Microwave, '80 M181
Breads
Caramel Ring, Easy, '85 M89
Cheese-Herb Bread, '84 M144
Chocolate Loaf Bread, '88 M188
Coffee Cake, Cinnamon, '83 M203
Coffee Cake, Orange, '85 M88
Coffee Cake Ring, '85 M89
Coffee Ring, Sugarplum, '83 M37
Muffins, Apple-Bran, '85 M89
Muffins, Cheesy Cornbread, '88 M275
Muffins, Cinnamon-Nut, '85 M88
Muffins, Corn, '82 M282
Muffins, Cranberry Streusel Cake,
'88 M274
Muffins, Lemon, '88 M275
Muffins, Whole Wheat Bran, '88 M274
Pumpkin Bread, Harvest, '90 M215
Rolls, Cherry-Almond, '84 M198
Rolls, Dinner, '93 M326
Rolls, Easy Orange, '89 M131
Toast, Easy French, '82 M172
Whole Wheat-Rye Bread, '83 M37
Chutney, Autumn Fruit, '88 M230
Croutons, '86 M288
Croutons, Microwave, '86 M227
Desserts
Apple Crumble, Whole Wheat-,
'90 M213
Apple Dessert, Honey-Baked, '90 M213
Apple-Nut Crunch, '82 M238
Apple Rings, Cinnamon, '82 M237
Apples and Cream, Brandied, '82 M237
Apples, Caramel, '89 M231
Apples, Caramel-Peanut, '93 M244
Apples, Easy Baked, '82 M238
Bananas Foster, '83 M114
Bars, Blackberry Jam, '82 M185
Bars, Chewy Peanut, '80 M172
Bars, Date-Oat, '80 M172
Bars, Peanut Butter-and-Fudge,
'80 M172
Bavarian Cream, '86 M165
Blueberry Dessert, Easy, '89 M130
Brie, Almond-Raspberry, '94 M89
Brownies, Biscuit Mix, '94 M51
Brownies, Chocolate-Mint, '85 M294
Brownies, Mississippi Mud, '89 M25
Brownies, Nutty Fudge, '80 M171
Brownies, Quick, '87 M302
Cake, Fruit and Spice, '87 M97
Cake, Fudge, '94 M293
Cake, German Chocolate, '83 M233
Cake, No-Egg Chocolate Marshmallow,
'87 M97
Cake, Old-Fashioned Carrot, '83 M232
Cake, Peanut Butter, '83 M233
Candies, Turtle, '93 M41
Charlotte Russe, '82 M142
Cheesecake, Chocolate-Amaretto,
'85 M294
Cheesecake, Luscious Lemon,
'90 M196
Cheesecake, Pear-Berry, '82 M141
Cherries Jubilee, Quick, '82 M100
Chocolate-Marshmallow Squares,
'92 M50

Chocolate-Mint Parfaits, '90 M15
Chocolate-Peanut Butter Bites,
'92 M317
Chocolate Peanutty Swirls, '94 M330
Cobbler, Apple-Pecan, '84 M198
Cookies, Chocolate-Almond Surprise,
'88 M45
Cookies, Doubly-Good Chocolate,
'82 M185
Cookies, Keyboard, '94 M330
Cookies, Nutty Oatmeal-Chocolate Chip,
'82 M185
Cookies, Spice, '87 M278
Cookies, Spider, '93 M166
Cookies, Wedding, '82 M185
Cream, Vanilla, '83 M115
Crème, Orange-Tapioca, '82 M283
Crust, Chocolate, '90 M15
Crust, Graham Cracker, '88 M45;
'91 M234
Crust, Microwaved Graham Cracker,
'82 M141
Cupcakes, Cinnamon-Chocolate,
'81 M139
Custard, Chocolate-Topped Amaretto,
'87 M37
Divinity, Peanut, '87 M278
Frosting, Buttery Cinnamon, '81 M139
Frosting, Caramel, '81 M289
Frosting, Chocolate, '80 M171;
'83 M233; '87 M97; '89 M25
Frosting, Coconut-Pecan, '83 M233
Frosting, Cream Cheese, '83 M233
Fudge, Double-Good, '79 M263
Fudge, Double Good, '87 M278
Fudge, Microwave, '91 M92
Fudge, Microwave Chocolate, '92 M50
Fudge, Quick-and-Easy, '88 M190
Glaze, Chocolate, '91 M296
Ice Cream Cake for Grown-Ups,
'88 M192
Jam Squares, '81 M289
Jellyrolls, Raspberry, '93 M255
Kahlúa Delight, Make-Ahead, '84 M89
Kahlúa Velvet Dessert, '85 M294
Millionaires, '79 M262
Oatmeal Cherry-Apple Crisp, '90 M16
Oranges, Wine-Poached, '84 M323
Pastry, Basic, '84 M268
Pastry, Basic Microwave, '82 M142;
'85 M113
Pastry, Double-Crust, '82 M298
Peaches, Gingersnap, '85 M329
Peach Melba, '83 M114
Peanut Brittle, '79 M263
Peanut Butter Slice-and-Bakes,
'82 M185
Peanut-Fudge Bites, '91 M231;
'92 M68
Pears with Dark Chocolate Sauce,
Poached, '90 M141
Pecan Brittle, '91 M272
Pecan-Coconut Clusters, '86 M251
Pie, Best-Ever Chocolate, '88 M45
Pie, Caramel-Banana, '86 M165
Pie, Cranberry-Apple Holiday,
'81 M269
Pie, Double Chocolate, '82 M282
Pie, Easy Cherry, '82 M299
Pie, Festive Pumpkin, '81 M269
Pie, Fluffy Eggnog, '81 M269

Microwave, Desserts *(continued)*

Pie, Frosty Pumpkin-Praline, **'91** M234
Pie, Glazed Strawberry, **'82** M142
Pie, Lemon Meringue, **'85** M112
Pie, Microwave Chocolate, **'90** M15
Pie, Nutty Cranberry, **'82** M298
Pie, Old-Fashioned Apple, **'82** M299
Pie, Old-Fashioned Pecan, **'81** M269
Pie, Quick Pumpkin, **'88** M230
Plums, Poached, **'90** M141
Pots de Crème, **'84** M145
Pots de Crème, Mocha, **'88** M45
Pralines, **'86** M288
Pralines, Old-Fashioned, **'89** M318
Pralines, Southern, **'79** M263
Pudding, Bread, **'89** M130
Pudding, Brown Sugar-Pecan, **'86** M165
Pudding, Butternut Squash, **'89** M313;
'90 M19
Pudding, Chocolate-Almond, **'82** M142
Pudding, Creamy Banana, **'89** M130
Pudding, Mandarin-Almond, **'85** M12
Pudding, Pecan-Mocha, **'89** M130
Pudding, Pumpkin, **'89** M313; **'90** M20
Soufflé, Brandy Alexander, **'83** M114
Sundaes, Cocoa-Kahlúa, **'83** M58
Sundaes, Hot Strawberry, **'81** M5
Sundaes, Spicy Apple Ice Cream,
'86 M195
Tart, Caramel Turtle Truffle, **'93** M131
Toffee, Microwave, **'92** M317
Toffee, Nutty, **'79** M263
Truffles, Yule Street, **'90** M242
Eggs and Omelets
Baked Eggs Florentine, **'86** M12
Benedict, Easy Eggs, **'80** M268
Benedict, Light Eggs, **'93** M68
Casserole, Saucy Scrambled Egg,
'89 M213
Creamed Eggs in Patty Shells, **'80** M267
Medley, Cheddar Egg, **'81** M176
Olé Omelet, **'87** M124
Sausage Omelet, Puffy, **'80** M268
Scramble, Bacon-and-Eggs, **'80** M267
Scrambled Eggs, Creamy Onion,
'83 M203
Vegetable Omelet, Golden, **'82** M123
Fruit Bake, Cranberry-Mustard, **'90** M287
Fruit Compote, Hot, **'90** M124
Fruit Mélange, **'88** M295
Grits, Quick Cheese, **'83** M203
Jam, Freezer Blackberry, **'84** M181
Jam, Freezer Peach, **'84** M182
Jam, Freezer Plum, **'89** M156
Jam, Raspberry Freezer, **'84** M181
Jam, Strawberry Freezer, **'84** M182
Jelly, Christmas Freezer, **'86** M288
Jelly, Quick Grape, **'89** M156
Jelly, Red Pepper, **'89** M156
Macaroni and Cheese, **'83** M7;
'88 M147, M190
Main Dishes
Beans and Franks, Jiffy, **'91** M172
Beans-and-Franks, Polynesian, **'84** M11
Beef Casserole, Easy, **'86** M58
Beef Casserole, Layered, **'82** M203
Beef Roast, Easy, **'89** M65
Beef with Pea Pods, Oriental, **'86** M328
Broccoli-Ham au Gratin, **'90** M239

Burgers, Blue Cheese, **'89** M66
Casserole, Mexi, **'83** M87
Casserole, Mexican, **'92** M22
Casserole, Microwave Mexican,
'90 M231
Catfish, Microwave, **'89** M52
Catfish, Spicy-Seasoned, **'89** M66
Chicken alla Romano, **'83** M58
Chicken-and-Broccoli Stroganoff,
'89 M248
Chicken and Cashews, Ginger, **'85** M11
Chicken and Dumplings with Vegetables,
'85 M56
Chicken and Pasta, Pesto, **'89** M132
Chicken and Spinach Rollups, **'82** M68
Chicken-and-Vegetable Platter, **'88** M52
Chicken and Vegetables Vermouth,
'87 M37
Chicken-Asparagus Rolls, **'86** M211
Chicken, Barbecued, **'89** M167
Chicken Breasts, Breaded, **'89** M196
Chicken Breasts, Herb-Seasoned,
'93 M325
Chicken, Crispy Parmesan, **'80** M76
Chicken, Crunchy Spiced, **'85** M57
Chicken Dinner, Hot-and-Spicy,
'94 M94
Chicken Divan, **'80** M10; **'87** M218
Chicken Divan Casserole, **'82** M203
Chicken Divan Quiche, **'88** M125
Chicken, Easy, **'89** M129
Chicken, Ginger-Nut, **'90** M33
Chicken in a Bag, **'86** M57
Chicken Kabobs, Marinated, **'84** M144
Chicken Kabobs, Pineapple-,
'86 M328
Chicken Lasagna, **'87** M302
Chicken, Lemon, **'81** M138
Chicken, Lemon-Garlic, **'89** M132
Chicken Mexicana, **'91** M127
Chicken, Orange, **'86** M140
Chicken, Pineapple, **'83** M194
Chicken, Tangy Herbed, **'87** M302
Chicken Teriyaki, **'80** M76
Chicken Tetrazzini, **'80** M75
Chicken Tetrazzini, Cheesy, **'83** M87
Chicken Toss, Quick, **'87** M124
Chicken, Vegetable-Stuffed, **'89** M65
Chicken with Noodles, Sesame,
'88 M125
Chicken with Pecan-Rice Dressing,
'85 M57
Chicken with Tomato-Basil Pasta,
Basil-Stuffed, **'94** M204
Chicken with White Barbecue Sauce,
'89 M84
Chicken with Wild Rice, Elegant,
'80 M76
Chicken, Zesty Barbecued, **'80** M76
Chiles Rellenos with Walnut Cream
Sauce, Havarti-and-Corn-Stuffed,
'93 M275
Chili-Cheese Dogs, **'81** M176
Chili, Microwave, **'91** M232
Chili, Turkey-Bean, **'88** M213
Cornish Hens, Orange-Glazed Stuffed,
'84 M89
Crab Imperial, Pineapple-, **'84** M286
Crabmeat and Mushrooms on Toast
Points, **'82** M91
Crabmeat Imperial, Speedy, **'90** M112

Crab, Shrimp, and Artichoke au Gratin,
'90 M240
Crêpes, Sherried Beef, **'85** M29
Dinner, Easy Steamed, **'83** M314
Eggs, Cheddar, **'94** M141
Filet Mignon Patties, Mock, **'82** M68
Fillets, Apple-Carrot Stuffed, **'88** M192
Fillets, Lemon-Coated, **'80** M53
Fillets, Parmesan, **'86** M112
Fillets, Spanish-Style, **'86** M112
Fish Amandine, Fillet of, **'80** M54
Fish-and-Potato Platter, **'89** M248
Fish-and-Vegetable Dinner, **'91** M196
Fish, Creole, **'87** M79
Fish Delight, **'86** M212
Fish, Easy Italian, **'86** M112
Fish, Herb-Coated, **'86** M112
Fish in Creamy Swiss Sauce, Poached,
'80 M53
Fish Rolls, Vegetable-Filled, **'86** M251
Fish Steaks, Soy, **'86** M112
Fish, Sweet-and-Sour, **'80** M54
Fish with Greek Sauce, Poached,
'91 M183
Flounder Amandine, **'89** M196
Flounder, Baked, **'90** M316
Frankfurters, Barbecued, **'84** M12
Grits, Sausage-Cheese, **'90** M238
Grouper Fillets, Breaded, **'89** M36
Grouper with Confetti Vegetables,
'88 M189
Grouper with Sautéed Vegetables,
'90 M233
Haddock Fillets with Zucchini Stuffing,
'88 M191
Haddock Italiano, **'81** M4
Halibut Steaks Italiano, **'88** M191
Halibut with Swiss Sauce, **'83** M195
Ham and Apples, Baked, **'82** M237
Ham and Chicken, Creamed, **'81** M74
Ham-Asparagus Dinner, **'80** M10
Hamburger Patties, **'82** M172
Ham Casserole, Macaroni-, **'81** M177
Ham Loaf, Cranberry-, **'82** M77
Ham Loaf, Saucy, **'86** M328
Ham, Marmalade-Glazed, **'89** M196
Ham Ring, Chili-Sauced, **'81** M122
Ham Roll Casserole, **'91** M127
Ham Slice, Fruited, **'83** M317
Ham Steak, Glazed, **'91** M13
Ham, Sweet-and-Sour Glazed, **'88** M15
Ham Tetrazzini, **'82** M77
Ham Towers, Cheesy, **'82** M77
Ham with Raisin Sauce, **'82** M76
Kabobs, Shish, **'85** M112
Kielbasa and Cabbage, **'89** M196
Lasagna, **'83** M6
Lasagna, Easy, **'92** M197; **'93** M24
Lasagna, Lots of Noodles, **'91** M127
Lasagna, One-Step, **'89** M129
Lasagna, Quick 'n Easy, **'80** M10
Lasagna Rolls, Pepper-Topped, **'89** M36
Lasagna, Zesty, **'87** M188
Manicotti, Stuffed, **'83** M6
Meat Loaf, Basic, **'88** M14
Meat Loaf, Cheesy Pizza, **'81** M121
Meat Loaf, Easy, **'88** M214
Meat Loaf, Oriental, **'81** M122;
'83 M194
Meat Loaf, Swedish, **'81** M121
Meat Loaf, Vegetable, **'85** M29

Microwave, Main Dishes *(continued)*

Monkfish, Greek-Style, **'87** M79
Mussels Linguine, **'90** M112
Orange Roughy with Spinach Pesto,
 '88 M192
Oysters on the Half Shell, Dressed,
 '87 M79
Paella, Party, **'88** M189
Papillote, Ocean, **'84** M287
Patties, Cracked Pepper, **'89** M131
Peppers, Beef-Stuffed, **'91** M127
Peppers, Hearty Stuffed, **'88** M214
Pie, Country Breakfast, **'93** M328
Pineapple Loaves, Individual, **'81** M121
Pizza Casserole, Microwave, **'89** M248
Pizza, Jiffy Jazzed-Up, **'83** M314
Pizza, Taco, **'89** M177
Pork Casserole, Cheesy, **'81** M74
Pork Chop, Saucy, **'86** M140
Pork Chops, Lemon-Herb, **'89** M132
Pork Chops, Pineapple, **'87** M124
Pork Chops with Apricot Glaze, Stuffed,
 '89 M36
Pork Loin Roast with Red Currant Sauce,
 '89 M84
Potatoes, Frank-Filled, **'84** M11
Pot Roast, Basic, **'81** M208
Pot Roast, Company, **'88** M14
Pot Roast with Vegetables, **'81** M208
Pot Roast with Vegetables, Marinated,
 '88 M52
Quiche, Benedict, **'80** M107
Quiche, Crab, **'82** M122
Quiche Lorraine, **'80** M108
Quiche, Spicy Sausage, **'80** M108
Quiche, Spinach-Mushroom, **'81** M74
Quiche, Vegetable, **'87** M219
Ribs, Sweet-and-Sour, **'89** M84
Round Steak over Rice, Burgundy,
 '90 M33
Salmon Patties, Open-Faced, **'87** M218
Sausage and Rice Casserole, Oriental,
 '82 M123
Sausage Casserole, Easy, **'87** M189
Sausage Dinner, Beefy, **'80** M9
Sausage-Egg Casserole, **'86** M12
Sausage Jambalaya Casserole, **'82** M203
Shrimp Creole, **'90** M220
Shrimp, Garlic-Buttered, **'86** M226
Shrimp in Cream Sauce, **'84** M286
Shrimp, Quick Curried, **'84** M198
Shrimp, Sweet-and-Sour, **'90** M112
Sloppy Joes, Pocket, **'85** M328
Snapper Provençal, **'91** M170
Sole, Saucy, **'82** M68
Sole with Cucumber Sauce, **'84** M286
Spaghetti, Easy, **'83** M317
Spaghetti Pie, **'81** M32
Spinach-Tenderloin Pinwheels,
 '88 M118
Steak, Onion-Smothered, **'87** M189
Taco Pies, Individual, **'82** M282
Tacos, Jiffy, **'83** M318
Tacos, Microwave, **'88** M213
Tortilla Pie, **'85** M211
Trout, Sunshine, **'84** M286
Tuna Casserole, Easy, **'82** M203
Turkey Breast and Gravy, Savory
 Seasoned, **'89** M309
Turkey Casserole, Crunchy, **'89** M282
Turkey Divan, Creamy, **'90** M34
Turkey-Noodle-Poppyseed Casserole,
 '90 M239
Veal and Carrots in Wine Sauce,
 '86 M139
Veal, Italian Style, **'82** M68
Welsh Rarebit with Tomatoes and Bacon,
 '92 M159
Zucchini, Beef-Stuffed, **'86** M139
Marmalade, Orange-Pineapple, **'89** M156
Mustard, Coarse-and-Sweet, **'86** M288
Noodles, Cheesy Parmesan, **'83** M7
Pastry, Microwaved Quiche, **'81** M74;
 '82 M122
Pastry, Quiche, **'80** M107
Peaches, Bay Laurel, **'90** M124
Peaches with Rum, Ginger, **'84** M323
Pears, Gingered, **'89** M231
Pears, Marmalade Breakfast, **'83** M203
Pears, Spiced Fall, **'89** M231
Pineapple, Scalloped, **'84** M323
Pizza on a Bagel, **'93** M94
Pumpkin, Cooked Fresh, **'88** M230
Pumpkin Seeds, Seasoned, **'91** M234
Pumpkin Seeds, Toasted, **'88** M230
Relish, Cranberry-Orange, **'81** M289
Relish, Quick Corn, **'90** M13
Relish, Spicy Apple, **'84** M323
Relish, Tipsy Cranberry, **'92** M310
Rice, Almond, **'85** M112
Rice, Basic Long-Grain, **'83** M285
Rice, Basic Quick-Cooking, **'83** M285
Rice, Chicken-Flavored, **'84** M144
Rice, Curry-Spiced, **'86** M226
Rice, Herb, **'91** M257
Rice, Herbed, **'83** M285
Rice, Jiffy Spanish, **'90** M176
Rice, Oriental, **'85** M12, 146
Rice, Parsleyed, **'83** M58
Rice with Almonds, Curried, **'83** M285
Salads
 Artichokes with Orzo Salad, **'88** M193
 Beef Salad, Tangy, **'87** M218
 Chef Salad, Microwave, **'90** M146
 Chicken Salad, Special, **'88** M193
 Chicken Taco Salad, **'94** M136
 Fast-and-Easy Salad, **'85** M328
 Fruit Salad with Mint Sauce, **'88** M96
 Green Beans-and-Cheese Salad,
  '91 M159
 Pork-and-Spinach Salad, Mandarin,
  '88 M126
 Potato Salad, Chunky, **'81** M138
 Potato Salad, German-Style, **'88** M194
 Spinach Salad, Sweet-Sour, **'85** M112
 Spinach Salad, Wilted, **'81** M4
 Taco Salad Cups, **'85** M29
 Tuna Salad, Cheese-Sauced, **'87** M124
Sandwiches
 Asparagus-and-Ham Melt Sandwiches,
  '88 M96
 Breakfast Pita Pockets, **'89** M21
 Breakfast Sandwiches, **'82** M123;
  '89 M230
 Brown Bread-Cream Cheese
  Sandwiches, **'87** M6
 Burgers, Pizza, **'80** M201
 Crabmeat Sandwiches, Deluxe,
  '81 M74
 Frankfurter Sandwiches, **'84** M11
Fruit-and-Cheese Breakfast Sandwiches,
 '89 M21
Grilled Cheese Sandwiches, **'82** M172
Hot Brown Sandwiches, **'80** M202
Pita Sandwiches, Denver, **'86** M12
Pita Sandwiches, Hot, **'87** M6
Pizza Sandwiches, Open-Face,
 '84 M198
Pork Sandwiches, Party, **'88** M273
Reuben Sandwiches, **'80** M201
Sausage-Cheese Muffin Sandwiches,
 '92 M212
Tuna Sandwiches, Hot, **'86** M194
Sauces and Gravies
 Almond-Vanilla Custard Sauce,
  '88 M177
 Amaretto-Strawberry Sauce, **'87** M165
 Apple Dessert Sauce, **'87** M165
 Barbecue Sauce, Lemony, **'88** M177
 Béchamel Sauce, **'84** M239
 Blueberry Sauce, **'89** M130
 Cheese Sauce, **'79** M156; **'82** M123
 Cheese Sauce, Guilt-Free, **'93** M95
 Cheesy Vegetable Sauce, **'92** M134
 Cherry Sauce, Elegant, **'79** M156
 Chocolate Cherry Sauce, **'87** M165
 Chocolate Mint Sauce, Quick, **'86** M58
 Chocolate-Peanut Butter Sauce,
  '79 M156
 Chocolate-Praline Sauce, **'85** M295
 Chocolate Sauce, Creamy, **'88** M177
 Crab Marinara Sauce, Quick, **'85** M151
 Cream Sauce, Sherried, **'85** M152
 Curry Sauce, **'79** M156; **'84** M71
 Dill Sauce, **'84** M70
 Dill Sauce, Creamy, **'79** M156
 Garlic-Cheese Sauce, **'84** M70
 Hollandaise Sauce, **'80** M107, M268;
  '88 M177
 Horseradish-Mustard Sauce, Creamy,
  '88 M177
 Horseradish Sauce, **'88** M273
 Lemon Dessert Sauce, **'87** M165
 Mint Sauce, **'88** M96
 Mushroom Sauce, **'84** M70
 Mustard Sauce, **'84** M70
 Orange Sauce, **'84** M286
 Orange Sauce, Sweet, **'93** M325
 Parsley-Garlic Sauce, **'84** M70
 Peach-Berry Sauce, **'87** M165
 Peanut Dessert Sauce, **'86** M251
 Pineapple Ice Cream Sauce, **'81** M289
 Praline Ice Cream Sauce, Southern,
  '86 M227
 Sour Cream Sauce, **'82** M68
 Swiss Sauce, **'83** M195
 Taco Sauce, **'82** M283
 Tomato Sauce, Herbed Fresh, **'85** M151
 Tomato Sauce, Italian, **'82** M68
 Vegetable-Cheese Sauce, **'85** M152
 White Sauce, Basic, **'79** M156
Sausage in a Bun, **'89** M22
Soups and Stews
 Bacon-Beer Cheese Soup, **'87** M7
 Beef Stew with Parsley Dumplings,
  '85 M246
 Broccoli Soup, **'86** M194
 Broccoli Soup, Cream of, **'80** M225
 Carrot-Mint Soup, Chilled, **'90** M168
 Carrot Soup, Creamy, **'92** M218
 Cauliflower Soup, Cream of, **'87** M7

Microwave, Soups and Stews *(continued)*

Cheese Soup, Bacon-Topped, **'80** M224
Cheese Soup, Monterey Jack, **'85** M211
Chicken Broth, Easy Microwave,
  '90 M167
Chicken Soup, Quick, **'86** M72
Chili, Basic, **'82** M11
Chili, Beefy Sausage, **'82** M11
Chili, Cheese-Topped, **'82** M11
Chili, Chunky, **'82** M11
Chili with Rice, **'82** M11
Chowder, Corn, **'84** M38
Chowder, Creamy Ham, **'88** M53
Chowder, Fish, **'84** M38
Chowder, New England Clam, **'86** M72
Crab Soup, Creamy, **'80** M224
Cucumber Soup, Dilled, **'90** M167
Egg-Drop Soup, **'85** M12
Garden Harvest Soup, Italian, **'90** M167
Mushroom Soup, **'86** M73
Mushroom Soup, Curried, **'84** M89
Onion Soup, French, **'86** M212
Onion Soup, Shortcut French, **'85** M328
Oyster-and-Artichoke Soup, Louisiana,
  '92 M81
Pea Soup, Spring, **'88** M96
Potato-Bacon Soup, **'84** M38
Potato Soup, Cream of, **'80** M224
Potato-Yogurt Soup, **'92** M217
Strawberry Soup Supreme, **'81** M144
Tomato-Celery Soup, **'83** M58
Tomato-Vegetable Soup, **'81** M177
Vegetable Soup, Beefy, **'84** M38
Vegetable Soup, Chunky, **'89** M283
Spread, Peachy Cream Cheese, **'90** M215
Topping, Streusel, **'88** M275
Vegetables
  Acorn Rings, Easy Glazed, **'81** M231
  Artichokes, **'92** M107
  Artichokes, Stuffed, **'91** M117
  Asparagus-Carrot-Squash Toss,
    '91 M45
  Asparagus in Lemon Butter, **'80** M123
  Asparagus, Lemon-Sesame, **'91** M31
  Asparagus-Pea Casserole, **'88** M294
  Asparagus with Almond Sauce,
    '91 M117
  Asparagus with Lemon Butter,
    '87 M151
  Beans, Marinated Italian, **'86** M226
  Beets, Harvard, **'83** M195
  Beets with Sour Cream Dressing,
    '88 M295
  Black-Eyed Peas, Fresh, **'81** M165
  Broccoli au Gratin, **'82** M20
  Broccoli, Chinese, **'85** M12
  Broccoli Goldenrod, Lemon-, **'84** M89
  Broccoli, Marinated Fresh, **'81** M139
  Broccoli-Swiss Cheese Casserole,
    '85 M211
  Carrots-and-Celery, Scalloped,
    '84 M112
  Carrots, Orange-Fennel, **'92** M133
  Carrots, Orange-Glazed, **'81** M165;
    '90 M98
  Carrots, Peach-Glazed, **'90** M13
  Carrots, Spice-Glazed, **'83** M58
  Corn-and-Bean Casserole, **'90** M208
  Corn Fix-Up, Quick, **'81** M4

Corn, Mexi-, **'82** M21
Corn on the Cob, Microwaved,
  '80 M122
Corn on the Cob, Parmesan, **'88** M187
Corn on the Cob, Spicy, **'87** M151
Corn, Parslied, **'90** M155
Corn, Seasoned Fresh, **'83** M147
Corn, Southern-Style Creamed,
  '81 M165
Eggplant, Easy, **'87** M151
Fresh Vegetables, Microwaving,
  '82 M138
Garden Harvest, **'85** M142
Green Beans, **'87** M151
Green Beans Amandine, **'82** M20
Green Beans, Bacon-Topped, **'80** M123
Green Beans, Baked, **'91** M159
Green Beans, French, **'90** M208
Green Beans, Garlic, **'91** M159
Green Beans, Herbed, **'83** M147;
  '88 M190
Green Beans, Nutty, **'88** M187
Green Beans Oriental, **'91** M158
Green Beans, Tangy, **'85** M142
Green Beans with Marjoram, Fresh,
  '91 M159
Green Peas, Company, **'91** M31
Julienne Vegetables with Walnuts,
  '86 M251
Kabobs, Marinated Vegetable,
  '83 M195
Leeks in Dilled Lemon-Butter, **'90** M98
Medley, Garden Vegetable, **'91** M45
Medley, Vegetable, **'89** M129
Mixed Vegetables, **'83** M195
Okra and Tomatoes, Fresh, **'81** M165
Okra, Corn, and Peppers, **'87** M151
Okra Medley, **'88** M185
Onion-Potato Bake, **'83** M195
Onions and Peppers, Sautéed, **'83** M148
Onions, Micro-Baked, **'82** M32
"Pasta," Garden-Fresh, **'94** M134
Peas and Peppers, Minted, **'90** M99
Peas in a Potato Nest, **'84** M239
Peas with Almonds, Curried, **'88** M294
Pepper Cups, Hot Vegetable, **'88** M188
Platter, Vegetable, **'88** M187
Potato Casserole, Creamy, **'84** M113
Potatoes, Basil-Cheese, **'90** M316
Potatoes, Blue Cheese Stuffed,
  '92 M228
Potatoes, Broccoli-Shrimp Stuffed,
  '92 M228
Potatoes, Cheesy Bacon-Stuffed,
  '81 M61
Potatoes, Chili-Cheese, **'90** M62
Potatoes, Cottage, **'93** M92
Potatoes, Creamy Cheese, **'88** M146
Potatoes, Hearty Stuffed, **'89** M282
Potatoes, Herbed New, **'83** M148
Potatoes, Jalapeño-Ham Stuffed,
  '81 M61
Potatoes, Micro-Baked, **'81** M61
Potatoes, Orange-Baked Sweet,
  '88 M294
Potatoes, Parmesan, **'90** M62;
  '92 M341; **'93** M46
Potatoes, Quick Baked, **'92** M134
Potatoes, Quick Browned, **'82** M172
Potatoes, Seasoned New, **'87** M151
Potatoes, Shrimp-Sauced, **'81** M61

Potatoes, Soufflé, **'90** M14
Potatoes, Summertime, **'86** M195
Potatoes, Taco-Topped, **'93** M18
Potatoes, Twice-Baked, **'91** M185
Potatoes with Béchamel Sauce, Stuffed,
  '84 M239
Potatoes with Chives, **'81** M61
Potatoes with Hot Bacon Dressing,
  '88 M294
Potatoes, Zesty Stuffed, **'94** M46
Potato Fans, Parmesan, **'84** M240
Potato Fans, Parmesan-, **'88** M190
Potato, Twice-Baked, **'90** M295
Potato Wedges, **'94** M119
Potato Wedges, Lemony, **'90** M61
Snow Peas and Tomatoes, Basil, **'88** M185
Spinach Casserole, **'91** M31
Spinach Delight, **'84** M144
Squash-and-Pepper Toss, Crisp,
  '87 M152
Squash, Apple-Stuffed Butternut,
  '81 M232
Squash Bake, Cheddar-, **'84** M113
Squash Casserole, Jiffy, **'81** M144
Squash, Country Club, **'88** M16
Squash, Cranberry-Filled Acorn,
  '81 M231
Squash Medley, Fresh, **'81** M165
Squash Mexican, Stuffed, **'90** M200
Squash Ring, Butternut, **'81** M232
Squash, Sausage-Stuffed Acorn,
  '81 M231
Squash, Stuffed White, **'90** M201
Squash Stuffed with Spinach Pesto,
  '89 M133
Squash Toss, Simple, **'85** M142
Squash with Meat Sauce, Spaghetti,
  '88 M180
Steamed Herbed Vegetables, **'93** M303
Stir-Fry, Vegetable, **'82** M172
Sweet Potatoes, Applesauce, **'91** M292;
  '92 M256
Tomatoes with Walnut-Rice Stuffing,
  '91 M102
Tomatoes, Zippy Mustard, **'86** M226
Zucchini and Carrots, Julienne, **'90** M14
Zucchini Boats, **'85** M143
Zucchini-Egg Casserole, **'84** M113
Zucchini, Italian, **'83** M147
Zucchini, Stuffed, **'89** M133
Vinaigrette Dressing and Croutons,
  '86 M288
Waffles, Honey-Buttered Peanut Butter,
  '94 M206
Mincemeat
Apples, Baked Mincemeat-Filled, **'80** 276
Bars, Mincemeat-Spice, **'88** 231; **'89** 22
Cake, Mincemeat Spice, **'79** 246
Cakes, Mini-Mincemeat Nut, **'88** 257
Cookies, Mincemeat, **'79** 51
Cookies, Mincemeat Drop, **'79** 246
Cookies, Mincemeat Sweetheart, **'87** 293
Cookies, Pear Mincemeat, **'84** 264
Homemade Mincemeat, **'79** 245
Peaches, Mincemeat, **'85** 178
Peaches with Mincemeat, Brandied, **'81** 47
Pear Mincemeat, **'79** 196; **'84** 264; **'88** 226
Pie, Apple-Mincemeat, **'85** 316
Pie, Holiday Mincemeat, **'80** 282; **'87** 213
Pie, Mincemeat-Cheese, **'80** 253
Pie, Mincemeat Chiffon, **'79** 245

Mincemeat *(continued)*

Pie, Mincemeat-Peach, **'80** 295; **'81** 188
Pie, Pear-Mince, **'81** 271
Pie, Pear Mincemeat, **'84** 264; **'88** 226
Pie, Spirited Mince, **'92** 316
Pudding, Steamed Mincemeat, **'80** 264
Salad, Holiday Mincemeat, **'85** 263
Salad, Mincemeat, **'94** 282

Mousses

Amaretto-Chocolate Mousse, **'86** 50
Amaretto-Chocolate Mousse, Elegant, **'86** 337
Amaretto Mousse, **'86** 188
Apricot Mousse, **'82** 72; **'91** 297
Asparagus Mousse Salad, **'86** 252
Butterscotch Mousse, **'93** 254
Cake, Chocolate Mousse, **'87** 264
Catfish Mousse, **'92** 327
Caviar Mousse, **'82** 71; **'85** 86; **'92** 83
Chocolate-Almond Mousse, **'93** 316
Chocolate Mousse, **'88** 280
Chocolate Mousse au Grand Marnier, **'91** 296
Chocolate Mousse Baked Alaska, **'85** 195
Chocolate Mousse, Blender, **'82** 71
Chocolate Mousse, Blender-Quick, **'80** 269
Chocolate Mousse, Brandy-, **'85** 102
Chocolate Mousse, Creamy, **'87** 133
Chocolate Mousse, Honeyed, **'87** 223
Chocolate Mousse, Kid-Pleasin', **'90** 271
Chocolate Mousse Parfait, **'94** 90
Chocolate Mousse, Quick, **'85** 87
Chocolate Mousse Roll, **'88** 280
Chocolate-Orange Mousse, **'81** 16, 205
Chocolate Rum Mousse, **'86** 189
Coconut-Pineapple Mousse, **'94** 198
Coffee Mousse, **'84** 126
Coffee-Nut Mousse, **'86** 319
Crabmeat Mousse, **'90** 190; **'91** 244; **'94** 159
Crab Mousse, **'79** 117
Cran-Apple Mousse, **'93** 255
Crème de Menthe Mousse, **'80** 109
Cucumber Mousse, **'79** 11; **'88** 121
Horseradish Mousse, **'84** 126
Lemon Cloud Mousse, **'90** 90
Lemon Mousse with Raspberry Sauce, **'91** 96; **'92** 130
Lime Mousse Freeze, Luscious, **'81** 173
Mocha Mousse, **'94** 232
Mustard Mousse, **'84** 127; **'86** 184
Orange Mousse, **'86** 69; **'94** 198
Oyster Mousse, **'81** 245
Oyster Mousse, Smoked, **'84** 320
Peach Macaroon Mousse, **'80** 153
Peach Mousse, **'85** 54
Peppermint Candy Mousse, **'82** 71; **'94** 198
Peppermint Mousse, **'93** 315
Pie, Chocolate-Amaretto Mousse, **'80** 180; **'81** 30
Pie, Chocolate Mousse, **'81** 136
Pineapple Mousse, Elegant, **'79** 230
Pumpkin Mousse, **'91** 96; **'92** 130
Quick-as-a-Wink Mousse, **'84** 311
Raspberry Mousse, **'81** 34
Raspberry Mousse in Chocolate Crinkle Cups, **'93** 270
Rhubarb Mousse, **'88** 93
Roquefort Mousse, **'82** 71
Salmon Dill Mousse, **'81** 21

Salmon Mousse, Irresistible, **'79** 284
Sherried Mousse, **'81** 247
Shrimp Mousse, **'79** 57; **'87** 196, 251
Strawberry-Lemon Mousse, **'82** 128
Strawberry Mousse, **'81** 95
Strawberry Mousse, Fresh, **'82** 72
Tuna Mousse, **'80** 275
Watercress Mousse, **'88** 104
Watermelon Mousse, Frozen, **'91** 96; **'92** 130
White Chocolate Mousse, **'91** 247; **'93** 315

Muffins

All-Bran Oat Bran Muffins, **'91** 134
Almond Muffins, **'90** 87
Almond Muffins, Peachy-, **'86** 301
Apple-Bran Muffins, **'85** M89
Apple-Carrot Muffins, **'91** 213
Apple-Cinnamon Oat Bran Muffins, **'89** 106
Apple Muffins, **'83** 96; **'84** 193; **'87** 23
Apple Muffins, Fresh, **'84** 264
Apple Muffins, Spiced, **'79** 60
Apple-Oat Muffins, Spicy, **'86** 45
Applesauce Muffins, **'84** 284; **'91** 141
Applesauce Muffins, Bite-Size, **'82** 104
Applesauce Spice Muffins, **'88** 236
Bacon-and-Cheese Muffins, **'89** 205
Banana Bran Muffins, **'83** 48
Banana-Chocolate Chip Muffins, Jumbo, **'93** 339
Banana-Chocolate Muffins, **'94** 197
Banana-Honey-Nut Muffins, **'88** 62
Banana Muffins, **'80** 88; **'84** 75
Banana-Nut Muffins, **'93** 140
Banana Oat Bran Muffins, **'89** 106
Banana-Oatmeal Muffins, **'84** 20
Banana-Oat Muffins, **'87** 188
Banana-Orange Muffins, **'84** 148
Banana-Poppyseed Muffins, **'89** 205
Banana-Raisin Muffins, **'89** 218
Banana Surprise Muffins, **'82** 105
Basic Cupcake Muffins, **'90** 87
Blueberry-Bran Muffins, **'89** 23
Blueberry Buttermilk Muffins, **'80** 16
Blueberry-Cream Cheese Muffins, **'86** 14
Blueberry Ice Cream Muffins, **'82** 143
Blueberry-Lemon Muffins, **'79** 7
Blueberry Muffins, **'80** 143; **'91** 140, 203
Blueberry Muffins, Easy, **'81** 197
Blueberry Muffins, Golden, **'79** 235
Blueberry Muffins, Old-Fashioned, **'86** 161
Blueberry Muffins with Streusel Topping, **'88** 129
Blueberry Oat Bran Muffins, **'89** 106
Blueberry-Oatmeal Muffins, **'87** 24
Blueberry-Oat Muffins, **'92** 119
Blueberry Streusel Muffins, **'80** 46
Bran-Buttermilk Muffins, **'85** 7
Bran Muffins, **'84** 53

Bran Muffins, Easy, **'83** 55
Bran Muffins, Ever-Ready, **'81** 106
Bran Muffins for Two, **'84** 211
Bran Muffins, Freezer, **'91** 141
Bran, Muffins Made of, **'86** 103
Bran Muffins, Maple-, **'90** 66
Bran Muffins, Quick, **'86** 85
Bran Muffins, Refrigerator, **'79** 6
Bran Muffins, Sour Cream-, **'87** 98
Bran Muffins, Spiced, **'84** 229
Breakfast Bites, **'86** 15
Caraway-Cheese Muffins, **'91** 213
Carrot-and-Raisin Muffins, **'87** 24
Carrot-Date-Nut Muffins, **'86** 262
Carrot-Pineapple Muffins, **'81** 6
Carrot-Wheat Muffins, **'88** 9
Cheddar Muffins, **'89** 15
Cheddar-Raisin Muffins, **'91** 51
Cheese-and-Pepper Muffin Mix, **'89** 330
Cheese-and-Pepper Muffins, **'84** 139
Cheese Muffins, Marvelous, **'83** 96
Cherry Muffins, **'82** 105
Cherry Muffins, Dried, **'94** 59
Cherry-Nut Muffins, **'90** 87
Chive Muffins, **'91** 34
Chocolate Chip Muffins, **'90** 87
Cinnamon-Nut Muffins, **'85** M88
Cinnamon-Pecan Muffins, **'84** 219
Coconut-Molasses Muffins, **'82** 210
Coffee Cake Muffins, **'79** 7
Cornbread Muffins, Cheesy, **'88** M275
Cornbread Muffins, Southern, **'85** 201
Cornbread Muffins, Spicy, **'90** 59
Cornmeal Muffins, **'80** 90; **'88** 92; **'91** 19
Cornmeal Muffins, Miniature, **'93** 119
Cornmeal Yeast Muffins, **'92** 49
Corn Muffins, **'82** M282; **'84** 16
Corn Muffins, Blue, **'89** 145; **'92** 52
Corn Muffins, Jalapeño-, **'93** 164
Corn Muffins, Quick, **'88** 15
Corn Muffins, Sage-, **'83** 207
Corn Muffins, Tex-Mex, **'92** 253; **'93** 144
Corn Muffins, Tomato, **'81** 137
Corn-Oat Muffins, **'89** 108
Cranberry Muffins, **'81** 249
Cranberry Muffins, Miniature, **'90** 294
Cranberry Oat Bran Muffins, **'89** 107
Cranberry-Pecan Muffins, **'84** 269
Cranberry Streusel Cake Muffins, **'88** M274
Date Muffins, **'79** 142
Date Muffins, Surprise, **'79** 216
Date-Nut Muffins, **'84** 75
Dino-Mite Muffins, **'94** 197
Egg Muffins, One-, **'83** 9
English Muffins, **'87** 49; **'88** 76
English Muffins, Raisin, **'80** 75
Fiber Muffins, High-, **'85** 250
Fig Muffins, **'86** 206
Gingerbread Muffins, **'81** 285
Gingerbread Muffins, Last-Minute, **'82** 105
Grain Muffins, Four-, **'80** 46
Ham-and-Cheese Muffins, **'92** 252; **'93** 144
Honey Bran Muffins, **'88** 171
Honey-Bran Muffins, **'89** 250
Honey-Oatmeal Muffins, **'84** 229
Honey-Wheat Muffins, **'83** 96; **'88** 263
Jam Muffins, **'79** 7
Jelly-Filled Muffins, **'80** 16
Kiwifruit Muffins, **'87** 255
Lemon Muffins, **'88** 119, M275
Lemon Muffins, Fresh, **'79** 161

Muffins *(continued)*

Lemon-Raspberry Muffins, **'92** 119
Magic Muffins, **'79** 244
Mayonnaise Muffins, **'83** 57; **'86** 16
Merry Muffins, **'82** 253
Mix, Quick, **'94** 167
Mix, Quick Bread, **'81** 90
Monster Muffins, **'94** 256
Morning Glory Muffins, **'93** 327
Muffins, **'81** 90
Nut Crunch Muffins, Best Ever, **'82** 65;
    '83 106
Nut Muffins, Tasty, **'79** 208
Nutty Muffins, **'86** 141
Oat Bran-Banana Muffins, **'91** 18
Oat Bran Muffins, **'89** 106
Oatmeal Bran Muffins, **'81** 236
Oatmeal-Bran Muffins, **'91** 83
Oatmeal-Honey Muffins, **'83** 95
Oatmeal Muffins, **'82** 129, 210; **'84** 72, 140;
    '92 163
Oatmeal Muffins, Best-Ever, **'84** 242
Okra Muffins, Fresh, **'93** 161
Onion-Dill Muffins, **'92** 253; **'93** 144
Orange-Date Muffins, **'92** 119
Orange-Ginger Muffins, **'89** 41
Orange-Honey Muffins, **'88** 284
Orange Juice Muffins with Honey Spread,
    '81 229
Orange Muffins, **'79** 236; **'81** 107; **'83** 54;
    '89 205
Orange Muffins, Streusel-Topped, **'84** 74
Orange-Oatmeal Muffins, **'85** 202
Orange-Pecan Muffins, **'83** 96
Peach Muffins, Special, **'84** 74
Peanut Butter-Chocolate Chip Muffins,
    '94 167
Peanut Butter-Honey Muffins, **'82** 56
Peanut Butter Muffins, **'80** 86; **'87** 158
Peanut Muffins, **'91** 223
Pear-Ginger Muffins, **'91** 240
Pecan Muffins, **'80** 16
Pecan Muffins, Chunky, **'88** 9
Pecan Muffins, Country, **'83** 222
Pineapple Muffins, **'81** 14, 250
Plum Good Muffins, **'83** 96
Poppy Seed Muffins, **'81** 63; **'91** 34
Prune Muffins, Miniature, **'85** 223
Pumpkin Muffins, **'79** 206, 275; **'81** 272
Pumpkin Muffins, Nutty, **'86** 291
Raisin Muffins, Breakfast, **'84** 59
Raisin-Nut Muffins, **'92** 46
Raisin Oat Bran Muffins, **'89** 106
Raisin-Pecan Ginger Muffins, **'88** 9
Rum-Nut Muffins, **'90** 87
Sandwiches, Sausage-Cheese Muffin,
    '92 M212
Sausage-Cheese Muffins, **'86** 213
Sausage Muffins, **'88** 52
Sausage Muffins, Cheesy, **'92** 252; **'93** 144
Sesame-Cheese Muffins, **'86** 16
Sour Cream Muffins, **'90** 283
Sour Cream Muffins, Mini, **'88** 283
Southwestern Muffins, **'91** 34
Squash Muffins, **'91** 69
Squash Muffins, Yellow, **'81** 163
Sunshine Muffins, **'86** 9
Sweet Potato Muffins, **'81** 224; **'85** 6;
    '87 280; **'92** 31

Tea Muffins, **'82** 105
Tropical Muffins, **'84** 299
Wheat Germ-Prune Muffins, **'81** 106
Wheat Muffins, Fruited, **'79** 93
Whole Wheat Bran Muffins, **'88** M274
Whole Wheat Raisin Muffins, **'85** 207
Yam Muffins, **'79** 7
Yeast Muffins, Quick, **'84** 69
Yogurt-Muesli Muffins, **'90** 215
Yogurt Muffins, **'88** 55
Zucchini Muffins, **'83** 121; **'86** 146

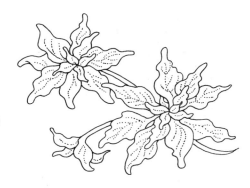

Mushrooms
Acorn Squash-Mushroom Puree, **'93** 305
à la King, Mushrooms, **'89** 285
Appetizers, Chicken-Mushroom, **'88** 210
Asparagus and Mushrooms, **'85** 108
au Gratin, Mushrooms, **'81** 108
Aztec Mushrooms, **'82** 51
Bake, Cheesy Macaroni-Mushroom, **'81** 243
Baked Mushrooms, Creamy, **'87** 127
Bake, Mushroom-Chicken, **'89** 147
Bake, Windsor Mushroom, **'88** 132
Balls, Cheese and Mushroom, **'79** 63
Beef Tenderloin with Mushrooms, **'87** 115
Bisque, Brisk Mushroom, **'81** 190
Bundles, Chicken-Mushroom, **'80** 157
Burgers, Mushroom, **'89** 164
Canapés, Mushroom, **'80** 285
Casserole, Crab-and-Mushroom, **'89** 96
Casserole, Egg-Mushroom, **'83** 49
Casserole, Mushroom-Artichoke, **'87** 241
Casserole, Mushroom-Cheese, **'83** 216
Casserole, Mushroom-Potato, **'84** 5
Casserole, Sausage-Mushroom Breakfast,
    '86 95
Champignons au Vin, **'79** 47
Cheesecake, Spinach-Mushroom, **'92** 326
Chicken and Mushrooms in Wine Sauce,
    '81 109
Chicken Livers with Mushrooms, **'81** 133
Chicken-Mushroom Dinner, **'81** 3
Chicken with Artichokes and Mushrooms,
    '90 35
Chowder, Mushroom, **'79** 16
Chowder, Mushroom-Potato, **'92** 331
Consommé aux Champignons, **'79** 48
Crabmeat and Mushrooms on Toast Points,
    '82 M91
Creamed Mushrooms in Wild Rice Ring,
    '80 270
Creamed Mushrooms on Toast, **'81** 190
Creamed Oyster Mushrooms, **'89** 61
Crêpes, Cheese and Mushroom, **'81** 88
Crêpes, Coquilles St. Jacques, **'83** 13

Crêpes, Mushroom-Cheese, **'87** 289;
    '88 135
Curried Mushrooms, **'84** 214
Dip, Hot Mushroom, **'89** 48
Dressing, Whole Wheat-Mushroom, **'84** 283
Drunk Mushrooms, **'83** 174
Egg Delight, Mushroom-, **'83** 14
Eggplant, Mushroom-Stuffed, **'83** 136
Filling in a Peel, Mushroom, **'84** 214
Filling, Mushroom, **'81** 89; **'82** 259; **'83** 51;
    '88 84
Filling, Spinach-Mushroom, **'80** 215
Fluted Mushrooms, **'82** 280
Fresh Mushrooms, Savory, **'85** 268
Fried Mushrooms, French-, **'82** 78
Fried Mushrooms with Tartar Sauce,
    French-, **'86** 233
Gravy, Baked Quail with Mushroom, **'89** 273
Green Beans, Mushroom-Bacon, **'91** 291;
    '92 255
Green Beans with Bacon and Mushrooms,
    '92 13
Green Beans with Mushrooms, **'82** 21;
    '93 89
Heavenly Mushrooms, **'87** 281
Herbed Mushrooms, **'84** 214; **'88** 176
Logs, Mushroom, **'84** 206
Marinated Herb Mushrooms, **'86** 327
Marinated Mushroom Caps, **'83** 128
Marinated Mushrooms, **'80** 82, 270; **'81** 69;
    '86 135; **'91** 306; **'92** 328
Marinated Mushrooms, Easy, **'86** 217
Marinated Mushrooms, Mexican, **'81** 66
Marinated Mushrooms, Special, **'83** 13
Marsala, Veal-and-Mushrooms, **'89** 44
Muffin Stacks, Mushroom-Topped, **'80** 271
Newburg, Mushroom, **'88** 252
Noodles and Mushrooms, Cheesy, **'79** 84
Omelet, Broccoli-Mushroom, **'85** 45
Omelet, Rolled Mushroom, **'82** 70
Panuchos, Mushroom, **'83** 51
Pastry Cups, Mushroom-Almond, **'88** 210
Pâté de Champignon, **'93** 171
Pâté in Pastry, Turkey-Mushroom, **'92** 327
Pâté, Mushroom, **'89** 157
Patty Shells, Mushrooms and Eggs in,
    '85 143; **'88** 197
Patty Shells, Mushrooms in, **'80** 283
Peas and Mushrooms, **'83** 141
Peas and Mushrooms, Buttered, **'82** 204
Peas with Mushrooms, Creamy, **'84** 196
Peas with Mushrooms, Green, **'80** 101
Pepper-Mushroom Medley, **'90** 98
Phyllo Bites, Sausage-Mushroom-, **'89** 284
Piroshki, **'92** 84
Pizza, Cheese-and-Mushroom, **'83** 226
Pork Loin with Apples and Mushrooms,
    Roast, **'92** 218
Pork Loin with Mushrooms and Garlic,
    Roasted, **'92** 301
Potatoes, Mushroom-Dill-Topped, **'86** 41
Potatoes, Mushroom Scalloped, **'87** 191
Pot Roast, Mushroom, **'79** 17
Quail with Mushrooms, **'85** 138
Quail with Mushrooms, Baked, **'81** 259
Quiche, Ham-and-Mushroom, **'81** 11
Quiche Lorraine, Mushroom-, **'86** 242
Quiche, Mushroom, **'80** 222; **'81** 244;
    '89 285
Quiche, Spinach-Mushroom, **'81** M74
Quiches, Wild Rice-and-Mushroom, **'93** 237

Mushrooms *(continued)*

Quiche, Zucchini-Mushroom, **'79** 127
Ragoût of Wild Mushrooms with Creamy
  Grits, **'92** 238
Rice, Baked Mushroom, **'92** 170
Rice, Easy Mushroom, **'89** 286
Rollups, Mushroom, **'85** 318
Salad, Fabulous Mushroom, **'81** 190
Salad, Fresh Mushroom, **'93** 65
Salad, Marinated Mushroom, **'88** 215;
  '90 181
Salad, Mushroom-and-Pepper, **'86** 68
Salad, Mushroom-Zucchini, **'85** 8
Salad, Quick Cheesy-Mushroom, **'89** 128
Salad, Spinach and Mushroom, **'80** 112
Salad, Spinach-Enoki, **'89** 62
Salad, Watercress-and-Mushroom, **'88** 104
Salad with Fresh Mushrooms, Rice, **'80** 231
Salmon with Mushrooms and Green Onions,
  Fresh, **'93** 180
Samurai 'shrooms, **'93** 258
Sandwiches, Toasted Mushroom, **'87** 281
Sauce, Beef Tenderloin with Mushroom,
  '88 3
Sauce, Beef Tenderloin with
  Mushroom-Sherry, **'87** 306
Sauce, Broiled Tomatoes with Mushroom,
  '81 103
Sauce, Chanterelle Brown, **'89** 62
Sauce, Chicken Florentine with Mushroom,
  '87 250
Sauce, Eggs Baked in Mushroom, **'93** 47
Sauce, Filet Mignon with Mushroom, **'94** 250
Sauce, Green Beans in Sherried Mushroom,
  '93 206
Sauce, Mushroom, **'81** 90, 200; **'82** 46;
  '83 71, 205, 212; **'84** M70; **'85** 40;
  '86 198; **'87** 36, 186, 284; **'91** 221
Sauce, Mushroom-Cheese, **'83** 190; **'86** 48
Sauce, Mushroom-Dill, **'80** 271
Sauce, Mushroom-Wine, **'84** 84; **'86** 24
Sauce, Onion-Mushroom, **'85** 224; **'86** 84
Sauce, Spicy Sherried Mushroom, **'89** 239
Sauce, Steak with Ham-and-Mushroom,
  '83 109
Sauce, Steak with Mushroom, **'83** 212
Sauce Supreme on Vermicelli, Mushroom,
  '86 158
Sauce, Zucchini-Mushroom, **'93** 71
Saucy Mushrooms and Eggs, **'79** 138
Sauté, Asparagus-and-Mushroom, **'93** 115
Sautéed Mushrooms, **'84** 35
Sautéed Mushrooms, Easy, **'81** 131
Sautéed Mushroom Spectacular, **'83** 206
Sautéed Peppers and Mushrooms,
  Herb-Stuffed Chicken with, **'91** 26
Sauté, Mixed Mushroom, **'89** 62
Sauté, Veal-Cepe, **'89** 62
Scallops and Mushrooms, Creamy, **'83** 144
Seasoned Mushrooms, **'83** 291
Sherried Mushroom Eggs, **'83** 49
Sherried Mushrooms, **'83** 13
Shrimp and Mushrooms with Angel Hair
  Pasta, **'92** 34
Shrimp-Mushroom Italienne, Green Pasta
  with, **'79** 170
Soufflés, Mushroom, **'87** 282
Soup, Chicken, Artichoke, and Mushroom,
  '92 324

Soup, Chunky Mushroom, **'88** 12
Soup, Cream of Mushroom, **'84** 5;
  '85 93, 261
Soup, Creamy Avocado-Mushroom, **'85** 25
Soup, Creamy Mushroom, **'79** 243; **'81** 307
Soup, Curried Mushroom, **'84** M89
Soup, Elegant Mushroom, **'83** 99
Soup, Fresh Mushroom, **'81** 109; **'90** 190
Soup, Mushroom, **'82** 286; **'86** M73; **'94** 54
Soup, Mushroom-Onion, **'80** 25
Soup, Mushroom-Rice, **'90** 32
Soup, Oyster-and-Mushroom, **'87** 39
Sour Cream-Dill Sauce, Mushrooms in,
  '84 215
Spaghetti with Mushrooms, Spicy, **'85** 2
Sparkling Mushrooms, **'94** 24
Spinach with Mushrooms, **'80** 19
Spread, Eggplant-Mushroom, **'92** 156
Spread, Hot Mushroom, **'81** 190
Squash, Mushroom-Stuffed Yellow, **'84** 154
Steak and Mushrooms, Flank, **'87** 61
Stems, Mushrooms with, **'86** 258
Stir-Fried Mushrooms with Bacon, **'80** 123
Stir-Fry, Shiitake-Chicken, **'89** 61
Stroganoff, Mushroom, **'81** 298
Stroganoff, Mushroom-Meatball, **'85** 85
Stuffed Mushroom Appetizers, **'88** 210
Stuffed Mushroom Caps, Crab-, **'84** 160
Stuffed Mushroom Delight, **'87** 281
Stuffed Mushrooms, **'79** 212; **'81** 239;
  '83 13, 66, 126, 136; **'86** 258
Stuffed Mushrooms, Black Olive-, **'86** 258
Stuffed Mushrooms, Cheese 'n' Bacon-,
  '86 258
Stuffed Mushrooms, Chicken-, **'80** 162
Stuffed Mushrooms, Crab-, **'81** 190
Stuffed Mushrooms, Crawfish-, **'86** 258
Stuffed Mushrooms, Elegant Cheese-,
  '81 57
Stuffed Mushrooms, Flavor-, **'85** 288
Stuffed Mushrooms Florentine, **'82** 270
Stuffed Mushrooms, Italian Sausage-,
  '83 127
Stuffed Mushrooms, Parmesan, **'83** 115
Stuffed Mushrooms, Pâté-, **'85** 118
Stuffed Mushrooms, Pecan-, **'84** 261
Stuffed Mushrooms, Pesto-, **'85** 150
Stuffed Mushrooms, Pistachio-, **'86** 141
Stuffed Mushrooms, Ricotta-, **'85** 20
Stuffed Mushrooms, Sausage-, **'80** 248;
  '91 164
Stuffed Mushrooms, Seasoned, **'84** 206
Stuffed Mushrooms, Shrimp-, **'80** M135
Stuffed Mushrooms, Spinach-, **'86** 81;
  '88 131, M261; **'89** M133
Stuffed with Crab, Mushrooms, **'82** 249
Supreme, Mushrooms, **'84** 214
Tarts, Hot Sherried Mushroom, **'83** 78
Tart, Smoked Portabello Mushroom,
  '94 163
Tarts, Mushroom, **'88** 161
Tipsy Mushrooms, **'84** M216
Tomatoes, Mushroom-Stuffed, **'86** 218
Turnovers, Hot Mushroom, **'89** 285
Turnovers, Tiny Mushroom, **'86** 24
Vegetable Mushroom Caps, **'81** 246
Venison Loin, Mushroom-Crusted, **'94** 302
Vermicelli with Mushrooms, **'79** 195
Vermouth, Mushrooms in, **'89** 203
Wild Rice and Mushrooms, **'83** 278
Wild Rice with Morels, **'89** 62

Wine Sauce, Mushrooms with, **'85** 292
Zesty Mushrooms, **'93** 218
Zucchini with Mushrooms, Sautéed, **'94** 135
Mustard
Bourbon Mustard, **'93** 240
Brie, Honey-Mustard, **'91** 252
Brussels Sprouts with Shallots and Mustard,
  '85 258
Chicken, Mustard, **'93** 239
Coarse-and-Sweet Mustard, **'86** M288
Compote, Baked Mustard Fruit, **'85** 47
Dressing, Dijon-Honey, **'89** 45
Dressing, Honey-Mustard, **'90** 55, 111, 146
Dressing, Mustard, **'80** 112
Dressing, Tangy Mustard, **'93** 323
Flounder Dijon, **'85** 95
Fruit Bake, Mustard, **'90** 291
Glaze, Game Hens with Chutney-Mustard,
  '93 66
Glaze, Roast Chicken with Pineapple-
  Mustard, **'89** 83
Herbed Mustard, **'87** 134
Homemade Mustard, **'81** 77
Homemade Mustard, Zesty, **'82** 55
Honey Mustard, Hot, **'93** 240
Horseradish Mustard, **'93** 240
Horseradish Mustard, Lower Sodium,
  '86 325
Hot German Mustard, **'82** 298
Hot Mustard, Chinese, **'85** 12
Hot Sweet Mustard, **'85** 12
Jalapeño Mustard, **'93** 240
Key Lime Mustard, **'94** 278
Marinade, Honey-Mustard, **'93** 103
Mousse, Mustard, **'84** 127; **'86** 184
Sauce, Champagne-Poached Chicken with
  Creamy Mustard, **'94** 24
Sauce, Chilled Asparagus in Mustard, **'88** 130
Sauce, Chutney-Mustard, **'89** 242
Sauce, Creamy Horseradish-Mustard,
  '88 M177
Sauce, Creamy Mustard, **'80** 272; **'86** 257;
  '87 232; **'93** 240
Sauce, Easy Mustard, **'94** 83
Sauce, Extra-Special Mustard, **'79** 82
Sauce, Honey-Lemon Mustard, **'84** 275
Sauce, Honey-Mustard, **'85** 13
Sauce, Hot Mustard, **'93** 240
Sauce, Leg of Lamb with Mustard, **'89** 71
Sauce, Light Mustard, **'82** 178
Sauce, Mild Mustard, **'85** 224; **'86** 84
Sauce, Mock Mustard-Hollandaise, **'87** 269
Sauce, Mustard, **'80** 222, 283; **'83** 21, 321;
  '84 M70, 289; **'85** 148; **'86** 185; **'87** 22;
  '89 122, 333; **'90** 19, 97; **'92** 302;
  '93 118
Sauce, Mustard Cream, **'88** 61
Sauce, Mustard-Sour Cream, **'81** 68
Sauce, Sausage Sandwiches with Mustard,
  '84 250
Sauce, Shrimp with Mustard-Vinegar,
  '93 240
Sauce, Smoked Ribs with Honey-Mustard,
  '92 168
Sauce, Stone Crab Mustard, **'80** 3
Sauce, Sweet Mustard, **'85** 12
Sauce, Tangy Mustard, **'92** 201
Sauce, Turkey Cutlets with
  Tarragon-Mustard, **'93** 239
Spread, Chive-Mustard, **'91** 12
Spread, Mustard, **'86** 105

Mustard (continued)

Vegetables, Honey-Mustard Marinated, **'93** 236
Vinaigrette, Baby Lettuces with Mustard, **'93** 67
Vinaigrette, Honey-Mustard, **'94** 249

Nectarines

Apple Juice, Nectarines in, **'83** 183
Butter, Nectarine, **'79** 175
Cocktail, Nectarine, **'85** 107
Royale, Nectarines, **'85** 132
Salad, Nectarine Chicken, **'79** 175
Sherbet, Nectarine, **'89** 199

Noodles
Bake, Hamburger-Noodle, **'81** 140
Bake, Pork-and-Noodle, **'88** 98
Bake, Sausage-Noodle, **'81** 92
Bake, Sour Cream-Noodle, **'79** 55
Bake, Taco Beef-Noodle, **'81** 141
Bake, Turkey Noodle, **'93** 243
Beef and Noodles, Easy, **'83** 288
Caraway Buttered Noodles, **'87** 230
Casserole, Beef-and-Noodles, **'84** 72
Casserole, Chicken and Green Noodle, **'80** 32
Casserole, Chicken-Noodle, **'94** 286
Casserole, Eggplant and Noodle, **'82** 230
Casserole, Ham and Noodle, **'80** 300
Casserole, Sausage and Noodle, **'82** 123
Casserole, Shrimp-and-Noodle, **'90** 240
Casserole, Turkey-Noodle-Poppyseed, **'90** 239
Casserole, Vegetable Noodle, **'91** 30
Cheesy Noodles and Mushrooms, **'79** 84
Chicken with Noodles, Sesame, **'88** M125
Chili with Noodles, **'81** 282; **'82** 57
Crispy Noodles, Chow Mein over, **'85** 286
Dinner, Beefy Noodle, **'81** 179
Dinner, Creamy Liver and Noodle, **'80** 11
Dinner, Pork-and-Noodles Skillet, **'88** 199
Green Noodles, **'80** 211
Ham and Swiss on Noodles, **'87** 108
Italian Sauce with Noodles, **'84** 250
Kugel, Apricot Noodle, **'92** 251
Kugel, Nu Awlins, **'94** 229
Kugel, Sweet, **'90** 254
Lasagna, Lots of Noodles, **'91** M127
Orange Noodles, **'84** 177
Parmesan Noodles, **'83** 118
Parmesan Noodles, Cheesy, **'83** M7
Parslied Noodles, **'85** 31
Rice Noodles, Shredded Beef over, **'85** 74
Ring, Noodle, **'85** 285
Salad, Ham-Noodle, **'85** 249
Salad, Ramen Noodle, **'88** 41
Scallops and Pasta, Fresh, **'83** 164
Shrimp and Noodles, Creamy, **'92** 100
Skillet, Ham-Noodle, **'87** 78
Soup, Chicken Noodle, **'80** 264
Soup Mix, Turkey-Noodle, **'89** 330
Soup, Turkey-Noodle, **'91** 312

Spinach Noodles, Chicken and, **'82** 19
Spinach with Noodles, Creamed, **'84** 29
Stew with Noodles, Hungarian, **'80** 263
Veal Sauce, Noodles with, **'80** 236
White Noodles, **'80** 211

Oatmeal

Applesauce Oatmeal, **'89** 108
Bake, Pear-Oatmeal, **'89** 208
Bars, Apricot-Oatmeal, **'86** 216
Bars, Chocolate-Topped Oatmeal, **'86** 110
Bars, Date-Oat, **'80** M172
Bars, Layered Oatmeal-Date, **'85** 10
Bars, Oatmeal-Caramel, **'85** 247
Bars, Yummy Fudge, **'87** 158
Biscuits, Oatmeal, **'89** 108
Bread, Blueberry-Oatmeal, **'83** 139
Bread, Caraway-Raisin Oat, **'86** 44
Bread, Dill-Oat, **'91** 95
Bread, Honey-Oat, **'89** 107
Bread, Honey Oatmeal, **'80** 60
Bread, Oatmeal, **'81** 236, 300; **'92** 212
Bread, Oatmeal Raisin, **'81** 14
Bread, Oatmeal-Raisin, **'83** 59
Bread, Oat-Molasses, **'82** 139
Bread, Round Oatmeal, **'84** 20
Bread, Whole Wheat-Oatmeal, **'87** 85
Breakfast Oatmeal Surprise, **'93** 178
Breakfast Oatmeal, Swiss Style, **'81** 49
Brownies, Oat, **'89** 59
Brownies, Oatmeal, **'87** 199
Brownies, Oat 'n' Crunch, **'91** 233
Buns, Honey Oatmeal, **'83** 154
Cake, Applesauce-Oatmeal, **'92** 119
Cake, Dutch Oatmeal, **'83** 95
Cake, Golden Apple-Oatmeal, **'86** 301
Cake, Honey-Oatmeal, **'87** 222
Cake, Oatmeal-Coconut Coffee, **'83** 312
Cereal, Full-of-Fiber Hot, **'89** 208
Chocolate Chippers, Oatmeal-, **'90** 218
Cookies, Apple-Nut, **'80** 228
Cookies, Apple-Oatmeal, **'85** 215; **'90** 218
Cookies, Banana Oatmeal, **'79** 217
Cookies, Chocolate Chip-Oatmeal, **'84** 119
Cookies, Chocolate-Oatmeal, **'80** 105
Cookies, Cinnamon Oatmeal, **'84** 72
Cookies, Crispy Coconut-Oatmeal, **'93** 80
Cookies, Crispy Oat, **'88** 203; **'90** 311
Cookies, Crispy Oatmeal, **'89** 328
Cookies, Crunchy Oatmeal, **'85** 202
Cookies, Date-Filled Oatmeal, **'86** 314
Cookies, Easy Oatmeal, **'80** 105
Cookies, Frosted Oatmeal-Raisin, **'79** 290
Cookies, Giant Oatmeal-Spice, **'80** 105
Cookies, Lace, **'86** 8
Cookies, Nutty Oatmeal, **'81** 130
Cookies, Nutty Oatmeal-Chocolate Chip, **'82** M185
Cookies, Oatmeal, **'92** 82
Cookies, Oatmeal-Carrot, **'94** 292
Cookies, Oatmeal-Coconut, **'80** 218
Cookies, Oatmeal-Date, **'82** 109
Cookies, Oatmeal-Date Sandwich, **'83** 257
Cookies, Oatmeal-Peanut Butter, **'85** 171
Cookies, Oatmeal-Peanut Butter Chocolate Chip, **'92** 207
Cookies, Oatmeal-Raisin, **'87** 221; **'93** 127

Cookies, Oatmeal Sunshine, **'89** 59
Cookies, Oats-and-Peanut, **'89** 60
Cookies, Old-Fashioned Oatmeal, **'80** 106; **'85** 250
Cookies, Orange-Glazed Oatmeal, **'80** 60
Cookies, Peanut Butter-Oatmeal, **'81** 218; **'84** 72
Cookies, Peanutty Oatmeal, **'80** 106; **'83** 95
Cookies, Slice-and-Bake Oatmeal, **'80** 105
Cookies, Special Oatmeal, **'81** 236
Cookies, Spicy Oatmeal, **'81** 197
Cookies, Take-Along Breakfast, **'84** 59
Cookies, Toasted Oatmeal, **'92** 273
Crackers, Oatmeal-Wheat Germ, **'84** 236
Crispies, Oat, **'83** 96
Crispies, Oatmeal Nut, **'80** 208
Crisp, Oatmeal Cherry-Apple, **'90** M16
Crust, Nutty Oat, **'89** 251
Fruited Oatmeal, **'88** 19
Granola Bars, **'83** 305
Granola, Crunchy, **'81** 218; **'84** 144
Granola, Easy, **'81** 49
Granola, Fruity, **'84** 148
Granola, Homemade, **'84** 58
Granola, Sunny Orange, **'84** 212
Ice Cream Sandwiches, Oatmeal Crispy, **'93** 199
Krispies, Oatmeal, **'85** 115
Loaf, Banana-Oat Tea, **'87** 256
Loaf, Pumpkin-Oatmeal, **'81** 49
Mix, Rolled Oats, **'84** 72
Muesli, **'89** 208
Muesli, Homestyle, **'91** 315
Muffins, Banana-Oat, **'87** 188
Muffins, Banana-Oatmeal, **'84** 20
Muffins, Best-Ever Oatmeal, **'84** 242
Muffins, Blueberry-Oat, **'92** 119
Muffins, Blueberry-Oatmeal, **'87** 24
Muffins, Corn-Oat, **'89** 108
Muffins, Honey-Oatmeal, **'84** 229
Muffins, Oat Bran, **'89** 106
Muffins, Oat Bran-Banana, **'91** 18
Muffins, Oatmeal, **'82** 129, 210; **'84** 72, 140; **'92** 163
Muffins, Oatmeal Bran, **'81** 236
Muffins, Oatmeal-Bran, **'91** 83
Muffins, Oatmeal-Honey, **'83** 95
Muffins, Orange-Oatmeal, **'85** 202
Muffins, Spicy Apple-Oat, **'86** 45
Pancakes, Oat, **'89** 227
Pancakes, Oatmeal, **'80** 44; **'89** 107
Pancakes, Oatmeal-Brown Sugar, **'88** 203
Pancakes, Whole Wheat-Oat, **'93** 16
Piecrust, Crisp Cereal, **'83** 100
Piecrust, Oatmeal, **'79** 79
Snowballs, Macadamia-Oat, **'92** 274
Topping, Oat Crunch, **'89** 108
Waffles, Banana-Oatmeal, **'94** 206
Waffles, Oatmeal, **'89** 107
Waffles, Oatmeal-Nut, **'83** 96

Okra
Bake, Okra-and-Tomato, **'89** 173
Bake, Okra-Tomato, **'80** 298; **'81** 26
Casserole, Okra, **'79** 160
Cheese, Okra with, **'80** 185
Chowder, Quick Okra, **'80** 185
Corn, and Peppers, Okra, **'87** M151
Cream, Okra and Corn in, **'79** 160
Creole, Corn-and-Okra, **'89** 127
Creole, Meatball-Okra, **'83** 156
Creole Okra, **'81** 182

Okra (continued)

Creole, Okra-Corn, '83 157
Deep-Fried Okra, '90 154
Fingers, Okra, '85 196
Fresh Okra and Tomatoes, '87 89
Fried Okra, '79 122; '86 211; '87 89;
    '88 111
Fried Okra and Green Tomatoes, '93 160
Fried Okra, Crispy, '86 169
Fried Okra, French-, '82 126
Fried Okra, Fritter-, '86 218
Fried Okra, Old-Time, '80 185
Fritters, Okra, '79 160; '92 133
Fry, Okra-Potato, '81 159
Goulash, Okra, '93 160
Gumbo, Deep South Okra, '79 48
Gumbo Freezer Mix, Okra, '86 210
Gumbo, Light Seafood-Okra, '86 155
Gumbo, Okra, '86 210; '91 206
How to Can Okra, '80 127
Medley, Okra, '88 M185
Medley, Okra-Corn-Tomato, '81 159
Muffins, Fresh Okra, '93 161
Oven-Fried Okra, '91 121
Pickles, Okra, '81 173
Pilaf, Okra, '80 185; '82 126; '93 160
Plantation Okra, '82 126
Puffs, Okra, '83 157
Salad, Okra, '90 155
Sautéed Corn and Okra, '84 158
Soup, Charleston Okra, '87 156
Soup, Okra-and-Shrimp, '94 323
Soup, Sausage and Okra, '80 209
Stewed Okra, Southern, '82 134
Stew, Old-Fashioned Okra, '84 158
Surprise, Okra, '79 160; '84 158
Tomato Combo, Okra-, '83 157
Tomatoes and Okra, '86 170; '87 164
Tomatoes, Fresh Okra and, '81 M165
Tomatoes, Okra and, '80 185; '81 139;
    '92 215
Tomatoes, Okra and Green, '79 160
Tomatoes with Okra, '85 106
Vinaigrette, Okra-Corn-and-Tomato, '90 173

Olives

Antipasto, Easy, '85 114
Appetizers, Cheesy Olive, '85 113
Appetizers, Cheesy-Olive, '87 246
Ball, Blue Cheese-Olive, '82 248
Ball, Olive Cheese, '80 258
Black Olives, Shrimp Spaghetti with, '85 13
Black Olive-Stuffed Mushrooms, '86 258
Bread, Olive, '93 78
Bread, Olive-Dill Casserole, '92 16
Butter, Olive, '91 295
Casserole, Turkey-Olive, '87 268
Chalupas, Chicken-Olive, '81 227
Chicken-and-Rice Valencia, '85 113
Filling, Chicken-Olive, '81 227
Ham-and-Swiss Rollups, '85 113
Lemon-Garlic Olives, '94 118
Marinated Olives, Herb-, '92 176
Potatoes, Olive, '80 114
Salad, Doodles Olive, '94 35
Salad, Italian Olive, '94 35
Salad, Mexican Olive, '85 84
Salad Mix, Muffy, '94 34
Salad, Olive Clubhouse, '81 114
Salad, Olive-Potato, '85 114

Salad with Sherry Vinaigrette, Shrimp,
    Orange, and Olive, '93 177
Snack, Open-Faced Cheese-and-Olive,
    '89 97
Spread, Antipasto, '81 25
Spread, Cheese-Olive, '79 82
Spread, Cream Cheese-Olive, '82 35
Spread, Creamy Olive, '81 290
Spread, Tomatoes with Olive, '85 114
Stuffed Olives, Almond-, '88 95
Tapenade, '92 194
Toss, Cauliflower-Olive, '85 198; '86 147
Toss, Tomato-Olive Pasta, '86 209

Omelets

Apple Omelet Stack, '94 50
Baked Omelets, '94 50
Broccoli-Mushroom Omelet, '85 45
Cheese Omelet, Herbed, '93 47
Cheese Omelet, Puffed, '89 227
Cheese Omelet, Zippy, '87 287
Cheesy Picante Omelet, '86 95
Chicken Liver Omelet, '82 44
Country Omelets, '91 128
Creole Sauce, Omelets with, '89 228
Filling, Greek Omelet, '80 68
Filling, Spanish Omelet, '80 68
Fluffy Omelet, '84 56
George's Omelets, '80 68
Ham and Cheese Omelet, '79 262; '80 123
Mexican Omelet, '79 128; '81 225
Mushroom Omelet, Rolled, '82 70
Mushroom Sauce, Puffy Omelets with, '85 40
Olé Omelet, '87 M124
Olé, Omelet, '94 31
Oyster Omelets, Smoked, '84 96
Potato Omelet, Family-Size, '94 31
Potato-Sprout Omelet, '79 128
Primavera, Omelet, '87 71
Rising Sun Omelet, '82 281; '83 42
Rolled Omelet, '89 228
Sandwich, Omelet, '86 95
Sausage Filling, Omelet with, '81 43
Sausage Omelet, Puffy, '80 M268
Shrimp-and-Cheddar Omelet, '84 57
Shrimp-and-Cheese Omelet, '94 31
Sour Cream-Ham Omelet, '79 261
Spanish Omelet, '81 201; '83 243; '84 101
Spanish-Style Omelets, '83 188
Spinach-Cheese Omelet, '83 119
Strawberry-Sour Cream Omelet, '89 229
Sunrise Omelet, '83 289
Swiss Oven Omelet, '80 189
Tarragon Omelet, '89 144
Tex-Mex Omelet con Carne, '81 209
Vegetable Omelet, Beefy, '83 188
Vegetable Omelet, Cheddar-, '83 205
Vegetable Omelet, Cheesy, '85 49
Vegetable Omelet, Fresh, '84 211
Vegetable Omelet, Golden, '82 M123
Vegetable Omelet, Puffy, '83 188
Vegetarian Omelet, '84 111
Wine Omelet, White, '79 103
Yogurt-Avocado Omelet, '81 33
Zucchini Omelet, '81 99

Onions

Appetizers, Bacon-Onion, '94 290
Bake, Cheese Onion, '82 32
Baked Onions, Micro-, '82 M32
Baked Onions, Spicy, '84 65
Baked Onions, Sweet-and-Sour, '90 34
Baked Sweet Onions, '91 79

Bake, Four Onion, '93 304
Bake, Onion-Potato, '83 M195
Bake, Romano Onion, '90 98
Barbecued Onions, '88 86
Beans and Scallions, Fresh Lima, '82 133
Bean Sauce, Pork-and-Onions with, '85 76
Beef and Onions, Smothered, '85 293
Beef Burgundy with Pearl Onions, '81 108
Blossom, Onion, '94 226
Bread, Easy Onion, '81 162
Bread, Easy Onion-Dill, '85 5
Bread, French Onion, '91 90
Bread, Onion-Cheese, '79 180; '81 8
Bread, Onion-Cheese French, '89 29
Bread, Onion-Cheese Supper, '83 112
Bread, Onion-Herb, '90 165
Bread, Onion-Parmesan, '84 284
Bread, Toasted Onion-Herb, '83 266
Buns, Cheesy Onion, '85 5
Buns, Onion-Cheese, '88 218
Burgers, Open-Faced Chicken-Onion,
    '94 139
Butter, Onion, '86 253
Butter, Sweet Onion, '93 124
Carrots with Bacon and Onion, Glazed,
    '87 200
Casserole, Cheesy Onion, '79 101
Cheese Onions, Sherried, '82 32
Chicken, Onion-Crusted, '88 40
Chutney, Kiwifruit-Onion, '93 125
Confit, Roasted Shallot-Garlic, '94 303
Cornbread, Onion, '88 283
Cornbread, Onion-Topped, '84 153
Creole Onions, '82 32
Crunch Sticks, Onion Crescent, '90 206
Curried Onions, '90 34
Deluxe, Broccoli-Onion, '81 75
Dip, Cheesy Onion, '83 145
Dip, Chunky Onion, '84 257
Dip, Cream Cheese-Onion, '79 236
Dip, Curry-Onion, '93 313
Dip, Onion, '94 21
Dressing, Green Pepper-Onion Salad, '84 12
Dressing, Onion-French, '84 283
Eggs, Creamy Onion Scrambled, '83 M203
Focaccia, Mustard-and-Onion, '90 321;
    '92 97
Focaccia, Onion, '93 77
Fried
    Beer-Battered Onion Rings, '92 52
    Crisp Fried Onion Rings, '84 65
    Crispy Fried Onion Rings, '80 108
    Crispy Onion Rings, '86 110
    Deluxe Fried Onion Rings, '80 108
    Easy Onion Rings, '80 108
    Favorite Fried Onion Rings, '81 86
    French-Fried Onion Rings, '88 111
    French-Fried Onion Rings Supreme,
        '80 109
    Green Onions, Fried, '81 106
    Leonard's-Style Onion Rings, '90 120
    Rings, Fried Onion, '83 85; '85 69
Glazed Carrots and Onions, '83 25; '87 128
Glazed Onions, '84 104
Glazed Pearl Onions, '85 258
Gourmet Onions, '81 86
Gravy, Fried Quail with Onion, '82 214
Green Beans with Roasted Red Peppers and
    Pearl Onions, '93 260
Green Onion Canapés, '84 M216
Green Onion-Cheese Spread, '92 24

Onions (continued)

Green Onion Hoecakes, **'88** 112
Green Onion Quiche, Cheesy, **'83** 194;
 '84 42
Green Onion Relish, **'84** 65
Green Onion Teasers, **'82** 42
Grilled Squash and Onion, **'79** 150
Herbed Carrots and Onions, **'87** 31
Herbed Onions, **'84** 149
Honey Onions, **'81** 86
Honey-Paprika Sweet Onions, **'92** 52
Hush Puppies, Onion, **'85** 14
Hush Puppies, Tomato-Onion, **'91** 201
Italian Dressing, Tomato, Onion, and
 Cucumber in, **'81** 83
Jelly, Onion, **'93** 135
Kale with Tomato and Onion, **'92** 244
Kuchen, Onion, **'90** 34
Loaves, Onion Twist, **'84** 300
Marinated Bermuda Onions, **'92** 194
Muffins, Onion-Dill, **'92** 253; **'93** 144
Parmesan Onions, **'93** 170
Pearl Onions, Snap Peas and, **'89** 280
Peas with Onions, Buttered, **'80** 242
Pickled Cocktail Onions, **'89** 197
Pickled Refrigerator Onion Rings, **'84** 265
Pie, Onion, **'82** 191
Pie, Onion-Cheese, **'88** 86
Quiche, Onion, **'83** 121
Relish, Onion, **'91** 79
Relish, Pepper-Onion, **'84** 180
Relish, Sweet Onion, **'93** 124
Rice, Seasoned Onion, **'82** 166
Rings, Crispy Baked Onion, **'93** 247
Rolls, Onion Twist, **'89** 288
Rolls, Poppy Seed Onion, **'81** 63
Salad Bowl, Spinach-and-Onion, **'81** 157
Salad, Lemon-Onion, **'85** 252
Salad, Marinated Orange-Onion, **'91** 231;
 '92 68
Salad, Orange-Onion, **'89** 41
Salad, Tomato-Cucumber-Onion, **'81** 239
Salad, Vidalia-Tomato, **'84** 65
Salmon with Mushrooms and Green Onions,
 Fresh, **'93** 180
Salsa, Fiesta Onion, **'94** 82
Sandwiches on Salt-Rising Bread, Vidalia,
 '79 145
Sauce, Brussels Sprouts in Onion, **'81** 308
Sauce, Onion, **'82** 72; **'87** 248
Sauce, Onion Cream, **'87** 232
Sauce, Onion-Mushroom, **'85** 224; **'86** 84
Sauce, Onion-Parsley, **'85** 148
Sauce, Pepper-Onion, **'84** 125
Sautéed Apples, Onions, and Pears over
 Spinach, **'94** 212
Sautéed Onions and Peppers, **'83** M148
Scallions, Cukes and, **'91** 168
Selecting and Storing Onions, **'84** 65
Shells, Cheese and Limas in Onion, **'81** 86
Shortcake, Onion, **'92** 51
Soufflé, Onion, **'79** 247
Soup
 Cheese Onion Soup, Double-, **'85** 227
 Cheese Soup, Onion-, **'87** 81
 Classic Onion Soup, **'84** 65
 Creamy Onion Soup, **'90** 211
 Double Cheese-Topped Onion Soup,
  '79 49

Easy Onion Soup, **'85** 226
French Onion-Beef Soup, **'87** 54
French Onion Soup, **'79** 49; **'80** 188;
 '83 126; **'85** 226; **'86** M212; **'90** 31;
 '93 246
French Onion Soup, Shortcut, **'85** M328
French Onion Soup, Toasty, **'81** 306
Green Onion Soup, **'84** 112
Green Onion Soup, Creamed, **'83** 82
Mushroom-Onion Soup, **'80** 25
Oven-Browned Onion Soup, **'79** 49
Potato Soup, Creamy Onion-and-, **'92** 51
Rich Onion Soup, **'85** 226
Superb Onion Soup, **'81** 86
Vichyssoise, **'86** 181
Sour Cream, Cucumber and Onion in, **'81** 69
Spread, Braunschweiger-Onion, **'79** 82
Squares, Creamy Onion, **'79** 48
Squares, Sausage-Onion, **'83** 112
Steak, Onion-Smothered, **'87** M189
Stew, Beef-and-Onion, **'87** 18
Stuffed Baked Onions, **'82** 32
Stuffed Onions and Wine, **'85** 268
Stuffed Onions, Baked, **'83** 135
Stuffed Onions, Broccoli-, **'84** 154
Stuffed Onions, Cheese-, **'90** 34
Stuffed Sweet Onions, **'91** 79
Stuffed Vidalia Onions, **'89** 172
Stuffed with Peas, Onions, **'84** 68
Stuffing, Rice-and-Onion, **'88** 246
Sweet-Hot Onions, **'85** 139
Sweet Onions, Balsamic Caramelized Florida,
 '94 163
Turnips and Onions, **'83** 242
Veal and Onions, Herbed, **'79** 108
Vidalia Deep Dish, **'89** 120
Vidalia Onion Sauté, **'89** 119
Vidalia Onions with Pecans and Roasted
 Carrots, Roasted, **'92** 340
Vidalias, Marinated, **'89** 119
Vinaigrette, Spinach Salad with Apple-Onion,
 '94 276
Vinegar Sauce, Whole Onions with Warm,
 '94 172
On The Light Side. *See* Living Light.
Oranges
Appetizer, Orange-Berry, **'85** 81
Apples, Orange-Glazed, **'82** 51
Asparagus with Orange Butter Sauce, **'85** 43
Asparagus with Orange Sauce, **'83** 46
Bake, Butternut-Orange, **'86** 295
Baked Fruit, Ginger-Orange, **'93** 313
Baked Oranges, **'79** 247; **'89** 41
Baked Orange Slices, **'89** 88
Bake, Sweet Potato-Orange, **'83** 226
Baskets, Orange, **'93** 286
Beets, Orange, **'91** 219
Beets, Orange-Ginger, **'80** 137
Beets, Orange-Glazed, **'81** 167; **'85** 289;
 '86 187
Beets, Spicy Orange, **'94** 280
Beverages
 Blush, Orange, **'80** 51
 Breakfast Eye-Opener, **'87** 199
 Champagne with Orange Juice, **'91** 71
 Cider, Apple-Orange, **'92** 20
 Citrus Cooler, **'82** 160
 Cocktail, Orange-Champagne, **'79** 39
 Cocktail, Tomato-Orange Juice, **'83** 169
 Coffee, Viennese Orange, **'84** 54
 Flip, Orange-Banana, **'82** 48

 Flips, Orange Blossom, **'80** 51
 Frosty, Orange, **'86** 101
 Frosty Sours, **'81** 156
 Jogger's Sunrise, **'93** 213
 Juicy, Orange, **'90** 178
 Lemonade, Orange-Mint, **'88** 82
 Liqueur, Orange, **'81** 287
 Magnolia Blossoms, **'87** 72
 Magnolias, **'82** 196
 Mist, Orange-Lemon, **'79** 288; **'80** 35
 Nog, Orange Spiced, **'82** 48
 Pick-Me-Up, Orange, **'80** 232
 Pineapple Drink, Orange-, **'89** 35
 Punch, Citrus Party, **'83** 141
 Punch, Orange Blossom, **'83** 142
 Punch, Orange-Lime, **'82** 160
 Punch, Orange-Mint, **'82** 121
 Punch, Orange Sherbet Party, **'83** 142
 Punch, Orange Soda, **'87** 214
 Punch, Pineapple-Orange, **'85** 236
 Punch, Refreshing Orange, **'81** 39
 Refresher, Grapefruit-Orange, **'82** 174
 Sangría, **'81** 67
 Sangría, Easy Citrus, **'80** 218
 Sangría, Orange, **'81** 237
 Shake, Orange Milk, **'84** 166
 Shake, Peachy Orange, **'81** 156
 Shake, Strawberry-Orange Breakfast,
  '87 186
 Shake, Tropical, **'87** 200
 Slush, Banana-Orange, **'80** 48; **'81** 155
 Slush, Orange, **'82** 49
 Slush, Strawberry-Orange, **'83** 172
 Slush, Vodka-Orange, **'89** 92
 Smoothie, Mango-Orange, **'86** 216
 Smoothie, Tropical, **'81** 50
 Soda, Cranberry-Orange, **'79** 148
 Sunshine Fizz, **'92** 44
 Whiskey Sours, Frozen Orange-, **'92** 67
Breads
 Anise-Orange Bread, **'83** 295
 Apricot-Orange Bread, **'92** 285
 Baba au Orange, **'86** 138
 Biscuits, Orange, **'88** 85
 Blueberry-Orange Bread, **'87** 140
 Breakfast Ring, Orange, **'81** 229
 Coffee Cake, Cranberry-Orange,
  '82 283
 Coffee Cake, Orange, **'85** M88
 Coffee Cake, Orange Butter, **'89** 229
 Coffee Cake, Orange Marmalade Swirl,
  '81 107
 Coffee Cake, Orange-Pecan, **'86** 86
 Coffee Ring, Caramel-Orange, **'80** 45
 Cranberry Bread, Orange-, **'85** 266
 Cranberry-Orange Bread, **'87** 244
 Cream Cheese Bread, Orange-, **'82** 210
 Muffins, Banana-Orange, **'84** 148
 Muffins, Orange, **'79** 236; **'81** 107;
  '83 54; **'89** 205
 Muffins, Orange-Date, **'92** 119
 Muffins, Orange-Ginger, **'89** 41
 Muffins, Orange-Honey, **'88** 284
 Muffins, Orange-Oatmeal, **'85** 202
 Muffins, Orange-Pecan, **'83** 96
 Muffins, Streusel-Topped Orange, **'84** 74
 Muffins with Honey Spread, Orange
  Juice, **'81** 229
 Nut Bread, Blueberry-Orange, **'84** 141
 Nut Bread, Cranberry-Orange, **'80** 288
 Nut Bread, Orange-, **'82** 75

Oranges, Breads *(continued)*

Nut Loaf, Orange, **'80** 226
Pecan Bread, Glazed Orange-, **'81** 250
Pecan Bread, Orange-, **'79** 148
Pecan Loaves, Orange-, **'79** 215
Puffs, Upside-Down Orange, **'83** 57
Pumpkin Bread, Orange-, **'87** 300
Rolls, Easy Orange, **'89** M131
Rolls, Frosted Hot Orange, **'80** 257
Rolls, Glazed Orange, **'90** 194
Rolls, Luscious Orange, **'86** 298
Rolls, Orange, **'80** 22; **'82** 17; **'88** 79
Rolls, Orange Butter, **'82** 206; **'83** 33
Rolls, Speedy Orange, **'89** 287
Rye Bread, Swedish Orange-, **'85** 111
Scones, Orange-Pecan, **'94** 215
Tea Bread, Orange, **'79** 234
Toast, Orange French, **'83** 292; **'84** 78;
  '86 329
Toast, Orange Praline, **'79** 36
Toast Topper, Orange, **'79** 36
Toast with Orange Sauce, French,
  '82 47
Whole Wheat Orange Bread, **'85** 5
Broccoli, Easy Orange, **'85** 267
Broccoli with Orange Sauce, **'80** 243
Broiled Orange Halves, **'85** 288
Brussels Sprouts, Orange, **'84** 34
Butter, Honey-Orange, **'79** 36; **'85** 19
Butter, Orange, **'81** 8, 42; **'90** 323; **'92** 319;
  '94 115
Butter, Orange-Pecan, **'84** 75
Butter, Prune-Orange, **'92** 49
Butter, Tomato-Curry-Orange, **'93** 159
Candied Orange Peel, **'81** 286
Carrots and Turnips, Sunset Orange,
  '94 213
Carrots in Orange Sauce, **'82** 107
Carrots, Orange-Fennel, **'92** 133
Carrots, Orange-Glazed, **'79** 12; **'81** M165;
  '90 M98
Carrots, Orange-Raisin, **'80** 24
Carrots, Orange-Spiced, **'88** 18
Carrot Strips, Orangy, **'89** 312
Catfish Amandine, Mandarin, **'84** 183
Celery in Orange Sauce, **'79** 70
Chicken à l'Orange, **'84** 277
Chicken à l'Orange, Stir-Fry, **'83** 82
Chicken Breasts with Orange Sauce, **'79** 77
Chicken Breasts with Parslied Rice, Orange,
  '87 242
Chicken, Crispy Mandarin, **'86** 119
Chicken Drummettes, Orange-Pecan,
  '93 158
Chicken, Grilled Ginger-Orange, **'91** 26
Chicken in Orange-Almond Sauce, **'79** 219;
  '80 13
Chicken in Orange Sauce, **'83** 8
Chicken Livers in Orange Sauce, **'82** 218
Chicken, Orange, **'83** 278; **'86** M140
Chicken, Orange-Avocado, **'80** 38
Chicken, Orange Barbecued, **'88** 123
Chicken Stir-Fry, Kyoto Orange-, **'87** 96
Chicken Stir-Fry, Orange-, **'84** 68
Chutney, Cranberry-Orange, **'79** 292
Chutney, Orange-Cranberry, **'86** 266
Cornish Hens, Orange-Glazed, **'83** 267
Cornish Hens, Orange-Glazed Grilled,
  '86 250

Cornish Hens, Orange-Glazed Stuffed,
  '84 M89
Cornish Hens with Cranberry-Orange Sauce,
  '86 119
Cornish Hens with Orange Glaze, **'79** 244
Cream Cheese, Orange, **'91** 177
Cream, Orange, **'90** 126
Crêpes, Chocolate-Orange, **'85** 263
Desserts
Alaska, Orange, **'83** 177
Ambrosia, Pineapple-Orange, **'88** 252
Baked Apples, Orange-Pecan, **'85** 45
Baked Apples with Orange Sauce,
  '84 314
Baked Bananas with Orange Sauce,
  '79 115
Baked Orange Elegance, **'80** 13
Balls, Orange, **'94** 331
Bananas Foster, Orange-Glazed, **'91** 91
Bars, Pineapple-Orange, **'82** 129
Baskets, Orange, **'81** 308
Cake, Chocolate-Orange Pound, **'89** 94
Cake, Fresh Orange, **'83** 300
Cake, Fresh Orange Chiffon, **'88** 179
Cake, General Robert E. Lee
  Orange-Lemon, **'88** 92
Cake, Mandarin Orange, **'83** 24
Cake, Mandarin-Rum, **'84** 150
Cake, Orange, **'86** 61
Cake, Orange Chiffon, **'91** 56
Cake, Orange-Coconut Angel Food,
  '94 294
Cake, Orange-Cranberry, **'85** 314
Cake, Orange-Date, **'94** 60
Cake, Orange Liqueur, **'87** 84
Cake, Orange Marmalade, **'85** 53
Cake, Orange Meringue, **'86** 336;
  '87 84
Cake, Orange Nut, **'80** 70
Cake, Orange-Nut Butter, **'80** 254
Cake, Orange-Pecan Crunch, **'83** 10
Cake, Orange-Pecan Pound, **'93** 13
Cake, Orange Pound, **'87** 84, 221;
  '92 69
Cake, Orange Rum, **'79** 2
Cake, Orange-Slice, **'81** 264
Cake, Orange Streusel, **'88** 10
Cake, Rum-Orange Coconut, **'88** 224
Cake, Sour Cream-Orange Pecan Pound,
  '89 207
Cake Squares, Apple-Orange, **'84** 150
Cake Squares, Orange, **'81** 34
Cake Squares, Orange-Pumpkin,
  '83 242
Cake, Williamsburg Orange, **'81** 120;
  '82 23
Champagne Oranges, **'93** 83
Cheesecake, Orange, **'81** 84; **'85** 38
Chiffon Dessert, Orange, **'93** 295
Chocolate-Orange Delights, **'93** 52
Chocolate-Orange Roll, **'87** 21
Cookies, Carrot-Orange, **'83** 149
Cookies, Frosted Orange, **'83** 114
Cookies, Orange-Chocolate, **'83** 113
Cookies, Orange-Glazed Oatmeal,
  '80 60
Cookies, Orange-Pecan, **'88** 119
Cookies, Orange Refrigerator, **'86** 230
Cookies, Orange-Slice, **'89** 294
Cookies, Orange Sugar, **'89** 329
Cran-Orange Surprise, **'94** 143

Cream Dessert, Orange, **'80** 254;
  '84 165
Cream, Orange, **'81** 12
Cream, Orange Chantilly, **'84** 156
Cream, Orange-Coconut, **'84** 24
Cream, Orange-Mallow, **'94** 295
Cream, Orange Whipped, **'88** 83
Crème, Orange-Tapioca, **'82** M283
Crêpes, Amaretto-and-Orange, **'86** 260
Crêpes, Orange Dream, **'82** 183
Crispies, Orange, **'84** 205
Crisp, Orange-Apple, **'80** 295
Delight, Pumpkin-Orange, **'86** 321
Dip, Creamy Orange, **'84** 117
Filling, Lemon-Orange, **'81** 71
Filling, Orange, **'79** 229; **'86** 336;
  '87 84; **'88** 224
Fingers, Orange, **'87** 57
Flambé, Dessert Orange, **'85** 313
Flan, Orange, **'84** 95
Frosted Oranges, **'83** 270
Frosting, Creamy Orange, **'83** 24, 241
Frosting, Orange, **'81** 7; **'86** 61;
  '88 119
Frosting, Orange Butter, **'83** 300
Frosting, Orange Buttercream, **'80** 70
Frosting, Orange Cream, **'81** 207;
  '82 14
Frosting, Orange-Cream Cheese,
  '81 70; **'82** 16; **'92** 19
Frosting, Orange-Lemon, **'88** 92
Frozen Orange Dessert, **'92** 44
Fruit Dessert Orange, **'84** 314
Fudge, Orange-Walnut, **'92** 288
Glazed Oranges and Pineapple, **'86** 318
Grand Marnier, Oranges, **'92** 82
Granita, Orange, **'88** 118
Ice Cream, Orange-Pineapple, **'86** 117
Ice, Strawberry-Orange, **'86** 196
Ice, Tart Cranberry-Orange, **'86** 317
Juice, Strawberries with Brandied
  Orange, **'82** 160
Kiwi-and-Orange Dessert, **'93** 295
Molded Dessert, Orange, **'83** 302
Mousse, Chocolate-Orange, **'81** 16, 205
Mousse, Orange, **'86** 69; **'94** 198
Parfaits, Chilled Orange, **'80** 219
Parfaits, Orange Cream, **'94** 198
Peanut Brittle, Orange, **'80** 302
Pears Flambé, Orange-Poached,
  '85 313
Pears in Orange Sauce, Poached, **'82** 19
Pears, Orange Poached, **'80** 218
Pie, Coconut-Orange Chess, **'89** 169
Pie, Florida Orange, **'91** 43
Pie, Frosty Orange, **'90** 296
Pie, Lemon-Orange, **'85** 172
Pie, Orange Ambrosia, **'80** 237
Pie, Orange Chess, **'88** 204
Pie, Orange Chiffon, **'87** 260
Pie, Orange-Coconut, **'90** 90
Pie, Orange-Coconut Cream, **'94** 208
Pie, Orange Meringue, **'81** 12, 309
Pie, Orange-Pecan, **'79** 282; **'83** 222
Pie, Sweet Potato-Orange, **'88** 207
Poached Oranges, Wine-, **'84** M323
Pops, Hawaiian Orange-Pineapple,
  '94 143
Pops, Orange-Banana, **'82** 129
Pralines, Orange, **'92** 313; **'93** 51
Pudding, Mandarin-Almond, **'85** M12

Oranges, Desserts (continued)

Pudding, Orange, '81 85; '82 111; '83 153
Pudding, Orange Custard, '88 174
Rice Cream with Mandarin Oranges, '85 317
Roulage, Chocolate-Orange, '94 314
Sherbet Ambrosia Cups, '82 159
Sherbet, Banana-Orange, '83 162
Sherbet, Orange, '79 155
Sherbet with Blackberry Sauce, Orange, '94 232
Shortbread Madeleines, Orange, '88 242
Shortbread, Orange, '91 272
Shortcake, Fresh Orange, '80 100
Slices, Burgundy-Spiced Orange, '93 294
Sorbet, Banana-Orange, '88 117
Sorbet, Fresh Orange, '92 143
Soufflé, Chilled Orange, '84 317; '86 189
Soufflé, Frozen Orange, '79 211
Soufflé, Grand Marnier, '79 281
Soufflé, Orange Dessert, '83 206
Special, Orange Blossom, '79 48
Squares, Orange-Crunch, '86 136
Tapioca Fluff, Orange, '87 31
Tarts, Frozen Orange, '80 154
Tarts, Orange Curd, '92 193
Topping, Whipped Orange, '80 254
Dip, Creamy Orange, '87 247
Dip, Orange Sour Cream, '79 208
Dip, Spicy Orange, '85 230
Doughnuts, Orange Spiced, '79 136
Dressing, Cranberry-Orange, '91 287
Dressing, Mandarin, '89 137
Dressing, Marmalade-Fruit, '84 171
Dressing, Orange, '81 141
Dressing, Orange Blossom, '82 266
Dressing, Orange-Coconut, '80 158
Dressing, Orange-Curd, '93 22
Dressing, Orange-Poppy Seed, '87 187
Dressing, Orange-Yogurt, '85 304
Duck, Chafing Dish Orange, '79 226
Filling, Cheese-and-Orange, '93 159
Filling, Orange, '89 287
Filling, Orange-Cheese, '90 47
Fish à l'Orange, Fillet of, '89 180
Fritters, Puffy Orange, '81 169
Granola, Sunny Orange, '84 212
Gravy, Orange, '81 259; '89 323
Grits, Orange, '81 47
Halibut with Orange-Curry Sauce, '87 91
Ham, Cranberry-Orange Glazed, '81 295
Ham, Orange-Glazed, '89 324
Honey Yogurt, Orange Slices with, '91 68
Jelly, Pineapple-Orange Mint, '92 105
Lamb Chops, Orange, '83 35
Lobster Tails with Spiced Orange Sauce, '86 155
Marmalade, Orange, '81 42
Marmalade, Orange-Pineapple, '82 150; '89 M156
Marmalade, Peach-Orange, '82 150
Marmalade, Pork Tenderloin with Orange, '91 49
Noodles, Orange, '84 177
Nuts, Sherry-Orange, '86 M289

Pancakes, Orange-Yogurt, '87 225
Pears and Oranges, Spicy, '89 305
Pears, Marmalade Breakfast, '83 M203
Pears, Orange-Glazed, '79 247
Pecans, Orange, '84 299; '87 292
Popcorn, Orange, '86 230
Porc à l'Orange, '80 242
Pork Chops, Orange, '84 81
Pork Chops, Orange-Cranberry, '86 335; '87 84
Pork Chops, Orange-Glazed, '81 234; '82 52; '83 39; '91 84
Prunes, Orange-Spiced, '85 224
Relish, Cranberry-Orange, '81 M289; '88 254
Rice à l'Orange, '90 236
Rice, Orange, '79 43; '81 175; '82 200
Rice, Orange-Herb, '89 286
Roast, Orange Marinated Chuck, '85 179
Salads
Ambrosia Supreme, Orange, '79 37
Aspic, Orange-and-Carrot, '86 199
Avocado-Orange Salad, '91 44
Beet Salad, Orange-and-, '88 43
Broccoli-Orange Salad, '94 281
Carrot Salad, Orange-, '80 89; '84 325
Carrot-Tangerine Salad, '83 316; '84 16
Cauliflower Salad, Orange-, '82 266
Cherry-Orange Salad, '79 74; '82 56
Chicken-and-Orange Salad, Curried, '87 144
Chicken Salad, Persian, '81 12
Congealed Salad, Pineapple-Orange, '83 218
Cottage Cheese Salad, Orange-, '79 44
Cranberry-Orange Delight, '90 168
Creamy Orange Salad, '84 124
Cup, Orange Fruit, '91 277
Cups, Citrus Salad in Orange, '85 47
Cups, Orange, '86 92
Cups, Orange Salad, '85 40
Frosted Orange Salad, '81 154; '83 123
Grapefruit-Orange Salad, '91 276
Grapefruit Salad, Orange-, '93 294
Honey-Berry Dressing, Orange Salad with, '89 250
Honey Dressing, Orange Salad with, '89 14
Jeweled Orange Salad, '83 210
Jicama-and-Orange Salad, '88 246
Jicama-Orange Salad, '86 83; '90 122
Lobster and Orange Salad, '82 207
Mandarin Chicken, Carousel, '79 88
Mandarin Ham-and-Rice Salad, '87 145
Mandarin Orange and Pineapple Salad, '82 266
Mandarin Orange-Lettuce Salad, '92 79
Mandarin Orange Salad, '81 252; '84 161
Mandarin Orange Salad, Congealed, '89 327
Mandarin Orange Tossed Salad, '92 303
Mandarin Pork-and-Spinach Salad, '88 M126
Mandarin Rice Salad, '88 271
Mandarin Salad, Broccoli-, '93 325
Mandarin Salad Molds, '85 54
Mandarin Spinach Salad, '85 163
Mandarin Tossed Salad, '89 12

Marinated Orange-Onion Salad, '91 231; '92 68
Minted Orange Salad, '92 105
Onion Salad, Orange-, '89 41
Pear Salad, Orange-, '84 164
Quick Orange Salad, '87 80
Red Cabbage Citrus Salad, '94 72
Romaine Salad, Orange-, '84 325; '87 239
Sesame-Citrus Green Salad, '86 33
Sherbet Salad, Orange, '81 154
Shrimp-and-Orange Rice Salad, Zesty, '87 155
Shrimp, Orange, and Olive Salad with Sherry Vinaigrette, '93 177
Shrimp Salad, Orange-, '84 197
Slaw, Cabbage-Orange, '79 135
Spinach-and-Orange Salad, '86 15
Spinach Salad, Orange-, '83 316; '84 16
Strawberry Salad with Orange-Curd Dressing, Orange-, '93 22
Sunshine Delight, '86 117
Surprise Salad, Orange, '79 12
Tropical Orange Salad, '92 97
Turkey-in-the-Orange Salad, '93 21
Walnut Salad, Orange, '80 246
Sauces and Glazes
Butter Glaze, Orange, '90 194
Chicken in Orange Sauce, Skillet, '94 252
Chicken with Orange, Lime, and Ginger Sauce, '92 123
Chocolate-Orange Sauce, '86 165; '94 314
Coconut-Orange Sauce, '85 189
Dessert Sauce, Orange, '86 337; '87 58
Duck with Orange Sauce, Grilled, '94 305
Fresh Orange Glaze, '88 179
Fresh Orange Sauce, '85 209
Hard Sauce, Orange, '88 225
Honey-Orange Sauce, '85 108
Leeks in Orange Sauce, '88 86
Liqueur Sauce, Orange, '86 142
Mandarin Orange Sauce, '89 204
Mandarin Sauce, '84 60
Nutty Orange Glaze, '80 45
Orange Glaze, '79 2; '80 257; '81 34, 107; '82 75, 206; '83 33, 114, 140, 267; '84 161; '86 298; '92 263
Orange Sauce, '82 47; '83 10, 277; '84 M286; '86 294
Peas in Orange Sauce, Green, '88 97
Pineapple Glaze, Orange-, '81 60
Pineapple-Orange Sauce, '84 14
Raspberry-Orange Sauce, '88 22; '92 154
Sweet Orange Sauce, '93 M325
Syrup, Orange, '80 228; '89 254
Scampi, Orange, '85 303
Slices, Spicy Orange, '81 12
Snapper à l'Orange, Baked, '85 181
Snapper, Orangy, '88 23
Soup, Carrot-Orange, '79 172
Spareribs, Orange-Glazed, '84 296
Spareribs with Orange Barbecue Sauce, '83 11
Special, Orange Blossom, '88 158
Spread, Orange Cheese, '87 292

Oranges *(continued)*

Squash à l'Orange, **'85** 230
Squash Brûlée, Orange-, **'94** 267
Sweet Potatoes, Coconut-Orange, **'84** 252
Sweet Potatoes in Orange Cups, **'82** 272
Sweet Potatoes, Orange, **'86** 279
Sweet Potatoes, Orange-Baked, **'88** M294
Sweet Potatoes, Orange-Glazed, **'81** 223;
'83 280
Sweet Potato-Stuffed Orange Cups,
'81 223
Swordfish Steaks, Orange-Ginger Marinated,
'93 271
Turkey Breast with Orange-Raspberry Glaze,
'91 253
Turkey-Orange Skillet, Oriental, **'86** 284
Turkey Slices, Orange-, **'90** 53
Vinaigrette Dressing, Tangy Orange,
'93 46
Vinaigrette, Honey-Orange, **'91** 255

Orzo
Marinara on Beds of Spinach and Orzo,
'93 320
Primavera, Orzo, **'92** 192
Salad, Artichokes with Orzo, **'88** M193
Salad, Confetti Orzo, **'92** 173
Salad, Peppers Stuffed with Shrimp-and-Orzo,
'91 203

Oysters
Annapolis, Oysters, **'89** 195
Bacon, Oysters in, **'83** 211
Baked Oysters, Bacon-, **'86** 132
Baked Oysters Bienville, **'90** 27
Baked Oysters Italiano, **'89** 97
Baked Oysters on the Half Shell, **'93** 269
Baked Oysters over Toast Points, **'84** 214
Bake, Oyster-and-Corn, **'83** 34; **'84** 44
Barbecued Oysters, **'82** 247
Bienville, Oysters, **'79** 182; **'93** 257
Bisque, Oyster, **'83** 252
Brochette, Oysters, **'80** 56
Buccaneer, Oysters, **'87** 40
Casino on Cornbread, Oysters, **'79** 34
Casino, Oysters à la, **'80** 296
Casserole, Oyster, **'79** 228
Casserole, Oyster-and-Spinach, **'83** 34;
'84 44
Casserole, Oyster-and-Wild Rice, **'83** 34;
'84 44
Casserole, Wild Rice-Oyster, **'86** 256
Chesapeake, Oysters, **'92** 254
Chowder, Oyster, **'83** 229
Chowder, Oyster-Corn, **'83** 211
Creamed Oysters, **'92** 254
Creamed Oysters, Pan-Fried Grits with,
'93 62
Creamy Oysters and Crabmeat, **'83** 211

Crêpes, Virginia, **'79** 264
Dip, Smoked Oyster, **'79** 233
Dressed Oysters on the Half Shell,
'87 M79
Dressing, Oyster, **'79** 250
Dressing, Oyster Bread, **'82** 251
Fresh Oysters, Preparing, **'82** 127
Fried Oyster Bubbles, **'80** 296
Fried Oysters, **'85** 104
Fried Oysters, Delicious, **'83** 212
Fried Oysters, Southern, **'88** 111
Fried Raw Oysters, **'81** 135; **'82** 14
Fritters, Oyster, **'79** 31
Fry, Hangtown, **'80** 297
Gino, Oysters à la, **'81** 126
Grilled Oysters Mornay, **'89** 195
Gumbo, Chicken and Oyster, **'81** 198
Gumbo, Duck, Oyster, and Sausage,
'79 226
Gumbo, Seafood, **'83** 90; **'87** 210
Ham, Edwards' Oysters and, **'86** 253
Johnny Reb, Oysters, **'82** 42
Landmark, Oyster, **'84** 88
Loaf, Crusty Oyster, **'92** 254
Loaves, Spinach-Oyster, **'84** 213
Mornay, Seafood, **'83** 67
Mousse, Oyster, **'81** 245
Mousse, Smoked Oyster, **'84** 320
Nachos, Texas Oyster, **'87** 39
Omelets, Smoked Oyster, **'84** 96
Patty Shells, Oysters in, **'83** 212;
'85 257
Pie, Creole Oyster, **'84** 214
Pie, Turkey-and-Oyster, **'82** 267
Poor Boys, Oyster-and-Bacon, **'87** 40
Rockefeller, Southern Oysters, **'80** 212
Sandwich, Oyster Submarine, **'80** 92
Sautéed Oysters, **'86** 132
Sautéed Seafood Platter, **'83** 89
Scalloped Oysters, **'79** 225; **'84** 213;
'86 132; **'90** 249
Scalloped Oysters with Macaroni,
'80 297
Shrimp Sauce, Oysters in, **'87** 40
Smoked Oysters, Deviled Eggs with,
'84 161
Smoky Oysters Supreme, **'87** 60
Soup, Chicken, Ham, and Oyster,
'79 198
Soup, Louisiana Oyster-and-Artichoke,
'92 81
Soup, Oyster, **'79** 228; **'83** 211
Soup, Oyster-and-Mushroom, **'87** 39
Soup, Oyster-Cheese, **'84** 213
Soup, Oyster-Turnip, **'94** 328
Spinach Salad with Oysters and Red Wine
Vinaigrette, **'94** 327
Spread, Smoked Oyster, **'91** 64
Stew, Company Oyster, **'80** 297
Stewed in Cream, Oysters, **'93** 50
Stew, Golden Oyster, **'86** 132
Stew, Holiday Oyster, **'85** 264
Stew, Oyster, **'80** 221
Stew, Oyster-Broccoli, **'89** 242
Stew, Oyster-Sausage, **'89** 242
Stew, Potato-Oyster, **'89** 243
St. Jacques, Oysters, **'80** 103
Stuffed Oysters, Crabmeat, **'94** 328
Stuffing, Roast Turkey with Oyster,
'80 251
Wild Rice and Oysters, **'92** 339

Pancakes

Ambrosia Pancakes with Orange Syrup,
'89 254
Apple Pancakes with Cider Sauce, Spicy,
'87 224
Applesauce Pancakes, **'79** 114
Apple-Topped Pancakes, **'93** 339
Apricot Delight, **'81** 42
Black Bean Pancakes with Gazpacho Butter,
'92 86
Blueberry Buttermilk Pancakes, **'79** 114
Blueberry Pancakes, **'85** 152; **'89** 138
Blueberry Pancakes, Sour Cream, **'81** 164
Blue Cornmeal-Blueberry Pancakes, **'94** 115
Bran Pancakes with Cinnamon Syrup,
'91 315
Buttermilk Griddle Cakes, **'81** 120; **'82** 22
Buttermilk Pancakes, **'83** 243; **'84** 101
Buttermilk Pancakes with Fruit Topping,
'89 50
Cornmeal Batter Cakes, **'87** 16
Cornmeal Pancakes, Hearty, **'88** 129
Corn Pancakes, **'93** 43
Cottage Cheese Pancakes, **'79** 115
Dessert Ginger Pancakes, **'88** 153
Dessert Pancakes, Luau, **'88** 154
Easy Pancakes, **'92** 203
Filled Pancake, Apple-, **'86** 96
Fluffy Pancakes, **'86** 137
Fruit Topping, Pancakes with, **'81** 42
Gingerbread Pancakes, **'84** 242
Ham Griddle Cakes, **'89** 255
Honey Pancakes, **'91** 139
Island Pancakes, **'87** 225
Latkes, **'90** 254
Maple-Bacon Oven Pancake, **'89** 255
Oatmeal-Brown Sugar Pancakes, **'88** 203
Oatmeal Pancakes, **'80** 44; **'89** 107
Oat Pancakes, **'89** 227
Orange-Yogurt Pancakes, **'87** 225
Oven-Baked Pancake for Two, **'89** 227
Pancakes, **'81** 90
Potato Pancake, **'85** 20
Potato Pancakes, **'79** 115; **'89** 144
Potato Pancakes, Moist, **'80** 36
Potato Pancakes, Sweet, **'87** 280
Pumpkin Pancakes, **'80** 228
Quick Bread Mix, **'81** 90
Refrigerator Pancakes, Overnight, **'93** 196
Rice Pancakes, **'85** 147
Sauce, Cinnamon-Pecan-Honey Pancake,
'88 46
Sauce, Peach-Blueberry Pancake, **'82** 177
Sausage Rollups, Pancake-, **'83** 246;
'84 42
Sausage Wedges, Pancake-, **'93** 196
Sour Cream Pancakes, **'79** 213
Sour Cream Pancakes, Fluffy, **'79** 209
Sour Cream Pancakes with Fruit Topping,
'90 142
Squash Pancakes, Granola-, **'94** 267
Strawberry Pancakes, **'84** 219
Supper Pancake, **'86** 242
Vegetable Pancakes, **'88** 297
Vegetable-Rice Pancakes, **'93** 43
Wheat Germ-Banana Pancakes, **'79** 114
Wheat Germ Pancakes, **'86** 242
Wheat Pancakes, Shredded, **'84** 59
Wheat Quick Pancakes, **'85** 278
Whole Grain Pancakes, **'93** 123

Pancakes (continued)

Whole Wheat-Oat Pancakes, '93 16
Whole Wheat Pancakes, '83 18
Zucchini Pancakes, '93 43
Parsnips
Candied Parsnips, '86 224
Glazed Parsnips, '91 220
Soufflé, Golden Parsnip, '83 266
Sugar-Crusted Parsnips, '88 229
Pastas. *See also* specific types.
Angel Hair Pasta, Shrimp and Mushrooms
  with, '92 34
Angel Hair Pasta with Shrimp and Asparagus,
  '92 100
Angel Hair Pasta with Tomato Cream Sauce,
  '93 292
Antipasto, Pasta, '85 286
Artichoke Hearts, Pasta with, '86 209
Basil Pasta, Fresh Tomato Sauce over,
  '93 176
Bean-Salami Pasta Toss, Kidney, '85 165
Bites, Pesto-Cheese Pasta, '87 251
Bow-Tie Pesto, '94 231
Bow-Tie with Marinara, '94 64
Broccoli and Sausage, Pasta with, '87 109
Broccoli Pasta, '84 176
Cannelloni, '85 60; '92 17
Catfish and Artichokes, Pasta with, '90 123
Cavatini, '94 214
Cheeses, Pasta Stuffed with Five, '88 197
Chicken-and-Broccoli Pasta, '87 286
Chicken and Pasta, Pesto, '89 M132
Chicken and Pasta, Quick, '93 14
Chicken, Bird's-Nest, '88 152
Chicken with Pasta, Dijon, '90 318
Clam Sauce, Pasta with, '84 291
Collards and Sausage, Pasta with, '94 230
Crab Bake, Quick, '87 192
Dressing, Pasta Salad, '86 121
Frittata, Firecracker Pasta, '94 230
Frittata, Pasta, '85 286
Garden Pasta, '82 199
Garden Pasta Medley, '89 256
Garlic Pasta with Marinara Sauce, '92 78
Green Pasta with Shrimp-Mushroom
  Italienne, '79 170
Kabobs, Antipasto, '94 144
Mexican Luncheon, '87 192
Minestrone, Dixie, '94 230
Mostaccioli Alfredo, '91 47
Oregano Pasta, '84 176
"Pasta," Garden-Fresh, '94 M134
Peas and Pasta, '93 139
Pepperoni Pasta, '83 105
Pepper Pasta, '89 321
Peppers and Broccoli, Pasta with, '91 69
Peppery Pasta, '94 164
Pesto and Pasta, '92 98
Pie, Broccoli-and-Turkey Pasta, '88 269
Pie, Spinach-Pasta, '85 286
Pimiento Pasta, '84 176
Platter, Cold Pasta, '88 42
Potpourri, Pasta, '94 33
Primavera, Almost Pasta, '86 38
Primavera, Chicken-Pasta, '91 72
Primavera, Garden Spiral, '91 30
Primavera, Pasta, '85 86; '89 105; '93 168
Primavera, Smoked Turkey Pasta, '90 84
Primavera, Tomato-Pasta, '86 209

Prosciutto, Party Pasta with, '94 176
Provençale, Pasta, '88 90
Ravioli, Homemade, '87 230
Ravioli, Mediterranean, '93 301
Ravioli Pasta, Homemade, '87 231
Ravioli with Creamy Pesto Sauce, '92 79
Rotelle, Chicken and Tomato with, '87 108
Rotelle, Shrimp, '85 165
Rotini Romano, '87 193
Salad, Acini di Pepe, '83 163
Salad, Artichoke-Pasta, '94 180
Salad, Broccoli-Cauliflower Pasta, '88 269
Salad, Chicken Pasta, '88 89
Salad, Crabmeat-Shrimp Pasta, '86 208
Salad, Crunchy Pasta, '85 166
Salad, Crunchy Rotelle, '86 209
Salad, Easy Confetti-Pasta, '92 220
Salad, Fruited Pasta, '92 108
Salad, Garden Pasta, '86 188
Salad, Grilled Chicken-Pasta, '94 64
Salad, Ham-and-Pasta, '90 128
Salad, Ham-Dijon Pasta, '92 191
Salad, Ham-Pecan-Blue Cheese Pasta, '90 62
Salad, Herbed Pasta-and-Tomato, '92 144
Salad, Italian, '87 145
Salad, Luncheon Pasta, '90 191
Salad, Main-Dish Pasta, '82 199
Salad, Marinated Bean-Pasta, '94 167
Salad, Oriental Pasta, '90 63
Salad, Overnight Pasta, '82 276
Salad, Pasta, '84 139; '86 120; '87 36;
  '89 217; '90 62, 91
Salad, Pasta-and-Shrimp, '83 163
Salad, Pasta-Bean, '86 169
Salad, Pistachio-Pasta, '86 141
Salad, Presto Pasta, '90 63
Salad, Ranch-Style Turkey 'n' Pasta,
  '94 184
Salad, Ratatouille Pasta, '90 74
Salad, Rotini, '88 42
Salad, Salmon-Pasta, '87 9
Salad, Seafood Pasta, '90 62
Salad, Seashell, '86 209
Salad, Shrimp Vermicelli, '88 139
Salad, Southwestern Pasta, '94 278
Salad, Tarragon Pasta-Chicken, '87 155
Salad, Tuna-Pasta, '91 43; '92 141
Salad, Tuna Pasta, '92 108
Salad, Vegetable Pasta, '89 256; '91 143
Salad, Vegetable-Pasta, '92 167
Salad, Vermicelli Vinaigrette, '82 189
Salad with Ham, Pasta, '92 108
Salad, Ziti-Cheddar, '85 165
Salmon Carbonara, '83 43
Sauerkraut Salad, Crunchy, '87 9
Sausage and Mixed Vegetables, Pasta with,
  '84 249
Scallops and Pasta, Fresh, '83 164
Seafood and Pasta, '90 234
Seafood Delight, '86 208
Seashell-Provolone Casserole, '80 189
Seashells Florentine, Jumbo, '79 6
Shell Salad, Tossed, '91 256
Shells, Cheesy Beef-Stuffed, '83 217
Shells, Mexican Stuffed, '91 87
Shells, Salmon Salad, '85 286
Shells, Southwestern Stuffed, '93 234
Shells, Spinach-Stuffed, '85 60; '87 20
Shrimp and Pasta, '91 207
Shrimp and Pasta, Herbed, '92 329
Shrimp Élégante, '83 48

Shrimp Marinara, '84 233
Shrimp-Pasta Medley, '88 302
Snappy Pasta, '83 164
Soup, Bean and Pasta, '94 220
Spinach-Mustard Twist, '86 209
Spinach-Peanut Pesto and Pasta, '93 212
Spinach Pesto-Pasta, '91 314
Straw and Hay Pasta, '80 211
Tetrazzini, Chicken, '79 268
Tetrazzini, Ham, '82 M77
Tomato-Basil Pasta, '94 204
Tomatoes, Quick Pasta and, '92 180
Tomato-Garlic Pasta, '94 177
Tomato-Olive Pasta Toss, '86 209
Tomato Pasta, Caribbean, '93 201
Tomato Pasta, Italian, '93 201
Tomato Pasta, Southwestern, '93 201
Tortellini Carbonara, '91 47
Tortellini, Italian Sausage Soup with, '88 46
Tortellini-Pesto Salad, '92 22
Tortellini Salad, '89 237
Tortellini Salad, Chicken, '87 288
Tortellini Salad, Garden, '91 44
Tortellini, Shrimp and, '92 34
Tortellini with Parsley-Caper Sauce, '93 175
Tortellini with Rosemary-Parmesan Sauce,
  '92 284
Tortellini with Tomato Sauce, Spinach,
  '88 302
Toss, Pasta-Basil, '87 33
Tricolor Pasta with Clam Sauce, '93 272
Tuna Pasta, Stuffed Tomato with, '88 54
Turkey-Basil Pasta, Creamy, '89 216
Vegetables and Pasta, Roasted, '93 184
Vegetable Sauce, Pasta with, '83 163
Vegetables, Pasta and, '89 255
Vegetables, Pasta and Garden, '87 192
Verde, Pasta, '84 201
Vermicelli, Anchovy-Garlic Sauce over,
  '86 158
Vermicelli and Sprouts with Red Clam Sauce,
  '86 143
Vermicelli, Lemon, '84 329
Vermicelli, Mushroom Sauce Supreme on,
  '86 158
Vermicelli, Salmon-Pesto, '92 200
Vermicelli, Scallop-Vegetable, '87 143
Vermicelli, Shrimp and Feta Cheese on,
  '87 108
Vermicelli Soup with Quenelles, Veal-, '94 14
Vermicelli with Clam Sauce, '85 295
Vermicelli with Fresh Spinach Sauce, '89 256
Vermicelli with Mushrooms, '79 195
Vermicelli with Tomato Sauce, '83 164
Vinaigrette, Italian Pasta, '92 78
Ziti, Baked, '94 65
Pâtés. *See* Appetizers/Pâtés.
Peaches
Alaska, Peachy Melba, '88 266
Ambrosia, Peach, '83 53
Baked Peaches, '92 179
Baked Peaches and Sausage, '82 50
Baked Peaches, Spicy, '86 39
Baked Peaches with Ginger, Oven-, '82 170
Bay Laurel Peaches, '90 124
Bellinis, '88 77
Bellini Spritzers, '90 110
Bombe with Raspberry Sauce, Creamy,
  '89 322
Brandied Peaches with Mincemeat, '81 47
Brandy Peaches, '85 275

Peaches *(continued)*

Bread, Georgia Peach, '79 161
Bread, Peach, '82 170
Butter, Golden Peach, '91 178
Butter, Peach, '82 308
Cake, Fresh Peach, '85 178
Cake, Peach-Almond Pound, '89 86
Cake, Peaches and Cream, '80 142
Cake, Peach Upside-Down, '87 8
Cake, Peachy Almond-Butter, '90 107
Cake, Peachy Picnic, '79 178
Caramel Peaches, '93 134
Cardinale, Peach, '89 155
Champagne, Peaches, '79 146
Charlotte, Peach, '79 68
Cheesecake, Peaches 'n' Cream, '88 137
Chicken Breasts, Peach-Stuffed, '79 177
Chicken Peach Dinner, '79 77
Chicken, Peachy, '90 212
Chutney, Peach, '84 179
Cobbler, Cranberry-Peach, '92 322
Cobbler, Fresh Peach, '82 139; '89 154
Cobbler, Grenadine-Peach, '85 178
Cobbler, Lattice-Topped Peach, '79 154
Cobbler, No-Dough Blueberry-Peach,
  '86 177
Cobbler, Old-Fashioned Peach, '82 170
Cobbler, Peach, '83 175; '84 178; '90 219
Cobbler, Peach-Caramel, '86 300; '87 178
Cobbler, Peachy Blueberry, '80 143
Cobbler, Quick Peach, '79 215; '81 142
Cobbler, Spicy Peach, '85 178
Cobbler Supreme, Peach, '81 184; '90 313
Cobbler with Praline Biscuits, Peach, '92 180
Compote, Berry-Peach, '82 133
Compote, Peach-Berry, '89 112
Conserve, Peach, '79 120
Cooler, Peach, '85 198; '86 6
Crabapple Peaches, Broiled Pork Chops with,
  '81 83
Cream, Bavarian Peach, '82 171
Cream Cheese, Peachy, '92 289
Cream, Honeyed Peaches 'n', '93 134
Cream, Peach Almond, '82 108
Cream, Peaches 'n' Almond, '86 229
Cream, Peachy-Apricot, '86 163
Crêpes, Fresh Peach, '84 186
Crêpes, Peach, '82 184
Crinkle, Peach, '91 20
Crisp, Peach, '83 113; '92 13; '93 134
Crumble, Easy Peach, '83 116
Curried Ham and Peaches, '82 60
Custard Dessert, Fresh Peach, '86 162
Daiquiris, Peach, '90 322
Dessert, Peach-Blueberry, '92 184
Dessert, Peachy Melt-Away, '87 298
Dessert, Quick Peach, '85 178
Dip, Creole Peach, '80 142
Dip, Peachy, '92 179
Dressing, Peach, '90 180
Dumplings, Peach, '80 143; '85 177
Filling, Peach, '89 154; '90 107
Flambé, Banana-Peach, '85 316
Flambé, Peach Sundaes, '81 88
Flip, Peach, '79 217
Foster, Peaches, '86 240
Freeze, Creamy Peach, '82 144
Frost, Peach, '84 164; '89 155
Frosty, Peach, '81 156; '83 318

Fuzz Buzz, '82 160
Ginger Peaches with Rum, '84 M323
Gingersnap Peaches, '85 M329
Ham Roast, Peachy, '86 118
Honey-Lime Whip, Peaches with, '85 108
Honey-Sweet Peaches, '85 107
Ice Cream, Creamy Peach, '85 177
Ice Cream, Deluxe Peach, '80 176; '90 314
Ice Cream, Peach, '81 184; '82 171;
  '83 159; '86 15; '93 135
Ice Cream, Peach-Almond, '89 156
Ice, Peach, '81 178
Ice, Peach-Yogurt, '84 83
Jam, Freezer Peach, '83 182; '84 M182
Jam, Peach, '93 135
Jam, Peach-Plum Freezer, '85 130
Jam, Rosy Peach-Banana, '80 142
Marinated Peaches, '91 91
Marmalade, Peach-Orange, '82 150
Melba, Peach, '81 83; '83 M114
Meringues, Peach Melba, '87 76
Mincemeat Peaches, '85 178
Mold, Peachy Berry Cream, '83 130
Mousse, Peach, '85 54
Mousse, Peach Macaroon, '80 153
Muffins, Peachy-Almond, '86 301
Muffins, Special Peach, '84 74
Nest, Peaches in a Garden, '87 154
Parfait, Peach, '82 166
Pears, Peaches and, '85 106
Petals, Peach, '90 104
Pickled Peaches, Perfect, '85 178
Pickles, Peach, '85 177
Pick-Me-Up, Peach, '89 183
Pie, Blueberry-Peach, '94 158
Pie, Fresh Peach, '82 170
Pie, Luscious Peach, '81 136
Pie, Mincemeat-Peach, '80 295; '81 188
Pie, Peach-and-Blackberry, '89 136
Pie, Peach Chiffon, '89 155
Pie, Peach-Cranberry, '83 249
Pie, Peaches-and-Cream, '81 184
Pie, Peach Praline, '89 136
Pie, Quick Peach, '89 252
Pie, Rhubarb-Peach, '86 140
Pies, Delicious Fried, '83 84
Pies, Easy Peach Fried, '85 178
Pies, Fried Peach, '81 272
Pies, Little Peach, '86 303
Pork Chops, Peachy, '89 310
Pork Steaks, Peachy, '79 166
Preserves, Cream Cheese and Peach,
  '84 264
Preserves, Honeyed Peach, '85 130
Preserves, Old-Fashioned Peach, '82 150
Preserves, Peach, '81 147; '89 140
Pudding, Peachy Bread, '88 175
Puffs, Peach Sweet Potato, '87 280
Refresher, Peach, '86 103
Relish, Peach, '85 136
Ring, Spicy Peach-Cranberry, '85 264
Salad, Frosted Peach, '82 145
Salad, Frozen Peach, '82 54
Salad, Georgia Peach, '80 142
Salad, Georgia Summer, '92 179
Salad, Peach-and-Kiwi, '90 180
Salad, Peaches-and-Cream, '83 108
Salad, Peach Party, '84 290
Salad, Peach Pinwheel, '79 11
Salad, Peachy Fruit, '89 206
Salad, Pickled Peach, '80 104; '85 264

Salad, Spiced Peach, '94 68
Salad Supreme, Easy Peach, '79 177
Salsa, Peach, '91 183
Sauce, Creamy Fresh Peach, '79 177
Sauce, Creamy Peach, '85 189
Sauce, Fresh Peach, '87 167
Sauce, Peach, '84 144; '92 203
Sauce, Peach-Berry, '87 M165
Sauce, Peach-Blueberry, '81 170
Sauce, Peach-Blueberry Pancake, '82 177
Sauce, Peach-Praline, '85 161
Sauce, Strawberry-Peach, '92 154
Shake, Peach Melba Sundae, '93 134
Shake, Peachy Orange, '81 156
Shake, Pep, '79 38
Sherbet Cooler, Peachy, '91 187
Sherbet, Peach, '90 179
Shortcakes, Spicy Peach, '89 154
Slaw, Party Peach, '86 250
Smash, Peach, '88 161
Smoothie, Strawberry-Peach, '89 182
Sorbet, Peach, '93 153
Soup, Peach, '83 120, 180
Soup, Peach-Plum, '87 157
Spareribs, Peach-Glazed, '86 14
Spiced Peach Dessert, '83 9
Spiced Peaches, '91 72, 148
Spiced Peaches, Brandy, '80 142
Spiced Peaches, Ginger, '86 15
Spiced Peaches with Nutty Dumplings,
  '87 164
Split, Peach, '85 277
Spread, Peachy Cream Cheese, '90 M215
Spread, Peachy-Raisin, '86 326
Strawberry Sauce, Peaches with, '85 8
Stuffed Peaches, Macaroon-, '79 178
Stuffed Peach Halves, '86 196
Sweet Potatoes and Peaches, '86 11
Tart, Kiwifruit-Peach, '88 20
Tart, Peach Cream, '90 173
Tarts, Peachy Keen, '91 118
Topping, Peach, '94 22
Topping, Raspberry-Peach, '87 126
Torte, Frozen Peach, '93 135
Trifle, Peach, '92 179
Wine Sauce, Peaches in, '79 184
Yogurt, Frozen Fresh Peach, '90 139

Peanut Butter

Apple, Piggy, '94 194
Balls, Chocolate-Peanut Butter, '80 87
Balls, No-Cook Candy, '85 14
Balls, Peanut Butter-Chocolate, '80 269
Bars, Peanut Butter, '84 243; '93 166
Bars, Peanut Butter-and-Fudge, '80 M172
Bars, Peanut Butter 'n' Jelly, '83 305
Bites, Chocolate-Peanut Butter, '92 M317
Bites, Peanut Butter Elf, '91 275
Bread, Peanut Butter, '86 171; '88 64
Brownies, Chocolate Chip-Peanut Butter,
  '84 73
Brownies, Chocolate-Peanut Butter Chip,
  '91 306
Brownies, Frosted Peanut Butter, '92 272
Brownies, Peanut Butter, '87 199
Cake, Chocolate-Peanut Butter, '84 240
Cake, Fudgy Peanut Butter, '85 91
Cake, Peanut Butter, '79 51; '83 M233
Cake, Peanut Butter-and-Jelly, '85 34
Cake, Peanut Butter-Banana, '80 87
Cake, Peanut Butter Swirl, '86 109
Candy, Peanut Butter, '93 166

Peanut Butter *(continued)*

Cheese Ball, Peanut Butter-, '86 136
Cheesecake, Peanut Butter, '94 142
Chicken, Peanut Butter-Marmalade, '81 282; '82 30
Chocolate Peanutty Swirls, '94 M330
"Concrete," All Shook Up, '94 114
Cones, Chocolate-Peanut Butter, '85 14
Cookies, Chocolate-Peanut Butter, '85 90
Cookies, Choco-Peanut Chip, '92 318
Cookies, Choco Surprise, '80 60
Cookies, Crisp Peanuttiest, '88 65
Cookies, Double Chip, '81 301
Cookies, Double-Chip Peanut Butter, '89 169
Cookies, Double Peanut Butter, '80 209
Cookies, Easy Peanut Butter, '92 272
Cookies, Freezer Peanut Butter-Chocolate Chip, '86 230
Cookies, Miracle, '83 149
Cookies, Monster, '84 36
Cookies, No-Bake Peanut Butter, '94 197
Cookies, Oatmeal-Peanut Butter, '85 171
Cookies, Oatmeal-Peanut Butter Chocolate Chip, '92 207
Cookies, Peanut Butter, '82 56; '87 58
Cookies, Peanut Butter and Chocolate Chunk, '94 169
Cookies, Peanut Butter-Chocolate Kiss, '86 49
Cookies, Peanut Butter-Cinnamon, '84 30
Cookies, Peanut Butter-Coconut, '83 113
Cookies, Peanut Butter-Oatmeal, '81 218; '84 72
Cookies, Peanut Truffle, '93 212
Cookies, Quick Peanut Butter, '86 109
Cooler, Peanut Butter, '84 115
Creams, Peanut Butter, '79 273
Crisps, Peanut Butter, '79 50
Cupcakes, Chocolate Surprise, '85 91
Cups, Chocolate-Peanut Butter, '85 14
Dessert, Crunchy Peanut-Buttery, '92 204
Dessert, Peanut Butter, '92 164
Dip, Peanut Butter, '86 135
Dip, Peanut Butter-Honey, '85 19
Dip, Peanut Butter Lovers', '93 162
Drops, Chocolate-Peanut Butter, '92 322
Eggs, Peanut Butter Easter, '87 86
Fingers, Peanut Butter, '79 256
French Toast, Peanut Butter, '93 166
Frosting, Chocolate-Peanut Butter, '84 240; '87 222
Frosting, Creamy Peanut, '80 87
Frosting, Peanut Butter, '83 223; '84 153; '85 34
Frosting, Peanut Butter-Fudge, '87 184
Frosting, Peanut Butter Swirl, '86 109
Frosts, Peanut Butter, '84 153
Frozen Peanut Butter Delight, '88 137
Fudge Bites, Peanut-, '91 M231; '92 M68
Fudge, Chocolate-Peanut Butter, '87 257; '90 311
Fudge, Creamy Peanut Butter, '92 240
Fudge, Diamond, '92 193
Fudge, Double-Good, '79 M263
Fudge, Double Peanut, '85 91
Fudge, Four Chips, '92 318
Fudge, Marbled Peanut Butter, '88 65
Fudge, Peanut Butter, '80 302; '89 307
Granola, Peanut Butter, '82 296

Ice Cream, Chocolate Chunk-Peanut Butter, '85 297; '86 120
Ice Cream, Peanut Butter, '81 103; '88 64, 203
Ice Cream Sandwiches, Peanut Butter Cookie, '93 199
Jam Bars, Peanut Butter-, '94 291
Logs, No-Bake Peanut Butter, '84 211
Milkshakes, Peanut Butter, '85 198
Muffins, Peanut Butter, '80 86; '87 158
Muffins, Peanut Butter-Chocolate Chip, '94 167
Muffins, Peanut Butter-Honey, '82 56
Napoleons, Peanut Butter-and-Chocolate, '94 121
Parfaits, Crunchy Peanut Butter, '79 176; '80 6
Pie, Chocolate-Peanut Butter, '85 91
Pie, Chocolate-Peanut Butter Swirl, '87 262
Pie, Fluffy Peanut Butter, '94 246
Pie, Peanut Butter, '85 275; '86 109; '89 252
Pie, Peanut Butter Cream, '79 50; '88 65
Pie, Peanut Butter Meringue, '84 30
Pie, Tin Roof, '85 91
Pie, "Working for Peanuts," '93 115
Pinecones, Peanut Butter-Suet, '93 286
Pizza, Peanut Butter-Fruit, '94 60
Pralines, Chocolate-Peanut Butter, '92 313; '93 51
Pralines, Peanut Butter, '92 313; '93 51
Pudding, Peanut Butter, '85 95; '88 32
Pudding, Peanut Butter-Banana, '93 340
Sandwiches, Peanut Butter-and-Jelly "Fish," '91 177
Sandwiches, Peanut-Cheese-Raisin, '88 140
Sandwiches, Spider, '93 193
Sandwich, Peanut Butter Breakfast, '82 55
Sauce, Chocolate-Peanut Butter, '79 91, M156
Sauce, Peanut Butter Barbecue, '81 233
Sauce, Peanut Butter Ice Cream, '84 30
Shake, PBJ, '93 292
Shake, Peanut Butter, '82 48
Slice-and-Bakes, Peanut Butter, '82 M185
Snacks, Chocolate-Peanut Butter, '90 226
Snaps, Peanut Butter, '81 237
Soup, Cream of Peanut, '92 193; '93 288
Soup, Cream of Peanut Butter, '84 29
Soup, Creamy Peanut, '79 50
Soup, Peanut Butter, '89 28
Spread, Peanut Butter, '92 21
Squares, Chocolate Chip-Peanut Butter, '84 118
Squares, Peanut Butter, '83 116
Squares, Peanut Butter-Chocolate Candy, '82 56
Tarts, Chocolate-Peanut Butter, '92 277
Temptations, Peanut Butter, '84 29
Tiger Butter, '86 48
Waffles, Honey-Buttered Peanut Butter, '94 M206
Yummies, Peanut Butter, '83 223

Peanuts

Apples, Caramel-Peanut, '93 M244
Apples, Peanutty Stuffed, '85 25
Balls, Peanut-Date, '81 92
Bananas, Nutty, '79 251
Bars, Chewy Peanut, '80 M172
Bars, Fruit and Nut Granola, '81 49
Bars, Peanut, '89 307

Bread, Peanut, '87 184
Bread, Peanut Lover's, '93 211
Brittle, Golden Peanut, '83 223
Brittle, Never-Fail Peanut, '79 273
Brittle, Orange Peanut, '80 302
Brittle, Peanut, '79 M263; '80 87; '84 298; '92 240
Brittle with Crushed Peanuts, '87 184
Cake, Chocolate-Caramel-Nut, '83 23
Cake, Chocolate-Peanut Cluster, '87 184
Cakes, Nutty, '89 50
Cake, Super Peanutty Layer, '83 222
Candied Popcorn and Peanuts, '82 295
Chesapeake Nuts, '93 269
Chicken, Ginger-Nut, '90 M33
Chicken with Peanuts, Oriental, '82 236
Chili Nuts, Hot, '81 254
Chocolate-Peanut Crispies, '93 80
Clusters, Chocolate-Peanut, '81 16
Clusters, Nut, '81 254
Clusters, Peanut, '87 184; '92 288
Clusters, Peanutty, '83 143
Cookies, Chocolate-Peanut, '83 223
Cookies, Crisp Peanuttiest, '88 65
Cookies, Oats-and-Peanut, '89 60
Cookies, Peanutty Oatmeal, '80 106; '83 95
Cookies, Salted Peanut, '87 92
Crunchy Munchies, '94 196
Crust, Peanut-Graham Cracker, '79 50
Crust, Sweet Potatoes with Peanut, '93 212
Dessert, Fudge-Peanut Ice Cream, '88 167
Dessert, Peanut-Chocolate, '80 86
Divinity, Peanut, '85 233; '87 M278
Dressing, Roast Turkey with Peanut, '79 283
Filling, Nut, '91 35
Filling, Peanut, '93 211
Frosting, Creamy Peanut, '80 87
Fruit Dressing, Nutty, '88 68
Fudge, Double Peanut, '85 91
Granola, Crunchy Peanut, '90 48
Ice Cream, Chocolate-Covered Peanut, '88 203
Ice Cream, Peanut, '92 132
Mix, Nutty Snack, '92 22
Muffins, Peanut, '91 223
Pesto and Pasta, Spinach-Peanut, '93 212
Pie, Caramel-Nut Crunch, '94 244
Pie, Caramel-Peanut, '86 259
Pie, Peanut Raisin, '79 85
Pie, Peanutty Ice Cream, '82 56
Pie, "Working for Peanuts," '93 115
Puff Nibbles, '84 191
Salad, Broccoli-Peanut, '92 35
Salad, Green Bean-Peanut, '86 117
Salad, Nutty Cabbage, '87 42
Salad, Nutty Green, '87 168
Salad, Peanut-Apple, '80 5
Sauce, Hot Indonesian Peanut, '93 211
Sauce, Peanut Dessert, '86 M251
Sauce, Peanut Hot, '86 305
Sauce, Pork Chops with Peanut, '83 29
Sauce, Shrimp with Peanut, '93 303
Slaw, Banana-Nut, '86 250
Slaw, Chinese Peanut, '93 212
Slaw, Nutty Cabbage, '88 218
Slaw, Peanut, '85 139
Slaw, Peanutty-Pear, '86 250
Snack, Toasted Cereal, '85 215
Soup, Chilled Peanut, '79 130
Soup, Creamy Peanut, '79 50
Soup, Peanut, '87 184

Peanuts (*continued*)

Spiced Nuts, '91 M316
Spicy Nuts, '82 161
Squares, Caramel-Peanut, '85 247
Sugared Peanuts, '82 249

Pears
Amaretto Pears with Meringue, '90 M58
Baked Pears Elegant, '91 48
Baked Pears, Honey-, '93 47
Bake, Pear-Oatmeal, '89 208
Belle Helene, Pears, '86 164
Blue Cheese Sauce, Brunch Pears with, '90 142
Bread, Pear, '80 218
Breakfast Pears, Marmalade, '83 M203
Breakfast Treat, Pear, '87 72
Butter, Pear, '85 130
Butter, Spiced Pear, '80 218
Cake, Pear Preserve, '85 52
Cake, Upside-Down Sunburst, '87 9
Cake with Caramel Drizzle, Pear, '86 247
Casserole, Pear-Sweet Potato, '86 280
Cheesecake, Pear-Berry, '82 141
Cheesecake, Pear-Glazed, '79 67
Chutney, Pear-Apple, '89 141
Cobbler, Best Ever Pear, '82 194
Coconut Pears, Spicy, '83 207
Cookies, Pear Mincemeat, '84 264
Cream, Pears in Orange, '84 245
Crème Chantilly, Holiday Pears with, '91 297
Crème de Menthe Pears, '94 50
Crisp, Cranberry-Pear, '83 207
Crisp, Raspberry-Pear, '89 109
Crumble, Pear, '85 221
Delight, Pineapple-Pear, '82 54
Dressing, Pear, '83 146
en Croûte, Pears, '93 210
Filled Pears, Cheese-, '81 268
Flaming Pears, '84 313
Fritters, Ol' Timey Pear, '86 51
Gingered Pears, '89 M231
Glazed Pears, Orange-, '79 247
Gratin, Pear-Blue Cheese, '93 328
Honey, Pear, '90 159
Jam, Paradise Pear, '84 300
Marmalade, Pear, '79 196
Meringues, Baked Pear, '85 232
Mincemeat, Pear, '79 196; '84 264; '88 226
Muffins, Pear-Ginger, '91 240
Muscadine Sauce, Pears in, '88 216
Oranges, Spicy Pears and, '89 305
Peaches and Pears, '85 106
Pickles, Mustard Pear, '79 196
Pie, Apple-Pear, '83 249
Pie, Backyard Pear, '93 237
Pie, Deep-Dish Pear, '80 219
Pie, Delicious Pear, '88 226
Pie, Double-Crust Pear, '82 194
Pie, French Pear, '87 213
Pie, Ginger-Pear, '93 48
Pie, Natural Pear-Apple, '88 226
Pie, Pear Crumble, '83 207
Pie, Pear-Macadamia, '93 260
Pie, Pear-Mince, '81 271
Pie, Pear Mincemeat, '84 264; '88 226
Pie, Pear Streusel, '83 234; '84 244
Pie, Tennessee Pear, '85 230
Pineapple-Honey Pears, '86 94
Plate, Pretty Pear, '89 225

Poached in Red Wine, Pears, '83 302
Poached Pear Fans with Raspberry-Orange Sauce, '88 22
Poached Pears Flambé, Orange-, '85 313
Poached Pears in Custard, '88 20
Poached Pears in Orange Sauce, '82 19
Poached Pears in Wine, '82 194
Poached Pears, Lemon, '82 74
Poached Pears, Orange, '80 218
Poached Pears, Vanilla, '90 57
Poached Pears with Berry Sauce, Wine-, '86 144
Poached Pears with Dark Chocolate Sauce, '90 M141
Poached Pears with Honey-Yogurt Sauce, '92 306
Poached Pears with Raspberry Sauce, '84 213; '87 69; '88 223
Preserves, Pear, '82 195
Puree, Grapefruit with Pear-Berry, '89 213
Relish, Cranberry-Pear, '85 232
Relish, Pear, '79 196
Relish, Peppery Pear, '89 141
Ruby Pears, '81 288
Salad, Blue Cheese-Pear-Apple, '81 224
Salad, Crunchy Pear, '83 234; '84 244
Salad, Festive Fruit, '94 244
Salad, Festive Pear-and-Spinach, '85 131
Salad, Golden Pear, '91 58
Salad, Orange-Pear, '84 164
Salad, Pear-and-Celery, '87 56
Salad, Pear-Lime, '84 152
Salad, Pear-Swiss Cheese, '91 237
Salad, Royal Pear, '84 265
Sauce, Pear, '92 164
Sautéed Apples, Onions, and Pears over Spinach, '94 212
Sautéed Pears, Spinach Salad with, '94 237
Shake, Strawberry-Pear, '92 139
Shortcake, Pear, '94 215
Slaw, Peanutty-Pear, '86 250
Slaw, "Think Pink," '94 247
Sorbet, Pear-Lemon, '88 116
Soup, Pumpkin-Pear, '92 234
Spiced Fall Pears, '89 M231
Spiced Pears, '89 305
Spread, Pear-Cream Cheese, '93 80
Stuffed Pears, Almond-, '83 207
Stuffed with Cheese, Pears, '82 290
Sugared Pears, Maple-, '81 232
Sundaes, Quick Pear, '86 71
Tart, Pear, '82 304; '92 72
Tart with White Caramel Sauce, Pear, '92 195
Whip, Pear, '89 94
Wild Rice, Cranberry-Pear, '83 279
Wine, Pears in Red, '82 254

Peas
Baked Peas, Chinese-Style, '86 305
Black-Eyed
    Best Ever Plain Ole Peas, '88 2
    Cajun Peas, '88 3
    Casserole, Reunion Pea, '87 11
    Caviar, Texas, '86 218
    Chinese Peas, '88 3
    Creole Black-Eyed Peas, '86 252
    Creole Black-Eyes and Rice, '85 6
    Delight, Tomato-Pea, '84 196
    Dinner, Black-Eyed Pea Skillet, '86 6
    Dip, Black-Eyed Pea, '81 8

Dip, Chili-and-Black-Eyed Pea, '92 155
Flips, Pea, '80 7
Fresh Black-Eyed Peas, '81 M165
Gravy, Black-Eyed Pea, '87 12
Ham Hocks, Black-Eyed Peas with, '79 122; '89 16
Hearty Black-Eyed Peas, '85 7
Hopping Good Peas, '80 7
Hopping John, '80 7; '90 12
Hopping John, Skillet, '79 10
Hopping John with Grilled Pork Medaillons, '93 229
Hopping John with Ham, '81 7
Hummus, Black-Eyed Pea, '94 123
Jalapeño Black-Eyed Peas, '88 166
Jambalaya, Black-Eyed Pea, '92 70
Jambalaya, Good Luck, '87 11
Marinated Black-Eyed Peas, '82 156; '88 101
Mexican Black-Eyed Peas, '84 327
Mexicano, Black-Eyed Peas, '79 10
Mexi-Peas, '88 3
Passion Peas, '89 17
Pâté, Black-Eyed Pea, '91 12; '93 97
Peas, Black-Eyed, '93 180
Pickled Black-Eyed Peas, '79 10
Pinwheels, Black-Eyed Pea, '85 300; '86 18
Rice, Black-Eyed Peas with, '83 12; '90 208; '91 13
Rice with Black-Eyed Peas, '93 66
Salad, Black-Eyed Pea, '80 112; '86 225; '88 92, 221; '90 173
Salad, Hot Bacon and Black-Eyed, '85 7
Salad, Marinated Black-Eyed Pea, '93 190
Salad, Mexi-Pea, '81 7
Salad, Overnight Black-Eyed Pea, '81 280
Salad, Plentiful P's, '87 12
Salsa, Black-Eyed Pea, '93 164
Sausage, Black-Eyed Peas with, '86 7
Seasoned Black-Eyed Peas, '85 138
Soup, Beefy Black-Eyed, '85 6
Southern-Style Black-Eyed Peas, '82 107
South-of-the-Border Black-Eyed Peas, '86 7
Spaghetti, Black-Eyed Pea, '81 7
Special, Black-Eyed Pea, '86 7
Spicy Black-Eyed Peas, '92 23
Spicy Black-Eyed Peas, Hot-and-, '84 9
Spicy Hot Black-Eyed Peas, '81 8
Spicy-Hot Black-Eyed Peas, '90 135
Spread, Black-Eyed Pea, '86 77
Stew, Ham-and-Black-Eyed Pea, '93 20
Sweet-and-Sour Black-Eyed Peas, '85 290
Sweet-and-Sour Peas, '88 3
Tasty Black-Eyed Peas, '89 68
Vinaigrette, Black-Eyed Pea, '86 7
Zesty Black-Eyed Peas, '89 147
Casserole, Curry Pea, '87 154
English
    Baked Tuna and Peas in Wine Sauce, '83 196
    Braised Belgian Endive and Peas, '93 22
    Braised Rice and Peas, '79 101
    Broil, Tomato-English Pea, '83 192
    Buttered Peas and Mushrooms, '82 204
    Buttered Peas with Onions, '80 242

Peas, English *(continued)*

Carrots and Peas, Mint-Glazed, **'90** 291
Casserole, Asparagus-and-English Pea,
  '86 324
Casserole, Asparagus and Peas, **'80** 152
Casserole, Asparagus-Pea, **'88** M294
Casserole, Cauliflower-Pea, **'85** 260
Casserole, Cheesy English Pea, **'83** 216
Casserole, English Pea-Pimiento,
  '83 207
Casserole, Quick Fresh English Pea,
  '84 145
Casserole Supreme, Pea, **'82** 281;
  '83 32
Cauliflower and Peas with Curried
  Almonds, **'79** 221; **'80** 82
Cauliflower, Peas and, **'82** 288
Celery, Deluxe Peas and, **'81** 267
Celery, Peas and, **'93** 289
Chilled Dilly Peas, **'90** 143
Company Green Peas, **'91** 31
Continental, Peas, **'84** 254
Country-Style Peas, **'80** 101
Country Style Peas, **'81** 101
Creamed Peas and New Potatoes,
  '79 102
Creole Peas, Quick, **'84** 123
Curried Peas with Almonds, **'88** M294
Deluxe English Peas, **'84** 68
Deviled Peas in Toast Cups, **'86** 280
Dumplings, Green Peas and, **'80** 102
Glazed English Peas, **'83** 111
Italian Peas, **'81** 83
Lettuce Peas, French, **'86** 62
Medley, English Pea, **'85** 236
Medley, Spring Peas, **'83** 141
Minted Peas, **'83** 141; **'87** 56
Mushrooms, Creamy Peas with, **'84** 196
Mushrooms, Green Peas with, **'80** 101
Mushrooms, Peas and, **'83** 141
Onions Stuffed with Peas, **'84** 68
Orange Sauce, Green Peas in, **'88** 97
Party Peas, **'79** 102
Perfection, Peas to, **'94** 321
Pignoli, Peas, **'83** 190
Potato Nest, Peas in a, **'84** M239
Rice, Holiday Peas and, **'86** 328
Rice, Peas and, **'88** 97
Rice with Green Peas, **'87** 45
Salad, Cauliflower-Pea, **'87** 231
Salad, Cheddar-Pea, **'84** 82
Salad, Chicken-Pea, **'83** 218
Salad, Corn-and-Pea, **'90** 181
Salad, Creamy Pea, **'80** 111
Salad, Crunchy Pea, **'90** 143
Salad, English Pea, **'81** 280; **'90** 143
Salad, English Pea-and-Apple, **'87** 24
Salad, Lettuce-English Pea, **'91** 208
Salad, Marinated English Pea, **'82** 54
Salad, Marinated Pea, **'81** 204
Salad, Minted Pea, **'91** 119
Salad, Peas-and-Asparagus, **'83** 141
Salad, Rice-Pea, **'85** 163
Salad, Savory Cauliflower and Pea,
  '81 280
Salad, Special Pea, **'83** 239
Sauce, Green Pea, **'83** 22
Sautéed Peas and Bacon, **'89** 331
Scallions, Peas and, **'80** 101

Sherry, Peas with, **'80** 102
Soup, Chilled Pea, **'84** 181
Soup, Cold Curried Pea, **'91** 120
Soup Élégante, Pea, **'79** 53
Soup, Fresh Pea, **'86** 181
Soup, Peppery Pea, **'82** 271
Soup, Potato-Pea, **'94** 90
Soup, Spring Pea, **'88** M96
Special Peas, **'88** 97
Ham, Southern Peas and, **'85** 138
Medley, Peas-and-Corn, **'85** 138
Pasta, Peas and, **'93** 139
Pigeon Peas, Rice with, **'92** 157
Salad, Three Pea, **'84** 290
Snap Peas and Pearl Onions, **'89** 280
Snow
    Basil Snow Peas and Tomatoes,
      '88 M185
    Beef and Snow Peas, Oriental, **'79** 105
    Beef with Pea Pods, Oriental, **'86** M328
    Cashew Pea Pods, **'92** 343
    Chicken with Snow Peas, **'83** 137
    Chinese Peas, Easy, **'83** 206
    Crunchy Snow Peas and Dip, **'86** 62
    en Papillote, Fish with Snow Peas,
      '86 144
    Medley, Cauliflower-Snow Pea, **'87** 305
    Peas and Snow Peas, **'88** 67
    Peppers, Minted Peas and, **'90** M99
    Pineapple, Snow Peas and, **'91** 120
    Piquant, Snow Peas, **'79** 21
    Red Pepper, Snow Peas with, **'90** 102
    Sesame Snow Peas and Red Pepper,
      '84 175
    Shrimp Combo, Snow Pea-, **'79** 57
    Shrimp with Snow Peas, **'85** 75
    Skillet Snow Peas with Celery, **'84** 123
    Stir-Fried Peas and Peppers, **'87** 51
    Stir-Fry, Beef and Pea, **'82** 98
    Stir-Fry Beef and Pea Pods, **'80** 19
    Stir-Fry, Beef and Snow Pea, **'82** 98
    Stir-Fry Beef and Snow Peas, **'83** 22
    Stir-Fry, Potato-Snow Pea, **'86** 173
    Stuffed Snow Peas, **'84** 80
    Stuffed Snow Peas, Crab-, **'85** 288
    Tomatoes, Snow Peas and, **'83** 111
    Vegetable Medley, Spring, **'86** 115
Soup, Country-Style Pea, **'86** 267
Soup, Cream Pea, **'90** 211
Soup, French Market, **'94** 317
Soup Mix, French Market, **'94** 317
Soup, Pea-and-Watercress, **'93** 162
Soup, Split Pea, **'88** 235; **'89** 17; **'90** 198;
  '94 322
Soup, Split Pea and Frankfurter, **'79** 64
Sugar Peas with Dip, **'86** 170
Sugar Snap Dip, **'88** 91
Sugar Snap Pea Appetizers, **'86** 115
Sugar Snap Pea Salad, **'86** 115
Sugar Snap Peas, Potato Salad with, **'91** 120
Sugar Snap Peas with Basil and Lemon,
  '93 66
Sugar Snaps and Carrots, Creamed, **'93** 139
Sugar Snaps and Peppers, **'93** 139

Pecans
Apples, Orange-Pecan Baked, **'85** 45
Ball, Date-Nut, **'92** 326
Ball, Deviled Pecan, **'80** 258
Ball, Party Pecan Cheese, **'81** 235
Ball, Pecan Cheese, **'83** 127
Balls, Date-Nut, **'85** 10

Ball, Tuna-Pecan, **'87** 94
Barbecued Pecans, **'83** 222
Bars, Butter Pecan Turtle, **'90** 70
Bars, Gooey Pecan, **'94** 133
Bars, Pecan, **'82** 209
Beans, Nutty Green, **'88** M187
Biscuits, Nutty Tea, **'89** 210
Bites, Cheesy Pecan, **'82** 248
Bread, Apple-Nut, **'85** 281
Bread, Applesauce Nut, **'81** 305
Bread, Applesauce-Pecan, **'90** 66
Bread, Banana-Nut, **'86** 8, 70
Bread, Banana-Nut-Raisin, **'81** 59
Bread, Bourbon-Pecan, **'93** 308
Bread, Cheddar-Nut, **'85** 41
Bread, Cherry Nut, **'81** 306; **'82** 36
Bread, Chocolate Date-Nut, **'81** 284
Bread, Glazed Orange-Pecan, **'81** 250
Bread, Kahlúa Fruit-Nut, **'79** 235
Bread, Lemon-Pecan, **'83** 54
Bread, Maraschino Cherry Nut, **'79** 234
Bread, Orange-Nut, **'82** 75
Bread, Orange-Pecan, **'79** 148
Bread, Persimmon Date-Nut, **'82** 218
Bread, Pineapple-Nut, **'79** 215
Bread, Pineapple-Pecan Loaf, **'87** 256
Bread, Prune-Nut, **'87** 255; **'91** 55
Bread, Pumpkin-Nut, **'83** 294
Bread, Pumpkin-Pecan, **'87** 221
Bread, Quick Cherry-Nut, **'85** 55
Bread, Strawberry-Nut, **'79** 24
Bread, Wine-Date Nut, **'82** 253
Brie, Kahlúa-Pecan, **'92** 289
Brittle, Chocolate, **'83** 315
Brittle, Pecan, **'91** 272
Broccoli with Lemon Sauce and Pecans,
  '86 71
Brownies, Chocolate-Pecan, **'81** 64
Brownies, Nutty Blonde, **'81** 64
Brownies, Nutty Cocoa, **'81** 64
Brownies, Nutty Fudge, **'80** M171
Buns, Nutty, **'86** 290
Buttered Pecans, Green Beans with, **'92** 61
Butter, Orange-Pecan, **'84** 75
Cake, Apple-Pecan, **'92** 167
Cake, Apple-Pecan Coffee, **'84** 242
Cake, Banana-Nut, **'92** 120
Cake, Bourbon-Pecan, **'84** 25
Cake, Bourbon-Pecan Pound, **'91** 270
Cake, Butter Pecan, **'80** 229
Cake, Butterscotch-Pecan Pound, **'92** 153
Cake, Caramel-Filled Butter Pecan, **'88** 278
Cake, Cinnamon-Pecan Coffee, **'87** 69
Cake, Date Nut, **'79** 176; **'80** 5
Cake, Kentucky Pecan, **'84** 263
Cake, Marbled Pecan Pound, **'93** 313
Cake, Orange Nut, **'80** 70
Cake, Orange-Nut Butter, **'80** 254
Cake, Orange-Pecan Coffee, **'86** 86
Cake, Orange-Pecan Crunch, **'83** 10
Cake, Orange-Pecan Pound, **'93** 13
Cake, Pecan-Topped Coffee, **'81** 41
Cake, Pineapple-Pecan Upside-Down, **'84** 25
Cake, Praline Pound, **'82** 88
Cake, Rich Chocolate-Nut, **'86** 8
Cake, Sour Cream-Orange Pecan Pound,
  '89 207
Cake with Praline Glaze, Pecan, **'82** 196
Candied Nuts, **'81** 261
Candy, Chocolate-Nut Log, **'86** 335
Caramel Corn, Nutty, **'92** 317

Pecans (*continued*)

Carrots and Celery with Pecans, '84 254
Casserole, Carrot-Pecan, '93 44
Catfish Pecan, '85 53
Cheesecake, Butter Pecan, '86 61
Cheesecake, Chocolate-Caramel-Pecan,
   '91 197
Cheesecake, Pecan, '85 38
Chesapeake Nuts, '93 269
Chews, Chocolate-Nut, '81 92
Chicken, Buttermilk-Pecan, '89 166
Chicken Drummettes, Orange-Pecan,
   '93 158
Chicken Fingers, Buttermilk-Pecan, '93 165
Chicken, Nutty Oven-Fried, '85 160
Chicken, Oven-Fried Pecan, '84 288
Chicken, Pecan, '90 54
Chicken, Sweet-and-Sour, '79 106
Chocolate Date-Nut Delight, '88 168
Christmas Eve Pecans, '91 276
Clusters, Pecan, '81 266
Clusters, Pecan-Coconut, '86 M251
Clusters, Roasted Pecan, '85 233; '90 310
Cobbler, Apple-Pecan, '84 M198
Coconut-Pecan Coils, '90 196
Coffee 'n' Spice Pecans, '88 256
Cookies, Brown Sugar-Pecan, '91 236
Cookies, Butter Pecan, '82 139
Cookies, Butter Pecan Shortbread, '80 282
Cookies, Butterscotch-Pecan, '84 36
Cookies, Cherry Pecan, '82 136
Cookies, Chocolate-Nut Freezer, '88 217
Cookies, Easy Pecan, '80 208
Cookies, Nutty Oatmeal, '81 130
Cookies, Nutty Oatmeal-Chocolate Chip,
   '82 185
Cookies, Orange-Pecan, '88 119
Cookies, Pecan-Butter, '83 113
Cookies, Pecan Crescent, '85 324
Cookies, Pecan Pie, '92 289
Cornbread, Pecan, '94 169
Crispies, Oatmeal Nut, '80 208
Crispies, Pecan-Cheese, '87 168
Crisps, Sugar Pecan, '86 230
Crunch, Apple-Nut, '82 M238
Crunchy Munchies, '94 196
Crust, Nutty Oat, '89 251
Crust, Pecan, '86 317; '89 291
Crust, Spiced Nut, '87 295
Cupcakes, Apple-Nut, '82 279
Curried Pecans, '91 208
Dainties, Lemon Pecan, '80 208
Dessert, Maple Nut, '81 84
Dessert, Nutty Fudgy Frozen, '94 28
Deviled Nuts, '93 118
Dressing, Chicken with Pecan-Rice, '85 M57
Dressing, Fruit-and-Pecan, '84 252
Dressing, Pecan-Sage, '80 262
Dressing, Watermelon Salad with Celery-Nut,
   '80 182
Dumplings, Spiced Peaches with Nutty,
   '87 164
Eggs, Pecan-Stuffed, '80 78
Fettuccine, Chicken-Pecan, '86 52
Filling, Fruit-Nut, '80 289
Filling, Nut, '91 35
Fritters, Chocolate-Covered Pecan, '79 205
Frosting, Banana-Nut, '79 115
Frosting, Butter Pecan, '80 229

Frosting, Chocolate Nut, '80 140
Frosting, Coconut-Pecan, '81 296;
   '83 M233; '84 43, 322
Frosting, Nutty Coconut, '86 8
Frosting, Nutty Cream Cheese, '85 117
Frosting, Pecan, '86 86
Fudge, Cherry Nut, '83 315
Fudge, Creamy Pecan, '84 321
Fudge, Nutty White, '81 253
Fudge, Quick Nut, '83 316
Funnel Cakes, Nutty, '91 233
Glazed Nuts, '88 222
Glazed Pecans, '81 254; '82 136
Glaze, Honey-Nut, '87 15
Goose, Fruit- and Pecan-Stuffed, '83 268
Granola, Nutty, '90 95
Honeycomb Pecans, '84 300
Hot-and-Spicy Pecans, '89 161
Hot Pepper Pecans, '85 4
Ice Cream, Butter Pecan, '80 176; '86 129;
   '88 202
Ice Cream, Cherry-Nut, '86 129
Ice Cream, Cherry-Pecan, '88 203
Ice Cream, Straw-Ba-Nut, '80 177
Ice Cream, Strawberry-Banana-Nut, '88 203
Loaf, Date-Nut, '85 10
Loaf, Orange Nut, '80 226
Loaf, Tasty Apricot-Nut, '82 10
Loaves, Orange-Pecan, '79 215
Log, Chicken-Pecan, '81 290
Log, Roquefort Pecan, '89 247
Log, Toasted Pecan Cheese, '86 M288
Maple-Nut Coffee Twist, '86 290
Muffins, Banana-Nut, '93 140
Muffins, Cherry-Nut, '90 87
Muffins, Chunky Pecan, '88 9
Muffins, Cinnamon-Nut, '85 M88
Muffins, Cinnamon-Pecan, '84 219
Muffins, Country Pecan, '83 222
Muffins, Cranberry-Pecan, '84 269
Muffins, Nutty Pumpkin, '86 291
Muffins, Orange-Pecan, '83 96
Muffins, Pecan, '80 16
Muffins, Raisin-Nut, '92 46
Muffins, Raisin-Pecan Ginger, '88 9
Muffins, Rum-Nut, '90 87
Mushrooms, Pecan-Stuffed, '84 261
Nippy Nuts, '93 301
Nuggets, Cherry Nut, '81 286
Onions with Pecans and Roasted Carrots,
   Roasted Vidalia, '92 340
Orange Nuts, Sherry-, '85 M289
Orange Pecans, '84 299; '87 292
Pepper Pecans, '87 137; '93 79
Pie, Bourbon-Pecan, '85 90
Pie, Bourbon-Pecan Pumpkin, '87 264
Pie, Caramel-Pecan, '88 282
Pie, Caramel-Pecan Apple, '85 247
Pie, Cherry-Pecan, '92 30
Pie, Chocolate-Banana-Pecan Cream,
   '94 210
Pie, Chocolate Pecan, '80 237; '83 12;
   '90 184
Pie, Chocolate-Pecan, '91 272
Pie, Chocolate-Pecan Chess, '93 251
Pie, Choco-Pecan, '82 86
Pie, Coconut Pecan, '81 161
Pie, Coconut-Pecan Chess, '81 248
Pie, Coffee Pecan, '82 74
Pie, Cranberry-Pecan, '92 316
Pie, Custard Pecan, '87 184

Pie, Date-Pecan, '80 15
Pie, Frozen Bourbon-Pecan, '89 251
Pie, Golden Pecan, '81 266
Pie, Grandmother's Pecan, '86 269
Pie, Holiday Pecan, '81 296
Pie, Layered Pecan, '83 305
Pie, Lemon-Pecan, '93 251
Pie, Louisiana Pecan, '92 83
Pie, Maple-Pecan, '81 266
Pie, Molasses-Pecan, '86 259
Pie, Nutty Cranberry, '82 298
Pie, Nutty Ice Cream, '91 180
Pie, Nutty Pumpkin, '82 67
Pie, Old-Fashioned Pecan, '81 M269
Pie, Orange-Pecan, '79 282; '83 222
Pie, Pecan, '79 251; '80 57; '85 255;
   '90 312; '92 234
Pie, Pumpkin-Pecan, '85 233, 282
Pie, Raisin-Pecan, '87 213
Pies, Honey-Pecan Finger, '90 184
Pies, Individual Pecan, '85 295
Pies, Miniature Pecan, '79 205; '86 13
Pie, Spicy Pecan, '84 240
Pies, Tiny Pecan, '79 225
Pie, Sweet Potato-Pecan, '83 90
Pie, Texas Pecan, '83 159
Pie, Texas Star Pecan, '90 184
Pie, Turtle Pecan, '93 250
Popcorn Balls, Nutty, '88 227
Popovers, Giant Pecan, '83 208
Pork Loin, Apricot-Pecan Stuffed, '94 274
Praline Brownies, '93 243
Praline Cheesecake, '83 270; '89 93
Praline Clusters, Dark, '86 313
Praline Cookies, '91 271
Praline Delights, Spicy, '84 299
Praline-Flavored Coffee, '87 69
Praline Freeze, '89 60; '90 48
Praline Fruit Compote, Warm, '85 260
Praline Glaze, '82 196
Praline Grahams, '92 239
Praline Ham, '85 302
Praline Ice Cream, '89 318
Praline Ice Cream Cake, '80 84
Praline Ice Cream Sauce, '85 189
Praline Ice Cream Sauce, Southern,
   '86 M227
Praline Pastries, '89 318
Praline Pie, Chocolate-, '86 259
Praline Pie, Peach, '89 136
Praline Pound Cake, '82 88
Pralines, '79 272; '86 M288; '89 60; '90 48
Pralines and Cream Ice Cream, '82 184;
   '83 159
Praline Sauce, '83 25; '84 143; '89 95;
   '92 282; '94 206, 312
Praline Sauce, Bourbon, '81 170
Praline Sauce, Chocolate-, '85 M295
Praline Sauce, Peach-, '85 161
Pralines, Basic, '92 313; '93 50
Pralines, Bourbon, '92 313; '93 51
Pralines, Butterscotch, '81 253
Pralines, Café au Lait, '92 313; '93 51
Pralines, Chocolate, '92 313; '93 51
Pralines, Chocolate-Mint, '92 313; '93 51
Pralines, Chocolate-Peanut Butter, '92 313;
   '93 51
Pralines, Creamy, '80 198; '92 289
Pralines, Dark, '83 52
Praline Shortbread Cookies, '88 242
Pralines, Hot Spicy, '92 313; '93 51

Pecans *(continued)*

Pralines, Maple-Pecan, **'83** 222
Pralines, Mocha, **'92** 313; **'93** 51
Pralines, New Orleans-Style, **'86** 335
Pralines, Old-Fashioned, **'89** 318
Pralines, Orange, **'92** 313; **'93** 51
Pralines, Original Pecan, **'81** 11
Pralines, Peanut Butter, **'92** 313; **'93** 51
Pralines, Plantation Coffee, **'86** 241
Pralines, Southern, **'79** M263
Pralines, Texas-Size, **'79** 186
Pralines, Vanilla, **'92** 313; **'93** 51
Praline Thumbprint Cookies, **'89** 328
Praline Toast, Orange, **'79** 36
Pudding, Brown Sugar-Pecan, **'86** M165
Pudding, Pecan-Mocha, **'89** M130
Pudding, with Hot Rum Sauce, Apple-Nut, **'79** 86
Quiche, Chicken-Pecan, **'91** 206
Rice, Nutted, **'85** 269
Rice, Pecan, **'85** 53
Rice, Shrimp-and-Scallop Sauté with Pecan, **'90** 317
Roll, Banana-Nut, **'85** 112
Roll, Date Nut, **'79** 249
Rolls, Buttered Rum-Nut, **'86** 291
Rolls, Caramel-Nut, **'86** 312
Rolls, Easy Cinnamon-Pecan, **'89** 307
Rolls, Pecan, **'79** 285; **'81** 62
Roughy with Brown Butter Sauce, Pecan, **'91** 64
Roulade, Pecan, **'87** 183
Roulage, Toffee-Pecan, **'94** 312
Salad, Apple-Nut, **'80** 226
Salad, Beet-Nut, **'79** 74
Salad, Cantaloupe-Pecan, **'86** 178
Salad, Creamy Carrot-Nut, **'86** 331
Salad, Endive, Bacon, and Pecan, **'89** 12
Salad, Ham-Pecan-Blue Cheese Pasta, **'90** 62
Salad, Spinach-Pecan, **'89** 128
Salad, Strawberry-Nut, **'94** 132
Salted Pecans, Southern, **'80** 285
Sauce, Butter Pecan, **'91** 174
Sauce, Butterscotch-Pecan, **'82** 212
Sauce, Cinnamon-Pecan-Honey Pancake, **'88** 46
Sauce, Date-Nut Sundae, **'82** 167
Sauce, Éclairs with Pecan, **'83** 219
Sauce, Pecan, **'83** 219
Sauce, Pecan-Butter, **'91** 65
Scones, Orange-Pecan, **'94** 215
Shortcake, Banana-Pecan, **'93** 43
Special, Old Pecan Street, **'93** 251
Spiced Nuts, **'91** M316
Spiced Pecans, **'79** 296; **'80** 31; **'81** 286
Spicy Curried Nuts, **'82** 250
Spicy Pecans, **'81** M289; **'93** 279
Spread, Honey-Nut, **'87** 157
Spread, Nutty Carrot, **'94** 123
Spread, Nutty Cream Cheese, **'89** 327
Squares, Butter Pecan Pie, **'81** 262
Squares, Easy Pecan, **'79** 292; **'81** 230
Squares, Lemon-Pecan, **'89** 124
Squares, Pecan, **'79** 205; **'90** 69
Squares, Twice-Baked Pecan, **'79** 291
Squash, Apple-and-Pecan-Filled, **'88** 228
Squash with Molasses and Pecans, Acorn, **'85** 205

Stuffing, Chicken Breasts with Pecan-Sausage, **'94** 212
Stuffing, Pecan, **'79** 292; **'80** 32
Stuffing, Wild Duck with Pecan, **'85** 269
Sugar-and-Honey Pecans, **'86** 319
Sugar and Spice Pecans, **'82** 297
Sugar-and-Spice Pecans, **'86** 121; **'94** 272
Sugared Pecans, **'82** 167
Sugar Pecans, Brown, **'81** 266
Sugarplums, Pecan Shortbread, **'83** 298
Sweet-and-Spicy Pecans, **'92** 321
Syrup, Chunky Pecan, **'85** 278
Syrup, Maple-Nut, **'80** 228
Tarts, Apple-Pecan, **'80** 282
Tarts, Easy Pecan, **'84** 313
Tarts, Pecan, **'81** 266
Tarts, Special Pecan, **'87** 224
Tart with Caramel Sauce, Chocolate-Pecan, **'93** 296; **'94** 234
Tart with Praline Cream, Pecan, **'90** 256
Tassies, Teatime, **'84** 321
Toasted Chili Pecans, **'85** 154
Toasted Pecans, **'84** 321; **'86** 229
Toasted Pecans, Buttery, **'88** 77
Toffee, Microwave, **'92** M317
Toffee, Nutty, **'79** M263
Topping, Apple-Nut, **'93** 162
Topping, Cinnamon-Pecan, **'85** 277
Topping, Nutty, **'85** 256
Topping, Pecan, **'94** 36
Torte, Carob-Pecan, **'85** 218
Torte, Chocolate-Pecan, **'89** 42
Torte, Heavenly Pecan, **'81** 266
Torte, Mocha-Pecan, **'86** 26
Turkey Cutlets, Pecan-Crusted, **'94** 282
Wafers, Pecan-Cheese, **'81** 119
Wafers, Sage-Pecan Cheese, **'93** 12
Waffles, Pecan, **'87** 225
Waffles, Pumpkin-Nut, **'86** 96
Waffles, Southern Chicken-Pecan, **'82** 231
Wild Rice, Pecan-Lemon, **'92** 211
Zucchini with Pecans, **'87** 31

Peppermint
Bavarian, Peppermint, **'80** 153
Brownies, Chocolate-Peppermint, **'88** 262
Brownies, Pistachio-Mint, **'94** 50
Brownies, Southern Chocolate-Mint, **'93** 216
Cake, Peppermint Candy, **'89** 254
Cheesecake, Frozen Peppermint, **'94** 143
Chocolate Mint Freeze, **'88** 167
Cookies, Peppermint Candy, **'88** 286
Cookies, Peppermint Sandwich, **'92** 277
Dessert, Peppermint Wafer, **'79** 176; **'80** 7
Dessert, Triple Mint Ice-Cream Angel, **'93** 86
Filling, Peppermint, **'81** 119; **'89** 254
Flip, Hot Peppermint, **'86** 329
Fondue, Peppermint, **'94** 332
Frosting, Mint Cream, **'93** 216

Frosting, Pink Peppermint Birthday Cake, **'92** 269
Hot Cocoa Mix, Minted, **'91** 316
Ice Cream, Peppermint, **'80** 176; **'86** 129
Mints, Party, **'79** 273; **'81** 119
Mousse, Peppermint, **'93** 315
Mousse, Peppermint Candy, **'82** 71; **'94** 198
Parfait, Peppermint, **'93** 315
Parfaits, Chocolate-Peppermint, **'88** 65
Patties, Peppermint, **'86** 278
Pie, Peppermint Candy-Ice Cream, **'87** 260
Pralines, Chocolate-Mint, **'92** 313; **'93** 51
Rounds, Peppermint, **'94** 19
Sauce, Chocolate-Peppermint, **'94** 205
Snowball Surprises, **'93** 315
Soufflé, Chocolate Mint, **'81** 16
Squares, Chocolate-Peppermint, **'81** 119
Twists, Mint, **'86** 106
Wreaths, Melt-Away Peppermint, **'85** 324
Peppers
Chicken Sauté, Sweet Pepper-, **'89** 104
Chicken Scallopini with Peppers, **'85** 78
Chile
    Beef Kabobs, Chile-, **'94** 251
    Casserole, Chile-Cheese, **'82** 90
    Casserole, Chile 'n' Cheese Breakfast, **'88** 57
    Casserole, Chiles Rellenos, **'79** 84; **'84** 31, 234; **'92** 18
    Casserole, Chili-Corn, **'88** 266
    Casserole, Chili-Rice, **'79** 54
    Casserole, Corn-and-Green Chile, **'89** 68
    Casserole, Green Chile-and-Fish, **'84** 32
    Casserole, Mexican Rice, **'83** 31
    Casserole, Sausage-Chile Rellenos, **'88** 52
    Cheesecake, Chicken-Chile, **'92** 42
    Chicken with Salsa, Baked Chile, **'88** 147
    Chimichangas (Fried Burritos), **'81** 196; **'85** 244
    con Queso, Chile, **'80** 194
    con Queso Supreme, Chile, **'80** 265
    Cream, Ancho Chile, **'87** 121
    Dip, Cheese-and-Chile, **'83** 31
    Dip, Hot Chile, **'82** 248
    Dip, Hot Chile-Beef, **'83** 218
    Egg Rolls, Chiles Rellenos, **'86** 296
    Eggs, Chile, **'88** 80
    Enchiladas, Green Chile-Sour Cream, **'84** 234
    Enchiladas, New Mexican Flat, **'85** 245
    Green Chile-Cornbread Dressing, **'93** 306
    Jelly, Chile Piquín, **'94** 28
    Light Chile Verde, **'88** 148
    Pie, Green Chile-Cheese, **'84** 234
    Powder, Red Chile, **'85** 245
    Puerco en Adobo, **'88** 116
    Quiche, Chile Pepper, **'82** 224
    Quiche, Green Chile, **'83** 31
    Quiche, Shrimp, **'83** 50
    Quiche, Squash-and-Green Chile, **'88** 143
    Red Chile Sauce, **'94** 251
    Rellenos, Chiles (Stuffed Chiles), **'82** 220; **'83** 150; **'88** 116; **'89** 226
    Rellenos with Tomatillo Sauce, Roasted Chiles, **'94** 203

Peppers, Chile (continued)

Rellenos with Walnut Cream Sauce, Havarti-and-Corn-Stuffed Chiles, '93 M275
Rice and Green Chiles, '83 152
Rice, Chili-Cheesy, '79 43
Salad, Spicy Chile-Tomato, '88 121
Salsa with Homemade Tostados, Hot Chile, '88 115
Sauce, Ancho Chile, '87 122
Sauce, Green Chile, '82 220
Sauce, Red Chile, '85 245
Sauce, Red Chile Enchilada, '85 245
Sauce, Verde, '93 275
Serrano Chile Blue Cornbread, '94 114
Squash, Chile, '84 77
Squash, Mexican, '83 31
Squash with Green Chiles, Stuffed, '83 148
Stuffed Green Chiles, '93 208
Tamales, Hot, '83 51
Tamales, Sweet, '83 52
Turnovers, Chile-Ham, '88 64
Waffles, Corn-Chile, '94 206
Chutney, Jeweled Pepper, '94 316
Combo, Cucumber-and-Pepper, '88 176
Cups, Hot Vegetable Pepper, '88 M188
Curried Peppers, Chicken Breasts with, '90 227
Dip, Pepperoncini-Cream Cheese, '91 252
Flank Steak with Sweet Peppers, Grilled, '90 138
Green
Beef and Green Peppers, '79 104
Beefed-Up Peppers, '82 186
Bread, Pepper, '85 156
Casserole, Peppered Pork Chop, '82 25
Chicken Peppers, Devilish, '80 65
Cups, Potato Salad in Pepper, '79 78
Deluxe, Peppers, '81 159
Dressing, Green Pepper-Onion Salad, '84 12
Fried Pepper Strips, '82 208
Jelly, Pepper, '79 121
Jelly, Unusual Green Pepper, '82 132
Mexican Green Peppers, '80 65
Muffins, Cheese-and-Pepper, '84 139
Pizza Peppers, '83 135
Potato Salad 'n' Peppers, '83 135
Ratatouille, '85 92
Relish, Pepper, '83 183
Relish, Pepper-Onion, '84 180
Salad, Ruby-and-Emerald, '85 79
Sauce, Pepper-Onion, '84 125
Sausage and Peppers, Italian, '84 9
Sautéed Onions and Peppers, '83 M148
Sauté, Tomato-Pepper, '84 142
Soup, Green Pepper, '88 250
Stacks, Pepper-Cheese, '87 80
Steak and Rice, Pepper, '81 17
Steak, Pepper, '81 273; '85 57; '88 113
Steak, Pepper-Beef, '85 21
Stir-Fried Sweet Peppers with Tomatoes, '93 207
Stir-Fry Steak, Pepper, '81 240
Stuffed Green Peppers, Beefy, '81 86
Stuffed Green Peppers, Ham-, '80 65
Stuffed Pepper Medley, '82 131

Stuffed Peppers, '81 239; '83 66; '84 202
Stuffed Peppers, Beef-, '84 154; '85 146
Stuffed Peppers, Corn-, '84 104
Stuffed Peppers, Curried Chicken-, '87 19
Stuffed Peppers for Two, '80 84
Stuffed Peppers, Ham-and-Corn, '81 87
Stuffed Peppers, Hearty, '88 M214
Stuffed Peppers, Macaroni-and-Cheese-, '80 65
Stuffed Peppers, Rice-, '80 65
Stuffed Peppers, Shrimp-, '80 162; '86 131, 197
Stuffed Peppers, Spinach-, '82 180
Stuffed Peppers with Rice and Ham, '82 131
Stuffed with Beef, Peppers, '84 72
Taco Peppers, '81 86
Turkey with Peppers, '92 182
Veal and Peppers, Spaghetti with, '81 201; '82 14
Jalapeño
Biscuits, Cornmeal-Jalapeño, '94 214
Black-Eyed Peas, Jalapeño, '88 166
Bread, Jalapeño Pepper, '83 121
Casserole, Jalapeño Corn, '83 256
Casserole, Jalapeño Rice, '81 66
Celery, Jalapeño Stuffed, '79 70
Cheese, Shrimp with Herbed Jalapeño, '87 112
Cheesy Jalapeño Peppers, '80 195
Chicken, Grilled Jalapeño, '93 213
Chicken, Grilled Lime-Jalapeño, '91 87
Chicken Jalapeño, Easy, '92 310
Chicken Legs, Jalapeño Oven-Fried, '94 94
Cornbread, Beefy Jalapeño, '82 142
Cornbread, Cheddar-Jalapeño, '85 3
Cornbread, Jalapeño, '85 200; '94 78
Grits, Jalapeño Cheese, '85 43
Hominy, Jalapeño, '82 51
Jelly, Jalapeño, '92 230
Loaf, Jalapeño-Cheese, '84 76
Muffins, Jalapeño-Corn, '93 164
Mustard, Jalapeño, '93 240
Open-Faced Jalapeño Heroes, '90 144
Pickled Jalapeño Peppers, '93 136
Potatoes, Jalapeño, '84 39
Potatoes, Jalapeño-Ham Stuffed, '81 M61
Puffs, Cajun Hot, '94 277
Quiche, Cheesy Jalapeño, '84 31
Quiche, Jalapeño-Corn, '85 122
Quiche Squares, Cheesy Hot, '79 124
Rice, Jalapeño, '79 43
Rice, Jalapeño Hot, '80 126
Salsa Picante, '84 108
Salsa Picante, Homemade, '81 67
Sauce, Hot Chile, '92 156
Sauce, Jalapeño, '80 193; '93 230
Sauce, Jalapeño-Cranberry, '92 310
Sauce, San Antonio Hot, '84 291
Spread, Jalapeño-Cheese, '82 248
Squares, Jalapeño Cheese, '80 195
Stuffed Jalapeños, Fiery Fried, '90 118
Stuffed Jalapeños, Shrimp-, '88 115
Vinegar, Southwest, '94 200
Kabobs, Pretty Pepper, '90 166
Marinated Roasted Peppers, '92 176

Meatballs with Pineapple and Peppers, '90 145
Medley, Pepper-Mushroom, '90 98
Medley, Rainbow Pepper, '91 126
Okra, Corn, and Peppers, '87 M151
Parmesan Pepper Toss, '93 208
Pasta, Peppery, '94 164
Pasta with Peppers and Broccoli, '91 69
Peas and Peppers, Minted, '90 M99
Pesto, Pepper, '89 103; '90 97
Pizza, Roasted Pepper, '94 218
Red or Green Pepper Sauce, '91 85
Red Pepper and Watercress Salad, Roasted, '90 55
Red Pepper Jelly, '89 M156
Red Pepper Puree, '93 275
Red Pepper Rings, Broccoli in Sweet, '94 322
Red Pepper Round Steak, '88 214
Red Pepper Salad, Broccoli and, '83 224
Red Pepper Salad, Tuna-and-, '93 143
Red Peppers and Pearl Onions, Green Beans with Roasted, '93 260
Red Pepper Sauce, Linguine with, '93 127
Red Pepper, Sesame Snow Peas and, '84 175
Red Pepper, Snow Peas with, '90 102
Red Pepper Soup, Chilled Sweet, '93 69
Red Peppers, Potatoes with Sweet, '87 192
Relish, Confetti Pepper, '91 195
Rice, Hot Pepper, '92 310
Roasted Peppers, Marinated, '87 90
Roasted Peppers with Balsamic Vinaigrette, '94 128
Salad, Chilled Turkey-and-Pepper Stir-Fry, '88 140
Salad, Mixed Pepper, '89 103
Salad, Mushroom-and-Pepper, '86 68
Salad, Three-Pepper, '91 162
Salsa, Double Chile, '91 182
Salsa, Mixed Pepper, '91 181
Salsa, Pepper, '88 26
Salsa, Yellowfin Tuna with Corn, Pepper, and Tomato, '94 164
Sandwiches, Smoked Turkey-Roasted Pepper, '94 66
Sautéed Peppers and Mushrooms, Herb-Stuffed Chicken with, '91 26
Sautéed Sweet Peppers, '89 102
Sauté, Julienne Pepper, '89 104
Soup, Bell Pepper, '89 103
Soup, Roasted Pepper-and-Chicken, '90 58
Soup, Spicy Pepper, '93 98
Soup, Sweet Pepper, '93 277
Spread, Roasted Pepper, '94 123
Stir-Fried Peas and Peppers, '87 51
Strips, Green Beans and Pepper, '86 170
Stuffed Peppers, Beef-, '91 M127
Stuffed with Shrimp-and-Orzo Salad, Peppers, '91 203
Sugar Snaps and Peppers, '93 139
Topping, Rainbow Pepper, '90 117
Toss, Crisp Squash-and-Pepper, '87 M152
Persimmons
Bread, Persimmon, '80 228
Bread, Persimmon Date-Nut, '82 218
Cake, Persimmon, '79 205
Cookies, Persimmon-Raisin, '85 232
Pie, Persimmon, '79 206
Pudding, Persimmon, '79 206
Salad, Persimmon Fruit, '79 206
Pheasant
Muscatel, Pheasant, '85 269
Port Wine Sauce, Pheasants with, '84 252

Pickles and Relishes

Acorn Squash-and-Bourbon Butter, '94 266
Antipasto Relish, '86 327
Apple-Celery Relish, '89 141
Apple Relish, Spicy, '84 M323
Artichoke Relish, Jerusalem, '89 197
Asparagus, Pickled, '83 46
Avocado Relish, '87 120
Beet Pickles, '81 210
Beet Relish, '84 179
Beet Relish, Colorful, '85 136
Beets, Easy Pickled, '80 137
Beets, Pickled, '81 216
Black Bean-Tomatillo Relish, '87 121
Broccoli, Pickled, '81 308
Cabbage Relish, '83 260
Cantaloupe, Sweet Pickled, '89 197
Carrots, Pickled, '93 12
Chow Chow, '82 196
Chowchow, '87 150
Chutney
   Apple Chutney, '92 309
   Commander's Chutney, '87 245
   Cranberry-Amaretto Chutney with
     Cream Cheese, '87 244
   Cranberry Chutney, '80 243; '83 260;
     '84 265
   Cranberry-Orange Chutney, '79 292
   Fruit Chutney, Autumn, '88 M230
   Kiwifruit-Onion Chutney, '93 125
   Mango Chutney, '89 141
   Orange-Cranberry Chutney, '86 266
   Pâté, Chutney-Cheese, '84 152
   Peach Chutney, '84 179
   Pear-Apple Chutney, '89 141
   Pepper Chutney, Jeweled, '94 316
   Plum Chutney, '84 179
   Rhubarb Chutney, '87 245
   Roll, Chutney, '83 259
   Rosy Chutney, '80 120
   Sauce, Chutney-Mustard, '89 242
   Tomato-Apple Chutney, '84 180
Confit, Roasted Shallot-Garlic, '94 303
Corn Relish, '81 129, 175; '83 189; '84 107;
   '85 136; '87 120, 245; '92 241
Corn Relish, Easy, '83 260
Corn Relish, Quick, '90 13
Corn Relish, Summer, '89 127
Corn Relish, Sweet, '93 119
Corn Relish, Virginia, '79 283
Cran-Apple Relish, '84 300
Cranberry Conserve, '79 243
Cranberry-Nut Relish, '86 275
Cranberry-Orange Relish, '81 M289;
   '88 254
Cranberry-Pear Relish, '85 232
Cranberry Relish, '81 275; '83 144;
   '85 258, 264; '86 283; '87 245; '91 257;
   '92 341
Cranberry Relish, Holiday, '88 304
Cranberry Relish, Lemony, '79 243
Cranberry Relish, Old-Fashioned, '82 297
Cranberry Relish, Tipsy, '92 M310
Cucumber Chips, '85 176
Cucumber Pickles, Sour, '85 176
Cucumber Relish, '85 176
Cucumber Rounds, Easy Pickled, '90 143
Cucumber Sandwich Pickles, '81 174
Dill Pickles, '81 174
Dill Pickles, Fried, '84 206
Dills, Lazy Wife, '87 149

Eggs, Beet Pickled, '84 287
Eggs, Spiced Pickled, '84 288
Figs, Pickled, '79 140
Fire-and-Ice Pickles, '94 316
Garden Relish, '83 259
Garden Relish, End-of-the-, '80 179
Icicle Pickles, Sweet, '85 176
India Relish, '84 179
Jalapeño Peppers, Pickled, '93 136
Kraut Relish, '91 232
Mango Relish, '89 198
Mixed Pickles, '81 174
Okra Pickles, '81 173
Onion Relish, '91 79
Onion Relish, Green, '84 65
Onion Relish, Sweet, '93 124
Onion Rings, Pickled Refrigerator, '84 265
Onions, Pickled Cocktail, '89 197
Orange Slices, Spicy, '81 12
Papaya-Basil Relish, '94 82
Peaches, Perfect Pickled, '85 178
Peach Pickles, '85 177
Peach Relish, '85 136
Pear Pickles, Mustard, '79 196
Pear Relish, '79 196
Pear Relish, Peppery, '89 141
Pepper-Onion Relish, '84 180
Pepper Relish, '83 183
Pepper Relish, Confetti, '91 195
Pineapple, Pickled, '79 24
Problem Chart, Pickle, '85 176
Prune Relish, Peppy, '90 227
Raisin Relish, '92 310
Salad, Relish, '84 121
Salsa, '80 196
Salsa Cruda, '87 180
Salsa, Fresh Summer, '87 89
Salsa, Hot Mexican, '85 136
Salsa Picante, '84 108
Salsa Picante, Homemade, '81 67
Salsa, Spicy Corn, '93 322
Salsa, Tomato, '87 120
Salsa, Yellow Tomato, '87 122
Sauerkraut Relish, '85 136
Squash, Pickled Yellow, '93 136
Squash Pickles, '81 174; '87 150
Squash Pickles, Chayote, '89 197
Summer Squash Relish, Pollock with, '92 200
Sweet Pickles, Quick, '87 149
Tomato Pickles, Green, '87 134
Tomato Relish, '85 188
Tomato Relish, Easy, '80 126
Tomato Sweet Relish, Green, '93 136
Vegetable Relish, '90 147
Vegetable Relish, Eight-, '84 179
Watermelon Rind Pickles, '81 174; '84 106
White Bean Relish, '93 229
Zucchini, Dilled Fresh, '81 174
Zucchini Relish, '87 200

Pies and Pastries

Almond Combs, '84 136
Almond Pie, Toasted, '86 163
Almond Tassies, Lucky, '91 13
Ambrosia Pie, '79 284
Angel Pie, '79 123; '80 238
Apple
   Amandine Pie, Apple-, '89 215
   American Apple Pie, '91 197
   Autumn Apple Pie, '79 205
   Berry-Apple Pie, '88 251
   Blackberry-Apple Pie, '87 130

   Brandy-Apple Pie, '86 301
   Brandy Raisin-Apple Pie, '83 192
   Cake, Apple Pie, '82 226
   Chess Pie, Apple-Lemon, '86 220
   Cider Pie, Apple, '84 227
   Cinnamon Sauce, Apple Pie with Hot,
     '88 210
   Covered Apple Cake, '89 317
   Cran-Apple Pie, '92 304
   Cranberry-Apple Holiday Pie, '81 M269
   Cranberry-Apple Pie, '79 264
   Cream Cheese Pie, Apple-, '81 247
   Custard Pie, Apple, '88 236
   Danish, Deep-Dish Apple, '86 161
   Dumplings, Old-Fashioned Apple,
     '84 226
   Dutch Apple Pie, '81 105; '82 273
   Easy-Crust Apple Pie, '87 11
   Flan, Apple, '81 309
   Foldovers, Apple, '84 136
   Fresh Apple Pie, '84 178
   Fried Apple Pies, '81 217; '86 302;
     '88 112, 225; '94 61
   Fried Apple Turnovers, '81 161
   Grandmother's Apple Pie, '87 212
   Grated Apple Pie, '83 304
   Holiday Apple Pie, '87 260
   Lemon-Apple Pie, Tart, '80 100
   Mexican Apple Pie, '94 97
   Mincemeat Pie, Apple-, '85 316
   No-Crust Apple Pie, '88 204
   Old-Fashioned Apple Pie, '82 M299;
     '88 94
   Pear-Apple Pie, Natural, '88 226
   Pear Pie, Apple-, '83 249
   Raisin Brandy Pie, Apple-, '89 58
   Red Apple Pie, '79 282
   Roll, Apple, '82 178
   Rolls, Luscious Apple, '88 225
   Squares, Apple, '92 311
   Strudel, Apple, '85 259; '89 267;
     '92 269
   Turnovers, Delicious Apple, '86 25
   Turnovers, Puffy Apple, '87 276
   Upside-Down Southern Apple Pie,
     '88 226
Apricot Fried Pies, '86 269
Apricot Pastries, '83 297
Apricot Pies, Special, '94 60
Apricot Pie, Yogurt-, '85 132
Apricot Pinwheels, '87 276
Apricot Surprise Pie, '88 99
Banana Cream Pie, '84 48; '87 207
Banana Cream Pie, Hawaiian, '90 105
Banana Pie with Hot Buttered Rum Sauce,
   '88 204
Bavarian Cream Pie, '79 281
Blackberry Cream Pie, '81 132
Blackberry Pie, '84 141; '86 152
Blackberry Pie, Creamy, '88 179
Blackberry Roll, '82 178
Blueberry-Banana Pie, '93 115
Blueberry-Cream Cheese Pie, '88 154
Blueberry Cream Pie, '84 142
Blueberry Cream Pie, Fresh, '80 144
Blueberry Kuchen, '80 143
Blueberry-Peach Pie, '94 158
Blueberry Pie, Chilled, '89 136
Blueberry Pie, Fresh, '83 183; '85 152
Blueberry Pie, Old-Fashioned, '89 136
Blueberry-Sour Cream Pie, '83 183

Pies and Pastries *(continued)*

Blueberry Streusel Pie, Fresh, '89 137
Boston Cream Pie, '83 220
Bourbon Pie, Kentucky, '84 87
Boysenberry Pie, '82 133
Brownie Pie, Crustless, '82 33
Buttermilk Chess Pie, '92 214
Buttermilk-Coconut Pie, '94 246
Buttermilk-Lemon Cream Pie, '88 99
Buttermilk Lemon Pie, '81 120; '82 23
Buttermilk-Lemon Pie, '88 297
Buttermilk Pie, '82 53; '83 158; '88 93; '92 95
Buttermilk Pie, Old-Fashioned, '79 72
Butterscotch Cream Pie, '84 48; '87 207
Butterscotch Meringue Pie, '83 158
Cannoli, '80 58
Cantaloupe Cream Pie, '79 177
Cantaloupe Meringue Pie, '88 182
Cantaloupe Pie, '86 163
Caramel-Banana Pie, '86 M165
Caramel Banana Pie, Luscious, '79 115
Caramel-Nut Crunch Pie, '94 244
Caramel-Peanut Pie, '86 259
Caramel Pie, Burnt, '82 53
Carrot Custard Pie, '79 45
Caviar Pie, '79 154
Cheese
 Camembert Bars, '86 58
 Cottage Cheese Pie, '82 85
 Cream Puffs with Chicken Salad, Cheesy, '86 260
 Date-Filled Cheese Pastries, '83 259
 Fruited Cheese Pie, '92 228
 Hors d'Oeuvre Pie, Cheesy, '88 91
 Lemon Cheese Pie, '81 136; '82 146
 Lemon-Cottage Cheese Pie, '79 44
 Lemon Cottage Cheese Pie, '81 143
 Make-Ahead Cheesecake Pie, '81 233
 Mincemeat-Cheese Pie, '80 253
 Phyllo-Cheese Triangles, '87 246
 Puffs, Mexican Cheese, '87 8
 Tartlets, Cheese, '88 211
 Yogurt-Cheese Pie, '82 121
Cherry-Berry Pie, '92 316
Cherry Confetti Pie, No-Bake, '93 114
Cherry Cream Pie with Almond Pastry, '92 30
Cherry Pie, Coconut Crumb, '92 30
Cherry Pie, Easy, '82 299
Cherry Pie, Fresh, '88 178
Cherry Pie, Lemony, '92 30
Cherry Pie, Prize-Winning, '82 57
Cherry Pie, Red, '83 192
Cherry Pie, Scrumptious, '83 250
Chess Pie, Brown Sugar, '86 220
Chess Pie, Old-Fashioned, '86 220
Chicken Puffs, Appetizer, '85 72
Chocolate
 Almond Pie, Creamy Chocolate-, '85 102
 Amandine, Chocolate Pie, '83 300
 Amaretto Mousse Pie, Chocolate-, '80 180; '81 30
 Banana-Pecan Cream Pie, Chocolate-, '94 210
 Bavarian Pie, Chocolate, '89 326
 Berry Pie, Heavenly Chocolate-, '85 102

Best-Ever Chocolate Pie, '88 M45
Black Bottom Pie, '82 53
Bourbon Pie, Chocolate, '88 99
Cake, Chocolate Pastry, '91 196
Chess Pie, Chocolate, '81 161; '86 220; '92 13
Chilled Chocolate Pie, '88 99
Chip Pie, Chocolate, '85 114
Coffee Cream Pie, '94 209
Cream Cheese Pie, Chocolate-, '80 69
Cream Cheese Pie, Chocolate, '92 240
Cream Pie, Chocolate, '83 192; '84 49; '87 208; '94 208
Creamy Chocolate Pie, '85 298; '86 119
Double Chocolate Pie, '82 M282
Easy Chocolate Pie, '83 158
French Silk Pie, '80 247
Frozen Chocolate Pie, '80 154
Frozen Chocolate Pie with Pecan Crust, '89 291
Fudge Pie, '87 168; '89 252
Fudge Pie, Sweetheart, '86 316; '90 313
German Chocolate Pie, '93 129
Heavenly Chocolate Pie, '87 260
Ice Cream Pie, Chocolate-, '87 224
Meringue Pie, Chocolate, '80 238; '82 206; '83 158; '92 216
Meringue Pie, Chocolate-Filled, '86 121
Microwave Chocolate Pie, '90 M15
Mocha Crunch Pie, Chocolate-, '81 136
Mocha Pie, '94 168
Mousse Pie, Chocolate, '81 136
Mud Pie, Decadent, '89 252
Mud Pie, Mississippi, '89 26
Mud Pie, Tipsy, '80 255
Peanut Butter Pie, Chocolate-, '85 91
Peanut Butter Swirl Pie, Chocolate-, '87 262
Praline Pie, Chocolate-, '86 259
Silk Pie, Chocolate, '88 67
Strawberry-Chocolate Truffle Pie, '89 112
Whipped Cream Pie, Chocolate, '79 124
White Chocolate-Banana Cream Pie, '94 314
Christmas Pie, White, '88 281; '93 289
Cobblers
 Apple Cobbler, Easy, '83 174
 Apple Cobbler for Two, '85 261
 Apple Cobbler, New-Fashioned, '91 221
 Apple Crisp, '84 122
 Apple Crisp, Tart, '92 226
 Apple-Pecan Cobbler, '84 M198
 Apple Walnut Cobbler, '79 154
 Apple-Walnut Cobbler, '81 248
 Apricot Cobble Up, '82 138
 Berry-Cherry Cobbler, '83 270
 Berry Crisp, '83 130
 Blackberry-Almond Cobbler, '81 132
 Blackberry Cobbler, '82 139; '83 175
 Blackberry Cobbler, Deep-Dish, '80 186
 Blackberry Cobbler, Deluxe, '81 132
 Blackberry Cobbler, Juicy, '89 137
 Blackberry Cobbler, New-Fashioned, '87 164
 Blackberry Cobbler, Southern, '81 132
 Blueberry Buckle, '85 30
 Blueberry Cobbler, '83 175
 Blueberry Cobbler, Easy, '83 183
 Blueberry Cobbler, Fresh, '80 144

Blueberry Cobbler, Peachy, '80 143
Blueberry Crisp, '84 177
Blueberry Crunch, Fresh, '82 143
Blueberry, Huckle-Buckle, '86 151
Blueberry-Peach Cobbler, No-Dough, '86 177
Blueberry Pinwheel Cobbler, '87 140
Blueberry Slump, Quick, '91 20
Boysenberry Cobbler, '82 133
Cherry Cobbler, '82 91, 139
Cherry Cobbler, Colossal, '89 137
Cherry Cobbler, Fresh, '84 178
Cherry Crisp, '91 20
Cherry Slump, '83 139
Cranberry-and-Apple Cobbler, '84 306; '90 294
Cranberry Cobbler, '81 275
Cranberry Cobbler, Easy, '86 260
Cranberry Cobbler Roll, '80 288; '81 248
Cranberry-Peach Cobbler, '92 322
Cranberry-Pear Crisp, '83 207
Fig Cobbler, '79 140
Fig Cobbler, Cajun, '94 196
Fig Cobbler, Super, '86 206
Fruit Cobbler, Quick, '91 20
Grenadine-Peach Cobbler, '85 178
Peach-Caramel Cobbler, '86 300; '87 178
Peach Cobbler, '83 175; '84 178; '90 219
Peach Cobbler, Fresh, '82 139; '89 154
Peach Cobbler, Lattice-Topped, '79 154
Peach Cobbler, Old-Fashioned, '82 170
Peach Cobbler, Quick, '79 215; '81 142
Peach Cobbler, Spicy, '85 178
Peach Cobbler Supreme, '81 184; '90 313
Peach Cobbler with Praline Biscuits, '92 180
Peach Crinkle, '91 20
Peach Crisp, '83 113; '92 13; '93 134
Peach Crumble, Easy, '83 116
Pear Cobbler, Best Ever, '82 194
Pear Crumble, '85 221
Pineapple-Apple Betty, '85 46
Plum Cobbler, Crunchy, '88 152
Raspberry-Cherry Cobbler, '93 230
Strawberry-Rhubarb Cobbler, '88 93
Strawberry-Rhubarb Cobbler, Rosy, '79 154
Coconut-Caramel Pies, '87 260
Coconut Chess Pie, '86 220
Coconut Cloud, '80 70
Coconut Cream Pie, '80 238; '81 136; '82 85; '84 49; '87 207; '89 236; '90 312
Coconut Cream Pie, Fresh, '80 289
Coconut Cream Pie, Surprise, '92 43
Coconut Crunch Pie, '90 105
Coconut Custard Pie, '82 33
Coconut Macaroon Pie, '88 204
Coconut-Orange Chess Pie, '89 169
Coconut Pie, '93 115
Coconut Pie, Blender, '84 236
Coconut Pie, French, '90 162
Coconut Pie, Magic, '79 53
Coconut Pie, Mock, '86 200
Coconut Pie, Quick, '83 115
Coconut Pie, Toasted, '90 105
Coconut-Pineapple Pie, '84 256
Coconut Puffs, '87 277

Pies and Pastries (continued)

Coffee Cream Pie, '94 209
Cracker Pie, '79 113
Cranberry-Cherry Pie, Tart, '87 299
Cranberry Freezer Pie, Festive, '84 306
Cranberry Pie, Frosty, '79 249
Cranberry Pie, Nutty, '82 M298
Cranberry Pie, Walnut-, '87 259
Cranberry-Raisin Pie, '80 283; '85 316
Cran-Raspberry Pie, '87 244
Cream Horns, '84 137
Cream Pie, Texas, '81 181
Cream Puffs, Captivating, '81 180
Cream Puffs, Java, '81 187
Cream Puffs, Lemon, '93 254
Cream Puffs, Strawberry, '81 95
Cream Puffs, Strawberry-Lemon, '87 75
Cream Puffs, Tutti-Frutti, '79 231
Crème de Menthe Pie, Quick, '88 127
Custard Pie, Old-Fashioned Egg, '82 261
Custard Pie, Perfect, '82 92
Daiquiri Pie, '79 68
Daiquiri Pie, Daring, '92 191
Danish Pastry Puffs, '85 311
Dream Pie, '80 90
Éclairs, Pistachio-Cream, '91 296
Éclairs with Pecan Sauce, '83 219
Eggnog Chiffon Pie, '86 281
Eggnog Pie, '80 254; '83 205; '86 317; '87 295
Eggnog Pie, Fluffy, '81 M269
Empanadas, '92 156
Empanadas de Calabaza (Pumpkin Empanadas), '94 28
Fig Snacks, Sliced, '86 206
Fried Pies, Delicious, '83 84
Fruitcake Pie, '80 237
Fruit Pie, Crispy-Crust, '88 68
Fruit Pie, Dried, '83 249
Fruit Pie, Japanese, '80 238
Fruit Pies, Baked, '84 7
Fruit Puff, Giant, '85 72
Grape Juice Pie, '79 123
Grape Pie, '85 212
Grasshopper Freeze, Creamy, '81 180
Grasshopper Pie, '83 145
Guava Puffs, '92 247
Heavenly Pie, '83 158
Ice Cream Delight, '80 69
Ice Cream Pie, Absolutely Divine, '82 181
Ice Cream Pie, Caramel, '82 181
Ice Cream Pie, Carrot, '86 200
Ice Cream Pie, Chocolate, '91 56
Ice Cream Pie, Chocolate-Mint, '81 144
Ice Cream Pie, Coffee, '79 231
Ice Cream Pie, Double-Delight, '89 72
Ice Cream Pie, Heavenly, '82 181
Ice Cream Pie, Kona, '83 189
Ice Cream Pie, Lemon, '80 70
Ice Cream Pie, Nutty, '91 180
Ice Cream Pie, Peanutty, '82 56
Ice Cream Pie, Peppermint Candy-, '87 260
Ice Cream Pie, Pumpkin, '81 272
Ice-Cream Pie Spectacular, '90 314
Ice Cream Pie with Meringue-Pecan Crust, '88 127
Ice Cream Pie with Rum-Fruit Sauce, '84 312
Ice Cream Sundae Pie, '94 244
Kahlúa Pie, '83 191

Key Lime Pie, '91 42
Lemonade Pie, '91 42
Lemonade Pie, Frozen, '92 101
Lemon-Buttermilk Pie, '91 272
Lemon Chess Pie, '79 32; '82 196
Lemon Cream Pie, Frozen, '82 86
Lemon Fluff Pie, '92 342; '93 46
Lemon in Pastry Shell, '84 137
Lemon Meringue Pie, '85 M112; '86 130
Lemon Meringue Pie, Best-Ever, '94 208
Lemon Meringue Pie, Deluxe, '81 172; '90 313
Lemon-Orange Pie, '85 172
Lemon Parfait Pie, '94 310
Lemon Pie, Buttermilk, '81 120; '82 23
Lemon Pie, Slice of, '84 23
Lemon Pie, Tart, '91 275
Lemon Pie, Whipped, '79 124
Lemon-Sour Cream Pie, '82 169
Lemon Sponge Pie, '83 192
Lemon-Strawberry Pie, '88 127
Lemon Twirl Pie, '84 94
Lime Chiffon Pie, '86 130
Lime Fluff Pie, '84 43
Lime Party Pies, '92 65
Macadamia Pie, '80 238
Magnolia Pie, '94 210
Main Dish
    Artichoke Pie, '79 25
    Beef Pies, Carry-Along, '80 224; '81 56
    Beef Pot Pie, Oriental, '92 253
    Beef Pot Pies with Yorkshire Pudding Topping, '93 45
    Beef Roast Pot Pie, '88 296
    Breakfast Pie, '86 242
    Breakfast Pie, Country, '93 M328
    Broccoli-and-Turkey Pasta Pie, '88 269
    Broccoli-Beef Pie, '83 196
    Burrito Pie, Mexican, '87 287
    Cheese-Beef Pie, '85 33
    Cheeseburger Pie, '89 121
    Cheese Pie, Mexican, '82 9; '83 69
    Chicken Breasts in Phyllo Pastry, '91 105
    Chicken Breasts Wellington, '84 22
    Chicken, Company Creamed, '82 84
    Chicken in Pastry, '86 122
    Chicken in Phyllo, '87 286
    Chicken in Puff Pastry, Spinach-Stuffed, '92 125
    Chicken Liver Turnovers, '79 141
    Chicken Phyllo Pie, Greek, '92 328
    Chicken Pie, '81 281; '82 31
    Chicken Pie, Biscuit-Topped, '86 157, 264
    Chicken Pie, Cheesy Mexican, '82 142
    Chicken Pie, Deluxe, '88 298
    Chicken Pie, Double-Crust, '87 111
    Chicken Pie, Egg-Stra Special, '86 264
    Chicken Pie, Nana's, '90 25
    Chicken Pie, Savory Southern, '90 24
    Chicken Pot Pie, '81 210; '82 114; '84 21; '94 21
    Chicken Pot Pie, Double-Crust, '90 220
    Chicken Pot Pie, Easy, '83 156; '89 218
    Chicken Pot Pie, Old-Fashioned, '92 271
    Chicken Pot Pie, Thick 'n' Crusty, '87 267; '88 102; '89 67
    Chicken Pot Pie with Cheese Crust, '86 264

Chicken Salad in Cream Puff Bowl, '86 232
Chicken Tarts, Deviled, '94 14
Chicken-Vegetable Pot Pie, '81 281; '82 30
Chile-Cheese Pie, Green, '84 234
Chili-Tamale Pie, '82 9; '83 68
Cornbread-Sausage-Apple Pie, '87 171
Cornbread-Tamale Pie, '92 123
Corn Burger Pie, '83 156
Country Pie, '83 155
Enchilada Pie, '83 155
Fish in a Crust, '84 294
Game Pot Pie with Parmesan Crust, '94 304
Grits-and-Ham Pie, Crustless, '86 103
Grits Fiesta Pie, '92 43
Hamburger Pie, '81 92; '84 13
Ham Pie, Golden, '87 78
Ham Pie with Cheese Crust, '80 286
Ham Pot Pie, '90 25
Ham Tart, Supreme, '84 22
Ham Towers, Cheesy, '82 77
Lamb Pie, '90 26
Meat-and-Potato Pie, '84 23
Meat Loaf in a Wrap, '89 122
Meat Pie, Italian, '89 109
Meat Pie, Mexicali, '81 194
Meat Pie, Old-Fashioned, '82 110
Meat Pie, Reuben, '80 189
Meat Pies, Cornish, '84 23
Meat Pies, Natchitoches, '84 21; '91 241
Meat Turnovers, '86 326
Oyster Pie, Creole, '84 214
Pancake, Supper, '86 242
Pea Flips, '80 7
Pineapple-Chicken Salad Pie, '80 138
Roast Beef Turnovers, '88 273; '89 180
Salmon-Spinach Turnovers, '83 44
Sausage-and-Cornbread Pie, '90 25
Sausage-Cheese Turnovers, '88 231
Sausage Log, Phyllo, '84 294
Sausage Pizza Pie, Link-, '85 33
Seafood Pie, Hot, '80 32
Shepherd Pie, '83 116
Shepherd's Pie, '92 168
Shrimp Puffs, Luncheon, '85 72
Sombrero Pie, '81 140
Spaghetti-Ham Pie, '93 19
Spaghetti Pie, '81 32
Spanakópita, '86 58
Spinach-Pasta Pie, '85 286
Taco Pie, '88 256
Taco Pie, Crescent, '80 80
Taco Pie, Double-Crust, '88 272; '89 180
Taco Pies, Individual, '82 M282
Tarts, Picadillo, '91 279
Torta Mexican Style, '89 122
Tortilla Pie, '85 M211
Tortilla Pie, Montezuma, '83 199
Tuna Pie with Cheese Roll Crust, '80 286
Tuna-Rice Pie, '84 123
Turkey-and-Dressing Pie, '84 326
Turkey-and-Oyster Pie, '82 267
Turkey-Cheese Pie, '88 264
Turkey Pie, '80 285
Turkey Pie, Crumb-Crust Curried, '86 265

Pies and Pastries, Main Dish *(continued)*

Turkey Pie, Golden, **'79** 253
Turkey Pie, Lattice-Topped, **'81** 277;
   '82 7
Turkey Pie, Potato-Topped, **'86** 265
Turkey Pot Pie, **'86** 265; **'90** 24; **'93** 45
Turkey Turnovers, Home-Style, **'94** 325
Vegetable-Beef Pies, **'80** 286
Zucchini-Ham-Cheese Pie, **'80** 272
Mango-Ginger Pie, **'88** 138
Mango Pie, Green, **'79** 137
Maple Cream Coffee Treat, **'90** 50
Mexican Fiesta Confection, **'82** 223
Mincemeat Chiffon Pie, **'79** 245
Mincemeat-Peach Pie, **'80** 295; **'81** 188
Mincemeat Pie, Holiday, **'80** 282; **'83** 250;
   '87 213
Mincemeat Pie, Pear, **'84** 264; **'88** 226
Mince Pie, Spirited, **'92** 316
Mint Pie, Candy-Crust, **'92** 191
Mocha Meringue Pie, **'80** 242; **'88** 163
Molasses Pie, **'86** 20
Muscadine Pie, **'82** 202
Mushroom-Almond Pastry Cups, **'88** 210
Napoleons, **'84** 138
Napoleons, Berry, **'94** 120
Napoleons, Blueberry-Lemon, **'94** 122
Napoleons, Peanut Butter-and-Chocolate,
   '94 121
Napoleons, Strawberry, **'81** 126
Nesselrode Pie, Fluffy, **'87** 261
Orange Ambrosia Pie, **'80** 237
Orange Blossom Special, **'79** 48
Orange Chess Pie, **'88** 204
Orange Chiffon Pie, **'87** 260
Orange-Coconut Cream Pie, **'94** 208
Orange-Coconut Pie, **'90** 90
Orange Meringue Pie, **'81** 12, 309
Orange Pie, Florida, **'91** 43
Orange Pie, Frosty, **'90** 296
Orange Shortcake, Fresh, **'80** 100
Palmiers, **'87** 277
Papaya Pie, **'86** 53
Papaya-Pineapple Roll, **'94** 18
Pastries and Crusts
   Almond Pastry, **'85** 177; **'89** 317;
      '92 30
   Basic Microwave Pastry, **'82** M142;
      '85 M113
   Basic Pastry, **'79** 282; **'81** M268;
      '82 114; **'84** 48; **'89** 215; **'91** 119;
      '94 210
   Brown Sugar Crust, **'92** 118
   Butter Crust, **'90** 173
   Butter Pastry, Golden, **'84** 22
   Cereal Piecrust, Crisp, **'82** 209;
      '83 100
   Cheddar Cheese Pastry, **'80** 219;
      '82 194
   Cheddar Pastry, **'86** 206
   Cheese Crust, **'80** 286; **'86** 264
   Cheese Pastry, **'88** 56
   Cheese Rolls, **'80** 286
   Chocolate-Coconut Crust, **'87** 261
   Chocolate-Coconut Pie Shell, **'82** 210;
      '83 100
   Chocolate Crumb Crust, **'87** 261
   Chocolate Crust, **'87** 264; **'90** M15
   Chocolate Cups, **'80** 207

Chocolate Pastry Shell, **'87** 262
Chocolate Wafer Crust, **'89** 42, 93
Cinnamon Meringue Shell, **'82** 263
Citrus Pastry, Hint-of-, **'93** 260
Coconut Crust, **'89** 160
Cookie Crust, Spicy, **'88** 7
Cornmeal Pastry, **'81** 140
Cornmeal Pastry Cups, **'90** 69
Cracker Crust, **'88** 97
Cream Cheese Pastries, **'80** 250
Cream Cheese Pastry, **'82** 39;
   '86 24, 78; **'89** 136
Cream Cheese Pastry Shells, **'86** 13
Cream Cheese Pastry Shells, Miniature,
   '87 190
Cream Cheese Patty Shells, **'81** 266;
   '82 249
Cream Cheese Shells, **'79** 2
Crumb Crust, Cheesy, **'88** 86
Crust, **'89** 272
Decorating Pie Crusts, **'83** 248
Deluxe Piecrust, **'79** 79
Double-Crust Pastry, **'81** 105;
   '82 85, M298; **'83** 248; **'85** 191;
   '87 299; **'88** 94, 178
Double-Crust Pastry, Flaky, **'82** 57
Flaky Pastry, **'80** 224; **'81** 56, 210;
   '83 156
German Pastries, **'86** 78
Ginger Snap Crust, **'88** 138
Gingersnap Crust, **'89** 93; **'90** 296
Graham Cracker Crust, **'79** 45; **'86** 32;
   '87 139, 243; **'88** M45, 55, 67;
   '89 93, 326; **'90** 296;
   '91 197, M234, 308; **'94** 310
Graham Cracker Crust, Microwaved,
   '82 M141
Graham Cracker Crust, Peanut-, **'79** 50
Heart Tart Pastry, **'87** 14
Italian Sweet Crust, Plum Pie with,
   '79 162
Lattice Crust, **'90** 294
Light Pastry, **'92** 95
Make-Ahead Pastry, **'82** 209; **'83** 100
Mocha Pastry Shell, **'81** 136
Never Fail Pastry, **'79** 79
Nut Crust, Spiced, **'87** 295
Nutty Oat Crust, **'89** 251
Oatmeal Piecrust, **'79** 79
Parmesan Crust, **'94** 304
Paste Pastry, Common, **'94** 17
Pastry, **'82** 85, 139, 259;
   '83 84, 91, 175; **'84** 21, 23;
   '86 24, 25, 242, 259, 303, 326;
   '87 212, 267; **'88** 103, 198, 225;
   '89 67, 137, 154, 214, 267;
   '91 23, 241; **'92** 84, 157
Pastry Shell, **'93** 289; **'94** 158
Pâté Pastry, **'86** 65
Pecan Crust, **'86** 317; **'89** 291
Perfect Pastry Mix, **'81** 142
Perfect Pastry Shell, **'81** 142
Perfect Piecrust, Making, **'82** 234
Phyllo Baskets, Walnut-, **'93** 210
Pizza Crust, **'80** 233; **'83** 226; **'86** 77
Pizza Crust, Crispy, **'87** 181
Processor Pastry, **'87** 67
Processor Pie Dough, Quick Food,
   '84 219
Puff Pastry, Basic, **'84** 135
Puff Pastry Baskets, **'93** 177

Puff Pastry, Cream, **'85** 72
Puff Pastry, Quick, **'84** 207
Quiche Pastry, **'80** M107
Quiche Pastry, Microwaved, **'81** M74;
   '82 M122
Rice-Cheese Shell, **'82** 49
Rice Crust, Crispy, **'84** 43
Savory Pastry, **'90** 24
Seasoned Pastry, **'79** 253
Sesame Pastry Shell, **'82** 67
Shell, Pastry, **'84** 31, 127; **'87** 262;
   '89 236
Shells, Pastry, **'83** 93
Shortcake Pastry, **'80** 100
Spice Crust, **'82** 298
Sugar Cookie Crust, **'93** 131
Sugar Cookie Pastry, **'91** 119
Tart Crust, **'84** 178; **'90** 58
Tart Pastry, **'89** 232; **'90** 92; **'91** 118
Tart Shell, **'87** 77; **'88** 20
Tart Shells, **'82** 304; **'83** 279; **'85** 300;
   '86 18, 105; **'88** 4; **'90** 84; **'91** 13
Tart Shells, Cheese, **'88** 88
Tart Shells, Cheese Pastry, **'85** 216
Tart Shells, Tea, **'85** 120
Timbale Shells, **'82** 108
Triple-Crust Pastry, **'80** 186
Vegetable Oil Pastry, **'91** 204
Whole Wheat Crust, **'82** 298
Whole Wheat Pastry, **'81** 229
Pâté in Pastry, Turkey-Mushroom,
   '92 327
Peach-and-Blackberry Pie, **'89** 136
Peach Chiffon Pie, **'89** 155
Peach-Cranberry Pie, **'83** 249
Peach Cream Pie, Dried, **'84** 146
Peaches-and-Cream Pie, **'81** 184
Peach Fried Pies, Easy, **'85** 178
Peach Pie, Fresh, **'82** 170
Peach Pie, Luscious, **'81** 136
Peach Pie, Quick, **'89** 252
Peach Pies, Fried, **'81** 272
Peach Pies, Little, **'86** 303
Peach Praline Pie, **'89** 136
Peanut Butter Cream Pie, **'79** 50;
   '88 65
Peanut Butter Meringue Pie, **'84** 30
Peanut Butter Pie, **'85** 275; **'86** 109;
   '89 252
Peanut Butter Pie, Fluffy, **'94** 246
Peanut-Raisin Pie, **'79** 85
Peanuts" Pie, "Working for, **'93** 115
Pear Crumble Pie, **'83** 207
Pear-Macadamia Pie, **'93** 260
Pear Mincemeat Pie, **'84** 264;
   '88 226
Pear-Mince Pie, **'81** 271
Pear Pie, Backyard, **'93** 237
Pear Pie, Deep-Dish, **'80** 219
Pear Pie, Delicious, **'88** 226
Pear Pie, Double-Crust, **'82** 194
Pear Pie, French, **'87** 213
Pear Pie, Ginger-, **'93** 48
Pear Pie, Tennessee, **'85** 230
Pears en Croûte, **'93** 210
Pear Streusel Pie, **'83** 234; **'84** 244
Pecan
   Bourbon Pecan Pie, **'85** 90
   Bourbon-Pecan Pie, Frozen,
      '89 251
   Butter Pecan Pie Squares, **'81** 262

Pies and Pastries, Pecan (continued)

Caramel-Pecan Apple Pie, '85 247
Caramel-Pecan Pie, '88 282
Cherry-Pecan Pie, '92 30
Chocolate-Banana-Pecan Cream Pie,
 '94 210
Chocolate-Pecan Chess Pie, '93 251
Chocolate Pecan Pie, '80 237; '83 12;
 '90 184
Chocolate-Pecan Pie, '91 272
Choco-Pecan Pie, '82 86
Coconut-Pecan Chess Pie, '81 248
Coconut Pecan Pie, '81 161
Coffee Pecan Pie, '82 74
Cranberry-Pecan Pie, '92 316
Custard Pecan Pie, '87 184
Date-Pecan Pie, '80 15
Golden Pecan Pie, '81 266
Grandmother's Pecan Pie, '86 269
Holiday Pecan Pie, '81 296
Honey-Pecan Finger Pies, '90 184
Individual Pecan Pies, '85 295
Layered Pecan Pie, '83 305
Lemon-Pecan Pie, '93 251
Louisiana Pecan Pie, '92 83
Maple-Pecan Pie, '81 266
Miniature Pecan Pies, '79 205; '86 13
Molasses-Pecan Pie, '86 259
Old-Fashioned Pecan Pie, '81 M269
Orange-Pecan Pie, '79 282; '83 222
Pecan Pie, '79 251; '80 57; '85 255;
 '90 312; '92 234
Pumpkin-Pecan Pie, '85 233, 282
Raisin-Pecan Pie, '87 213
Special, Old Pecan Street, '93 251
Spicy Pecan Pie, '84 240
Sweet Potato-Pecan Pie, '83 90
Texas Pecan Pie, '83 159
Texas Star Pecan Pie, '90 184
Tiny Pecan Pies, '79 225
Turtle Pecan Pie, '93 250
Persimmon Pie, '79 206
Phyllo Cheesecakes, Little, '87 275
Phyllo Nests, Nutty, '87 277
Pineapple-Coconut Chess Pie, '92 214
Pineapple Phyllo Bundles, '87 277
Pineapple Pie, '80 237; '89 252
Pineapple Pie, Double-Crust, '82 85
Pineapple Pie, Fresh, '91 178
Piroshki, '92 84
Pistachio Pie, '80 56
Plum Cream Pie, Easy, '86 174
Plum Kuchen, '79 161
Plum Pie, Streusel-Topped, '88 153
Plum Pie with Italian Sweet Crust, '79 162
Praline Pastries, '89 318
Preserve-Filled Foldovers, '80 7
Profiteroles, '84 208
Puff Pastry Baskets, Tropical, '93 177
Puffs, Cocktail, '91 106
Puffs, Sweet, '89 91
Pumpkin Chiffon Pie, '84 312
Pumpkin Empanadas, '82 223
Pumpkin-Ice Cream Pie, '87 243
Pumpkin Pie, Autumn, '87 213
Pumpkin Pie, Bourbon-Pecan, '87 264
Pumpkin Pie, Festive, '81 M269
Pumpkin Pie, Fluffy, '80 283
Pumpkin Pie in Spiced Nut Crust, '87 295

Pumpkin Pie, New-Fashioned, '90 296
Pumpkin Pie, Nutty, '82 67
Pumpkin Pie, Quick, '88 M230
Pumpkin Pie, Rich, '86 292
Pumpkin Pie, Sour Cream-, '84 263
Pumpkin Pies, Spicy, '84 322
Pumpkin Pie Supreme, '82 217
Pumpkin Pie, Traditional, '85 256
Pumpkin Pie with Meringue, '92 268
Pumpkin Praline Pie, '80 244
Pumpkin-Praline Pie, Frosty, '91 M234
Raisin Pastry Bites, '90 86
Raisin Pie, '83 220
Raisin Pie, Spiced, '84 148
Raspberry Cream Pie, '94 209
Raspberry-Nut Strudel, '83 304
Raspberry Party Puffs, '90 170
Ravioli, Sweet, '91 107
Rhubarb-Peach Pie, '86 140
Rhubarb-Raisin Pie, '79 112
Rugelach, '85 276
Rum Bisque Pie, '79 123
Rum Cream Pie, '85 212
Samosas, '89 266
Scuppernong Pie, '88 216
Sopaipillas, '89 268
Sour Cream Pie, '86 260
Sour Cream Pie, Tropical, '79 176; '80 6
Strawberry Angel Pie, '88 136
Strawberry-Banana Glazed Pie, '81 181
Strawberry-Glaze Pie, '81 141
Strawberry Pie, Chilled, '82 112
Strawberry Pie, Glazed, '82 M142
Strawberry Yogurt Pie, '80 232
Strawberry-Yogurt Pie, '85 122; '86 124
Strudel, Fruit Basket, '87 276
Strudels, Spinach, '93 249
Tarts
 Almond Tart, '89 232
 Almond Tea Tarts, '85 120
 Apple Cream Tart, '84 207
 Apple-Pecan Tarts, '80 282
 Apple Tart, Creamed, '94 17
 Apple Tart, Deluxe, '84 227
 Apple Tart with Cheese Pastry,
  '88 225
 Apricot-Apple Crumb Tart, '94 60
 Apricot Tarts, '79 282; '88 281
 Berry Tartlets, Fresh, '91 98
 Berry Tart, Pick-a-, '91 118
 Blackberry Pudding Tarts, '93 200
 Black Bottom Mocha-Cream Tart,
  '92 304
 Blue Cheese Appetizer Tarts, '85 300;
  '86 18
 Bouilli, Tarte à la, '83 92
 Caramel Tarts, '82 43
 Caramel Turtle Truffle Tart, '93 M131
 Cheese Tart, Herb-, '87 98
 Cherry and Blackberry Tart, '83 225
 Cherry Tarts, Cheery, '80 238
 Chess Tarts, '90 83
 Chicken Salad Tarts, '84 257
 Chicken Tarts, Deviled, '94 14
 Chocolate-Amaretto Heavenly Tarts,
  '88 4
 Chocolate Chess Tarts, '92 214
 Chocolate-Peanut Butter Tarts, '92 277
 Chocolate-Pecan Tart with Caramel
  Sauce, '93 296; '94 234
 Chocolate Tarts, Bluegrass, '90 84

 Cranberry-Cream Cheese Tarts,
  '80 154
 Cranberry Holiday Tarts, '83 279
 Cranberry-Nut Tart, '84 305
 Cranberry Tartlets, Fresh, '87 244
 Cran-Raspberry Meringue Tarts,
  '92 286
 Cream Cheese Tarts, '84 74; '90 312
 Derby Tarts, Miniature, '90 92
 Eggnog Tarts, Creamy, '79 255
 French Silk Tarts, '79 236
 Fruit Tart, Fancy, '82 128; '91 119
 Fruit Tart, Fresh, '84 178; '90 58
 Fruit Tartlets, Fresh, '93 96
 Fruit Tart, Open-Face, '84 207
 Fruit Tart, Rainbow, '82 304
 Fruit Tarts, Bowl-Me-Over Fresh,
  '93 200
 Grape Tart, Green, '87 77
 Grasshopper Tarts, '80 220; '89 275
 Ham-and-Cheese Tart, '92 332
 Heart Tarts, '87 14
 Kentucky Derby Tarts, '79 102
 Key Lime Tart in Coconut Crust,
  '89 160
 Kiwifruit-Peach Tart, '88 20
 Kiwifruit Tart, '89 232
 Lady Baltimore Tarts, '88 282
 Lemon-Cheese Tarts, '79 2
 Lemon Ice Cream Tarts, '80 152
 Lemon-Sour Cream Tarts, '81 304
 Lemon Tarts, '82 156; '83 79
 Lemon Tarts, Berry Good, '91 119
 Lemon Tarts, Dainty, '82 304
 Lemon Tarts, Golden, '85 191
 Lemon Tart Shells, '88 195
 Lime-Pineapple Tart, '88 6
 Little Bits, '79 196
 Milan, Tart, '87 70
 Mushroom Tarts, '88 161
 Orange Curd Tarts, '92 193
 Orange Tarts, Frozen, '80 154
 Peach Cream Tart, '90 173
 Peachy Keen Tarts, '91 118
 Pear Tart, '82 304; '92 72
 Pear Tart with White Caramel Sauce,
  '92 195
 Pecan Tarts, '81 266
 Pecan Tarts, Easy, '84 313
 Pecan Tarts, Special, '87 224
 Pecan Tart with Praline Cream, '90 256
 Pommes, La Tarte aux, '80 125
 Portabello Mushroom Tart, Smoked,
  '94 163
 Prune Tarts, Brandied, '85 223
 Puddin' Pies, President Tyler's, '80 43
 Pumpkin Tarts, No-Bake, '86 291
 Sausage 'n' Cheese Tarts, '88 51
 Seafood Tartlets, '87 247
 Shrimp Tart, '87 70
 Strawberry Dream Tart, '92 118
 Strawberry-Lemon Tart, '89 111
 Strawberry Tart, '84 138; '89 272
 Strawberry Tarts, '80 70
 Teatime Tassies, '84 321
 Tomato-Cheese Tart, Dried, '90 203
Tin Roof Pie, '85 91
Transparent Pie, '80 238
Turnovers, Baked Apple, '93 338
Turnovers, Cheesy Sesame Seed, '91 252
Turnovers, Fried Apricot, '86 24

Pies and Pastries *(continued)*

Turnovers, Fruit, **'79** 150
Turnovers, Party Ham, **'82** 39
Turnovers, Reuben, **'94** 253
Vanilla Cream Pie, Fruit-Topped, **'84** 49
Vegetable
  Bean Pie, Pinto, **'80** 40
  Broccoli-Cheese Pie, **'84** 235
  Carrot Pie, **'83** 117
  Cauliflower-Carrot Pie, **'82** 191
  Corn Pie, Quick and Cheesy, **'82** 191
  Florentine Crêpe Pie, **'79** 34
  Mushrooms in Patty Shells, **'80** 283
  Mushroom Tarts, Hot Sherried, **'83** 78
  Mushroom Turnovers, Hot, **'89** 285
  Mushroom Turnovers, Tiny, **'86** 24
  Onion-Cheese Pie, **'88** 86
  Onion Pie, **'82** 191
  Portabello Mushroom Tart, Smoked,
    '94 163
  Ratatouille Pie, **'88** 198
  Scallopini Pie, **'94** 133
  Spinach Pie, **'82** 191; **'88** 56
  Spinach Pie, Greek, **'85** 59
  Spinach, Pie Pan, **'94** 195
  Spinach Tarts, **'82** 249
  Squash Chiffon Pie, Butternut, **'83** 296;
    '84 285
  Squash Pie, Butternut, **'80** 40; **'87** 212
  Squash Pie, Spaghetti, **'80** 186
  Squash Pie, Spicy, **'85** 9
  Squash Pie, Spicy Butternut, **'80** 296
  Sweet Potato Cream Pie, Southern,
    '87 260
  Sweet Potato Meringue Pie, **'81** 126;
    '83 225
  Sweet Potato-Orange Pie, **'88** 207
  Sweet Potato Pie, **'79** 207; **'85** 255,
    275; **'86** 269; **'89** 289
  Sweet Potato Pie, Carolina, **'89** 295
  Sweet Potato Pie, No-Crust, **'84** 236
  Sweet Potato Pie, Old-Fashioned, **'79** 9
  Sweet Potato Pie, Speedy, **'90** 219
  Sweet Potato Pone Pie, **'80** 288
  Tomato Pie, **'88** 198
  Tomato Pie, Green, **'79** 195
  Vegetable Turnovers, **'86** 24
  Yam Pie, Louisiana, **'81** 223
  Zucchini Pie, Cheesy, **'82** 191
  Zucchini Pie, Italian-Style, **'83** 43

Pimiento
Ball, Pimiento Cheese, **'80** 258
Bread, Pimiento-Cheese, **'85** 223
Casserole, English Pea-Pimiento, **'83** 207
Cheese, Chunky Pimiento, **'86** 295
Cheese, Creamy Pimiento, **'86** 296
Cheeses, Pimiento and Three, **'86** 296
Cheese, West Texas Pimiento, **'84** 9
Eggs, Pimiento-Deviled, **'84** 143

Hoagies, Bacon, Pimiento, and Cheese,
  '90 144
Pasta, Pimiento, **'84** 176
Popovers, Pimiento, **'79** 138
Sandwiches, Pimiento Cheese, **'82** 278
Sauce, Cauliflower with Pimiento, **'87** 232
Spread, Creamy Pimiento Cheese, **'92** 159
Spread, Garlic Pimiento Cheese, **'79** 58
Spread, Ham and Pimiento, **'80** 285; **'81** 56
Spread, Low-Calorie Pimiento Cheese,
  '85 215
Spread, Pimiento Cheese, **'82** 35; **'83** 93;
  '86 127
Topping, Pimiento, **'83** 93

Pineapple
Ambrosia, Pineapple-Orange, **'88** 252
Appetizer, Shrimp-Pineapple, **'85** 80
Bacon-Wrapped Pineapple Chunks, **'84** 25
Baked Pineapple, **'83** 261; **'84** 287
Baked Pineapple with Natillas Sauce, **'83** 179
Bake, Ham-Potato-Pineapple, **'93** 302
Bake, Pineapple, **'79** 251
Bake, Pineapple-Cheese, **'79** 106
Ball, Pineapple Cheese, **'81** 160
Ball, Pineapple-Cheese, **'84** 26
Bars, Pineapple-Orange, **'82** 129
Basket, Summer Berry, **'84** 158
Beans and Franks, Hawaiian Baked, **'80** 136
Beans, Hawaiian-Style Baked, **'86** 210
Beefburgers Hawaiian, **'86** 137
Beets with Pineapple, **'79** 249; **'82** 204
Betty, Pineapple-Apple, **'85** 46
Blue Woo-Woo, **'94** 226
Boat Aloha, Pineapple, **'80** 102
Boats Ahoy, Pineapple, **'80** 148
Bread, Carrot-Pineapple, **'82** 210
Bread, Pineapple, **'83** 139
Bread, Pineapple-Apricot, **'84** 7
Bread, Pineapple-Carrot, **'79** 106
Bread, Pineapple-Nut, **'79** 215
Bread, Pineapple-Pecan Loaf, **'87** 256
Buns, Easy Pineapple, **'85** 14
Burgers, Pineapple, **'82** 169
Cake, Cajun, **'87** 138
Cake, Coconut-Pineapple, **'89** 56
Cake, Coconut-Pineapple Layer, **'80** 140
Cake, Heavenly Pineapple, **'83** 303
Cake, Lemon-Pineapple, **'86** 60, 239
Cake, Pineapple-Coconut Coffee, **'94** 49
Cake, Pineapple-Pecan Upside-Down,
  '84 25
Cake, Pineapple Pound, **'79** 148
Cake, Pineapple Upside-Down, **'80** 102;
  '88 10
Cake Roll, Coconut-Pineapple, **'84** 304
Cake, Skillet Pineapple Upside-Down,
  '85 242
Cake, Stacked Pineapple Upside-Down,
  '86 239
Carrots, Pineapple, **'83** 198
Charlotte, Pineapple, **'90** 288
Cheesecake, Pineapple, **'81** 32
Cheesecake, Ultimate Pineapple, **'85** 38
Chicken and Pineapple, **'81** 281; **'82** 30
Chicken Bake, Pineapple, **'82** 120
Chicken, Hawaiian Sesame, **'81** 106
Chicken, Oriental Pineapple, **'84** 288
Chicken, Piña Colada, **'86** 21
Chicken, Pineapple, **'83** M194; **'85** 3
Chicken Stir-Fry, Pineapple-, **'89** 176
Chicken with Pineapple, Oriental, **'86** 42

Chocolate-Drizzled Pineapple with Raspberry
  Sauce, **'90** 57
Chops, Pineapple-Curry Glazed, **'82** 106
Citrus, Pineapple and Fresh, **'89** 206
Coleslaw, Curried Pineapple, **'88** 172
Cookies, Pineapple, **'79** 216
Cooler, Pineapple, **'90** 207
Crab Imperial, Pineapple-, **'84** M286
Cream, Pineapple 'n', **'88** 202
Crêpes, Mango-Pineapple, **'86** 216
Curried Carrots and Pineapple, **'90** 228
Delight, Pineapple-Almond, **'85** 96
Delight, Pineapple-Pear, **'82** 54
Dessert Chimichangas, Pineapple, **'86** 4
Dip, Cheesy Pineapple, **'80** 249
Dip, Pineapple-Ginger, **'86** 104
Doughnuts, Pineapple Drop, **'83** 95
Dressing, Fruit Salad with Pineapple, **'85** 207
Dressing, Pineapple Cream, **'83** 81
Dressing, Pineapple-Poppy Seed, **'85** 55
Drink, Coconut-Pineapple, **'83** 172
Drink, Hot Buttered Pineapple, **'91** 260
Drink, Orange-Pineapple, **'89** 35
Filling, Pineapple, **'80** 140; **'83** 179;
  '84 153; **'89** 57
Float, Pineapple Sherbet, **'79** 148
Franks, Hawaiian, **'81** 202
Frappé, Hawaiian, **'81** 178
Fresh Pineapple Boats, **'83** 153
Fresh Pineapple Delight, **'79** 111
Fried Pineapple, **'81** 232
Fritters, Pineapple, **'88** 112
Frozen Tropical Paradise, **'89** 206
Glazed Oranges and Pineapple, **'86** 318
Glaze, Orange-Pineapple, **'81** 60
Glaze, Pineapple, **'83** 143; **'84** 26; **'85** 38
Glaze, Roast Chicken with Pineapple-
  Mustard, **'89** 83
Gratin, Pineapple, **'93** 328
Ham, Citrus-and-Spice, **'88** 40
Ham, Pineapple-Baked, **'86** 48
Ham, Pineapple-Flavored, **'87** 160
Hawaiian Dream Boats, **'86** 151
Ice Cream, Orange-Pineapple, **'86** 117
Ice Cream, Pineapple-Mint, **'84** 186
Jam, Pineapple, **'81** 147
Jelly, Pineapple-Orange Mint, **'92** 105
Kabobs, Pineapple-Beef, **'83** 212
Kabobs, Pineapple-Chicken, **'86** M328
Lemonade, Pineapple, **'93** 194
Loaf, Hawaiian, **'80** 225
Loaf, Pineapple Upside-Down Ham, **'79** 253
Loaves, Individual Pineapple, **'81** M121
Marmalade, Orange-Pineapple, **'82** 150;
  '89 M156
Marmalade, Strawberry-Pineapple, **'85** 130
Meatballs, Chinese, **'87** 194
Meatballs, Polynesian, **'80** 207
Meatballs with Pineapple and Peppers,
  '90 145
Meringue-Topped Pineapple, **'84** 178
Milkshake, Pineapple, **'87** 199
Mold, Minted Pineapple, **'85** 240
Mousse, Coconut-Pineapple, **'94** 198
Mousse, Elegant Pineapple, **'79** 230
Muffins, Carrot-Pineapple, **'81** 6
Muffins, Morning Glory, **'93** 327
Muffins, Pineapple, **'81** 14, 250
Muffins, Sunshine, **'86** 9
Nectar, Hot Pineapple, **'90** 21
Nog, Speedy Breakfast, **'82** 47

Pineapple (continued)

Papaya-Pineapple Roll, **'94** 18
Parfait, Pineapple, **'84** 83
Patties, Pineapple-Ham, **'80** 110
Pears, Pineapple-Honey, **'86** 94
Phyllo Bundles, Pineapple, **'87** 277
Pickled Pineapple, **'79** 24
Pie, Coconut-Pineapple, **'84** 256
Pie, Double-Crust Pineapple, **'82** 85
Pie, Fresh Pineapple, **'91** 178
Pie, Pineapple, **'80** 237; **'89** 252
Pie, Pineapple-Chicken Salad, **'80** 138
Pie, Pineapple-Coconut Chess, **'92** 214
Pops, Hawaiian Orange-Pineapple, **'94** 143
Pops, Pineapple-Yogurt, **'91** 173
Pork and Pineapple, Polynesian, **'83** 102
Pork Chops, Hawaiian, **'86** 212
Pork Chops, Pineapple, **'87** M124
Pork, Pineapple, **'82** 60
Pork, Pineapple Sweet-and-Sour, **'82** 120
Pork Roast, Pineapple, **'79** 41
Pot Roast, Hawaiian, **'81** 298
Pot Roast, Polynesian, **'80** 59
Preserves, Mango-Pineapple, **'79** 137
Pudding, Pineapple, **'80** 102
Punch, False-Kick, **'82** 121
Punch, Frosty Pineapple, **'91** 66
Punch, Hot Pineapple, **'82** 264
Punch, Lime-Pineapple, **'83** 142
Punch, Pineapple, **'79** 174; **'80** 128
Punch, Pineapple-Mint, **'88** 209
Punch, Pineapple-Orange, **'85** 236
Punch, Spiced Pineapple, **'83** 33; **'92** 66
Rice with Pineapple, Curried, **'79** 142
Rolls, Cranberry-Pineapple, **'86** 275
Rolls, Pineapple Angel, **'89** 72
Salad, Carrot-Pineapple, **'91** 83
Salad, Cucumber-Pineapple, **'84** 124
Salad Dressing, Pineapple, **'81** 36
Salad, Frosty Pineapple, **'89** 278
Salad, Frozen Cranberry-Pineapple, **'91** 237
Salad, Heavenly Frosted, **'79** 286
Salad, Icy Pineapple-Fruit, **'87** 9
Salad, Mandarin Orange and Pineapple,
    '82 266
Salad, Pineapple-Buttermilk, **'82** 80
Salad, Pineapple-Celery, **'85** 95
Salad, Pineapple-Cucumber Congealed,
    '83 118
Salad, Pineapple Daiquiri, **'84** 232
Salad, Pineapple-Lime, **'84** 320
Salad, Pineapple Macaroni, **'79** 220
Salad, Pineapple-Nut Chicken, **'83** 80
Salad, Pineapple-Orange Congealed, **'83** 218
Salad, Pineapple Waldorf, **'92** 97
Sandwich Loaf, Pineapple-Ham, **'91** 167
Sangría, Pineapple, **'91** 176
Sauce, Banana-Pineapple, **'83** 48
Sauce, Jezebel, **'81** 29; **'82** 55
Sauce, Pineapple, **'84** 236; **'92** 203
Sauce, Pineapple-Curry, **'79** 252
Sauce, Pineapple Ice Cream, **'81** M289
Sauce, Pineapple-Orange, **'84** 14
Sauce, Pineapple-Rhubarb, **'88** 94
Sauce, Pineapple-Rum, **'84** 275
Sauce, Raisin-Pineapple, **'82** 177
Sauce, Sweet-and-Sour Pineapple, **'85** 66
Scalloped Pineapple, **'79** 106; **'82** 254;
    '84 M323

Shake, Banana-Pineapple Milk, **'84** 59
Shake, Pineapple-Banana, **'85** 215
Shake, Pineapple Milk, **'94** 113
Shake, Strawberry-Pineapple, **'84** 166
Sherbet, Creamy Pineapple, **'79** 155
Sherbet, Easy Pineapple, **'92** 199
Sherbet, Pineapple, **'81** 177; **'84** 83;
    '89 199
Skewered Pineapple and Strawberries,
    '84 251
Slaw, Apple-Pineapple, **'79** 241
Slaw, Cabbage-Pineapple, **'92** 182
Slaw, Colorful Pineapple, **'86** 250
Slaw, Pineapple, **'94** 49
Slaw, Pineapple-Almond, **'92** 171
Slicing Pineapples, Instructions for, **'82** 94
Slush, Pineapple, **'88** 82
Slush, Pineapple-Banana, **'90** 14
Slush, Pineapple-Strawberry, **'94** 227
Smoothie, Quick Banana-Pineapple, **'93** 195
Snow Peas and Pineapple, **'91** 120
Soda, Pineapple, **'90** 179
Sopaipillas, Pineapple, **'83** 179
Soufflé, Pineapple Dessert, **'80** 153
Spiced Pineapple, **'80** 102
Spiced Pineapple Sparkle, **'92** 322
Spread, Coconut-Pineapple, **'93** 309
Spread, Hawaiian Cheese, **'87** 158
Spread, Pineapple-Cheese, **'86** 126; **'91** 167
Spread, Pineapple-Cream Cheese, **'82** 35
Spread, Pineapple Sandwich, **'84** 166
Spritz, Pineapple, **'86** 94
Squash, Pineapple-Stuffed Acorn, **'84** 255
Sundaes, Mauna Loa, **'80** 126
Tart, Lime-Pineapple, **'88** 6
Tea, Pineapple, **'93** 165
Topping, Cherry-Pineapple, **'87** 126
Topping, Lemon-Pineapple, **'86** 60
Topping, Pineapple, **'86** 239
Trifle, Pineapple Angel Food, **'93** 86
Tropical Snow, **'86** 34
Wassail, Pineapple-Apricot, **'83** 275
Yogurt Whirl, Pineapple, **'91** 132

Pizza

Appetizer Pizzas, **'89** M118
Artichoke and Prosciutto, Pizza with,
    '87 182
Bagel, Pizza on a, **'93** M94
Beef-and-Sausage Pizza, Double Cheesy,
    '86 77
Bobolis, Easy Cheesy, **'92** 278
Bread, Pizza Batter, **'85** 56
Breakfast Pizza, **'85** 44; **'88** 288;
    '90 140, 178
Burger, Pizza, **'87** 185
Burgers, All-American Pizza, **'92** 148
Burgers, Easy Pizza, **'82** 190
Burger Snacks, Pizza-, **'84** 30
Burgers, Pizza, **'80** M201; **'81** 73; **'89** 165
Calzone, **'85** 94
Casserole, Microwave Pizza, **'89** M248
Casserole, Pizza, **'88** 273; **'89** 181
Casserole, Quick Pizza, **'83** 266
Cheese-and-Mushroom Pizza, **'83** 226
Chicken Pizza, **'94** 218
Chocolate Pizza, **'91** 298
Clam Pizza, Baby, **'87** 182
Cocktail Pizzas, **'79** 110
Cookie, Pizza, **'90** 49
Crust, Crispy Pizza, **'87** 181; **'89** 64
Crust, Parmesan Pizza, **'93** 58

Crust, Pizza, **'80** 233; **'83** 226; **'85** 243;
    '86 77
Crust, Special Pizza, **'90** 139
Crusts, Skillet Pizza, **'94** 218
Crust, Thick, **'81** 214
Crust, Thin, **'81** 214
Crust, Whole Wheat, **'94** 78
Crust, Whole Wheat Pizza, **'93** 58
Cups, Pizza, **'81** 215
Deep-Dish Mediterranean Pizza, **'80** 163
Deep-Dish Pizza Luncheon Pie, **'80** 286
Deep-Dish Vegetarian Pizza, **'85** 243
Easy Pizza, **'92** 181
Eggplant Pizza, **'85** 221
French Bread, Pizza on, **'82** 131
Garden Pizza, **'89** 108
Grilled Pizzas, **'93** 178
Gruyère-Chicken Pizza, **'87** 182
Ham-and-Eggs Crescent Pizza, **'93** 47
Hamburger Pizza, Quick, **'85** 243
Herb Pizza, Easy, **'92** 99
Homemade Pizza, Best Ever, **'80** 233
Horns, Pizza, **'89** 214
Hot Dog Pizzas, **'93** 78
Italian-Style Pizza, Original, **'87** 182
Jazzed-Up Pizza, Jiffy, **'83** M314
Kiwi-Berry Pizza, **'86** 198; **'87** 55
Kiwifruit Pizza, **'89** 306
Lasagna Pizza, **'85** 285
Meatballs, Pizza, **'85** 86
Meat Loaf, Cheesy Pizza, **'81** 121
Mexican Pizza, **'94** 218, 327
Pan Pizza, Quick, **'86** 160
Party Pizzettes, **'80** 192
Peanut Butter-Fruit Pizza, **'94** 60
Pepperoni Pizza, Thick 'n' Crusty, **'85** 244
Pepper Pizza, Roasted, **'94** 218
Peppers, Pizza, **'83** 135
Pesto Pizza, **'87** 182; **'94** 218
Phyllo Pizza, **'94** 91
Pie, Pizza, **'91** 23
Pita Pizzas, **'89** 19
Pita Pizza Snack, **'94** 193
Pocket Pizzas, Easy, **'90** 168
Popcorn, Pizza-Flavored, **'85** 236
Quiche, Pizza, **'86** 53
Quick Little Pizzas, **'88** 227
Salad Pizza, **'87** 182
Sandwiches, Open-Face Pizza, **'82** 3; **'83** 85;
    '84 M198; **'85** 22
Sandwich, Giant Pizza, **'80** 93
Sauce, Pizza, **'84** 33; **'85** 285
Sausage-Pepperoni Pizza, Spicy, **'83** 226
Sausage Pizza Pie, Link-, **'85** 33
Shellfish Pizza, **'91** 224
Shrimp Pizza Wedges, **'89** 158
Slices, Pizza, **'84** 269
Snacks, Pizza Party, **'86** 262
Snacks, Tasty Little Pizza, **'79** 248
Speedy Pizza, **'81** 214
Squares, Pizza, **'87** 168
Strawberry Pizza, **'79** 94
Sunburst, Pizza, **'94** 245
Supreme, Pizza, **'81** 214
Taco Pizza, **'89** M177
Tostada Pizza, **'81** 16; **'82** 13
Turkey-Vegetable Pizza, **'90** 139
Turnovers, Little Pizza, **'85** 327
Two-Way Pizza, **'79** 93
Upside-Down Pizza, **'91** 185
Vegetable Pizza, **'89** 64; **'94** 218

Pizza *(continued)*

Vegetarian Processor Pizza, '89 225
Veggie Pizza, '94 78
Whole Wheat Pizza, '84 33
Wide-Eyed Pizzas, '90 94
Zucchini Pizzas, '88 212

Plums

Bread, Sugar Plum, '80 256
Butter, Plum, '88 152
Chutney, Plum, '84 179
Cobbler, Crunchy Plum, '88 152
Crunch, Layered Plum, '86 174
Fajitas, Plum Good, '94 115
Ham, Plum, '80 110
Jam, Freezer Plum, '89 M156
Jam, Peach-Plum Freezer, '85 130
Jam, Plum Refrigerator, '89 139
Jelly, Plum, '82 150
Kuchen, Plum, '79 161
Muffins, Plum Good, '83 96
Pie, Easy Plum Cream, '86 174
Pie, Streusel-Topped Plum, '88 153
Pie with Italian Sweet Crust, Plum,
    '79 162
Poached Plums, '90 M141
Pudding, Flamed Plum, '84 276
Pudding-Gelatin Mold, Plum, '86 300;
    '87 178
Pudding, Light Plum, '86 318
Pudding, Old-Fashioned Plum, '80 264
Pudding, Plum, '79 281
Sauce, Chinese Plum, '82 237
Sauce, Fresh Plum, '94 129
Sauce, Gingered Plum, '87 175
Sauce, Plum, '80 249; '82 40; '88 152
Sauce, Quail with Red Plum, '80 48
Sauce, Spicy Plum, '86 11
Slush, Plum, '84 139
Soup, Chilled Purple Plum, '79 162
Soup, Peach-Plum, '87 157
Soup, Plum, '85 107

Popcorn

Bacon-Cheese Popcorn, '86 74
Balls, Marshmallow Popcorn, '90 226
Balls, Nutty Popcorn, '88 227
Cake, Popcorn-Gumdrop, '87 262
Candied Popcorn and Peanuts, '82 295
Caramel Corn, '88 64
Caramel Corn, Baked, '81 218
Caramel Corn Candy, '84 243
Caramel Corn, Nutty, '92 317
Caramel Corn, Oven-Made, '91 233
Caramel Popcorn, '79 219; '86 M212
Caramel Popcorn, Crispy, '85 247
Chili Popcorn, '91 17
Cinnamon-Popcorn Crunch, '86 136
Garlic Popcorn, '83 M315
Ghoul's Hands, '94 256
Harvest Popcorn, '84 300
Herb-Seasoned Popcorn, '94 122
Honey-and-Spice Crunch, '94 290
Mix, Curried Popcorn, '86 326
Nutty Popcorn, '85 208
Orange Popcorn, '86 230
Oriental Popcorn, '86 74
Pizza-Flavored Popcorn, '85 236
Pizzazz, Popcorn with, '93 245
Pretzel Popcorn, '84 30
Scramble, Popcorn, '87 185

Sesame-Cheese Popcorn, '79 220
Spiced Popcorn Snack, '87 8

Pork. *See also* Bacon, Ham, Sausage.

Backbones, Smoked Country-Style, '82 162
Bake, Pork-and-Noodle, '88 98
Bake, Pork Spaghetti, '81 11

Barbecue

    Bannister's Barbecue, '92 166
    Chops, Barbecued Pork, '81 10
    Chops, Marinated Barbecued Pork,
       '79 90
    Chops, Oven-Barbecued Pork, '81 234;
       '82 26; '83 40
    Home-Style Barbecue, '88 145
    Pork, Barbecued, '80 72
    Ribs, Apple Barbecued, '80 111
    Ribs, Barbecued, '80 111; '85 159
    Ribs, Country-Style Barbecued, '79 42
    Ribs, Herbed Barbecued, '86 185
    Ribs, Oven-Barbecued Pork, '88 132
    Ribs, Smoky Barbecued, '80 111
    Ribs, Tangy Barbecued, '83 160
    Roast, Barbecued Pork, '82 11
    Roast, Barbecue Pork, '82 97; '83 104
    Roast, Berry Barbecued Pork, '80 288
    Shoulder, Barbecued Pork, '81 111;
       '82 11
    Spareribs, Barbecued, '81 112; '82 12;
       '86 232
    Spareribs, Barbecued Country-Style,
       '80 73
    Spareribs, Easy Barbecued, '82 97;
       '83 104
    Spareribs, Saucy Barbecued, '79 14
    Spareribs, Southern Barbecued, '79 90
    Spareribs, Spicy Barbecued, '84 93
    Spareribs, Tangy Barbecued, '82 106
    Spareribs with Orange Barbecue Sauce,
       '83 11
    Spicy Barbecued Pork, '84 296

Bean Sauce, Pork-and-Onions with, '85 76
Brunch Eggs, '85 44
Burgers, Hearty Sauced Pork, '84 125
Burgoo, Five-Meat, '87 3
Burgoo, Harry Young's, '87 3
Burritos, '80 196
Burritos, Meat-and-Bean, '81 194
Calabaza Guisada con Puerco (Pumpkin
    Cooked with Pork), '80 193
Casserole, Cheesy Pork, '81 M74
Casserole, Pork, '83 116
Chalupa, Bean, '80 223
Chalupas, Pork, '83 160
Chile Verde, Light, '88 148
Chili, Double-Meat, '79 269; '80 12

Chops

    Apple-Kraut Pork Chops, '84 50
    Apple Pork Chops, '91 198
    Apple Pork Chops, Spicy, '87 230
    Apricot-Sauced Pork Chops, '85 22
    Arlo, Pork, '87 229
    Baked Pork Chops and Apples, '81 10
    Bake, Fiesta Pork, '79 265
    Beans, Pork Chops with Baked, '93 18
    Braised Pork Chops, Bourbon-, '85 89
    Broiled Pork Chops, '89 191
    Broiled Pork Chops with Crabapple
      Peaches, '81 83
    Carne Adovada, '91 162
    Casserole, Peppered Pork Chop,
      '81 235; '82 25; '83 39

Casserole, Pork Chop, '94 255
Cheesy Pork Chops, '83 102
Chili Chops, '87 10
Cider-Sauced Pork Chops, '86 213;
    '87 81
Company Pork Chops, '85 109
Costillas Rellenos (Stuffed Pork Chops),
    '82 219
Country Pride Pork Chops, '79 159
Cranberry Pork, '90 293
Cranberry Pork Chops, '80 288; '90 53
Creamy Gravy, Pork Chops and, '81 207
Creole Pork Chops, '83 102
Creole-Style Pork Chops, '91 49
Curried Apricot Pork Chops, '89 191
Dill-Cream Gravy, Pork Chops with,
    '84 81
Dinner, Pork Chop, '80 84; '81 180;
    '88 25
Fiesta, Pork Chops, '86 118
Fruited Pork Chops, '87 194
Fruit-Topped Pork Chops, '94 41
Glazed Apple Pork Chops, '86 300
Glazed Chops, Pineapple-Curry, '82 106
Glazed Pork Chops, '86 185
Glazed Pork Chops, Apple-, '84 212;
    '87 35
Glazed Pork Chops, Orange-, '81 234;
    '82 25; '83 39; '91 84
Glazed Pork Chops with Rice, Fruit-,
    '82 73
Glazed Pork Steaks, '83 178
Gourmet Pork Chops, '79 180
Gravy, Pork Chops in, '91 137
Grilled Pork Chops, '88 113
Grilled Pork Chops, Hawaiian, '85 159
Grilled Pork Chops, Marinated, '81 110
Hawaiian Pork Chops, '86 212; '87 82
Honey-Lime Pork Chops, '91 33
Italiano, Pork Chops, '80 72
Italian, Pork Chops, '79 47
Jardinière, Pork Chops, '81 112; '82 12
Lemon-Herb Pork Chops, '84 81;
    '89 M132
Lemony Pork Chops, '88 118
Marinated Pork Chops, '89 249
Meal for Two, Pork Chop, '81 273
Mustard-Apricot Pork Chops, '89 225
Orange-Cranberry Pork Chops, '86 335;
    '87 84
Orange-Glazed Pork Chops, '84 234
Orange Pork Chops, '84 81
Oriental Pork Chops, '84 81; '90 212
Parmesan Pork Chops with Apples,
    '93 338
Peachy Pork Chops, '89 310
Peanut Sauce, Pork Chops with, '83 29
Pineapple Pork Chops, '87 M124
Pleasing Pork Chops, '79 125
Polynesian Pork and Pineapple, '83 102
Rice, Pork Chops and Spanish, '83 103;
    '85 293
Risotti, Pork Chops, '81 234; '82 26
Saucy Company Pork Chops, '83 102
Saucy Pork Chop, '86 M140
Sauerkraut, Pork Chops and, '88 98
Savory Pork Chops, '87 194
Scallop, Pork Chops and Potato, '82 114
Sherry-Apple Pork Chops, '88 40
Sherry, Chops in, '79 125
Skillet Dinner, Pork Chop, '79 125

Pork, Chops *(continued)*

Skillet Pork Chops, Easy, **'79** 255
Sour Cream Sauce, Pork Chops with, **'83** 102
Special, Pork Chop, **'79** 81
Stuffed Baked Pork Chops, **'79** 222; **'80** 64
Stuffed Chops, Barbecued, **'87** 229
Stuffed Pork Chops, **'84** 195; **'86** 89
Stuffed Pork Chops, Apple-, **'79** 125
Stuffed Pork Chops, Apple-Crumb, **'81** 234; **'82** 26; **'83** 39
Stuffed Pork Chops, Apricot-, **'86** 76; **'92** 219
Stuffed Pork Chops, Braised, **'87** 249
Stuffed Pork Chops, Cheese-, **'84** 81
Stuffed Pork Chops, Easy, **'81** 10
Stuffed Pork Chops, Fruit-, **'82** 136
Stuffed Pork Chops, Fruited, **'86** 197
Stuffed Pork Chops, Rice-, **'83** 102
Stuffed Pork Chops with Apricot Glaze, **'89** M36
Stuffed with Prunes, Pork Chops, **'84** 7
Sweet-and-Sour Pork Chops, **'83** 160
Vegetable Casserole, Pork Chop-, **'90** 208
Vegetable Pork Chops, Skillet, **'85** 179
Vegetables, Golden Chops with, **'89** 218
Vegetables, Pork Chops and Garden, **'88** 297
Chow Mein, Pork, **'80** 208; **'90** 101
Combo, Vegetable-Pork, **'85** 113
Curry, Hurry, **'79** 103
Cutlets, Apple-Glazed Pork, **'92** 181
Dinner, Pork-and-Noodles Skillet, **'88** 199
Egg Rolls, **'86** 81
Eggrolls, Shrimp and Pork, **'82** 240; **'83** 18
Eggs, Tulsa, **'87** 95
Hominy, Mexican, **'86** 255
Hot-and-Spicy Pork, **'81** 228
Kabobs, Spicy Pork, **'82** 182
Leg of Pork with Cranberry Glaze, **'88** 244
Loin Stuffed with Wild Rice, Pork, **'84** 35
Marinated Pork Strips, **'92** 219
Meatballs in Gravy, **'79** 136
Meatballs, Sauerkraut, **'86** 257
Meatballs, Tangy Hawaiian, **'79** 129
Meat Loaf
Family-Style Meat Loaf, **'93** 18
Glazed Ham Loaf, **'79** 187
Ham Loaf, **'79** 180
Italian Meat Loaf, **'79** 187
Mozzarella-Layered Meat Loaf, **'79** 71
Pineapple Upside-Down Ham Loaf, **'79** 253
Savory Meat Loaf, **'87** 216
Skillet Liver Loaf, **'80** 11
Stuffed Meat Loaf, **'79** 187
Supreme Ham Loaf, **'79** 242
Swedish Meat Loaf, **'81** 121
Triple Meat Loaf, **'79** 186
Veal Meat Loaf, **'93** 292
Meat Mixture, Basic, **'92** 241
Medaillons of Pork with Vegetables, **'88** 223
Oriental, Pork, **'81** 212
Paella, Chicken-Pork-Shrimp, **'82** 245
Pâté, Country, **'86** 66
Pâté en Croûte, **'86** 65
Pâté with Spinach and Cream, Pork, **'83** 224

Picadillo II, **'93** 72
Pies, Natchitoches Meat, **'84** 21; **'91** 241
Pie, Sombrero, **'81** 140
Pilaf, Fruited Pork, **'82** 246
Pineapple Pork, **'82** 60
Polynesian Pork, **'85** 78
Ribs
Apple-Barbecue Spareribs, **'90** 160
Baby Loin Back Ribs, John Wills's, **'90** 120
Baked Ribs, Easy, **'86** 20
Baked Ribs, Lemon, **'81** 166
Barbecued Ribs, **'91** 205
Barbecue Sauce, Ribs with Blender, **'90** 12
Chinese Spareribs, **'81** 10
Glazed Spareribs, **'88** 98
Glazed Spareribs, Honey-, **'82** 163
Glazed Spareribs, Orange-, **'84** 296
Glazed Spareribs, Peach-, **'86** 14
Grilled Ribs, Lemon, **'81** 154
Lemony Sweet Spareribs, **'80** 73
Oven Ribs, Smoky, **'81** 166
Plantation Ribs, **'84** 217
Puerco en Adobo, **'88** 116
Saucy Oven Spareribs, **'80** 207
Saucy-Sweet Ribs, **'81** 166
Smoked Ribs, **'88** 169
Smoked Ribs with Honey-Mustard Sauce, **'92** 168
Smoky Ribs, **'84** 172
Spicy Spareribs, **'89** 168
Stuffed Spareribs, Fruit-, **'79** 14
Sweet-and-Sour Ribs, **'89** M84
Sweet-and-Sour Spareribs, **'83** 21
Rice, Pork Fried, **'89** 99
Risotto, Pork, **'82** 60
Roasts
à l'Orange, Porc, **'80** 242
Apples and Mushrooms, Roast Pork Loin with, **'92** 218
Arista of Pork, **'81** 260
Barbecued Pork Loin Roast, **'93** 34
Braised Pork, Brown Sugar, **'84** 36
Chinese Roast Pork, **'91** 308
Crown Pork Roast, Stuffed, **'89** 272
Crown Roast of Pork, Royal, **'80** 252
Crown Roast of Pork, Stuffed, **'86** 323
Crown Roast of Pork with Cranberry-Sausage Stuffing, **'88** 49
Glazed Pork Loin, **'87** 229
Glazed Pork Roast, Cherry-, **'91** 84
Grilled Pork, Honey-and-Herb, **'90** 148
Grilled Pork Loin, Honey-, **'92** 219
Indonesian Pork Roast, **'81** 227
Italian Pork Roast, **'91** 238; **'92** 27
Loin of Pork, Roast, **'84** 276
Loin, Roast Pork, **'88** 221
Loin Roast with Red Currant Sauce, Pork, **'89** M84
Mandarin Pork Roast, **'83** 47
Marinated Pork Roast, **'80** 71; **'84** 260
Oven-Barbecued Pork Roast, **'91** 50
Pernil (Pork Roast), **'92** 157
Pineapple Pork Roast, **'79** 41
Pineapple Sweet-and-Sour Pork, **'82** 120
Rio Grande Pork Roast, **'84** 35, 296
Roasted Pork Loin with Mushrooms and Garlic, **'92** 301
Smoked Pork Loin Mahogany, **'91** 148
Smoked Pork Shoulder, **'82** 225

Spiced Cherry Sauce, Roast Pork with, **'89** 324
Stuffed Crown Pork Flambé, **'83** 263
Stuffed Pork Loin, Apricot-Pecan, **'94** 274
Stuffed Pork Loin Roast, Prune-, **'80** 29
Stuffed Pork Rib Roast, Sausage, **'94** 240
Stuffed Pork Roast, **'81** 111; **'82** 12; **'85** 229
Stuffed Pork Shoulder, **'81** 11
Stuffed Pork, Spinach-and-Herb, **'89** 193
Tomato Sauce, Pork Roast with, **'87** 249
Zesty Pork Roast, **'85** 179
Salad, Mandarin Pork-and-Spinach, **'88** M126
Salad, Oriental Pork, **'92** 140
Salad, "Pig in the Garden," **'92** 255
Salad, Pork-'n'-Bean, **'87** 83
Sandwiches, Party Pork, **'88** M273
Sausage, Pork, **'81** 55
Sauté, Plum Delicious Pork, **'89** 105
Sesame Pork Rounds, **'89** 122
Sloppy Joes, Pork, **'86** 294
Soup, Guadalajara, **'88** 30
Soup, Homemade, **'79** 198
Steaks, Herbed Pork, **'80** 72
Steaks, Peachy Pork, **'79** 166
Stew, Bama Brunswick, **'87** 4
Stew, Breeden Liles's Brunswick, **'91** 14
Stew, Brunswick, **'80** 264
Stew, Dan Dickerson's Brunswick, **'91** 16
Stew, Easy Brunswick, **'92** 280
Stew, Georgian Brunswick, **'92** 35
Stew, Pancho Villa, **'94** 44
Stew, Sonny Frye's Brunswick, **'87** 4
Stew, Virginia Ramsey's Favorite Brunswick, **'91** 16
Stir-Fried Pork, **'87** 51
Stir-Fried Pork in Garlic Sauce, **'84** 141
St. Tammany, Pork, **'82** 260
Swedish Porkburgers, **'79** 42
Sweet-and-Pungent Pork, **'86** 118
Sweet-and-Sour Pork, **'79** 42; **'80** 72, 227; **'81** 26, 104, 111; **'82** 12; **'84** 218; **'85** 34, 194; **'86** 241; **'90** 317; **'92** 219
Tamales, **'80** 195
Tamales, Hot, **'83** 51
Tempting Twosome, **'81** 240
Tenderloin
Apple-Ginger Pork Tenderloin, **'86** 75
Blue Cheese, Pork Tenderloin with, **'86** 76
Curried Pork Tenderloin, **'86** 76
Danish Pork Tenderloin, **'82** 186
Glazed Pork Tenderloin, **'90** 315
Grilled Marinated Pork Tenderloin, **'91** 199
Grilled Pork Tenderloin, **'88** 98; **'91** 163; **'94** 88
Grilled Pork Tenderloin, Garlic, **'90** 172
Grilled Pork Tenderloins, **'94** 158
Grilled Pork Tenderloin with Brown Sauce, **'89** 32
Grilled Pork with Salsa, **'90** 128
Grilled Tenderloins, Honey-, **'92** 199
Marinated Pork Tenderloin, **'84** 175
Marsala, Pork, **'90** 35
Medaillons, Grilled Pork, **'93** 229
Medaillons in Mustard Sauce, Pork, **'90** 96

Pork, Tenderloin *(continued)*

Medaillons with Chutney Sauce, Pork, '87 35
Mustard Sauce, Pork Tenderloin with, '92 302
Orange Marmalade, Pork Tenderloin with, '91 49
Parmigiana, Easy Pork, '94 57
Peking Pork Tenderloin, '93 173
Picatta, Pork Tenderloin, '86 76
Piccata, Pork, '94 57
Pinwheels, Herbed Pork, '92 23
Pinwheels, Spinach-Tenderloin, '89 M118
Platter, Tenderloin, '79 42
Roast Pork Tenderloin, '84 35
Sandwiches, Beef and Pork Tenderloin, '80 175
Scaloppine Marsala, Pork, '94 57
Scaloppine, Olive-Pork, '89 191
Stuffed Pork Tenderloins, Fruit-, '87 270
Stuffed Pork Tenderloin, Spinach-and-Bacon, '94 81
Sunrise Pork Tenderloin, '79 103
Towers, Pork Tenderloin, '86 75
Terrine, Jeweled Pork, '84 130
Terrine of Pork and Veal, '93 287
Wontons, Crispy Fried, '83 21

Potatoes
Appetizers, Potato Shell, '89 M119
au Gratin, Potatoes, '93 90, 217
au Gratin, Potatoes and Eggs, '79 107
au Gratin, Potatoes-and-Zucchini, '84 5
au Gratin, Shredded Potatoes, '89 69
Bacon Dressing, Potatoes with Hot, '88 M294
Bake, Chive-Potato, '82 229
Bake, Creamy Potato, '82 201; '88 41
Baked
Avocado-Topped Potatoes, '83 3
Beef and Chicken-Topped Potatoes, Creamed, '83 210
Broccoli-and-Almond-Topped Potatoes, '83 3
Broccoli-Topped Baked Potatoes, '86 17
Cheese Potato Skins, '84 M239
Cheese Sauce, Baked Potatoes with, '83 239
Cheesy Frank-Topped Potatoes, '83 3
Cheesy Potato Skins, '82 78
Chili-Topped Potatoes, '83 3
Crabmeat-Topped Potatoes, '83 3
Frank-Filled Potatoes, '84 M11
Garden Potato Cups, '83 76
Garden-Topped Potatoes, '83 4
Mexican-Topped Potatoes, '83 3
Micro-Baked Potatoes, '81 M61
Million Dollar Potatoes, '83 210
Mushroom-Dill-Topped Potatoes, '86 41
Mushroom Filling in a Peel, '84 214
New Potatoes, Baked, '90 90
Oven-Baked Potatoes, Easy, '82 202
Pleated Potatoes, Baked, '93 54
Quick Baked Potatoes, '92 M134
Salmon-Topped Potatoes, '84 124
Skins, Baked Potato, '86 81
Sweet-and-Sour-Topped Potatoes, '83 4
Taco-Baked Potatoes, '84 119
Taco-Topped Potatoes, '93 M18
Bake, Ham-Potato-Pineapple, '93 302
Bake, Herbed Fish and Potato, '79 287; '80 34
Bake, Onion-Potato, '83 M195
Bake, Potato, '83 209
Bake, Potato-Broccoli-Cheese, '80 114
Bake, Potato-Tomato, '86 17
Barbecued Potatoes, '91 311; '92 26
Basil-Cheese Potatoes, '90 M316
Baskets, Potato, '86 193
Basque-Style Potatoes, '79 46
Beans and Potatoes, Down-Home, '85 254
Beets, Potato-Stuffed, '83 234
Biscuits, Potato-Bacon, '94 214
Bisque, Spinach-Potato, '86 66
Bread Dough, Potato Sourdough, '94 324
Bread, Old-Fashioned Potato, '86 57
Bread, Potato, '85 56
Bread, Potato Sourdough, '94 325
Breakfast, Farmer's, '81 44
Breakfast Potatoes, '91 68
Breakfast Potatoes, Mexican, '81 209
Broiled Marinated Potatoes, '93 54
Browned Potatoes, Quick, '82 M172
Brunch for a Bunch, '88 57
Candy, Potato, '79 273
Caraway Potatoes, '85 85
Caraway Potatoes, Cheesy, '86 17
Casserole, Cheesy Ham-and-Potato, '84 326
Casserole, Cheesy Potato, '80 244; '83 53; '92 229
Casserole, Cheesy Potato-Egg, '84 5
Casserole, Creamy Potato, '84 M113
Casserole, Easy Potato, '80 114
Casserole, Fluffy Potato, '80 268
Casserole, Ham-and-Potato, '83 M87
Casserole, Hash Brown Potato, '81 40
Casserole, Holiday Potato, '92 302
Casserole, Irish Potato, '81 263
Casserole, Italian, '80 81
Casserole, Mashed Potato, '85 296
Casserole, Mushroom-Potato, '84 5
Casserole, Potato, '87 190
Casserole, Potato Breakfast, '80 52
Casserole, Potato-Cheese, '79 101
Casserole, Potato-Eggplant, '87 166
Casserole, Processor Potato, '86 159
Casserole, Saucy Potato, '81 276
Casserole, Saucy Potato-Tomato, '79 46
Casserole, Sausage-Potato, '86 217
Caviar Potatoes, '84 80
Caviar Potatoes, Appetizer, '86 223
Charcoal Potatoes, '88 129
Cheese Dream, Potato-, '91 307
Cheese Potatoes, Creamy, '88 M146
Cheese Potatoes, Double-, '86 6
Cheese Potatoes, Two-, '80 114
Cheesy Potatoes, '82 211
Chicken Livers and Potatoes, '82 218
Chili-Cheese Potatoes, '90 M62
Chili, Savory Potato, '83 284
Chips, Homemade Potato, '82 25
Chive Potatoes, Cheesy, '79 46
Chives, Potatoes with, '81 M61
Chowder, Mushroom-Potato, '92 331
Chowder, Potato-Corn, '94 66
Christmas Potatoes, '88 252
Colcannon, '90 64
Cottage Potatoes, '89 69; '93 M92
Crab Burgers, Potato-Crusted, '94 139
Creamed Potatoes, '83 25
Cream-Wine Sauce, Potatoes in, '86 18
Creamy Potatoes and Broccoli, '92 61
Creamy Potatoes with Ham Bits, '87 191
Creole Potatoes, '87 138
Croquettes, Parmesan Potato, '84 210
Croquettes, Potato, '87 116
Deviled Potatoes, Hot, '84 296; '85 196
Doughnuts, Chocolate-Glazed Potato, '85 6
Doughnuts, Old-Fashioned Potato, '84 56
Duchesse, Potatoes, '84 210
Duchess Potatoes, '93 288
Dumplings, Venison Stew with Potato, '87 304
Eggs and Meat, Potatoes with, '91 311; '92 26
Fans, Parmesan Potato, '84 M240
Feta Cheese, Potatoes with, '84 295; '85 196
Fish-and-Potato Platter, '89 M248
Fluffy Potatoes, '84 296; '85 196
French Fries, Herb, '82 211
French Fries, Oven, '91 122
Fried Potatoes, Almond-, '82 25
Fried Potatoes, Herb-, '82 25
Fried Potatoes, Oven-, '82 25
Fried Potatoes, Southern-, '82 25
Fried Potato Patties, '82 25; '93 54
Fries, Cheesy Oven, '91 187
Frittata, Potato, '89 145
Fry, Okra-Potato, '81 159
Garlic-Parsley Potatoes, '90 290
Garlic Potatoes, '84 296; '85 196
Gourmet, Potatoes, '80 114
Gratin, Dual Potato, '93 328
Green Beans and Potatoes, '91 221
Greens and Potatoes, Mustard, '86 224
Grilled Herb Potatoes, '84 172
Gruyère Potatoes, '83 193
Hash Brown Cheese Bake, '82 50
Hash Brown Potatoes, '81 48
Hash Browns, Company, '79 268; '80 14
Hash Browns, Franks and, '80 166
Hash Brown Skillet Breakfast, '82 5
Herb Butter, Potatoes with, '81 276
Herbed Potatoes, '91 220
Herb Potatoes, '88 134
Italiano, Potatoes, '89 174
Italian-Style Potatoes, '89 69
Jalapeño Potatoes, '84 39
Latkes, '84 318; '90 254
Lemon and Nutmeg Potatoes, '80 36
Lemony Potato Wedges, '90 M61
Lightbread, Potato, '80 225
Loaves, Potato, '86 162
Lorraine, Potatoes, '87 190

Potatoes *(continued)*

Mashed Potatoes, Basic, '92 330
Mashed Potatoes, Blue Cheese, '92 330
Mashed Potatoes, Chive-Cream Cheese, '92 330
Mashed Potatoes, Dill-Sour Cream, '92 330
Mashed Potatoes, Feta, '92 330
Mashed Potatoes, Fix-Ahead, '89 70
Mashed Potatoes, Garlic, '92 330; '93 328
Mashed Potatoes, Good Old, '92 215
Mashed Potatoes, Herbed Lemon, '93 208
Mashed Potatoes, Jazzy, '87 192
Mashed Potatoes, Mexican, '92 330
Mashed Potatoes, Old-Fashioned, '89 234
Mashed Potatoes, Pesto, '92 330
Mashed Potatoes, Quick-and-Easy, '93 41
Mashed Potato Nests, '94 141
Medley, Potato, '92 61
Mexican-Style Potatoes, '91 78
Missy Potatoes, '85 259
Moussaka, Potatoes, '93 44
Mustard Potatoes, '79 32
Nest, Peas in a Potato, '84 M239
Nests with Savory Shavings, Potato, '84 209
New Potatoes, Browned, '86 244
New Potatoes, Cheesy, '85 156
New Potatoes, Creamed Peas and, '79 102
New Potatoes, Garden, '91 80
New Potatoes, Garlic, '92 54
New Potatoes, Green Beans with, '87 164
New Potatoes, Ham-Stuffed, '88 211
New Potatoes, Herbed, '81 102; '83 9, M148
New Potatoes, Lemon-Buttered, '84 149; '90 268
New Potatoes, Lemony, '82 158
New Potatoes, Parsley, '79 122
New Potatoes, Roasted, '90 138
New Potatoes, Seasoned, '87 M151
New Potatoes with Basil Cream Sauce, '91 46
New Potatoes with Lemon Sauce, '86 130
New Potatoes with Parsley-Chive Sauce, '84 212
New Potato Medley, '90 279
Olive Potatoes, '80 114
Omelet, Family-Size Potato, '94 31
Omelet, Potato-Sprout, '79 128
Omelets, Country, '91 128
Oven Potatoes, Crispy, '82 96
Pancake, Potato, '85 20
Pancakes, Moist Potato, '80 36
Pancakes, Potato, '79 115; '89 144
Parmesan Potatoes, '82 270; '90 M62; '92 M341; '93 M46
Parmesan-Potato Fans, '88 M190
Parslied Potatoes, '86 18
Patties, Thunderbolt Potato, '94 213
Peppers, Potatoes with Sweet Red, '87 192
Pie, Country Breakfast, '93 M328
Pie, Meat-and-Potato, '84 23
Pie, Potato-Topped Turkey, '86 265
(Plantain Chips), Tostones de Platano, '92 158
Potage, Subtle Potato, '80 78
Pudding, Carrot-Potato, '94 279
Puffs, Celeried Potato, '89 279
Puffs, Potato, '80 36
Quiche, Crustless Potato, '83 49

Quick Potatoes, '94 283
Roasted Potatoes, Carrots, and Leeks, '94 276
Rolls, Easy Potato, '89 287
Rolls, Feathery Light Potato, '81 305; '82 36
Rolls, Homemade Potato, '82 252
Rolls, Potato, '81 300
Rolls, Potato Sourdough, '94 325
Rolls, Potato Yeast, '87 53
Rolls, Refrigerated Potato, '83 254
Rolls, Refrigerator Potato, '87 15
Rolls, Southern Potato, '86 299
Rolls, Super Potato, '85 145
Rolls, Supreme Potato, '82 130
Rolls, Whole Wheat Potato, '89 50
Rosemary, Potatoes Anna with, '84 209
Roses, Potato, '81 246
Sage Potatoes, '94 320
Salads
 Any Day Potato Salad, '81 154
 Bacon-Topped Potato Salad, '85 59
 Basil Potato Salad, '94 178
 Bean Salad, Potato-, '82 301
 Blue Cheese-Potato Salad, '91 208
 Broccoli-Potato Salad, Hot, '85 23
 Chunky Potato Salad, '81 M138
 Confetti Potato Salad, '80 5; '88 16
 Corned Beef-Potato Salad, '85 213
 Corned Beef Salad, Potato-, '81 36
 Cottage Cheese-Potato Salad, '79 147, 285
 Creamy Potato Salad, '80 178; '88 171; '92 241
 Deluxe Potato Salad, '80 155
 Dill-and-Sour Cream Potato Salad, '93 105; '94 100
 Dill Potato Salad, '85 213; '94 179
 Dill Potato Salad, Hot, '79 78
 Dutch Potato Salad, Hot, '86 297; '87 176
 Festive Potato Salad, '89 315
 Fish-Potato Salad, Smoked, '84 233
 French-Style Potato Salad, '88 171
 Fruity Potato Salad, '85 214
 Garden Patch Potato Salad, '84 82
 German Potato Salad, '82 134, 239; '84 18; '92 169
 German Potato Salad, Hot, '79 78; '94 254
 German-Style Potato Salad, '83 23; '88 M194
 Grecian Potato Salad, '82 55
 Green Bean-Potato Salad, '83 80
 Ham-and-Egg Potato Salad, '86 84
 Ham and Potato Salad, '80 272
 Herbed Potato Salad, '87 171; '94 164
 Hot-and-Light Potato Salad, '93 90
 Hot Potato Salad, '79 78; '81 276; '86 10
 Hot Potato Salad Supreme, '79 78
 Layered Creamy Potato Salad, '81 23
 Marinated Potato Slices, '93 98
 Mustard Potato Salad, '86 302
 New Potato Salad, '84 120, 139; '94 162
 New Potato Salad, Asparagus-and-, '86 69
 Olive-Potato Salad, '85 114
 Parmesan Potato Salad, Hot, '79 78
 Parslied Potato Salad, '85 240
 Patio Potato Salad, '90 160

 Pepper Cups, Potato Salad in, '79 78
 Peppers, Potato Salad 'n', '83 135
 Pesto Potato Salad, '90 164
 Pickle-Potato Salad, Sweet, '85 213
 Pole Bean-Potato Salad, Hot, '79 74
 Potato Salad, '90 122; '94 160
 Red Potato Salad, '93 119
 Salmon-Potato Salad, '87 285
 Saucy Potato Salad, '87 123
 Savory Potato Salad, '80 30
 Sour Cream Potato Salad, '79 104; '80 79
 Sour Cream-Potato Salad, '84 149
 South-of-the-Border Potato Salad, '94 178
 Spring Salad, Mediterranean, '80 148
 Sugar Snap Peas, Potato Salad with, '91 120
 Sweet and Sour Potato Salad, '80 152
 Sweet-and-Sour Potato Salad, '92 106
 Tri Club Potato Salad, '92 166
 Tuna-Potato Salad, '84 289
Saucy Potatoes for Company, '82 202
Scalloped Potatoes, '82 300; '83 211; '92 48
Scalloped Potatoes and Turnips, '85 235
Scalloped Potatoes, Cheesy, '83 82
Scalloped Potatoes, Light, '89 311
Scalloped Potatoes, Mushroom, '87 191
Scalloped Potatoes, Party, '87 191
Scalloped Potatoes, Skillet, '79 46
Scalloped Potatoes, Special, '88 162
Scalloped Potatoes, Wayside, '79 283
Scalloped Potatoes with Pimiento, '81 75
Scalloped Potatoes with Sweet Marjoram and Parmesan Cheese, '91 246
Scallop, Pork Chops and Potato, '82 114
Seasoned Potatoes, '87 253
Shavings, Savory, '84 209
Shoestring Potato Tuna Bake, '82 211
Shrimp-Sauced Potatoes, '81 M61
Skillet Potatoes, Oregano-and-Lemon, '93 54
Skillet Potatoes, Peppy, '86 110
Skillet, Potato-Vegetable, '92 61
Skins, Baked Potato, '86 81
Skins, Cheesy Potato, '82 78
Skin Snack, Potato, '91 18
Slims, Potato, '81 276
Snow-Capped Potatoes, '84 255
Soufflé, Cheesy Potato, '89 332
Soufflé Potatoes, '84 295; '85 196; '90 14
Soup, Asparagus-Potato, '85 23
Soup, Baked Potato, '91 311; '92 26
Soup, Celery-and-Potato, '84 279
Soup, Cheesy Potato-and-Wild Rice, '89 16
Soup, Chilled Cucumber-Potato, '85 93
Soup, Cold Potato-Cucumber, '88 160
Soup, Cream of Potato, '80 M224; '82 21
Soup, Creamy Onion-and-Potato, '92 51
Soup, Creamy Potato, '81 19, 98; '84 112
Soup, Easy Potato, '92 17
Soup, Golden Cream of Potato, '86 302
Soup, Holiday Potato, '79 236
Soup, Leek-and-Potato, '84 112
Soup, Potato, '82 278; '83 292; '92 263
Soup, Potato-Bacon, '84 M38
Soup, Potato-Beet, '88 156
Soup, Potato-Carrot, '88 297
Soup, Potato-Pea, '94 90
Soup, Potato-Yogurt, '92 217
Soup, Sausage-Potato, '80 25
Soup, Special Potato, '82 3

Potatoes (continued)

Soup, Three-Potato, **'86** 16
Sour Cream Potatoes, **'84** 39
Sourdough Cinnamon Rolls, Potato,
  '94 325
Sourdough Starter, Potato, **'94** 324
Special Potatoes, **'83** 169
Starter Food, **'94** 324
Steak 'n Potatoes, Skillet, **'81** 18
Steamed Potatoes, Lemon-, **'86** 177
Stew, Potato-Oyster, **'89** 243
Stir-Fry, Potato, **'93** 240
Stir-Fry, Potato-Snow Pea, **'86** 173
Stuffed
  Alfredo, Potatoes, **'89** 204
  Bacon-Stuffed Potatoes, **'86** 193
  Bacon-Stuffed Potatoes, Cheesy,
    '81 M61
  Bacon-Topped Blue Cheese Potatoes,
    '79 46
  Baked Potatoes, Stuffed, **'83** 322
  Baked Stuffed Potatoes, **'84** 38
  Béchamel Sauce, Stuffed Potatoes with,
    '84 M239
  Blue Cheese Stuffed Potatoes, **'81** 276;
    '92 M228
  Blue Cheese-Stuffed Potatoes, **'89** 69
  Broccoli-Shrimp Stuffed Potatoes,
    '92 M228
  Cheese Sauce, Stuffed Potatoes with,
    '87 192
  Chicken-Cheese Stuffed Potatoes,
    '86 55
  Chive-Stuffed Baked Potatoes, **'79** 52
  Chive-Stuffed Potatoes, Cheesy,
    '91 128
  Chive-Stuffed Potatoes, Creamy,
    '80 268
  Crab-Stuffed Potatoes, **'91** 311;
    '92 26
  Crab-Stuffed Potatoes, Cheesy, **'86** 17
  Creamy Stuffed Baked Potatoes,
    '86 55
  Creamy Stuffed Potatoes, **'79** 211
  Fish-Stuffed Potatoes, **'92** 306
  Fluffy Stuffed Potatoes, **'86** 223
  Franks and Potatoes, Stuffed, **'81** 202
  Ham Stuffed Potatoes, **'79** 210
  Hearty Stuffed Potatoes, **'89** M282
  Herb Stuffed Potatoes, **'79** 211
  Jalapeño-Ham Stuffed Potatoes,
    '81 M61
  Lemon-Herb Stuffed Potatoes, **'83** 173
  Mexican-Stuffed Potatoes, **'91** 131
  Patchwork Potatoes, **'86** 54
  Potatoes, Stuffed, **'89** 173
  Roquefort, Potatoes, **'79** 211
  Savory Stuffed Potatoes, **'81** 101
  Shrimp Boats, **'79** 57
  Shrimp-Stuffed Potatoes, Creamy,
    '80 36
  South-of-the-Border Stuffed Potatoes,
    '86 54
  Tuna Stuffed Potatoes, **'79** 210
  Twice Baked Cottage-Style Potatoes,
    '91 135
  Twice-Baked Potato, **'90** M295
  Twice-Baked Potatoes, **'83** 227;
    '91 185

Vegetable-Topped Stuffed Potatoes,
    '85 235
  Yogurt-Stuffed Potatoes, **'88** 24
  Zesty Stuffed Potatoes, **'94** M46
Summertime Potatoes, **'86** M195
Tacos, Breakfast, **'91** 316
Thunderbolt Potatoes, **'94** 213
Toast, Potato-Crusted Texas, **'94** 142
Topping, Mashed Potato, **'89** 243
Tortilla Campesina, **'89** 85
Tortilla Española, **'92** 175
Turnips and Potatoes, **'79** 254
Turnips, Southern, **'87** 190
Vichyssoise, **'86** 181
Vinaigrette, Potato-Broccoli, **'85** 84
Wedges, Beer-Batter Potato, **'83** 211
Wedges, Lemon Potato, **'88** 21
Wedges, Potato, **'94** M119
Whipped Celery Potatoes, **'94** 305
Yeast, Potato, **'87** 53

Potatoes, Sweet
Applesauce Sweet Potatoes, **'91** 292;
    '92 256
Apple Shells, Sweet Potatoes in, **'85** 206
Apple-Stuffed Sweet Potatoes, **'88** 207
Apricot Glaze, Sweet Potatoes with, **'89** 331
Apricot Sweet Potatoes, **'82** 228
Bake, Holiday Sweet Potato, **'90** 291
Bake, Southern Sweet Potato, **'85** 229
Bake, Sweet Potato, **'80** 287
Bake, Sweet Potato-Apple, **'83** 25; **'86** 282
Bake, Sweet Potato-Apricot, **'85** 206
Bake, Sweet Potato-Orange, **'83** 226
Balls, Sweet Potato, **'86** 312
Biscuits, Sweet Potato, **'80** 287; **'84** 140;
    '89 210
Biscuits, Sweet Potato Angel, **'93** 312
Boats, Sweet Potato, **'80** 287
Boniato Chips, **'92** 247
Bourbon Sweet Potatoes, **'86** 324; **'87** 280
Bread Pudding, Sweet Potato, **'94** 241
Broiled Sweet Potatoes, Coconut-, **'84** 231
Cake, Sweet Potato, **'79** 207; **'89** 295
Cake, Sweet Potato Loaf, **'81** 224
Cake, Sweet Potato Pound, **'83** 85
Cake, Sweet Potato Surprise, **'80** 287
Candied Sweet Potatoes, **'79** 9, 251;
    '86 111; **'88** 207
Casserole, Glazed Sweet Potato, **'90** 250
Casserole, Pear-Sweet Potato, **'86** 280
Casserole, Sweet Potato, **'79** 289; **'80** 26;
    '85 256; **'89** 279
Casserole, Sweet Potato-and-Apple, **'94** 280
Casserole, Sweet Potato-Banana, **'86** 276
Casserole, Sweet Potatoes-and-Apple,
    '90 228
Casserole, Sweet Potatoes-and-Berries,
    '84 231
Casserole, Sweet Potato-Rum, **'84** 231
Cheesecake, Sweet Potato, **'80** 287
Cheesecake, Yam, **'81** 224
Chips, Sweet Potato, **'91** 138; **'93** 332
Chips with Blue Cheese, Sweet Potato,
    '93 290
Coconut-Orange Sweet Potatoes, **'84** 252
Croquettes, Sweet Potato, **'81** 223
Cups, Sunshine Sweet Potato, **'82** 195
Delight, Sweet Potato, **'86** 335; **'87** 83
Festive Sweet Potatoes, **'80** 244
Fried Sweet Potatoes, **'83** 226
Fried Sweet Potatoes, French-, **'81** 223

Fried Sweet Potato Strips, **'94** 238
Fritters, Golden Sweet Potato, **'79** 9
Fritters, Sweet Potato, **'88** 44
Glazed Sweet Potatoes, **'85** 206; **'89** 274
Glazed Sweet Potatoes, Apple-, **'82** 303
Glazed Sweet Potatoes, Apricot-, **'81** 295
Glazed Sweet Potatoes, Orange-, **'81** 223;
    '83 280
Glazed Sweet Potatoes, Tropical, **'83** 226
Gravy, Roast Duck with Sweet
    Potato-Eggplant, **'83** 90
Grilled Sweet Potatoes, **'93** 213
Hash, Sweet Potato, **'92** 337
Mashed Sweet Potatoes, **'85** 25
Muffins, Sweet Potato, **'81** 224; **'85** 6;
    '87 280; **'92** 31
Muffins, Yam, **'79** 7
Orange-Baked Sweet Potatoes, **'88** M294
Orange Cups, Sweet Potatoes in, **'82** 272
Orange Cups, Sweet Potato-Stuffed, **'81** 223
Orange Sweet Potatoes, **'86** 279
Oven-Fried Sweet Potatoes with Chutney,
    '93 241
Pancakes, Sweet Potato, **'87** 280
Peaches, Sweet Potatoes and, **'86** 11
Peanut Crust, Sweet Potatoes with, **'93** 212
Pie, Carolina Sweet Potato, **'89** 295
Pie, Louisiana Yam, **'81** 223
Pie, No-Crust Sweet Potato, **'84** 236
Pie, Old-Fashioned Sweet Potato, **'79** 9
Pie, Southern Sweet Potato Cream, **'87** 260
Pie, Speedy Sweet Potato, **'90** 219
Pie, Sweet Potato, **'79** 207; **'85** 255, 275;
    '86 269; **'89** 289
Pie, Sweet Potato Meringue, **'81** 126;
    '83 225
Pie, Sweet Potato-Orange, **'88** 207
Pie, Sweet Potato-Pecan, **'83** 90
Pie, Sweet Potato Pone, **'80** 288
Pudding, Sweet Potato, **'79** 244; **'80** 228;
    '86 52
Puffs, Peach Sweet Potato, **'87** 280
Puffs, Sweet Potato, **'87** 253
Puff, Sweet Potato, **'85** 235
Puree, Carrot-and-Sweet Potato, **'94** 56
Puree, Carrot-Sweet Potato, **'92** 90
Puree, Sweet Potato, **'92** 306
Raspberry Sweet Potatoes, **'87** 280
Rolls, Sweet Potato, **'93** 172
Roll, Sweet Potato Log, **'82** 227
Royale, Sweet Potatoes, **'91** 250
Salad, Fresh Sweet Potato, **'86** 226
Salad, Hawaiian Ham-Sweet Potato, **'82** 232
Scallop, Yam-and-Apple, **'91** 199
Sherry and Walnuts, Sweet Potatoes with,
    '86 286
Slaw, Sweet Potato-Currant, **'93** 246
Soufflé, Sweet Potato, **'82** 286; **'86** 121;
    '93 325
Soup, Sweet Potato, **'88** 250
Stuffed Baked Sweet Potatoes, **'79** 207;
    '84 231
Stuffed Sweet Potatoes, **'86** 224
Stuffed Sweet Potatoes, Bacon-, **'86** 224
Stuffed Sweet Potatoes, Coconut-, **'82** 204
Stuffed Sweet Potatoes, Fluffy, **'79** 9
Stuffed with Apples, Sweet Potatoes, **'82** 228
Supreme, Sweet Potato, **'94** 196
Surprise, Holiday Sweet Potato, **'84** 254
Surprise, Sweet Potato, **'81** 267
Tzimmes, Sweet Potato-Beef, **'92** 234

Potatoes, Sweet (*continued*)

Velouté, Sweet Potato, **'94** 238
Waffles, Sweet Potato, **'88** 208
Waffles with Orange Butter, Sweet Potato, **'90** 323
Yam Rolls, Golden, **'86** 299
Yams, Bourbon, **'90** 232
Yams, Brandied, **'94** 273
Yams Cointreau, **'92** 192
Yams, Cornwallis, **'79** 276
Yams, Rosemary-Garlic, **'93** 174

Pralines
Bananas, Praline, **'84** 313
Basic Pralines, **'92** 313; **'93** 50
Bourbon Pralines, **'92** 313; **'93** 51
Brownies, Praline, **'93** 243
Buns, Praline, **'90** 195
Butterscotch Pralines, **'81** 253
Café au Lait Pralines, **'92** 313; **'93** 51
Cake, Praline, **'81** 162
Cake, Praline Ice Cream, **'80** 84
Cake, Praline Pound, **'82** 88
Cheesecake, Praline, **'83** 270; **'89** 93
Chocolate-Mint Pralines, **'92** 313; **'93** 51
Chocolate-Peanut Butter Pralines, **'92** 313; **'93** 51
Chocolate Pralines, **'92** 313; **'93** 51
Clusters, Dark Praline, **'86** 313
Coffee, Praline-Flavored, **'87** 69
Coffee Pralines, Plantation, **'86** 241
Compote, Warm Praline Fruit, **'85** 260
Cookies, Praline, **'91** 271
Cookies, Praline Shortbread, **'88** 242
Cookies, Praline Thumbprint, **'89** 328
Creamy Pralines, **'80** 198; **'92** 289
Dark Pralines, **'83** 52
Delights, Spicy Praline, **'84** 299
Filling, Praline, **'89** 328
Freeze, Praline, **'89** 60; **'90** 48
Glaze, Praline, **'82** 196
Ham, Praline, **'85** 302
Hot Spicy Pralines, **'92** 313; **'93** 51
Ice Cream, Praline, **'89** 318
Ice Cream, Pralines and Cream, **'82** 184; **'83** 159
Maple-Pecan Pralines, **'83** 222
Mocha Pralines, **'92** 313; **'93** 51
New Orleans-Style Pralines, **'86** 335
Old-Fashioned Pralines, **'89** 318
Orange Pralines, **'92** 313; **'93** 51
Pastries, Praline, **'89** 318
Peanut Butter Pralines, **'92** 313; **'93** 51
Pecan Pralines, Original, **'81** 11
Pie, Chocolate-Praline, **'86** 259
Pie, Frosty Pumpkin-Praline, **'91** M234
Pie, Peach Praline, **'89** 136
Pie, Pumpkin Praline, **'80** 244
Pralines, **'79** 272; **'86** M288; **'89** 60; **'90** 48
Sauce, Bourbon Praline, **'81** 170
Sauce, Chocolate-Praline, **'85** M295
Sauce, Peach-Praline, **'85** 161
Sauce, Praline, **'83** 25; **'84** 143; **'89** 95; **'92** 282; **'93** 214; **'94** 206, 312
Sauce, Praline Ice Cream, **'85** 189
Sauce, Southern Praline Ice Cream, **'86** M227
Southern Pralines, **'79** M263
Texas-Size Pralines, **'79** 186
Toast, Orange Praline, **'79** 36

Torte, Chocolate Praline, **'84** 165
Vanilla Pralines, **'92** 313; **'93** 51

Pretzels
Brownies, Saucepan Pretzel, **'85** 171
Chocolate-Covered Pretzels, **'82** 295
Dressing, Pretzel, **'86** 280
Frosted Pretzels, **'92** 280
Garlands, Pretzel, **'93** 286
Herb Pretzels with Lower Sodium Horseradish Mustard, **'86** 325
Homemade Pretzels, **'84** 159; **'91** 185
Popcorn, Pretzel, **'84** 30
Soft Pretzels, **'83** 18
Soft Pretzels, Chewy, **'87** 159
Whole Wheat Pretzels, **'89** 20

Prunes
Bavarian, Prune, **'86** 223
Bread, Prune-Nut, **'87** 255; **'91** 55
Butter, Prune-Orange, **'92** 49
Cake and Sauce, Prune, **'85** 118
Cake, Prune, **'85** 223
Cake, Spicy Prune, **'79** 136
Compote, Baked Prune, **'94** 50
Muffins, Miniature Prune, **'85** 223
Muffins, Wheat Germ-Prune, **'81** 106
Pork Chops Stuffed with Prunes, **'84** 7
Pork Loin Roast, Prune-Stuffed, **'80** 29
Raspberry Prunes, **'82** 124
Relish, Peppy Prune, **'90** 227
Spiced Prunes, Orange-, **'85** 224
Stuffed Prunes, **'85** 47
Tarts, Brandied Prune, **'85** 223

Puddings. *See also* Custards.
Apple-Nut Pudding with Hot Rum Sauce, **'79** 86
Applesauce-Graham Cracker Pudding, **'81** 34
Banana-Mallow Pudding, **'86** 139
Banana Pudding, **'82** 53; **'84** 94; **'85** 255; **'88** 16, 32
Banana Pudding, Almost, **'88** 174
Banana Pudding, Basic, **'81** 59
Banana Pudding, Creamy, **'89** M130
Banana Pudding, Delicious, **'80** 9
Banana Pudding, No-Bake, **'91** 172
Banana Pudding, Old-Fashioned, **'92** 94
Banana Pudding, Surprise, **'86** 7
Biscuit Pudding, **'79** 86; **'93** 51
Blackberry Pudding Tarts, **'93** 200
Bread Pudding, **'89** M130; **'90** 219
Bread Pudding, Amish, **'80** 8
Bread Pudding, Apple-Raisin, **'88** 175
Bread Pudding, Apricot, **'85** 24

Bread Pudding, Blueberry, **'88** 154
Bread Pudding, Cheesy, **'83** 68
Bread Pudding, Chocolate, **'80** 8
Bread Pudding, Chocolate Biscuit, **'94** 215
Bread Pudding, French, **'85** 231
Bread Pudding, Old-Fashioned, **'83** 213; **'88** 175
Bread Pudding, Old-Fashioned Lemon, **'88** 95
Bread Pudding, Peachy, **'88** 175
Bread Pudding, Raisin, **'94** 215
Bread Pudding, Spiced, **'93** 52
Bread Pudding, Sweet Potato, **'94** 241
Bread Pudding with Bourbon Sauce, Tennessee, **'93** 51
Bread Pudding with Rum Sauce, Old-Fashioned, **'88** 32
Bread Pudding with Whiskey Sauce, **'80** 58; **'90** 230; **'92** 93
Brownie Pudding, **'79** 265; **'80** 295
Brown Sugar-Pecan Pudding, **'86** M165
Butternut Squash Pudding, **'89** M313; **'90** M19
Cake, Carrot Pudding, **'83** 24
Cake, Danish Pudding, **'91** 269
Cake, Lemon Pudding, **'83** 106
Cake Pudding, Chocolate, **'81** 99
Cake Pudding, Hot Fudge Sundae, **'88** 167
Cake Pudding, Lemon, **'92** 96
Cake Pudding, Wine, **'79** 230
Carrot-Potato Pudding, **'94** 279
Cheese Pudding, Baked, **'86** 78
Chocolate-Almond Pudding, **'82** M142; **'88** 24
Chocolate Pudding, Creamy, **'83** 106
Chocolate-Rum Dessert, **'81** 247
Christmas Pudding, **'79** 230
Christmas Pudding, Flaming, **'85** 312
Christmas Pudding with Brandy Sauce, Baked, **'88** 279
Corn-Cheese Pudding, **'80** 244
Corn Pudding, **'79** 276; **'81** 128; **'86** 192; **'90** 219
Corn Pudding, Baked, **'83** 314
Corn Pudding, Creamy, **'81** 267
Corn Pudding, Easy, **'83** 280
Corn Pudding, Fresh, **'80** 157, 165; **'89** 172
Cranberry Pudding, **'84** 306
Frozen Ozark Pudding, **'88** 127
Fruit Pudding Compote, Fresh, **'86** 151
Fudge Pudding, Hot, **'81** 208
Hansel Pudding, **'80** 9
Holland Rusk Pudding, Yia Yia's, **'93** 124
Kugel, Nu Awlins, **'94** 229
Lemon Fluff Pudding, **'85** 304
Lemon Pudding, **'79** 86; **'81** 99
Lemon Pudding, Layered, **'82** 128
Mandarin-Almond Pudding, **'85** M12
Orange Custard Pudding, **'88** 174
Orange Pudding, **'81** 85; **'82** 111; **'83** 153
Orange-Tapioca Crème, **'82** M283
Peanut Butter-Banana Pudding, **'93** 340
Peanut Butter Pudding, **'85** 95; **'88** 32
Pecan-Mocha Pudding, **'89** M130
Persimmon Pudding, **'79** 206
Pineapple Pudding, **'80** 102
Plum Pudding, **'79** 281
Plum Pudding, Flamed, **'84** 276
Plum Pudding-Gelatin Mold, **'86** 300; **'87** 178
Plum Pudding, Light, **'86** 318

Puddings (continued)

Plum Pudding, Old-Fashioned, '80 264
Pumpkin Pudding, '89 M313; '90 M20
Pumpkin Pudding, Baked, '80 244
Raisin-Pumpkin Pudding, '84 315
Raisin-Rice Pudding, '87 46
Raspberry Pudding, '92 92
Rice Pudding, Amaretto, '86 334
Rice Pudding, Apple, '91 217
Rice Pudding, Brown, '85 77
Rice Pudding, Creamy, '81 51, 205
Rice Pudding, Fruited, '81 205; '86 95
Rice Pudding, Fudgy, '81 205
Rice Pudding, Old-Fashioned, '85 147
Rice Pudding, Velvety, '81 205
Rum Pudding with Raspberry Sauce, '82 288
Snowflake Pudding, '85 30
Snow White Pudding, '85 77
Squash Pudding, '82 277; '83 15
Steamed Date Pudding, '79 86
Steamed Holiday Pudding, '84 275
Steamed Mincemeat Pudding, '80 264
Sweet Potato Pudding, '79 244; '80 228;
   '86 52
Tipsy Pudding, Parson's, '80 156
Turnip Pudding, '94 213
Vanilla Pudding, '88 32
Vanilla Pudding, Creamy, '83 227
Woodford Pudding, '79 86
Yorkshire Pudding, '80 252
Pumpkin
Baked Pumpkin, '82 217
Bars, Pumpkin, '80 40
Bars, Pumpkin Nut, '82 217
Bisque, Spicy Pumpkin, '86 67
Bread, Harvest Pumpkin, '90 M215
Bread, Moist Pumpkin, '80 245
Bread, Orange-Pumpkin, '87 300
Bread, Pumpkin, '81 8
Bread, Pumpkin-Coconut, '87 255
Bread, Pumpkin-Nut, '83 294
Bread, Pumpkin-Pecan, '87 221
Bread, Spiced Pumpkin, '91 233
Bread with Cream Cheese and Preserves,
   Pumpkin, '84 264
Cake Bars, Pumpkin, '80 245
Cake, Pumpkin, '81 272; '93 303
Cake, Pumpkin Date, '79 251
Cake, Pumpkin Kahlúa, '86 292
Cake, Pumpkin Layer, '80 245
Cake, Pumpkin Pound, '92 235
Cake Squares, Orange-Pumpkin, '83 242
Calabaza Guisada con Puerco (Pumpkin
   Cooked with Pork), '80 193
Cheesecake, Pumpkin, '80 254; '85 280
Chiffon, Pumpkin, '82 216; '86 283; '88 260
Cooked Fresh Pumpkin, '88 M230
Cookies, Frosted Pumpkin-Walnut, '82 217
Cookies, Great Pumpkin, '91 234
Cookies, Jack-O'-Lantern, '87 214
Cookies, Peppy Pumpkin, '89 253
Cookies, Pumpkin-Chocolate Chip, '93 235
Cookies, Pumpkin Drop, '79 206
Cupcakes, Pumpkin, '85 121
Custard, Pumpkin, '88 279
Delight, Pumpkin-Orange, '86 321
Dessert, Frozen Pumpkin, '88 167
Dessert, Pumpkin Chiffon, '88 128
Doughnut Drops, Pumpkin, '90 323

Empanadas de Calabaza (Pumpkin
   Empanadas), '94 28
Empanadas, Pumpkin, '82 223
Flan, Pumpkin, '82 217
Gingerbread with Caramel Sauce, Pumpkin,
   '93 235
Loaf, Harvest Pumpkin, '85 232
Loaf, Pumpkin-Oatmeal, '81 49
Mold, Pumpkin, '82 311
Mousse, Pumpkin, '91 96; '92 130
Muffins, Monster, '94 256
Muffins, Nutty Pumpkin, '86 291
Muffins, Pumpkin, '79 206, 275; '81 272
Pancakes, Pumpkin, '80 228
Pie, Autumn Pumpkin, '87 213
Pie, Bourbon-Pecan Pumpkin, '87 264
Pie, Festive Pumpkin, '81 M269
Pie, Fluffy Pumpkin, '80 283
Pie, Frosty Pumpkin-Praline, '91 M234
Pie in Spiced Nut Crust, Pumpkin, '87 295
Pie, New-Fashioned Pumpkin, '90 296
Pie, Nutty Pumpkin, '82 67
Pie, Pumpkin Chiffon, '84 312
Pie, Pumpkin Ice Cream, '81 272
Pie, Pumpkin-Ice Cream, '87 243
Pie, Pumpkin-Pecan, '85 233, 282
Pie, Pumpkin Praline, '80 244
Pie, Quick Pumpkin, '88 M230
Pie, Rich Pumpkin, '86 292
Pie, Sour Cream-Pumpkin, '84 263
Pies, Spicy Pumpkin, '84 322
Pie Supreme, Pumpkin, '82 217
Pie, Traditional Pumpkin, '85 256
Pie with Meringue, Pumpkin, '92 268
Pudding, Baked Pumpkin, '80 244
Pudding, Pumpkin, '89 M313; '90 M20
Pudding, Raisin-Pumpkin, '84 315
Roll, Pumpkin, '79 206; '91 297
Rolls, Pumpkin, '87 254
Sauce, Pumpkin Seed, '88 246
Seeds, Seasoned Pumpkin, '91 234
Seeds, Toasted Pumpkin, '88 M230
Soup, Cream of Pumpkin, '93 234
Soup, Pumpkin, '79 48
Soup, Pumpkin-Pear, '92 234
Soup, Pumpkin-Tomato, '86 291
Swirl, Easy Pumpkin, '93 234
Tarts, No-Bake Pumpkin, '86 291
Waffles, Pumpkin-Nut, '86 96
Waffles with Mandarin Orange Sauce, Dessert
   Pumpkin, '89 204

Quail

Baked Quail with Cornbread Stuffing,
   '94 305
Baked Quail with Mushroom Gravy,
   '89 273
Baked Quail with Mushrooms, '81 259
Breasts, Southern Quail, '85 270
Currant Jelly Sauce, Quail with, '86 94
Foxfire Quail, '89 240
Fried Quail, '82 45
Fried Quail, Seasoned, '88 220
Fried Quail with Onion Gravy, '82 214
Gravy, Georgia Quail with, '87 240
Grilled Breakfast Quail, '88 220
Grilled Quail, '92 90
Hatcreek Quail, '89 270
J.W. Quail, '89 240

Magnificent, Quail, '82 214
Marinated Quail, '80 221
Mushrooms, Quail with, '85 138
Orange Sauce in Potato Baskets, Quail with,
   '86 193
Pepper Feet, '93 258
Plum Sauce, Quail with Red, '80 48
Smoked Quail, '93 236
Stuffed Quail, Hawkeye-, '89 241
Stuffed with Cornbread Dressing, Quail,
   '93 280
Superb, Quail, '81 303
Quiches
Artichoke Quiche, '91 71
Asparagus-Tomato Quiche, '88 198
Bacon-Cheese Quiches, Miniature, '83 93
Bacon Quiche, '85 60
Benedict Quiche, '80 M107
Blue Cheese Quiche, '84 52
Broccoli Quiche, Easy, '82 34
Broccoli Quiche, Italian, '85 45
Broccoli-Rice Quiche, '81 228
Cauliflower Quiche, '83 86
Cheddar-Leek Quiche, '88 198
Cheese Pie, Mexican, '83 69
Cheese Quiches, Miniature, '80 150
Cheese-Vegetable Quiche, '81 228
Chicken Divan Quiche, '88 M125
Chicken-Pecan Quiche, '91 206
Chile Pepper Quiche, '82 224
Chile Quiche, Green, '83 31
Clam Quiche, '83 215
Crab Quiche, '82 M122, 243
Crab Quiche, Almond-Topped, '79 127
Crab Quiche, Quick, '84 96
Crab Quiche, Sherried, '83 180
Crab Quiche, Simple, '85 207
Eggless Quiche, '87 220
Fiesta Quiche, '92 47
Ham-and-Grits Crustless Quiche, '94 89
Ham-and-Mushroom Quiche, '81 11
Ham-and-Vegetable Quiche, '84 326
Ham-Cheese Quiche, '79 26
Ham Quiche, '80 110
Ham Quiche, Cheesy, '79 127
Ham Quiche, Country, '87 287
Ham Quiche, Crustless, '84 235
Jalapeño-Corn Quiche, '85 122
Jalapeño Quiche, Cheesy, '84 31
Lorraine, Classic Quiche, '81 131
Lorraine, Mushroom-Quiche, '86 242
Lorraine, Peppery Quiche, '81 228
Lorraine, Perfect Quiche, '79 127
Lorraine, Quiche, '79 40; '80 M108
Mexicali Quiche with Avocado Topping,
   '93 309; '94 96
Mushroom Quiche, '80 222; '81 244;
   '89 285
Noël, Quiche, '82 310
Olive Quiche Appetizers, '86 159
Onion Quiche, '83 121
Onion Quiche, Cheesy Green, '83 194;
   '84 42
Pastry, Microwaved Quiche, '81 M74;
   '82 M123
Pastry, Quiche, '80 M107
Pizza Quiche, '86 53
Potato Quiche, Crustless, '83 49
Salmon Quiche, '82 87; '87 38
Sausage-Apple Quiche, Crustless, '87 70
Sausage-Cheddar Quiche, '79 26

Quiches *(continued)*

Sausage Quiche, Easy, '79 261
Sausage Quiche, Italian, '81 200
Sausage Quiche, Spicy, '80 M108
Shrimp Miniquiches, '87 146
Shrimp Quiche, '83 50
South-of-the-Border Quiche, '93 321
Spinach-Mushroom Quiche, '81 M74
Spinach Quiche, '81 44; '85 49; '91 204
Spinach Quiche, Cheesy, '81 228
Spinach Quiche, Crustless, '84 235
Spinach Quiche, Greek, '86 10
Spinach Quichelets, '87 67
Spinach Quiche, No-Crust, '90 142
Spinach Quiches, Individual, '86 38
Spinach Quiches, Miniature, '82 38
Springtime Quiche, '83 122
Squares, Cheesy Hot Quiche, '79 124
Squares, Quiche, '84 222
Squash-and-Green Chile Quiche, '88 143
Swiss Alpine Quiche, '90 18
Swiss-Zucchini Quiche, '82 49
Tarragon Cocktail Quiches, '84 127
Tasty Quiche, '82 264
Vegetable Quiche, '87 M219
Wild Rice-and-Mushroom Quiches, '93 237
Zucchini Frittata, '86 103
Zucchini-Mushroom Quiche, '79 127
Zucchini Pie, Italian-Style, '83 43
Zucchini Quiche, Cheesy, '83 312
Zucchini-Sausage Quiche, '83 122

Raisins

Bars, Raisin, '94 228
Biscuits, Buttermilk-Raisin, '92 338
Biscuits, Cinnamon-Raisin Breakfast,
  '93 159
Biscuits, Glazed Raisin, '89 210
Bread, Banana-Nut-Raisin, '81 59
Bread, Butternut-Raisin, '79 25
Bread, Caraway-Raisin Oat, '86 44
Bread, Cinnamon Raisin, '80 22
Bread, Curried Chicken Salad on Raisin,
  '85 96
Bread, Homemade Raisin, '87 300
Bread, Oatmeal Raisin, '81 14
Bread, Oatmeal-Raisin, '83 59
Bread, Raisin-Cranberry, '81 305; '82 36
Bread, Raisin-Whole Wheat, '93 77
Bread, Round Raisin, '89 230
Bread, Salt-Free Raisin Batter, '86 33
Buns, Rum-Raisin, '80 22
Butter, Raisin, '81 272
Cake, Cinnamon-Raisin Coffee, '93 180
Cake, Spicy Raisin Coffee, '88 63
Cake, Spicy Raisin Layer, '79 230
Carrots, Orange-Raisin, '80 24
Chocolate-Bran Raisin Jumbos, '91 142
Cookies, Alltime Favorite Raisin, '80 24
Cookies, Frosted Oatmeal-Raisin, '79 290
Cookies, Nugget, '79 291
Cookies, Oatmeal-Raisin, '87 221;
  '93 127
Cookies, Persimmon-Raisin, '85 232
Filling, Raisin, '90 86
Gingersnaps, Raisin, '85 324

Granola Gorp, '89 59
Granola Treats, Raisin-, '92 22
Gravy, Currant, '83 276
Ham, Raisin, '80 124
Mix, Raisin-Nut Party, '83 60
Muffins, Banana-Raisin, '89 218
Muffins, Breakfast Raisin, '84 59
Muffins, Carrot-and-Raisin, '87 24
Muffins, Cheddar-Raisin, '91 51
Muffins, Raisin English, '80 75
Muffins, Raisin-Nut, '92 46
Muffins, Raisin-Pecan Ginger, '88 9
Muffins, Whole Wheat Raisin, '85 207
Pastry Bites, Raisin, '90 86
Pie, Apple-Raisin Brandy, '89 58
Pie, Brandy Raisin-Apple, '83 192
Pie, Cranberry-Raisin, '80 283; '85 316
Pie, Peanut-Raisin, '79 85
Pie, Raisin, '83 220
Pie, Raisin-Pecan, '87 213
Pie, Rhubarb-Raisin, '79 112
Pie, Spiced Raisin, '84 148
Pudding, Apple-Raisin Bread, '88 175
Pudding, Raisin Bread, '94 215
Pudding, Raisin-Pumpkin, '84 315
Pudding, Raisin-Rice, '87 46
Pull-Aparts, Raisin Cinnamon, '82 205;
  '83 32
Relish, Raisin, '92 310
Rice with Curry, Raisin, '85 83
Rolls, Raisin Cinnamon, '81 107
Rolls, Raisin-Cinnamon, '91 240
Rollups, Sweet Raisin, '86 290
Salad, Carrot-Raisin, '83 117; '84 174;
  '87 10
Salad, Creamy Broccoli-Raisin, '92 106
Salad, Curried Apple-Raisin, '80 24
Sandwiches, Peanut-Cheese-Raisin, '88 140
Sandwich, Raisin Country, '91 168
Sauce, Baked Ham with Cranberry-Raisin,
  '88 244
Sauce, Caramel-Raisin, '88 127
Sauce, Ham with Raisin, '82 M76
Sauce, Raisin, '83 59, 215; '84 91, 275;
  '87 127; '89 58
Sauce, Raisin-Pineapple, '82 177
Sauce, Rum-Raisin, '84 7; '94 295
Scones, Currant, '84 117; '92 332
Scones, Lemon-Raisin, '87 69
Shake, Amazin' Raisin, '86 195
Slaw, Sweet Potato-Currant, '93 246
Spread, Creamy Raisin, '90 36
Spread, Peachy-Raisin, '86 326
Teacakes, Currant, '80 88

Raspberries
Appetizer, Orange-Berry, '85 81
Bars, Raspberry, '82 209; '84 212
Bavarian, Raspberry-Strawberry, '89 15
Biscuits, Raspberry-Almond, '93 160
Bisque, Banana-Raspberry, '93 161
Brie, Almond-Raspberry, '94 M89
Brie in Rye, Raspberry, '93 252
Brownies, Raspberry, '92 274
Cake, Chocolate-Raspberry, '92 173
Cake, Lemon-Raspberry, '91 247
Cake, Raspberry Coffee, '83 112
Cheesecake, Chocolate-Raspberry Truffle,
  '91 270
Chocolate Cups, Miniature, '87 132
Chocolates, Raspberry Cream, '91 36
Cobbler, Berry-Cherry, '83 270

Cobbler, Raspberry-Cherry, '93 230
Compote, Berry, '81 275
Compote, Berry-Peach, '82 133
Compote, Spicy Grapefruit-Berry, '91 19
"Concrete," Foxtreat, '94 113
Cookies, Raspberry Swirl, '90 111
Cooler, Raspberry, '89 171
Crêpes, Raspberry, '87 126
Crêpes Suzette, Raspberry, '84 84
Crêpes with Yogurt Filling, Fresh Raspberry,
  '93 123
Crisp, Raspberry-Pear, '89 109
Custard with Raspberries, Almond Crème,
  '88 174
Custard with Raspberries, Amaretto,
  '86 152
Dessert, Frozen Raspberry, '84 192
Dessert, Raspberry-Jellyroll, '85 95
Dessert, Raspberry Sauce, '80 147
Dream, Raspberry, '83 108
Dressing, Bibb Salad with Raspberry-Maple,
  '91 246
Dressing, Raspberry, '87 153
Dressing, Raspberry Cream, '94 321
Filling, Raspberry, '90 111
Fizz, Rosy Raspberry, '90 179
Fluff, Raspberry, '89 198
Glaze, Turkey Breast with Orange-
  Raspberry, '91 253
Granita, Raspberry Liqueur, '88 117
Ice Cream, Fresh Raspberry, '86 152
Ice Cream, Raspberry, '80 176
Ice, Raspberry, '92 268
Jam, Berry Refrigerator, '89 139
Jam, Raspberry Freezer, '84 M181
Jellyrolls, Raspberry, '93 M255
Kir, Raspberry, '86 183
Lemon Curd with Berries, '90 102
Mold, Raspberry Holiday, '84 253
Mounds, Raspberry Fruit, '79 35
Mousse in Chocolate Crinkle Cups,
  Raspberry, '93 270
Mousse, Raspberry, '81 34
Muffins, Lemon-Raspberry, '92 119
Napoleons, Berry, '94 120
Parfait, White Chocolate-Raspberry Swirl,
  '93 315
Party Puffs, Raspberry, '90 170
Pie, Cherry-Berry, '92 316
Pie, Cran-Raspberry, '87 244
Pie, Raspberry Cream, '94 209
Prunes, Raspberry, '82 124
Pudding, Raspberry, '92 92
Punch, Raspberry-Rosé, '87 242
Punch, Raspberry Sparkle, '84 57
Puree, Fruit Compote with Raspberry,
  '88 81
Salad Dressing, Raspberry, '94 158
Salad, Frozen Raspberry, '79 287; '80 35
Salad, Marinated Chicken-Raspberry,
  '93 190
Salad, Raspberry, '86 286
Salad, Raspberry Ribbon, '87 236
Salad, Raspberry-Walnut, '94 158
Salad, Raspberry-Wine, '91 256
Sauce, Berry, '94 130
Sauce, Berry Mimosa, '90 315
Sauce, Crimson Raspberry, '79 91; '85 30
Sauce, Duck Breasts with Raspberry,
  '87 240
Sauce Flambé, Raspberry, '84 142

Raspberries *(continued)*

Sauce, Fresh Berries with Raspberry
    Custard, **'88** 163
Sauce, Fresh Raspberry, **'93** 120
Sauce, Melba, **'87** 77
Sauce, Peach-Berry, **'87** M165
Sauce, Poached Pears with Raspberry,
    '87 69; **'88** 223
Sauce, Raspberry, **'82** 289; **'83** 108;
    '84 73, 213; **'87** 69, 117, 183; **'88** 267;
    '89 183, 322; **'91** 96, 180, 270; **'92** 130;
    '93 82, 99, 315; **'94** 295
Sauce, Raspberry-Amaretto, **'88** 130
Sauce, Raspberry-Orange, **'88** 22; **'92** 154
Sauce, Tea-Berry, **'94** 130
Shake, Peach Melba Sundae, **'93** 134
Shake, Raspberry-and-Banana, **'89** 183
Sherbet, Raspberry, **'83** 162
Soufflé, Raspberry, **'86** 188
Soufflé, Raspberry-Topped, **'85** 317
Soup, Chilled Raspberry, **'81** 130
Soup, Sherry-Berry Dessert, **'91** 180
Strudel, Raspberry-Nut, **'83** 304
Sweet Potatoes, Raspberry, **'87** 280
Tartlets, Fresh Berry, **'91** 98
Tart, Pick-a-Berry, **'91** 118
Tarts, Berry Good Lemon, **'91** 119
Tarts, Cran-Raspberry Meringue, **'92** 286
Tea Cake, Raspberry, **'91** 271
Tea, Sangría, **'94** 131
Topping, Raspberry, **'85** 317
Topping, Raspberry-Peach, **'87** 126
Trifle, Raspberry, **'88** 259
Vinaigrette, Raspberry, **'94** 249
Vinegar, Raspberry-Lemon, **'87** 134
Vinegar, Raspberry Wine, **'93** 191
Watermelon-Berry Slush, **'90** 137
Relishes. *See* Pickles and Relishes.
Rhubarb
Ambrosia, Rhubarb, **'88** 93
Bavarian, Rhubarb-Strawberry, **'86** 140
Chutney, Rhubarb, **'87** 245
Cobbler, Rosy Strawberry-Rhubarb, **'79** 154
Cobbler, Strawberry-Rhubarb, **'88** 93
Crisp, Rhubarb, **'91** 146; **'92** 130
Mousse, Rhubarb, **'88** 93
Pie, Rhubarb-Peach, **'86** 140
Pie, Rhubarb-Raisin, **'79** 112
Salad, Rhubarb, **'91** 146; **'92** 129
Salad, Rhubarb Congealed, **'86** 140
Salad, Tart Rhubarb, **'91** 146; **'92** 129
Sauce, Chilled Rhubarb, **'88** 94
Sauce, Pineapple-Rhubarb, **'88** 94
Squares, Rhubarb, **'91** 146; **'92** 129
Squares, Rosy Rhubarb, **'79** 111
Whip, Rhubarb, **'79** 112
Rice
Almond Rice, **'81** 195; **'85** M112; **'89** 100;
    '91 291
à l'Orange, Rice, **'90** 236
Apple-Cinnamon Rice, **'86** 249
Arabic Rice, **'94** 200
Asparagus, Rice and, **'93** 324
au Gratin, Rice, **'83** 129
au Gratin Supreme, Rice, **'86** 78
Bacon-Chive Rice, **'83** 129
Bake, Creole Sausage-and-Rice, **'88** 58
Baked Rice, **'94** 270
Bake, Egg and Rice, **'83** 119

Bake, Ham-Rice-Tomato, **'87** 78
Balls, Rice, **'81** 51
Basic Long-Grain Rice, **'83** M285
Basic Molding Rice, **'86** 221
Basic Quick-Cooking Rice, **'83** M285
Basic Rice, **'79** 64
Beans and Rice, Black, **'80** 222; **'89** 178;
    '91 82
Beans and Rice, Cajun Red, **'83** 26
Beans and Rice, Creole, **'80** 223
Beans and Rice, Easy Red, **'90** 220
Beans and Rice, Red, **'80** 58; **'83** 89; **'84** 37;
    '87 45; **'90** 27
Beans and Rice, South Texas, **'85** 252
Beans, and Rice, Texas Sausage, **'84** 296
Beans and Yellow Rice, Easy Black, **'92** 308
Beef and Cauliflower over Rice, **'93** 94
Beef and Rice, Spiced, **'84** 285
Beef and Rice, Spicy, **'83** 231
Beef Rollups with Rice, Royal, **'79** 105
Beef Tips on Rice, **'85** 87
Black-Eyed Peas, Rice with, **'93** 66
Black-Eyed Peas with Rice, **'83** 12; **'90** 208;
    '91 13
Black-Eyes and Rice, Creole, **'85** 6
Boudin, Old-Fashioned, **'85** 250
Braised Rice and Peas, **'79** 101
Broccoli with Rice, Holiday, **'87** 252
Brown Rice, **'82** 275
Brown Rice Bake, Chicken-, **'91** 314
Brown Rice, Calico, **'86** 33
Brown Rice Casserole, **'87** 118
Brown Rice, Cornish Hens with, **'82** 275
Brown Rice Parmesan, **'84** 196
Brown Rice Pilaf, **'90** 136; **'91** 82
Brown Rice Pudding, **'85** 77
Brown Rice, Roast Chicken and, **'83** 268
Brown Rice, Spanish, **'84** 196
Brussels Sprouts and Rice, **'79** 288; **'80** 26
Cabbage Rolls, Stuffed, **'88** 18
Cacciatore, Quick Chicken-and-Rice, **'88** 38
Calas, Easy, **'92** 89
Calico Rice, **'85** 83
Casserole, Broccoli-Rice, **'81** 101
Casserole, Chicken and Rice, **'80** 260
Casserole, Chicken-Rice, **'86** 52
Casserole, Chili-Rice, **'79** 54
Casserole, Colorful Rice, **'82** 199
Casserole, Cornish Hens-and-Rice, **'92** 267
Casserole, Ham-and-Rice, **'84** 75
Casserole Italiano, Zucchini-Rice, **'89** 146
Casserole, Jalapeño Rice, **'81** 66
Casserole, Lentils-and-Rice, **'93** 301
Casserole, Mexican Rice, **'83** 31
Casserole, Oriental Sausage and Rice,
    '82 M123
Casserole, Rice, **'87** 45
Casserole, Rice-and-Chicken, **'87** 154
Casserole, Sausage-Rice, **'82** 50; **'83** 75
Casserole, Shrimp and Rice, **'79** 228
Casserole, Shrimp-and-Rice, **'94** 328
Casserole, Spanish Rice, **'79** 192
Chantilly, Rice, **'86** 82
Cheese-Parslied Rice, **'89** 99
Chicken and Rice, Creole, **'92** 262
Chicken and Rice, Shortcut, **'90** 220
Chicken and Rice, Spicy, **'88** 200
Chicken-and-Rice Valencia, **'85** 113
Chicken Caruso and Rice, **'89** 177
Chicken-Flavored Rice, **'84** M144
Chicken Livers and Rice Dish, **'82** 218

Chicken Livers with Rice, **'80** 200; **'81** 58;
    '84 292
Chicken over Rice, Cajun, **'88** 102; **'89** 67
Chicken, Rice-Stuffed, **'81** 4
Chicken, Rice-Stuffed Roasted, **'88** 38
Chicken with Rice, Sherry, **'81** 97
Chiles, Rice-and-Cheese con, **'89** 99
Chiles, Rice and Green, **'83** 152
Chili-Cheesy Rice, **'79** 43
Chili with Rice, **'82** 11
Confetti Rice, **'89** 146
Consommé Rice, **'80** 246
Cornish Hens, Rice-Stuffed, **'82** 302
Cream with Mandarin Oranges, Rice, **'85** 317
Creole Rice, **'90** 183
Cumin Rice, **'85** 83
Curried Beef and Rice, **'88** 164
Curried Rice, **'90** 183
Curried Rice and Shrimp, **'83** 231
Curried Rice, Quick, **'86** 81
Curried Rice with Almonds, **'83** M285
Curried Rice with Pineapple, **'79** 142
Curry-Spiced Rice, **'86** M226
Custard, Baked Rice, **'92** 308
Dinner, Jollof Rice, **'91** 230; **'92** 325
Dinner, Mexican Beef-and-Rice, **'88** 199
Dirty Rice, **'86** 142
Dirty Rice, Hot, **'93** 219
Dressing, Chicken and Rice, **'79** 288
Dressing, Chicken with Pecan-Rice, **'85** M57
Dressing, Mexican Rice, **'87** 253
Dressing, Rice, **'91** 217
Dressing, Roast Turkey with Rice, **'82** 286
Fiesta Rice, **'84** 76
French Rice, **'83** 24
Fried Rice, **'83** 129; **'84** 197; **'88** 67
Fried Rice, Bacon, **'80** 115
Fried Rice, Easy, **'84** 76
Fried Rice, Egg, **'79** 252; **'80** 19
Fried Rice for Two, **'81** 31
Fried Rice, Pork, **'89** 99
Fried Rice Special, **'80** 56
Fried Rice, Turkey, **'83** 282
Fried Rice with Sausage, **'83** 12
Fruited Rice, Far East, **'81** 175
Garden Rice, **'92** 12
Ginger Rice, Fluffy, **'83** 102
Glorified Rice, **'83** 129
Golden Rice, **'79** 270
Grape Leaves, Stuffed, **'94** 48
Green Rice Bake, **'79** 43
Green Rice, Celebrity, **'81** 207
Ham-Rice Toss, **'82** 40
Ham Rolls, Rice-Stuffed, **'83** 190
Ham with Rice, Curried, **'80** 111
Herbed Rice, **'83** M285; **'93** 278
Herb Rice, **'91** 257
Honey Rice, **'85** 83
Hopping John, Skillet, **'79** 10
Indian Rice, **'79** 64
Jalapeño Hot Rice, **'80** 126
Jalapeño Rice, **'79** 43
Lamb Curry with Rice, **'80** 83; **'81** 10
Lemon Rice, **'89** 166
Lentil-and-Rice Supper, **'84** 202
Lime-Flavored Rice, **'84** 175
Lyonnaise, Rice, **'83** 151
Mango-Beef and Rice, **'88** 138
Meatballs Paprikash with Rice, **'85** 31
Medaillons in Pepper Pesto, Chicken-Rice,
    '90 97

Rice *(continued)*

Medley, Rice, **'79** 270
Mélange, Rice, **'87** 240
Mexican Rice, **'83** 85; **'85** 147; **'91** 217
Mexican Rice, Spicy, **'88** 149
Mix, Fruited Curry-Rice, **'86** 326
Mix, Fruited Rice, **'90** 267
Mix, Herb-Rice, **'91** 257
Mix, Paella Rice, **'94** 168
Mold, Chile-Rice, **'86** 221
Mold, Curried Rice, **'85** 36
Mold, Saffron Rice, **'86** 221
Mushroom Rice, Baked, **'92** 170
Mushroom Rice, Easy, **'89** 286
Noodles, Shredded Beef over Rice, **'85** 74
Nutted Rice, **'85** 269
Orange-Herb Rice, **'89** 286
Orange Rice, **'79** 43; **'81** 175; **'82** 200
Oriental Rice, **'85** M12, 146
Oven Rice, **'83** 89
Paella, Chicken-Pork-Shrimp, **'82** 245
Paella, Garden, **'82** 245
Paella, Seafood, **'82** 245
Paella, Spanish, **'85** 26
Paella Valenciana, **'82** 246
Pancakes, Rice, **'85** 147
Pancakes, Vegetable-Rice, **'93** 43
Parsleyed Rice, **'83** M58
Parsley Rice, **'84** 197; **'85** 95
Parslied Rice, **'87** 167, 243
Parslied Rice, Creamy, **'88** 255
Peas and Rice, **'88** 97
Peas and Rice, Holiday, **'86** 328
Peas, Cajun, **'88** 3
Peas, Rice with Green, **'87** 45
Pecan Rice, **'85** 53
Pecan Rice, Shrimp-and-Scallop Sauté with, **'90** 317
Peppered Rice, **'82** 4
Pepper Rice, Hot, **'92** 310
Peppers, Beef-Stuffed, **'85** 146
Peppers, Rice-Stuffed, **'80** 65
Pepper Steak and Rice, **'81** 17
Peppers with Rice and Ham, Stuffed, **'82** 131
Pie, Tuna-Rice, **'84** 123
Pigeon Peas, Rice with, **'92** 157
Pilaf, Browned Rice, **'87** 305
Pilaf, Chicken, **'82** 246
Pilaf, Chicken Breasts with Fruited Rice, **'92** 307
Pilaf, Fruit-and-Vegetable Rice, **'84** 196
Pilaf, Fruited Pork, **'82** 246
Pilaf Mold, Ham, **'86** 222
Pilaf, Near-Eastern, **'82** 246
Pilaf, Okra, **'80** 185; **'82** 126; **'93** 160
Pilaf, Rice, **'86** 82; **'87** 229; **'88** 42; **'89** 286
Pilaf, Rice-and-Lentil, **'88** 17
Pilaf, Savory, **'83** 93
Pilaf, Shrimp, **'82** 246
Pilaf, Turkey-Asparagus, **'88** 200
Pilaf, Turkey-Rice, **'86** 284
Pilaf, Turkish, **'79** 184
Pork Chops, Rice-Stuffed, **'83** 102
Pudding, Amaretto Rice, **'86** 334
Pudding, Apple Rice, **'91** 217
Pudding, Creamy Rice, **'81** 51, 205
Pudding, Fruited Rice, **'81** 205; **'86** 95
Pudding, Fudgy Rice, **'81** 205
Pudding, Old-Fashioned Rice, **'85** 147

Pudding, Raisin-Rice, **'87** 46
Pudding, Velvety Rice, **'81** 205
Quiche, Broccoli-Rice, **'81** 228
Raisin Rice with Curry, **'85** 83
Red Rice, **'92** 235
Red Rice Jambalaya, **'91** 18
Red Rice, Savannah, **'80** 119; **'89** 286
Refried Rice, Shrimp and, **'89** 176
Ring, Oregano Rice, **'86** 222
Ring, Rice-Carrot, **'79** 246
Ring, Shrimp Creole in a Rice, **'86** 222
Ring with Beets, Rice, **'79** 225
Risotto alla Milanese, **'85** 228
Risotto, Southwestern, **'92** 211
Rolls, Crunchy Cabbage-Rice, **'85** 32
Saffron Rice, **'79** 43; **'93** 282
Saffron Rice Mold, **'86** 221
Salads
    Artichoke-Chicken-Rice Salad, **'94** 132
    Artichoke Hearts, Rice Salad with, **'80** 232
    Artichoke-Rice Salad, **'80** 178; **'81** 41; **'85** 81
    Avocado Salad, Rice-and-, **'89** 146
    Bacon, Rice Salad with, **'79** 52
    Bean-and-Rice Salad, Marinated, **'87** 152
    Bean Salad, Rice-and-, **'85** 22
    Beans-and-Rice Salad, **'91** 44
    Brown Rice-and-Vegetable Salad, **'84** 202
    Brown Rice Confetti Salad, **'94** 174
    Chicken-and-Rice Salad, Hot, **'83** 22
    Chicken-Rice Salad, **'81** 203
    Chicken-Rice Salad, Nutty, **'83** 157
    Chutneyed Rice Salad, **'88** 100
    Colorful Rice Salad, **'81** 253
    Confetti Rice Salad, **'80** 232
    Crunchy Rice Salad, **'82** 302
    Curried Chicken-Rice Salad, **'92** 190
    Curried Rice Salad, **'80** 84; **'85** 147, 220
    Curry Rice Salad, **'89** 146
    Egg-Rice Salad, **'84** 18; **'86** 169
    Gazpacho-Rice Salad, Molded, **'86** 221
    Ham-and-Rice Salad, Colorful, **'90** 319
    Ham-and-Rice Salad, Mandarin, **'87** 145
    Hearty Rice Salad, **'82** 233
    Lentils-and-Rice Salad, **'90** 197
    Mandarin Rice Salad, **'88** 271
    Mardi Gras Rice, **'91** 217
    Mushrooms, Rice Salad with Fresh, **'80** 231
    Paella Salad, **'86** 207
    Pea Salad, Rice-, **'85** 163
    Pebble Salad, **'91** 27
    Red Rice Salad, Charleston, **'79** 146
    Rice Salad, **'79** 74; **'81** 51
    Salmon-Rice Salad, **'84** 289
    Shrimp-and-Orange Rice Salad, Zesty, **'87** 155
    Shrimp and Rice Salad, **'80** 231; **'82** 207
    Shrimp-and-Rice Salad, **'92** 307
    Shrimp-Rice Salad, Baked, **'83** 22
    Shrimp-Rice Salad, Tangy, **'84** 66
    Shrimp Salad, Rice-, **'79** 270; **'92** 142
    Shrimp Salad, Rice-and-, **'83** 82
    Spinach-Rice Salad, **'94** 63
    Tuna-Rice Salad, **'87** 202
    Vegetable-Rice Salad, **'80** 148; **'83** 198; **'85** 87
    Vegetable Salad, Rice-and-, **'86** 42

Wild Rice Salad, Oriental Salmon-and-, **'94** 173
    Zesty Rice Salad, **'81** 23
Sausage and Rice, Italian, **'86** 53
Savory Rice, **'89** 201
Seasoned Onion Rice, **'82** 166
Seasoned Rice, **'79** 244; **'83** 212
Shell, Rice-Cheese, **'82** 49
Shrimp and Rice, Oriental, **'90** 183
Shrimp and Sausage Rice, **'79** 64
Soufflé, Rice-Cheese, **'79** 270
Soup, Chicken-and-Rice, **'88** 236
Soup, Mushroom-Rice, **'90** 32
Soup, Tomato-and-Rice, **'85** 24
Soup, Turkey-Rice, **'90** 89
Southern Rice, **'90** 250
Southwestern Rice, **'90** 121
Spanish Rice, **'81** 51; **'83** 209; **'90** 183; **'94** 27
Spanish Rice, Jiffy, **'90** 176
Spanish Rice, Pork Chops and, **'83** 103; **'85** 293
Spanish Rice with Tofu, **'88** 26
Spanish-Style Rice, **'83** 152
Spicy Rice, **'83** 215; **'85** 256
Spinach Rice, **'85** 146
Squares, Creamed Chicken over Confetti Rice, **'81** 282; **'82** 31
Steamed Rice, Oven-, **'89** 226
Stew, Lentil-Rice, **'82** 232
Strata, Cheese-Rice, **'81** 176
Stuffing, Rice-and-Onion, **'88** 246
Stuffing, Tomatoes with Walnut-Rice, **'91** 102
Timbales, Rice, **'94** 32
Timbales, Spinach-Rice, **'88** 271
Vegetable-Rice Toss, **'91** 309
Vegetables and Rice, **'93** 91
Vegetables, Rice with, **'79** 64; **'85** 83
Waldorf Rice, **'84** 281
Wild Rice
    Almond Wild Rice, **'86** 50
    Belvedere, Wild Rice, **'86** 82
    Bulgur, Wild Rice, **'91** 83
    Casserole, Chicken-Wild Rice, **'84** 241; **'85** 65
    Casserole, Duck and Wild Rice, **'79** 224
    Casserole, Oyster-and-Wild Rice, **'83** 34; **'84** 44
    Casserole, Sausage and Wild Rice, **'83** 196
    Casserole, Sausage-Wild Rice, **'84** 250
    Casserole, Veal and Wild Rice, **'79** 180
    Casserole, Wild Rice, **'82** 199
    Casserole, Wild Rice-Oyster, **'86** 256
    Chicken and Wild Rice, **'79** 248
    Chicken-Fried Wild Rice, **'89** 24; **'91** 132
    Chicken Rollups, **'88** 38
    Chicken, Wild Rice-Stuffed, **'79** 219
    Chicken-Wild Rice Supreme, **'79** 77
    Chicken with Wild Rice, Elegant, **'80** M76
    Cranberry-Pear Wild Rice, **'83** 279
    Creole, Wild Rice-and-Shrimp, **'84** 292
    Dressed-Up Wild Rice, **'92** 60
    Eggs with Wild Rice, Scrambled, **'80** 42
    Gourmet Wild Rice, **'89** 271
    Morels, Wild Rice with, **'89** 62
    Mushrooms, Wild Rice and, **'83** 278
    Oysters, Wild Rice and, **'92** 339
    Pecan-Lemon Wild Rice, **'92** 211

Rice, Wild Rice *(continued)*

    Popped Wild Rice, '85 65
    Pork Loin Stuffed with Wild Rice, '84 35
    Quiches, Wild Rice-and-Mushroom,
      '93 237
    Ring, Creamed Mushrooms in Wild Rice,
      '80 270
    Ring, Wild Rice, '83 253
    Salad, Crab and Wild Rice, '79 116
    Salad, Crab-Wild Rice, '86 207
    Salad, Oriental Salmon-and-Wild Rice,
      '94 173
    Salad, Springtime Wild Rice, '88 100
    Salad, Wild Rice, '85 65; '89 147;
      '93 191
    Salad, Wild Rice-Chicken, '83 146
    Salad, Wild Rice-Green Apple, '92 90
    Sausage and Wild Rice, '85 65
    Sausage, Wild Rice and, '86 268
    Scallops and Wild Rice, '90 129
    Soup, Cheesy Potato-and-Wild Rice,
      '89 16
    Stuffing, Cornish Hens with Wild Rice,
      '79 222; '80 64; '82 136
  Yellow Rice, '91 136
  Yellow Rice, Black Beans with, '82 2
  Yellow Rice with Water Chestnuts, '85 24
Rolls and Buns. *See also* Breads.
  Anise Rolls, '89 91
  Apple Pinwheel, Quick, '85 42
  Basic Angel Rolls, '89 72
  Big-Batch Rolls, '88 289
  Blueberry Buns, Deluxe, '81 164
  Blueberry Pinwheels, '82 205
  Bolillos, '88 247
  Bran Rolls, '85 145
  Bran Yeast Rolls, '87 116
  Broccoli-Cheddar Rolls, '91 21
  Butter-and-Herb Rolls, '86 306
  Buttered Rum-Nut Rolls, '86 291
  Butterhorn Rolls, '89 288
  Butterhorns, '84 267
  Buttermilk Rolls, Quick, '83 155
  Butterscotch Pinwheels, '90 49
  Caramel Breakfast Rolls, '79 193
  Caramel-Nut Rolls, '86 312
  Caramel Rolls, Easy, '90 195
  Caraway Puffs, '82 174
  Centerpiece Rolls, '94 276
  Cheese-Apricot Sweet Rolls, '90 195
  Cheese Buns, Hurry-Up, '81 300
  Cheese Crescents, '82 18
  Cherry-Almond Rolls, '84 M198
  Chocolate-Cinnamon Buns, '85 5
  Chocolate Sticky Buns, '81 300; '82 124
  Cinnamon Buns, '91 68
  Cinnamon Crisps, '81 113
  Cinnamon-Pecan Rolls, Easy, '89 307
  Cinnamon Rolls, '79 80; '88 290; '92 270
  Cinnamon Rolls, Easy, '85 290
  Cinnamon Rolls, Glazed, '86 312
  Cinnamon Rolls, Old-Fashioned, '86 298;
    '90 196; '92 226
  Cinnamon Rolls, Potato Sourdough, '94 325
  Cinnamon Rolls, Spiral, '82 205; '83 32
  Cinnamon Sticky Buns, '83 244
  Cinnamon Tea Rolls, '92 263
  Cinnamon Twists, '83 53
  Cloverleaf Refrigerator Rolls, '80 256

Cloverleaf Rolls, '82 18
Cloverleaf Rolls, Light, '83 290
Coconut-Pecan Coils, '90 196
Cornmeal Rolls, '79 60; '89 184
Cornmeal Yeast Rolls, '86 177
Cottage Cheese Rolls, '81 78
Cranberry-Pineapple Rolls, '86 275
Cream Cheese Pinches, '87 85
Crescent Rolls, '84 267; '89 235
Crescent Rolls, Almond, '90 283
Crescent Rolls, Butter-Rich, '81 211
Crescent Rolls, Buttery, '83 180
Crescent Rolls, Deep South, '82 309; '83 16
Crescent Rolls, Easy, '79 60
Crescent Rolls, French-Style, '82 288
Crescent Rolls, Yogurt, '91 123
Crescents, Apricot, '90 181
Crescents, Festive, '80 281
Croissants, '83 54
Croissants, Cream Cheese, '92 159
Dinner Rolls, '79 251; '89 312; '93 M326
Dinner Rolls, Fancy, '86 299
Dinner Rolls, Freezer, '90 251
Dinner Rolls, How to Shape, '83 323
Dinner Rolls, Italian, '83 254
Dinner Rolls, Italiano, '85 32
Dinner Rolls, Refrigerator, '81 78
Dinner Rolls, Whole Wheat, '91 53
Dough, Basic Roll, '82 17
Dough, Sweet Roll, '79 80
Fantan Rolls, French, '80 276
Finger Rolls, '83 254
Garlic Rolls, Easy, '86 234
Hard Rolls, '86 85, 306
Holiday Sparkle Rolls, '83 296
Honey Oatmeal Buns, '83 154
Honey Rolls, Super, '80 115
Honey Wheat Rolls, '83 278
Honey-Wheat Rolls, Dilled, '83 254
Hot Cross Buns, '81 77
Icebox Rolls, '80 242
Jam Kolaches, '85 290
Jam Teasers, '81 8
Lemon Knots, Glazed, '86 290
Lemon Spirals, French, '81 94
Mayonnaise Rolls, '90 283
Moravian Feast Buns, '83 295
Nutty Buns, '86 290
Onion Buns, Cheesy, '85 5
Onion-Cheese Buns, '88 218
Onion Rolls, Poppy Seed, '81 63
Onion Twist Rolls, '89 288
Orange Butter Rolls, '82 206; '83 33
Orange Rolls, '80 22; '82 17; '88 79
Orange Rolls, Easy, '89 M131
Orange Rolls, Frosted Hot, '80 257
Orange Rolls, Glazed, '90 194
Orange Rolls, Luscious, '86 298
Orange Rolls, Speedy, '89 287
Overnight Rolls, '86 233
Pan Rolls, '88 76
Pan Rolls, Brown-and-Serve, '91 52
Parker House Refrigerator Rolls, '82 310;
  '83 17
Parkerhouse Rolls, Super, '81 78
Parmesan Rolls, '79 181
Parsley-Garlic Rolls, '93 319
Pecan Rolls, '81 62
Pepperoni Rolls, Ground-, '83 244
Pineapple Angel Rolls, '89 72
Pineapple Buns, Easy, '85 14

Pinwheel Rolls, Sweet, '90 46
Potato Rolls, '81 300
Potato Rolls, Easy, '89 287
Potato Rolls, Feathery Light, '81 305; '82 36
Potato Rolls, Homemade, '82 252
Potato Rolls, Refrigerated, '83 254
Potato Rolls, Refrigerator, '87 15
Potato Rolls, Southern, '86 299
Potato Rolls, Super, '85 145
Potato Rolls, Supreme, '82 130
Potato Rolls, Whole Wheat, '89 50
Potato Sourdough Rolls, '94 325
Potato Yeast Rolls, '87 53
Praline Buns, '90 195
Pull-Apart Buns, Easy, '83 100
Pumpkin Rolls, '87 254
Raisin Cinnamon Pull-Aparts, '82 205; '83 32
Raisin Cinnamon Rolls, '81 107
Raisin-Cinnamon Rolls, '91 240
Raisin Rollups, Sweet, '86 290
Refrigerator Rolls, '82 287; '91 53
Refrigerator Rolls, Buttermilk, '81 120;
  '82 22
Refrigerator Rolls, Low-Sodium, '82 67
Refrigerator Rolls, Party, '79 248
Refrigerator Rolls, Three-Day, '86 306
Refrigerator Yeast Rolls, '91 80
Reuben Buns, '88 298
Romano Sesame Rolls, '87 144
Rounds, Individual Bread, '83 159
Rum Buns, '81 299
Rum-Raisin Buns, '80 22
Rum Rolls, Easy, '79 287; '80 35
Saffron Rolls, '83 296
Sesame Buns, '82 17
Sesame Knots, '89 29
Snack Buns, '87 279
Sour Cream Rolls, '80 71
Sour Cream Yeast Rolls, '85 259; '90 17;
  '93 232
Sourdough Hot Rolls, '82 201
Special Rolls, Extra-, '88 257
Spoon Rolls, '87 15; '91 275
Sticky Buns, '80 23
Sweet Potato Rolls, '93 172
Sweet Rolls, Mexican, '81 285
Sweet Rolls, Quick Breakfast, '90 195
Sweet Rolls, Yummy, '80 281
Tasty Rolls, '90 85
Toasted Rolls with Herb Butter, '89 70
Twists, Austrian, '80 45
Wheat Feather Rolls, Shredded, '82 309;
  '83 16
Wheat Rolls, Light, '87 254
Whole Grain Pan Rolls, '89 256
Whole Wheat Bread and Rolls, Hearty, '79 92
Whole Wheat Buns, '86 236
Whole Wheat Rolls, '79 275; '90 111
Whole Wheat Rolls, Easy, '86 286; '87 74
Whole Wheat Rolls, Petite, '85 146
Whole Wheat Rolls, Wholesome, '92 31
Yam Rolls, Golden, '86 299
Yeast Rolls, Best-Ever, '90 46
Yeast Rolls, Buttermilk, '79 59
Yeast Rolls, Easy, '81 78; '86 16
Yeast Rolls, Hurry-Up, '90 90
Yeast Rolls, Low-Sodium, '84 228
Yeast Rolls, Quick, '84 267
Yeast Rolls, Refrigerator, '81 296, 307;
  '82 309; '83 17, 118
Yeast Rolls, Speedy, '82 309; '83 17

Rutabagas

au Gratin, Rutabaga, '79 254
Bacon, Rutabaga with, '83 243
Boiled Rutabagas, '86 224
Buttered Rutabagas, '81 274
Creamy Rutabaga, '79 254
Glazed Rutabaga, '88 229
Honey Rutabaga, '91 220
Mashed Rutabagas, '86 295
Simple Rutabaga, '83 243
Steamed Rutabagas, '81 274

Salad Dressings

Almond Salad Dressing, '81 37
Apple Dressing, '83 181; '92 216
Apple-Onion Vinaigrette, Spinach Salad with,
 '94 276
Artichoke Dressing, '84 126
Avocado Cream, '92 158
Avocado Dressing, '80 15; '92 321
Avocado Fruit Salad Dressing, '82 93
Bacon Dressing, Hot, '84 12
Barbecue Salad Dressing, '80 74
Barbecue Salad Dressing, Cheesy-,
 '92 255
Basil-and-Garlic Dressing, '94 55
Basil Dressing, '88 24
Basil Vinaigrette, '93 106
B. B.'s Salad Dressing, '91 65
Blender Dressing, '80 78
Blue Cheese Dressing, '79 69; '82 166;
 '86 233; '90 286
Blue Cheese Dressing, Apple Salad with,
 '87 103
Blue Cheese Dressing, Creamy, '81 150;
 '91 307
Blue Cheese Dressing, Special, '80 30
Blue Cheese Dressing, Tangy, '87 81
Blue Cheese Dressing, Zesty, '79 104
Blue Cheese Salad Dressing, '82 94
Blue Cheese Salad Dressing, Creamy,
 '86 123
Blue Cheese Vinaigrette, '89 45; '90 55, 280
Blue Cheese Vinaigrette, Mixed Greens with,
 '89 274
Buttermilk Dressing, Down-Home,
 '84 114
Buttermilk Salad Dressing, '79 69
Caesar Salad Dressing, '82 94
Caper Vinaigrette, '91 310
Celery-Honey Dressing, '80 42
Celery Seed Dressing, '82 265
Celery Seed Dressing, Grapefruit-Banana
 Salad with, '91 237
Celery Seed Salad Dressing, '82 94
Cheese Fluff Dressing, '91 256
Chili-Lime Dressing, Spinach Salad with,
 '94 63
Cilantro-Lime Vinaigrette, '94 77
Citrus-Cilantro Dressing, '93 310; '94 97
Citrus Dressing, '85 92
Citrus Dressing, Fruit Salad with, '88 6
Coconut Dressing, '87 251
Coconut-Fruit Dressing, Tangy, '84 171
Cooked Salad Dressing, '90 231
Cranberry-Orange Dressing, '91 287
Creamy Dressing, '79 159; '83 81; '85 26;
 '92 45, 241; '93 318
Creamy Salad Dressing, '83 181

Cucumber-Curry Dressing, '89 179
Cucumber Dressing, '80 74; '90 144
Cucumber-Mint Dressing, '87 153
Cucumber Salad Dressing, Creamy, '82 79
Curried Dressing, '84 115
Curry Dressing, '80 242; '82 78
Curry Vinaigrette, Warm, '93 107
Dairy Land Salad Dressing, '86 85
Date Dressing, '87 57
Delightful Salad Dressing, '83 181
Dijon Dressing, '94 282
Dijon-Honey Dressing, '89 45
Dill Dressing, '88 182
Dill Dressing, Creamy, '91 213
Dilly Dressing, '80 74
Dried Tomato Vinaigrette, '93 272
Egg Dressing, '86 79
French Dressing, '89 46
French Dressing, Creamy, '81 60; '90 286
French Dressing, Grapefruit, '80 101
French Dressing, Green Salad with Lemony,
 '85 67
French Dressing, Honey, '87 81
French Dressing, Miracle, '82 79
French Dressing, Onion-, '84 283
French Dressing, Piquant, '87 202; '88 43
French Dressing, Spicy, '81 150; '86 123
French Dressing, Sweet, '82 94
French Dressing, Tangy, '84 12
French Dressing, Tomato-Honey, '81 105
Fruit Dressing, Fluffy, '79 69
Fruit Dressing, Fresh, '87 134
Fruit Dressing, Marmalade-, '84 171
Fruit Dressing, Sweet-and-Sour, '84 125
Fruit Dressing, Whipped Cream, '79 270
Fruit Salad Dressing, '79 69; '93 184
Fruit Salad Dressing, Creamy, '82 94
Fruit, Salad Dressing for, '86 40
Fruit Salad, Dressing for, '87 81
Fruit Salad Dressing, Red, '83 231
Garden Dew Dressing, '86 50
Garden Dressing, Spring, '85 157
Garlic-Blue Cheese Vinaigrette, '92 57
Garlic-Chive Vinaigrette, '91 44
Garlic Dressing, '79 269; '80 14
Garlic-Ginger Vinaigrette Dressing, '92 195
Garlic-Herb Salad Dressing, Creamy, '84 66
Garlic Salad Dressing, '86 123
Ginger Dressing, '82 194; '88 61; '90 160;
 '93 290
Ginger-Yogurt Dressing, '81 302
Grapefruit Salad Dressing, '84 262
Greek Goddess Dressing, '81 150
Greek Salad Dressing, '90 286
Guacamole Dressing, '92 64
Herb Dressing, '80 122
Herbed Salad Dressing, '88 29
Herb-Mayonnaise Sauce, '85 73
Herb Salad Dressing, '86 40
Honey-Berry Dressing, Orange Salad with,
 '89 250
Honey Dressing, '79 242; '83 146; '87 129
Honey Dressing, Orange Salad with, '89 14
Honey Dressing, Spinach Salad with, '90 16
Honey-Lemon Dressing, Fruit Salad with,
 '93 21
Honey-Lime Dressing, '83 139; '93 71
Honey-Mustard Dressing, '90 55, 111, 146
Honey-Mustard Vinaigrette, '94 249
Honey-Orange Vinaigrette, '91 255
Honey-Walnut Dressing, '93 107

Honey-Yogurt Dressing, '93 172
Horseradish Dressing, '87 152; '91 32
Horseradish Dressing, Vegetable Salad with,
 '92 85
Italian-American Salad Dressing, Creamy,
 '79 69
Italian Cream Dressing, '89 83
Italian Dressing, '79 52; '85 261; '89 166
Italian Dressing, Sour Cream, '89 45
Italian Dressing, Special, '79 190
Italian Dressing, Tomato, Onion, and
 Cucumber in, '81 83
Italian Salad Dressing, '80 82; '84 12
Lemon-and-Herb Dressing, '92 108
Lemon-Basil Vinaigrette, '94 205
Lemon Cream Dressing, '82 170
Lemon Dressing, Chilled Broccoli with,
 '88 270
Lemon Dressing, Creamy, '88 M193
Lemon-Herb Salad Dressing, '82 67
Lemon-Pepper Dressing, '87 55
Lemon Salad Dressing, '79 8
Lemon-Yogurt Dressing, '93 17
Lemon-Yogurt Slaw or Salad Dressing, '88 54
Lime Dressing, '79 2; '83 120
Lime-Honey Dressing, '92 213
Lime-Honey Fruit Salad Dressing, '87 81
Lime-Parsley Dressing, '85 131
Lime Sherbet Dressing, '80 221
Magnificent Seven Salad Dressing, '89 45
Margarita Dressing, '94 107
Marinara Vinaigrette, '94 64
Mayonnaise Dressing, '86 11
Mayonnaise Dressing, Herbed-, '86 119
Mayonnaise, Easy Homemade, '84 12
Mayonnaise, Homemade, '80 155
Mayonnaise, Hot Wine, '81 83
Mayonnaise, Parmesan, '86 79
Mayonnaise, Russian, '80 137
Mint Dressing, '80 183
Mint Dressing, Fresh, '84 126
Mustard Dressing, '80 112
Mustard Dressing, Tangy, '93 323
Mustard Vinaigrette, Baby Lettuces with,
 '93 67
Olive Oil Dressing, '84 266
Olive Oil, Flavored, '89 193
Orange Blossom Dressing, '82 266
Orange-Coconut Dressing, '80 158
Orange Cream, '90 126
Orange-Curd Dressing, '93 22
Orange Dressing, '81 141
Orange-Poppy Seed Dressing, '87 187
Orange Vinaigrette Dressing, Tangy,
 '92 341; '93 46
Orange-Yogurt Dressing, '85 304
Oregano Dressing, '86 141
Oregano-Vinaigrette Dressing, '79 113
Oriental Dressing, '91 277
Paprika Dressing, '86 191
Parmesan Dressing, '86 192
Pasta Salad Dressing, '86 121
Peach Dressing, '90 180
Pear Dressing, '83 146
Pepper Dressing, '80 174
Pepper-Onion Salad Dressing, Green, '84 12
Peppery Salad Dressing, '79 69
Pesto Salad Dressing, '86 150
Pimiento Dressing, Lettuce Wedges with,
 '84 212
Pineapple Cream Dressing, '83 81

Salad Dressings *(continued)*

Pineapple Dressing, Fruit Salad with, **'85** 207
Pineapple-Poppy Seed Dressing, **'85** 55
Pineapple Salad Dressing, **'81** 36
Poppy Seed Dressing, **'80** 152; **'81** 63, 252;
  '83 153, 316; **'84** 16; **'86** 123, 305;
  '88 78; **'91** 169; **'92** 191; **'93** 65, 168
Poppy Seed Dressing, Blender, **'79** 176
Poppy Seed Dressing, Spinach Salad with,
  '91 210
Poppy Seed Vinaigrette, **'94** 249
Raspberry Cream Dressing, **'94** 321
Raspberry Dressing, **'87** 153
Raspberry-Maple Dressing, Bibb Salad with,
  '91 246
Raspberry Salad Dressing, **'94** 158
Raspberry Vinaigrette, **'94** 249
Red Wine Vinaigrette, **'94** 327
Rémoulade Dressing, **'86** 123
Romano Dressing, **'80** 174
Roquefort Dressing, **'79** 85; **'80** 74;
  '93 128
Roquefort Dressing, Creamy, **'84** 12
Rosemary Dressing, **'81** 131
Rum Dressing, **'80** 139
Russian Dressing, **'80** 4
Russian Dressing, Spinach Salad with,
  '79 144
Russian Sour Cream Dressing, **'79** 55
Russian-Style Dressing, **'83** 181
Russian-Style Salad Dressing, **'86** 305
Salad Dressing, **'90** 161
Sesame Seed Dressing, **'87** 81
Sesame-Soy Dressing, **'93** 106
Sherry Dressing, Cherry Salad with, **'79** 165
Sour Cream Dressing, **'82** 164; **'86** 331
Sour Cream Dressing Deluxe, Lettuce with,
  '88 48
Sour Cream Sauce, **'87** 233
Southwestern Dressing, Spicy, **'94** 136
Southwestern Salad Dressing, Creamy,
  '94 278
Soy Dressing, **'86** 191
Soy-Sesame Dressing, **'87** 153
Spicy Dressing, **'80** 55
Spinach Salad Dressing, **'83** 181; **'93** 250
Stay Trim Dressing, **'86** 40
Strawberry Dressing, Creamy, **'84** 161
Sweet-and-Sour Dressing, **'80** 247; **'84** 70,
  161; **'85** 163; **'87** 305; **'89** 62; **'91** 126;
  '94 281
Sweet-Sour Dressing, **'80** 246
Tangy Dressing, **'83** 9
Tangy Red Dressing, **'86** 191
Tangy Salad Dressing, **'80** 146; **'84** 115
Tarragon Dressing, **'90** 55
Tarragon Vinaigrette, **'94** 201
Thousand Island Dressing, **'80** 74; **'81** 104;
  '83 135; **'86** 123
Thousand Island Dressing, Special, **'82** 79
Tomato-Cream Cheese Dressing, Garden
  Salad with, **'79** 173
Tomato Salad Dressing, Fresh, **'83** 193
Tossed Salad Dressing, **'84** 115
Touchdown Salad Dressing, **'81** 197
Vanilla Oil, **'94** 243
Vanilla Vinaigrette, **'94** 242
Vinaigrette, **'94** 179
Vinaigrette, Basic, **'94** 249

Vinaigrette Dressing, **'79** 171; **'87** 138;
  '89 12, 220, 256; **'90** 173; **'92** 303;
  '93 41
Vinaigrette Dressing and Croutons,
  '86 M288
Vinaigrette, Herbed, **'93** 120
Vinaigrette, Versatile, **'93** 140
Whipped Cream Salad Dressing, **'82** 145
White Wine Vinaigrette, **'89** 46
Wine Dressing, Creamy, **'85** 20
Wine Vinegar Dressing, **'92** 91; **'93** 126
Yogurt Dressing, **'85** 59, 215; **'88** 27
Yogurt Dressing, Sweet-Hot, **'86** 40
Yogurt Dressing, Turkey Waldorf Salad with,
  '88 53
Yogurt-Herb Dressing, **'92** 96
Yogurt-Honey Poppy Seed Dressing, **'83** 177
Yogurt Salad Dressing, **'79** 69
Zesty Salad Dressing, **'92** 60

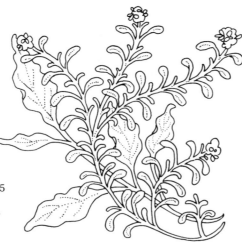

Salads
Acini di Pepe Salad, **'83** 163
Alfalfa-Celery Salad, Overnight, **'82** 97
Ambrosia
  Anytime Ambrosia, **'86** 182
  Baked Ambrosia, **'83** 303
  Bowl, Ambrosia, **'80** 138; **'84** 313
  Brunch Ambrosia, **'83** 57
  Carrot-Ambrosia Salad, **'81** 252
  Carrot-Marshmallow Ambrosia, **'80** 5
  Chicken Salad Ambrosia, **'85** 216
  Citrus Ambrosia, **'82** 287
  Fantastic Ambrosia, **'91** 277
  Fruit Ambrosia, Fresh, **'88** 184
  Fruit Ambrosia, Mixed, **'83** 10
  Grandma's Ambrosia, **'90** 254
  Honey Bee Ambrosia, **'83** 267
  Layered Ambrosia, **'88** 304
  Mold, Ambrosia, **'79** 241
  Mold, Ambrosia Cream Cheese, **'79** 249
  Old-Fashioned Ambrosia, **'80** 5
  Orange Ambrosia Supreme, **'79** 37
  Peach Ambrosia, **'83** 53
  Pineapple-Orange Ambrosia, **'88** 252
  Rhubarb Ambrosia, **'88** 93
  Salad, Ambrosia, **'83** 231; **'94** 271
  Sherried Ambrosia, **'84** 324; **'86** 317
  Tropical Ambrosia, **'79** 74

Antipasto, Easy, **'85** 114
Antipasto, Pasta, **'85** 286
Antipasto Salad, **'84** 66; **'89** 145
Antipasto Salad, Layered, **'92** 220
Apple-Beet Salad, **'91** 237
Apple-Bran Salad, Lemony, **'86** 223
Apple-Carrot Salad, **'85** 22
Apple-Cream Salad, Frozen, **'82** 80
Apple-Nut Salad, **'80** 226
Apple-Raisin Salad, Curried, **'80** 24
Apple Ring Salad, Stuffed, **'91** 198
Apple Salad, **'87** 233
Apple Salad, Cheesy, **'86** 301
Apple Salad, Crunchy, **'80** 138
Apple Salad, Double, **'84** 227
Apple Salad, Fresh, **'81** 207
Apple Salad, Spicy, **'85** 215
Apple Salad, Stuffed, **'92** 266
Apple Salad, Summer, **'80** 149
Apple Salad, Swiss-, **'84** 81
Apple Salad with Blue Cheese Dressing,
  '87 103
Apple Snow Salad, **'81** 224
Apple Toss, Sesame-, **'88** 21
Apple Wedges with Poppyseed Dressing,
  '86 131
Apricot Salad, Frosted, **'80** 248
Artichoke-Pasta Salad, **'94** 180
Artichoke-Rice Salad, **'80** 178; **'81** 41;
  '85 81
Artichoke Salad, **'86** 333
Artichoke Salad, Marinated, **'83** 241
Artichokes Vinaigrette, **'88** 101
Artichokes with Orzo Salad, **'88** M193
Artichoke-Tomato Salad, **'82** 239
Asparagus-and-Egg Salad, **'86** 305
Asparagus-Artichoke Salad, **'85** 162
Asparagus-Horseradish Salad, **'87** 80
Asparagus, Marinated, **'83** 46; **'86** 92
Asparagus Medley, Marinated, **'91** 105
Asparagus Salad, **'94** 67
Asparagus Salad Cups, **'83** 47
Asparagus Salad, Easy, **'88** 131
Asparagus Salad, Marinated, **'79** 20
Asparagus Salad Vinaigrette, **'88** 56
Asparagus Vinaigrette, **'80** 77; **'90** 138
Asparagus Vinaigrette, Light, **'82** 50
Asparagus with Tarragon Marinade, **'83** 47
Asparagus with Yogurt Dressing, **'79** 66
Aspic
  Apple Aspic, Sunshine, **'81** 73
  Basic Aspic for Garnishing, **'84** 189
  Beet Aspic, **'90** 123
  Coating, White Aspic, **'85** 151
  Cucumber-Curry Dressing, Aspic with,
    '89 178
  Fish Aspic, **'84** 190
  Fish 'n Aspic, **'84** 190
  Gazpacho Aspic, **'89** 179
  Grapefruit Aspic, **'80** 297; **'82** 112;
    '83 153
  Madeira Aspic, **'86** 65
  Orange-and-Carrot Aspic, **'86** 199
  Shrimp-Coleslaw Aspic, **'79** 88
  Shrimp-Cucumber Aspic, **'83** 108
  Sunshine Aspic, **'80** 103
  Three-Layer Aspic, **'88** 120
  Tomato-Artichoke Aspic, **'84** 320;
    '86 92
  Tomato Aspic, Bloody Mary-, **'81** 77
  Tomato Aspic, Chicken in, **'84** 190

Salads, Aspic *(continued)*

Tomato Aspic, Chili Sauce, **'85** 252
Tomato Aspic, Classic, **'91** 229
Tomato Aspic, Herbed, **'81** 73
Tomato Aspic, Layered, **'90** 99
Tomato Aspic, Light, **'85** 83
Tomato Aspic, Ranch, **'83** 218
Tomato Aspic, Spicy, **'81** 40; **'89** 288
Tomato Aspic, Tangy, **'83** 124
Tomato Aspic with Shrimp, **'79** 241
Tomato-Crab Aspic, **'85** 287
Two, Aspic for, **'83** 209
Vegetable Aspic, Cheesy, **'81** 73
Vegetable Aspic with Horseradish
   Dressing, Crisp, **'87** 152
Australian Outback Salad, **'92** 45
Avocado Acapulco, **'83** 2
Avocado and Zucchini Salad, Creamy, **'79** 208
Avocado Garbanzo Salad, **'81** 33
Avocado-Grapefruit Salad, **'85** 26; **'93** 282
Avocado-Melon Salad, **'82** 164
Avocado-Orange Salad, **'91** 44
Avocado Salad, **'81** 195; **'82** 9; **'83** 69;
   '92 246
Avocado Salad, Citrus-, **'82** 265
Avocado Salad, Spanish, **'87** 41
Avocados, Salmon-Stuffed, **'86** 74
Avocados, Shrimp-Filled, **'83** 2
Avocado with Crabmeat, **'86** 119
Bacon and Black-Eyed Salad, Hot, **'85** 7
Banana Salad, **'87** 80
Banana Salad, Frozen, **'82** 80, 132
Bananas, Nutty, **'79** 251
Barley-Broccoli Salad, **'90** 135
Barley Salad, **'92** 212
Bean
   Black Bean-and-Barley Salad, **'94** 174
   Black Bean-and-Cheese Salad, **'92** 217
   Black Bean Salad, **'89** 217
   Chilled Bean Salad, **'80** 178
   Cucumber-Bean Salad, **'83** 81
   Five-Bean Salad, Hot, **'81** 149
   Four-Bean Salad, **'79** 20; **'84** 82
   Full o' Beans Salad, **'81** 38
   Garbanzo Salad, **'82** 2
   Garbanzo Salad, Avocado-, **'81** 33
   Green Bean-and-Tomato Salad, **'86** 180
   Green Bean-Peanut Salad, **'86** 117
   Green Bean-Potato Salad, **'83** 80
   Green Bean Salad, **'87** 90
   Green Bean Salad, Cold, **'84** 106
   Green Bean Salad, Crispy, **'82** 239
   Green Bean Salad, German, **'92** 169
   Green Bean Salad, Hot, **'86** 298;
      '87 176
   Green Bean Salad, Lettuce and, **'80** 79
   Green Bean Salad, Paprika-, **'86** 191
   Green Bean Salad, Pickled, **'82** 239
   Green Bean Salad, Speedy, **'84** 283
   Green Beans-and-Cheese Salad, **'91** 159
   Green Beans, Marinated, **'83** 145
   Green Beans Vinaigrette, **'83** 25
   Hacienda Salad, **'81** 67
   Hot German-Style Bean Salad, **'91** 314
   Kentucky Wonder Green Beans
      Vinaigrette, **'94** 158
   Kidney Bean-Salami Pasta Toss, **'85** 165
   Lima Beans, Chilly, **'81** 206
   Lima Bean-Tomato Salad, **'85** 137

Marinated Bean-and-Rice Salad, **'87** 152
Marinated Bean-Pasta Salad, **'94** 167
Marinated Bean Salad, **'85** 137, 296;
   '89 314; **'93** 312; **'94** 167
Marinated Bean Salad, Crunchy, **'84** 197
Marinated Corn-Bean Salad, **'87** 9
Mexican Salad, **'81** 113
Mexican-Style Salad, **'83** 240
Mexican Tossed Salad, **'81** 280
Mixed Bean Salad, **'83** 217
Niçoise, Salad, **'86** 35
Overnight Fiesta Salad, **'83** 80
Pasta-Bean Salad, **'86** 169
Pinto Salad, **'86** 169
Pole Bean-Potato Salad, Hot, **'79** 74
Pork-'n'-Bean Salad, **'87** 83
Potato-Bean Salad, **'82** 301
Quick Bean Salad, **'89** 128
Rice-and-Bean Salad, **'85** 22
Rice Salad, Beans-and-, **'91** 44
Sandwiches, Bean Salad, **'81** 243
Saucy Bean Salad, **'84** 18
Sausage Salad, Bean-and-, **'91** 313
Six-Bean Salad, Colorful, **'87** 82
Southwest Salad, **'81** 113
Sprout Salad, Bean, **'82** 113
Supreme Bean Salad, **'91** 202
Sweet-and-Sour Bean Salad, **'85** 198;
   '86 147
Sweet-and-Sour Beans with Sprouts,
   '86 32
Beef-and-Broccoli Salad, **'87** 187
Beef-Cauliflower Salad, Corned, **'83** 16
Beef Fajita Salad, **'91** 70
Beef-Potato Salad, Corned, **'85** 213
Beef Salad, Gingered, **'88** 61
Beef Salad, Peking, **'88** 60
Beef Salad, Potato-Corned, **'81** 36
Beef Salad, Roast, **'80** 223; **'81** 56
Beef Salad, Tangy, **'87** M218
Beef Salad, Vegetable-Corned, **'80** 148
Beef Salad, Western-Style, **'93** 321
Beef Salad, Zesty, **'79** 56
Beet Salad, Marinated, **'83** 216
Beets and Cauliflower, Chilled, **'80** 137
Berry Grapefruit Cup, **'79** 242
Black Cherry Salad, Frozen, **'89** 163
Black-Eyed Pea Salad, Marinated, **'93** 190
Black-Eyed Peas, Zesty, **'89** 147
Blue Cheese-Pear-Apple Salad, **'81** 224
Blue Cheese Salad, **'88** 48
Boats, Salad, **'80** 93
Broccoli and Cauliflower Salad, **'81** 280
Broccoli and Cauliflower Salad, Creamy,
   '81 23
Broccoli and Cauliflower Toss, Crunchy,
   '83 25
Broccoli and Red Pepper Salad, **'83** 224
Broccoli-Cauliflower Pasta Salad, **'88** 269
Broccoli-Cauliflower Salad, **'92** 97
Broccoli-Corn Salad, **'87** 24
Broccoli-Mandarin Salad, **'93** 325
Broccoli, Marinated, **'81** 40
Broccoli Medley, **'81** 206
Broccoli 'n' Cauliflower Salad, **'90** 32
Broccoli-Orange Salad, **'94** 281
Broccoli-Peanut Salad, **'92** 35
Broccoli-Raisin Salad, Creamy, **'92** 106
Broccoli Salad, **'82** 24; **'85** 249; **'90** 292
Broccoli Salad, Creamy, **'79** 143
Broccoli Salad, Crunchy, **'83** 39

Broccoli Salad, Curried, **'86** 225
Broccoli Salad, Fresh, **'82** 34; **'87** 103
Broccoli Salad, Marinated, **'83** 240
Broccoli Salad Supreme, **'83** 260
Broccoli Salad, Warm, **'92** 35
Brown Rice Confetti Salad, **'94** 174
Brussels Sprouts Salad, **'87** 233
Cabbage and Fruit Salad, **'79** 286
Cabbage Salad, **'87** 120, 233
Cabbage Salad, Chinese, **'81** 271
Cabbage Salad, Garden, **'81** 210
Cabbage Salad, Nutty, **'87** 42
Cabbage Salad, Overnight, **'79** 83
Cabbage Salad, Tangy, **'82** 55
Cabbage Salad, Wilted, **'94** 281
Cabbage, Sweet-Sour Red, **'79** 5
Caesar Margarita Salad, **'94** 107
Caesar Salad, Maui, **'94** 107
Caesar Salad, Oriental, **'94** 107
Caesar Salad, Southern, **'94** 106
Caesar Salad, Turkey, **'93** 320
Caesar Salad with White Beans, **'93** 30
Cantaloupe-Cheese Salad, **'88** 184
Cantaloupe Cooler Salad, **'79** 176
Cantaloupe-Pecan Salad, **'86** 178
Cantaloupe Salad, **'86** 182
Carrot-and-Seed Salad, Fruity, **'86** 223
Carrot-and-Zucchini Salad, **'83** 240
Carrot-Caraway Salad, **'89** 105
Carrot-Fruit Toss, **'82** 235
Carrot-Raisin Salad, **'83** 117; **'84** 174;
   '87 10
Carrot Ring, Festive, **'82** 16
Carrot Salad, Favorite, **'80** 33
Carrot Salad, Harvest, **'89** 128
Carrot Salad, Honey-Sweet, **'89** 161
Carrot Salad, Shredded, **'80** 178
Carrot Salad, Simple, **'82** 101; **'84** 152
Carrot Salad, Sunshine, **'82** 132
Carrots, Creamy Marinated, **'87** 200
Carrot-Tangerine Salad, **'83** 316; **'84** 16
Cauliflower and Pea Salad, Savory, **'81** 280
Cauliflower-Broccoli Crunch, **'88** 216
Cauliflower-Broccoli Salad, **'79** 20
Cauliflower-Broccoli Toss, **'82** 54
Cauliflower-Broccoli Toss, Italian, **'88** 269
Cauliflower-Brussels Sprouts Salad, **'83** 240
Cauliflower-Olive Toss, **'85** 198; **'86** 147
Cauliflower-Pea Salad, **'87** 231
Cauliflower Salad, **'79** 221; **'80** 83; **'81** 225;
   '84 291; **'85** 240, 279; **'92** 36
Cauliflower Salad, Creamy, **'82** 102
Cauliflower Salad, Crunchy, **'80** 4; **'82** 75
Cauliflower Salad, Layered, **'83** 240
Cauliflower Salad, Marinated, **'82** 303;
   '84 232
Cauliflower Salad, Sweet-and-Sour, **'81** 2
Cauliflower-Vegetable Salad, **'85** 158
Celery-and-Cauliflower Salad, **'83** 39
Celery Salad, **'79** 70
Cheese-Banana Splits, Cottage, **'87** 56
Cheesy Italian Salad, **'84** 33
Chef Salad, Mexican, **'85** 84; **'92** 64
Chef Salad, Microwave, **'90** M146
Chef's Garden Salad, **'83** 146
Chef's Salad, **'86** 186
Chef's Salad Bowl, **'84** 66
Chef's Salad, Combination, **'86** 47
Chef's Salad, Vinaigrette, **'81** 9
Cherry-Orange Salad, **'79** 74; **'82** 56
Cherry Salad, Delicious Frozen, **'81** 252

Salads *(continued)*

Cherry Salad, Fresh, **'83** 120
Cherry Salad, Frozen, **'79** 126
Cherry Salad with Honey-Lime Dressing,
  '83 139
Cherry Salad with Sherry Dressing, **'79** 165
Chicken
  Almond-Chicken Salad Shanghai,
    '90 160
  Almond Salad, Chicken-, **'81** 133
  Aloha Chicken Salad, **'80** 297
  Amandine, Chicken Salad, **'81** 37
  Ambrosia, Chicken Salad, **'85** 216
  Apple Salad, Chicken-, **'90** 216
  Artichoke-Chicken-Rice Salad, **'94** 132
  Artichokes, Chicken Salad with, **'86** 186
  Asparagus-Chicken Salad, **'89** 83
  Aspic-Topped Chicken Salad, **'88** 88
  Avocado-Chicken Salad, **'87** 107
  Avocado Salad, Chicken-, **'80** 139
  Avocado Salad, Fruited Chicken,
    '82 101
  Avocado Salad Platter, Chicken-, **'83** 2
  Avocado Salad, Tossed Chicken-, **'80** 4
  Avocados, Chicken Salad in, **'85** 216
  Baked Chicken Salad, **'86** 297; **'87** 176
  Basil-Chicken-Vegetable Salad, **'92** 162
  BLT Chicken Salad, **'87** 144
  Blue Cheese Chicken Salad, **'94** 81
  Broccoli-Chicken Salad, **'90** 129
  Celery Salad, Chicken-, **'81** 187
  Chicken Salad, **'86** 232, 261
  Chop Suey Salad, **'81** 37
  Chutney-Chicken Salad, **'87** 74
  Chutney Salad, Chicken, **'82** 108
  Coleslaw, Chicken, **'84** 2
  Cream Puff Bowl, Chicken Salad in,
    '86 232
  Crunchy Chicken Salad, **'86** 157, 207
  Curried Chicken-and-Orange Salad,
    '87 144
  Curried Chicken-Rice Salad, **'92** 190
  Curried Chicken Salad, **'79** 219; **'84** 66;
    '85 96; **'86** 131; **'89** 176
  Curried Chicken Salad on Raisin Bread,
    '85 96
  Curried Chicken Salad with Asparagus,
    '81 36
  Dilled Chicken Salad, **'91** 212
  Fancy Chicken Salad, **'79** 55
  Filling, Chicken Salad, **'87** 106
  Fried Chicken Ginger Salad, **'93** 290
  Fruit, Chicken Salad with, **'82** 171
  Fruited Chicken Salad, **'84** 25, 290;
    '88 88; **'90** 318
  Fruited Chicken Salad in Avocados,
    '87 41
  Fruit Salad, Chicken-, **'82** 79; **'90** 234
  Fruity Chicken Salad, **'83** 157
  Grapes, Chicken Salad with, **'86** 117
  Green Salad with Chicken, Mixed,
    '80 54
  Hot Chicken Salad, **'81** 201; **'83** 196
  Hot Chicken Salad, Country Club-Style,
    '86 10
  Hot Chicken Salad, Crunchy, **'80** 138
  Hot Chicken Salad Pinwheel, **'80** 139
  Italian, Chicken Salad, **'89** 18
  Layered Chicken Salad, **'89** 162

Lettuce Folds, Thai, **'94** 47
Macadamia Chicken Salad, **'80** 138
Macaroni-Chicken Salad, **'85** 296;
  '86 302
Macaroni-Chicken Salad, Dilled, **'92** 142
Mama Hudson's Chicken Salad, **'93** 238
Mandarin Chicken, Carousel, **'79** 88
Mango, Chicken Salad with, **'86** 215
Marinated Chicken-Grape Salad, **'85** 74
Marinated Chicken-Raspberry Salad,
  '93 190
Mexican Chicken Salad, **'85** 84;
  '88 272
Minted Chicken Salad, **'92** 104
Nectarine Chicken Salad, **'79** 175
Old-Fashioned Chicken Salad, **'83** 79
Oriental Chicken Salad, **'85** 216;
  '88 271
Oriental, Chicken Salad, **'90** 146
Oriental Chicken Salad, **'91** 43
Pasta-Chicken Salad, Tarragon, **'87** 155
Pasta Salad, Chicken, **'88** 89
Pasta Salad, Grilled Chicken-, **'94** 64
Pea Salad, Chicken-, **'83** 218
Persian Chicken Salad, **'81** 12
Pineapple-Chicken Salad Pie, **'80** 138
Pineapple-Nut Chicken Salad, **'83** 80
Pocket, Chicken Salad in a, **'88** 139
Polynesian Chicken Salad, **'88** 272
Poulet Rémoulade, **'87** 144
Rice Salad, Chicken-, **'81** 203
Rice Salad, Hot Chicken-and-, **'83** 22
Rice Salad, Nutty Chicken-, **'83** 157
Roasted Chicken Salad, **'93** 14
Sandwiches, Chicken-Salad Finger,
  '85 119
Southwestern Chicken Salad, **'88** 88
Spaghetti Salad, Chicken-, **'90** 146
Special Chicken Salad, **'85** 82; **'87** 183;
  '88 M193
Spinach Tossed Salad, Chicken-and-,
  '83 157
Spread, Chicken Salad Party, **'88** M8
Stack-Up Salad, Chicken, **'83** 80
Summer Chicken Salad, **'83** 145
Super Chicken Salad, **'82** 174
Supreme, Chicken Salad, **'79** 107, 152;
  '89 176
Taco Salad, Chicken, **'94** M136
Tahitian Chicken Salad, **'84** 120
Tarragon Chicken Salad, **'90** 199
Tarts, Chicken Salad, **'84** 257
Tortellini Salad, Chicken, **'87** 288
Tropical Chicken Boats for Two,
  '82 186
Tropical Chicken Salad, **'85** 216
Twist, Chicken Salad with a, **'84** 221
Vegetable-Chicken Salad, **'91** 287
Walnut-Chicken Salad, **'89** 14
Walnut Salad, Sunburst Chicken-and-,
  '93 91
Wild Rice-Chicken Salad, **'83** 146
Chili Salad, Spicy, **'86** 71
Citrus-Blue Cheese Salad, **'92** 220
Citrus Salad, **'87** 103
Citrus Salad Bowl, **'86** 335; **'87** 83
Citrus Salad in Orange Cups, **'85** 47
Citrus Salad, Southern-Style, **'84** 262
Citrus Salad, Tangy, **'89** 34
Citrus Vinaigrette Salad, **'86** 192
Committee, Salad by, **'87** 288

Congealed
  Apple-Apricot Salad, **'88** 121
  Apple Cider Salad, **'83** 123
  Apple Cider Salad Mold, **'85** 54
  Apple Crunch Salad, **'84** 232; **'86** 331
  Apple Salad, Congealed, **'85** 252
  Apple Salad, Triple, **'88** 122
  Apricot Fruit Salad, **'82** 132
  Apricot Nectar Salad, **'83** 218; **'87** 236
  Apricot Salad, **'81** 251; **'83** 123
  Apricot Salad, Creamy, **'85** 263
  Asheville Salad, **'86** 199
  Asparagus-Cucumber Mold, **'85** 252
  Asparagus Mold, **'80** 104
  Asparagus Mousse Salad, **'86** 252
  Asparagus Salad, **'88** 121
  Asparagus Salad, Congealed, **'83** 260
  Asparagus Salad, Creamy Lemon-,
    '93 116
  Asparagus Salad, Tart, **'81** 203
  Avocado Crunch Salad, Congealed,
    '85 26
  Avocado Salad, Congealed, **'84** 266
  Avocado Salads, Congealed, **'87** 42
  Bean Salad, Molded Green, **'85** 252
  Beef Salad, Corned, **'80** 104
  Beef Salad, Molded Corned, **'82** 86
  Beet-Nut Salad, **'79** 74
  Beet Salad Mold, **'82** 267
  Beet Salad, Pickled, **'83** 234
  Beet Salad, Tangy, **'86** 199
  Berry Salad, Layered, **'79** 173
  Broccoli Salad, Congealed, **'84** 124
  Cantaloupe, Southern Plantation,
    '82 179
  Carrot-Nut Salad, Creamy, **'86** 331
  Carrot-Pineapple Salad, **'91** 83
  Carrot Salad, **'82** 137
  Cauliflower-Lemon Salad, **'81** 23
  Cheese Molds, Snowcap, **'79** 242
  Cherry-Apple Salad, **'86** 31
  Cherry Cola Salad, **'80** 104
  Cherry-Cola Salad, **'91** 224
  Cherry-Salad, Best, **'82** 302
  Cherry Salad, Congealed, **'89** 278
  Cherry Salad, Festive, **'84** 265
  Cherry Salad, Port Wine-, **'86** 11
  Cherry Salad, Sweet, **'89** 326
  Cherry-Wine Salad, Elegant, **'82** 56
  Chicken-Cucumber Mold, **'80** 175
  Chicken Jewel Ring Salad, **'83** 282
  Chicken-Pea Salad, **'83** 218
  Chicken Salad Mold, **'83** 80; **'84** 163
  Chicken Salad Ring, **'90** 123
  Chile-Tomato Salad, Spicy, **'88** 121
  Christmas Salad, **'88** 249
  Christmas Snow Salad, **'82** 266
  Citrus Mold, Sparkling, **'86** 331
  Citrus Salad Mold, Golden, **'85** 303
  Crabmeat-and-Asparagus, Congealed
    Salad with, **'84** 86
  Cranberry-Apple Mold, **'89** 277
  Cranberry Congealed Salad, **'91** 296
  Cranberry Gelatin Mold, **'92** 271
  Cranberry Mold, **'79** 250
  Cranberry-Orange Delight, **'90** 168
  Cranberry Ring, **'90** 291
  Cranberry Salad, Congealed, **'90** 124
  Cranberry Salad, Festive, **'81** 264, 296
  Cranberry Salad, Frosted, **'90** 288
  Cranberry Salad, Holiday, **'82** 266, 288

Salads, Congealed (continued)

Cranberry Salad, Jellied, '83 279;
  '85 281
Cranberry Salad, Layered, '84 322;
  '86 325
Cranberry Salad Ring, '80 247
Crème de Menthe Salad, '82 122
Creole Salad, '79 147
Cucumber Mold, Creamy, '84 164
Cucumber Mousse, '88 121
Cucumber-Pineapple Salad, '84 124
Cucumber Salad, Creamy, '86 147;
  '92 97
Cucumber Salad Mold, '82 111;
  '83 81, 253
Eggnog Christmas Salad, '86 281
Egg Salad, Deviled, '83 124
Emerald Salad, '81 143
Emerald Salad, Snowy, '87 311
Fall Salad with Ginger Dressing, '82 194
Frosted Salad, Heavenly, '79 286
Fruit Mold, Sherried, '90 124
Fruit Salad, Cherry, '87 236
Fruit Salad, Sparkling, '82 266
Fruit Salad, Spiced Autumn, '87 228
Garden-Patch Salad Molds, '86 283
Garden Salad, Molded, '86 199
Gazpacho Molded Salad, '92 323
Gazpacho Salad Mold, '87 311
Gazpacho Salad, Molded, '79 159
Gazpacho Salad with Avocado Cream,
  Congealed, '92 158
Grape-Cantaloupe Mold, Double,
  '79 173
Grapefruit Congealed Salad, '83 190
Grapefruit-Orange Salad, '91 276
Grapefruit Salad, '83 124; '84 325;
  '88 122
Grapefruit Salad, Congealed, '84 325;
  '85 279
Grape Salad Mold, '83 120
Green Spring Salad, '83 124
Ham Salad, Congealed, '81 36
Holiday Jewel Salad, '81 252
Horseradish Salad, '85 66
Layered Congealed Salad, '81 143
Layered Holiday Salad, '81 252
Layered Salad, Make Ahead, '81 296
Layer Mold, Three-, '82 54
Lemon-Cheese Salad, '85 240
Lemon-Cranberry Congealed Salad,
  '87 311
Lemon-Cream Salad, '88 250
Lemon-Cucumber Mold, '87 90
Lemon Mold, Cheesy, '79 241
Lemon-Onion Salad, '85 252
Lemon-Tomato Salad, Congealed,
  '89 178
Lemon-Vegetable Congealed Salad,
  '85 22
Lime-Carrot Salad, '92 65
Lime-Cheese Salad, Frosted, '79 286
Lime Sherbet Salad, '80 104
Mandarin Orange Salad, Congealed,
  '89 327
Mandarin Salad Molds, '85 54
Melon Ball Salad, Congealed, '84 125
Mincemeat Salad, '94 282
Mincemeat Salad, Holiday, '85 263

Molds, Perfection, '81 153
Mosaic Salad, '89 313
Orange-Pear Salad, '84 164
Orange Salad, Creamy, '84 124
Orange Salad, Frosted, '81 154;
  '83 123
Orange Salad, Jeweled, '83 210
Orange Sherbet Salad, '81 154
Orange Surprise Salad, '79 12
Peach-Cranberry Ring, Spicy, '85 264
Peaches-and-Cream Salad, '83 108
Peach Frost, '84 164
Peach Party Salad, '84 290
Peach Salad, Pickled, '80 104; '85 264
Peach Salad, Spiced, '94 68
Peachy Berry Cream Mold, '83 130
Pear-Lime Salad, '84 152
Pear Salad, Royal, '84 265
Pimiento Salad, Sunshine, '84 124
Pineapple-Buttermilk Salad, '82 80
Pineapple-Cucumber Congealed Salad,
  '83 118
Pineapple Daiquiri Salad, '84 232
Pineapple-Lime Salad, '84 320
Pineapple Mold, Minted, '85 240
Pineapple-Orange Congealed Salad,
  '83 218
Pineapple-Pear Delight, '82 54
Raspberry Fruit Mounds, '79 35
Raspberry Holiday Mold, '84 253
Raspberry Ribbon Salad, '87 236
Raspberry Salad, '86 286
Raspberry-Wine Salad, '91 256
Rhubarb Congealed Salad, '86 140
Rhubarb Salad, '91 146; '92 129
Rhubarb Salad, Tart, '91 146; '92 129
Roquefort Salad, Creamy, '79 73
Ruby-and-Emerald Salad, '85 79
Salmon Salad, Chilly, '80 104
Sangría Salad, '86 331
Shrimp Salad, '84 221
Strawberry-Nut Salad, '94 132
Strawberry Salad, Hidden Treasure,
  '79 11
Strawberry-Wine Salad Mold, '83 261
Sunshine Delight, '86 117
Tomato Mold, Tangy, '79 74
Tomato Ring, Tangy, '84 164
Tomato Salad, Frozen, '84 52
Tomato-Vegetable Ring, '81 302
Tuna-Cheese Mold, Creamy, '81 135
Tuna Ring, Creamy, '80 275
Tuna Salad, Congealed, '84 163
Tuna Salad, Creamy, '82 87, 208
Tuna Salad, Luncheon, '81 135
Vegetable Congealed Salad, Cheesy-,
  '86 199
Vegetable Congealed Salad, Fresh,
  '91 229
Vegetable Relish Salad, '82 267
Vegetable Salad, Congealed, '79 276
Vegetable Salad, Congealed Fresh,
  '82 240
Waldorf Salad, Congealed, '82 80
Waldorf Salad, Molded, '84 326
Corn-and-Pea Salad, '90 181
Cornbread Salad, '87 172
Corn-in-the-Shuck Salad, '93 236
Corn Salad, '80 247; '81 139; '85 236;
  '91 27
Corn Salad, Chilled, '79 20

Corn Salad, Festive, '92 263
Corn Salad, Fresh, '91 126; '94 162
Corn Salad, Marinated, '89 126
Corn Salad, Shoepeg, '81 23
Corn Salad, Tangy, '88 176
Corn Salad, Tasty, '84 289
Cottage Cheese Salad, Different, '85 328;
  '86 22
Cottage Cheese Salad in Tomatoes, '86 208
Cottage Cheese Salad, Out-of-This-World,
  '79 44
Cottage-Tomato Salad, '85 163
Couscous Salad, Curried, '91 44
Crab-and-Asparagus Salad, '92 141
Crab-and-Endive Salad, Marinated, '93 22
Crab and Wild Rice Salad, '79 116
Crab-Avocado Salad, '81 114
Crabmeat Luncheon Salad, '82 207
Crabmeat Salad, '91 169
Crabmeat-Shrimp Pasta Salad, '86 208
Crab Mousse, '79 117
Crab Salad, Chesapeake, '89 195
Crab Salad, Delightful, '87 145
Crab-Wild Rice Salad, '86 207
Cranberry-Cheese Ribbon Salad, '79 241
Cranberry Christmas Salad, '79 243
Cranberry Cloud, '90 287
Cranberry Holiday Salad, '89 277
Cranberry Oriental, '79 126
Cranberry-Pineapple Salad, Frozen, '91 237
Cranberry Salad, '88 250
Cranberry Salad, Tart, '79 286
Cranberry-Whipped Cream Salad, '83 261
Crawfish Salad, Dilled, '83 126
Crunchy-Creamy Salad, '88 100
Cucumber-Almond Salad, '86 147
Cucumber and Tomato Salad, Dilled, '81 153
Cucumber Cooler, Simple, '86 147
Cucumber Mousse, '79 11
Cucumber-Roast Beef Salad, '89 162
Cucumber Salad, Dilled, '82 229; '92 72;
  '93 65
Cucumber Salad, Marinated, '82 111
Cucumbers and Artichokes, Marinated,
  '82 111
Cucumbers, Cool, '84 152
Cucumbers in Sour Cream, '79 52; '80 178
Cucumber-Tomato Salad, '90 144
Cucumber-Vinaigrette Oriental, '85 198;
  '86 147
Cucumber-Yogurt Salad, '87 33
Cukes and Scallions, '91 168
Curry Salad, Hot Indian, '83 23
Dude Ranch Salad, '80 15
Eggplant Salad, '90 99
Egg-Rice Salad, '84 18; '86 169
Egg Salad, Bacon-Horseradish, '94 181
Egg Salad, Green Vegetable and, '79 191
Egg Salad Spread, Cottage-, '82 146
Egg Salad Tacos, Mexican, '94 181
Egg Salad, Yolkless, '94 181
Endive, Bacon, and Pecan Salad, '89 12
Endive-Tomato Starburst Salad, '93 323
Escarole-and-Bacon Salad, '84 85
Extravaganza, Salad, '87 233
Fast-and-Easy Salad, '85 M328
Fennel Salad, Marinated, '93 56
Freezer Salad, '94 118
Fruit
  Ambrosia, Mixed Fruit, '83 10
  Avocado Fruit Salad, '87 41

Salads, Fruit *(continued)*

Avocado-Fruit Salad with Honey-Yogurt Dressing, '93 172
Banana Split Salad, '91 58
Chef Salad, Fruited, '85 222
Chef's Fruit Salad, '86 35
Chilled Fruit with Dressing, '85 222
Citrus-Cilantro Dressing, Fruit Salad with, '93 310; '94 97
Citrus Dressing, Fruit Salad with, '88 6
Coconut Fruit Bowl, '83 111
Coconut Salad, Chunky Fruit-and-, '84 24
Colorful Fruit Salad, '82 113
Cottage Cheese-and-Fruit Salad, '86 16
Cottage-Fruit Split, '86 169
Cream Dressing, Fruit Salad with, '89 277
Creamy Fruit Salad, '84 265
Creamy Holiday Fruit Salad, '90 251
Cups, Royal Fruit, '81 146
Cups, Sangría Fruit, '89 34
Cups with Pineapple Cream Dressing, Fruit, '83 81
Curried Fruit Salad, '85 107
Date Dressing, Fruit Salad with, '87 57
Delight, Fruit, '86 131
Dressed-Up Fruit, '82 5
Easy Fruit Salad, '80 221
Easy Patio Fruit Salad, '88 184
Festive Fruit Salad, '80 16
Fresh Fruit Bowl, Sparkling, '80 146
Fresh Fruit Cup with Mint Dressing, '80 183
Fresh Fruit Salad, '82 165
Fresh Fruit Salad with Celery-Honey Dressing, '80 42
Fresh Fruit Salad with Poppy-Seed Dressing, '80 137
Fresh Fruit Salad with Poppy Seed Dressing, '91 168
Fresh Fruit with Lemon Sauce, '82 290
Frisky Fruit Salad, '85 46
Frozen Fruit Salad, '83 110
Frozen Fruit Salad, Dreamy, '79 126
Frozen Fruit Salad, Luscious, '81 204
Frozen Fruit Salad, Summertime, '89 111
Frozen Salad, Christmas Wreath, '79 241
Glazed Fruit Salad, '83 48; '84 290
Green Fruit Salad with Honey-Lime Dressing, '93 71
Hawaiian Fruit Dish, '82 112
Heavenly Salad, '81 252
Holiday Fruit Salad, '87 236
Honeydew Fruit Boats, '81 147
Honeydew Fruit Bowl, '84 186
Honey Dressing, Fruit Salad with, '87 129
Honey Fruit Salad, '80 276
Honey-Lemon Dressing, Fruit Salad with, '93 21
Hurry-Up Fruit Salad, '87 236
Jicama-Fruit Salad, '86 83
Layered Fruit Salad, '84 290; '89 277; '91 58
Lemonade Fruit Salad, '84 24
Lemon Freeze, Fruity, '82 145

Lettuce and Fruit Salad with Poppy Seed Dressing, '80 152
Main Dish Fruit Salad, '83 119
Marinated Fruit Bowl, '80 297
Marinated Fruit Deluxe, '81 146
Medley, Chilled Fruit, '84 60
Medley, Fruit Cup, '85 47
Mélange Delight, Fruit, '81 302
Minted Fruit Medley, '80 182
Mint-Gin Fruit Salad, '92 92
Mint Sauce, Fruit Salad with, '88 M96
Mixed Fruit Cup, '87 233
Mixed Fruit Salad, Banana-, '79 270
Multi-Fruit Salad, '93 184
Nut Salad, Cheesy Fruit-'n'-, '87 56
Old-Fashioned Fruit Salad, '82 80
Orange Cream, Fresh Fruit Salad with, '90 126
Orange Fruit Cup, '91 277
Oriental Dressing, Fruit Salad with, '91 277
Pasta Salad, Fruited, '92 108
Peachy Fruit Salad, '89 206
Persimmon Fruit Salad, '79 206
Picks, Fruit on, '80 159
Pineapple Dressing, Fruit Salad with, '85 207
Pineapple-Fruit Salad, Icy, '87 9
Platter, Fresh Fruit, '92 213
Platter, Fruit Salad, '83 261
Poppy Seed Dressing, Fruit Salad with, '88 78
Quick-and-Easy Fruit Salad, '81 99
Refreshing Fruit Salad, '85 92
Rhapsody, Fruit, '80 158
Rum, Fruit Cup with, '83 55
Salad, Fruit, '83 209; '89 277
Sherried Fruit Mélange, '80 158
Shrimp Salad, Fruited, '86 156
Sour Cream Fruit Salad, '80 138
Springtime Fruit Salad, '81 96
Summer Fruit Salad, '82 164; '92 171
Summer Salad, Favorite, '80 158
Sunny Fruit Salad, '91 58
Sunny Salad, '80 138
Sweet-and-Sour Fruit Salad, '80 13; '84 125
Tossed Fruit Salad, '92 106
Tropical Fruit Salad, '89 306
Tropical Fruit Salad with Fresh Mint Dressing, '84 126
Turkey Salad, Fruit-and-, '89 176
Vanilla Fruit Cup, '80 183
Watermelon Fruit Basket, '84 161
Wine, Fruit in White, '81 48
Winter Fruit Delight, '80 243
Winter Fruit Salad, '80 248; '82 23
Wreath, Della Robbia Fruit, '87 294
Yogurt Fruit Salad, '81 114
Yogurt-Granola Fruit Medley, '91 58
Garden Salad, '89 166
Gazpacho Salad, '91 313
Grapefruit-and-Shrimp Salad, '88 5
Grapefruit-Apple Salad, '89 41
Grapefruit-Avocado Salad, '83 316; '84 16; '89 41
Grapefruit-Banana Salad with Celery Seed Dressing, '91 237
Grapefruit Combo Salad, '80 50
Grapefruit-Cucumber Salad, '80 100
Grapefruit Winter Salad, '84 24

Greek Salad, '87 103; '93 208; '94 160, 202
Greek-Style Salad, '91 27
Green. *See also* Salads/Spinach.
  Apple and Brie, Salad Greens with, '93 241
  Balsamico, Insalata, '94 46
  B.B.'s Salad Dressing, Green Salad with, '91 65
  Bibb Salad, Tossed, '87 128
  Bibb Salad with Raspberry-Maple Dressing, '91 246
  Boston Lettuce and Watercress Salad, '93 65
  Bouquet, A Salad, '91 44
  Caesar Salad, '80 112; '86 80; '92 71
  Caesar Salad, Easy, '87 116
  Caesar Salad, Flippo, '87 61
  Caesar Salad, Mock, '92 283
  California Green Salad, '81 84
  Cantaloupe Green Salad, '91 126
  Chef's Salad. *See* Salads/Chef.
  Chinese Green Salad, '88 48
  Citrus Green Salad, '85 304
  Citrus Salad, Southern-Style, '84 262
  Combination Salad Bowl, '85 132
  Combo Salad Bowl, '81 9
  Company's Coming Salad, '79 113
  Cranberry-Topped Green Salad, '87 311
  Crimson Greens, '87 153
  Crunchy Green Salad, '89 321
  Endive Salad, Avocado-, '94 88
  Endive-Watercress Salad, '93 22
  Fenron Salad, '79 85
  Garden Salad, '85 92; '92 60
  Garden Salad Centerpiece, '83 171
  Garden Salad, Herbed, '85 328; '86 22
  Garden Salad, Summer, '87 153
  Garden Salad Toss, '81 9
  Garden Salad with Rosemary Dressing, Fresh, '81 131
  Garlic-Tarragon Green Salad, '92 79
  Goat Cheese and Greens, '90 54
  Grecian Green Salad, '84 266
  Grecian Tossed Salad, '79 174
  Hill Country Salad, '81 9
  Lemony French Dressing, Green Salad with, '85 67
  Lettuce, Cheesy Stuffed, '79 175
  Lettuce, Confetti-Stuffed, '87 24
  Lettuce, Delicate Garden, '87 62
  Lettuce-English Pea Salad, '91 208
  Lettuce, Garden-Stuffed, '83 135
  Lettuce Salad, Blue Cheese Stuffed, '94 202
  Lettuce Salad, French, '84 187
  Lettuce Salad, Tennessee-Killed, '88 86
  Lettuce Salad, Wilted, '82 302
  Lettuce Salad, Wilted Bacon-and-, '85 69
  Lettuces with Mustard Vinaigrette, Baby, '93 67
  Lettuce Wedges with Pimiento Dressing, '84 212
  Lettuce, Wilted, '86 269
  Lettuce with Sour Cream Dressing Deluxe, '88 48
  Marinated Cheese Dressing, Green Salad with, '93 206
  Mediterranean Salad, '90 99
  Mesclun with Tarragon Dressing, '90 55
  Mint-Fresh Green Salad, '92 105
  Mixed Green Salad, '90 230
  Mixed Green Salad, Wilted, '85 69

Salads, Green *(continued)*

Mixed Green Salad with Chicken, '80 54
Mixed Greens Salad, '87 62
Mixed Greens with Blue Cheese Vinaigrette, '89 274; '90 280
Nutty Green Salad, '87 168
Oriental, Green Salad, '85 92
Red-and-Green Salad, '90 55
Robust Salad, '90 181
Romaine Salad, Tangy, '80 155
Romaine-Spinach Salad, '89 123
Romaine with Caper Vinaigrette, Hearts of, '91 310
Salmagundi Salad, '83 146
Savory Green Salad, '82 74
Sensational Salad, '84 320
Sesame-Citrus Green Salad, '86 33
Shrimp, Green Salad with, '88 49
Simply Good Salad, '85 131
Soy Dressing, Green Salad with, '86 191
Spring Salad, '87 62
Spring Salad, Mediterranean, '80 148
Spring Salad Wedges, '87 62
Summer Salad, Crisp, '85 92
Summertime Salad, '79 143; '84 195
Sweet-and-Sour Green Salad, '94 281
Tangy Wilted Salad, '85 69
Tossed Mixed Green Salad, '84 126
Tossed Salad, Blue Cheese, '84 195
Tossed Salad, Boston, '84 85
Tossed Salad, Colorful, '90 55
Tossed Salad, Radish-Dressed, '79 104
Watercress-and-Mushroom Salad, '88 104
Watercress Salad, Roasted Red Pepper and, '90 55
Guacamole Salad, '80 14; '87 181
Guacamole-Tomato Salad, '81 302
Ham-and-Apple Salad, '88 139
Ham-and-Cheese Salad, '88 138
Ham and Cheese Toss, '79 55
Ham and Macaroni Salad, '79 220
Ham-and-Pasta Salad, '90 128
Ham-and-Rice Salad, Colorful, '90 319
Ham-and-Rice Salad, Mandarin, '87 145
Ham-Dijon Pasta Salad, '92 191
Ham 'n Egg Salad, '81 36
Ham-Noodle Salad, '85 249
Ham-Rice Toss, '82 40
Ham Salad, Crunchy Baked, '83 23
Ham Salad, Fruited, '81 36, 146
Ham Salad, Hearty, '82 40
Ham Salad Sandwich, Tangy, '80 272
Ham Salad, Spicy Italian, '85 74
Ham Salad Spread, '87 92
Ham Salad, Tropical, '89 175
Ham-Sweet Potato Salad, Hawaiian, '82 232
Hearts of Palm Salad, '81 252; '89 276
Hearts-of-Palm Salad, '87 138
Hearts of Palm Salad with Basil-and-Garlic Dressing, '94 55
Herb Salad, '87 90
Hominy-Bean Salad, '88 266
Honeydew Salad with Apricot Cream Dressing, '84 191
Ice Cream Salad, '79 126
Italian Salad, '87 145
Jicama-and-Orange Salad, '88 246

Jicama-Orange Salad, '86 83; '90 122
Jicama Salad, '87 123
Layered Overnight Salad, '90 319
Layered Salad, '86 35, 79
Layered Salad, Cheesy, '81 37
Layered Salad Deluxe, '81 153
Layered Salad, Hearty, '86 79
Layered Salad, Majestic, '86 79
Layered Salad, Make-Ahead, '81 296
Layered Salad, Overnight, '81 188
Legumes, Marinated, '90 197
Lentils-and-Rice Salad, '90 197
Lobster and Orange Salad, '82 207
Lobster Salad, '89 249; '90 69
Macaroni-Cheese Salad, Dilled, '86 208
Macaroni-Crabmeat Salad, '81 153
Macaroni-Ham Salad, '85 218
Macaroni Salad, '87 92
Macaroni Salad, Barbecue, '82 276
Macaroni Salad, Confetti, '82 132; '85 297
Macaroni Salad, Crunchy, '82 24
Macaroni Salad, Dilled, '89 161
Macaroni Salad for Two, '81 31
Macaroni Salad, Garden, '84 290; '92 64
Macaroni Salad, Gourmet, '81 253
Macaroni Salad, Hearty, '84 90
Macaroni Salad, Pineapple, '79 220
Macaroni Salad, Refreshing, '80 177
Macaroni Salad, Shell, '92 163
Macaroni Salad, Spiral, '82 276
Macaroni Salad, Sweet-and-Sour, '85 166
Macaroni Salad, Taco, '85 165
Macaroni Salad Véronique, '85 164
Macaroni-Salmon Salad, '82 232
Macaroni Shell Salad, '87 38
Macaroni-Shrimp Salad, '85 121
Macaroni-Shrimp Salad, Festive, '85 165
Macaroni Toss, Corkscrew, '83 163
Macaroni-Tuna Salad, Whole Wheat, '84 193
Macaroni-Vegetable Salad, '86 209
Madras Salad, '86 82
Magnolia Blossom Salad, '89 123
Main-Dish Salad, '86 191
Mandarin, Salad, '84 231
Mandarin Spinach Salad, '85 163
Mandarin Tossed Salad, '89 12
Mango Salad, '79 137
Mango Salad, Fresh, '84 126
Marinated Salad, '83 170
Marinated Salad, Zesty, '90 90
Meal-in-One Salad, '86 188
Melon-and-Prosciutto Salad, '92 191
Melon Balls in Watermelon Sauce, '79 177
Melon Balls, Minted, '87 162
Melon-Berry Salad, '90 180
Melon-Citrus Mingle, '79 177
Melon Cocktail, Minted, '81 146
Melon Cooler, '81 146
Melon Mélange, '84 139
Melon Salad, Summertime, '82 101
Melon Salad with Dill Dressing, '88 182
Mexican Salad, '94 202
Mexican Salad in a Shell, '86 4
Mexican Salad Supper, '82 9; '83 68
Mexican Salad with Avocado Dressing, '92 321
Middle Eastern Salad, '87 107
Minestrone Salad, '79 220
Mix, Muffy Salad, '94 34

Mozzarella-Tomato-Basil Salad, Fresh, '93 131
Mushroom-and-Pepper Salad, '86 68
Mushroom Salad, Fabulous, '81 190
Mushroom Salad, Fresh, '93 65
Mushroom Salad, Marinated, '88 215; '90 181
Mushroom Salad, Quick Cheesy-, '89 128
Mushroom-Zucchini Salad, '85 8
Noodle Salad, Ramen, '88 41
Okra-Corn-and-Tomato Vinaigrette, '90 173
Okra Salad, '90 155
Olive Clubhouse Salad, '81 114
Olive Salad, Doodles, '94 35
Olive Salad, Italian, '94 35
Olive Salad, Mexican, '85 84
Orange-and-Beet Salad, '88 43
Orange and Pineapple Salad, Mandarin, '82 266
Orange-Carrot Salad, '80 89; '84 325
Orange-Cauliflower Salad, '82 266
Orange-Cottage Cheese Salad, '79 44
Orange Cups, '86 92
Orange-Grapefruit Salad, '93 294
Orange-Lettuce Salad, Mandarin, '92 79
Orange-Onion Salad, '89 41
Orange-Onion Salad, Marinated, '91 231; '92 68
Orange-Romaine Salad, '84 325; '87 239
Orange Salad Cups, '85 40
Orange Salad, Mandarin, '81 252; '84 161
Orange Salad, Quick, '87 80
Orange Salad, Tropical, '92 97
Orange-Shrimp Salad, '84 197
Orange-Spinach Salad, '83 316; '84 16
Orange-Strawberry Salad with Orange-Curd Dressing, '93 22
Orange Tossed Salad, Mandarin, '92 303
Orange Walnut Salad, '80 246
Oriental Salad Bowl, '87 153
Orzo Salad, Confetti, '92 173
Paella Salad, '86 207
Party Freeze Salad, '82 145
Pasta-and-Shrimp Salad, '83 163
Pasta-and-Tomato Salad, Herbed, '92 144
Pasta Medley, Garden, '89 256
Pasta Platter, Cold, '88 42
Pasta Salad, '84 139; '86 120; '87 36; '90 62, 91
Pasta Salad, Crunchy, '85 166
Pasta Salad, Easy Confetti-, '92 220
Pasta Salad, Garden, '86 188
Pasta Salad, Ham-Pecan-Blue Cheese, '90 62
Pasta Salad, Luncheon, '90 191
Pasta Salad, Main-Dish, '82 199
Pasta Salad, Oriental, '90 63
Pasta Salad, Overnight, '82 276
Pasta Salad, Presto, '90 63
Pasta Salad, Ratatouille, '90 74
Pasta Salad, Seafood, '90 62
Pasta Salad, Southwestern, '94 278
Pasta Salad with Ham, '92 108
Pasta, Snappy, '83 164
Pasta Vinaigrette, Italian, '92 78
Pea-and-Apple Salad, English, '87 24
Peach-and-Kiwi Salad, '90 180
Peaches in a Garden Nest, '87 154
Peach Pinwheel Salad, '79 11
Peach Salad, Frosted, '82 145
Peach Salad, Frozen, '82 54
Peach Salad, Georgia, '80 142

Salads (*continued*)

Peach Salad Supreme, Easy, '79 177
Peanut-Apple Salad, '80 5
Pear-and-Celery Salad, '87 56
Pear-and-Spinach Salad, Festive, '85 131
Pear Plate, Pretty, '89 225
Pear Salad, Crunchy, '83 234; '84 244
Pear Salad, Golden, '91 58
Pear-Swiss Cheese Salad, '91 237
Pea Salad, Black-Eyed, '80 112; '86 225;
    '88 92, 221; '90 173
Pea Salad, Cheddar-, '84 82
Pea Salad, Creamy, '80 111
Pea Salad, Crunchy, '90 143
Pea Salad, English, '81 280; '90 143
Pea Salad, Marinated, '81 204
Pea Salad, Marinated English, '82 54
Pea Salad, Mexi-, '81 7
Pea Salad, Minted, '91 119
Pea Salad, Overnight Black-Eyed, '81 280
Pea Salad, Special, '83 239
Pea Salad, Sugar Snap, '86 115
Pea Salad, Three, '84 290
Peas-and-Asparagus Salad, '83 141
Peas, Marinated Black-Eyed, '82 156
Pea Vinaigrette, Black-Eyed, '86 7
Pebble Salad, '91 27
Pepper-Cheese Stacks, '87 80
Pepperoni-and-Broccoli Salad, '83 216
Pepper Salad, Mixed, '89 103
Pepper Salad, Three-, '91 162
"Pig in the Garden" Salad, '92 255
Pineapple Boat Aloha, '80 102
Pineapple Boats Ahoy, '80 148
Pineapple Boats, Fresh, '83 153
Pineapple-Celery Salad, '85 95
Pineapple Salad, Frosty, '89 278
Pineapple Waldorf Salad, '92 97
Pistachio-Pasta Salad, '86 141
Pita Salad Sandwiches, '83 134
Pizza, Salad, '87 182
Plentiful P's Salad, '87 12
Pork-and-Spinach Salad, Mandarin, '88 M126
Pork Salad, Oriental, '92 140
Potato
    Any Day Potato Salad, '81 154
    Asparagus-and-New Potato Salad,
        '86 69
    Bacon-Topped Potato Salad, '85 59
    Basil Potato Salad, '94 178
    Bean Salad, Potato-, '82 301
    Blue Cheese-Potato Salad, '91 208
    Broccoli-Potato Salad, Hot, '85 23
    Chunky Potato Salad, '81 M138
    Confetti Potato Salad, '80 5; '88 16
    Corned Beef-Potato Salad, '85 213
    Corned Beef Salad, Potato-, '81 36
    Cottage Cheese-Potato Salad,
        '79 147, 285
    Creamy Potato Salad, '80 178; '88 171;
        '92 241
    Deluxe Potato Salad, '80 155
    Dill-and-Sour Cream Potato Salad,
        '93 105; '94 100
    Dill Potato Salad, '85 213; '94 179
    Dill Potato Salad, Hot, '79 78
    Dutch Potato Salad, Hot, '87 176
    Festive Potato Salad, '89 315
    Fish-Potato Salad, Smoked, '84 233

French-Style Potato Salad, '88 171
Fruity Potato Salad, '85 214
Garden Patch Potato Salad, '84 82
German Potato Salad, '82 134, 239;
    '84 18; '92 169
German Potato Salad, Hot, '79 78;
    '94 254
German-Style Potato Salad, '83 23;
    '88 M194
Grecian Potato Salad, '82 55
Green Bean-Potato Salad, '83 80
Ham-and-Egg Potato Salad, '86 84
Ham and Potato Salad, '80 272
Herbed Potato Salad, '87 171; '94 164
Hot-and-Light Potato Salad, '93 90
Hot Dutch Potato Salad, '86 297
Hot Potato Salad, '79 78; '81 276;
    '86 10
Hot Potato Salad Supreme, '79 78
Layered Creamy Potato Salad, '81 23
Marinated Potato Slices, '93 98
Mustard Potato Salad, '86 302
New Potato Salad, '84 120, 139;
    '94 162
Olive-Potato Salad, '85 114
Parmesan Potato Salad, Hot, '79 78
Parslied Potato Salad, '85 240
Patio Potato Salad, '90 160
Pepper Cups, Potato Salad in, '79 78
Peppers, Potato Salad 'n', '83 135
Pesto Potato Salad, '90 164
Pickle-Potato Salad, Sweet, '85 213
Pole Bean-Potato Salad, Hot, '79 74
Potato Salad, '90 122; '94 160
Salmon-Potato Salad, '87 285
Saucy Potato Salad, '87 123
Savory Potato Salad, '80 30
Sour Cream Potato Salad, '79 104;
    '80 79
Sour Cream-Potato Salad, '84 149
South-of-the-Border Potato Salad,
    '94 178
Spring Salad, Mediterranean, '80 148
Sugar Snap Peas, Potato Salad with,
    '91 120
Sweet and Sour Potato Salad, '80 152
Sweet-and-Sour Potato Salad,
    '92 106
Sweet Potato Salad, Fresh, '86 226
Tri Club Potato Salad, '92 166
Tuna-Potato Salad, '84 289
Raspberry Salad, Frozen, '79 287; '80 35
Raspberry-Walnut Salad, '94 158
Red Cabbage Citrus Salad, '94 72
Red, White, and Green Salad, '90 18
Relish Salad, '84 121
Rice-and-Avocado Salad, '89 146
Rice-and-Shrimp Salad, '83 82
Rice-and-Vegetable Salad, Brown, '84 202
Rice-Carrot Ring, '79 246
Rice-Green Apple Salad, Wild, '92 90
Rice, Mardi Gras, '91 217
Rice-Pea Salad, '85 163
Rice Salad, '79 74; '81 51
Rice Salad, Charleston Red, '79 146
Rice Salad, Chutneyed, '88 100
Rice Salad, Colorful, '81 253
Rice Salad, Confetti, '80 232
Rice Salad, Crunchy, '82 302
Rice Salad, Curried, '80 84; '85 147, 220

Rice Salad, Curry, '89 146
Rice Salad, Hearty, '82 233
Rice Salad, Mandarin, '88 271
Rice Salad, Molded Gazpacho-, '86 221
Rice Salad, Springtime Wild, '88 100
Rice Salad, Vegetable-, '80 148; '83 198;
    '85 87
Rice Salad, Wild, '85 65; '89 147; '93 191
Rice Salad with Artichoke Hearts, '80 232
Rice Salad with Bacon, '79 52
Rice Salad with Fresh Mushrooms, '80 231
Rice Salad, Zesty, '81 23
Rice-Shrimp Salad, '79 270; '92 142
Roast Beef Salad, '90 318
Rolls, Hearty Salad, '81 206
Rolls, Picnic Salad, '79 127
Rotelle Salad, Crunchy, '86 209
Rotini Salad, '88 42
Salmon-and-Macaroni Salad, '81 114
Salmon on Mixed Greens with Creamy Dill
    Dressing, '93 143
Salmon-Pasta Salad, '87 9
Salmon-Rice Salad, '84 289
Salmon Salad, '89 99
Salmon Salad, Broiled, '92 108
Salmon Salad, Crunchy, '81 148
Salmon Salad Shells, '85 286
Salmon Salad, Simple, '91 23
Salmon Salad, Summertime, '82 207
Salmon-Spinach Salad, '87 145
Sauerkraut Salad, '80 178
Sauerkraut Salad, Crunchy, '87 9
Seafood Salad, '90 88
Seafood Salad, Baked, '86 10
Seafood Salad, Hot, '79 117; '80 164
Seafood Salad, Polynesian, '79 57
Seafood Salad, Smoky, '84 46
Seafood Salad Sussex Shores, '93 98
Seashell Salad, '86 209
Sesame-Almond Salad, '89 123
Shell Salad, Tossed, '91 256
Shrimp and Avocado Salad, '80 266
Shrimp-and-Black Bean Salad, Caribbean,
    '93 143
Shrimp-and-Egg Salad Sandwiches, '94 182
Shrimp-and-Orange Rice Salad, Zesty,
    '87 155
Shrimp-and-Orzo Salad, Peppers Stuffed with,
    '91 203
Shrimp and Rice Salad, '80 231; '82 207
Shrimp-and-Rice Salad, '92 307
Shrimp Bowl, Mediterranean, '80 174
Shrimp-Egg Salad, Tossed, '80 4
Shrimp-Endive Salad, '85 73
Shrimp Macaroni Salad, '79 220
Shrimp-Macaroni Salad, '85 219
Shrimp Mousse, '79 57
Shrimp, Orange, and Olive Salad with Sherry
    Vinaigrette, '93 177
Shrimp Rémoulade, '90 255
Shrimp-Rice Salad, Baked, '83 22
Shrimp-Rice Salad, Tangy, '84 66
Shrimp Rotelle, '85 165
Shrimp Salad, '81 94; '86 186; '93 238
Shrimp Salad, Avocado Stuffed with, '82 207
Shrimp Salad, Creamy, '79 56
Shrimp Salad Filling, '87 106
Shrimp Salad in Pastry, '86 105
Shrimp Salad, Layered, '88 100
Shrimp Salad, Marinated, '85 82; '93 321
Shrimp Salad on the Half Shell, '86 73

Salads *(continued)*

Shrimp Salad, Oriental, '91 313
Shrimp Salad Sandwiches, '90 178
Shrimp Salads, Individual, '83 146
Shrimp Salad, Super, '81 37
Shrimp Salad, Vegetable-, '79 190
Shrimp Vermicelli Salad, '88 139
Sirloin Salad, Grilled, '94 129
Slaws
    Apple-Carrot Slaw, '92 243
    Apple Coleslaw, '89 315
    Apple-Pineapple Slaw, '79 241
    Apple Slaw, Fresh, '81 63
    Bacon Coleslaw, '83 58
    Banana-Nut Slaw, '86 250
    Bean Slaw, Red, '79 247
    Blue Cheese Coleslaw, '89 13
    Broccoli Slaw, Zesty, '93 246
    Cabbage-and-Apple Slaw, Red, '87 31
    Cabbage-Orange Slaw, '79 135
    Cabbage-Pineapple Slaw, '92 182
    Cabbage Slaw, Fresh, '85 139
    Cauliflower Slaw, '92 167
    Chicken Coleslaw, '84 2
    Chili Coleslaw, '80 178
    Chinese Cabbage Slaw, '89 312
    Coleslaw, '79 152; '82 135
    Confetti Slaw, '89 48
    Corn and Cabbage Slaw, '79 135
    Cottage Coleslaw, '80 64
    Country-Style Coleslaw, '83 59
    Creamy Coleslaw, '83 170
    Crunchy Coleslaw, '86 295
    Cucumber Slaw, Creamy, '89 49
    Curried Coleslaw, '85 139
    Freezer Coleslaw, '89 49
    Freezer Slaw, '81 279; '82 24; '83 154
    Frozen Coleslaw, '82 102
    Fruit Coleslaw, Three-, '86 250
    Fruited Coleslaw, '83 209; '85 139
    Grape-Poppy Seed Slaw, '86 225
    Grapes and Almonds, Coleslaw with,
     '83 59
    Guacamole Mexican Coleslaw, '82 302
    Ham Coleslaw, '84 195
    Healthy Slaw, '92 183
    Hot-and-Creamy Dutch Slaw, '87 127
    Hot-and-Sour Chinese Slaw, '85 139
    Hot Slaw, '89 49
    Kentucky Coleslaw, '81 216
    Layered Coleslaw, '86 180
    Layered Slaw, '93 214
    Light and Creamy Coleslaw, '93 318
    Make-Ahead Coleslaw, '81 155
    Mango Slaw, '93 31; '94 71
    Marinated Coleslaw, '79 135
    Marinated Slaw, '91 229
    Memphis Slaw, '91 28
    Mexicali Coleslaw, '84 18
    Mexican Coleslaw, '89 48
    Old-Fashioned Coleslaw, '80 120;
     '82 225
    Old-Fashioned Slaw, '84 149
    Old-Fashioned Sweet Coleslaw, '93 128
    Overnight Cabbage Slaw, '81 88; '82 7
    Overnight Coleslaw, '79 135
    Overnight Slaw, '79 5; '92 280
    Peach Slaw, Party, '86 250
    Peanut Slaw, '85 139

    Peanut Slaw, Chinese, '93 212
    Pear Slaw, Peanutty-, '86 250
    Pineapple-Almond Slaw, '92 171
    Pineapple Slaw, '94 49
    Pineapple Slaw, Colorful, '86 250
    Polka Dot Slaw, '83 59
    Red Cabbage-and-Apple Slaw, '91 309
    Seafood Slaw, '79 56
    Silks, Slaw, '93 236
    Sour Cream Slaw, '87 10
    Swedish Slaw, '79 135
    Sweet and Crunchy Slaw, '79 104
    Sweet-and-Sour Hot Slaw, '92 63
    Sweet-and-Sour Slaw, '81 237
    Sweet Cabbage Slaw, '79 76
    Sweet Potato-Currant Slaw, '93 246
    Tangy Coleslaw, '83 59
    "Think Pink" Slaw, '94 247
    Tomatoes, Coleslaw with, '80 34
    Turnip Slaw, '89 245
    Vegetable Slaw, '81 280
    Zesty Slaw, '82 127
    Zucchini Coleslaw, Fiesta, '91 168
Spaghetti Salad, '82 277; '84 205
Spaghetti Squash Salad, Marinated, '94 134
Spinach and Bacon Salad, '81 143
Spinach and Mushroom Salad, '80 112
Spinach-and-Onion Salad Bowl, '81 157
Spinach-and-Orange Salad, '86 15
Spinach and Sun-Dried Tomato Salad, '93 250
Spinach-Apple Salad, '90 89; '92 13
Spinach-Apricot Salad, '94 63
Spinach-Beet Salad, '83 227
Spinach-Blue Cheese Salad, '82 166
Spinach-Enoki Salad, '89 62
Spinach-Kiwifruit Salad, '87 305
Spinach-Lamb Salad, '85 58
Spinach-Lettuce Salad, Layered, '84 266
Spinach-Mustard Twist, '86 209
Spinach-Pecan Salad, '89 128
Spinach, Pickled, '81 69
Spinach-Rice Salad, '94 63
Spinach Salad, '82 102; '86 302; '87 62;
  '88 299; '92 281, 341; '93 46, 65
Spinach Salad, Arranged, '91 210; '92 160
Spinach Salad, Citrus, '90 59
Spinach Salad, Combination, '85 327; '86 22
Spinach Salad, Creamy, '83 60
Spinach Salad, Crunchy, '80 147; '81 225
Spinach Salad, Curry, '80 242
Spinach Salad Delight, Fresh, '80 146
Spinach Salad, Dijon, '89 282
Spinach Salad, Easy, '91 249
Spinach Salad, Festive, '80 247
Spinach Salad, French, '79 8
Spinach Salad, Fresh, '82 73; '83 240;
  '84 15, 77; '86 130
Spinach Salad, Green, '79 142
Spinach Salad, Layered, '80 5; '89 163
Spinach Salad, Minted, '94 63
Spinach Salad, Oriental, '82 23
Spinach Salad, Sesame, '90 292
Spinach Salad, Southern, '80 55
Spinach Salad, Special, '80 78
Spinach Salad, Springtime, '81 114
Spinach Salad, Strawberry-, '91 169; '93 168
Spinach Salad, Supreme, '79 243
Spinach Salad, Sweet-Sour, '85 M112
Spinach Salad, Tropical, '90 231
Spinach Salad, Wilted, '81 M4; '89 123;
  '91 210; '92 160; '93 125

Spinach Salad with Apple-Onion Vinaigrette,
  '94 276
Spinach Salad with Chili-Lime Dressing,
  '94 63
Spinach Salad with Citrus Dressing, '88 133
Spinach Salad with Creamy Dressing, Crisp,
  '83 81
Spinach Salad with Dried Tomato Vinaigrette,
  '93 272
Spinach Salad with Garlic-Ginger Vinaigrette
  Dressing, '92 195
Spinach Salad with Honey Dressing, '90 16
Spinach Salad with Hot Bacon Dressing,
  '82 211
Spinach Salad with Orange Dressing, '87 187
Spinach Salad with Oysters and Red Wine
  Vinaigrette, '94 327
Spinach Salad with Poppy Seed Dressing,
  '91 210; '92 160
Spinach Salad with Raspberry Cream
  Dressing, '94 321
Spinach Salad with Russian Dressing, '79 144
Spinach Salad, Zesty, '79 88
Spinach-Sesame Salad, '91 211; '92 160
Spinach-Sprout Salad, Fresh, '82 281; '83 42
Spinach with Spicy Dressing, Fresh, '80 55
Sprout Salad, '90 137
Sprout Salad, Spanish, '85 327; '86 22
Steak Salad Cups, Pepper, '86 206
Steak Salad, Greek, '92 107
Strawberry Salad, Frozen, '94 119
Strawberry Yogurt Salad, '80 232
Summer Salad, '93 179
Summer Salad, Georgia, '92 179
Summer Salad with Citrus Marinade, '92 133
Tabbouleh, '85 148; '93 70
Tabbouleh Salad, '91 70; '92 212; '94 174
Taco Salad, '79 56; '83 145; '84 221;
  '85 84; '89 332; '90 20
Taco Salad Cups, '85 M29
Taco Salad, Meatless, '81 204
Taco Salad, Spicy, '87 287
Tex-Mex Salad, Marinated, '93 106
Tofu Salad, '88 27
Tomato-and-Cucumber Salad, Marinated,
  '92 216
Tomato-and-Cucumber Summer Salad,
  '93 141
Tomato-Asparagus Salad, '92 79
Tomato-Avocado Salad, '86 74
Tomato-Basil Vinaigrette, '87 89
Tomato Couscous Salad, Basil-and-, '94 175
Tomato-Cucumber-Onion Salad, '81 239
Tomato-Cucumber Salad, '86 218; '92 199
Tomato-Cucumber Salad with Yogurt-Herb
  Dressing, '92 96
Tomatoes, Avocado-Stuffed, '82 101
Tomatoes, Cold Stuffed, '80 100
Tomatoes, Herbed, '83 173
Tomatoes, Marinated, '85 156, 163;
  '89 174, 202
Tomatoes, Marinated Salsa, '82 164
Tomatoes, Oregano, '83 145
Tomatoes Stuffed with Sea Slaw, '89 96
Tomatoes Vinaigrette, '84 106
Tomato-Feta Salad, '81 246; '91 168
Tomato Flower Salad, '89 128
Tomato-Herb Salad, '89 220
Tomato-Mozzarella Salad, '89 220
Tomato Petal Salad, '79 88
Tomato Refresher, '81 94

Salads (continued)

Tomato Relish Salad, '83 111
Tomato Salad, Artichoke-Stuffed, '82 101
Tomato Salad, Cherry, '87 156
Tomato Salad, Crab-Stuffed, '80 148
Tomato Salad, Oriental-Stuffed, '82 101
Tomato Salad, Summer, '94 201
Tomato Salad, Vidalia-, '84 65
Tomato Slices, Marinated, '83 193
Tomato Slices with Lemon Dressing, '87 167
Tomato Treat, Summer, '79 143
Tortellini-Pesto Salad, '92 22
Tortellini Salad, '89 237
Tortellini Salad, Garden, '91 44
Tossed Salad with Parmesan Dressing,
  '86 192
Tropical Salad, '85 91
Tuna
  Cannellini Bean Salad, Tuna-and-,
    '86 143
  Cheese-Sauced Tuna Salad, '87 M124
  Chef Salad, Tuna, '82 78
  Company Tuna Salad, '87 201
  Confetti Salad, '80 4
  Crunchy Tuna Salad, '87 201
  Curried Tuna Salad, '86 208
  Curried Tuna Salad with Grapes, '87 201
  Egg Salad, Tuna-, '81 135
  Favorite Tuna Salad, '82 208
  Flavorful Tuna Salad, '81 37
  Greens and Tuna Salad, Fresh, '80 55
  Layered Tuna Salad, '84 221
  Macaroni Salad, Tuna, '83 44
  Macaroni Salad, Tuna-, '83 145; '84 66
  Pasta Salad, Tuna-, '91 43; '92 141
  Pasta Salad, Tuna, '92 108
  Potato Salad, Tuna-, '84 289
  Red Pepper Salad, Tuna-and-, '93 143
  Rice Salad, Tuna-, '87 202
  Rolls, Hot Tuna Salad, '84 281
  Swiss Tuna Salad, '86 186
  Taco Salad, Tuna-, '87 145
  Tomatoes, Tuna-Mac in, '87 188
  Whole Wheat Macaroni-Tuna Salad,
    '84 193
Turkey-and-Pepper Stir-Fry Salad, Chilled,
  '88 140
Turkey-Apple Salad, '88 123; '90 181
Turkey-Carrot Salad, '86 283
Turkey-Fruit Salad, '79 56
Turkey Fruit Salad, '83 233; '84 244
Turkey-in-the-Orange Salad, '93 21
Turkey Macaroni Salad, '83 282
Turkey 'n' Pasta Salad, Ranch-Style, '94 184
Turkey Salad, '90 318
Turkey Salad Bake, '79 253
Turkey Salad, Curried, '88 140
Turkey Salad, Fruit-and-Spice, '94 325
Turkey Salad, Fruitful, '84 197
Turkey Salad, Holiday, '84 320
Turkey Salad, Honey-Mustard, '92 309
Turkey Salad, Hot, '86 10, 297; '87 176
Turkey Salad, Layered, '86 332; '92 220
Turkey Salad Pita Sandwiches, '87 202;
  '88 43
Turkey Salad, Polynesian, '87 285
Turkey Salad, Southwestern, '91 313
Turkey Salad with Hot Bacon Dressing,
  '87 285

Turkey Salad with Sautéed Walnuts, '86 117
Turkey Waldorf Salad with Yogurt Dressing,
  '88 53
Turkey-Zucchini Salad, '85 74
Turnip-and-Carrot Salad, '91 212
Turnip Salad, '85 235
Turnip Salad, Irish, '94 178
Vegetable. *See also* Salads/Congealed.
  Antipasto, Vegetable, '85 263
  Boats, Salad, '80 93
  Calico Salad, '82 35
  Chinese Salad, '80 4
  Composée, Salad, '79 171
  Composé, Salad, '93 126
  Creamy Vegetable Salad, '79 47
  Creole Salad, '79 147
  Crunchy Vegetable Salad, '79 11;
    '80 217; '83 216
  Different Vegetable Salad, '82 143
  Easy Vegetable Salad, '83 316; '84 16
  Garden Marinade, '81 23
  Garden Medley Salad, '80 122
  Garden Salad, '87 62
  Garden Salad Bowl, '82 239
  Garden Salad with Tomato-Cream
    Cheese Dressing, '79 173
  Greek Salad, Garden, '86 173
  Green-and-White Vegetable Salad,
    '79 286
  Green Vegetable Salad, Overnight,
    '80 5
  Grilled Vegetable Salad, '94 203
  Horseradish Dressing, Vegetable Salad
    with, '92 85
  Italian Vegetable Salad, '81 253;
    '82 19
  Luncheon Salad, '84 232
  Marinade, Fresh Vegetable, '83 209
  Marinade, Garden, '81 23
  Marinade, Medley, '79 20
  Marinade, Tossed Vegetable, '84 266
  Marinated Combo Salad, '82 267
  Marinated Garden Vegetables, '87 252
  Marinated Mixed Vegetables, '89 276;
    '92 106
  Marinated Salad, '91 186
  Marinated Salad, Eight-Vegetable,
    '80 218
  Marinated Summer Salad, '81 153
  Marinated Vegetable-Bacon Bowl,
    '79 191
  Marinated Vegetable Patch Salad,
    '84 232
  Marinated Vegetables, '79 146;
    '81 239; '85 67; '88 4, 170
  Marinated Vegetable Salad, '79 106, 143;
    '81 280; '82 163; '83 260;
    '84 13; '87 243; '92 64, 91
  Marinated Vegetable Salad, Crispy,
    '84 193
  Marinated Vegetable Salad, Fresh,
    '86 173
  Marinated Vegetables, Sweet-and-Sour,
    '83 266
  Marinated Vegetables, Zesty, '82 272
  Marinate, Fresh Vegetable, '80 33;
    '81 230
  Meal-in-One Salad, '82 232
  Medley Salad, Vegetable, '88 86
  Mexican Salad, '81 36, 113
  Minted Vegetable Salad, '88 23

  Mixed Vegetable Salad, '80 115;
    '81 302; '82 239; '83 317; '84 16;
    '86 136
  Next-Day Vegetable Salad, '83 81
  Oriental Salad, Make-Ahead, '82 163
  Oriental Vegetable Salad, '84 290
  Overnight Vegetable Salad, '90 33
  Party Vegetable Salad, '86 79
  Pasta and Vegetables, '89 255
  Pasta Salad, Vegetable, '89 256;
    '91 143
  Pasta Salad, Vegetable-, '92 167
  Primavera Salad, '93 140
  Quick Summer Italian Salad, '92 79
  Rainbow Vegetable Salad, '83 111
  Refrigerated Vegetable Salad, '84 120
  Rice-and-Vegetable Salad, '86 42
  Riviera, Salade, '89 12
  Rolls, Vegetable Salad, '82 278
  Senator's Salad, '79 191
  Seven-Layer Vegetable Salad, '79 88
  Spring Vegetable Salad, '88 48
  Swedish Vegetable Salad, '82 23
  Sweet-and-Sour Vegetable Salad, '81 25
  Tangy Vegetable Toss, '79 144
  Tarragon-Vegetable Salad, '85 288
  Variety Salad, '79 113
  Vinaigrette Salad, Vegetable-Chicken,
    '86 135
  Vinaigrette, Vegetables, '82 225, 290
  Walnuts, Vegetable Salad with, '86 118
  Winter Vegetable Salad, '86 42
Vermicelli Vinaigrette Salad, '82 189
Waldorf Salad, '89 278
Waldorf Salad, Creamy, '87 311
Waldorf Salad, Deluxe, '83 81
Waldorf Salad, Frozen, '79 126; '82 145
Waldorf Salad, Jiffy, '88 100
Waldorf Salad, New Wave, '92 36
Waldorf Salad, Old-Fashioned, '81 295
Waldorf Salad, Overnight, '81 309
Waldorf Salad, Southern Classic, '92 36
Waldorf Salad, Tropical, '89 12
Watercress Salad, '79 144
Watercress-Tomato Salad, '85 132
Watermelon Salad with Celery-Nut Dressing,
  '80 182
Watermelon Sparkle, '84 191
Wheat Berry-and-Roasted Corn Salad,
  '94 175
Wild Rice Salad, Oriental Salmon-and-,
  '94 173
Yogurt-Cucumber Salad, '82 122
Yogurt Salad, Frozen, '92 303
Ziti-Cheddar Salad, '85 165
Zucchini-Artichoke Salad, '91 229
Zucchini Chef's Salad, '83 143
Zucchini, Marinated, '80 33
Zucchini Salad, '82 104; '87 103; '89 128
Zucchini Salad, Marinated, '82 164; '90 32
Salmon
Avocados, Salmon-Stuffed, '86 74
Ball, Salmon, '80 149; '86 262
Ball, Smoky Salmon Cheese, '82 247
Barbecued Salmon, '81 181
Burgers, Salmon, '89 98
Carbonara, Salmon, '83 43
Casserole, Salmon, '81 22
Chilled Salmon with Dill Sauce, '84 285
Croquettes, Baked Salmon, '81 22
Fettuccine, Salmon, '90 123

Salmon (continued)

Fillets with Red Wine Garlic Sauce, Salmon, '94 250
Fillets with Sweet Corn Relish, Salmon, '93 119
Florentine, Salmon, '83 43
Kabobs, Salmon, '81 182
Loaf, Easy Salmon, '80 4
Loaf, Savory Salmon, '92 33
Loaf with Cucumber-Dill Sauce, Salmon, '86 5
Log, Salmon, '81 22
Mixed Greens with Creamy Dill Dressing, Salmon on, '93 143
Mousse, Irresistible Salmon, '79 284
Mousse, Salmon, '83 79
Mousse, Salmon Dill, '81 21
Mushrooms and Green Onions, Fresh Salmon with, '93 180
Patties, Cheesy Salmon, '89 99
Patties, Open-Faced Salmon, '87 M218
Patties, Salmon, '92 215
Patties with Lemon-Cheese Sauce, Salmon, '91 24
Patties with Sauce, Salmon, '88 164
Poached Salmon, '83 35
Poached Salmon with Emerald Sauce, '90 63
Poached Salmon with Horseradish Sauce, '91 183
Potatoes, Salmon-Topped, '84 124
Quiche, Salmon, '82 87; '87 38
Roll, Salmon Party, '83 127
Salad, Broiled Salmon, '92 108
Salad, Chilly Salmon, '80 104
Salad, Crunchy Salmon, '81 148
Salad, Macaroni-Salmon, '82 232
Salad, Oriental Salmon-and-Wild Rice, '94 173
Salad, Salmon, '89 99
Salad, Salmon-and-Macaroni, '81 114
Salad, Salmon-Pasta, '87 9
Salad, Salmon-Potato, '87 285
Salad, Salmon-Rice, '84 289
Salad, Salmon-Spinach, '87 145
Salad Shells, Salmon, '85 286
Salad, Simple Salmon, '91 23
Salad, Summertime Salmon, '82 207
Scalloped Salmon, '81 273
Scalloped Salmon for Two, '89 98
Scaloppine with Vegetable Confetti and Pernod Sauce, Salmon, '94 172
Smoked Salmon, Drizzled, '88 91
Soufflé, Fresh Salmon, '81 182
Spread, Salmon, '81 149
Spread, Salmon-and-Horseradish, '87 146
Spread, Smoked Salmon, '84 324
Steaks, Baked Salmon, '85 54
Steaks, Glazed Salmon, '86 256
Steaks, Grilled Herbed Salmon, '93 176
Steaks, Grilled Salmon, '94 278
Steaks, Marinated Salmon, '87 6
Steaks, Oven-Fried Salmon, '81 181
Steaks with Dill Sauce, Salmon, '85 164
Steaks with Tarragon Butter, Salmon, '87 155
Terrine, Layered Salmon-and-Spinach, '84 132
Turnovers, Salmon-Spinach, '83 44
Vermicelli, Salmon-Pesto, '92 200

Sandwiches

Alfalfa Pocket Bread Sandwiches, '82 282; '83 41
Amberjack Sandwiches, Grilled, '91 195
Apple Breakfast Sandwiches, '92 332
Apple-Cinnamon Breakfast Sandwiches, '85 298
Apple Party Sandwiches, '92 234
Apple Sandwiches, '79 164; '80 130
Asparagus-and-Ham Melt Sandwiches, '88 M96
Asparagus Grill Sandwiches, '79 164; '80 130
Asparagus Spear Sandwiches, '84 165
Avocado, Bacon, and Cheese Sandwiches, '87 279
Avocado-Crabmeat Sandwiches, '83 2
Bacon, Cheese, and Tomato Sandwiches, '84 14
Bacon-Cheese Sandwiches, Grilled, '83 242
Bacon, Pimiento, and Cheese Hoagies, '90 144
Bacon Sandwiches, Open-Faced Cheesy, '80 78
Bagel, Breakfast on a, '94 66
Bagels, Meal-in-One, '88 159
Bar, Super Summer Sandwich, '91 143
Basket of Sandwiches, Bread, '86 126
Bean Salad Sandwiches, '81 243
Beef-and-Kraut Sandwich, '91 167
Beef and Pork Tenderloin Sandwiches, '80 175
Beef-Eater Sandwiches, '86 72
Beef Pocket Sandwich, Saucy, '80 92
Beef Salad Pocket Sandwiches, '83 267
Beef Sandwiches, Barbecued, '81 25; '82 31; '83 34
Beef Slice, French, '79 125
Beef Tenderloin Picnic Sandwiches, '90 91
BLT Croissants, '93 158
BLT in Pita Pockets, '93 158
BLT Sandwiches, Curried, '93 158
BLT's, Cheesy, '85 92
Breakfast Sandwiches, '80 52; '82 M123; '89 M230
Breakfast Sandwiches, Cheesy, '90 140
Breakfast Sandwiches, Open-Faced, '92 140
Brown Bread-Cream Cheese Sandwiches, '87 M6
Bunwiches, '80 92
Calla Lily Sandwiches, '91 106
Calzone, '85 94
Cheese-and-Ham Striped Tea Sandwiches, Cheshire Claret, '94 16
Cheeseburger Biscuits, '79 194
Cheese-Ham Sandwiches, Creamy Blue, '87 279
Cheese Sandwiches, Grilled, '82 M172; '94 167
Cheese Sandwiches, Hot French, '82 3
Cheese Sandwiches, Leafy, '90 56
Cheese Sandwich, Mexican Grilled, '92 63
Cheese Tea Sandwiches, '92 276
Chef's Salad, '86 186
Chicken-Almond Pocket Sandwiches, '81 240; '83 69
Chicken-and-Cheese Sandwiches, Toasted, '85 242
Chicken Club Sandwiches, '86 160
Chicken Croissants, Chutney-, '92 22
Chicken in a Sandwich, Marinated, '86 185

Chicken Parmigiana Sandwich, '94 65
Chicken Pita, Oriental, '89 216
Chicken-Salad Finger Sandwiches, '85 119
Chicken Salad in a Pocket, '88 139
Chicken Salad on Raisin Bread, Curried, '85 96
Chicken Salad with Artichokes, '86 186
Chicken Sandwich, Crispy, '81 114
Chicken Sandwiches, Baked, '79 164; '80 130; '84 165
Chicken Sandwiches, Cheesy, '82 190
Chicken Sandwiches, Hot, '83 291
Chicken Sandwiches, Marinated, '86 M45
Chicken Sandwiches, Puffed, '82 35
Chicken Spread, Tasty, '84 193
Chick-Wiches, Saucy, '81 25; '82 31; '83 34
Christmas Tree Sandwiches, '92 279
Club Sandwich Bar, Easy, '91 279
Club Sandwiches, Double-Decker, '91 231; '92 68
Club Sandwiches, Tangy, '80 93
Club Sandwich, South Seas, '84 282
Confetti Sandwiches, '79 236
Corned Beef and Cheese Sandwich, '79 214
Corned Beef Sandwiches, '83 291; '85 242; '92 23
Corned Beef Sandwiches, Barbecued, '83 130
Corned Beef Sandwiches, Grilled, '87 54
Crab-and-Cheese Sandwiches, Hot, '87 279
Crab Burgers, Potato-Crusted, '94 139
Crabmeat Sandwiches, '84 285
Crabmeat Sandwiches, Deluxe, '81 M74
Crab Sandwiches, Open-Faced, '87 106
Crab Sandwiches, Puffy, '83 291
Crab Tomato Sandwiches, Open-Face, '81 29
Croissant Eggwiches, '91 160
Croissant Sandwiches, '89 161
Crostini, Feta-Tomato, '92 159
Cucumber Pinwheel Sandwiches, '85 120
Cucumber Sandwiches, '88 159; '90 81; '94 14
Cucumber Sandwiches, Dainty, '81 119
Curried Tea Sandwiches, '91 314
Date-Nut Lettuce Sandwich, '94 202
Deviled Delight, '83 130
Eggplant Sandwiches, Baked, '82 230
Egg Sandwiches, Open-Face, '83 292; '84 78; '86 160
Egg Sandwiches, Open-Faced Cheesy, '86 67
Egg Sandwiches, Saucy, '91 160
Eggsclusive Sandwiches, '79 164; '80 130
Eggs-Tra Special Sandwiches, '81 240; '83 69
English Muffin Delight, '82 45
Frankfurter Sandwiches, '84 M11
French Toast Sandwiches, Strawberry-, '91 160
Fruit-and-Cheese Breakfast Sandwiches, '89 M21
Fruit Sandwiches, Glazed Breakfast, '93 178
Garden Sandwiches, Open-Faced, '87 105
Garden, The, '83 134
Grilled Sandwiches, Tasty, '84 30
Grinder Sandwich, '85 299
Guacamole Sandwiches, '82 9; '83 68
Guacamole Subs, '84 293
Gumbo Joes, '88 158
Ham-and-Cheese Pita Sandwiches, '87 202
Ham-and-Cheese Rolls, '82 3

Sandwiches (*continued*)

Ham-and-Cheese Sandwiches, Hot, '85 299
Ham-and-Cheese Sandwich Round, '94 326
Ham-and-Cheese Sandwich, Tex-Mex, '86 4
Ham and Eggs à la Swiss, '88 158
Ham and Swiss in the Pocket, '83 31
Ham-and-Swiss Sandwiches, Tangy, '85 164
Ham-and-Turkey Specials, Cheesy, '84 14
Ham Hideaways, '81 29
Ham Hot Rods, '86 136
Ham Loaves, Country, '86 255
Ham Salad Sandwich, Tangy, '80 272
Ham Sandwiches, Baked, '81 29
Ham Sandwiches, Hot, '79 214
Ham Sandwiches, Open-Face, '82 40; '85 8
Ham Sandwiches, Virginia, '80 155
Hearts of Palm Sandwich, '92 191
Heroes, Healthy, '90 177
Heroes, Neptune, '84 281
Hero, E-Z, '92 63
Hot Brown Sandwiches, '80 M202
Italian Pesto Sandwich, Grilled, '94 170
Jalapeño Heroes, Open-Faced, '90 144
Lamb Pockets with Dilled Cucumber Topping, '87 104
Loaf, Big Wheel, '84 281
Meal-in-One Sandwiches, '80 218
Meatball Sandwich, Giant, '92 196
Monte Cristo Sandwiches, '83 134
Muffaletta-Style Po-Boys, '83 230
Muffin Stacks, Mushroom-Topped, '80 271
Muffuletta, Doodles, '94 35
Muffuletta, Napoleon House, '94 35
"Muffy" Sandwich, Fertitta's, '94 34
Mushroom Sandwiches, Toasted, '87 281
Omelet Sandwich, '86 95
Open-Faced Sandwiches, '79 214
Open-Face Sandwiches, '84 13
Orange Blossom Special, '88 158
Oyster-and-Bacon Poor Boys, '87 40
Oyster Submarine Sandwich, '80 92
Party Sandwiches, Double-Filled, '93 159
Peanut Butter-and-Jelly "Fish" Sandwiches, '91 177
Peanut Butter-and-Jelly Sandwiches, Christmas Tree, '85 319
Peanut Butter Breakfast Sandwich, '82 55
Peanut-Cheese-Raisin Sandwiches, '88 140
Pimiento Cheese Sandwiches, '82 278
Pineapple-Ham Sandwich Loaf, '91 167
Pita Pockets, Breakfast, '89 M21
Pita Pockets, Ham-and-Cheese, '90 271
Pitas, Acadian Stuffed, '90 177
Pita Salad Sandwiches, '83 134
Pita Sandwiches, '84 139
Pita Sandwiches, Bavarian, '83 31
Pita Sandwiches, Denver, '86 M12
Pita Sandwiches, Dried Beef, '86 160
Pita Sandwiches, Ham-and-Cheese, '88 44
Pita Sandwiches, Hot, '83 217; '87 M6
Pita Sandwiches, Turkey Salad, '88 43
Pita Sandwiches, Vegetarian, '84 193
Pitas, Curried Beef, '85 220
Pitas, Spinach-Walnut, '88 43
Pitas, Taco, '83 31
Pita, Stuffed, '89 87
Pizza Sandwiches, Open-Face, '82 3; '83 85; '84 M198; '85 22
Pizza Sandwich, Giant, '80 93

Po-Boy, Pain-Perdu, '93 291
Pocket Sandwiches, Hearty, '80 93
Pockets, Oriental Stuffed, '79 14
Pork Sandwiches, Party, '88 M273
Pound Cake Dessert Sandwich, Grilled, '94 171
Raisin Country Sandwich, '91 168
Rarebit, Tangy Welsh, '88 159
Rarebit, Uptown Welsh, '87 279
Rarebit with Tomatoes and Bacon, Welsh, '92 M159
Reuben Sandwiches, '80 M201
Reuben Sandwiches, Broiled, '81 240; '83 69
Reuben Sandwiches, Crispy, '85 299
Reuben Sandwiches, Grilled, '81 206
Reuben Sandwiches, Open-Face, '91 199
Reubens, Party, '90 61
Roast Beef Hero Sandwich, '91 167
Salad Boats, '80 93
Salad Rolls, Hearty, '81 206
Salami Sandwiches, Open-Faced, '87 279
Sausage and Pepper Loaves, Italian, '83 11
Sausage-Cheese Loaves, '88 235
Sausage-Cheese Muffin Sandwiches, '92 M212
Sausage Sandwiches with Mustard Sauce, '84 250
Sausage Sandwich, Italian, '80 92
Sausage Sloppy Joes, Italian, '86 160
Sausage-Stuffed French Loaf, '90 19
Seafood Hot Brown, '88 158
Sebastian, The, '94 184
Shrimp-and-Egg Salad Sandwiches, '94 182
Shrimp-Cheese Sandwiches, '85 242
Shrimp Destin, '82 29
Shrimp Salad, '86 186
Shrimp Salad Sandwiches, '90 178
Sloppy Joe Pocket Sandwiches, '81 200
Sloppy Joes, '91 172
Sloppy Toms, '91 51
Snack Buns, '87 279
Snackwiches, '88 172
Spider Sandwiches, '93 193
Spinach Fondue Sandwich, Grilled, '94 171
Spinach-Oyster Loaves, '84 213
Spinach Sandwiches, Fresh, '85 59
Spinach-Walnut Pitas, '87 202
Sprout Sandwiches, Polynesian, '85 51
Stacking Sandwiches, '86 127
Steaks, Greek Pocket, '81 262
Steak Stroganoff Sandwiches, '85 110
Stromboli, '88 272
Submarine Sandwiches, Superb, '84 250
Taco Joes, '91 167
Tea Sandwiches, Gingered, '84 116
Tempting Twosome, '81 240; '83 69
Tofu-Veggie Sandwiches, Open-Face, '86 5
Tomatillo Sandwiches, Open-Faced, '92 246
Tomatoes with Cheese Sauce over Toast, '88 159
Tortilla Stack-Ups, '92 196
Tuna Burgers, Zippy, '81 135
Tuna Cheesies, '82 191
Tuna Club Sandwiches, '83 134
Tuna-in-a-Pita Pocket, '87 202
Tuna Melts, Tempting, '88 158
Tuna Pockets, '88 139
Tuna Salad Rolls, Hot, '84 281
Tuna Salad, Swiss, '86 186
Tuna Sandwich Boats, '91 166

Tuna Sandwiches, French Toasted, '80 275
Tuna Sandwiches, Hot, '85 299; '86 M194
Tuna Waffle-Wich, '88 272; '89 181
Turkey-Cheese Puffs, '87 301
Turkey Hero Sandwiches, '92 196
Turkey Hero with Garlic Sauce, '90 145
Turkey-in-the-Slaw Sandwich, '90 177
Turkey-Mozzarella Rounds, '82 3
Turkey Open-Facers, '82 190
Turkey-Roasted Pepper Sandwiches, Smoked, '94 66
Turkey Salad Pita Sandwiches, '87 202
Turkey Sandwich, Hot, '93 306
Turkey Sandwich, Waffle-Grilled, '94 170
Vegetable Garden Heroes, '84 14
Vegetable Pockets, '85 215
Vegetable Puff Sandwich, '85 51
Vegetable Salad Rolls, '82 278
Vegetarian Melt, Open-Faced, '87 106
Veggie Sandwich, Big, '92 196
Victoria Sandwiches, '94 16
Vidalia Sandwiches on Salt-Rising Bread, '79 145
Wake-Up Sandwiches, '84 58
Watercress Sandwiches, '90 82
Wreath, Festive Sandwich, '86 333
Yummy Sandwiches, '81 229
Zucchini Sandwiches, Open-Faced, '88 159

Sauces. *See also* Desserts/Sauces.
Alfredo Sauce, '94 84
Almond Sauce, Asparagus with, '91 117
Anchovy-Garlic Sauce over Vermicelli, '86 158
Apple-Horseradish Sauce, '82 229
Apricot Sauce, '87 172
Apricot-Sauced Pork Chops, '85 22
Avgolemono Sauce, '94 48
Avocado Sauce, '80 198; '83 200
Barbecue
    Bannister's Barbecue Sauce, '92 166
    Beer Barbecue Sauce, '84 173
    Bourbon Barbecue Sauce, '85 90
    Dressed-Up Barbecue Sauce, '84 173
    Eastern-Style Barbecue Sauce, '88 145
    Easy Barbecue Sauce, '79 90; '82 178
    John Wills's Barbecue Sauce, '92 255
    Lemon Barbecue Sauce, Herbed, '94 154
    Maple Syrup Barbecue Sauce, '94 154
    Mustard Barbecue Sauce, '84 173
    Oven Barbecue Sauce, '82 233
    Paprika Barbecue Sauce, '79 90
    Peanut Butter Barbecue Sauce, '81 233
    Piquant Barbecue Sauce, '79 159
    Sauce, Barbecue, '84 172; '86 153; '88 218; '91 16, 205; '93 129; '94 27
    Savory Barbecue Sauce, '86 153
    Special Barbecue Sauce, '82 177
    Spicy Southwest Barbecue Sauce, '94 154

Sauces, Barbecue *(continued)*

Thick and Robust Barbecue Sauce, '94 95
Thick and Sweet Barbecue Sauce, '94 95
Thin and Tasty Barbecue Sauce, '94 95
Tomato Barbecue Sauce, Fresh, '84 172
Western-Style Barbecue Sauce, '88 145
White Barbecue Sauce, '94 95
White Barbecue Sauce, Chicken with, '89 M84
Zippy Barbecue Sauce, '92 166
Basil and Cream Sauce, '90 118
Basil-Brown Butter Sauce, '93 92
Basil Cream, '89 159
Basil Cream Sauce, New Potatoes with, '91 46
Basil Sauce, '90 85
Basil Sauce, Asparagus with, '86 33
Basil-Tomato Sauce, '92 198
Bean Sauce, Pork-and-Onions with, '85 76
Béarnaise Sauce, '83 138; '85 37; '86 193; '89 201
Béarnaise Sauce, Blender, '81 90
Béarnaise Sauce, Classic, '86 244
Béarnaise Sauce, Quick, '82 84
Béchamel Sauce, '80 190; '83 277; '84 M239; '87 286; '91 94
Black Bean Sauce, '93 59
Blueberry Sauce, '80 144; '86 248
Bordelaise Sauce, '83 138, 262
Bouillon Sauce, '80 8
Brandy-Butter Sauce, '79 230
Brandy Sauce, Carrots in, '83 86
Brandy Sauce, Lemony-Butter Steak with, '85 78
Broccoli Sauce, '91 85
Brown Butter Sauce, '91 65
Brown Sauce, '89 32; '94 15, 240
Buttermilk Sauce, '84 6
Butter Sauce, '86 268
Butter Sauce, Vegetable, '86 174
Catsup Sauce, '81 228
Catsup Topping, '81 170
Champagne-Saffron Sauce, Scallops with, '93 177
Champagne Sauce, '90 29
Champagne Sauce, Chicken Breasts with, '86 49
Chanterelle Brown Sauce, '89 62
Cheese
  Blue Cheese Sauce, '90 142; '94 320
  Brussels Sprouts with Cheese Sauce, '79 246
  Cheddar Cheese Sauce, '91 286
  Cottage Cheese Sauce, '87 232
  Cream Sauce, Cheesy, '82 79
  Easy Cheese Sauce, '79 22
  Garlic-Cheese Sauce, '84 M70
  Guilt-Free Cheese Sauce, '93 M95
  Lemon-Cheese Sauce, '91 24
  Lemony Cheese Sauce, '84 183
  Monterey Jack Sauce, '84 293
  Mornay Sauce, '80 120; '81 90; '83 138; '84 295; '89 195
  Mushroom-Cheese Sauce, '83 190; '86 48
  Parmesan Cheese Sauce, '79 165; '80 162; '85 143

Rich Cheese Sauce, '81 89
Roquefort Sauce, '89 321
Sauce, Cheese, '79 M156; '81 43, 44, 225; '82 M123; '83 49, 138, 188; '84 57; '85 92; '86 241; '88 78, 272; '89 181, 229; '90 235; '93 48
Seafood Cheese Sauce, '89 240
Swiss Cheese Sauce, '79 35; '87 289; '88 135
Swiss Sauce, '83 M195
Swiss Sauce, Creamy, '80 M53
Topper, Vegetable-Cheese Potato, '86 6
Turnips in Cheese Sauce, '84 229
Vegetable-Cheese Sauce, '85 M152
Vegetable Sauce, Cheesy, '92 M134
Cherry Sauce, '83 276; '84 91; '91 67
Cherry Sauce, Elegant, '79 M156
Cherry Sauce, Roast Ducklings with, '86 312
Cherry Sauce, Roast Pork with Spiced, '89 324
Cherry Sauce, Royal, '85 224; '86 83
Cherry Sauce, Spicy, '83 244
Chervil-and-Savory Sauce, '90 117
Chervil Sauce, '83 128
Chicken Curry Sauce, '90 117
Chicken Sauce, Creamy, '81 91
Chile Cream, Ancho, '87 121
Chile Sauce, Ancho, '87 122
Chile Sauce, Green, '82 220
Chile Sauce, Hot, '92 156
Chile Sauce, Red, '94 251
Chili Meat Sauce, '83 4
Chili Sauce, '81 175; '94 287
Chili Sauce, Chunky, '85 188
Chili Sauce, Red, '85 245
Chili Sauce, Spicy, '87 127
Chive Sauce, Steamed Broccoli with Tangy, '83 101
Chutney-Mustard Sauce, '89 242
Cider Sauce, '87 224
Cilantro Cream, '87 121
Citrus Sauce, Stuffed Flounder Rolls with, '85 180
Clam Sauce, Tricolor Pasta with, '93 272
Cocktail Sauce, '87 128; '90 242
Cocktail Sauce, Boiled Shrimp with, '79 151
Cocktail Sauce, Coastal, '92 254
Cocktail Sauce, Delta, '91 147
Cocktail Sauce, French Fried Zucchini with, '86 146
Cocktail Sauce, Spicy, '83 258
Country Ham Sauce, '90 117
Cranberry-Apple Sauce, '92 203
Cranberry-Apricot Sauce, Fresh, '87 243
Cranberry Juice Sauce, '85 224; '86 83
Cranberry-Raisin Sauce, Baked Ham with, '88 244
Cranberry Sauce, '92 269
Cranberry Sauce, Baked, '88 257
Cranberry Sauce, Cornish Hens with, '79 180
Cranberry Sauce, Fresh, '79 283; '84 275
Cranberry Sauce, Tart, '83 261
Cranberry Wine Sauce, '83 276
Cream Sauce, '85 291; '93 157
Cream Sauce, Brandied, '82 70
Cream Sauce, Peppery, '88 206
Cream Sauce, Sherried, '84 210; '85 M152
Cream Sauce, Shrimp in, '84 M286
Cream Sauce, Spicy, '82 45

Cream-Wine Sauce, Potatoes in, '86 18
Creamy Sauce, '79 41
Creolaise Sauce, '83 91, 262
Creole Sauce, '89 228; '90 28; '92 87
Cucumber Cream Sauce, '92 33
Cucumber-Dill Sauce, '86 5; '91 62; '92 51
Cucumber Dipping Sauce, '94 47
Cucumber Sauce, '82 111; '84 M286; '92 41
Cucumber Sauce, Lemony, '89 245
Cumberland Sauce, '92 309
Currant Jelly Sauce, Quail with, '86 94
Currant Sauce, '87 240
Curried Cream Sauce, Turkey Slices with, '91 60
Curried Rum Sauce, '91 164
Curried Sour Cream Sauce, '90 174
Curry Sauce, '79 M156; '83 138; '84 M71; '94 54
Curry Sauce, Asparagus with, '90 17
Custard Sauce, '89 291
Devonshire Cream, Mock, '81 288
Devonshire Sauce, Processor, '86 337; '87 58
Dill Sauce, '84 M70, 107; '85 39; '88 162
Dill Sauce, Chilled Salmon with, '84 285
Dill Sauce, Creamy, '79 M156; '94 42
Dill Sauce, Salmon Steaks with, '85 164
Egg Foo Yong Sauce, '86 232
Emerald Sauce, '90 63
Enchilada Sauce, '81 194
Enchilada Sauce, Red Chile, '85 245
Florentine Sauce, '93 48
Foo Yong Sauce, '80 223
French Sauce, Broccoli with, '81 295
Fruit Sauce, '81 177
Fruit Sauce, Grand Marnier, '90 93
Fruit, Tangy Sauce for, '90 161
Garlic Buerre Blanc Sauce, '88 222
Garlic-Chive Butter Sauce, '90 96
Garlic-Ginger Butter Sauce, '94 89
Garlic Sauce, '92 56
Garlic Sauce, Stir-Fried Pork in, '84 141
Garlic Sauce, Turkey Hero with, '90 145
Ginger-Soy Sauce, '91 33
Goat Cheese Sauce, Asparagus with, '93 116
Grape Sauce, Mahimahi in, '91 218
Grape Sauce, White, '80 38
Greek Sauce, '91 183
Green Sauce, Herbed, '86 244
Guacamole, '89 226
Ham-and-Mushroom Sauce, Steak with, '83 109
Heather Sauce, '84 182
Herb Butter Sauce, Corn with, '79 150
Herb-Mayonnaise Sauce, '85 73
Herb Sauce, '91 29
Herb Sauce, Green, '83 36
Hollandaise Sauce, '80 M107, M268; '81 90; '83 137; '85 295; '86 94; '87 195; '88 58, M177, 222; '89 24; '92 93
Hollandaise Sauce, Blender, '79 39; '82 84, 234
Hollandaise Sauce, Broccoli with, '79 244, 276
Hollandaise Sauce, Broccoli with Mock, '82 272
Hollandaise Sauce, Classic, '88 53
Hollandaise Sauce, Easy Dilled, '92 107
Hollandaise Sauce, Lime, '93 121
Hollandaise Sauce, Mock, '85 49; '93 68

Sauces (*continued*)

Hollandaise-Shrimp Sauce, Flounder with, '86 234
Hollandaise, Tangy, '85 148
Honey-Butter Sauce, '85 18
Honey-Lemon Mustard Sauce, '84 275
Honey-Lime Sauce, '82 85
Honey-Mustard Sauce, '85 13
Honey-Mustard Sauce, Smoked Ribs with, '92 168
Honey-Poppy Seed Sauce, '93 13
Honey Sauce, Chicken in, '89 82
Horseradish-Mustard Sauce, Creamy, '88 M177
Horseradish Sauce, '84 190; '85 224; '86 83; '87 127; '88 207, M273; '91 183; '93 215
Horseradish Sauce and Curried Bananas, Fillets with, '85 230
Horseradish Sauce, Broccoli with, '81 2; '83 206; '84 33
Horseradish Sauce, Carrots and Broccoli with, '91 246
Horseradish Sour Cream, '86 244
Hot Diggity Dog Sauce, '93 198
Hot Sauce, '79 185; '83 74
Hot Sauce, Kleberg, '94 28
Hot Sauce, San Antonio, '84 291
Italian Sauce, '80 63; '90 67
Italian Sauce, Quick, '82 230
Italian-Style Sauce, '83 250
Jalapeño-Cranberry Sauce, '92 310
Jalapeño Sauce, '80 193
Jezebel Sauce, '81 29; '82 55; '93 331
Juniper Sauce, '93 278
Lemon-Butter Sauce, '84 252; '92 337
Lemon-Celery Sauce, Baked Fillets in, '84 91
Lemon-Cheese Sauce, '91 24
Lemon Cream Sauce, Braised Chicken Breast in, '94 184
Lemon Garlic Sauce, Shrimp in, '83 67
Lemon-Herb Sauce, Hot, '91 286
Lemon Meunière Sauce, '88 222
Lemon Parsley Sauce, '81 106
Lemon-Parsley Sauce, '93 48
Lemon Sauce, '82 290
Lemon Sauce, Asparagus with, '86 62
Lemon Sauce, Chicken Scallopini with, '86 156
Lime-Saffron Sauce, '94 71
Mahogany Sauce, '91 148
Mandarin-Almond Cream Sauce, '84 183
Mandarin Sauce, '84 60
Marinade, '86 153; '92 283
Marinade, Cinnamon-Soy, '93 103
Marinade, Citrus, '93 103
Marinade, Garlic-Basil, '94 160
Marinade, Garlic-Honey, '93 102
Marinade, Honey-Mustard, '93 103
Marinade, Lemon-Soy, '91 194
Marinade, Minty, '92 105
Marinade, Oriental, '93 102
Marinade, Southwestern, '93 102
Marinade, Sweet-and-Sour, '86 113
Marinade, Tangy Beef, '86 113
Marinade, Tangy Light, '82 178
Marinade, Teriyaki, '86 114; '93 102
Marinade, Vegetable, '92 231

Marinara Sauce, '82 178; '89 239; '92 18; '94 64
Meat Sauce, Italian, '83 193
Mediterranean Sauce, '94 83
Meunière Sauce, '80 57
Mexican Sauce, '80 198
Microwaving Sauces, '84 M70
Mimosa, Sauce, '88 288
Mint Sauce, '84 107; '88 M96
Mint Sauce over Vegetables, '92 104
Mushroom-Dill Sauce, '80 271
Mushroom Sauce, '81 90, 200; '82 46; '83 71, 205, 212; '84 M70; '85 40; '86 198; '87 36, 186, 284; '91 221
Mushroom Sauce, Eggs Baked in, '93 47
Mushroom Sauce, Filet Mignon with, '94 250
Mushroom Sauce, Spicy Sherried, '89 239
Mushroom Sauce Supreme on Vermicelli, '86 158
Mushroom-Wine Sauce, '84 84; '86 24
Mustard Cream Sauce, '88 61
Mustard Cream Sauce, Chicken in, '92 181
Mustard-Hollandaise Sauce, Mock, '87 269
Mustard Sauce, '80 222, 283; '83 21, 321; '84 M70; '86 185; '87 22; '89 122, 333; '90 19, 97; '92 302; '93 118
Mustard Sauce, Creamy, '80 272; '86 257; '87 232; '93 240
Mustard Sauce, Extra-Special, '79 82
Mustard Sauce, Hamburger Steaks with, '84 230
Mustard Sauce, Hot, '93 240
Mustard Sauce, Leg of Lamb with, '89 71
Mustard Sauce, Light, '82 178
Mustard Sauce, Mild, '85 224; '86 84
Mustard Sauce, Sausage Sandwiches with, '84 250
Mustard Sauce, Scallops with, '84 163
Mustard Sauce, Smoked Sausages with, '81 56
Mustard Sauce, Sweet, '85 12
Mustard Sauce, Tangy, '92 201
Mustard-Sour Cream Sauce, '81 68
Mustard-Vinaigrette Sauce, '84 174
Mustard-Vinegar Sauce, Shrimp with, '93 240
Natillas Sauce, '83 179
Olive-Butter Sauce, Broccoli with, '83 118
Onion Cream Sauce, '87 232
Onion-Mushroom Sauce, '85 224; '86 84
Onion-Parsley Sauce, '85 148
Onion Sauce, '82 72; '87 248
Onion Sauce, Brussels Sprouts in, '81 308
Orange-Almond Sauce, Chicken in, '79 219; '80 13
Orange Butter Sauce, Asparagus with, '85 43
Orange, Lime, and Ginger Sauce, Chicken with, '92 123
Orange Liqueur Sauce, '86 142
Orange Sauce, '82 47; '83 10, 277; '84 M286
Orange Sauce, Asparagus with, '83 46
Orange Sauce, Brussels Sprouts in, '86 55
Orange Sauce, Celery in, '79 70
Orange Sauce, Chicken Breasts with, '79 77
Orange Sauce, Grilled Duck with, '94 305
Orange Sauce, Lobster Tails with Spiced, '86 155
Orange Sauce, Sweet, '93 M325
Pancake Sauce, Cinnamon-Pecan-Honey, '88 46

Parmesan Sauce, '92 17
Parsley-Caper Sauce, Tortellini with, '93 175
Parsley-Chive Sauce, '84 212
Parsley-Garlic Sauce, '83 138; '84 M70
Parsley Sauce, '82 248; '86 108
Peach-Blueberry Pancake Sauce, '82 177
Peach-Blueberry Sauce, '81 170
Peach Sauce, '92 203
Peach Sauce, Creamy Fresh, '79 177
Peanut Hot Sauce, '86 305
Peanut Sauce, Hot Indonesian, '93 211
Peanut Sauce, Shrimp with, '93 303
Pea Sauce, Green, '83 22
Pecan-Butter Sauce, '91 65
Pepper-Onion Sauce, '84 125
Pesto, '80 242
Pesto and Pasta, '92 98
Pesto and Pasta, Spinach-Peanut, '93 212
Pesto, Bow-Tie, '94 231
Pesto, Dried Tomato, '90 204; '94 249
Pesto, Fettuccine and Shrimp with Dried Tomato, '94 249
Pesto, Fresh, '86 150
Pesto, Garlic, '84 108
Pesto-Pasta, Spinach, '91 314
Pesto, Pepper, '89 103; '90 97
Pesto Sauce, '89 280; '91 94
Pesto, Tomatoes, '86 150
Picante Sauce, '94 116
Picante Sauce, Homemade, '90 205
Picante Sauce, Processed, '91 257
Pico de Gallo, '79 185; '86 19
Pineapple-Curry Sauce, '79 252
Pineapple-Rhubarb Sauce, '88 94
Pineapple Sauce, '84 236; '92 203
Pizza Sauce, '80 163; '84 33; '85 285
Plum Sauce, '80 249; '82 40; '88 152
Plum Sauce, Chinese, '82 237
Plum Sauce, Gingered, '87 175
Plum Sauce, Red, '80 49
Plum Sauce, Spicy, '86 11
Port Wine Sauce, '84 252
Pumpkin Seed Sauce, '88 246
Raisin-Pineapple Sauce, '82 177
Raisin Sauce, '83 59, 215; '84 91, 275; '87 127; '89 58
Raisin Sauce, Ham with, '82 M76
Rancheros Sauce, '88 148
Red Hot Sauce, '93 158
Red or Green Pepper Sauce, '91 85
Red Sauce, Zippy, '91 147
Red Wine Garlic Sauce, '94 250
Rémoulade Sauce, '80 58; '81 89; '82 178; '91 147; '93 280; '94 139
Rémoulade Sauce, Shrimp with, '91 29
Rhubarb Sauce, Chilled, '88 94
Rosemary-Parmesan Sauce, Tortellini with, '92 284
Rum Sauce, Mango-Spiced, '86 215
Salsa, '80 196; '87 217; '88 147
Salsa, Avocado, '91 182
Salsa, Avocado-Corn, '94 201
Salsa, Black Bean, '93 155; '94 161
Salsa, Black Bean-and-Corn, '94 80
Salsa, Black-Eyed Pea, '93 164
Salsa, Chunky, '86 130; '90 206
Salsa, Creamy Green, '91 162
Salsa Cruda, '87 180; '88 148
Salsa, Double Chile, '91 182
Salsa, Fiesta Onion, '94 82
Salsa, Fresh Tomato, '91 182

Sauces *(continued)*

Salsa, Garden, **'91** 182
Salsa, Hot Kiwifruit, **'94** 82
Salsa, Hot Mexican, **'85** 136
Salsa, Mango, **'91** 182
Salsa, Mexi-Corn, **'91** 182
Salsa, Mixed Pepper, **'91** 181
Salsa, Papaya, **'94** 173
Salsa, Peach, **'91** 183
Salsa, Pepper, **'88** 26
Salsa Picante, Homemade, **'81** 67
Salsa Picante with Shrimp, **'92** 210
Salsa, Poblano, **'91** 135
Salsa, Red, **'90** 172
Salsa, Southwest Kale with, **'94** 246
Salsa, Three Tomato, **'93** 138
Salsa, Tomatillo, **'92** 245
Salsa, Tomato-Avocado, **'94** 83
Salsa, Tropical Rainbow, **'94** 161
Salsa Verde, **'91** 182
Salsa with Homemade Tostados, Hot Chile, **'88** 115
Salsa, Yellowfin Tuna with Corn, Pepper, and Tomato, **'94** 164
Sauerbraten Sauce, **'93** 16
Savory Sauce, **'84** 196
Seafood
    Clam Sauce, Linguine with, **'84** 124; **'88** 90; **'89** 178
    Clam Sauce, Pasta with, **'84** 291
    Clam Sauce, Vermicelli and Sprouts with Red, **'86** 143
    Clam Sauce, Vermicelli with, **'85** 295
    Clam Sauce with Linguine, **'84** 9
    Crab and Shrimp Sauce Piquante, **'83** 92
    Crab Marinara Sauce, Quick, **'85** M151
    Delight, Seafood Sauce, **'82** 91
    Linguine with Seafood Sauce, **'83** 232
    Sauce, Seafood, **'79** 3; **'82** 84; **'83** 36; **'86** 304; **'89** 239
    Shrimp-and-Almond Sauce, **'87** 282
    Shrimp Sauce, **'87** 138, 232
    Shrimp Sauce, Broccoli and Cauliflower with, **'84** 248
    Shrimp Sauce, Flounder Fillets in, **'83** 227
    Stone Crab Mustard Sauce, **'80** 3
    Stone Crab Sauce, Tangy, **'80** 3
Sesame Sauce, Vegetables with, **'83** 112
Sherry Sauce, **'87** 96
Sofrito, **'92** 158
Sour Cream-Dill Sauce, Mushrooms in, **'84** 215
Sour Cream-Horseradish Sauce, **'88** 4
Sour Cream-Lime Sauce, **'91** 286
Sour Cream, Mock, **'83** 71, 205
Sour Cream Sauce, **'82** 68; **'84** 132; **'87** 233; **'93** 162
Sour Cream Sauce, Broccoli with, **'87** 127
Soy Sauce, Grilled Trout with Ginger and, **'85** 228
Spaghetti Meat Sauce for 4, Easy, **'92** 244
Spaghetti Meat Sauce for 25, Easy, **'92** 245
Spaghetti Sauce, Beer, **'85** 13
Spaghetti Sauce, Dried Tomato, **'90** 202
Spaghetti Sauce, Grisanti, **'94** 194
Spaghetti Sauce, Herbed, **'85** 13
Spaghetti Sauce, Lentil, **'90** 198
Spaghetti Sauce, Thick, **'84** 118

Spaghetti Sauce, Turkey, **'85** 13
Spicy Sauce, **'84** 77
Spinach Pasta Sauce, **'93** 71
Spinach Pesto Sauce, **'93** 59
Spinach Sauce, Fettuccine with, **'84** 329
Spinach Sauce, Vermicelli with Fresh, **'89** 256
Strawberry-Banana Sauce, **'81** 41
Sunshine Sauce, **'87** 96
Sweet-and-Sour Sauce, **'80** 20; **'85** 12, 34; **'86** 240
Taco Sauce, **'82** M283; **'93** 69; **'94** 30
Tarragon-Mustard Sauce, Turkey Cutlets with, **'93** 239
Tarragon Sauce, **'83** 56; **'84** 190; **'87** 229
Tarragon-Tomato Sauce, **'84** 131
Tartar Sauce, **'79** 184; **'81** 134; **'82** 135; **'86** 233; **'91** 147
Tartar Sauce, Boiled Shrimp with Green Peppercorn, **'94** 144
Tartar Sauce, Bold-and-Spicy, **'86** 180
Tartar Sauce, Creamy, **'80** 164
Tartar Sauce, Quick, **'87** 128
Tempura Sauce, Basic, **'81** 68
Teriyaki Sauce, **'93** 258
Tomatillo Sauce, **'94** 231
Tomatillo Sauce, Roasted Chiles Rellenos with, **'94** 203
Tomato Basil Sauce, **'91** 85
Tomato-Basil Sauce, **'92** 180
Tomato-Caper Sauce, Turkey Cutlets with, **'91** 61
Tomato Cream, **'94** 70
Tomato Cream Sauce, Angel Hair Pasta with, **'93** 292
Tomato-Cream Sauce, Linguine with, **'86** 158
Tomato Sauce, **'85** 193, 244; **'87** 249; **'88** 116
Tomato Sauce, Basil-, **'93** 25, 48, 65
Tomato Sauce, Creamy, **'93** 71
Tomato Sauce, Fish in, **'85** 75
Tomato Sauce for Spaghetti, Italian, **'81** 134
Tomato Sauce, Fresh, **'83** 224; **'87** 171
Tomato Sauce, Herbed, **'86** 277
Tomato Sauce, Herbed Fresh, **'85** M151
Tomato Sauce, Italian, **'82** M68; **'92** 57
Tomato Sauce, Italian-Style, **'87** 182
Tomato Sauce over Basil Pasta, Fresh, **'93** 176
Tomato Sauce, Red Pepper-, **'93** 59
Tomato Sauce, Refrigerator, **'85** 188
Tomato Sauce, Seasoned, **'83** 150
Tomato Sauce, Spicy, **'84** 294; **'88** 19
Tomato Sauce, Vermicelli with, **'83** 164
Tomato Sauce with Green Chiles, **'81** 196
Vanilla Wine Sauce, Pan-Fried Grouper with, **'94** 241
Vegetable Sauce, **'89** 98
Vegetable Sauce, Greek Fish with, **'82** 72
Vegetable Sauce, Pasta with, **'83** 163
Vegetable Sauce, Tangy, **'89** 280
Velouté Sauce, **'84** 22
Venison Reduction Sauce, **'94** 303
Verde Sauce, **'93** 275
Vinaigrette, Versatile, **'93** 141
Vinegar Basting Sauce, **'91** 205
Walnut Cream Sauce, **'93** 275
Walnut Sauce, Spaghetti with Parsley and, **'80** 30
Watercress Sauce, **'91** 85
Whiskey Sauce, **'80** 58

White Butter Sauce, **'92** 107
White Sauce, **'82** 269; **'83** 138, 245; **'87** 166
White Sauce, Asparagus, **'80** 147
White Sauce, Basic, **'79** M156; **'81** 89
White Sauce, Low-Calorie, Medium, **'87** 26
White Sauce, Medium, **'93** 48
White Sauce, Thick, **'82** 42
Wine Reduction Sauce, **'94** 270
Wine Sauce, Beef Cubes in, **'79** 264
Wine Sauce, Broccoli with, **'84** 187
Wine Sauce, Chicken in, **'80** 8
Wine Sauce, Marsala, **'81** 77
Wine Sauce, Mushrooms with, **'85** 292
Wine Sauce, Red Snapper in, **'85** 138
Wine Sauce, Skillet Steak in Red, **'85** 21
Wine Sauce, Veal and Carrots in, **'86** M139
Wine Sauce, White, **'84** 132; **'89** 24; **'92** 41; **'93** 49
Yogurt-Horseradish Sauce, **'85** 66
Yogurt Sauce, **'89** 283
Yogurt Sauce, Creamy, **'91** 238; **'92** 28
Yogurt Sauce, Lamb Meatballs with, **'85** 132
Zesty Sauce, **'94** 82
Zippy Sauce, **'86** 44
Zucchini-Mushroom Sauce, **'93** 71
Zucchini Sauce, Spaghetti with, **'81** 38

Sauerkraut
Beany Kraut and Franks, **'79** 64
Bratwurst and Sauerkraut, **'84** 250
Cake, Sauerkraut, **'94** 254
Homemade Sauerkraut, **'81** 216
Meatballs, Sauerkraut, **'86** 257
Pork Chops and Sauerkraut, **'88** 98
Relish, Kraut, **'91** 232
Relish, Sauerkraut, **'85** 136
Salad, Crunchy Sauerkraut, **'87** 9
Salad, Sauerkraut, **'80** 178
Sandwich, Beef-and-Kraut, **'91** 167
Sausage and Kraut, **'83** 11

Sausage
Andouille, **'92** 242
Appetizers, Party Rye, **'86** 262
Bake, Creole Sausage-and-Rice, **'88** 58
Baked Peaches and Sausage, **'82** 50
Baked Sausage Patties, **'90** 82
Baked Zucchini and Sausages, **'80** 300
Bake, Eggplant-Sausage, **'85** 221
Bake, Hominy-Sausage, **'88** 51
Bake, Sausage-Cheese, **'88** 58
Bake, Sausage Egg, **'81** 225
Bake, Sausage-Noodle, **'81** 92
Bake, Smoked Sausage-Egg, **'85** 248
Balls in Cheese Pastry, Sausage, **'80** 248
Balls, Sausage-Apple, **'90** 85
Balls, Venison Sausage, **'80** 42
Barbecued Sausage, **'86** 153
Basic Sausage, **'88** 104
Beans, and Rice, Texas Sausage, **'84** 296
Beans, Spicy-Hot, **'89** 17
Biscuit Bites, Sausage, **'84** 95
Biscuits, Cheesy Sausage, **'80** 78
Biscuits, Southern Sausage and, **'82** 43
Biscuits with Sausage, Angel Heart, **'87** 156
Boudin, Old-Fashioned, **'85** 250
Bratwurst and Sauerkraut, **'84** 250
Bratwurst Dinner, Krause's Café, **'87** 238
Bratwurst, Grilled, **'94** 253
Breakfast Delight, **'93** 195
Breakfast Dish, Sausage-Apricot, **'82** 10
Brunch for a Bunch, **'88** 57
Bun, Sausage in a, **'89** M22

Sausage *(continued)*

Burgers, All-American Pizza, **'92** 148
Burgers, Sausage, **'83** 212
Burritos, Breakfast, **'84** 57; **'90** 192
Cabbage, Italian Stuffed, **'84** 294
Cabbage Rolls, Hot-and-Spicy, **'84** 249
Cabbage, Sausage-Sauced, **'81** 271
Cabbage, Stuffed, **'84** 282
Calzone, **'85** 94
Casserole, Breakfast, **'91** 285
Casserole, Brunch, **'82** 124
Casserole, Cheesy Sausage, **'82** 124
Casserole, Country Sausage, **'79** 192
Casserole, Crunchy Sausage, **'81** 288
Casserole, Easy Sausage, **'87** M189
Casserole, Eggplant-Sausage, **'84** 215
Casserole, Grits-Sausage, **'84** 75; **'86** 241
Casserole, Ground Beef and Sausage, **'80** 260
Casserole, Hawaiian Sausage, **'85** 42
Casserole, Italian, **'90** 238
Casserole, Oriental Sausage and Rice, **'82** M123
Casserole, Sausage, **'81** 112; **'82** 12
Casserole, Sausage and Broccoli, **'80** 33
Casserole, Sausage-and-Egg, **'94** 284
Casserole, Sausage and Noodle, **'82** 123
Casserole, Sausage and Wild Rice, **'83** 196
Casserole, Sausage Breakfast, **'81** 270
Casserole, Sausage-Chile Rellenos, **'88** 52
Casserole, Sausage-Egg, **'86** M12
Casserole, Sausage Jambalaya, **'82** M203
Casserole, Sausage-Mushroom Breakfast, **'86** 95
Casserole, Sausage-Potato, **'86** 217
Casserole, Sausage-Rice, **'82** 50; **'83** 75
Casserole, Sausage-Wild Rice, **'84** 250
Casserole, Spanish Rice, **'79** 192
Casserole, Swiss Sausage, **'80** 209
Chicken Rolls Élégante, **'80** 210
Chile con Queso Supreme, **'80** 265
Chili, Beefy Sausage, **'82** 11
Chili, Company, **'82** 311
Chili con Carne, Beef and Sausage, **'83** 284
Chili con Queso Dip, **'86** 81
Chili Goes Southwest, Basic, **'93** 326
Chili, Hearty Kielbasa, **'91** 28
Chili, Hotto Lotto, **'89** 316
Chili-I-Cious, **'89** 315
Chili, Lolly's Pop, **'89** 316
Chili, Sausage-Beef, **'86** 232
Chili, Texas-Style, **'82** 311; **'83** 30
Chorizo, **'92** 241
Chorizo and Egg Tortillas, **'81** 193
Chorizo, Breakfast, **'91** 77
Chorizo, Carbonara, **'94** 230
Chorizo (Spicy Spanish Sausage), **'81** 193
Chorizo Substitute, **'87** 238
Chowder, Clam-and-Sausage, **'94** 104
Chowder, Sausage-Bean, **'83** 20
Cocktail Sausages, Saucy, **'87** 173
Cocktail Smoky Links, **'90** 168
Country Sausage, **'88** 104; **'92** 242
Country Sausage, Spiced, **'88** 104
Crêpes, Cheesy Sausage, **'82** 240; **'83** 71
Crêpes, Sausage, **'88** 295
Crêpes, Sausage-Filled, **'79** 39
Dinner, Beefy Sausage, **'80** M9
Dinner, Sausage-Vegetable, **'84** 250

Dip, Braunschweiger-and-Beer, **'85** 69
Dressing, Cajun, **'82** 307
Dressing, Cornbread-and-Sausage, **'83** 213
Dressing, Cornbread-Sausage, **'82** 307; **'85** 280
Dressing, Harvest Sausage, **'88** 254
Dressing, Sausage, **'86** 280
Dressing, Sausage-Apple, **'93** 305; **'94** 296
Dressing, Turkey with Sausage-Cornbread, **'83** 287
Eggplant Parmesan, **'86** 53
Eggplant, Sausage Stuffed, **'81** 204
Eggplant, Sausage-Stuffed, **'91** 211
Eggs Creole, **'92** 86
Eggs, Scotch, **'79** 261; **'83** 289
Filling, Omelet with Sausage, **'81** 43
Garlic Sausage, **'88** 104
Gravy, Sausage, **'92** 271; **'94** 20
Grits and Sausage, Country, **'83** 54
Grits Italiano, **'92** 43
Grits, Sausage, **'86** 92
Grits, Sausage-Cheese, **'90** 238
Gumbo, Chicken-and-Sausage, **'89** 275; **'90** 256; **'94** 20
Gumbo, Dove and Sausage, **'81** 199
Gumbo, Duck, Oyster, and Sausage, **'79** 226
Gumbo, The Gullah House, **'92** 237
Gumbo Ya Ya, **'87** 210
Gumbo z' Herbes, **'94** 239
Homemade Sausage, Spicy, **'84** 320
Hominy-Sausage Skillet, **'81** 29
Italian Meat Sauce, **'83** 193
Italian Sauce with Noodles, **'84** 250
Italian Sausage, **'88** 104; **'92** 242
Italian Sausage and Pepper Loaves, **'83** 11
Italian Sausage and Peppers, **'84** 9
Italian Sausage and Rice, **'86** 53
Italian Sausage Brunch, **'88** 57
Italian Sausage Dinner, **'91** 218
Italian Sausage Quiche, **'81** 200
Italian Sausage Sandwich, **'80** 92
Italian Sausage Sloppy Joes, **'86** 160
Italian Sausage Soup, **'84** 235
Italian Sausage Soup with Tortellini, **'88** 46
Italian Sausage-Stuffed Mushrooms, **'83** 127
Italian Sausage Supper, **'88** 164
Italian Sausage-Zucchini Soup, **'84** 4
Italian Turkey Sausage, Marinara Sauce with, **'89** 239
Jambalaya, Chicken-and-Sausage, **'88** 200; **'91** 216
Jambalaya, Creole, **'81** 51
Jambalaya de Covington, **'87** 211
Jambalaya, Northshore, **'87** 45
Jambalaya, Oven, **'84** 44
Jambalaya, Sausage, **'80** 210; **'84** 249
Jambalaya, Trail, **'93** 179
Kielbasa, **'92** 242
Kielbasa and Cabbage, **'85** 67; **'89** M196
Kielbasa, Cabbage, **'87** 42
Kielbasa, Sweet-and-Sour, **'89** 327
Kielbasa-Vegetable Dinner, **'91** 274
Kraut, Sausage and, **'83** 11
Lasagna Florentine, Creamy, **'91** 94
Lasagna Maria, **'90** 191
Lasagna Rollups, Sausage-, **'80** 236
Lasagna, Sausage, **'83** 288
Lasagna Sausage Pinwheels, **'79** 6
Loaf, Hawaiian Ham, **'79** 71
Loaf, Sausage-Stuffed French, **'90** 19
Loaf, Skillet Liver, **'80** 11

Loaves, Sausage-Cheese, **'88** 235
Log, Phyllo Sausage, **'84** 294
Log, Stuffed Beef, **'79** 71
Main Dish, Sausage-Eggplant, **'80** 211
Manicotti, Saucy Stuffed, **'83** 288
Meatballs and Sausage, Spicy, **'79** 163
Meatballs, Chestnut, **'79** 110
Meatballs, Crisp German, **'92** 326
Meatballs, Sweet-and-Sour, **'82** 247
Meat Loaf, Mozzarella-Layered, **'79** 71
Mexican Luncheon, **'87** 192
Muffins, Cheesy Sausage, **'92** 252; **'93** 144
Muffins, Sausage, **'88** 52
Muffins, Sausage-Cheese, **'86** 213
Mushrooms, Sausage-Stuffed, **'80** 248; **'91** 164
Omelet, Puffy Sausage, **'80** M268
Onions, Baked Stuffed, **'83** 135
Pancake-Sausage Wedges, **'93** 196
Pasta with Broccoli and Sausage, **'87** 109
Pasta with Collards and Sausage, **'94** 230
Pasta with Sausage and Mixed Vegetables, **'84** 249
Patties, Apples on Sausage, **'82** 120
Peas Mexicano, Black-Eyed, **'79** 10
Peas with Sausage, Black-Eyed, **'86** 7
Pepperoni-and-Broccoli Salad, **'83** 216
Pepperoni and Cheese Loaf, **'82** 32
Pepperoni Biscuits, **'84** 95
Pepperoni Pasta, **'83** 105
Pepperoni Rolls, Ground-, **'83** 244
Pepperoni-Squash Toss, **'84** 127
Phyllo Bites, Sausage-Mushroom-, **'89** 284
Pie, Breakfast, **'86** 242
Pie, Cornbread-Sausage-Apple, **'87** 171
Pie, Sausage-and-Cornbread, **'90** 25
Pintos and Sausage, Hearty, **'88** 296
Pinwheels, Sausage, **'80** 209; **'93** 238
Pita Pockets, Breakfast, **'89** M21
Pizza, Breakfast, **'85** 44; **'88** 288
Pizza, Double Cheesy Beef-and-Sausage, **'86** 77
Pizza Luncheon Pie, Deep-Dish, **'80** 286
Pizza Peppers, **'83** 135
Pizza Pie, Link-Sausage, **'85** 33
Pizza Sandwich, Giant, **'80** 93
Pizza Snacks, Tasty Little, **'79** 248
Pizza, Speedy, **'81** 214
Pizza, Spicy Sausage-Pepperoni, **'83** 226
Pizza, Thick 'n' Crusty Pepperoni, **'85** 244
Polenta with Sausage, **'93** 32
Polish Sausage, Cabbage with, **'83** 104
Pork Rib Roast, Sausage Stuffed, **'94** 240
Pork Sausage, **'81** 55
Pork Sausage Ring, **'80** 49
Potatoes, Mexican-Topped, **'83** 3
Potatoes with Eggs and Meat, **'91** 311; **'92** 25
Puffs, Cajun Hot, **'94** 277
Quesadillas, Sausage, **'90** 118
Quiche, Crustless Sausage-Apple, **'87** 70
Quiche, Easy Sausage, **'79** 261
Quiche, Pizza, **'86** 53
Quiche, Sausage-Cheddar, **'79** 26
Quiche, South-of-the-Border, **'93** 321
Quiche, Spicy Sausage, **'80** M108
Quiche with Avocado Topping, Mexicali, **'93** 309; **'94** 96
Quiche, Zucchini-Sausage, **'83** 122
Ratatouille, Sausage, **'89** 248
Rice, Shrimp and Sausage, **'79** 64

Sausage *(continued)*

Rice with Sausage, Fried, **'83** 12
Rolls with Sweet-and-Sour Sauce, Sausage, **'83** 74
Rollups, Pancake-Sausage, **'83** 246; **'84** 42
Rollups, Sausage-Bacon, **'88** 51
Roll-Ups, Spicy Egg, **'90** 140
Ryes, Sausage Party, **'89** 315
Salad, Bean-and-Sausage, **'91** 313
Salami-Corn Casserole, **'80** 209
Salami Rollups, **'90** 226
Salami Sandwiches, Open-Faced, **'87** 279
Sandwiches, Breakfast, **'80** 52
Sandwiches, Sausage-Cheese Muffin, **'92** M212
Sandwiches with Mustard Sauce, Sausage, **'84** 250
Shrimp and Sausage over Creamy Grits with Tasso Gravy, Spicy, **'92** 236
Skillet Dinner, Sausage, **'83** 29
Skillet Express, Sausage, **'83** 117
Skillet, Mexican-Style, **'83** 12
Skillet Supper, Sausage, **'85** 293
Smoked Sausage, **'86** 154
Smoked Sausage, Chicken Gumbo with, **'81** 199
Smoked Sausage, Jambalaya, **'79** 42
Smoked Sausage Stew, **'82** 231
Smoked Sausages with Mustard Sauce, **'81** 56
Soup, Sausage and Okra, **'80** 209
Soup, Sausage-Bean, **'85** 88
Soup, Sausage-Potato, **'80** 25
Soup, Spicy Sausage-Bean, **'83** 229
Spaghetti Dinner, Sausage, **'79** 194
Spaghetti, Italian, **'81** 38
Spaghetti, Italian Zucchini, **'85** 2
Spaghetti, Real Italian, **'81** 233
Spaghetti, Sausage, **'83** 160
Spicy Sausage, Dieters', **'85** 49
Squares, Chile-Sausage, **'86** 297
Squares, Sausage-Onion, **'83** 112
Squash, Harvest, **'80** 214
Squash, Sausage-Stuffed, **'81** 183
Squash, Sausage-Stuffed Acorn, **'81** 231; **'83** 296; **'84** 285
Squash, Sausage-Stuffed Turban, **'80** 214
Squash with Sausage, Acorn, **'85** 9
Stew, Frogmore, **'92** 236
Stew, Oyster-Sausage, **'89** 242
Stew, Venison Sausage, **'87** 238
Sticks, Beef, **'93** 331
Stir-Fry, Sausage, **'82** 236
Stir-Fry Sausage and Vegetables, **'86** 213; **'87** 82
Strata, Sausage, **'83** 243; **'84** 101
Stuffing, Chicken Breasts with Pecan-Sausage, **'94** 212
Stuffing, Crown Roast of Pork with Cranberry-Sausage, **'88** 49
Supper, Cabbage, **'89** 314
Supper, Sausage-Bean, **'86** 52
Surprise, Sausage, **'83** 245; **'84** 42
Sweet-and-Sour Sausage, **'88** 296
Tacos, Breakfast, **'80** 43
Taquitos, Breakfast, **'87** 237
Tarts, Sausage 'n' Cheese, **'88** 51
Tomatoes, Sausage-Stuffed, **'80** 47
Tortilla Campesina, **'89** 85
Tortillas, Egg-and-Sausage, **'83** 246; **'84** 42
Turnovers, Sausage-Cheese, **'88** 231; **'89** 22
Vegetables and Sausage, Spicy, **'80** 82
Venison-Vegetable Bake, **'87** 304
Waffles, Sausage, **'83** 50
Wild Rice and Sausage, **'86** 268
Wild Rice, Sausage and, **'85** 65
Zucchini and Sausage, Sautéed, **'83** 289

Scallops
Appetizer, Scallop, **'86** 155
Appetizers, Flaky Scallop, **'86** 327
Artichokes Stuffed with Shrimp and Scallops, **'84** 174
Bacon-Wrapped Scallops, **'87** 94
Baked Gruyère Scallops, **'92** 57
Broiled Scallops, **'91** 170
Broiled Scallops with Tartar Sauce, **'80** 164
Broth with Black Beans and Cilantro, Southwestern Scallop, **'87** 123
Casserole, Scallop, **'79** 228
Ceviche (Marinated Raw Fish), **'82** 220
Champagne-Saffron Sauce, Scallops with, **'93** 177
Cheese Scallops, Chip and, **'80** 301
Coquilles Saint Cyrano, **'86** 90
Creamy Scallops and Mushrooms, **'83** 144
Crêpes, Coquilles St. Jacques, **'83** 13
Fresh Scallops and Pasta, **'83** 164
Grilled Orange Scallops with Cilantro-Lime Vinaigrette, **'94** 77
Grilled Scallops, Marinated, **'84** 171
Kabobs, Grilled Scallop, **'83** 101
Kabobs, Grilled Shrimp-and-Scallop, **'92** 210
Kabobs, Scallop-Bacon, **'81** 111
Kabobs, Sea Scallop, **'82** 162
Mornay, Scallops, **'80** 164
Mustard Sauce, Scallops with, **'84** 163
Provençal, Scallops, **'85** 66
Salad, Hot Seafood, **'80** 164
Sautéed Scallops with Cranberry Relish, **'83** 144
Sauté, Scallop, **'88** 28
Sauté, Shrimp-and-Scallop, **'85** 103
Sauté with Pecan Rice, Shrimp-and-Scallop, **'90** 317
Savannah, Scallops, **'79** 145
Sherried Scallops, **'83** 281
Stir-Fry, Scallop, **'94** 32
Supreme, Seafood, **'82** 284
Tostada, Grilled Scallops, **'87** 120
Vegetable Nests, Scallops in, **'91** 70
Vegetables, Bay Scallops with, **'84** 233
Vegetables, Scallops en Brochette with, **'80** 163
Vermicelli, Scallop-Vegetable, **'87** 143
Véronique, Scallops, **'83** 144
Wild Rice, Scallops and, **'90** 129
Wine, Scallops in, **'91** 48
Seafood. *See also* specific types and Fish.
Appetizer, Layered Seafood, **'88** 2
Bisque, Seafood, **'86** 66
Boil, Low Country Seafood, **'80** 119
Boil, Southern Shellfish, **'93** 258
Bouillabaisse, Florida, **'79** 158
Brochette, Seafood, **'87** 96
Broiled Shellfish, Quick, **'79** 228
Casserole, Seafood, **'87** 109; **'89** 63
Chowder, Curried Seafood, **'94** 103
Chowder, Seafood, **'85** 9; **'92** 122
Chowder, Southern Seafood, **'83** 20
Cioppino, Gulf Coast, **'94** 102
Crawfish Étouffée, **'94** 239
Delight, Seafood, **'86** 208
Dip, Hot Artichoke-Seafood, **'80** 241
Dip, Hot Artichoke Seafood, **'85** M212
Dip, Hot Cheesy Seafood, **'84** 221
Dip, Seafood, **'79** 3
Dip, Super Seafood, **'90** 292
Eggplant, Seafood Stuffed, **'79** 187
Gumbo, Cajun Seafood, **'94** 238
Gumbo, Champion Seafood, **'86** 293
Gumbo, Chicken-Ham-Seafood, **'81** 6
Gumbo, Creole, **'86** 228
Gumbo, Creole Seafood, **'82** 278
Gumbo, Ham and Seafood, **'81** 199
Gumbo, Light Seafood-Okra, **'86** 155
Gumbo, Quick Creole, **'82** 87
Gumbo, Seafood, **'79** 198, 286; **'80** 34; **'81** 5; **'83** 90; **'84** 87, 92; **'87** 210; **'90** 154
Gumbo, Spicy Seafood, **'91** 207
Gumbo with Whole Crabs, Seafood, **'85** 2
Hot Brown, Seafood, **'88** 158
Imperials, Individual Seafood, **'84** 162
Jambalaya, Three-Seafood, **'82** 126
Linguine, Seafood, **'79** 227
Manicotti, Seafood, **'94** 195
Mayonnaise, Seafood with Dill, **'86** 234
Mold, Chilled Seafood, **'86** 70
Mornay, Seafood, **'83** 67
Mussels Linguine, **'90** M112
Mussel Soup, **'93** 259
Paella, Chicken-Seafood, **'88** 68
Paella, Party, **'88** M189
Paella, Seafood, **'82** 245
Papillote, Ocean, **'84** M287
Pasta, Seafood and, **'90** 234
Pie, Hot Seafood, **'80** 32
Salad, Baked Seafood, **'86** 10
Salad, Hot Seafood, **'79** 117; **'80** 164
Salad, Paella, **'86** 207
Salad, Polynesian Seafood, **'79** 57
Salad, Seafood, **'90** 88
Salad, Seafood Pasta, **'90** 62
Salad, Seaside, **'86** 183
Salad, Smoky Seafood, **'84** 46
Salad Sussex Shores, Seafood, **'93** 98
Sauce Delight, Seafood, **'82** 91
Sauce, Linguine with Seafood, **'83** 232
Sauce, Seafood, **'79** 3; **'82** 48; **'86** 304; **'89** 239
Sauce, Seafood Cheese, **'89** 240
Sautéed Seafood Platter, **'83** 89
Seasoning Blend, Bay Seafood, **'92** 121
Seasoning Blend, Fish-and-Seafood, **'88** 28
Seasoning Rub, Seafood, **'93** 101
Slaw, Seafood, **'79** 56
Spread, Seafood, **'86** M58; **'87** 146
Spread, Seafood Sandwich, **'82** 87
Stew, Seafood, **'84** 280
Stock, Seafood, **'94** 238
Supreme, Seafood, **'82** 284
Tartlets, Seafood, **'87** 247

Seafood *(continued)*

Tempura, Basic, **'81** 68
Tempura, Cornmeal, **'81** 68
Seasonings
Adobo, **'92** 158
Bay Seafood Seasoning Blend, **'92** 121
Blend, Seasoning, **'82** 296
Creole Rub, **'93** 101
Creole Seasoning Blend, **'92** 121
Fish-and-Seafood Seasoning Blend, **'88** 28
Five-Spice Powder Blend, **'92** 121
Garlic, Herbed Roasted, **'94** 177
Garlic Puree, Roasted, **'92** 55
Garlic, Roasted, **'94** 177
Greek Seasoning Blend, **'92** 121
Ground Seasoning Blend, **'92** 121
Herb Rub, **'93** 102
Herbs Seasoning Blend, **'92** 121
Jerk Rub, **'93** 101
Meat Seasoning Blend, **'88** 29
Mexican Rub, **'93** 102
Mix, GOPPS Seasoning, **'92** 305
Mix, Seasoning, **'91** 64
Poultry Seasoning Blend, **'88** 28
Salt, Gourmet Seasoning, **'82** 297
Sazon, **'92** 157
Seafood Seasoning Rub, **'93** 101
Vanilla Extract, **'94** 243
Vanilla Oil, **'94** 243
Vanilla Sugar, **'94** 243
Vegetable Seasoning Blend, **'88** 29
Sherbets. *See* Ice Creams and Sherbets.
Shrimp
Appetizer, Artichoke-and-Shrimp, **'93** 271
Appetizer, Layered Seafood, **'88** 2
Appetizer, Shrimp-Pineapple, **'85** 80
Appetizers, Zucchini-Shrimp, **'89** 311
Ariosto, Shrimp and Chicken, **'79** 31
Artichokes, Shrimp-Stuffed, **'84** 67; **'87** 55
Artichokes, Shrimp Stuffed, **'94** 62
Artichokes Stuffed with Shrimp and Scallops, **'84** 174
Aspic, Shrimp-Coleslaw, **'79** 88
Aspic, Shrimp-Cucumber, **'83** 108
Aspic with Shrimp, Tomato, **'79** 241
au Gratin, Crab, Shrimp, and Artichoke, **'90** 240
au Gratin, Shrimp, **'85** 79
Avocados, Shrimp-Filled, **'83** 2
Baked Shrimp, **'87** 35
Balls, Curried Shrimp, **'94** 180
Ball, Shrimp-Cheese, **'85** 208
Barbecued Shrimp, **'82** 74; **'84** 93; **'90** 28
Barbecued Shrimp, Cajun, **'87** 95
Bayou, Shrimp, **'88** 261
Bisque, Shrimp-Chile, **'94** 272
Bisque, Shrimp-Cucumber, **'79** 172
Bisque, Shrimp-Vegetable, **'82** 313; **'83** 66
Bisque, Tomato-Shrimp, **'86** 66
Boats, Shrimp, **'79** 57
Boiled Shrimp, **'79** 3
Boiled Shrimp, Ray Kidd's, **'84** 87
Boiled Shrimp, Special, **'83** 36
Boiled Shrimp, Spicy, **'83** 320; **'84** 289
Boiled Shrimp Supper, **'94** 200
Boiled Shrimp with Cocktail Sauce, **'79** 151
Boiled Shrimp with Green Peppercorn Tartar Sauce, **'94** 144

Breakfast Shrimp, Classic Charleston, **'93** 60
Broiled Shrimp, Beer-, **'87** 142
Broiled Shrimp, Garlic-, **'83** 193
Broiled Shrimp, Lemon-Garlic, **'82** 29; **'86** 182
Broiled Shrimp Supreme, **'79** 3
Butter, Shrimp, **'92** 91
Cajun Shrimp, **'89** 283
Cajun Shrimp, Fiery, **'91** 218
Canapés, Shrimp, **'84** 116
Canapés, Shrimp-and-Cucumber, **'93** 164
Cashew Shrimp Supreme, **'83** 29
Casserole, Chayotes and Shrimp, **'80** 230
Casserole, Crab-and-Shrimp, **'84** 71
Casserole, Shrimp, **'85** 240
Casserole, Shrimp-and-Chicken, **'91** 102
Casserole, Shrimp-and-Noodle, **'90** 240
Casserole, Shrimp and Rice, **'79** 228
Casserole, Shrimp-and-Rice, **'94** 328
Casserole, Turkey-and-Shrimp Florentine, **'92** 122
Catfish, Crown Room's Shrimp-Stuffed, **'84** 182
C'est Bon, Shrimp, **'94** 195
Cheese Ball, Curried Shrimp, **'86** 135
Cheesecake, Shrimp-and-Gruyère, **'92** 57
Cheese, Shrimp with Herbed Jalapeño, **'87** 112
Chowder, Shrimp, **'89** 218
Chowder, Shrimp and Corn, **'79** 199
Chow Mein, Shrimp, **'82** 30
Cocktail, Shrimp, **'87** 173
Coconut-Beer Shrimp, **'85** 230; **'89** 23
Combo, Snow Pea-Shrimp, **'79** 57
Cream Sauce, Shrimp in, **'84** M286
Creole in a Rice Ring, Shrimp, **'86** 222
Creole, Shrimp, **'86** 256; **'87** 18; **'90** M220; **'93** 282
Creole, Special Shrimp, **'87** 172
Creole, Spicy Shrimp, **'79** 181
Creole, Wild Rice-and-Shrimp, **'84** 292
Curried Rice and Shrimp, **'83** 231
Curried Shrimp, **'84** 110
Curried Shrimp, Quick, **'84** M198
Curried Shrimp, West Indian, **'79** 227
Curry, Charleston-Style Shrimp, **'84** 109
Curry, Creamy Shrimp, **'90** 145
Curry, Polynesian Shrimp, **'89** 23
Curry Sauce, Hawaiian Shrimp with, **'94** 54
Curry, Shrimp Malai, **'84** 110
Curry, Sour Cream and Shrimp, **'81** 10
Curry, Sour Cream Shrimp, **'80** 83
Dee-Lish, Shrimp, **'90** 216
de Jonghe, Shrimp, **'79** 228
Delight, Shrimp, **'79** 192
Destin, Shrimp, **'82** 29
Dijonnaise, Shrimp, **'87** 91
Dilled Sauced Shrimp, **'86** 88
Dilled Shrimp, **'88** 150
Dip, Hot Cheesy Seafood, **'84** 221
Dip, Hot Shrimp, **'87** 190
Dippers, Shrimp, **'84** 324
Dip, Quick Shrimp, **'79** 153
Dip, Shrimp, **'86** 84; **'88** M261
Dip, Zesty Shrimp, **'80** 150
Egg Foo Yong, Shrimp, **'83** 22
Eggplant, Shrimp-Stuffed, **'92** 99
Eggrolls, Shrimp and Pork, **'82** 240; **'83** 18
Eggs, Saucy Shrimp-Curried, **'84** 143
Eggs, Shrimp and Crab Scrambled, **'79** 261

Élégante, Shrimp, **'83** 48
en Papillote, Shrimp Cancun, **'91** 136
en Papillote, Shrimp with Asparagus, **'86** 145
Étouffée, Crab-and-Shrimp, **'89** 96
Étouffée, Shrimp, **'79** 4; **'90** 229
Fettuccine and Shrimp with Dried Tomato Pesto, **'94** 249
Fettuccine, Shrimp, **'94** 84
Filling, Shrimp, **'89** 320
Filling, Shrimp Salad, **'87** 106
Fish with Shrimp, Veracruz, **'86** 130
Flambé, Prawns, **'89** 24
Florentine, Chicken-and-Shrimp, **'89** 64
Flounder Stuffed with Shrimp, **'88** 51
Fondue, Shrimp, **'86** 244
French Shrimp, **'80** 85
Fresh Shrimp, Preparing, **'82** 127
Fried Marinated Shrimp with Mango Slaw, **'93** 31
Fried Shrimp, French-, **'79** 4
Fried Shrimp, Golden, **'82** 29
Fried Shrimp, Gulf Coast, **'91** 29
Fried Shrimp, Puffy, **'79** 4
Fried Shrimp with Apricot Sauce, **'87** 172
Garlic-Buttered Shrimp, **'86** M226
Garlic Shrimp, **'79** 268; **'80** 14
Gazpacho, Shrimp-Cream Cheese, **'94** 137
Grilled Shrimp, **'85** 103
Gumbo, Crab and Shrimp, **'81** 200
Gumbo, Quick Shrimp, **'86** 71
Gumbo, Shrimp, **'81** 199
Honeyed Shrimp, Tangy, **'94** 32
Jalapeños, Shrimp-Stuffed, **'88** 115
Jambalaya, Creole Shrimp, **'92** 99
Kabobs, Appetizer Shrimp, **'91** 251
Kabobs, Grilled Shrimp-and-Scallop, **'92** 210
Kabobs, Marinated Shrimp, **'84** 276; **'85** 158
Kabobs, Shrimp, **'80** 150, 184
Kabobs, Steak-and-Shrimp, **'80** 184
Key West Shrimp, **'94** 278
Lamb Chops with Shrimp, **'88** 58
Lemon Butter, Shrimp in, **'84** 163
Lemon Garlic Sauce, Shrimp in, **'83** 67
Lemon Shrimp, Luscious, **'88** 150
Linguine, Spicy Shrimp and, **'92** 34
Manale, Shrimp, **'86** 268
Marinara, Shrimp, **'84** 233
Marinated and Grilled Shrimp, **'87** 141
Marinated Shrimp and Cucumber, **'91** 166
Marinated Shrimp, Grilled, **'87** 173
Marinated Shrimp, Icy, **'84** 215
Marinated Shrimp, Zesty, **'87** 173
Mediterranean Shrimp Bowl, **'80** 174
Medley, Eggplant-Shrimp, **'79** 188
Melba, Shrimp, **'84** 86
Miniquiches, Shrimp, **'87** 146
Mold, Shrimp, **'87** 94
Mold with Asparagus, Shrimp, **'93** 214
Mousse, Shrimp, **'79** 57; **'87** 196, 251
Mushrooms, Shrimp-Stuffed, **'80** M135
Mushrooms with Angel Hair Pasta, Shrimp and, **'92** 34
Mustard-Vinegar Sauce, Shrimp with, **'93** 240
Noodles, Creamy Shrimp and, **'92** 100
Omelet, Shrimp-and-Cheddar, **'84** 57
Omelet, Shrimp-and-Cheese, **'94** 31
Paella, Chicken-Pork-Shrimp, **'82** 245
Paella, Shrimp-and-Chicken, **'94** 168
Pasta, Herbed Shrimp and, **'92** 329
Pasta Medley, Shrimp-, **'88** 302

Shrimp *(continued)*

Pasta Primavera, Shrimp with, '93 168
Pasta, Shrimp and, '91 207
Pasta with Shrimp and Asparagus, Angel Hair, '92 100
Pasta with Shrimp-Mushroom Italienne, Green, '79 170
Pâté with Dill Sauce, Shrimp, '85 39
Patties, Shrimp, '92 128
Peanut Sauce, Shrimp with, '93 303
Peas, Shrimp with Snow, '85 75
Peppers, Shrimp-Stuffed, '80 162; '86 131, 197
Pickled Shrimp, '79 3; '94 182
Pickled Shrimp, New Orleans, '79 145
Pickle, Shrimp-in-a-, '86 326
Pilaf, Shrimp, '82 246
Pizza Wedges, Shrimp, '89 158
Polynesian Shrimp, '79 3
Potatoes, Broccoli-Shrimp Stuffed, '92 M228
Potatoes, Creamy Shrimp-Stuffed, '80 36
Potatoes, Shrimp-Sauced, '81 M61
Puffs, Gouda-Shrimp, '79 234
Puff, Shrimp-Crab, '79 57
Puffs, Luncheon Shrimp, '85 72
Quesadillas with Shrimp and Brie, '94 173
Quiche, Shrimp, '83 50
Rémoulade Sauce, Shrimp with, '91 29
Rémoulade, Shrimp, '83 173; '90 255
Rice, Oriental Shrimp and, '90 183
Rice, Shrimp and Refried, '89 176
Rice, Shrimp and Sausage, '79 64
Rock Shrimp Conga, '80 2
Rock Shrimp Tails, Batter-Fried, '80 2
Rock Shrimp Tails, Broiled, '80 3
Rock Shrimp Tails, Sweet-and-Sour, '80 3
Rollups, Shrimp-Stuffed, '82 234
Rotelle, Shrimp, '85 165
Sailor Shrimp for Two, '82 276
Salad, Avocado Stuffed with Shrimp, '82 207
Salad, Baked Shrimp-Rice, '83 22
Salad, Caribbean Shrimp-and-Black Bean, '93 143
Salad, Crabmeat-Shrimp Pasta, '86 208
Salad, Creamy Shrimp, '79 56
Salad, Festive Macaroni-Shrimp, '85 165
Salad, Fruited Shrimp, '86 156
Salad, Grapefruit-and-Shrimp, '88 5
Salad in Pastry, Shrimp, '86 105
Salad, Layered Shrimp, '88 100
Salad, Macaroni-Shrimp, '85 121
Salad, Marinated Shrimp, '85 82; '93 321
Salad on the Half Shell, Shrimp, '86 73
Salad, Orange-Shrimp, '84 197
Salad, Oriental Shrimp, '91 313
Salad, Pasta-and-Shrimp, '83 163
Salad, Peppers Stuffed with Shrimp-and-Orzo, '91 203
Salad, Rice-and-Shrimp, '83 82
Salad, Rice-Shrimp, '79 270; '92 142
Salad Sandwiches, Shrimp, '90 178
Salad, Shrimp, '81 94; '84 221; '86 186; '93 238
Salad, Shrimp and Avocado, '80 266
Salad, Shrimp and Rice, '80 231; '82 207
Salad, Shrimp-and-Rice, '92 307
Salad, Shrimp-Endive, '85 73
Salad, Shrimp Macaroni, '79 220

Salad, Shrimp-Macaroni, '85 219
Salad, Shrimp Vermicelli, '88 139
Salad, Shrimp-Walnut, '86 182
Salads, Individual Shrimp, '83 146
Salad, Super Shrimp, '81 37
Salad, Tangy Shrimp-Rice, '84 66
Salad, Tossed Shrimp-Egg, '80 4
Salad, Vegetable-Shrimp, '79 190
Salad with Sherry Vinaigrette, Shrimp, Orange, and Olive, '93 177
Salad with Shrimp, Green, '88 49
Salad, Zesty Shrimp-and-Orange Rice, '87 155
Salsa Picante with Shrimp, '92 210
Sandwiches, Shrimp-and-Egg Salad, '94 182
Sandwiches, Shrimp-Cheese, '85 242
Sauce, Broccoli and Cauliflower with Shrimp, '84 248
Sauce, Flounder Fillets in Shrimp, '83 227
Sauce, Flounder with Hollandaise-Shrimp, '86 234
Sauce, Oysters in Shrimp, '87 40
Sauce Piquante, Crab and Shrimp, '83 92
Sauce, Shrimp, '87 138, 232
Sauce, Shrimp-and-Almond, '87 282
Sausage over Creamy Grits with Tasso Gravy, Spicy Shrimp and, '92 236
Sautéed Shrimp, '79 3
Sauté, Shrimp-and-Grouper, '87 91
Sauté, Shrimp-and-Scallop, '85 103
Sauté with Pecan Rice, Shrimp-and-Scallop, '90 317
Scampi, Easy, '84 291
Scampi, Orange, '85 303
Scampi, Quick, '88 301
Scampi, Shrimp, '84 230; '92 117; '93 70
Shells, Creamy Shrimp, '79 4
Sherried Garlic Shrimp, '92 175
Sirloin Supreme, Shrimp and, '81 131
Skillet, Quick Shrimp, '87 50
Soufflé Roll, Shrimp, '89 320
Soup, Okra-and-Shrimp, '94 323
Soup, Shrimp-and-Corn, '84 88
Soup, Shrimp Enchilada, '94 103
Soup, Shrimp-Mushroom, '85 87
Spaghetti, Shrimp-and-Vegetable, '91 170
Spaghetti with Black Olives, Shrimp, '85 13
Spread, Chunky Shrimp, '85 300; '86 18
Spread, Curried Shrimp, '87 158
Spread, Shrimp, '81 306; '85 135; '87 111; '93 205
Spread, Shrimp-Cucumber, '79 81
Spread, Tempting Shrimp, '79 57
Spread, Zippy Shrimp, '90 36
Squash, Shrimp-Stuffed Yellow, '84 194
Steak and Shrimp, '88 123
Stew and Grits, Shrimp, '80 118
Stewed Shrimp with Dumplings, '79 31
Stew over Grits, Shrimp, '88 126; '89 47
Stew, Shrimp, '83 4
Stir-Fry, Beef-and-Shrimp, '93 32
Stir-Fry, Cajun Shrimp, '92 127
Stir-Fry Shrimp and Vegetables, '87 91
Stock, Shrimp, '93 60
Stroganoff, Oven-Baked Shrimp, '81 297
Stroganoff, Shrimp, '79 81
Stuffed Shrimp Bundles, Crab-, '81 176
Stuffed Shrimp, Crab-, '84 259
Stuffed Shrimp, Parmesan-, '85 103
Sweet-and-Sour Shrimp, '83 278; '90 M112

Sweet-and-Sour Shrimp and Chicken, '87 267; '88 103; '89 66
Szechuan Shrimp, '86 173
Tart, Shrimp, '87 70
Toast, Shrimp, '86 91
Topping, Shrimp, '93 291
Tortellini, Shrimp and, '92 34
Tostadas, Shrimp-and-Black Bean, '93 204
Tree, Shrimp, '83 320; '84 288; '85 318
Vegetables, Shrimp and, '82 6
Vermicelli, Shrimp and Feta Cheese on, '87 108
Versailles, Shrimp, '90 233

Soufflés
Apricot Soufflé, Baked, '88 267
Asparagus Soufflé, '79 66; '83 265; '89 89
Banana Daiquiri Soufflé, '84 317
Blintz Soufflé, '88 155
Blue Cheese Soufflé, '91 244
Brandy Alexander Soufflé, '82 173; '83 M114
Bread Pudding Soufflé, Creole, '92 87
Broccoli Soufflé, '81 24
Broccoli Soufflé, Golden, '84 283
Butternut Soufflé, '83 266
Carrot Puff, '89 89
Carrot Soufflé, '79 73; '83 265
Cauliflower Soufflé, '82 76; '89 279; '90 17
Cheese Soufflé, '79 72, 261; '94 116
Cheese Soufflé, Cream, '88 11
Cheese Soufflé for Two, '81 226
Cheese Soufflé, Rolled, '89 13
Cheese Soufflé, Three-Egg, '87 234
Chicken-Chestnut Soufflé, '79 107
Chocolat Cointreau, Soufflé au, '94 56
Chocolate Mint Soufflé, '81 16
Chocolate Soufflé, '84 317; '94 46
Chocolate Soufflé, Light, '83 278
Coconut Soufflé, '79 73; '85 212
Corn-and-Cheese Soufflé, '88 122
Crab Soufflé Spread, '85 4
Cranberry-Topped Holiday Soufflé, '84 306
Cups, Hot Soufflé, '85 284
Daiquiri Soufflé, Elegant, '80 69
Devonshire Soufflé, Chilled, '88 279
Egg Soufflé Casserole, '83 55
Egg Soufflés, Little, '83 57
Frozen Soufflés, Individual, '80 52
Grand Marnier Soufflé, '79 281
Grand Marnier Soufflés, '89 290
Grasshopper Soufflé, '81 248; '86 188
Grits Soufflé, '80 30
Grits Soufflé, Mexican, '79 55
Ham Breakfast Soufflé, Virginia, '93 121
Ham Soufflé with Cucumber Sauce, '92 41
Individual Soufflés, '80 190
Kahlúa Soufflé, '82 173
Lemon-Lime Soufflé, Cold, '84 24
Lemon Sauce Soufflés, Quick, '88 43
Lemon Soufflé, '82 170, 252; '94 199
Lemon Soufflé, Tart, '85 82
Lemon Soufflé with Raspberry-Amaretto Sauce, Frozen, '88 130
Mushroom Soufflés, '87 282
Onion Soufflé, '79 247
Orange Dessert Soufflé, '83 206
Orange Soufflé, Chilled, '84 317; '86 189
Orange Soufflé, Frozen, '79 211
Parsnip Soufflé, Golden, '83 266
Pineapple Dessert Soufflé, '80 153
Potatoes, Soufflé, '84 295; '85 196; '90 14

Soufflés (*continued*)

Potato Soufflé, Cheesy, **'89** 332
Potato Soufflé, Sweet, **'82** 286; **'86** 121
Raspberry Soufflé, **'86** 188
Raspberry-Topped Soufflé, **'85** 317
Rice-Cheese Soufflé, **'79** 270
Salmon Soufflé, Fresh, **'81** 182
Shrimp Soufflé Roll, **'89** 320
Sour Cream Soufflé, **'80** 43
Spinach Soufflé, **'79** 73; **'81** 304; **'84** 78;
  '85 248; **'86** 108
Spinach Soufflé, Cheesy, **'81** 53
Spinach Soufflé Deluxe, **'79** 8
Spinach Soufflé Roll, **'80** 215
Squash Soufflé, Cheesy, **'82** 146
Squash Soufflé, Yellow, **'89** 89
Sweet Potato Soufflé, **'93** 325
Turkey Soufflé, **'80** 271
Turnip Soufflé, **'79** 254
Vanilla Soufflé, Frozen, **'79** 230; **'82** 173
Vanilla Soufflés with Vanilla Crème Sauce,
  '94 242
Zucchini-and-Corn Soufflé, **'83** 265
Zucchini Soufflé, **'79** 157
Soups. *See also* Chili, Chowders, Gumbos,
  Stews.
Acorn Squash Soup, **'91** 294
Acorn Squash Soup, Cream of, **'94** 268
Almond Soup, **'79** 48
Artichoke Cream Soup, **'94** 62
Artichoke Soup, **'89** 269
Artichoke Soup, Cream of, **'82** 232
Asparagus Soup, **'84** 67
Asparagus Soup, Cream of, **'84** 111
Asparagus Soup, Creamy, **'94** 225
Avocado-Banana-Yogurt Soup, **'80** 78
Avocado-Mushroom Soup, Creamy, **'85** 25
Avocado Soup, **'88** 160
Avocado Soup, Chilled, **'81** 34; **'87** 37;
  '93 108
Avocado Soup, Creamy, **'79** 107
Avocado Soup, Sherried, **'84** 181
Bacon-Beer Cheese Soup, **'87** M7
Bacon, Lettuce, and Tomato Soup, **'91** 207
Bean and Bacon Soup, **'83** 26
Bean-and-Barley Soup, Hearty, **'86** 304
Bean and Pasta Soup, **'94** 220
Bean-and-Turkey Soup, **'93** 319
"Bean Counter" Soup, **'92** 80
Beanolla Soup, **'94** 248
Bean Pot, White, **'86** 194
Bean Soup, **'80** 25
Bean Soup, Black, **'88** 30, 266; **'89** 28;
  '93 231
Bean Soup, Capitol Hill, **'80** 222
Bean Soup, Carolina Black, **'92** 139
Bean Soup, Chunky Navy, **'83** 291
Bean Soup, Cream of Green, **'84** 111
Bean Soup, Drunken, **'87** 283
Bean Soup, Ham-and-, **'84** 4
Bean Soup, Leafy, **'86** 223
Bean Soup, Navy, **'84** 280
Bean Soup, Sausage-, **'85** 88
Bean Soup, Savory Navy, **'87** 282
Bean Soup, Spicy Sausage-, **'83** 229
Bean Soup, Spicy Three-, **'91** 28
Bean Soup, Spicy White, **'94** 225
Bean Soup, Three-, **'89** 17
Bean Soup, White, **'83** 229

Beer-Cheese Soup, **'84** 246
Bell Pepper Soup, **'89** 103
Bisque, Banana-Raspberry, **'93** 161
Bisque, Brisk Mushroom, **'81** 190
Bisque, Clam, **'86** 228
Bisque, Crab, **'88** 251
Bisque, Crab-and-Corn, **'87** 137
Bisque, Make-Ahead Tomato-Basil, **'93** 322
Bisque, Oyster, **'83** 252
Bisque, Seafood, **'86** 66
Bisque, Shrimp-Chile, **'94** 272
Bisque, Shrimp-Cucumber, **'79** 172
Bisque, Shrimp-Vegetable, **'82** 313; **'83** 66
Bisque, Spicy Pumpkin, **'86** 67
Bisque, Spinach-Potato, **'86** 66
Bisque, Squash, **'84** 280
Bisque, Tomato-Shrimp, **'86** 66
Bisque, Tuna, **'79** 76
Black-Eyed Soup, Beefy, **'85** 6
Borscht, Crawfish, **'92** 84
Borscht, Ruby Red, **'83** 176
Bouillabaisse, Florida, **'79** 158
Bouillon, Redfish Court, **'83** 290; **'84** 93
Bouillon, Tomato, **'83** 8
Broccoli-and-Chicken Soup, **'90** 202
Broccoli Soup, **'86** 161, M194; **'87** 288
Broccoli Soup, Cheesy-, **'86** 258
Broccoli Soup, Creamed, **'85** 24
Broccoli Soup, Cream of, **'79** 130; **'80** 188,
  M225; **'82** 314; **'83** 66; **'86** 259
Broccoli Soup, Cream-of-, **'88** 56
Broccoli Soup, Creamy, **'81** 75; **'82** 13;
  '83 99; **'91** 307
Broccoli Soup, Easy, **'81** 307
Broccoli Soup, Fresh, **'91** 86
Broccoli Soup, Hot, **'81** 235; **'83** 44
Broccoli Soup, Light Cream of, **'93** 17
Broccoli Soup, Mock Cream of, **'85** 288
Broccoli-Swiss Soup, **'86** 6
Butternut-and-Apple Soup, Creamed,
  '88 228
Cabbage Soup, **'83** 291; **'85** 88
Cabbage Soup, Sweet-and-Sour, **'89** 314
Cantaloupe Soup, **'83** 120; **'88** 160
Cantaloupe Soup, Chilled, **'81** 156
Cantaloupe Soup, Fresh, **'84** 190
Carrot-and-Tomato Soup, Cream of, **'94** 176
Carrot Cream Soup, **'90** 210
Carrot-Leek Soup, **'86** 34
Carrot-Mint Soup, Chilled, **'90** M168
Carrot-Orange Soup, **'79** 172
Carrot Soup, **'80** 88; **'89** 146
Carrot Soup, Cheesy, **'81** 262
Carrot Soup, Cream of, **'81** 307; **'88** 46;
  '91 69
Carrot Soup, Creamy, **'92** 218
Carrot Soup, Curried, **'82** 157
Carrot Soup, Savory, **'84** 107
Cauliflower and Caraway Soup, **'82** 264
Cauliflower and Watercress Soup, Cream of,
  '83 126
Cauliflower Soup, **'90** 211
Cauliflower Soup, Cream of, **'87** M7; **'88** 12
Cauliflower Soup, Creamy, **'82** 76
Cauliflower Soup, Fresh, **'84** 279
Celery Soup, Burnet-, **'84** 107
Celery Soup, Cream of, **'79** 71; **'90** 210
Celery Soup, Light Cream-of-, **'82** 279
Cheese-and-Broccoli Soup, **'89** 276
Cheese Soup, Bacon-Topped, **'80** M224
Cheese Soup, Cream of, **'83** 99

Cheese Soup, Gazebo, **'90** 158
Cheese Soup, Hearty, **'84** 4
Cheese Soup, Monterey Jack, **'81** 112;
  '85 M211
Cheese Soup, Uncle Ed's Favorite, **'94** 228
Cheese Velvet Soup, **'80** 74; **'92** 193
Cheesy Anytime Soup, **'81** 307; **'82** 314;
  '83 66
Chicken-Almond Cream Soup, **'92** 21
Chicken-and-Rice Soup, **'88** 236
Chicken, Artichoke, and Mushroom Soup,
  '92 324
Chicken Broth, Easy Microwave, **'90** M167
Chicken Enchilada Soup, **'86** 22
Chicken, Ham, and Oyster Soup, **'79** 198
Chicken Noodle Soup, **'80** 264
Chicken-Noodle Soup, Chunky, **'88** 12
Chicken Soup, **'81** 98
Chicken Soup, Cream of, **'85** 243
Chicken Soup, Curried, **'86** 34
Chicken Soup, Homemade, **'82** 34
Chicken Soup, Mexican, **'84** 234
Chicken Soup, Quick, **'86** M72
Chicken-Vegetable Soup, **'88** 18
Chill-Chaser Soup, **'87** 282
Cioppino, Gulf Coast, **'94** 102
Clam Florentine Soup, **'85** 23
Consommé aux Champignons, **'79** 48
Corn-and-Bourbon Soup, **'92** 194
Corn-and-Crab Soup, Fresh, **'92** 183
Corned Beef Soup, **'83** 16
Corn Soup, **'80** 56; **'85** 243; **'87** 156
Corn Soup, Cream of, **'90** 210
Corn Soup, Favorite, **'85** 155
Corn Soup, Grilled, **'87** 121
Corn Soup, Pimiento-, **'89** 126
Crab-and-Leek Bisque, **'94** 104
Crabmeat Soup, **'84** 123
Crab Soup, Beaufort, **'92** 238
Crab Soup, Cream of, **'88** 302
Crab Soup, Creamy, **'80** M224
Crab Soup, Elegant, **'80** 188
Crab Soup, Old-Fashioned, **'90** 71
Crab Soup, Plantation, **'92** 237
Crab Soup, Quick, **'84** 279
Crab Soup, Steamboat's Cream of, **'81** 127
Cucumber Soup, Chilled, **'79** 144
Cucumber Soup, Cold, **'79** 130; **'81** 130
Cucumber Soup, Cold Minted, **'86** 34
Cucumber Soup, Cream of, **'81** 98
Cucumber Soup, Creamy, **'80** 171
Cucumber Soup, Dilled, **'90** M167
Cucumber Vichyssoise, **'94** 90
Cucumber-Yogurt Soup, **'82** 157; **'83** 205
Curried Soup, **'81** 130
Dill Soup, Cold, **'84** 107
Egg Drop Soup, **'83** 21; **'86** 16
Egg-Drop Soup, **'85** M12
Egg Flower Soup, **'81** 307; **'82** 313; **'83** 65
Eggplant Soup, Herbed, **'90** 173
Eggplant Supper Soup, **'85** 221
Fire Water, **'80** 188
Fish Soup with Garlic Mayonnaise, Rich,
  '92 56
French Market Soup, **'85** 277; **'92** 49;
  '94 317
Fruit Soup, **'87** 98
Fruit Soup, Chilled Fresh, **'88** 160
Fruit Soup, Cold Fresh, **'87** 157
Fruit Soup Dessert, **'79** 172
Fruit Soup, Dried, **'79** 23

Soups *(continued)*

Fruit Soup, Swedish, '82 313; '83 65
Garden Harvest Soup, Italian, '90 M167
Garden Soup, '85 241
Gazpacho, '79 172; '80 266; '81 98; '82 73;
　'84 112; '85 164; '91 94; '92 64; '93 215
Gazpacho, Blender, '85 93
Gazpacho, Chilled, '84 138
Gazpacho, Classy, '89 220
Gazpacho, Cool, '83 140
Gazpacho, Saucy, '82 157
Gazpacho, Secret, '93 161
Gazpacho, Smoked Vegetable, '93 156
Gazpacho, Spring, '81 112
Gazpacho, Summer, '84 181
Green Pepper Soup, '88 250
Greens Soup, Cream with, '94 277
Guadalajara Soup, '88 30
Ham-and-Bean Soup, Spicy, '94 322
Hamburger Soup, '80 263
Ham Soup, Hearty, '82 4
Harvest Soup, '79 101
Homemade Soup, '79 198
Hot-and-Sour Soup, '83 68; '91 50
Jambalaya, '84 282
Jambalaya, Black-Eyed Pea, '92 70
Jambalaya, Chicken-and-Sausage, '88 200;
　'91 216
Jambalaya, Creole, '81 51; '87 210
Jambalaya, Creole Shrimp, '92 99
Jambalaya de Covington, '87 211
Jambalaya, Good Luck, '87 11
Jambalaya, Oven, '84 44
Jambalaya, Red Rice, '91 18
Jambalaya, Sausage, '80 210; '84 249
Jambalaya, Smoked Sausage, '79 42
Jambalaya, Three-Seafood, '82 126
Jambalaya, Trail, '93 179
Jambalaya, Tuna, '83 44
Lemon-Egg Drop Soup, '93 81
Lemon Soup, '85 94
Lentil Soup, '83 292; '86 304; '91 28
Lentil Soup, Beefy, '87 282
Lime Soup, '88 31
Lobster Soup, Spicy Thai, '94 102
Melon Soup, '80 182
Melon Soup, Swirled, '87 162
Minestrone, '82 4
Minestrone, Dixie, '94 230
Minestrone Soup, '84 202; '86 144; '91 258
Minestrone Soup Mix, '91 258
Mix, French Market Soup, '85 277; '94 317
Mushroom-Onion Soup, '80 25
Mushroom-Rice Soup, '90 32
Mushroom Soup, '82 286; '86 M73; '94 54
Mushroom Soup, Chunky, '88 12
Mushroom Soup, Cream of, '84 5;
　'85 93, 261
Mushroom Soup, Creamy, '79 243; '81 307
Mushroom Soup, Curried, '84 M89
Mushroom Soup, Elegant, '83 99
Mushroom Soup, Fresh, '81 109; '90 190
Mushroom Soup, Shrimp-, '85 87
Mussel Soup, '93 259
Mustard Green Soup, Cream of, '93 280
Okra-and-Shrimp Soup, '94 323
Okra Soup, Charleston, '87 156
Onion-and-Potato Soup, Creamy, '92 51
Onion-Beef Soup, French, '87 54

Onion-Cheese Soup, '87 81
Onion Soup, Classic, '84 65
Onion Soup, Creamed Green, '83 82
Onion Soup, Creamy, '90 211
Onion Soup, Double-Cheese, '85 227
Onion Soup, Double Cheese-Topped, '79 49
Onion Soup, Easy, '85 226
Onion Soup, French, '79 49; '80 188;
　'83 126; '85 226; '86 M212; '90 31;
　'93 246
Onion Soup, Green, '84 112
Onion Soup, Oven-Browned, '79 49
Onion Soup, Rich, '85 226
Onion Soup, Shortcut French, '85 M328
Onion Soup, Superb, '81 86
Onion Soup, Toasty French, '81 306
Oyster-and-Artichoke Soup, Louisiana,
　'92 81
Oyster-and-Mushroom Soup, '87 39
Oyster-Cheese Soup, '84 213
Oyster Soup, '79 228; '83 211
Oyster-Turnip Soup, '94 328
Pea-and-Watercress Soup, '93 162
Peach-Plum Soup, '87 157
Peach Soup, '83 120, 180
Peanut Butter Soup, '89 28
Peanut Butter Soup, Cream of, '84 29
Peanut Soup, '87 184
Peanut Soup, Chilled, '79 130
Peanut Soup, Cream of, '92 193; '93 288
Peanut Soup, Creamy, '79 50
Pea Soup, Chilled, '84 181
Pea Soup, Cold Curried, '91 120
Pea Soup, Country-Style, '86 267
Pea Soup, Cream, '90 211
Pea Soup Élégante, '79 53
Pea Soup, Fresh, '86 181
Pea Soup, Peppery, '82 271
Pea Soup, Spring, '88 M96
Pepper-and-Chicken Soup, Roasted, '90 58
Pepper Soup, Spicy, '93 98
Pepper Soup, Sweet, '93 277
Plum Soup, '85 107
Plum Soup, Chilled Purple, '79 162
Potato-and-Wild Rice Soup, Cheesy, '89 16
Potato-Bacon Soup, '84 M38
Potato-Beet Soup, '88 156
Potato-Carrot Soup, '88 297
Potato-Cucumber Soup, Cold, '88 160
Potato-Pea Soup, '94 90
Potato Potage, Subtle, '80 78
Potato Soup, '82 278; '83 292; '92 263
Potato Soup, Asparagus-, '85 23
Potato Soup, Baked, '91 311; '92 26
Potato Soup, Celery-and-, '84 279
Potato Soup, Chilled Cucumber-, '85 93
Potato Soup, Cream of, '80 M224; '82 21
Potato Soup, Creamy, '81 19, 98; '84 112
Potato Soup, Easy, '92 17
Potato Soup, Golden Cream of, '86 302
Potato Soup, Holiday, '79 236
Potato Soup, Leek-and-, '84 112
Potato Soup, Sausage-, '80 25
Potato Soup, Special, '82 3
Potato Soup, Three-, '86 16
Potato-Yogurt Soup, '92 217
Pot-of-Gold Soup, '86 259
Pumpkin-Pear Soup, '92 234
Pumpkin Soup, '79 48
Pumpkin Soup, Cream of, '93 234
Pumpkin-Tomato Soup, '86 291

Raspberry Soup, Chilled, '81 130
Red Pepper Soup, Chilled Sweet, '93 69
Sausage and Okra Soup, '80 209
Sausage Soup, Italian, '84 235
Sausage Soup with Tortellini, Italian, '88 46
Sausage-Zucchini Soup, Italian, '84 4
Scallop Broth with Black Beans and Cilantro,
　Southwestern, '87 123
She-Crab Soup with Marigold, '79 32
Sherry-Berry Dessert Soup, '91 180
Shrimp-and-Corn Soup, '84 88
Shrimp-Cream Cheese Gazpacho, '94 137
Shrimp Enchilada Soup, '94 103
Sopa de Lima, '79 211
Southwest Soup, '86 255
Spinach Soup, Cream of, '82 38; '90 211
Spinach Soup, Hot Cream of, '84 29
Spinach Soup, Oriental, '83 151
Spinach Soup with Meatballs, Italian, '92 331
Split Pea and Frankfurter Soup, '79 64
Split Pea Soup, '88 235; '89 17; '94 322
Squash Soup, '94 134
Squash Soup, Chilled, '92 173
Squash Soup, Cold Cream of, '81 130
Squash Soup, Cream of, '81 246
Squash Soup, Perky, '85 20
Squash Soup, Summer, '83 99; '84 193;
　'85 136
Stock, Brown Meat, '90 31
Stock, Homemade Fish, '92 237
Stock, Light Poultry, '90 31
Stock, Seafood, '94 238
Stock, Vegetable, '90 31
Stock, Venison, '94 302
Strawberry-Banana Soup, '86 181
Strawberry Soup, '88 160
Strawberry Soup, Cold, '82 157
Strawberry Soup Supreme, '81 M144
Sweet Potato Soup, '88 250
Sweet Potato Velouté, '94 238
Taco Soup, '94 225
Tomatillo Soup with Crunchy Jicama, '92 245
Tomato-and-Rice Soup, '85 24
Tomato-Celery Soup, '83 M58
Tomato Consommé, '88 250
Tomato-Cream Soup, Dried, '90 203
Tomato Cream Soup, Refreshing, '79 172
Tomato Juice Soup, Hot, '86 302
Tomato Potage, '79 250
Tomato Soup, '81 236; '83 44; '89 217
Tomato Soup, Appetizer, '86 258
Tomato Soup, Chilled, '82 155
Tomato Soup, Cold, '88 160
Tomato Soup, Creamy, '83 267; '86 258
Tomato Soup, Easy, '84 14
Tomato Soup, Fresh, '83 140
Tomato Soup, Iced, '79 170
Tomato Soup, Icy-Spicy Mexican, '90 155
Tomato Soup Plus, '88 170
Tomato Soup, Savory, '94 91
Tomato Soup, Sour Cream-Topped, '80 246
Tomato Soup, Summer, '79 130
Tomato Soup with Parmesan Cheese, Cream
　of, '86 161
Tomato-Vegetable Soup, '81 M177; '86 9
Tortilla Soup, '88 31, 245; '90 201; '93 197,
　274; '94 136
Tortilla Soup, Spicy, '90 32; '93 108
Turkey-Barley Soup, '91 312
Turkey Carcass Soup, '86 284
Turkey-Noodle Soup, '91 312

Soups (*continued*)

Turkey-Noodle Soup Mix, **'89** 330
Turkey-Rice Soup, **'90** 89
Turkey Soup, Curried, **'86** 332
Turkey Soup, Williamsburg, **'90** 287
Turkey-Vegetable Soup, **'84** 4; **'88** 264;
    '91 312
Turnip Soup, **'92** 217
Turnip Soup, Creamy, **'84** 279
Turtle Soup, **'92** 92
Turtle Soup au Sherry, **'80** 56
Veal-Vermicelli Soup with Quenelles, **'94** 14
Vegetable-Bean Soup, **'83** 317
Vegetable-Beef Soup, **'88** 296
Vegetable-Beef Soup, Hearty, **'84** 102
Vegetable-Beef Soup, Spicy, **'88** 11
Vegetable Broth, Savory, **'81** 230
Vegetable-Burger Soup, **'82** 6
Vegetable-Cheese Soup, **'89** 15
Vegetable-Cheese Soup, Creamy, **'81** 244
Vegetable Cheese Soup, Creamy, **'83** 230
Vegetable Soup, **'80** 128; **'84** 148; **'85** 106;
    '86 187; **'87** 83, 123; **'88** 266; **'93** 157
Vegetable Soup, Beef-and-Barley, **'89** 31
Vegetable Soup, Beefy, **'79** 113; **'84** M38
Vegetable Soup, Cheesy, **'80** 73
Vegetable Soup, Chili, **'94** 157
Vegetable Soup, Chunky, **'89** M283
Vegetable Soup, Clear, **'79** 130
Vegetable Soup, Cold Garden, **'84** 197
Vegetable Soup, Down-Home, **'90** 32
Vegetable Soup, Garden, **'83** 140; **'86** 160
Vegetable Soup, Hearty, **'80** 26
Vegetable Soup, Leek-, **'86** 304
Vegetable Soup, Light, **'84** 280
Vegetable Soup, Marvelous, **'82** 3
Vegetable Soup Mix, **'84** 148
Vegetable Soup, Old-Fashioned, **'86** 304
Vegetable Soup, Quick, **'79** 190; **'85** 24, 32
Vegetable Soup, Quick Beefy, **'80** 25
Vegetable Soup, Spicy, **'79** 198; **'93** 293
Veggie Soup, Quick, **'91** 31
Venison Soup, **'82** 216
Vichyssoise, **'86** 181
Vichyssoise, Velvety Roquefort, **'83** 223
Watercress-and-Leek Soup, **'86** 161
Watercress Soup, **'79** 82; **'88** 104
White Bean Soup, **'90** 201
Yogurt Fruit Soup, **'86** 176
Zucchini Soup, **'82** 104; **'84** 181; **'86** 181;
    '89 14
Zucchini Soup, Chilled, **'87** 90
Zucchini Soup, Cold, **'85** 265; **'92** 64
Zucchini Soup, Cream of, **'83** 99
Zucchini Soup, Creamy, **'83** 140
Zucchini Soup, Dilled, **'90** 88
Zucchini Soup, Watercress-, **'91** 72
Zucchini Soup with Cilantro, **'93** 130

Spaghetti

Bacon Spaghetti, **'86** 213; **'87** 82
Black Bean Spaghetti, **'92** 217
Carbonara, Salmon, **'83** 43
Carbonara, Spaghetti, **'85** 34; **'87** 167
Carbonara, Spaghetti alla, **'81** 38
Casserole, Asparagus-Spaghetti, **'80** 77
Casserole, Chicken-Spaghetti, **'84** 15
Casserole, Italian, **'90** 238
Casserole, Spaghetti, **'84** 241
Casserole, Spaghetti and Beef, **'79** 129

Cheese Spaghetti, Three-, **'83** 105
Chicken Spaghetti, **'83** 105; **'87** 221
Chicken-Vegetable Spaghetti, **'92** 281
Chili-Spaghetti, Herbed, **'84** 222
Chorizo Carbonara, **'94** 230
Crawfish Spaghetti, **'85** 104
Easy Spaghetti, **'83** M317; **'84** 72; **'92** 66
Etcetera, Spaghetti, **'83** 105
Ham Spaghetti Skillet, **'83** 283
Herbal Dressing, Spaghetti with, **'86** 158
Hot Dog and Spaghetti Skillet, **'83** 144
Italian Spaghetti, **'81** 38
Italian Spaghetti, Real, **'81** 233
Meatballs, Spaghetti-and-Herb, **'84** 75
Meatballs, Spaghetti with, **'81** 38
Meat Sauce, Quick Spaghetti and, **'94** 64
Meaty Spaghetti, **'82** 19
Mushrooms, Spicy Spaghetti with, **'85** 2
Parmesan Noodles, Cheesy, **'83** M7
Parsley and Walnut Sauce, Spaghetti with,
    '80 30
Parsley, Spaghetti with, **'80** 236
Pea Spaghetti, Black-Eyed, **'81** 7
Pepperoni Pasta, **'83** 105
Pepperoni Spaghetti, Quick, **'88** 40
Pie, Spaghetti, **'81** M32
Pie, Spaghetti-Ham, **'93** 19
Pizzazz, Spaghetti with, **'80** 85
Pork Spaghetti Bake, **'81** 11
Pot Roast with Spaghetti, **'80** 59
Salad, Chicken-Spaghetti, **'90** 146
Salad, Spaghetti, **'82** 277; **'84** 205
Sauce, Beer Spaghetti, **'85** 13
Sauce for Spaghetti, Italian Tomato, **'81** 134
Sauce, Grisanti Spaghetti, **'94** 194
Sauce, Herbed Spaghetti, **'85** 13
Sauce, Pasta with Vegetable, **'83** 163
Sauce, Spaghetti with Zucchini, **'81** 38
Sauce, Thick Spaghetti, **'84** 118
Sauce, Turkey Spaghetti, **'85** 13
Sausage Spaghetti, **'83** 160
Sausage Spaghetti Dinner, **'79** 194
Shrimp-and-Vegetable Spaghetti, **'91** 170
Shrimp Spaghetti with Black Olives, **'85** 13
Szechuan Noodle Toss, **'91** 30
Tetrazzini, Chicken, **'79** 268; **'80** 75;
    '83 288
Tetrazzini, Ham, **'82** 77; **'84** 241
Tetrazzini, Herbed Turkey, **'86** 47
Thick-and-Spicy Spaghetti, **'83** 287
Tomatoes and Garlic, Spaghetti with, **'91** 47
Veal and Peppers, Spaghetti with, **'81** 201;
    '82 14
Veal Spaghetti, **'84** 276
Vegetables, Spaghetti with, **'85** 67
Vegetables with Spaghetti, Fresh, **'86** 257
Vegetables with Spaghetti, Sautéed, **'81** 89
Zucchini Spaghetti, **'83** 160
Zucchini Spaghetti, Italian, **'85** 2

Spice

Balls, Decorative Ribbon-Spice, **'84** 325
Blend, Five-Spice Powder, **'92** 121
Dry Spices, **'90** 120
Mix, Mulled Wine Spice, **'85** 266
Mix, Tex-Mex Spice, **'94** 135

Spinach

Apples, Onions, and Pears over Spinach,
    Sautéed, **'94** 212
Bake, Creamy Spinach, **'89** 68
Baked Spinach, Gourmet, **'82** 180
Bake, Spinach-Cheese, **'88** 10

Bake, Spinach-Ricotta, **'88** 97
Bisque, Spinach-Potato, **'86** 66
Bread, Spinach, **'83** 121; **'87** 144
Cannelloni, **'85** 60; **'92** 17
Casserole, Cheesy Spinach, **'81** 263
Casserole, Cottage Cheese-and-Spinach,
    '84 77
Casserole, Creamy Crab and Spinach, **'80** 3
Casserole, Creamy Spinach, **'86** 111
Casserole, Oyster-and-Spinach, **'83** 34;
    '84 44
Casserole, Spinach, **'79** 265; **'91** 31
Casserole, Spinach and Artichoke, **'81** 103
Casserole, Spinach and Beef, **'79** 192
Casserole, Spinach-and-Celery, **'84** 294
Casserole, Spinach and Egg, **'82** 270
Casserole, Spinach-Artichoke, **'88** 252;
    '93 44
Casserole, Spinach-Beef-Macaroni, **'83** 313
Casserole, Spinach-Cheese, **'83** 216; **'89** 64
Casserole, Spinach-Parmesan, **'82** 281;
    '83 32
Casserole, Turkey-Spinach, **'84** 71
Cheese Bites, Spinach-, **'94** 23
Cheesecake, Spinach-Mushroom, **'92** 326
Cheesecake, Spinach Pesto, **'90** 175
Cheesy Topped Spinach, **'84** 85
Chicken Breasts, Fried Spinach-Stuffed,
    '88 206
Chicken, Garlic-Spinach, **'92** 56
Chicken in Puff Pastry, Spinach-Stuffed,
    '92 125
Chicken Rolls, Spinach-Stuffed, **'86** 248
Chinese Spinach, **'79** 179; **'82** 39
Chinese Spinach Sauté, **'83** 208
Company Spinach, **'89** 280
con Queso, Easy Spinach, **'88** 101
Creamed Spinach, **'81** 54; **'86** 110
Creamed Spinach in Pastry Shells, **'89** 280
Creamed Spinach with Noodles, **'84** 29
Creamy Spinach, **'85** 289
Crêpes, Spinach-Ricotta, **'81** 52
Cups, Cottage Cheese-Spinach, **'87** 190
Delight, Spinach, **'84** M144
Dip, Cheesy Spinach, **'82** 59
Dip, Creamy Spinach, **'88** 132
Dip, Hot Spinach, **'80** 249
Dip, Hot Spinach-Cheese, **'89** 48
Dip in Cabbage, Spinach, **'82** 155
Dip, Spinach, **'80** 86; **'86** 159; **'87** 25, 214;
    '93 324
Eggs Sardou, **'92** 93
Enchiladas, Chicken-and-Spinach, **'91** 222
Enchiladas, Spinach, **'83** 60; **'84** 14
Fantastic, Spinach, **'93** 173
Fettuccine and Spinach, **'88** 90
Fettuccine, Easy Chicken with Spinach,
    '88 89
Fettuccine, Fresh Spinach, **'83** 60
Fettuccine, Spinach, **'82** 179
Fettuccine with Mustard Greens, Spinach,
    '94 247
Filling, Spinach, **'79** 34
Filling, Spinach-Mushroom, **'80** 215
Filling, Spinach-Ricotta, **'81** 53
Florentine, Baked Eggs, **'86** M12
Florentine Casserole, Turkey-and-Shrimp,
    '92 122
Florentine, Cheesy Trout, **'85** 53
Florentine, Chicken, **'93** 107
Florentine, Chicken-and-Shrimp, **'89** 64

Spinach (*continued*)

Florentine, Creamy Lasagna, **'91** 94
Florentine Crêpe Cups, **'89** 44
Florentine Crêpe Pie, **'79** 34
Florentine, Crêpes, **'80** 190
Florentine, Eggs, **'79** 39; **'83** 56
Florentine, Fish, **'86** 35
Florentine in Parchment, Fish, **'87** 22
Florentine, Jumbo Seashells, **'79** 6
Florentine, Lasagna, **'88** 196
Florentine, Salmon, **'83** 43
Florentine Sauce, **'93** 48
Florentine, Stuffed Mushrooms, **'82** 270
Florentine-Style Eggs, **'82** 38
Florentine, Turkey, **'88** 264
Florentine with Mushroom Sauce, Chicken, **'87** 250
Frittata, Spinach, **'81** 53
Garden, The, **'83** 134
Greek Sunburst, **'94** 245
Grits, Garlicky Ham-and-Spinach, **'94** 177
Lasagna, Cheesy Spinach, **'80** 32; **'83** 204
Lasagna, Spinach, **'79** 25; **'81** 243
Lasagna, Spinach-Bean, **'92** 96
Lemon Spinach, Creamy, **'82** 302
Lemon Spinach with Feta, **'85** 190
Linguine with Spinach, **'91** 30
Loaves, Spinach-Oyster, **'84** 213
Madeleine in Chafing Dish, Spinach, **'85** 319
Manicotti, Spinach, **'82** 199
Manicotti, Spinach-Stuffed, **'88** 255
Marinara on Beds of Spinach and Orzo, **'93** 320
Mushrooms, Spinach-Stuffed, **'86** 81; **'88** 131, M261; **'89** M133
Mushrooms, Spinach with, **'80** 19
Nests, Baked Eggs in Spinach, **'82** 70
Noodles, Chicken and Spinach, **'82** 19
Omelet, Spinach-Cheese, **'83** 119
Parmesan, Spinach, **'93** 72
Parmesan Spinach, Savory, **'85** 68
Pasta Bites, Pesto-Cheese, **'87** 251
Pasta Verde, **'84** 201
Pasta with Shrimp-Mushroom Italienne, Green, **'79** 170
Pâté with Spinach and Cream, Pork, **'83** 224
Peppers, Spinach-Stuffed, **'82** 180
Pesto and Pasta, Spinach-Peanut, **'93** 212
Pesto, Orange Roughy with Spinach, **'88** M192
Pesto-Pasta, Spinach, **'91** 314
Pesto, Squash Stuffed with Spinach, **'89** M133
Phyllo Triangles, Spinach-Filled, **'84** 52
Phyllo Triangles, Spinach-Ricotta, **'88** 212
Pie, Greek Spinach, **'85** 59
Pie Pan Spinach, **'94** 195
Pie, Spinach, **'82** 191; **'88** 56
Pie, Spinach-Pasta, **'85** 286
Pinwheels, Spinach-Tenderloin, **'89** M118
Pitas, Spinach-Walnut, **'87** 202; **'88** 43
Pork, Spinach-and-Herb Stuffed, **'89** 193
Pork Tenderloin, Spinach-and-Bacon Stuffed, **'94** 81
Puffs, Cheese-and-Spinach, **'87** 246
Puff, Spinach-Cheese, **'84** 96
Quiche, Cheesy Spinach, **'81** 228
Quiche, Crustless Spinach, **'84** 235
Quiche, Greek Spinach, **'86** 10

Quichelets, Spinach, **'87** 67
Quiche, No-Crust Spinach, **'90** 142
Quiches, Individual Spinach, **'86** 38
Quiches, Miniature Spinach, **'82** 38
Quiche, Spinach, **'81** 44; **'85** 49; **'91** 204
Quiche, Spinach-Mushroom, **'81** M74
Rice Bake, Green, **'79** 43
Rice, Spinach, **'85** 146
Ring au Fromage, Spinach, **'79** 8
Roll, Feta Cheese-Spinach, **'91** 22
Rolls, Spinach-Ham, **'88** 78
Rollups, Chicken and Spinach, **'80** 90; **'82** M68
Roll-Ups, Ham and Spinach, **'81** 143
Rollups, Spinach-and-Ham, **'86** 84
Salad Dressing, Spinach, **'83** 181; **'93** 250
Salads
   Apple-Onion Vinaigrette, Spinach Salad with, **'94** 276
   Apple Salad, Spinach-, **'90** 89; **'92** 13
   Apricot Salad, Spinach-, **'94** 63
   Arranged Spinach Salad, **'91** 210; **'92** 160
   Bacon Dressing, Spinach Salad with Hot, **'82** 211
   Bacon Salad, Spinach and, **'81** 143
   Beet Salad, Spinach-, **'83** 227
   Blue Cheese Salad, Spinach-, **'82** 166
   Chicken-and-Spinach Tossed Salad, **'83** 157
   Chili-Lime Dressing, Spinach Salad with, **'94** 63
   Citrus Dressing, Spinach Salad with, **'88** 133
   Citrus Spinach Salad, **'90** 59
   Combination Spinach Salad, **'85** 327; **'86** 22
   Creamy Spinach Salad, **'83** 60
   Crisp Spinach Salad with Creamy Dressing, **'83** 81
   Crunchy Spinach Salad, **'80** 147; **'81** 225
   Curry Spinach Salad, **'80** 242
   Dijon Spinach Salad, **'89** 282
   Dried Tomato Vinaigrette, Spinach Salad with, **'93** 272
   Easy Spinach Salad, **'91** 249
   Enoki Salad, Spinach-, **'89** 62
   Festive Spinach Salad, **'80** 247
   French Spinach Salad, **'79** 8
   Fresh Spinach Salad, **'82** 73; **'83** 240; **'84** 15, 77; **'86** 130
   Fresh Spinach Salad Delight, **'80** 146
   Fresh Spinach with Spicy Dressing, **'80** 55
   Garden Salad Toss, **'81** 9
   Garlic-Ginger Vinaigrette Dressing, Spinach Salad with, **'92** 195
   Green Spinach Salad, **'79** 142
   Honey Dressing, Spinach Salad with, **'90** 16
   Kiwifruit Salad, Spinach-, **'87** 305
   Lamb Salad, Spinach-, **'85** 58
   Layered Salad, Make-Ahead, **'81** 296
   Layered Spinach-Lettuce Salad, **'84** 266
   Layered Spinach Salad, **'80** 5; **'89** 163
   Mandarin Spinach Salad, **'85** 163
   Minted Spinach Salad, **'94** 63
   Mushroom Salad, Spinach and, **'80** 112
   Onion Salad Bowl, Spinach-and-, **'81** 157
   Orange Dressing, Spinach Salad with, **'87** 187

   Orange Salad, Spinach-and-, **'86** 15
   Orange-Spinach Salad, **'83** 316; **'84** 16
   Oriental Spinach Salad, **'82** 23
   Oysters and Red Wine Vinaigrette, Spinach Salad with, **'94** 327
   Pears, Spinach Salad with Sautéed, **'94** 237
   Pecan Salad, Spinach-, **'89** 128
   Pickled Spinach, **'81** 69
   Poppy Seed Dressing, Spinach Salad with, **'91** 210; **'92** 160
   Pork-and-Spinach Salad, Mandarin, **'88** M126
   Raspberry Cream Dressing, Spinach Salad with, **'94** 321
   Rice Salad, Spinach-, **'94** 63
   Romaine-Spinach Salad, **'89** 123
   Russian Dressing, Spinach Salad with, **'79** 144
   Salmon-Spinach Salad, **'87** 145
   Sesame Salad, Spinach-, **'91** 211; **'92** 160
   Sesame Spinach Salad, **'90** 292
   Southern Spinach Salad, **'80** 55
   Special Spinach Salad, **'80** 78
   Spinach Salad, **'82** 102; **'86** 302; **'87** 62; **'88** 299; **'92** 281, 341; **'93** 46, 65
   Springtime Spinach Salad, **'81** 114
   Sprout Salad, Fresh Spinach-, **'82** 281; **'83** 42
   Strawberry-Spinach Salad, **'91** 169; **'93** 168
   Sun-Dried Tomato Salad, Spinach and, **'93** 250
   Supreme, Spinach Salad, **'79** 243
   Sweet-Sour Spinach Salad, **'85** M112
   Tropical Spinach Salad, **'90** 231
   Twist, Spinach-Mustard, **'86** 209
   Vinaigrette Spinach, **'79** 8
   Wilted Spinach Salad, **'81** M4; **'89** 123; **'91** 210; **'92** 160; **'93** 125
   Zesty Spinach Salad, **'79** 88
Sandwiches, Fresh Spinach, **'85** 59
Sandwich, Grilled Spinach Fondue, **'94** 171
Sauce, Emerald, **'90** 63
Sauce, Fettuccine with Spinach, **'84** 329
Sauce, Herbed Green, **'86** 244
Sauce, Spinach Pasta, **'93** 71
Sauce, Spinach Pesto, **'93** 59
Sauce, Vermicelli with Fresh Spinach, **'89** 256
Sautéed Spinach, **'93** 250
Sauté, Fresh Spinach, **'93** 55
Scalloped Spinach with Cheese, **'79** 8
Shells, Spinach-Stuffed, **'85** 60; **'87** 20
Soufflé, Cheesy Spinach, **'81** 53
Soufflé Deluxe, Spinach, **'79** 8
Soufflé Roll, Spinach, **'80** 215
Soufflé, Spinach, **'79** 73; **'81** 304; **'84** 78; **'85** 248; **'86** 108
Soup, Cream of Spinach, **'82** 38; **'90** 211
Soup, Cream with Greens, **'94** 277
Soup, Hot Cream of Spinach, **'84** 29
Soup, Oriental Spinach, **'83** 151
Soup with Meatballs, Italian Spinach, **'92** 331
Spanakópita, **'86** 58
Spread, Parmesan-Spinach, **'93** 55
Spread, Savory Spinach, **'82** 180
Spread, Spinach, **'88** 132

Spinach (*continued*)

Spread, Spinach-Bacon, **'92** M310
Squares, Spinach, **'88** 131
Squash, Spinach-Stuffed, **'82** 4; **'91** 14
Stir-Fry Spinach, **'81** 182
Strudels, Spinach, **'93** 249
Supreme, Layered Spinach, **'82** 38
Supreme, Spinach, **'84** 77
Surprise, Spinach, **'82** 42
Tart Milan, **'87** 70
Tarts, Spinach, **'82** 249
Tenderloin, Spinach-Stuffed, **'89** 311
Terrine, Layered Salmon-and-Spinach,
   '84 132
Timbales, Spinach, **'84** 29
Timbales, Spinach-Rice, **'88** 271
Tomatoes, Baked Spinach, **'90** 92
Tomatoes, Spinach-Stuffed, **'89** 203; **'93** 281
Tomatoes, Spinach-Stuffed Baked, **'86** 14
Tomatoes, Spinach-Topped, **'88** 265;
   '94 321
Tortellini with Tomato Sauce, Spinach,
   '88 302
Triangles, Phyllo-Spinach, **'87** 53
Turnovers, Salmon-Spinach, **'83** 44
Wontons, Spinach, **'83** 74
Zucchini Boats with Spinach, **'82** 252

Spreads. *See also* Appetizers/Spreads.
Aioli, Shortcut, **'93** 157
Almond Cheese Spread, **'87** 292
Aloha Spread, **'83** 93
Ambrosia Spread, **'92** 50
Antipasto Spread, **'81** 25
Apple-Date Spread, **'91** 231; **'92** 67
Apricot Brie Spread, **'86** 275
Apricot-Cream Cheese Spread, **'87** 158
Artichoke-Crab Spread, Hot, **'85** 81
Artichoke Hearts with Caviar, **'79** 142
Artichoke Spread, Hot, **'79** 110
Beef Spread, Hot, **'83** 50
Beer Cheese Spread, **'94** 123
Boursin Cheese Spread, Buttery, **'94** 301
Boursin Cheese Spread, Garlic, **'94** 301
Braunschweiger-Onion Spread, **'79** 82
Bread Spread, Party, **'82** 161
Broccamoli Curry Spread, **'88** 55
Caraway Spread, **'85** 276
Carrot Spread, Nutty, **'94** 123
Caviar Spread, Creamy, **'92** 58
Cheese, Herbed, **'88** 152
Cheese-Horseradish Spread, **'84** 222
Cheese-Olive Spread, **'79** 82
Cheese-Olive Spread, Cream, **'82** 35
Cheese Spread, **'86** 135
Cheese Spread, Apricot-Cream, **'82** 161
Cheese Spread, Bacon-, **'83** 241
Cheese Spread, Beer, **'81** 69
Cheese Spread, Beer-, **'85** 69
Cheese Spread, Caviar-Cream, **'84** 256
Cheese Spread, Chile-, **'86** 297
Cheese Spread, Confetti, **'84** 256
Cheese Spread, Cottage, **'87** 107
Cheese Spread, Creamy Sweet, **'79** 264
Cheese Spread, Cucumber and Cream,
   '82 140
Cheese Spread, Deviled Cream, **'81** 235
Cheese Spread, Fruit and, **'81** 245
Cheese Spread, Garlic Pimiento, **'79** 58
Cheese Spread, German, **'79** 82

Cheese Spread, Gouda, **'90** 36
Cheese Spread, Hawaiian, **'87** 158
Cheese Spread, Herb-Cream, **'83** 24
Cheese Spread, Herbed, **'87** 247
Cheese Spread, Jalapeño-, **'82** 248
Cheese Spread, Low-Calorie Pimiento,
   '85 215
Cheese Spread, Make-Ahead, **'93** 324
Cheese Spread, Mexican, **'90** 119
Cheese Spread, Pimiento, **'82** 35; **'83** 93;
   '86 127
Cheese Spread, Pineapple-Cream, **'82** 35
Cheese Spread, Tipsy, **'80** 150
Cheese Spread, Tomato-, **'81** 157
Cheese Spread, Zesty, **'82** 140
Cheese Spread, Zippy, **'85** 4
Cheesy Beer Spread, **'87** 196
Cherry Spread, **'93** 309
Chicken Salad Party Spread, **'88** M8
Chicken Spread, Festive, **'87** 158
Chicken Spread, Low-Fat, **'82** 290
Chicken Spread, Tasty, **'84** 193
Chili Cheese Spread, **'93** 242
Chive-Mustard Spread, **'91** 12
Chocolate Cheese Spread, **'87** 292
Chocolate Chip Cheese Loaves, **'91** 299;
   '92 264
Chutney Spread, Curried, **'89** 283
Clam Spread, Creamy, **'91** 274
Coconut-Cranberry Cheese Spread,
   '92 328
Coconut-Pineapple Spread, **'93** 309
Corned Beef Spread, **'87** 196
Crabmeat-Horseradish Spread, **'90** 292
Crabmeat Spread, **'79** 81
Crabmeat Spread, Layered, **'83** 127
Crab Soufflé Spread, **'85** 4
Crab Spread, **'93** 167
Crab Spread, Baked, **'80** 86
Crab Spread, Superb, **'81** 255
Cranberry Salsa with Sweet Potato Chips,
   '93 332
Cream Cheese Spread, Nutty, **'89** 327
Cream Cheese Spread, Peachy, **'90** M215
Cucumber Spread, **'79** 295; **'80** 31; **'93** 158
Curry Spread, **'93** 159
Date Spread, Breakfast, **'84** 7
Date-Walnut Spread, **'87** 292
Deviled Delight, **'83** 130
Edam-Sherry Spread, **'84** 257
Eggplant Spread, **'86** 278
Egg Salad Spread, **'86** 127
Egg Salad Spread, Cottage-, **'82** 146
Egg, Sour Cream, and Caviar Spread,
   '85 279
Fruit-and-Cheese Spread, Nutty, **'87** 246
Fruit Spread, **'85** 135
Fruit Spread, Sugarless, **'84** 60
Garden Spread, **'86** 135
Garlic Puree, Roasted, **'92** 55
Garlic Spread, **'85** 111
Green Onion-Cheese Spread, **'92** 24
Gruyère-Apple Spread, **'81** 160
Guacamole Spread, **'90** 119
Ham-and-Egg Spread, **'79** 59
Ham and Pimiento Spread, **'80** 285; **'81** 56
Ham Spread, **'86** 126
Ham Spread, Cold, **'82** 248
Ham Spread, Country, **'87** 8
Ham Spread, Deviled, **'79** 81
Ham Spread, Hawaiian, **'87** 106

Hearts of Palm Spread, **'90** 293
Herb-Cheese Spread, **'91** 124
Honey-Nut Spread, **'87** 157
Honey Spread, **'81** 229
Horseradish-Ham Spread, **'91** 167
Horseradish, Homemade, **'92** 25
Horseradish Spread, **'90** 243
Italian Spread, **'85** 135
Liver Spread, **'89** 161
Liver Spread, Sherried, **'80** 86
Mushroom Spread, Hot, **'81** 190
Mustard Spread, **'86** 105
Olive Spread, Creamy, **'81** 290
Olive Spread, Tomatoes with,
   '85 114
Orange Cheese Spread, **'87** 292
Orange Toast Topper, **'79** 36
Oyster Spread, Smoked, **'91** 64
Peanut Butter Spread, **'92** 21
Pear-Cream Cheese Spread, **'93** 80
Pepper Spread, Roasted, **'94** 123
Pimiento Cheese Spread, Creamy,
   '92 159
Pineapple-Cheese Spread, **'86** 126;
   '91 167
Pineapple Sandwich Spread, **'84** 166
Radish Spread, Fresh, **'84** 166
Raisin Spread, Creamy, **'90** 36
Raisin Spread, Peachy-, **'86** 326
Relish Spread, Creamy, **'93** 217
Salad Dressing Spread, **'82** 140
Salmon-and-Horseradish Spread, **'87** 146
Salmon Spread, **'81** 149
Salmon Spread, Smoked, **'84** 324
Sandwich Spread, Benedictine, **'80** 299
Sandwich Spread, Chunky, **'82** 140
Sandwich Spread, Home-Style, **'80** 179
Seafood Sandwich Spread, **'82** 87
Seafood Spread, **'86** M58; **'87** 146
Shrimp-Cucumber Spread, **'79** 81
Shrimp Spread, **'81** 306; **'85** 135; **'87** 111;
   '93 205
Shrimp Spread, Chunky, **'85** 300
Shrimp Spread, Curried, **'87** 158
Shrimp Spread, Tempting, **'79** 57
Shrimp Spread, Zippy, **'90** 36
Smoked Fish Spread, **'92** 305
Sombrero Spread, **'87** 111
Spinach-Bacon Spread, **'92** M310
Spinach Spread, **'88** 132
Spinach Spread, Savory, **'82** 180
Strawberry Spread, Light, **'85** 55
Sweet 'n' Sour Spread, **'86** 184
Swiss Cheese Spread, **'90** 60
Tomato-Cheese Spread, Dried, **'90** 204
Tomato-Cheese Spread, Fiery, **'87** 196
Tomato Spread, **'94** 123
Trout Spread, Smoked, **'84** 47
Tuna Spread, **'83** 174; **'91** 305
Tuna Spread, Chunky, **'89** 147
Turkey Party Spread, **'83** 282
Turkey Spread, Curried, **'92** 16
Vegetable-Egg Spread, **'87** 106
Vegetable Party Spread, **'84** 166
Vegetable Sandwich Spread, **'83** 174;
   '85 135
Vegetable Spread, **'90** 144
Watercress Spread, **'88** 103
White Bean Spread, **'93** 30
Whitefish Spread, Smoked,
   '92 58

Sprouts
Beans with Sprouts, Sweet-and-Sour, **'86** 32
Beef and Bean Sprouts, **'82** 281; **'83** 42
Meat Loaf, Sprout, **'85** 51
Omelet, Potato-Sprout, **'79** 128
Omelet, Rising Sun, **'82** 281
Patties, Ham-Sprout, **'85** 51
Salad, Bean Sprout, **'82** 113
Salad, Fresh Spinach-Sprout, **'82** 281; **'83** 42
Salad, Spanish Sprout, **'85** 327; **'86** 22
Salad, Sprout, **'90** 137
Sandwiches, Alfalfa Pocket Bread, **'82** 282; **'83** 41
Sandwiches, Polynesian Sprout, **'85** 51

Squash. *See also* Zucchini.
Acorn
Apple-and-Pecan-Filled Squash, **'88** 228
Bake, Acorn Squash, **'83** 280
Baked Acorn Squash, **'81** 24
Baked Sweet Dumpling Squash, **'94** 266
Bake, Squash, **'82** 107
Bread, Squash, **'79** 210
Butter, Acorn Squash-and-Bourbon, **'94** 266
Delight, Acorn Squash, **'81** 267
Deluxe Acorn Squash, **'80** 215
Filled Acorn Squash, Cranberry-, **'81** M231
Filled Acorn Squash, Custard-, **'86** 334
Fruited Acorn Squash, **'85** 235; **'90** 228
Molasses and Pecans, Acorn Squash with, **'85** 205
Nutmeg, Acorn Squash with, **'85** 267
Orange Squash Brûlée, **'94** 267
Pancakes, Granola-Squash, **'94** 267
Puppies, Acorn Squash, **'94** 268
Puree, Acorn Squash-Mushroom, **'93** 305
Puree, Basic Acorn Squash, **'94** 267
Rings, Easy Glazed Acorn, **'81** M231
Rings, Glazed Acorn, **'80** 214
Sausage, Acorn Squash with, **'85** 9
Sherried Acorn Squash, **'85** 9
Soup, Acorn Squash, **'91** 294
Soup, Cream of Acorn Squash, **'94** 268
Stuffed Acorn Squash, **'82** 277; **'83** 15
Stuffed Acorn Squash, Apple-, **'83** 296; **'84** 285
Stuffed Acorn Squash, Fruit-, **'81** 295
Stuffed Acorn Squash, Ham-, **'81** 239; **'83** 66
Stuffed Acorn Squash, Pineapple-, **'84** 255
Stuffed Acorn Squash, Sausage-, **'81** M231; **'83** 296; **'84** 285
Stuffed Baked Squash, **'85** 206
Stuffed Squash, Apple-, **'85** 206
Stuffed Squash, Maple-Flavored, **'85** 205
Baby Squash, **'93** 118
Butternut
Bake, Butternut-Orange, **'86** 295
Baked Butternut Squash, **'85** 205
Bake, Squash and Apple, **'79** 210
Bisque, Squash, **'84** 280
Bread, Butternut-Raisin, **'79** 25
Bread, Squash, **'79** 210
Casserole, Butternut, **'83** 280
Casserole, Butternut Squash, **'79** 210

Casserole, Squash and Apple, **'79** 209
Casserole, Sweet Butternut, **'83** 256
Harvest Squash, **'80** 214
Medley, Harvest Squash, **'94** 268
Pie, Butternut Squash, **'80** 40; **'87** 212
Pie, Butternut Squash Chiffon, **'83** 296; **'84** 285
Pie, Spicy Butternut Squash, **'80** 296
Pie, Spicy Squash, **'85** 9
Pudding, Butternut Squash, **'89** M313; **'90** M19
Pudding, Squash, **'82** 277; **'83** 15
Puff, Butternut Squash, **'85** 205
Ring, Butternut Squash, **'81** M232
Sauté, Savory Butternut, **'85** 205
Skillet Butternut and Bacon, **'85** 9
Soufflé, Butternut, **'83** 266
Soup, Creamed Butternut-and-Apple, **'88** 228
Stir-Fry, Honey-Butternut, **'93** 184
Stuffed Butternut Squash, Apple-, **'81** 232
Sunshine Squash, **'85** 205
Whipped Butternut Squash, **'94** 302
Whipped Squash, Tasty, **'82** 277; **'83** 15
Cajun Squash, **'88** 142
Casserole, Calico Squash, **'90** 290
Casserole, Squash, **'87** 163; **'89** 159; **'90** 161; **'92** 342
Casserole, Two-Squash, **'79** 101
Chayote Squash Pickles, **'89** 197
Chayote, Stuffed, **'92** 247
Chile Squash, **'84** 77
con Crema, Squash, **'89** 148
Delight, Squash, **'90** 236
Dressing, Turkey with Squash, **'87** 248
Greek-Style Squash, **'92** 26
Hubbard Squash, Tart, **'80** 214
Marinated Squash Medley, **'94** 126
Medley, Carrot-Lima-Squash, **'80** 123
Medley, Fresh Squash, **'81** M165
Medley, Sautéed Vegetable, **'83** 101
Medley, Squash, **'81** 139; **'84** 128
Mirliton Balls, **'90** 217
Mirlitons, Stuffed, **'90** 217; **'93** 278
Muffins, Squash, **'91** 69
"Pasta," Garden-Fresh, **'94** M134
Pattypan Squash, Stuffed, **'82** 103; **'85** 136; **'88** 142
Pattypan-Zucchini Skillet, **'82** 103
Pickles, Squash, **'87** 150
Pie, Mock Coconut, **'86** 200
Pie, Scallopini, **'94** 133
Puff, Golden Squash, **'82** 288
Relish, Pollock with Summer Squash, **'92** 200
Rosemary, Summer Squash with, **'88** 143
Sauté, Squash, **'82** 67
Scallop, Green-and-Gold, **'81** 159
Skillet Squash, **'82** 195
Spaghetti Squash, **'92** 340
Spaghetti Squash and Chicken Skillet Casserole, **'94** 134
Spaghetti Squash, Asian, **'94** 268
Spaghetti Squash Lasagna, **'84** 127
Spaghetti Squash Pie, **'80** 186
Spaghetti Squash Salad, Marinated, **'94** 134
Spaghetti Squash, Sautéed Vegetables with, **'84** 128
Spaghetti Squash with Meat Sauce, **'88** M180
Spaghetti Squash with Sesame Eggplant, **'92** 252

Stir-Fried Squash Medley, **'80** 123
Stir-Fry, Squash, **'80** 184
Stir-Fry, Two-Squash, **'86** 174
Stuffed Squash, Crumb-, **'89** 148
Tomatoes, Squash-Stuffed, **'82** 102
Tomato Squash, **'86** 111
Toss, Pepperoni-Squash, **'84** 127
Turban Chicken Curry, **'94** 266
Turban Squash, Glazed, **'81** 24
Turban Squash, Sausage-Stuffed, **'80** 214
Turban Squash, Stuffed Turks, **'88** 228
White Squash, Stuffed, **'90** M201
Yellow
à l'Orange, Squash, **'85** 230
Bacon-Flavored Squash, **'82** 158
Bake, Cheddar-Squash, **'84** M113, 128
Bake, Cheesy Squash, **'80** 183
Beans, and Tomatoes, Squash, **'83** 148
Bread, Spicy Squash, **'83** 121
Bread, Yellow Squash, **'84** 140
Buttered Summer Squash, **'81** 84
Cake, Squash, **'86** 200
Casserole, Baked Squash, **'83** 149
Casserole, Blender Squash, **'81** 212
Casserole, Cheesy Squash, **'79** 123; **'82** M21
Casserole, Company Squash, **'81** 183
Casserole, Crunchy Squash, **'84** 293
Casserole, Fresh Squash, **'82** 204
Casserole, Jiffy Squash, **'81** M144
Casserole, Squash and Egg, **'80** 146
Casserole, Squash-Carrot, **'81** 157
Casserole, Summer Squash, **'81** 102, 184
Casserole, Yellow Squash, **'79** 179; **'85** 135; **'88** 166
Casserole, Zippy Squash, **'80** 183
Country Club Squash, **'79** 158; **'88** M16
Croquettes, Squash, **'79** 157; **'83** 148; **'88** 142
Dip, Yellow Squash-Zucchini, **'89** 48
Dressing, Squash, **'83** 315; **'86** 280
Fiesta Squash, **'82** 102
Fried Yellow Squash, **'86** 211
Fritters, Squash, **'89** 68
Greek-Style Squash, **'91** 285
Grilled Squash and Onion, **'79** 150
Grilled Vegetables, **'84** 172
Marinated Cucumbers and Squash, **'86** 146
Medley, Summer Garden, **'84** 158
Mexican Squash, **'82** 103
Muffins, Yellow Squash, **'81** 163
Nicholas, Squash, **'94** 236
Nosh, Squash, **'90** 147
Pats, Squash, **'80** 298; **'81** 25
Patties, Squash, **'79** 158
Patties, Summer Squash, **'81** 184
Pickled Yellow Squash, **'93** 136
Pickles, Squash, **'81** 174
Plantation Squash, **'79** 225
Posh Squash, **'81** 159
Puffs, Yellow Squash, **'82** 103
Puppies, Squash, **'83** 170
Quiche, Squash-and-Green Chile, **'88** 143
Rings, Asparagus in Squash, **'87** 68
Skillet Squash, **'92** 62
Skillet Summer Squash, **'82** 96
Soufflé, Cheesy Squash, **'82** 146
Soufflé, Yellow Squash, **'89** 89

Squash, Yellow *(continued)*

Soup, Chilled Squash, **'92** 173
Soup, Cold Cream of Squash, **'81** 130
Soup, Cream of Squash, **'81** 246
Soup, Perky Squash, **'85** 20
Soup, Squash, **'94** 134
Soup, Summer Squash, **'83** 99; **'85** 136
South-of-the-Border Squash, **'89** 148
Stir-Fried Squash Medley, **'80** 123
Stuffed Squash, Beef-, **'83** 134
Stuffed Squash Boats, Parmesan-,
   '79 156
Stuffed Squash, Cheesy, **'82** 134
Stuffed Squash Mexican, **'90** 200
Stuffed Squash, Sausage-, **'81** 183
Stuffed Squash, Spinach-, **'82** 4; **'91** 14
Stuffed Squash, Vegetable-, **'84** 104
Stuffed Squash with Green Chiles,
   '83 148
Stuffed with Spinach Pesto, Squash,
   '89 M133
Stuffed Yellow Squash, Garden-, **'84** 106
Stuffed Yellow Squash, Italian, **'86** 111
Stuffed Yellow Squash, Mushroom-,
   '84 154
Stuffed Yellow Squash, Shrimp-, **'84** 194
Stuffed Yellow Squash with Cheese
   Sauce, **'80** 162
Summer Squash, **'80** 127; **'85** 105
Toss, Asparagus-Carrot-Squash, **'91** 45
Toss, Crisp Squash-and-Pepper,
   '87 M152
Toss, Simple Squash, **'85** M142
Vegetable-Herb Trio, **'83** 172
Stews. *See also* Chili, Gumbos, Soups.
Bean Pot, White, **'86** 194
Beef-and-Onion Stew, **'87** 18
Beef and Vegetable Stew, Sweet-and-Sour,
   '85 87
Beef Stew, **'86** 51; **'90** 230
Beef Stew, Burgundy, **'88** 234
Beef Stew, Company, **'83** 85
Beef Stew, Oven, **'79** 222; **'80** 64
Beef Stew, Quick, **'86** 302; **'92** 71
Beef Stew, Spicy, **'86** 228
Beef Stew with Dumplings, **'84** 3
Beef Stew with Parsley Dumplings, **'81** 76;
   '82 13; **'85** M246
Brown Stew, **'85** 239
Brunswick Stew, **'80** 264
Brunswick Stew, Aunt Willette's, **'85** 320
Brunswick Stew, Bama, **'87** 4
Brunswick Stew, Blakely, **'87** 4
Brunswick Stew, Breeden Liles's, **'91** 14
Brunswick Stew, Dan Dickerson's, **'91** 16
Brunswick Stew, Easy, **'92** 280
Brunswick Stew, Gay Neale's, **'91** 17
Brunswick Stew, Georgian, **'92** 35
Brunswick Stew, Jeff Daniel's, **'91** 16
Brunswick Stew, Sonny Frye's, **'87** 4
Brunswick Stew, Van Doyle's Family-Size,
   '91 14
Brunswick Stew, Virginian, **'92** 34
Brunswick Stew, Virginia Ramsey's Favorite,
   '91 16
Burgoo, Five-Meat, **'87** 3
Burgoo, Harry Young's, **'87** 3
Burgoo, Kentucky, **'88** 235
Burgoo, Old-Fashioned, **'87** 3

Burgundy Stew with Drop Dumplings,
   '83 125
Caldo de Rez (Mexican Beef Stew), **'89** 276
Catfish Stew, Cajun-Style, **'88** 12
Chicken Ragout with Cheddar Dumplings,
   '94 44
Chicken Stew and Dumplings, **'84** 4
Chicken Stew, Brunswick, **'87** 4
Chicken Stew, Chili-, **'90** 319
Fish-and-Vegetable Stew, **'87** 220
Fisherman's Stew, **'81** 98
Frogmore Stew, **'92** 236
Game Pot Pie with Parmesan Crust,
   '94 304
Ham-and-Black-Eyed Pea Stew, **'93** 20
Hamburger Oven Stew, **'84** 4
Hungarian Stew with Noodles, **'80** 263
Hunter's Stew, **'85** 270
Irish Stew, **'90** 64
Lamb Stew, **'79** 293; **'88** 58
Lamb Stew-in-a-Loaf, **'85** 37
Lamb Stew with Popovers, **'94** 43
Lentil-Rice Stew, **'82** 232
Meatball Stew, **'79** 198
Mexican Stew, **'82** 231
Mexican Stew Olé, **'86** 296
Minestrone Stew, **'93** 184
Okra Stew, Old-Fashioned, **'84** 158
Oyster-Broccoli Stew, **'89** 242
Oyster-Sausage Stew, **'89** 242
Oyster Stew, **'80** 221
Oyster Stew, Company, **'80** 297
Oyster Stew, Golden, **'86** 132
Oyster Stew, Holiday, **'85** 264
Pancho Villa Stew, **'94** 44
Pollo en Pipián, Mexican, **'88** 31
Potato-Oyster Stew, **'89** 243
Rib-Tickling Stew, Campeche Bay,
   '89 317
Sausage Stew, Smoked, **'82** 231
Seafood Stew, **'84** 280
Shrimp Creole, **'93** 282
Shrimp Creole, Spicy, **'79** 181
Shrimp Creole, Wild Rice-and-, **'84** 292
Shrimp Stew, **'83** 4
Shrimp Stew and Grits, **'80** 118
Shrimp Stew over Grits, **'88** 126; **'89** 47
Strader Stew, **'89** 28
Turkey Stew, Hearty, **'79** 252
Turkey-Tomato Stew, **'90** 279
Tzimmes with Brisket, Mixed Fruit, **'93** 114
Veal-and-Artichoke Ragout, **'94** 43
Vegetable-Beef Stew, **'94** 323
Vegetable-Beef Stew, Shortcut, **'89** 218
Vegetable Stew, Mixed, **'84** 13
Venison Sausage Stew, **'87** 238
Venison Stew, **'86** 294
Venison Stew with Potato Dumplings, **'87** 304
White Wine Stew, **'82** 228
Strawberries
Almond Cream Dip with Strawberries,
   '92 164
Arnaud, Strawberries, **'93** 50
Banana-Berry Flip, **'88** 215; **'89** 20
Bars, Strawberry, **'81** 301
Bavarian, Raspberry-Strawberry, **'89** 15
Bavarian, Rhubarb-Strawberry, **'86** 140
Beets, Strawberry-Glazed, **'83** 234
Brandied Orange Juice, Strawberries with,
   '82 160
Bread, Strawberry, **'81** 250; **'83** 140; **'84** 49

Bread, Strawberry Jam, **'79** 216
Bread, Strawberry-Nut, **'79** 24
Butter, Strawberry, **'79** 36; **'81** 286; **'91** 71
Cake Roll, Strawberries 'n Cream Sponge,
   '81 95
Cake Roll, Strawberry, **'79** 49; **'83** 129;
   '84 305; **'85** 172
Cake, Strawberry Coffee, **'85** 46
Cake, Strawberry Cream, **'86** 61
Cake, Strawberry Crunch, **'79** 288; **'80** 35
Cake, Strawberry Delight, **'85** 30
Cake, Strawberry Meringue, **'86** 240
Cake, Strawberry Yogurt Layer, **'94** 85
Cake with Strawberries and Chocolate Glaze,
   White, **'87** 76
Calypso, Coco-Berry, **'89** 171
Carousel, Strawberry, **'91** 247
Cheesecake, Almost Strawberry, **'86** 32
Cheesecake, Pear-Berry, **'82** M141
Cherry-Berry on a Cloud, **'79** 94
Christmas Strawberries, **'87** 293; **'94** 331
Cobbler, Rosy Strawberry-Rhubarb, **'79** 154
Cobbler, Strawberry-Rhubarb, **'88** 93
Combo, Strawberry-Chocolate, **'85** 96
Compote, Peach-Berry, **'89** 112
Cookie Tarts, Strawberry, **'89** 112
Coolers, Strawberry, **'92** 67
Cooler, Strawberry, **'83** 56; **'84** 51
Cooler, Strawberry-Mint, **'84** 57
Cream, Chocolate Baskets with Berry,
   '92 118
Cream Dip, Fresh Strawberries with, **'90** 86
Cream Puffs, Strawberry, **'81** 95
Cream Puffs, Strawberry-Lemon, **'87** 75
Cream, Strawberries and, **'82** 100; **'92** 132
Cream, Strawberries in, **'89** 88
Cream, Strawberries 'n', **'90** 30
Cream, Strawberries 'n Lemon, **'85** 120
Cream, Strawberries with Chocolate, **'85** 81
Cream, Strawberries with French, **'83** 191
Cream, Strawberries with Strawberry,
   '84 108
Cream, Strawberry, **'88** 153
Cream with Fresh Strawberries, Almond,
   '87 93
Crêpes, Nutritious Brunch, **'80** 44
Crêpes, Strawberry Dessert, **'83** 122
Crêpes with Fruit Filling, **'81** 96
Daiquiris, Creamy Strawberry, **'91** 66
Daiquiris, Strawberry, **'90** 125
Daiquiri, Strawberry, **'81** 156
Delight, Frozen Strawberry, **'82** 112, 174
Delight, Strawberry, **'81** 85
Delight, Strawberry Cheese, **'79** 50
Delight, Strawberry Yogurt, **'85** 77
Dessert, Chilled Strawberry, **'84** 164
Dessert, Glazed Strawberry, **'84** 33
Dessert, Honeydew-Berry, **'83** 120
Dessert, Strawberry, **'83** 123
Dessert, Strawberry-Cream Cheese, **'83** 123
Dessert, Strawberry-Lemon, **'86** 162
Dessert, Strawberry-Yogurt, **'90** 295
Dessert, Summer Strawberry, **'92** 143
Dessert, Sweet-and-Sour Strawberry, **'92** 54
Dipped Strawberries, **'94** 17
Divinity, Strawberry, **'91** 272
Dressing, Creamy Strawberry, **'84** 161
Float, Strawberry-Banana, **'87** 160
French Toast Sandwiches, Strawberry-,
   '91 160
Fried Strawberries, Deep-, **'84** 109

Strawberries (*continued*)

Frost, Banana-Strawberry, '87 199
Frosting, Strawberry, '89 184
Frost, Strawberry, '81 279; '82 24; '83 154
Frozen Strawberry Cups, '91 173
Frozen Strawberry Refresher, '93 213
Fudge Balls, Strawberry, '93 80
Glaze, Strawberry, '80 35; '83 142
Ham, Strawberry-Glazed, '91 84
Ice Cream Crêpes, Strawberry, '87 290;
    '88 135
Ice Cream, Fresh Strawberry, '89 111
Ice Cream, Homemade Strawberry, '84 184
Ice Cream, Old-Fashioned Strawberry,
    '79 94
Ice Cream Roll, Strawberry, '84 105
Ice Cream, Straw-Ba-Nut, '80 177
Ice Cream, Strawberry, '80 177
Ice Cream, Strawberry-Banana-Nut, '88 203
Ice Cream Torte, Chocolate-Strawberry,
    '79 7
Ice Cream, Very Strawberry, '81 155
Ice Milk, Fresh Strawberry, '92 94
Ice Mold, Strawberry, '91 278
Ice Ring, Strawberry, '94 176
Ice, Strawberry, '84 175; '85 108
Ice, Strawberry-Orange, '86 196
Jamaica, Strawberries, '85 161; '93 239
Jam, Christmas, '88 288
Jam, Strawberry, '89 138
Jam, Strawberry Freezer, '84 M182
Jellyroll, Easy, '82 176
Jelly, Strawberry, '81 147
Juliet, Strawberries, '84 82
Lemonade, Berry Delicious, '93 205
Lemonade, Strawberry, '80 160
Lemon Cream, Strawberries with, '90 170
Marmalade, Strawberry-Pineapple, '85 130
Marsala, Strawberries, '88 171
Melon, Berry-Filled, '86 93
Meringues, Strawberry, '84 188
Milkshake, Fresh Strawberry, '82 113
Mimosa, Sparkling Strawberry, '88 169
Mousse, Fresh Strawberry, '82 72
Mousse, Strawberry, '81 95
Mousse, Strawberry-Lemon, '82 128
Napoleons, Strawberry, '81 126
Nests, Strawberry Coconut, '88 136
Omelet, Strawberry-Sour Cream, '89 229
Pancakes, Strawberry, '84 219
Parfait, Crunchy Strawberry-Yogurt, '79 124
Parfaits, Frosty Strawberry, '85 213
Parfaits, Strawberry-Lemon, '84 198
Parfait, Strawberry, '79 99
Parfait, Surprise Strawberry, '86 151
Pie, Chilled Strawberry, '82 112
Pie, Glazed Strawberry, '82 M142
Pie, Heavenly Chocolate-Berry, '85 102
Pie, Lemon-Strawberry, '88 127
Pie, Strawberry Angel, '88 136
Pie, Strawberry-Banana Glazed, '81 181
Pie, Strawberry-Chocolate Truffle, '89 112
Pie, Strawberry-Glaze, '81 141
Pie, Strawberry Yogurt, '80 232
Pie, Strawberry-Yogurt, '85 122; '86 124
Pizza, Kiwi-Berry, '86 198; '87 55
Pizza, Strawberry, '79 94
Popsicles, Smoothie Strawberry, '82 112
Preserves Deluxe, Strawberry, '82 150

Preserves, Freezer Strawberry, '82 112
Preserves, Strawberry, '79 120; '81 96
Puff, Strawberry, '82 5
Punch, Berry, '92 67
Punch, Creamy Strawberry, '86 195
Punch, Strawberry, '90 273
Punch, Strawberry Champagne, '90 315
Punch, Strawberry-Lemonade, '85 116;
    '91 175
Raspberry Custard Sauce, Fresh Berries
    with, '88 163
Ring, Strawberry-Cheese, '86 14
Rock Cream with Strawberries,
    Old-Fashioned, '90 125
Roll, Heavenly Strawberry, '82 176
Roll, Strawberry, '82 120
Romanoff, Strawberries, '84 108; '88 95;
    '91 126; '94 68
Ruby Strawberries, '82 100
Sabayon, Strawberries, '79 94
Salad, Frozen Strawberry, '94 119
Salad, Hidden Treasure Strawberry, '79 11
Salad Mold, Strawberry-Wine, '83 261
Salad, Strawberry-Nut, '94 132
Salad, Strawberry-Spinach, '91 169; '93 168
Salad, Strawberry Yogurt, '80 232
Salad with Orange-Curd Dressing,
    Orange-Strawberry, '93 22
Sangría, Teaberry, '87 147
Sauce, Amaretto-Strawberry, '87 M165
Sauce, Berry, '87 290; '88 135
Sauce, Berry Mimosa, '90 315
Sauce, Brandied Strawberry, '88 196
Sauce, Fresh Strawberry, '82 177
Sauce, Melon Wedges with Berry, '86 178
Sauce, Old-Fashioned Strawberry, '94 130
Sauce, Peaches with Strawberry, '85 8
Sauce, Strawberries Arnaud, '93 50
Sauce, Strawberry, '84 144; '87 93, 198;
    '92 85; '94 121
Sauce, Strawberry-Banana, '81 41
Sauce, Strawberry-Peach, '92 154
Sauce with Crunchy Topping, Strawberry,
    '81 170
Sauce with Dumplings, Strawberry, '84 314
Shake, Strawberry-Banana, '89 35
Shake, Strawberry-Cheesecake, '92 44
Shake, Strawberry Milk, '94 113
Shake, Strawberry-Orange Breakfast,
    '87 186
Shake, Strawberry-Pear, '92 139
Shake, Strawberry-Pineapple, '84 166
Shake, Strawberry-Yogurt, '87 199
Sherbet, Strawberry, '82 112, 160
Shortcake, A Favorite Strawberry, '88 136
Shortcake, Chocolate-Strawberry, '89 216
Shortcake, Elegant Strawberry, '88 37
Shortcake Jubilee, Strawberry, '88 209
Shortcake Shells, Strawberry, '88 196
Shortcake Squares, Strawberry, '86 124
Shortcakes, Strawberry Crispy, '93 42
Shortcake, Strawberry, '81 96; '83 122;
    '92 184; '94 162
Shortcake, Strawberry Pinwheel, '89 112
Skewered Pineapple and Strawberries,
    '84 251
Slurp, Strawberry, '81 96
Slush, Pineapple-Strawberry, '94 227
Slush, Strawberry-Orange, '83 172
Smoothie, Strawberry, '86 183
Smoothie, Strawberry-Banana, '81 59

Smoothie, Strawberry-Peach, '89 182
Smoothie, Tropical, '81 50
Soda, Old-Fashioned Strawberry,
    '79 149
Soda, Strawberry, '84 115
Sorbet, Strawberry, '88 117; '93 153
Sorbet, Strawberry-Champagne, '83 162
Sorbet, Strawberry Margarita, '89 111
Sorbet, Very Berry, '90 85
Soup, Cold Strawberry, '82 157
Soup, Sherry-Berry Dessert, '91 180
Soup, Strawberry, '88 160
Soup, Strawberry-Banana, '86 181
Soup Supreme, Strawberry, '81 M144
Spread, Light Strawberry, '85 55
Spritzer, Strawberry, '90 14
Spumoni and Berries, '91 204
Squares, Strawberry Shortcake, '85 122
Stuffed Strawberries with Walnuts, '85 122;
    '86 124
Sundaes, Hot Strawberry, '81 M5
Supreme, Banana-Berry, '81 205
Swirl, Strawberry, '84 108
Tartlets, Fresh Berry, '91 98
Tarts, Berry Good Lemon, '91 119
Tarts, Strawberry, '80 70
Tart, Strawberry, '84 138; '89 272
Tart, Strawberry Dream, '92 118
Tart, Strawberry-Lemon, '89 111
Tea, Sparkling Strawberry, '94 131
Tea, Strawberry, '88 248
Topping, Pound Cake with Strawberry-
    Banana, '89 200
Topping, Strawberry, '86 32; '90 142
Topping, Strawberry-Banana, '87 125
Torte, Spring, '91 57
Torte, Strawberry Meringue, '88 136
Treasure, Berried, '89 124
Trifle, Easy Strawberry, '88 201
Whip, Strawberry, '89 198
White Chocolate, Strawberries Dipped in,
    '90 83
Zabaglione, Strawberries, '81 95
Stroganoff
Beef Burgundy Stroganoff, '85 31
Beef Stroganoff, '79 163; '81 179; '91 134;
    '93 18
Beef Stroganoff, Ground, '84 71
Beef Stroganoff, Light, '86 36
Beef Stroganoff, Quick, '92 20
Chicken Livers Stroganoff, '80 200; '81 57
Chicken Livers Supreme, '81 298
Crab Stroganoff, '79 116
Crawfish Stroganoff, '91 89
Hamburger Stroganoff, '82 108, 110
Hamburger Stroganoff, Easy, '79 208
Ham Stroganoff, '82 40
Liver Stroganoff, '79 54
Meatballs, European Veal, '85 30
Meatballs Paprikash with Rice, '85 31
Meatball Stroganoff, '81 297
Mushroom-Meatball Stroganoff, '85 85
Mushroom Stroganoff, '81 298
Quickie Stroganoff, '81 200
Shrimp Stroganoff, '79 81
Shrimp Stroganoff, Oven-Baked, '81 297
Sirloin Stroganoff, '81 297
Steak Stroganoff Sandwiches, '85 110
Steak Stroganoff with Parslied Noodles,
    '85 31
Tofu, Stroganoff, '84 202

Stroganoff *(continued)*

Turkey Stroganoff, **'91** 61
Veal Stroganoff, **'79** 108

Stuffings and Dressings
Apple-Crumb Stuffing, **'81** 234; **'82** 26; **'83** 39
Cajun Dressing, **'82** 307
Chicken and Dressing, Baked, **'79** 296
Chicken Cornbread Dressing, **'90** 159
Cornbread-and-Sausage Dressing, **'83** 213
Cornbread-Biscuit Dressing, **'79** 296
Cornbread Dressing, **'86** 286; **'88** 254; **'92** 267
Cornbread Dressing, Fruited, **'80** 262
Cornbread Dressing, Green Chile-, **'93** 306
Cornbread Dressing, Herb-Seasoned, **'83** 315
Cornbread Dressing, Kentucky, **'86** 281
Cornbread Dressing, Light, **'92** 324
Cornbread Dressing, Old-Fashioned, **'84** 321
Cornbread Dressing, Quail Stuffed with, **'93** 280
Cornbread Dressing, Roast Turkey and, **'89** 324
Cornbread Dressing, Sage-, **'84** 283
Cornbread Dressing, Savory, **'88** 303
Cornbread Dressing, Texas, **'82** 243
Cornbread Dressing, Turkey with Sausage-, **'83** 287
Cornbread-Sage Dressing, **'80** 262
Cornbread-Sausage Dressing, **'82** 307; **'85** 280
Cornbread Stuffing, **'94** 305
Corn Dressing Balls, Zesty, **'82** 307
Crabmeat Stuffing, **'94** 68
Crabmeat Stuffing, Chicken Breasts with, **'85** 302
Cranberry-Sausage Stuffing, Crown Roast of Pork with, **'88** 49
Crawfish Dressing, Louisiana, **'90** 103
Eggplant Dressing, **'90** 236
Fruit-and-Pecan Dressing, **'84** 252
Fruit Dressing, Baked, **'87** 253
Fruited Stuffing, Cornish Hens with, **'90** 191
Fruited Stuffing Mix, **'89** 331
Giblet Dressing, **'91** 255
Grandmother's Dressing, **'91** 254
Green Chile-Cornbread Dressing, **'94** 296
Grits Dressing, **'93** 306; **'94** 296
Low-Sodium Stuffing, **'82** 66
Oyster Bread Dressing, **'82** 251
Oyster Dressing, **'79** 250
Oyster Stuffing, Roast Turkey with, **'80** 251
Peanut Dressing, Roast Turkey with, **'79** 283
Pecan-Rice Dressing, Chicken with, **'85** M57
Pecan-Sage Dressing, **'80** 262
Pecan-Sausage Stuffing, Chicken Breasts with, **'94** 212
Pecan Stuffing, **'79** 292; **'80** 32
Pecan Stuffing, Wild Duck with, **'85** 269
Pretzel Dressing, **'86** 280
Rice-and-Onion Stuffing, **'88** 246
Rice Dressing, **'91** 217
Rice Dressing, Chicken and, **'79** 288
Rice Dressing, Mexican, **'87** 253
Rice Dressing, Roast Turkey with, **'82** 286
Sausage-Apple Dressing, **'93** 305; **'94** 296
Sausage Dressing, **'86** 280
Sausage Dressing, Harvest, **'88** 254

Seasoned Dressing, Stuffed Turkey Breast with, **'83** 320; **'84** 128
Spoonbread Dressing, Southwestern-Style, **'94** 273
Squash Dressing, **'83** 315; **'86** 280
Squash Dressing, Turkey with, **'87** 248
Tangerine Stuffing, **'90** 16
Turkey and Dressing, Easy, **'79** 296
Turkey-and-Dressing Pie, **'84** 326
Turkey Dressing, **'85** 298
Walnut-Rice Stuffing, Tomatoes with, **'91** 102
Whole Wheat-Mushroom Dressing, **'84** 283
Wild Rice Stuffing, Cornish Hens with, **'79** 222; **'80** 64; **'82** 136
Zucchini Dressing, **'86** 282

Sweet-and-Sour
Asparagus, Sweet-and-Sour, **'89** 159
Beans and Carrots, Sweet-and-Sour Green, **'83** 6
Beans, Sweet-and-Sour, **'87** 197
Beans, Sweet-and-Sour Green, **'79** 184; **'81** 158; **'82** 90; **'91** 250
Beans, Sweet-and-Sour Snap, **'89** 173
Beans with Sprouts, Sweet-and-Sour, **'86** 32
Beets, Sweet-and-Sour, **'81** 167; **'82** 22; **'89** 314
Burgers, Sweet-and-Sour, **'90** 128
Cabbage, Sweet-and-Sour, **'86** 295; **'87** 189
Cabbage, Sweet-Sour Red, **'79** 5
Carrots, Sweet-and-Sour, **'82** 137
Chicken Nuggets, Sweet-and-Sour, **'90** 168
Chicken, Sweet-and-Sour, **'79** 106; **'86** 217, 240; **'90** 161; **'91** 202
Chicken, Sweet-and-Sour Lemon, **'84** 93
Chicken Wings, Sweet-and-Sour, **'90** 206
Dessert, Sweet-and-Sour Strawberry, **'92** 54
Dressing, Sweet-and-Sour, **'80** 247; **'84** 70, 161; **'85** 163; **'87** 305; **'89** 62; **'91** 126; **'94** 281
Dressing, Sweet-and-Sour Fruit, **'84** 125
Dressing, Sweet-Sour, **'80** 246
Fish, Sweet-and-Sour, **'80** M54
Ham, Sweet-and-Sour Glazed, **'88** M15
Ham, Sweet-Sour Glazed, **'83** 311
Kale, Sweet-and-Sour, **'80** 298
Kielbasa, Sweet-and-Sour, **'89** 327
Liver, Sweet-and-Sour, **'81** 277
Marinade, Sweet-and-Sour, **'86** 113; **'87** 115
Meatballs, Sweet-and-Sour, **'82** 233, 247; **'86** 240
Meatballs, Sweet-and-Sour Party, **'79** 233
Onions, Sweet-and-Sour Baked, **'90** 34
Peas, Sweet-and-Sour, **'88** 3
Peas, Sweet-and-Sour Black-Eyed, **'85** 290
Pork Chops, Sweet-and-Sour, **'83** 160
Pork, Pineapple Sweet-and-Sour, **'82** 120
Pork, Sweet-and-Sour, **'79** 42; **'80** 72, 227; **'81** 26, 104, 111; **'82** 12; **'84** 218; **'85** 34, 194; **'86** 241; **'90** 317; **'92** 219
Potatoes, Sweet-and-Sour-Topped, **'83** 4
Pot Roast, Sweet-and-Sour, **'83** 8
Riblets, Sweet-and-Sour, **'85** 276
Ribs, Sweet-and-Sour, **'89** M84
Salad, Sweet-and-Sour Bean, **'85** 198; **'86** 147
Salad, Sweet-and-Sour Cauliflower, **'81** 2
Salad, Sweet-and-Sour Fruit, **'80** 13; **'84** 125
Salad, Sweet-and-Sour Green, **'94** 281
Salad, Sweet-and-Sour Macaroni, **'85** 166
Salad, Sweet and Sour Potato, **'80** 152
Salad, Sweet-and-Sour Potato, **'92** 106

Salad, Sweet-and-Sour Vegetable, **'81** 25
Salad, Sweet-Sour Spinach, **'85** M112
Sauce, Sausage Rolls with Sweet-and-Sour, **'83** 74
Sauce, Sweet-and-Sour, **'80** 20; **'85** 12, 34; **'86** 240
Sauce, Sweet-and-Sour Pineapple, **'85** 66
Sausage, Sweet-and-Sour, **'88** 296
Shrimp and Chicken, Sweet-and-Sour, **'87** 267; **'88** 103; **'89** 66
Shrimp, Sweet-and-Sour, **'83** 278; **'90** M112
Shrimp Tails, Sweet-and-Sour Rock, **'80** 3
Slaw, Sweet-and-Sour, **'81** 237
Slaw, Sweet-and-Sour Hot, **'92** 63
Soup, Sweet-and-Sour Cabbage, **'89** 314
Spareribs, Sweet-and-Sour, **'83** 21
Spread, Sweet 'n' Sour, **'86** 184
Steaks, Sweet-and-Sour Marinated, **'83** 110
Stew, Sweet-and-Sour Beef and Vegetable, **'85** 87
Turkey, Sweet-and-Sour, **'79** 252
Turnips, Sweet-and-Sour, **'81** 274
Vegetables, Sweet-and-Sour Marinated, **'83** 266
Sweet Potatoes. *See* Potatoes, Sweet.
Swiss Chard
Bundles, Swiss Chard, **'94** 48
Buttered Chard, **'83** 36
Tomatoes, Swiss Chard with, **'83** 36
Syrups
Almond Syrup, **'82** 47
Anise Sugar Syrup, **'86** 248
Apple Syrup, Spiced, **'79** 114
Apricot Fruit Syrup, **'82** 10
Barbecue Sauce, Maple Syrup, **'94** 154
Caramel Syrup, **'82** 43
Cherry-Lemonade Syrup, **'86** 214
Cinnamon Syrup, **'91** 315
Citrus Syrup, Sweet, **'86** 270
Fruit Syrup, **'86** 176
Kirsch Syrup, **'80** 280
Maple-Honey-Cinnamon Syrup, **'85** 19
Maple-Nut Syrup, **'80** 228
Maple Syrup, **'81** 120; **'82** 23; **'93** 16
Maple Syrup, Homemade, **'79** 114
Mint Syrup, **'90** 89
Orange Syrup, **'80** 228; **'89** 254
Pecan Syrup, Chunky, **'85** 278
Sugar Syrup, **'93** 29

Tacos
al Carbón, Tacos, **'86** 19
al Carbón, Tailgate Tacos, **'79** 185
Appetizer, Layered Taco, **'84** 206
Bake, Taco Beef-Noodle, **'81** 141
Basic Tacos, **'83** 199
Beef Tacos, Soft, **'91** 88
Biscuit Bites, Taco, **'91** 89
Breakfast Tacos, **'80** 43; **'91** 316
Casserole, Taco, **'80** 33
Chicken-and-Bean Tacos, **'93** 293
Corn Chip Tacos, **'81** 67
Deep-Dish Taco Squares, **'91** 88
Dip, Hot Taco, **'93** 238
Egg Salad Tacos, Mexican, **'94** 181
Jiffy Tacos, **'83** M318
Joes, Taco, **'91** 167
Lentil Tacos, **'88** 197

Tacos *(continued)*

Lobster Taco with Yellow Tomato Salsa and
  Jicama Salad, Warm, **'87** 122
Microwave Tacos, **'88** M213
Navajo Tacos, **'84** 246
Peppers, Taco, **'81** 86
Pie, Crescent Taco, **'80** 80
Pie, Double-Crust Taco, **'88** 272;
  '89 180
Pies, Individual Taco, **'82** M282
Pie, Taco, **'88** 256
Pitas, Taco, **'83** 31
Pizza, Taco, **'89** M177
Potatoes, Taco-Topped, **'93** M18
Salad, Chicken Taco, **'94** M136
Salad Cups, Taco, **'85** M29
Salad, Meatless Taco, **'81** 204
Salad, Spicy Taco, **'87** 287
Salad, Taco, **'79** 56; **'83** 145; **'85** 84;
  '89 332; **'90** 20
Salad, Taco Macaroni, **'85** 165
Salad, Tuna-Taco, **'87** 145
Sauce, Taco, **'82** M283; **'93** 69;
  '94 30
Soup, Taco, **'94** 225
Tacos, **'80** 196

Tamales
Bake, Cornbread Tamale, **'79** 163
Casserole, Quick Tamale, **'94** 255
Chicken Tamales, **'88** 151
Hot Tamales, **'83** 51
Mango Dessert Tamales, **'94** 190
Meatballs, Tamale, **'80** 194
Miniature Tamales, **'85** 154
Pie, Chili-Tamale, **'82** 9; **'83** 68
Pie, Cornbread-Tamale, **'92** 123
Sweet Tamales, **'83** 52
Tamales, **'80** 195

Tea
Almond-Lemonade Tea, **'86** 229
Almond Tea, **'85** 43; **'86** 329; **'89** 212
Apple-Cinnamon Tea, Hot, **'87** 57
Apricot Tea, Hot Spiced, **'88** 248
Brew, Quilter's, **'85** 43
Citrus-Mint Tea Cooler, **'92** 105
Citrus Tea, Hot, **'83** 275
Citrus Tea, Iced, **'85** 162
Cranberry-Apple Tea, **'88** 169
Cranberry Tea, **'94** 131
Cubes, Frozen Tea, **'85** 161
Fruited Tea Cooler, **'94** 131
Fruit Tea, Christmas, **'83** 275
Fruit Tea, Hot Spiced, **'87** 242
Ginger-Almond Tea, **'94** 131
Ginger Tea, **'81** 100
Granita, Mint Tea, **'88** 117
Grapefruit Tea, **'92** 67
Grape Juice Tea, White, **'87** 57
Grape Tea, Spiced, **'79** 174
Hawaiian Tea, **'87** 57
Honey Tea, **'81** 105
Iced Tea, Bubbly, **'81** 168
Johnny Appleseed Tea, **'85** 23
Lemon-Mint Tea, **'85** 162
Lemon Tea, **'82** 156
Long Island Iced Tea, Southern, **'90** 207
Minted Tea, **'86** 101; **'88** 163; **'92** 54
Mint Tea, **'87** 107; **'90** 89
Mint Tea, Easy, **'91** 187

Mint Tea, Frosted, **'84** 161
Mint Tea, Fruited, **'88** 79; **'91** 81
Mint Tea, Iced, **'83** 170
Mix, Deluxe Spiced Tea, **'88** 257
Mix, Friendship Tea, **'83** 283
Mix, Spiced Tea, **'86** 32
Mix, Sugar-Free Spiced Tea, **'91** 258
Pineapple Tea, **'93** 165
Punch, Apple-Tea, **'85** 82
Punch, Bourbon-Tea, **'87** 57
Punch, Citrus-Tea, **'85** 116
Punch, Cran-Grape-Tea, **'92** 209
Punch, Spiked Tea, **'86** 101
Punch, Tea, **'90** 143, 207
Sangría Tea, **'94** 131
Sangría, Teaberry, **'87** 147
Sauce, Tea-Berry, **'94** 130
Spiced Iced Tea, **'91** 209
Spiced Tea Cooler, **'83** 55
Spiced Tea, Hot, **'83** 244
Strawberry Tea, **'88** 248
Strawberry Tea, Sparkling, **'94** 131
Summer Tea, **'85** 162
Summertime Tea, **'81** 167
Sun Tea, Southern, **'81** 168
Yaupon Tea, **'79** 31

Tempura
Basic Tempura, **'81** 68
Chicken Tempura Delight, **'85** 66
Cornmeal Tempura, **'81** 68
Sauce, Basic Tempura, **'81** 68
Sauce, Mustard-Sour Cream, **'81** 68
Vegetable Tempura, **'79** 112

Terrines
Black Bean Terrine with Fresh Tomato Coulis
  and Jalapeño Sauce, **'93** 230
Black Bean Terrine with Goat Cheese,
  '87 120
Cheese Terrine, Italian, **'93** 64
Chicken-Leek Terrine, Cold, **'92** 145
Chicken Terrine Ring, **'84** 132
Chicken-Vegetable Terrine, **'84** 131
Pork and Veal, Terrine of, **'93** 287
Pork Terrine, Jeweled, **'84** 130
Salmon-and-Spinach Terrine, Layered,
  '84 132
Veal Terrine with Mustard Sauce, **'93** 118
Vegetable-Chicken Terrine, **'83** 224

Timbales
Cheesy Mexicali Appetizer, **'82** 108
Chicken Chutney Salad, **'82** 108
Corn-and-Zucchini Timbales, **'92** 100
Grits Timbales, **'88** 223
Grits Timbales, Chives-, **'90** 172
Hamburger Stroganoff, **'82** 108
Peach Almond Cream, **'82** 108
Rice Timbales, **'94** 32
Shells, Timbale, **'82** 108
Spinach-Rice Timbales, **'88** 271
Spinach Timbales, **'84** 29

Tofu
Dip, Tofu, **'86** 109
Drink, Tofruitti Breakfast, **'88** 26
Lasagna, Tofu, **'83** 312
Rice with Tofu, Spanish, **'88** 26
Salad, Tofu, **'88** 27
Sandwiches, Open-Face Tofu-Veggie, **'86** 5
Stroganoff Tofu, **'84** 202

Tomatillos
Beef Saltillo (Beef with Tomatillos), **'82** 219
Fillets Tomatillo, **'94** 135

Relish, Black Bean-Tomatillo, **'87** 121
Salsa, Tomatillo, **'92** 245
Sandwiches, Open-Faced Tomatillo, **'92** 246
Sauce, Roasted Chiles Rellenos with Tomatillo, **'94** 20
Sauce, Tomatillo, **'94** 231
Soup with Crunchy Jicama, Tomatillo, **'92** 245

Tomatoes
Asparagus and Tomatoes, Fresh, **'94** 162
Aspic, Bloody Mary-Tomato, **'81** 77
Aspic, Chicken in Tomato, **'84** 190
Aspic, Chili Sauce Tomato, **'85** 252
Aspic, Classic Tomato, **'91** 229
Aspic, Herbed Tomato, **'81** 73
Aspic, Layered Tomato, **'90** 99
Aspic, Light Tomato, **'85** 83
Aspic, Ranch Tomato, **'83** 218
Aspic, Spicy Tomato, **'81** 40; **'89** 288
Aspic, Tangy Tomato, **'83** 124
Aspic, Tomato-Artichoke, **'84** 320; **'86** 92
Aspic, Tomato-Crab, **'85** 287
Aspic with Shrimp, Tomato, **'79** 241
au Gratin, Zucchini and Tomato, **'82** 208
Bake, Chicken-Tomato, **'83** 35
Baked Cheddar Tomatoes, **'85** 43
Baked Ranch Tomatoes, **'94** 72
Baked Spinach Tomatoes, **'90** 92
Baked Tangy Tomatoes, **'81** 168
Baked Tomatoes, **'83** 53; **'87** 197
Baked Tomatoes, Spinach-Stuffed, **'86** 14
Baked Tomatoes with Corn, **'80** 161
Baked Tomato Halves, Zippy, **'81** 182
Bake, Ham-Rice-Tomato, **'87** 78
Bake, Okra-and-Tomato, **'89** 173
Bake, Okra-Tomato, **'80** 298; **'81** 26
Bake, Potato-Tomato, **'86** 17
Bake, Tomato-and-Artichoke Heart, **'85** 81
Bake, Zucchini and Tomato, **'82** 158
Basil, Zucchini and Tomatoes, **'89** 147
Bean-and-Tomato Skillet, **'90** 316
Beans and Tomatoes, Basil, **'83** 172
Beans with Tomatoes, Green, **'85** 137
Beef with Tomatoes and Artichokes, **'92** 282
Biscuits, Tomato, **'86** 72
Biscuits, Tomato-Herb, **'94** 215
Bisque, Make-Ahead Tomato-Basil, **'93** 322
Bisque, Tomato-Shrimp, **'86** 66
Bites, Tomato, **'84** 80
Bouillon, New Year's Tomato, **'94** 24
Bouillon, Tomato, **'83** 8
Bowl, Tomato, **'81** 69
Bread, Herbed Tomato-Cheese, **'88** 143
Broiled Tomatoes, **'80** 152
Broiled Tomatoes, Quick, **'79** 153
Broiled Tomatoes, Romano, **'80** 42
Broiled Tomatoes with Dill Sauce, **'80** 161
Broiled Tomatoes with Mushroom Sauce,
  '81 103
Broil, Tomato-English Pea, **'83** 192
Buffet Tomatoes, **'82** 180
Butter, Tomato, **'86** 128
Butter, Tomato-Curry-Orange, **'93** 159
Cabbage and Tomatoes, **'83** 104
Cabbage and Tomatoes, Tasty, **'86** 72
Cacciatore, Chicken, **'86** 42
Canning Tomatoes, **'80** 128; **'85** 106
Casserole, Corn and Tomato, **'81** 127
Casserole, Corn-and-Tomato, **'84** 145
Casserole, Eggplant-and-Tomato, **'83** 187
Casserole, Saucy Potato-Tomato, **'79** 46
Casserole, Scalloped Tomato, **'88** 144
Casserole, Zucchini-and-Tomato, **'88** 265

Tomatoes (*continued*)

Catsup, Spicy Tomato, '83 182
Caviar Tomatoes, '91 12
Cheese Herbed-Topped Tomatoes, '86 108
Cheese Sauce over Toast, Tomatoes with, '88 159
Cheese-Topped Tomatoes, '81 160
Cheesy Puff-Top Tomatoes, '86 187
Cherry Tomatoes, Cheesy, '83 135
Cherry Tomatoes, Crab-Stuffed, '82 289; '88 78
Cherry Tomatoes, Cucumber-Stuffed, '88 262
Cherry Tomatoes, Green Beans with, '86 177
Cherry Tomatoes, Herbed, '82 128
Cherry Tomatoes in Brown Butter Sauce, '81 168
Cherry Tomatoes, Marinated Dried, '93 23
Cherry Tomatoes, Stuffed, '84 160; '88 95, 212; '92 25
Cherry Tomatoes, Tuna-Stuffed, '89 214
Cherry Tomatoes with Rum, '83 192
Cherry Tomato Salad, '87 156
Chicken, Tomato-Baked, '81 281; '82 30
Chowder, Tomato-Clam, '84 251
Chutney, Tomato-Apple, '84 180
Cioppino, Gulf Coast, '94 102
Cocktail, Tomato, '83 M203
Cocktail, Tomato-Clam, '87 252
Cocktail, Tomato Juice, '79 212; '83 230; '90 12
Cocktail, Tomato-Orange Juice, '83 169
Cocktail, Zesty Tomato Juice, '83 289
Coleslaw with Tomatoes, '80 34
Consommé, Tomato, '88 250
Coulis, Fresh Tomato, '93 230
Cream, Tomato, '94 70
Creole-Style Tomatoes-and-Corn, '84 142
Croissants, BLT, '93 158
Crostini, Feta-Tomato, '92 159
Cucumber on Tomatoes, Dilled, '84 142
Cups, Turkey-Tomato, '84 119
Delights, Tomato, '81 140
Delight, Tomato-Pea, '84 196
Dip, Bacon-and-Tomato, '90 147
Dip, Cottage Cheese Sun-Dried Tomato, '93 13
Dressing, Fresh Tomato Salad, '83 193
Dressing, Garden Salad with Tomato-Cream Cheese, '79 173
Dressing, Tomato-Honey French, '81 105
Dried Tomato-Cheese Spread, '90 204
Dried Tomato-Cheese Tart, '90 203
Dried Tomato-Cream Soup, '90 203
Dried Tomato Focaccia, '94 65
Dried Tomato Pesto, '90 204; '94 249
Dried Tomato Pesto, Fettuccine and Shrimp with, '94 249
Dried Tomato Spaghetti Sauce, '90 202
Dried Tomato Vinaigrette, '93 272
Dumplings, Tomato, '88 144
Eggs Benedict, Bacon-and-Tomato, '87 195
Fettuccine, Chicken-and-Tomatoes over, '90 204
Fire-and-Ice Tomatoes, '87 92
Fried Herb Tomatoes, '88 144
Fried Red Tomatoes, '81 102
Fried Ripe Tomatoes, '81 168
Fried Ripe Tomatoes with Gravy, '82 180

Fried Tomatoes with Bacon, Saucy, '81 210
Fried Tomatoes with Gravy, '86 211
Gravy, Tomato, '93 18
Green Tomato Cheeseburgers, Fried, '94 138
Green Tomatoes, Curried, '93 138
Green Tomatoes, Fried, '79 123; '80 178; '81 210; '85 214
Green Tomatoes, "Fried," '89 174
Green Tomatoes, Fried Okra and, '93 160
Green Tomatoes, Herb-Baked, '85 214
Green Tomatoes, Italian-Sauced, '85 214
Green Tomatoes, Okra and, '79 160
Green Tomatoes, Oven-Fried, '82 107; '91 122
Green Tomato Jam, '79 121
Green Tomato Pickles, '87 134
Green Tomato Pie, '79 195
Green Tomato Sweet Relish, '93 136
Grilled Tomatoes, '85 158
Grilled Tomatoes, Cheesy, '79 150
Herbed Tomatoes, '81 102; '82 49; '83 173
Herbed Tomato Slices, '89 173
Hot Tomatoes, '93 138
Hush Puppies, Tomato-Onion, '91 201
Italian Dressing, Tomato, Onion, and Cucumber in, '81 83
Italiano, Tomatoes, '88 29
Juice, Homemade Tomato, '81 50
Juice, Spicy Tomato, '85 189
Kale with Tomato and Onion, '92 244
Lemon Dressing, Tomato Slices with, '87 167
Lima and Tomato Combo, Hot, '83 219
Marinade, Bright Tomato, '88 176
Marinated Salsa Tomatoes, '82 164
Marinated Sliced Tomatoes, '92 173
Marinated Tomatoes, '85 156, 163; '89 174, 202
Marinated Tomato Slices, '82 134; '83 193
Medley, Okra-Corn-Tomato, '81 159
Medley, Tomato, '81 159
Mold, Tangy Tomato, '79 74
Muffins, Tomato Corn, '81 137
Mustard, Green Beans and Tomatoes with, '87 83
Mustard Tomatoes, Zippy, '86 M226
Okra and Tomatoes, '80 185; '81 139; '92 215
Okra and Tomatoes, Fresh, '81 M165; '87 89
Okra-Tomato Combo, '83 157
Okra, Tomatoes and, '86 170; '87 164
Okra, Tomatoes with, '85 106
Olive Spread, Tomatoes with, '85 114
Oregano Tomatoes, '83 145
Parmesan Tomatoes, '80 161
Pasta and Tomatoes, Quick, '92 180
Pasta, Caribbean Tomato, '93 201
Pasta, Italian Tomato, '93 201
Pasta, Southwestern Tomato, '93 201
Pasta, Tomato-Basil, '94 204
Pasta, Tomato-Garlic, '94 177
Pasta Toss, Tomato-Olive, '86 209
Peas and Tomatoes, Basil Snow, '88 M185
Peas and Tomatoes, Snow, '83 111
Pesto, Bow-Tie, '94 231
Pesto, Dried Tomato, '90 204; '94 249
Pesto, Tomatoes, '86 150
Pie, Tomato, '88 198
Pita Pockets, BLT in, '93 158

Potage, Tomato, '79 250
Primavera, Tomato-Pasta, '86 209
Provençal, Tomatoes, '82 181
Puffs, Tomato Cheese, '81 48
Puree, Seasoned Tomato, '83 182
Quiche, Asparagus-Tomato, '88 198
Ratatouille, '84 105, 243; '85 92
Ratatouille-Bran Stuffed Eggplant, '86 44
Ratatouille, Eggplant-Zucchini, '81 205
Ratatouille, Niçoise, '81 22
Ratatouille, Quick-and-Easy, '80 212
Ratatouille-Stuffed Eggplant, '83 187
Refresher, Tomato, '81 94; '83 318
Relish, Easy Tomato, '80 126
Relish, End-of-the-Garden, '80 179
Relish, Tomato, '85 188
Rice, Red, '92 235
Ring, Tangy Tomato, '84 164
Ring, Tomato-Vegetable, '81 302
Roma Tomatoes, Sautéed, '92 338
Rose, Tomato, '82 51; '85 338
Rotelle, Chicken and Tomato with, '87 108
Salad, Artichoke-Stuffed Tomato, '82 101
Salad, Artichoke-Tomato, '82 239
Salad, Basil-and-Tomato Couscous, '94 175
Salad, Congealed Lemon-Tomato, '89 178
Salad, Cottage-Tomato, '85 163
Salad, Crab-Stuffed Tomato, '80 148
Salad, Cucumber-Tomato, '90 144
Salad, Dilled Cucumber and Tomato, '81 153
Salad, Endive-Tomato Starburst, '93 323
Salad, Fresh Mozzarella-Tomato-Basil, '93 131
Salad, Frozen Tomato, '84 52
Salad, Gazpacho, '91 313
Salad, Guacamole-Tomato, '81 302
Salad, Herbed Pasta-and-Tomato, '92 144
Salad in Tomatoes, Cottage Cheese, '86 208
Salad, Lima Bean-Tomato, '85 137
Salad, Marinated, '83 170
Salad, Marinated Tomato-and-Cucumber, '92 216
Salad, Oriental-Stuffed Tomato, '82 101
Salad, Red, White, and Green, '90 18
Salad, Ruby-and-Emerald, '85 79
Salad, Spicy Chile-Tomato, '88 121
Salad, Summer Tomato, '94 201
Salad, Tomato-and-Cucumber Summer, '93 141
Salad, Tomato-Asparagus, '92 79
Salad, Tomato-Avocado, '86 74
Salad, Tomato-Cucumber, '86 218; '92 199
Salad, Tomato-Cucumber-Onion, '81 239
Salad, Tomato-Feta, '81 246; '91 168
Salad, Tomato Flower, '89 128
Salad, Tomato-Herb, '89 220
Salad, Tomato-Mozzarella, '89 220
Salad, Tomato Petal, '79 88
Salad, Tomato Relish, '83 111
Salad, Vidalia-Tomato, '84 65
Salad, Watercress-Tomato, '85 132
Salad with Citrus Marinade, Summer, '92 133
Salad with Yogurt-Herb Dressing, Tomato-Cucumber, '92 96
Salsa, '88 147
Salsa, Chunky, '86 130; '90 206
Salsa, Fresh Tomato, '91 182
Salsa, Red, '90 172
Salsa, Three Tomato, '93 138

Tomatoes *(continued)*

Salsa, Tomato, '87 120
Salsa, Tomato-Avocado, '94 83
Salsa, Yellowfin Tuna with Corn, Pepper, and Tomato, '94 164
Salsa, Yellow Tomato, '87 122
Sandwiches, Bacon, Cheese, and Tomato, '84 14
Sandwiches, Curried BLT, '93 158
Sandwiches, Open-Face Crab Tomato, '81 29
Sauce, Angel Hair Pasta with Tomato Cream, '93 292
Sauce, Asparagus with Tomato, '83 46
Sauce, Basil-Tomato, '92 198; '93 25, 48, 65
Sauce, Chili, '94 287
Sauce, Chunky Chili, '85 188
Sauce, Creamy Tomato, '93 71
Sauce, Creole, '89 228
Sauce, Fish in Tomato, '85 75
Sauce for Spaghetti, Italian Tomato, '81 134
Sauce, Fresh Tomato, '83 224; '87 171
Sauce, Hamburgers with Tomato, '81 73
Sauce, Herbed Fresh Tomato, '85 M151
Sauce, Homemade Picante, '90 205
Sauce, Italian-Style Tomato, '87 182
Sauce, Italian Tomato, '82 M68; '92 57
Sauce, Kleberg Hot, '94 28
Sauce, Linguine with Tomato-Cream, '86 158
Sauce, Marinara, '94 64
Sauce over Basil Pasta, Fresh Tomato, '93 176
Sauce, Quick Crab Marinara, '85 M151
Sauce, Rancheros, '88 148
Sauce, Red Pepper-Tomato, '93 59
Sauce, Refrigerator Tomato, '85 188
Sauce, Seasoned Tomato, '83 150
Sauce, Spicy Tomato, '84 294; '88 19
Sauce, Spinach Tortellini with Tomato, '88 302
Sauce, Tarragon-Tomato, '84 131
Sauce, Tomato, '85 193, 244; '87 249; '88 116
Sauce, Tomato Basil, '91 85
Sauce, Tomato-Basil, '92 180
Sauce, Turkey Cutlets with Tomato-Caper, '91 61
Sauce, Turkey Patties in Vegetable-Tomato, '87 18
Sauce, Vermicelli with Tomato, '83 164
Sauce with Green Chiles, Tomato, '81 196
Sauté, Tomato-Pepper, '84 142
Scalloped Tomatoes, '84 142
Scalloped Tomato Slices, '81 168
Sesame Tomatoes, '84 142
Sipper, Peppy Tomato, '94 227
Skillet, Cabbage-and-Tomato, '86 110
Skillet Tomatoes, '81 108
Skillet, Zucchini-Tomato, '93 206
Soup, Appetizer Tomato, '86 258
Soup, Bacon, Lettuce, and Tomato, '91 207
Soup, Chilled Tomato, '82 155
Soup, Cold Tomato, '88 160
Soup, Cream of Carrot-and-Tomato, '94 176
Soup, Creamy Tomato, '83 267; '86 258
Soup, Easy Tomato, '84 14
Soup, French Market, '94 317
Soup, Fresh Tomato, '83 140
Soup, Hot Tomato Juice, '86 302
Soup, Iced Tomato, '79 170

Soup, Icy-Spicy Mexican Tomato, '90 155
Soup Plus, Tomato, '88 170
Soup, Pumpkin-Tomato, '86 291
Soup, Refreshing Tomato Cream, '79 172
Soup, Savory Tomato, '94 91
Soup, Sour Cream-Topped Tomato, '80 246
Soup, Summer Tomato, '79 130
Soup, Tomato, '81 236; '83 44; '89 217
Soup, Tomato-and-Rice, '85 24
Soup, Tomato-Celery, '83 M58
Soup, Tomato-Vegetable, '81 M177; '86 9
Soup with Parmesan Cheese, Cream of Tomato, '86 161
Spaghetti with Tomatoes and Garlic, '91 47
Spicy Tomato Sipper, '86 229
Spinach-Topped Tomatoes, '88 265; '94 321
Spread, Fiery Tomato-Cheese, '87 196
Spread, Home-Style Sandwich, '80 179
Spread, Tomato, '94 123
Spread, Tomato-Cheese, '81 157
Squash, Beans, and Tomatoes, '83 148
Squash, Tomato, '86 111
Stack-Ups, Jiffy Tomato, '80 161
Stewed Tomatoes, '83 182
Stew, Turkey-Tomato, '90 279
Stir-Fried Sweet Peppers with Tomatoes, '93 207
Stir-Fry, Italian, '92 126
Stir-Fry, Tomato-Zucchini, '80 158
Stir-Fry, Zucchini-and-Tomato, '85 108
Strata, Tomato-Cheese, '81 209
Stuffed Eggs-and-Tomato Slices, '84 152
Stuffed Scalloped Tomatoes, '90 29
Stuffed Tomatoes, '83 252
Stuffed Tomatoes, Avocado-, '82 101
Stuffed Tomatoes, Bacon-and-Egg-, '80 162
Stuffed Tomatoes, Baked, '88 162
Stuffed Tomatoes, Bean-, '84 34
Stuffed Tomatoes, Broccoli-, '83 136; '93 216
Stuffed Tomatoes, Cheese-, '91 69
Stuffed Tomatoes, Cheesy, '80 161
Stuffed Tomatoes, Chile-Cheese, '94 141
Stuffed Tomatoes, Cold, '80 100
Stuffed Tomatoes, Corn-, '82 270
Stuffed Tomatoes, Crab-and-Avocado, '94 141
Stuffed Tomatoes, Easy, '82 264
Stuffed Tomatoes, Maque Choux, '87 89
Stuffed Tomatoes, Mushroom-, '86 218
Stuffed Tomatoes, Parmesan-, '92 182
Stuffed Tomatoes, Sausage-, '80 47
Stuffed Tomatoes, Spinach-, '89 203; '93 281
Stuffed Tomatoes, Squash-, '82 102
Stuffed Tomatoes, Turkey, '94 140
Stuffed Tomatoes, Vegetable, '94 141
Stuffed Tomato with Tuna Pasta, '88 54
Stuffed with Sea Slaw, Tomatoes, '89 96
Sun-Dried Tomatoes and Herbs, Meat Loaf with, '92 192
Sun-Dried Tomatoes and Rosemary, Goat Cheese with, '93 175
Sun-Dried Tomatoes, Cheese Balls with, '94 317
Sun-Dried Tomato Salad, Spinach and, '93 250
Swiss Chard with Tomatoes, '83 36
Treat, Summer Tomato, '79 143
Tuna-Mac in Tomatoes, '87 188
Venison and Tomatoes, '85 270

Vinaigrette, Marinara, '94 64
Vinaigrette, Okra-Corn-and-Tomato, '90 173
Vinaigrette, Tomato-Basil, '87 89
Vinaigrette, Tomatoes, '94 200
Vinegar, Tomato-Herb, '94 200
Walnut-Rice Stuffing, Tomatoes with, '91 102
Welsh Rarebit with Tomatoes and Bacon, '92 M159
Zucchini and Tomato with Herbs, '92 182
Tortillas. *See also* Burritos, Enchiladas, Tacos.
Appetizers, Tex-Mex Tortilla, '86 297
Bake, Cheesy Beef-and-Bean, '82 89
Bake, Chicken Tortilla, '82 89
Bake, Texas Tortilla, '94 285
Baskets, Tortilla, '94 97
Beef Roll-Ups, Mexican, '90 176
Buñuelos, '80 199
Buñuelos, King-Size, '86 5
Burgers, Tortilla, '94 138
Campesina, Tortilla, '89 85
Casserole, Chicken Tortilla, '81 166
Casserole, El Dorado, '81 140
Casserole, Mexican Chicken, '82 143
Chalupas, Bean, '83 313
Chalupas, Chicken, '79 185
Chalupas, Chicken-Olive, '81 227
Chalupas, Texas Turkey, '80 196
Cheese Tortilla Snack, Two-, '90 119
Cheesy Tortillas, '81 62
Chicken Acapulco, '84 32
Chicken-Tortilla Stack, Cheesy, '86 3
Chicken Tostadas, '93 204
Chilaquiles, '82 220
Chilaquiles con Pollo, '81 66
Chimichangas, '86 114
Chimichangas, Oven-Fried Beef, '92 124
Chimichangas, Pineapple Dessert, '86 4
Chips, Corn Tortilla, '91 17
Chips, Light Tortilla, '90 278; '91 257
Chips, Tortilla, '91 137
Chorizo and Egg Tortillas, '81 193
Dippers, Rolled Tortilla, '86 4
Egg-and-Sausage Tortillas, '83 246; '84 42
Eggs Sonora, '80 196
Española, Tortilla, '92 175
Fajitas, '84 233
Fajitas, Favorite, '86 114
Flautas, '83 199
Flautas with Guacamole, Chicken, '89 226
Flour Tortillas, '81 303
Flour Tortillas, Never-Fail, '80 198
Franks, Mexican, '93 78
Ham Appetillas, '93 63
Huevos Rancheros, '91 77
Migas, '94 26
Picadillo, '84 118
Pie, Mexican Cheese, '82 9; '83 69
Pie, Montezuma Tortilla, '83 199
Pie, Tortilla, '85 M211
Quesadillas, Quick, '89 87
Quesadillas, Sausage, '90 118
Rollups, Tortilla, '89 87
Salad in a Shell, Mexican, '86 4
Sandwiches, Guacamole, '82 9; '83 68
Sandwich, Tex-Mex Ham-and-Cheese, '86 4
Snacks, Pesto Tortilla, '89 19
Soup, Spicy Tortilla, '90 32; '93 108
Soup, Tortilla, '88 31, 245; '90 201; '93 197, 274; '94 136
Stack-Ups, Tortilla, '92 196

Tortillas (continued)

Tacoritos, '90 133
Tostada Compuestas, '81 194
Tostadas, Crab, '93 203
Tostadas, Crispy, '83 2
Tostadas, Shrimp-and-Black Bean,
  '93 204
Tostadas, Super, '83 199
Triangles, Tortilla, '94 107

Tuna
Baked Tuna and Peas in Wine Sauce, '83 196
Bake, Shoestring Potato Tuna, '82 211
Ball, Tuna-Pecan, '87 94
Barbecued Tuna, '80 275
Bisque, Tuna, '79 76
Boats, Cucumber Tuna, '83 136
Broiled Tuna with Rosemary, '93 127
Burgers, Zippy Tuna, '81 135
Casserole, Biscuit-Topped Tuna, '79 113
Casserole, Easy Tuna, '82 M203
Casserole, Nippy Tuna, '84 241
Casserole, Tangy Tuna-Broccoli, '83 75
Casserole, Tuna, '82 119
Casserole, Tuna Vegetable, '81 135
Casserole with Cheese Swirls, Tuna, '88 256
Cheesies, Tuna, '82 191
Chopsticks, Tuna, '94 255
Croquettes, Tuna-Egg, '80 275
Croquettes with Parsley Sauce, Tuna,
  '86 108
Dip, Low-Cal Tuna, '87 25
Dip, Tuna-Curry, '84 31
Eggs, Tuna-Stuffed, '83 83
Grilled Florida Tuna, '93 128
Grilled Tuna with Poblano Salsa, '91 135
Jambalaya, Tuna, '83 44
Lasagna, Tuna, '83 44; '84 123
Macaroni Treat, Tuna-, '82 131
Melts, Tempting Tuna, '88 158
Mold, Creamy Tuna-Cheese, '81 135
Mound, Tuna, '80 276
Mousse, Tuna, '80 275
Mustard Sauce, Tuna with Tangy, '92 201
Pasta, Stuffed Tomato with Tuna, '88 54
Pie, Tuna-Rice, '84 123
Pie with Cheese Roll Crust, Tuna, '80 286
Pita Pocket, Tuna-in-a-, '87 202
Pockets, Tuna, '88 139
Potatoes, Tuna-Stuffed, '79 210
Ring, Creamy Tuna, '80 275
Salad, Cheese-Sauced Tuna, '87 M124
Salad, Company Tuna, '87 201
Salad, Confetti, '80 4
Salad, Congealed Tuna, '84 163
Salad, Creamy Tuna, '82 87, 208
Salad, Crunchy Tuna, '87 201
Salad, Curried Tuna, '86 208
Salad, Favorite Tuna, '82 208
Salad, Flavorful Tuna, '81 37
Salad, Fresh Greens and Tuna, '80 55
Salad, Layered Tuna, '84 221
Salad, Luncheon Tuna, '81 135
Salad, Meal-in-One, '82 232
Salad Rolls, Hot Tuna, '84 281
Salad, Swiss Tuna, '86 186
Salad, Tuna-and-Cannellini Bean, '86 143
Salad, Tuna-and-Red Pepper, '93 143
Salad, Tuna Chef, '82 78
Salad, Tuna-Egg, '81 135

Salad, Tuna Macaroni, '83 44, 145
Salad, Tuna-Macaroni, '84 66
Salad, Tuna-Pasta, '91 43; '92 141
Salad, Tuna Pasta, '92 108
Salad, Tuna-Potato, '84 289
Salad, Tuna-Rice, '87 202
Salad, Tuna-Taco, '87 145
Salad, Whole Wheat Macaroni-Tuna, '84 193
Salad with Grapes, Curried Tuna, '87 201
Sandwich Boats, Tuna, '91 166
Sandwiches, French Toasted Tuna, '80 275
Sandwiches, Hot Tuna, '85 299; '86 M194
Sandwiches, Tuna Club, '83 134
Spread, Chunky Tuna, '89 147
Spread, Tuna, '83 174; '91 305
Steaks, Grilled Tuna, '90 129
Steaks on Mixed Greens with Lemon-Basil
  Vinaigrette, Seared Tuna, '94 205
Steaks with Tarragon Butter, Tuna, '92 328
Tomatoes, Tuna-Mac in, '87 188
Tomatoes, Tuna-Stuffed Cherry, '89 214
Waffle-Wich, Hot Tuna, '88 272; '89 181
Yellowfin Tuna with Corn, Pepper, and
  Tomato Salsa, '94 164

Turkey
Appetizers, Turkey, '91 314
Baked Turkey, Cider, '83 263
Bake, Layered Ham and Turkey, '79 252
Bake, Turkey Noodle, '93 243
Barbecue, Turkey, '90 158
Braised Turkey Breast, '84 260
Breast and Gravy, Savory Seasoned Turkey,
  '89 M309
Breast, Herb Butter-Basted Turkey, '86 285
Breast, Herbed Turkey, '92 266
Breast, Smoky Turkey, '89 323
Breast with Orange-Raspberry Glaze,
  Turkey, '91 253
Buffet Turkey, '80 29
Burgers, All-American Pizza, '92 148
Burgers, Grilled Turkey, '91 61
Casserole, Crunchy Turkey, '89 M282
Casserole, Golden Turkey, '80 271
Casserole, Stuffed Turkey, '88 246
Casserole, Turkey, '84 327
Casserole, Turkey-and-Broccoli, '86 332
Casserole, Turkey-and-Shrimp Florentine,
  '92 122
Casserole, Turkey-Asparagus, '86 284
Casserole, Turkey-Noodle-Poppyseed,
  '90 239
Casserole, Turkey-Olive, '87 268
Casserole, Turkey-Spinach, '84 71
Casserole, Turkey-Swiss, '86 283
Chalupas, Texas Turkey, '80 196
Chili, Turkey-Bean, '88 M213
Chowder, Turkey, '85 10; '91 312
Chowder, Turkey-Corn, '81 98
Creamed Turkey, Southern, '80 272
Crêpes, Elegant Turkey, '83 282
Crêpes, Turkey, '92 41
Cups, Turkey-Tomato, '84 119
Curried Cream Sauce, Turkey Slices with,
  '91 60
Cutlets, Pecan-Crusted Turkey, '94 282
Cutlets with Pepper Salsa, Spicy Turkey,
  '88 26
Cutlets with Tarragon-Mustard Sauce,
  Turkey, '93 239
Cutlets with Tomato-Caper Sauce, Turkey,
  '91 61

Deep-Fried Turkey, '92 339
Divan, Creamy Turkey, '90 M34
Divan, Quick Turkey, '89 178
Divan, Turkey, '82 268
Dressing, Easy Turkey and, '79 296
Dressing, Turkey, '85 298
Drumsticks, Grilled Turkey, '89 168
Fast-and-Savory Turkey, '87 306
Florentine, Turkey, '88 264
Galantine of Turkey, '85 150
Garlic Sauce, Turkey Hero with, '90 145
Giblet Dressing and Turkey Gravy, Turkey
  with, '91 254
Gravy, Savory Turkey and, '94 326
Gravy, Turkey, '91 255; '94 306
Gumbo, Turkey, '82 268; '85 258
Ham-and-Turkey Specials, Cheesy, '84 14
Herbed Turkey-in-a-Bag, '91 253
Indian Turkey, '85 302
Italiano, Turkey, '91 62
Kabobs, Turkey-and-Fruit, '88 140
Lasagna, Turkey, '83 239; '91 130
Lazy Day Turkey, '93 93
Loaf, Cranberry-Glazed Turkey, '86 171
Loaf, Ground Turkey, '86 171
Loaf, Turkey, '92 33
Marinated Turkey Breast, Citrus-, '94 272
Meatballs, Turkey, '89 237
Meat Mixture, Basic, '92 241
Mix, Ground Meat, '89 143
Nachos, Turkey, '90 118
Open-Facers, Turkey, '82 190
Oriental Turkey, '82 268
Oven-Fried Turkey Cutlets, '91 121
Parmesan, Turkey, '82 268
Parmigiana, Turkey, '87 193
Pasta, Creamy Turkey-Basil, '89 216
Pâté in Pastry, Turkey-Mushroom, '92 327
Patties in Vegetable-Tomato Sauce, Turkey,
  '87 18
Patties, Stuffed Ground Turkey, '86 171
Peppers, Turkey with, '92 182
Picatta, Turkey, '91 137
Pie, Broccoli-and-Turkey Pasta, '88 269
Pie, Crumb-Crust Curried Turkey, '86 265
Pie, Golden Turkey, '79 253
Pie, Lattice-Topped Turkey, '81 277; '82 7
Pie, Potato-Topped Turkey, '86 265
Pie, Turkey, '80 285
Pie, Turkey-and-Dressing, '84 326
Pie, Turkey-and-Oyster, '82 267
Pie, Turkey-Cheese, '88 264
Pie, Turkey Pot, '86 265; '90 24; '93 45
Pilaf, Turkey-Asparagus, '88 200
Pilaf, Turkey-Rice, '86 284
Pizza, Turkey-Vegetable, '90 139
Primavera, Smoked Turkey Pasta, '90 84
Puffs, Turkey-Cheese, '87 301
Rice, Turkey Fried, '83 282
Roast Turkey, '79 250; '80 262; '86 47;
  '88 253; '90 321
Roast Turkey and Cornbread Dressing,
  '89 324
Roast Turkey and Giblet Gravy, '94 308
Roast Turkey Breast and Gravy, '88 303
Roast Turkey Breast with Special Gravy,
  '86 282
Roast Turkey, How to, '83 286
Roast Turkey with Grandmother's Dressing,
  Madeira, '91 254
Roast Turkey with Oyster Stuffing, '80 251

Turkey *(continued)*

Roast Turkey with Peanut Dressing, **'79** 283
Roast Turkey with Rice Dressing, **'82** 286
Rollups, Turkey, **'86** 198
Rounds, Turkey-Mozzarella, **'82** 3
Salad Bake, Turkey, **'79** 253
Salad, Chilled Turkey-and-Pepper Stir-Fry,
    '88 140
Salad, Curried Turkey, **'88** 140
Salad, Fruit-and-Spice Turkey, **'94** 325
Salad, Fruit-and-Turkey, **'89** 176
Salad, Fruitful Turkey, **'84** 197
Salad, Holiday Turkey, **'84** 320
Salad, Honey-Mustard Turkey, **'92** 309
Salad, Hot Turkey, **'86** 10, 297; **'87** 176
Salad, Layered Turkey, **'86** 332; **'92** 220
Salad Pita Sandwiches, Turkey, **'87** 202;
    '88 43
Salad, Polynesian Turkey, **'87** 285
Salad, Ranch-Style Turkey 'n' Pasta,
    '94 184
Salad, Southwestern Turkey, **'91** 313
Salad, Turkey, **'90** 318
Salad, Turkey-Apple, **'88** 123; **'90** 181
Salad, Turkey Caesar, **'93** 320
Salad, Turkey-Carrot, **'86** 283
Salad, Turkey-Fruit, **'79** 56
Salad, Turkey Fruit, **'83** 233; **'84** 244
Salad, Turkey-in-the-Orange, **'93** 21
Salad, Turkey Macaroni, **'83** 282
Salad, Turkey-Zucchini, **'85** 74
Salad with Hot Bacon Dressing, Turkey,
    '87 285
Salad with Sautéed Walnuts, Turkey,
    '86 117
Salad with Yogurt Dressing, Turkey Waldorf,
    '88 53
Sandwiches, Smoked Turkey-Roasted
    Pepper, **'94** 66
Sandwiches, Turkey Hero, **'92** 196
Sandwich, Hot Turkey, **'93** 306
Sandwich, Turkey-in-the-Slaw, **'90** 177
Sandwich, Waffle-Grilled Turkey, **'94** 170
Sauce, Turkey Spaghetti, **'85** 13
Sausage-Cornbread Dressing, Turkey with,
    '83 287
Sausage, Marinara Sauce with Italian Turkey,
    '89 239
Sauté, Creamy Turkey, **'93** 19
Sauté, Turkey, **'89** 105
Schnitzel, Turkey, **'84** 230
Skillet, Oriental Turkey-Orange, **'86** 284
Skillet Turkey Dinner, **'91** 61
Slices, Orange-Turkey, **'90** 53
Sloppy Toms, **'91** 51
Smoked Turkey, **'79** 293; **'84** 160; **'85** 258;
    '90 249
Smoked Turkey Breast, **'88** 169
Smoked Turkey Medley, **'90** 128
Soufflé, Turkey, **'80** 271
Soup, Bean-and-Turkey, **'93** 319
Soup, Curried Turkey, **'86** 332
Soup Mix, Turkey-Noodle, **'89** 330
Soup, Turkey-Barley, **'91** 312
Soup, Turkey Carcass, **'86** 284
Soup, Turkey-Noodle, **'91** 312
Soup, Turkey-Rice, **'90** 89
Soup, Turkey-Vegetable, **'84** 4; **'88** 264;
    '91 312

Soup, Williamsburg Turkey, **'90** 287
Spread, Curried Turkey, **'92** 16
Spread, Turkey Party, **'83** 282
Squash Dressing, Turkey with, **'87** 248
Steaks, Grilled Marinated Turkey, **'93** 170
Stew, Hearty Turkey, **'79** 252
Stew, Turkey-Tomato, **'90** 279
Stir-Fry, Turkey-Broccoli, **'91** 62
Stock, Light Poultry, **'90** 31
Stroganoff, Turkey, **'91** 61
Stuffed Turkey Breast, **'87** 270; **'89** 322
Stuffed Turkey Breast with Seasoned
    Dressing, **'83** 320; **'84** 128
Sweet-and-Sour Turkey, **'79** 252
Tarragon Cream, Turkey with, **'91** 60
Tenderloins, Lime-Buttered Turkey,
    '92 127
Tetrazzini, Herbed Turkey, **'86** 47
Tomatoes, Turkey Stuffed, **'94** 140
Topping, Turkey-Vegetable, **'94** 22
Treats, Turkey, **'93** 256
Turnovers, Home-Style Turkey, **'94** 325
Wild Turkey, Country-Fried, **'94** 306

Turnips

au Gratin, Turnip, **'79** 289
au Gratin, Turnips, **'84** 229; **'88** 229;
    '89 244
Boiled Turnips, **'83** 242
Braised Turnips, **'91** 219
Casserole, Baked Turnip, **'82** 274
Casserole, Turnip, **'83** 242; **'84** 229
Cheese Sauce, Turnips in, **'84** 229
Collard Greens, Turnip-and-, **'92** 215
Cooked Turnips, Creamy, **'86** 224
Dip, Turnip Green, **'91** 13
Fried Turnips, Shoestring, **'81** 274
Gingered Turnips, **'82** 274
Glazed Turnips, **'81** 274
Greens and Ham Hock, Southern Turnip,
    '80 119
Greens, Fresh Turnip, **'92** 339
Greens, Old-Fashioned Turnip, **'85** 255
Greens, Turnip, **'90** 13, 232
Greens with Turnips, Turnip, **'84** 230
Hash Brown Turnips, **'79** 254
Julienne, Turnips and Carrots, **'86** 295
Onions, Turnips and, **'83** 242
Orange Carrots and Turnips, Sunset,
    '94 213
Parsleyed Turnips and Carrots, **'79** 253
Party Turnips, **'84** 230
Potatoes, Turnips and, **'79** 254
Pudding, Turnip, **'94** 213
Salad, Irish Turnip, **'94** 178
Salad, Turnip-and-Carrot, **'91** 212
Saucy Turnips, **'85** 289
Sauté, Carrot-Turnip, **'93** 241
Scalloped Potatoes and Turnips, **'85** 235
Scalloped Turnips, **'79** 254
Slaw, Turnip, **'89** 245
Soufflé, Turnip, **'79** 254
Soup, Creamy Turnip, **'84** 279
Soup, Oyster-Turnip, **'94** 328
Soup, Turnip, **'92** 217
Southern Turnips, **'87** 190
Supreme, Turnip, **'79** 254
Sweet-and-Sour Turnips, **'81** 274

Turtle

Fried Cooter (Soft-Shell Turtle), **'80** 99
Soup au Sherry, Turtle, **'80** 56
Soup, Turtle, **'92** 92

Vanilla

Almond Crunch, Vanilla, **'93** 243
Cake, Vanilla Chiffon, **'79** 266
Cheesecake, Creamy Vanilla, **'89** 93
Cookies 'n' Cream Dessert, Gold-Dusted,
    '94 271
Cookies, Vanilla Slice-and-Bake, **'85** 171
Cream, Vanilla, **'81** 248; **'83** M115
Crescents, Vanilla, **'82** 307
Cupcakes, Golden Vanilla, **'85** 121
Cupcakes, Vanilla, **'92** 14
Custard, Baked Vanilla, **'82** 129
Dessert, Glorified Vanilla Sherry, **'81** 85
Extract, Home-Brewed Vanilla, **'83** 228
Extract, Homemade Vanilla, **'83** 228
Extract, Vanilla, **'94** 243
Frosting, Vanilla, **'84** 36; **'85** 236;
    '92 14, 274
Frosting, Vanilla Buttercream, **'92** 239;
    '94 99
Frosting, Vanilla-Rum, **'85** 324
Frosty, French Vanilla, **'79** 148
Fruit Cup, Vanilla, **'80** 183
Glaze, Vanilla, **'85** M89; **'89** 211
Helado, Caramel-Vanilla (Caramel-Vanilla Ice
    Cream), **'81** 67
Ice Cream, Basic Vanilla, **'88** 202
Ice Cream, Country Vanilla, **'82** 143
Ice Cream Spectacular, Vanilla, **'82** 166
Ice Cream, Vanilla, **'80** 176; **'86** 129;
    '91 174
Ice Cream, Vanilla Custard, **'92** 148
Oil, Vanilla, **'94** 243
Pears, Vanilla Poached, **'90** 57
Pie, Fruit-Topped Vanilla Cream, **'84** 49
Pralines, Vanilla, **'92** 313; **'93** 51
Pudding, Creamy Vanilla, **'83** 227
Pudding, Vanilla, **'88** 32
Sauce, Almond-Vanilla Custard, **'88** M177
Sauce, Pan-Fried Grouper with Vanilla Wine,
    '94 241
Sauce, Vanilla Crème, **'94** 243
Shortbread, Scottish, **'94** 242
Soufflé, Frozen Vanilla, **'79** 230; **'82** 173
Soufflés with Vanilla Crème Sauce, Vanilla,
    '94 242
Sugar, Vanilla, **'94** 243
Vinaigrette, Vanilla, **'94** 242

Veal

Amaretto-Lime Veal, **'93** 54
Amelio, Veal, **'86** 142
au Madeira, Veal, **'81** 131
Birds, Veal, **'84** 260
Burgoo, Five-Meat, **'87** 3
Casserole, Veal and Wild Rice, **'79** 180
Casserole, Veal Cutlet, **'79** 109
Chops, Apple Veal, **'87** 220
Chops Mediterranean, Veal, **'79** 108
Company Veal and Carrots, **'85** 22
Cordon Bleu, Veal, **'87** 219
Cutlets, Stuffed Veal, **'92** 329
Delight, Veal, **'79** 109
Herbed Veal and Onions, **'79** 108
Herbed Veal with Wine, **'86** 193
Italian Style, Veal, **'82** M68
Lemon Veal, **'93** 35
Lemon Veal Piccata, **'86** 118
Lemon Veal with Artichoke Hearts, **'87** 219
Marsala, Veal, **'91** 218, 310
Marsala, Veal-and-Mushrooms, **'89** 44

Veal *(continued)*

Meatballs, European Veal, '85 30
Meat Loaf, Italian, '79 187
Meat Loaf, Savory, '87 216
Meat Loaf, Triple, '79 186
Meat Loaf, Veal, '93 292
New Orleans Veal with Crabmeat, '86 94
Paprika, Veal, '88 113
Parmigiana, Veal, '81 227
Peppercorns, Veal with Green, '87 220
Picante, Veal, '87 31
Piccata, Veal, '92 181
Piccata with Capers, Veal, '87 142
Ragout, Veal-and-Artichoke, '94 43
Roast, Best Baked Veal, '87 219
Roast with Vegetables, Veal, '89 71
Sauce, Noodles with Veal, '80 236
Sauté, Veal-Cepe, '89 62
Savory Veal, '83 281
Scallopini à la Marsala, Veal, '79 109
Scallopini Marsala, Veal, '85 295
Scallopini of Veal al Sorriso, '79 85
Scallopini, Veal, '83 8, 125
Schnitzel, Swiss, '80 189
Skillet Veal, '83 200
Soup with Quenelles, Veal-Vermicelli,
  '94 14
Spaghetti, Veal, '84 276
Spaghetti with Veal and Peppers, '81 201;
  '82 14
Steak, Veal, '82 276
Stock, Brown Meat, '90 31
Stroganoff, Veal, '79 108
Supreme, Veal, '85 109
Sweetbreads, Creamed, '90 82
Swirls, Veal-and-Smithfield Ham, '86 253
Terrine of Pork and Veal, '93 287
Terrine with Mustard Sauce, Veal, '93 118
Wine Sauce, Veal and Carrots in, '81 31;
  '86 M139
Vegetables. *See also* specific types.
à la Grill, Vegetables, '88 130
Antipasto, Easy, '92 24
Antipasto, Vegetable, '85 263
Appetizer, Hot Vegetable Juice, '93 324
Appetizer, Tarragon Vegetable, '83 277
Aspic, Cheesy Vegetable, '81 73
Bake with Sweet Bacon Dressing,
  Vegetable-Chicken, '93 108
Barley and Vegetables, '91 81
Beef and Vegetables, Company, '88 234
Beef and Vegetables in a Noodle Ring,
  '85 285
Beef and Vegetables, Savory, '79 163
Beef Kabobs with Vegetables, '90 148
Beef with Chinese Vegetables, '81 211
Bites, Veggie, '91 171
Blanching Chart, Microwave, '80 M181
Bread, Breakaway Vegetable, '82 74
Bread, Herb-Vegetable-Cheese, '88 172
Bundles, Vegetable, '93 181
Buñuelos, '93 29
Burgers, Beef-and-Vegetable, '84 125
Burgers, Vegetable, '89 164
Burritos, Vegetable, '80 197; '90 134;
  '92 138
Burritos, Vegetarian, '93 319
Burritos with Avocado Sauce, Vegetable,
  '83 200

Buttermilk Sauce, Vegetables with, '84 6
Cabbage Rolls, Vegetarian, '91 86
Canapés, Vegetable, '91 252
Casserole, Beef and Vegetable Chow Mein,
  '83 313
Casserole, Beefy Vegetable, '79 248
Casserole, Cheesy Vegetable, '81 103
Casserole, Fresh Vegetable, '82 225
Casserole, Garden, '82 168; '88 122
Casserole, Layered Vegetable, '91 286;
  '92 27
Casserole, Mixed Vegetable, '83 208, 256;
  '86 327
Casserole, Mixed-Vegetable, '87 154
Casserole, Tuna Vegetable, '81 135
Casserole, Vegetable-and-Ham, '84 91
Casserole, Vegetable-Curry, '91 286; '92 27
Casserole, Vegetable Lasagna, '92 198
Casserole, Vegetable Noodle, '91 30
Casserole, Veggies, '88 123
Cheesecake, Layered Vegetable, '91 62;
  '92 51
Chicken and Dumplings with Vegetables,
  '85 M56
Chicken-and-Vegetable Platter, '88 M52
Chicken and Vegetables, '88 165
Chicken and Vegetables, Almond, '86 21
Chicken and Vegetables, Chinese, '81 212
Chicken and Vegetables, Creamed, '91 90
Chicken and Vegetables, Lemon, '88 118
Chicken and Vegetables, Roast, '81 3
Chicken and Vegetables, Walnut, '85 194
Chicken and Vegetables with Ginger-Soy
  Sauce, '91 32
Chicken Breast with Turned Vegetables and
  Chive Sauce, Poached, '94 309
Chicken Strips and Vegetables, Marinated,
  '90 110
Chicken, Vegetable-Stuffed, '89 M65
Chili, Mom's, '93 292
Chili, Vegetable, '91 28
Chili, Vegetarian, '84 280, 327; '91 284
Chinese Vegetable Pouches, '94 34
Chops with Vegetables, Golden, '89 218
Chowder, Creamy Chicken-Vegetable,
  '92 20
Chowder, Hearty Vegetable, '88 56
Cocktail, Fresh Vegetable, '82 165
Cornish Hens with Vegetables, Tarragon
  Roasted, '94 79
Creamed Spring Vegetables, '87 127
Crêpes, Chicken-Vegetable, '83 70
Crêpes, Vegetable-Filled Bran, '86 44
Croutons, Vegetable-Flavored, '84 148
Curried Vegetables, '89 219
Dilled Vegetable Sticks, '88 179
Dinner, Jollof Rice, '91 230; '92 325
Dip, Creamy Vegetable, '83 180
Dip, Cucumber-Cheese Vegetable, '83 128
Dip, Fresh Vegetable, '80 249
Dip, Herb Vegetable, '89 269
Dip, Starburst Vegetable, '82 248
Dip, Tangy Vegetable, '87 196
Dip, Vegetable, '79 52; '82 161
Dip, Vegetable Garden, '85 215
Dip, Zippy Vegetable, '84 256
Egg Rolls, Vegetarian, '86 148
Enchiladas, Meatless, '93 106
Enchiladas, Vegetable-Cheese, '94 42
en Papillote, Chicken and Vegetables, '86 145
Fennel, Braised, '88 46

Fennel, Italian-Style Braised, '93 56
Fennel with Garlic Butter, Steamed, '93 56
Fettuccine Primavera, '89 238; '94 85
Fettuccine, Vegetable, '83 312
Fish-and-Vegetable Dinner, '91 196
Fish and Vegetables, Cheesy, '94 254
Fish and Vegetables, Grilled, '89 179
Fish Rolls, Vegetable-Filled, '86 M251
Fish with Vegetables, Poached, '89 332;
  '90 18
Flounder Rolls, Vegetable-Stuffed, '87 6
Flounder-Vegetable Medley, '85 217
Freezing Chart, Vegetable, '85 185
Fresh Vegetable Party Tray, '82 122
Fresh Vegetable Potpourri, '79 208
Fresh Vegetables, Parsley-Dill Dip with,
  '85 79
Fried Vegetables, Skillet-, '88 156
Frittata, Fresh Vegetable, '93 140
Frittata, Vegetable, '92 48; '93 183
Garden Combo, '86 172
Garden Harvest, '85 M142
Garden Surprise, '83 112
Garnishes, '82 280; '85 338, 339
Gazpacho, Smoked Vegetable, '93 156
Grilled Vegetables, '84 172; '92 124, 231
Grilled Vegetables, Italian-Style, '92 143
Grilled Vegetable Skewers, '94 160
Grouper with Confetti Vegetables, '88 M189
Ham-and-Vegetables, Skillet, '84 90
Herbed-Smoked Vegetables, '85 145
Heroes, Vegetable Garden, '84 14
Juice Delight, Vegetable, '84 58
Julienne Vegetables, '93 31
Julienne Vegetables with Walnuts, '86 M251
Kabobs, Beef-and-Vegetable, '91 148
Kabobs, Fresh Vegetable, '81 158; '92 101
Kabobs, Grilled Vegetable, '93 170
Kabobs, Marinated Vegetable, '83 M195
Kabobs, Tangy Marinated Vegetable, '88 142
Kabobs, Vegetable, '87 116
Kielbasa-Vegetable Dinner, '91 274
Lamb with Vegetables, Fillets of, '85 36
Lasagna Casserole, Vegetable, '93 25
Lasagna, Cheesy Vegetable, '79 84
Lasagna, Colorful Vegetable, '87 19
Lasagna, Garden, '83 119
Lasagna, Vegetable, '84 201; '93 320
Lemon Vegetables, '93 83
Limping Susan, '90 155
Liver with Vegetables, Calf's, '85 219
Loaf, Beef-Vegetable, '79 164
Loaf, Pureed Vegetable-Cheese, '85 297
Marinade, Fresh Vegetable, '83 209
Marinade, Vegetable, '92 231
Marinated Vegetable Medley, '85 319;
  '89 14
Marinated Vegetables, '79 146; '81 239;
  '85 67; '86 286; '94 183
Marinated Vegetables, Honey-Mustard,
  '93 236
Marinated Vegetables Italian, '90 242
Marinated Vegetables, Sweet-and-Sour,
  '83 266
Marinated Vegetables, Zesty, '82 272
Marinated Vegetable Toss, '82 113
Marinated Veggies, '91 46
Meatballs and Vegetables with Horseradish
  Dressing, '91 32
Meat Loaf, Vegetable, '85 M29
Medley, Baked Vegetable, '81 75

Vegetables *(continued)*

Medley Bake, Vegetable, '81 268
Medley, Chinese Vegetable, '84 33
Medley, Crunchy Vegetable, '84 254
Medley, Fresh Vegetable, '85 155
Medley, Garden Vegetable, '91 45
Medley, Green Vegetable, '79 287; '80 34
Medley, Italian Vegetable, '88 143
Medley, Masala Vegetable, '94 56
Medley, Mixed Vegetable, '82 126
Medley, Sautéed Vegetable, '83 101
Medley, Skillet Vegetable, '81 134
Medley, Spring Vegetable, '86 115
Medley, Summer Garden, '84 158
Medley, Summer Vegetable, '83 208
Medley, Vegetable, '79 102; '83 112;
 '86 327; '89 M129
Microwaving Fresh Vegetables, '82 M138
Mint Sauce over Vegetables, '92 104
Mixed Vegetables, '83 M195
Mixed Vegetables, Pasta with Sausage and,
 '84 249
Mushroom Caps, Vegetable, '81 246
Nachos, Vegetable, '91 17
Nests, Scallops in Vegetable, '91 70
Olive Butter, Vegetables Tossed in, '91 295
Omelet, Beefy Vegetable, '83 188
Omelet, Cheddar-Vegetable, '83 205
Omelet, Cheesy Vegetable, '85 49
Omelet, Fresh Vegetable, '84 211
Omelet, Golden Vegetable, '82 123
Omelet Primavera, '87 71
Omelet, Puffy Vegetable, '83 188
Omelet, Vegetarian, '84 114
Open-Faced Vegetarian Melt, '87 106
Orange Roughy, Vegetable-Topped, '93 67
Orange Roughy with Vegetables, Basil-,
 '92 98
Oriental Vegetables, '84 26; '85 108
Oriental Vegetables, Beef with, '84 140
Orzo Primavera, '92 192
Paella, Garden, '82 245
Paella, Spanish, '85 26
Pancakes, Vegetable, '88 297
Pancakes, Vegetable-Rice, '93 43
Pasta and Garden Vegetables, '87 192
Pasta, Garden, '82 199
Pasta Potpourri, '94 33
Pasta Primavera, '85 86; '89 105; '93 168
Pasta Primavera, Almost, '86 38
Pâté, Vegetable-Chicken, '86 66
Pepper Cups, Hot Vegetable, '88 M188
Pie, Chicken-Vegetable Pot, '81 281; '82 30
Pies, Vegetable-Beef, '80 286
Pilaf, Barley-Vegetable, '91 33
Pizza, Deep-Dish Vegetarian, '85 243
Pizza, Garden, '89 108
Pizza, Turkey-Vegetable, '90 139
Pizza, Vegetable, '89 64; '94 218
Pizza, Vegetarian Processor, '89 225
Pizza, Veggie, '94 78
Platter, Curry Dip and Vegetable, '89 327
Platter, Fresh Vegetable, '92 60
Platter, Vegetable, '88 M187
Pockets, Vegetable, '85 215
Pork Chops and Garden Vegetables, '88 297
Pork Chops, Skillet Vegetable, '85 179
Pork Combo, Vegetable-, '85 113
Pork with Vegetables, Medaillons of, '88 223

Potatoes, Vegetable-Topped Stuffed, '85 235
Pot Roast Medley, Vegetable-, '83 319
Pot Roast with Vegetables, '80 59; '81 M208
Pot Roast with Vegetables, Marinated,
 '88 M52
Primavera, Chicken-Pasta, '91 72
Primavera, Garden Spiral, '91 30
Punch, Hot Vegetable, '93 12
Puree, Smoked Vegetable, '93 156
Quiche, Cheese-Vegetable, '81 228
Quiche, Ham-and-Vegetable, '84 326
Quiche, Vegetable, '87 M219
Ragoût, Vegetable, '89 172
Ratatouille, '84 105, 243; '85 92; '89 174
Ratatouille-Bran Stuffed Eggplant, '86 44
Ratatouille, Eggplant-Zucchini, '81 205
Ratatouille Niçoise, '81 22
Ratatouille Pie, '88 198
Ratatouille, Quick-and-Easy, '80 212
Ratatouille, Sausage, '89 248
Ratatouille Supreme, '86 172
Relish, Eight-Vegetable, '84 179
Relish, Garden, '83 259
Relish Tree, Christmas, '84 257
Relish, Vegetable, '90 147
Rice, Garden, '92 12
Rice Pilaf, Fruit-and-Vegetable, '84 196
Rice Toss, Vegetable-, '91 309
Rice, Vegetables and, '93 91
Rice with Vegetables, '79 64; '85 83
Ring, Tomato-Vegetable, '81 302
Roasted Vegetables and Pasta, '93 184
Roasted Vegetables, Traveling Linguine with,
 '93 178
Salads
 Aspic with Horseradish Dressing, Crisp
  Vegetable, '87 152
 Boats, Salad, '80 93
 Calico Salad, '82 35
 Cauliflower-Vegetable Salad, '85 158
 Chicken Salad, Vegetable-, '91 287
 Chicken-Vegetable Salad, Basil-, '92 162
 Chinese Salad, '80 4
 Composée, Salad, '79 171
 Composé, Salad, '93 126
 Congealed Fresh Vegetable Salad,
  '82 240
 Congealed Salad, Cheesy-Vegetable,
  '86 199
 Congealed Salad, Fresh Vegetable,
  '91 229
 Congealed Vegetable Salad, '79 276
 Corned Beef Salad, Vegetable-, '80 148
 Creamy Vegetable Salad, '79 47
 Creole Salad, '79 147
 Crunchy Vegetable Salad, '79 11;
  '80 217; '83 216
 Different Vegetable Salad, '82 143
 Easy Vegetable Salad, '83 316; '84 16
 Fennel Salad, Marinated, '93 56
 Freezer Salad, '94 118
 Garden Medley Salad, '80 122
 Garden Salad, '87 62
 Garden Salad Bowl, '82 239
 Greek Salad, '93 208
 Greek Salad, Garden, '86 173
 Green-and-White Vegetable Salad,
  '79 286
 Green Vegetable and Egg Salad, '79 191
 Green Vegetable Salad, Overnight, '80 5
 Grilled Vegetable Salad, '94 203

 Horseradish Dressing, Vegetable Salad
  with, '92 85
 Italian Vegetable Salad, '81 253; '82 19
 Lemon-Vegetable Congealed Salad,
  '85 22
 Luncheon Salad, '84 232
 Macaroni-Vegetable Salad, '86 209
 Marinade, Garden, '81 23
 Marinade, Medley, '79 20
 Marinade, Tossed Vegetable, '84 266
 Marinated Combo Salad, '82 267
 Marinated Garden Vegetables, '87 252
 Marinated Mixed Vegetables, '89 276;
  '92 106
 Marinated Salad, '91 186
 Marinated Salad, Eight-Vegetable,
  '80 218
 Marinated Summer Salad, '81 153
 Marinated Vegetable-Bacon Bowl,
  '79 191
 Marinated Vegetable Patch Salad,
  '84 232
 Marinated Vegetables, '88 4, 170
 Marinated Vegetable Salad, '79 106,
  143; '81 280; '82 163; '83 260;
  '84 13; '87 243; '92 64, 91
 Marinated Vegetable Salad, Crispy,
  '84 193
 Marinated Vegetable Salad, Fresh,
  '86 173
 Marinate, Fresh Vegetable, '80 33;
  '81 230
 Meal-in-One Salad, '82 232
 Medley Salad, Vegetable, '88 86
 Mexican Salad, '81 113
 Minted Vegetable Salad, '88 23
 Mixed Vegetable Salad, '80 115;
  '81 302; '82 239; '83 317; '84 16;
  '86 136
 Next-Day Vegetable Salad, '83 81
 Oriental Salad, Make-Ahead, '82 163
 Oriental Vegetable Salad, '84 290
 Overnight Vegetable Salad, '90 33
 Pasta and Vegetables, '89 255
 Pasta Salad, Vegetable, '89 256;
  '91 143
 Pasta Salad, Vegetable-, '92 167
 Pebble Salad, '91 27
 Primavera Salad, '93 140
 Quick Summer Italian Salad, '92 79
 Rainbow Vegetable Salad, '83 111
 Ratatouille Pasta Salad, '90 74
 Refrigerated Vegetable Salad, '84 120
 Relish Salad, Vegetable, '82 267
 Rice-and-Vegetable Salad, '86 42
 Rice-and-Vegetable Salad, Brown,
  '84 202
 Rice Salad, Vegetable-, '80 148;
  '83 198; '85 87
 Riviera, Salade, '89 12
 Rolls, Vegetable Salad, '82 278
 Senator's Salad, '79 191
 Seven-Layer Vegetable Salad, '79 88
 Shrimp Salad, Vegetable-, '79 190
 Slaw, Layered, '93 214
 Slaw, Vegetable, '81 280
 Spring Vegetable Salad, '88 48
 Summertime Salad, '79 143
 Swedish Vegetable Salad, '82 23
 Sweet-and-Sour Vegetable Salad, '81 25
 Tangy Vegetable Toss, '79 144

Vegetables, Salads *(continued)*

Tarragon-Vegetable Salad, **'85** 288
Tortellini Salad, Garden, **'91** 44
Variety Salad, **'79** 113
Vinaigrette Salad, Vegetable-Chicken, **'86** 135
Vinaigrette, Vegetables, **'82** 225, 290
Walnuts, Vegetable Salad with, **'86** 118
Winter Vegetable Salad, **'86** 42
Salmon Scaloppine with Vegetable Confetti and Pernod Sauce, **'94** 172
Salsa, Garden, **'91** 182
Sandwich, Big Veggie, **'92** 196
Sandwiches, Open-Face Tofu-Veggie, **'86** 5
Sandwiches, Vegetarian Pita, **'84** 193
Sandwich, Vegetable Puff, **'85** 51
Sauce, Cheesy Vegetable, **'92** M134
Sauce, Greek Fish with Vegetable, **'82** 72
Sauce, Pasta with Vegetable, **'83** 163
Sauce, Tangy Vegetable, **'89** 280
Sauce, Turkey Patties in Vegetable-Tomato, **'87** 18
Sauce, Vegetable, **'89** 98
Sauce, Vegetable Butter, **'86** 174
Sauce, Vegetable-Cheese, **'85** M152
Sausage Vegetable Dinner, **'84** 250
Sauté, Cajun Vegetable, **'92** 62
Sautéed Vegetables, Grouper with, **'90** M233
Sautéed Vegetables with Spaghetti, **'81** 89
Sautéed Vegetables with Spaghetti Squash, **'84** 128
Sauté, Garden, **'87** 90
Sautéing Fresh Vegetables, **'82** 138
Sauté, Tossed Vegetable, **'92** 138
Scalloped Mixed Vegetables, **'83** 5
Scallops en Brochette with Vegetables, **'80** 163
Scallops with Vegetables, Bay, **'84** 233
Seasoning Blend, Vegetable, **'88** 29
Sesame Sauce, Vegetables with, **'83** 112
Shrimp and Vegetables, **'82** 6
Skillet, Potato-Vegetable, **'92** 61
Skillet, Vegetable-Beef, **'86** 172
Soups
Bean Soup, Vegetable-, **'83** 317
Beef-and-Barley Vegetable Soup, **'89** 31
Beef Soup, Hearty Vegetable-, **'84** 102
Beef Soup, Spicy Vegetable-, **'88** 11
Beef Soup, Vegetable-, **'88** 296
Beefy Vegetable Soup, **'79** 113; **'84** M38
Beefy Vegetable Soup, Quick, **'80** 25
Burger Soup, Vegetable-, **'82** 6
Cheese Soup, Creamy Vegetable-, **'81** 244
Cheese Soup, Creamy Vegetable, **'83** 230
Cheese Soup, Vegetable-, **'89** 15
Cheesy Vegetable Chowder, **'80** 25; **'83** 20
Cheesy Vegetable Soup, **'80** 73
Chicken-Vegetable Soup, **'88** 18
Chili Vegetable Soup, **'94** 120
Chunky Vegetable Soup, **'89** M283
Clear Vegetable Soup, **'79** 130
Down-Home Vegetable Soup, **'90** 32
Garden Soup, **'85** 241

Garden Vegetable Soup, **'83** 140; **'86** 160
Garden Vegetable Soup, Cold, **'84** 197
Gazpacho, **'84** 112; **'85** 164
Gazpacho, Chilled, **'84** 138
Gazpacho, Cool, **'83** 140
Gazpacho, Spring, **'81** 112
Gazpacho, Summer, **'84** 181
Harvest Chowder, **'83** 317
Harvest Soup, **'79** 101
Hearty Vegetable Soup, **'80** 26
Homemade Soup, **'79** 198
Leek-Vegetable Soup, **'86** 304
Light Vegetable Soup, **'84** 280
Marvelous Vegetable Soup, **'82** 3
Mix, Vegetable Soup, **'84** 148
Old-Fashioned Vegetable Soup, **'86** 304
Quick Vegetable Soup, **'79** 190; **'85** 24, 32
Quick Veggie Soup, **'91** 31
Savory Vegetable Broth, **'81** 230
Shrimp-Vegetable Bisque, **'82** 313; **'83** 66
Spicy Vegetable Soup, **'79** 198; **'93** 293
Stock, Vegetable, **'90** 31
Tomato-Vegetable Soup, **'81** 177; **'86** 9
Turkey-Vegetable Soup, **'84** 4; **'88** 264; **'91** 312
Vegetable Soup, **'80** 128; **'84** 148; **'85** 106; **'86** 187; **'87** 83, 123; **'88** 266; **'93** 157
Spaghetti, Chicken-Vegetable, **'92** 281
Spaghetti, Fresh Vegetables with, **'86** 257
Spaghetti, Shrimp-and-Vegetable, **'91** 170
Spaghetti with Vegetables, **'85** 67
Spicy Vegetables and Sausage, **'80** 82
Spread, Garden, **'86** 135
Spread, Garden Vegetable, **'93** 184
Spread, Vegetable, **'90** 144
Spread, Vegetable-Egg, **'87** 106
Spread, Vegetable Party, **'84** 166
Spread, Vegetable Sandwich, **'83** 174; **'85** 135
Squash, Vegetable-Stuffed, **'84** 104
Steak with Vegetables, Skewered, **'81** 124
Steak with Vegetables, Swiss, **'81** 273
Steamed and Minted Garden Toss, **'83** 173
Steamed Dinner, Easy, **'83** M314
Steamed Fish and Vegetables, **'91** 32
Steamed Garden Vegetables, **'93** 155
Steamed Herbed Vegetables, **'93** M303
Steamed Vegetable Medley, **'86** 50; **'90** 29
Steamed Vegetables with Garlic-Ginger Butter Sauce, **'94** 89
Steamed Vegetables with Mustard Sauce, **'83** 208
Steaming Fresh Vegetables, **'82** 138, 183
Stew, Fish-and-Vegetable, **'87** 220
Stew, Minestrone, **'93** 184
Stew, Mixed Vegetable, **'84** 13
Stew, Shortcut Vegetable-Beef, **'89** 218
Stew, Sweet-and-Sour Beef and Vegetable, **'85** 87
Stew, Vegetable-Beef, **'94** 323
Stir-Fried Beef and Vegetables, **'88** 301
Stir-Fried Vegetables, **'79** 217; **'83** 193; **'90** 136
Stir-Fried Vegetables with Curry, **'87** 51
Stir-Fry, Almond-Vegetable, **'86** 222
Stir-Fry, Beef-and-Vegetable, **'81** 211; **'87** 22

Stir-Fry Beef-and-Vegetables, **'84** 141
Stir-Fry, Chicken and Vegetable, **'82** 237
Stir-Fry Chicken and Vegetables, **'86** 249
Stir-Fry Chicken-and-Vegetables, **'86** 68
Stir-Fry, Chicken-Vegetable, **'83** 151; **'84** 13, 141
Stir-Frying Fresh Vegetables, **'82** 138
Stir-Fry Medley, **'88** 156
Stir-Fry, Mixed Vegetable, **'79** 268; **'80** 14
Stir-Fry, Orange Roughy-and-Vegetable, **'91** 50
Stir-Fry Sausage and Vegetables, **'86** 213; **'87** 82
Stir-Fry Shrimp and Vegetables, **'87** 91
Stir-Fry, Steak-and-Vegetable, **'84** 8
Stir-Fry, Three-Vegetable, **'86** 174
Stir-Fry, Vegetable, **'79** 214; **'82** M172, 208; **'84** 104
Stir-Fry, Vegetable Medley, **'85** 109
Stir-Fry Vegetables with Chicken, **'84** 195
Succotash, **'85** 106
Succotash, Easy, **'80** 165
Succotash, Summer, **'86** 170
Summer Vegetables, **'91** 136
Supper, Vegetarian, **'86** 222
Tempura, Basic, **'81** 68
Tempura, Cornmeal, **'81** 68
Tempura, **'79** 112
Terrine, Chicken-Vegetable, **'84** 131
Terrine, Vegetable-Chicken, **'83** 224
Tomatoes, Vegetable Stuffed, **'94** 141
Topper, Vegetable-Cheese Potato, **'86** 6
Topping, Turkey-Vegetable, **'94** 22
Topping, Vegetable, **'79** 79
Torte, Layered Vegetable, **'84** 52
Trio, Vegetable-Herb, **'83** 172
Turkey Pasta Primavera, Smoked, **'90** 84
Turnovers, Vegetable, **'86** 24
Veal Roast with Vegetables, **'89** 71
Venison-Vegetable Bake, **'87** 304
Vermicelli, Scallop-Vegetable, **'87** 143
Vermouth, Chicken and Vegetables, **'87** M37
Vinaigrette, Grilled Chicken with Vegetables, **'91** 26
Wine-Soaked Vegetables, Baked Chicken with, **'84** 277
Yuca Con Mojo, **'93** 29

Venison
Appetizers, Venison Tenderloin, **'88** 249
Bake, Venison-Vegetable, **'87** 304
Balls, Venison Sausage, **'80** 42
Burgers, Venison, **'87** 304
Chili, Double-Meat, **'79** 269; **'80** 12
Chili, Hot Venison, **'91** 283
Chili, Venison, **'82** 216; **'86** 3; **'87** 304
Chutney-Mustard Sauce, Bostick Venison with, **'89** 242
Fried Venison, Country-, **'81** 233
Gumbo, Wild Game, **'91** 290
Kabobs, Venison, **'82** 215; **'88** 249
Loin, Mushroom-Crusted Venison, **'94** 302
Pot Pie with Parmesan Crust, Game, **'94** 304
Roast, Grilled Venison, **'93** 278
Roast, Lillie Bell's Venison, **'89** 242
Roast, Venison, **'82** 226
Roast with Red Wine Gravy, Venison, **'85** 270
Sauce, Venison Reduction, **'94** 303
Soup, Venison, **'82** 216
Steak, Country-Fried Venison, **'83** 262
Steaks, Country-Style Venison, **'82** 215

Venison *(continued)*

Steaks, Grilled Venison, **'82** 215
Stew, Venison, **'86** 294
Stew, Venison Sausage, **'87** 238
Stew with Potato Dumplings, Venison, **'87** 304
Stock, Venison, **'94** 302
Tomatoes, Venison and, **'85** 270

Vinegars

Basil Vinegar, **'93** 218
Cranberry Vinegar, **'91** 288
Dill-and-Chive Vinegar, **'84** 300
Garlic-Basil Vinegar, **'85** 124
Herb Vinegar, Five-, **'85** 124
Herb Vinegar, Homemade, **'79** 100
Herb Vinegar, Mixed, **'84** 107
Lemon-Mint Vinegar, **'85** 124
Mint Vinegar, **'92** 104
Oregano-Lemon Vinegar, Spicy, **'85** 124
Raspberry-Lemon Vinegar, **'87** 134
Shallot-Tarragon-Garlic Vinegar, **'93** 191
Southwest Vinegar, **'94** 200
Tarragon-Dill Vinegar, **'85** 124
Tarragon Vinegar, **'84** 107; **'89** 194; **'94** 201
Tomato-Herb Vinegar, **'94** 200

Waffles

Banana-Ginger Waffles, **'86** 96
Banana-Oatmeal Waffles, **'94** 206
Banana Split Waffles, **'89** 205
Belgian Waffles, **'94** 206
Chicken-Pecan Waffles, Southern, **'82** 231
Chocolate Waffles with Strawberry Cream, **'88** 153
Club Soda Waffles, **'94** 206
Cornbread Waffles, **'79** 265; **'91** 90
Corn-Chile Waffles, **'94** 206
Cornmeal Waffles, **'85** 201; **'94** 22
Crunchy Brunch Waffles, **'81** 41
French Toast, Waffled, **'82** 47
French Waffles, **'86** 138
Fudge Waffles, **'94** 205
Gingerbread Waffles, **'91** 68
Ham Waffles, **'80** 44
Light Waffles, **'91** 139
Oat Bran Waffles, **'92** 139
Oatmeal-Nut Waffles, **'83** 96
Oatmeal Waffles, **'89** 107
Peanut Butter Waffles, Honey-Buttered, **'94** M206
Pecan Waffles, **'87** 225
Pumpkin-Nut Waffles, **'86** 96
Pumpkin Waffles with Mandarin Orange Sauce, Dessert, **'89** 204
Quick Bread Mix, **'81** 90
Quick Mix Waffles, **'86** 9
Refrigerator Waffles, Best Ever, **'87** 225
Sausage Waffles, **'83** 50
Sorghum-Ginger Waffles, **'85** 239
Southern Waffles, **'87** 225
Sweet Potato Waffles, **'88** 208
Sweet Potato Waffles with Orange Butter, **'90** 323
Tuna Waffle-Wich, Hot, **'88** 272; **'89** 181
Wacky Waffles, **'93** 195
Waffles, **'81** 90

Walnut Waffles, Crunchy, **'85** 48
Whole Wheat Dessert Waffle, **'79** 92
Whole Wheat Waffles, **'84** 228

Walnuts

Apple-Date-Nut Ring, **'90** 212
Bonbons, Coconut-Black Walnut, **'82** 307
Bread, Apple-Nut, **'79** 12
Bread, Applesauce-Honey Nut, **'87** 300
Bread, Apricot-Nut, **'79** 24
Bread, Carrot-Walnut, **'88** 284
Bread, Cherry Nut, **'81** 306; **'82** 36
Bread, Chocolate Date-Nut, **'81** 284
Bread, Cinnamon-Nut Bubble, **'80** 22
Bread, Cranberry-Orange Nut, **'80** 288
Bread, Date-Nut, **'85** 306
Bread, Fresh Apple-Nut, **'87** 256
Bread, Walnut, **'93** 77
Bread, Wine-Date Nut, **'82** 253
Brie, Walnut-Baked, **'93** 241
Brie, Walnut-Fried, **'86** 244
Broccoli, English Walnut, **'89** 68
Brownies, Chocolate-Walnut, **'89** 325
Brownies, Walnut-Cream Cheese, **'84** 240
Burgers, Nutty, **'87** 185
Burgers, Walnut, **'89** 163
Cake, Apple-Nut, **'87** 76
Cake, Apple-Walnut, **'94** 242
Cake, Black Walnut, **'80** 253; **'84** 316; **'90** 308
Cake, Black Walnut Pound, **'92** 16
Cake, Cranberry-Nut Coffee, **'81** 250
Cake, Orange Nut, **'80** 70
Cake, Orange-Nut Butter, **'80** 254
Cake Roll, Date-Nut, **'89** 94
Cakes, Mini-Mincemeat Nut, **'88** 257
Cake, Sour Cream-Walnut Coffee, **'79** 209
Cake, Walnut Coffee, **'93** 124
Cake, Yogurt-Lemon-Nut, **'89** 169
Candied Nuts, **'81** 261
Carrots with Walnuts, Julienne, **'84** 188
Cheese, Nutty Date Dessert, **'87** 299
Chicken and Vegetables, Walnut, **'85** 194
Chicken-and-Walnut Salad, Sunburst, **'93** 91
Chicken Breasts, Walnut-Stuffed, **'85** 293
Chicken, Crispy Walnut, **'90** 89
Chicken, Deep-Fried Walnut, **'87** 175
Chicken, Walnut, **'85** 126
Chocolate-Nut Chews, **'81** 92
Cobbler, Apple-Walnut, **'79** 154; **'81** 248
Cookies, Apple-Nut, **'80** 228
Cookies, Frosted Pumpkin-Walnut, **'82** 217
Cookies, Nutty Oatmeal, **'81** 130
Cookies, Rich Date-Nut Chocolate Chip, **'92** 207
Cookies, Simply Walnut, **'91** 236
Cookies, Walnut, **'81** 301
Cupcakes, Apple-Nut, **'82** 279
Cups, Chocolate-Walnut, **'85** 213
Dressing, Green Beans with Walnut, **'94** 279
Dressing, Honey-Walnut, **'93** 107
Filling, Honey-Walnut, **'80** 21
Fried Walnuts, Chinese, **'81** 254
Frosting, Nutty Coconut, **'86** 8
Fruit, Cheese, and Nuts, **'93** 324
Fudge, Nutty White, **'81** 253
Fudge, Orange-Walnut, **'92** 288
Green Beans, Lemon-Walnut, **'93** 304
Honey-Walnut Swirl, **'80** 21
Ice Cream Balls, Nutty, **'89** 72

Loaf, Apricot-Nut, **'81** 8
Loaf, Blue Ribbon Date-Walnut, **'80** 15
Loaf, Nutty Wheat, **'90** 65
Meatballs, Mock, **'81** 243
Mousse, Coffee-Nut, **'86** 319
Muffins, Carrot-Date-Nut, **'86** 262
Muffins, Nutty Pumpkin, **'86** 291
Phyllo Baskets, Walnut-, **'93** 210
Pie, Walnut-Cranberry, **'87** 259
Pitas, Spinach-Walnut, **'87** 202; **'88** 43
Salad, Orange Walnut, **'80** 246
Salad, Raspberry-Walnut, **'94** 158
Salad, Shrimp-Walnut, **'86** 182
Salad, Walnut-Chicken, **'89** 14
Salad with Walnuts, Vegetable, **'86** 118
Sandwich, Date-Nut Lettuce, **'94** 202
Sauce, Apricot-Walnut Hard, **'88** 153
Sauce, Spaghetti with Parsley and Walnut, **'80** 30
Sauce, Walnut Cream, **'93** 275
Sautéed Walnuts, Turkey Salad with, **'86** 117
Sherry-Orange Nuts, **'86** M289
Slaw, Nutty Apple, **'88** 216
Spice Kisses, Walnut, **'89** 295
Spread, Date-Walnut, **'87** 292
Spread, Nutty Fruit-and-Cheese, **'87** 246
Strawberries with Walnuts, Stuffed, **'85** 122; **'86** 124
Stuffing, Tomatoes with Walnut-Rice, **'91** 102
Sweet Potatoes with Sherry and Walnuts, **'86** 286
Syrup, Maple-Nut, **'80** 228
Topping, Nutty, **'86** 16
Twists, Fruit-Nut, **'82** 253
Vegetables with Walnuts, Julienne, **'86** M251
Waffles, Crunchy Walnut, **'85** 48
Zucchini with Walnuts, **'84** 213

Watermelon. *See* Melons.

Wheat Germ

Biscuits, Wheat Germ, **'86** 261
Bread, Banana Wheat, **'81** 14
Crackers, Oatmeal-Wheat Germ, **'84** 236
Crisps, Sesame Wheat, **'81** 106
Muffins, Carrot-Wheat, **'88** 9
Muffins, Wheat Germ-Prune, **'81** 106
Pancakes, Wheat Germ, **'86** 242
Pancakes, Wheat Germ-Banana, **'79** 114
Squares, Spicy Wheat Germ, **'80** 44

Wild Rice. *See* Rice/Wild Rice.

Wok Cooking

Asparagus and Mushrooms, **'85** 108
Asparagus, Stir-Fried, **'87** 52
Bean Medley, Green, **'85** 108
Beans, Stir-Fried Green, **'85** 148
Beef and Asparagus, Stir-Fry, **'91** 124
Beef and Broccoli, Quick, **'91** 123
Beef and Broccoli, Stir-Fry, **'79** 47
Beef-and-Broccoli Stir-Fry, **'91** 46
Beef and Pea Pods, Stir-Fry, **'80** 19
Beef-and-Shrimp Stir-Fry, **'93** 32
Beef and Snow Peas, Oriental, **'79** 105
Beef and Snow Peas, Stir-Fry, **'83** 22
Beef and Snow Pea Stir-Fry, **'82** 98
Beef and Vegetables, Stir-Fried, **'88** 301
Beef-and-Vegetables, Stir-Fry, **'84** 141
Beef-and-Vegetable Stir-Fry, **'81** 211; **'87** 22
Beef, Chinese-Style, **'87** 50
Beef, Mongolian, **'85** 2, 75
Beef, Oriental, **'85** 20
Beef over Rice Noodles, Shredded, **'85** 74

Wok Cooking *(continued)*

Beef Stew, **'86** 51
Beef, Stir-Fried, **'84** 26
Beef Stir-Fry, Chinese, **'83** 151
Beef Stir-Fry, Lime-Ginger, **'92** 65
Beef Stir-Fry, Mongolian, **'89** 25
Beef with Chinese Vegetables, **'81** 211
Beef with Oriental Vegetables, **'84** 140
Bok Choy-Broccoli Stir-Fry, **'84** 2
Broccoli and Beef, Stir-Fry, **'83** 110
Broccoli, Jade-Green, **'80** 12
Broccoli, Stir-Fried, **'83** 227
Broccoli, Stir-Fry, **'80** 19
Broccoli with Sesame, **'80** 13
Broccoli with Sesame Seeds, **'82** 34
Brussels Sprouts Stir-Fry, **'81** 308
Cabbage, Lemon-Butter, **'88** 156
Cabbage, Stir-Fried, **'81** 75, 271; **'85** 109
Catfish Stir, **'84** 184
Cheese Wontons with Hot Sauce, **'83** 74
Chicken à l'Orange, Stir-Fry, **'83** 82
Chicken and Vegetables, Almond, **'86** 21
Chicken and Vegetables, Chinese, **'81** 212
Chicken-and-Vegetables, Stir-Fry, **'86** 68
Chicken and Vegetable Stir-Fry, **'82** 237
Chicken and Vegetables, Walnut, **'85** 194
Chicken, Braised Bourbon, **'86** 51
Chicken-Broccoli Stir-Fry, **'82** 33
Chicken, Cashew, **'79** 255; **'83** 21
Chicken Chinese, **'94** 33
Chicken Curry, Stir-Fried, **'87** 51
Chicken-in-a-Garden, **'80** 18
Chicken in Soy and Wine, **'84** 26
Chicken, Lemon, **'86** 173
Chicken, Princess, **'86** 122
Chicken Stir-Fry, Chinese, **'90** 100
Chicken Stir-Fry, Easy, **'91** 124
Chicken Stir-Fry, Herb-, **'89** 177
Chicken Stir-Fry, Hurry-Up, **'91** 124
Chicken Stir-Fry, Kyoto Orange-, **'87** 96
Chicken Stir-Fry, Orange-, **'84** 68
Chicken Stir-Fry, Pineapple-, **'89** 176
Chicken, Stir-Fry Vegetables with, **'84** 195
Chicken, Sweet-and-Sour, **'86** 240
Chicken, Szechwan, **'83** 85
Chicken Tempura Delight, **'85** 66
Chicken-Vegetable Stir-Fry, **'83** 151; **'84** 13, 141
Chicken, Walnut, **'85** 126
Chicken with Cashews, **'79** 207
Chicken with Cashews, Szechwan, **'81** 212
Chicken with Peanuts, Oriental, **'82** 236
Chicken with Pineapple, Oriental, **'86** 42
Chicken with Plum Sauce, **'82** 236
Chicken, Zesty Stir-Fried, **'83** 82
Chicken-Zucchini Stir-Fry, **'84** 50
Chinese-Style Dinner, **'84** 26
Egg Rolls, **'86** 81
Eggrolls, Shrimp and Pork, **'82** 240; **'83** 18
Egg Rolls, Vegetarian, **'86** 148
Greens, Stir-Fried, **'94** 33
Ham and Zucchini Stir-Fry, **'79** 47
Ham Stir-Fry, Easy, **'86** 332
Hungarian Stir-Fry, **'93** 64
Indian Stir-Fry, **'92** 126
Italian Stir-Fry, **'92** 126
Meatballs, Sweet-and-Sour, **'86** 240
Medley, Stir-Fry, **'88** 156
Mexican Stir-Fry, **'92** 126

Mushrooms with Bacon, Stir-Fried, **'80** 123
Orange Roughy-and-Vegetable Stir-Fry, **'91** 50
Pasta Potpourri, **'94** 33
Pear Fritters, Ol' Timey, **'86** 51
Peas and Peppers, Stir-Fried, **'87** 51
Pork-and-Onions with Bean Sauce, **'85** 76
Pork, Hot-and-Spicy, **'81** 228
Pork in Garlic Sauce, Stir-Fried, **'84** 141
Pork Oriental, **'81** 212
Pork, Stir-Fried, **'87** 51
Pork, Sweet-and-Sour, **'79** 42; **'80** 227; **'81** 26; **'85** 34, 194
Pork Tenderloin, Curried, **'86** 76
Potato Pudding, Sweet, **'86** 52
Potato-Snow Pea Stir-Fry, **'86** 173
Rice, Easy Fried, **'84** 76
Rice, Egg Fried, **'80** 19
Rice Special, Fried, **'80** 56
Rice with Sausage, Fried, **'83** 12
Sausage Rolls with Sweet-and-Sour Sauce, **'83** 74
Sausage Stir-Fry, **'82** 236
Scallop Stir-Fry, **'94** 32
Shiitake-Chicken Stir-Fry, **'89** 61
Shrimp and Refried Rice, **'89** 176
Shrimp and Sirloin Supreme, **'81** 131
Shrimp and Vegetables, Stir-Fry, **'87** 91
Shrimp Skillet, Quick, **'87** 50
Shrimp Stir-Fry, Cajun, **'92** 127
Shrimp, Szechuan, **'86** 173
Shrimp, Tangy Honeyed, **'94** 32
Shrimp with Snow Peas, **'85** 75
Spinach, Chinese, **'79** 179
Spinach, Stir-Fry, **'81** 182
Spinach with Mushrooms, **'80** 19
Spinach Wontons, **'83** 74
Squash Medley, **'84** 128
Squash Medley, Stir-Fried, **'80** 123
Squash Stir-Fry, **'80** 184
Squash Stir-Fry, Two-, **'86** 174
Steak, Chinese Pepper, **'82** 236
Steak, Fast-and-Easy Stir-Fried, **'87** 50
Steak, Pepper Stir-Fry, **'81** 240
Steak Sukiyaki, Flank, **'88** 233
Sugar Flips, **'83** 74
Teriyaki Stir-Fry, **'83** 110
Tomato-Zucchini Stir-Fry, **'80** 158
Turkey-Broccoli Stir-Fry, **'91** 62
Vegetable Medley, Chinese, **'84** 33
Vegetable Medley Stir-Fry, **'85** 109
Vegetable Pouches, Chinese, **'94** 34
Vegetables, Oriental, **'84** 26; **'85** 108
Vegetables, Skillet-Fried, **'88** 156
Vegetables, Stir-Fried, **'79** 217; **'83** 193; **'90** 136
Vegetable Stir-Fry, **'82** 208; **'84** 104
Vegetable Stir-Fry, Mixed, **'79** 268; **'80** 14
Vegetable Stir-Fry, Three-, **'86** 174
Vegetables with Curry, Stir-Fried, **'87** 51
Wontons, Tex-Mex, **'87** 196
Zucchini-and-Tomato Stir-Fry, **'85** 108
Zucchini, Italian-Style, **'80** 123
Zucchini Pesto, **'84** 194
Zucchini Toss, Stir-Fry, **'88** 156

Wontons
Cheese Wontons with Hot Sauce, **'83** 74
Chicken Wontons, **'92** 284
Chips, Baked Wonton, **'91** 138
Chips, Cinnamon-and-Sugar Wonton, **'91** 138
Chips, Garlic Wonton, **'91** 138

Chips, Lemon-and-Herb Wonton, **'91** 138
Chips, Parmesan Cheese Wonton, **'91** 138
Fried Wontons, Crispy, **'83** 21
Fruit-Filled Wontons, **'85** 287
Nibbles, Wonton, **'85** 287
Preparation Techniques, **'83** 74
Sausage Rolls with Sweet-and-Sour Sauce, **'83** 74
Spinach Wontons, **'83** 74
Sugar Flips, **'83** 74
Tex-Mex Wontons, **'87** 196

Yogurt

Apples, Honey-Yogurt, **'92** 46
Avocado Yogurt with Candied Lime Strips, Frozen, **'94** 137
Bars, Lemon Yogurt Wheat, **'79** 93
Breakfast-in-a-Bowl, **'89** 87
Cake, Strawberry Yogurt Layer, **'94** 85
Cake, Yogurt-Lemon-Nut, **'89** 169
Cake, Yogurt Pound, **'84** 10
Carambola-Yogurt Calypso, **'90** 169
Chicken, Grilled Yogurt-Lemon, **'81** 111
Chicken, Savory Yogurt, **'91** 238; **'92** 28
Chicken, Yogurt-Sesame, **'90** 216
Chocolate Yogurt, Mocha Sauce with, **'92** 243
Dessert, Strawberry-Yogurt, **'90** 295
Dip, Curry, **'85** 132
Dip, Fruited Yogurt, **'84** 171
Dip, Yogurt, **'94** 21
Dip, Yogurt Herring, **'80** 232
Dressing, Asparagus with Yogurt, **'79** 66
Dressing, Ginger-Yogurt, **'81** 302
Dressing, Honey-Yogurt, **'93** 172
Dressing, Lemon-Yogurt, **'93** 17
Dressing, Orange-Yogurt, **'85** 304
Dressing, Sweet-Hot Yogurt, **'86** 40
Dressing, Turkey Waldorf Salad with Yogurt, **'88** 53
Dressing, Yogurt, **'85** 59, 215; **'88** 27
Dressing, Yogurt-Herb, **'92** 96
Dressing, Yogurt-Honey Poppy Seed, **'83** 177
Dressing, Yogurt Salad, **'79** 69
Filling, Fresh Raspberry Crêpes with Yogurt, **'93** 123
Fruit Medley, Yogurt-Granola, **'91** 58
Honey Yogurt, Orange Slices with, **'91** 68
Ice, Apricot Yogurt, **'81** 177
Ice Milk, Banana Yogurt, **'89** 199
Ice, Peach-Yogurt, **'84** 83
Lemon-Chiffon Frozen Yogurt, **'85** 54
Muffins, Yogurt, **'88** 55
Muffins, Yogurt-Muesli, **'90** 215
Nectarines Royale, **'85** 132
Omelet, Yogurt-Avocado, **'81** 33
Pancakes, Orange-Yogurt, **'87** 225
Parfait, Crunchy Strawberry-Yogurt, **'79** 124
Peach Yogurt, Frozen Fresh, **'90** 139
Pie, Strawberry Yogurt, **'80** 232
Pie, Strawberry-Yogurt, **'85** 122; **'86** 124
Pie, Yogurt-Apricot, **'85** 132
Pie, Yogurt-Cheese, **'82** 121
Pineapple-Yogurt Whirl, **'91** 132
Pops, Pineapple-Yogurt, **'91** 173
Potatoes, Yogurt-Stuffed, **'88** 24
Rolls, Yogurt Crescent, **'91** 123
Salad, Crème de Menthe, **'82** 122
Salad, Cucumber-Yogurt, **'87** 33

(...ntinued)

Salad, Frozen Yogurt, **'92** 303
Salad, Strawberry Yogurt, **'80** 232
Salad, Yogurt-Cucumber, **'82** 122
Salad, Yogurt Fruit, **'81** 114
Sauce, Creamy Yogurt, **'91** 238; **'92** 28
Sauce, Honey-Yogurt, **'92** 307
Sauce, Lamb Meatballs with Yogurt, **'85** 132
Sauce, Yogurt, **'89** 283
Sauce, Yogurt-Horseradish, **'85** 66
Shake, Strawberry-Yogurt, **'87** 199
Slaw or Salad Dressing, Lemon-Yogurt, **'88** 54
Smoothie, Fruited Honey-Yogurt, **'88** 231; **'89** 23
Snack, Yogurt, **'88** 55
Soup, Avocado-Banana-Yogurt, **'80** 78
Soup, Cucumber-Yogurt, **'82** 157; **'83** 205
Soup, Potato-Yogurt, **'92** 217
Soup, Yogurt Fruit, **'86** 176
Strawberry Yogurt Delight, **'85** 77
Topping, Yogurt-Cheese, **'88** 55
Vanilla Frozen Yogurt, **'87** 125

Zucchini
Appetizers, Zucchini-Shrimp, **'89** 311
au Gratin, Potatoes-and-Zucchini, **'84** 5
au Gratin, Zucchini and Tomato, **'82** 208
Bake, Corn-Zucchini, **'79** 178
Baked Zucchini, **'83** 209
Baked Zucchini and Sausages, **'80** 300
Baked Zucchini Fans, **'87** 243
Bake, Squash, **'82** 107
Bake, Zucchini and Tomato, **'82** 158
Bake, Zucchini-Beef, **'86** 146
Bars, Zucchini, **'85** 77
Basil, Zucchini and Tomatoes, **'89** 147
Beans with Zucchini, Green, **'84** 128
Bites, Crab-Zucchini, **'84** M216
Boats with Spinach, Zucchini, **'82** 252
Boats, Zucchini, **'85** M143
Bread, Banana-Zucchini, **'85** 326
Bread, Chocolate-Zucchini, **'93** 308
Bread, Spiced Zucchini, **'79** 161; **'86** 162
Bread, Spicy Zucchini, **'81** 305; **'82** 36
Bread, Zucchini, **'85** 111; **'86** 93
Bread, Zucchini-Apple, **'87** 255
Bread, Zucchini-Carrot, **'83** 190
Bread, Zucchini-Honey, **'89** 143
Broiled Zucchini, Quick-and-Easy, **'86** 169
Buttered Zucchini and Carrots, **'83** 252
Cajun Squash, **'88** 142
Cake, Chocolate-Zucchini, **'85** 156
Cake, Zucchini, **'79** 24
Cake, Zucchini-Carrot, **'93** 20
Calabaza Guisada con Puerco (Pumpkin Cooked with Pork), **'80** 193
Calabaza Mexicana (Mexican Squash), **'81** 196
Carrots and Zucchini, **'84** 262
Carrots, Zucchini with Baby, **'88** 24
Casserole, Carrot and Zucchini, **'83** 256
Casserole, Cheese-Egg-Zucchini, **'84** 114
Casserole, Cheesy Zucchini, **'82** 168; **'84** 145
Casserole Italiano, Zucchini-Rice, **'89** 146
Casserole, Italian Zucchini, **'85** 59

Casserole, Zucchini, **'79** 157; **'87** 154
Casserole, Zucchini-and-Tomato, **'88** 265
Casserole, Zucchini-Egg, **'84** M113
Casserole, Zucchini-Jack, **'85** 296
Caviar, Zucchini, **'88** 212
Coleslaw, Fiesta Zucchini, **'91** 168
Combo, Zucchini-Corn, **'86** 218
Corn and Zucchini, **'83** 190
Corn, Zucchini and, **'86** 177
Crêpes, Zucchini, **'79** 157
Delight, Zucchini-Basil, **'85** 267
Dilled Fresh Zucchini, **'81** 174
Dilled Zucchini and Corn, **'83** 173
Dip, Yellow Squash-Zucchini, **'89** 48
Dressing, Zucchini, **'86** 282
Easy Zucchini, **'87** 167
Eggplant and Squash, **'83** 187
Eggplant and Zucchini, Italian-Style, **'79** 289; **'80** 26
Eggplant and Zucchini, Sautéed, **'82** 96
Fans, Baked Zucchini, **'88** 246
Fans, Herb Butter Zucchini, **'90** 201
Fans, Zucchini, **'91** 33
Fried Zucchini, Oven-, **'86** 211
Fried Zucchini Strips, **'81** 184
Fried Zucchini with Cocktail Sauce, French, **'86** 146
Fries, Zucchini, **'90** 147
Fries, Zucchini French, **'82** 78
Frittata, Corn-and-Squash, **'89** 144
Frittata, Zucchini, **'86** 103
Fritters, Cheesy Zucchini, **'88** 44
Fritters, Zucchini, **'81** 163
Fruitcake, Zucchini, **'88** 284
Fry, Zucchini, **'81** 102
Grilled Zucchini Fans, **'89** 200
Herbed Zucchini, **'84** 104
Hors d'Oeuvres, Zucchini, **'80** 151
Italiano, Zucchini, **'81** 183
Italian Squash, **'79** 158
Italian-Style Zucchini, **'80** 123
Italian Zucchini, **'83** M147
Julienne Zucchini and Carrots, **'90** 14
Lasagna, Garden, **'83** 119
Lasagna, Zucchini, **'85** 194
Lemon-Garlic Zucchini, **'89** 226
Manicotti, Zucchini, **'84** 194
Marinated Squash Medley, **'94** 126
Marinated Zucchini, **'80** 33; **'89** 102
Medley, Zucchini-and-Corn, **'80** 298; **'81** 25
Mexican Squash, **'83** 31
Mexican Style, Zucchini, **'80** 184
Muffins, Zucchini, **'83** 121; **'86** 146
Omelet, Zucchini, **'81** 99
Oven-Fried Zucchini Spears, **'91** 121
Pancakes, Zucchini, **'93** 43
Parmesan Zucchini, **'81** 234
Parmesan, Zucchini, **'81** 108; **'82** 103
Pecans, Zucchini with, **'87** 31
Pesto, Zucchini, **'84** 194
Pie, Cheesy Zucchini, **'82** 103
Pie, Italian-Style Zucchini, **'83** 43
Pie, Zucchini-Ham-Cheese, **'80** 272
Pizzas, Zucchini, **'88** 212
Pollo con Calabacita (Mexican Chicken with Zucchini), **'82** 219
Provençal, Zucchini, **'86** 146
Quiche, Cheesy Zucchini, **'83** 312
Quiche, Swiss-Zucchini, **'82** 49
Quiche, Zucchini-Mushroom, **'79** 127

Quiche, Zucchini-Sausage, **'83** 122
Ratatouille, **'84** 105, 243; **'85** 92
Ratatouille, Eggplant-Zucchini, **'81** 205
Ratatouille Niçoise, **'81** 22
Ratatouille, Quick-and-Easy, **'80** 212
Ratatouille-Stuffed Eggplant, **'83** 187
Relish, Pollock with Summer Squash, **'92** 200
Relish, Zucchini, **'87** 200
Rosemary, Summer Squash with, **'88** 143
Salad, Carrot-and-Zucchini, **'83** 240
Salad, Creamy Avocado and Zucchini, **'79** 208
Salad, Marinated Zucchini, **'82** 164; **'90** 32
Salad, Mushroom-Zucchini, **'85** 8
Salad, Turkey-Zucchini, **'85** 74
Salad, Zucchini, **'82** 104; **'87** 103; **'89** 128
Salad, Zucchini-Artichoke, **'91** 229
Salad, Zucchini Chef's, **'83** 143
Sandwiches, Open-Faced Zucchini, **'88** 159
Sauce, Spaghetti with Zucchini, **'81** 38
Sauce, Zucchini-Mushroom, **'93** 71
Sautéed Zucchini, **'83** 86; **'92** 60
Sautéed Zucchini and Carrots, **'92** 62, 99
Sautéed Zucchini and Sausage, **'83** 289
Sautéed Zucchini with Mushrooms, **'94** 135
Sauté, Zucchini, **'81** 183; **'84** 35
Scalloped Zucchini Bites, **'91** 165
Scallop, Green-and-Gold, **'81** 159
Scramble, Zucchini-Basil, **'87** 34
Skillet, Pattypan-Zucchini, **'82** 103
Skillet, Squash, **'82** 195
Skillet, Zippy Zucchini, **'82** 158
Skillet, Zucchini-Tomato, **'93** 206
Soufflé, Zucchini, **'79** 157
Soufflé, Zucchini-and-Corn, **'83** 265
Soup, Chilled Zucchini, **'87** 90
Soup, Cold Zucchini, **'85** 265; **'92** 64
Soup, Cream of Zucchini, **'83** 99
Soup, Creamy Zucchini, **'83** 140
Soup, Dilled Zucchini, **'90** 88
Soup, Italian Sausage-Zucchini, **'84** 4
Soup, Summer Squash, **'84** 193
Soup, Watercress-Zucchini, **'91** 72
Soup with Cilantro, Zucchini, **'93** 130
Soup, Zucchini, **'82** 104; **'84** 181; **'86** 181; **'89** 14
South-of-the-Border Zucchini, **'85** 135
Spaghetti, Italian Zucchini, **'85** 2
Spaghetti, Zucchini, **'83** 160
Squares, Zucchini, **'82** 103
Stir-Fried Squash Medley, **'80** 123
Stir-Fry, Chicken-Zucchini, **'84** 50
Stir-Fry, Ham and Zucchini, **'79** 47
Stir-Fry, Squash, **'80** 184
Stir-Fry, Tomato-Zucchini, **'80** 158
Stir-Fry, Two-Squash, **'86** 174
Stir-Fry, Zucchini-and-Tomato, **'85** 108
Stir-Fry Zucchini Toss, **'88** 156
Stuffed Zucchini, **'86** 54, 187; **'89** M133
Stuffed Zucchini, Beef-, **'86** M139
Stuffed Zucchini, Ham and Cheese, **'79** 157
Stuffed Zucchini, Italian, **'84** 119
Stuffed Zucchini Main Dish, **'79** 215
Stuffed Zucchini, Savory, **'80** 161
Stuffed Zucchini Supreme, **'83** 136
Stuffing, Haddock Fillets with Zucchini, **'88** M191
Timbales, Corn-and-Zucchini, **'92** 100
Tomato with Herbs, Zucchini and, **'92** 182
Toss, Zucchini, **'91** 292